An Tuil

Mar chuimhne air m' athair, Eideard Màrtainn MacilleDhuibh (1896–1967), a fhritheil a dhùthaich tron dà Chogadh Mhór ann an trì seirbheisean a' Chrùin — Arm, Cabhlach agus Feachd Adhair

In memory of my father, Edward Martin Black AMIMechE (1896–1967), who served his country through both World Wars in the three services of the Crown — Army, Navy and Air Force

An Tuil

Duanaire Gàidhlig an 20mh Ceud

air a dheasachadh le

Raghnall MacilleDhuibh

Polygon

boillsgeadh dhen tuil tha gar toirt leatha
thar slèibhtean is còmhnardan eachdraidh

glimpses of the flood that carries us
over the mountains and plains of history

— *Ruaraidh MacThòmais, 'Seanairean' (dàn 208)*

Bidh 'n t-aoibhneas seo gam chur gu ceòl
'S b'e sin an ceòl tha barraichte,
Is bristidh e a-mach mar thuil
Is togaidh e bhon talamh mi.

This joy sets me music-making
And marvellous music it is too,
For it bursts out like a flood
And lifts me up above the ground.

— *Catrìona NicDhòmhnaill, 'An t-Aoibhneas a tha staigh sa Chridhe' (dàn 222)*

agus thuirt an nighean a bha seo / an
nighean leis a' ghràdh 'na sùilean /
'Gabhaidh tu ris' / 's thuirt mise /
'Gabhaidh mi ri dé?' / agus thuirt i
a-rithist anns an aon ghuth chiùin /
'Gabhaidh tu ris / ris an tuil / ris a'
chiùine / ris na sìthichean / 's ri daoine'

and this girl said / the girl with love in
her eyes / 'You will accept it' / and I said
/ 'I will accept what?' / and she said
again in the same calm voice / 'You will
accept it / accept the flood / accept the
calmness / accept the otherworld people
/ and accept human beings'

— *Maoilios M Caimbeul, 'Agus mar sin car a' Mhuiltein' (dàn 287)*

An Tuil

Anthology of 20th Century Scottish Gaelic Verse

edited by

Ronald I M Black

Polygon

Acknowledgments and Copyright

Selection, 'Introduction', 'Background' and all other editorial material © Ronald Black 1999

Grateful acknowledgment is made to poets and their next-of-kin for permission to translate and reprint their work. While every effort has been made to trace copyright holders, who are duly identified in 'Background', if it is brought to the Publishers' attention that they have overlooked anyone they will be glad to rectify this in any future edition.

Copyright of original Gaelic poems remains with their authors or their authors' estates or publishers. All English translations in this work are by the author of the original poem or by the Editor of *An Tuil*. Where the translation is by the author (shown in 'Background' as 'Author's trl.'), copyright of the translation belongs to the author or the author's estate or publisher. Where the translation is by the Editor of *An Tuil* (shown in 'Background' as 'Editor's trl.'), copyright of the translation belongs to him. Requests for permission to reproduce poems, translations or other parts of the text of *An Tuil*, and all other enquiries, should be addressed in the first instance to Polygon.

The publisher acknowledges subsidy from the Faculty Group Research Committee for Arts, Divinity and Music, University of Edinburgh, towards the publication of this volume.

A CIP record is available

ISBN 0 7486 6219 7

Published by Polygon
22 George Square
Edinburgh

1999
Reprinted 2002

Set in Horley Old Style by Edderston Book Design, Peebles
Printed and bound in Great Britain by Creative Print and Design, Ebbw Vale, Wales

Clàr-Innse / Contents

Roimh-Ràdha xix
Foreword xx
Introduction xxi

CATRÌONA NICPHÀIDEIN (CATHERINE MACFADYEN) 1819–1913
   1 *Am Peinsean* (The Pension) 2

ALASTAIR MACGILLEMHÌCHEIL (ALEXANDER CARMICHAEL) 1832–1912
   2 *Ora nam Buadh* (The Invocation of the Graces) 2

CATRÌONA NICGHILLE-BHÀIN (KATHERINE WHYTE) 1845–1928
   3 from *Céilidh Dhùn-Ì* (The Ceilidh of Dùn-Ì) 6
   4 *Iomram Bean na Bainnse* (The Bride's Oar-Song) 8
   5 *Briseadh na Fàire* (The Breaking of the Dawn) 10

ALASDAIR CAMSHRON (ALEXANDER CAMERON) 1848–1933
   6 *An Sgàileagan* (The Umbrella) 14

GILLEASBAIG MAC AN T-SAOIR (ARCHIBALD MACINTYRE) 1854–1922
   7 from *Òran Ghlinne Chrò* (The Song of Glen Croe) 16

DÒMHNALL MACÌOMHAIR (DONALD MACIVER) 1857–1935
   8 *An Ataireachd Àrd* (The Sea's Lofty Roar) 18

SEONAIDH CAIMBEUL (JOHN CAMPBELL) 1859–1947
   9 *Òran a' Pheinsean* (The Song of the Pension) 22

AONGHAS MOIREASDAN (ANGUS MORRISON) 1865–1942
  10 from *Alba Saor* (Scotland Free) 28
  11 *Nam biodh agam moisein bodaich* (If I had an old meanie of a mannie) 34
  12 from *Smuaintean air Mórachd Ìmpireachd Bhreatainn* (Thoughts on the
       Greatness of the British Empire) 36
  13 *Madainn na Sàbaid* (The Sabbath Morning) 38

AONGHAS MACEACHARNA (ANGUS MACKECHNIE) 1870–1944
  14 *Iorram nan Ìtheach* (The Iona Boatsong) 42

AN T-URR. COINNEACH MACLEÒID (REV. KENNETH MACLEOD) 1871–1955
  15 *An Fhuar-Bheinn* (The Cold Hill) 44

AN T-URR. NIALL ROS (REV. NEIL ROSS) 1871–1943
  16 *Dunkirk* (from *Armageddon*) 44

AONGHAS MACDHONNCHAIDH (ANGUS ROBERTSON) 1871–1948

17   *An Dà Latha* (The Two Days) 48
18   *Maorach is Feamannadh* (Shell-Fishing, Seaweed-Cutting) 50

RUAIRIDH MACAOIDH (RODERICK MACKAY) 1872–1949

19   *Òran aig Toiseach Cogadh Mór na h-Eòrpa* (Song at the Start of the Great
     European War) 52
20   *Òran na Caillich Bhuana* (The Song of the Cailleach of Harvest) 54

TEÀRLACH MACNÌMHEIN (CHARLES MACNIVEN) 1874–1944

21   *Òran Bainnse* (Wedding Song) 58
22   from *Seinnidh mis' an duanag* (I'll sing the lovesong) 62
23   *Banais Chòrsabuil* (The Wedding at Corsapol) 62

DONNCHADH MACDHUNLÉIBHE (DUNCAN LIVINGSTONE) 1877–1964

24   from *Cogadh agus Sìth* (War and Peace) 64
25   *Rannan Callainne* (Festive Verses) 68
26   *Cath Fairge Monte Video* (The Battle of the River Plate) 68
27   *Am Bullaphant* (The Bullaphant) 70
28   *Feasgar an Duine Ghil* (The Evening of the White Man) 72
29   *Bean Dubh a' Caoidh a Fir a Chaidh a Mharbhadh leis a' Phoileas* (A Black
     Woman Mourns her Husband Killed by the Police) 74
30   *Togalach an Aonaich* (The Union Buildings) 78

AONGHAS MACGILL-FHAOLAIN (ANGUS Y MACLELLAN) 1879–1962

31   *An Sgiobair Ùr* (The New Skipper) 82
32   *Fàilte na h-Aimsir do D.D.* (Season's Greetings to D.D.) 84
33   *Am Bùth aig Maitiu* (Matthew's Shop) 86

SEUMAS MACLEÒID (JAMES MACLEOD) 1880–1947

34   *A' Cheist* (The Question) 88

DONNCHADH MACNÌMHEIN (DUNCAN MACNIVEN) 1880–1955

35   *Cadal* (Sleep) 90
36   *Far 'n do chaith mi 'n oidhch'* (Where I spent last night) 94

CIORSTAI NICLEÒID (CHRISTINA MACLEOD) 1880–1954

37   *Cuimhneachan 1914-1918* (In Memory of 1914–1918) 96
38   *An Dubhsgaile* (The Blackout) 100

MURCHADH MACLEÒID (MURDO MACLEOD) 1881–1907

39   *Gràdh m' Fhear-Saoraidh* (The Love of my Redeemer) 102

DONNCHADH MACIAIN (DUNCAN JOHNSTON) 1881–1947

40   *Càrn air a' Mhonadh* (A Cairn on the Moor) 110

AN T-URR. AONGHAS MACFHIONGHAIN (REV. ANGUS MACKINNON) 1885–1957

41   *Deireadh Òrdugh Ghleann Dail* (The End of the Glendale Communion) 110
42   *Am Mac Stròdhail* (The Prodigal Son) 112

Dòmhnall Mac na Ceàrdaich (Donald Sinclair) (1885–1932)
43 Slighe nan Seann Seun (The Way of the Old Spells) 114

Eachann MacFhionghain (Hector MacKinnon) 1886–1954
44 Fuath an t-Saoghail (The World's Hatred) 116
45 Lìon an Damhain-Allaidh (The Spider's Web) 120

Dòmhnall Ruadh Chorùna (Donald Macdonald) 1887–1967
46 Òran Arras (The Song of Arras) 122
47 Air an Somme (On the Somme) 124
48 Dh'fhalbh na gillean grinn (Off went the handsome lads) 126
49 Òran a' Phuinnsein (The Song of the Poison) 130
50 Nam bithinn mar eun (Were I like a bird) 132
51 Tha mi duilich, cianail, duilich (I am sorry, anguished, sorry) 134
52 Cha b'e gunna mo nàmhaid (It was not my enemy's gun) 138
53 Òran an H-Bomb (The Song of the H-Bomb) 144
54 Motor-Boat Heillsgeir (The Heisgeir Motor-Boat) 146

Seumas MacThòmais (James Thomson) 1888–1971
55 A' Ghaoth (The Wind) 148

Domhnall Mac an t-Saoir (Donald Macintyre) 1889–1964
56 from Aeòlus agus am Balg (Æolus and the Bellows) 150
57 Thug mi 'n oidhche raoir glé shàmhach (I spent last night very quiet) 152
58 Aoir Mhusolinidh (In Dispraise of Mussolini) 156
59 Òran na Cloiche (The Song of the Stone) 166
60 Nuair chaidh a' Chlach a Thilleadh (When the Stone was Returned) 176
61 Bùth Dhòmhnaill 'IcLeòid (Donald MacLeod's Pub) 180
62 from Fàilte an Diabhail don Droch Dhuine (The Devil's Welcome to the bad Man) 184
63 from Aoir an Luchd-Riaghlaidh (The Satire of the Ruling Class) 188
64 Nuair a thàinig am Buroo do Dhùthaich nam Beann (When the Buroo came to the Land of the Mountains) 196
65 O, faighibh suas an Cogadh (O, get ye up the War) 206

Ùisdean Laing (Hugh Laing) 1889–1974
66 Seann Éipheiteach ann an Tìr Airsnealach (An Ancient Egyptian in a Weary Land) 210

Pàdraig Moireasdan (Peter Morrison) 1889–1978
67 Òran don Chogadh (A Song to the War) 212

Iain Rothach (John Munro) 1889–1918
68 Ar Tìr (Our Land) 214
69 Ar Gaisgich a Thuit sna Blàir (Our Heroes who Fell in Battle) 214
70 Air sgàth nan sonn (For the sake of the warriors) 218

Murchadh Moireach (Murdo Murray) 1890–1964
71 Luach na Saorsa (The Value of Freedom) 220

DONNCHADH FIONNLASAN (DUNCAN FINLAYSON) 1897–1966
 72   Òran Hitler (The Song of Hitler) 220

AN T-URR. AONGHAS FIONNLASAN (REV. ANGUS FINLAYSON) 1897–1973
 73   Dùrachd Teachdaire Chrìost (The Wish of a Messenger of Christ) 224

IAIN ÈIRDSIDH MACASGAILL (IAIN ARCHIE MACASKILL) 1898–1933
 74   Mì-Chliù nan Daoine Dubha, 1930 (The Ill-Fame of the Black Men, 1930) 228

SEONAG NICCOINNICH (JOAN MACKENZIE) 1900–72
 75   Òran Clach Stèineagaidh (The Song of Steinigie Stone) 234

MURCHADH MACPHÀRLAIN (MURDO MACFARLANE) 1901–82
 76   Naoi Ceud Deug 's a Ceithir Deug (Nineteen Fourteen) 236

CALUM MACNEACAIL (MALCOLM NICOLSON) 1902–78
 77   Cùmhnantan Sìthe Pharis (The Paris Peace Treaties) 240
 78   Blàr Chaol Àcainn (The Battle of Kyleakin) 244

DÒMHNALL GRANND (DONALD GRANT) 1903–70
 79   from An Uilebheist is na Foghlamaich (The Monster and the Experts) 246

RUAIRIDH MACLEÒID (RODERICK MACLEOD) 1903–65
 80   An Cùlaibh Éirinn (At the Back of Ireland) 252

AONGHAS CAIMBEUL, 'AM PUILEAN' (ANGUS CAMPBELL) 1903–82
 81   Deargadan Phóland (The Fleas of Poland) 254
 82   Ciod E? (Who is He?) 258

IAIN MACNEACAIL (JOHN NICOLSON) 1903–99
 83   An t-Each Iarainn (The Iron Horse) 260
 84   Nochd gur luaineach mo chadal (Fitful's my sleep tonight) 262
 85   Òran do Teonaidh Hellinga (Song to Johnnie Hellinga) 264

TORMOD MACLEÒID (NORMAN MACLEOD) 1904–68
 86   Raoir chunna mi (Last night I saw) 266
 87   An 'Sus' a Shàraich Mi (The "Sus" that Vexed Me) 268
 88   Bàgh Leumrabhaigh (Lemreway Bay) 270
 89   Faoin Achain (An Idle Wish) 272
 90   Dubh is Geal (Black and White) 272
 91   An t-Àite bho Dheireadh (The Last Place) 272
 92   Thuit mo leannan (My love's fallen) 274

SEÒRAS MOIREASDAN (GEORGE MORRISON) 1906–88
 93   An t-Earrach (The Spring) 274

DÒMHNALL AILEAN MACDHÒMHNAILL (DONALD ALLAN MACDONALD) 1906–92
 94   Ceud Fàilt' air Gach Gleann (A Hundred Greetings to Each Glen) 278

AONGHAS CAIMBEUL, 'AM BOCSAIR' (ANGUS CAMPBELL) 1908–49
 95   Caithris nam Bodach (The Old Men's Night-Watch) 282

MÌCHEAL MAC A' PHEARSAIN (MICHAEL MACPHERSON) 1910–84

96   *Cumha Mhaighstir Nèill* (The Lament for Father Neil) 284

SOMHAIRLE MACGILL-EAIN (SORLEY MACLEAN) 1911–96

97   *Dàin do Eimhir II: A Chiall 's a Ghràidh* (Reason and Love) 288

98   *Dàin do Eimhir IV: Gaoir na h-Eòrpa* (The Cry of Europe) 290

99   *Dàin do Eimhir X: Theagamh nach eil i 'nam chàs* (Perhaps it's not part of
my destiny) 290

100   *Dàin do Eimhir XIII: A' Bhuaile Ghréine* (The Sunny Fold) 292

101   *Dàin do Eimhir XIV: Reic Anama* (The Selling of a Soul) 294

102   *Dàin do Eimhir XXV: B' fheàrr leam na goid an teine* (I'd prefer to
the stealing of fire) 296

103   *Dàin do Eimhir XXIX: Coin is Madaidhean-Allaidh* (Dogs and Wolves) 296

104   *Dàin do Eimhir XXXVIII: Labhair mi* (I spoke) 298

105   *Dàin do Eimhir XLIV: Ged chuirinn dhiom éideadh* (Should I even strip off) . . .298

106   *Dàin do Eimhir XLIX: Fo Sheòl* (Under Sail) 298

107   *Dàin do Eimhir LIII: Gur suarach leam* (Insignificant to me) 300

108   *Dàin do Eimhir LIV: Camhanaich* (Dawn) 300

109   *Dàin do Eimhir LVIII: A nighean 's tu beairteachadh* (O girl who enriches) 300

110   *Dàin do Eimhir LIX: MhicGilleMhìcheil . . . (Carmichael . . .)* 302

111   *Dàin do Eimhir LX: Nuair chunna mi* (When I saw) 304

112   *Dàin do Eimhir: Dimitto* 304

113   *Dàin Eile I: Ban-Ghaidheal* (A Highland Woman) 306

114   *Dàin Eile XVI: Trì Slighean* (Three Paths) 308

115   *Dàin Eile XVII: 'N e d' mhiann* (Is it your wish) 308

116   *Dàin Eile XVIII: An Dùn Éideann 1939* (In Edinburgh 1939) 308

117   *Dàin Eile XIX: Gabh a-mach ás mo bhàrdachd* (Get out of my poetry) 310

118   *Dàin Eile XXI: An Seann Òran* (The Old Song) 310

119   *Dàin Eile XXIII: Thug Yeats dà fhichead bliadhna* (Yeats spent two
score of years) 314

120   *Dàin Eile XXIV: An uair a thig an teannachadh* (When the tightness comes) . .314

121   *Dàin Eile XXVI: An-seo an gaol* (Here is love) 316

122   *Éisgeachd I: An Dùn 'na Theine* (The Castle on Fire) .316

123   *Éisgeachd II: Air an Adhbhar Cheudna* (On the Same Topic) 316

124   *Éisgeachd IV: Do Mgr Niall Mac an t-Seumarlain* (To Mr Neville
Chamberlain) 318

125   *Éisgeachd VI: Don Bhreitheamh a thubhairt ri Iain MacGhill-Eathain
gum b'e Gealtair a bh' ann* (To the Judge who told John Maclean
that he was a Coward) 318

126   *Éisgeachd VII: Road to the Isles* 318

127   *Glac a' Bhàis* (Death Valley) 320

128   from *An Cuilithionn* (The Cuillin) 322

129   *An t-Àilleagan* (The Little Jewel) 328

130   *A' Bheinn* (The Hill) 330

131   *Mhag mo reusan* (My reason mocked) 332

132   *Feasgar Samhraidh: Linne Ratharsair* (A Summer's Evening: The Sound
of Raasay) 332

133   from *Uamha 'n Òir* (The Cave of Gold) 332

DÒMHNALL MACDHÒMHNAILL (DONALD MACDONALD, ERISKAY) 1912–89
  134 Òran na Politician (The Song of the Politician) 334

CALUM IAIN MACLEÒID (CALUM I N MACLEOD) 1913–77
  135 An Giùlan (The Funeral Procession) 338

CARSTÌONA ANNA STIÙBHART (CHRISTINA STEWART) 1914–83
  136 Taigh Dubh mo Sheanar (My Grandfather's Black House) 340

AN T-URR. COINNEACH ROS (REV. KENNETH ROSS) 1914–90
  137 Fògradh Cogaidh sna h-Innsean (Wartime Exile in India) 342
  138 O a Ghaidhealtachd Till (O my Gaeldom Return) 342
  139 Farmad (Envy) 344

DEÒRSA MAC IAIN DEÒRSA (GEORGE CAMPBELL HAY) 1915–84
  140 Siubhal a' Choire (The Voyaging of the Corrie) 344
  141 Òran don Oighre (A Song to the Heir) 346
  142 An t-Sàbaid (The Sabbath) 346
  143 Ceithir Gaothan na h-Albann (The Four Winds of Scotland) 348
  144 from Mochtàr is Dùghall (Mokhtâr and Dougall) 348
  145 Atman 366
  146 Còmhradh an Alldain (The Wee Burn's Talk) 370
  147 Bisearta (Bizerta) 376
  148 An t-Òigear a' Bruidhinn on Ùir (The Young Man Speaking from the Grave) . .378
  149 Meftah Bâbkum es-Sabar? 380
  150 from Tilleadh Uilìseis (The Return of Ulysses) 384
  151 Achmhasain (Rebukes) 384
  152 Ors a' Bhéist Mhór ris a' Bhéist Bhig (Said the Big Beast to the Little Beast) . . .386
  153 An Ciùran Ceòban Ceò (The Smirry Drizzle of Mist) .386
  154 Uladh (Ulster) 388
  155 Suas gun Sìos (Up with no Down) 388
  156 Ionndrainn na Sìne (Longing for the Tempest) 388
  157 Guidhe an Iasgair (The Fisherman's Prayer) 390
  158 Bloigh Lebensraum (A Spot of Lebensraum) 390
  159 Na Ràtaichean 's a' Bhàrdachd (The Rates and Poetry) 390
  160 Dùrachdan Nollaige (Christmas Greetings) 392
  161 Dùrd a' Ghlinne (The Hum of the Glen) 392

IAIN PEATARSON (IAN PATERSON) 1916–90
  162 Turas an Ànraidh (Stormy Voyage) 392
  163 Uisge Phìob (Piped Water) 400
  164 Bogsa Diùc (Juke Box) 400
  165 Bó Dhearg (Red Cow) 402
  166 Cearcall Hùla (Hula Hoop) 402

AN T-URR. CAILEIN T MACCOINNICH (REV. COLIN N MACKENZIE) 1917–94
  167 An Seanchaidh (The Shennachie) 404

AN T-URR. IAIN MACLEÒID (REV. JOHN MACLEOD) 1918–95
168   Bantrach Cogaidh (War Widow) 410
169   Bàs Baile (The Death of a Township) 412
170   Aideachadh (Confession) 416

DÒMHNALL IAIN MACDHÒMHNAILL (DONALD JOHN MACDONALD) 1919–86
171   Òran an Fheamnaidh (The Song of the Seaweed-Cutting) 418
172   An Guth á Broinn na Màthar (The Voice from the Mother's Womb) 420
173   Taigh a' Bhàird (The Poet's House) 424
174   Do Mhaighstir Niall (To Father Neil) 426
175   Geata Tìr nan Òg (The Gate of the Land of the Young) 428

DOMHNALL R MACGILLEMHOIRE (DONALD R MORRISON) 1919—
176   from Fàilte don Phrionnsa Teàrlach 's a' Bhana-Phrionnsa Diàna a dh'Eilean
       Sgalpaigh na Hearadh, 2.7.85 (Prince Charles' and Princess Diana's Welcome
       to the Isle of Scalpay, Harris, 2.7.85) 430

AN T-URR. RUAIRIDH MACDHÒMHNAILL (REV. RODERICK MACDONALD) 1920–98
177   from Turas don Ghealaich (Journey to the Moon) 432
178   Taibhs (Ghost) 434
179   Meirg (Rust) 436
180   Seotal (Shottle) 438

MÀIRI M NICGHILLEATHAIN (MARY M MACLEAN) 1921—
181   Do Bheinn Eubhal (To Ben Eaval) 438
182   Glòir no Dórainn? (Glory or Agony?) 442

AN T-OLL. RUARAIDH MACTHÒMAIS (PROF. DERICK THOMSON) 1921—
183   Teallaichean (Hearths) 446
184   Sgòthan (Clouds) 446
185   from Mu Chrìochan Hòil (In the Vicinity of Hòl) 448
186   Na Cailleachan (The Old Women) 450
187   Clann-Nighean an Sgadain (The Herring Girls) 452
188   Srath Nabhair (Strathnaver) 452
189   Bùrn is Mòine 's Coirc (Water and Peats and Oats) 454
190   Am Bodach-Ròcais (Scarecrow) 454
191   Murdag Mhòr 456
192   Làmhan (Hands) 456
193   Earrach '74 (Spring '74) 458
194   Ceud Bliadhna san Sgoil (A Hundred Years in School) 458
195   An Crann (The Plough (or Cross/Mast/Lot/Harp-Key/Saltire etc.)) 460
196   Earail air Luchd-Adhraidh a' Bheòil-Aithris (A Warning for
       Folklore Worshippers) 466
197   Alba v. Argentina, 2/6/79 (Scotland v. Argentina, 2/6/79) 466
198   from Àirc a' Choimhcheangail (The Ark of the Covenant) 468
199   from Air Sràidean Ghlaschu (On Glasgow Streets) 476
200   Madainn Diar-Daoin, ann an Oifis Puist an Glaschu (Thursday Morning, in
       a Glasgow Post Office) 478
201   Na h-Iongnan (The Nails) 480

202   A' Ghaidhealtachd (The Highlands) 480
203   Pioghaid (Magpie) 482
204   Deireadh an t-Saoghail (The End of the World) 482
205   Teagamh (Doubt)..484
206   from Gormshuil (Gormshuil/Blue-Eye)..................................484
207   from Meall Garbh 486
208   Seanairean (Grandparents) 488
209   from An t-Anam-Fàis (The Vegetative Soul) 490
210   Ròidean Rwanda (The Rwanda Roads) 490

UILLEAM NÈILL (WILLIAM NEILL) 1922—
211   from Sealg Ulaidh (Treasure Hunt) 492
212   Plus ça change 492
213   Aghaidh ri Aghaidh (Face to Face) 494
214   Sealltainn thar Chluaidh (Looking over Clyde) 494
215   Cumha Bhaltair Cinneide 1450–1508 (In Memory of Walter
      Kennedy 1450–1508) 496
216   Stuth Toirmisgte (Contraband) 496

CALUM DÒMHNALLACH (MALCOLM MACDONALD) 1922—
217   Gu Dé Thachair dha m' Thìr? (What's Happened to my Land?) 498

TORCUIL MACRATH, 1923—
218   Cead Deireannach Àirnis (Last Farewell to Arnish) 498
219   Cor na Tìr (The Country's State) 502

NEIL B MACKINNON (NIALL B MACFHIONGHUIN) 1925—
220   A' Chlach Ionmhainn (The Dear Stone) 502

CATRÌONA NICDHÒMHNAILL (CATHERINE MACDONALD) 1925—
221   Cum Sinn Dlùth (Hold Us Close) 504
222   An t-Aoibhneas a tha staigh sa Chridhe (The Joy that is inside the Heart) 506

DOMHNALL AONGHAIS BHÀIN (DONALD MACDONALD) 1926—
223   Am Faoilteach (January) from Mìosan na Bliadhna (The Months of the Year) ..508
224   Moladh Mnathan-Eiridinn Ospadal an Rathaig Mhóir, Inbhir Nis (In Praise
      of the Nurses of Raigmore Hospital, Inverness) 510
225   A' Mhaighdeann Chriadhadh (The Doll) 512

TORMOD CALUM DÒMHNALLACH (NORMAN MALCOLM MACDONALD) 1927—
226   Eathar Angaidh (Angie's Boat) 512

IAIN MAC A' GHOBHAINN (IAIN CRICHTON SMITH) 1928–98
227   Tha thu air aigeann m' inntinn (You are at the bottom of my mind) 514
228   Aig a' Chladh (At the Cemetery) 516
229   An Litir Àraid (The Strange Letter) 516
230   An t-Òban (Oban) 518
231   Na Seanfhacail (The Proverbs) 520
232   Coinnichidh sinn (We will meet) 520
233   Mas e Ghàidhlig an cànan (If Gaelic is the language) 520

234   *Innsidh mi dhut mar a thachair* (I'll tell you how it happened) 524
235   *A' Ghaoth* (The Wind) 526
236   *Aig an Doras* (At the Door) 528
237   *An TV* (The TV) 528
238   *Na h-Eilthirich* (The Emigrants) 530
239   *Dealachadh* (Parting) 532

MÀIRI NICDHÒMHNAILL (MÀIRI MACDONALD)
240   *Ghrad-leum cù-geàrd a h-inntinn* (The watchdog of her mind) 532

CAIRSTÌONA ANNA NICAOIDH (CHRISTINA A MACKAY) 1928—
241   *An t-Earrach* (Spring) 534

GARBHAN MACAOIDH (GIRVAN MCKAY) 1929—
242   *Bealltainn ann am Fàcland* (Maytime in the Falklands) 534

ANTHONY DILWORTH, 1929—
243   from *Successa Petronia* 536

VICTOR PRICE, 1930—
244   *An déidh aimhreit* (After a struggle) 538

AN T-OLL. DÒMHNALL MACAMHLAIGH (PROF. DONALD MACAULAY) 1930—
245   *Rabhd Eudochais* (Cry of Despair) 540
246   *A' Cheiste* (Question) 540
247   *Do Fhear-Sgrìobhaidh Ainmeil* (To a Famous Writer) 542
248   *Féin-Fhìreantachd* (Selfrighteousness) 542
249   *A' Ghiblinn troimh thrì Sùilean* (April through three Eyes) 544
250   *Soisgeul 1955* (Gospel 1955) 544

DONNCHADH MACLEÒID (DUNCAN MACLEOD) 1934—
251   *Samhla* (Illustration) 546

IAIN MOIREACH (JOHN MURRAY) 1938—
252   *Ar n-Airgead 's ar n-Òr* (Our Silver and our Gold) .548
253   *An t-Acras* (Hunger) 552

TORMOD MACGILL-EAIN (NORMAN MACLEAN) 1938—
254   *Maol Donn* (MacCrimmon's Sweetheart) 554

AONGHAS MACNEACAIL, 1942—
255   from *sireadh bradain sicir* (seeking wise salmon) 560
256   from *an cathadh mór* (the great snowbattle) 562
257   *teist* (testimony) 566
258   *acras* (hunger) 566
259   *an eilid bhàn* (the white hind) 568
260   *dàn bealltainn* (beltane poem) 570
261   *samhla* (appearance) 574
262   *marilyn monroe* 576
263   *fòrladh dhachaigh* (home vacation) 578

264   from *Sgàthach* 578
265   from *An Turas Sìos gu Tìr nam Marbh*
        (The Journey Down to the Land of the Dead) 580

CALUM GREUM (CALUM GRAHAM) 1942—
266   *Daoine bha an Leódhas uaireigin* (Lewis Heroes) .584

TORMOD CAIMBEUL (NORMAN CAMPBELL) 1942—
267   *Mi Fhìn agus a' Revolution agus mo Bhata-Darach* (Me and the Revolution
        and my Oaken Stick) 584

DOMHNALL IAIN MACÌOMHAIR (DONALD JOHN MACIVER) 1942—
268   *Mathanas* (Forgiveness) 592
269   *Indira* 594
270   *Cladh* (Graveyard) 596
271   *Dàin* (Poems) 598

MAOILIOS M CAIMBEUL (MYLES M CAMPBELL) 1944—
272   *Dòchas* (Hope) 598
273   *Do Chròcus air a Shlighe a Nèamh* (To a Crocus on its Way to Heaven) 600
274   *An Referendum air son Pàrlamaid ann an Alba 1/3/79* (The Referendum
        for a Scottish Assembly 1/3/79) 602
275   *An t-Aran* (Bread) 604
276   *Na Liopan* (The Lips) 604
277   *An t-Eilean 'na Bhaile* (The Island a Town) 606
278   *An Clamhan* (The Buzzard) 608
279   *Am Fear-Turais* (The Tourist) 608
280   *Glaschu* (Glasgow) 608
281   *Borgh Leódhais* (Borve, Lewis) 610
282   *Gealach na Sultain* (September Moon) 610
283   from *Haiku* 612
284   *A' Càradh an Rathaid* (Mending the Road) 612
285   *Ceartas Coma a' Bhàis* (The Indifference of Death) 614
286   *An Éibhleag* (The Ember) 616
287   from *Agus mar sin car a' Mhuiltein* (And so Somersault) 616

IAIN MACDHÒMHNAILL (IAN MACDONALD) 1946—
288   *Hearach* (Harrisman) 616
289   *Turas* (Once) 618
290   *An t-Uisge* (The Rain) 620
291   *Ainmeannan* (Names) 620

CATRÌONA NICGUMARAID (CATRIONA MONTGOMERY) 1947—
292   *Gealladh Gaoil* (The Promise of Love) 622
293   *Sireadh* (Seeking) 622
294   *An Ceusadh* (The Crucifixion) 624

FEARGHAS MACFHIONNLAIGH, 1948—
295   *An Geiréiniam* (The Geranium) 624
296   *Medusa, an Cuclopach, 's an Daily Record*

    (Medusa, the Cyclops, and the *Daily Record*) 626
297 *An Tuagh* (The Axe) 628
298 *Flùrannan* (Flowers) 630
299 from *A' Mheanbhchuileag* (The Midge) 632
300 from *Iolair, Brù-Dhearg, Giuthas* (Eagle, Robin, Pine) 638
301 from *Bogha-Frois san Oidhche* (Rainbow in the Night) 640

DÒMHNALL GREUMACH (DONALD GRAHAM) 1949—
302 *Superloo Steòrnabhaigh* (The Stornoway Superloo) 648

MÒRAG NICGUMARAID (MORAG MONTGOMERY) 1950—
303 *Uaireannan tha eagal orm* (Sometimes I'm afraid) 650
304 *Geamhradh* (Winter) 650
305 *Coilleag ghlan gheal chadalach* (Pure white sleepy cockle) 650
306 *Dùisgidh mi aon mhadainn* (I'll wake up one morning) 650
307 *An t-Amadan* (The Fool) 652
308 *Muilemhàgag* (Toad) 654

DONNCHADH MACLABHRAINN (DUNCAN MACLAREN) 1950—
309 *Clydebank* 654

JULIAN RONAY, 1951—
310 *Bi air t' Fhaiceall* (Be Careful) 656
311 from *A' Dràibheadh ann an Ameireaga* (Driving in America) 656
312 *Féin-Mhort, Lunnainn a-Deas* (Suicide, South London) 658

CRÌSDEAN WHYTE (CHRISTOPHER WHYTE) 1952—
313 *Ro-dh'aithnich mi* (I foresaw) 658
314 *Thug thu cead dhomh* (You gave me permission) 662
315 *Fontana Maggiore* 662
316 *An Daolag Shìonach* (The Chinese Beetle) 666
317 Two sections of *Bho Leabhar-Latha Maria Malibran* (From the Diary of
    Maria Malibran) 668

AONGHAS PÀDRAIG CAIMBEUL (ANGUS PETER CAMPBELL) 1954—
318 *Ràdar Beinn Sheaval* (The Radar of Beinn Sheaval) 672
319 *Gearraidh na Mònadh á Smeircleit* (Garrynamonie from Smerclate) ...674
320 *Oidhche Chullaig* (Hogmanay Night) 674
321 *Farpais Réidio nan Gaidheal* (The Gaelic Radio Quiz) 676

MÀIRI NICGUMARAID (MARY MONTGOMERY) 1955—
322 *Sgillinn leis nach Ceannaichear Càil* (A Penny that Buys Nothing) .678
323 *Do Dhol-a-Mach* (Your Carry-On) 678
324 *Soraidh Leibh* (Farewell) 680

MEG BATEMAN, 1959—
325 *Dealbh mo Mhàthar* (Picture of my Mother) 682
326 *Do Sgoilear Àraidh* (To a Certain Academic) 682
327 *Ceist* (Question) 684
328 *Cìocharan* (Breastling) 684

329 *Ath-Chruthachadh* (Transformation) 684
330 *Cuireadh dhan Bheatha* (Invitation to Life) 686
331 from *Do Fhear-Pòsta* (To a Married Man) 686

RODY GORMAN, 1960—
332 *Air Bàs Charles Bukowski* (On the Death of Charles Bukowski) 688
333 *Ìomhaighean* (Images) 688
334 *Ubhal* (An Apple) 690
335 *Deich Bliadhna* (Ten Years) 690
336 *Leumadair Bungee* (Bungee Jumper) 692
337 *Rodeo* 692
338 *Gnìomhair is Cuspair* (Verb and Subject) 692
339 *An Oidhch' Ud* (That Night) 694

PEADAR MORGAN, 1960—
340 *Dùn Dà Làmh* 694
341 *Coinneal* (Candle) 696
342 *Trafaig Oidhche* (Night Traffic) 696

DÒMHNALL ROTHACH (DONALD MUNRO) 1962—
343 *Madainn Sneachda* (Snowy Morning) 696

CAILEIN MACFHIONGHAIN (COLIN MACKINNON) 1963—
344 *Cothrom Peanais* (Penalty) 698

ALASDAIR BARDEN, 1963–98
345 *An Teaghlach Sìonach* (The Chinese Family) 700

DÒMHNALL UILLEAM STIÙBHART, 1967—
346 *Bù tu mo mhuir gun stiùireadh* (You my unsteerable sea) 700
347 *Latha Eadar-Dhà-Shian* (A Day Between Two Storms) 702

ANNA FRATER (ANNE FRATER) 1967—
348 *Aon Phòg* (One Kiss) 702
349 *Clann a-Màireach* (Tomorrow's Children) 704
350 *Bill* 704
351 *Ceist* (Question) 706

Notes to the Poems 708
Cùl-Cinn / Background 709
General Bibliography 820
The Bardic Crown 821
Index to Poems 823

Roimh-Ràdha

Chan eil e furasta ceartas a dhèanamh do cheud bliadhna de bhàrdachd. Chan eil an-seo ach taghadh; bhiodh taghadh diofraichte aig duine sam bith eile a thogadh an dùbhlan. Tha de bheairteas ann nan robh mi a' tòiseachadh as ùr 's gum faodainn cruinneachadh a dhèanamh de 351 dàn eile a bhiodh a-cheart cho math sa h-uile dòigh.

Dh'fhiach mi ri dàin a thaghadh a sheasadh a-mach gu math ann an clò fuar 's a bhruidhneadh gu sònraichte mun fhicheadamh linn seach mu chùisean neo-thìmeil mar ghràdh, nàdar, bòidhchead, bàs. Se sin as coireach mar eisimpleir gu bheil Dòmhnall Ailean Dhòmhnaill na Bainich air a riochdachadh le 'Ceud Fàilt' air gach Gleann' seach 'Gruagach Òg an Fhuilt Bhàin' air a bheil muinntir Uibhist cho eòlach. Gu bith ann an leabhar mar seo feumaidh 'greim' a bhith aig bàrdachd gun a bhith idir an eisimeil a' chiùil. Tha greim 'Ceud Fàilt' air gach Gleann' anns na chanas am bàrd mu dheidhinn fhéin 's mu dheidhinn chàich 's e a' fàs suas mu àm a' Chiad Chogaidh. Se an aon adhbhar seo as coireach gu bheil bàird ann a tha air leth measail aig an t-sluagh ach nach d'fhuair a-staigh dhan duanaire seo — leithid Uilleim Dhòmhnaill 'ic Coinnich, Bàrd Chnoc Chusbaig, ged a tha mi làn tuigsinn gur ann taobh bhos 1900 a rinn e a' chuid mhór dhe na h-òrain aige. Chan eil mi a' faireachdainn gun rachadh gu math leotha mar bhàrdachd lom, agus dh'fhailicheadh orm Beurla shnasail a chur orra. Dh'fhiach mi corrag a chur air òrain bu ghlan a thigeadh Beurla riutha, leithid 'An Ataireachd Àrd' agus 'An Cùlaibh Éirinn'. Bha greis as déidh dhomh 'An Ataireachd Àrd' eadar-theangachadh mun d'fhuair mi a-mach gur ann mar bhàrdachd lom a rugadh e, 's gur e duin' eile — 's cha bu Leódhasach e! — a rinn òran dheth.

Tha mi an dòchas gu bheil rudeigin ri ionnsachadh bho *An Tuil* mu eachdraidh an fhicheadamh linn. Tha eachdraidh ri lorg an dà chuid sna dàin agus ann am beathannan nam bàrd. Seall mar eisimpleir cor na dùthcha eadar an dà Chogadh: mar thill saighdearan (an fheadhainn a bha beò) bho na trainnsichean, mar gheibheadh iad cosnadh bhon Mhorair Leverhulme, mar a chaidh na sgeimichean aigesan mu làr, mar thug móran òigridh Canada orra, mar a bh' aig càch an uair sin ri obair a ghabhail far am faigheadh iad i. Bha buaidh aige sin uile air cruth na Gaidhealtachd — 'bàs baile', mar th' aig aon bhàrd, Iain MacLeòid.

Bàrdachd a tha math seasaidh i leatha fhéin. Ach cha dèan cron beagan ionnsachadh mun duine 's mun tachartas air a cùl. Uairean nuair tha fios dhen t-seòrsa sin agad théid bàrdachd mhath 'na bàrdachd mhór. Sann mar siud a tha 'A' Cheist' aig Seumas MacLeòid, a tha s dòcha 'na dhàn gaoil cho math 's a rinneadh an Gàidhlig air feadh an fhicheadamh linn, 'Dàin do Eimhir' ann neo ás. Ach bidh a bheachd fhéin aig gach leughadair.

Tha iomadh seòrsa bàrdachd san leabhar eadar aoirean, laoidhean, moladh dùthcha 's an t-uabhas eile. Ach aon seòrsa nach do lorg mi rùm ceart air a shon se bàrdachd cloinne. Gun teagamh tha pìosan aig Aonghas Moireasdan 's Iain Peatarson aig a bheil nàdar na bàrdachd cloinne, 's tha bàird eile an-seo leithid Dhòmhnaill Éirisgich 's Iain Mhic a' Ghobhainn a rinn iomadh rann math cloinne 'nan ré. Ach tha cunntas fhathast ri dhèanamh air bàrdachd cloinne, 's nuair a nithear sin tha mi an dòchas gum bi urram air a thoirt do *Rannan Éibhinn Cloinne* le 'Màiri Tàilleir' 's do na rannan aig Eibhrig NicLeòid á Beàrnaraigh na Hearadh.

> Mach 's a-steach don Phanamà, dé bha siud sa ghaoith?
> Gunna mór a' breabadaich 's a' sabaid ris an Rìgh,
> Hu hu hi ar ó, hu hu hi ar ì,
> Mach 's a-steach don Phanamà, siud na chunnaic mì . . .

Mur bàrdachd i seo aig Eibhrig chan eil fhios agamsa dé th' ann bàrdachd.

Raghnall MacilleDhuibh, Baile nam Puball, 21 Dàmhair 1999

Foreword

When Cairns Craig asked me in 1986 to write about Gaelic poetry in the twentieth century — 'everyone except Sorley' — for his forthcoming *History of Scottish Literature*, he supplied a provisional list of chapters. It was full of imaginative-sounding titles. 'Cabbage and Turnips — The Kailyard Poets.' Things like that. Ever anxious to oblige, I called mine 'Thunder, Renaissance and Flowers: Gaelic Poetry in the Twentieth Century'.

When the volume was published I found to my dismay that nobody else had followed Cairns's lead. The Kailyard Poets came out as 'The Kailyard'. As a friend pointed out when I ruefully told him what had happened, I was the only one in fancy dress at the party.

Despite my embarrassment the chapter was well received, and another idea began to take root. I had found it difficult to present Gaelic literature properly to a non-Gaelic readership without extensive quotation. Why not do an anthology to illustrate the chapter?

That was the genesis of *An Tuil*. My first criterion for selecting items was simply that they were mentioned in 'Thunder, Renaissance . . .' My next was that poems by Sorley MacLean had to be added. Then I brought the selection up to date to complete the century. Finally I added some more for the sake of balance. Or because I liked them. In the end, 'Thunder . . .' has had to be roughly doubled in size in order to serve as the Introduction.

When biographies started to come in, poets took over from poems. The biographies found their own length. I soon realised I was receiving the kind of information that might well be unobtainable in another few years, and I began positively to encourage it. Fortunately at the same time my wife Máire developed a passion for genealogical research. She spent many long days in New Register House and other resource centres. The result is that, taken together with the poems, the 'Background' section serves as an ethnological record of the experience of the Gael in the twentieth century. I hope it will encourage students to research the lives of other poets, writers, singers and so on in the same way. If only someone had done this at the end of the seventeenth, eighteenth, nineteenth centuries!

I am profoundly grateful to everyone who provided information, gave permission to reproduce poems, or helped me with translations. They are individually thanked in the appropriate places. I would also like to thank Mary Beith, Jean Cooper, Angus Dickson, Anja Gunderloch, Catherine Johnson, Bill Lawson, Allan MacDonald, Ian MacDonald, Dr John MacInnes, Wilson McLeod, Ivor Normand, Tim Rideout, Laura Sugg, and the staffs of the National Library of Scotland, Edinburgh University Library, Edinburgh Central Library, New Register House and the Scottish Genealogical Society.

Special thanks must also go to John Campbell, Castlebay, for first setting me on the path that led to this; to Professor Derick Thomson, for inspiring me with a love of Gaelic poetry, editing *Gairm* (my most important source) and dispatching me to the Islands in the 1960s with books to sell, so enabling me to meet many of the poets in this book; to Professor William Gillies, for asking me in 1980 to teach Twentieth Century Poetry and recommending me to Cairns Craig; to my Honours students over all the years since then, in particular the class of 1996 whom I asked to visualise this book (I'm sorry I wasn't able to take up all their excellent suggestions); and to Máire, not only for her research but for her love, patience, support, commonsense — and typesetting. Finally my thanks are due to Polygon, especially in the form of Marion Sinclair (a relative of the poet Donald Sinclair) and her successor Alison Bowden, both of whom showed unwavering commitment to the project, never blanching on any of the occasions when I confessed it had got still bigger.

Ronald Black, Peebles, 21 October 1999

Introduction

The twentieth century in Gaelic verse may be conveniently summarised according to its four quarters, all offering variations on the theme of tradition and innovation. The first was ushered in by the 'parnassian spring' of *Carmina Gadelica*, an idyll smashed by the realism of the First World War. This realism is at its best in the poems of Dòmhnall Ruadh Chorùna. The second was dominated by the Second World War and the economic and political events that led to it; its outstanding products were the poems of Donald Macintyre, Sorley MacLean and George Campbell Hay. Each of these poets stands at a different point in the spectrum of tradition and innovation.

The third quarter brought a thirst for new beginnings. Dominated by Derick Thomson, it threw up a great deal of satire and witnessed a battle royal for the soul of Gaelic, sometimes bad-tempered, often witty. By the end of the third quarter it is possible, with the benefit of hindsight, to see tradition and innovation coming close together, even in poets as different as Iain Crichton Smith and Donald John MacDonald. Finally, the innovators of the third quarter became the traditionalists of the fourth, as they discovered that a new generation of poets, including more learners of Gaelic than ever before, appeared to have little interest in capturing the traditional soul of Gaelic, and were forging out in quite independent directions for themselves.

Probably the most important event in the history of Gaelic poetry in the twentieth century was the publication in 1943 of MacLean's *Dàin do Eimhir*. It can be described as the third great landmark of Gaelic publishing, the first two being John Carswell's translation of Knox's liturgy in 1567 (the first book to be printed in the Gaelic of either Scotland or Ireland) and the *Aiseirigh* of 1751, by which the redoubtable Alexander MacDonald (*Alastair mac Mhaighstir Alastair*, c.1698–c.1770) became the first Gaelic poet to publish his work.

Dàin do Eimhir was little known until after the war, however, and was in any case in advance of its time. Hay's *Fuaran Sléibh* of 1947 was hailed as the most important volume of Gaelic poetry for a century and a half, Hay himself as the best Gaelic poet since mac Mhaighstir Alastair.[1] A great deal of what was published during the first half of the century was not very good, and a great deal of what was very good was not yet published. This was to change in 1952 with the founding of the all-Gaelic quarterly *Gairm*, and it is fascinating to reflect that before that *annus mirabilis* was out *Gairm* had already published Thomson's gently disturbing picture of 'Na Cailleachan' (poem 186), Smith's existentialist 'Tha thu air aigeann m' inntinn' (poem 227), and 'Ròs na Cluaine' ('The Rose of the Field') by Anthony Dilworth, q.v.:

Grian cheathach cùl na beinne	Misty sun behind the mountain
'Cur san t-sneachda tuar an teine —	Casts gleam of fire upon the snow —
Se mo thàladh.	It's my temptation.
Dithist lòn fo ghorm adhar	Twin pools rest under azure sky
'Dian-bhoillsgeadh anns a' mhachair	Gleaming brightly in the plain —
Se as àille.	It's what's most lovely.
Mìn-ròs chùbhraidh anns a' chluain,	A smooth rose fragrant in the field,
Dealt 'na bile,	Dew in her leaf,
Mi ga òl is i 'na suain —	I drink it while she lies asleep —
Mèirleach mise.[2]	I am a thief.

An archaic keynote had been struck in 1900 by the appearance of the traditional incantations that made up Alexander Carmichael's *Carmina Gadelica*, followed in 1909 by the first volume of Marjory Kennedy-Fraser's *Songs of the Hebrides* (see p. 721). I present a piece from *Carmina* at the start of my anthology (poem 2) in order to acknowledge Carmichael's creative role in polishing these gems of antiquity, and in order to indicate the source of the first discernible trend of twentieth-century Gaelic verse, a trend that is echoed in the work of Kenneth Macleod (poem 15), Duncan Johnston (poem 40) and Donald Sinclair (poem 43). From Johnston a line of poetic descent can also be traced to George Campbell Hay. The trend may be called romanticism. Its influence would probably have been much greater had the First World War not crushed it so brutally, but it can still be detected as late as 1938 in the unfortunate (and misleading) title chosen for the poems of Roderick Mackay (q.v.), *Oiteagan á Tìr nan Òg* ('Breezes from the Land of the Young'), and in that same year Sorley MacLean identified its exponents as the most prominent figures in the Gaelic poetry of the century so far.

> Such Gaelic verse as is being now produced I consider very insignificant. I have already indicated my opinion that the fine talent of Kenneth Macleod was dissipated in the fogs of Celtic Twilight, a purely foreign non-Celtic development. As far as I know the only poet of consequence in the 20th century was the late Donald Sinclair, whose talent again was outwith the main stream of Gaelic poetry.[3]

The whole point is I think effectively (if accidentally) underlined by the editors of a servicemen's pocket anthology of spiritual verse, *A' Chruit Òir* (1919), through their inclusion in it of no less than five prayers from *Carmina*, all attributed not to folklore or to tradition but to Alexander Carmichael in person, with grateful thanks to his widow.[4]

For the people of the Highlands and Islands the real beginning of the twentieth century did not come until 1919 in any case. Successive censuses recorded a catastrophic fall in the Gaelic-speaking population of Scotland from 210,000 in 1891 to 65,000 in 1991, but the fall between 1911 and 1921 was far bigger than the usual decennial drop of 10,000 or so. Between those years the decline was from 184,000 to 149,000, a loss of 35,000 speakers. The Education Act (Scotland) of 1872 had swept away a modest structure of Gaelic-medium schools and imposed a much larger system of universal English-medium primary education (see poem 194), while the Crofting Act of 1886 had provided the Gaelic-speaking people with something resembling a constitution, under which they might dwell in peace and earn a living — or rather half a living — from the land. These measures took a generation to make a difference, but in 1914 the slow wheel of history had begun to turn faster. Huge numbers of young men from the Highlands and Islands were swept into the War, partly for their skills as seamen, partly by the atavistic attraction of the Highland regiments, partly because the militia system had given many of them their only chance to carry a gun or spend a while away from home (poems 52, 76; pp. 734, 742, 747). A privilege suddenly became a duty, and the island of Lewis, in particular, "is said to have lost proportionately more lives in the First World War than any other community in the British Empire. From a population of 29,500, 6,700 young men joined the forces (22.7%) and 1,151 died (17% of the recruits)."[5]

As if this were not enough, the steamship *Iolaire* went down on 1 January 1919 in the approach to Stornoway harbour with the loss of over 200 returning servicemen, drowned within sight of their homes after surviving Armageddon.[6] Our poem 168 is one of many reactions in verse to this disaster. Few Lewis poets of the twentieth century failed to touch upon it in one way or another, and it is still as real to the people of Lewis as on the day it happened.

There followed a loss of collective confidence throughout Gaelic Scotland, compounded by disappointment over hopes of more land being released for crofting. Those who returned brought materialistic attitudes and a first-hand knowledge of English. This marks the beginning of real linguistic and cultural decline in what was now the Gaelic heartland, the Western Isles. Celtic performance rituals came to an end, such as parading around the houses in animal skins to bring in the New Year (cf. poem 320), or playing shinty on winter holidays (poem 25). In many places football took the place of shinty (poem 344). In another generation even the transmission of oral knowledge weakened to breaking point. By now there was no such thing as Gaelic society: a knowledge of Gaelic could not be taken for granted among all people at all levels in a given community. This had linguistic and literary consequences. Vocabulary changed rapidly,[7] upper registers disappeared, and language acquisition by outsiders became unnecessary and artificial, the only obligation felt being upon insiders to learn English. In such an atmosphere the novel was an unrealistic and unusual genre, and verse and short stories carried the whole burden of literary creativity.[8]

The final stage in the process is reached in the child born c.2000, who may have no Gaelic at all, or, following educational developments, a 'school' Gaelic distinct from that of its parents. Such a child has replaced vertical genealogical links to the past with horizontal electronic links to the present, and has also lost that *third* dimension which John Lorne Campbell defined as the 'ever-present sense of the reality and existence of the other world of spiritual and psychic experience'.[9]

With the exception of MacLaren's of Glasgow, entrepreneurial Gaelic publishing collapsed after the First World War. Throughout the first four decades of the century the collections of Gaelic verse that received the lion's share of public attention were those which harked back to the nineteenth century and beyond, such as Sinton's *Poetry of Badenoch* (1906), *The MacDonald Collection* (1911), Calder's edition of Donnchadh Bàn (1912), John N Macleod's *Bàrdachd Leódhais* (1916), W J Watson's *Bàrdachd Ghàidhlig* (1918), *The Poems of Alexander MacDonald* (1924), Cameron's *Tiree Bards* (1932), John Lorne Campbell's *Highland Songs of the '45* (1933), J Carmichael Watson's *Gaelic Songs of Mary MacLeod* (1934), *Ewen MacLachlan's Gaelic Verse* (1937), Calder's edition of William Ross (1937), W J Watson's *Scottish Verse from the Book of the Dean of Lismore* (1937), MacColl's *Clàrsach nam Beann* (1937), Matheson's *Songs of John MacCodrum* (1938), and Neil Ross's *Heroic Poems from the Book of the Dean of Lismore* (1939). All this was in addition to the volumes of *Carmina Gadelica* which appeared in 1900, 1928, 1940 and 1941, and of *The Songs of the Hebrides*, which appeared in 1909, 1917, 1921 and 1929.

It was all songs and scholarship, and beside it contemporary poetry had very little impact, despite the efforts of An Comunn Gaidhealach as an organisation, of Hector MacDougall (in particular) as an editor of contemporary verse, and of those like Donald MacCallum and Thomas MacDonald who published their own work. MacLean and Hay were seen about 1950 as the last gleam of the Gaelic sky,[10] and it seemed that Gaelic verse was all past and no future, so what happened after 1952 stands out the more as deserving the title of renaissance.

Throughout the first half of the century An Comunn Gaidhealach — founded in 1891 to run an annual festival called the Mod — made prodigious efforts, enthusiastically supported by a cadre of individuals, to nurture Gaelic verse, and in 1923 their president Angus Robertson (q.v.) amalgamated their poetry competitions into a single contest for a Bardic Crown (see p. 821). The overall aim was twofold: to rehearse and preserve the riches of Gaelic vocabulary and idiom, and to search for a new medium that could be as faithful to the needs and rhythms of Gaelic as free verse was to those of English. Items from the first half of the century whose roots are in activism of this kind include poems 3–5, 8, 10–13, 14, and 16–18; one (13) is in free verse. And it is in this context that we may view the curious little prose-poems that appeared from time to time in the pages of An Comunn Gaidhealach's monthly magazine *An Gaidheal*. Here is one example:

Oidhche bha siud bha m' anam an sàs anns a' bhoglaich agus gun rian agam air subhachas a
thoirt do mo chridhe. Chunna mi gu tric an iomall na h-uarach àilleagan nan sùilean gorma a
thréig mi. Bha i 'na seasamh air bilean uaine na bruaiche faisg air Réidhlean an Teampaill, agus
bha a sùil gu màirnealach air a' chuan. Bha i air a sgeadachadh ann an gùn de shìoda na
Gailbhinn agus bha crios òir ga teannachadh. Bha gaoth fhuaraidh an taibh a' sìomanaich mu a
casan beaga, rùisgte, ach ged bu nimheil a' ghaoth mhothaich mi gun robh a gnùis ciùin mar an
driùchd. Ged bu bheag a pearsa, bu mhór a cridhe: ged bu bheag a sùil, bu bhlàth a lainnir: ged
bu bheag a bial, bu mhilis a pòg. Fhreagair an fhaoileag beucail na mara; fhreagair an damh mac-
alla nam beann; ach tha ainnir nan sùilean gorma fhathast a' feitheamh ri marcach ciamhair nan
tonn a sheòl air falbh thar bàirlinn barrgheal gu tìr a' chruidh-bhainne.[11]

("That night my soul was stuck in the bog and I could not summon any cheer to my heart. I often
saw upon the outside edge of the moment the blue-eyed beauty whom I had forsaken. She was
standing on the green margin of the slope hard by the Temple Sward, gazing fixedly at the ocean.
She was dressed in a gown of Galway silk with a golden belt around her waist. The cold wind of
the sea swirled around her small, naked feet, but although the wind was sharp I noticed that her
expression was as calm as the dew. Though small was her person, big was her heart: though small
was her eye, warm was her radiance; though small was her mouth, sweet was her kiss. The
seagull answered the roar of the sea; the stag answered the echo of the mountains; but the blue-
eyed maiden still awaits the weary rider of the waves who sailed away over white-crested billow
to the land of the milk cows.")

There are traces here of the language of traditional tales and of *Carmina Gadelica*, but if we
were to break the sentences into short lines we would have something approximating to free
verse. It is curious how similar this is to Myles Campbell's 'Agus mar sin car a' Mhuiltein'
(poem 287) of half a century later. Nor is the style very far from Robertson's extraordinary
prose in his novel *An t-Ogha Mór*.

A possible line of descent for such pieces is suggested by the item which won one of the
two main literary prizes at the Rothesay Mod in 1908. The larger prize ($\pounds$3.3s), for the best
elegy on the Rev. Dr Robert Blair, was won by Duncan MacNiven, q.v. The smaller prize
($\pounds$2) was for a poem on any subject not exceeding 100 lines, and was won by Donald
Macdonald (*Dòmhnall Chràisgein*, 1861–1916), blacksmith at Barvas in Lewis, with a
curious effort called 'Pòsadh Eoghainn ri Iseabail' ('Ewen's Marriage to Isabel'). Described
as an òran ('song'), it consists of five stanzas of eight long lines alternating with five prose
passages of between 100 and 200 words. It may be that it reflects a continuing Gaelic
tradition of alternating prose and verse going back through burlesque like 'Croit an
Droighinn' to the *crosanachd* of Scotland and the *crosántacht* of Ireland.[12]

Turning to verse made by soldiers who served in the trenches and by songmakers steeped
in tradition, we meet the unselfconscious verse of the real world, whose purpose was to
communicate. Poets who fought in the First World War include the Lewismen John Munro
(poems 68–70) and Murdo Murray (poem 71), and, from Uist, Dòmhnall Ruadh Chorùna
(poems 46–54), Donald Macintyre (poems 58, 63) and Peter Morrison (poem 67). Munro
fell on 16 April 1918 after three-and-a-half years at the front, leaving his thoughts on his
fallen comrades in tortured free verse full of reminiscence-of-rhyme; forty more years were
to pass before free verse became widespread in Gaelic. However, Dòmhnall Ruadh
Chorùna is the outstanding Gaelic poet of the trenches. His best-known song, 'An Eala
Bhàn' ('The White Swan'), was produced there for home consumption, but in a remarkable
series of ten other compositions he describes what it looked, felt, sounded and even smelt
like to march up to the front (poem 46), to lie awake on the eve of battle (47), to go over the
top (48), to be gassed (49), to wear a mask (50), to be surrounded by the dead and dying
remains of Gaelic-speaking comrades (51), and so on. Others of his compositions contain
scenes of deer-hunting, a symbolically traditional pursuit of which he happened to be
passionately fond, and which he continued to praise all his life. At its best his versification
is controlled yet fresh, for unlike most of his contemporaries he knew the virtues of brevity

and variety. He lived to express his horror of weapons of mass destruction in 'Òran an H-Bomb' (poem 53), which stands in contrast to the gung-hoism with which a younger poet, Malcolm Nicolson, celebrated Hiroshima and threatened the 'atomic' on Molotov (poem 77).

Among the traditional songmakers represented in An Tuil from the first half of the century — some of whom survived well into the second — are Catherine Macfadyen from Tiree (poem 1), Alexander Cameron from Gairloch in Wester Ross (poem 6), Archibald Macintyre from Lochfyneside (poem 7), John Campbell, Donald Allan MacDonald and Michael MacPherson from South Uist (poems 9, 94, 96), Roderick Mackay from North Uist (poems 19–20), the brothers Charles and Duncan MacNiven from Islay (poems 21–3 and 35–6), Duncan Finlayson and John Nicolson from Skye (poems 72, 83–5), and Joan MacKenzie from Harris (poem 75). These are outstanding poets from a variety of locations, but they are far from unique for their time; a hundred others were just as good, though in some cases less fortunate in being recorded or published. Despite the heroic efforts of the School of Scottish Studies, of the BBC, and of countless individual scholars and enthusiasts like the late John MacMillan (Iain Sgobaidh), the Rev. Fr John Angus Macdonald and Tom McKean, this part of our literature has been slipping away from us — witness, to give two small examples from these pages, the loss of the songs of Iain Campbell, S. Uist (p. 717), and of Malcolm MacKinnon, Barra (p. 736). Typically, one poet's next-of-kin reported to me in July 1999 that a television crew was on its way to Lewis and then on to Canada to make a film of the great man's life, and that she wished she had paid more attention to him when he was alive. Given the perishing of the oral tradition and the poor state of Gaelic education, it has been impossible to keep up with the rate of loss; it is to be hoped that the electronic media, especially, can now keep up with what remains, and that surviving manuscripts of Gaelic songs and poems are preserved, no matter how poor their condition. Ideally, they should be copied by libraries or passed into their care. There must be no more burnings of the type which Donald Macintyre nearly inflicted, and which other poets like Hector MacKinnon, Angus MacKinnon and Sorley MacLean really did inflict, on all or part of their work.

Satire is a particular concern. Only now, with a slow return to codes of tolerance scarcely experienced in the Highlands since the eighteenth century, are the deep roots and subtle conventions of traditional satire beginning to be understood through systematic study of the scatology of Alastair mac Mhaighstir Alastair, a master of the art. Great flights of twentieth-century verse satire are still remembered and savoured, and I have been buttonholed with some prime examples, but getting them recorded and into print is another matter. In fact, it is probably right to place on record here that two good examples of the genre (poems 81 and 95) were denounced to me by a relative of the poets in question as 'this coarse piece' and 'a trifling parody' respectively.

At the request of John Nicolson (q.v.), Tom McKean withheld from publication a 'humorously scathing' satire on a local character of his youth.[13] When his mother discovered her son's talent, Dòmhnall Ruadh Chorùna promised her never to make satires, a promise which he kept. As is pointed out at p. 714, Alexander Cameron was careful to avoid satire, studiously avoiding the controversial path trodden by his neighbour Duncan Mackenzie. Mary Maclean (q.v.) says,

> Soon after I wrote my first poem [about age 12] I wrote another about some potatoes that got stolen in the village. To this day it remains unpublished. I recited it to my family but they got very nervous and said such a poem should never pass beyond our walls.[14]

And Kenneth MacLeod from Bayble (Coinneach Ruadh Choinnich Ruaidh, 'Red', 1899–1977) concluded a song on a reckless sailing expedition to Lochs:

> Cha téid mi gu ur moladh — sann a choisinn sibh ur càineadh,
> Ged tha sinn uile toilichte ur faighinn dhachaigh sàbhailt';
> 'S mur b'e dhòmhs' na choisneadh e ur n-eachdraidh thoirt an àirde,
> Dheigheadh e don phàipear gus an leught' e anns gach ceàrnaidh.[15]

("I'll not try to praise you — you deserve to be criticised, / Though we're all delighted that you've got home in safety; / And if it weren't for what I'd suffer for bringing up your story, / It would go into the paper to be read in every district.")

Having thus despaired of securing even one sustained piece of character assassination with a less obvious target than Hitler or Mussolini (poems 58, 72), it was with great delight that I discovered on opening *Bàrdachd Dhòmhnaill Alasdair* that not only was the pre-Christian tradition of Gaelic satire — satire so strong that it could bring out boils on a man's face, or kill him — still alive at the beginning of the twentieth century, but that it was still alive at the end, though admittedly the poet (who comes from Garrabost in Point, Lewis) was now 80 years of age.[16] His primeval ire was directed at my fellow *Scotsman* writer Tom Morton — 'Columnist of the Year', no less, in the 1994 Bank of Scotland Press Awards — who had claimed in the paper on 4 May 1994 that Gaelic had no future, lacked modern relevance, and depended for its culture on 'one or two sorrowing poets and an endless grim howl of lamenting singers, all chundering on endlessly about the Clearances to audiences crying whisky tears by the bottleful'.[17] Dòmhnall Alasdair's response came a little late for entry to the parlour, but I hereby admit it to the porch.

> Tha Tòmas 'na sgrìobhaiche ainmeil,
>   Tha 'ainm san *Albannach* tric;
> Ge bith cia ás a bha sheanmhair,
>   Chan eil a shearmon mun chànan sa glic.
>
> Am bruidhinn am bodach ar cànan?
>   An cual' e ar dàin nach eil gann?
> Ma chuala, s cinnteach g' eil nàr air —
>   Dlieil a chluas cho tàireil ri cheann?
>
> S lìonmhor nàimhdean na Gàidhlig,
>   Gu h-àraidh an tìr nam beann,
> Fir brathaidh sa h-uile ceàrnan,
>   'S tràillean mar Tòmas le pheann.
>
> Ged a choisneadh e 'n duais as àirde
>   Agus moladh bho chàirdean gu léir,
> Mar neoni e 'n sùilean a' bhàird sa —
>   Mar Iùdas grànda, gun spéis.
>
> San uaigh bidh Tòmas a' cnàmh
>   'S mallachd nan àl 'na dhéidh,
> Ach bidh Gaidhil a' seinn sa Ghàidhlig —
>   Ri gàgail Thòmais chan éist.
>
> S iomadh cat a rinn oirre tàire,
>   Eadar piseagan gràineil is tòmais,
> Ach bidh Gàidhlig beò a's an àite
>   Fada 'n déidh bàs nan dòlais.[18]

> Tom is a famous writer,
>   His name's in *The Scotsman* a lot;
> Wherever his grandmother came from,
>   His sermon is not worth a jot.
>
> Does this fellow speak our language?
>   Has he heard our abundant verse?
> If so, he must be embarrassed —
>   Is his ear as bad as his head?
>
> Gaelic has many enemies,
>   Not least in the land of the bens,
> With traitors in every corner
>   And hacks like Tom with his pen.
>
> Who cares if he won the top prize
>   And unanimous praise from his friends?
> In the eyes of this poet he's nothing —
>   Like vile Judas, with no respect.
>
> In the grave our Tom will be rotting
>   While the curse of generations torments him,
> But Gaels will be singing in Gaelic —
>   To Tom's babble they'll pay no attention.
>
> Many a cat has insulted it,
>   Ugly kittens as well as toms,
> But Gaelic will still be spoken
>   When the devils are long dead and gone.

That is in the tradition of the Rev. Donald MacCallum (1849–1929). MacCallum, from Craignish in Argyll, was a Church of Scotland minister who had made his name in the nineteenth century as an orator in the cause of land reform and the defence of the people.

Sorley MacLean called him 'not much of a poet', but I am not so sure.[19] He is the most brilliant exponent of anti-landlordism in Gaelic verse. His principal achievement is 'Domhnullan', a poem of 1,670 lines arranged in four cantos. It tells how young Domhnullan ('Donnie') takes the King's shilling and leaves his heart in the care of his sweetheart Catriona. While he is becoming a hero in the trenches, a vision of his death is seen at home in Innis-Bhrògaig. Catriona buries his heart at the foot of *Craobh a' Gheallaidh*, 'the Tree of Promise', and marries another. When Donnie comes home from the War, Catriona assumes that he is a ghost come to collect the heart, and tells him where it is. When he retrieves it, it is broken.

Donnie becomes a drover, and is not very good at it, so he consults the idol Mammon. Mammon laughs fit to burst at his tale, and tells him that if he leaves his heart with him he will do well. Heartless once again, Domhnullan succeeds beyond his dreams in the world of business, and becomes:

SIR DOMHNULL, TRIATH-NAM-BINNEAN

SIR DONALD, LAIRD-OF-THE-PINNACLES

Nuair chruthaicheadh an cruinne-cé chaidh crò
Dha fhéin a chur a-mach san astar ghorm
Gu ruith a réis, is crìochan air nach bìodh
Aig rionnag còir bhith briseadh steach gu sìor
Mar sin gu bith, mar Thighearn' Tìr; nuair dh'éibh
A Mhóralachd, an Rìgh, an curaidh treun,
Mu'm bheil mo dhuan, bha oighreachd air thoirt dhà,
Gu saor, 's do shliochd 'na dhéidh gu latha bràth;
Le còir bhith gairm air Cabhalaich an Rìgh,
Is armachd, fòs, o reubaltaich g'a dhìon
'Na bhaidealan; oir feuch! o iomairt dhòbh
Na dròbhaireachd, nach tug e fhéin dà shoitheach mhòr,
An *Dràgon* 's a' *Maclàmhaich*, 'chuir a-sìos
Gu grunnd a' chuain na dh'éirich ann an slìgh
An dìth-mhilleadh gu cath; 's b'e 'n titil àrd,
'Na chruthachadh a bhuilicht' air an t-sàr:
"Sir Domhnull, Triath-nam-Binnean", 's chum 's gum bìodh
Mo laochan, mar ri bodaich mhór na tìr'
'Na iodhal-adhraidh aig an t-sluagh, is tùis
An cràbhaidh dha gum bi 'na fhàile cùbhr'
Ag éirigh suas, a Mhóralachd an Rìgh
Thug àithn' do sheanachaidh, air seiche laoigh,
Bhiodh oibrichte le coslas fìor sheann aois,
Don Triath, ùr-chruthaichte, bhith cur air dòigh
Seann sinnsearachd, 'nan uabhas bheireadh glòir
D'a ainm; 's a thogadh e gu cathair àrd
Nan Uachdaran gu dèanamh leis mar b' àill
Is, O! 'nan reachdarachd, an olcas gnìomh,
Na b' oillt á Iuthairne cha b' urrainn bhith.

On creation of the universe, a special place
Was set apart for him out in the blue expanse
To run his race, with bounds which other stars
Would have no right forever to invade
At any time, as Lord of Land; and when
His Majesty the King proclaimed the knight
Of whom I sing, in freedom an estate
Was given him and his heirs in perpetuity;
With right to call upon the Royal Navy
And his army too, from rebels to defend him
In his battlements; for see! from droving's
Shady deals he took two vessels of some size,
The *Dragon* and *Sea-Devil*, which despatched
Down to the sea-bed anything that challenged them
To battle and destruction; and his title was
A new creation specially for him:
"Sir Donald, Laird-of-Pinnacles", and to make of him,
My warrior, with all the great men of the land,
An idol worshipped by the people, and make sure
The incense of their piety for him in fragrance
Rises up, His Majesty the King
Commands a wise man to devise an ancient
Pedigree on calfskin worked with all the marks
Of genuine antiquity for him, the new-
Created Lord, whose awfulness would glorify
His name; and raise him to the stately throne
Of Landlords so that he could do with it
Whate'er he liked, and O! in arbitrary rule and evil deed
From Hell itself comes nothing more disgusting.

Donnie's money has been made in the States, which suggests that there is a little bit in him of Andrew Carnegie (1835–1919), although one might have thought that a more obvious model was Sir James Matheson (1796–1878), proprietor of Lewis, who had made his money in Hong Kong from the Chinese opium trade. Anyway, Donnie finds no happiness in his wealth, and for his depression and insomnia three physicians are consulted. One prescribes medicine, one travel, one hunting and feasting. None of these work, but while being ignored by his guests at a feast, he has a vision of his long-dead comrade from the trenches, Gilleasbaig Bàn, who advises him to go to Mammon and get his heart back. This Donnie does, and when 'all his riches have melted in his generosity like snow' he and his friend Calum Beag buy a fishing-boat with what is left. He lives out the rest of his life in happiness, and God, having repaired the crack in his heart, keeps it next to His own.

Although an old man's poem, 'Domhnullan' has verve, humour, variety, lyric power, and great philosophical integrity.[20]

In 1921 Thomas Donald MacDonald (1864–1937), from Appin in Argyll, published a 458-line poem called 'An Déidh a' Chogaidh' ('After the War').[21] It begins impressively.

An ainm na sìth, dhomh crathadh de d' làimh,
Dùrachdan math 'nar cridhe a ghnàth;
Dèanamaid eadhoin a' ghuidhe do'r nàmh
    Sonas is àgh is rèite.
Is càirdean sinn uile gu léir 's is caoin
Ma chumar a' chòir, oir chan eil aon
Lagh no crìoch a' dealachadh dhaoin'
    San t-saogh'l os ceann nan speuran.

In the name of peace, let me shake your hand,
With goodwill forever in our hearts;
Let us wish even our enemy
    Comfort and joy and accord.
We're all kin to each other, and friends
If justice is done, for no law
Or boundary separates men
    In the world above the skies.

Cinnidhean 's rìoghachdan air bheag céill,
Iad uile a' strìth an aghaidh a-chéil',
Gan tabhairt 'nan ìobairtean gu léir —
    Biodh tàmh air an streup gun tròcair!
Luingeas neo-sgàthach, an cuirear oirr' feum,
No bàta-fo-uisg' a' tabhairt a beum,
A' sgriosadh nan neo-chiontach 'na ceum?
    Cha bhi iad an nèamh nan sòlas.

Tribes and kingdoms of little sense
All competing against each other,
Being presented as sacrifices —
    Let their merciless fighting cease!
Fearless fleet, will it be needed,
Or submarine with her knockout blow,
Destroying the innocents in her path?
    They'll not be in the heaven of joys.

Bha airm ann an uidheam, gunnachan-mòr'
Ri sgrios agus milleadh, gun aithn' air a' chòir,
Carbadan-adhair ri fair' anns na neòil
    Ré nam bliadhnachan cràidhteach, dòbhaidh!
Aonadh nam Fineachan, an tig e gu buil?
No 'n toir e gu crìch an dòrtadh air fuil?
An do thuig sinn an leasan a thàinig mar thuil
    A smàladh 's a sgiùrsadh an domhain?

Armies in uniform, field artillery
Wreaking destruction, not heeding what's right,
Aeroplanes on watch in the sky
    Through those painful, terrible years!
The League of Nations, will it come to fruition?
Or will it bring to an end the spilling of blood?
Did we grasp the lesson that came as a flood
    Choking and scourging the world?

MacDonald goes on to make his political stance clear. It is not that of MacCallum, whom he probably regarded as subversive. He says, *Tha eadhoin a' Ghàidhlig ga dèanamh 'na cleòc / Gu craobh-sgaoladh air creideamh 'tha sgiùrsail.* "Even Gaelic's made into a cloak / For broadcasting a sinister creed." And he footnotes the first of these two lines in one word: *Boilsibheachd.* 'Bolshevism.'

What activity he is referring to I am not sure. It may have been the very prolific writings of MacCallum, it may have been the teachings of John Maclean, Bolshevik consul in Glasgow; it may be that, in places like Glasgow, some of the Socialist and Communist Sunday Schools of which Angus Morrison speaks in poem 13 (see p. 720) were conducted in Gaelic. He goes on to blame *rag-mhuinealachd Shasainn* ('English intransigence') for the dreadful situation in Ireland, and to speak eloquently of those who profit from war. This brings him back to the use of new military technology such as submarines and aeroplanes, and to his belief that the popularity of Marxism/Leninism is due to these frightening changes in warfare.

Thaobh cuid diubh ris a' chreideamh sgiùrsail
    A rinn an Ruis 'na dìol-déirce,
Léirsinn chumh'nn gan dèanamh brùideil,
    Mì-rùn 's amharas 'gineadh feirge.

Some of them took to the sinister creed
    That has made of Russia a beggar,
Narrow philosophy making them brutish,
    Ill-will and suspicion begetting wrath.

But, he says, he wants to learn from these experiences. He starts with the Highlands.

Tha iarratas air còirichean	There's a demand for justice
A dhìoladh dhaibhs' tha còmhla rinn,	To be done to those who're with us,
'S gum biodh am fonn air son nan sonn	And for land fit for heroes
Air òrdachadh mar 's còir da bhith.	To be provided as is proper.

Tha acraichean air fàsachadh	There are acres of desert
Far 'm b' àbh'st am pòr bhith gràinneachadh,	Where grain used to ripen,
Gu luachrach bog, gach dìg 'na lod,	Of rushes and bog, each ditch waterlogged,
Is aonarachd sna làraichean . . .	While dwellings stand forsaken . . .

Tha 'n fhàistneachd mu shaoghal ùr fhath'st	The prophecy of a new world remains
Gun choilionadh, 's mì-shuaimhneas ann;	Unfulfilled, instead there's discontent;
An tìr fo bhròn le gainnead lòn	The country's depressed by shortage of food
Is ceistean mòr' gun fhuasgladh ann.	And big questions remain unresolved.

Finally he discusses Turkey, Greece, Germany, Russia and Ireland, while desperately superimposing the images of peace over those of war.

Ceileireadh san speur os cionn a' bhlàir,	Birdsong in the sky above the field,
Thairis air sgrios na còmhraig ghairbh,	Over the débris of violent strife,
Thar an àit' 'san cluinnear guth a' bhàis.	Over the place where the voice of death is heard.
Tha eun an gorm nan neòil á sealladh —	A bird's out of sight in the blue of the skies —
Thar chobhanan aingidh nan diathan céin	Over wicked covens of alien gods
Tha esan a' seinn a ghaol d'a chéil'.	He sings his love of his mate.

MacDonald thus produced a long poem, rooted in the Highlands, which looked beyond the mountains to survey the condition of humanity in other countries, and was glued together by passages of lyric power. This idea was to be taken up in 'An Cuilithionn' (poem 128) by Sorley MacLean, with whom, it has been claimed, 'Gaelic poetry in one step moves triumphantly into the contemporary world'.[22]

MacLean was born in 1911 in Raasay. His people had included poets and pipers for four generations, and were immersed in history and storytelling. On his mother's side it was said that they had lost their land because of their loyalty to Prince Charles; his grandfather had taken part in the disturbances in the Braes in 1882, while his grandfather's uncle acted as spokesman for the people, much as MacCallum had done when minister of Waternish in 1884–7. His great-grandfather was the only one of his family who had not been evicted to Canada or Australia during the Raasay clearance of 1852–4, and two of his paternal uncles had been friends and fellow-workers of John Maclean, whom MacLean once described as 'the last word in honesty and courage . . . a terrific man'.[23]

From 1929 to 1933 MacLean attended Edinburgh University, where he took a first class Honours degree in English, sitting at the feet of Professor Herbert Grierson, the rediscoverer of John Donne and the other metaphysical poets. This made a great impression, as did the politics of the day. Communism was the norm among the students, the Nationalists of the day tending to be romantics and Catholics in the mould of Donald Sinclair, q.v. Most Highland students preferred to put their trust in the ideals of the Land League and of John Maclean's Scottish Socialist Republic. This radicalism can be seen clearly in poems 113, 122, 123 and 128.

From 1934 to 1940 he taught in Portree, Tobermory, Edinburgh and Hawick. As a MacLean, he did not enjoy his year in Tobermory.

I remember going about on a bicycle and asking a postman somewhere near Ulva Ferry, "Is it a Mull man lives on that farm?" meaning a man of genuine Mull stock, "or this one, or that one?" He said, "No." And then asking him, "Can you think of any farm in the north of Mull (there were no crofters then) at which there is a Mull name?" And he said, "No."[24]

He volunteered for the Army on the first day of the War in 1939, but was not deployed on active service until 1941 (see poem 111). He was badly wounded at El Alamein in 1943, and the introduction to *Dàin do Eimhir* speaks for itself:

> Meanwhile Somhairle had gone to Egypt, where he was blown up at El Alamein, and I myself was cast into prison by the British authorities, where I was not permitted to correct proofs . . . The purpose of this note is to show the vicissitudes of the publication. Douglas Young, May 1943.

Dàin do Eimhir [*DE*] was little known until after the war, and has never been understood by the many Gaelic-speakers who do not wish to understand it. Those with a more open cast of mind were struck down by it one by one with an experience that can only be likened to religious conversion. Dr John MacInnes has rightly written that we all remember exactly where we were on first opening the book.[25] In my own case it was in John Smith's bookshop; I was a Glasgow schoolboy with a smattering of Gaelic but a romantic taste in literature, and I found William Crosbie's surrealist illustrations so repulsive that the book dropped out of my hand. When I became a student the poems were explained to me, and I came to respect the illustrations greatly as of a piece with the verse. By contrast, the late Rev. Donald N MacDonald of the Iona Community, a churchman in the MacCallum mould, who found the book in the Celtic Class Library of Glasgow University, felt like a man fired at with both barrels and sat reading it over and over for a week.[26]

For a third gut reaction we may turn to a review of *Dàin do Eimhir* written early in 1944 by another Established Church clergyman, Malcolm Macleod (1881–1946), a native of Uig in Lewis who was minister of Balquhidder in Perthshire and editor of *An Gaidheal*. Macleod's regular reviews of (and comments on) Gaelic verse suggest that he had a pedagogic taste in literature, which made him a dangerous reviewer of *Dàin do Eimhir*. But he sensed its importance.

> The marrow and true spirit of poetry are in the book. Profundity of thought and lyricism, genuine feeling and lucid imagination — the strands that make up poetry that lives and will last — are here; and these strands are woven together so smoothly and so attractively that no-one alive will imagine that they consist of anything other than one extraordinary force. And the poet Maclean uses language that matches the pith and substance of the verse — Gaelic that is fresh, strong, supple. It's a relief to us that he does not rely merely on the pleasant sound of words without the food and fuel of poetry behind them. We are indebted to him for this; for some of the Highland poets rely on the pleasant sound of words, without there being much substance behind them. But no-one who understands great poetry, and the best and choicest of Gaelic, will accuse Maclean of that.

He goes on to praise the internationalism and universality of the verse, quoting with approval quatrains about Lenin's patience and his wrath[27] and Europe's anguish 'from the Slave Ship to the slavery of the masses' (poem 98). Turning to the question of love he says, very justifiably:

> The poems addressed to Eimhir are as if to a beautiful woman — perhaps to his sweetheart — or to the muses. No matter, they suit them both. There are no less than 60 songs to lovely Eimhir, both large and small; and there are 26 'Other Poems' in the book. These poems are on many subjects, such as Highland Woman — on the toil and sufferings of the Highland female — a song that is true, and incisive. One on Calvary, one on The Tree of Strings — for George Campbell Hay — one on The Island, one on The Heron, one on The Head of Loch Eynort, and one on Glen Eyre, and another on The Woods of Raasay. I spent some time the other afternoon in the woods of Raasay and I cannot recall having a more pleasant afternoon for many a year.

Hay gets a mention because he had been a lively contributor to *An Gaidheal* in the years before the War. Macleod quotes our poem 122 as an example of satire *cho làidir agus cho leamh 's a bha i aig na seann bhàird Ghaidhealach*, 'as strong and impudent as was practised by the old Highland poets', and goes on:

> There is another on 'The Road to the Isles', and I would wish that every semi-Gael in the Lowlands and in the Highlands would read it. The satires are as satire should be, true and sharp and impudent. There is one quatrain in the book about which we are very sorry that it was ever printed. It reflects no credit upon the poet, or upon anyone else connected with the book, that it was printed.

What could it be that had so upset the minister of Balquhidder? My first thought on reading this was of poem 126 (MacLean's satire on the author of *The Road to the Isles*, who was Macleod's Established Church colleague and a distinguished literary figure). But Macleod has gone far out of his way to praise that poem. My second was of 'Bana-Ghaidheal', its strident anticlericalism and its address to Christ as 'great Jew / Who art called the One Son of God' (poem 113), but Macleod has been careful to commend it highly. My next was of how Eimhir is preferred to Christ in stanzas such as:

<table>
<tr><td>Cha do chuir de bhuaireadh riamh
No thrioblaid dhian 'nam chré
Allaban Chrìosda air an talamh
No muillionan nan speur.</td><td>Never has such turmoil
Nor vehement trouble been put in my flesh
By Christ's suffering on the earth
Or by the millions of the skies. (*DE* 12, 97)</td></tr>
</table>

Blasphemy? But this is in the very poem praised by Macleod for its reference to Lenin. Surely, by the same token, the objection could hardly be to praise of John Maclean the Bolshevik. Could it then be to the mocking of some *political* hero of Macleod's? But the Chamberlain satire (poem 124) has only three lines, and anyway Macleod has singled out the satires for approval. What then does MacLean say about women? Surely Macleod was not being prudish about a quatrain mentioning

<table>
<tr><td>Na seann siùrsaichean beaga breòite
A chunnaic Baudelaire 'na ònrachd. (*DE* 65)</td><td>The little old decrepit prostitutes
Whom Baudelaire saw in his loneliness.</td></tr>
</table>

After all, this is in 'The Tree of Strings' which he seemed to like. But the word *breòite* brought to my mind those disturbing references to an abused female body which tend to appear in the unpublished poems (see p. xxxiii below). Do they surface in the book? There are small hints of them in 'Coilltean Ratharsair' (*DE* 76–82), but again, Macleod singled out this poem for praise. Finally I hit upon it. What Macleod objected to so strenuously was not a quatrain about abortion but one about the place where every young man would like to be, one which earned its place in *An Tuil* as a delightful little lyric (poem 115).

Macleod's words serve as a reminder, then, of how the climate in which Gaelic literature operates has changed back and forth. In his formal adjudication of the literary competitions at the 1908 Mod, in a category which he called 'Unfortunate choice of subject', the Rev. George Calder wrote:

> A poem on Jus primæ noctis — a custom which is said to have been the origin of, as it was superseded by, mulierum mercheta, or marriage casualty — however well handled, cannot at this time of day escape the charge of bad taste. The poem may be good in everything — except the subject, which refuses to be dealt with artistically.[28]

Ten years later Professor Watson wrote in his anthology that 'the tone of modern [i.e. *post* 1600] Gaelic poetry is clean and virile . . . the total amount of Gaelic poetry unfit *virginibus puerisque* is so small that we are left with a strong sense of the clean-mindedness and good taste of its composers . . .' And he underlined his point by silently omitting from the seventeenth-century poem 'Tuirseach dhùinne ri port' a stanza with an obscenity in it.[29] Poem 115 is in fact extremely tame compared to a great deal of what Alastair mac Mhaighstir Alastair published in 1751; in 1971 John Lorne Campbell wrote that the only line of mac Mhaighstir Alastair's likely now to give offence was *Hotentots bhreuna*, 'stinking Hottentots',[30] but it is only in the first decade of the twenty-first century that we can expect to see his scatological poems reprinted with English translation.[31]

The illustrations in *Dàin do Eimhir* made as great an impact on Malcolm Macleod as they did upon me.

There are ten pictures in the book drawn by William Crosbie, I suppose in order to explain some of the poet's thoughts. When I first opened the book and viewed them the words of the Psalmist came to my mind:

Tha an t-eòlas so ro iongantach,	This knowledge is too wonderful,
'S ormsa tha e cruaidh;	It's difficult for me;
Cha ruig mi air, oir tha e àrd	I can't attain it, for it's high
R'a thuigsinn is r'a luaidh.	To understand and speak.

I remember when I was a lad a tinker came to the village. He had a terrier and the terrier would be chasing everyone he saw, and barking at the top of his voice. *Cuir*, said one of the old men to the tinker, *rian air do chù*. "Put your dog in order." *Tha*, said the tinker, *an cù 'na rian fhéin*. "The dog is in his own order." I deduce that that is how the pictures are — *'nan rian fhéin*, in their own order. The book is well printed, and pleasant to handle. It is published by William MacLellan, 240 Hope Street in Glasgow, and sold at 10/6. We hope that Gaelic-speakers will buy the book and get acquainted with modern Gaelic poetry at the height of its powers.[32]

Three months later, in the section of *An Gaidheal* set apart for the youth movement Comunn na h-Òigridh, Hector MacDougall reported on a letter that had come in from the Rev. Malcolm MacLean, Conon (1895–1961). "Our friend feels, children, that you should get to know his kinsman Sorley Maclean's book, about which the Editor wrote in *An Gaidheal* after it came out." The Rev. Malcolm enclosed a friendly but rather allusive poem of congratulation in five stanzas, entitled 'Dàin do Eimhir', of which these are the first two.

Fhir dhuinn a thug am munadh ort	Brown-haired lad who set off up the slope
'S a chunnaic mise tràth,	And whom I've known of old,
Bu dìreach rinn thu 'm mullach dheth	You've made it straight up to the summit
Gun buil a thoirt bho chàch;	And done it on your own;
Is thug thu dhachaigh ulaidh leat	And what a treasure you've brought back
Gu ullachadh nam bàrd:	To enrich the bardic trade:
Tha sitheann agus ceòl againn	We've got venison and music
O leòn a rinn an gràdh.	From a wound that love has made.
Té bhuidhe thuirt thu, Shomhairle,	A golden-haired girl you said, Sam,
Té chomharraicht', 's i bàn,	An outstanding girl, who's blonde,
Té ghuanach, uasal, fhoghainteach,	A fine, fun-loving, upright girl,
'S na dh'fhoghainn dhuit 'na dàil;	With every quality you sought;
Cha choma — ach s math chothaich thu	Good — but how well you've striven
Ri reothairt is muir-tràigh:	Against spring-tide and low tide:
Rinn t' inntinn fuachd is reodhadh dhuinn	Your mind's turned frost and cold for us
'Nan gabhail sheòid is dhàn.[33]	To treasure-trove of jewels and poems.

Which brings us to Eimhir. Is this one girl? Or two? Or even three? As a symbol of the deep-rooted, Irish-rooted, non-Christian tradition of the Gaelic language and its literature, she is the wife of the stunted hero Cù Chulainn. As a real woman she is, apparently, an amalgam of two, and these two are distinguished with particular clarity in poem 116: a red-haired Scottish girl and a fair-haired Irish girl. In a sense these women's identity is unimportant; they were a catalyst — as long as MacLean had a face in his mind's eye, he could make poetry for it out of the gifts he possessed. But as the verse contains specific references to the two relationships (e.g. poems 111, 116), it will be helpful to say something about them here, based on an interview given by the poet to Colin Nicholson in 1986. Wrote Nicholson:

> For a year or two in the early thirties he loved a woman he had first met at the beginning of the decade. Then, in August 1937, he met an Irish woman to whom he was irresistibly drawn, but to whom he could never make any kind of advances. The difficulty lay in the fact that MacLean was under the mistaken impression that one of his greatest friends, who was responsible for the poet first meeting the woman in question, wanted to marry her himself. Under such circumstances, MacLean saw no choice but to hold off.

The identity of the first of these women has become a matter of oral tradition. The fairest thing to say is that it is in dispute. The second was the Irish scholar Nessa Ní Sheaghdha (1916–93), who visited the National Library of Scotland in 1937 to begin work on texts to be published by the School of Celtic Studies of the Dublin Institute for Advanced Studies as *Leabhair ó Láimhsgríbhnibh*. As Mrs Nessa Doran, she was still a woman of unusual beauty and dignity of bearing when I met her in the Royal Irish Academy in 1970, and when she died the first eight lines of our poem 100 were cited in her obituary in the School's newsletter to exemplify the impression that she made on the poet.[34] Nicholson continues:

> The Irish woman got married in December 1939; nor did she marry MacLean's friend. It transpired that there had never been any question of that marriage taking place. In that same December, MacLean was led to believe that the woman he had loved much earlier for a year or two, had suffered a very great disability in consequence. Also in that fateful December, the wife of MacLean's brother John began her last illness. She was to die in January, 1940. "Her last illness coincided with me finding out about this terrible misfortune of this other woman; and the point is that I was so touched by the revelation that this woman had made to me, about her own condition, that I became madly devoted." There began a black and wretched melancholy. References in several of the poems about this time to a woman's wounded and mutilated body are to be taken literally. "I was wrong about this, too, but I had no way at all, as far as I can see, of finding out, because between one thing and another, I saw her only once between December 1939 and late July or early August 1941."[35]

Such, then, are the elements that formed MacLean's poetry: a strong and radical traditional background; the intellectual stimulation of Edinburgh; the cataclysmic political events of the time; love; and, I would argue, innovative trends within Gaelic literature set in motion by An Comunn Gaidhealach, Donald MacCallum and Thomas MacDonald. It is tempting to suggest, as Iain Crichton Smith has done, that an outpouring of poetry was inevitable, but these elements, even love, were merely the firework waiting to be lit. The combustible elements in the match may be defined using terms got by MacLean himself from William Ross, a great Gaelic love poet of the past: *an aigne thorrach* ('creative intellect'); *an iargain* ('passion').

Dàin do Eimhir is in three parts — the 'Poems to Eimhir' themselves, the 'Other Poems' and the 'Satires'. Seemingly the poet composed 61 'poems to Eimhir', of which 49 are in the book, and three more have been published since. MacLean's work as a whole may be conveniently divided into five parts: the 61 'Poems to Eimhir', 1930–40; the 31 'Other Poems' and 'Satires', 1930–40; the long poem 'An Cuilithionn', 1939 (poem 128); the war poems, 1940–5 (about 26 in number, with our poem 127 probably the outstanding item); and the post-war poems, 1945–96 (about 25 in number, represented here by poem 133). This body of work offered a yardstick with which, for the first time, Gaelic tradition could be compared with that of the outside world. If MacLean looks to Gaelic poets of the sixteenth and seventeenth centuries like Murchadh Mór mac 'ic Mhurchaidh for his substance, he looks to Murchadh's contemporary John Donne for his philosophy. For example, the exquisite lines *Air dara tobhta 'n fhuaraidh / Shuidh thu, luaidh, 'nam chòir / Agus do ròp laist cuailein / Mu m' chrìdh 'na shuaineadh òir* (poem 106) echo Murchadh's words

Air bharraibh nan stuagh	On the tips of the waves
Cur daraich 'na luas	Sending oak timbers speeding
'S buill-tharraing nan dual 'nan dòrn.[36]	With plaited halyards in their fists.

But the poet's pleasure at having his loved one in his boat is such that with Donne's help the plaited halyards join his heart to her golden hair. Similarly, for every mention of Pàdraig Mór MacCrimmon there is one of Beethoven; for every mention of William Ross there is one of Baudelaire; for every mention of MacCallum and the Glendale Martyrs there is one of Julian Cornford; for every mention of Christ there is one of Lenin; and so on. Out of the rich vocabulary of the early poetry, the terse but passionate eloquence of popular song, and the subtle abstractions of Presbyterian religious terminology, MacLean had created a new and exciting instrument of poetic expression.

He may perhaps be said to have three major topics, and three more which do not surface so often. The major topics are: politics and the world's conscience (e.g. poems 98, 124); literature, tradition and the making of poetry (e.g. 99, 114); and eternity (e.g. 103, 112).[37] The minor topics are: the conflict between love and reason (e.g. 97, 105, 131); wit and the soul (e.g. 101); and the lyric, or the pleasure that comes of being in love (e.g. 106, or 108, which has a sting in the tail worthy of Heine himself, or 118). But the shape of the poems is unendingly fluid, dynamic, changing. The poet constantly returns to some point made earlier, picks it up and carries it in a different direction (e.g. 104). The examples I have given here are central with regard to subject-matter, but many poems (e.g. 102, 107, 116) offer a synthesis of themes, and indeed there are those which may be regarded as central to a particular synthesis (e.g. 115).

Unity is given to the poetry by the passion of love and the Spanish Civil War. The poems are full of symbols and paradoxes. The face is the symbol used over and over for the presence of his love (poems 107, 109, 117, 119); the poems are like horses, *eachraidh fhiadhaich bhàrd* ('a wild cavalry for bards', *DE* 31, 99), constantly running. It is no surprise that MacLean once wrote, "Symbolism . . . is the most impressive 'ism' that I know of in this century."[38] Iain Crichton Smith summed up MacLean's contribution like this:

I would say that he taught us how to speak out clearly and passionately (though most of us haven't done this as well as he has); that he taught us how necessary it is to fuse the new with the old; that he taught us deep feeling rather than cleverness; that he taught us to transcend parochialism (in the same way as Macdiarmid taught Scottish, non-Gaelic poets); that he taught us that one can at the same time be both musical and intelligent; and, above all, that he taught us how to make it new without losing the resonance of the language and its essential genius. He has, I think, also taught us that poetry is not an affair of the will, that it requires luck (however agonising). He has taught us the virtues of authenticity.[39]

It is an important analysis, which raises some fundamental questions about MacLean himself, the generation that followed him, and the generation after that. Did MacLean himself always avoid cleverness? I think not. However, it is noticeable that when the seminal passions of the 1930s and 1940s left him, and he was faced with practising cleverness as an alternative, he fell silent. Did the generation after him learn these lessons? Yes. MacLean inspired a great flowering of Gaelic writing after the war, and items like our poem 293 are full of echoes of his work for all the best of reasons. But are these lessons known to the newest generation of Gaelic poets? Yes and no: there are problems, or issues, with regard to the resonance of the language and its essential genius, as I will show later (p. lxiv).

MacLean's poetry, like Thomas MacDonald's, radiates from the Highlands to take in the entire world, and in this respect he was representative of his generation. For the twentieth-century Highlander, place of origin was one thing, place of residence might well be another. Such men's knowledge of the world, through war, migration, or a life on the high seas, was considerable. This simple set of statistics, gleaned in 1934 from telephone directories, tells its own story.[40]

	Vancouver	Glasgow
Camerons	105	150
Campbells	249	271
MacDonalds	347	210

Our poets' biographies reveal some of the realities behind the worldwide quest for jobs and prosperity. Murdo Macleod (poem 39) saw the world as a merchant seaman, fell victim to drink, and was left injured in a foreign port without a penny. Angus MacKinnon (poems 41–2) emigrated to Canada in 1908 to work variously as docker, deep-sea fisherman, track-layer for the Canadian Pacific Railway, and warehouseman; in Vancouver he received a permanent injury from a falling log, and experienced the religious conversion which led to his returning home to become a minister. Hector MacKinnon (poems 44–5) had a similarly life-altering experience when his ship was sunk by enemy action in the Dardanelles. Donald Macintyre (poems 56–65) saw action as a piper at the Battle of Loos and lived for many years in Paisley, from which he is often referred to as *Dòmhnall Ruadh Phàislig* or just *Bàrd Phàislig*. A bricklayer, he might equally be called the 'Red Clydesider' of Gaelic. Angus Campbell ('Am Bocsair'), George Morrison, 'the Brieve' (poem 93), and Donald Grant (poem 79) all lived many years in Glasgow. Morrison and Grant became headmasters, while Campbell worked as a nurse: 'Caithris nam Bodach' (poem 95), perhaps his most interesting piece of work, was composed at Hawkhead Asylum, now Leverndale Hospital.

Murdo MacFarlane (poem 76) returned to Melbost in Lewis from the prairies of Manitoba, as he put it himself, 'nearly as poor as I left, but a little wiser'.[41] He went on to gain a reputation as 'the Cole Porter of Gaeldom' from his ability to set his material to original airs;[42] the label does little justice to his formidable intellect, and the fresh wind of his imagination barks through his songs. Roderick MacLeod from Harris, a merchant seaman, composed one of the truly great sea songs of the Second World War, 'An Cùlaibh Éirinn' (poem 80), and died tragically on board ship in 1965. Ian Paterson from Berneray, Harris (poems 162–6), nearly lost his life at sea in the Second World War, became a teacher in Fife, and went on to live in Edinburgh. Angus Campbell ('Am Puilean', poems 81–2) and Donald John MacDonald (poems 171–5) were prisoners of war. Calum I N MacLeod (poem 135) emigrated to Nova Scotia to work in Gaelic education there; in addition to his own output he collected and published much of the Gaelic poetry of the province, past and present. Of poets born in Nova Scotia, the most significant is the lighthouse-keeper Angus Y MacLellan, who began to lay the foundations of a creative Cape Breton Gaelic literature in both prose and verse (poems 31–3).

The life of Norman Malcolm Macdonald (poem 226) followed a reverse pattern from that of Calum MacLeod. Born at Thunder Bay on the shores of Lake Superior, he was brought home by his parents to the security of their native island during the Great Depression; he spent time in New Zealand, but eventually settled down in Lewis to immerse himself in literature and scrape a living as a playwright. Iain Archie MacAskill emigrated from Berneray, Harris, to farm in Western Australia, where his nostalgia gained colouring from storms, drought and aborigines (poem 74). Western Australia also became the home of Hugh Laing from South Uist, who made Gaelic versions of material from various languages, one of which is our poem 66. MacAskill and Laing both lie today in Karrakatta Cemetery in Perth. Most remarkable of all, perhaps, was Duncan Livingstone, a stonemason from Mull who emigrated to South Africa immediately after the Boer War (poems 24–30). A deeply read man, he experimented with free verse and other forms, and in a series of mould-breaking works, notably poem 28, savaged the imperialistic ethos and surveyed its legacy throughout the world (compare poem 12). On 21 March 1960, at Sharpeville near Johannesburg, the South African police fired into a crowd demonstrating against the apartheid state's notorious 'pass laws', killing 69 and injuring 186. Livingstone put the spine-chilling words of a black woman mourning her husband who had been killed by the police (poem 29) into a very traditional Gaelic verse-form to warn his readers of the dangers of racism. A deeply religious man, he recognised apartheid at work in Christ's birth in a stable.[43] Well over 100 of his earlier poems lie in a manuscript in Cape Town, while his later ones are scattered through journals published in South Africa, Scotland and Canada.

It is but a short step from Livingstone to George Campbell Hay (poems 140–161). For thirty years our judgement of Hay's work was based almost entirely on his collections *Fuaran Sléibh* (1947) and *O na Ceithir Àirdean* (1952, dedicated to MacLean). For many, including MacLean, that judgement was of a brilliant virtuoso: one who loved ideas well, but words more. However, when 'Mochtàr is Dùghall' (poem 144) appeared in 1982 the judgement had to be reversed. Africa had made the difference.

Hay grew up in Kintyre hearing English, Scots and Gaelic, and came to make translations into Gaelic from French, Greek, Welsh, Irish, Arabic and Italian. Thanks to a linguist's ear, a phenomenal memory and a deep reading of the literatures of many periods, his verse is invested with rich lexical and metrical music, and an uncanny instinct for the right word; only occasionally, in the way that learners are apt to do, does he push a word beyond the bounds of normal usage, e.g. *ag osnaich luchd nan linn a' fàs*, 'sighing its burden of centuries ever increasing', where he makes an intransitive verb transitive.[44]

Hay's nationalist verse (e.g. poem 143) is a cry for unity of purpose, straight from the heart, unsullied by ideology, and of a piece with its time. Its intention is to inspire, just as Hay himself, many years an exile, was inspired by the thought of how 'when the Prince's army reached the soil of England after fording the river, they turned round, every man unsheathed his sword and they looked silently on Scotland for a while'.[45] Poem 149 is an argument against political fatalism which ends by warning that Scotland may become 'A mean thing of no account hidden away in a corner / Which another people drained dry and forgot'; if it is his best patriotic poem, it is so for the 'wrong' reasons — above all, its supercharged North African beginning.

A phrase from the same poem, *draoidheachd cheòlmhor fhacal lìomhta* ('the musical wizardry of polished words'), sums up for us Hay's outstanding achievement as a poet of Kintyre and of nature. 'Siubhal a' *Choire*' (poem 140) and 'An Ciùran Ceòban Ceò' (poem 153) have to be spoken for the full savour of their assonance and alliteration — the one declaimed, the other whispered. 'An Ciùran Ceòban Ceò' is an ethereal celebration of the kind of weather that many an expatriate would kill for, introducing the name of a scrap of arable — *am Paiste Beag*, 'the Wee Patch' — on the Kintyre shore, used as a mark by the fishermen. "We're on the run o' the Paiste Beag," a member of the crew said to young George one night at sea, pointing to the spot, and George 'looked in on the land and saw what was meant'.[46] The *Corrie* was actually a yacht chartered by Hay and some friends in 1935 for a Clyde cruise, but he had spent many hours of his youth with the ringnet fishermen of Loch Fyne; perhaps only Dòmhnall Ruadh Chorùna, in poem 54, and Ian Paterson, in poem 162, have achieved the effect of buffeting waves to the same degree.

This is the appropriate place to mention 'Mac a Sheanar' ('His Grandfather's Son') by

Roderick Campbell, Bragar, Lewis, who had won the Bardic Crown at the Dunoon Mod in 1930 (see p. 821). 'Mac a Sheanar' contains an extended passage of sea-imagery, e.g.:

An Rògh an-iardheas, lìonadh mara,	Butt of Lewis to south-west, swelling of sea,
Gleann gad bhiathadh dian gu'n earthu',	Valley feeding you fast to the north-east,
Iùnnrais speur a' séideadh bagraidh,	Storm in the firmament blowing a threat,
Tonnan leòideach leomh'nnt ag caradh.[47]	Towering waves that wrestle like lions.

The terse, verbally impacted style of the poem makes it a thrill to read but very difficult to translate. It is in the same metre and idiom as 'Siubhal a' Choire'. Campbell was schoolmaster at Minard on Loch Fyne. 'Siubhal a' Choire' was written in 1936. 'Mac a Sheanar' was published in 1944, 'Siubhal a' Choire' in 1947. When was 'Mac a Sheanar' written? What was the relationship between these two men and their work?[48]

War broke out shortly after Hay had completed his education at Edinburgh and Oxford. In 1940 he appeared twice as a Nationalist conscientious objector before an Appellate Tribunal in Edinburgh. After eight months on the run and a few days in Saughton jail, he joined up, spending 1942–5 with the Royal Army Ordnance Corps in Tunisia, Algeria and Italy, followed by a spell in 1945–6 as a sergeant in the Education Corps in Macedonia. Wherever he was he spent his free time mixing with the local community and soaking up their language. In 'Atman' (poem 145) he introduces his friend ('brother') of that name, married, with five children, possessor of some goats, an ass, a cow and a plot of rye, who gave him wit, and tales, and praised the form and colour of Jebel Yussuf; stricken by hunger, Atman stole, lied to the judge to get off, and was reviled, whipped and imprisoned. But Atman, says Hay, is a man, and alive, two things which the judge is not; and he reminds us that Christ, whom he refers to by the Arabic Sidna Aissa, was crucified with thieves. It is scarcely surprising that in Civil War conditions in Greece Hay was taken for a communist, which he was not.[49] The result was tragic. A rightist gang made an attempt on his life, and a fierce fight ensued with knives and guns from which Hay emerged physically unharmed but mentally scarred. Like MacLean, then, he is a great pacifist poet: his most personal statement is poem 148, in which he talks of a cloud rising from the overthrown villages of Africa and the crushed towns of Italy and blowing in the eyes of those who do not care, 'Even as the dark dust cloud choked us / And quenched the young sun of our day'.

Hay's most praised poem has tended to be 'Bisearta' (poem 147). This Tunisian city suffered intensive bombing, and the poet's concern is to show how war goes beyond human control and becomes a realisation of all that has been called evil. On night guard many miles away, the young soldier whose brother was Atman saw the sky ablaze, knew the sounds of it but could not hear them, knew the people of common blood who were struggling among stones and fallen beams but could not see them. Humanity has become anonymous, and inhumanity begins to take on human features as observed in the flames. "I see Evil as a pulse / And a heart declining and leaping in throbs." It is the very picture that Hay's father had painted in his novel Gillespie of the fishing fleet in Brieston (Tarbert) harbour — the flames "took a hundred fantastic shapes . . . Some titanic maleficent power was abroad . . . The red foam of hell was being brewed upon the tortured face of the night."[50]

It took little imagination to see in Bizerta the image of Clydebank, to see in Atman the image of the Gael, to see in Tunisia or Algeria the colonial experience of Scotland, or to find among the Arabs some of the lost world of the Highlands that was so dear to Hay. This is the inspiration of 'Mochtàr is Dùghall' (poem 144).

After the War Hay lived a largely reclusive life in Edinburgh, consisting of bouts of mental illness alternating with lively poetic activity (e.g. poems 159, 161). He met Derick Thomson for the first time, for example (at a Comunn Gaidhealach function in the city), as late as 1978. This may make it easier to understand why the existence of a long poem begun in the 1940s was only discovered by the Kintyre poet Angus Martin when interviewing him for a chapter in his book *Kintyre: The Hidden Past* in November 1980. Written mainly in Italy, and added to in Macedonia and Tarbert during 1946–7, it was published by Thomson as *Mochtàr is Dùghall* [*MD*] in 1982, with the sub-heading 'Sgeula-Dhàn Fada Neochrìochnaichte' ('An Unfinished Epic Poem'). Incomplete though it is, with over 1,200 lines it is longer than mac Mhaighstir Alastair's 'Birlinn Chlann Raghnaill' and Donnchadh Bàn's 'Beinn Dóbhrain' put together, and must stand with them as one of the great sustained achievements of Gaelic literature. In monorhymed paragraphs interspersed with other metres, it has philosophical depth, music, humour, atmosphere, colour, excitement, and a conceptual richness that takes the breath away.

Mokhtâr represents the world of the Arab, Dougall of the Gael. We learn at the beginning that they have been killed together by a German soldier in the desert. Their two cultures are synthesised.

Chan eil foirfeach no *marbat*   There is no elder or marabout
A thearbas sibh le 'eòlas,   Who can estrange you with his knowledge,
Tàileab, iomàm no ministear   Taleb, imam or minister
Chuireas iongnadh, crith no bròn oirbh. To fill you with wonder, or trembling or sorrow.
                                                   (*MD* 6, 47)

Pacifism is expressed with tight-lipped irony.

Fear-réite treun is tìoranach   A powerful, tyrannous reconciler
Deagh shìbhealtachd na h-Eòrpa!   Is the goodly civilisation of Europe! (*MD* 7, 47)

The bulk of the poem as we have it consists of a spectacular presentation of the heritage of Mokhtâr — son of Obaïd the blessed prophet, son of Omar the traveller of the Sahara, son of Ahmad who was in the 'sanctified hosts' of Abd el-Qader (the self-styled Emir of the Faithful, who proclaimed a *Jehad* against the French shortly after they had captured Algiers, and fought them for over ten years).[51] The section of the poem which I have selected for quotation at length concerns Omar. It is full of that delight in detail which characterises Gaelic verse at its best; through the behaviour of Arab and Touareg, but employing traditional vocabulary, it recaptures the flavour of a stage in society well within the traditional memory of the Gael, to the extent that it is easy to see in the Touareg leader some liminal figure like, say, Ailean nan Sop, or Mac Iain 'ic Sheumais who fought the battle of Carinish in N. Uist in 1601.

The Dougall section consists mainly of some vestigial sketches — 'The Wee Bay', 'The Fisherman's Wife', 'The Sea', 'The Woman Speaks' — amounting to an epitome of Hay's Kintyre poetry. It is doubtful in any case whether the reader of Gaelic poetry needs to be told of Dougall's antecedents; this is the weakness of the original plan, but the strength of the work as we have it. Mokhtâr's genealogy offers an allegory of Highland history: for Ahmad read the heroic age, for Omar read emigration, for Obaïd read Calvinism, for Mokhtâr — an ordinary twentieth-century human being — read Dougall. Hay's philosophical purpose, clarified at the end of the poem (pp. 362–7 below), is to show how speech, tradition and history accumulate genetically and otherwise in the individual, and how the untimely death of an individual in war is therefore a cultural act. It may be suggested, all in all, that now that the old Gaelic world of the ringnet fishermen had died, Hay had found his soul in Algeria, and that this great but lopsided poem shows us that Hay was not so much a 'Bard of Kintyre' as a 'Bard of Africa'.

Hay died in 1984 unmarried and alone, but much loved by those of us who were privileged to know him. It could be argued that he had not brought Gaelic poetry forward, that he had merely embellished it wondrously, but I would prefer to say that 'Mochtàr is

Dùghall' permanently broadened the range of Gaelic verse. After Hay any kind of subject-matter was possible, and in this respect the line of poetic succession passed from him to Christopher Whyte (see below, p. lxiv).

At this halfway point I would like to consider two anthologies which might be expected to sum up the first part of the century for us: James Thomson's *An Dìleab* (1932) and Lachlan Mackinnon's *Cascheum nam Bàrd* (1939). How much attention did these pay to contemporary work?

An Dìleab contains 39 poems. In his introduction Thomson (q.v.) described it as a collection of 'modern Gaelic poetry' for schools, even though it includes such items as the seventeenth-century 'Crodh Chailein' and 'Cead Deireannach nam Beann' by Duncan Bàn Macintyre (1724–1812). It also includes Donald Maciver's 'An Ataireachd Àrd' (poem 8), a genuinely twentieth-century item which by 1991 was being described as 'an old song' in the same breath as such venerable relics as 'Seathan Mac Rìgh Éireann' and 'A Mhairead Òg, s tu rinn mo leòn'.[52] Almost half of the poets in *An Dìleab* lived wholly or partly in the twentieth century, including six who feature in *An Tuil* (Maciver, Kenneth Macleod, James MacLeod, John Munro, Murdo Murray and Thomson himself). It should also be noted that the three Munro items (poems 68–70) are in primitive free verse. This was a courageous step for Thomson to take, clearly enabled by the respect which his generation in Lewis had for their fallen comrade. Thomson wrote:

> Many a young lad in Lewis was sorrowful when he heard news of the death of Lt John Munro in the year 1918. He fell in France. He was born and bred in Aignish, in Lewis. When the Great War broke out he was in Aberdeen studying to be a minister. He was a celebrated scholar, and as a poet in both English and Gaelic he was outstanding.[53]

On the debit side, it is noticeable that Thomson included verse by six poets from Lewis and several from Argyll, but not a single one from what are nowadays called 'the southern isles' — Uist and Barra. Why is this, I wonder?

Cascheum nam Bàrd contains 111 poems. Its editor, Lachlan Mackinnon (1903–91) from Breakish in Skye, defined its purpose like this:

> Intended for use in schools, it presents pieces representative of all aspects of Gaelic poetry, *e.g.*, heroic ballads, hunting songs, labour songs, lullabies, laments, songs of nature, rowing songs, love songs, &c. As well as poems of the present day and of the immediate past, there are included a few of the compositions of the first rank poets of the Eighteenth Century.

Cascheum succeeded where *An Dìleab* failed, and, more importantly, failed where it succeeded. Of the 42 poets in it, 12 may be described as twentieth-century figures. Eight of them are in *An Tuil*: Donald Maciver, Angus Robertson, Angus Mackechnie, Kenneth Macleod, Angus Morrison, Kirsty Macleod, Neil Ross and Donald MacDonald (Eriskay). The other four are Neil Shaw (Jura), Hector MacDougall (Coll), Donald MacMillan (Lochaber) and Donald MacLeod (Sutherland). Perhaps to make amends for Thomson's partiality, these 12 represent an impressively wide range of districts: Lewis (2), Uist, Skye (2), Eigg, Sutherland, Ullapool, Lochaber, Coll, Tiree and Jura. That is the credit side. On the debit side, Mackinnon's choice stands as a memorial to the fact that the greatest Gaelic poets of the first half of the twentieth century — Dòmhnall Ruadh Chorùna, Donald Macintyre, MacLean, Hay — were still unpublished, unknown, or unregarded. More culpably, he failed in his typological aims. There are no examples of free verse, of nineteenth- or twentieth-century war poetry, or indeed of anything exciting whatever from the twentieth century. Mackinnon's thematic choices display a preference for 'safe' subjects: nature, landscape, the sun (but not the moon, a less suitable role-model), 'Tìr nan Òg' (the title of poems by both the Rev. Kenneth Macleod and the Rev. Neil Ross); and, above all, birds. From our 12 twentieth-century poets alone, there are poems on the lark (Mackechnie and Shaw) and the robin (Shaw again), while a glance further back in time reveals two cuckoos, a thrush and another lark. A boring choice, even to an ornithologist.

'Tìr nan Òg' was also made the subject of a poem by the Rev. Colin T Mackenzie (q.v.), published in the *annus mirabilis*.[54] If any of these talented churchmen had used their gifts actually to explore this Celtic idea of a unitary otherworld as an alternative to orthodox Christian eschatology, they might have produced something memorable, for, as the Rev. Archibald MacDonald pointed out in 1908, 'in the traditions of Islesmen fifty years ago there were echoes of a fading faith in an island in the Western Sea, *an t-eilean uaine*, the green isle, to which the notions of a Celtic Elysium were attached'.[55] Wrote Macleod:

Bàs no bròn cha bheò 'nad loinn-thìr,	Death and grief don't live in your lovely land,
Ùir air foill 's air gò,	Buried are lies and guile,
Sàir sìor-òl do dheò 's do choibhneis,	Heroes hard-drinking your kindness and spirit,
Aoibhneas snàmh sna neòil;	Happiness swims in the clouds;
Reultan àrda là 's a dh'oidhche	Stars upon high by day and by night
Boillsgeadh sèimh tro cheò,	Gently shining through mist,
Teudan tlàtha fàs ad' choilltean,	Melodious harpstrings grow in your forests,
O Thìr nan Òg.[56]	O Land of the Young.

So the abolition of Hell had to wait, and the otherworld of traditional belief was sanitised into an alliterative, harp-twanging Christian heaven, pending its poetic resurrection in different forms later in the century (poems 175, 198, 287).

All in all, then, the choice of poets and poems in *Cascheum*, while outwardly appealing, actually represents a falling away from relatively adventurous standards set by Thomson. There is no common ground whatsover between the last reprint of *Cascheum* (1957) and the next educational anthology of Gaelic verse to appear, Donald MacAulay's *Nua-Bhàrdachd Ghàidhlig* of 1976, which consisted of poems by MacLean, Hay, Thomson's son Derick, Iain Crichton Smith, and MacAulay himself. In 19 short years the public face of Gaelic poetry had been entirely transformed.

Derick Thomson (poems 183–210) has been the long rumble of thunder to Sorley MacLean's flash of lightning. Born in Lewis in 1921, his work offers a full commentary on the Gaelic experience of the twentieth century. He is the father of modern Gaelic publishing, and the founder (in 1968) of the Gaelic Books Council. *Gairm* ('Cry', or perhaps better 'Call'), founded by Thomson with Finlay J MacDonald in 1952, began mainly as a family magazine with something of the look and feel of its contemporary, *Picture Post*; under his sole editorship since 1964, it has increasingly stressed its role as a vehicle for new and experimental writing. This development reflects a decline in competition from other Gaelic periodicals; an increase in competition from the non-Gaelic media, notably tabloids and television; the decline of Gaelic as an everyday language, and its virtual extinction since 1952 over large areas of the Highlands; and the emergence of a new market of highly-educated Gaelic learners.

Two great paradoxes can be detected in Derick Thomson's work. One is public, the other personal. The public one has to do with Thomson as teacher and propagandist. He has indefatigably put forward a modern, cosmopolitan view of the Gaelic world. He is justifiably proud of his work in translating a biology textbook into Gaelic,[57] and has expressed disappointment at the failure of others to follow this lead. His *Companion to Gaelic Scotland* (1983, 1994), over which he exercised rigorous editorial control, made Gaelic studies an open book where once they were closed, but presents a determinedly multicultural view of Gaeldom that seems to prefer castles to domestic architecture, painting to craftsmanship, Charles Rennie Mackintosh to the ceilidh-house, Mendelssohn to the shieling. His 'Earail air Luchd-Adhraidh a' Bheòil-Aithris' ('A Warning for Folklore Worshippers', poem 196) may helpfully be seen in this context. His purpose is the same as that of Alexander Carmichael (who equally sought to avoid identifying the Gael with Hallowe'en), namely the presentation of his people in the best possible cultural light. Like Carmichael, then, he can be absolved of any charge of élitism, and indeed for name-dropping (albeit in the best possible taste) we must go to Sorley MacLean or Fearghas MacFhionnlaigh.

The personal paradox is the other side of the same coin. Thomson is Lewis's greatest poet ever, in precisely the way that Hay is the bard of Algeria rather than of Kintyre, for he celebrates not the landscape or seascape of Lewis but her people. However, the people of Lewis will never fully embrace her secular poets and thinkers until their culture is in tatters, for it is nothing if not a spiritual culture; there are many in the island to whom 'a good book' means a religious one, and who would rather conceal social evils than expose them to light. Blinkered as such attitudes may be, they are representative of cultural values in Lewis in the past two centuries. Do away with such values, and you lose the linguistic and institutional props that have shored them up; what then is left? A tattered economy, the English language, materialism, the *Daily Record*, social security, television. That is surely why Thomson says of Bayble Hill and Hòl in 'Sgòthan' (poem 184) that he 'went away from them on a tether / As far as love goes from hate'. This poem, entirely traditional in form but with a very modern sting in the tail, could have been written by MacLean to Eimhir.

The paradoxes are synthesised, I think, in 'Bùrn is Mòine 's Coirc' (poem 189). These three words, spoken by a stranger in a city street, represent the 'public' paradox, for they symbolise the Lewis that Thomson loves, yet is estranged from. They bring him to this conclusion, the 'personal' paradox: "The heart tied to a tethering-post, round upon round of the rope / till it grows short / and the mind free. / I bought its freedom dearly."

The tethering-post, the round upon round of the shortening rope, and the freedom of Thomson's mind offer a paradigm of the development of his work through six published collections. *An Dealbh Briste* of 1951 is the tethering-post. In it there is love and cultural patriotism, the apprenticeship of this master craftsman: metre-bridled, disciplined verse showing MacLean's influence. *Eadar Samhradh is Foghar* [ESF] of 1967 focuses more closely on Lewis and on the human condition, and loanwords begin to creep in. 'Mu Chrìochan Hòil' (poem 185) is a 'Cottar's Saturday Night' of a poem, Gaelic seasonal poetry in the best tradition of mac Mhaighstir Alastair, but in the mesmeric rhythms of iambic pentameters.

At its best, Thomson's writing moves slowly, with an irresistible movement towards some truth or other. His picture of 'Na Cailleachan' (poem 186), for example, draws us inexorably through images of scarcity, boredom and evil, and touches of deliberate banality — using that archetypal picture of a 'black house' interior and its inhabitants which one seeks in vain in *The Companion to Gaelic Scotland* — to its ringing conclusion:

> O shaoghail, is goirid do chuairt, 's is lom an cridhe,
> is tana an sgàile, is dlùth oirnn nimh an fhuaraidh.

("O life, short is your course, bare is the heart, / frail is the shelter, close to us is the venom of the cold wind.")

Thomson's third collection, *An Rathad Cian* [RC] of 1970, is named for the road of history which learning can follow, and for the even longer one that stretches seven miles through and between the teeming communities of Point from Stornoway to the sea. He coins and transmutes language, experiments with free verse and new rhythms, and achieves the medium that is to become his trademark, the three-part lyrical allegory consisting of picture, thought and conclusion. In 'Troimh uinneig a' chithe' ('When this fine snow is falling', *ESF* 23, 73–4) the picture is of snow piled high outside, the thought is of when Lewis communities were self-sufficient, the conclusion is that he wastes his forebears' strength *a' treabhadh ann an gainneamh* ('ploughing in the sand'), a theme later picked up by Shawbost headmaster Charles Macleod in his novel *Devil in the Wind* (Edinburgh 1979). In 'Cisteachan-Laighe' ('Coffins', *ESF* 67–8, 89–90) the picture is of his grandfather, a maker of coffins, being put in one himself; the thought is of the coffins being prepared to receive his culture; the conclusion is that he can already feel the nails going through him. 'Srath Nabhair' (poem 188) vies with MacLean's over-symbolistic 'Hallaig' to be (by nineteenth-century default) our best poem of the Clearances: the picture is of 'the year we thatched the house with snowflakes', the thought is of the otherworldly religion that allowed such things to happen, the conclusion is that this religion survives today, still seeking martyrs in preference to justice.[58]

Lack of that extra lifetime needed to pursue all their talents is the tragedy that has befallen many fine minds caught up in the Gaelic movement of the second half of the twentieth century. Had Thomson had time he would have made a superb novelist. He has patience, sensitivity, strength, an all-seeing painter's eye and a photographic memory. These qualities are as evident in his few short stories, such as the superbly understated 'Bean a' Mhinisteir' ('The Minister's Wife'), as in his verse.[59] In his criticism he is fond of drawing on a range of art-forms for his terminology — verse, for example, has 'texture', and may be 'well-moulded', 'hard', 'flabby', 'held taut by a spring', or 'shot through with emotional shrapnel'. His own verse lends itself to the terminology of drawing and painting. In addition to large canvases teeming with life he paints brilliant portraits of groups like the herring-girls (poem 187) and of individuals like Murdag Mhòr ('Mucka'), the cleaner at Bayble School where his father was head (poem 191), and also leaves us little etchings like 'Làmhan' (poem 192), often adding intellect to observation such as in 'Teallaichean' (poem 183), where *sùilean m' eagail* ('my fear's eyes') turn the fire and its embers into symbols of youth and decline. This ability to paint a clear picture with a few deft strokes puts him in the mainstream of the Gaelic verse tradition at its best.

Thomson is a highly disciplined poet, and when he breaks out of the bonds of self-discipline one knows that something has troubled him greatly; down through the years he has done this with increasing frequency. By 1970 he was moving towards puns, loanwords, throwaway lyrics, bitterness, descriptions of city life; in tune with the 1960s, the Gaelic literature of the past was irreverently placed at the disposal of humour, and he deliberately set out to shock. His fourth collection, *Saorsa agus an Iolaire* (1977), marks a shift towards ideology; the book is about his relationship with Lewis, as always, but also freedom of all kinds, North Sea Oil, drink and religion. Three different poems offer three different metaphors for Scotland resurgent (spider, thistle, eagle), while 'An Crann' (poem 195) is a tour-de-force of layered meaning. A *crann* can be practically anything pole-shaped — a plough, symbolising land; a cross, symbolising religion; a mast, symbolising the sea; a lot (sticks or poles were used in drawing lots), symbolising fortune, fate, future; a harp-key, symbolising cultural tradition; a saltire, symbolising Scottish Nationalism; an oilrig, symbolising North Sea Oil; and there is an erotic symbolism too. It is hard to believe that such a multilayered structure could get off the ground, yet it soars.

Another feature that emerged after 1970 was the influence of the public stage. It was a long time since Neil Ross had brought the first Mod to life in 1892 with his rendering of 'Chan fhaigh a' Ghàidhlig bàs' (p. 722). Since then the custom of declaiming verse had effectively lapsed, so that the only poetry of performance in Gaelic was the kind that was sung — in church, at mods, at concerts, at public ceilidhs, or at private gatherings of one kind or another. Even at the Mod the speaking of verse was restricted to children, and the verse of MacLean or Hay belonged entirely to the printed page. Suddenly, however, there were opportunities for poets like Thomson to read their work in public, mainly in the cities, but also in Gaelic-speaking areas. The chief impetus for this was annual tours of Scotland and Ireland by Gaelic poets, singers and musicians from the two countries, organised by the Scottish Arts Council and Comhdháil Náisiúnta na Gaeilge. These began in 1971, and the encouragement that they offered cannot be overestimated. As noted at p. 766, the whole strange quickening coincided with MacLean's retirement from teaching in 1972; it may even have been partly caused by it, because he proved to be a formidable troubadour. He and Thomson were the first Scottish Gaelic poets to go on the new *cuairt* to Ireland. The most tangible outcome of the *cuairtean* was the 1993 anthology *Sruth na Maoile*, which includes 55 poems by 22 Scottish Gaelic poets (all of whom, as it happens, are represented in *An Tuil*), 'all chosen initially with public reading in mind — in village halls, theatres, schools, colleges and universities, from Dingle to Stornoway'. This is why, as Iain Crichton Smith points out in his critical introduction to the book, "These poems are on the whole clear and easily understood. They are not ironical, nor are they, like Eliot's *The Waste Land*, opaque." The less tangible results were summed up by the late Col. Eoghan Ó Néill, who was for many years the organising genius behind the *cuairtean*:[60]

> The effects, influence and results of this cultural exchange scheme have been rewarding, far-reaching and lasting. There is now an appreciative audience for contemporary Gaelic literature in both countries, not just amongst poets, critics, academics and enthusiasts, but amongst a wide cross-section of the general public, hitherto perhaps out of contact or largely unaware of its existence. Courts of poetry and poetry readings are now a common feature at gatherings and festivals throughout both countries.

The long-term result, as seen in Derick Thomson's work, is verse of immediate impact — aural, in the case of alliterative poems like the untranslatable 'Gaol is Gràdh' ('Love and Love', 1977) and 'Fuaim-Dhàn' ('Sound-Poem', 1982),[61] both of which play on the sound G; and political, in the case of items like 'Earrach '74' (poem 193) and 'Alba *v.* Argentina, 2/6/79' (poem 197). This is a popularisation of poetry which no-one need regret, an assumption by the innovators of the mantle of the so-called *bàrd baile* (see pp. lxi–lxiii). Audiences were getting what they wanted to hear. The wheel was coming back full circle.

Thomson's fifth collection is represented by the 23 new poems in his collected verse, *Creachadh na Clàrsaich* (1982). Of these, the sequence 'Àirc a' Choimhcheangail' (poem 198) is as good, and as fundamental to his art, as anything he has ever done. The title is that of a hymn by the Lewis poet Murdo MacLeod, *Murchadh a' Cheisteir* (1837–1914),[62] and indeed one section is devoted to a *ceistear* (catechist); denotatively it means 'The Ark of the Covenant', connotatively it means 'The Synthesis of the Relationship'. The relationship in question is of course with Lewis; in an incandescent sweep of his net Thomson echoes his best work of the past while surging forward to make new statements. *Ged a ghabh sinn caochladh shlighean, / ged nach b'e 'n aon chrois a bh' air a' chrann againn . . .* ('Though we took different roads, / though it was not the same cross we had on our shields'), he goes on to find that Lewis religion has confidence, strength, profound traditional and emotional roots: *Rut 's Naòmi am bun na lota, / Iòseph a chaidh a dhìth air an Iolaire* ('Ruth and Naomi at the foot of the croft, / Joseph who was lost on the *Iolaire*'); it has the virtues of sweetness and total familiarity, everlasting life, for example, offering 'butter and fish / and good company, / hymns and psalms, / favours under the blanket / and porridge in the morning'. This is 'Tìr nan Òg' deromanticised.

Living as the Lewisman does in an environment dominated by sea and rock, Thomson can understand the pull on him of one who recruited burly fishermen to His cause, turned stones into bread and moved a huge rock from the mouth of His grave. Thinking back, he remembers what was good about the Sabbath in his maternal grandfather's home at Keose, expressing it principally in terms of sound: the clock strikes ten, his grandfather jabs words into the racket, a lark sings, rowlocks creak in the bay, eggs make a fearful din jumping in the pan. He describes the church, plaintively, conceding with mild embarrassment that it is its eschewal of beauty that set him against it. "Why did you put me off?" he seems to say. "There were occasional people / who took their beauty in and out of it / without its going up in flames." And the beauty of Lewis is, of course, its people: some of those who got religion he proceeds to describe in an ineffable series of cameos: Iain son of Calum son of Ewen, from Flesherin, a good family man, Calum son of Murdo son of Finlay, from Bayble, a wild spirit who contracted TB and was 'brought in' by his mother and sister, Neil son of Alexander son of Norman, from Garrabost, a shopkeeper and speculator who smoked heavily and had nightmares, Mary daughter of Big Hector, from Knock, who mourned for 61 years a sweetheart lost in the Trenches. Above all, perhaps, he finds the perfect synthesis in the man who recalls, as he speaks to the Question on communion Fridays, his experience of conversion in a bar at the English fishing: this sort of thing happened to many, but, as the poet says with admiration, *Có chailleadh cuimhn' air a leithid?* "Who would forget the like of that?" *Thu* (thou) turns to *sibh* (ye) as he reflects that Glasgow was the Egypt from which Lewis folk in general were recalled to the Land of Promise, and so at the end (pp. 476–7 below) he returns, uncomfortably, to himself: "My prayer / that I be not found, / one day, in extremity, / on my knees, / praying." So Thomson doubts doubt, while putting beyond doubt that his was the major voice of Gaelic poetry in the second half of the twentieth century.

His latest two collections, *Smeur an Dòchais* (1991) and *Meall Garbh* (1995), continue his measured but incisive commentary on the world about him: the former a notably urban collection, the latter (following his retirement) a strongly rural one. They throw up yet another powerful allegory, 'Gormshuil', and much else of importance besides (poems 199–210). He continues to edit *Gairm*, and to publish new poems in it.

The development from traditional to modern styles and attitudes, and thence towards a synthesis, seems smooth enough in such a study of Thomson's work, but it would be a mistake to imagine that such a revolution could be achieved across the board without letting of blood. In fact during the quarter-century between the founding of *Gairm* and the appearance of *Saorsa agus an Iolaire* (1952–77) a holy war was fought between tradition and innovation for the soul of Gaelic poetry. However, many of those most firmly on the side of tradition were an ageing breed. They were perhaps typified by Norman Murray, a Lewisman who emigrated to British Columbia, and who wittily lampooned the new verse under the title 'Bàrdachd an-diugh' ('Poetry today').

Tha meall math den bhàrdachd an-diugh	There's a great deal of poetry today
A tha Gallda 'na stuth is 'na cruth	That's Lowland in content and shape
Gun lathailt gun rian	With no skill to command it
Cha tuig sinne sìon	We can't understand it
Ma tha d' eanchainn mar m' eanchainn-sa tiugh.[63]	If like me you haven't the brains.

They had already sold the pass however by their failure to 'understand' MacLean's poetry, even though he used traditional metres, traditional vocabulary, and traditional symbols, only his subjects and attitudes being relatively new; their blindness was akin to that of the many Gaelic speakers who not only would not, but literally could not, read anything in Gaelic except the Bible. In the words of the innovators' guru, Donald MacAulay, they were 'the ones who have chosen / deafness and blindness — / and are facing dumbness' (poem 245).

Traditional poetry is thirled to rhyme and generally sung; its patterns can be mesmeric, and at its worst it certainly follows clichés like railway tracks. In a song by Michael

MacPherson the burial ground at Hallin in South Uist is *Cnoc Hàllainn taobh a' chuain*, 'Hallin Hill beside the sea' (poem 96), while a younger poet, with no loss of rhyme or rhythm, calls it *machair ìosal do-shàsaicht' Hàllainn*, 'the low insatiable plain of Hallin' (poem 318). By the 1960s the art and practice of poetry had ceased to be the living heritage of the generation brought up since the Second World War, as the ceilidh-house died and its cultural role was usurped by secondary education and the media. As Iain Crichton Smith remarked in poem 237 of nobody in particular, "He is closer to Humphrey Bogart / than he is to Tormod Mór — / since he got the TV." Perhaps the best description of this change is Morag MacLeod's.

> The introduction of hydro-electric power has probably had the most long-reaching effect on the social organisation, combined with improvements in the financial status of people in rural areas. Beautiful light-coloured carpets, which became practical because they could be kept clean by electric vacuum cleaners, are discouraging to courteous visitors who are afraid they might dirty them. With electricity came facilities for television reception, and soon every household had a set. This not only caused people to stay at home instead of going to visit friends, but it discouraged them from visiting, because when they did so the television set was often not even switched off in the house they were visiting. The céilidh-house gradually became a very rare commodity.[64]

The biographies at the end of this book contain various examples of the response of individual poets to this situation. Angus Campbell, 'Am Puilean' (poems 81–2), did his best to re-invent the ceilidh-house tradition in more basic accommodation, but the idea got out of hand, fell foul of the church, and his little ceilidh-houses turned into the rural drinking-dens well known to the English-medium press in the 1960s as 'bothans'. Donald John MacDonald (poems 171–5) simplified the vocabulary of his hymns, which retained a public audience, while maintaining demanding standards in his secular verse, which became more personal. His uncle Donald Macintyre (poems 56–65) despaired of his work reaching anyone any more, and attempted to consign it to the flames. Donald Allan MacDonald (poem 94) ceased composing altogether and became that contradiction in terms, a dumb poet: as he did not write his material, his legacy is now full of gaps. Duncan Finlayson (poem 72) wrote down his songs as best he could. Dòmhnall Aonghais Bhàin (poems 223–5) disseminates his work through the print media, but needs a little reassurance now and again that it is being read. Donald R Morrison (poem 176) does likewise, and is willing to write in English if requested; his substitute for oral memory is libraries, to which he regularly sends his work. Curiously, the change worked slightly to the advantage of poets who were not singers: Ian Paterson (poems 162–6) found a suitable audience for his poems in the family kitchen whenever he went home to Berneray. Finally, the act of composition could be stimulated by regular motion (see p. 759), a curious example being that of Malcolm MacDonald (poem 217), who spent his working life in England as a British Railways guard — songs would come to him while the green of the landscape or the black of the night rolled by. But they were inspired not by England but by thoughts of his native Harris.

Donald MacAulay (poems 245–50) was, by contrast, a university lecturer. He had observations to make, experiences to recount, and feelings to express, about poetry and language, Lewis, religion and exile, love and people, his period of national service in Turkey, peace, war and disarmament, and to do this he chose a style of verse which was as new to Gaelic as that of Pound to English in the decades between the Wars. It is uncompromising poetry, with few concessions to convention, understanding, sound, optimism, even humour; a theoretical linguist, he does not love words, but respects them greatly, selecting them carefully and with judicious use of blank space to represent the vagaries and deficiencies of his intellect as accurately as possible without pretending to resolve anything. This is seen particularly well in poem 246. He seems quite deliberately to eschew rhythm, rhyme and musicality, although capable of introducing any of these when it suits his purpose. Here, then, was a fluent Gaelic speaker with a very traditional poetic urge, whose work nevertheless demanded an entirely new definition of poetry. In printing it for the first time in 1956, the editors of *Gairm* invited correspondence on such new verse.[65]

At first the silence was deafening. Staunch traditionalists like John A ('Jake') MacDonald of Jordanhill College (a Skyeman from Camustianavaig) preferred to ignore the new verse in the hope that it would go away. But the battle-lines were quietly being drawn up. Despite the risk of caricature, here is a little checklist to categorise the opposing forces.

Tradition	Innovation
The poetry	
Rhyme	Free verse
Sung	Written
Some religious bigotry	Some artistic snobbery
Occasional intellectual inconsistency	Either tight logic or no logic at all
Obscurities caused by wordiness	Obscurities caused by symbolism
Target audience: local community or anyone	Target audience: anyone
Subject-matter: anything	Subject-matter: anything
Field of reference: global	Field of reference: global
The poet	
Often living at home	Seldom living at home
Little experience of secondary or higher education	University-trained
Often non-literate (but never illiterate) in Gaelic	Highly literate in Gaelic
English sometimes poor	English always excellent

Some of these points require comment. With regard to 'bigotry' I am thinking of the treatment of Jews in the work of Donald Macintyre: his *Iùdhaich*, 'Jews', cannot always be explained away as meaning capitalists. I am also thinking of the treatment of the Catholic Church in some Presbyterian spiritual verse, as for example in John MacRae's elegy on the Rev. Angus Finlayson (q.v.):

> Bha shùil air Taigh na Pàrlamaid He watched the House of Commons
> 'S air innleachdan a' Phàp', And the Pope's machinations,
> Mar tha iad faighinn àite How they keep gaining ground
> An eaglais 's ann an stàit.[66] In church and in state.

And inconsistency: every so often in a corpus of traditional verse it strikes one that the poet seems to be saying the opposite of something he said before. Sorley MacLean called it 'pathetic confusion', referring to some lines by John Campbell (1823–97) of Ledaig in Benderloch: "Sometimes there is a pathetic confusion, as in John Campbell's 'Is toigh leam a' Ghàidhealtachd', in which he says:

> Nis tha dùthaich ar gaoil fo chaoraich 's fo fhéidh,
> Sinn 'gar fuadach thar sàile mar bhàrrlach gun fheum.

('Now the land of our love is under sheep and deer, / Ourselves being driven away like useless scum.') But he goes on to declare that, no matter what happens, the Gael will always be available for military duty as he was of yore, smashing Napoleon and Czar Nicholas and giving freedom to India. Imperialist dope had badly muddled John Campbell."[67]

In the same way, after reading Dòmhnall Alasdair's demolition of Tom Morton it comes as a shock when he declares in a poem called 'An Clachan' that 'Gaelic is wheezing in its throat there / And coming close to death' (*Tha Ghàidhlig leis an tùchadh ann / 'S i dlùthadh ris a' bhàs*).[68] He can't really have it both ways. But this has something to do with target audience. The traditional poet is a little like an advertiser, more inclined than the innovator to give his audience what they want to hear. (Poem 33 actually *is* an advertisement!) Intellectual inconsistency within a single poem is obviously more serious.

Finally, with regard to choice of subject-matter and field of reference, I have chosen to stress that there is basically no difference between traditional and innovative verse; perhaps the simplest proof of that is our two ceilidh-house poems (57, 167). I might have added, however, that traditional poets seem to have fewer inhibitions than innovative ones about raising practical issues — note, for example, the discussion of Old Age Pensions and Unemployment Benefits in poems 1, 9 and 64. And with regard to two particularly common subjects, religion and the homeland, there is a very major difference in attitude.

With religion, especially, the battle was on the classic ground of Gaelic dialectic, and during the third quarter of the century it was difficult to stand simultaneously on traditional ground with regard to belief and on modern ground with regard to the means of expression. An anonymous contributor to *Gairm* in 1966 hammered home the message that 'Gaelic will not live without Bible' (*Cha bhi Gàidhlig beò gun Bhìobull*) in traditional stanzas, but showed willingness to experiment when dealing with purely moral themes.[69] The 1960s brought to the consciousness of Gaelic poets the kind of fashionable iconoclasm gently satirised by Charles Coventry:[70]

Chan eil Dia ann idir; tha mise an aghaidh a h-uile rud, chan eil duine tha gam thuigsinn.	There's no God at all; I'm against everything, there's nobody who understands me.

It became a characteristic innovative trend to point out that Calvinism is an alien aberration in Gaelic culture, to the extent that, as Meg Bateman has pointed out, rejection of established religion, 'often for 1940s nihilism', became 'almost . . . an orthodoxy amongst Gaelic *literati*'.[71] MacAulay's well-balanced 'Soisgeul 1955' (poem 250) finds a psalm-tune as mysterious as the voyage of Maol Dùin, a prayer as his people's access to poetry, but a sermon to be so vicious, alien and embarrassing that he gets pins and needles in his feet. His 'Féin-Fhìreantachd' (poem 248) talks in a nicely-sustained image of being drubbed in the washing-tub of alien philosophy and confidently hung out to dry in the heavens. Thomson's 'Am Bodach-Ròcais' (poem 190) tells how the scarecrow of the title came into the ceilidh-house with middle-eastern tales and Genevan philosophy, sweeping the fire from the middle of the floor and putting instead a 'bonfire in our breasts', while in Iain Crichton Smith's 'Coinnichidh Sinn' (poem 232) the pious man's view of an innocent heaven sounds to the woman like a frozen one and her bosom goes cold.

Strong as it may seem, however, this was tame compared to the existing religious battlegrounds of Gaelic verse. Even in the limited space which I have felt able to give to spiritual poetry in this anthology, we find a reformed sinner pouring out his love for God as he faces Him on his deathbed at the age of 26 (poem 39), an experience of religious conversion in the warehouses and lumber-yards of Vancouver (poem 42), and an evocation of one of the huge outdoor communions often called 'holy fairs' (poem 41); one can also compare the vivid teaching of an inspired saint of the church (poems 44–5) with the soul-searching of an ordained minister experiencing the anguish of doubt (poem 73). In this context, the Rev. Roderick Macdonald (q.v.) once wrote:

> Ri taobh nan sruthan coimheach   Beside the alien streams
> Shuidh mi agus ghuil mi;   I sat down and wept;
> Ghuil mi chionns gun d'chaill mi   I wept because I'd lost
> Creideamh làidir mo luchd-dàimhe.[72] The strong faith of my kinsfolk.

There are also studies of the very special relationship that can exist between a woman and Christ: the warmth of Catherine Macdonald's 'Cum Sinn Dlùth' (poem 221), the ecstasy of 'An t-Aoibhneas a tha staigh sa Chridhe' (222), the agony of having to choose between the spiritual life and the secular (182), the tragedy of Mary at the crucifixion (294).

The 'homeland' issue was best put into perspective, I think, by Donald John MacLeod (b. 1943), a Marxist from Ardhasaig in Harris who first established his credentials by securing the Bardic Crown at the 1964 Mod with a poem about freedom of conscience that was only modestly subversive (see p. 822). He went on to make a series of increasingly virulent attacks on the seemingly indivisible target of traditional verse, religion, and entrenched cultural attitudes.[73] In 'Ràithean na Bliadhna' ('The Seasons of the Year') he turns a line of a simple aphorism into a torrent of prose castigating his forefathers for knuckling under to capitalism, and finishes with the ultimate heresy: *An eilean mo luaidh, is fuath leam eilean mo ghràidh*, "In the isle of my heart, I hate the isle of my love".[74]

> Tha 'n geamhradh fo shian,
> Tha 'n t-earrach fo shìol,
> Tha 'n samhradh fo ghrian,
> 'S tha am foghar làn de dh'eallaich mhùchail fheòir
> 's de dh'fhallas goirt 's gun aon sgillinn ruadh aig
> duine air a shon ach aig "fear nan aeroplanes" aig a
> bheil not san acair sa bhliadhna 'son a' chraicinn
> ùrach seo (reiceadh Ceann a-Tuath na Hearadh an
> 1834 'son £60,210) bhon do dh'fhògradh mo
> shìnseanair (am fear ainmeil eaglais sin) trì uairean,
> 's tha daoine air a bhith ga fhàgail on uair sin gan
> deòin 's gan ainneoin is, an déidh sin 's 'na dhéidh
> ge-tà, "ann an eilean mo ghaoil bidh daoine
> fuireach gu bràth" —
> Sin agad a' bhliadhn'.

> The winter's under storm,
> The spring's under seed,
> The summer's under sun,
> And the autumn's full of the stifling burden of
> hay and bitter sweat and nobody gets as much
> as a penny for it but the "aeroplane man" who
> has a pound per acre per year for this skein of
> soil (North Harris was sold in 1834 for
> £60,210) from which my great-grandfather
> (that celebrated man of the church) was cleared
> three times, and people have been leaving it
> ever since voluntarily and otherwise and, for all
> that and all that however, "in the isle of my love
> folk will forever live" —
> That's the year for you.

> Chan eil comhardadh slàn
> Anns a' bhàrdachd ud shuas,
> 'S nach mór a' chùis nàir
> Gum biodh mearachd an duan
> Mu eilean mo ghràidh.

> There's no perfect rhyme
> In the above poem,
> And isn't it disgraceful
> That there should be a mistake in a song
> About the isle of my love.

> An eilean mo luaidh, is fuath leam eilean mo ghràidh.   In the isle of my heart, I hate the isle of my love.

This is of course the same as Derick Thomson's straying from Lewis 'as far as love goes from hate'. Disjunction has set in: the innovative poet's relationship with his homeland (an island, usually, nearly always Lewis or Harris, seldom Uist or Skye) can, in a very post-modern way, involve mixtures of love and hate, passion and doubt, estrangement and divorce.

The Lewismen John Murray and Norman Campbell (a son of 'Am Bocsair') pulled the revolution in a less ideological direction. Murray's comic imagination sizzles in ferment as he satirises the traditionalists' pavlovian reactions in poem 252, while Campbell's 'Mi Fhìn agus a' Revolution agus mo Bhata-Darach' (poem 267) conveys a glorious picture of traditional stanzas marching along Princes Street while the drunken poet, 'as happy as a bottle of Parozone', runs along behind the crowd and jumps up and down yelling irreverent comments.

One day in 1964, the Rev. (later Rt Rev.) T M Murchison, editor of the Gaelic supplement to the Church of Scotland's monthly magazine *Life and Work* (1951–80) and former editor of *An Gaidheal* (1946–58), attacked modern trends in art, sculpture and literature in his weekly column 'Còmhradh Cagailte, le Dòmhnall Donn' ('Fireside Chat, by Brown Donald') in *The Stornoway Gazette*.[75] It was what Thomson had been waiting for. In *Gairm*, under the title 'Cagailte Còmhradh, le Donn Dòmhnall', he selected the most relevant part of the article, and reversed it. Here is a literal translation.

TOO poetry is this, poetry is poetry modern today's of lot a if and, are they that say would others but, poetry are they that say wouldn't I. minute very this, together lines four these put who myself is it that confessed shamefully be to has it, Now. leaves the tossing is wind the where tree a in nest a in birds little of chirping the of were it as conscious is He ?about thinking he is what and, purring and, moment very this at doing is Tom Ginger the as just, fire the of front in sitting cat a of picture a is line urth-fo the In. nation-imagi and mind same the in pictures are they that except them between whatsoever connection no is there and, included been have "pictures mind" or (say poets the as) "images" nine or eight lines four those In.

".ghaoith a' anns bigeil is cait Crònan   ".wind the in chirping and purring cat's A
:ciùin cuan air reach-loinn, aobrann 'nam Cràdh   :sea calm on kling-spar, ankle my in Pain
:sàil 'na toll, aosda Bròg   :heel its in hole a, boot old An
:dusd air gréin deàrrsadh, dhonn Cathair"   :dust on shining sun, chair Brown"

:ple-exam for this Take. another and line one between connection any without, words of lines eight you give who poets are There
 mind your to comes that title any be could it deed-In. "Evening mer-Sum" or "Death" or "Life" is picture the of title or name the and, head his of top the from tree a like rises hand left his while arm his on eyes his and som-bo his on is ear right his that except, man a of figure the, say, is which in, drawn-hand been has which, picture a see You
 .writers and, tors-sculp, artists amongst today fashionable are which approaches new behind is that view the is This !you around are that people the or things the than certain more or true more is nation-imagi your in or dream a in see you thing the that believe who people are there that iced-not be also should it, further step a issue this take To
WE WILL AWARD *ALBA* (1946), OR PERHAPS *NA SÉ BONNAICH BHEAGA*, TO THE FIRST PERSON WHO MAKES SENSE OF THE ABOVE, AND SENDS US AN EXPLANATION BY LETTER.[76]

Thomson devoted a page of his next issue to solving the 'mystery'.[77] The first of the two responses printed was from Murdo MacLeod, Glasgow, who chose to reflect upon the societal implications of the challenge.

Starting at the bottom and reading back up to the top you can make sense of what's written in the Chat on page 65 (Winter *Gairm*). Perhaps eventually you'll see poetry and prose written like this. Given the world we live in, and the people who're shaping it, space, sputniks, computers, some folk's minds are going into orbit (*a' dol a mach air raointean*) pretty much the way sputniks do. But, but, what are they, or what's going to come of it all? You're just as likely to find the answer by starting at the bottom and carrying on up to the top.

Then, under the words *Sgrìobh fear eile mar so* ('Another man wrote as follows'), Thomson printed his own reply (again, I translate):

I'm quite happy with the meaning I took out of this page by reading it as it was. Although I tried to turn the chat this way and the other no better meaning came to the surface. This is exactly the way firesides have of chatting: *dranndan teallaich*, 'hearth's hum', as Donnchadh Bàn said. Is it Donald John MacAulay Smith that composed the poetry that was in the Chat? If not, it was surely Hugh Laing, translating aboriginal verse from Australia. It's hard to grasp the images stored in this poetry:

    :sàil 'na toll, aosda Bròg   :heel its in hole a, boot old An
    :dusd air gréin deàrrsadh, dhonn Cathair,   :dust on shining sun, chair Brown"

but beyond any doubt there is beauty in these words.

Three years later Donald John MacLeod put on the gloves for another round. The location was the Glasgow student magazine *Ossian*, of which I was editor at the time. The article, if that is the right word for it, was an anonymous and supposedly seamless piece of satire headed 'Prògram Ghàidhlig air TV: Carson a tha a' Ghàidhlig a' dol bàs?'[78] If I recall correctly, the first three pages were by Angus John Smith (Barvas, Lewis), the last four-and-a-half by MacLeod (who was a lecturer at the time), the introduction and other stitching (in shamelessly bad Gaelic) by myself. Returning to it after more than thirty years, I find that Smith and MacLeod both turned in a brilliant piece of work. Smith wittily probes the reluctance of the Lewis crofter to take the slightest responsibility for anything to do with his language, then MacLeod weighs in with poetry. His part of the 'TV programme' takes the form of a discussion, chaired by "Marischall's Mick Luhan", featuring half-a-dozen eccentric and more or less recognisable characters representing six different points on the spectrum of tradition and innovation.[79]

On Luhan's right, "Dan ('Dìreach') MacDonald, of East Kilbride and South Uist" comes across as a strange mixture of people like Tom Murchison, Donald John MacDonald (poems 171–5) and Norman Maclean (poem 254), with a bit thrown in of all the old-style upholders of tradition such as Donald Grant (poem 79). "William ('Tawse') Williams of Fort William, who has been a Gaelic master in an island school for thirty years", a hard man to put down, behaves very like 'Jake' MacDonald. "John Brown, of Surbiton, a learner of Gaelic" sounds like a poke at the late Seumas Mac a' Ghobhainn of Surbiton, but the siting of the token learner on the 'soft right' of the argument is, I think, prophetic.

On Luhan's left, "Dom. L. ('Domb') O'Huntin, a folklorist from Ireland who, however, resides for part of the year in Eriskay" represents the late John Lorne Campbell and almost anyone in the School of Scottish Studies: his is the ethnological approach to Gaelic literature (for which see for example poems 20, 57, 136, 167, 196, 260 and 320 and p. lvii below). I have to confess that by making the learner and the folklorist join hands, as it were, across the middle of the debate, Donald John MacLeod anticipated by thirty years my perspective in *An Tuil*. Next is "Karl A. Camacellany, poet", whose name fails to disguise a brilliant caricature of Donald MacAulay (poems 245–50); and finally, on the hard left, "the irreverent [sic] young satirist, Donnchadh Bàn Mac-an-Aoir, better known simply as 'Mag'" is basically MacLeod himself, though we can just as easily see him as John Murray (poems 252–3) or Norman Campbell (poem 267) if we prefer.

These, then, are MacLeod's protagonists; here, in translation, is the middle part of his satire.

Luhan: . . . Mr Camacellany, I'm now going to ask you to give us your opinions on this topic: Why is Gaelic dying?
Camacellany: What do you mean 'dying'? Is Gaelic dying?
Luhan: A good question. Is Gaelic dying? What do all the rest think?
The rest: Yes.
Luhan: Well, Mr Camacellany, you heard that yourself. What's your opinion of why it is dying?
Camacellany: . . . Well, . . .
Williams: It's laziness. There are too many folk around who are too free with their advice and their moaning: and you don't even see their faces at a ceilidh or a Highland gathering more than once a year. Let the complainers do more for Gaelic themselves . . . That's what's wrong!
Luhan: Right. Well, now, some would have it, Mr Camacellany, that things aren't improved by not teaching modern literature — what's easiest about it anyway — in the schools. What do you think?

Camacellany: . . . Well . . .

Williams: We teach *Bàrdachd Ghàidhlig* in the schools and *Bàrdachd* only reaches 1900.[80] I think that answers your question.

Luhan: Well, we have one of the modern poets here. Mr MacDonald, I'm sure you have a song about the state of Gaelic?

Dàn: Yes.

Cainnt mo mhàthar Gàidhlig Bharraidh,	The Gaelic of Barra's my mother's language,
Cainnt mo ghràidh i Gàidhlig Bharraidh,	The Gaelic of Barra's my beloved language,
Chaoidh cha bhàsaich Gàidhlig Bharraidh,	The Gaelic of Barra will never perish,
No Gàidhlig Uibhist, Gàidhlig m' athar.[81]	Or the Gaelic of Uist, my father's language.

O'Huntin: Marvellous.

Luhan: And Mr Camacellany is a poet too. On you go, my friend.

Camacellany:

Dh'fhàg an oidhch ud	That night left
clais 'san inntinn	a ditch in the mind
far eil bùrn electric a' ruith ma sgaoil	where piped water runs amok
a bheothaich aon uair	which once quickened
talamh glas gu torradh,	fallow land to fertility,
buntàta (dh'fheumas bàrr),	potatoes (which need cropping),
lus-a-chorracha-mille is eala-bhì —	bitter vetch and St John's wort —
feum is bòidhchead.	function and beauty.
Air an deas, geamhradh nan creagan blian	To the south, the winter of lean rocks
is lusan;	and herbs;
air an tuath, carraighean-cuimhne	to the north, monuments
is fiar fiadhaich as cinn nan uaigh.	and wild grass that is gravestones.

Mag:

Ugh	(an ceann beag)	A	(the small end)
circ fraoich		grouse's egg	
air a' fhraoch ghorm		on the purple heather	
na h-eòin ann an Glascho		for the birds in Glasgow	
tha an àile ro fhuar		the air's much too cold	
airson breith		for laying without	
gun ghur	(an ceann mór)	hatching	(the big end)

Luhan: Quite so. Well, now we've heard your opinions on the schools, laziness, literature — what are your views on the Church? Mr Camacellany?

Camacellany: That night left a ditch in the mind where piped water runs amok which once quickened fallow land to fertility, potatoes (which need cropping), bitter vetch and St John's wort — function and beauty. To the south, the winter of lean rocks and herbs; to the north, monuments and wild grass that is gravestones, as I said before on this topic.

Luhan: Quite so.

(Short silence)

Williams: Give me Donnchadh Bàn any day. At least a man could understand him.

O'Huntin: The unlettered man could understand him, the ordinary crofter, the warm-hearted, generous and civil workers of the land. That's everything. That's literature!

Williams: Listen to Donnchadh Bàn on Beinn Dòbhrain — Gu stobanach, stacanach, slocanach, laganach, cnocanach, crapanach, caiteanach, ròmach, pasganach, badach, bachlagach, bòidheach, a h-aiseireine carrach 'nam farraichean mollach.[82]

Mag: (pinnacled)²; (groovy)²; (lumpy)² . . . and so on, whoever can understand the rest of it.

In 1974 Donald John MacLeod, reviewing Donald John MacDonald's *Sguaban Eòrna*, spluttered that it was "so . . . well, *Uibhisteach* (Uist)", and compared it unfavourably with Smith's work.[83] When, next year, a poet of a still later generation (Duncan MacLaren, a learner of Gaelic, see poem 309) could find nothing good at all to say of Smith's brilliant

Eadar Fealla-Dhà is Glaschu, we sense that a new era is dawning.[84] But by then the posthumous publication, in 1968, of *Sporan Dhòmhnaill* [*SD*], the collected work of Donald Macintyre (poems 56–65), had provided the first real opportunity to assess the case for twentieth-century 'traditional' verse on its merits; to me at least, this book arrived like a bombshell, blowing up into the air all the certainties about the superiority of the 'new' verse that I had imbibed since arriving at university in 1964.

As I have said, Macintyre was a S. Uist man who lived in Paisley and worked as a bricklayer. His work amounts to about 10,000 lines, and the subjects mentioned in his account of a ceilidh (poem 57) amount to a degree course in Celtic Studies.[85] As is normal with traditional poets, his most popular pieces are not necessarily his best. His song on the removal of the Stone of Destiny in 1950, for example (poem 59), does not have the depth of the one he made in praise of Kay Matheson, the Gaelic-speaking teacher from Inverasdale in Wester Ross who played a major part in the affair (*SD* 144–6). He displays a huge and limpid vocabulary, and that uncanny facility of expression which has died with the monoglot Gaelic world. Paisley he calls *an crò charbad seo*, 'this cattlefold of vehicles' (pp. 198–9 below). A gift has *còrn de phàipear glas air*, / *snasmhor air a lùbadh*, 'a horn (roll) of brown paper on it, / snazzily wrapped' (*SD* 289). He tells of a man *A ghabh air muin an eich-iarainn*, / *'S a shluig an ceò às ar fianais* 'Who mounted the iron horse [a bicycle, cf. poem 83] / And whom the mist swallowed from our sight' (*SD* 219). The bicycle has *acfhainn-mhiadhoin tri-fillt' ann*, / *Deas, ullamh, iasgaidh gu dìreadh* / *'S gu teàrnadh*, 'three-speed gears in it, / Ready, efficient, flexible for climbing / And descending' (*SD* 219). These examples are full of *mots justes* which we might not think of using today, and give an idea of how, through enlightened educational policies applied at the right time, Gaelic could have evolved organically into the twentieth-century world rather than being wrenched into it by an English-oriented society and all its media and institutions.

Macintyre's instincts are rooted in the seventeenth century. This has something to do with being a South Uist Catholic. Thoughts of the part played by Dr John MacCormick (whose Scottish Covenant secured over two million signatures for Home Rule in 1949–50) in the return of the Stone of Destiny to the authorities in 1951 remind him of the collusion between Covenanters and Cromwellians that led to the massacre of Highland troops at Inverkeithing in 1651 (poem 60), and he describes a Glasgow pub in poem 61 as if he had just fallen through a time-warp. He even includes the 'Gents'. Such a seventeenth-century view of the twentieth is in contrast to the twentieth-century view of the seventeenth that we find in Thomson's book *An Introduction to Gaelic Poetry*, in which, for example, it is suggested (p. 135) that the reputation of Màiri nighean Alastair Ruaidh has been greatly inflated. It is a surreal experience to read seven stanzas of Macintyre's 'Dìth nan Cungaidhean' ('The Shortage of Cosmetics') in which a young woman's behaviour does not breach the bounds of seventeenth-century terminology, then to find her in the eighth *a' nochdadh leugan de chalpa* / *Cho cuimir, dealbhach ri Gàrbo*, 'showing a smasher of a leg / As neat and shapely as Garbo'.[86] In poem 58, Macintyre revels in the violence of Mussolini's death in a way which would have turned even Iain Lom's stomach.[87] By contrast, in 'O, faighibh suas an Cogadh' (poem 65) Macintyre ranges over international politics with a gently left-wing irony that eluded even his editor (*SD* 378). He is perhaps clearer elsewhere: *Tha muinntir an airgid is dealbh 'nan sealladh* / *Air Ruisianaich dhearga 's an fhearg gan dalladh*, "The capitalists have a picture in view / Of red Russians blinded with rage" (*SD* 297). His very popular song on the coming of the rocket-range to Uist warns of the coming of plague to the Western Isles, and is chillingly prophetic in tone (*SD* 294, cf. poem 318). *Tha 'n Donas ann mu sgaoil*, / *Thug e 'n taod thar a làmh*. "The Devil's on the loose there, / He's got the halter off his hands."

He seems to be anti-racist: borrowing a line from mac Mhaighstir Alastair he says, *biodh iad dubh, no geal, no grìsfhionn,* / *Dh'fhuasgail E bhon chìs mar aon iad,* 'Be they black, or white, or grizzly, / He redeemed them all from sin' (*SD* 191). Yet anti-semitism shows through repeatedly. The same intellectual inconsistency can perhaps be found in the contrast between his three poems on the Stone of Destiny and his two fulsome elegies of George VI, a deeply superstitious man who regarded the removal of the Stone as a personal affront — he 'knew privately that he had only a few months to live, and wanted to be sure that his daughter would be properly crowned, on the Stone'.[88] But there again, in seventeenth-century terms it was no inconsistency at all to uphold a king's right to rule while opposing everything he tried to do; and anyway, in the tradition of Gaelic verse, Macintyre was a craftsman whose services could be bought no less than could those of physician, tailor or stonemason — his George VI elegies were commissioned by the BBC, and duly printed in *Gairm*.

It is in fact quite hard to substantiate charges of intellectual slackness against Macintyre. Poem 64 stands in critical contrast to generations of verse that romanticise the past: "The floor was just mud / Stamped underfoot, / Save that they'd shake a dash of sand on it, / And dampness streamed / Down the sooty walls — / Which today they're most loth to mention." In other words, there is an innovatory sensibility at work — this is not what his audience wanted to hear. Items like poem 62 offer symbolism as profound and thoughtful as any in innovatory verse, and only a lyrical imagination of startling originality could see the Gaelic language *Mar churra chnàmhach air mullach fàsaich* / *'S nach fuiling càch dhi bhith tighinn 'nan ceann,* 'As a bony heron on top of a wilderness / That no others will allow near them' (*SD* 142). He shows a sound grasp of history, a big-hearted sense of humour, a capacity for self-mockery; arguably, however, he is at his best when he simply uses to exuberant fullness the riches of his linguistic inheritance, as in his translations of Burns's 'Tam O' Shanter' (*SD* 315–26) and 'The Brigs of Ayr' (*SD* 98–9) and his brilliant satire on two lazy crofters, 'MacPhàil is MacThòmais' (*SD* 102–23).

One of Macintyre's most enjoyable poems, '"Bàrdachd nam Beann"' ('"The Poetry of the Bens"', *SD* 232–4), tells of his disappointment upon buying a book of that title in MacLaren's shop. "When I looked inside it / And read the verses, / I said to myself, 'Who's this bungler? / Who's this blubbering bard / Who raised you on high, / Attempting a craft when incompetent?' / What I'd call it is not / The poetry of the bens / That would suit the sons of the mountains, / But verses and lines / Without strength, without life, / Adequate for idiots and Lowlanders.

"There was an epoch / In the Land of the Mountains, / Before the times grew so sorrowful, / When if their ears had heard / Rubbish so awful, / The people would surely have shot him. / I chucked it away / To lie in a corner, / I couldn't bear to see it any longer; / No use would it be / Save for cleaning the rear / Of a man rushing off with diarrhoea." I have argued that the target of this priceless piece of literary criticism was in fact *Òrain nam Beann* (1913, reissued 1932, 1946), the first collection of Angus Morrison (poems 10–13).[89] I suspect that Morrison was already dead by the time Macintyre bought his book, but that the complaints would have been familiar to him, for he learned his lessons quickly and well — his *Dàin agus Òrain Ghàidhlig* of 1929 is a far better book, and seems to have sold out quite quickly, while the offending *Òrain nam Beann* could still be bought from Gairm Publications for £2 in 1999.

Macintyre's work offers fecund comparisons with innovatory verse. If for example we set his 'Aoir an Luchd-Riaghlaidh' (poem 63) against John Murray's Vietnam War piece 'An t-Acras' (poem 253), we find that both note the contrasting eating habits of the rich capitalist and the soldier who fights his wars for him; Macintyre sketches in the political and social context at great length, however, and touches on solutions, while Murray offers only some carefully-balanced central imagery with hints that both men may be equally unhappy.

And if we compare Macintyre's 'Aeòlus agus am Balg' (poem 56) with Iain Crichton Smith's 'A' Ghaoth' (poem 235) and James Thomson's a characteristically restrained little piece of the same name (poem 55), we have three poems about wind, one huge, two tiny; while Macintyre offers words and pictures on a cosmic scale, including damage to property and a moral and religious message, Smith just paints the same picture in a line or two then asks six unanswered questions which make the wind sound like an unruly adolescent. Thomson's can best be described as contemplative: he gives no answers, neither does he describe nor criticise. The balance of clarity favours Smith, yet it is clearly Macintyre who has composed the greatest poem.

Smith contributed a steady flow of poetry to *Gairm* from its beginning. In a way he was the Betjeman of Gaelic verse. Ordinary people and everyday objects flit in and out of his work. He watches television, sees *The Sound of Music* at the pictures. He makes much use of platitudes and commonplaces, but his work is never dull. He fires poems like machine-guns, spraying symbols and images everywhere. He expresses in a word what formerly took a stanza, being a master conductor who blends images, memories and ideas into an effortless symphony. *Orchestra mo ghaoil* ('The orchestra of my love'), he writes,[90] and calls up tradition with a nod to woodwind: *éiridh camhanaich no dhà*, 'a dawn or two will rise',[91] or *Co-dhiù thug e gu m' chuimhne / cruachan-mònach, muir is teine, / etcetera*. ('Anyway it brought to my memory / peat-stacks, sea and fire, / etcetera', poem 234.)

The fundamental tone and technique of a Smith poem changed little from the moment his first collection, *Bùrn is Aran* [*BA*], appeared in 1960. He rejoices in rhyme and rhythm but is no slave to them. Vocabulary is simple, ideas complex. His world is of the interior as Donnchadh Bàn's was of the exterior, and he observes and cherishes the intricacies of human behaviour as Donnchadh Bàn did that of the deer in 'Moladh Beinn Dòbhrain' (of which Smith published a translation).[92] To him the real world is the world as the mind sees it, so he retails experience not directly, like Derick Thomson or (sometimes) a camera, but as filtered and distorted by mind, memory, culture, language, imagination and so on, not to mention the pen, paper, books and other paraphernalia that surround him. He sits *air tulach inntinn* ('on a hillock of the mind', *BA* 61, *NBG* 174–5) or *air fàire m' inntinn* ('on the horizon of my mind', *BA* 60). A church opens, and *shuidh mi sìos innte 'nam inntinn*: 'I sat down inside it in my mind' (poem 230). Sailing over the Minch, he sees *clann-nighean naidhlon aig doras, / clachan Woolworth anns a' bhàgh* ('nylon girls in a doorway, / Woolworth's stones in the bay', *BSR* 25). Even the moon is likened to an indoor phenomenon, *truinnsear air balla* ('a plate on a wall', poem 238). He is capable of a lyric peak like *lainnir a' chuain mhóir 's a ghàire* ('the gleam of the great ocean and its laugh', *BA* 69), yet shrugs it off, almost as if this were MacLean talking and not himself.[93] He employs the symbolism of stark colours — white for purity, green for beauty, red for death, black for religion and hypocrisy, orange for exoticism and so on. He opposes static symbols of order and stability (*bìoball* 'bible', *ad* 'hat', *dìthean* 'flower', *laighe* 'lying down') to dynamic ones of disorder and instability (*seinn* 'singing', *danns* 'dancing', *ceòl* 'music', *dòrtadh* 'pouring', *slaodadh* 'pulling', *leum* 'leaping', *ruith* 'running', *falbh* 'travelling', *seòladh* 'sailing', *losgadh* 'burning', *teine* 'fire', *lasair* 'flame').[94] In poem 228 these are mixed and balanced to a degree reminiscent of the doctrine of the humours. *Cuan a' seinn* ('sea singing'), *Bìoball a' losgadh ann an làmhan / Gaoithe 's gréine* ('A Bible burning in the hands / Of wind and sun'), *Is grian a' dòrtadh, cuan a' dòrtadh* ('Sun pouring, sea pouring'), *Adan dubh' gu dorch a' seòladh* ('Black hats darkly sailing'), and so on — these paint a dynamic picture of a static scene to express the unity of the cosmos with private grief.

Smith once wrote that 'any form of ideology . . . always seems to me bad for an artist', but this does not mean that his work lacks coherence. His second collection, *Bìobuill is Sanasan-Reice* [*BSR*] of 1965, presents a consistently serious and deromanticised view of a world which had increasingly become confused, monocultural, monolingual and materialistic. His native Lewis is no longer the real world (*BA* 61, *NBG* 174–7), but provides the means of expression while the outside world (symbolised at random by Hiroshima and Pasternak) provides stimulation (*BSR* 19, *NBG* 180–1). 'An Litir' ('The Letter', *NBG* 186–9) offers a basic philosophical statement. Why did God crucify Christ and the men of the *Iolaire*, he asks? *Car son a dh'fhàg thu an iolair 'na h-aonar / ann an nead de sgòthan / crochte le ròpan / air a piocadh le tairgnean?* "Why did you leave the *iolair* (eagle) alone / in a nest of clouds / hanging from ropes / transfixed by nails?" He finds that in addition to His boxer's face and rusty helmet, God has a book with a steel fastening and an edge red as a rose — this rose, this symbol of beauty and stability, offers hope. Perhaps his best poem, however, is 'An t-Òban' (poem 230), which paints an atmospheric picture of the litter-strewn, rain-soaked promenade while exuding faint whiffs of Gaelic tradition: *'s air pàipear na rainn gan gearradh* ('with my verses being cut on paper') evokes a line of William Ross's valedictory 'Òran Eile', and *dh'fhalbh a' chuibhle leatha fhéin* ('the wheel has gone off by itself') doubles as the big wheel of the carnival and the 'wheel of fortune' beloved of poets like the *Clàrsair Dall*.[95] Everything seems reduced to paper, to advertisements — lions and tigers on circus posters, the town, the sea, the Gael (himself) who appears on the street now the tourists have gone, and is turned red and green by the traffic-lights until his bones appear as if in an X-ray. The circus posters make him feel that the Gael and his culture is being swallowed up by the modern world as surely as the Christians were fed to the lions in Palestine.

Smith's insights on the human menagerie were complemented by his free-verse studies of animal personality for children in *Na h-Ainmhidhean* (1979). His previous two collections, *Rabhdan is Rudan* [*RR*] of 1973 and *Eadar Fealla-Dhà is Glaschu* [*EFDG*] of 1974, showed his increasingly humorous bent. *RR* is for children, *EFDG* for adults, but both are enormously entertaining, and even a children's poem like 'Solas uaine, solas dearg' ('Green light, red light', *RR* 11) can offer a nice commentary on his use of symbolism. *EFDG* is full of cartoons in words, such as a delightful picture of when the Jehovah's Witnesses came to call (poem 236); words themselves often take a major role, as when he visualises proverbs as *baile de shiùil dhonna* ('a city of brown sails', poem 231). 'Mas e Ghàidhlig an Cànan' (poem 233) deals acutely with contemporary issues of culture and religion and is no less important for being gentle, amusing, and in rhyme. And since Smith loves scattering symbols, he takes to the haiku like a duck to water.

> Nighean le naidhlons
> gabhail seachad air prìosan —
> bàrdachd Uilleim Rois. (*EFDG* 14)

> A girl with nylons
> walking past a prison —
> the poetry of William Ross.

It is a style taken up later by Myles Campbell (poem 283) and, less explicitly, by Rody Gorman (poems 332–9).

Na h-Eilthirich [*NE*] of 1983 is a quiet collection of no great complexity, in which Smith reflects on youth, memory and the passage of time. It is in such contemplative work that his slightly manic faculty for picking the most unexpected word or phrase comes to the fore. Bonnie Prince Charlie is *a' seargadh sìos an subway* ('disappearing down the subway', *NE* 10), emigrant ships are *mar neapaigearan 'nar cuimhne* ('like handkerchiefs in our memory', poem 238), birds taking off and landing have *sgiathan sgaoilt is paisgt* ('wings spread and folded', *NE* 28). His Gaelic poetry is perhaps not as important as his Gaelic prose, in which he had fewer rivals, but it stands out for its stylistic sharpness, its questioning intelligence, its easygoing biculturalism, and its wit.

In 1985 the Scottish Poetry Library counted 40 living poets writing in Gaelic.[96] The full total was, and is, more like double this, but probably not over a hundred. In 1900 there would have been thousands, and indeed there were more Gaelic poets in the single island of

Tiree at the close of the nineteenth century than in the whole of Scotland at the close of the twentieth. But poetry of all kinds has continued to be written, and on all sorts of subjects, including for example Princess Diana (poem 176), the Falklands War (242), Marilyn Monroe (262), Indira Gandhi (269), pornography (296, 333), homosexuality (314) and football (344).

Of poets who emerged in the final quarter of the century the most representative voice is that of Myles Campbell. The obvious influences on his work are Thomson and Smith: his voice is thoughtful, probing, experimental, his subjects both private and public, and through several collections he has offered a wry commentary on his times. He makes his points with a succinct and passionate clarity.

> Tha an saoghal gam shealg The world is pursuing me
> on dh'fhalbh Seonaidh, since Johnnie left,
> on a chaidh e mach since he went out
> 'na dheise bhuidhe ghiuthais in his yellow pine suit
> 's na putanan cumha.[97] with the . . . buttons.

This is a blend of ancient and modern. Traditional motifs are quickened by the suit and buttons, and the last line is impossible to translate because the buttons are not of *umha* ('brass') but of *cumha* ('grief').

Campbell's 'An Referendum air son Pàrlamaid ann an Alba' (poem 274) is brilliantly constructed in two halves — on Referendum day, and on the day after. Snow-covered Scotland is seen as a virgin going to her wedding. By the end of the second half he has moved from St Matthew's oil-less virgin (Matt. xxv) to a firmly atavistic referent — the picture of keening women who clap and rub their hands until their palms are bleeding and blistered is central to the Gaelic elegiac tradition. Curiously, Fearghas MacFhionnlaigh provides a fresh twist to this personification of Scotland:

> Se siùrsach na Roinn Eòrpa th' annad, You are the whore of Europe,
> le mascara gorm is craos deargsmeurt' with blue mascara and red-smeared mouth
> is làmh iarrtasach sìnt' a-mach, and soliciting hand outstretched,
> gun cuimhn'ad idir, a réir coltais, oblivious, apparently,
> gun robh thu uair 'nad òigh 's 'nad bhànrigh. that you once were a virgin and a queen.[98]

A little like Smith, Campbell lived most of his life away from his native island (Skye, though he has Lewis connections too) without going so far as to settle in the city: his choice was Tobermory in Mull, a location that gave him many opportunities to reflect on the wreck of Gaeldom (e.g. poem 277). For some modern poets the relationship with the homeland continues to be of prime importance in their work; others, like MacFhionnlaigh and Aonghas MacNeacail (poems 255–65), offer a highly global outlook.

MacNeacail has examined the condition of his beloved language through the fecund symbolism of nature, love and sexual desire. Sea and land teem cosmically with life in the long poems 'Sireadh Bradain Sicir' (poem 255) of 1983 and 'An Cathadh Mór' (poem 256) of 1984, while his collections *An Seachnadh* (1986) and *Oideachadh Ceart* (1996) exude the electric quality of hard-won personal experience more than any other book of Gaelic verse since *Dàin do Eimhir*. Darwin and Frazer are his heroes, not Marx or Christ, and as for Freud, he 'unlocked nothing that was not in my loins' (poem 257). Emotion is both whetted by nature and reinterpreted in terms of it. In 'Acras' (poem 258) the woman — or the Gaelic language — is the sea, rising red-lipped at dawn to offer food before retreating; in 'An Eilid Bhàn' (poem 259) she becomes a white hind, loved by him but stalked and gralloched by others like the deer of Donnchadh Bàn's 'Beinn Dòbhrain'. A passionately committed writer of robust, sensuous verse that owes something to the past for its imagery while being strikingly modern in form, MacNeacail first succeeded Hay as the leading nature poet in Gaelic, then went on to become a librettist (poems 264–5), using exciting mixtures of innovative and traditional forms to bring Gaelic verse to a larger public audience than it had ever enjoyed before (if we exclude the lyrics of the rock band Runrig, that is).

Before returning finally to the central theme of tradition and innovation, we should note three distinct trends in the last quarter. The first is a return to mythology. The second is what I think we may call the 'refeminisation' of Gaelic verse. And the third is the arrival of learners, that is, those for whom Gaelic is not their mother tongue.

I referred at p. xxii to what I called the 'romanticism' of the first quarter. It was fuelled by mythology (cf. poems 3, 40), backed up by *Carmina Gadelica* and *The Songs of the Hebrides*, and epitomised by poems about *Tìr nan Òg* (p. xl). Shorn of romanticism, the mythological strand survived in the poets of the second quarter — one can point to MacLean's celebration of the name Eimhir and to the density of mythological allusion in such items as poems 100 and 118. Hay, with his Classical training, applied a more broadly-based mythology (poem 150), while Donald Macintyre and Joan MacKenzie knew the mythological tales of the ceilidh-house (poems 57, 75); Macintyre enjoyed pointing to the mythic significance of the Stone of Destiny (poem 59). Others, like Roderick Mackay, still lived in a society in which superstition and pre-Christian ritual retained their place alongside orthodox Christianity (poem 20). The poets of the third quarter appeared to reject everything of this kind, Derick Thomson issuing his 'Warning against Folklore Worshippers' (poem 196). In the fourth quarter, however, it became acceptable to re-examine eschatological concepts and push them forward (poems 175, 198, 287). William Neill and Christopher Whyte picked up the broader mythological strand where Hay had left it off, indeed Whyte's first collection was called *Uirsgeul* ('Myth'). Aonghas MacNeacail explored cosmological ideas in a manner strongly influenced by mythologies while untrammeled by religion or humanism (poems 255–9); he returned with eagerness to the great themes and characters of Gaelic mythology for his librettos (poems 264–5), and both he and Angus Peter Campbell wrote studies of calendar ritual (poems 260, 320). It is clear, then, that by the end of the century Gaelic verse was willing to engage squarely with mythology while firmly rejecting romanticism. It had got Kenneth Macleod (poems 15, 126) out of its system without losing the heroic memory of Alexander Carmichael (poems 2, 110, 129, and see p. lxvi).

The female voice, mostly anonymous, was once dominant enough in Gaelic verse to set the prevailing tone. The imagery and passion of women's worksong and lament were so strong that other genres were drawn magnetically towards them. Formal panegyric was at its best in the sincere little concluding stanzas that the classical poets of the sixteenth and seventeenth centuries dedicated to the wives and daughters of the chiefs. Under vernacular influence, Scottish classical verse edged away from its Irish exemplars and took on the sound and colouring of its natural surroundings; vernacular panegyric took on the feel of worksong when great female poets such as Màiri nighean Alastair Ruaidh and Mairearad nighean Lachainn got to work on it. In the fierce competition that existed for patronage, both of these women appear to have been deeply resented by their male opponents for their evident popularity and success. Many of the great songs that influenced MacLean (and were repeatedly praised by him in print) were women's songs, and Roxanne Reddington-Wilde has drawn attention to the ways in which male poets such as Iain Lom would adopt the female voice to achieve a particular purpose — most specifically, in calling for revenge upon those who murdered MacDonald of Keppoch and his brother in 1663. "He felt able, from the stance of a feminised lament, to criticise the clan as a whole about their actions (or lack of them) towards their chief."[99] It was precisely this authoritative female voice that Duncan Livingstone evoked to such effect after the Sharpeville Massacre (poem 29).

It is usually, as I have said, an anonymous voice, but once or twice in every century it has taken on the power of flesh and blood for us, in the form for example of Aithbhreac inghean Coirceadail in the fifteenth century, Marion Campbell in the sixteenth, the two whom I have mentioned in the seventeenth, Sìleas na Ceapaich and Bean Torra Dhamh in the eighteenth, and Mary MacPherson (*Màiri Mhòr nan Òran*, 'Big Mary of the Songs', 1821–98, the much-loved propagandist of the Land Reform movement) in the nineteenth.[100] *An Tuil* begins (poem 1) with a woman poet, but after the death in 1928 of Katherine Whyte (poems 3–5) the influence of women seems to dissipate (except as mediated by MacLean). Only four women ever won the Bardic Crown (pp. 821–2). Women 're-emerge' in our collection in the personae of Christina Macleod from Bayble in Lewis (poems 37–8), Joan MacKenzie from Harris (poem 75), Christina Stewart, again from Bayble (poem 136), Mary M Maclean from Grimsay (poems 181–2), Catherine Macdonald from Staffin in Skye (poems 221–2), and Christina A MacKay from Achmore in Lewis (poem 241).[101] What this suggests (I think) is that Gaelic literature, as a natural product of a complete society, had experienced a form of death in 1919 (see pp. xxii–xxiii above), the subsequent *tuil* being the artificial creation of a hugely successful men's club.

In the last quarter of the century, the female voice finally regained some of that strength and clarity that had perished with Màiri Mhór in 1898. Beginning with *A' Choille Chiar* in 1974, the work of Catriona and Morag Montgomery (two sisters from Skye) shows at first the influence of MacLean, then develops along individual paths (poems 292–4, 303–8). In 1985 Màiri Macdonald from Grimsay produced a collection, *Mo Lorgan Fhìn*, full of the ghosts of the past and of the future (see poem 240). Mary Montgomery from Arivruaich in Lewis (who is also a highly accomplished Gaelic novelist) began to write with great intelligence and wit on language, culture and nationalism (poems 322–4). Her work can be difficult but rewarding. With the gifted Meg Bateman and Anne Frater in addition (poems 325–31, 348–51), it is clear that in the final quarter, female poets were beginning to catch up. Also worth noting here is the experience of secondary schools and universities at the close of the twentieth century that Gaelic was becoming 'a girls' subject'.

If the term is to have any meaning, of course, 'refeminisation' is about more than the existence of female poets. It is about the greater empowerment of poetry through the application of female qualities. While it is hard to deduce examples of this from the twentieth century as specific as Reddington-Wilde's from the seventeenth, it seems to me that poems 76, 273 and 317 provide starting-points for an examination of the concept.

The third trend to note is the increasing prominence of learners. For almost the first time, it is now possible to find work which would get slightly better marks for content than for form (e.g. poems 220, 299, 345, 347). Such people learn as they write, and their verse can grow steadily in assurance. The early Gaelic work of the doyen of the group, William Neill, for whom the acquisition of Gaelic was the expiation of guilt (poem 211), concerned the state of Scotland and the symbols which unite and divide her — kilt, haggis, Edinburgh, landlords, grouse-moors, city Gaels — as well as the early literature and mythology of Scotland, Ireland, Rome and Greece. It has been pointed out that 'a greater concern about symbols than reality' is the Scottish people's abiding fault; but then, symbolism is above all a poet's job.[102] In fact, thanks to his habit of dating his poems, it is possible to trace Neill's development, not to say emergence, as a Gaelic poet, and after about 1980 the virtues of simplicity, modesty and humour appear as his eye focuses on objects and individuals rather than ideas and clichés. His return to the land of his roots in south-west Scotland may have something to do with this — he begins to notice things like *cnàmhan dhaoine is cnàmhan bragsaidh fon fhraoch*, 'bones of men and bones of braxy under the heather'. An element of Smith-like unpredictability appears, too: *Gàidhlig is Albais is Beurla / 'nan Sliabh an t-Siorraim buan dhomh*, 'Gaelic and Scots and English / an eternal Sheriffmuir to me'.[103] He inherits Hay's one-nation left-wing nationalism, and can be trusted to comment pungently on the 'white settler' phenomenon, as does Catriona Montgomery.[104] But he came to the language too late. His Gaelic verse lacks music.

Another learner, Fearghas MacFhionnlaigh (poems 295–301), is an explosively good poet with a very distinctive voice. He tells us a little bit about himself in one of his long poems.

Thogadh mi faisg air Toronto,	I grew up near Toronto,
a' tilleadh a dh'Alba aig deich bliadhna dh'aois.	returning to Scotland at the age of ten.
'Nam inntinn òg shaoil mi	In my young mind I thought
nach bitheadh droch-chainnt idir	there would be no bad language
am measg nan Albannach;	among the Scots;
nach bitheadh sgeulachdan salach acasan	they would have no dirty stories
a bha air taobh thall a' chuain.	on the other side of the ocean.
Cha robh fios agam aig an àm sin	I didn't know at that time
air Ceirbearas agus a chaochladh chinn.	about Cerberus and his various heads.[105]

His is the Gaelic of the computer age, the extension (one might say) of Thomson's biology textbook, full of compounds, assimilated loanwords and international scientific terms. He makes no concessions to lexical tradition. (In this he stands diametrically opposed to Donald Macintyre and Sorley MacLean, who took pride in employing the existing resources of the language.) An art teacher by profession, his work has instant visual impact. A typical beginning is *siet-phlèan a' sàthadh* 'jet-plane thrusting'.[106] A poem about de Bohun at Bannockburn starts *thàinig e oirbh mar shrònadharcach 'na dheann*, 'he came at you like a rhinoceros at speed' (poem 297), while one on Humpty-Dumpty ends laconically with the English words *eggshell finish*.[107] Flowers may be described as *neon-dhearg* 'neon-red' or *factoraidhean foto-cho-chur a' beò-ghlacadh na gréine* 'photosynthesis factories seizing the sun alive' (poems 295, 298).

His principal field of reference is art, his cultural background cosmopolitan, his reading wide. His passions are God, art and nationalism; these and other themes are examined in 'A' Mheanbhchuileag' (poem 299), a 708-line philosophical treatise of considerable depth and power. Its unifying theme is *so-leòntachd*, 'vulnerability': the poet sees a midge caught in a spider's web, a symbol of strength and weakness, power and martyrdom. His thoughts, thus provoked, range broadly over religion, history, art and politics. In the middle of the poem are the epigraphic words: *AM FEAR A DHIÙLTAS SO-LEÒNTACHD, THÉID E 'NA CHLACH!* "THE MAN WHO REFUSES VULNERABILITY WILL BECOME A STONE!" He is fond of small things — like Gaelic, like Scotland — so, at the end, in God's name, he picks up a knife and releases the midge, concluding that the dynamic of the universe is 'vulnerability and power; / and mercy'. There is meat and music in it (unfortunately not always at the same time) and it is undoubtedly an important poem.

Subsequent long poems have added further still to MacFhionnlaigh's reputation. Provoked by his mother's death, 'Iolair, Brù-Dhearg, Giuthas' (poem 300) offers a very sharply-focused symbolism on the relationships between matter, existence, time and eternity. His vitality has been increasingly tested by the real world: 'Bogha-Frois san Oidhche' (poem 301) is an account of how his seven-year-old son was struck down by a virus in the brain. The dreams in it are those of a child, the nightmares those of an adult. The world is an entirely modern one, and MacFhionnlaigh's normally substantial poetic bibliography is reduced to little more than *The Wizard of Oz* — the Judy Garland film, presumably, as well as Frank Baum's book — and the Bible.[108]

Other learners have included California's Gaelic poet Dennis King, who expresses the instability of his environment in poems like 'Trocadero Transfer, San Francisco';[109] the Ulsterman Victor Price, whose view of the Highlands is that of the most kindly and intelligent type of tourist (poem 244); Peadar Morgan, who brought into the fold of modern verse a part of the world (Badenoch) recently lost to the language, thus demonstrating a type of service to which the learner, being 'territorially neutral', is well suited (poem 340); Alasdair Barden, who died tragically in 1998 with a great deal still to give (poem 345); and Meg Bateman, already mentioned.

One learner making rapid strides at the close of the century was Rody Gorman, whose work is full of sardonic humour, irony and whimsy (poems 332–9). Displaying quite the opposite of Morgan's historical instincts, he epitomises the moment of time in which he lives. The mixtures of love and hate, passion and doubt, estrangement and divorce in his work do not seem to apply to religion or to homeland — as far as it is possible to judge, when he refers in his poetry to a relationship with a woman, the subject is just that. His collection *Cùis-Ghaoil* contains over 150 short poems in which such a relationship is obsessively and exhaustively examined through over 150 different images. The contrast is not merely with Morgan but with MacLean and MacNeacail, whose preoccupations are clearly multi-layered. What Gorman provides in good measure, however, like the *bàrd baile* of old and the TV set of today, is entertainment. He has something of Smith's sense of the ridiculous, allied to a talent for self-mockery also found in Myles Campbell (poem 276). His verse is a delight.

In the third quarter, as I have shown, there was on the one hand an exciting legacy of spiritual verse and on the other that resentful anti-Calvinism epitomised by Smith's *adan dubha* ('black hats', poem 228). At the end of the fourth quarter Catherine Macdonald's hymns lay unsold in large numbers along the shelves of the Stornoway Religious Bookshop, while poets like Derick Thomson and Myles Campbell were left in their maturity to present a probing and far from unsympathetic view of religion — Thomson doubting doubt, while Campbell saw himself as 'I who am afraid / to be a Christian, / who am afraid / to be a sinner' (poem 275). Donald John Maciver's verse is as guilt-ridden as his short stories, but not as morbid: "Will you give me forgiveness / for seeking forgiveness, / even for forgiveness / of forgiveness?" (poem 268). Angus Peter Campbell is of some interest here as the first 'modernist' Gaelic poet to come from an island Catholic background; in a manner characteristic of the third quarter he abandoned religion, in a manner characteristic of the fourth he rediscovered it. There are other Catholic voices, of different kinds, in contemporary Gaelic verse, mainly however those of people without an island background, such as Anthony Dilworth and Christopher Whyte. In poem 309 Duncan MacLaren, who later became director of the Scottish Catholic International Aid Fund, depicts the sectarianism of urban west central Scotland in graphic terms.

It was all highly symptomatic of how the gap between traditional and innovatory verse had closed. Poets like MacLean and Hay who once seemed *avant garde* could now be seen to occupy various parts of the middle ground. With the benefit of hindsight, one realised that the subject of a poem like Calum Graham's innovatory 'Daoine bha an Leòdhas uaireigin' (poem 266) could be traced back in a straight line through, for example, the likes of 'Ho-ro siùdaibh i' by Murdo Murray (q.v.) to 'Sgoil a' Chruadail' by John Smith of Iarshader in the nineteenth century and 'Birlinn Chlann Raghnaill' in the eighteenth.[110] And as Donald John MacDonald of Peninerine cast off what remained of the mantle of the *bàrd baile* to express serious global concerns in stately but varied metres, Derick Thomson picked it up by playing to his new-found gallery and sparking off delightful modernist ditties on trivial-sounding events.

Although by the last quarter the ceilidh-house tradition was gone (or almost gone, see p. 788), traditional poetry survived. Hymns, elegies, lovesongs, popsongs, praise of places and comic songs were all still being made, and satires too. The death of such a respected clergyman as Mgr Neil Mackellaig of Daliburgh remained capable of provoking two or three elegies (poems 96, 174). Items like these might circulate orally, in photocopied manuscript, in typescript, in a parish newsletter, in a community newspaper such as *Dé Tha Dol?* in Harris or *Am Pàipear* in Uist, or in *The Stornoway Gazette*. And traditional verse can take a long time to appear in print. Poem 134, a definitive verse account of the 'Whisky Galore' saga of 1941, took forty years.

As the century reached its end an acceleration appeared to take place in the rate of publication of such poetry. In 1998 there appeared *Chì Mi*, the collected poems of Donald John MacDonald, q.v.; *Moch is Anmoch*, the poems of Donald A MacNeill, Colonsay (1924–95), whose 'Mo Charaid Balbh' (then called 'Cù an t-Sealgair') came second to Norman Maclean's 'Maol Donn' (poem 254) at the 1967 Mod; and *Òrain Red*, the songs of Kenneth MacLeod (1899–1977) from Bayble in Point, Lewis, which are full of incisive and humorous reflections on the nature of change in a crofting community and the strategies by which people adapt to it. In 1999 there appeared *Òrain Dhòmhnaill Ailein*, the collected poems of Donald Allan MacDonald (q.v.), and *Bàrdachd Dhòmhnaill Alasdair*, the poetry of Dòmhnall Alasdair Dòmhnallach from Garrabost in Point, Lewis, who spent half of his working life in the RAF and the other half caring for the blind in the Western Isles — a poetry expressing modern concerns in traditional metres, musing if the Western Isles were ever an Eden, while reliving over and over the trauma of the Wartime gunner in Bomber Command.

Spreadhadh tric gar n-iathadh,	Flak often surrounding us,
Sgailc aig' air gach cliathaich,	Rattling on each side,
A' tolladh 's a' riabadh	Piercing and tearing
Na h-iarmailt 'nar sealladh;	The sky in our sights;
'Nar cuinnlean neo-chùbhraidh	Not sweet in our nostrils
Bhiodh fàileadh an fhùdair,	Was the scent of powder,
Solais-lorg a' tighinn dlùth	Searchlights coming close
'S ar sùilean dhan dalladh.	And blinding our eyes.

Also in 1999 came Tim Neat's *The Voice of the Bard*, which attempted for almost the first time to lay open this 'hidden Scotland' of twentieth-century traditional verse to the non-Gaelic reader, and finally, almost as if in deliberate contrast, an eye-opener for the connoisseur — the remarkable *Tiugainn do Sgalpaigh*, the collected work of John Morrison, *Seonaidh Fhionnlaigh* from Scalpay, Harris (b. 1914), now living in Grangemouth, whose songs were already popular but whose many elegies turned out to combine a modern sensitivity with a traditional craftsmanship so profound, so perfect, that the effect on opening the book was rather like turning the corner to go to the supermarket and discovering that a renaissance cathedral had appeared overnight in its place.

This then is a good place to emphasise my dislike for the Gaelic term *bàrd baile* and the equivalent English term 'bard' — I have used 'bard' just twice in this essay, at pp. xxxviii and xli. They were used as loaded weapons in the tradition–innovation wars of the 1960s. What they seek to imply is that such a person is a laureate of a small community and therefore narrow in his (or her) view of the world. In practice, however, such poets have typically fought a war, sailed seven seas, or otherwise sweated blood far and wide for a living, and their view of their community is by no means uncritical or lacking in global perspective. What they reflect is the value of 'community' itself, in a sense which came to be far better appreciated at the end of the century than ever before. MacLean called the term 'village poetry' a 'snobbish classification' on the grounds that 'the light-hearted village poetry of Charles Matheson of Braes had a sure and consistent brilliance of phrase and rhythm that made him a master of the mock-heroic'.[111] John MacInnes translated *bàrd baile* as 'poet of a township' and remarked: "Traditionally, the phrase described verse and rhyme-makers whose reputation was never likely to extend beyond the bounds of their own townships. It now seems to designate all versifiers who live in the Gaelic-speaking areas . . ."[112]

Between his thesis of 1983 and his book of 1999 Fr John Angus Macdonald shifted somewhat from 'village poet' to 'local poet', while in both works he pointed out that 'despite very strong and clearly discernible ties with his homeland of South Uist, Donald MacIntyre composed his poetry for the "village" of the Gaelic-speaking community of Scotland's Central Belt, where he spent most of his adult life'.[113] That, in my opinion, is the way we must look at it: either no poet is a *bàrd baile*, or every poet is a *bàrd baile*; either no poet is a bard, or every poet is a bard.

Aonghas MacNeacail shares my distaste for the distinction. Speaking of the growing interest in the 'village bards' in the last quarter of the century he describes it as "a term I dislike, as it seems to contain them in a box. 'Social poetry' might define the work better, if what such poets do needs to be categorised differently from the work of any other poet."[114] In the course of these two sentences there is a subtle shift of emphasis — it is certainly better to speak of poetry than of poets, of *bàrdachd* than of *bàird*. If we see twentieth-century Gaelic poetry as a rainbow, poems at the cutting edge of innovation (such as MacNeacail's own) are a pot of gold at one end, songs in the purity of the oral tradition are a pot of gold at the other.

The unfortunate mutual alienation of the two extremes is highlighted I think by the following two opinions. First, 'modern' verse seen from a 'traditional' viewpoint:

> I must say, too, that some of the poetry written by Sammy (as we used to say) is far, far beyond my understanding. I don't understand at all why he is doing as he is. If the brilliance of the poetry is so strong why doesn't he write in English? He would be more famous and he would make money! But perhaps he isn't so worldly![115]

Next, 'traditional' verse seen from a 'modern' viewpoint:

> One of the crucial features of these songs was their transience, a concept that is hard for most Western Europeans to grasp, used as we are to the permanence of the written word. They were oral both in use and in nature and were never meant to be written. By being transcribed, they have been so divorced from their function that they are transformed into different entities and judged by inappropriate criteria.[116]

The biggest difference, then, appears to be between poetry and song, or, to use Gaelic terms, between poetry that is 'written' and poetry that is 'made'. This difference (and the transience of song) is entirely familiar to all Western Europeans. And the distinction was a functional one in traditional Gaelic literary criticism. For example, referring to the work of Murdo MacFarlane, of all people, John Nicolson (q.v.) once said: "It's not for singing, it's *bàrdachd*. Songs and *bàrdachd* are two different things."[117]

In an oral tradition, singing was synonymous with publication, a poem unsung was a poem kept to oneself and forgotten, so ultimately the distinction is between public and private. The resolution of the issue therefore lies, I think, in a view attributed to Myles Campbell:

> Maoilios sees a distinction between community verse (*bàrdachd coimhearsnachd*) and personal verse (*bàrdachd phearsanta*). The two always existed, but there was not previously such a big gulf between them. The first kind of poetry often confirms feelings and thoughts that already exist in the community. The second kind is confidential, personal and apart from the community, and emerges from values held by the individual. This conflict is evident in the arts throughout the world — conflict between tradition/community on the one hand and a personal view on the other.[118]

We may note that he avoids the term *bàrdachd baile*, that the term *coimhearsnachd* ('neighbourhood', hence 'community') is open nowadays to a very broad definition, and that, since he speaks of *bàrdachd* and not of *bàird*, he also leaves open the possibility — or likelihood, or inevitability — that *bàrdachd coimhearsnachd* and *bàrdachd phearsanta* will be composed by one and the same person. His view that the gulf between personal and public verse is growing, not diminishing, is of great interest; it is a gulf, as he suggests, that exists within the work of poets of all kinds, and the reader can only be left to wonder what 'personal' means, exactly, if it refers to verse written for publication.

For Gaelic in general, the final quarter of the twentieth century was one of revival, but that revival took place in education, the mass media, and various forms of prose — not in its use as a community language, and not in poetry, whose renaissance arrived earlier and may be said to have provoked the rest. However, the 'tradition v. innovation' debate took another intriguing twist. In the third quarter, as we have seen, it had been between those who stood for traditional metres and traditional religious beliefs on the one side, and those who practised free verse and humanism on the other. By the 1970s these barriers were breaking down, and Christian poets such as the Rev. Roderick Macdonald and Duncan MacLeod were becoming perfectly willing to express religious belief in free verse (poems 179, 251), while Fearghas MacFhionnlaigh has been called 'the most innovative and exciting of contemporary religious poets in Gaelic' by a critic who sees the poet's knife as the invading grace of God cutting through existentialism and materialism.[119] In the last quarter, with the empowerment of learners, tradition came to mean the expression of a Gaelic literary sensibility, and innovation the *lack* of such a sensibility (or, rather, its replacement by other sensibilities). One of the earliest and bluntest expressions of this polarity came from Julian Ronay in 1975 (poem 310): in stark contrast to the innovators of the third quarter, Gaelic and the Western Isles have to him no necessary connection, and his concern is solely with the health of the former. Crudely put, it is the old Scottish (and Irish) syndrome of Gael and Gall. It must not be seen as surprising, however, that the 'guru' of innovation in the third quarter, Donald MacAulay, became the champion of tradition in the fourth, because it was always the innovators' claim that they were expressing a Gaelic literary sensibility better than were the traditionalists.

The crucial text of this debate is MacAulay's *Gairm* review of Christopher Whyte's 'last-quarter' anthology *An Aghaidh na Sìorraidheachd*, which contained verse by MacNeacail, Myles Campbell, Catriona Montgomery, MacFhionnlaigh, Whyte himself, Mary Montgomery, Bateman, and Frater.[120] Prof. MacAulay has kindly read and corrected my translation of the key passage.

> I think a good deal of this poetry is not very Gaelic (*Gaidhealach*) although it is in Gaelic, and does not have much connection with the tradition, with Gaelic convention (*ris an traidisean, ri gnàthas na Gàidhlig*). I am not speaking particularly with reference to language. There is a gain and a loss in that respect. The gain is the substantial expansion in words representing new concepts (*coincheapan ùra*) and the freedom with which they are used; the loss is the weakness and disjunction that can be seen, especially in the accidence (*an lapachd agus am mì-amladh a tha ri fhaicinn gu sònraichte san deilbheachd*). The biggest gulf to be discerned is that between the basic codes of this poetry and the basic codes of traditional verse (*bun-riochd na bàrdachd ghnàthasaich*) — and between their respective accents (*eadar blas na dhà aca*); perhaps that is a linguistic matter!
>
> That change of accent is to be found in spite of the mimicking of convention and of 'modern' Gaelic verse (*an atharrais air a' ghnàthas agus air an 'nua-bhàrdachd' Ghàidhlig*) that is to be seen throughout the book (except perhaps in the poetry of Christopher Whyte). Although that new verse, as seen in the other anthology *Nua-bhàrdachd Ghàidhlig*, for example, has brought about a metamorphosis (*cruth-atharrachadh*) in many ways, it never lost the flavour of the tradition (*blas a' ghnàthais*). Much of this book is a step away from it.
>
> But that is only natural. Gaelic, and its poetry, is being drawn out into the current of the world

as a whole by its users, both native speakers (*luchd dùthchais*) and learners. That brings its own flavour. (*Bheir sin a bhlas fhèin oirre.*) And perhaps, with time, it will establish a new tradition. Although that is not yet at the stage at which we can discern its shape there is enough innovation (*annas*) and food for thought (*adhbhar smaoineachaidh*) in this collection to keep us talking and thinking for a long time (What is translation, for example?). There is mental stimulation (*toileachas inntinn*) in it too, of many kinds, if we read it with a mind that is open and flexible . . .

What MacAulay seemed to regard as missing above all was Gaelic convention (*gnàthas na Gàidhlig*). It would be useful to have a clear definition of *gnàthas na Gàidhlig*, which is I think an important concept; perhaps it involves, for example, Gaelic preoccupations with regard to subject-matter (religion, language, homeland); Gaelic social assumptions (small is beautiful, the weak must be helped); Gaelic modes of expression (the inheritance of the 'panegyric code' with, for example, its pervasive tree-imagery). But then, there is a very different argument that says, "So what?" It is an argument based on the identity of the poet as an individual human being rather than as a member of a cultural community.

Whyte's poetic response was strong and clear. It has to be said, however, that it appeared at first in his work that the potential difficulties brought to Gaelic verse by the new wave of learners were coming to a head. Items like 'Fontana Maggiore' (poem 315) happened to read beautifully in English, but sprang entirely from non-Gaelic models and sensitivities, and appeared not to have an independent Gaelic existence, to the extent that the Gaelic versions could not easily be understood without reference to the English. As my friend Dr John MacInnes once memorably said, "It loses something in the original."

Whyte was well aware of such difficulties, however. "I'm only beginning, my lips / are clumsy and stammering . . ." (poem 313). In the final decade of the century his Gaelic voice grew in assurance (thanks to much practice in both original work and translation). He is a George Campbell Hay with a background which lacks Hay's Highland element but makes up for it with a strong, not to say exotic, cosmopolitanism. 'Fontana Maggiore', placed in the mouth of the sculptor Giovanni Pisano, hints strongly at Whyte's belief in poetry as craftsmanship, while 'An Daolag Shìonach' (poem 316) expresses his aims: it is, in effect, the literary purpose of 'Mochtàr is Dùghall' without the philosophising. 'Bho Leabhar-Latha Maria Malibran' (poem 317) is a deliberate (and hugely successful) attempt to write in Gaelic without a trace of *gnàthas na Gàidhlig*, and his belligerent conclusion to that poem picks up more or less where Julian Ronay left off in 1975.

In 1998 a debate took place on the translation of Gaelic poetry.[121] It had clearly become an issue. The initiative was taken by Wilson McLeod, an American learner of Gaelic, who pointed out that over thirty years since the 1960s the profile of the English language in collections of Gaelic poetry had typically risen from translations of a small number of poems at the back to facing-page translations of every item. "There is thus no space in which Gaelic poetry exists on its own, to be considered and assessed on its own terms: from the first moment of exposure to the world it is over-shadowed and usurped."

There is an element of exaggeration here. Many collections still appear in Gaelic only. Myles Campbell's *Bailtean* of 1987 included facing English translations, his *A' Gabhail Ris* of 1994 (also from Gairm Publications) did not. And the principal fora for informed critical assessment are *Gairm* (in Gaelic), *The Scotsman* (in Gaelic), radio (in Gaelic), *The West Highland Free Press* (in English), its insert *An Gaidheal Ùr* (in Gaelic), *The Stornoway Gazette* (in Gaelic or English), *Cothrom* (in Gaelic *and* English), *Chapman* (in English). But there are certainly things to worry about.

Firstly, the books without translations are usually 'traditional', the books with translations are usually 'innovative'. There is an imbalance.

Secondly, Donald MacAulay wrote in 1967 in *Seòbhrach ás a' Chlaich*, in which 27 out of 78 poems were translated, "An attempt has been made to preserve the spirit, and the content and lay-out as far as this proved possible, of the poems translated. Where this proved impossible, translations are not given." If it is so possible to translate things nowadays, what has changed? Could it be that poems are written with translation in mind? Alternatively, could it be that those who feel as MacAulay did in 1967 are inhibited from producing collections?

Thirdly, as McLeod pointed out, in 1998 Aonghas MacNeacail was awarded a 'Scottish Writer of the Year' prize for *Oideachadh Ceart* (1996) by a panel of judges none of whom were able to understand the Gaelic originals in that book. Seemingly they had not come across Sorley MacLean's dictum, "Gaelic poetry that is published with English translations cannot be assessed on its translation alone even by the most honest and perceptive of critics who do not know Gaelic."[122] My concern however is not that justice was not done in this case, but that Mary Montgomery, for example, was presumably disenfranchised by the fact that her collection *Ruithmean 's Neo-Rannan* (1997) was published in Scottish and Irish Gaelic, without any English. This took some of the gloss off MacNeacail's well-deserved success, which is a shame.

McLeod's article was answered by MacNeacail himself:

> I believe it is, at present, not only possible but imperative for Gaelic poets to communicate with a wider audience than our own language community can provide. That very question of numbers is a crucial factor. At the basic economic level, it makes our books more viable and we, surely, are as entitled as any other serious writers to seek viability. By doing so, we also offer yet another door, however narrow, for those who are curious about Gaelic to peer in, and perhaps eventually to step into our world. It should also be remembered that a high proportion of Gaels, particularly older Gaels, cannot comfortably read their own language.

This does not, of course, answer the point that the writer who is willing to 'give in' to English translation is making things difficult for those who do not wish to make such a concession, or have not been invited to do so. Poets may have a variety of reasons for not wishing to translate their own work: for example, at least one Gaelic poet who is not a native speaker of the language has chosen never again to translate his work into English, apparently after suffering the humiliation of being told that his English translations are better than his Gaelic originals.

A third, and entirely neutral, contribution to the debate came from Peter France, who spoke of how a translation can become a source of insight, but also pointed out that translation from a minority into a majority language can be seen as a political act: one of aggression, of colonisation, in which 'the translator is a raider, bringing home booty which is then made available like tea or sugar to consumers in the dominant cultures'. By this argument poets who translate their own work are quislings.

One small point made by McLeod which neither MacNeacail nor myself can accept is that the left-hand pages of a book are 'less prominent' than the right-hand pages. If there is anything in this theory at all, I would suggest that it is only true in the first half of a book, and that the reverse is true in the second half. In *An Tuil* the Gaelic texts appear on the left-hand page because they came first and because we read from left to right.

In his conclusion McLeod says:

> The publishing practices of even recent decades show a range of options — printing translations in less privileged typeface in less privileged places, translating some poems in a collection but not all, publishing some collections without translation.

These are three good options, and distinguishing between line-by-line and 'prose' translations would add two more. Full parallel translation is another, and there are three more options still. One is the addition of glosses to the page, on the same line as the text to which they refer, as is often done with Scots poetry such as that of Burns. Another is to provide endnotes: Angus Morrison did this in his *Dàin is Òrain Ghàidhlig* of 1929, for example. Yet another is the provision of a full glossary. These are all enhancements which would make poetry collections attractive to the learner, add to their permanent value, and make them more saleable.

If it is claimed that such things would make poetry-books look like textbooks, I would argue that that is no less true of parallel translation, which was slow to reach contemporary Gaelic verse precisely because of its pedagogic appearance — it was first made familiar by the academic works listed at p. xxiii above. The first contemporary Gaelic verse to be published with parallel translation was, I think, Ross's *Armageddon* of 1950. There was then a gap until MacAulay's *Nua-Bhàrdachd Ghàidhlig* and MacLean's *Reothairt is Contraigh* appeared in quick succession in 1976 and 1977. This clearly marked the commercialisation of Gaelic poetry. None of Derick Thomson's four collections down to that point had included parallel translation, while all of his three subsequent collections did so.

As the century ends, there are still poets in the Gaelic-speaking communities who have found ways of adapting to a ceilidh-less environment, varying from the shy and romantic Dòmhnall Aonghais Bhàin (poems 223–5) to the tough and outgoing Torcuil MacRath (poems 218–9). At the other end of the age-spectrum, it is a delight to find that young poets are being born and made just as young poets have always been born or made. These are of three or four types. If I may state my personal experience, there are those who approach you diffidently with a sheaf of experiments that they have typed out on their computer (Dòmhnall Uilleam Stiùbhart, poems 346–7, is my example). There are those send you a poem or two for publication on some contemporary topic that has moved them greatly (I am thinking here of Alick O'Henley, whose poems on the Kosovo war of 1999 appeared in *The Herald*, *Am Pàipear*, and *Gairm*). Then there are the poems you read and enjoy in some new book or magazine, finally discovering with surprise that the name at the end belongs to some young person whom you never suspected of having poetic leanings. I am thinking here of Michael Newton's tribute in Alec Finlay's little anthology *Carmichael's Book — A Homage to Alexander Carmichael's 'Carmina Gadelica'* (1998):

Sgrìobh thu air duilleagan bàna glana
crònain bhleoghainn
gun pholl mu'r casan
gun chuileagan gar sàrachadh.

You wrote upon clean white leaves
milking croons
with no mud round our feet
or flies tormenting us.

And finally there are the little jewels that you discover in school magazines and collections of young people's work, and you think: will he (or she) keep practising these skills and become an adult poet of the twenty-first century?

So the last quarter of the century has proved as distinct and as exciting as each of the others. In fact, Gaelic poetry has found commercial success. Stephanie Wolfe Murray of Edinburgh publishers Canongate wrote in 1983:

We have published quite a few original works by Scottish authors and poets although not as many as I would have liked. It is a hard slog, financially unrewarding. With the exception of Gaelic poetry, our poetry books do not make money.[123]

Above all, there is a promising pack of seven or eight poets who are battling hard against a climate in which poetry itself has declined in status. Most of them have poetic voices which are extremely clear and distinctive. Those who find the tools to win the battle, as did Sorley MacLean, can become giants in their turn in the new millennium.

Notes to Introduction

1   Deòrsa Caimbeal Hay, *Fuaran Sléibh* (Glasgow 1947), dust-jacket quotations.

2   *Gairm* 2 (An Geamhradh 1952) 76. Editor's trl.

3   Samuel MacLean, 'Realism in Gaelic Poetry', *Transactions of the Gaelic Society of Inverness* 37 (1934–6) 80–114: 114, reprinted in Somhairle MacGill-Eain, *Ris a' Bhruthaich* (Stornoway 1985) 15–47: 46–7.

4   Rev. Malcolm MacLennan and Rev. Donald MacLean (eds), *A' Chruit Òir* (Stornoway 1919) v, 141. The collection was 'the nineteenth and last of a series of books, specially prepared and edited, under the ægis of a joint Committee of the Churches, for the use of Highland sailors and soldiers serving in H.M.'s Forces during the great and terrible war of 1914–18'. The prayers chosen were 'Athair Naomha na Glòir', 'Ìosa bu Chòir a Mholadh', 'Achanaich Gràis', 'An Ùrnuigh Chadail', and 'Ùrnuigh Mhaduinn'.

5   Frank Thompson, *History of An Comunn Gaidhealach: The First Hundred (1891-1991)* (Inverness 1992) 53.

6   See Tormod Calum Dòmhnallach (q.v.), *Call na h-Iolaire* (Stornoway 1978), and the study of the religious poet Kenneth John Smith, Earshader, Lewis, whose father was another of those drowned, in Timothy Neat's *The Voice of the Bard* (Edinburgh 1999) 94–107.

7   A curious weakening even enters the system of *sloinneadh* which is so much to the fore in the biographies at pp. 709–819 below: in the patronymics of children born after *c.*1900 the words *mac* ('son') and *nighean* ('daughter') are dropped, leaving intact the genitive *'ic* (for *mhic*) for previous generations, so that a man who would have been *Dòmhnall mac Aonghais 'ic Iain 'ic Ruairidh* ('Donald son of Angus son of John son of Roderick') if born in 1850 is merely *Dòmhnall Aonghais 'ic Iain 'ic Ruairidh* ('Donald of Angus son of John son of Roderick') if born in 1900.

8   "Henry James has written that the novel 'needs the concept of a normal society'. This we do not have in Gaelic at present . . ." (Donald John MacLeod, 'Gaelic Prose', *Transactions of the Gaelic Society of Inverness* 49 (1974–6) 198–230: 218). Other than during a brief period at the end of the third quarter (see p. 800), verse remained the pre-eminent medium of literary expression in Gaelic throughout the twentieth century.

9   J L Campbell (ed.), *Tales of Barra Told by the Coddy* (Edinburgh 1960) 25. On the distinction between a 'vertical' and a 'horizontal' consciousness see further J L Campbell and Trevor H Hall, *Strange Things* (London 1968) 7, and Norman Maclean's remarks in Neat's *The Voice of the Bard* 290.

10   *Tha còrr agus deich bliadhna fichead ann o thuirt fear às an Apainn, nuair a bha bhàrdachd aig Somhairle Mac Gill-eain is aig Deòrsa Caimbeul Hay ùr nodha, gur e seo am boillsgeadh gréine ma dheireadh a chìte air speur na Gàidhlig gu bràch.* ("More than thirty years ago an Appin man said, when the poetry of Sorley Maclean and George Campbell Hay was brand new, that this was the last gleam of sunshine that would ever be seen on the sky of Gaelic.") Dr John MacInnes, reviewing Aonghas Caimbeul, *A' Suathadh ri Iomadh Rubha*, *Gairm* 87 (An Samhradh 1974) 279.

11   Calum I N MacLeòid (q.v.), 'Rosg-Bàrdachd', *An Gaidheal* 33 (1937–8) 194–5. Editor's trl. Other examples of the genre may be found in *An Gaidheal* 34 (1938–9) 5 (by 'Fonn', seemingly a Lewisman) and *An Gaidheal* 36 (1940–1) 11 (by 'Saighdear', who from internal evidence is clearly Calum I N MacLeod again).

12   *An Deo-Gréine* 4 (1908–9) 7, 38–9; Domhnull Macdhomhnuill, *Bard Bharabhais* (Glasgow 1920) 39–43. A piece very similar in structure, 'Domhnull an Gille', appears at *Bard Bharabhais* 33–8. See Alexander Campbell, *The Grampians Desolate* (Edinburgh 1804) 265–8; R MacilleDhuibh, 'The Dance of the Thorny Croft', *West Highland Free Press*, 19 October 1990; R Black, 'The Genius of Cathal MacMhuirich', *Transactions of the Gaelic Society of Inverness* 50 (1976–8) 327–66: 335–7; Alan Harrison, *An Chrosántacht* (Dublin 1979); Alan Harrison, *The Irish Trickster* (Sheffield 1989).

13   Thomas A McKean, *Hebridean Song-Maker* (Edinburgh 1997) xiv, 217 note 132.

14   Timothy Neat (ed.), *The Voice of the Bard* (Edinburgh 1999) 60.

15   Coinneach MacLeòid, *Òrain Red* (Stornoway 1998) 37. Editor's trl.

16   For eighteenth- and nineteenth-century traditions of satire that could kill, see R MacilleDhuibh, 'The Song that Killed a Man', *West Highland Free Press*, 6 November 1998, and John Shaw, 'The Ethnography of Speaking and Verbal Taxonomies', in R Black, W Gillies and R Ó Maolalaigh (eds), *Celtic Connections: Proceedings of the Tenth International Congress of Celtic Studies*, vol. 1 (E. Linton 1999) 309–23: 320.

17   Quoted by Farquhar Macintosh, 'The Prospects for Gaelic', in Black et al., *Celtic Connections*, 457–69: 458.

18   Dòmhnall Alasdair Dòmhnallach, *Bàrdachd Dhòmhnaill Alasdair* (Stornoway 1999) 98. Editor's trl.

19   Sorley MacLean, *Ris a' Bhruthaich* (Stornoway 1985) 67.

20   Domhnull Mac Chalum, *Domhnullan: Dàn an Ceithir Earrannan* (Glasgow 1925). See also: Donald MacCallum, *English Translation of the First Canto of Domhnullan, A Gaelic Epic in Four Cantos* (Glasgow 1927); R MacilleDhuibh, 'How Donnie gave his heart to Mammon' and 'Sir Donald, Laird-of-the-Pinnacles', *West Highland Free Press*, 8 and 22 October 1999.

21   T D Macdhomhnuill, *An Dèidh a' Chogaidh* (Glasgow and Oban 1921) 11–29. Editor's trl. There are five other poems in the book, three of them translations.

22   Dr John MacInnes, 'Sorley Maclean: the harvest of his genius', *The Scotsman*, 23 April 1977.

23   Raymond J Ross and Joy Hendry (eds), *Sorley MacLean: Critical Essays* (Edinburgh 1986) 18. See also note on poem 125, p. 769 below.

24   Ann Matheson, *Somhairle MacGill-Eain: Sorley MacLean* (exhibition catalogue, National Library of

Scotland, Edinburgh 1981) 23.
25 'Sorley Maclean: the harvest of his genius', *The Scotsman*, 23 April 1977; 'The Tunes of his own Mind', in Sorley MacLean, *Poems 1932–82* (Philadelphia 1987) 9–13: 9.
26 Dòmhnall Iain MacLeòid, 'A' Còmhradh ris an Urr. Dòmhnall Tormod Dòmhnallach', *Gairm* 97 (An Geamhradh 1976–7) 65–73: 73.
27 From 'Dàin do Eimhir III: Cha do chuir de bhuaireadh riamh', *Dàin do Eimhir* [*DE*] 12, 97.
28 *An Deo-Gréine* 4 (1908–9) 53.
29 W J Watson (ed.), *Bàrdachd Ghàidhlig: Specimens of Gaelic Poetry 1550–1900* (Inverness 1918) xxiv, xxv, 230–2. The omission was pointed out by Sorley MacLean, *Ris a' Bhruthaich* 204.
30 J L Campbell, 'The Expurgating of Mac Mhaighstir Alasdair', *Scottish Gaelic Studies* 12 (1971) 59–76: 76.
31 By Sarah Fraser of Edinburgh University.
32 *An Gaidheal* 39 (1943–4) 70–1. Editor's trl. Macleod's quotation is from Ps. 139: 6.
33 *An Gaidheal* 39 (1943–4) 105. Editor's trl.
34 Máirtín Ó Murchú, in *Newsletter of the School of Celtic Studies*, no. 6 (May 1993) 8.
35 Colin Nicholson, 'To sing a people's fate . . .', *The Scotsman*, 25 October 1986.
36 W J Watson (ed.), *Bàrdachd Ghàidhlig* (3rd edn, Inverness 1959) 218. Editor's trl.
37 Poem 103 was composed 'during sleep or in a state between sleeping and waking', see John MacInnes, 'Sorley Maclean: the harvest of his genius', *The Scotsman*, 23 April 1977.
38 Sorley MacLean, 'Old Songs and New Poetry', in Karl Miller (ed.), *Memoirs of a Modern Scotland* (London 1970) 121–135: 127, reprinted in *Ris a' Bhruthaich* (Stornoway 1985) 106–119: 111.
39 'The Poetry of Sorley Maclean', *The Glasgow Review*, vol. 4, no. 3 (1973) 38–41: 40.
40 *An Gaidheal* 30 (1934–5) 42–3.
41 *Cha mhór cho bochd 's a dh'fhalbh mi, ach beagan na bu ghlice*: Murchadh MacPhàrlain, *An Toinneamh Dìomhair* (Stornoway [1973]) [5].
42 See for example his brief obituary in *The Scotsman*, 8 November 1982.
43 'Laoidh Nollaige' ('A Christmas Carol'), *Gairm* 39 (An t-Earrach 1962) 248.
44 In 'Tilleadh Uiliseis', *Fuaran Sléibh* 44, cf. poem 150 below.
45 Introduction to 'Feachd a' Phrionnsa' ('The Prince's Army'), *O na Ceithir Àirdean* 20–1.
46 Angus Martin, *Kintyre: The Hidden Past* (Edinburgh 1984) 59.
47 *An Gaidheal* 39 (1943–4) 116–7. Editor's trl.
48 For Campbell see also Morag MacLeod, 'A Lewis Man's Song Notebook', *Scottish Studies* 32 (1998) 70–88.
49 It would be correct to call him a left-wing nationalist. He describes Dougall in 'Mochtàr is Dùghall' as a Gael, a Scot and a man, in that order.
50 John Macdougall Hay, *Gillespie* (3rd edn, Edinburgh 1979) 253–4.
51 Deòrsa Caimbeul Hay, *Mochtàr is Dùghall* (Glasgow 1982) [*MD*] 61.
52 Maoilios Caimbeul, 'Ath-Sgrùdadh (15): An Dà-rìribh agus Mire na h-Ealain (2)', *Gairm* 156 (Am Foghar 1991) 338–46: 342.
53 *An Dìleab* 47, translated.
54 *Gairm* 2 (An Geamhradh 1952) 22.
55 Rev. Archibald MacDonald, 'Tìr nan Òg', *An Deo-Gréine* 3 (1907–8) 160.
56 Rev. Kenneth Macleod, 'Tìr nan Òg', *Cascheum nam Bàrd* 143. Editor's trl. The second line, more literally 'Earth upon lies and guile', actually contains a verbal echo of the well-known story about how Calum Cille buried St Oran alive so that he could get a glimpse of the afterlife. After three days and nights the grave is opened and Oran says, "Heaven's not as they say, / Nor is Hell as alleged, / No good man's always happy / And no bad man's always sad." Oran had clearly found the Celtic otherworld, not the Christian Heaven or Hell, and Calum Cille said: *Ùir, ùir air sùil Odhrain, mun dùisg e 'n còrr carmaisg!* "Earth, earth on Oran's eye, before he wakens more controversy!" (Alexander Nicolson (ed.), *Gaelic Proverbs* (Edinburgh 1882) 376–7; Alexander Carmichael (ed.), *Carmina Gadelica* 2 (2nd edn, Edinburgh 1928) 338–40.) The seventh line contains the idea of *Craobh nan Teud*, 'the Tree of Strings', used to great effect by Sorley MacLean in his poem of that name, which I believe refers to a tradition of a great tree whose branches are played upon by the giants of the *Féinn* as more ordinary mortals would play upon the harp, cf. the pipe tune 'Cumha Craobh nan Teud', known in English as 'The Lament for the Harp Tree'. According to tradition there is a place in Skye called Rubha Chraoibh nan Teud, where pipers gathered to compete (The Pìobaireachd Society, *Pìobaireachd*, book 12 (London 1970) 365).
57 Raghnall MacLeòid, *Bith-Eòlas: A' Chealla, Gintinneachd is Mean-Fhàs* (Glasgow 1976).
58 For 'Hallaig' see *Gairm* 8 (An Samhradh 1954) 360–1; MacAulay, *Nua-Bhàrdachd Ghàidhlig* 84–9; MacGill-Eain, *O Choille gu Bearradh* 226–31; etc. In 1997, according to a National Poetry Day survey organised by Book Trust Scotland and James Thin Ltd, 'Hallaig' was the only Gaelic item among Scotland's 20 favourite poems. Burns's 'Tam O'Shanter' was no. 1 ('National treasures', *The Scotsman*, 4 October 1997).
59 *Gairm* 22 (An Geamhradh 1957) 177–81; Dòmhnall Iain MacÌomhair (ed.), *Eadar Peann is Pàipear* (Glasgow 1985) 139–44.
60 Michael Davitt and Iain MacDhòmhnaill (eds), *Sruth na Maoile: Modern Gaelic Poetry from Scotland and Ireland* (Edinburgh and Dublin 1993) xiii, xix, xxiii.
61 Derick Thomson, *Creachadh na Clàrsaich* (Edinburgh 1982) 238, 252–4.
62 For his work see *Bàrdachd Mhurchaidh a' Cheisdeir*, ed. by Angus Duncan and Jane Mary Duncan (Edinburgh 1962).

63 *Gairm* 67 (An Samhradh 1969) 273. Editor's trl.
64 Morag MacLeod, 'The Folk Revival in Gaelic Song', in Ailie Munro, *The Folk Music Revival in Scotland* (London 1984) 191–204: 196.
65 'Bàrdachd an là-an-diugh', *Gairm* 15 (An t-Earrach 1956) 250.
66 Iain MacRath, *Tuireadh agus Dìoghlum* (Habost, Lochs, Lewis 1982) 16. Editor's trl.
67 Samuel Maclean, 'The Poetry of the Clearances', *Transactions of the Gaelic Society of Inverness* 38 (1937–41) 293–324: 314. Reprinted in Somhairle MacGill-Eain, *Ris a' Bhruthaich* (Stornoway 1985) 48–74: 66.
68 Dòmhnall Alasdair Dòmhnallach, *Bàrdachd Dhòmhnaill Alasdair* (Stornoway 1999) 110.
69 Aibhear O Du-mhal, 'Spreòdadh' and 'Gàradh', *Gairm* 55 (An Samhradh 1966) 260, 267.
70 'Eachdraidh Bheò', *Gairm* 70 (An t-Earrach 1970) 160. Coventry's extended verse description of St Andrews, 'Cill Rìmhinn', *Gairm* 77 (An Geamhradh 1971) 24–31, makes delightful reading. It is a pity that he appears to have written little Gaelic poetry since.
71 Meg Bateman, 'Women's Writing in Scottish Gaelic since 1750', in Douglas Gifford and Dorothy McMillan (eds), *A History of Scottish Women's Writing* (Edinburgh 1997) 659–76: 667.
72 'Daorach', Ruairidh MacDhòmhnaill, *Traoghadh is Lìonadh* (Insch 1991) 22. Editor's trl.
73 See for example his witty satirical essay 'Gaisgich, 1967: Sgialachd 1', *Gairm* 58 (An t-Earrach 1967) 165–6.
74 *Gairm* 56 (Am Foghar 1966) 327. The first verse of the popular Lewis song 'Eilean mo Ghaoil' by Dòmhnall Chràisgein (for whom see p. xxiv above) ends: *An Eilean an Fhraoich bidh daoine fuireach gu bràth, / An eilean mo ghaoil, is caomh leam eilean mo ghràidh* ('In the Isle of Heather people will always live, / In my darling isle, how I love my beloved isle'). See James Thomson and Duncan MacDonald (eds), *Eilean Fraoich: Lewis Gaelic Songs and Melodies* (2nd edn, ed. by Duncan M Morison *et al.*, Stornoway 1982) 15–16.
75 'An Dràma Nodha', *The Stornoway Gazette*, 17 October 1964.
76 *Gairm* 49 (An Geamhradh 1964) 65. The broken words like *reach-loinn* ('kling-spar') actually result from Thomson's typist reproducing the *Gazette*'s frequent end-of-line breaks as if they were necessary hyphenations, but they are satirically effective, and I have retained them in my translation. *Alba: A Scottish Miscellany in Gaelic and English, No. 1*, ed. by Malcolm MacLean and T M Murchison, appeared in 1948, not 1946. No more were issued. J F Campbell's *Na Sé Bonnaich Bheaga, and other Easy Gaelic Fairy Tales* was reissued in 1946.
77 *Gairm* 50 (An t-Earrach 1965) 151. Editor's trl.
78 'Gaelic Programme on TV: Why is Gaelic dying?' *Ossian* (1968) 36–43.
79 Marshall McLuhan (1911–80) was a Canadian academic who gained fame in the 1960s with his proposal that the electronic media, especially television, were creating a 'global village' in which 'the medium is the message'.
80 The reference is to W J Watson's anthology *Bàrdachd Ghàidhlig: Specimens of Gaelic Poetry 1550–1900* (Inverness 1918, 1932, 1959, repr. 1976), and the comment is perfectly accurate. *Bàrdachd Ghàidhlig* was still a standard textbook when I was taught Gaelic at school in the early 1960s, and remained a standard textbook at the University of Edinburgh (though not of Glasgow) until the 1990s. It is the Gaelic equivalent of Palgrave's *Golden Treasury*, and it has to be admitted that it has reinforced to generations of young people the impression that real poetry stopped dead in 1900 and gave way immediately to the practice of worthless ditties and incomprehensible free verse. Aonghas MacNeacail's experience was worse still: "As far as school was concerned Gaelic poetry died out around the beginning of the 19th century" ('Being Gaelic and otherwise', *Chapman* 89–90 (1998) 152–7: 152).
81 'Cainnt mo mhàthar Gàidhlig Bharraigh', by Alastair Ruairidh Lachlainn, won Norman Maclean (q.v.) the Gold Medal for singing at the Glasgow National Mod in 1967. It is published in Colm Ó Lochlainn (ed.), *Deoch-Slàinte nan Gillean* (Dublin 1948) 4. The words here are pastiche, developed from a single line of the original song.
82 The reference is to 'Moladh Beinn Dòbhrain' by Duncan Macintyre (*Donnchadh Bàn*, 1724–1812). The quote is slightly different from the text in Angus MacLeod's edition, *The Songs of Duncan Ban Macintyre* (Edinburgh 1952) 216–7, but Angus MacLeod's translation will stand: "with pillars and rock-stacks, / with hillocks and hummocks, / with pits and depressions, / shaggy, rough-coated, / clumpy and tufted, / ringlety, lovely; / her rugged defiles / are rich pastures of tall grass".
83 *Gairm* 88 (Am Foghar 1974) 378.
84 *Gairm* 91 (An Samhradh 1975) 279–80.
85 Other than what appears in Thomson's *Introduction to Gaelic Poetry* 257–9 and in *An Tuil*, very little of his work appears to have been translated (at least in print), but see my articles 'From *seanchas* to shoes' and 'All the way from baking to weaving', *West Highland Free Press*, 31 May and 28 June 1996.
86 *SD* 209. Macintyre comments elsewhere on Hollywood lifestyles, but on the whole film stars are more at home in the Gaelic poetry of the 1970s than of the 1940s, as in this haiku of Smith's: *Cailleach a' nighe / steapaichean taigh-dhealbh — / os a cionn Greta Garbo*. "A wifie washing / cinema steps — / above her Greta Garbo" (Iain Mac a' Ghobhainn, *Eadar Fealla-Dhà is Glaschu* (Glasgow 1974) 14).
87 The reference is to John MacDonald (*Iain Lom, c.*1625–*post*1707), who danced in verse upon the graves of his defeated Campbell enemies after the battle of Inverlochy: "A plague on you if I regret your treatment / As I listen to the distress of your children; / The object of the dog-howling of the Argyll women / Is to keen the softies that were in the field of slaughter." Thus does he turn the Campbell men into waulking-women (*pannal*), and their women into bitches. See Annie M Mackenzie (ed.), *Òrain Iain Luim: Songs of John MacDonald, Bard of Keppoch* (Edinburgh 1964) 24, and poem 142 below. There is a little of the same sadism

in poems 72 and 80, while in 81 it is lightened by humour; it is a product of war, both actuality and propaganda.

88 SD 253–7; Pat Gerber, The Search for the Stone of Destiny (Edinburgh 1992) 9.

89 R MacilleDhuibh, '"Bàrdachd nam Beann"', West Highland Free Press, 24 September 1999.

90 'Òran', in Iain Mac a' Ghobhainn, Na h-Eilthirich (Glasgow 1983) [NE] 8.

91 'A' Dol Dhachaigh' ('Going Home'), in Iain Mac a' Ghobhainn, Bùrn is Aran (Glasgow 1960) [BA] 61 and Donald MacAulay (ed.), Nua-Bhàrdachd Ghàidhlig (Edinburgh 1976) [NBG] 175.

92 Ben Dorain (Newcastle upon Tyne 1969, repr. 1988).

93 Cf. MacLean's lainnir a' chuain, coille-bionain na h-oidhche ('the glitter of the sea, the phosphorescence of night'), in 'Coilltean Ratharsair' (Dàin do Eimhir 78).

94 Douglas Sealy, review of Eadar Fealla-Dhà is Glaschu, in Lines Review 51 (1974) 47.

95 For Smith's translation of the 'Òran Eile' see Derick Thomson's Introduction to Gaelic Poetry 215–6, and for the original see Thomson's Gaelic Poetry in the Eighteenth Century (Aberdeen 1993) 156–8. For the 'wheel of fortune' see p. 770 (note on poem 128).

96 'List of Living Poets Writing in Gaelic', Scottish Poetry Library Information Sheet no. 3, August 1985.

97 From 'Caochladh' ('Dying/Changing'), Maoilios M Caimbeul, Eileanan (Glasgow 1980) 43. Editor's trl.

98 MacFhionnlaigh, A' Mheanbhchuileag (Glasgow 1980) 17–19, orig.; Cencrastus 10 (1982) 31, trl.

99 Roxanne Reddington-Wilde, 'Violent Death and Damning Words: Women's Lament in Scottish Gaelic Poetry', in Black et al. (eds), Celtic Connections, 265–86: 282.

100 See Catherine Kerrigan (ed.), An Anthology of Scottish Women Poets (Edinburgh 1991) 12–113, 336–43; Rev. Alexander Macrae (ed.), Mary Macpherson (Mrs Clark) Bean Torra Dhamh: The Religious Poet of Badenoch (Glasgow [1935]); Dòmhnall E Meek (ed.), Màiri Mhòr nan Òran (2nd edn, Edinburgh 1998).

101 The contribution of Bayble is astonishing. It also nurtured Donald Maciver and James Thomson, and produced Derick Thomson, Iain Crichton Smith and Anne Frater, not to mention more traditional poets like Kenneth MacLeod ('Red'). See p. 773 below. Other crofting townships, such as Balephuil in Tiree, may have rivalled Bayble in numbers of poets, but this emergence of Bayble poets in such numbers into the European mainstream is unparalleled in Gaelic Scotland. Has any village in Europe given more to literature?

102 Alan Clements, Kenny Farquharson and Kirsty Wark, Restless Nation (Edinburgh 1996) 23.

103 Uilleam Nèill, Cnù à Mogaill (Glasgow 1983) 44, 43.

104 Poem 212, cf. poem 158; 'Ròdhag, anns a' Bhliadhna 2000', in Michael Davitt and Iain MacDhòmhnaill (eds), Sruth na Maoile (Edinburgh and Dublin 1993) 226–7, repr. in Catrìona NicGumaraid, Rè na h-Oidhche (Edinburgh 1994) 78–9.

105 MacFhionnlaigh, A' Mheanbhchuileag (Glasgow 1980) 25, orig.; Cencrastus 10 (1982) 32, trl.

106 'Eun Neònach', in Christopher Whyte (ed.), An Aghaidh na Sìorraidheachd (Edinburgh 1991) 82–3.

107 'Fear Humptaidh-Dumptaidh', Gairm 91 (An Samhradh 1975) 235.

108 For discussion of the poem's use of symbolism see Fearghas MacFhionnlaigh, 'Oz agus Uz: rathad breigeach buidhe gu slàinte?', The Scotsman, 28 August 1998.

109 Gairm 113 (An Geamhradh 1980–1) 85.

110 Murchadh Moireach, Luach na Saorsa (Glasgow 1970) 65–6; Iain N MacLeòid (ed.), Bàrdachd Leòdhais (Glasgow 1916) 121; Derick S Thomson (ed.), Alasdair Mac Mhaighstir Alasdair: Selected Poems (Edinburgh 1996) 132–65.

111 Somhairle MacGill-Eain, O Choille gu Bearradh (Manchester 1989) xii; see also his Ris a' Bhruthaich (Stornoway 1985) 47: 'Charles Matheson, who had real and original brilliance of language and technique, but whose matter was mainly local and trivial'.

112 John MacInnes, 'The Bard Through History', in Timothy Neat (ed.), The Voice of the Bard (Edinburgh 1999) 321–52: 337.

113 'The Songs of Donald Allan MacDonald (MLitt thesis, Aberdeen 1983) 15; Bàrdachd Dhòmhnaill Ailein (Benbecula 1999) 43.

114 West Highland Free Press, 28 May 1999.

115 Feumaidh mi ràdh, cuideachd, gu bheil pàirt de bhàrdachd Thamaidh (mar a chanamaid), fada, fada os cionn mo thuigse. Cha n'eil mi a' tuigsinn idir ciarson a tha e 'deanamh mar a tha e. Ma tha boillsgeadh na bàrdachd cho làidir ciarson nach sgrìobh e am Beurla? Bhiodh e na b' ainmeile agus dheanadh e airgiod! Ach 's dòcha nach eil e cho saoghalta! Hugh MacAskill, Shelley, Yorkshire (a brother-in-law of Sorley MacLean), personal communication, 22 November 1982.

116 Thomas A McKean, Hebridean Song-Maker: Iain MacNeacail of the Isle of Skye (Edinburgh [1997]) 129.

117 Hebridean Song-Maker 160. "Part of the Sgiobair's definition of the term rhyme . . . is that a song must flow smoothly and rhythmically off the tongue and MacFarlane does not always measure up." I suspect therefore that what he was referring to was MacFarlane's tendency to invert syntax, a Lewis habit which is also very prominent in the work of the Rev. Donald MacCallum, and perhaps derives ultimately from the psalms.

118 Maoilios M Caimbeul, A' Gabhail Ris (Glasgow 1994), back cover, translated.

119 Kenneth MacDonald, in Thomson's Companion to Gaelic Scotland (1983, 1994) 301.

120 Gairm 157 (An Geamhradh 1991–2) 93–4.

121 Chapman 89–90 (1998) 149–151 (Wilson McLeod, 'The Packaging of Gaelic Poetry'), 152–7 (Aonghas MacNeacail, 'Being Gaelic, and Otherwise'), 158–60 (Peter France, 'Bilingual Poetry').

122 Ris a' Bhruthaich 14.

123 Letter to The Scotsman, 15 October 1983.

Duanaire

Anthology

The verse is presented in such a way as to provide the non-Gaelic reader with signals as to the structure of the originals. Poems full of regular indents and lines beginning with upper-case letters are in traditional metres; unindented poems whose lines mostly begin with lower-case letters are in free verse. Mixed signals indicate mixed structures. Indents represent rhyme-schemes, and translations are always indented identically to originals, so although translations are seldom themselves in rhyme, the 'ghost' of rhyme shows through them.

The translations are by the poets or myself, though I have sought extra help wherever it seemed most necessary. The source of both originals and translations is indicated in the 'Background' section. My principles of translation have been well stated by Norman Maclean (Neat, *The Voice of the Bard* 289): "The academic who delights to put bardachd into deliberately clumsy English in the name of literal meaning does a great tradition a real disservice. If a thing is worth translating, it must be worth presentation with either linguistic precision or with some kind of poetic force. Sense must be made and at best the translation will carry something of the music of the original bardachd."

R.B.

Catrìona NicPhàidein (1819–1913)

1   *Am Peinsean*

Tha mi mall ann am' choiseachd,
   'S fad air ais ann am' léirsinn,
Tha mo chlaisteachd gam fhàgail
   'S buadhan nàdair gam thréigsinn,
Ach tha 'n Tighearna dlùth dhomh,
   Aon ungta nan nèamhan,
'S bheir E sàbhailt' mi dhachaigh
   'Thìr a' Gheallaidh 's cha tréig mi.

Fhuair mise crùn airgid
   A tha dearbhte bhon Rìgh dhomh,
Ach cha dèan e bonn stàth dhomh
   Nuair bheir mo chàirdean don chill mi:
An Tì a dh'fhuiling 'nam àite,
   Mur dèan mi tàir air an Fhìrinn,
Bheir E crùn a bhios buan dhomh
   'S oighreachd shuas ann an Sìon.

Alastair MacGilleMhìcheil (1832–1912)

2   *Ora nam Buadh*

Ionnlaime do bhasa
Ann am frasa fiona,
Ann an liu nan lasa,
Ann an seachda siona,
Ann an subh craobh,
Ann am bainne meala,
Is cuirime na naoi buaidhean glana caon,
Ann do ghruaidhean caomha geala,
   Buaidh cruth,
   Buaidh guth,
   Buaidh rath,
   Buaidh math,
   Buaidh chnoc,
   Buaidh bhochd,
   Buaidh na rogha finne,

Catherine Macfadyen (Caolas, Tiree)

The Pension

I'm slow in my walking,
　My eyesight is failing,
My hearing's deserting me
　And I'm losing my faculties,
But the Lord is beside me,
　The heavens' anointed,
He'll bring me home safely
　To Promised Land unforsaken.

Crown of silver's been given me
　Confirmed by the King,
But no good will it do me
　When buried by my kin:
He who suffered in my place,
　If I scorn not the Scriptures,
Will give me crown that's eternal
　And inheritance in Zion.

Alexander Carmichael (Lismore)

The Invocation of the Graces

I bathe thy palms
In showers of wine,
In the lustral fire,
In the seven elements,
In the juice of the rasps,
In the milk of honey,
And I place the nine pure choice graces
In thy fair fond face,
　The grace of form,
　The grace of voice,
　The grace of fortune,
　The grace of goodness,
　The grace of wisdom,
　The grace of charity,
　The grace of choice maidenliness,

Buaidh na fior eireachdais,
Buaidh an deagh labhraidh.

Is dubh am bail ud thall,
Is dubh na daoine th'ann,
Is tu an eala dhonn,
Ta dol a steach 'n an ceann.
Ta an cridhe fo do chonn,
Ta an teanga fo do bhonn,
'S a chaoidh cha chan iad bonn
    Facail is oil leat.

Is dubhar thu ri teas,
Is seasgar thu ri fuachd,
Is suilean thu dha'n dall,
Is crann dh' an deoraidh thruagh,
Is eilean thu air muir,
Is cuisil thu air tir,
Is fuaran thu am fasach,
    Is slaint dha'n ti tha tinn.

Is tu gleus na Mnatha Sithe,
Is tu beus na Bride bithe,
Is tu creud na Moire mine,
Is tu gniomh na mnatha Gréig,
Is tu sgeimh na h-Eimir aluinn,
Is tu mein na Dearshul agha,
Is tu meanm na Meabha laidir,
    Is tu taladh Binne-bheul.

Is tu sonas gach ni eibhinn,
Is tu solus gath na greine,
Is tu dorus flath na feile,
Is tu corra reul an iuil,
Is tu ceum feidh nan ardu,
Is tu ceum steud nam blaru,
Is tu seimh eal an t-snamhu,
    Is tu ailleagan gach run.

Cruth aluinn an Domhnuich
Ann do ghnuis ghlain,
An cruth is ailinde
Bha air talamh.

The grace of whole-souled loveliness,
The grace of goodly speech.

Dark is yonder town,
Dark are those therein,
Thou art the brown swan,
Going in among them.
Their hearts are under thy control,
Their tongues are beneath thy sole,
Nor will they ever utter a word
     To give thee offence.

A shade art thou in the heat,
A shelter art thou in the cold,
Eyes art thou to the blind,
A staff art thou to the pilgrim,
An island art thou at sea,
A fortress art thou on land,
A well art thou in the desert,
     Health art thou to the ailing.

Thine is the skill of the Fairy Woman,
Thine is the virtue of Bride the calm,
Thine is the faith of Mary the mild,
Thine is the tact of the woman of Greece,
Thine is the beauty of Emir the lovely,
Thine is the tenderness of Darthula delightful,
Thine is the courage of Maebh the strong,
     Thine is the charm of Binne-bheul.

Thou art the joy of all joyous things,
Thou art the light of the beam of the sun,
Thou art the door of the chief of hospitality,
Thou art the surpassing star of guidance,
Thou art the step of the deer of the hill,
Thou art the step of the steed of the plain,
Thou art the grace of the swan of swimming,
     Thou art the loveliness of all lovely desires.

The lovely likeness of the Lord
Is in thy pure face,
The loveliest likeness that
Was upon earth.

An trath is fearr 's an latha duit,
An la is fearr 's an t-seachdain duit,
An t-seachdain is fearr 's a bhliadhna duit,
A bhliadhn is fearr an domhan Mhic De duit.

Thainig Peadail 's thainig Pol,
Thainig Seumas 's thainig Eoin,
Thainig Muiril is Muir Oigh,
Thainig Uiril uile chorr,
Thainig Airil aill nan og,
Thainig Gabriel fadh na h-Oigh,
Thainig Raphail flath nan seod,
'S thainig Micheal mil air sloigh,
  Thainig 's Iosa Criosda ciuin,
  Thainig 's Spiorad fior an iuil,
  Thainig 's Righ nan righ air stiuir,
  A bhaireadh duit-se graidh is ruin,
    A bhaireadh duit-se graidh is ruin.

Catrìona NicGhille-Bhàin (1845–1928)

3 bho *Céilidh Dhùn-Ì*

"'S am freumh tha snaimte teann san talamh, chan ann air a spìonadh
 Glan ás a bhun gu h-an-iochdmhor," fhreagair gu h-ealamh an Draoidh,
"'S mar luibheannach sguabt' air falbh gu cinntinn, theagamh, no crìonadh,
 Rinneadh e tric air ar cinneadh, se seo as adhbhar do m' chaoidh:
Ciod tha sa Ghaidhealtachd ach cniota, ball-cluiche fo chasan nan uaibhreach —
 Uaislean bhlàr-réis nan steud-each, uachd'rain a' bhuideil 's an stòp?
An dùthaich a ghléidh sinn tre chruadal, nach faigheadh aon choigreach uainn i,
 Nach faigheadh e 'm-feasta le 'chlaidheamh — mhealladh i uainn tre a phòc.

"Càit an-diugh bheil an sluagh a bha fialaidh, misneachail, cridheil?
 Càit an-diugh bheil na bàird a thogadh gu ceòlmhor na dàin?
Càite na sàir a bha ciallach, gnìomhach le briathr' air am bilibh
 Fallain mar fhìor-uisg an fhuarain a' sruthadh sa chéitein on bhràigh,
 Cùbhraidh mar anail nan lòintean fo throm-dhriùchd na maidne sa Mhàigh?
Dh'fhalbh iad siud mar an driùchd, agus có 'nan àite th' air tighinn?
 Ginealach lag, neo-stéidheil, do shògh agus uabhar 'na thràill,
Luchd-frithealaidh dìblidh uaislean, ag ionaltradh chaorach is shitheann —
 Seotaichean agus cha *seòid* sinn, le'r cridhe cho ìosal ri'r sàil!

The best hour of the day be thine,
The best day of the week be thine,
The best week of the year be thine,
The best year in the Son of God's domain be thine.

Peter has come and Paul has come,
James has come and John has come,
Muriel and Mary Virgin have come,
Uriel the all-beneficent has come,
Ariel the beauteousness of the young has come,
Gabriel the seer of the Virgin has come,
Raphael the prince of the valiant has come,
And Michael the chief of the hosts has come,
And Jesus Christ the mild has come,
And the Spirit of true guidance has come,
And the King of kings has come on the helm,
To bestow on thee their affection and their love,
To bestow on thee their affection and their love.

Katherine Whyte (Oban)

from *The Ceilidh of Dùn-Ì*

"And the root is firmly knotted in the soil, not mercilessly plucked
    Clean out of the ground," the Druid answered readily,
"And like weeds swept away to grow, perhaps, or wither,
    So has our race often been treated, this is the cause of my lament:
What are the Highlands but a football, a plaything under the feet of the proud —
    The doyens of the racecourse, the bottle and the stoup?
The land we defended through hardship, that no stranger could get from us,
    Could ever get with his sword — we've been cheated of it by his pocket.

"Where today are the folk who were generous, courageous, warm-hearted?
    Where today are the poets who so musically made the poems?
Where are the leaders who were sensible, active, with words on their lips
    As healthy as the pure spring water flowing downhill in early summer,
    As sweet as the scent of meadows under heavy morning dew in May?
They have gone like the dew, and who has come in their place?
    A weak, vacillating generation, in thrall to luxury and pride,
Vile servants of aristocrats, mere herders of sheep and venison —
    Chumps we are, not *champs*, with our hearts as low as our heels!

"Nan cluinnt' an-diugh iomradh air Fionn, chuireadh Bantighearna fios air d'a lùchairt
    Gu fastadh a chur air an laoch gu marcachd sa charbad 'na còir,
Chan ann aig a taobh, ach a cùlaibh, gu modhail a shuidhe 'na ùspair
    Le còta gu 'shàil air is briogais, ad àrd agus putain gu leòir.
Is ghabhadh am fleasgach gu càirdeil deagh thairgse na bean-uasail mhàlda —
    Gheibheadh i curaidh nan Gaidheal cho meata 's cho sìobhalt ri uan;
Reiceadh e 'shè troighean àirde gu tionndadh 'na lunndaire callda,
    B' fheàrr leis marcachd mar thràill na bhith 'm bochdainn a' treabhadh nan cruach."

"Stad ort, a charaid!" ars' Calum, "nach eil thu 'nad ruith tuillidh 's ealamh?
    Càite bheil adhbhar air talach mur faigheadh duin' obair a b' fheàrr?
Mur faigh mi an obair bu mhath leam, nach gabh mi an rud thig am' charamh?
    Is feàrr e gu mòr na bhith falamh, is có a their rium, 'Tha thu ceàrr!'
Mar mheanbhchuileag bhaoth anns an fheasgar tha mac an duin' air an talamh,
    Chan eil ann a bheatha ach latha, tha cinneas a ghineil on dé,
'S an glac a' mhì-fhoidhidinn fhaoin sinn mur téid e le'r dùthaich 's le'r daoine
    Cho math 's a bu toil leinn no 'shaoil sinn, 's an leaghar ar cridhe mar chéir?
Air gràdh ar Dé chan eil caochladh, a cheartas bith-bhuan cha dèan claonadh,
    'S na rùnaich a ghliocas d'ar taobh-ne, se bheir E gu crìch gu léir."

4 *Iomram Bean na Bainnse*

Dubhghorm an t-iar-chuan
    Fo ghuirme nan speuran,
Gaoth mhòr an ear-thuath
    Le fuar-fhead a' séideadh,
Tonnan a' luasgadh
    Fo bhuaireas a' beucadh,
Eòin mhara luaineach
    Mun cuairt orra, 'g éigheach.

Faic feadh nam bàth-thonn,
    A' teàrnadh 's a' dìreadh,
Bàta ga sàrachadh —
    S fhada o thìr i;
Féitheach na gàirdeana,
    Calma na daoine
Tha nis ann an gàbhadh
    A' sireadh a' chaolais.

Faic anns an deireadh,
    Le a maighdeann air chòmhla,
Rìbhinn nan eileana,

"If Fingal were heard of today, some lady would summon him to her palace
   To employ the hero to ride in the coach in her presence,
Not at her side but behind her, a lackey sitting politely
   With a heel-length coat and breeches, high hat and buttons galore.
And the warrior would amiably accept the gentle lady's fine offer —
   She'd find the champion of the Gael as meek and mild as a lamb;
He'd sell his six feet of height to become a domestic scrounger,
   For he'd rather ride as a slave than plough the hillsides in poverty."

"Stop, my friend!" said Columba, "aren't you running too fast?
   Where is there cause of reproach if no better work can be found?
If I can't get the work I would like, won't I take whatever comes by?
   It's far, far better than nothing, and who will tell me, 'You're wrong!'
Like an evanescent midge in the evening is the son of man on the earth,
   His life's but a day, his race began only yesterday,
And will vain impatience trap us if our land and people don't prosper
   As well as we'd like or we thought, and will our hearts be melted like wax?
The love of our God is unchanged, His eternal truth never fails,
   And what His wisdom decreed for us, that He will do in full."

The Bride's Oar-Song

Sleek black's the west sea
   Under skies that are leaden,
Shrill blows the icy
   Nor'-easterly gale,
Waves are being tossed
   Under turbulent roaring,
Sea-birds are wheeling
   About them, and calling.

See in the massive waves,
   Descending and climbing,
A boat being tormented —
   She's far out from land;
Sinewed the arms,
   Brave are the men
Who're now in great danger
   Seeking the kyles.

See in the stern,
   With her maid in attendance,
Màiri, nighean Dòmhnaill,

Màiri, nighean Dòmhnaill:
Air Raghnall a h-aire,
    A dòchas a' traoghadh,
"Mo thruaigh, bidh ar banais
    Measg ròd agus fhaochag."

Smiorail na gillean,
    Is tàireil leo strìochdadh,
Ach spionnadh na gaillinn
    Bheir barrachd san strì seo:
Cho dlùth air a' mhòrthir,
    An sealladh an càirdean,
Gun lùth tha na h-òigfhir
    Air ùrlar a' bhàta.

Ràmh ghlac na h-òighean
    'S gach dòrnag 'nan àite,
"Suas leatha, Mhòrag
    A ghràidh," arsa Màiri;
Suas i don chamas
    Air barra nam bàirlinn —
Sàbhailt sa chala
    Tha Raghnall agus Màiri.

5   *Briscadh na Fàire*

Nuair a dh'éirich a' ghrian
    Air a' chamas fo fhiath
Bu bhriagh laigh na soithichean mòr'
    A' tulgadh air luinn,
    'S iad gu bàrraibh an croinn
Mar òg mhaighdean-bainnse fo shròl.

O gach àras air tìr,
    O gach bothan bochd crìon,
Bha suaicheantas Bhreatainn ri srann:
    Cha robh smid air a ràdh,
    Cha robh fuaim air an t-sràid
Ach caisimeachd 's gliogarsaich lann.

A' marcachd nan stuadh
    A-staigh ás a' chuan
Ruith an *Canada*, uaibhreach mar steud;

Star of the islands:
Her gaze fixed on Ronald,
    Her hope sinking low,
"I'm afraid we'll be married
    In seaware and winkles."

The lads are so hardy,
    They're loth to give up,
But the strength of the storm
    Requires more than they've got:
So close to the mainland,
    In sight of their kinsfolk,
The heroes collapse
    On the floor of the boat.

The girls seized an oar
    In their place in each fistie,
"Up with her, Morag
    My darling," says Màiri,
In she goes to the bay
    On the tops of the breakers —
Safe in the harbour
    Are Ronald and Mary.

The Breaking of the Dawn

When the sun arose
On the calm of the bay
The great ships lay in beauty
    Rocking on the swell,
    Right up to their mastheads
Like a young bride in her wedding-dress.

From each dwelling on land,
    From each poor little hut,
The flag of Britain was fluttering:
    With no syllable spoken,
    No sound on the street
But march of feet and rattle of swords.

Riding the billows
    In from the ocean
Ran the *Canada*, proud as a horse;

Air a' cheadha mun cuairt
Dh'fheith maithean an t-sluaigh
Le an Ceannard gu rìomhach 'na éid'.

Gun othail gun fhuaim
Mar a' ghrian ás a' chuan
Thàin' an sonn ris an d'fheith iad a-nìos;
Dh'éirich iolach an àigh
Dhùisg mac-talla nam bràigh
A' co-fhreagairt ri muir agus tìr.

"Mìle fàilte don t-sàr
O luchd-sìochaint 's luchd-àir!"
Tha gach cridh' agus teanga ag ràdh,
"Mìle fàilte don Iarl'
On ear, deas is iar,
Aon an gràdh do dh'fhear-buaidh Chandahàr!"

Tha na h-òg-mhnathan uaisl',
Rudhadh aoibh air an gruaidh,
Tighinn le blàithean is pailme 'na làthair;
Shuas air mala na bruaich'
Chithear trusadh nan uan,
Gach leanaban le bratach 'na làimh.

Le féith-ghàire blàth
Dhearc a' ghrian air a' mhàgh,
Clann a' bhaile 'nan treudan sa chrò —
Uain dubha, uain donn,
Le uain gheal' air an lòn,
Le aon chridhe don aoidh a' toirt còmh'il.

Òigh an òr-fhuilt mar eala
'Na sgèimh-éididh geala,
Òigh nan Innsean le sùil mar an reul,
Isean mear an dubh-aogaisg
Le sìor-ghàir' air a bhraoisgein,
Uile 'mireag le chéil' 'nan aon treud.

Thog iad uile an ceòl
Le aon ghuth ás am beòil
Don aon Dia air thalamh 's air nèamh:

On the quay round about
Stood the people's commanders
With their Governor grand in his uniform.

Without bustle or noise
Like the sun from the sea
Up came the hero they'd waited for;
    A cry of glory arose
    That woke the echo of the slopes
Responding to ocean and land.

"A thousand welcomes to the hero
From men of peace and of battle!"
Each heart and each tongue is crying,
    "A thousand welcomes to the Earl
    From the east, south and west,
United in love for the victor of Kandahar!"

The young ladies come,
    Flush of joy in their cheeks,
With blossoms and palms to greet him;
    Up on top of the hill
    Are seen gathered the lambs,
All the infants with flags in their hands.

With her welcoming smile
Gazed the sun on the plain,
The town's children in flocks in the fold —
    Black lambs, brown lambs,
    And white lambs on the meadow,
With one heart for meeting the guest.

Blonde-haired girl like a swan
In her lovely white garments,
Girl of India with eyes like the stars,
    Lively black-faced young chicken
    With a huge grin forever,
All playing in one flock with each other.

They all started to sing
    With one voice from their mouths
To the one God on heaven and earth:

"Ar Banrigh 's ar crùn,
    Ar poball 's ar dùth'ich
Beannaich Thusa, a Thighearna, 's glèidh!"

Tha sa chraoibh os ar ceann
    Dreollan teas'aidh ri srann,
Cridh' an t-samhraidh a' dranndail san fhonn;
    Tha crònan ait binn,
    Fàilt' na sìth' do ar linn,
Ag éirigh gu sàmhach on tonn.

Tha 'n òg-mhadainn chiùin
    A' deàlradh as ùr
Air gorm-chrios nan sléibht' fad' an céin,
    Gealladh fàire na sìth',
    Madainn aonachd na tìr'
An déidh oidhche a' bhuaireis 's na péin.

Alasdair Camshron (1848–1933)

6   *An Sgàileagan*

Beannachd do *Phàipeir an t Sluaigh*
A chuir thugam mar mo dhuais
Sgàileagan den t-sìoda luaidht'
    Gus mo ghuaillibh chòmhdach.

Rathad mór gu Ceann Loch Iùbh,
Rathad mór gu Ceann Loch Iùbh,
Rathad mór gu Ceann Loch Iùbh,
    Rathad ùr gu Geàrrloch.

Móran taing don ghaisgeach ghrinn
Chuir am fasgadh os mo chinn —
Ged bhiodh frasan ann gun dìth
    Cha tig nì 'nam chòir-sa.

Sìoda dubh air aisnean iarainn,
Gàirdeanan den mhiotailt chiadna,
Cas den aiteann nach gabh fiaradh,
    Cearcall briagh òir oirre.

"Our Queen and our crown,
Our people and our land,
Bless them and keep them, O Lord!"

In the tree up above us
A grasshopper's chirping,
The summer's heart humming on shore;
A joyful musical murmur,
Peace's greeting to our century,
Rises gently from ocean wave.

The calm early morning
Is shining anew
On the blue ring of hills far away,
Dawn promising peace,
Day uniting the land
After night of commotion and pain.

Alexander Cameron (Tournaig, Gairloch)

The Umbrella

A blessing on *The People's Journal*
Who have sent me as my prize
An umbrella of well-thickened silk
To protect my shoulders.

High road to Kinlochewe,
High road to Kinlochewe,
High road to Kinlochewe,
New road to Gairloch.

Many thanks to the gallant lad
Who put the shelter over me —
Even if there's showers aplenty
Nothing will come near me.

Black silk upon iron ribs,
Arms of identical metal,
And juniper handle that can't be bent,
With a beautiful band of gold on her.

Tha i taitneach anns an làimh,
Nì i bata air an làr,
Nì i taigh nuair théid i 'n àird'
     Is gheibh mo nàbaidh sgeòd dhith.

Dh'ainneoin stoirm a thig den mhunadh
Cha chuir i idir ormsa cunnart,
Nì i stairirich air a mullach
     Ach cha bhuin i dhòmhsa.

Neiptiun fiadhaich is 'eòlas greannach
Roimhe dh'fheuch ris an *Dubh-Ghleannach*
Cha chuir fiamh orm no aimheal —
     Théid iad seachad dòigheil.

Beannachd uam le m' uile chridhe
Phàipeir an t-Sluaigh an Dùn Dèagh —
Gun robh buannachd, duais is dlighe
     Air am fighe còmh' ris.

Gilleasbaig Mac an t-Saoir (1854–1922)

7   bho *Òran Ghlinne Chrò*

Gur beag mo shannta
Bhith nis sa ghleann seo
'S gach taigh is fang
     A' dol glan ás òrdugh
'S gach lianag uaine
As tric a bhuain mi
Gun ann ach cluaran
     An àit' an eòrna.

Chan ionn 's mar bhà e
Nuair bha mi 'm phàiste,
Bha cur is àiteach
     Aig daoine còire;
E nis 'na fhàsach
Is féidh gun àireamh
Toirt spurt do ghàrlaich
     'S do dhaoine neònach.

She feels pleasant to the hand,
She makes a stick upon the ground,
She makes a house when she goes up
    And my neighbour gets a nook of her.

Whatever storm comes off the moor
Can put me at no risk at all,
It rattles away upon her roof
    But it will never touch me.

Wild Neptune and his surly witchcraft
That once challenged the *Dubh-Ghleannach*
Won't frighten me or vex me —
    They'll fly past in good order.

I bless with all my heart
The People's Journal in Dundee —
May prosperity, reward and right
    Combine together in it.

Archibald Macintyre (Inveraray)

from *The Song of Glen Croe*

Small is my wish
To be now in this glen
With each house and each fank
    Going out of repair
And every green pasture
Which often I reaped
Yielding nothing but thistles
    In place of the barley.

It's not how it was
When I was a child,
Being sown and being tilled
    By civilised folk;
It's now just a desert
With deer beyond number
Giving sport to rapscallions
    And some very strange people.

Bidh féidh nam fuar-bheann
A-nis air ghluasad
Is gràisg de dh'uabhraich
   A' dol 'nan còmhdhail;
Bidh màidsear cuagach
A' caitheamh luaidh' orr'
'S gruing is gruaim air
   Mur dèan e 'n leònadh.

Ma thig an nàmhaid
A-nis don àite
Bidh féidh nan àrd-bheann
   A' cur ri crònan;
Bu mhaith 'nan àite
A-nis na Gàidhil
A chur nam blàr leinn
   Gu duineil dòigheil.

Se forsair grànda
A rinn mo shàrach'
On chuir e sgànradh
   An-diugh 'nam dhròbh-sa;
Ma gheibh mi slàinte
'S a bhith 'nam àbhaist
Gun dèan mi fàidh
   Mas duine beò mi.

Dòmhnall MacÌomhair (1857–1935)

8 *An Ataireachd Àrd*

An ataireachd bhuan,
Cluinn fuaim na h-ataireachd àird,
   Tha torann a' chuain
Mar chualas leams' e 'nam phàist —
   Gun mhùthadh gun truas
A' sluaisreadh gaineamh na tràghad:
   An ataireachd bhuan,
Cluinn fuaim na h-ataireachd àird.

   Gach làd le a stuadh
Cho luaisgeach faramach bàn,

The deer of the cold hills
Are now on the move
With a rabble of toffs
    Going out to meet them;
Some ungainly major
Scattering lead at them
And going sour and surly
    If he doesn't wound them.

Should the enemy come now
To the district
The deer of the mountains
    Will be roaring away;
Good now in their place
Would be the Gael
To fight our battles
    With courage and cheer.

A loathsome gamekeeper's
Caused my vexation
Since he dispersed
    My drove today;
If I have my health
And stay as I am
I'll be a prophet
    As long as I live.

Donald Maciver (Crowlista, Uig, Lewis)

The Sea's Lofty Roar

Endless surge of the sea,
Hear the sound of the sea's lofty roar,
The thundering swell
That I heard as a child long ago —
    Without change or compassion
Dragging the sand of the shore:
    Endless surge of the sea,
Hear the sound of the sea's lofty roar.

All the waves crashing down
Are trembling, loud-sounding and white,

'Na chabhaig gu cruaidh,
'S e gruamach dosrach gun sgàth;
    Ach strìochdaidh a luaths
Aig bruaich na h-uidhe bh' aig càch
    Mar chaochail an sluagh
Bha uair sa bhaile sa tàmh.

    Sna coilltean a-siar
Chan iarrainn fuireach gu bràth,
    Bha m' inntinn 's mo mhiann
A-riamh air lagan a' bhàigh;
    Ach iadsan bha fial
An gnìomh, an caidreamh 's an àgh
    Air sgapadh gun dìon
Mar thriallas ealtainn roimh nàmh.

    Seileach is luachair,
Cluaran, muran is stàrr
    Air tachdadh nam fuaran
'N d'fhuair mi iomadh deoch-phàit';
    Na tobhtaichean fuar'
Le buathallan 's cuiseag gu'm bàrr
    'S an fheanntagach ruadh
Fàs suas sa chagailt bha blàth.

    Ach chunnaic mis' uair
'M bu chuannar beathail an t-ait',
    Le òigridh gun ghruaim
Bha uasal modhail 'nan càil,
    Le màthraichean suairc'
Làn uaill 'nan companaich gràidh
    Le caoraich is buar
Air ghluas'd moch mhadainn nan tràth.

    Ag amharc mun cuairt
Cha dual dhomh gun a bhith 'm pràmh:
    Chan fhaic mi an tuath
Dom b' shuaicheant' carthannas tlàth —
    'Nam fògarraich thruagh'
Chaidh 'm fuadach thairis air sàl
    'S cha chluinn iad gu buan
Mór fhuaim na h-ataireachd àird.

So hurried and cruel,
Grim and spuming without taking fright;
 But their speed falls away
At the same destination each time
 As the people have perished
Who once dwelt in this village of mine.

In the forests of the west
I've never requested to stay,
 My mind and ambition
Set firm on the hollow of the bay;
 But those who were generous
In effort, in friendship and fame
 Are scattered defenceless
Like birds in their enemy's way.

Rushes and willow,
And thistle, and marram and grass
 Have choked up the springs
Where I'd find many thirst-quenching draughts;
 The ruins are so cold
With ragwort and dockens growing high
 While the red nettle swarms
Where warm is the ghost of the hearth.

But I've seen an age
When the place was both snug and alive,
 With youngsters unbowed
Whose manner was proud but polite,
 Their mothers serene
Well pleased with their partners in life
 With sheep and with cows
Setting out at the morning's first light.

But looking around
My spirits are bound to be low:
 I don't see the tenants
Whose warm generosity flowed —
 As exiles in misery
They've been driven away from our shores
 And they'll never now hear
The great sound of the sea's lofty roar.

Fir-sgiùrsaidh an t-sluaigh,
Cha bhuan iad bharrachd air càch —
Bu chridheil an uaill
Gar ruagadh mach gun chion-fàth
Ach sannt agus cruas;
An duais tha aca mar-thà
Mór dhiomb is droch luaidh,
An uaigh le mallachd nan àl.

Ach siùbhlaidh mi uat,
Cha ghluais mi tuilleadh 'nad dhàil:
Tha m' aois is mo shnuadh
Toirt luaidh air giorrad mo là;
An àm dhomh bhith suaint'
Am fuachd 's an cadal a' bhàis,
Mo leabaidh dèan suas
Ri fuaim na h-ataireachd àird.

Seonaidh Caimbeul (1859–1947)

9 Òran a' Pheinsean

S iomadh fear a bhios ag ràdha
Mar a thà e cho falamh,
Nach e an cosnadh a theirig?
Chan eil cealp 's chan eil stamh ann —
Théid iad sìos far a bheil Ruairidh
'S gheibh iad cuaraidh no meatail,
'S b'e sin obair na truaighe:
Cha bhithinn suas leis aon latha
Gu'n teichinn ás.

B' fheàrr leam fhìn a bhith 'g iasgach
Ged bhiomaid riaslach air uairibh:
Fliuch a dh'oidhche 's do latha,
An sgor sa chladach no 'n uaimh —
Nuair a thigeadh a' mhadainn
Bhiodh rud againn no bhuainn;
Nuair bhiomaid treis san taigh-òsta
Bhiodh ar dòchas an uair sin
A-cheart cho math.

Those who've wielded the lash
Won't outlast the folk they have cleared —
Lusting for glory
They drove us out for no reason
But power and desire;
The prize they've won for their deed
Is disgust and ill fame,
The grave with the curse of the seed.

But I must go away,
I can't stay with you any more:
My age and appearance
Reveal that I've not far to go;
When I'm finally seized
By the sleep of perpetual cold,
In my bed lay me down
To the sound of the sea's lofty roar.

John Campbell (S. Lochboisdale, S. Uist)

The Song of the Pension

It's many a man that is saying
How desperately short he is,
Hasn't employment disappeared?
There's no kelp and there's no tangles —
They go down to see Roderick
And get quarrying or roadmaking
And wretched work it would be:
I wouldn't stand it for a single day
Till I got out.

I'd much prefer to be fishing
Though we used to find it tough at times:
Soaking wet both night and day,
The boat propped up in shore or cave —
When the morning came at last
We might get a catch or we might not;
But after a spell in the inn
Our optimism would then
Be fully restored.

S mór an cothrom a thànaig
   Seach an uair a bha mise 'g iasgach;
Cha robh socair no tàmh ach
   Anns a h-uile h-àite ga iarraidh —
A' cur nan lìon 's ris an fhaochaig,
   'S a h-uile h-aon dhiubh cho riaslach
Seach falbh a dh'iarraidh a' Pheinsean
   A h-uile madainn Di-Haoine
     Ach mi bhith gu math.

S mór an cothrom 's an t-saoirsne
   A th' aig seann daoin' anns gach àite
Nuair a fhuair iad am Peinsean
   'S e an déidh a cheangal gu bràch dhaibh
Nuair a dh'fhàsas iad aosta
   'S nach bi h-aon dhiubh ro làidir;
'S tha e math cuideachd dhan òigridh
   Ma bhios iad còmhla ri'n càirdean
     Nuair bhios iad sean.

Chan eil bodach no cailleach
   A th' eadar Arainn is Cnòideart,
Tha eadar ceann a-deas Bharraigh
   'S Caol na Hearadh is Leòdhas
Nach bi tric air an glùinean
   'S iad ag ùrnaigh gu deònach
Air son a' chiad fhear a dh'éirich
   Gu cur mu dheidhinn, 's a thòisich
     Ri thoirt a-mach.

Dh'fhàg e mios air na bodaich
   'S thug e socair do chailleachan,
Ged a bhiodh iad car oglaidh
   A-null mu oirean a' ghealbhain,
Nas lugha na dh'fhàsas iad pròiseil
   A' cumail còmhstri ri seanchas,
Ag ràdh, "Fhuair mise am Peinsean,
   Sann bhios tu agam 'nad shearbhana" —
     Sin am beachd.

Nuair a théid thu dhan bhùthaidh
   Bidh do shùil gu dé a chì thu,
Chan eil cuimhn' air an diùideachd

Great is the chance that has come
   Since the time I was fishing myself;
There was no ease or rest but
   Just seeking it everywhere —
Setting the nets and gathering winkles,
   And each of these was vexatious
Compared to fetching the Pension
   Every Friday morning
     As long as I'm well.

Great is the chance and the freedom
   That old folk have everywhere
When they've got the Pension
   Permanently allotted to them
When they grow old
   And none of them's too strong;
And it's good for the young folk too
   To be with their kin
     When they are old.

There's not an old man or old woman
   Between Arran and Knoydart,
Between the south end of Barra
   And the Sound of Harris and Lewis
That doesn't frequently kneel
   And most willingly pray
For the first man who got up
   To set about it, and began
     To give it out.

He gained the old men respect
   And the old women comfort,
Forbidding though they might be
   When glowering from the fireside,
Unless they grow uppity
   Keeping pace with the gossip,
Saying, "I've got the Pension,
   I'll have you as a servant" —
     That's what they think.

When you go to the shop
   You look to see what to buy,
Forgetting the diffidence

A chum fad ùin' thu cho ìseal;
Bidh am marsanta deònach
    A bhith riut an-còmhnaidh am briotal
Nuair a chì e na bhios agad
    A bhuinn dà thastan, 's e cinnteach
        Thu rud thoirt leat.

S mòr a dh'atharraich rudan
    Seach mar a chunnaic mi fhìn iad
Bho chionn trì fichead bliadhna,
    'S cha chan mi sian ach an fhìrinn:
Cha robh Dól ann no Peinsean
    A gheibheadh dad bhiodh a dhìth ort
Gu'n tigeadh là na féilleadh,
    Ach gu dé mar a bhitheadh
        Mar a chreic thu an damh.

S iomadh rud a bha as do dheoghaidh
    Gad chumail fodha gun dìreadh —
Ged bhiodh prìs air na gamhna
    'S gun ghin ann dhiubh ach aoinfhear;
Ged bhiodh e urad ri tarbh
    An déidh dhut falbh leis, ma dh'fhaoidte,
Nuair a ruigeadh tu an fhéill
    Gur h-ann a dh'fheumadh tu saod air
        A philleadh leat.

Thig am bàillidh 's an clachair,
    An gobha tarsainn 's an saor ort,
Thig fear dianamh nan cliabh
    'S cha bhiodh tus' ach riaslach ás aonais;
Thig an griasaiche 's an tàilleir
    'S cha bhiodh tu blàth gun an t-aodach,
'S nuair thig fear airgead nam bochd
    Gura gann a nochdas tu t' aodann —
        Cha ruig thu leas.

Nuair a dh'fhalbhas iad uile
    'S nach bi guth air a h-aon dhiubh,
Fàsaidh t' inntinne socair
    Ged bhiodh tu 'g osnaich 's a' smaointinn;
'S tu 'nad shuidh' air a' chnoc
    A' faicinn collas an t-saoghail

That kept you long in subjection;
The shopkeeper's willing
    To make small talk forever
When he sees you've a number
    Of two-shilling pieces, for he's sure
        There's something you'll buy.

So many things have changed
    From how I've seen them myself
Over sixty years past,
    And I'll speak only the truth:
There was no Dole or Pension
    To get what you wanted
Until the fair-day arrived,
    And even then it depended
        On selling the bullock.

Many things conspired
    To keep you down and out —
Like a good price for stirks
    When there was only one there;
Be he as big as a bull
    Once you'd set off, let us say,
When you arrived at the fair
    You'd just have to turn him around
        And bring him back.

You meet the factor, the mason,
    The blacksmith and carpenter,
The creelmaker approaches
    And you'd be stuck without him;
The shoemaker and tailor come over,
    And you'd be cold without clothes,
And when the poor-law collector comes
    You scarcely show your face —
        You needn't bother.

When they've all gone away
    And there's no word of any of them,
Your mind will relax
    Even if you were sighing and worrying;
There you sit in the open
    Contemplating the scene

Gu'n tig am marsanta bho d' chùl ort
    'S gun can e an diùrais, "A laochain,
        Do chreic thu an damh?"

Canaidh tu le guth beag ris,
    "Cha do chreic mis' an-dràst e,
Chan eil prìs air na daimh —
    Se sin tha iad ag ràdha;
Bho nach digeadh fear dùthcha
    A chumadh ùin' ann am pàirc e
Còmh' ri leithidean eile,
    'S gum biodh e rud beag na b' fheàrr
        Fiach an seas e a-mach."

Saoilidh móran dhan òigridh
    G'eil cuid dhan òran 'na bhriagan,
Sann a bhios iad glé dheònach
    Bhith cur sgleò air mo bhriathran —
Nuair a tha an Dól 's an Transitional
    Air am mios ris an riaghailt
Agus Peinsean na h-Aoise
    Nach dig air caochladh gu sìorraidh,
        Se sin tha math.

Aonghas Moireasdan (1865–1942)

10   bho *Alba Saor*

Cha nàimhdeas do Shasann
A dhùisg mi gu ealaidh
No tnù ri cuid beairteas,
    A mórachd 's a cliù,
Ach bhith sealltainn air Alba
'S i sìor dhol an ceannas
Gus an caill i mu dheireadh
    A toil gu bhith saor —
O éiribh, mo dhaoine,
Gu còmhstri 's chan aithreach,
A' chòmhstri nach fuilteach,
    Is sibhse mar aon
Gus am buidhinn an t-saorsa
Tha brath dol á sealladh

Till the shopkeeper comes up from behind
   And says confidentially, "My friend,
      Did you sell the bullock?"

You say quietly to him,
   "No, not for the moment,
There's no price for bullocks —
   That's what they say;
Since no countryman came
   Who'd graze him awhile
With others of his like,
   It might be preferable
      To keep him out of the sale."

Many young folk will think
   That the song is partly lies,
They'll be more than willing
   To gloss over my words —
When the Dole and Transitional
   Are worked out automatically
And the Old Age Pension
   Is made fully permanent,
      That is what's good.

Angus Morrison (Ullapool)

from *Scotland Free*

No malice for England
Has aroused me to song
Nor any greed for her wealth,
   Her grandeur and fame,
But just looking at Scotland
Bit by bit taken over
Till she loses at last
   Her desire to be free —
O rise up, my people,
To fight unrepentant,
Without shedding of blood,
   Together as one
Till you gain independence
That drops out of sight

'Nur suain anns a' chadal
Ás am mithich gun dùisg.

Tha airgead is òr
Ro bhuailteach bhur mealladh
Gus an dèan e bhur ceangal
    Le slabhraidhean ùr,
Ged nach cruaidh mar an t-iarann
Ach bog mar an canach,
Gidheadh nì iad daingeann
    Bhur cumail an daors;
Tha meatachd is uabhar
Tric fuaigheal na bannaidh
Leis an ceangail an t-umaidh
    Chuid ionmhais gu dlùth —
Biodh dìlseachd d'ur dùthaich
A ghnàth air bhur n-aire
'S cha bhi sibh mar thràillean
    'S mar ablaich gun diù.

O Alba, mo dhùthaich
A dh'àraich na gallain
Tha ainmeil an eachdraidh,
    Bha meanmnach gu spàirn,
A dh'fhàg dhuinn mar dhìleab
An t-saorsa ro bheannaicht' —
An dèan sinn an iomlaid
    Gu daors' chur 'na h-àit?
Ma chuirear gu dìochuimhn'
Leinn Brus agus Uallas
'S na fiùrain nach maireann
    A bhuidhinn ar gràdh,
Gun thoill sinn san uair sin
Ar sgiùrsadh 's ar feannadh,
'S gun iomradh oirnn tuille
    Uaith' seo gu là bhràth.

Ged as adhbhar bhith taingeil
Gu bheil Albainn is Sasann
An co-bhuinn a-chéile
    Am bagraidh do nàmh,
Ar guidhe 's ar dòchas
An cùmhnant bhith maireann

While you stay in that sleep
  From which it's time to awake.

With silver and gold
You're so easily tempted
Until you're tied up
  With chains that are new,
Though not hard like iron
But soft like bog-cotton,
They keep you for all that
  Firmly in thrall;
Cowardice and pride
Often sew up the bands
That are used by the boor
  To secure all his riches —
If love of your country
Remains in your mind
You won't be like slaves
  Or a bare heap of bones.

O Scotland, my country
Which nurtured the heroes
Who're famous in history,
  Courageous in combat,
Who bequeathed as their legacy
Freedom most blessed —
Will we make the exchange
  And put chains in its place?
If we let Bruce and Wallace
Slip out of our minds
With other past warriors
  Who've earned our affection,
We deserve when that happens
To be whipped, to be flayed,
And never remembered
  From here to eternity.

Though there's cause to be grateful
That Scotland and England
Are working together
  To threaten our enemies,
We hope and we pray
That the contract will last

'S nach tig an là tuille
    'S sinn roinnte air blàr;
Gidheadh, tha e soilleir
'S na bliadhnan dol tharainn
Alb' bhith ga cuingleachadh
    Seach mar a bhà,
'S am Pàrlamaid Bhreatainn
Gur tearc is gur annamh
Na laghan a dhealbhar
    G'a feabhas 's gach ceàrn.

Gur mithich dhuinn éirigh
'S ar cùisean chur dìreach —
'S Alba an deis-làimh
    'S a daoine ga dìth,
Luchd ciùird 's tuath-cheatharn'
Ga fàgail 'nam mìltean,
A' Ghaidhealtachd gu sònraicht'
    'Na fàsach 's 'na frìth;
Ar druim air a chromadh
Mheud 's a tha chìs oirnn
'S nach fhios leinn cuin idir
    A leagar iad sìos:
Mura comas an dìoladh
Do dhruideadh am prìosan
Aig maor agus siorram
    Gad fhòirneart gun sgìths.

Tha còmhlan 'nar dùthaich
Ag iarraidh le dùrachd
Gun tig Alba as ùr gu
    A Pàrlamaid fhéin,
'S an deagh ghean ri Sasann,
Gach rìoghachd gu aonaicht'
San Ìmpireachd allail
    'S an laghan g'an réir;
Nam biodh an sluagh uile
A' tagradh gun faochadh,
Bhiodh Pàrlamaid ullamh
    D'an iarrtas bhith réidh —
'S an-sin bhiodh ar dùthaich
Is aitreabh ar saorsa
Le ceartas mar bhunait
    Air rogha cloich-stéidh.

And the day won't return
  When we're divided on battlefield;
However, it's clear
As the years roll on by
That Scotland's being strangled
  More than ever before,
It being rare and unusual
In the Parliament of Britain
For laws to be framed
  Entirely to her benefit.

It's time we arose
And put right our affairs —
Scotland's neglected
  And losing her people,
Craftsmen and labourers
Forsaking her in thousands,
The Highlands especially
  A desert and hunting-ground;
Our backs are so bent
With the burden of taxes
That we haven't a clue
  When they're going to be lowered:
If unable to pay them
You're thrown into prison
With bailiff and judge
  Harassing you tirelessly.

There's a group in our land
Who're earnestly seeking
For Scotland to have her own
  Parliament again,
Every country united
With goodwill to England
In the excellent Empire
  With laws that are right for them;
If all their people
Petitioned unceasingly,
Parliament would agree
  To grant their request —
And thus would our country
And the seat of our freedom
Be with justice erected
  On the best of foundation-stones.

Tha Pàrlamaid Bhreatann
Air fàs cho mì-chumadhta,
Mar ghearran ri ùinich
  'S a luchd ga chur ceàrr:
Gum b' fheàrr a bhith sireadh
Bhith 'g imeachd gun ùspairt
'S ro chudrom an lod
  Ga roinn mar a b' fheàrr;
Mar sin nam biodh Albainn
A' réiteach a cùisean
Is Sasann gu fuasgailte
  Seach i bhith 'n sàs,
Bhiodh ceartas is cothrom
A' stiùireadh ar cùrsa
'S ar siùil air an séideadh
  Le deagh-ghean is gràdh.

11 *Nam biodh agam moisein bodaich*

Nam biodh agam moisein bodaich
  Bhogainn anns an allt e,
Mur biodh e glan nuair bheirinn ás e
  Chuirinn rithist ann e,
Bhogainn e is thogainn e
  Is chuirinn rithist ann e,
'S mur biodh e glan nuair bheirinn ás e
  Chuirinn rithist ann e.

Nam biodh agam moisein bodaich
  Chuirinn e fo cheannsal,
An tuba dhomhain bhith ga loireadh,
  Siabann bog gun taing air,
Rubainn anns an tuba e,
  Rubainn rithist gu teann e,
Mur biodh e glan nuair bheirinn ás e
  Chuirinn rithist ann e.

Nam biodh agam moisein bodaich
  Chuirinn gus an Fhraing e,
Mur biodh e glan nuair bheirinn ás e
  Chuirinn rithist ann e,

The Parliament of Britain
Has grown as unwieldy
As a pony that stumbles
    When its load puts it wrong:
It's better to seek
To proceed without strife
While the weight of the load
    Is distributed sensibly;
In that way if Scotland
Could run her affairs
With England released
    And no longer involved,
Justice and opportunity
Would navigate our course
While our sails would be filled
    With goodwill and love.

If I had an old meanie of a mannie

If I had an old meanie of a mannie
    I'd dip him in the burn,
If he wasn't clean when I took him out
    I'd put him in again,
I'd dip him in and I'd lift him out
    And I'd put him in again,
And if he wasn't clean when I took him out
    I'd put him in again.

If I had an old meanie of a mannie
    I'd get him under my thumb,
In a deep bath I'd force him to wallow,
    Soft soaping him against his will,
I'd rub him in the bath,
    I'd rub him hard again,
And if he wasn't clean when I took him out
    I'd put him in again.

If I had an old meanie of a mannie
    I'd send him off to France,
If he wasn't clean when I took him out
    I'd send him there again,

Chuirinn-sa gu Lunnainn e,
Chuirinn rìs don Fhraing e,
'S mur biodh e glan nuair bheirinn ás e,
Chuirinn rithist ann e.

12 bho *Smuaintean air Mórachd Ìmpireachd Bhreatainn*

Cia lìonmhor feart as leat o d' theachd gu d' thriall,
A ghréin as oirdheirc siubhal bhon ear gu'n iar;
Cia lìonmhor subhailc fialaidh ann ad' ghnùis,
Cia lìonmhor beannachd dòrtadh air gach taobh!
Air Ìmpireachd Bhreatainn 'freastal oirr' a-ghnàth
An ear no 'n iar, an tuath no 'n deas gun tàmh,
Cha laigh an dùbhlachd oirre seo gu léir —
Do sholas deàlrach 'soills an àird nan speur
An àiteigin 's a' bhratach togt' ri crann
An-siud no 'n-seo is thusa gràsail ann;
Mi 'n dòchas nach tig ortsa caochladh rian,
Is thusa maireann, Breatann, mar an ciand'.

Có chuireadh smal air Breatann aoigheil, chòir?
Ar màthair thu rinn còmhnadh oirnne 's fòir,
Muim-altram thu gach dùthcha tha fon ghrian;
Do thabhairt suilbhir cha d'rinn bochd thu riamh,
Sgaoil thu do dhuilleag ghorm thar bhàrr gach fonn —
Do fhreumh, do stoc, do mheanglain làidir buan;
Mar s mòid do thabhartas ro mhòid do mhaoin,
Cha robh thu balbh ri feumalachd cloinn daoin';
An t-eilean beag a' boillsgeadh anns a' chuan
Mar sheud ro phrìseil sgapas foidhneal uaith',
Mar lòchran deàlrach tilgeil solas-iùil
Do mhuilleanan air seachran cuan an t-saoghail;
Do mhuirichinn sgaoileadh iad air raon is bheann
Mun iadh a' ghrian an sliochd gum faighear ann
Is aitreabh thogadh leo is bailtean mòr'
Le laghan ceart gun fiaradh clì on chòir,
Le grìd is spìd air taille dìchill chruaidh;
Ge cruaidh an gleac, gu diongmhalt' ràinig buaidh,
Gun chìosnaich daoine borba 's coille 's fonn,
An colann slàn 's an inntinn làn de chonn —
Ged fhuair iad freumh is sìol an dùthaich ùir,
Air am màthair Breatainn cha do thionndaidh cùl.

I'd send him off to London,
   I'd send him back to France,
And if he wasn't clean when I took him out
   I'd send him there again.

from *Thoughts on the Greatness of the British Empire*

How manifold your strength from your coming to your going,
O sun whose course from east to west is so magnificent;
How manifold the generous virtues in your countenance,
How manifold the blessings pouring on each side!
Upon the British Empire shining always
In east or west or north or south unceasing,
The dark will not descend on it entire —
Your brilliant light is shining in the skies
On some place where the flag is raised
Here or there where gracefully you are;
I hope no change of state befalls you ever,
And that you, O Britain, will be no less lasting.

Who would besmirch hospitable, kind Britain?
You are our mother who gave us help and succour,
Fostermother you are of every land on earth;
Your cheerful giving never made you poor,
Across the surface of each land you've spread your foliage green —
Your root, your trunk, your branches strong and lasting;
The more you give away the more your wealth increases,
You were not dumb to needs of human beings;
The little island shining in the sea
Like priceless jewel that sparkles far and wide,
Like shining lantern casting guiding light
On millions scattered across the oceans of the world;
Your offspring have been spread on hill and plain
Until where sun encompasses their progeny is found
And homesteads built by them and cities too
With proper laws unbending from the right,
With excellence and energy resulting from sound diligence;
Though hard the struggle, triumph was firmly reached,
They conquered savages and wood and land,
Their bodies healthy and their minds replete with sense —
Yet for all their roots and seed in pastures new,
On their mother Britain they've not turned their back.

13 *Madainn na Sàbaid*

Cia bòidheach sèimh madainn na Sàbaid,
gu sònraichte air an dùthaich,
co-ainm an là air an d'éirich
ar Slànaigheir bho uaigh a bhàis,
's 'na dhéidh sin an ùine gheàrr
chaidh e suas 'na ghlòir
gu deas-làmh na Cathrach.
Gu ruig an là sin,
là deireannach na seachdain
bho chruthachadh an t-saoghail,
's mar chuimhneachan air aiseirigh
goirear dheth a' chiad là den t-seachdain
gu ruig deireadh na cruinne.
Ar leam gu bheil na diasan arbhair
cromadh an ceann le beic spéiseil,
a' toirt urraim don mhadainn
mhaiseach chiùin-bhog ghrinn,
a' ghrian mhór-gheal bheannaichte
ag òradh mullach nan cruach
is binnean nam beann
air dhòigh barraichte 's an t-alltan
ri m' thaobh le crònan nas mìlse
na 'n àbhaist air a shlighe
troimhn àilean gus an sluigear e
am beul a' chuain bhith-bhuan.
Tha an t-ainmhidh fhéin
a' mealtainn na fois bheannaichte,
's an t-each gu sicir seasgair
san stàball 'na laigh gun charachadh,
's e cho mothachail, mo thruaigh,
ri cuid den chinne-daoine
air sochairean spéiseil an là seo.
Tha 'n duine air fois fhaotainn bho obair lathail,
's gu dleasail ma tha e air sligh' a dhleasnais
a' triall don eaglais gu ìota a riarachadh
le deoch ùrail á tobar prìseil na slàinte
gheibh e bhon aoghair chràbhach,
's e gu deas uidheamaichte,
ma tha e san spiorad togarrach
gu sin a thoirt dha.
Tha dleasaileachd is dleasaileachd ann.

The Sabbath Morning

How lovely and quiet is the Sabbath morning,
especially in the country,
named for the day when our Saviour
arose from the grave of his death,
and a short time after that
he went up in his glory
to the right hand of the Throne.
Until that day
the last day of the week
since the creation of the world,
and in memory of resurrection
it will be called the first day of the week
until the end of the globe.
It seems to me that the ears of corn
are bending their heads in respectful bow,
honouring the morning
that's lovely, calmly-soft and elegant,
the brilliant blessed sun
gilding the tops of the hills
and the mountain peaks
in a splendid way while the burn
beside me croons more sweetly
than usual on its way
through the meadow till it's swallowed
in the mouth of the eternal sea.
Even the animal
enjoys the blessed rest,
with the horse sensible and snug
in the stable lying motionless,
he being as aware, sad to say,
as some of mankind
of the treasured benefits of this day.
Man has got rest from his daily toil,
and dutifully if he is on the path of duty
he goes to church to satisfy his thirst
with a refreshing drink from the precious well of salvation
which he gets from the pious shepherd,
he being ready and prepared,
if he is in spirit liberated
to give him that.
There's duty and there's duty.

Iain còir 's am fuar-chràbhadh
air ruigheachd thar bhàrr do smige
cha d'fhàiltich mi air madainn na Sàbaid,
ged bha thu coibhneil gu leòir
nuair thachair mi ort air madainn Di-Luain,
's do choimhearsnach a choisicheas
na mìltean don eaglais
's nach gabh sochair 'carbad-coise' —
iad seo 'nan eisimpleir air beachdan cuid
mar as còir an t-Sàbaid a naomhachadh,
lagh nan deas-ghnàth air faotainn
barrachd àite 'nan cridhe na feartan
an spioraid a dh'ath-bheothaicheas.
Sealladh eile.
Na mìltean cur là na Sàbaid
fo'n casan gu dàna ladarna,
's an là chaidh ullachadh air an son
gu fois a ghabhail cho tàireil 'nan sùil
ris a' mheanbhchuileig.
Beachdan ceàrr air tighinn am follais
is sgoilean mì-Chrìostail air an là naomh
air togail cinn an-siud 's an-seo
anns a bheil cuspairean air an càramh
ri cridheachan na h-òigridh
tha calg-dhìreach an aghaidh teagasg a' Bhìobaill,
cluiche dìbhearsan spors feala-dhà
air fàs cho cumanta, 's a dh'fhaodas a bhith
ceadaichte 's iomchaidh air làithean eile,
mar gum b'e crìoch àraidh an duine
ith òl 's bi subhach.
Dìomhanas nan dìomhanas.
Ciamar ma-tà a their thu
as còir don t-Sàbaid
bhith air a cumail?
Mar èarlas air an fhois shìorraidh
chaidh ullachadh dhaibhsan
aig a bheil gràdh do Dhia.

Honest John whose hypocrisy
has stretched past the tip of your chin
greeted me not on the Sabbath morning,
though you were decent enough
when I met you on Monday morning,
and your neighbour who walks
miles to church
and won't make use of a tramway car —
these are examples of some folk's opinions
of how the Sabbath should be kept holy,
the ceremonial law having found
more room in their hearts than the virtues
of the spirit which brings back to life.
Another view.
The thousands trampling the Sabbath
underfoot with brazen impudence,
the day prepared for them
to take their rest as contemptible in their eyes
as the midge.
Wrong opinions have come to light
with un-Christian schools on the holy day
appearing here and there
in which subjects are drummed
into young people's hearts
which are totally opposed to the teaching of Scripture,
games entertainment sports amusement
have become so common, and which may be
permissible and proper on other days,
as if man's chief end were
eat drink and be merry.
Vanity of vanities.
How then do you say
the Sabbath ought
to be kept?
As a pledge of the eternal rest
that has been prepared for those
who have love for God.

Aonghas MacEacharna (1870–1944)

14 *Iorram nan Ìtheach*

Iomraibh ho, suas i, fheara,
   Ràimh ri gearan, cnead aig àbrain;
Iomraibh ho, théid i dh'ainneoin,
   Siad nach fannaich, na fir làidir.

Frasan cruaidh a-nuas bho Ghrìoban
   'S i 'na sìoban bho Cheann Tràighe,
Ach na fleasgaich cha dèan strìochdadh —
   Ruigidh sinn an cala sàbhailt'.

Eilean Ì nan sìthean grianach,
   Nam fear fialaidh 's nam ban àlainn,
E mar sheud air bhàrr nan siantan,
   'S crònan a' chuain shiar ga thàladh.

S iomadh maighdeann bhanail ghuamach
   'S maraich' cruaidh a chaidh ann àrach,
S iomadh rìgh 's ceann-cinnidh uasal
   Tha san Réilig shuas aig tàmh ann.

Saoghal buan don t-saor chuir suas dhuinn
   Iùbhrach chruaidh thug buaidh air sàile,
'Ghiubhas Lochlannach 's e fuaighte
   Leis a' chopar ruadh nach fàilnich.

Deòrsa th' air an ailm gu h-uallach
   'S e ri fuaradh cumail càir oirr' —
Siud am fleasgach sheasadh cruadal,
   Shiùbhladh cuan air slige bàirnich.

Càirdean th' air an tràigh gu lìonmhor,
   Tàirngidh iad air tìr gun dàil i
'S iad ri gàirdeachas bhon thill sinn —
   Se mo dhìth nach eil MacPhàil ann.

Angus Mackechnie (Hynish, Tiree)

The Iona Boatsong

Row ye ho, up with her, lads,
  Oars complaining, patches grinding;
Row ye ho, she'll go regardless,
  They'll not weaken, those strong men.

Sudden squalls come down from Gribun
  Spindrift driving from Ceann Tràighe,
But the warriors never yield —
  We will reach the harbour safely.

Iona's isle of sun-blessed otherworlds,
  Generous men and lovely women,
Like a jewel atop the elements,
  Crooned to sleep by the western sea.

Many a fine and charming girl
  And hardy sailor has been reared there,
Many a king and noble chieftain
  Lies up there resting in the Reilig.

Long life to the wright who built for us
  A hardy vessel that vanquished the sea,
Made of Norwegian pine and riveted
  With red-coloured copper that never fails.

George sits dignified at the helm
  Driving her into the foam to windward —
That's the hero who'd stand any hardship,
  Who'd travel the sea on a limpet shell.

Kinsfolk lining the strand aplenty
  Draw her up on the land right away
Delighted that we've returned in safety —
  My one regret's that MacPhail isn't there.

An t-Urr. Coinneach MacLeòid (1871–1955)

15   *An Fhuar-Bheinn*

A-raoir bha mo bhruadar, mo bhruadar, mo bhruadar,
   'S a-nochd bidh mo bhruadar am fuar-bheinn a' cheò,
Gach oidhche mo bhruadar san fhuar-bheinn, san fhuar-bheinn,
   Is t' fhuaran a' nuallan am' chluais ri mo bheò.

Tha m' ionndrainn 's mo bhruadair san fhuar-bheinn, san fhuar-bheinn,
   Is fìor-uisg' a fuarain a' nuallan tre cheò,
A' ghrian is na reultan a' pògadh a ciabhan
   Is mise ga h-iargain 's ga h-iarraidh ri m' bheò.

Ged as cian mi air m' aineol on dachaigh fon fhuar-bheinn
   Is miann le mo bhruadar, mo bhruadar bhith 'd cheò,
Do dhuan ris na h-àrdaibh 's do ghàir ris na cuanta
   Is t' fhuaran a' nuallan am' chluais ri mo bheò.

An t-Urr. Niall Ros (1871–1943)

16   *Dunkirk* (bho *Armageddon*)

Siud am baile mu dheireadh, Dunkirk, an làmhan nan Càirdean,
Frangaich dhìon e bhon iar, 's bhon ear na Breatannaich spracail,
Thog iad an ionad san t-sreath a sgaoileas guineadach gaisgeil
Deas gu Armentières, tre Dhixmude gu àr-achadh Ypres.

Roinn-feachd Caogadamh 's Aon, Roinn Armachd, 's caochladh de bhuidhnean,
Thionail taobh deas an trannsa, sgarte bho'n dàimhich am Flanders;
Sheas iad air raon Saint Valery, dh'iadh an nàmhaid mu'n cùlaibh:
Braighdean cogaidh an cor, an comaidh ri dosgainn na Frainge.

Còmhrag duineil bho'n cùl thug laoich nan Càirdean gun ghéilleadh,
Dhealbh iad ceàrnan cliùiteach, gearastan teann ceithir-shlisneach,
Cóig mìle deug ri tràigh is sia air leud chun na dùthcha,
Deagh chlaisean-uisge mu'n coinneamh bho Bhergues gu Furnes agus Nieuport.

Eadhon mar chìtear tric an glinn na Gaidhealtachd bheanntaich
Fraoch gu maiseach fo bhlàth air feasgar Liùnastail bruicheil,
Gathan na gréin' fo dhubhar le sgaoth de chuileagan meanbha,
Cùis a dh'adhbhraicheas cràdh do dhream air thuras gun dìdeann:

Rev. Kenneth Macleod (Eigg)

The Cold Hill

Last night my dream was, my dream was, my dream was,
    And tonight it will be in the cold hill of mist,
Each night my dream's in the cold hill, the cold hill,
    With the roar of your spring in my ear while I live.

My desire and my dreams in the cold hill, the cold hill,
    With her pure spring water roaring down through a mist,
The sun and the starlight kissing her tresses
    While I want her and crave her as long as I live.

Though I'm far from my home in the lee of the cold hill
    My dream seeks to be, seeks to be in your mist,
Your song to the heights and your cry to the oceans
    With the roar of your spring in my ear while I live.

Rev. Neil Ross (Glendale, Skye)

Dunkirk (from *Armageddon*)

Now remains Dunkirk alone in the hands of the Allies,
Held to the west by the French, to the east by the confident British,
Manning the desperate line whose hard-kept boundary reaches
South to Armentières, through Dixmude and war-battered Ypres.

Armoured and Fifty-First, with units of other divisions,
Join south-west of the breach, though torn from comrades in Flanders;
Soon their stand at Saint Valery saw their cohort surrounded:
Captives of war for France, they share her subsequent fortunes.

Waging a rearguard fight, the unbroken ranks of the Allies
Form the famed perimeter shaped like a garrisoned oblong,
Fifteen miles on the beach by six which penetrate inland,
Moated in front by canals from Bergues to Furnes and to Nieuport.

As in a Highland valley among precipitous mountains
Out of the bell-covered heath on a sultry even of August,
Midget myriads rise, obscuring the rays of the sunlight,
Causing discomfort and pain to pilgrims lacking protection:

Hunaich le nàdar an treud ghabh misneach bho mheudachd an àireamh,
Muinghin an truimead an slògh, le taic bho thaghadh gach cothruim —
Sgiathalain, tancaichean, gunnachan, airm is uidheam am pailteas —
Dhòirt an corraich gu cas air ùr ghleus-catha nan Càirdean.

Eilean beag aonranach Hiort, an uaigneas fàsail na mara,
Cumaidh a ghnùis cloich-theine ri tuinn is fearg na h-Atlantic;
Amhail a bhuanaich treun an ceàrnan bunailteach daingeann —
Gnìomh is cruadal arm gun choimeas an iomradh nan cogadh.

Dh'fhàgadh treas-roghainn cruaidh aig laochraidh Bhreatann 's na Frainge:
Cathaich gu bàs, no géill, no falmhaich feachdan air uisge.
Taisgeachan stòir is ola gu léir a' lasadh mar fhùirneis,
Teas rinn cala Dhunkirk do-ghiùlanta teinntidh gu iomairt.

Chòrd cath-innleachd Ghort ri earail Àrd Chomhairle Bhreatann:
"Sàbhail am feachd air tùs do bhrìgh an t-suidheachaidh ghàbhail.
Cathaich do shlighe gu cuan, is ullaich do bhannal gu seòladh —
Greasaidh a' Chabhlach luingeis, is Arm an Adhair bheir dìdeann."

Thàinig iad fann gu tràigh, na suinn bu chlaoidhte le cogadh,
Chathaich iad sia latha deug air bheagan de chadal no àrach;
Stòlda, sàmhach, ciùin, fo shligean is pheileirean spreadhaidh —
Sreathadan fiar air ghaineamh b'e 'n rian a lughdachadh millidh.

Itealain chàirdeil shuas, nach faicte le sùil air a' chladach,
Choinnich an nàmh a' tighinn, is dhìol dha call ceithir-fillte;
Làdaichean guineach bho airm a loisg air sgiathalain nàimhdeil,
Gunnachan Frangach is Breatannach dhìon le'n lasair an ceàrnan.

Sàr 'Ghnìomh Comasach' siud, aon dèanadas iongantach ainmeil,
Ùghdarras Dhùbrium ghairm air cabhlach iomadh is neònach —
Eithear gu iomain is méin is trusadh is eile 'nan ceudan,
Drochaid air flod, long aiseig, long slaodaidh, birlinn is milltear.

Astar mhìltean ri tràigh, le grinneal is tolmanan murain,
Còrsachan còmhnard mìn fo bhàrcadh cobharach tuinne —
Bàtaichean staoin a-mhàin a dh'aisig na fiùrain bho chladach,
Chaidh iad air bòrd na luingeis a sheòl gu Sasainn is tearmann.

Dh'ainneoin gach ionnsaigh is call, ar soithichean ghiùlain do Shasainn
Mìltean trì deug thar fhichead is naodh fichead mìle le Breatann,
Trì mìle fichead is ceud de mhìltean àireamh nam Frangach:
'Iongantas Naodh Latha' siud, bhios maireann an eachdraidh nan linntean.

So the gregarious Hun, encouraged by prodigal numbers,
Marshalled in mass formation, backed by total advantage —
Aircraft, tanks, artillery, all in superabundance —
Dashes his hurricane rage on the new-formed Allied positions.

Firm in the ocean waste the lonely isle of St Kilda
Holds its front of basalt against the savage Atlantic;
So the perimeter stands, a bastion steady and solid —
Marking a feat of arms unmatched in the records of warfare.

Three contingent courses remain to the French and the British:
Fight to the death, or yield, or quit by evacuation.
Heat from stores and oil-tanks burning fierce like a furnace
Render the Dunkirk docks unfit for the purpose of transport.

Gort's own plan of action accords with the Cabinet mandate:
"Safety predominates now in view of the stern situation.
Fight your way to the sea, prepare the troops for embarking —
Navy will furnish the ships, and the Air Force render protection."

So to the beach they came, those grim war-weary campaigners,
Sixteen days they fought on little of rations or slumber;
Bombed and shelled with malice, yet calm, deliberate, silent —
Marshalled in curving lines on the sands to mitigate slaughter.

Fighters friendly, unseen by wistful eyes from the beaches,
Punish the oncoming Hun, inflicting quadruple losses;
Anti-aircraft guns maintain a cannonade constant,
British and French artillery keep the perimeter blazing.

One 'Operation Dynamo', one amazing performance,
Dover Command convenes a huge fantastic flotilla —
Mine-sweepers, drifters, trawlers, manifold craft by the hundred,
Cross-channel steamers and tugs, pontoons, destroyers and barges.

Miles of low-lying shore, with bent grass tufts on the sand dunes,
Stretches of even coast with crested surf on the shallows —
Only smaller boats can ferry the troops to the offing,
There to enter the vessels that make for safety and England.

Spite of attack and loss, the muster carries to England
Thousands ninety and three and a hundred thousand of British,
Thousands twenty-three and a hundred thousand of Frenchmen:
'Nine Days Wonder' this, endures to all generations.

Sgeul air Liubhairt Dhunkirk bidh buan an cuimhne nan cinneach
Amhail am mìorbhail aithnicht', am feart bho chumhachd Iehovah,
Sgoilt a' Mhuir Ruadh a tuinn mar labhair a theachdair' am facal,
Thàrr Clann Israel ás bho fheirg is bhraighdeanas Phàroh.

Aonghas MacDhonnchaidh (1871–1948)

17 *An Dà Latha*

'S iomadh latha math a bh'agam:
  Seadh, is latha tàireil.
'S iomadh latha math a bh'agam;
  Seadh, is latha tàireil.
'S iomadh latha math a bh'agam:
  Seadh is latha tàireil,
Gearradh feamann anns a' chladach,
  Is a cur am bàta

Nuair a theann e stigh an t-Earrach,
  Cha b'e dad a b' fhearr e.
Nuair a theann e stigh an t-Earrach,
  'S latha cur bhuntàta;
Nuair a theann e stigh an t-Earrach,
  Cha b'e dad a b' fhearr e:
Cur an clais' ri clacha-meallain,
  'S crodhanan 'g am fàsgadh

Togail fhaochag ris an reothairt,
  Agus buain nam bàirneach;
Togail fhaochag ris an reothairt
  As a gheodh' am fàs iad;
Togail fhaochag ris an reothairt,
  Cha b'e rogha ceaird e,
'S bogadh leathaig air a' bhogha —
  Fodhail na seol-tràghad

'S iomadh latha math a bh'agam:
  Seadh, is latha spàirneil.
'S iomadh latha mear a bh'agam
  Ruith air feadh nan cairdean.
'S iomadh latha gean a bh'agam
  Rùdhrachadh nan àbhaist,

So the Dunkirk Deliverance lives in memory human
Like that marvel of old, the sign of the might of Jehovah,
When by His messenger's word the Red Sea waters dividing,
Israel's host escaped the chains and fury of Pharaoh.

Angus Robertson (Breakish, Strath, Skye)

The Two Days

Many happy days I had,
　　Yes, and many vile ones,
Many happy days I had,
　　Yes, and many vile ones;
Many happy days I had,
　　Yes, and many vile ones,
Cutting seaweed in the shore
　　And putting it in a boat.

When it turned into the spring
　　It wasn't one bit better,
When it turned into the spring
　　And time to plant potatoes,
When it turned into the spring
　　It wasn't one bit better —
Filling trenches in a hailstorm
　　And wringing paws together.

Picking winkles at the springtide
　　And collecting limpets,
Picking winkles at the springtide
　　In the inlet where they're growing;
Picking winkles at the springtide,
　　No-one's favourite employment,
Exposing flounder on the reef —
　　The tribute of the ebbtide.

Many happy days I had,
　　Yes, and many hard ones,
Many lively days I had
　　Going from friend to friend;
Many cheerful days I had
　　Scouring well-loved places

Far am minig fhuair mi giomach,
  Claba-dubh' is càrnag

Far am minig fhuair mi giomach,
  Claba-dubh is càrnag;
Agus minig fhuair mi tumadh
  Ann an glumaig sàile;
Far am minig fhuair mi tumadh,
  Agus cunnart bàthaidh —
Call nan casan ann am ghurrach
  Siubhal air mo mhàgan

18   *Maorach is Feamannadh*

Bi' maorach is feamannadh
  Le ùprait an Earraich ann.
Bi' maorach is feamannadh
  Le saothair an Earraich ann.
Bi' maorach is feamannadh
  Le ùprait an Earraich ann —
Fire faire! dol is cabhag
  Ann am bad an fheamannaidh

Fir a' bhaile dol 'nan cabhaig
  Ann am bad an fheamannaidh;
Fir a' bhaile cumail faire
  Ann am plath na camhanaich;
Fir a' bhaile cur mu'n cais'eart
  Mar a b' fhearr a b'aithne dhaibh —
Cliabh is corran ann an oisein,
  'S ràmh am bac a' snagadaich

Cliabh is corran anns an eathair
  Airson sac nan cladaichean:
Seol na mara gabhail ealla
  Riuth' nach toir an aire dha.
Seol na mara greasad cabhaig;
  Rang fo chorrain tanachadh;
Fir air bharradh tarruing eallach'
  Mun tig casadh mar' orra

Where I often found a lobster,
   Clabbie-doo and sand-eel.

Where I often found a lobster,
   Clabbie-doo and sand-eel,
And I often got a ducking
   In a briny puddle,
Where I often got a ducking
   And came close to drowning —
Losing foothold, on my hunkers,
   Crawling on all fours.

Shell-Fishing, Seaweed-Cutting

There'll be shell-fishing, seaweed-cutting
   With all the riot of spring in it,
There'll be shell-fishing, seaweed-cutting
   With all the toil of spring in it;
There'll be shell-fishing, seaweed-cutting
   With all the riot of spring in it —
Haste and hurry, going and coming,
   Where the seaweed-cutting's done.

Township men go in a panic
   Where the seaweed-cutting's done,
Township men keep a lookout
   In the dawn's first glimmer;
Township men augment their footgear
   The best way they know how —
Creel and sickle in a corner
   And oar in tholepins grating.

Creel and sickle in the boat
   To rob the shores of seaware,
Tidal movements lie in wait
   For such as may neglect them;
Tidal movements causing haste,
   Swathe for sickles shallowing —
Men atop it dragging burdens
   Before the tide can catch them.

Ruairidh MacAoidh (1872–1949)

19   *Òran aig Toiseach Cogadh Mór na h-Eòrpa*

Horo ho hi horo chlann,
Horo chlann éiribh,
Horo ho hi horo chlann.

Anns a' mhadainn 's mi dùsgadh
   Bidh mi tùrsach trom deurach.

Anns gach feasgar gun othail
   'N àm dol fodha na gréine

'S mi ri ionndrainn nam fiùran
   Rinn mo dhùthaich a thréigsinn.

Gur e 'Ceusfhear' na mallachd
   Chuir an dorran gu léir oirnn.

Gus a chumhachd a thilleadh
   Feumar gillean nan sléibhtean.

Tha luchd-àitich nan gleann
   A' tarraing lann air an gleusadh,

Tarraing lanntan cruaidh sgaiteach
   'S iad mar ealtainn air ghéiread.

Siud na fir nach till mùiseag
   Gus an sgiùrs iad an Ceusfhear,

Gus am fàg iad 'na chorp e
   Tollte fosgailte creuchdach,

'S feòil a' chealgair a' biathadh
   Biataich fhiadhaich an t-sléibhe.

Luchd nam boineidean gorma,
   Bhon a dh'fhalbh sibh, cha ghéill sibh.

Bhon a dh'fhalbh sibh, cha tàmh sibh
   Gu'm bi Berlin agus séist ris,

Roderick Mackay (Illeray, N. Uist)

Song at the Start of the Great European War

> *Horo ho hi horo my children,*
> *Horo my children arise,*
> *Horo ho hi horo my children.*

When I wake in the morning
  I'm sad, mournful and weeping.

When it's quiet every evening
  And the sun is going down

How I miss the lads
  Who've departed my district.

It's the damned 'Crucifier'
  That's filled us with anger.

To repel his attack
  They need the lads from the hillsides.

The dwellers of the glens
  Are drawing blades that they've sharpened,

Drawing slashing steel blades
  As sharp as a razor.

No threat will repulse them
  Till they've routed the Crucifier,

Till they leave him a corpse
  Riddled with open wounds,

The scoundrel's flesh feeding
  The scavengers of the hillside.

You boys with blue bonnets,
  Since you've gone, you won't yield.

Since you've gone, you won't rest
  Till Berlin's under siege,

Gu'm bi shràidean caol crotach
'S iad air flod le fuil bhéistean.

Nuair a bhagras an nàmhaid,
Air a' Ghàidheal a dh'éighear —

Bidh gach morair is iarla
Guidhe dian leibh gu éirigh,

Bidh sibh measail aig diùcan
'S bheir an Crùn a chuid fhéin dhuibh;

Ach nuair cheanglar an t-sìth leibh
Cha bhi cuimhn' air bhur feum dhaibh,

Cha bhi cuimhn' air mar smàladh
Thar sàl do thìr chéin sibh,

Mar chaidh fearann a dhiùltadh
'S mar a chum iad na féidh bhuaibh,

Mar a chum iad an t-iasg bhuaibh
Agus ianlaith nan speuran.

Chan àm cuimhneachadh dhuibh air,
Bhon tha 'n Rìoghachd 'na h éiginn!

20   *Òran na Caillich Bhuana*

An cuala sibhse mun chaillich
    Th' air tighinn gu fearann na h-Àirde —
'N àm am beum a chur thairis
    Gun d'bhuail i spealan na Càrnaich?
Mur do mhealladh mo bharail
    Gun tug a' ghailleann am bàs dhi
Air a turas don Eilean,
    'S iad air deireadh mar b' àbhaist —
        Cha d'dhlùth iad dad.

Sann thuirt Ailean ri Ruairidh,
    "Chan eil tuairm' aig do bhriathran:

Till its hunched little alleyways
   Are awash with beasts' blood.

When the enemy threaten,
   It's the Gael who is called —

Each earl and each lord
   Implores you to rise,

Dukes show you respect
   And the Crown gives you its share;

But when peace is secured by you
   They'll forget how you served them,

They'll forget you were banished
   Far over the sea,

And how land was refused
   And they forbade you the deer,

And forbade you the fish
   And the birds of the air.

It's no time to remind you of it,
   Since the Kingdom's in need!

The Song of the Cailleach of Harvest

Did you hear about the cailleach
   Who came to Aird croftlands —
That when time for cutting came
   She struck the Carnach scythes?
If my view's not mistaken
   She was killed by the storm
On her way to the Island,
   They being behindhand as usual —
      They've brought nothing home.

Said Allan to Roderick,
   "Your words make no sense:

Sann tha 'turas mar as dual dhi,
   Dol gu tuath chun an iasgaich;
Nach seall thus' air a gualainn
   'S air a' chruaidh th' air a cliathaich —
S math gu sgailceadh 's gu bualadh i
   'N àm bhith ruagadh nam biastan
      'S gan cur fo smachd!"

Nuair a dh'éirich Iain Chaluim
   'S a rinn e amharc mun cuairt air,
Sann a chunnaic e chailleach
   A' gabhail fabhair gu gluasad;
Gun do thill e 'na dheannaibh,
   'S geilt air anam le uabhas —
Rinn e 'n doras a dhùnadh
   'S bhrist e lùdagan shuas air,
      Aig meud a' ghlag.

Siud a' chailleach bha fiadhaich,
   Sann air a fiacaill bha choltas
Bhith cho cruaidh ris an iarann,
   Bha i riamh anns a' bhochdainn;
Cha robh greim air a cnàmhan,
   Chaidh a h-àrach sa ghorta —
Bha gach cuisl' agus féithe
   Bha sa bhéist ud cho nochdte
      Ri spuir a' chait.

Mas e gillean an t-Samhla
   Chuir a-nall air a' bhàgh i
S olc an turas thug ann iad,
   Cha bhi 'geamhradh 'nam fàbhar;
'N àm dhol suas air an fhadhail,
   Ma nì iad tadhal sa Chàrnaich
Chan fhaigh iad aoigheachd no coibhneas
   Mun tùrn a rinn iad san Àird air —
      Cha robh i ceart.

Bha i 'n dùil an àm gluasad
   Gum biodh i cuairt an taigh Dhòmhnaill,
'S nuair thug i sùil thar a gualainn
   Bha 'chuid chruachan an òrdugh;
Sann a thug i 'n-sin leum aist',
   A' dol air chéilidh air Mòraig:

She's making her usual trip,
   Going north to the fishing;
Just look at her shoulder
   And the steel on her hip —
She's good for thumping and walloping
    When time comes to chase off the beasts
      And teach them a lesson!"

When Iain Chaluim got up
   And looked all around him,
He caught sight of the cailleach
   Getting ready to move;
He came back in a hurry,
   His soul petrified with fear —
He got the door shut
   And broke a hinge at the top of it,
     So big was the crash.

That cailleach was savage,
   Her teeth had the look
Of being as hard as iron,
   She'd been always in poverty;
Without meat on her bones,
   She'd been brought up in dearth —
Each artery and vein
   In that monster was as prominent
     As the claws of the cat.

If it's the lads of Samhla
   Who sent her over the bay,
It's an ill trip that brought them,
   Her winter won't favour them;
When crossing the ford,
   If they call in at Carnach
They'll get no welcome or kindness
   For the job they made in Aird of it —
     It wasn't right.

When time came to move she thought
   She'd spend a while in Donald's house,
And when she looked over her shoulder
   His stacks were in order;
She then made a leap,
   Going visiting Morag:

Thàinig bogs' uic' á Glaschu,
   Bha e pailt leis gach seòrsa,
   Agus mharbh i molt!

Ach am molt ged a mharbh i,
   Cha toir e gainmhein dheth, 'chreutair,
Théid a shailleadh gu dearbhte
   San tuba ghorm gu'n tig feum air;
Ach thug Aonghas mart làmhaig —
   'S chan eil i ceàrr — á Loch Eubhart,
Bheir e dhìse na h-àirnean
   'S bidh 'chuid as fheàrr aige fhéin dhith
     Air olc no math.

Bhon tha bàrr aige 'm-bliadhna
   Air ais am biadh, seach an-uiridh,
Na gabh tàmh mu na crìochan —
   S fheàrr dhuit triall ás na fuireach;
Gabh do chairtealan geamhraidh
   'N taobh ud thall dhen a' mhuileann,
Nì iad móran buntàta
   'S tha pailteas gràin aig gach duine
     Ged dh'fhalbh a' chearc.

Cha robh cailleach san dùthaich
   As motha dhùisg a dhroch sheanchas,
Gach fear-fearainn an diomb rithe
   'S mallachd dhaoine 'na h-earball;
Cuir glas air a mùiseag
   Bhon si diùbhaidh nan cailleachan —
Théid a glacadh 's a sgiùrsadh
   A-mach á dùthaich nan garbhchrìoch
     Gun tighinn air ais.

Teàrlach MacNìmhein (1874–1944)

21 *Òran Bainnse*

Siud a dh'fhàg mi 'n-diugh gun sunnd,
   Air mo dhìochuimhneachadh sa chabhaig;
Siud a dh'fhàg mi 'n-diugh gun sunnd
   Chionn nach d'fhuair mi thun na banais.

She'd got a box from Glasgow
    Full of all sorts of things
        And had killed a wedder!

But though she'd slaughtered the wedder,
    It will give nothing, the creature,
It will be thoroughly salted
    In the blue tub till it's needed;
But Angus brought a hatchet-cow —
    No error she — from Locheport,
He'll give Morag the kidneys
    And have the best of it himself
        For good or for ill.

Since he has a crop this year
    Food's back compared to last year,
Don't stay on in the district —
    You'd better leave and not stay;
Take up your winter quarters
    On the other side of the mill,
They'll grow lots of potatoes
    And they all have plenty grain
        Though the hen's gone.

No cailleach in the country
    Ever drew more adverse comment,
Every crofter's annoyed at her
    And people's curse goes around with her;
Put a stop to her bullying
    As she's the worst of all women —
She'll be captured and scourged
    From the land of the rough bounds
        Without coming back.

Charles MacNiven (Scoraig and Islay)

Wedding Song

That's what's left me sad today,
Being forgotten in the rush;
That's what's left me sad today,
Not getting to the wedding.

Bha sùil agam ri cuireadh fialaidh,
  Gun rachadh m' iarraidh thun na banais
'S gum faighinn cearc le forc is sgian
  Gu bhith ga h-ialladh — biadh ro bhlasta.

Gun do reamhraich mi 'n gèadh mòr
  Le min phònair thàin' á Glaschu,
'S nan do chuir mi e gu margadh
  Chuireadh e airgead dhomh am banca.

Cheannaich mi tiodhlac a bha fiachail,
  Deagh leab' iarainn a chuid Shasann,
Ach gun chuireadh mar bu mhiann leam
  Chaill iad fiachan nach bu mhaith leo!

Fhuair mi cùrainn a bha crùn,
  Air son flùr gun phàigh mi tastan —
Fhuair mi siud is casag chaol,
  Sgoltadh bha 'na cùl san fhasan.

Gléidhidh mi 'n tiodhlac nis domh fhéin
  'S cuiridh mise feum oirr' fhathast
Nuair a gheibh mi bean dhomh fhéin —
  Ach is ainmig iadsan gheibh gu m' bhanais!

Bu lìonmhor ann na daoine mòra
  Le 'n cuid charbad 's paidhir each annt',
Ach a' chuid aig nach robh carbad,
  Fhuair iad coingheal o MhacArtair.

Cha robh 'n coisiche gu stàth ann
  'S cha robh ann ach sàr nam marcaich —
Ach ged bha 'bhanais ud cho stràiceil,
  Se 'm biadh fhuair pàirt buntàta 's sgadan.

Bidh mi tighinn gu ceann le m' òran,
  A fhleasgaich òig, thoir thus' an aire,
Cuimhnich nuair a bhios thu pòsadh
  Gun iarr thu mo sheòrsa thun do bhanais.

I expected a generous invitation,
   That I'd be asked to the wedding,
That I'd get chicken with a fork and a knife
   To pick it up with — delicious food.

So I fattened the big gander
   With bean-meal got from Glasgow,
And if I'd sent it to market
   I'd have money in the bank.

I bought a valuable present,
   A good iron bed made in England,
But without the invitation I'd have liked
   They lost possessions they'll regret!

I bought clothes that cost a crown,
   For a flower I paid a shilling —
All that and a tailored coat,
   With the split behind that's in fashion.

Now I'll keep the gift for myself
   And I'll make use of it eventually
When I find myself a wife —
   Though *they're* unlikely to be at my wedding!

There were plenty of toffs there
   With their carriages and pairs,
While those without a carriage
   Got a loan from Macarthur.

Arriving on foot was inadequate
   And no-one was there but equestrians —
Yet despite that wedding being so swanky,
   Some were given tatties and herring.

I'll be bringing my song to a finish,
   But young bachelor, you be careful,
Don't forget when you get married
   To invite my sort to your wedding.

22   bho *Seinnidh mis' an duanag*

Chan eil san Eilean Ìleach
   Aon rìbhinn as maisiche,
Do ghaol cho buan 's am fìor-uisg',
   'S nam faighinn fhìn bhith cadal leat
Ged b'ann am bothan àirigh
   'S nàdar a bhith maille rium,
Fo dhìon 's fo sgàth nan àrd-bheann,
   Ged thigeadh àrd nan gailleannan,
Ged shéideadh oirnn na gaothan
   Agus smùid nan gailleannan,
Bhithinn sona leatsa, ghràidh,
   Is mo làmh bhith thairis ort
Ged b'e tom luachair, seadh, ar cluasag
   An gleann uaine glacagach
'S mi tarraing, ghràidh, ri m' thaobh thu —
   'S a ghaoil, cha bhiodh ort aithreachas.

23   *Banais Chòrsabuil*

B'i siud a' bhanais urramach a chruinnich ann an Còrsabol,
S iomadh aon fhuair cuireadh bha urramach ro mhòr ann;
   Dh'fhàg iad mis' am' aonarach is shaoilinn nach bu chòir dhaibh,
   Cha robh mi idir cianalach 's mi trang a' dèanamh òrain.

Bha gu leòir de bhiadh ac', oir fhuair iad fiadh á Pròaig,
Chuir iad molt á Sanaig agus gamhainn ás an Òtha,
   'S mun robh 'n dìnneir seachad ac' bha fallas air gach còcair' —
   Loisg iad tunna guail rithe, 's mo thruaighe a' chruach mhòna.

Bha còrr is dusan fidhleir ann, bha trì dhiubh á Dùn Éideann,
Ach thachair nì bha mìothlachdail, dhìochuimhnich iad na teudan,
   'S dh'ith a' mhuc am pìobaire 's e seinn, mas fìor an sgeula —
   Se 'n dòigh a rinn iad dannsadh a bhith canntaireachd ri chéile.

Bha dà fhichead òg-bhean ann is gillean òg' do réir sin,
Gach aon dhiubh 's cearc 'na achlais a' tarraing chum na féiste;
   Bha cuid aig an robh tunnag dhiubh, sann bha cearc-ghuir aig té dhiubh,
   'S bha fear ann a thug coileach leis, ach ghoideadh e á Gréineil.

from *I'll sing the lovesong*

In the whole Isle of Islay
     There's no girl that is prettier,
Your love eternal as spring water,
     And if I could sleep with you
Even in a shieling-hut
     Surrounded by nature,
Protected and sheltered by the mountains,
     Though the worst of storms arose,
Though the winds might blow on us
     And the spindrift of gales,
I'd be content with you, love,
     To have my arm around you
Though rushes, yes, were our pillow
     In a green glen of hollows
As I drew you, love, to my side —
     And darling, you would not regret it.

The Wedding at Corsapol

What a grand wedding party it was that gathered in Corsapol,
Many folk were invited who were most honourable guests;
     They left me by myself and I thought they really shouldn't have,
     But I didn't mind a bit as I was working hard on a song.

They had plenty of food, as they'd got a deer from Proaig,
They'd sent a wedder from Sanaig and a stirk from the Oa,
     And before the meal was over every cook was in a sweat —
     They burned a ton of coal on it, and I'm sorry for the peatstack.

There were over twelve fiddlers, with three of them from Edinburgh,
But an unfortunate thing happened, they forgot the strings,
     And the pig ate the piper as he played, or so I'm told —
     But they managed to dance by singing mouth tunes at each other.

There were forty young women there with enough young men to match them,
Each one arriving at the feast with a chicken in his oxter;
     There were some that brought a duck, one girl a broody hen,
     And one man brought a cockerel, but it was stolen from Greineil.

Ach guidheam don a' chàraid sin buan shlàint' 'nan laigh' 's 'nan éirigh,
Sìth, sonas dhaibh, is àghalachd, seadh ge b'e àit an téid iad;
    Tha 'm pòsadh dhìth san rìoghachd seo, se sin aon nì tha dearbhte,
    Tha feum air tuille shaighdearan chum oillt chur air a' Ghearmailt.

Donnchadh MacDhunléibhe (1877–1964)

24   bho *Cogadh agus Sìth*

Tha na fir air a' chuan agus tha a' chòisir a' seinn:

Tha cabhlach nan long a' marcachd nan tonn
    'S a' giùlan nan sonn thar chuan,

Tha 'n soirbheas 'nan déidh 's an gluasad d'a réir
    Ged nach feudar dhaibh bréid chur suas;

Tha iùbhraich na smùid' nach iarradh na siùil
    A' gabhail an cùrs' le luaths

Cho luath ris an fhiadh agus aghaidh ri sliabh
    Is gadhar gu dian ga ruag —

Tha torrann nan tonn ri sliosaibh nan long
    Tha a' giùlan nan sonn thar chuan.

Thàinig fios gun robh na Gàidhil ri aghaidh nàmhaid, agus tha màthair Sheumais a'
cur suas athchuinge agus a' seinn:

O Athair nan Gràs, 'n àm gleadhraich na spàirn'
Is teasaich a' bhlàir ann an tèarmann do làimh',
    Cum macan mo ghràidh o bheud;
    O Athair nam Feart, thoir fòir agus neart
    Do m' mhacan an gleac na streup.

O Athair nam Buadh, ri àm dha dol suas
Ri frasan na luaidhe 's ri faobhar na cruaidh',
    Cum tèaraint mo luaidh o bheum;
    O Athair an t-Saoghail, o dhoimhneachd do ghaoil
    Cum mo mhacan o bhaoghal 's on eug.

I wish that couple lifelong health both in going to bed and rising,
Peace, happiness, prosperity, yes wherever they may go;
   This country's short of marriages, that's one thing that's shown for certain,
   For more soldiers are essential now for frightening the Germans.

Duncan Livingstone (Reudle, Torloisk, Mull)

from *War and Peace*

The men are on the sea and the chorus sings:

> The flotilla of boats is coursing the waves
>   To carry the lads overseas,
>
> A breeze from astern is helping them on
>   Though they've no need to hoist any cloth;
>
> The galleys of steam independent of sails
>   Are setting their course with speed,
>
> As swift as a deer up the mountainside
>   With a hound in hot pursuit —
>
> The breakers snarl at the side of the craft
>   That carry the lads overseas.

Word has come that the Gael have been in action, and James's mother prays and sings:

> O Father of Graces, when armies clash
> With the rage of battle in the palm of Thy hand,
>   Keep the son of my love from harm;
>   O Father of Powers, give succour and strength
>   To my son in the tumult of strife.
>
> O Father of Powers, in going over the top
> Into showers of lead and blades of steel,
>   Don't let my darling be hit;
>   O Father of the World, from the depths of Thy love
>   Keep my son from peril and death.

O Athair na Sìth, air sgàth Ìosa Crìost,
An àm an dol sìos gu faobhar nam pìc
    Cum dìon air macan mo chléibh;
O Ìosa gun lochd, aon tèarmann nam bochd,
    Éist m' athchuing' a-nochd, O éist.

Fhuaireadh sanas gun robh cabhlach mhòr sgiathlain nàimhdeil a' dèanamh air a'
bhaile, agus tha am maor a' toirt rabhadh do gach neach agus a' seinn:

Bithibh fo dhìon, na feithibh ri nì,
Ach greasaibh a-sìos don fhasgadh —

Feuch trast nan speur cabhlach an éig,
Àr agus reub faisg oirnn;

Greasaibh, a chlann, na mnathan, 's na fann,
Treòraich an dall 's am bacach,

Greasaibh fon làr gun eagal gun sgàth
Ach cruadalach dàn' tapaidh.

Tha a' chabhlach sgiathlain a' pleasgadh a' bhaile, agus tha a' chòisir a' seinn:

Dararaich sadadh spadadh spreadhadh
Pleasgadh losgadh deataich thachdach
    Bàs a' spùtadh ás an adhar.

Ar taighean 'nan caoir theine,
Na ballachan a-sìos 'nan spruidhleach,
Am bail' air a léirsgrios
    Le bàs tha spùtadh ás an adhar.

Closaichean briste 'nam fuil 's 'nan gaorr,
Sgreamh agus oillt,
Uabhas nach fhaodar innseadh
An déidh a' bhàis
    A spùt oirnn ás an adhar.

Bha Mòrag a' cuideachadh na cloinne agus nam fann gu dìon, ach mun d'fhuair i
fhéin fasgadh chaidh i a leònadh gu goirt. Air a' chabhlach dol seachad, fhuaireadh i
'na sìneadh, agus tha màthair Sheumais a' toirt cobhair dhi agus a' seinn:

Och mo chreach, mo chreach 's mo léireadh,
Is mise màthair a' bhròin,

O Father of Peace, for Jesus' sake,
When it's time to face the bayonet blades
Protect the child of my womb;
O matchless Christ, sole resort of the poor,
Hear my prayer tonight, O hear.

Word came that a great fleet of enemy aircraft was making for the town, and the policeman warns everyone and sings:

Get under cover, don't wait for a thing,
Just hurry down into the shelter —

See crossing the skies the flotilla of death,
Slaughter and wounds are near us;

Hurry, children, the women, infirm,
Guide the blind and the crippled,

Get under the ground without panic or fear
But strong, courageous and cheerful.

The fleet of aircraft bombs the town, and the chorus sings:

Rattling thudding slaughter exploding
Crackling burning choking of smoke
Death spewing out of the sky.

Our houses become fireballs,
The walls collapse in rubble,
The town devastated
By death that's spewing out of the sky.

Carcases broken into flesh and gore,
Carnage and terror,
Unspeakable horror
After death
That spewed on us out of the sky.

Morag was helping the children and the infirm to get under cover, but before she herself could find shelter she was seriously injured. When the all-clear sounded, she was discovered lying on the ground, and James's mother tends her and sings:

O my anguish, anguish and torment.
I'm the mother of grief,

Seud nam beusan air a reubadh —
     Luaidh mo chléibh 's i leòint.

Fuil o creuchdan ruith 'na sruthan
     'S lùban dhith air làr,
O a Dhé, na tréig mi buileach —
     Tèarainn i on bhàs.

Dh'òrdaichear ar n-òigridh thapaidh
     Dhìonadh na Roinn Eòrp'
'S dh'fhàgar sinne lom gun fhasgadh —
     Mnathan 's daoine breòit'.

Ach nan d'fhuair ar gillean fuireach
     Air an tulaich fhéin
Cha robh sinne 'n càs no 'n cunnart
     O làr, o mhuir no speur.

25   Rannan Callainne

Se ar guidhe bhur Nollaig bhith cridheil le àgh
     Agus Bliadhna Mhath Ùr dhuibh le mùirn agus gràdh;
'S ged nach téid sinn le'r camain gu faiche no tràigh,
     Cha do dh'fhannaich ar tlachd air na cleachdainn a bhà.

Ar beannachd le'r dùrachd bhur Nollaig bhith sunndach
     Agus Bliadhna Mhath Ùr dhuibh le mùirn agus àgh;
Gach sonas oirbh riaraicht', gach sochair gu'r n-iarrtas —
     Gu solarach, rianach, le miadh agus gràdh.

26   Cath Fairge Monte Vìdeo

Fheara, biomaid sunndach is mùirneach is pròiseil
Mun sgeul seo as ùire air cliù ar fear òga,
Fheara, biomaid sunndach is mùirneach is pròiseil.

Thàinig air an fhrith-theud dhuinn
A-nall á Monte Vìdeo
An sgeul a thog ar cridheachan
     Mar dh'iomaineadh luchd fòirneirt.

The jewel of virtues torn apart —
    The love of my heart is maimed.

Blood from injuries running in streams
    With pools of it on the ground,
O my God, don't forsake me completely —
    Keep her away from death.

Our brave young men were conscripted to go
    To defend the continent of Europe
And we were left naked without protection —
    The women and the infirm.

But had our lads been allowed to remain
    Inside their own garden gate
We'd have been in no plight or peril
    From the ground, the sea or the air.

Festive Verses

We wish you a Christmas that's full of good cheer
    And a Happy New Year full of love and great joy;
And though we don't go playing shinty on field or on strand,
    Our delight in the ways of the past is still strong.

Our blessings and wishes for a Christmas that's cheerful
    And a Happy New Year full of joy and content;
May prosperity be yours, all ease as you wish it —
    Well-ordered, provisioned, with love and respect.

The Battle of the River Plate

Men, let's be happy and joyful and proud
    At this latest proof of our young men's repute,
Men, let's be happy and joyful and proud.

We heard on the wireless
From Montevideo
The news that delighted us
    Of how tyrants were repulsed.

Bha *Ajax* bheag an eireachdais
Mar abhag sàs an eleaphant
'S an *Achilles* gu dealasach
     Ri bearradh agus stròiceadh

'S a bhean mo chridhe *Exeter*
Bha frasadh dìle theachdairean —
An dìblidh chaidh a ghleacadh riut
     Gun mheataich thu le d' phòig e.

Bu gharg a' phòg o d' bhilean-sa,
Bu shearbh, 's bu choimheach nimheil i
Is lasair dhearg an dì-mhillidh
     A chlisge tighinn á d' sgòrnan.

Thug e cùl 's bu nàire dha
'S cha d'éist e bùir do thàirneanaich —
Bha eagal air gum bàthadh e
     Oir cha b'e ghnàths bhith seòladh.

A dh'ainneoin bòst nan Gearmailteach
Is cumhachd mhòr an armailtean,
Chuir sibhse gu féin-mharbhadh e
     Is sgàin sibh balg na bòilich.

Innsidh mi oir s fìrinn e
'S is cian on chaidh a sgrìobhadh oirnn —
Gur sinne dream nan dìbeargach
     On d'theich an long aig Nòah.

27   *Am Bullaphant*

Se m' eudail-sa am bullaphant, si m' eudail-sa chuir chugam e,
Tha gach neach an eud rium mar mheudaich mo chulaidh orm;
     Fhuair mi e o m' annsachd a-nuas o chois nam beanntan —
'S nuair dh'fhuasgail mi an t-sreang dheth gun dhanns mi na Tulaichean.

Se m' eudail am bullaphant, gur feumail an cuideachd e,
Tha mise nis gu spéiseil oir s éibhinn mo chugann-sa;
     Ged nì mi latha féille cha leig mi leas bhith gréidheadh —
'S ged thigeadh sluagh Dhùn Éideann bhiodh greim do na h-uile dhiubh.

The neat little *Ajax*
Like a terrier at an elephant
While the eager *Achilles*
    Went clipping and tearing

And my darling the *Exeter*
Fired her deluge of missives —
The wretch who came to grips with you
    You weakened with your kiss.

From your lips the kiss was savage,
Bitter, poisonous and cruel
With the scarlet flame of carnage
    Coming swiftly from your throat.

He turned his back and shamefully
Didn't listen to your thundering —
He was afraid that he'd be drowned
    For he wasn't used to sailing.

Despite the boast of the Germans
And the great power of their armies,
You drove him to suicide
    And burst the bag of bombast.

I'll tell it since it's true
And was long ago written of us —
We're the tribe of the pirates
    From whom Noah's ship fled.

The Bullaphant

My darling's the bullaphant, it's my darling that sent me it,
Everyone envies the growth in my provisions;
    It came from my beloved up in the foothills —
And when I'd undone the parcel I danced a Reel of Tulloch.

My darling's the bullaphant, it's useful in company,
I'm the toast of the town for having good things to eat;
    If I hold a party I don't have to bake for it —
And if all Edinburgh came they could still get a bite.

Se m' eudail am bullaphant air ghréidheadh le m' ulaidh-sa,
'S le cùram chuir i bréid 's nach éireadh aon tubaist dha;
     Gabhaidh mi le m' thì e is tairgidh mi le fìon e —
Is seo an t-sraibheag rìoghail as prìseile chunnaic mi.

Se m' eudail am bullaphant, gur h-éibhinn a chumasg-san,
S mise nach bi 'n éiginn 's an treun-fhear seo fuireach leam;
     Ithidh mi gu sòghail is nì mi cuirm gu dòigheil —
A Shatharn, Luan 's a Dhòmhnach mo bhòrd air dheagh shuidheachadh.

Se m' eudail am bullaphant 's na reusans air fhuineadh ann,
Is milis e fo m' dheudan, gun euradh gun uireasbhaidh;
     Tha mise nis gun chùram ciod e tha gann sna bùthan —
'S ged bhiodh na dorsan dùinte, 's mo bhrù làn den bhullaphant.

28   *Feasgar an Duine Ghil*

     "Tha ciaradh an fheasgair a' teagasg gach rùn,
     Is na nithean ri teachd am follais mo shùil."

A dhuine ghil, a luaisg an saoghal, is caochlaideach an-diugh do réim,
An cruinne-cé a-nis am baoghal, cuing na daorsa ann ad' cheum.
Luasgach, luaineach mar na gaothan séideadh thar taobh tuath na h-Eòrp,
Ghluais na daoine geal 'nan sgaothan; deasgainn anns an taois an treòir.
Cho innleachdach ri mac an diabhail; neo-thruacantach ri bochd no fann;
Neo-fhulangach air rian no riaghail; gun ùidh an ceart ach faobhar lann
Misneachail gun sgàth gun eagal; coimhdheas doininn dhoirbh no fèath;
Cinnteach, earbsach, is gun teagamh; maoin is ceannas an dà dhia.
Seòladairean nan luingeas gleusta (nuair a chithear long fo a siùil
Aoibhneas 's ìocshlainte do léirsinn, dreachdt 'na h-éideadh bréidgheal ùr).
An ionann cleachdainn anns gach iomall: a' daoradh slòigh 's a' togail cìs;
Na h-uachdarain dhligheach air an iomain; an sluagh a' saothrachadh gun phrìs.
A' slaodadh bathair, bìdh is ùmhladh ás gach dùthaich thar an lear;
An Iar Roinn Eòrpa bòcan dùbhlain do gach dùthchasaich fon ghréin.
Is a-nis air sgéith san iarmailt, a' seòladh fànas tha gun chrìoch
Le cumhachdan pleasgach, reubach, stiallach, le rocaidean fiadhaich udroighne.
Is shìos san aigeann, air tighinn fìor, tha an sgeul a dh'adhbharaich caochladh snuadh
Aig iomadh céilidh, a' toirt oirnn grìs: fomhairean ag éirigh ás a' chuan.

Fhuair an duine geal a chumhachd, is thugar ceannas dha le Dia;
Innleachd chum an t-saoghail a chumadh air a bhuileachadh air gu fial.
Ach bhrath e Dia agus an tàlann a fhuair e chum math an t-saoghail gu léir;

My darling's the bullaphant baked by my sweetheart,
And she wrapped it with care lest some accident befall it;
　　I'll take it with my tea and offer it with wine —
It's the rarest royal delicacy I've ever seen.

My darling's the bullaphant, successful is its recipe,
I'll never be stuck while this prizewinner stays with me;
　　I'm going to dine in luxury and have a proper feast —
From Saturday to Monday my table's complete.

My darling's the bullaphant with raisins baked into it,
It's sweet to my tooth, without stint or deficiency;
　　I no longer care whatever's scarce in the shops —
They might as well be shut, for my belly's full of bullaphant.

The Evening of the White Man

"Twilight reveals every secret,
And the future is clear to my eye."

O white man, who shook the world, unsteady today is your rule,
The universe now in danger, the yoke of slavery in your step.
Shifting, fleeting as the winds blowing over northern Europe,
The white men moved in swarms; yeast in the dough is their strength.
As devious as the devil's son; unmerciful to poor or weak;
Intolerant of order, rule; uninterested in law save blade of sword.
Courageous, fearless; indifferent to raging storm or calm;
Certain, confident, and free of doubt; with two gods, wealth and power.
Sailors of the speedy ships (when ship's seen under sail
Joy and balm to the sight, girt in her fresh white linen raiment).
The same custom in every corner: enslaving a people and raising tax;
Lawful leaders driven off; the people labouring without reward.
Extracting goods, food and submission from every land overseas;
Western Europe a challenging spectre to every native under the sun.
And now flying in the sky, penetrating outer space
With cracking, tearing, ripping forces, with wild exotic rockets.
And down in the deep, come true is the tale that turned faces pale
At many a ceilidh, making us shudder: monsters rising from the ocean.

The white man got his power from God, who gave him his authority;
A strategy to shape the world that was generously granted him.
But he betrayed God and the talent that he got for the sake of all the world;

Is rinn e an cinne-daonna a thràilleadh; 's an toradh uile ghléidh e fhéin,
Neo-thruacantach, ach cìocrach, lonach, dhìol e tròcair Dhé le cruas,
An tiodhlac a thug Dia chum sonais iompaichte gu adhbhar uaill.

Dìtear an crann a dhiùltas toradh, agus mallaichear an chraobh
Air nach cinn ach duilleach corrach. Gearrar sìos i. Théid i aog.
Tha an saoghal gu iomallan nis fo dhaorsa an duine ghil — ach éist an fhuaim:
Na fir dhathte 'n geall air saorsa, is sgìth de dhaorsairean thar chuain.
Tha Breatann mhòr an éis a cutadh; earball an pheucaig is e spìont;
Ameireaga 's i air a putadh gu tur 's gu buileach ás an t-Sìn;
An Fhraing uaibhreach is i a' tuisleadh; a daorsan ceannarcach gun rian
A' tulgadh mar an fhairge chuisleach; an Òlaint rùisgte gu a bian;
Cuprus, Ailgear, is Formósa mar neasgaidean thar sgil an léigh;
Lebanon 's Iòrdan 's iad a' sòradh ìoc o chumhachd ach iad fhéin;
Na h-Afracandaraich air bhàinidh, mar rìgh Cnut air oir na tràgh'd,
Don t-sruth-lìonaidh a' toirt àithne — ach a' teicheadh on tonn bhàtht.
Coimhfhlaitheachd a-nis na h-Innsean; Burma saor, is fòs Sailon;
Ghana nis air iùil do-innseadh; na h-Àrabaich aonaichte am bann.
An saoghal air udal is a' luasgadh mar bheinn-theine romh an àm
Anns an sgàin i oirnn a h-fhuath-bhas: aibhnean teinteach ruith 'nan deann.
Aibhnean nach bac cumhachd dhaoine; nach bac rocaid 's nach bac bom;
Tha ar cumhachdan nas faoine an aghaidh sin na borb-fhear lom.
A dhuine ghil, is e do dheasgainn a chuir atmhoireachd san taois;
Dh'fhalbh do latha, chiar ort feasgar; an oidhche dùnadh nis air t' aois.

29   Bean Dubh a' Caoidh a Fir
a Chaidh a Mharbhadh leis a' Phoileas

> Baba Inkòsi Sikelele, Baba Inkòsi Sikelele.
> Car son, a Dhé a tha san chathair,
> Car son an-diugh a rinn Thu 'n latha?
> > Baba Inkòsi Sikelele, Baba Inkòsi Sikelele.

> Mo-nuar gum faca mi a shoillse
> Ach a bhith gu bràth san oidhche.
> > Baba Inkòsi Sikelele, Baba Inkòsi Sikelele.

> Och, mo chràdh, mo chràdh 's mo léireadh
> An latha thug iad uam mo cheudghràdh.
> > Baba Inkòsi Sikelele, Baba Inkòsi Sikelele.

And he enslaved mankind; and he kept all the proceeds for himself,
Not merciful, but ravenous, greedy, he repaid God's mercy with harshness,
The gift God gave for happiness turned into cause of pride.

Condemned is the tree that bears no fruit, and cursed is the branch
On which only coarse foliage grows. It's cut down. It dies.
The world to its fringes is now enslaved by the white man — but listen to the sound:
Coloured men are seeking freedom and tired of masters overseas.
Great Britain's gutted like a fish; the peacock's tail's been plucked;
America's been thrown once and for all out of China;
Proud France is stumbling; her seditious captives out of control
Rocking like the streaming ocean; the Netherlands stripped to her skin;
Cyprus, Algeria, and Formosa like boils beyond physician's skill;
Lebanon and Jordan refusing protection from any power but themselves;
The Afrikaners crazy, like King Canute upon the beach,
Commanding the flowing tide — but fleeing the drowning wave.
India now a republic; Burma free, and Ceylon as well;
Ghana now on course to who knows where; the Arabs united in a pact.
The world shaken up and rumbling like a volcano before the time
When she'll explode her horror on us: fiery rivers running wild.
Rivers that power of men will not stop; that no rocket or bomb will stop;
Our powers are weaker against that than any naked savage.
O white man, it's your yeast that put swelling in the dough;
Your day has gone, dusk has fallen on you; night's now closing on your era.

A Black Woman Mourns her Husband Killed by the Police

Baba Inkòsi Sikelele, Baba Inkòsi Sikelele.
Why, O God upon the throne,
Why did you make the day today?
    Baba Inkòsi Sikelele, Baba Inkòsi Sikelele.

Alas that I ever saw its brightness,
I'd rather it were night forever.
    Baba Inkòsi Sikelele, Baba Inkòsi Sikelele.

Oh my pain, my pain, my torment's
The day they took my first love from me.
    Baba Inkòsi Sikelele, Baba Inkòsi Sikelele.

Do chorp donn an-sin 'na laighe,
Toll air tholl a' sileadh fala.
   Baba Inkòsi Sikelele, Baba Inkòsi Sikelele.

Am fear bòidheach laigh ri m' thaobh-sa
An-sin 's a mhionach ás a' slaodadh.
   Baba Inkòsi Sikelele, Baba Inkòsi Sikelele.

Aichbheil, aichbheil, sgrios is léireadh
Air an luchd a rinn mo cheusadh.
   Baba Inkòsi Sikelele, Baba Inkòsi Sikelele.

Éist ri m' ghuidhean, Rìgh nan Dùilean,
Éist ri m' athchuinge 's ri m' ùrnaigh.
   Baba Inkòsi Sikelele, Baba Inkòsi Sikelele.

Tha 'n luchd bàn an-diugh làn aigheir
'S tha mo phàistean-sa gun athair.
   Baba Inkòsi Sikelele, Baba Inkòsi Sikelele.

Is tha mo bheatha-sa nis falamh —
Ach ceadaich dhomh, mum fàg mi 'n talamh,
   Baba Inkòsi Sikelele, Baba Inkòsi Sikelele.

Air m' fhear-céile an-sin 'na shìneadh,
Nuair a thig mo mhic gu ìre,
   Baba Inkòsi Sikelele, Baba Inkòsi Sikelele.

An éirig dhuinn air son ar dòrainn,
Latha réidh a ghearradh sgòrnan,
   Baba Inkòsi Sikelele, Baba Inkòsi Sikelele.

Ghearradh sgòrnan nam fear fuileach,
Fuil mu m' dhòrnaibh suas gu uilinn,
   Baba Inkòsi Sikelele, Baba Inkòsi Sikelele.

A bhith gan reubadh is gam pianadh
Is deagh fhaobhar air mo sgian-sa:
   Baba Inkòsi Sikelele, Baba Inkòsi Sikelele.

Thoir latha dhuinn gu saor a' pàigheadh
Fhir is mhnathan agus phàistean
   Baba Inkòsi Sikelele, Baba Inkòsi Sikelele.

Your brown body lying before me,
Blood pouring out from wound on wound.
 Baba Inkòsi Sikelele, Baba Inkòsi Sikelele.

The handsome man who lay beside me
There with his intestines trailing loose.
 Baba Inkòsi Sikelele, Baba Inkòsi Sikelele.

Vengeance, vengeance, grief, destruction
On the people who've had me crucified.
 Baba Inkòsi Sikelele, Baba Inkòsi Sikelele.

King of the Elements, hear my oaths,
Listen to my petition and my prayer.
 Baba Inkòsi Sikelele, Baba Inkòsi Sikelele.

Today the whites are full of gladness
And my children have no father.
 Baba Inkòsi Sikelele, Baba Inkòsi Sikelele.

And my life is empty now —
But grant me, while I'm still on earth,
 Baba Inkòsi Sikelele, Baba Inkòsi Sikelele.

For my husband lying before me,
When my sons have come of age,
 Baba Inkòsi Sikelele, Baba Inkòsi Sikelele.

In compensation for our grief,
Some perfect day for cutting throats,
 Baba Inkòsi Sikelele, Baba Inkòsi Sikelele.

For cutting throats of bloody men,
Blood on my fists up to the elbow,
 Baba Inkòsi Sikelele, Baba Inkòsi Sikelele.

For tearing them and torturing them
With a good blade upon my knife:
 Baba Inkòsi Sikelele, Baba Inkòsi Sikelele.

Give us a day to pay back freely
The men, the women and the children
 Baba Inkòsi Sikelele, Baba Inkòsi Sikelele.

An luchd ghil a bhuail ar daoine;
Cuairt mu'n amhaichean de'n caolain —
     Baba Inkòsi Sikelele, Baba Inkòsi Sikelele.

Cuairt de'n caolain an àite chneapan,
Is siridh mi 'n-sin taobh do leapach,
     Baba Inkòsi Sikelele, Baba Inkòsi Sikelele.

Na fiachan uile air an dìoladh,
Fhir 's a ghràidh, 's tu 'n-sin ad' shìneadh.
     Baba Inkòsi Sikelele, Baba Inkòsi Sikelele.

30   *Togalach an Aonaich*

Aotrom, uallach air an leathad
     Tha thu suidhichte ad' loinn;
Òirdhearc thu, chan eil do leithid
     An leth-dheas an t-saoghail chruinn.

Do dhà thùr an àird a' ruigheachd
     Air an t-slighe naomh do Nèamh;
T' aogais shoitheamh, tàladh cridhe,
     Fiamh-ghaireach, is ciùin is sèimh.

Do chuilbh chumachdail, glan shnaidhte,
     Do bhoghachan, mar rannan dàin,
Sreath air shreath a' ruith gu snasmhor,
     Cumte le sàr ealadhain.

Rìomhach thu an lì 's an cumadh,
     Ìoc-shlainte don t-sùil as léir;
Grinneas gràbhalaidh do chulaidh
     Fo lainnir loinnreach shoillse gréin'.

Tha do mhaise dhomh do-innseadh,
     Dh'fheumainn mòran barrachd sgil;
Ach is e do dhealbh am' inntinn
     Ceòl mór reòdhte gu cloich ghil.

Is lìonmhor àireamh do luchd turais,
     Iomraideach thu 'n tìrean céin;
O fòid do bhuinn gu bàrr do mhullaich
     Chan eil nas luraiche r'a léir.

Of the white folk who struck our people
With a turn of their guts around their necks —
    Baba Inkòsi Sikelele, Baba Inkòsi Sikelele.

A turn of their guts instead of beads,
And then I'll seek the side of your bed,
    Baba Inkòsi Sikelele, Baba Inkòsi Sikelele.

All the debts having been paid,
Beloved husband, who's lying before me.
    Baba Inkòsi Sikelele, Baba Inkòsi Sikelele.

The Union Buildings

Light, majestic on the slope
    You lie there in your beauty;
Splendid you are, there is not your like
    In all the southern hemisphere.

Your twin towers rise up
    On the holy path to Heaven;
Your gentle face, heart's allurement,
    Soft-smiling, calm and lovely.

Your shapely columns, cleanly hewn,
    Your arches, like poetic stanzas,
Neatly coursing row on row,
    Formed by excellence of art.

Lovely you are in hue and form,
    Balm you are to the seeing eye;
The hewn splendour of your raiment
    Under stately sheen of shining sun.

Words for your beauty I cannot find,
    They'd need more skill than I possess;
But your image in my mind
    Is *ceòl mór* frozen in white stone.

Large is the number of your visitors,
    Famous are you in foreign lands;
From the turves of your foundations to the top of your roof
    Nothing more splendid can be seen.

'S chan fhaic iadsan ach na chì iad,
  Na tha léirsinneach don t-sùil;
Ach chì mise do luchd-céirde,
  Bu mi fhéin a thug dhaibh iùil.

Soilleir dhòmhsa ail an làmhan
  Air gach grinneas agus gréis,
Na fir fhòghlaimte 'chuir anam
  San chloich mhairbh le rùn an spéis.

Làmhchaireach gu cur an eagar,
  Gràbhailt', geàrrte, gleusta, slìom,
Air a cruadhs i, cloich na creige
  Fighte fìnealta mar stìom.

Bha an mhòr-roinn dhiubh á Albainn,
  Tha fhathast, ceòlmhor agus binn,
An Gàidhlig is am Beurla Albann,
  Ann am' chluasan an guth-cinn.

Chan e togalach tha annad
  Dhòmhsa, ach se taisbean Dhé
A thug soillse a chuir anam
  Ann am fiodh, an cloich, 's an cré.

'S an tùs na h-oibre thàinig Ise:
  An Òighe Mhuileach, reul nan reul,
Am blàth a b' àillidhe san lios seo,
  Barra-maise tìr-na-gréin'.

Is chunnaic i an aitreabh àlainn
  Clach air chloich a' dol ri chéil',
Is gach clach mar phonc o chlàrsaich
  Is ceòl mór àillidh dol an céill.

Is roinn i dhòmhsa mar mo chuibhreann
  Togalach nan colbh 's nan tùr
Agus thagh i, mar a roinn-se,
  An gàrradh, 's àillidheachd nam flùr.

A lùchairt sgiamhaich, chiataich, àlainn,
  Thug i cion dhuit agus gràdh
A chionn gum b'ann o iùil mo làimh-sa
  A dh'éirich baidealach thu 'n àird.

And they only see what they see,
   What the naked eye beholds;
But I can see your craftsmen,
   I it was who directed them.

Clear to me is their hands' impression
   On each subtlety and flourish,
Those men of skill who put a soul
   In dead stone with their calling's secret.

Dexterous to put in order
   Sculpted, hewn, trimmed and smooth,
For all its hardness, rock-born stone
   Delicately woven like a snood.

Most of them had come from Scotland,
   And even yet, musical and tuneful,
In Gaelic and in Lowland Scots
   Their voices echo in my head.

No building you are at all
   To me, but God's revelation
That put soul-creating brightness
   Into wood, and stone, and clay.

And in the start of the work She came:
   The girl from Mull, star among stars,
Loveliest blossom in this garden,
   Topmost prize of the land of the sun.

And she saw that gorgeous edifice
   Coming together stone by stone,
Every stone like a note from a harp
   And splendid *ceòl mór* taking shape.

And she reserved as my own portion
   The building, its columns and its towers
While she chose as her own department
   The garden, the beauty of the flowers.

O palace, elegant, lovely, serene,
   She gave you love and admiration
Because it was with my hand's guidance
   That you rose up with all your pillars.

Tha thus' am bith, ged tha do dhruidhnich
   Am bith am' chuimhne-sa a-mhàin;
Sùil a' faicinn, cluas a' cluinntinn
   Saothair fhilidh 'cumadh dàin.

Sìneadh trast an leathaid, loinneil,
   Le t' aogais ghil as grinne lì,
Tha thu am' inntinn latha 's a dh'oidhche,
   Adhbhar aoibh is bristeadh-crìdh.

Aonghas MacGill-Fhaolain (1879–1962)

31   *An Sgiobair Ùr*

Biodh an deoch seo 'n làimh mo rùin,
Slàinte don sgiobair ùr;
Biodh an deoch seo 'n làimh mo rùin.

Sgiobair ùr air luing na Mòrroinn,
   Deagh MhacDhòmhnaill th' air an stiùir

Chuireas oirre gleus gu astar
   Le deagh acfhainn agus criù,

Chumas i gu seasgair tioram
   Anns an iomairt air an lunn,

Nach leig i air chòir nan creagan
   Ged bhiodh greadan teth m'a cùl,

Nuair a bhios na siantan fàbh'rach
   Chuireas 'n àird i fo làn shiùil

Ach nuair chì e coltas gaillinn
   A bheir faireachadh don chriù

Chum 's gun toir iad uaipe h-aodach
   Thoirt dhi faochadh ma thig brùchd,

A bheir i gu caladh sàbhailt
   'S bratach àrd a' snàmh os 'cionn.

You exist, although your craftsmen
    Survive in my memory alone;
An eye seeing, an ear hearing
    Poet's toil composing verse.

Stretched along the slope, so shapely,
    With your white visage elegant of hue,
You're in my mind both day and night,
    The cause of joy and breaking heart.

Angus Y MacLellan (S. W. Margaree, Cape Breton)

The New Skipper

Be this drink in my loved one's hand,
Here's health to the new skipper;
Be this drink in my loved one's hand.

A new skipper on the Provincial ship,
    It's good MacDonald that's at the helm

Who'll trim her to get under way
    With good tackle and good crew,

Who'll keep her watertight and dry
    In the struggle with the ocean,

Who'll hold her well away from rocks
    Even in a following gale,

And when the elements are kind
    Will guide her under every stitch of sail,

But when he sees a storm is coming
    Will give warning to the crew

So that they can reef her sails
    To slacken off before the blast,

Who'll guide her safely into harbour
    While noble banner flutters high.

Cha lean mi do shloinneadh mòrail —
  Fòghnaidh gur MacDhòmhnaill thù

'S faillean ùr á broilleach deàrrsach,
  Smior Chloinn Raghnaill, chanadh rium;

Fuil na Frainge mar an ciadna
  Glan a' sìoladh 'na do ghnùis;

Cha tuirt mi, nan leanainn céin thu,
  Nach tug thu á Éirinn drùchd.

Nall a' ghlaine, lìon gu'n stràc i,
  Suas air slàint an sgiobair ùir.

32   *Fàilte na h-Aimsir do D.D.*

Gun robh agad Nollaig Chridheil
  'S nuair a thig i, a' Bhliadhn' Ùr
A bhith giùlan iomadh beannachd
  A nì leanachd riut gu dlùth;
Móran cuid a bhith fo d' riaghladh
  'S tu le riaghailt air a cheann,
A' toirt fuasglaidh do na feumaich
  Nuair bhios iad 'nan éiginn teann.

Is coltach sinn 'nar cuairt san fhàsach
  Ris an luing air bhàrr nan stuadh,
Uair ga h-iomain anns a' ghàbhadh,
  Uair mar eala bhàin 'na suain,
Uair ga liodairt anns an an-shìd',
  Crith air anam na th' air bòrd,
Uair a' siubhal réidh gu caladh
  'S iolach chaithream aig a seòid.

Uair a' dlùth'chadh air na creagan,
  Diùltadh freagairt thoirt d'a stiùir,
Beinnean beucach bras ag éirigh
  Bagairt léirsgrios air a' chriù;
Amhail sin is mar tha sinne —
  Gheibh sinn tilleadh garbh air uair,
Ach 'nar dòchas bidh sinn làidir
  Gum bi leinn a-màireach buaidh.

I'll not trace your excellent pedigree —
   Suffice to say you're a MacDonald

And a fresh sprig from a radiant bosom,
   Clanranald's marrow, I've been told;

The blood of France on top of that
   Mantling nobly in your face;

I dare say, if I traced you far enough,
   You've taken a drop of blood from Ireland.

Pass over your glass, fill it to bursting,
   Here's to the health of the new skipper.

Season's Greetings to D.D.

Have a Merry Christmas
   And, when it comes, may New Year
Bring you countless blessings
   That will closely adhere;
With much at your command
   And you firmly in control,
Giving help to the needy
   When their stocks run low.

In our journey through the desert
   We're like a ship on the deep,
Now driven into danger,
   Now like a white swan asleep,
Now pummelled by bad weather,
   Every soul on board quivering,
Now gliding smoothly into port
   As her heroes cry victory.

Now closing on the rocks,
   Refusing to answer her helm,
As roaring pinnacles rise
   To threaten death to her men;
That's how it is for us —
   Sometimes forced to go about
While in our hope we're strong
   That tomorrow will be ours.

33   Am Bùth aig Maitiu

I hiuraibh o, i hiuraibh o,
Tiugainn mar seo ma tha cunnradh bhuat,
I hiuraibh o, i hiuraibh o,
     Se 'm bùth aig Maitiu as fheàrr.

Se Maitiu fear-gnothaich as ciataiche
Tha 'n-diugh an taobh staigh de na crìochan sa,
'Na sheasamh mu d' choinneamh gad riarachadh —
     Chan iarr e obair as fheàrr.

Ma tha cupa no bruis agus siabann bhuat
No na bhios ad' dhìth thoirt na fiasaig' dhiot,
No cungaidh a dh'ùraicheas d' fhiacalan,
     Se 'm bùth aig Maitiu as fheàrr.

Ma bhios tu a' sgrìobhadh gu nighneagan
'S ag innse do ghaoil dhaibh an dìomhaireachd,
Biodh agad am pàipear as finealta
     Ás a' bhùth aig Maitiu as fheàrr.

O chaileag mas math leat gach sùil bhith ort
'S na gillean air mhire gad ionnsaigh-sa,
Dèan cabhag is ceannaich am fùdar sa
     Tha sa bhùth aig Maitiu, se as fheàrr.

Gun tuit iad cho grad 's ged a bhuailteadh iad
Nuair chì iad cho grinn 's a tha 'n snuadh bhios ort
Ma chuireas tu pàirt air do ghruaidheanan —
     Se an rouge aig Maitiu as fheàrr.

Ma leagair le cnatan no fiabhras thu
'S tu fulang mar dhuine ga riaslachadh,
Gu deimhinn aig Maitiu tha ìocshlaint dhuit —
     Dèan fhiachainn 's bithidh tu nas fheàrr.

Ma bhuailear gu grad leis an déideadh thu
'S do chlaigeann a' dol ás a-chéile leis,
A bhurraidh, na fulaing is leigheas ann —
     Se 'm bùth aig Maitiu as fheàrr.

Matthew's Shop

I hiuraibh o, i hiuraibh o,
Come on here if you want a bargain,
I hiuraibh o, i hiuraibh o,
    Matthew's shop is the best.

Matthew's the handsomest businessman
That's inside these borders today,
Standing in front of you serving you —
    No better work can he ask.

If cup, brush and soap's what you're after
Or all that you need for a shave,
Or paste for refreshing your teeth with,
    Matthew's shop is the best.

If you're writing away to young ladies
And telling your love to them privately,
Use only the best quality paper
    From Matthew's shop which is best.

Young girl if you want every eye on you
And the lads going crazy pursuing you,
Make haste and purchase this powder
    That's in Matthew's shop, it's the best.

They'll fall down as if someone had hit them
When they see how lovely your face is
If you put on your cheeks just a bit of it —
    Matthew's rouge is the best.

If laid low by a cold or a fever
And feeling you're going through a mangle,
Matthew sure has a medicine for you —
    Try it and you will be better.

If you're suddenly seized by the toothache
And your skull is splitting apart with it,
Don't suffer, you clown, when relief's there —
    Matthew's shop is the best.

Tiugainnibh, tiugainnibh 'nur ciadan sibh
Is sgiathaibh cho luath ris na riabhagan leam —
Tha baile is baile 's gach bial a' glaodh,
  "Se 'm bùth aig Maitiu as fheàrr."

I hiuraibh o, i hiuraibh o,
Tiugainn mar seo ma tha cunnradh bhuat,
I hiuraibh o, i hiuraibh o,
  Se 'm bùth aig Maitiu as fheàrr.

Seumas MacLeòid (1880–1947)

34   *A' Cheist*

Cuin a thig thu?
'S mis' an-seo leam fhéin
  Ag éisteachd srann na gaoith';
Tha osag mhìn ag éirigh suas
  'Cur gluasaid anns gach cré,
A' ghrian le a h-àilleachd 's beatha nuadh
  Le plosgadh suas 's gach àit',
Is ceist nan ceist 'nam chridhe buan:
  "Feuch! Cuin a thig mo ghràdh?"

Cuin a thig thu?
'S mis' an-seo leam fhéin
  Air gleannan séimh nan sonn
Ag éisteachd còmhraidh ghrinn nan crann —
  Gun ghreann, le aiteas binn,
Ag aithris dhomhs' mun gheamhradh fhuar
  Chuir ruagadh air gach càil,
Is ceist nan ceist 'nam chridhe buan:
  "Feuch! Cuin a thig mo ghràdh?"

Cuin a thig thu?
'S mis' an-seo leam fhéin
  Aig torman séimh nan allt
Is còisir bhinn na mìle beul
  Làn suilt 's an t-eug air chall,
Ag aithris dhomhs' mar thug iad buaidh
  'S mar bhris iad suain a' bhàis,
Is ceist nan ceist 'nam chridhe buan:
  "Feuch! Cuin a thig mo ghràdh?"

Come on, come on in your hundreds
And fly as swift as the larks with me —
From town to town every mouth is shouting,
   "Matthew's shop is the best."

I hiuraibh o, i hiuraibh o,
Come on here if you want a bargain,
I hiuraibh o, i hiuraibh o,
   Matthew's shop is the best.

James MacLeod (Scalpay, Harris)

The Question

   When will you come?
For I'm here by myself
   Hearing the wind snore;
A gentle breeze is rising up
   Causing every being to stir,
The sun with her beauty and new life
   Up pulsating everywhere,
And the question of questions in my heart forever:
   "Watch! When will she come, my love?"

   When will you come?
For I'm here by myself
   In the heroes' quiet little glen
Hearing the trees' elegant murmur —
   Not surly, but cheerful, sweet-sounding,
Telling me about the cold winter
   That has banished everything
And the question of questions in my heart forever:
   "Watch! When will she come, my love?"

   When will you come?
For I'm here by myself
   In thrall to burns gently rippling
With the sweet choir of a thousand mouths
   Full of vigour now death's lost and gone,
Telling me how they triumphed
   And broke the sleep of death,
And the question of questions in my heart forever:
   "Watch! When will she come, my love?"

Cuin a thig thu?
'S mise an-seo leam fhéin
  Air tolman beag de fhraoch,
Canach mìn-gheal fàs ri m' chléith
  Mar shamhladh air do ghnùis;
Tha clachag òrbhuidh anns an allt
  Tha ruith gu fann gun tàmh,
Is ceist nan ceist 'nam chridhe buan:
  "Feuch! Cuin a thig mo ghràdh?"

  Cuin a thig thu?
'S mise an-seo leam fhéin
  Air machair dosrach dlùth,
Am bàrd a' gleusadh ceòl d'a chéil'
  Is is' a' leum le sùrd;
Mise an gleac ri aiteal tlàth —
  Do chruth, a dheilbh mo phràmh —
Is ceist nan ceist 'nam chridhe buan:
  "Feuch! Cuin a thig mo ghràdh?"

  Cuin a thig thu?
'S mis' an-seo leam fhéin
  Fa chomhair Dhé nan Dùl,
A' coistrig' m' anma as ùr don àit'
  Chuir fonn is àill 'nam ghnùis;
Ma bhrist thu 'r comhcheangal gu bràth
  'S nach fhaic mi, ghràidh, thu 'n tùs,
Bidh ceist nan ceist air uchdan Ràth
  Is mise a' tàmh fon ùir.

Donnchadh MacNìmhein (1880–1955)

35   *Cadal*

Nach sòlasach an nì an cadal,
  Guma beannaicht' gun robh thù:
Gur tric a rinn thu fhéin mo phasgadh
  Ann ad' ghlacaibh coibhneil, caomh;
O, thig a-nochd, na tréig mo chluasag,
  Paisg mi ann an suain ro chiùin —
O, sgaoil do chùirteinean mun cuairt dhomh,
  Na fan bhuam, thig 's dùin mo shùil.

When will you come?
For I'm here by myself
  On a little clump of heather,
Smooth white bog-cotton growing by my fence
  As a symbol of your face;
A golden pebble's in the burn
  That runs listless but unresting,
And the question of questions in my heart forever:
  "Watch! When will she come, my love?"

When will you come?
For I'm here by myself
  On a tufted sandy plain,
The poet composing for his spouse
  While she has spring in her step;
Myself engaging a faint sunbeam —
  Your form, which caused my pain —
And the question of questions in my heart forever:
  "Watch! When will she come, my love?"

When will you come?
For I'm here by myself
  Confronting God of the Elements,
Consecrating my soul anew to the place
  That gave my face spirit and form;
If you've broken our covenant forever
  So I may not see you, love, before then,
The question of questions will lie on Heaven's slope
  When under the sod I rest.

Duncan MacNiven (Scoraig and Islay)

Sleep

What a joyful thing is sleep,
  Much blessed may you be:
How often you've enfolded me
  In your gentle, kind embrace;
O come tonight, don't leave my pillow,
  Wrap me in most gentle rest —
O, draw your curtains round about me,
  Don't hold back, just come and close my eyes.

Gur tric a thug thu fois is sìth dhomh
   Nuair a bha mi sgìth fo leòn,
Nuair bha mo chogais fhéin gam dhìteadh
   Air son nithean nach bu chòir;
S iomadh oidhch' le m' uile dhùrachd
   Ghuidh mi air do shaorsa mhòr,
Thu thighinn, is fuasgladh bho throm thùrsa
   'S mi gam lot as ùr le bròn.

Gur tric a thug thu fois is sòlas
   Bho throm dhòrainn agus cràdh,
Bho throm thrioblaid agus tinneas
   S tric a thug thu rithist slàint';
Ged a b'e tom fraoich mo chluasag,
   Mar a thachair uair no dhà,
Cha d'rinn thu dìmeas orm an uair sin —
   Thug thu suain dhomh mar a bhà.

S tric a thug thu fois don mharaich'
   An déidh cunnairt, cath is spàirn,
S tric a thug thu fois don ghaisgeach
   Tacan mun do thòisich blàr;
S tric a chuir thu e 'na laighe,
   'Chlaidheamh glact' aige 'na làimh,
'S dh'ùraich thu e rithist le spionnadh
   Chum bhith dol an aghaidh nàmh.

S tric a thug thu dhomh am bruadar
   Nighean mo luaidh an gleann nan geug
'S mi ga faicinn air a' bhuaile
   'N àm bhith buachailleachd na spréidh,
Far an tric a shuidh sinn còmhladh
   'S mi ga pògadh beul ri beul —
Thoir dhomh i rithist a-nochd 'nam ghlacaibh
   Tacan ann am bruadar fhéin.

Cha dèan creutair feum ás t' eugmhais
   Anns an t-saoghal seo gu léir:
Tha thu feumail do na brùidean,
   Chan e clann nan daoin' a-mhàin,
Ach sìos gu ruig eòin bheag na h-ealtainn,
   Paisgidh iad an ceann fo'n sgéith —
Nach sòlasach an nì an cadal,
   'S guma beannaicht' gun robh è.

You often gave me rest and peace
  When I was tired and vexed,
When my conscience was condemning me
  For things that weren't right;
So many nights with all my heart
  I prayed for your great freedom,
For your coming, for release from pain
  When anguish came once more.

So often you've brought glad relief
  From heavy grief and torment,
From deep distress and sickness
  You've often nursed me back to health;
When heather hillock was my pillow,
  As has happened once or twice,
You were not scornful of me then —
  You gave me slumber as before.

You often gave the sailor peace
  From danger, storm and toil,
You often gave the soldier peace
  With battle close at hand;
You often laid him down to rest,
  His sword firm in his grasp,
And filled him up again with strength
  To face the foe anew.

You often gave me in a dream
  The girl I loved in leafy glen
So that I saw her by the fold
  At the herding of the cows,
Where we often sat together
  As I kissed her on the mouth —
Give me her in my arms tonight
  For a while but in a dream.

No creature can survive without you
  In this whole wide world of ours:
You are needed by the beasts,
  Not by humankind alone,
But down to little birds in flocks,
  Who tuck their head beneath their wing —
What a joyful thing is sleep,
  And much blessed may it be.

36 *Far 'n do chaith mi 'n oidhch'*

Dh'fhuirich mi a-raoir am' chaithris
   Far 'n do chaith mi 'n oidhch'
Leis an rìbhinn bhòidhich bhanail
   Far 'n do chaith mi 'n oidhch';
Nuair a fhuair mi i 'nam ghlacaibh
   Cha robh smal no oillt
Air nach deach an ruaig le cabhaig
   Far 'n do chaith mi 'n oidhch'.

Rinn mi air mo ghlùin a h-altram
   Far 'n do chaith mi 'n oidhch',
Bha mo làmh mu gualainn thairis
   Far 'n do chaith mi 'n oidhch',
Sheinn mi duanag dhi le caithream,
   Bhrùchd mi mach gun fhoill
Ann an dàn mo ghràdh don ainnir
   Far 'n do chaith mi 'n oidhch'.

Bha mi 'g éisteachd fuaim na gaillinn
   Far 'n do chaith mi 'n oidhch'
'S mi an seòmar beag gam gharadh
   Far 'n do chaith mi 'n oidhch',
Chluinninn fhéin na féidh le'n aighean
   Langanaich sa choill
Aig a' chaol ri taobh na mara
   Far 'n do chaith mi 'n oidhch'.

Bha 'na shòlas dhomh air thalamh
   Far 'n do chaith mi 'n oidhch',
Cha robh smuain air dol a chadal
   Far 'n do chaith mi 'n oidhch';
Theich ro luath na h-uairean beannaicht',
   Cha do dh'fhan iad ruinn,
Mar gum b'ann air sgiathan aingil
   Far 'n do chaith mi 'n oidhch'.

Tha mo dhùil ri tilleadh fhathast
   Far 'n do chaith mi 'n oidhch'
'S gheibh mi i gu teann 'nam ghlacaibh
   Far 'n do chaith mi 'n oidhch';

Where I spent last night

I did not go to sleep at all
    Where I spent last night
With the lovely charming girl
    Where I spent last night;
When I took her in my arms
    Every shade, every terror
Fled away at once
    Where I spent last night.

Caressing her upon my lap
    Where I spent last night,
My arm around her shoulder
    Where I spent last night,
I sang her praises from the heart,
    Pouring out undissembling
In song my passion for the lass
    Where I spent last night.

I heard the raging of the wind
    Where I spent last night
While snug in a little room
    Where I spent last night,
I heard even deer with their calves
    Belling in the wood
At the narrows by the sea
    Where I spent last night.

It was joy to me on earth
    Where I spent last night,
With no thought of going to sleep
    Where I spent last night;
The blessed hours flew by too fast,
    Without waiting for us,
As if on angels' wings
    Where I spent last night.

I hope to return
    Where I spent last night
And hold her tight in my arms
    Where I spent last night;

Is mas è 's gum bi sinn maireann
Ceanglaidh sinn an t-snaoim
Is cha bhi feum air dol air astar
Far 'n do chaith mi 'n oidhch'.

Ciorstai NicLeòid (1880–1954)

37   *Cuimhneachan 1914–1918*

Naidheachd na tìr'. Ciod naidheachd na tìr'?
'N e cogadh no sìth as brìgh do m' shealladh?
Oir chunnaic mi sluagh gun àireamh mu m' chuairt,
    Bha fuil air an gruaidh 's bha 'n gluasad fanant;
Bha onfhadh nan stuadh air ospaig a' chuain
    A' cagair am' chluais, "Is fuar mo leabaidh."
Ach naidheachd na tìr'. Ciod naidheachd na tìr'?
    'N e cogadh no sìth as brìgh do m' shealladh?

Briseadh air sìth s truagh naidheachd na tìr'.
    Bidh iomadh fear sìnt'. Sin brìgh mo sheallaidh.
Seo teachdair an rìgh gairm 'fheara gu strì.
    Faic gaisgich ar tìr' le aont' 'nan cabhaig.

        Cluinn a' phìob a' togail fuinn.
        Sin na balaich air am buinn,
        Spiorad fìor-ghlan tìr nam beann
            A' ruith 'na deann sna h-àrdaibh.
        Fuil an sinnsear ruith 'na leum
        Troimh gach cuisle tha 'nan cré,
        'S chan eil nàmhaid fon a' ghréin
            D'an géill iad mur dèan bàs e.

Faic na fir threun is luathas 'nan ceum
    Ach sùil as an déidh. Chan fheum iad maille.
Le cridhe fo thùrs ach gàir' air a gnùis
    Tha cailin le mùirn toirt sùil air fleasgach.
Tha màthair 's bean òg a' fàsgadh nan dòrn
    'S a' falach am bròin. Cha chòir dhaibh gearan.
As-creideamh gun stàth cha sheas iad sa chàs;
    Their dòchas na slàint', "Bheir dàn iad dhachaigh."
Tha bàta na smùid air togail a cùrs'.
    Sin eilean an rùin 's an dùbhlachd seachad.

And if it be that we're spared
We will tie the knot
And there'll be no need to go
Where I spent last night.

Christina Macleod (Bayble, Point, Lewis)

In Memory of 1914–1918

News of the land. What news of the land?
  Is war or peace the pith of my vision?
For I saw people unnumbered around me
  With blood on their cheeks and their movements halting;
The raging waves of the sighing sea
  Whispered in my ear, "Cold is my bed."
But news of the land. What news of the land?
  Is war or peace the pith of my vision?

Bad news of the land is the breaking of peace.
  Many men will be felled. That's the pith of my vision.
Here's the messenger of the king calling his men to the struggle.
  See the warriors of our land united in haste.

    Hear the pipe raise a tune.
    That's the lads on the march,
    The pure Highland spirit
      Running hard in the heights.
    Their ancestral blood leaping
    Through each vein in their body,
    And there's no foe on earth
      That they'll yield to but death.

See the brave men with speed in their step
  While looking behind them. They mustn't slow down.
With saddened heart but a smile on her face
  A girl with affection looks at a youth.
A mother and bride are wringing their hands
  And hiding their grief. They shouldn't complain.
Disbelief without point won't protect them in hardship;
  Hope of salvation says, "Fate will bring them home."
The steamship has set her course.
  That's the beloved island with the winter past.

O fhir an taobh tuath, sibh sìol dom bu dual
   Bhith fearail is cruaidh aig uair na gaillinn;
Se dìlseachd bith-bhuan is seasmhachd gu buaidh
   An dìleab a fhuair sibh nuas 'nar n-eachdraidh.

Naidheachd na tìr'. Ciod naidheachd na tìr'?
   'N e buaidh no strìochdadh brìgh mo sheallaidh?
Oir chunnaic mi sluagh 'nan sìneadh 's iad fuar
   Ach spiorad na buaidh' rinn gluasad m' aigne
'S bha ainglean na glòir le iolach is ceòl
   Ag aithris sna neòil, "Bidh mòrachd maireann."
Ach naidheachd na tìr'. Ciod naidheachd na tìr'?
   'N e buaidh no strìochdadh brìgh mo sheallaidh?

Na nàimhdean bha cruaidh. A' chòmhstri bha buan
   'S bha dòchas na buaidh aig uair air seachran;
Bha marbhadh is leòn a' glacadh an còir —
   Ach strìochdadh 's iad beò! Sin seòrs' de dh'fhacal
Rinn fulang fo thàir an reachdaibh nan sàr.
   Gu buaidh no gu bàs — deoch-slàint' gach gaisgeach.
Ach naidheachd na tìr'. Ciod naidheachd na tìr'?
   'N e buaidh no strìochdadh brìgh mo sheallaidh?

Buaidh agus sìth. Buaidh agus sìth!
   O naidheachd na tìr' as prìseil t' aithris.
Moladh don Tì a dheònaich dhuinn sìth
   'S a theasraig ar tìr bho dhaors' na madraidh.

Ach càit bheil na laoich? O càit bheil na laoich?
   An till iad a-rìst gu tìr nam beanna?
Cuid tha 'nan suain an leabaidh a' chuain
   Is cuid dhiubh tha fuar san uaigh 'nan laighe;
Ach spiorad gach tréin a dh'ìobair e fhéin
   Bidh 'n cuideachd a Dhé gach ré sna flaitheas.
Nuair choinnicheas sinn càch aig clachan no tràigh
   Bidh luaidh air gach sàr bhios 'àite falamh;
Is togaidh sinn càrn mar chuimhneachan gràidh,
   An euchdan air clàr don àl a leanas.

O men of the north, it's in the blood of your race
   To be manly and hard in the time of the storm;
Perpetual loyalty, constancy unto triumph
   Are the legacy that's come down to you from our history.

News of the land. What news of the land?
   Is triumph or surrender the pith of my vision?
For I've seen people stretched out so cold
   But the spirit of triumph caused my heart to move
While the angels of glory with shout and with music
   Proclaimed in the clouds, "Might will prevail."
But news of the land. What news of the land?
   Is triumph or surrender the pith of my vision?

The enemy were cruel. Strife was eternal
   And hope of triumph was at one time lost;
Killing and wounding were seizing their due —
   But surrender alive! That's a kind of a word
Which brought the suffering of contempt to the realms of the great.
   To victory or death — the toast of each hero.
But news of the land. What news of the land?
   Is triumph or surrender the pith of my vision?

Victory and peace. Victory and peace!
   O news of the land most priceless to tell.
Praise to the Lord who granted us peace
   And delivered our land from enslavement by hounds.

But where are the heroes? O where are the heroes?
   Will they come back to the land of the mountains?
Some are asleep in the bed of the ocean
   And some of them cold as they lie in the grave;
But the spirit of each warrior who sacrificed himself
   Will accompany his God at all times in the heavens.
When we meet others at township or ebb
   There'll be talk of each hero whose place is empty;
And we'll raise a cairn as a monument of love,
   Their deeds on a tablet for the next generation.

38 *An Dubhsgaile*

Gur doirbh a' chìs an dubhsgaile
    As ro chudromach thar chàch —
Os cionn gach dìth is uireasbhaidh
    Orr' uile thug i bàrr;
Ged s fiosrach mi gur neoni i
    Seach cruas is sgrios nam blàr,
Tha bioran innt' tha coimheach leam
    Aig mochthràth 's deireadh là.

Shaothraich mi gu làmhchuiseach
    Gu bratan-sgàil' chur suas,
Gach uinneag ann am' fhàrdaich-sa
    Bhith dubh mar làr na h-uaimh;
B'e sin mo mhiann mun d'fhàg mi iad
    'S mi sàsachadh le uaill
An reachd a dh'òrdaich Pàrlamaid
    Gu nàmh a chumail uainn.

O thaobh a-muigh mo bhallachan
    Gun saoileadh neach air chuairt
Gur taigh bha fàsail falamh e,
    A ghean fo chlos na h-uaigh'
Gun sholas coinnl' no teine ann
    Gun bhlàths bho shneachd no fhuachd,
An aoigheachd a bha maille ris
    Air teich' bho chagailt fhuair.

Ach fuirich agus beachdaich leam
    Air cùisean ceart mar thà 'd,
An duibhr' tha muigh cha sanas i
    Gur duibhr' ar solas àigh,
Ar lòchranan tha lasaichte,
    Ar bòrd le biadh tha làn
'S tha aoidh is bàidh an gealladh dhuit
    Nuair thig thu staigh cur fàilt'.

Nach lìonmhor smuain tha mearachdach
    Is sealladh nach eil fìor
A dh'fhaodas neach bhith 'g altramas
    Mur cleachd e tuigse 's ciall;

The Blackout

What a hard tax to bear is the blackout
　　Which is of paramount importance —
Above each scarcity and shortage
　　It has beaten all the rest;
Though well do I know that it's nothing
　　To the hardship and carnage of battle,
It pricks in a way I detest
　　At the start and the end of the day.

I've laboured with all my dexterity
　　To put curtain covers up,
To make all the windows in my home
　　As black as the depths of a cave;
It was my aim before I left them
　　To satisfy with pride
The law that was passed by Parliament
　　To keep the enemy at bay.

From the outside of my walls
　　The passer-by would imagine
It was a house deserted and empty,
　　Its good cheer in the quiet of the grave
With no candlelight or fire in it
　　Or protection from frost or snow,
The hospitality that came with it
　　Having fled from a hearth grown cold.

But stay and reflect with me
　　On matters just as they are,
The gloom outside is no signal
　　That the light of our joy is dark,
For our lamps inside are lit,
　　Our table is full of food
And you're certain of welcoming kindness
　　When you come in and say hello.

Many thoughts are mistaken
　　And many beliefs aren't true
That a person may be nurturing
　　If he applies no reason or sense;

Faodaidh gràs is ceanaltas
    Is gean cho blast' ri fìon
Bhith glaist' an cridhe socharach
    Nach nochdar dhuit gu fial.

Mur tig thu dlùth air onarach
    Gun olcas ann ad' dhùil,
Ach rùn do chrìdh gum b' airidh thu
    Air sealladh Dhé as ùr
'S gun tuigeadh tu 'nad aineolas
    An saoibhreas glan gun smùr
A dh'fhaodas a bhith falaicht' ort
    Mur sir thu e le mùirn.

Ach dh'ainneoin smuain a chuidich mi
    Gu m' fhulangas chur bàs
Cha déidh leam daors' an dubhsgaile
    'S cha thrus mi i le bàidh;
Le gràs ar Dé ma ghuinear leinn
    Ar n-eascairdean gu làr,
Gun las sinn coinn'l nach mùchar leinn
    'S bidh oidhch' mar mheadhan là.

Murchadh MacLeòid (1881–1907)

39   *Gràdh m' Fhear-Saoraidh*

Tha mi fo leòn 's mo threòir ri fannach',
    'Nam dheòraidh airsneulach truagh
Gun dòchas gu bràth ri slàint' air thalamh
    'S am bàs 'na chabhaig teachd dlùth;
'S gach lighich' fon ghréin cha leighis mo ghalair
    'S mo réis chaidh seachad mar dhriùchd —
'S tha galair mo chléibh gam reubadh dhachaigh
    'S le péin théid m' anam fa sgaoil.

S fheudar dhomh innseadh, 's mi fìor ga aithris,
    Tha dìteadh maille ri m' phéin:
Se misg agus pòit rinn òg mo mhealladh
    'Nam dheòraidh greannach gun chéill
Thug mise don ùir aig tùs mo latha
    'S mo ghlaodh 's gach cala fon ghréin

For even grace and kindness
    And charity sweet as wine
May be locked in a diffident heart
    That's not freely revealed to you.

Unless you approach a person of honour
    Without any evil intent,
As heart's desire you ought to hold
    A sight of God renewed
That you might know in your ignorance
    The riches unsullied and pure
That may be hidden away from you
    If you don't civilly seek them out.

But despite the thoughts that have helped me
    To keep my worries at bay,
I dislike the tyranny of the blackout
    And gather it with no affection;
With the grace of our God if we strike
    Our enemies to the ground,
We'll light a candle and not put it out
    So that night will resemble midday.

Murdo Macleod (Scalpay, Harris)

The Love of my Redeemer

I've been struck down and my strength is wasting,
    A vagrant tired and miserable
Without hope of recovering health in this world
    While death comes rapidly near;
No physician on earth can cure my sickness
    And my life has gone past like the dew —
The disease of my chest is clawing me homewards
    And in pain my soul will depart.

I have to be telling, for it's true to relate,
    That condemnation goes with my pain:
It's the drink and the drunkenness that lured me when young
    Into vagrancy miserable and foolish
That have brought me to the grave at the start of my lifetime
    With my cry in each port in the world

Gun seachainn sibh pòit 's taigh òst' nam mallachd
　　Mas deòin leibh beannachd ur Dé.

Thug E dhomh buadhan cruaidhe fallain
　　A bu thruagh a chaith mi gu léir
Gu'n do chaill mi mo lùths mar bhrùid gun anam
　　'S gun smaoin mu mhaise mo Dhé,
A' saltairt a ghaoil gun diù fo m' chasaibh
　　'S a rùn gam leantainn 's gach ceum;
'S ged thug mi gach tàir do ghràdh an Athar
　　Bha fhàbhar maireann dhomh fhéin.

Cliù don Uan thug buadh air thalamh
　　Air truaillidheachd, peacadh is bàs,
A choisinn an t-saors' do dhaoinibh grathail
　　Bha aognaidh, ceannairceach, grànd',
'S an lagh air an tòir le'n dòigh an sgaradh
　　Dhan Tophet fharsaing gu bràth —
Do dheatach na péin' bhios éigneach maireann
　　Mo ghné-sa b' airidh an t-àit'.

Cha do thoill mi na b' fheàrr na cràdh na lasair
　　Gu bràth an comann nan truagh
Rinn dìmeas is tàir air slàint' an anam
　　'S an gràdh a cheannaicheadh cho cruaidh;
An sonas tha saor an cùirt nam flaitheas
　　Mas diù leinn amharc air suas —
Chaidh a chrochadh air crann 's a cheann a' cromadh
　　'S mar allt shruth naomh-fhuil a-nuas.

Se peacaidhean mòr' an t-slòigh chaidh cheannach
　　A chòmhraig ceannard nam buadh:
Ged bhiodh iad cho breun 's gum b' oillt an aithris
　　Chaidh sgeul nam beannachd a luaidh;
Gach aon leis an àill troimh ghràs bhith gabhail
　　Mar sgàil gu falach an truaigh'
Nì fuil an Uain Chàisg 'nar n-àit' ar glanadh
　　A phàigh ar ceannairc le buaidh.

Is duilich leam fhéin mo léirs' bhith salach
　　'S nach léir dhomh aithris mu ghaol:
An Dia tha ro threun rinn nèamh is talamh
　　E fhéin mar charaid aig daoin',

That you all shun the drink and the inn that's accursed
  If you wish to be blessed by your God.

He gave me faculties hardy and strong
  That I totally wasted in wretchedness
Till I lost my strength like a soulless brute
  Without thought for the beauty of my God,
Heedlessly trampling His love underfoot
  While His will followed me in each step;
And though I've so much reviled the love of the Father
  His favour to me has remained.

Fame to the Lamb who triumphed on earth
  Over sin, corruption and death,
Who won freedom for loathsome humanity
  That was repulsive, rebellious, and vile,
While the law pursues those who wish to be separate
  Into Tophet's broad valley forever —
In the smoke of pain that tortures eternally
  My sort has earned its place.

I deserved no better than the anguish of flame
  Forever along with the wretches
Who miscalled and abused their souls' salvation
  And the love that was purchased so dearly;
The joy that is free in the court of the heavens
  If we trouble to lift up our eyes to it —
He was hung on a cross with His head bending down
  While His holy blood flowed like a stream.

It's the great sins of the people that have been bought
  Who fought the leader omnipotent:
Even if so vile that they were foul to relate
  The tale of blessings has been told;
All those of us who wish through grace to be going
  As a wraith to the burial of our viciousness
Will be cleansed in our stead by the Paschal Lamb's blood
  Who so efficaciously paid for our mutiny.

I regret for myself that my sight's so obscured
  That I see no telling of love:
The God so brave who made heaven and earth
  Himself as a friend to men,

A' siubhal fo thàir 's gach àit' ga agairt,
   'S b'e gràin nan sagart a ghnùis,
Is 'eisimpleir ghlòrmhor òirdheirc mhaiseach
   'Toirt leòn agus eallach dha'n smaoin.

Nuair chualas an sgeul á beul nan aingeal
   Rinn Herod cabhag le rùn,
'S e ceasnach' nan draoidh mun naoidhean bheannaicht'
   'S iad ag innse mun t-sealladh ro naomh
A chunnaic iad réidh air sléibh is machair,
   An reult bu lainnire cùrs' —
Gun do sheas i le deàrrs', 's a blàths a' lasadh
   Mun stàball, is beannachd fo cùrs'.

Tha cruas air mo chrìdh mar phìos á carraig
   'S mi sgìth de charaibh an Nàmh'
A dhall mo dhà shùil le dùsal cadail
   'S mo smaoin a' gearradh mo chàil
Gu meòrach' le ùidh mun t-saoghal mhaireann
   'S dé chùirt a bhios m' anam 'na phàirt —
San t-sìorraidheachd bhuain mo thruaigh' an t-anam
   Nach buannaich flaitheas troimh ghràs.

Sagart an àigh a phàigh 's a cheannaich
   Gu bràth chuir faileas air chùl —
Seann lagh nan deas-ghnàth chuir gràs air falach —
   San là 'n do chriothnaich an saoghal
Nuair a ghlaodh e le buaidh, 's bu chruaidh an sgal i,
   'S an uaigh toirt thairis a daoin'
A choisich mar chàch air sràid a' bhaile
   'Nan slàinte fallain gun ghaoid.

Sona gu bràth an àireamh bheannaicht'
   Fo sgàile Ceannard na Saors',
Cha chomasach cas no bas a sgaradh
   On ghràdh nach atharraich rùn;
'S nuair bhios iad le péin 's an eug gan teannach'
   'S iad éigneach, anshocrach, ciùrrt',
Bidh an t-anam ag òl á lòn a' gheallaidh
   Troimh Iòrdan dhachaigh a-null.

Bidh aingeal Mhic Dhé ro dhlùth don anam,
   Gun leum e dealaicht' on fheòil

Wandering reviled and accused in each place,
   His countenance loathed by the priests,
And his glorious shining lovely example
   Bringing sadness and gloom to their thoughts.

When the news was heard from the angels' mouths
   Herod quickly applied his plan,
Questioning the druids about the holy child
   As they told what a blessed sight
They had seen prepared on mountain and plain,
   The star most brilliant of motion —
How it stood there ablaze, its warmth illuminating
   The stable, so blessed was its course.

My heart is as hard as a splinter of rock
   And I'm tired of the wiles of the Devil
Who blinded my eyes with the torpor of sleep
   While my thoughts cut across my appetite
To ponder the questions of life eternal
   And of which court my soul will be part —
In lasting eternity pity the soul
   That wins not heaven through grace.

The magnificent priest who paid and redeemed
   Cast out a shadow forever —
The old law of ritual that put grace in concealment —
   On the day when the world was shaken
When He shouted in triumph, and loud was the cry,
   While the grave rendered up its inhabitants
Who walked like the rest on the streets of the town
   In salvation whole and unblemished.

Forever content are the blessed elect
   In the shade of the Master of Freedom,
Not a foot nor a palm can ever be parted
   From the love whose aim never falters;
And when they're in pain in the coils of death,
   Oppressed, uneasy, and wounded,
The soul will drink from the pool of promise
   Through Jordan and over to home.

When the Son of God's angel comes close to the soul,
   It will leap away from the body

Bha dhaibhsan 'na prìosan sgìth air thalamh
   A' strì 's a' cathach' le deòin
An aghaidh a gné, tha breun 'nan sealladh —
   Mas léir do dh'anam a chòir
Tha fhathast ro thruagh fo ruaig na nathrach
   'S mar uan measg mhathan an crò.

Nam faighinn mo mhiann is riarach' m' anam
   Gus an sgeul seo aithris le còir
Mu ghràdh 's mu thruas an Uain ro bheannaicht'
   Do thruaghain cheannairceach slòigh
On mhallachd gun leus ro oillteil salach
   Nach d'ghéill do gheallaidhean òg'
Bha saltairt a' ghaoil gun ghrunnd 'na aigeal —
   Tha saors' trìd fhala do'n seòrs'.

Tha mo dhòchas troimh ghràs ri slàint' do m' anam
   Oir phàigh an Ceannard cho daor
'Na éirig 'nar n-àite 's a ràdh air aithris
   'S gach cànain is teanga san t-saoghal;
Ma thig sinn dha dlùth 's sinn brùit' le eallach
   Nì naomhachd fhala a' chùis;
Troimh chreideamh na buaidh bidh suaimhneas flaithis
   Do thruaghain anshocrach chlaon.

Hosanna gu bràth do ghràdh an Athar
   Nach d'fhàg an talamh fon bhinn
Bho dheatach bith-bhuan 's bho thruaigh na lasair
   Do chuan gun aigeal a-chaoidh
Measg dhiabhailean breun 'nan gné ro ghrathail
   Le'n aoibhinn sgalaich nan daoi
Is corraich Mhic Dhé le meud gan sgathadh —
   'S a phéin, có dh'aithriseas ì?

Nach tuig sibh 'na thràth gur feàrr an rathad
   Tha teàrnadh dhachaigh gu glòir,
'S ged s cumhang an ceum 's neo-shèimh ri ghabhail
   Le éiginn is anshocair mhòr?
Is iomadach béist a' feitheamh ri faire
   'S iad treun gu gearradh na feòl',
Ach an eaglais bheir buaidh 's théid suas le caithream
   Far an siab an t-Athair a deòr'.

Which to them was a tiresome prison on earth
    As it struggled and battled with a will
Against the flesh, which is vile in their sight —
    If a soul, that is, can see its rights
When still very weak from the serpent's assault
    And like a lamb amongst bears in a fold.

If I had my desire it's the wish of my soul
    To tell this story aright
Of the love and the pity of the Lamb so holy
    For rebellious wretches of folk
Who from unremitting curse most loathsome and vile
    Did not yield to the promise of youth
And have trampled a love of unfathomable depth —
    There's freedom through His blood for their kind.

My hope through grace is my soul's salvation
    For the Master paid so dearly
His bloodprice in our stead while His message is told
    In each language and tongue in the world;
If we come close to Him when crushed down by care
    His holy blood will suffice;
Through efficacious faith heaven's joy will come
    To troubled souls who have strayed.

Hosanna forever to the love of the Father
    Who's not abandoned the world to the judgement
Of eternal smoke and the horror of flame
    Going to bottomless ocean forever
Amongst loathsome demons repulsive in nature
    Who enjoy the shrieks of the wicked
While the Son of God's wrath lops them off in its fury —
    And His pain, who can describe it?

Won't you realise in time how much better's the road
    That leads us homewards to glory,
Though narrow's the path and difficult to follow
    Through danger and great anxiety?
There's many a beast that's waiting and watching
    And fearless at cutting the flesh,
But the church will prevail and rise up with rejoicing,
    Its tears wiped away by the Father.

Donnchadh MacIain (1881–1947)

40   *Càrn air a' Mhonadh*

Togaibh an t-Arannach 's fàgamaid Ìle,
    Togaibh on talamh e, Aonghas mo ghràdh-sa;
Togaibh an t-Arannach 's leigibh a-sìos e —
    Arainn san t-sealladh dhuinn, togaibh an càrn!

Togaibh an carragh, gach caraid is dìleas,
    Togaibh an carragh air mullach Bheinn Bhàin,
Togaibh an carragh air talamh nan Ìleach —
    Arainn san t-sealladh dhuinn, togaibh an càrn!

Coma leibh caisealan astair a' ghiùlain,
    Coma leibh allaban mhonadh is chàthar;
Togaibh gu h-ealamh on talamh an diùlach
    Is dhachaigh do dh'Arainn thoiribh an sàr.

Dhachaigh do dh'Arainn O dèanaibh a ghiùlan,
    Esan bha airidh air cliù anns a' bhlàr;
Ruigibh an cala is greasaibh an iùbhrach
    Is rachadh i thairis le Aonghas mo ghràdh.

An t-Urr. Aonghas MacFhionghain (1885–1957)

41   *Deireadh Òrdugh Ghleann Dail*

    O tha mi muladach
    Ag ionndrainn na chunnaic mi,
    Dol dhachaigh don an teampall
       'S bho shamhlaichean 'fhulangasan.

    Gur mise bha gu brònach
    Air Di-Luain an òrduigh
    Cur m' aghaidh air an òtrach
       'S gun deòin agam pilleadh ris.

    Nuair sheall mi air mo chùlaibh
    Bha 'm pàilliun air a dhùnadh —
    Thug siud na deòir o m' shùilean
       'S mi 'g ionndrainn na chunnaic mi.

Duncan Johnston (Lagavulin, Islay)

A Cairn on the Moor

Lift up the Arranman and let us leave Islay,
  Lift up the Arranman, Angus my darling;
Lift up the Arranman, put him down carefully —
  Arran in sight of us, build up the cairn!

Build the memorial, kinsfolk and followers,
  Build the memorial on top of Beinn Bhàn,
Build the memorial on Islaymen's land —
  Arran in sight of us, build up the cairn!

Make light of obstacles blocking the portage,
  Make light of crossing the marshes and moors;
Lift up the warrior with ease from the ground
  And homeward to Arran carry the hero.

Homeward to Arran O take turns to carry him,
  He who deserved all his fame in the field;
Get to the harbour and loosen the galley
  And let her go over with Angus my love.

Rev. Angus MacKinnon (Glendale, Skye)

The End of the Glendale Communion

O I'm so sorrowful
Missing what I've seen,
Going home to the temple
    And from the symbols of His suffering.

I was filled with sadness
On communion Monday
Heading for the grind
    With no wish to go back to it.

When I looked behind me
The tent had been closed up —
Tears came to my eyes
    From missing what I'd seen.

Nuair sheall mi air gach taobh dhiom
Bha 'n coithional air sgaoileadh,
Bha sgapadh anns na caoraich
     Ri aodann nam firichean.

Bha fear na cuirm 'na làthair
Toirt cuireadh do na bràithribh,
'S cha mhòr nach togainn pàilliun
     Dha fhéin 's do Mhaois 's do dh'Elias.

Bha 'ghràs gar dèanamh làidir,
Bha 'anail a' cur blàths oirnn,
'S dhe 'aodach thàinig fàileadh
     Den àlos, mhirr is chassia.

Ach tha mi nise cràiteach
'S mi air a chuideachd fhàgail,
'S gum feudar teachd don fhàsach
     'S mi teàrnadh far na beinne ud.

Ach ithidh Mephibòset
An-còmhnaidh aig mo bhòrd-sa —
Se siud mo bharant dòchais
     'S mo chòmhnadh ro bhunaiteach.

B'e Pòl is Timotèus
Bha roinn an arain nèamhaidh,
'S chan fhuiligeadh Timotèus
     Gun Pòl a bhith air thoiseach air.

Bha Pòl gu h-ealamh eudmhor
Toirt cuireadh do na feumaich,
'S bu teth gu dèanamh sgeul e
     Air sheudan nam flaitheanas.

42   *Am Mac Stròdhail*

Se dhol do thìr na fadachd ás thug creachadh air mo mhaoin,
Se 'n truaillidheachd san d'ghabh mi tlachd a dh'fhàg mi 'm' mhac-na-daors';
Do bhrìgh mo lochd tha mi ro bhochd 's le ocras a' dol aog —
Gun sunnd gun sult am measg nam muc, 's a' feitheamh air am plaosg.

When I looked to each side of me
The congregation had gone,
The sheep were scattering
    Round the faces of the hills.

The controller of the feast was there
Inviting the brethren,
And I could have built a tent
    Just for him, Moses and Elias.

His grace gave us strength,
His breath gave us warmth,
And from his clothing came the scent
    Of aloes, myrrh and cassia.

But now I'm in anguish
After leaving his company,
Forced to face the wilderness
    As I descend that mountainside.

But Mephibosheth will always
Dine at my table —
That's my warrant of hope
    And my fundamental succour.

It was Paul and Timothy
Who broke the sacred bread,
With Timothy insisting
    That Paul go in front of him.

Paul was active and zealous
In inviting the needy,
And warm in describing
    The jewels of the heavens.

The Prodigal Son

It's going to a far distant land that's plundered my resources,
The corruption I took pleasure in has put me into bondage;
My sins have left me very poor and dying of starvation —
Thin and sad amongst the swine, and waiting for their leavings.

Dh'iarr mi mo mhaoin air m' athair gràidh 's dh'fhàg siud e rium an gruaim,
Dh'fhàg mi dachaigh bheartach bhlàth far nach robh càs no cruas;
Bha m' anamiann ag iarraidh sàth bho nithe gràineil truagh' —
Thug mi gu làr fo smàg mo nàmh 's gu dorsa bàis is uaigh.

Éiridh mi 's théid mi air m' ais a dh'aideachadh mo bhròn
Le colann rùisgte 's poca lom 's gun bhonn agam am' dhòrn;
Car son a bhiodh mo chridhe fann 's mo chnàmhan gann de dh'fheòil
'S gu leòir ri sheachnadh aig gach àm aig m' athair 'na thaigh stòir?

Mun tàinig mi do m' athair dlùth chunnaic a shùil mo chàs
'S 'nam chòmhdhail ruith e 's phòg e mi, 's 'na ghlacaibh mise dh'fhàisg;
An àite corraich bhith 'na ghnùis se bh' innte ciùine 's blàths
Is fhuair mi deagh ghean, 'n àite diomb, is gabhail rium 'na ghràdh.

Dh'iarr e culaidh dhomh a-mach bu taitneach bha 'na bhùth
Is rinn e maiseach mi gun dàil le fàinne 's brògan ùr'
Is fhuair mi sàth den fheòil a b' fheàrr dem bheil am fàileadh cùbhr'
'S bidh mi gu bràth le aoighean gràidh ag àrdachadh a chliù.

Dòmhnall Mac na Ceàrdaich (1885–1932)

43   *Slighe nan Seann Seun*

Saoibhir sìth nan sian a-nochd air Tìr an Àigh
Is ciùine ciùil nam fiath ag iadhadh Innse Gràidh,
Is èasgaidh gach sgiath air fianlach dian an Dàin
Is slighe nan seann seun a' siaradh siar gun tàmh.

Saoibhir com nan cruach le cuimhne làithean aost',
Sona gnùis nan cuan am bruadair uair a dh'aom;
Soillseach gach uair an aigne suaimhneach ghaoth —
O, làithean mo luaidh, ur n-uaill, ur n-uails', ur gaol!

O làithean geala gràidh le'r gnàthan glana còir',
O aimsirean an àigh le'r gàire, gean is ceòl,
O shaoghail nan gràs, nan gathan aithne 's eòil,
Cuime thréig 's nach d'fhàg ach àilte àin ur glòir'?

An iongnadh deòin is dùil bhith dol a-null 'nur déidh,
Ri ionndrainn nan rùn a lìon ur sgùird le spéis?
An iongnadh ceòl nan dùl bhith seinn air cliù ur réim'
Is fabhra crom gach sùl' bhith tais fo dhùbhradh leug?

By asking him to send my all I angered my dear father,
I'd left a prosperous warm home which knew no straits nor hardship;
My lusts sought their fulfilment from ugly wretched pleasures —
Stricken by my enemies' paw I reached the doors of death and burial.

I'll get up and go back home and confess to all my sorrows
With naked body, empty pocket and no money in my fist;
Why should my heart be failing with no flesh upon my bones
When my father always has a surplus of provisions in his storehouse?

Before I got near to my father he'd seen my poor condition
And he ran to meet me, kissed me and then wrapped me in embraces;
In place of anger in his face were calmness and affection
And I received goodwill, not rage, and full acceptance in his love.

For me he looked out clothing that was splendid in his shop
And made me handsome straight away with a ring and brand-new shoes
And I had my fill of the best meat of wonderful aroma
And forever with beloved guests I'll glorify his name.

Donald Sinclair (Barra)

The Way of the Old Spells

Rich is the peace of the elements tonight on the Land of Glory
As the musical quietness of calms envelops the Isle of Love,
Fleet is each wing of the vehement warriors of Fate
As the path of the old charms winds westward without rest.

Rich is the stomach of the stacks with the memory of ancient days,
Happy's the face of the seas in the dreams of a time that has gone;
Bright every hour in contented spirit of winds —
O darling days, your pride, nobility, and love!

O bright cherished days with your pure acts of kindness,
O glorious times with your laughter, gladness and music,
O world of graces, of darts of knowledge and of guidance,
Why did you pass leaving nought but the honoured shade of your glory?

Is it a surprise that energy and hope go over in your wake,
For lack of the emotions that filled your lap with esteem?
Is it a surprise for the music of the elements to sing of the fame of your rule
With each anxious eyebrow moist under fading jewels?

A làithean sin a thriall le ial-luchd àis mo shluaigh,
Cuime thàrr ur miann gach dias a b' fhiachmhor buaidh?
An iongnadh an iarmailt shiar bhith nochd fo shnuadh
'S ur n-àrosan an cian bhith laist' le lias bith-bhuan?

An iongnadh lom gach làir bhith 'luaidh air làn ur sgeòil?
An iongnadh cnuic is ràdh a chomha-thràth 'nam beòil?
An iongnadh cruit nan dàn bhith bìth fo sgàil' a neòil
Is ealaidh-ghuth nam bàrd gun seun, gun sàire seòil?

Cha neònach cill mo shluaigh an cois nan cuan bhith balbh,
Chan iongnadh uchd nan tuam bhith 'n tòic le luach na dh'fhalbh,
O shaoghail, s truagh nach till aon uair a shearg,
'S nach tàrr mo dheòin, ge buan, aon fhios á suain nam marbh!

Eachann MacFhionghain (1886–1954)

44 *Fuath an t-Saoghail*

Se briathran caomh' an t-Slànaigheir
　　Ri bhràithrean anns gach linn,
"O bithibh seasmhach làidir ann
　　'S na fàilnichibh a-chaoidh;
O feuch nach dèan sibh m' àicheadh ann
　　Ged shàraicheadh iad sìbh —
'S bidh fuath nan uile dhaoine dhuibh
　　'S nach ann dhen t-saoghal sìbh."

Se thubhairt an t-Àrd Bhuachaille,
　　"Tha sluagh agam le cinnt
A leanas mi san fhàsach seo,
　　Is gràdhaichidh iad mì,
Bhon thagh mi mar mo chaoraich iad
　　'S nach téid a h-aon dhiubh dhìth —
'S bidh fuath nan uile dhaoine dhuibh
　　'S nach ann dhen t-saoghal sìbh.

"Chreid iad seo gun tàinig mi
　　Gan teàrnadh anns gach linn
Is chreid iad gun do bhàsaich mi
　　'Nan àit' air Calbharì,

O all you days that passed away with a generation of my people's wisdom,
Why did your desire evoke each ear of corn of most valuable effect?
Is it a surprise that the western sky tonight is in gloom
And your far-off palaces lit up with glow eternal?

Is it a surprise that each floor's bareness speaks your tale in full?
Is it a surprise for hills to have dusk's sayings in their mouths?
Is it a surprise for lyres of poetry to be ever under the shadow of its clouds
When the poets' creative voice has no charm or excellence of method?

It's not strange that my people's graves at oceans' edge are dumb,
It's no surprise for the tombs' outsides to swell with the worth of what's gone,
O world, alas that that which withered once will not come back,
And that my will, though lasting, will evoke no word from dead men's slumbers!

Hector MacKinnon (Berneray, Harris)

The World's Hatred

The Saviour's gentle words
    To his brothers in each age
Are, "Be ye strong and steadfast there
    And do not ever fail;
See that you deny me not
    Despite all their harassments —
And all men will despise you
    For not being of the world."

Declared the Mighty Shepherd,
    "In this wilderness for sure
I have a host who'll follow me,
    And they will love me too,
For as my sheep I've chosen them
    And none will go astray —
And all men will despise you
    For not being of the world.

"They believed I came here
    To save them in each age
And they believed I died
    For them on Calvary,

Is chreid iad gur e màna mi
　　A shàsaicheas an crìdh —
'S bidh fuath nan uile dhaoine dhuibh
　　'S nach ann dhen t-saoghal sìbh.

"Bhon thagh mi anns an t-saoghal sibh,
　　'Mo chaoraich' their mi rìbh,
Is seallaidh mi na cluaintean dhuibh
　　San gluais sibh 'na mo shlìgh;
Ma dh'fhanas sibh an aonadh rium
　　Cha téid a h-aon dhibh clì —
'S bidh fuath nan uile dhaoine dhuibh
　　'S nach ann dhen t-saoghal sìbh.

"Có spìonas ás mo làmhan iad
　　Cha tàinig e le mnaoi,
'S iad sgrìobhte air mo dheàrnaibh-sa,
　　Siad àilleagain mo chrìdh;
Gun toir mi dhachaigh sàbhailt' iad
　　Gu fois is tàmh le sìth —
'S bidh fuath nan uile dhaoine dhuibh
　　'S nach ann dhen t-saoghal sìbh.

"Chan eagal dhuibh san fhàsach sin
　　Sa bheil ur tàmh car tìm:
Ma leanas sibh tro àmhghair mi,
　　Le m' àithntean air ur crìdh,
Gu cinnteach bidh sibh sàbhailte
　　Air gàirdeanan ur Rìgh —
'S bidh fuath nan uile dhaoine dhuibh
　　'S nach ann dhen t-saoghal sìbh.

"Tha rìogh'chd dhuibh air a h-òrdachadh
　　Gu còmhnaidh ghabhail innt',
'S chan abair an luchd-àiteachaidh
　　Gu bràth gu bheil iad sgìth
Nuair bheir mi null thar Iòrdain sibh
　　San àm a shònraich mì —
'S bidh fuath nan uile dhaoine dhuibh
　　'S nach ann dhen t-saoghal sìbh.

"Is deàrrsaidh sibh 'nam oighreachd-sa,
　　Na h-oighrichean bhios innt',

They believed I'm manna
   To satisfy their hearts —
And all men will despise you
   For not being of the world.

"As I chose you in the world,
   'My sheep' is what I'll call you,
To ye I'll show the pastures
   Where you'll move in my path;
If you stay at one with me
   None of you'll go wrong —
And all men will despise you
   For not being of the world.

"He who'll pluck them from my hands
   Has not been born of woman,
For they're written on my palms,
   They're the jewels of my heart;
I'll bring them safely home
   To rest in tranquil peace —
And all men will despise you
   For not being of the world.

"You needn't fear that wasteland
   Where you're living for a while:
If you follow me through pain,
   My commandments on your hearts,
You'll most certainly find safety
   In the arms of your King —
And all men will despise you
   For not being of the world.

"A kingdom's pre-ordained
   For ye to live in it,
And none of its inhabitants
   Ever say that they are tired
When I take ye over Jordan
   At the time I specified —
And all men will despise you
   For not being of the world.

"And you'll shine in my inheritance,
   As heirs that succeed to it,

Mar sholais ann an coinnleirean
     Is reultan boillsgeach sìbh,
Le trusgan geal mo bhainnse-sa
     Nach caith 's nach caill a lìth —
'S bidh fuath nan uile dhaoine dhuibh
     'S nach ann dhen t-saoghal sìbh.

"Nuair dh'fhoillsichear sna neulan mi
     Nuair mhiannaicheas an Rìgh,
Le ainglean air an sgiathan leam
     A dh'iarraidh mo chuid naoimh,
Cha dearmad mi an còmhlan sin
     A lean 's a ghlòraich mì —
'S bidh fuath nan uile dhaoine dhuibh
     'S nach ann dhen t-saoghal sìbh.

"Is bheir mi dhachaigh sàbhailt' iad
     Dhan àros tha gun dìth,
Na peathraichean 's na bràithrean sin
     A lean 's a ghràdhaich mì,
A' seinn ann air na clàrsaichean,
     'S gu bràth cha bhi iad sgìth —
'S bidh fuath nan uile dhaoine dhuibh
     Bhon se mo ghaol-sa sìbh."

45   *Lìon an Damhain-Allaidh*

Siud an lìon a tha breòite
     Anns nach eil dòchas ri fhaotainn,
Ged as maiseach a bhòidhchead
     Mar an t-òr air an raonaidh;
Se sin dòchas a' chealgair,
     Se sin anaman gun saoradh —
Bheir an oiteag air falbh e,
     A chuid dhealbhannan faoine,
          A-muigh 's a-mach!

Resembling candles in candlesticks
  And glittering stars,
With the white gown of *my* wedding
  That won't fray or lose its gloss —
And all men will despise you
  For not being of the world.

"When I'm revealed in the clouds
  At the King's desire,
Angels flying with me
  To seek my holy state,
I won't forget that company
  Who followed me and praised me —
And all men will despise you
  For not being of the world.

"And I'll bring them safely home
  To the palace of perfection,
Those sisters and brothers
  Who followed and loved me,
Playing their harps there,
  Although they'll never tire —
And all men will despise you
  Because you are my love."

The Spider's Web

There's the net that's defective
  And offers no hope,
Though great is its glory
  Like gold on the slope;
It's the hope of the scoundrel,
  It's souls without freedom —
The breeze will extinguish it,
  All its vain images,
        And blow it away!

Dòmhnall Ruadh Chorùna (1887–1967)

46 Òran Arras

'Illean, *march at ease!*
  Rìgh na Sìth bhith mar ruinn
A' dol chun na strì
  'S chun na cill aig Arras;
'Illean, *march at ease!*

Tha 'nochd, oidhche Luain,
  Teannadh suas ri faire,
A' dol chun na h-uaigh
  Far nach fhuasg'lear barrall;
'Illean, *march at ease!*

Tillidh cuid dhinn slàn,
  Cuid fo chràdh lann fala,
'S, mar a tha e 'n dàn,
  Roinn le bàs a dh'fhanas;
'Illean, *march at ease!*

Gus ar tìr a dhìon,
  Eadar liath is leanabh,
Mar dhaoin' ás an rian
  Nì sinn 'n sgian a tharraing;
'Illean, *march at ease!*

S lìonmhor fear is té
  Tha 'n tìr nan geug 'nan caithris
Feitheamh ris an sgeul
  Bhios aig a' chléir ri aithris;
'Illean, *march at ease!*

Gura lìonmhor sùil
  Shileas dlùth 's nach caidil
Nuair thig fios on Chrùn
  Nach bi dùil ri'm balaich;
'Illean, *march at ease!*

Donald Macdonald (Claddach Baleshare, N. Uist)

The Song of Arras

Lads, *march at ease!*
  The King of Peace be with us
Going to the strife
  And to the tomb at Arras;
Lads, *march at ease!*

Tonight, Monday night,
  Moving up to guard,
Going to the grave
  Where no bootlace is untied;
Lads, *march at ease!*

Some of us will return unscathed,
  Some in agony of bloody blade,
And, according to our fate,
  Some in company of death will stay;
Lads, *march at ease!*

To defend our land,
  From grey hairs to child,
Like men gone mad
  We will draw the knife;
Lads, *march at ease!*

Many men and women
  Lie awake in heroes' land
Waiting for the news
  That the clerk has to tell;
Lads, *march at ease!*

Many an eye will weep
  Profusely without sleep
When word comes from the Crown
  That their lads won't be expected;
Lads, *march at ease!*

47   Air an Somme

An oidhche mus deach sinn a-null
    Bha i drùidhteach a' sileadh,
Bha mi fhéin 'nam laighe 'n cùil
    'S thug mi sùil feadh nan gillean.

       Ochan ì, ochan ì,
       Tha sinn sgìth anns an ionad.
       Ochan ì, ochan ì.

Cuid 'nan suidhe 's cuid 'nan suain,
    Cuid a' bruadar 's a' bruidhinn
Gun robh mhadainn gu bhith cruaidh —
    "Saoil am buannaich sinn tilleadh?"

"Cha dèan biùgailear le bheul
    Ar pareudadh-ne tuilleadh;
Théid ar dealachadh bho chéil',"
    Thuirt mi fhéin far mo bhilean.

Agus mar a thubhairt b' fhìor,
    Chaidh na ciadan a mhilleadh,
Chaidh an talamh ás a rian
    'S chaidh an iarmailt gu mireag.

Dhubh an àird an-ear 's an-iar,
    Is an sliabh gun robh crith ann,
Is chan fhaighinn m' anail sìos —
    Àileadh cianail an tine.

Is cha chluinninn guth san àm
    Aig comanndair gar leigeil,
Bha na balaich 's iad cho trang
    Cumail thall na bha tighinn.

Bha gach fear a' caogadh sùl'
    'S e air cùlaibh a chruinneig
A' cur peileir glas a-null
    Le uile dhùrachd a chridhe.

On the Somme

The night before we went over
  It was pouring with rain,
I was lying in a corner
  And I looked round the lads.

    Ochan ì, ochan ì,
    We're tired of the place.
    Ochan ì, ochan ì.

Some sitting, some asleep,
  Some dreaming and saying
That the morning would be hard —
  "Think we'll manage to get back?"

"No bugler with his mouth
  Will parade us again;
We'll be parted from each other,"
  I murmured to myself.

And what I said came true,
  Hundreds were destroyed,
The earth dissolved in chaos
  And the sky went awry.

East and west turned black
  And the hill began to tremble,
I couldn't catch my breath —
  The acrid stench of fire.

And no voice could I hear
  Of officer commanding us,
For the lads were so busy
  Holding back what was coming.

Each man squinting an eye
  Through the sights of his darling
Sending grey bullet over
  With heartfelt sincerity.

48   *Dh'fhalbh na gillean grinn*

Dh'fhalbh na gillean grinn
    Fo'n cuid armaibh,
Sann rium fhìn a chòrdadh
    A bhith 'n còir nam balachan.
Dh'fhalbh na gillean grinn
Fo'n cuid armaibh.

Gun d'leum iad an truinnse,
Ruith an cùrsa dìreach,
'S dh'fhosgail teine-cinn orra
    Le innleachd na Gearmailt.

'S ged a leum iad sunndach,
Dol mar fhiadh sa bhùireadh,
Chaog an nàimhdean sùil riuth'
    'S rinn iad dhiùbhsan targaid.

'S gun robh fir mo rùin-sa
Tuiteam air gach taobh dhiom,
'S bha mo chridhe caoineadh
    Ged bha 'n caoch 'nam eanchainn.

Cuid dhiubh laighe sàmhach,
Roinn feadh shloc a' cràladh,
'S mòran ann an spàirn dhiubh
    'G iarraidh àite teanacsa.

Ach nuair fhuair sinn dìreadh
Am bruthach a mhill sinn,
Leum sinn uile dìgean
    'S gach fear dhinn air fhalachaig.

Nuair a fhuair sinn dlùth dhaibh
Far an robh na cùilean
'S mìltean dhiubh a' crùbadh,
    Dhùisg sinn iad le damnadh.

Sgrios sinn iad dhan t-sìorrachd,
Fear an-ear 's an-iar dhiubh,
'S cha robh mac am fianais
    Mun do chiar an t-anmoch.

Off went the handsome lads

Off went the handsome lads
  Shouldering their arms,
It's I who'd enjoy
  Being with the boys.
Off went the handsome lads
Shouldering their arms.

They leapt over the trench,
Running their straight course,
And head-fire opened up on them
  With all Germany's artifice.

And though they jumped happily,
Going like deer in rutting,
Their enemies squinted at them
  And made of them a target.

And the men I loved so much
Were falling each side of me,
And my heart was mourning
  Though my brain was in fury.

Some were lying quietly,
Some crawling through craters,
With many frantically
  Seeking place of safety.

But when we'd managed to climb
The brae that had shattered us,
We all leapt over ditches
  And each one of us took cover.

When we got close to them
Where the bunkers were
With thousands of them crouching,
  We woke them with damnation.

We blasted them to hell,
Some eastwards, some westwards,
No mother's son remained
  By the time dusk had fallen.

Dhubh an oidhch' oirnn cianail,
'S shil i oirnn gu fiadhaich,
'S cha b' urrainn dhuinn sian
   A dhèanamh ach bhith cearbach.

Sheas sinn mar a bhà sinn,
Ann an crèadh 's an clàbar,
'S bha 'n t-uisge cho àrd dhuinn
   Ann ri bàrr a' gharmain.

'S nuair a thuig ar nàmhaid
An tinnead mar bhà sinn,
Dh'fhosgail iad gach càil oirnn
   Rinn an làmh a dhearbhadh.

Thionndaidh iad le'n combaist
An gunnaichean trom oirnn,
'S thìodhlaig iad sa pholl sinn
   'S ar com air a sgealbadh.

Dealanach an fhùdair
Lasadh os ar cionn-ne
'S tàirneanach ri chùlaibh
   Brùchdadh ar fuil fheargach.

Nuair a fhuair sinn còmhla
Chaidh an rola chòileadh;
Gun robh 'mhadainn brònach
   Againn 'n còmhradh seanchais.

Bha gach fear a' feòrach
Mu chompanach eòlach:
"'M faca sibh ann beò e
   Measg nan leòn sa gharbhlach?"

Fhreagair fear 'n taobh shìos dhiom,
"Mharbhadh Eachann 's Iain,
Uilleam agus Niall,
   MacDhiarmaid agus Fearchar."

Fhreagair fear 'n taobh shuas dhiom,
"Mharbhadh Seonaidh 's Ruairidh,
Dòmhnall Bàn 's MacGuaire,
   Aonghas Ruadh is Tormod."

Night came on us wretchedly,
It was raining very hard,
There was nothing we could do
    But remain there feeling helpless.

We stood as we were,
In clay and in mud,
And the water rose as high on us
    As the breast-beam of a loom.

When our enemy discovered
The narrow straits we were in,
They opened up with everything
    That their hand had tested.

They turned with their compass
Their heavy guns upon us,
And buried us in mud
    With our bodies blown apart.

The lightning flash of powder
Bursting above us
With thunder behind it
    Exploding our angry blood.

When we got together
A roll-call was taken;
That the morning was grievous
    Was our conversation.

Every man was asking
About his boon companion:
"Did you see him there alive
    Amongst the wounded in the open?"

Replied someone down the line from me,
"Hector and John were killed,
And William and Neil,
    And MacDiarmid and Farquhar."

Replied someone up above me,
"Johnnie and Roddy were killed,
Dòmhnall Bàn and MacQuarrie,
    And Red Angus and Norman."

Dh'fhalbh na gillean grinn
Fo'n cuid armaibh,
Sann rium fhìn a chòrdadh
A bhith 'n còir nam balachan.
Dh'fhalbh na gillean grinn
Fo'n cuid armaibh.

49   *Òran a' Phuinnsein*

'Fhearaibh, a bheil cuimhn' agaibh
An là thàinig am puinnsean oirnn
'Nar seasamh anns na truinnsichean
    'S gun nì ann gus ar còmhdach?

O nach beag a shaoileamaid
Gun tigeadh nì as ùr oirnn —
An sruth tha ruith o'r sùilean
    'S sinn a' cùilearachd 's a' crònan.

Cha robh nì gu teanacsadh dhuinn
Ach làmh thoirt air an t-searbhadair
'S a cheangal gus nach fhalbhadh e
    Gu dearbhte mu ar srònan.

Cha shaoileamaid san àm bha siud
Gun robh am bàs cho teann oirnn —
Ar leamsa gur e meall a bh' ann
    Nuair theann e nall air còmhnard.

Sabaid 's cath cha dèanamaid
Ged nochdadh iad am fianais dhuinn,
Bha na deòir cho deuchainneach
    'S chan fhaicinn leus ach neònach.

Nam faighinn mar bu mhiannach leam
Dhan Ghearmailt gum b'e m' iarratas
Se teine thighinn on iarmailt oirr'
    Ga leaghadh sìos gun tròcair.

Off went the handsome lads
    Shouldering their arms,
It's I who'd enjoy
    Being with the boys.
Off went the handsome lads
    Shouldering their arms.

The Song of the Poison

Lads, do you remember
The day the poison came
As we stood in the trenches
    With nothing to protect us?

Oh how little we thought
A new thing would come at us —
Stream running from our eyes
    As we crouched and we wheezed.

There was no way to help ourselves
Except to grab a towel
And tie it so that it would stay
    Firmly round our noses.

At that point we hadn't thought
That death was so close to us —
I had taken it for a shower
    As it drifted across the ground to us.

Fighting and battle were impossible
Had they even approached us,
So painful were the tears
    While a weird glow was all I saw.

If I had things as I wanted
For Germany I'd ask
Fire raining from the sky on it
    To melt it without mercy.

50   *Nam bithinn mar eun*

Nam bithinn mar eun air sgiathan ealamh
    A dhèanadh cabhagach leum,
Shiùbhlainn an-iar 's cha dèanainn fantail
    San t-sliabh na b' fhaide le céinnt;
Nuair ruiginn an cuan gum fuarainn Sasainn,
    Bu shuarach agam i fhéin,
'S cha tiginn gu làr gu bràth gu anail
    Gu'n tàrrainn fearann nan geug.

Nuair chithinn mar sgòth bhuam ceò nam beannan
    Gan còmhdach thairis gu léir,
Eubhal fo cleòc is Rònaigh ghleannach
    Le còt' a chanach an t-sléibh,
Lì Deas agus Tuath, le fuarain ghlana
    'Nan luaths a' tarraing gu réidh,
On aigeal a-nuas, o ghruaim na stalla,
    Is luachair falach am beul,

Gun laighinn air bàrr a' chàrnain mhaisich
    Le bàidh 's le barrachd mo spéis,
An Eubhal mo ghràidh tha ghnàth air m' aire
    'S a dh'fhàg mi fad' as mo dhéidh;
Gun amhaircinn bhuam mun cuairt an sealladh
    Bu luachmhoir' agam fon ghréin,
Na lochan 's na bàigh fo chràgheoidh 's eala,
    'S an àird a' ghleanna, damh féidh.

Nuair dhèanainn treis tàmh 's a thàirninn m' anail
    Gun teàrnainn thairis mun cuairt,
Timcheall nam bàgh 's nan sràidean glana
    Le àileadh meala mu'm bruaich —
Chan ionnan 's mar thà san àraich charraich,
    Toirt slàinte 's fallaineachd bhuam,
Le boladh a' bhàis toirt plàigh le galair,
    'S gun àite falamh gun uaigh.

Ged bhithinn gun stòr gun òr gun fhearann,
    Gun chòmhnaidh agam no blàths
Ach toll ann am bruaich gun tuar gun teine,
    Gun truas gun charaid gun bhàidh,

Were I like a bird

Were I like a bird on supple wings
    Rising quickly into the sky,
I would travel west and wouldn't rest
    In foreign hills any longer;
When I reached the sea I'd leave England to leeward,
    For it means nothing to me,
And I'd not descend to catch my breath
    Till I reached the land of heroes.

When I saw like a cloud the mist of the mountains
    Covering them over completely,
Eaval becloaked and Rona of glens
    With their coat of moorland bog-cotton,
Lee South and North, with pure mountain springs
    Flowing swiftly to the plain,
From the depths of the earth, through the stubborn rock,
    With rushes hiding their mouths,

I'd land on the top of that beautiful rock
    With love and with all my affection,
On darling Eaval who's forever on my mind,
    And whom I've left so far behind me;
I'd gaze intent at the sight around me,
    Most precious to me in the world,
The lochs and the bays under sheldrake and swan,
    And the antlered stag up the glen.

When I'd stayed for a while and drawn my breath
    I'd go down and travel about,
Around the bays and the fertile walks
    With the scent of honey around their slopes —
Not at all like here in the blighted field
    Where one's robbed of fitness and health,
With the smell of death bringing sickness and plague
    And no empty space is without its grave.

Had I no wealth or gold or land,
    Without dwelling-place or warmth
But some hole in a bank without daylight or fire,
    Without kindness, friendship or love,

Gun léinidh mu m' chom 's mi lomnochd falamh,
    Gun bhonn gun aran 'nam làmh,
Ach bhith mar an t-eun tha 'g iasgach cladaich,
    Toirt trian dhe bheath' ás an tràigh —

Nuair thigeadh am fuachd, an cruas 's a' ghailleann
    On tuath a' frasadh le gaoth,
Gun rachainn dhan toll le fonn gu toilicht'
    Le bobhstair rainich fo m' thaobh;
Lìonainn gu dìonach beul an dorais
    Le fianaich mholaich 's le fraoch,
Gun eagal gun fhiamh roimh shian sa mhonadh
    Is sgian mo chogaidh 's i dùint'.

Chan fheumadh mo chluas bhith shuas a' caithris
    Ri fuaim a' chanain san àm,
No idir mo shùil bhith dlùth ag amharc
    Far chùl a' pharapaid ann
Mus tigeadh gas bàis a thàrradh m' anail —
    A-ghnàth am flanainn mu m' cheann,
'S an rubair mu m' bheul mar chìoch aig leanabh
    'S mi dian a' tarraing tro bann.

51 *Tha mi duilich, cianail, duilich*

Tha mi duilich, cianail, duilich,
    Tha mi duilich, s cianail thà mi
Bhon a chunna mi le m' shùilean
    Sealladh tùrsach mo chuid bhràithrean.

Gillean Gaidhealtachd na h-Alba,
    Feadhainn tha marbh is 'nan clàraibh
Anns an fhàsaich 's iad 'nan sìneadh,
    An neart 's an clì air am fàgail.

A luchd nan éilidhean tartain,
    A luchd nan gartannan sgàrlaid,
S duilich leam nach fhaod sibh dùsgadh,
    Sibhse, luchd nan glùinean àlainn.

With no shirt round my body, just bare and broke,
    Without coin or bread in my hand,
But to be like the bird that fishes the shore
    And takes a third of his food from the ebb —

When the cold would come, the hardship and storm
    From the north with a shower on the wind,
I'd get into the hole with contented mind
    And lie on my bolster of bracken;
I'd fill the entrance to keep out the draught
    With rough moor-grass and with heather,
Unafraid and unworried by anything in the moor
    And my battle-knife closed in its sheath.

No need for my ear to listen all night
    To the noise of the cannon's roar,
Or at all for my eye to be watching close
    Over the top of the parapet
Lest the gas of death would come and stop my breath —
    The flannel forever round my head,
With the rubber round my mouth like a child at the breast
    As I breathe heavily through gauze.

I am sorry, anguished, sorry

I am sorry, anguished, sorry,
    I am sorry and so anguished
Since I saw with my eyes
    The sad sight of my brothers.

The boys of the Scottish Highlands,
    Some who're dead and blown to pieces
Prostrate in the wilderness,
    Their energy and strength having left them.

O lads of the tartan kilts,
    O lads of the scarlet garters,
I'm sorry you can't awake,
    You lads of the shapely knees.

Tha mo chridhe brùite cianail,
    Tha mo shùil on deur air tràghadh,
'S nach aithnich mi sibh air ur n-ìomhaigh
    Bhon a riaghladh leis a' bhàs sibh.

Tha 'r leapannan fliuch, 's gur fuar iad,
    S cruaidh ur cluasagan gun chàradh,
Le uisge tàmh air an uachdar,
    S duilich leam an uair a thàrr sibh.

S trom an cadal th' air na fiùrain
    Chuireadh ormsa sunndach fàilte,
Le'm bu mhiann a bhith 'nam chòmhradh
    Cur mun cuairt nan òran Gàidhlig.

Chì mi roinn eile mun cuairt dhiubh,
    Crois air a cur suas aig pàirt dhiubh,
Ainm an laoich 'n-siud oirre sgrìobhte
    Dhèanadh innse dhuinn gun d'fhàg e.

Chì mi brògan agus aodach,
    Chì mi aodainn agus làmhan
Nochdte an talamh na Frainge
    Far 'n do chaill mi mo chuid bhràithrean.

Siud far am bi 'n latha brònach —
    Na faicibh neònach dhòmhs' a ràitinn:
Nuair a thilleas na bhios beò
    Se 'n roinn ro-mhòr bhios air am fàgail.

Ach nuair théid an t-sìth a dhùnadh,
    Gunnaichean gach aon dhiubh sàmhach,
Teine dealaichte bhon fhùdar,
    Nàimhdean cùl ri cùl a' màirdseadh —

Facal dhuibh gur anns an uair ud
    Théid an t-saighead chruaidh sa mhàthair,
Anns an athair, anns a' ghruagaich
    Dh'fhàgadh san uair seo gun bhràthair.

Siud nuair bhios an cridhe cianail,
    Siud nuair théid an sgian a shàth'dh ann,
Siud nuair ghealaicheas an ciabhag —
    Sann le deuchainnean a' bhlàir seo.

My heart is bruised and wretched,
　My eye's gone dry from tears,
For I can't recognise your appearance
　Since you were conquered by death.

Wet are your beds, and cold,
　Hard are your pillows unmade,
With brackish water on their surface,
　I regret the hour that caught you.

Deep is the sleep of the warriors
　Who'd greet me with cheerful welcome,
Who loved to converse with me
　And take turns at Gaelic songs.

I see others around them,
　Some with a cross erected,
The hero's name inscribed upon it
　To tell us he's departed.

I see boots, I see clothes,
　I see faces and hands
Showing in the soil of France
　Where I lost my brothers.

That's where the sad day will be —
　Don't see it strange for me to say:
When those who are alive return
　The greater number will be left behind.

But when peace is signed,
　When the guns of each side are at rest,
Fire separated from powder,
　And enemies marching away from each other —

Mark my words that at that time
　The cruel arrow's in the mother,
In the father, in the girl
　Who's now been left without a brother.

That's when the heart is desolate,
　That's when the knife is plunged in it,
That's when their locks of hair go white —
　Such are the trials of this war.

Ach misneachd do gach fear is té dhibh,
   Is leughaibh gu léir na h-àithntean
'S seallaibh Ris-san a rinn éirigh
   Ged a cheusadh E le nàmhaid.

Tha sibh dol gu léir 'nan déidh-san,
   Chan eil fear no té ri'm fàgail,
'S ma ghabhas sibh an nì tha saor dhuibh
   Gheibh sibh saorsa 's chì sibh fhath'st iad.

Chì a' bhantrach a fear-pòsta,
   Chì an t-òganach a mhàthair,
Tachraidh peathraichean le sòlas,
   Mar bu deònach leo, ri'm bràithrean.

An uair chì iad madainn Chéitein
   Eòin air géig 's an gleus gun tàmh ann,
Neònach mura tog iad fianais
   Leamsa gura fìor am bàrd mi.

Fhads a bhitheas mis' air m' fhaotainn
   Anns an t-saoghal seo air m' fhàgail
Bidh 'nam chridhe beò 's 'nam shùilean
   Sealladh tùrsach mo chuid bhràithrean.

52   *Cha b'e gunna mo nàmhaid*

Cha b'e gunna mo nàmhaid,
   Och, a b' àbhaist mo dhùsgadh
Ach a' cheilearachd bhòidheach
   Bh' aig na h-eòin an Corùna.

Ho ró shiùbhlainn ho ró.

Ach a' cheilearachd bhòidheach
   Bh' aig na h-eòin an Corùna,
Aig an uiseag 's an smeòrach
   'S druid a' crònan a brùndail,

Is aig màgail na lachainn
   Anns a' mhadainn bu chiùine

But may every one of you take courage,
   May you all read the commandments
And look at Him who rose
   Though He was crucified by foes.

All of you are following them,
   No male or female will be left,
And if you take what's freely offered
   You'll be free and you'll see them again.

The widow will see her husband,
   The youth will see his mother,
Sisters with joy will reunite,
   As they wanted, with their brothers.

When they see a Maytime morning,
   Birds on branches in ceaseless song,
They'll certainly agree with me
   That I'm a poet who speaks the truth.

As long as I'm to be found
   Remaining in this world
In my living heart and eyes will be
   The sad spectacle of my brothers.

It was not my enemy's gun

It was not my enemy's gun,
   Och, that used to awaken me
But the sweet serenade
   Of the birds in Corùna.

Ho ró I'd travel ho ró.

But the sweet serenade
   Of the birds in Corùna,
Of the lark and the thrush
   And the gossiping starling,

Of the quacking of duck
   In the calmest of mornings

Is aig gogail a' gheòidh ghlais,
Se thogadh Dòmhnall a shunnd ris.

An éirigh gréine bu toil leam
Goire coileach na fraoch-chirc

'S mac-an-fhéidh a' chùil dhonnaich
Am Beinn na Coille nan caorach.

Nuair bhiodh oidhcheannan reòt' ann
Sann leam bu bhòidheach a bhùirich.

A' toirt làmh air a' ghunna
Bhiodh an cuilean 's a shùil rium,

E ri miodal mun cuairt dhiom,
'S a chridhe bualadh le sùgradh,

Miann na fala 'na nàdar
'S tlachd de dh'fhàileadh an fhùdair;

Fear bu robaiche cluasan,
S tric san uair mi ga ionndrainn

'S cha b' iongnadh le càch e
Nam b' fhiosrach àd air ar sùgradh

Nuair a bhitheamaid còmhla
Air feadh na mòintich is sùrd oirnn

Le mo ghunna 'nam achlais
'S mi cumail fasgaidh on driùchd air

Gus am faicinn fear cabrach
Le chuid mheangannan ùr' air,

Sinn ag amharc le chéil' air —
Dé mar gheibheamaid dlùth ris

Air feadh chnocan is ghlaicean,
Air feadh chlachan is fhraochaibh

Gus an saoilinn gun dèanainn
Leis a' chiad té a' chùis air.

And the grey goose's honking
  Which cheered Donald so much.

At sunrise I loved
  The cry of the moorcock

And the tawny-rumped stag
  In Beinn na Coill' of the sheep.

When the nights of the frost came
  How I loved his great roaring.

As I reached for the gun
  The young dog would watch me,

Fawning around me,
  Palpitating with joy,

Blood lust in his nature
  And delight in the powder's smell;

The one with raggedest ears,
  Often now do I miss him

And no surprise that to others
  Had they known of our fun

When we'd be together
  Round the moor eagerly

With my gun in my oxter
  To protect it from dew

Till I saw an antlered stag
  With all his new points on him,

We both looking at him —
  How we'd get up close

Using hillocks and hollows,
  Using boulders and heather

Till I thought I could manage
  With one shot to drop him.

Readh, air gleusadh nam brag,
   An t-òrd a tharraing gu chùlaibh,

Is far bharran nan geugan
   Fear na h-euchda a stiùireadh

'S bhiodh an cuilean ag éisteachd,
   'S e feitheamh leum air mo chùlaibh.

Nuair a leiginn an t-sradag
   Dhan an deannan bha sunndach,

Bhiodh mac-an-fhéidh 's e 'na shìneadh
   Le osna thinn agus bhrùite

Agus lota 'na amhaich
   Far an d' dh'amhairc mi 'n t-sùil air.

Siud mar chuir mise seachad
   Iomadh latha gu sunndach

Agus oidhche 'nam chaithris
   Feadh nam beannanan cùbhraidh —

Nuair bhiodh càch 's iad 'nan cadal
   Bhiomaide mach 'na ar dùsgadh.

Is beag a shaoilinn an uair ud
   Gun robh 'n cruas seo gam ionnsaigh.

Se gaol na mosgaid a dh'fhàg
   Fo ghlas-làmh aig a' Chrùn mi —

An gaol a thug mi 'nam òige
   A bhith 'n-còmhnaidh ga stiùireadh —

Ach nuair rinn mis' a pòsadh
   Nochd rium bròn air a cùlaibh

'S thàinig mulad 'nam fhianais
   Is chan iarramaid fhaotainn

Nuair fhuair mi 'n tochradh o Sheòras
   Leis an ògbhannaich chaoil ud:

When the flints had been primed,
   And the hammer pulled back,

By the tips of the sights
   The champion was aimed

While the whelp listened,
   Keen to leap out behind me.

When the spark was applied
   To the shot that was lively,

The stag would collapse
   With a sigh sore and broken

And a wound in his neck
   Where I'd fixed my eye on him.

That's how I spent
   Many days of pleasure

And many nights without sleep
   Among sweet-scented mountains —

When the rest were abed
   Out we'd go wide awake.

I little thought at the time
   That these straits would befall me.

It's the love of the musket
   Has handcuffed me to the Crown —

The love I had in my youth
   For guiding her always —

But when we were married
   Grief reared up behind her

And a sorrow beset me
   That we'd never have sought

When I got George's dowry
   With yon slender young bride:

Bras is copar is feòdar,
Luaidhe, cordite is fùdar,

Botal ola 'na pòcaid
Gus bhith 'n-còmhnaidh ga sgùradh,

On a thug mi na bòidean
Gun dèanainn Mòrag a ghiùlan

Gus an tuiteamaid còmhla
Air neo dhan stòdhar a tionndadh.

53   *Òran an H-Bomb*

An t-inneal sgrios a rinn ar nàmhaid
Chum 's gum bàsaicheamaid còmhla,
S truagh nach d'thìodhlaig iad san t-sàl e,
An doimhneachd an làin a chòpadh.
B' fheàrr an saoghal bhith mar bhà e —
Ged bhiodh blàir ann agus còmhstri
Thilleadh cuid dhinn mar a b' àbhaist
Eadar a bhith slàn is leòinte.

Ach nam biodh tu air do chliathaich
Air an t-sliabh ud is tu leòinte
Thigeadh cuideachadh gad iarraidh
Nuair chromadh a' ghrian sna neòilibh;
Readh do ghiùlan mar bu mhiann leat,
Gillean èasgaidh leis a' chròileab,
Is readh do lotan a lìonadh —
Siud gu fìor mar dh'éirich dhòmhsa.

Ach dealanach an-diugh o d' nàmhaid,
Chan eil fàbhar dhan a' bheò ann,
Théid gach duine 's brùid a thàrradh
'S théid gach càil a smàladh còmhla;
Cha bhi nì air bith air fhàgail
Eadar tràigh is àird na mòintich,
'S ann an eileanan na Gàidhlig
Fear no dhà dhiubh 's bidh gu leòr ann.

Brass, copper and pewter,
    Lead, cordite and powder,

An oil-bottle in her pouch
    To be cleaning her always,

Since I gave my vows
    That I'd carry Morag

Till we fell side by side
    Or I turned her in to the store.

The Song of the H-Bomb

The means of destruction that our enemy made
    So that we'd die together,
Too bad they didn't bury it in the sea,
    Couping it in the depths of the high tide.
Better the world as it was —
    Even with battles and strife
Some of us would come back as usual
    Either healthy or wounded.

But if you were on your side
    Lying wounded on that hill
Help would come to seek you
    When the sun set in the clouds;
You'd be carried as you wished,
    Agile lads with the stretcher,
And your wounds would be dressed —
    That in truth's what happened to me.

But lightning today from your enemy,
    There's no bias to the living in it,
Each man and beast will be caught
    And everything snuffed out together;
Nothing at all will be left
    Between ebb and highest moorland,
And in Gaelic-speaking islands
    One or two will be thought plenty.

Ach saoil sib' fhéin an ceadaich Dia e —
   An sgrios chianail seo 'thighinn òirnne;
Ged as peacaich sinn 'na fhianais
   Gheall E fialaidh dhuinn a thròcair;
Chruthaich E sinn fhéin 'na ìomhaigh
   'S phàigh E ar fiachan mòra
Air a' chrann 's an lann 'na chliathaich
   'S na tàirnean an fhreumh a mheòirean.

54 *Motor-Boat Heillsgeir*

Soraidh leis a' bhàta a dh'fhàg leinn Port Ròigh
'S a chaidh leinn gu Màisgeir sàbhailte tron cheò;
Faoileag gheal an t-sàile fàlaireachd mu sròin,
Pliuthannan dhan phràisich oirre 'n àite sheòl.

A' dol seachad Stocaigh, cop oirre le spàirn,
Hìobhairean ag osnaich 's iad gun fhois gun tàmh,
Suaile trom gu socair leigeil roc am bàrr
'S nuallan aig gach oitir, roladh moil 's ga chnàmh.

Dol timcheall na h-Easgainn feasgar greannach fuar
Sann leam fhìn bu leisg e dol a shreap ri stuaigh,
Marannan a' cleasachd, tighinn on deas gu tuath,
Sùil air son na h-Eiste, 's eagal oirnn ro gruaim.

Sruth is gaoth a' còmhstri sa chòmhrag ri chéil' —
Cha robh 'n coltas bòidheach dol gam pògadh fhéin;
Clann Dòmhnaill mo luaidh ann ri guaillibh a-chéil',
Bristeadh geal mu sròin ga còmhdach as a déidh.

Ghabh i ris an fhuaradh, bhuail i ann le spàirn,
Gun d'sgoilt i le a gualainn rathad fuar fon t-sàl;
Dh'éirich i mar fhaoileag air a faobhar àrd,
Cuideam air a sliasaid, fiaradh air a sàil.

Seonaidh Mòr ga stiùireadh, 's gun robh shùil cho geur
Ri caiptean air criùsair dol a dh'ionnsaigh euchd;
Bha mise 's mi crùbadh ann an cùil leam fhéin,
'S an crodh ris an taobhstoc air an taodadh réidh.

But ask yourselves will God permit it —
　　This dreadful destruction coming on us;
Though we're sinners in His sight
　　Generously He promised us His mercy;
In His image He created us
　　And paid for us our greatest debts
On the cross with the lance in His side
　　And the nails in the root of His fingers.

The Heisgeir Motor-Boat

Farewell to the boat that left Port Ròigh with us
And went with us to Màisgeir safely through the mist;
The white crest of the ocean dancing round her prow,
With flippers of brass on her instead of sails.

Going past Stocaigh, foam on her with effort,
Heaving combers moaning, restless on the move,
A heavy swell gently bringing tangle to the surface
With all the shallows howling, rolling shingle and grinding it.

Going round the 'Eel' on a cold surly evening
It's I who was reluctant to face up to its waves,
Seas wrestling with each other, coming south to north,
Looking out for the Eist, we were afraid of its menace.

Wind and current wrestling in combat with each other —
They looked far from pretty moving in for the kiss;
My darling MacDonalds standing shoulder to shoulder,
White breakers at her bow raining down further aft.

She drove on to windward, struck with all her might,
Split with her forebreast a cold path through the brine;
She soared up like a seagull with her bow held high,
With her weight to one side, and her keel at a slant.

Big Johnnie steered her, and his eye was as sharp
As a cruiser captain's when sailing into battle;
I was crouched in a corner all by myself
With the cattle at the gunwale tethered neatly in line.

Chan eil gheat no criùsair no té shiùil fon ghréin
Gheibh 'nad uisge stiùrach 's tu fo shùrd do cheum;
Bidh iad dèanamh cùrs' ort, 'n dùil gum bi sibh réidh —
Fàgaidh tu gun diù iad is siùbhlaidh tu leat fhéin.

Copar agus cruaidhe fuaigheilte gu réidh,
Cnòintean air an uachdar gus nach gluais 's nach géill,
Peatarail gun sòradh, fuaim a bòrd gu treun,
Bataraidh ga suathadh is sradag uaine leum.

Ach thug mise bòidean nach seòlainn gu bràth
'S nach dèanainn a' bhòidse leis na seòid a bhà —
Ged a bha iad eòlach 's a Chlann Dòmhnaill àd,
Cha robh liad mo bhròige dhan chuairt-bheòil am bàrr.

Seumas MacThòmais (1888–1971)

55   *A' Ghaoth*

Anail chaoin tha siubhal mall
      'S nach fhaic mo shùil ri m' bheò,
Cuin a thòisich d' imeachd fann,
      'S an ruig thu d' uidh' air chòir?

Bheil cabhag ann am fannan speur
      Nach fan ri òrdugh rìgh?
Bheil dàn an tòir air slighe cheum'
      Gun tòiseachadh gun chrìch?

Nan innseadh tu gach sealladh faoin
      A chunnaic thu le d' shùil,
Nan aithriseadh gach facal baoth,
      Gach gealladh is sgeul-rùin,

Nach mòr an caoidh, nach buan an cràdh
      A mhosgladh ann an crìdh
Gach neach le mithich a bhith ghnàth
      'Na ionracan 's an sìth!

Ach dh'imich thu le athais bhuan
      Thar chluaintean gorm' an fheòir,
Is dh'fhalaich thu ad' chridhe suairc
      Gach gealladh baoth is bòid.

No yacht nor cruiser nor sailing-boat exists
Which can catch your rudder-wake when you're well under way;
They'll set a course for you, assuming you'll be easy —
But you'll leave them looking silly and press on by yourself.

Copper and steel amalgamated smoothly,
With nuts on their surface so they'll not shift or yield,
Petrol unstinting, her boards vibrating loudly,
Battery brought to life with green spark leaping.

But I have made a promise not to sail again
Or to make the voyage with the heroes of the day —
Despite their experience and for all they were MacDonalds,
Not the width of my shoe of the gunwale-board was showing.

James Thomson (Tong, Lewis)

The Wind

O gentle breath that slowly blows
　　Which my eye will never see,
When did your weak motion start,
　　And will you reach your goal all right?

Is there haste in the breeze aloft
　　Which awaits no king's command?
Does fate pursue it in its track
　　With no beginning or end?

If you told every foolish sight
　　You've observed with your eye,
Repeated every simple word,
　　Every promise, every secret,

Great were the grief, and lasting the pain,
　　That would awake in the heart
Of all whose time it is to know
　　Righteousness in peace!

But off you went in perpetual ease
　　Over pastures green with growth,
And in your gentle heart concealed
　　Each idle promise and oath.

Dòmhnall Mac an t-Saoir (1889–1964)

56   bho *Aeòlus agus am Balg*

Chunnaic mise bliadhna reimhid
   'S thug i leatha oirnn am fiar;
Cha do dh'fhàg i bior air balla,
   Sop air machair no air sliabh.

"Mas e màirnealaiche mise
   Tha nas miosa tighinn on iar,
Stoirm nach fhaca mac a rugadh" —
   'S dìreach mar a thubhairt, b' fhìor.

Thàinig dorchadas is ceò,
   Dhlùthaich neòil ri talamh glas;
Shaoileadh daoine gun robh ghrian
   Air an iarmailt a' dol ás.

Shéid i on iar-dheas is an uair sin
   (Is diocair dhòmhsa luadh an rann)
Sgread is fead na gaoithe cruaidh,
   Gaoir nach cuala cluas ach gann.

Iorghail uabhasach nan tonn,
   Le'm bilean crom a-steach gu tràigh,
Osnaich balg-séididh Aeòluis
   Gan toirt beò gu ceòthach bàn.

Dh'éirich suas gach sìlean gainmhich,
   Rùisg a' mhealbhach chun nan cnàmh,
Caorann is caol-dubh gan spìonadh
   Is an fhreumhaichean an sàs.

Cha robh bior air tobhta taighe,
   Taobhan no cabar no spàrr
Nach robh falbh aice 'na fiaclan
   Mar gum falbhadh ian le sràbh.

Chluinnte clachan-moil an aigeal
   Ann an aganaidh a' bhàis
'S iad a' bruanadh ris a' chladach,
   Air an cagnadh 's air an cnàmh.

Donald Macintyre (Snishival, S. Uist)

from *Æolus and the Bellows*

Once before I saw a year
　　When it took away our hay;
Not a rafter left on wall,
　　Nor wisp on machair or on hill.

"If I'm weather-wise at all
　　There's worse still coming from the west,
Storm that no son born has seen" —
　　And what was said was just what happened.

There came darkness, there came mist,
　　Clouds and soil rolled into one,
It seeemed to people that the sun
　　Had been extinguished in the sky.

It blew from south of west, and then
　　(It's hard for me to say in verse)
The screech and howl of vicious wind,
　　A cry like ear has seldom heard.

The dreadful tumult of the waves,
　　Their curling edges rolling beachward,
The sough as Æolus' bellows-bag
　　Turned them into live white mist.

Every grain of sand arose,
　　Stripping sand-dunes to the bone,
Rowan and small black willow plucked
　　Leaving roots stuck in the ground.

There wasn't a stick on the wall of a house
　　Not a beam nor a rafter or joist
That it didn't bear off between its teeth
　　As a bird might carry a straw.

You heard the shingle of the deep
　　In the agony of death
Being pounded hard against the shore,
　　Pulverised and turned to dust.

Mothar ann am bial gach uamha,
    Feadain a' cur suas 'nan spùt,
'S na h-eich bhàna teachd le turtar
    'S càch gam putadh air an cùl.

Ri bathais chloiche a' bualadh,
    'S a' tilleadh le nuallan garbh,
Bùirean aig corrain gan riasladh —
    Theich gach iasg a b' urrainn falbh.

Feusgain a' dinneadh an corrag
    Anns gach sgàineadh, sgor is eag,
Crith 'na slige air a' bhàirnich
    'S greim a bàis aic' air a' chreig.

Neiptiun a' brosnachadh 'armachd,
    A chuip mu'n earball 's mu'n ceann,
'S a chridhe sracadh le farmad —
    Cia air son a bhiodh Albainn ann?

Cuim' a dh'fhanainn air mo chrìochan?
    Cuim' nach leudaichear mo ghart?
Cuim' nach buannaichear an saoghal
    'S gun téid daonnan neart thar cheart?

57 *Thug mi 'n oidhche raoir glé shàmhach*

Thug mi 'n oidhche raoir glé shàmhach,
Thug mi 'n oidhche raoir gun diog
'S mi 'g éisteachd ri Móir bhig 's ri màthair,
    Thug mi 'n oidhche raoir glé shàmhach.

Feasgar geamhraidh 'n tùs na bliadhna,
Toiseach contraigh 's gaoith an-iardheas,
Chaidh mi mach dhan bheinn a dh'iasgach
    'S mi gun sìon leis a' bhuntàta.

Thug mi 'n oidhche raoir ag éisteachd
Ris na teangannan bu ghéire,
Bha iad a' cànran le chéile
    Coingeis am Beurla is an Gàidhlig.

A booming sound in every cave-mouth,
　　Streams being swollen into spouts,
White horses racing to the shore
　　As others push them from behind.

Striking the surface of a stone,
　　Bouncing back with raucous snarl,
Roar of sandspits being tortured —
　　Every fish that could has fled.

While the mussels wedge their fingers
　　In each crevice, notch and gap,
The limpet's shell's reduced to trembling
　　With death-like grip upon the rock.

Neptune's urging on his army,
　　His whip is on their tails and heads,
His heart is torn apart by envy —
　　Scotland, why should she exist at all?

Why should I stay within my bounds?
　　Why should my field not be enlarged?
Why should the whole world not be won
　　That might may always conquer right?

I spent last night very quiet

I spent last night very quiet,
I spent last night without a sound
Listening to little Mór and her mother,
　　I spent last night very quiet.

On a winter's night in the start of the year,
Neaptide beginning with a south-west wind,
I went out to the hills to fish
　　As I'd nothing to eat with the potatoes.

I spent last night listening
To the sharpest tongues of them all,
They were bickering with each other
　　As much in English as in Gaelic.

Teangannan sgaiteach gu còmhradh,
'S iad ag obair cearta còmhla,
'S chanadh aon té gu leòr dhiubh
    Ged nach tòisicheadh na dhà dhiubh.

S ioma rud a chuala mise
Bh' ann an duathar 's nach robh fios air —
Leag iad seann taigh Anna Shiosail,
    'S reic Iain Friseal an t-each spàgach.

Chuala mi mu ioma iongnadh
'S rud a bh' ann mu thùs an t-saoghail,
Aimhreitean bhiodh eadar dhaoine
    'S mar a bhreab Iain Maor an càidsear.

Chuala mi mu Chnoc nan Dos
'S cho àrd 's a mharcaich Mìcheal Scot
'S mar a thog an sluagh Niall Sgrob
    'S a dh'fhàg iad e aig gob Tràigh Bhàlaigh.

Dh'inns iad dhomh gach òirleach shìoda
A bh' aig MacLeòid sa bhratach shidhe,
'S mar chaidh Lachlann Mòr a dh'Ìle
    'S mar a loisg Dubh-Sìth air làmhach.

Chuala mi mun Chìrean Chròin
'S mun mheudachd a bhiodh anns an t-seòrsa —
Nam biodh 'earball aig an Òban
    Bhiodh a shròn aig Loch a' Chàrnain.

Gun robh 'n giolcam-daobhram sìnte
Ri bacan iosgaid na frìde
'S gun robh birlinn aig MacNìll
    'S nach robh e 'n taing bhith 'm broinn na h-Àirce.

Fhuair mi sgial mu Fhéill na Manchainn
'S cus de dh'òrain Iain Mhic Fhearchair,
'S chuala mi mu smuais na deargainn
    'S b'e mo ghalghad aig leum àrd i!

'S mar a bha Horus anns an Éipheit
'S mu fhuamhaire mòr na Gréige
'S mar a bha Crom Cruach an Éirinn
    'S daoine sleuchdadh air a' bhlàr.

Tongues scathing in conversation,
Working away simultaneously,
And one of them would say enough
    Even if the two of them didn't start.

It's many a thing I heard
That was unknown and in obscurity —
They've knocked down Anne Chisholm's old house,
    And John Fraser's sold the ungainly horse.

I heard of many a phenomenon
And much about the world's beginning,
Quarrels that folk would have
    And how John the Officer kicked the pedlar.

I heard about the battle of Knocknanoss
And how high was the ride of Michael Scot
And how Niall Sgrob was raised by the fairy host
    And left at the point of Vallay Strand.

They described to me every inch of silk
That MacLeod had in the fairy flag,
And how Lachlann Mór went to Islay
    And Duffie fired a shot at him.

I heard about the 'Crest from Hell'
And the size the species was —
If his tail were at Oban
    His nose would be at Loch Carnan.

That the animalcule nestled
In the curve of the fleshmite's hough,
And that MacNeil had a galley
    And had no need to be inside the Ark.

I got a story of Beauly Fair
And many songs by John MacCodrum,
And I heard about the strength of the flea
    And how she'd be my champion at the high jump!

And all about Horus in Egypt
And about the great giant of Greece
And all about Crom Cruach in Ireland
    With people prostrate on the ground.

Chuala mi gun deach Niall Bhuacair
Seachad le eallach a ghuailleadh
'S dh'fhàg e litir aig taigh Ruairidh
     'S eil fhios 'am fhìn có bhuaith' a bhà i?

Dh'inns iad mu Dhi-Dòmhnaich Caingis,
Mu Shàtan 's mar a thuit na h-ainglean,
'S mar chaidh athair Diùc Tharantum
     Null dhan Fhraing le Prionnsa Teàrlach.

Dh'inns iad mu Thuatha Dé Danann
'S mar thugadh an t-ainm air Manainn
'S chàin iad Seòras Dubh Both-Chanain
     A chionn bhith càineadh Banrigh Màiri.

Chuala mi mun torc 's mu Dhiarmad
'S mun bhòcan a bh' aig Loch Fhiarais
'S mar as e Peadair a' chiad fhear
     A chualas a bhith riamh 'na Phàpa.

Bha iad a' farraid dhe chéile
Co dhiùbh b' aosta Maois no Àron,
'S dé chuir Nebuchadnèasair
     Feadh na spréidh air a mhàgan.

Chuala mi mun iomairt lann
'S mar ghleac na famhairean aig Gabhra
'S mun fhear mhór a bh' air a' bhranndair
     Ceangailte le slabhraidh phràisich.

Dh'fhalbh mi ás mu mheadhan oidhche
An déidh na h-eachdraidhean a chluinntinn
     'S mar a chaidh mo cheann cho aimhreidh,
     Theab mi 'm pocan sùghain fhàgail!

58 *Aoir Mhusolìnidh*

Is aighearach leam fhìn mar tha gluasadan,
Mar tha Musolìnidh air fuarachadh.
     Thàinig e le sgraing
     Chogadh ris an Fhraing
'S cha robh gainne cainnteadh an uair sin air.

I heard that Neil Walker had gone
Past with his shoulder-sack
And left a letter at Roddy's house
    And do I know myself who it was from?

They told of Whitsunday,
About Satan and how the angels fell,
And how the Duke of Tarentum's father
    Went over to France with Prince Charlie.

They spoke about the Tuatha De Danann
And how the Isle of Man was named
And criticised Black George Buchanan
    Because he criticised Queen Mary.

I heard about the boar and Diarmad
And about the spectre of Loch Fhiarais,
And how St Peter is the first man
    Ever heard to have been Pope.

They were asking of each other
Whether Moses or Aaron was the older,
And what sent Nebuchadnezzar
    On all fours among the cattle.

I heard about the clash of swords
And how the giants fought at Gabhra
And of the big man on the gridiron
    Fastened down with chain of brass.

About midnight I took my leave
After hearing all the tales
And so disordered had my head gone,
    I nearly left the bag of sowens!

In Dispraise of Mussolini

I'm delighted how things have been going,
How Mussolini's out stiff as a poker.
    He came with a snarl
    To make war against France
And there was no lack of prattle in him then.

Thug e dhi bho cùl
Buille, tha mi 'n dùil,
Nach dèanadh a' mhiùl na bu shuaraiche —
Dùil aige san àm
Leis na caran cam
Gum faigheadh e dram aig an uaigh aice.

S beag a bha 'na bheachd nuair a bhuail e
Gun amaiseadh a ghleac bhith cho cruaidh dha.
Nach ann a bha 'na smaoin
Gun dèanadh e maoin
'S gun robh sinne air claonadh 'nar cruadalas.
Cha b'ann leis a' cheart
No idir le neart
Bu mhath leis am beartas a bhuannachd,
Ach colann bhith air bòrd
Is falairidh ga h-òl,
Siud an rud a chòrd ris, nan d'fhuair e e:

Leis an smigid mhóir a' cur bhuaithe
'S a' bruidhinn gus na bhodhair e ar cluasan,
A' bladaireachd 's a' bòst
Le clabastair beòil
'S teang' urad ri rò-seol sgoth thuathach,
'S an glagair' air each mòr,
Blaigeard na Roinn Eòrp',
Leithid sin de ròpladh cha chualas —
De sgailceadh leis an dòrn,
Slacaireachd ri bòrd,
Chan fhacas ri clò air cléith luaidh e.

'S e dol a chur na Fraingeadh 'na fuairnean
'S am fuigheall bhith gu fang air am fuadach
Dhe cladaichean 's dhe còrsa,
Dhe talamh is dhe còir,
Pìosan mòra mòr a thoirt bhuaipe
Gus ise chur gu bròn
Is esan a thighinn beò
Gu itheadh, gu òl is gus cur bhuaithe,
Gus cinneachadh dha phòr
Is sinne bhith fo spòig —
Sin agaibh na h-òrduighean nuadh agaibh.

From behind he bestowed
Upon her a blow
That not even a mule could excel for nastiness —
He supposed at the time
Sly tricks of that kind
Would get him a dram at her funeral.

Little did he reckon when he struck
That his assault would rebound so hard on him.
All he could think of
Was the money he would make
And how we had declined from our hardihood.
It wasn't by right
Or in any way by might
That he liked to earn his riches,
But with a corpse on the table
While folk drink the entertainment,
That's what he liked, if he could get it:

With enormous chin spitting forth
And talking till he deafened our ears,
Bawling and boasting
With a babbler of a mouth
And a tongue like a Norway skiff's topsail,
Prattler on big horse,
The blackguard of Europe,
Such vapouring has never been heard —
Such banging with the fist,
Beating on a board,
Was never seen with tweed on any waulking-frame.

As he tried to tie France to his warping-pin
While the leavings were driven to a fank
From her shores and her coast,
Her land and her property,
Taking big big pieces off her
To put her into mourning
And keep him alive
For eating, drinking and relieving himself,
To make his seed prosper
While we're under his thumb —
So there now you have your new orders.

Chruinnich e gu crìch gus a cuartachadh
Muilleanan is mìltean de shluagh aige
    'S troichein air an cinn,
    Isein deireadh linn,
Siud an rud a bhruidhneadh gu tuasaideach!
    Shaoilinn air a ghlòir
    ('S nach mò e na 'n dòrn)
Gun cuireadh e fògairt air fuamhaire —
    Bragadaich 's a' leum
    Is barail aig' air fhéin,
Fead is fuich is éibh, s fhad bho chual' thu e.
    Theagamh gum b'e spòrs,
    Bleidireachd is bòst,
Bheadagan le bhrògan gu chruachainn air;
    Breabadaich gun dòigh,
    Leibidean gun treòir,
Leagadh tu le d' mheòir air an suathadh ris.

Tha e 'n-diugh 's a dhaoin' air an sguabadh air
Mar gum biodh fear daoraich san tuainealaich,
    Puth aig' air an raon,
    Sruth a' tighinn bho mhaol
'S e dubh-shuileach, caog-shuileach, cuaranach:
    'S e chuideachd bhios daor,
    Dàn luidealach maol
A thug air a dhaoine an droch uachdaran —
    Tharraing iad gu raon,
    'S gu achadh na caoidh,
Gu tachartas sgaoilidh an tualasan.

Esan culaidh smaointean gun bhuaidh air,
A' dalladh a chuid daoine le tuairisgeul,
    Leantainn na droch smaoin
    Le mearan a' chaoich
A chinnich na smaointeanan duatharra;
    Se as cumha dha fhéin
    Nach b'e an-diugh an-dé,
Se ghuth a bhiodh reusanta, stuaime ruinn —
    Cha chluinneamaid beum
    Bhon bhurraidh gun bheus
Le ghunna air a ghleusadh gu buaireanta;
    Nan cumadh e a chéill
    'S a thuineachas fhéin
Bu lurach an geum air a bhuaile ann,

He gathered to the border to encircle it
Millions and thousands of his army
    With a dwarf at their head,
    Last chicken of the brood,
That's what would speak aggressively!
    I'd imagine from his voice
    (And he no bigger than your fist)
That it would send a giant packing —
    Strutting and leaping
    With so much self-importance
That it's long since you've heard such wheech, whistle and bawl.
    Maybe it's a joke,
    Blethering and boast,
His pretty boy with boots to his thigh on him;
    Prancing pointlessly,
    A pithless scrounger,
You'd knock him down by rubbing your fingers on him.

Today with his people swept away from him
He's like a drunkard for staggering,
    Snorting on the ground,
    Bleeding from his brow
And he black-eyed, cross-eyed and bootless:
    It's the company that's costly,
    A sorry profitless destiny
That imposed the bad leader on his people —
    They drew up to a field,
    To the plain of lamenting,
To the place for the spreading of their slanders.

Astonishingly lacking in virtue,
He blinded his followers with propaganda,
    Following ill doctrine
    With delirium of madness
That gave rise to sinister principles;
    It's unfortunate for him
    That today was not yesterday,
When his voice seemed sober and reasonable to us —
    We'd have not heard a word
    From the ill-behaved ass
With his gun aimed provocatively;
    If he'd kept to his senses
    And his own place of residence
There'd be sweet lowing on his cowfold there,

Seach dubhachas cheud
Bho mhullach nan speur —
Is muladach an ceum air na ghluais e iad.

Bha toiseach mo shaoghail-sa tuaireapach,
S tric a bha mi 'm baoghal, 's a fhuair mi ás:
      Bha mi air an raon
      Maille ris gach aon
'S dh'amais mi ri faobhar na cruadhach ann.
      Chaidh mi ann an sàs
      An iomadach càs,
Bha guileag a' bhàis ann am' chluasan ann —
      Gu barriall nam bròg
      Am fuil nam fear òg,
Gun tioma, gun deòir, b' fhada bhuaithe mi,
      Ach is beag orm glaodh
      Eagail phàistean maoth,
Sgreadail mhnathan aost' agus ghruagach
      Gan leagail ri m' thaobh
      Is theab iad Mac an t-Saoir.

Bhreithnich mi air aoir ('s their mi duan oirre)
Don fhear thug am foradh mu chluasan
Le chlaidheamh nuair a thàirneadh bhon truaill e:
      Se gliogaire nan sglàmh,
      Ridire Rìgh Màrs,
Seanalair nam blàr nach robh buadhmhor;
      Se sgriosadair nan àgh,
      Inisg air gach ceàrn,
Glaoic as culaidh-nàire na tuatha,
      Tha miodalaich ri ceàrd
      An ionad ro-àrd
Seach innean na ceàrdach bu dualchas dha.

'S e mar choileach gnù-cheannach, gruamach,
A ghoireadh air a dhùnan gu h-uallach,
      Le guib a spuirean cùil
      A' sgròbadh an smùir
'S e bogadh na stiùrach gu tuasaid
      Le gog is guli-gùg
      De ghoileam gun tùr —
Ge b' oil leam, cha chunntainn na chuala mi
      'S a choilleag 'na spùt
      Á goile gun ghrunnd
Mu choireannan dùthaich nam fuar-bheannan:

Instead of hundredfold mourning
From the roof of the skies —
Sad is the path that he set them on.

The start of my own life was turbulent,
I was often in danger, but survived it:
  I experienced the trenches
  As everyone else did
And encountered the sharp end of steel there.
  I frequently met with
  All sorts of extremity,
With the cry of death in my ears there —
  I was up to my bootlaces
  In the blood of young men,
Desensitised, tearless and distanced from it,
  Yet the cry I detest
  Is that of children in terror,
The screaming of old women and girls
  Being laid low at my side
  When they missed Macintyre.

I've devised a satire (and I'll put it into rhyme)
To the man who brought things crumbling round his ears
With his sword when it was drawn from the scabbard:
  He's the spouter of harangues,
  The Knight of King Mars,
The unvictorious battle commander;
  He's destroyer of joys,
  The disgrace of each place,
A bumpkin embarrassing the peasantry,
  Who sweet-talks some tinker
  In a place far exalted
From the blacksmith's anvil he was used to.

Like a rooster was he, po-faced and grim,
Who'd crow with such pride on his dunghill,
  The points of his hind claws
  Scratching the dust
While he ruffled his tail for the cockfight
  With a cock-a-doodle-doo
  Of complete ballyhoo —
Though disgusted, I'd not heed what I heard
  With his words tumbling out
  From a bottomless stomach
About the crimes of the land of cold mountains:

Bha sinne gun diù,
Fodha dheth co-dhiù,
Cha b' aithne dhuinn Iùdhaich a ruagadh
No smugaid chur 'nan sùil
No 'n cuid a thoirt dhiùbh.

Bilean beul-gun-fhàitheam a' fuaimneach'
Cho fileanta ri snàthad beairt-fhuaigheil,
Gun ghuth aig' ach a' gairm
Mu chumhachd 's mu airm,
Spriolag agus toirmeasg ga bhualadh,
Air bhiogairne gus falbh
An ugainn nan Dearg
'S chugainne le carbad na tuaighe
'S gum biomaid aige marbh
'S ar luingeas ga sealg
Thar mullach nam fairgeachan uaine.

Gun robh ochd muillean béigleid de chruaidh aige,
Cha tigeadh na Greugaich san fhuaradh air
Gus an deach e ann
Is, am bumailear fann,
Cha chumadh e cheann air a ghuaillean ann —
Chaith iad e dhan dìg
Is lathais air a dhruim,
Shalaich iad a chìrean 's a shuaicheantas;
Chabhagaich e buinn
Gus gléidheadh a chinn
'S chan fhaigheadh e cuidhteas na ruagairean:
Bha iad as a dhéidh
Mar fhaghaid an fhéidh
Bhiodh a' ruigheadh fhéithean gu luath-chasach
Le giorag 'na fheòil
Romh dhealann am beòil,
A' casachadh mòintich gu luasganach.

Ruitheadh e na glinn 's e gan cuartachadh,
Gan gearradh le sìnteagan uabhasach,
'S na fearaibh 'na luirg
Gus feannadh a' bhuilg
Mar gum biodh coin-sheilg 's madadh ruadh aca:
Thàinig iad mu cheann,
Thug iad ás na bh' ann,
Liodairt iad e, dh'fheann iad e, luairc iad e,

We were contemptible,
Beneath him in any case,
We'd no experience of persecuting Jews
Or spitting in their eye
Or confiscating their property.

Seamless-mouthed lips making noise
As fluently as sewing-machine needle,
With no message but shouting
About power and about armies,
A frustrated trouble-maker,
He'd be straining to set
At the Reds and ourselves
His fascist military machine
Till he'd have us all dead
And our fleet being pursued
Over the emerald wavetops.

Though he'd eight million bayonets of steel,
The Greeks wouldn't come where they'd smell him
Till he went there himself
And, weak bungler that he was,
Couldn't keep his head on his shoulders —
They threw him in the ditch
With a whip to his back
And muddied his coxcomb and insignia;
He hurried his steps
To preserve his head
But couldn't evade his pursuers:
They came at his heels
As if hunting the deer
That would stretch its sinews swift-footedly
With fear in its flesh
Of the baying of their mouths,
Traversing the moor with alacrity.

He ran from glen to glen to avoid them,
Taking short-cuts with leaps that were awesome,
With the men on his trail
For a stomach well flayed
Like hunting-dogs raising a fox:
They got him in a corner,
Stripped him of his all,
Beat him up, whipped him, knocked him down again,

Bhreab iad e mun bhreall,
Dh'fheadaraich iad rann
'S rinn iad maighstir dannsair nan cuaigean dheth
Gus an robh e mall,
Gus an robh e dall,
Gus an robh e call ma bha fual aige;
Dhroint iad air a dhroll,
Loint iad e sa pholl,
Spoth iad ás am ball a bha fuaighte ris,
Dh'fhàg iad smigid mhòr
Na bruidhinn 's na bòst
Gun urad de threòir ann 's gun gluaiseadh e,
'Na laighe ann an lòn,
Faghar air a shròin
'S 'aghaidh ris an Ròimh air a tuairneachadh.

59   Òran na Cloiche

I iù ro bha hó, e him bo hà,
E him bo ruaig thu i, e him bo hà;
I iù ro bha hó, e him bo hà.

A' Chlach a bha mo sheanmhair
'S mo sheanair oirre seanchas,
Air tilleadh mar a dh'fhalbh i —
Mo ghalghad a' Chlach!
'S gur coma leam i 'n Cearrara,
An Calasraid no 'n Calbhaigh
Cho fad 's a tha i 'n Albainn
Nan garbhlaichean cas'.
I iù ro bha hó, 7c.

Ga cur an àite tearmainn
A chumas i gu falchaidh
'S nach urrainn, nach dearg iad
Air sgealb dhith thoirt ás!
A' Chlach a chaidh a dhìth oirnn
Air faighinn ás an ingnean,
'S gu deimhinne ma thill i
Tha 'n nì sin gu math.
I iù ro bha hó, 7c.

Kicked him in the balls,
Then whistled up a tune
And made him play the splay-footed dancing-master
Till he went slow,
Till he went blind,
Till he was losing what piss was still in him;
Then they straightened out his back,
Rolled him in the mud,
Relieved him of the prick that was fixed to him,
And left the big chin
Of the blether and the swagger
Without enough strength in it for wagging,
Lying in a puddle
With a thump about his nose
And his face turned around towards Rome.

The Song of the Stone

I iù ro bha hó, e him bo hà,
E him bo ruaig thu i, e him bo hà;
I iù ro bha hó, e him bo hà.

The Stone that my grandmother
And grandfather spoke about,
Has come back as it went —
My darling's the Stone!
I don't care if it's in Kerrera,
In Callander or Calvay
As long as it's in Scotland
Of the steep high hills.
I iù ro bha hó, etc.

It's in a place of sanctuary
Which will hold it in secrecy
Where they can't or won't attempt
To take a chip of it away!
The Stone that was lost to us
Has been taken from their clutches,
And indeed if it's come back
It's a very good thing.
I iù ro bha hó, etc.

'S mo bheannachd air a' mhìlidh
A tharraing ás a' chill i,
'S a dh'aiseag, tha mi cinnteach,
          I mìltean a-mach;
A' Chlach a bha sna linntean
A' fantainn aig ar sinnsreadh
Bhon thàinig i dhan tìr seo
          An tìm nam fear breac.
I iù ro bha hó, 7c.

'S i measail ann bho ìslean
Gu ridirean is rìghrean
Tha 'n-diugh 'nan laighe 'n Ì
          Mar a dh'innseas an leac;
Gur iomadh baile fuadain
A dh'amais i air chuairt ann —
A' Chlach a bha cho buadhmhor
          Bu ruadh-bhuidhe dath.
I iù ro bha hó, 7c.

Nach faod mi tighinn mun cuairt
Air a buaidh, 's air a rath,
Bhon sguir i bhith 'na cluasaig
          Aig buachaill' a chleachd
Bhith cadal oirre suaimhneach,
'S a' faicinn ann am bruadar
Nan spioradan bho shuas
          A bhith nuas oirre teachd.
I iù ro bha hó, 7c.

'S mar thàinig i thar chuantan
Gum b' aithne do Choll' Uais i,
Bha treis aig Olla Ruadh dhi
          'S aig Duanach mac Earc;
'S car son a bhiomaid suarach
'S a leigeamaide bhuainn i
'S a liuthad àit' a bhuannaich
          Air chuairt dhi bhith ac'?
I iù ro bha hó, 7c.

Ma thàinig a' Chlach bhuadhach
Bho aiseirigh na h-uaghach,
Tha tamhasg Uilleam Uallais
          A' buannachd a' chath;

And my blessing on the warrior
Who dragged it from the churchyard,
Transporting it, I'm certain,
　　　Many miles away;
The Stone that for centuries
Had been with our ancestors
Since it entered this country
　　　In the time of painted men.
I iù ro bha hó, etc.

It was revered by common folk
And also knights and kings
Who now lie in Iona
　　　As their tombstone proclaims;
Through many vanished townships
It passed upon its tour —
The Stone that had such power
　　　With its reddish-yellow hue.
I iù ro bha hó, etc.

May I not now describe it
As powerful, effective,
Since it ceased to be a pillow
　　　For a shepherd who kept it
To sleep on it soundly,
When he saw a vision
Of spirits from heaven
　　　Landing on its top.
I iù ro bha hó, etc.

And since it crossed the oceans
Colla Uais has known it,
Olla Ruadh had a while of it
　　　As did Duanach mac Erc;
So why should we be churlish
And let it out of our hands
When so many places
　　　Deserve to have it to stay?
I iù ro bha hó, etc.

If the lucky Stone has come
From the grave resurrected,
The ghost of William Wallace
　　　Is winning the battle;

Gur milis le mo chluasan
Gach lideadh mar a chual' iad
'S tha mise dèanamh duanaig
    'S i uabhasach math!
I iù ro bha hó, 7c.

Mionnan air fear deàrnaidh,
    Gach màthair is mac,
Nach leig sinn ann an gàbhadh
Am fear a thug á sàs i
'S a mheantraig air a teàrnadh
    Á àite gun tlachd;
Ma chuireas iad an làmh air
Chan fhuilear dhuinn bhith làidir
Is buill' thoirt air a shàilleabh
    Le stàilinn a-mach.
I iù ro bha hó, 7c.

Togamaid ar bàrdachd
    An àirde le snas
Dhan ghineal thug bhon Spàinnt i,
'S ma thilleas iad gu Sgàin i
Bidh duinealas ar nàisein
    Nas fheàrr ann am blas,
Bhon rib iad i bhon ghràisg
A bha suidhe oirr' le màsan —
'S tha tuilleadh aig na gàrlaich
    Ri thàrradh air n-ais.
I iù ro bha hó, 7c.

Tha ioma rud a bhàrr air
A' chloich a bh' ann an Sgàin,
A dhraghadh sinn á làmhan
    Nan sglàmhaichean glas;
An duine bhios a' tàmhachd
An cuideachd nam meàirleach,
Chan fhuilear dha gach àirneis
    A chàradh fo ghlais.
I iù ro bha hó, 7c.

'S bha 'm Ministear cho tùirseach
Sa mhadainn nuair a dhùisg e,
'S praban air a shùilean
    A' tionndadh a-mach:

Such music to my ears
Is each syllable they've heard
That I'm making a ditty
          Which is totally superb!
I iù ro bha hó, etc.

Let each wellwisher swear,
          Every mother and son,
That we don't put in danger
The man who set it free
And dared to bring it out
          From an unpleasant place;
If they arrest him
We will have to be strong
And strike a blow on his behalf
          With sword unsheathed.
I iù ro bha hó, etc.

Exaltedly in verse
          Let's praise the generation
Who brought it here from Spain,
If they return it to Scone
The manhood of our nation
          Will improve much in flavour,
Since they snatched it from the rabble
Who sat their buttocks on it —
And that's not the only thing
          The rascals should return.
I iù ro bha hó, etc.

There's much else again
About the Stone that was in Scone,
Which we'd drag from the hands
          Of the pale-faced usurpers;
The person who lives
In the company of thieves,
He must stow his furniture
          Under lock and key.
I iù ro bha hó, etc.

How wretched was the Minister
When he woke in the morning,
His eyes were all bleary
          When he got out of bed:

E coiseachd feadh an ùrlair
Ag ochanaich 's ag ùrnaigh
'S a' coimhead air a' chùil
      Anns an d'ionndrainn e 'Chlach.
I iù ro bha hó, 7c.

Sin far an robh stàrachd
'S an ruith air feadh an làir ann
Gun smid aige ri ràitinn
      Ach "Càit 'n deach a' Chlach?"
'S "A Mhoire, Mhoire Mhàthair,
Gu dé nì mis' a-màireach?
Tha fios a'm gum bi 'Bhànrighinn
      A' fàgail a beachd."
I iù ro bha hó, 7c.

Gun tuirt e 's dath a' bhàis air,
"Cha chreidinn-sa gu bràth e,
Gun togadh fear bho làr e
      Na b' àirde na speach;
Tha rudeigin an dàn dhomh,
'S gun cuidicheadh an t-Àgh mi —
Bha 'n duine thug á sàs i
      Cho làidir ri each!"
I iù ro bha hó, 7c.

'S cha ruitheadh e ach lùigeach,
Bha 'luigheinean a' lùbadh,
Bha crith a' tighinn 'na ghlùinean
      'S e tionndadh cho lag;
Chan fhaiceadh e le 'shùilean,
Chan fhaigheadh e fo mhùigean,
Le corraig no le lùdaig,
      An dùdach no 'n glag.
I iù ro bha hó, 7c.

Ach ràinig e na diùidich
A' burralaich 's a' bùirich,
"Tha breitheanas a' dlùthadh oirnn —
      Spùilleadh a' Chlach!"
'S bha Sasann air a dùsgadh
'S an cathair air a rùsgadh
'S oileadhag mu na diùnlaich
      A ghiùlain a' chreach.
I iù ro bha hó, 7c.

He walked up and down the floor
Moaning and praying
And staring at the corner
      From which the Stone had fled.
I iù ro bha hó, etc.

That's when he panicked
And ran up and down the floor
With no words coming out
      But "What's happened to the Stone?"
And "Mary, Mary Mother,
What tomorrow will I do?
I know that the Queen will
      Register her view."
I iù ro bha hó, etc.

Turning pale as death he said,
"I'd never believe it,
That any man could lift it
      Higher than a wasp;
Something's in store for me,
And may Providence help me —
The man who set it free
      Was as strong as a horse!"
I iù ro bha hó, etc.

He could only run shakily,
His legs buckled under him,
His knees started to quiver
      And he turned very weak;
His eyes couldn't see,
He couldn't find for eyebrows,
With forefinger or pinkie,
      The horn or the bell.
I iù ro bha hó, etc.

But he reached the timid persons
Lamenting and roaring,
"Judgement is close to us —
      The Stone has been pinched!"
And England was aroused
As their throne was stripped bare
With a hunt on for the heroes
      Who carried out the raid.
I iù ro bha hó, etc.

Earraidean gu siùbhlach
A' farraid feadh na dùthcha
Bho Ghlaschu gu Diùraigh,
    Bho Mhùideart gu Peairt,
'S cha leig iad bàrr an dùirn
A dhol seachad air an sùilean,
Cha leig iad inneal-ùillidh
    No brùid air 'm bi cairt.
I iù ro bha hó, 7c.

'S na h-earraidean is colg orr'
Bho sholas gu rath-dorcha
Gun fhois orr' ach a' sporghail
    'S a' forfhais a-mach;
'S ged ruigeadh iad am morghan
An grinneal Abhainn Orchaidh
'S ged thigeadh na Fir Bholga,
    Cha lorg iad a' Chlach.
I iù ro bha hó, 7c.

Tha Deasaich agus Tuathaich
A' ceileireadh gu h-uallach,
Air mhire leis an uabhar
    Gun d'fhuair sinn a' Chlach;
Nuair thàinig i á Éirinn
Bha cantanas mu déidhinn
Gum fanamaid ri chéile
    Ma ghléidh sinn a' Chlach.
I iù ro bha hó, 7c.

'S nam faigheamaid le réit' i
Cha rachamaid san éirig,
Sann againne bha reusan
    Bhith 'g éigheach, "Mo chreach!"
Ach b' ainneoineach an ceum leoth' e,
'S b' annasach leam fhéin e —
Se barrantas an treud ud
    Gach seud thoirt a-mach.
I iù ro bha hó, 7c.

Ged ghealladh iad le'm beul e,
Cha dèanadh iad d'a réir sin —
An car a bha sa Bheurla
    Gur léir do gach neach.
I iù ro bha hó, 7c.

The police hurry on
Enquiring nationwide
From Glasgow to Jura,
     From Moidart to Perth,
And they don't let a fist's breadth
Escape examination,
They don't miss a motor-car
     Or an animal with a cart.
I iù ro bha hó, etc.

So angry policemen
Spend the length of a moon
Restlessly investigating
     And pursuing enquiries;
Even if they reached the gravel
At the bottom of the Orchy
And the Fir Bholga came,
     They won't find the Stone.
I iù ro bha hó, etc.

Lowlanders and Highlanders
Are celebrating mightily,
Rejoicing with pride
     That we've recovered the Stone;
When it came from Ireland
Word went round about it
That we'd stay together
     If we kept the Stone.
I iù ro bha hó, etc.

If we got it by agreement
We'd seek no compensation,
We certainly had reason
     To cry out, "Alas!"
But they were unwilling,
And I'd find it surprising —
It's the mark of that company
     To seize every prize.
I iù ro bha hó, etc.

Though they gave their promise orally,
They wouldn't act accordingly —
Their trickery of language
     Was clear to everyone.
I iù ro bha hó, etc.

60 *Nuair chaidh a' Chlach a Thilleadh*

Tha tigh'nn fodham, fodham, fodham,
Tha tigh'nn fodham, fodham, fodham,
Tha tigh'nn fodham, fodham, fodham,
    Tha tigh'nn fodham speuradh.

S mìchiatach le seanchaidhean
Feadh ìslich agus gharbhlaichean
Gun thill sibh Clach nan Albannach
    Gu ceannbhaile na Beurla.
Tha tigh'nn fodham, 7c.

Nuair leig sibh sìos gu'n nàimhdean i,
A' ghnìomh a bhios gu caillte dhuibh,
An robh sìol nan sonn gun chainnt aca
    'S na traoidhtearan ag eubhach?
Tha tigh'nn fodham, 7c.

Thig dìobhairt 'nan cuid uaghannan
Air sinnsreadh sìol nam fuarbheannan
Bhon shìn sibh dha'r luchd-fuath i
    A thug bhuaibh i leis an eucoir.
Tha tigh'nn fodham, 7c.

Tha ioma linn bhon spùill iad i
'S bhon dh'ìslich iad ri ùrlar i;
Mas rìoghail iad, ar liùmsa
    Gur e biùthas nam fear-bréige.
Tha tigh'nn fodham, 7c.

Se comharradh na rìoghalachd
Bhith gluasad seasrach fìrinneach,
'S gun dearbh am facal sgrìobhta
    Nach do dh'inntrig e fo léintean.
Tha tigh'nn fodham, 7c.

Nan d'fhuair mi fo mo mheòirean i
Nuair thàinig maor an tòir oirre,
Mum biodh i saor 's an t-òrd agam
    Bhiodh Seòras gun a dhéideag.
Tha tigh'nn fodham, 7c.

When the Stone was Returned

It behoves me, hoves me, hoves me,
It behoves me, hoves me, hoves me,
It behoves me, hoves me, hoves me,
    It behoves me to swear.

Historians are horrified
In Lowlands and in Highlands
That you've returned the Scottish People's Stone
    To the English-language capital.
It behoves me, etc.

When you released it to their enemies,
The deed that's your undoing,
Was the race of heroes speechless
    While the traitors cried for joy?
It behoves me, etc.

The cold-mountain people's ancestors
Will vomit in their graves
Since you gave it to your enemies
    Who wrongly took it from you.
It behoves me, etc.

It's a long time since they stole it
And lowered it to the floor;
If they're royal, it's my opinion
    That it's impostors' fame.
It behoves me, etc.

It's the mark of royalty
To move firmly and truthfully,
So the written word will show
    It came in under nobody's shirts.
It behoves me, etc.

If I'd got my hands on it
When the police came after it,
Before I'd finished with my hammer
    George would have lost his toy.
It behoves me, etc.

B'e Clach na Rìoghachd Albannaich
Tromh ioma linn is aimsir i,
'S mun sìninn do MhacCarmaig i
     Gun sgealbainn ás a-chéil' i.
Tha tigh'nn fodham, 7c.

Na suinn a chaidh ga h-eadraiginn,
Cha d'rinn iad ach an dleastanas,
'S bidh alladh oirbh am-feasta
     Nach do theasraig sibh fo'r sgéith iad.
Tha tigh'nn fodham, 7c.

Cha dèan Goill no Cùmhnantaich
Ach cleas nan rìghrean Stiùbhartach:
Thoir stoidhleadh Linne-an-Dùin dhaibh
     'S bidh an cùlaibh ri Dùn Éideann.
Tha tigh'nn fodham, 7c.

Cha rachainn fad mo bhuinn leotha,
Cha ruith iad cùrsa dìreach leibh,
Ach lùbaidh iad cho cinnteach
     'S a nì saoidhean air na h-éibhlean.
Tha tigh'nn fodham, 7c.

Sa h-uile cùis a chrom oirnn
'S a bhrùchd le buille throm oirnn,
Bha Cùmhnantaich is Crombalaich
     An companas a-chéile.
Tha tigh'nn fodham, 7c.

A shìol nan sonn 's nan àrdbheannan,
Na dèanaibh bann gu bràth riutha —
Cha sheas iad lom no làrach leibh,
     'S bha bhlàth aig Inbhir Chéitein.
Tha tigh'nn fodham, 7c.

Tha Albainn bhochd gun dòigh oirre,
Gun cheannabhaidh a bheir dòchas dhi
Bhon shearg air Craobh nan Dòmhnallach
     'S bhon dh'òl iad an deoch-sgléipidh.
Tha tigh'nn fodham, 7c.

It was the Scottish Kingdom's Stone
Through many an age and epoch,
And before I gave it to MacCormick
    I'd split it apart.
It behoves me, etc.

The heroes that released it,
They only did their duty,
And it will always be remembered
    How you failed to protect them.
It behoves me, etc.

Lowland Scots and Covenanters
Do the same as Stuart kings:
Give them a London title
    And their back's to Edinburgh.
It behoves me, etc.

I wouldn't go the length of my sole with them,
They won't run a straight course with you,
But they'll bend just as surely
    As a cuddy on the coals.
It behoves me, etc.

In each crisis that befell us
And burst with heavy blow on us,
Covenanters and Cromwellians
    Kept each other's company.
It behoves me, etc.

O race of heroes and high mountains,
Never ever make a pact with them —
They'll defend no hill or dale with you,
    As was seen at Inverkeithing.
It behoves me, etc.

Poor Scotland's in disarray,
With no leader to inspire her
Since Clan Donald's tree declined
    And they drank the drink of others.
It behoves me, etc.

61   *Bùth Dhòmhnaill 'IcLeòid*

E horo Chaluim Mhòir, thugainn còmh' rium gu dram
Nunn a bhùth Dhòmhnaill 'IcLeòid 's gheibh sinn stòpan de leann,
'S nuair a bhios sinn ga òl s math a chòrdas sinn ann,
Bidh ar n-inntinn air ceòl 's cha bhi òrain oirnn gann
       Ann am bùth Dhòmhnaill 'IcLeòid.

Bidh an seòmar cho blàth, bidh an t-àite cho briagh,
Air an ùrlar fo'r bonn dathan donn, dubh is liath;
Chì thu putan beag bàn air am fàisg thu do mhiar,
Thig fear-freasgairt mun cuairt 's na bheil bhuat a chur sìos
       Air do bhialaibh air bòrd.

Dhe gach seòrs' a théid òl bidh gu leòr fo do shùil,
Fear a' lìonadh nan stòp 's a' cur cròic air an liunn,
Chì thu fìon thig on Spàinnt, oirr' air fhàgail co-dhiù,
'S chì thu eun ann an cèidse shuas gu h-àrd os do chionn
       Ann am bùth Dhòmhnaill 'IcLeòid.

Chì thu togsaidean bhuat, bidh iad suas air an ceann,
Chì thu goc anns gach té leth na réiseadh o 'bonn,
Fear tha freasgairt na bùth tighinn gad ionnsaigh le dram,
'S their e 'n t-airgead a-nunn 's their e mùthadh a-nall
       Ann am bùth Dhòmhnaill 'IcLeòid.

Chì thu dìsnean is tàileasg gan càradh air bùird,
Bidh gach nì mar as còir eadar Dòmhnall 's a' bhùth,
Gheibh thu pàipear ri leughadh le speuclair dha d' shùil,
'S chì thu staidhre dol sìos, àit bhios riatanach dhuinn
       Ann am bùth Dhòmhnaill 'IcLeòid.

Gheibh thu searbhadair shìos, gheibh thu siabann is bùrn,
'S los gum falmhaich thu 'mhias tog a' chìochag 'na grunnd;
Chì thu sgàthan is cìr 's rud a shlìobas a-nunn
'S a their loinn air do cheann ged bhiodh sgall air gu chùl
       Ann am bùth Dhòmhnaill 'IcLeòid.

Ann am bùth Dhòmhnaill 'IcLeòid bidh gach seòrs' innte cruinn
Thig o thaobh Abhainn Chluaidh 's cuid tha nuas ás na glinn;
Bidh a' chàbraid cho cruaidh ann an cluasan do chinn
'S ged bhiodh bàrd ris gach gualainn dhiot 's fuaim ac' air seinn
       Ann am bùth Dhòmhnaill 'IcLeòid.

Donald MacLeod's Pub

E horo Big Malky, come on with me for a dram
Over to Donald MacLeod's pub to have a glass of beer,
And while we're drinking it it's well we'll agree there,
Our minds will be on music and we'll have plenty of songs
   In Donald MacLeod's pub.

The room will be so warm, the place will be so grand,
On the floor under our soles colours brown, black and blue;
You'll see a little white button that you press with your finger,
A waiter comes round to put down what you want
   On the table before you.

Of each kind people drink there is plenty to see,
A man filling the stoups and putting foam on the beer,
You'll see wine come from Spain, or so it is said,
And you'll see a bird in a cage upon high overhead
   In Donald MacLeod's pub.

You'll see hogsheads somewhere, they'll be upon their ends,
You'll see a tap in each one halfway up from its base,
The man who serves in the pub coming over with a dram
And he takes in the money and gives out the change
   In Donald MacLeod's pub.

You'll see dice and board-games placed upon tables,
Everything will be proper between Donald and the pub,
You'll get a paper to read with spectacles for your eye
And you'll see a stair going down, a place essential for us
   In Donald MacLeod's pub.

You'll find a towel down there, you'll find soap and water,
And to empty the basin lift the valve in its bottom;
You'll see mirror and comb and the stuff that slicks back
And smartens your head be it bald as a coot's
   In Donald MacLeod's pub.

In Donald MacLeod's pub folk of all sorts foregather
That come from the bank of the Clyde and down from the glens;
The babble's as loud in the ears of your head
As if you'd a poet at each shoulder singing his head off
   In Donald MacLeod's pub.

"Cuir a-nuas leth-té chruaidh," thuirt fear shuas mun cheann àrd,
"Gloine fìon," thuirt fear shìos air bheil fìor choltas ceàird;
"Happy Day, come away," labhair té chamhach bhàn
A bha bhlàth air a sròin gun do thòisich i tràth
           Ann am bùth Dhòmhnaill 'IcLeòid.

Chì thu deòraideach ruadh agus spuaic air a mhaol
'N déidh bhith Dòmhnach gu Luan glaiste suas aig na maoir;
Dh'fhalbh e 's dh'òl e té chruaidh 's ghabh an truaghan an caoch,
'S chuir e eòlas an uair sin g'eil smuais anns gach braon
           Th' ann am bùth Dhòmhnaill 'IcLeòid.

Nì sinn cinnteach mum falbh sinn á balgam no dhà
Thig á Ìle thar fairg' air eil dealbh an Eich Bhàin;
Toradh brìgheil an arbhair as ainmeile gràn —
Cha bhi rìoghachd na h-Alba neo-shealbhach gu bràth
           Fhads a dh'fhàsas innt' eòrn'.

Gloine mhòr dhen Each Bhàn 's i air clàr mar ri pinnt,
Théid an t-òran nas fheàrr leis gach làn a théid innt';
Cha bhi dhuilgheadas ann ach cho gann 's tha na buinn,
Cha bhiodh iongnadh ann leam sinn bhith 'g ionndrainn na tìm
           Nach robh 'phrìs aic' ach gròt'.

Air an aimsir a dh'aom bha mi smaointinn a-raoir,
O, sann oidhche Di-Haoin' bhios am maorach ga roinn,
'S mun do riaraich mi 'mhnaoi 's rud an t-aon thoirt don chloinn,
Cha b'e pòca cho aotrom a dh'fhaodainn air splaoid
           Thoirt gu bùth Dhòmhnaill 'IcLeòid.

Bha i fhéin anns an iorghaill 's i cruinneachadh a' mhàil,
Bhiodh am bàillidh mun cuairt 's e gu gruamach ag ràdh,
"Ma tha 'n t-airgead gad dhìth 's mura lìbhrig thu à
Gheibh thu dearbhadh le cinnt bhith 'nad shìneadh Di-Màirt
           Air an t-sràid air do thòin."

Their na làithean a dh'aom orm caoineadh nan diar —
Tha a bhlàth air an t-saoghal g'eil saorsa dol sìos
Nuair tha 'm bàrd 's e Di-Haoine gun bhraon théid 'na bhial
'S e air fhàgail cho daor aig na daoine gun chiall,
           An luchd-riaghlaidh a th' oirnn.

"Send over a small whisky," said a man up at the high end,
"Glass of wine," said a man down here with a real tinker's look on him;
"Happy Day, come away," said a talkative blonde
Who made clear by her nose that she started early
        In Donald MacLeod's pub.

You'll see a red-haired vagrant with a bruise on his forehead
Who'd been from Sunday to Monday locked up in a cell;
He went off and had a whisky and the wretch went crazy
And discovered then there's a punch in each drop
        That's in Donald MacLeod's pub.

We'll be sure before leaving to have a mouthful or two
That's crossed the sea from Islay under the White Horse label;
The substantial product of the corn whose grain is most famous —
The kingdom of Scotland will prosper forever
        As long as her barley grows.

A big glass of White Horse on a table with a pint,
The song gets better with each fill that goes in it;
There'll be no problem at all except shortage of coins,
It would be no surprise to me that we miss the time
        When it only cost fourpence.

Of times gone by I was thinking last night,
O, it's Friday night that the shellfish are shared,
And before I'd satisfied the wife and given the children something each,
It wasn't such a light pocket that I could have taken on a spree
        To Donald MacLeod's pub.

She was going hysterical scraping up the rent,
The bailiff would come round saying threateningly,
"If you don't have the money and don't hand it over
You'll be certain sure to be stretched out on Tuesday
        On the street on your backside."

Bygone days make me weep tears —
It seems from the world that freedom's on the decline
When the poet on a Friday puts not a drop in his mouth
For it's been made so expensive by senseless people,
        Those who rule over us.

Anns an aimsir a dh'fhalbh thug iad Albainn fo chìs,
Rinn iad ìocshlaint nam buadh a chur suas ann am prìs
Gus na gheàrr iad on t-sluagh e, mo thruaighe ri inns',
Gun do thràigh iad am fuaran bu dualach dhan tìr
     Bha na mìltean ag òl.

Thràigh iad fuaran nam buadh, dh'fhàg iad sluagh ann an càs,
Tha na ceàrnachan tuath 's iad air thuar a bhith fàs;
Tha na fàrdraichean fuar a bha uaireigin blàth,
'S chan eil àbhachd aig cluais mur eil fuaim a' mhuir-làin
     Far am b' àbhaisteach ceòl.

Tha na ceàrnachan tuath ac' air thuar a bhith fàs,
Sann tha àireamh an t-sluaigh a' dol suas tha 'nan tàmh;
Bidh am bàrd Mac an t-Saoir fhathast daonnan an sàs,
Ach ma thà, sann sa pholl agus toll air a mhàs,
     Ged tha iadsan air dòigh.

Ach fhuair mi airgead an-dé 's bha e feumail san àm,
Ruith an t-ainmhidh a réis 's fhuair e 'r éiginn a cheann
Chur air thùs air a' chòrr: bhuidhinn Dòmhnall an geall,
'S mi cho beartach ri *lord* — thugainn còmhla rium teann,
     Sguir a chnuasach do phòc!

62   bho *Fàilte an Diabhail don Droch Dhuine*

     Tapadh leat, a dhuine dhona!
       Tha mi toilicht' ás do ghluasad —
     Fhir a dhìobair taigh do mhàthar,
       Siud mo làmh dhut chum na guailleadh;
     Sann dhomh fhéin a thig bhith leòmach
       Gun do ghabh thu seòladh bhuamsa,
     'S glaodhar furan dhut is fàilte
       Bhon Lic Bhàin gu Sìg nan Cuaran.

     Glaodhar fàilte dhut le fialachd,
       Rinn thu 'n gnìomh ás bheil mi uasal:
     Thaisbein thu t' inntinn am-bliadhna
       'S tha na ciadan ort a' nuadal;
     Thionndaidh thu t' aghaidh gu d' chùlaibh,
       Leig thu cùrsa air dùthaich fhuadain
     Mach o lagh 's bho reachd nam fàintean —
       Gheàrr thu 'n càbla, 's thug thu 'n cuan dhi.

In times gone by they brought Scotland under tribute,
They raised the price of the magic elixir
Till they took it from the people, I'm sorry to say,
And dried up the well that was traditional to the land
　　　　　And that thousands drank.

They dried up the magic well, they left folk in a strait,
The northern districts are almost deserted;
The dwellings are cold that were formerly warm
And no ear has good cheer but the incoming tide
　　　　　Where once there was music.

They've made the northern districts almost deserted,
The proportion of people unemployed is going up;
The poet Macintyre will be still constantly busy,
But if he is, it's in mud with holes in his trousers,
　　　　　Though *they* are all fine.

But I got money yesterday and it was useful and timely,
The creature ran his race and just managed to put
His head in front of the rest: Donald won the bet,
And I'm as rich as a lord — come along with me,
　　　　　Stop searching your pocket!

from *The Devil's Welcome to the Bad Man*

My thanks to you, O man that's bad!
　I'm delighted with your move —
Man who forsook your mother's house,
　Here's my hand up to your shoulder;
It behoves me to be proud
　That you took advice from me,
And you'll be greeted, you'll be welcome
　From the Leac Bhàn to Sìg nan Cuaran.

You'll be generously welcomed,
　You did the deed that's made me proud:
You revealed your mind this year
　And folk in hundreds speak your name;
You turned your face around behind you,
　Set your course for foreign parts
Outside the law, outside commandments —
　You cut the cable, struck out to sea.

Gheàrr thu 'n càbla, 's thug thu 'n cuan dhi,
    Leig thu tuathail 's gaoth 'na cùl dhi,
Thug thu 'n stiùir á làimh na stuamachd,
    Thilg thu thar a guailleadh ùmhlachd;
S fhasa leis na dol gu fuaradh
    Nuair a dh'atas cuantan drùiseil
'S cha bhi guth air càit am buail i —
    Dol gu sìorrachd bhuan gu siùbhlach.

Gheàrr thu 'n càbla o Àirc a' Chùmhnaint,
    S mór mo shunnd 's an dìle ruadh ann;
Ged bhiodh bràithrean riut an diùmbadh,
    Leig do shùil air meud na duaise —
Gheibh thu àrdachadh sna cùirtean,
    Nì thu t' iùl am measg nan uaislean,
'S bidh mi fhìn a ghnàth gad stiùradh
    'S chan eil cùis nach tig gu d' bhuannachd.

Bidh mi fhìn a ghnàth mu d' thimcheall,
    Dhòmhsa s iomchaidh 's gur liùm thu,
Tha do cheum air sràid an iomraill
    Bhon a b' ionmhainn leat co-dhiù i;
Fillte ann an dubhailcean dorcha
    Sìor thighinn doirbh an cur gu cùl dhut,
'S tu mar long a chaill a h-aodach
    Fuadaichte romh ghaoth na Dùldachd.

Thu mar long an déidh a fuadach
    Ann an gailleann cruaidh a' gheamhraidh,
Tanalach leis air a guaillean,
    Miachd air an fhuaradh cha seall i,
Cudrom na fairge ga sìobadh,
    'S blad air a cliathaich gu h-aimhleas,
Gun acair a ghlacas grunnd dhi
    No chrochas air pluic an ceann dhi.

Bidh mi fhìn mu d' thimcheall daonnan,
    Fad do shaoghail bidh mi làmh riut;
Chan eil miann nach faigh a saorsa
    'S neartaichidh mi h-aon no dhà dhiubh;
Guma h-olc dhaibh fhéin 's dha naomhachd,
    Dh'fhalbhadh Maois e fhéin 's na fàintean —
Dé rud th' ann ach miod na faoineis
    A bhith smaointinn gu bheil bàs ann!

You cut the cable, struck out to sea,
　　Heading north with the wind astern,
You took the helm from sobriety's hand,
　　And cast humility overboard;
Easier it is than going to windward
　　When lustful oceans swell and fill
And there's no knowing where she'll strike —
　　Travelling fast to eternity.

You cut the cable from the Arc of the Covenant
　　In a biblical downpour, I'm happy to say;
Who cares if comrades are vexed at you,
　　Cast a glance at how great the reward is —
You'll get advancement in the courts,
　　You'll be a hit with the nobility,
And I'll be guiding you forever
　　To make sure you profit from each affair.

I will always be around you,
　　It's fair enough as you are mine,
Your step is on the primrose path
　　Since that is anyway what you wanted;
You're enfolded in dark vices
　　Steadily harder to give up,
You're like a ship that's lost her sails
　　Blown along by December winds.

Like a ship that's been driven along
　　In the fierce tempest of midwinter,
Shallows exposed at her shoulder,
　　While not a bit shows to windward,
The force of the sea propelling her
　　With a trough at her side to swallow her
And no anchor that holds sea-bottom
　　Or hangs from the blocks at her head.

I will always be around you,
　　All your life I'll be close by,
All desires will have their freedom
　　And one or two I'll fortify;
Bad luck to them and all their piety,
　　Off would go Moses with the commandments —
What is it but the height of folly
　　To believe there's such a thing as death!

63   bho *Aoir an Luchd-Riaghlaidh*

Chan ann am freastal bhuntàta
    Bhios fear tha 'm pàrlamaid Shasainn
Le brot de shùghadh nan cnàmhan
    Cha mhò, tràth anns a' mhadainn,
A chàirear ugh air a bhialaibh
    A dh'eug an t-ian o chionn fad' ann,
Cho luath 's a bhuaileas e spàin ann
    Gheibh am fàileadh a-mach ás
        A leagadh each.

Ach nuair a chuirear gu biadh e
    Chan fhaca crìostaidh a leithid,
Gheibh e chur air a bhialaibh
    De dh'airm na riaraicheadh seisear;
Gur gann gum b' urrainn mi àireamh
    Eadar spàinnean is sgeinean
Na bheir an duine ga ionnsaigh
    Mum faigh e 'n cùrsa mu dheireadh
        A chur a-steach.

Bidh brat beag geal air a ghlùinean
    Air son an smùrach a chumail
No shuas fo sprogan ga lùbadh
    'S e sìos 'na stiùp air a mhuineal;
Bidh na h-airm aig gach làimh dheth,
    'S e dol an greim on taobh muigh annt',
'S tuilleadh shuas air a bhialaibh
    Nuair bhios a' chiad fheadhainn ullamh
        Gus bhith 'nam bad.

Móran sheirbhiseach daonnan
    Aig na daoin' ud mun àite
Gus bhith gam freasgairt air ùrlar
    'S a' cumail sùl' air an àirneis:
Tha iad boireann is fireann ann
    Dhe gach fine agus nàisein
Gu ruige còcaire Frangach
    Nach fàgadh feann air mul-mhàgan
        Ris 'n can iad *chef*.

from *The Satire of the Ruling Class*

No man in England's parliament
   Is dependent on potatoes
With a broth of bone bree
   Nor, early in the morning,
Is an egg stuck in front of him
   Whose bird died long ago,
And which when pierced by a spoon
   Releases a scent that would
              Knock down a horse.

But when summoned to dine
   No christian's seen the like,
For in front of him's fixed
   Enough armaments for six;
I could scarcely compute
   What with knives and with spoons
What the man has picked up
   By the time he has tucked
              The last course away.

A little white cloth
   Catches crumbs on his knees
Or is turned under his chin
   Like a bib down his neck;
He has weapons both sides of him,
   Working in from the outside,
And more up to the front of him
   When the first lot are finished
              For going in to attack.

Such people have plenty
   Of servants around them
For coming and going
   And attending the tables:
There are females and males
   Of different races and nations
All the way to a French cook
   Who'd skin even a frog —
              He's called a *chef*.

Chan e muirsgian no srùban
  A nì chùis far bheil esan
Gam fàgail bramasach sunndach
  Ach làn mo sgùirdeadh de dh'eisir
'S rudan milis is cnòintean
  Is cus de sheòrsachan eile
Agus botal de dh'fhìona
    Bhios lethcheud bliadhn' ann an seilear
      Mun tig i ás.

A h-uile annlan bhios aca
  Gun toirinn seachdain gan àireamh:
Chan fhaighinn toradh na buaile
  A dh'ìm no uachdar no chàise
Gun chus de dh'ainmean neònach
  Air cus de sheòrsachan àraid
Eadar iasg agus ianlaith
    Nach fhac' thu riamh aig do mhàthair
      Ga chur sa phrais.

A Dhùghaill Chìobair, a nàbaidh,
  Cha b' fhealla-dhà leam a chunntais
A h-uile h-uan thug thu cràdh air
  'S e call gu bràth bhith 'na rùda,
Ach s beag a shaoil leat, a chrìostaidh,
  A liuthad biadh a bha sùghar
A thug thu asta le t' fhiaclan
    'S a thilg thu dh'ìochdar an dùnain
      Gun toirt fa-near.

Nach ort bhiodh an t-iongnadh
  Gum bi mi smaointinn air uairibh
Nam biodh tu oidhche dhe d' shaoghal
  A-muigh air aoigheachd aig uaislean —
'S tu faicinn maighdinn aig bòrd ann
  'S dath an òir air a cuailean
'Na suidhe, rùisgt' air do bhialaibh
  A com 's a cìochan 's a guaillean,
      'S i 'g ithe chlach.

Ach s ioma greim a tha neònach
  A bhios aig geòcairean craosach
Tha 'g iarraidh annas an-còmhnaidh
  Anns gach seòl air an smaoinich;

No cockle or razorfish
   Will suffice in his presence
To leave them fartingly happy
   But my lap full of oysters
And sweet things and nuts
   And lots of other ingredients
With a bottle of wine
   That's fifty years in a cellar
                     Before it comes out.

All the side-foods they have
   I'd take a week to relate:
I'd get no yield from the cowfold
   Of cream or butter or cheese
Without a host of strange names
   For a host of weird dishes
From fish through to poultry
   That you never saw your mother
                     Put in the pot.

O neighbour, Dugald the Shepherd,
   I'd find it no joke to count
Every lamb you castrated
   To prevent being a tup,
But you never guessed, christian,
   How many foods that were juicy
You removed with your teeth
   And threw on the dunghill
                     Without a thought.

It sometimes occurs to me
   How surprised you would be
If one night in your life
   You were asked out by gentry —
You'd see a girl at a table there
   With tresses of gold
With her throat, breasts and shoulders
   Sitting naked before you,
                     And she eating balls.

But there's many strange bites
   That such gluttons of greed take
Since they always seek novelty
   In every way thinkable;

Cha bu mhisd' iad ach b' fheàirrd' iad
   Traisg is càdamh na h-Aoine,
Feuch an sùghadh an stamag
   A tha le eallach gun traoghadh
         Air tighinn a-mach.

Nach ann tha 'n aon ghiorra-shaoghail
   Aig na daoin' bhios gam feitheamh,
'S nuair bhiomaid gu sgàineadh
   Nach bi na h-àrmainn ud leathach;
'S mi 'nan cuideachd nach iarradh,
   Cha ghabhainn miann air a leithid —
Gum b' fheàrr leam poit dhen bhuntàta
   Ga cumail blàth ris an teine
         Gu'm bruicheadh sgat.

An luchd-riaghlaidh a fhuair sinn,
   Och mo thruaighe ri aithris
Gur e sinn fhéin a chuir suas iad
   Tha 'n-diugh gar luaircneadh fo'n casan;
Dh'fhalbh ar sìth air an t-saoghal
   'S dh'fhalbh ar saorsa ri'r maireann
An latha leigeadh an t-òrdugh
   Gu bodach-ròcais na galladh —
         E fhéin 's an gamp.

Se 'bodach-ròcais' a thuirt mi,
   'S cha deach dùrd ann am mearachd,
Ged as Tòraidh gu chùl e,
   Le sròn an Iùdhaich a bharrachd;
Ach chuir an Gearmailteach fiamh air
   Nach fhaigh e 'm-bliadhn' ás a chlaigeann
Nuair thug e null e gu Munich —
   'S nach mise chunnaic an latha
         Tigh'nn air an staid.

Nach mise chunnaic an latha
   Nach fhaca m' athair 'na aimsir,
Nach fhaca linn a chaidh seachad
   Bhon cheangail Sasann ri Albainn:
Latha dh'adhbharaich masladh
   Do dhaoine chleachd a bhith calma,
'S a leig am follais le fìrinn
   Cho fad 's tha 'n ìmpireachd ainmeil
         Air dol air n-ais.

They'd be no worse, indeed better,
  Of fast and abstinence each Friday,
To try to rein in their stomachs
  Which with burden undrained
              Are bulging out.

All the folk who attend them
  Suffer shortness of life,
For when we're near bursting
  Those lads are just half full;
I'd have no wish to join them,
  I'd have no appetite for it —
Give me a pot of potatoes
  Being kept warm by the fire
              Till a skate boiled.

The rulers we're landed with,
  Oh how sad to relate
That's it's we who raised up
  Those who now trample us down;
Our peace went from the world
  And our freedom forever
The day the summons was given
  To that bloody scarecrow —
              Him and his gamp.

It's 'scarecrow' I said,
  And not a word was in error,
Though he's a Tory, true blue,
  With a Jew's nose for good measure;
But he got a fright from the German
  That he'll take a while to recover from
When he brought him to Munich —
  I've observed an event
              That changed how things stood.

I've observed an event
  Never seen by my father,
Seen by no generation
  Since England's union with Scotland:
A day that brought shame
  On people used to being brave,
And that revealed the stark truth
  Of how the once-celebrated empire
              Has declined.

An latha b' fheudar do cheannabhaidh
   Na rìoghachd airgeadach bheartach
A dhol gu dìblidh don Ghearmailt
   Gun urad armachd 's am bata
Gus guidhe 's griosad na sìth' ann —
   An nì bha cinnteach nach faighteadh
Bho fhear a dhearbh air na h-Iùdhaich
   Gum biodh ar dùthaich fon t-slacan
         Nam biomaid lag.

Am fear a mheall air a chàirdean,
   Am fear a dh'àicheadh a chùmhnant,
Am fear nach géill do na fàintean,
   A bhrosnaich nàdar na brùideadh;
Am fear a dh'éirich bhon t-salchar,
   Sann gu h-aimlisg a dhùisg e —
Am fear thug plàigh air an t-saoghal,
   A' saltairt saorsa gach dùthcha
         Na chuir e chas.

Fhuair e 'n t-Eadailteach còmh' ris
   A rinn am fòirneart cho gràineil
Air daoine dubha gun eòlas,
   Gun tuigse air seòltachd an nàisein,
A' mort le nimh ás an adhar
   A dh'fhir 's de mhnathan 's de phàistean,
'S nach do nochd dhaibh de thròcaire
   Am fear bhiodh leòint' anns an àraich
         A dh'fhaighinn ás.

Labhair Hitler ri 'aodann
   'S e 'n coltas aon bhiodh a' bagairt,
"Fhuair mi deas mo chuid daoine
   'S chan eil iad faoin anns an t-sabaid;
Mura càirich thu nall dhomh
   A h-uile bonn tha mi 'g agairt,
Chan fhàg mi clach ann an Lunnainn
   Nach cuir mi mhullach an adhair
         Mun dèan mi stad."

Sin ar duais agaibh cinnteach
   Air son na tìm a chaidh seachad
A dh'fhàg sibh riaghladh ar tìre
   An làmhan clìochdairean Shasainn

The day that the leader
   Of that rich capitalist kingdom
Went abjectly to Germany
   Armed with not even a stick
To negotiate for peace there —
   The thing certain not to be had
From a man who'd showed by the Jews
   How our land would be hammered
                  If we were weak.

The man who cheated his friends,
   Who reneged on his contract,
Who keeps no commandments,
   Who's encouraged brutality;
He who rose from the dirt
   Seeks to stir up disorder —
He's brought plague to the world,
   Trampling the freedom of each land
                  Where he's set foot.

With him's the Italian
   Who sent violence so loathsome
Against blacks who knew nothing
   Of the nation's duplicity,
Dropping poison from the air
   To slaughter men, women and children,
While showing not even the mercy
   Of letting wounded men flee
                  From the battlefield.

Hitler said to his face
   With a threatening manner,
"I've made my men ready
   And they are excellent soldiers;
Unless you sign over to me
   Every point I'm demanding,
There's no stone in London
   That I'll not blow sky high
                  Before I stop."

That's our certain reward for you
   For all the time that's gone by
While you left the governing of our country
   To the con-men of England

A dhùin ar sùilean 's ar cluasan
    'S a cheangail buarach m'ar casan —
Cho trang ag aimhreit mu stòras
    Gun d'fhalbh na h-eòin aig a' chlamhan
        An trod nan cearc.

Fichead bliadhn' thug a' ghràisg ud
    (An rud as nàir' dhuinn ri aithris)
A' còpadh muilleanan airgid
    Am pòca chealgairean carach
Le sluagh na dùthcha gun chosnadh
    Is gaoir na gort' air gach bealach —
A' falbh 'nan creutairean truagha,
    Le'n druim ga shuathadh ri balla
        Gun an deamhan car.

Fichead bliadhn' thoirt gun bhuaidh dhuinn
    An déidh na fhuair sinn de riasladh,
Gun ghuth air nì dhèanadh feum dhuinn
    Nan tigeadh éiginn san iar oirnn —
Gun ghuth air armailt no cabhlach
    No obair àitich no iasgaich
Fo bhinn MhicThormaid 's a chòmhlan
    A thoill an ròpa fo fhiasaig
        Bhig bhioraich ghlais.

An déidh na fhuair sinn de riasladh,
    Thug ceithir bliadhn' ann am fùirneis
A' cumail feachd agus fòirneirt
    A-mach bho chòrsa na dùthcha,
'S an ann gus uachdarain fearainn
    'S gach ceannabhaidh malairt is bùthadh
Bhith dùnadh dorsan na tròcair
    Air saighdear leòinte bochd brùite
        Bha muigh gun char?

64   *Nuair a thàinig am Buroo do Dhùthaich nam Beann*

Rìgh! Gur mis' tha fo phràmh,
    Cha tig aighear ri m' chàil
'S mi fad' o eilein nan àrd-gharbhlaichean.
    Se mo chuibhreann gu bràth
    Bhith air muinntearas chàich
Fhads a chumas an t-àgh anathadh rium.

Who closed our eyes and our ears
   And cow-fettered our feet —
So busy squabbling about wealth
   That the hawk snatched the chickens
      While the hens fought.

Twenty years have that rabble spent
   (It's our shame to relate)
Stuffing millions of pounds
   In the pockets of swindlers
While unemployment's been rife
   And hunger crying on each highway —
Folk wandering disconsolate,
   Their backs propping up walls
      With damn all to do.

Twenty years we have wasted
   Since we suffered such horrors,
Without suggestion for helping us
   Should the crisis come west on us —
No talk of army or navy
   Or agriculture or fishing
From that regime under Norman
   Who deserved a rope under the point
      Of his little grey beard.

Since we suffered such horrors,
   Spending four years in a furnace
To keep violence and armies
   From the shores of the country,
Is it for landed proprietors
   And each leader of trade and of commerce
To close the doors of compassion
   On a poor broken wounded soldier
      Demobbed without work?

When the Buroo came to the Land of the Mountains

Lord! I'm so very miserable,
I'm in no mood for mirth
And I so far from the isle of the high wildernesses.
   It's my portion forever
   To be at the service of others
As long as providence keeps puff in me.

Ach na dh'fhan ás mo dhéidh
'S a chum an dachaighean fhéin,
Dh'fhàs iad uile gu léir sealbhach ann,
Tighinn air n-adhart gu mòr
Ann an saidhbhreas 's an stòr
Ged tha mise sa chrò charbad seo.

Chan eil duine ri tràigh
Eadar Arcaibh nam bàgh
Agus Manainn mu'n gàir fairgeachan
Nach eil biadhta nas fheàrr
'S ann an sìochaint 's an tàmh
Nach robh riamh aig mo dhà sheanmhair-sa.
Sann tha mise 's mo chlann
Ann am meadhain nan Gall
'S tric m' aran gun feann armaidh air,
Agus Dùthaich nam Beann
A' cur thairis mu'n ceann —
Nuair bu chòir dhomh bhith ann dh'fhalbh mi ás.

S tric an osna tighinn bhuam,
S mi tha cosnadh mo dhuais
Gu lathte, lapanach, fuar, fearghasach,
Air mo rathad fo éis
A' cur seachad mo réis —
Nach ioma là bhios mo cheum falbhanach.
Chan eil troigh mu Chluaidh
'S am bi taigh ri chur suas
Nach bi 'm breigire ruadh 's cairbheas air
'S a' chlach-mheallain 'na deann
A' toirt snag air mo cheann
Gu'n do ragaich mo sheann fhailmeanan.

Nuair a chluinn mi 's a chì
Mar tha muinntir mo thìr'
S beag an t-iongnadh mi bhith farmadach —
Mura falbh iad air sgrìob
Air son bhith cnàmh an cuid bìdh,
Gu dé dh'fhàgas iad sgìth anfhainneach
A thig gu feasgar an là
'S iad gu seasgair 'nan tàmh?
Sann tha 'm peiteagan 's làn bhalg orra —
Nuair bhios mise san aol,
'S mi gun aighear, gun aoidh,
Ach gam fheannadh aig sgaoth mheanbhchuileag.

But those who stayed when I left
And kept their own homes,
They've all become terribly prosperous there,
Coming along splendidly
In wealth and possessions
While I'm in this cowfold of vehicles.

None live close to the shore
Between Orcadian bays
And Man where the oceans roar
Who're not better fed
And in rest and repose
That *my* two grandmothers never enjoyed.
Yet I and my offspring
In the midst of the Lowlanders
Find my bread with no spread of margarine on it,
While the Land of the Mountains
Overflows all around them —
When I should have been there I had left.

Many sighs are escaping me,
For I earn all my wages
By being numb, cold, faint and embittered,
Spending my life
Far behind on my road —
Many days is my step long and weary.
Each square foot near the Clyde
That has a house to go up in it
Has the red-haired brickie grimacing
As the hailstones rattle
And bang on my head
Till my old knee-pans give up on me.

When I hear and I see
How my compatriots are
It's no wonder I suffer from jealousy —
Except for going for a walk
To aid their digestion,
What tires out and weakens them
At the eve of their life
And they in comfort and ease?
It's how their waistcoats bulge out —
While I'm knee-deep in lime,
Melancholic, unsmiling,
And skinned alive by a swarm of midges.

Chan eil fear a chuir cliabh
Ann an roc an taobh siar
A thug dubhan á bial carbhanaich.
Chan eil fear a chuir lìon
Far an tuinicheadh iasg
Ged nach tugadh e riamh deargadh ás.
Nuair a thig iad gu aois
Cha bhi miodhairt no gaoid,
Cha chuir uisge no gaoth amaladh orr'.
Air an cumail nas fheàrr
Na tha mis' aig mo cheàird
Ged as tric air an t-sràid anmoch mi.

Tha gach fear agus mnaoi
Air an tachdadh le maoin,
Chan eil cailleach no aon seana-bhodach
Nach toir cobhair na h-aois'
Orra steach air gach taobh —
Nach ann an-siud tha na daoin' airgeadach!
Sann a chuireas iad geall
Ann an cas-chluich nam ball
O'm faigh iad uaireannan meall anabarrach,
'S nuair a dh'fhàsas iad mall
Gheibh iad cobhair nan dall
Bhon tha e nis aig gach seann fhearrabhalach.

Is mór an caochladh a th' ann
Seach an saoghal a bh' ann
Aig na daoin' anns na seann aimsirean.
S ioma là bha iad gann
Mun do dh'àraich iad clann,
Sann bha 'm màileidean fann falmhaichte.
Iad ri saothair gu dian
Gun an t-aodach no 'm biadh,
Cha robh aon bhonn-a-sia chalp' aca,
Ach 'nan culachan truais,
Fodha dh'ionnsaigh nan cluas,
Gus bhith bàtht' ann an cuan ainfhiachan.

Chunnaic mis' iad gu dian
Treis mun éireadh a' ghrian
Anns a' chladach a' sìor fheamnadh ás.
Gum b'e an t-srathair 's na cléibh
Inneal thàirnidh nan steud —
Cha robh 'n càrn ach gu glé ainmig ann.

No-one now who's set a creel
In the tangles of the west side
Has got a hook from the mouth of a sea-bream.
No-one now has set a net
Where the fish would collect
Without ever taking a fin of them.
When they come to old age
There'll be no misery or blemish,
Neither rain nor wind will hinder them.
They're better maintained
Than am I at my trade
Though often I'm late on the street.

Every husband and wife
Are stuffed up with wealth,
There's not a single old man or woman
Who won't bring in the pension
To them both from each side —
So they're just a bunch of old moneybags!
Down goes their stake
In the football pools
From which sometimes they scoop the jackpot,
And when they grow slow
They'll get blind person's dole
Now that every old codger is getting it.

How things have changed
From the world that was known
To the folk in the olden times.
Many days things were scarce
Before their kids came of age,
And their wallets were limp and empty.
They worked all the time
Without clothing or food,
Not sixpence of cash did they have,
But just objects of pity,
Up to the ears,
Almost drowned in a sea of debts

I've seen them at work
A while before sunrise
Bringing seaweed out of the shore.
Pack-saddle and creels
Were the horse-powered traction —
The slipe was seldom employed.

Falbh a dh'obair gu fiar
Air son ochd sgillinn diag —
Chan eil reusan dhomh 'm biadh ainmeachadh.
Chuireadh tuathanach còir
Caigeann thastan 'nan dòrn
Nuair a spealadh iad leòb arbhair dha.

Ged bu bhleideil na bàird
Gu cur ghaisgeach an àird
Chan eil teagamh g'eil dà sheanchas air.
Gur e cnotag is brà,
Corran-shìolag is tàbh
Inneal bhiathaidh nan sàr ainmeil sin.
Falbh le uibe 'nan làimh,
Bhiodh an sitigean làn
Dhe na sligean is càir dhearg orra,
'S iad a' cruadhachadh dhias
Ris an t-slabhraidh le cliabh,
Gum b'e 'n srùthan bu chiad theanacas dhaibh.

'Bhliadhna ghais am buntàt',
S mise dh'fhaodadh a ràdh,
Fhuair am maorach an dà shearbhag dheth.
Cha robh portan ri tràigh
Nach do chochlaich 'nan ràimh,
Chuir a' ghorta 's gach ceàrn fargradh orr'.
Chaidh na bàirnich air chrith
Leis a' ghàir a bha muigh,
"Och, a bhràithrean, thig sgrios marbhaidh oirnn!
Cha robh nàdarrachd glic
Chuir am fàs sinn air lic
Ann an sàs far an ruig sgealb oirnn."

Cha robh cudaig sna Hann
Ma bha gliocas 'na ceann
Nach do thuig gun robh 'n t-àm falbh aice.
Ghabh iad eagal a' bhàis,
'S cha b'e 'n t-iongnadh leam à,
S ioma laoiceann a bha sealg orra.
Cha robh bidean aig bàgh
Nach biodh dithis le tàbh
'S iad cho gionach ri dà sgarbh uice
Gus na dh'fhàs i cho gann
'S nach robh urad is lann
Eadar Nis agus Ceann Charadail.

Going to work at the hay
For one-and-sixpence a day —
The food wasn't worthy of mention.
Some kindly farmer would put
Two shillings in their fist
When they'd scythed a patch of corn for him.

Though the poets were forward
In elevating heroes
There are certainly two sides to the story.
Mortar and quernstone,
Sand-eel-sickle and hand-net
Were what fed those famous warriors.
Going with oatcake in hand,
Their dunghills were full
Of limpet shells red from roasting,
While they dried ears of grain
In a creel slung from the chain,
With the struan as their main salvation.

The year of potato blight,
It's I who could say it,
The shellfish had a doubly hard time of it.
All the crabs of the shores
Took to shell in their oars,
Universal starvation banished them.
The limpets were quaking
At the cry that was raging,
"O comrades, massacre will befall us!
Nature wasn't wise
To set us growing on slabs
Stuck where they'll prise us off."

Every cuddy in the Hann
That had sense in her pan
Twigged it was time to be going.
They got the fright of their lives,
Nor was that a surprise,
For many a young novice was after them.
If some scrap came to inlet
Some pair with a hand-net
Would give chase with the appetite of cormorants
Till fish grew so scarce
That not so much as a scale
Could be found from Ness down to Carradale.

S ioma fàrdach gun loinn
Air bheag àirneis 'na broinn
Bha eadar Arainn is Beinn Charbhaig,
Far am biodh an sparr-ghaoith
A' cur thairis le sùith
'S nach do ghlanadh bho linn Charmaig i.
Gum b'e 'n t-ùrlar am poll
Air a stampadh fo'm bonn,
Ach gun crathadh iad tonn ghainmhich air,
Agus fraighnigh 'na sruth
Leis na ballachan dubh' —
An rud as lugh' orra 'n-diugh ainmeachadh.

Ach nuair fhuair iad air dòigh
(Nach e 'm buaireadair stòr!)
Dh'fhàs na gruagaichean òg' anbharrach,
Coimhead sìos thar an sròin
'S iad air lìonadh le pròis
Gus nach dèan iad an còrr searbhantachd.
Cha bhi cuibheall no clòimh,
Cha bhi bior air am meòir,
S gann gun glac iad 'nan dòrn searbhadair,
Ach a' tionndadh an sùl'
Mar gum faiceadh tu gnùis
A bhiodh san uinneig aig bùth dealbhadair.

Chì thu gillean gun diù
'S iad 'nan ruith gu 'Buroo',
Gur ann a chuireadh a' chùis fearg orm.
Leis gach fasan as ùir'
Sann bhios gloin' air an sùil
A-cheart cho math ris an Diùc Earra-Ghaidhealach.
Cha bhi ruisgein mu'n ceann,
Chaidh a' Ghàidhlig air chall,
Fhuair iad cànain nan Gall, 's marbhphaisg air —
Còmhradh bleideil am beòil,
'S iad gu sgeith leis an leòm
Ged chaidh am breith ann an "Ò, falbhadh iad!"

       Countless dwellings without pride
       With little furniture inside
Existed from Arran to Beinn Charbhaig,
       With the cross-joint of their roof
       Overflowing with soot
And never cleaned since the rule of King Cormac.
       The floor was just mud
       Stamped underfoot,
Save that they'd shake a dash of sand on it,
       And dampness streamed
       Down the sooty walls —
Which today they're most loth to mention.

       But when things got better
       (O wealth's such a tempter!)
The young women grew demanding,
       Looking down their noses
       And puffed up with notions
So they'll never more go into service.
       They never touch spinning-wheel,
       Nor wool nor knitting-needle,
Scarce a dish-towel sullies their fingers,
       But rolling their eyes
       Like some face you might spy
In the shop window of a photographer.

       You see irresponsible youths
       Running to the 'Broo',
It all makes me quite infuriated.
       With every new fashion
       They put glass to their eyes
That's as good as the Duke of Argyll's.
       Their whiskers have gone,
       And Gaelic is lost,
They've got the Lowlanders' tongue, confound it —
       Snooty talk in their mouths,
       Near vomiting with cockiness
Despite their being born in "Oh, to hell with them!"

65   *O, faighibh suas an Cogadh*

O, faighibh suas an Cogadh,
E, faighibh suas an cogadh,
Briosgaidean is feòil nan crogan,
    Se an cogadh s docha lìnn.

Cuiribh Albainn ás a h-ànradh
Bhon tha 'crannchur mar a thà e —
Grodadh le caitheamh 'nan cnàmhan
    'S dol gu bàs le cion a' bhìdh.

Dheasaicheadh acfhainn sa Ghearmailt
Chuireas Glaschu 'na sgealban,
Fuil is gaorr is daoine marbh ann,
    Cuirp is anmannan a dhìth.

Bidh Ameireaga fo ghruaimean
Mura reic i móran cruadhach;
Chan eil sinne ach gortach truagh,
    Gur coingeis leinn tuasaid no sìth.

S beag an t-iongnadh ged bhiodh sòlas
Air gach aon anns an Roinn Eòrpa;
Gheibh iad gunnachan 'nan dòrn
    An àite flùr is feòil is ìm.

An nàmhaid a dh'fheuch ri'r marbhadh
Anns an iarmailt 's air an fhairge,
Togaibh suas as ùr a h-armailt
    'S cuiribh ceannabhaidh air an cinn.

Tha iad anabarrach am-bliadhna,
Chaidh droch ainm dhiubh leis na briagan;
Sann a bh' annta daoine ciallach
    Nach robh iarradach air strì.

Feumaidh sinn a dhol 'nan cleamhnas,
A bhith réidh riu aig an àm seo —
Tha na béistean tha 'n taobh thall dhiubh
    'S iad cho teann orra aig a' chrìch.

O, get ye up the War

Oh, get ye up the War,
Eh, get ye up the War,
Biscuits and tins of spam,
   It's war we prefer.

Put Scotland out of her misery
Because her fate is how it is —
Consumption's rot is in their bones
   And death from malnutrition.

Technology's developed in Germany
That will blow Glasgow to bits,
Blood and gore and corpses there,
   Bodies and souls gone west.

America will be in a depression
If she doesn't sell a lot of steel;
We're just starving and miserable,
   War and peace are all the same to us.

Little wonder happiness has come
To everyone all over Europe —
They'll get guns coming into their fists
   Instead of flour and meat and butter.

The enemy that tried to slaughter us
In the air and out upon the sea,
Build ye up again her army
   And put ye a leader at their head.

This year they've been outstanding,
Their bad reputation was all lies;
They were actually sensible folk
   With no desire at all for strife.

We must form with them an alliance,
And be nice to them for a while —
The monsters over on their other side
   Are massing on their boundary.

Seall sib' fhéin air cor an t-saoghail,
'S mar tha inntinnean nan daoine,
Móran sluaigh ag iarraidh saorsa
   'S nach biodh maoir gan toirt fo chìs.

Se na Ruisianaich ar nàmhaid
'S feumaidh sinne dhol gan smàladh,
S dearbh mun till sinn ás a' bhlàr sin
   Cha bhi cus air fhàgail dhìnn.

Rìoghachdan air chùl na gréine
'S iad a' diùltadh bhith toirt géill dhuinn;
Dùil aca mar mhuinntir Éireann
   Gur ann leotha fhéin tha 'n tìr.

Ged tha Sìona fad air falbh bhuainn,
Mìltean mìle bho chrìochan Albann,
Feumaidh sinne dhol gam marbhadh
   'S greasad oirnn mum marbh iad sìnn.

Théid na gillean òg' 'nan deann ann,
Théid na gruagaichean 'nan ceann ann;
Fàgaidh iad mi fhìn 's an t-seann té
   'S bidh an stall againn dhuinn fhìn.

Saoil nach sòlasach an ceartuair
Bhith fo òrdain aig MacArtair,
Rùsgadh phàistean feadh an t-sneachda
   'S bhith gan sgailceadh mu na cinn.

Saoil nach gasta bhith losgadh fùdair,
Bhith cur braidseil ris an dùthaich,
Mnathan òga 's sean gan rùsgadh —
   Thoill MacArtair crùn an rìgh.

See how the world is for yourselves,
How the minds of people are moving forward,
With many folk demanding to be free
  So no more bailiffs come along for rent.

O the Russians are our enemy
And we must go and choke them off,
Sure by the time we get back from that battle
  There won't be much of us left ourselves.

Countries behind the sun
Are refusing to submit to us;
Thinking like the Irish nation
  That their land belongs to them.

Though China's far away from us,
Thousands of miles from Scotland's borders,
We must go and kill them off
  In haste for fear they kill us first.

The young lads go off in a hurry,
The girls go off to join them;
The wife and I are left behind
  And we'll have the cowstall all to ourself.

O how happy to be just now
Under orders from MacArthur,
Abusing children in the snow
  And knocking them upon the head.

O how grand to be firing powder,
Putting the burning torch to the land,
Women old and young being raped —
  MacArthur's earned the crown of a king.

Ùisdean Laing (1889–1974)

66   *Seann Éipheiteach ann an Tìr Airsnealach*

Chan eil an dàn dhomh nis ach bàs —
   Tha mi 'nam thruaghan bochd is tinn
   A dh'éireas éiginneach, 's a chì
Ròs gheal a' fàs gun spàirn.

Chan eil an dàn dhomh ach am bàs —
   Tha mi mar ànrach air a' chuan
   Tha 'g ionndrainn ann an gaoir nan stuadh
Tlàth-ghaoth nan raon fo bhlàth.

Chan eil an dàn dhomh ach am bàs —
   Tha mi mar fhear san fhàsach theth
   A ruigeas lagan phailm 's nach faigh
Ach clàbar tais nan càmhal.

Chan eil an dàn dhomh ach am bàs —
   Tha mi mar thuiltean eadar stùc
   Tha gluasad chreagan mór' 'nan cùrs'
'S a' call an cruth san t-sàil.

Chan eil an dàn dhomh ach am bàs —
   Tha mi mar shealgair dian an fhéidh
   A mhothaicheas air uachdar sléibh
Cròic 's iad crìon a' cnàmh.

Se sin a' chrìoch,
An-dé, an-diugh, gu sìor,
   Ri teas is fuachd,
   Bho dheas gu tuath.
   Se sin ar duais:
      Am Bàs
   Le'm bi a' bhuaidh
      'Nar càs.

Hugh Laing (Stoneybridge, S. Uist)

An Ancient Egyptian in a Weary Land

There's nothing in store for me now but death —
  I'm just a poor and sickly wretch
  Who rises in distress, and sees
A white rose that grows with ease.

There's nothing in store for me but death —
  I'm like a wanderer on the sea
  That yearns amidst the screaming waves
For the soft breath of blossomed fields.

There's nothing in store for me but death —
  I'm like a man in the desert's heat
  Who finds on reaching a dell of palms
Just sodden mud of camels.

There's nothing in store for me but death —
  I'm like floods between the lofty heights
  That move great boulders in their course
Then lose their form in brine.

There's nothing in store for me but death —
  I'm like the bold hunter of the deer
  Who notices on mountain-top
Withered antlers rotting.

That is the end,
Yesterday, today, forever,
  In heat and cold,
  From south to north.
  That's our reward:
    Death
  Who triumphs
    In our plight.

Pàdraig Moireasdan (1889–1978)

67 Òran don Chogadh

Guma slàn do na gillean tha MacShimidh a' sireadh,
  Guma slàn do na gillean tha leinne san àm;
Mo bheannachd le dùrachd air na dh'fhàg iad fo mhulad
  Oir tha mòran dhiubh bhuineas a dh'Uibhist nam beann.

Fhearaibh th' aig baile 's a' céilidh nan taighean,
  Ag éigheachd[1] gach naidheachd mar tha tachairt san Fhraing,
Gur garadh gu dòigheil aig teine math mònadh,
  Sann leinne bu deòin a bhith còmh' ribh san àm.

Chan ionann is mise 's an còrr de na gillean
  Tha mach fon an t-sileadh a dh'uisgeachan trom
Fo luaidhe nan Turcach 's fo shligeannan muirte
  A' dòrtadh mar thuiltean gun sgur air ar ceann.

Ged gheibhinn car tacain cead sìneadh fon phlaididh
  Cha luaith' nì mi cadal — cha tarraing mi srann —
Nuair chluinneas mi 'n t-òrdugh bhith dol ann an òrdugh
  Chum losgadh is leònadh, 's a' chòmhstri tighinn teann.

Nuair thòisicheas buaireas thig stoirm mu ar cluasan,
  Tha 'n talamh mun cuairt dhinn air ghluasad fo'r bonn,
Bidh gillean gun ghruaman le'n gunna ri'n gualainn
  A' leagadh nan uaibhreach, 's a' bhuaidh bidh i leinn.

Bidh peileirean snaidhte mun cuairt oirnn am pailteas,
  Am fuaim a' dol seachad neo-thlachdmhor an srann;
Bidh gillean bha tapaidh a' tuiteam gun fhacal
  'S iad crioslaicht' an acfhainn gu batal nan lann.

Chan ionann 's nuair b' òg mi bhith seòladh na geòla
  Le mo chompanach còir a bu deòin a bhith leam,
Le m' ghunna glan bòidheach 's mo chù air an t-sòile —
  Nuair dhèanainn-sa leònadh bhiodh Dòmhnall 'na dheann.

Cha bhi mi ri gearan no caoidh anns an earrainn
  Ach seasaidh mi daingeann ris a' chath a tha teann
Le Gaidhil a' chruadail tha treun agus buadhach,
  Nì Turcaich a sguabadh far uachdar nam beann.

Peter Morrison (Grimsay, N. Uist)

A Song to the War

Here's to the lads that Lord Lovat's recruiting,
    Here's to the lads that are with us just now;
My heartfelt blessing to those they've left sorrowful
    For many of them belong to Uist of the mountains.

O men who're at home going the rounds of the houses,
    Announcing each news of what's happening in France,
Warming yourselves happily at a blazing peat fire,
    It's we who'd be glad to be with you just now.

How different from me and the rest of the lads
    Who're exposed to the drenching of downpours of rain
Under fire from the Turks with their murderous shelling
    Ceaselessly pouring like floods on our heads.

Though allowed now and then to rest under a blanket
    I've no sooner slept — I've not snored even once —
Than I hear the command to fall into line
    For firing and wounding, as conflict approaches.

When battle begins our ears are assaulted,
    The earth round about us moves under our feet,
Lads without sadness with guns to their shoulders
    Lay the mighty ones low, and it's we who will win.

Sharp-pointed bullets surround us aplenty,
    Their noise going past is an unpleasant whine;
Lively lads fall without uttering a word
    Though richly caparisoned for battling with blades.

Not at all like my youth when out sailing my boat
    With my dear companion who wished to be with me,
With my lovely smart gun and my dog on the sternseat —
    When I wounded a bird it's Donald would run.

I will not complain or lament at my share
    But will stand firm to face the battle that's close
With Gael that are hardy, brave and triumphant,
    Who'll sweep away Turks from the top of the slopes.

Tha sinne an earbsa ma laigheas an t-sealga
   Gun ruig sinne Stambal ged as fada e thall,[2]
Am baile 'm bheil dòchas aig réisimeid Lòbhait
   An dramaichean òl le òran nach gann.[3]

Mun crìochnaich mi 'n t-òran, mo bheannachd le deòin dhuibh,
   Ceud soraidh gu Flòraidh, an òigh as barraichte th' ann:[4]
Tha mi fhathast an dòchas gun coinnich sinn còmhla
   'S air m' fhacal bidh pòg ann cur an t-sòlais gu ceann.

Iain Rothach (1889–1918)

68   Ar Tìr

Brat shneachda air mullach nam beann,
currachd ceòtha mar liath-fhalt m'an ceann,
feadain is sruthain mòintich
a' leum 's a' dòrtadh,
's le torman a' sporgail measg garbhlach nan gleann,
a' sporgail air ùrlar nan gleann,
aig còsan 's mu shàilean nam mòr-bheann;
féidh ruadh', fir na cròice,
air sliosaibh fraoich ruadh-dhonn —
si Tìr nan Gaisgeach a th' ann,
Tìr nam Beann, nan Gaisgeach, 's nan Gleann,
si Tìr nan Gaisgeach a th' ann.

69   Ar Gaisgich a Thuit sna Blàir

S iomadh fear àlainn òg sgairteil,
ait-fhaoilt air chinn a bhlàth-chrìdh,
tric le ceum daingeann làidir,
ceum aotrom, glan, sàil-ghlan,
dhìrich bràigh nam beann móra,
chaidh a choinneamh a' bhàis —
tric ga fhaireach' roimh-làimh —
a chaidh suas chum a' bhlàir;
's tha feur glas an-diugh 'fàs
air na dh'fhàg innleachdan nàmh,
innleachdan dhubh-sgrios an nàmh a chòrr dheth.

We're confident if the bombardment dies down
   That we'll reach Istanbul though it's far over there,
The city where Lovat's regiment hopes
   To be drinking their drams with many a song.

Before ending the song, I'll send you my blessings,
   A hundred greetings to Flora, the best girl there is:
I still live in hope that we'll meet with each other
   And my word there'll be kisses to bring joy to a climax.

John Munro (Swordale, Point, Lewis)

Our Land

Mantle of snow on the tops of the hills,
capped with mist like grey hair on their heads,
moorland burns and streams
leaping and gushing,
and noisily rummaging through the wilds of the glens,
rummaging through the floors of the glens,
tucked in the mountains' crevices and rounding their heels;
red deer, antlered stags,
on russet-brown heathered slopes —
such is the Land of the Heroes,
the Land of the Mountains, the Heroes, the Glens,
such is the Land of the Heroes.

Our Heroes who Fell in Battle

Many a handsome young man full of energy
openly welcoming from the warmth of his heart,
so often with step firm and strong,
step light, fresh and clean-heeled,
who climbed the slope of the high mountains,
who went to face death —
often sensing it beforehand —
who went up to the battlefield;
and green grass grows today
on what enemy engines left
on what enemy engines of total destruction left over.

Ged bha cuid dhiubh, nuair bu bheò iad,
tric nach b' mhìn réidh sinn còmhla,
O! thuit iad air Còmhnard na Strì.
Fhuair sinn sìnt' iad le'm bàs-leòintean
an dust eu-dreach', na bha chòrr dhiubh,
an laighe 'sìneadh mar mheòir-shìnt' —
smèideadh, stiùireadh,
sparradh ùr-oidhirpean òirnne,
strì air n-adhart, strì còmhla,
an taobh a thuit iad dol còmhl' ruinn,
null thar Còmhnard na Strì.

Bi am' chuideachd gearr-ùin',
dùin do rosg-sgàilean air d' shùil
'n seòmar ionmhais do smaoin
's caoin sholas òg-mhaidne, ciùin-mhaidne, òg-mhéis
ga lìonadh, a' briseadh tre uinneag a' chùil —
'n àite taighe, tadhal d' anma,
fasgadh cuspairean a' mhùirn,
an-sin — tog, taisg dealbh orra
'nan laighe mar thuit san raon,
fairich, cluinn,
"Bi'bh deas gu leum 'n àirde
le'r ceum gaisgeil, neo-sgàthach, dàna,
bi'bh null Còmhnard na Strì,
na lagaichibh, bi'bh làidir,
bi'bh 'nam badaibh is pàighibh,
am féin-mhuinghinn leag gu làr dhaibh,
air adhart, air adhart;
seo an rathad,
cuir a' Bhratach an sàs
daingeann àrd
air Sliabh Glòrmhor Deagh-Sìth!"
An sméideadh, an cainnt ruinn,
'n rùn-gnìomh air an tug iad an deò
suas, 'nan càradh
air an àr-làr,
air a ghléidheadh dhuinn beò
mar gun snaidheadh fear seòlt'
cuimhneachain cloiche-gun-phrìs.

Though there were those, when alive,
with whom we often disagreed,
O! they fell on the Battlefield.
We found them lying with their fatal wounds
in formless dust, what was left of them,
lying stretched out like pointing fingers —
beckoning, guiding,
spurring us on to fresh efforts,
pressing forward, pressing together,
the very way where they fell when with us
they crossed the Battlefield.

Stay with me for a moment,
close the lids on your eyes
in the treasure-house of your thoughts
with the soft light of young-morning, calm-morning, June-morning
filling, breaking through the back window —
instead of house, penetrating your soul,
enveloping the objects of love,
then — make, store a picture of them
lying as they fell in the field,
feel, hear,
"Be ready to leap up
with your heroic, fearless, brave step,
cross the Battlefield,
don't weaken, be strong,
get at them and pay them back,
deflate their self-confidence,
onward, onward;
this is the way,
plant the standard
firm and high
on the Glorious Hill of Good Peace!"
Their beckoning, their speech to us,
the reflex in which they
expired, fixed
on the battle-floor,
preserved for us alive
as if some sculptor had hewn
marble memorials.

70 *Air sgàth nan sonn*

Air sgàth nan sonn nach fhaic mo shùil
tuilleadh ri m' bheò
's nach cuir blàth-phlac gu m' chrìdh nas mò
le greim an làmh, le tlàths an gnùis,
le fàilte 's furan am beòil —
O s minig a ghléidheadh le'n sgeòil
mi o dhubh-ghearan gruamach na h-ùine
's a rinneadh mo throm-uallach aotrom
le'n cuideachd 's am blàth-chridheas dòigh:
ach sguiream de Och is O!
Cuiream mo bhròn a thaobh,
's air sgàth balachain ar fàrdaich
a dhearbh an làn chridhe laoich,
air sgàth ar n-òg-ghillean maiseach,
dhearbh cridhe agus làmh-dheas maraon,
agus air sgàth nam fear duineil
a dh'fhàg na h-uiread air chùl —
dh'fhalbh iad uainn uile, leig sinn slàn leo,
gun againn ach tuairmeas air cùis
no adhbhar na h-eubh' air son cobhrach
bha cruinneach' feachd-dìon air son dùthch'
air an sgàth-s' chaidh an coinneamh nan uabhas
o bhalachain gu fir mheadhan là —
na gràidhein nach till a dh'fhalbh uainn,
seadh, 's fuigheall brist' an àir —
air an sgàth-s' iarram tapachd,
spìd innt'neil is corp'rail;
cumadh mo chridhe buille sgairteil,
na géilleam roimh chruaidh nì;
catham tre chruadail is dhoilgheas,
's nuair ruigeas Deuchainn a h-àirde
's gur e h-eubha rium "Fàilnich, strìochd,"
'n-sin cuimhnicheam Leódhas, m' àit-àraich,
is gléidheadh mo làmh a clì.

For the sake of the warriors

For the sake of the warriors whom my eye won't see
for the rest of my life
and who'll no more set my heart beating faster
with the grip of their hand, the warmth of their countenance,
the goodwill and welcome of their mouth —
O so often was I kept by their stories
from the grim black complaint of time
and since my heavy burden was lightened
by their company and warm-hearted ways:
but let me cease from Och and O!
I'll set aside my grief,
and for the sake of the boys of our dwelling
who proved all their heroic heart,
for the sake of our handsome young lads
who proved both their heart and their ready hand,
and for the sake of the brave men
who left so much behind —
they left us all, we bade them farewell
though we could scarcely guess at the cause
or the reason for the cry for assistance
that gathered a country's defence-force
which went for them to face horrors
from young boys to middle-aged men —
the loved ones who left never to return,
yes, and the broken remnant of slaughter —
for their sake I seek courage,
alertness of mind and body;
may my heart beat strongly,
may I flinch not under pressure;
may I fight through hardship and grief,
and when Adversity reaches her height
and cries to me, "Give in, surrender,"
then may I remember Lewis, where I was reared,
and may my hand keep its strength.

Murchadh Moireach (1890–1964)

71   *Luach na Saorsa*

Stad tamall beag, a pheileir chaoil,
Tha dol gu d' uidhe; ged as faoin
Mo cheist — am beil 'nad shraon
     Ro-ghuileag bàis?
'M beil bith tha beò le anam caoin
     Ro-sgart' o thàmh?

An làmh a stiùir thu air do chùrs',
An robh i 'n dàn do chur air iùil
A dh'fhàgadh dìlleachdain gun chùl
     An taigh a' bhròin,
Is cridhe goirt le osann bhrùit'
     Aig mnaoi gun treòir?

An urras math do chlann nan daoin'
Thu guin a' bhàis le d' rinn bhig chaoil
A chur am broilleach fallain laoich
     San àraich fhuair?
'Na eubha bàis am beil an t-saors'
     O cheartas shuas?

Freagairt

'Nam shraon tha caoin bhith sgart' o thàmh,
'Nam rinn bhig chaoil ro-ghuileag bàis,
'S an làmh a stiùir bha dhi san dàn
     Deur goirt don truagh;
Ach s uil' iad ìobairt-saors' on àird —
     Tron Bhàs thig Buaidh.

Donnchadh Fionnlasan (1897–1966)

72   *Òran Hitler*

Gur e sinn tha air ar pianadh leis an fhiadh-bheathach gun fhàbhar
Tha ri glaodhaich air an t-sliabh is e ag iarraidh le làmh-làidir
Gus an saoghal mun iadh grian a bhith a' strìochdadh fo 'spàgan
Is daoine bha an saorsa riamh ac' bhith 'nan ìochdarain 's 'nan tràillean.

Murdo Murray (Back, Lewis)

The Value of Freedom

Stop a little, slender bullet,
While speeding to your end; though vain
My question — is there in your wail
    The forecry of death?
Is anyone alive with gentle soul
    Pre-parted from rest?

The hand that sent you on your way,
Was it predestined to put you on a course
That would leave unsupported orphans
    In the house of grief,
And a bitter heart with sigh tormented
    In a powerless wife?

Is it good surety for mankind
That your slender tip should fatally pierce
Some warrior's healthy breast
    In the cold battlefield?
With his death-cry does there come freedom
    From judgement above?

Answer

My wail is a keen for being parted from rest,
In my slender tip is forecry of death,
And the guiding hand was predestined to bring
    Bitter tears to the damned;
But they are all freedom's sacrifice from above —
    For through Death comes Triumph.

Duncan Finlayson (Aird Bernisdale, Skye)

The Song of Hitler

We're all sick and tired of that unprepossessing creature
That howls on the mountainside demanding with violence
That the world the sun encircles should yield under his paws
And that people always free should become inferiors and slaves.

Gur e Pòland fhuair do dhiombadh, rinn thu oirre ionnsaigh ghàbhaidh,
A cuid bhailtean mòra smùideach rinn thu smùrach dhiubh is càrnach;
Mar na *lòcusts* feadh na dùthcha bha cead siùbhlach aig do dhràgoin
Gus na dh'fhàg an cliù 's an giùlain sùilean srùlach aig a' Phàpa.

Na Gearmailtich bha ainmeil riamh mun Chreideamh Chrìostail, 's ghabh iad tràth ris,
'S bhiodh iad cùramach ga dhìon nuair a bhiodh e riaslaicht' sàraicht';
Iad an tràth seo ás an ciall, a' leigeil srian le rian 's le'n nàire —
Gur e bh' ann gun dh'fhàg iad Dia nuair a rinn iad dhìotsa Dàgon.

A bhalgaire tha cealgach lùbach, rinn thu air na h-Iùdhaich tàire,
Thug thu bhuap' an còir 's an ionntas 's chuir thu t' ùmaidhean 'nan àite:
Iad gun bhiadh, gun dìon 's leth-rùisgte, 'nan cuis-bhùirt air feadh nan sràidean,
'S nuair a rinn thu iad a spùilleadh sgiùrs thu iad gu cùl do ghàrraidh.

Nuair a chaidh thu dhan an Òlaind ghabh thu orr' a' chòir a b' àbhaist dut —
Thug thu uatha an cuid lòin 's dh'fhàg thu iad gu brònach cràiteach;
Gura h-ann a bha an dòrainn dol gu spòrs is fealla-dhà dhuit
Nuair a shuidh thu sìos gu dòigheil aig an ròic nach d'rinn thu phàigheadh.

Cha chreid mi gun d'fhuair thu rùpail ùghdarrais bhon an Àrd-Fhear
Gus gach ceàrn 's na chuir thu ùidh a bhith ga brùthadh fo do shàilean —
Sann a tha E ann an diomb riut 's do chuid tùise 'na dhroch fhàileadh
Bhon an là a chuir thu cùl ris dhèanamh cùmhnantan ri Sàtan.

S bochd an nì gun ghineadh riamh thu no gun d'fhuair thu cìoch o d' mhàthair,
S truagh, hi rì, nach d'bhuail a' ghrian thu, ga do chrìonadh gu math tràth ás
Mun do dh'fhàs annad an cìocras thug na gnìomharran gu àirde
A rinn t' fhàgail 'nad chùis-deuchainn, is mar leus air aghaidh nàdair.

Thig a-nise le t' *invasion*, do chuid breunachais is stàirnich,
Théid ur smàladh anns na speuran, 'nur n-éibhlean chon nam blàraibh;
S iomadh fear a bhios 'na éiginn 's an ratreut ga ghearradh tràth dheth —
Cha téid aon ás dhe do *légions* null le sgeul nam breug gu 'chàirdean.

Nuair a chuireas tu d' chuid mhìltean le'n cuid innleachd oirnn thar sàile,
Sin an là a nì dhuit innse mar chaidh thu clì nach d'rinn thu tràth e:
Chan eil gàrlach 'na do thìr-sa a bheir sìnteag gu na tràghadh —
'S théid do chabhlach chur 'na mìrean, s cinnteach leam nach till dhith *bàirge*.

Nuair a nì a' chuibhle tionndadh, bidh na cùisean a' dol ceàrr ort,
Bidh thu thall aig ceann do chùrsa, 's bheir do bhùidsearan am bàs dhuit;
Théid do chàradh gu neo-mhùirneach air an dùnan smùideach ghràineil
'S tàrraidh iolairean do dhùthcha do chuid shùilean ás an àite.

Poland got your bile, and you viciously attacked her,
You reduced her smoky cities to dust and to rubble;
Like locusts swarming through the land you let your shock-troops roam
Till their reputation and behaviour left the Pope with weeping eyes.

Always noted for Christianity, the Germans took to it early,
And were attentive in defending it when it suffered oppression;
They're losing their senses, forsaking order and their principles —
Indeed they abandoned God when they made *you* into Dagon.

You parasite that's lying and crooked, you abused the Jews,
You took away their property and wealth and put your boors in their place:
You left them starving, defenceless, half-naked and mocked through the streets,
And when you'd plundered them you drove them to the back of your enclosure.

When you marched into Holland they suffered your usual impositions —
You took away their livelihood and left them wretched and anguished;
For to you their grief was just a bit of fun and amusement
While you sat smugly down to the feast you hadn't paid for.

I don't believe you had the slightest authority from God
For each land that took your fancy to be crushed under your heels —
Indeed He's in a rage at you and your odour is disgusting
Since the day you turned your back on Him to make a pact with Satan.

It's a shame you were conceived at all or suckled by your mother,
Too bad the sun didn't strike you young, and shrivel you to nothing
Before the avarice could grow in you that brought those deeds to a climax
That made you a tormentor, a painful boil on nature's face.

Come now with your invasion, and all your filth and clamour,
You'll all be blasted from the skies to fall as cinders on the landscape;
Many men will be trapped with their retreat cut off behind them —
Not one of your legions will get out to take back lies to their comrades.

When you send your thousands across the sea at us with all their armaments,
That's the day that will tell you you went wrong not doing it early:
There's not a youth in your country that will leap towards the beach-head —
Your navy blown to bits, I'm sure with not a barge of it returning.

When the wheel of fortune turns, things will start going wrong for you,
You'll have reached the end of your course and your butchers will slaughter you;
You'll be put unceremoniously on the loathsome reeking dunghill
And the eagles of the fatherland will pick your eyes from their sockets.

An t-Urr. Aonghas Fionnlasan (1897–1973)

73   *Dùrachd Teachdaire Chrìost*

Tha sgeul agam ri h-aithris
    'S chan eil fad' agam ri luaidh,
'S dh'ainneoin buaireadh Shàtain
    'S dh'ainneoin tàire sluaigh,
B'e siud mo mhiann is m' iarrtas
    'S dh'iarrainn e gach uair —
Gun tugadh Dia 'na fhàbhar dhomh
    Gach tràth bhith air a luaidh.

Na leigeadh Dia gun sgìthichinn
    An tìm bhith dèanamh sgeul
Air prìsealachd nan geallaidhean
    Mar bharantas don treud
Is éifeachd shìorraidh bhuadhach
    Fuil an Uain a choisinn e,
'S eadarghuidh' a' Bhuachaille
    Thug buaidh 'na uile dhreuchd.

O moladh, moladh sìorraidh Dhuit
    Gun robh E ìosal truagh,
'S air Dha bhith dìoladh m' fhiachan-sa
    Gun riaraich E an uaigh
'S gun sgar E uaipe 'n t-ùghdarras
    Bha aic' bho thùs air sluagh —
'S fa-dheòidh gun éirich m' Aiseirigh
    Le caithream a bhios buan:

"Leag mise 's chuir mi cuideachadh
    Air Curaidh treun nam buadh!"
'S tha E nis air àrdachadh
    Mar Shlànaighear a shluaigh;
'S ged a bhrùth a nàmhaid
    A shàil le iomairt chruaidh,
Rinn Esan briseadh maireann
    Air a chlaigeann greannach cruaidh.

Is maisich', O is maisich' Thu
    Na clann mo shluaigh gu léir,
Is mìlse leam do bhriathran
    Na fìon bho mhil nan geug;

Rev. Angus Finlayson (Marvig, Lochs, Lewis)

The Wish of a Messenger of Christ

I have news to relate
  Without much time to tell it,
And for all Satan's tempting
  And a multitude's mockery,
That were my wish and desire
  And I'd ask it each time —
That God grant me the favour
  Always to have praised Him.

May God not let me tire
  At the time of explaining
The value of the promises
  As a warrant to the flock
And the lasting efficaciousness
  Of the Lamb's blood that achieved it,
And the Shepherd's intercession
  That brought success in all His aims.

O praise, praise eternally be Thine
  That He was laid so low,
And after He has paid my debts
  He will arrange the grave
And remove the authority
  It always had on people —
And my Resurrection comes at last
  With a cry to last forever:

"I've relied for assistance
  On the brave all-powerful Hero!"
And He has now been raised
  To be the Saviour of his flock;
And though his foe has pressed
  A fierce attack upon his heel,
He has crushed for ever
  His hard and ugly skull.

More radiant, more radiant art Thou
  Than all my people's children,
To me sweeter are Thy words
  Than wine from honeyed boughs;

Tha boltrach chùbhraidh, òirdhearc
   Lìonadh seòmair m' anam' fhéin
Nuair dhearcainn troimh na sgòthan
   Air do ghlòir aig deas làimh Dhé.

'Nam fheòil-sa chan eil fallaineachd,
   'S aig m' anam chan eil sìth,
'S a dh'ainneoin bòidean 's aideachaidh
   Tha 'n anshocair 'nam chrìdh;
'S mo nàimhdean guineach àrdanach,
   Cha tàrr mi 'n cur fo chìs —
Gu cogadh tha iad togarrach
   An sìth 'n tràth labhras mì.

Se dh'fhàg san àm seo cianail mi
   'S mi riaraicht' air gach dòigh
An seannduin' a bhith miannachadh,
   'S e 'g iarraidh gu bhith mòr;
Tha sgealb san fheòil gam shàrachadh
   Gach là le iomadh deòir:
Och och is duine truagh mi —
   Có dh'fhuasglas air mo leòn?

Ach ged as treun an seannduine
   'S ged dh'fhàg e mall mo cheum,
'S ged as lìonmhor teanntachdan
   An-seo an gleann nan deur,
Thig an t-àm 's an caochlaidhear
   Gach aon gu àite fhéin,
'S bidh mise troimh an t-sìorraidheachd
   A' mealtainn ìomhaigh Dhé.

Bha càirdean agam uaireigin
   Nuair bha mi 'n cruas na daors',
Ach s fhad bho rinn iad m' fhuathachadh —
   Is suarach mi 'nan sùil;
Ach Caraid caomh nan truaghan,
   Tha E suairc rium anns gach cùis,
'S cha tréig E ri mo bheò mi
   'S aig sruth Iòrdain bidh mi saor.

Ach falbhadh iad no fuireadh iad,
   Is Tusa Fear mo Ghràidh,
Sann ort a bhios mo smuaintean
   Nuair as cruaidhe bhios am blàr;

A fragrant, wonderful scent
  Would fill the chambers of my soul
As I glimpsed between the clouds
  At God's right hand Thy glory.

In my flesh there's no salvation,
  In my soul there's no content,
And despite vows and confession
  There's worry in my heart;
My cruel vainglorious enemies
  I cannot bring to heel —
For war's their inclination
  When I converse in peace.

What's left me anxious for the time
  Though with good reasons to be glad
Is the old man's ambition,
  Desiring to be grand;
In my flesh a skelf torments me
  With many tears each day:
O what a wretched man I am —
  Who will relieve my pain?

But although the old man's mighty
  And has left my step so slow,
And though frequent are the crises
  Here in the vale of tears,
The time will come for changing
  Each person to his place,
While I through all eternity
  Enjoy the sight of God.

I had friends in former times
  When tight encased in bonds,
But they've long found cause to hate me —
  I'm worthless in their eyes;
But the kind Friend of the needy,
  He is always good to me,
He'll not forsake me all my life
  And at Jordan I'll be free.

But let them go or stay,
  Thou art the One I Love,
It's Thou whom I think of
  When the battle's at its height;

Mo dhaingneach treun 's gach cruadal Thu,
　Mo bhuaidh Thu anns gach càs,
'S a' Charraig air an d'fhuaireadh mi —
　Cha ghluaisear i gu bràth.

A' chlach a dhiùlt na clachairean,
　Clach-chinn na h-oisinn ì —
O anam, feuch nach suidhich thu
　Air bunait eil' ach ì
Air eagal nuair a dhearbhar thu
　Am meidhean feirg an Uain,
Gum faigh thu duais nan cealgairean
　An dorchadas bith-bhuan.

Mo bhràithrean caomh, na sgìthichibh,
　'S bithibh dìleas anns gach àm —
Ged tha sibh fulang mìcheartas
　Is mìorùn air gach làimh,
Nuair chruinnicheas E na dìobairich
　Ás na tìrean bhos is thall
Bidh gach dìblidh bochd a chuidich leis
　An culaidh bean na bainns'.

Iain Èirdsidh MacAsgaill (1898–1933)

74　*Mì-Chliù nan Daoine Dubha, 1930*

Tha daoine gnuadh gam chuartachadh
　Cho dubh ri sluagh Shliochd Àroin,
A dh'éirich suas mar bhuatharlain
　Á goirte chruaidh nam fàsach.

Nuair nochd an treud 'nam ionnsaigh ann
　Gun d'chaill mo lùths gun dàil mi,
'S an ceannard tairgse fùidse dhomh
　Is murt 'na shùilean deàrrsach.

Dh'iarr e deoch is biadh orm
　Gu socair, fiaichte, sàmhach,
'S e drannadh faobhar fhiaclan rium
　A chriathradh mar a' chàth mi.

Thou art my stronghold in each hardship,
 My triumph in each plight,
And the Rock that I was found on —
 It never can be moved.

The stone the masons rejected
 Is the bridge's cornerstone —
O soul, mind you don't fasten
 On some foundation elsewhere
For fear that when you're weighed
 In the Lamb's wrathful measure,
You'll get the evildoers' reward
 In the dark that lasts forever.

My dear brethren, tire not,
 And be faithful at all times —
Though you suffer injustice
 And malice on all sides,
When He gathers exiles
 From countries near and far
Every poor outcast that helped Him
 Will wear a bridal gown.

Iain Archie MacAskill (Berneray, Harris)

The Ill-Fame of the Black Men, 1930

Surly men surround me,
 As black as Aaron's tribe,
Who rose up like ragworts
 From the harsh famine of the deserts.

When the band appeared approaching me
 My strength drained out at once,
And their leader challenged me
 With murder in his shining eyes.

He asked me for food and drink
 In a gentle, calm, still voice,
Showing me teeth that were so sharp
 They'd riddle me like chaff.

Nuair sheall mi liad nan sgiathag dha
  'S gun dias ann air son làn dith,
Gun ghairm e dhan fhear sgiathach mi
  'S e 'g òrdan pian a' bhàis dhomh.

Theann mi 'n-seo ri chiallachadh
  'S gun dlò no sìol a' fàs dhuinn,
'S gun cuireadh iad fo fhiachan mi
  Bhiodh snìomhte gu là bhràth rium,

Gu'n robh mi sgìth ga thruaslionadh
  'S am feasgar gruamach geàrrte,
'S cha chumadh tu le buailtean iad
  Bho theine guail 'nam àrdraich.

Gheall mi uisge 's siabann dhaibh,
  Tombaca 's iasg is càise
Nan caidleadh iad gu sìochail
  Fo cheann iarainn bial na bàthchadh.

Se 'n cadal ud bha dùisgeallach
  'S iad ùpraideach ri stàrachd,
'S a' godail mar na h-Iùdhaich ann
  Gun fhois gun diù gun nàire.

Sa mhadainn nuair a dh'éirich mi
  Bha fear 'na leum mar gheàrr dhiubh,
'S fear eile slaoid na léine dheth
  'S e sealltainn béas a' mhàis dhuinn.

Bha aon dhiubh thall ga aonagraich
  Air leide chaol an àraidh,
Fo dhìon 'na sheice ghaoisideach
  'S e caochlaideach ga càrdadh.

Dòigh cha toireadh fuasgladh dhomh
  A dh'fhuadaicheadh on àit iad,
'S ged bhrisinn sròin nam buaistearan
  Cha ghluaiseadh iad o m' làthair.

Sin chuimhnich làithean m' òige dhomh
  Mo sheanair còir bha 'm Beàrn'raigh,
'S mar lìon e poca mònadh ann,
  Bha dhìth na tòin, dhan Tàilleir.

When I showed him the allotment's breadth
  With not an ear of corn in it,
He wished me to Beelzebub
  And summoned down my death-pangs.

I tried to make him understand
  That not a handful of our seed was growing,
That they'd put me into debts
  Which would last me all my days,

Till my sympathy ran out for him
  And the grim evening ended,
And you couldn't keep them with sheepfolds
  From the coal fire in my dwelling.

Water and soap I promised them,
  Tobacco, fish and cheese,
If only they'd sleep peacefully
  Under the cowshed's iron roof.

That night's sleep was fitful
  As they went about noisily
Chanting there like Jews
  Without rest nor heed nor shame.

When I got up in the morning
  One was leaping like a hare,
Another pulled off his clothing
  To show the base of his buttocks.

One was stretched out over there
  On the narrow ladder-bed,
Covered by a shaggy hide,
  Occasionally carding it.

I had no means of solving it
  That would drive them away,
Even if I broke the beggars' noses
  They'd never leave me alone.

Then youthful memories brought back to me
  My dear grandfather in Berneray,
And how he filled a peatbag there,
  That had no bottom, for the Tailor.

Gun d'lìon mi bac-cléibh sùganach
  Le flùr is ùr-bhuntàta,
'S cho tric 's gun gluaiseadh Ùistean e
  Gun srùileadh iad gu làrach.

Thriall iad uam 's bu tùrsach iad
  Gun mhin gun sùgh gun chàise,
'S b'e 'n innleachd gin cho cùramach
  'S a dh'ionnsaich iad o m' làmhan.

Siud far robh na suatharain
  Bha sleamhainn luath gu meàirle,
Gun ghoid iad ormsa 'n t-uaireadair
  'S deise ruadh mo bhràthar.

Mo mhollachd aig na plunndairean
  'S aig sluige chinn a' chàrsain
A chlaimhich uam an cìreanach
  Bu phrìseile sa cheàrn seo.

B' éiginn a bhith cuairtealan
  Le cabar cruaidh fo m' ghàirdean,
Mu thimcheall chearc gam buachailleachd
  'S na coin air thuar an tàrradh.

Bu taitneach leam 's b'e m' iarratas
  Bhith 'n-diugh air thriall le bàta
'S i stiùireadh tarsainn fiarach linn
  Gu tìr nan ciar-bheann àrda.

Bu chaomh leam pìob nan garbh-dhos ann
  Air ghleusadh tallanach làidir,
'S bhiodh meòir a' pògadh stararaich ghlan
  'S ceòl neo-shearbh ga fàgail.

Chan iongnadh ged a dh'iarrainn-sa
  Dhan eilean chiatach àlainn
Far robh mi òg 's mi miastath ann
  'S gu tric a' pianadh Phàdraig.

I filled a straw pannier
   With flour and raw potatoes
And as often as Hugh moved it
   They streamed to the floor.

They deserted me in sadness
   Without meal or juice or cheese,
And the trick was one as artful
   As they learnt from my hands.

Those were the thieving beggars
   Who were slippery and quick to steal,
They took my watch from me
   And my brother's brown suit.

My curse upon the plunderers
   And the gulping wheezy throat
That stole from me a rooster
   That had no equal in these parts.

I had to make a tour
   With a stout club in my oxter
Around the hens to guard them
   With the dogs primed to catch them.

My joy and my delight would be
   To set off by ship today,
Travelling the ocean
   To the land of high grey mountains.

I'd love to hear the pipe of drones
   Tuned both echoing and strong,
Fingers leaping in rippling notes
   And sweet music coming out.

It's not surprising if I desire
   To go back to the lovely island
Where I was young and so full of fun
   And often pestering Pàdraig.

Seonag NicCoinnich (1900–72)

75   *Òran Clach Stèineagaidh*

Bhon bha mi 'nam leanabh
   Gun do chleachd mi bhith 'g éisteachd
Mun chlach mhór bh' anns a' bhaile
   Ris an cante Clach Stèineagaidh.

Tha i dlùth ri mo dhachaigh
   'S gun aon fhacal bréige,
Gum bu tric mi 'nam chaileig
   A' ruith is a leum aice.

Their cuid anns a' bhaile
   (Mas e fìrinn neo breug e)
Gur clach-chinn i bh' air ceannard
   Ann an cogadh na Féinne.

Ma bhios armachd is eallach
   A-rithist ag éirigh
Nach e gheibh an damaist
   Tighinn a-mach fo Chlach Stèineagaidh!

An àm treabhaidh as t-earrach
   Bhiodh an t-amall tighinn dlùth oirr';
S tric a chunnaic mi geal i,
   'Na h-àit'-analach fhaoileag.

S iomadh caora le Calum
   A bhlais air bileig ghlain ùir aic',
S iomadh bó agus gamhainn
   A thachais an taobh rith'.

S iomadh fear a leig anail
   An àm gearradh an fheòir aic',
S iomadh gill' agus caileag
   A bha greis aice còrdte.

S iomadh bodach is cailleach
   Fhuair fasgadh fon t-sròin aic',
S iomadh pìob chaidh a smocadh,
   S iomadh botal chaidh òl aic'.

Joan MacKenzie (Scarista, Harris)

The Song of Steinigie Stone

Since I was a child
   I've been used to be hearing
Of the big stone in this township
   Called Steinigie Stone.

She's close to my home
   And without a word of a lie,
When a girl I would frequently
   Run and skip round about her.

Some say in the township
   (Be it truth or a lie)
She's the headstone of a chief
   In the war of the Féinn.

If his arms and equipment
   Are to rise up again
He'll not come undamaged
   From under Steinigie Stone!

In ploughing time each spring
   The swingle came close;
I often saw her white,
   Being where gulls took a rest.

Many sheep owned by Calum
   Tried her pure fresh young blade,
Many cows and stirks used her
   For scratching their sides.

Many men rested by her
   When cutting their hay,
And it's many boys and girls
   She introduced for a while.

Many old men and women
   Sheltered under her nose,
Many pipes she's seen smoked,
   Many bottles seen drunk.

Thig samhradh, thig earrach,
   Thig foghar, thig dùbhlachd,
Thig oidhcheannan fada
   Le frasan is gaothan,

Théid gach duine dha leabaidh
   A chadal gu saoirsneil,
Ach bidh 'chlach mhór cumail faire
   Air an fhearann aig Fionnlagh.

Murchadh MacPhàrlain (1901–82)

76 *Naoi Ceud Deug 's a Ceithir Deug*

Nuair bhiodh òganaich cruinn
   Dhèanta grìosach bhuntàt;
"Siùdaibh, seasaibh," siud chluinnt,
   "Ach am faic sinn eil àird
A' mhalisi nis òirnn
   'S gu Fort Dheòrs théid ma-thà
     A mhalisi an rìgh."

Ghabh mo ghràdh-sa Di-Màirt
   Do mhalisi Fort Dheòrs;
Féileadh beag 's seacaid bhàn
   Air bidh 'n àit pheitein mhòir
'S briogais thartain ghlan-gheàrrt
   Air an àit na té chlò
     Am malisi an rìgh.

"Cha bhi uat mi ach ràith,"
   Thuirt e 'n sgath bhlàth na cruaich;
"Bidh mi còmh riut, a ghràidh,
   Mun tig càch ás a' Bhruaich —
S dòch gum fiach mi mo làmh
   Ann an gàrraidhean Chluaidh
     Ma bhios rigears gan dìth."

Sheòl i, *Sìle* nan stuadh,
   'S móran sluaigh innt air bòrd —
Cuid gu iasgach na Bruaich
   'S tuath gu Sealtainn nan òb,

Come summer, come spring,
    Come autumn, come doldrums,
Come long winter nights
    With showers and winds,

People go to their beds
    To sleep in content,
But the big stone keeps watch
    Over Finlay's estate.

Murdo MacFarlane (Melbost, Lewis)

Nineteen Fourteen

When lads gathered around
    There'd be frying potatoes;
"Go on, stand up," would be heard,
    "Till we see if we're up
To militia height yet
    And go then to Fort George
        To the king's militia."

My love joined on Tuesday
    The Fort George militia;
He'll have kilt and white jacket
    In place of his waistcoat
And clean-cut tartan trews
    In place of the homespuns
        In the king's militia.

"I'll be gone but a season,"
    Said he in peatstack's warm shelter;
"I'll be with you, my love,
    Before the rest come from the Bruach —
Perhaps I'll try my hand
    In the Clyde shipyards
        If riggers are in demand."

She sailed, *Sheila* of the waves,
    With many people on board —
Some to the fishing of the Bruach
    And north to Shetland of the creeks,

'S cuid a' falbh mar mo luaidh
   A' chiad uair gu Fort Dheòrs
     A mhalisi an rìgh.

Fhuair mi dhealbh an céis dhùint
   'S chroch sa chùlaist le uaill,
Agus litir ag inns,
   "Tha gach nì dhomh cho nuadh —
Moch gar dùsgadh bidh phìob
   Nuair as fìor throm ar suain
     Am malisi an rìgh.

"On tha 'n cosnadh car gann,"
   Thuirt e rium, "dhomh is fheàrr
Ghallaibh dhol nuair bhios m' àm
   Anns a' champa seo 'n àird
Agus gabhail aig na Goill
   'Na mo chuibhlear am bàt —
     Seadh, ma ghabhas iad mì."

Naoi ceud deug 's ceithir deug,
   Tigh'nn fo dhias nuair bha 'n t-eòrn,
Caismeachd airm chualas cian,
   Geilt is fiamh chuir e òirnn:
Teachd tha stoirm, dhubh e ghrian,
   Mar bheul oidhch rinn tràth-nòin
     'S e ri fògradh ar sìth.

Bhris an stoirm, 's an tuil dhòirt
   'S air an Eòrpa rinn tigh'nn:
Tuil fhuil dhearg nam fir òg —
   Seadh, fir òg nan ciabh mìn;
Thraogh is thràigh chun an fheòir
   Fuil an cuislean 's an crìdh;
     Dh'fhuairich, reòdh 's chaill a clì.

Cuig a-riamh ghabh mo ghràdh
   Tastan eàrlais an rìgh?
S gann gun bhris fo làn bhlàth
   'S bha sa bhlàr 'na thost sìnt;
Air a' bhuaidh s daor a phàigh
   Le fuil bhlàth dhearg a chrìdh —
     S daor thu, bhuaidh, daor do phrìs.

And some going like my love
   For the first time to Fort George
      To join the king's militia.

I got his picture enclosed in an envelope,
   And hung it with pride in the closet,
With a letter that said,
   "Everything is so new to me —
The pipe wakes us early
   When our sleep's at its soundest
      In the king's militia.

"Since employment seems scarce,"
   He said to me, "I'd better go
To Caithness when my time
   In this camp is up
And get a job from the Lowlanders
   On a boat as a winchman —
      That is, if they'll have me."

In nineteen fourteen,
   When the barley was ripening,
The call to arms, heard afar,
   Caused us alarm and fear:
The storm's on its way, it's blackened the sun,
   And turned noon into evening
      As it banished our peace.

The storm broke, the flood poured
   And overwhelmed Europe:
The flood of young men's red blood —
   Yes, young men of soft hair;
To the grass ebbed and drained
   Their veins' and hearts' blood;
      It grew cold, froze and lost force.

Why did my love ever take
   The king's shilling for arles?
When just come to full bloom
   He lay still on the field;
He paid dear for victory
   With his heart's warm red blood —
      Dear you are, victory, dear is your price.

Thuit blàth bhraon air an raon
  'S nigh aog-aodann nan òg;
Shéid a' chaomh osag chaoin
  Orra 's thiormaich is phòg
'S i ri osnaich os cionn
  Òigfhir ghrinn an fhuilt òir —
    O mhalisi mo chrìdh!

Colla, Fionnlagh is Dòmhnall,
  Ruairidh Òg is Iain Bàn,
Aonghas, Ùistean 's Niall Mòr
  (Chòrr cha shloinn mi am' dhàn)
'N-dé 'nam balachain san dròbh,
  'N-diugh gun deò anns an àr —
    O mhalisi mo chrìdh!

Tha chruach mhòna 'na luath,
  Theich am fuachd, thill am blàths,
Thill luchd-cutaidh na Bruaich;
  S fhada buan leam tha 'n ràith
Gheall mo ghràdh bhiodh e bhuam
  Aig a' chruaich, 'n oidhch a dh'fhàg —
    O mhalisi mo chrìdh.

Chaidh na geòidh tarsainn tuath,
  Thug na geòidh mach an àil;
Thill gu deas mar as dual
  Àrd le 'n àil air an sàil,
Ach cha phill e, mo luaidh,
  Ach 'nam bhruadar a-mhàin —
    O mhalisi mo chrìdh.

Calum MacNeacail (1902–78)

77   Cùmhnantan Sìthe Pharis

Tha rìoghachdan an t-saoghail seo
  A' saothrachadh gach là
Ag iarraidh sìth is saoirsne
  Do chlann nan daoin' gu bràth;
Am baile mór na Frainge
  Tha ceannardan gach àit'
A' dol a dhèanamh còrdadh
  'S gum faigh Roinn Eòrpa tàmh.

Blossom-dew fell on field,
   Washed the young men's death-faces;
A soft gentle breeze blew
   Which dried them and kissed them
As it sighed for the beautiful
   Golden-haired youth —
      O my darling militia!

Coll and Finlay and Donald,
   Young Roddy and Fair John,
Angus, Hugh and Big Neil
   (I'll name no more in my song)
Yesterday boys in the gang,
   Today lifeless in battlefield —
      O my darling militia!

The peatstack is ashes,
   Cold has gone, warmth returned,
The gutters are back from the Bruach;
   Forever for me is the season
That my love swore to be gone
   At the stack, that last night —
      O my darling militia.

The geese went over northwards,
   And brought forth their young;
They went back south as ever
   Followed high by their brood,
But my love won't return
   Except in my dreams —
      O my darling militia.

Malcolm Nicolson (Braes, Skye)

The Paris Peace Treaties

The kingdoms of this world
   Are toiling day by day
Seeking peace and freedom
   For mankind forever;
In the capital of France
   The leaders of each place
Are trying to reach agreement
   To give Europe a rest.

Dh'fhalbh á Rìoghachd Bhreatainn
   Mgr Attlee is MacNèil,
Daoine fiosrach, eòlach,
   Daoine còire, sèimh;
Nì iad sìth is còrdadh —
   Sin an dòchas aig gach treubh:
'S biodh freastal beannaicht' còmhla riuth'
   Gan treòrachadh 'nam feum.

Tha aon fhear leo tha mallaichte,
   Se Molotov dha s ainm:
E dìblidh cumail conais riuth',
   'S gam brosnachadh gu fearg;
Ach mura gabh e comhairle
   Gun coinnich e ri stoirm —
Is feuchaidh iad *Atomic* air
   'S bheir sin gu fois a ghairm.

Riamh o thùs an t-saoghail seo,
   Bha seòrsa dhaoin' ann riamh
Nach b' urrainn a bhith còrdte riuth',
   Nach gabhadh dòigh no rian;
Bha iad ri àm Noah ann
   Nach do ghabh on dòrtadh dìon —
B' fheàrr leo bhith gam bàthadh
   'S a bhith sàsachadh am miann.

Nuair thàinig àm an t-Slànaigheir
   Bha aige dà dhuin' dheug
Bha dìleas dleasail bàidheil ris
   Gach àite an d'rinn e triall;
Bha fear a bha 'na shàtan dhiubh
   B'e 'n t-airgead grànd' a mhiann —
Is dhiùlt e bhunait ghràsmhor ud,
   Is bhàsaich e 'na bhiast.

Nuair chruthaicheadh an talamh seo
   Air aithris e, 's gu fìor,
Gun crìochnaicheadh 'na lasair e
   'S gum paisgte suas gach neul;
Ach tha sìth ri mhealtainn air
   Cho fad' ri mìle bliadhn' —
S dòch' gun tig a' bheannachd sin
   Á Paris oirnn am-bliadhn'.

From the Kingdom of Britain
  Went Mr Attlee and MacNeil,
Experienced, knowledgeable men,
  Decent, civilised men;
They'll make peace and agreement —
  That's the hope of each nation:
Blessed providence be with them
  To guide them in their task.

One man's with them who's cursed,
  Molotov is his name:
He vilely disagrees with them,
  Provoking them to rage;
But if he takes no counsel
  He'll be facing a storm —
They'll drop on him an A-bomb
  That will silence his call.

Ever since this world was made
  There's been a type of people
Whom no-one could get on with,
  Irresponsive to control;
There were those in Noah's time
  Who took no shelter from the flood —
They would rather be drowned
  While fulfilling their desires.

When the Saviour's time arrived
  He had twelve with faith in him
Who were dutiful and loving
  No matter where he went;
There was one of them a demon
  Who desired but filthy lucre —
And refusing elemental grace,
  He died a soulless brute.

When this planet was created
  It's said, and with some truth,
That it would finish up in flames
  With clouds all joined together;
But peace can be enjoyed on it
  Throughout a thousand years —
Perhaps this year that blessing
  Will come to us from Paris.

Se seo gach guidhe 's achanaich
   A th' aig gach neach fon ghréin,
Gum biodh sìth gu bràth aca
   'S dhan àl tha tighinn 'nan déidh;
'S gum biomaid uil' 'nar bràithrean
   Is gràdh againn dha chéil'
A thòisich anns a' ghàradh
   A bha aig Àdhamh 's aig Eubh.

78 Blàr Chaol Àcainn

Bha 'n t-Sàbaid riamh san Eilean Sgitheanach
   Air a cumail diadhaidh glan ann —
Bha o chionn cheudan bliadhna
   Le sìth is sìochaint is beannachd;
Thàinig taisbeanadh am-bliadhna
   O gu sìorraidh a nì magadh,
Nuair thàinig luchd-turais na Sàbaid
   Nall a Chaol Àcainn air madainn.

Thàinig iad sin gu dearbha,
   Agus s doirbh an nì a thachair:
Choinnich fir na h-Eaglais Shaoir riu,
   Bodaich fhaoin' a' dol a shabaid:
Cuid de dh'eildirean ag iarraidh
   ('S O nach cianail seo ga labhairt)
Iad a thoirt leo claidheamhnan meirgeach —
   'N e daoine mharbhadh bu mhath leo?

Nach e seo na fir bha làidir —
   Saoil 'n e gràs a ghluais na balaich?
Chuala mi e air a ràdha
   Gun robh pàirt dhiubh air 'n robh drama;
Na boireannaich a' gul 's ag éigheach,
   "Go away, you Sabbath-breakers!"
Nam b'e madainn Di-Luain bh' ann
   Bhiodh bùird suas le "Bed and Breakfast".

Thug iad Di-Sathairn' a-nuas iad
   Mun d'readh an truailleadh le peacadh
Do dhaoine a bha fada na b' fheàrr na iad
   'Nan cànan 's 'nan caitheamh-beatha;

It's the prayer and petition
   Of all people in the world
To have peace forever more
   For themselves and their children,
That we may all be brothers
   With that love for each other
Which began in the garden
   Where dwelt Adam and Eve.

The Battle of Kyleakin

The Sabbath was always in the Isle of Skye
   Kept both pious and pure —
It has enjoyed for hundreds of years
   Peace and quiet and blessing;
A demonstration came this year
   Which brings forever mockery,
When Sabbath visitors came over
   To Kyleakin in the morning.

Oh yes they did indeed,
   And cruel's the fate that befell them:
To be met by the Wee Frees,
   Silly asses spoiling for a fight:
Some elders even asked them
   (And oh how terrible to relate)
To bring their rusty swords —
   Was it people killed they wanted?

O how strong they were, these men —
   Could grace have moved the beggars?
Actually I heard it said
   That some of them had drink in them;
Women weeping, crying out,
   "Go away, you Sabbath-breakers!"
If it had been Monday morning
   There'd be signs saying "Bed and Breakfast".

On Saturday they took them down
   In case sin might corrupt them
For people far better than themselves
   In their language and way of life;

Chan fhaigheadh iad greim air Shàbaid,
　　Chan fhaigheadh iad àite gu fantainn —
Sann tearc tha 'mhuinntir seo san àite,
　　Taing dhan Àgh nach eil iad pailt ann!

Ùghdar na h-aimhreit 's na mì-riaghailt,
　　Nach e sin an Diabhal 's a mhollachd,
'S nach e sin a bha 'n Caol Àcainn
　　'Mhadainn Shàbaid seo rinn crois ann,
Rinn cùis-mhagaidh dhen an àite
　　Anns gach ceàrna th' air an domhan?
'S gun cumamaid cuimhne gu bràth air
　　Blàr Chaol Àcainn — mo bhonaid!

Dòmhnall Grannd (1903–70)

79　bho *An Uilebheist is na Foghlamaich*

Bu chiùin Loch Nis ré iomadh linn
　　Gun ghoil no gàirich thonn,
Bha neart nam beann ga dìon bho stoirm,
　　Cha b' ionann 's cuan le greannd;
A dh'ainneoin sin bu tric a' ghaoth
　　A' greasad nuas gach gleann
A mhilleadh sgàthan réidh an uisg'
　　Le cuairteig nach bu ghann.

Cha b' ainneamh breac a' leum le plub
　　Air feasgar ciùin an àird,
Cha b' ainneamh eala bhàn le céil'
　　Bho thaobh gu taobh a' snàmh;
Cha b' ainneamh fear an geòla chaoil
　　A' sìneadh air dà ràmh,
Cha b' ainneamh eadhon bàt' na smùid'
　　Sna làithean seo a chàidh.

Bha uair nach robh ach sin san loch
　　Cho fads a b' fhiosrach leò,
Cha robh ri fhaotainn air Loch Nis
　　Ach sàmhchair mar bu nòs;

They'd not get a bite on the Sabbath,
    They'd not get a place to stay —
Such people are thin on the ground here,
    Thank Goodness they're not plentiful!

The source of discord and misrule,
    Isn't it the Devil and his curse,
And isn't that what was in Kyleakin
    On this Sabbath that caused a fuss,
That made a mockery of the place
    In every corner of the world?
So let's remember forever
    The Battle of Kyleakin — my hat!

Donald Grant (Camuscross, Sleat, Skye)

from *The Monster and the Experts*

Loch Ness was calm for many an age
    Without churning or roaring of waves,
The mountains served as a shield from storm,
    Avoiding the ocean's rage;
Nevertheless the bustling wind
    Often hurried down each glen
To break that surface as smooth as glass
    Into eddies from shore to shore.

Not infrequent the trout that leapt on high
    In the evening calm with a plop,
Not infrequent the white-downed swan with her mate
    Swimming across the loch;
Not infrequent the man in a slender boat
    Pulling upon two oars,
Not even infrequent the steam-powered ship
    In days not so long ago.

Once that was *all* there was in the loch
    As far as the people knew,
All that there was to be found on Loch Ness
    Was tranquillity all day through;

Ach thàinig beothach mór ro threun
   'S na fir seo air a thòir —
An t-Ollamh Caol, an t-Uasal Maol
   'S an Dotair Mac Iain Ghròt.

Cha b' aon fhear do'm bu léir a' bhiast —
   Cha b'eadh, no dhà, no trì;
Cha tug mi feairt air feadhainn dhiubh
   A bha dhen eaglais chlì,
Ach nuair a chuala mi an sgeul
   Bho neach dhe m' eaglais fhìn,
Cha b' urrainn dhomh gun aideachadh
   Gun robh an t-iomradh fìor.

Ach bha gach fear a' faicinn cruth
   Nach faca neach de chàch —
Bha cuid a chunnaic adhaircean,
   Cuid eile ceann maol bàn;
Thuirt cuid gun robh i mìl' am fad,
   Cuid eile slat no dhà:
A h-astar uair cho luath ri fiadh,
   I rìs cha mhór 'na tàmh.

Bha sligean carrach air a druim
   Cheart uiread ri do dhòrn,
Ach beagan làithean as a dhéidh
   Bha i cho slìom ri ròn;
Air tùs bha 'druim 'na fhichead snaim,
   A-rìs a trì bu dòch';
Aon fhear ga faicinn staigh air tìr,
   Smùid aic' air ithe 'n fheòir.

Se thuirt riumsa fear na sgeig
   Nuair chual' e brìgh mo sgeòil,
"Is math an stuth tha 'n Inbhir Nis
   Ma chithear siud le seòid."
Ach s neònach leam a ghabhail a-steach
   Gun robh iad uil' ga òl,
Oir tha 'nam measg na h-éildearan
   Nach blaiseadh deur ri'm beò.

Ach tha e soilleir dhuinn co-dhiù
   Gun d'rinn am beothach feum,
'S gun d'ràinig daoine taobh Loch Nis
   Nach cuala roimh' m'a déidh;

But there came a great and valiant beast
   With these men in hot pursuit —
Professor Thin, the Hon. Mr Bald
   And Dr McJohn o' Groats.

It wasn't one man that saw the beast —
   No indeed, nor two, nor three;
I paid no heed to certain folk
   Who were of an errant creed,
But when I heard the selfsame tale
   From a man in the same church as me,
I had to admit that from that moment on
   The report must be believed.

But every man was seeing a shape
   Different from all the rest —
Some were certain that they'd seen horns,
   Some a polled white head;
Some said that she was a mile in length,
   Some just a yard or two:
Her speed now likened to a deer,
   Or else she'd hardly moved.

Knobbly shells were on her back
   The same size as your fist,
Or just a few days after that
   She was slippery like a seal;
At first her back had twenty coils,
   Later more like three;
One man saw her upon dry land,
   Eating the grass with glee.

There was a wit who when he heard
   My story said to me,
"The whisky's good in Inverness
   If that's what people see."
But I'm reluctant to accept
   That drink's behind it all,
For among them are church elders
   Who'd never touch a drop.

It's clear to us however
   That the beast has been of benefit,
For folk have come to see Loch Ness
   Who'd never previously heard of it;

Their Sasannach, "Sann air son seo
    A thog an sluagh an sgeul."
Tha Goill an dùil gu bheil gach neach
    Cho breugach riutha fhéin.

Is nì cho iongantach 's a bh' ann
    Ri fhaicinn anns an tìr
Mar thàinig biastan eile beò
    Gach seachdain fad na tìd':
An loch nach cumadh biast no dhà
    Gu dearbh cha b' fhiach i nì —
Bha iad cho pailt ri sgadan sìos
    Loch Aillse gu Loch Fìn.

Cha chuala tus' a leithid riamh
    De dh'ùpraid measg an t-sluaigh:
An dara taobh a' mionnachadh
    Gun robh rud ann a ghluais,
Cuid eil' an aghaidh sin gu dian —
    An cual thu dad cho truagh?
O làithean an Ath-Leasachaidh
    Cha robh ann cath cho cruaidh.

Gach neach a thuirt nach biast a bh' ann,
    Bha beachd aige dha fhéin,
B'e iarratas gach fir gum biodh
    A bheachd-san ùr gu léir;
'S gun cluinnteadh barail bhuaithsan,
    Ge beag bhiodh innt' de chéill,
Mar nach biodh ann ach faileas bheann
    Ga chluich fhéin ris a' ghréin.

'S ma bha mìle eanchainn
    A' cnuasach air a' chùis,
Gu deimhinn chluinnte mìle beachd
    Nan éisteadh daoine riù;
Gach pàipeir-naidheachd beag is mór
    Làn bhiastan fad na h-ùin' —
Is sgrìobhadh eadhon leabhraichean
    A tha nis àrd an cliù.

An Englishman says, "But this is why
   People made up the tale."
Non-Highlanders think that everyone's
   As mendacious as themselves.

One of the most surprising things
   To be seen throughout the land
Was how other beasts had sprung to life
   With every week that passed:
The loch without a beast or two
   Wasn't worth a dime —
They became as thick as herring were
   From Lochalsh down to Loch Fyne.

Of such a public controversy
   The likes you've never heard:
One side swearing blind
   There was something there that stirred,
Others denying it strenuously —
   Have you heard anything so weird?
Ever since the Reformation
   No debate has been so fierce.

Each one who said it wasn't a beast
   Had an individual view,
Each man desiring his idea
   To be completely new;
From him you'd hear the theory,
   Though little sense it made,
That it was just the mountains
   Playing with sun and shade.

And if there were a thousand brains
   All pondering the issue,
A thousand views might well be heard
   If anyone wished to listen;
Each newspaper big and small
   Full of monsters all the time —
Even books have now been written
   That are famous far and wide.

Ruairidh MacLeòid (1903–65)

80　An Cùlaibh Éirinn

Tha mi fo chùram an cùlaibh Éirinn,
Tha mi fo chùram air bòrd na h-iùbhraich
'S i gar giùlain a-null don Éipheit:
Tha mi fo chùram an cùlaibh Éirinn.

An té bh' aig fuaradh, an uair a bhuail i,
Bha cuid 'nan suain innt', 's cha d'fhuair iad éirigh:
Tha mi fo chùram an cùlaibh Éirinn.

Bha glaodh a' bhàis air gach taobh den bhàta
'S mo chrìdh gu sgàineadh le cràdh gan éisteachd:
Tha mi fo chùram an cùlaibh Éirinn.

Chithinn pàirt dhiubh le seacaid àirce,
Bha 'n fhairge làidir, 's cha do shàbhail creutair:
Tha mi fo chùram an cùlaibh Éirinn.

Ach théid gach cealgair a tha sa Ghearmailt
Chur sìnte marbh, bodhar balbh, gun éirigh:
Tha mi fo chùram an cùlaibh Éirinn.

Théid Musolìnidh chur don a' phrìosan
'S le cromadh cinn cluinnidh e 'bhinn ga leughadh:
Tha mi fo chùram an cùlaibh Éirinn.

Théid croich an òrdan is crochar beò e
'S bidh coin na Ròimhe toirt 'fheòil o chéile:
Tha mi fo chùram an cùlaibh Éirinn.

Gach inneal marbhaidh a bh' aig a' Ghearmailt
Bha siubhal na fairge 's a' falbh nan speuran:
Tha mi fo chùram an cùlaibh Éirinn.

O cha dìochuimhnich mi gu sìorraidh
Oidhche Chiadaoin an-iar air Éirinn:
Tha mi fo chùram an cùlaibh Éirinn.

Tha mi fo chùram air bòrd na h-iùbhraich
'S i gar giùlain a-null don Éipheit:
Tha mi fo chùram an cùlaibh Éirinn.

Roderick MacLeod (Kyles Stockinish, Harris)

At the Back of Ireland

I'm sick with anxiety at the back of Ireland,
I'm sick with anxiety aboard the vessel
   That's bringing us over the sea to Egypt:
   I'm sick with anxiety at the back of Ireland.

The one to windward, when she finally struck,
   Some were asleep in her, and couldn't get up:
   I'm sick with anxiety at the back of Ireland.

The cry of death was on each side of the boat
   With my heart torn apart in anguish at hearing them:
   I'm sick with anxiety at the back of Ireland.

I could see some of them with their cork jackets on,
   The sea was strong, not one of them survived:
   I'm sick with anxiety at the back of Ireland.

Every one of those criminals in Germany
   Will be laid out dead, deaf and dumb, without rising:
   I'm sick with anxiety at the back of Ireland.

Mussolini will be sent to prison
   And with bowed head will hear his sentence being read:
   I'm sick with anxiety at the back of Ireland.

They'll fix up a gallows and hang him alive
   And the dogs of Rome will tear apart his flesh:
   I'm sick with anxiety at the back of Ireland.

Every instrument of death that Germany possessed
   Has been coursing the ocean and flying through the skies:
   I'm sick with anxiety at the back of Ireland.

O I'll never forget as long as I live
   Wednesday night to the west of Ireland:
   I'm sick with anxiety at the back of Ireland.

I'm sick with anxiety aboard the vessel
   That's bringing us over the sea to Egypt:
   I'm sick with anxiety at the back of Ireland.

Aonghas Caimbeul, 'Am Puilean' (1903–82)

81 *Deargadan Phóland*

Deargadan dubha na dunaidh 's na dòrainn,
Gu dearbha cha tugainn mo chruth ga mo dheòin dhiubh —
S mairg dhan a' chuid thig fo phlucadh na h-òrdaig
  'S muirt-bhith làmh sgròbadh na sgobaig 'na cùl.

Freiceadan falachaidh nam plaide 's nan cuibhrig
Ri breacadh nan amhach, nan asainn, 's nan uillnean,
Spealairean ladarna carach nan cruinnleum,
  Camanachd bhuill fear cadail 'na rùit.

Sealgairean giobach a' griobadh 's a' grobadh,
A' bolgadh, a' bìdeadh, a' bioradh, 's a' brodadh,
Calpa ga chlipeadh 's cas dhioglach nam bonnan
  Toirt clisgeadh air colainn 's gun norrag an sùil.

Nàdar a' ghadaiche, faire gu foillbheart,
Là fo anail 's a' caithris na h-oidhche,
Cràdhlot mo thaisean le gathan is saighdean,
  Tachais mo dhruim le spuirean mo dhùirn.

Bidh criomag á camais, is glamadh á sliasaid,
Dh'fhidir is dh'fhairich mi cnamhadh nam biastan;
S tric iad ag amais air bad mu nach iarrainn
  Aithris a dhèanamh mun caillinn mo chliù.

Balgairean ciar-dhonn as sgiathalta spionnadh
Tha conablaich mo chliabh 's droch dhìol air mo mhuineal,
Ri borbadh mo bhial-sa gu grìosaidh is mionnan
  'S nach iarrainn-sa fulang mo chiùrradh aig cù.

"Oidhche mhath leat," their caraide, Ruairidh,
Crùbadh 'na cheirsle 's a' phlaide mu chnuacan;
Truillich nan grad-leum cha stad iad a bhruadar,
  'S mis' ann an suain na h-eadar-dha-lionn.

Cluinnidh mi Murchadh san dorcha ri gearain,
Ri dùsgadh le colg air, 's e sporghail nan casan,
Se adhbhar a' bhròin ged bu deòin leis an cadal
  Nach fhaigh e ach mabladh tha anshocair ciùrrt.

Angus Campbell (Swainbost, Ness, Lewis)

The Fleas of Poland

The confounded fleas of mischief and grief,
I'm not at all willing to lose my health to them —
Woe betide all who fall to thumb's squeezing
  And death-dealing backswipe of scratching hand.

Hidden watchers of blankets and coverings
Blotching the necks, the ribs and the elbows,
Bold crafty scythemen with springs in their heels
  Playing riotous shinty on sleeping man's limbs.

Shaggy hunters nibbling and biting,
Blistering, stinging, jabbing and goading,
The calf being gnawed and the soles being tickled
  Makes the body twitch without sleep in the eye.

In the manner of thieves, on the lookout for mischief,
Resting by day and awake all the night,
Wounding my soft spots with stings and with arrows
  As I claw at my back with a fistful of fingernails.

Morsel from inner thigh, mouthful from outer one,
I've perceived and I've felt the gnawing of the beasts;
They often aim for a place I wouldn't like to name
  For fear of not retaining my good reputation.

Dark dusky vermin very strong in flight
Who lacerate my trunk and ill-treat my neck,
Inciting my mouth to such cursing and swearing
  That I wouldn't wish my injuries even on a dog.

"Good night to you," says Roddy, a friend,
Crouching in his clew with his blanket round his noddle;
The prancing scavengers will not interrupt his dream,
  While I lie languishing in fitful reverie.

I hear Murdo in the darkness complaining,
Waking in a rage, scrabbling with his feet,
The cause of his grief being that while he craves sleep
  He gets only aggravation and painful unease.

Bidh Donnchadh an Òbain ag osnaich fon aodach,
Cuilbheartaich gheòir-ghob an dólais ga chaobadh,
Sultmhorachd feòil-bheathach òg 's e cho daor dhaibh
    Ri c[ro]gladh na daorsa a shaobhadh bho'n cùrs.

Glòir Bheniàmon troimh chàirean gun fhiaclan
Ag òrdachadh mèirlich bìd-mhàs agus chiasan
Do sheòmar dubh dàithte 'na smàl theine grìosaich
    'S e fasgadh na siamaich á ìochdair a bhrù.

Nan tuigeadh sibh Ghàidhlig an àite na Pòlais
Bhiodh innleachd 'nur gnàth, agus tàlann is seòltachd
An àit' bhith dol bàs air do stàrr-chruth gun lòn
    Nuair tha 'n t-àgh 'na làn stòrais a' còmhnaidh ribh dlùth.

Seall Ruairidh Mór, nach eil cóig chlachan deug ann,
Reamhaireachd an t-sògh-bheatha òg ann an Siadar,
Annlan is lòn dhèanadh beòshlainte 's biadh dhuibh
    A dh'fhòghnadh fad bliadhna nan riaghladh sibh chùis.

Tha Curly tiugh tuilear le sult bloinig bhog air,
Se goile gun slugan nach glugadh le sogan
Air cuirm de dh'fheòil ruiteach ga ithe gu sgogadh
    Bheir brùchd air ur slogaid le toileachadh brù.

Faic am fear ruadh, tha ceann uachdrach is tòin air
Cho cruinn thiugh ri buacaire buanna nan geòcair,
Seasgair dhuibh suaineadh ri fuachd agus reòtachd
    'Na chuaileanan òir 's am bheil còsan is 'curl'.

Tha Murchadh cho snasmhor, 'na bhagan cho toinnte,
Crannchur gu beannachd air basgaid is cuibhreann —
S iomadh té spaideil a chaithriseadh oidhche
    San achlais tha sibhse cur air bheag diù.

Ach cha sguir sibh, a riabhaich, a chliathadh mo chlàran
Gu'n lùb mo cheann iarach 's gu'n liath an ceann àrd dhiom —
Mar sgruit sgrath-gu-siaman chlèith fhiar cham taigh àirigh
    Bidh 'n ciaran aig Màiri, 's e grànda co-dhiù.

Nan tàrrainn ur cròdhadh 's ur stòdhadh am baraill
'S am fàbhar 'nam sheòl gus bhur treòireach gu Adolph,
Measg cràbais nam pùg agus bógais nam peallag
    Dheadh a dhòirteadh mu chlaigeann 's a ghlasadh 'na rùm.

Duncan from Oban sighs under the bedclothes
As pincer-beaked tricksters of misery chomp him,
For they've a high regard for young flesh in all its plumpness
       While famine's grip's being shifted from their path.

Benjamin's voice comes out through toothless gums
Consigning marauders who bite buttocks and hips
To a chamber singed black by flaming embers of fire
       As he squeezes the blackguards from his lower belly.

If you understood Gaelic instead of Polish
You'd have native resourcefulness, subtlety and skill
Instead of dying on your threshold for lack of nourishment
       When bountiful providence is so close at hand.

Look at Ruairidh Mór, doesn't he weigh fifteen stone,
All the girth of a well-fed upbringing in Shader,
Main course and side one to give you livelihood and eating
       That would last you all year if you organised the matter.

Stout Curly's afloat in soft blubbery fat,
It's a gorgeless stomach that wouldn't cluck with delight
At a feast of red meat being eaten to bursting
       Bringing belch to your gullets through bellyfuls of pleasure.

See the one with red hair, his top end and his backside
Are as round and as fat as any gluttonous layabout's,
You'll find it cosy to sleep when it's cold and it's frosty
       In his golden ringlets with their hollows and curls.

Murdo's so neat, such a compact little blob,
Life's lottery has blessed him in shape and amount —
Many fine women would spend the night gladly
       In the oxter you regard as of little account.

But you won't stop, you demons, harrowing my surfaces
Till my bottom bends over and my top becomes grey —
Like the mouldering divots when the shieling roof's collapsed
       Will be Mary's old darling, who's ugly in any case.

If I could round you all up and stow you in a barrel
And were I blessed with the means to guide you to Adolf,
Mixed with body-hugging crablice and bugs from the rugs
       I'd have it poured about his skull and he'd be locked in his room.

Bhiodh ana-ghalair oillteil, bhiodh teinn agus dórainn,
Toirt searg agus claoidh air sgaoth shaighdeach an dólais —
Gu'm fàiling mo chuimhne, bidh braighdeanas Phóland
    Le dheargadan geòcach tighinn beò ri mo smuain.

82   *Ciod E?*

Nuair shluigeas beul a' chiaraidh a' ghrian lasrach
'S a dhruideas duibhre na h-oidhch' m'a bathais,
Thig bandia eadar-shoillse le laoidh cagair
    A thàladh a taigh-tasgaidh, flaitheas cruinne.
    Àilleagain a h-altram gu latha dìlinn,
        Seudan glòir a h-aisridh, maise h-ìomhaigheachd,
        Deiltreadh céis a cearcaill le slat-draoidheachd,
Neamhnaidean a rìgh-choran 's e fallain.
Uinneagan nan nèamh se leus ri fadadh,
    Reultan tha so-mhaireann ri fad tìmeil
Rìomhachadh nan speur air leud is farsainn —
    Leugan a dubh-bhrat 'na lainnir fìor-ghlan.

O, ar n-iomraill 's ro-bheag cuimse ar gliocais —
Có 'na uamhrachd dhèanadh uaill á fhiosrachd?
Imchéin na bith-bhuantachd air nach ruig sinn
    A thòimhsean a chrioslachadh no 'chrìochadh,
    Neo-bhrigh, neonitheachd làn bois ar dìoghlaim
    Tighinn fa chomhair riochdaileachd cho-shìorraidh,
    Glòir na mórachd mheòmhrachadh le ciallachd.
Àirde, fad is leudachd tha do-thuigsinn,
Suim na tha do-rannsaicht' an an-fhios dhuinn,
    'M boillsg ar beatha dhiomain, mionaid iasaid,
Iteal luath ar bith an co-ruith ri tìm,
    Falamhachd is dìth ar strìthean dìomhain.

Ceistean sgrùdail: ùghdar mo chion-fàth-se,
Có, car son no cuime, cuin no càite,
Ciod e Cumadair — làmh-chruth no Àrd Fhlath,
    Ulaidh uile-làthaireachd no ceannabhrat?
    Teagamhan ag agairt air mo dhearbh-bheachd,
    Creideamh m' oilean ann an slochd ana-ceist,
    Rùdhraich far nach coisich mo mhac-meanmna,
Cuimseachadh air dealbh nach tog mo sgàthan,
Dìomhaireachd nach criathair m' uile thàlann,

Only dreadful disease, and hardship and agony,
Brought decline and defeat on that barbed swarm of evil —
Till my memory fails, the Polish captivity
    Will come alive in my thoughts with its ravenous fleas.

What is He?

When the mouth of the gloaming swallows the shining sun
And the gathering gloom of the evening touches its brow,
The goddess of twilight comes with whispering chant
    To lull her storehouse to sleep, the principality of the globe.
    Jewels are her rearing to the day of judgement,
    Glorious gems her abode, the beauty of her face,
    The gilding of her circle's frame by a magic wand,
Pearls are her crown in its regal perfection.
The windows of the heavens are a gleam akindled,
    Stars which survive unto endless time
Measuring the skies both in length and in breadth —
    The jewels of her black mantle gleam in all their purity.

O, so narrow our horizons and the aims of our wisdom —
Who in his vanity would take pride in such knowledge?
The distance of eternity which we cannot reach,
    Taking or enclosing its measurements,
    Insignificance, nothingness is the handful we have gleaned
    Compared to co-eternal reality,
    The glory of greatness pondered with ingenuity.
Height, length and breadth incomprehensible,
The total unsearched is unknown to us,
    In a gleam's our transient life, a minute borrowed,
The swift flight of our existence in comparison with time,
    The empty irrelevance of our foolish strivings.

Searching questions: author of my senses,
Who, why or how, when or where,
What is Creator — moulder or High King,
    Essence of omnipresence or mere canopy?
    Doubts pressing in upon my certainty,
    The faith of my upbringing in the slough of dilemma,
    Grope where my imagination cannot walk,
Trying to see an image which my mirror cannot grasp,
A mystery which all my talents cannot analyse,

Toiseach, iùl is fàs, is tàth na gineamhain,
Tòimhseachain nach ruig ach iomaill tràigh dhomh,
Farsaingeachd thar fàire ruigheachd eanchainn.

Socraich aidmheil, strì is barail dhaoine,
Eud is roinnean, an-iùl 's aire 'n smaointean,
Beud an ceannais, raige an easaonachd —
Sal an sannt gu maoin, 's an claoin gu aimhreit.
Dian 'na ruith gu aois is aog an tàimh,
Air smùirnean stùr de Shaoghal an co-shamhl'
Ri anabarr tùr do-mhùint' gun tùs gun cheann
Tha 'g iathadh na ro-aibheil air gach taobh dhinn.
Sinne 'n iorpais-gleac an neart ar saobh-ghlòir,
Srian ar beachdan faoin air thaoid gun cheannsail,
Dian ri beartadh gràbhalachd na daorsa,
Fiamh is fuath tha caochladh gaoil gu gamhlas.

Iain MacNeacail (1903–99)

83 An t-Each Iarainn

Chuala sibh mun each iarainn,
    S mìorbhail e san t-saoghal seo —
Cha chuir e feum air deoch no biadh,
    Chan iarr e srian no taod chur ann;
Nì mi falbh leis nuair as miann leam,
    S luaith' na fiadh an aonaich e,
Cha ghearain e air a dhroch dhìol
    'S cha drùidh sìon an aonaich air.

Seo an t-each dha bheil an t-iongnadh,
    Gur iomadh aon tha eòlach air:
Gun fheòil gun ghaoiseid air a chnàmh,
    E lom gun àite còmhnaidh aig';
Chan ionnan e is eich an t-sléibh',
    Sann dh'fheumas tu gach dòigh thoirt dhaibh —
Gur tric a bhios tu air do phianadh
    A' cur dìon mun phòr aca.

Ach seo am fear nach iarr aon nì
    De shlìobadh mar an seòrsa sin:
Chan eil mìothlachd air ri inns'
    'S gura grinn an òrdugh e;

Beginning, course and growth, and joining of conception,
Puzzles which can only reach the farthest ebb for me,
Breadth beyond the brain's attainable horizon.

Calm down confession, strife and men's opinion,
The distrust and divisions that lead astray their thoughts,
The harm done by their power, their disunity's stubbornness —
Filth is their cupidity, their tendency to strife.
Running madly to old age and on to peaceful death,
They may be likened to an atom of Earth's dust
Practising intractable genius with no beginning and no end
And circling the atmosphere on every side of us.
We sit shiftily in our false confidence,
Tethering our vain beliefs with some unjustified halter,
Busily equipping the loathsomeness of bondage,
The fear and the hatred which put malice in love's place.

John Nicolson (Uig, Skye)

The Iron Horse

You've all heard of the iron horse,
What a wonder he is in this world —
No need has he for drink or fodder,
No reins nor halter he wants fitted;
I ride him whenever I want to,
He's faster than deer on the heather,
He doesn't grouse at bad handling
And no moorland storm will drench him.

This is the horse that's incredible,
There's many a one that knows him:
Without flesh or hair upon his bone,
He's bare and has no stable;
He's not like the hillside horses,
Whose every whim you must humour —
You're frequently driven demented
Protecting their delicate pores.

But here's the one that has no need
Of pampering like that other breed:
There's no unpleasantness to tell of
For he's splendidly conceived;

Gu h-aotrom gluaisidh e a cheum,
   Cha toir e leum ron bhòcan ás —
Chan fhaic thu e ri gearradh shìnteag,
   Cha téid e aig spìd mar s deòin a chur.

Nuair a leumas mi 'na dhìollaid
   Se nach iarr an t-sràc thoirt da:
Nì e siubhal leam 'na dheann,
   Cha chrom e cheann san làr orm;
Cha tig braon air a dh'fhallas,
   'Anail cha dèan fàilneachadh —
Chan eagal leis ro nì air thalamh
   Dh'ainneoin 's na bheir tàire dha.

84   *Nochd gur luaineach mo chadal*

Nochd gur luaineach mo chadal,
Fliuch fuar tha mo leabaidh
'S mi 'nam shìneadh gun fhasgadh
   Air achadh na Fraing;
Gach cunnart is gàbhadh
O'm bheil mi a' tàrsainn
Bidh 'nam chuimhne gu bràth
   Fad bhios tàlant 'nam cheann.

Mìle mallachd don Ghearmailt
Dhùisg an cogadh le farmad
Nach déid leinn air dearmad
   Gun bhith searbh dhaibh dh'a réir
'Son nam mìltean a mharbhadh
De ar n-òigridh bu chalma
'S bailtean móra bha dealbhach
   Chaidh a spealg' ás a-chéil'.

Sann a thòisicheadh còmhraig
Ag iarraidh gu Pòland,
'N dùil gum faigheadh iad còir
   Na Roinn Eòrpa gu léir,
'S gach rìoghachd 'nan crìochan
Gun dug iad gu strìochdadh —
Cur dhaoin' ann an iarainn
   'S gam pianadh gu geur.

Lightly does he move his step,
   No ghost makes him refuse —
You don't see him frisk about,
   His speed's not self-dictated.

When I jump into his saddle
   There's no need to give him a clout:
Off he goes with me at a gallop,
   His head doesn't bend to the ground;
Not a drop of sweat comes upon him,
   And his breath can never fail —
Nothing on earth will frighten him
   No matter what gets in the way.

Fitful's my sleep tonight

Fitful's my sleep tonight,
Wet and cold is my bed
As I lie without shelter
   On the field of France;
Every danger and peril
From which I'm escaping
I'll remember forever
   While I still have my senses.

A thousand curses on Germany
Who caused war with her envy
Which we'll not overlook
   Without well-deserved bitterness
For killing in thousands
Our bravest young men
And blasting to smithereens
   Our beautiful cities.

Strife was commenced
By invasion of Poland,
Expecting to conquer
   Europe entirely,
And each neighbouring country
They forced to submit —
Putting people in irons
   And making them suffer.

Gu bheil innealan sgriosail
Tigh'nn 's na speuran gun fhios oirnn,
Air an talamh toirt clisgeadh
    'S a' bristeadh o chéil';
Longaibh adhair mar dhruidean
Feadh na h-iarmailt air uidil
'S gu bheil deatach bho ghunna
    Cur a dubhair air gréin.

Ach bròn de gach sealladh
Faicinn òigridh gan sgathadh,
'S iad leònt' air gach machair
    A' sileadh bho'n creuchd:
Na raointean tha dathte
Le fuil chraobhach nan gaisgeach
Nach tilleadh le athadh
    Ach chaidh gaisgeil san t-sreup.

Gu bheil móran rinn falbh dhiubh
Á Gaidhealtachd Alba —
B'iad taghadh ar n-armailt,
    'S a dhearbh e 'nan euchd;
Ar nàimhdean bu ghairge
Gun chuir iad gu farbhas:
Chaidh an sgapadh mar mheanbh-spréidh
    Feadh gharbhlach an t-sléibh'.

Ach thoir beannachd gu m' mhàthair
'S do luchd-eòlais 's do m' chàirdean,
'S dèan inns' dhaibh gur slàn mi
    Ged as ànrach mo cheum;
Gun till mi rithist sàbhailt'
Nuair théid crìoch air na blàran
'S a bhios sìth dhuinn air fhàgail
    'S do gach àl thig 'nar déidh.

85 *Òran do Teonaidh Hellinga*

Se seo an sgeul tha taitneach leinn
    Nì thachair anns an dùthaich —
Gun deachaidh oighreachd Bhatairnis
    A cheannach leis an Dùidseach.

Destructive devices
Come out of the blue at us,
Exploding on impact
    And breaking apart;
Aircraft like starlings
Buck and weave through the sky
While smoke from artillery
    Blackens the sun.

But the worst of all sights
Is seeing youngsters being injured,
Lying hurt on each greensward
    Bleeding from wounds:
The fields that are stained
With the tree-blood of heroes
Who'd not turn round in fear
    But bravely attacked.

Many of them came
From the Highlands of Scotland —
The flower of our army,
    They proved it with heroism;
The most fierce of our enemies
They despatched to perdition:
They were scattered like sheep
    Over mountain terrain.

But say hello to my mother
And my kinsfolk and friends,
Say to them that I'm well
    Though forlorn is my step;
That I'll come back in safety
When the battles are over
And we get peace established
    For all generations to come.

Song to Johnnie Hellinga

The news we've heard from Waternish
    Has echoed through the Highlands —
That the noble Dutchman
    Has bought part of our island.

Gun tàinig e bhon Òlaind
   Le chuid stòrais agus ionntais,
Is cheannaich e bhon Dòmhnallach
   Gach òirleach bha de ghrunnd aig'.

Se 'n t-ainm dha Teonaidh Hellinga,
   Tha e bho chinneadh cliùiteach,
'S their gach neach tha eòlach air
   Gur h-e duine còir gu chùl e.

Gu bheil na mìltean acair ann
   De dh'fhearann torrach sùghmhor
Le spréidh tha iad ag àrachadh
   Cha déid nas fheàrr gu bùidsear.

Na croitearan bidh uaill orra
   Gu bheil uachdaran ùr ac',
'S tha fearann dhaibh mar s deòin leo —
   Gun bòid bhith orr', no cùmhnant.

Crìochnaichidh mi 'n t-òran seo
   Le deagh dhòchas is deagh dhùrachd;
Guma fada buan e còmhnaidh leinn —
   'S gach sòlas bhith 'na lùchairt.

Tormod MacLeòid (1904–68)

86 *Raoir chunna mi*

Raoir chunna mi, troimh dhual-chuailean
   Na gruagaich uasail mhàld',
A' ghealach ùr is crùb oirre,
   Tigh'nn cùl nan cnoc air fàth.

'N e h-aonrachd fhéin chuir sgoinn oirre
   Gu farchlais air ar luaidh,
I naomhachadh le h-òr-bhoillsgeadh
   An ceòl cridhe bh' òirnn mun cuairt?

Ailleanachd air m' eudail
   'S a crìdh air sgéith 'na sùil,
Iongnadh air a tlàth-bhilean
   'S ar gràdh 'na shàmhchair ciùil.

He sailed across from Holland
   With dollars and with guilders,
He bought from the MacDonald laird
   His land, his stock, his buildings.

His name is Johnnie Hellinga,
   His fame has gone before him,
From all that I have seen and heard
   Both young and old extol him.

Here the crops are heaviest,
   The cattle are the finest
And when they go to market
   They're unequalled in the Highlands.

The crofters now are full of joy
   The laird is on their side now,
He gives them land as they desire —
   No tax, no rent will bind them.

I end my song and wish him well,
   May peace and joy attend him;
His stay with us be content and long —
   Ceud mìle fàilt' we'll send him.

Norman MacLeod (Aird, Point, Lewis)

Last night I saw

Last night I saw, through the curly locks
   Of the modest gentle girl,
The new moon crouched stealthily,
   Peeping from behind the hills.

Was it loneliness that brought it
   To eavesdrop on our talk
As it sanctified with its aura
   The heart's music enfolding us?

How perfect is my darling
   With her heart on wing in her eye,
Wondrous are her gentle lips
   When our love is musical silence.

A Rìgh, ged dheadh gach bliadhna dhomh
    A shnìomh 'na linn 's 'na ré,
Bidh h-ìomhaigh chaoin 's a sèimhealachd
    'Na naomhachd shìor 'nam chré.

87   An 'Sus' a Shàraich Mi

Bha mise 's M—— triall le sunnd
    'S a' conaltradh gu càirdeil
Nuair bhuail i làmh air clàr a cuim
    Is thug i sgal a' bhàis aist'.
"Gu dé, mo chreach," thuirt mi, "tha ceàrr,
    'N e cràidh tha 'nad appendix?"
Sin fhreagair i 's i tionndadh bàn,
    "Sann dh'fhosgail mo suspender."

"Gu dé thug ort," thuirt mi le feirg,
    "Mo chridhe-sa chur tuathail
Air son ma bhrist na galairsean
    Tha cumail drabhars suas dhut?
Gam fhaicinn fhìn mar neach le deoch
    A' siaradh suas air cabhsair,
'S tu tarsainn air cùl m' amhach bhochd
    Mar dhò-bhliadhnach de ghamhna!"

"O, s beag tha dh'fhios agad," thuirt i,
    "An éiginn bhios ann dhòmhsa —
Mo 'sus' le siùdan teanga gleoc
    Diog-diog eadar mo ghlùinean;
'S ma bheir mi ceum, gun tuit e sìos
    'Na shlaod mar earball-sàile,
'S cha choisicheadh tu 'n t-slighe leam
    'S e 'g uideal ri mo shàilean.

"'S chan fhaigh mi air a cheannsachadh
    Gun mis' mi fhìn a rùsgadh,
'S ged chuireadh tus' do chùlaibh rium
    Tha cus de dhaoine dlùth oirnn.
Sann bheir sinn ceum gu cabhagach,
    'S nuair ruigeas e mo shàilean,
Sin seasaidh tus' gu h-ealamh air
    Is slaodaidh sinn ás 'àit e."

O King, should every year for me
  Be spun into era and age,
Her gentle face and softness
  Will still sanctify my clay.

The 'Sus' that Vexed Me

M——— and I were strolling along
  And amicably chatting
When she clapped her hand upon her front
  And gave a deathly cry.
"What on earth," says I, "is wrong,"
  Is it a pain in your appendix?"
At which she answered, turning pale,
  "My suspender belt has opened."

"What made you," angrily says I,
  "Put my heart going crosswise
Just for galluses that broke
  While holding up your drawers?
I'm made to look like someone drunk
  Staggering on a pavement
While you're round the back of my poor neck
  Like a stirk two years of age!"

"Oh little do you know," she says,
  "What a problem this is for me —
My 'sus' with clock-tongue pendulum
  Going tick-tick between my knees;
If I take a step, down will it fall
  And drag along like a sea-tail
And you wouldn't want to walk with me
  As it bobs around my heels.

"I've no way of controlling it
  Without my stripping naked,
And even if you turned your back
  Too many folk are near us.
What we'll do is walk at speed
  And when it reaches my heels,
You'll stand on it immediately
  And we'll pull it out of there."

Sin dìreach rud a rinn sinn —
   Thug i mach le ceum an t-saighdeir
Is mise, le luaths analach,
   Dol troigh gu leth bho 'naidhlons,
'S mi cumail sùil gu fuirealach
   Ri cluigean thighinn am fàire;
Nochd stiallag ruadh mar siobhag
   'S rud man dubhan air a' bhàrr aic'.

"An aire," dh'éigh mi 'n uair sin
   'S mi toirt cruinnleum suas gu cùlaibh;
Sheas mi air an dubhan ud
   'S chaidh is' gu spàirn ri slaodadh.
B'e dubhan dubh nam mallachd e
   Nuair thug i tarraing teann air —
Bha m' fhad 's mo leud air talamh
   'S bha mi crochaid ri suspender.

"Nì siud a' chùis," thuirt mise rith'
   'S mi suidhe suas, gu diumbach:
Le sùilean dùinte rug mi
   Air an 'sus' os cionn nan glùinean.
Bha lastaig anns an t-siobhaig ud
   Agus leum i ás mo làimh-sa
'S thug i sgealp do rudeigin
   Tha ionmhainneach aig maighdeann.

Le sporghail rug mi rithist oirr'
   Is ghreimich mi gu dlùth rith';
Bha iadsan a bha 'g amharc oirnn
   Ri lachanaich gu'n cùlaibh.
Chuir mi dà shnaim caillich oirr'
   'S gu daingeann rinn mi teann i
Le prìne meirgeach banaltraim
   A thog mi feir a' chabhsair.

88 Bàgh Leumrabhaigh

Iùbhrach fo sheòl an òr-shruth na gealaich,
   Osann na mar' air an tràigh;
An oiteag bho thìr gu mìn tigh'nn thairis,
   Gu fann toirt fannadh don bhàt';
Aiteal á doimhne cuimhne m' earraich
   Fa m' chomhair am foghar mo là.

That is just what we did —
    She took off with the stride of a soldier
While I followed, breathing hard,
    A foot and a half from her nylons,
Keeping an eagle eye open
    For an object revealing itself;
A red strip like a wick appeared
    With some kind of a hook at its end.

"Look out," I cried straight away
    As I leaped up just behind her;
I managed to stand on that hook
    And then she strained to pull it.
The devil's own hook it turned out to be
    When she finally drew it tight —
I was laid out flat upon the ground
    Hanging from a suspender.

"That's enough of that," I said to her
    As I sat up, much annoyed:
I closed my eyes and made a grab
    At the 'sus' above her knees.
That wick contained elastic
    And it jumped out of my hand
And gave a skelp to something
    That's much treasured by a virgin.

By groping I recaptured it
    And gripped it very tightly;
The people who were watching us
    Were laughing fit to burst.
I put two granny knots in it
    And firmly made it fast
With a rusty safety pin
    That I picked up off the pavement.

Lemreway Bay

A boat under sail in the moon's golden path,
    Ocean's sigh upon strand;
The breeze from the land wafting gently across,
    Weakly propelling the craft;
A gleam from the deep is my memory of spring
    Recalled in the autumn of life.

89 *Faoin Achain*

Guirmead nan reul 'nad shùilean,
   Ròs fon driùchd 'nad àilleachd,
Do chorrag bheag an greim mo lùdaig —
   Achain dìon is sgàth bhuat.

O, na cuir annamsa do mhuinighin,
   Naoidhein earbsaich ghràdhaich,
Is Khrushchev, Ike 's MacGhilleMhaoil
   Snìomh trioblaidean 'nad dhàn-sa.

90 *Dubh is Geal*

Bha luachair ceann Loch Bhat an Dìb
   Faoin ghluasad anns a' ghaoith;
Gun dhearc mi maighdeann 'g imeachd ann
   'S an là air theich' roimhn oidhch'.

Air uisge balbh na linne dhuirch
   Bha lili-bhàite bhàn;
Aig fois ri oir bha 'mhaighdeann sheang,
   Dorch fhalt an glas an là.

O, s fhada s fhada leam an oidhch'
   'S an cadal dhomh dol clì,
A' faicinn loinn na maighdinn sheang
   Faoin ghluasad anns a' ghaoith':

A' faicinn 'na mo shùilean dùint'
   Bòidhchead gil' a bràgh'd
Air uisge balbh na linne dhuirch
   Mar lili-bhàite bhàn.

91 *An t-Àite bho Dheireadh*

Air oidhche ghrod gheamhraidh tighinn a-nall ás a' bhaile
   Ged bha charbaid le cabhaig bha mo smuain na bu luaith',
Air an lìonadh le fadachd gun ruiginn mo dhachaigh
   Far am faighinn an carthannas 's seasgair bhon fhuachd.

An Idle Wish

The blue of the stars is your eyes,
    A dew-drenched rose is your beauty,
Your tiny finger clutching my pinkie —
    Your plea for defence and protection.

O, don't put your confidence in me,
    My child that's so trusting and loving,
When Khrushchev, Ike and Macmillan
    Are spinning troubles in your future.

Black and White

The rushes at Loch Bhat an Dìb
    Moved gently in the breeze;
I saw a maiden walking there
    As the day escaped the night.

On dumb water of dark pool
    A white lily grew;
At rest by its edge was the slender girl,
    Dark hair in the dawning day.

O, long, long I found the night
    With sleep evading me,
As I saw the shape of the slender girl
    Move gently in the breeze:

Seeing in my eyes though closed
    The fair brightness of her bosom
On dumb water of dark pool
    Like a white lily growing.

The Last Place

On a foul winter's night coming back from the town
    Though the bus was at speed my thoughts were still faster,
Looking forward immensely to getting back home
    To have kindness and warmth and be out of the cold.

Arsa mise ri Tormod, fear stiùiridh na carbaid,
  "Am bi thu dol timcheall nam bailtean tha thall?"
Mus d'fhuair e air labhairt, thuirt caileag bha làimh ris,
  "An t-àite bho dheireadh, tha mise dol ann."

Sheall mi le uabhas an aodann na gruagaich,
  Bha h-ìomhaigh fo cuailean gu suairceil is réidh;
"Is minig," thuirt mise, "chaidh mo sgiorradh don droch-àit',
  Ach s tu 'chiad té le fios dhomh dh'iarr ann le 'toil fhéin."

Fhreagair a' mhaighdeann le gàire bha aoibhneach,
  "Do Thormod, ar dràibhear, se ubhal a shùl',
Is ged as e 'n t-àite bho dheireadh as ainm air,
  Nach eil fhios agad fhéin gur mór a nì 'n gaol?"

Thuig mi gun fhacail bhon t-sealladh bha tlùsar
  Leis na chuir esan aonta ri briathran na pàist'
Gun robh 'n t-àite bho dheireadh, ge b' fhad ás no dlùth e,
  'Na tharraing 's 'na mhùirn do dh'òigridh an gràdh.

92   *Thuit mo leannan*

Thuit mo leannan orm don teine,
  'S chan eil agam dhith ach luath;
Cha leig mo chridhe dhomh 'n teine bhrodadh
  Ged tha 'n rùm a' fàs glé fhuar.

Seòras Moireasdan (1906–88)

93   *An t-Earrach*

Ma chì thu cailleach
Le dronnag is toill innt'
Falbh le sgoinn le cliabh agus gràp;
Ma chì thu bodach
Le briogais làn bhrèidean
Falbh le drèin a chur a' bhuntàt'
— Sin an t-earrach.

Ma chì thu each
A tha peallach o gheamhradh,
Duine 'na cheann agus sruth ás a shròin;

I said to Norman, who was driving the bus,
   "Will you be going round those villages there?"
Before he could speak, a girl close to him said,
   "The last place, that's where I am going."

With horror I looked in the face of the girl,
   Under her hair her expression was sweet;
"I've often," says I, "been consigned to the Bad Place,
   But you're the first I recall volunteering."

The girl replied with a laugh that was cheerful,
   "To Norman, our driver, it's the apple of his eye,
And though the last place is the name that they've given it,
   Don't you know for yourself that love conquers all?"

I silently twigged from the look of affection
   With which he agreed with the words of the girl
That the last place, no matter if distant or near,
   Was a pleasant attraction for young ones in love.

My love's fallen

My love's fallen in the fire,
   All I have of her is cinders;
I don't feel that I should poke it
   Though the room is getting chilly.

George Morrison (North Tolsta, Lewis)

The Spring

If you see an old woman
   With a creel-pad with holes in it
Going off energetically with creel and with graip;
   If you see an old man
   With breeks full of patches
Going off with a girn to plant the potatoes
   — That's the spring.

If you see a pony
   Left shaggy by winter,
A man at his head and a stream from his nose;

Ma chì thu crodh
Mar a chunnacas le Phàraoh,
Crùibte ri gàrradh 'g ithe nam bròg
— Sin an t-earrach.

Ma chì gille
Le ceumannan aotrom,
'Cròthadh nan caorach aig a bheil uain;
Ma chì caileag
Le beannag is còta,
'Nighe nam bòtan 's i dol thar chuan
— Sin an t-earrach.

Ma chì thu sgiobadh
Le spaid agus tairisgear,
'Cladhach gu calma 'm meadhon a' bhlàir;
Ma chì 'm barr-fhad
'S an corr-fhad 's an caoran,
Sgaoilt' air an raon aig deireadh an là
— Sin an t-earrach.

Ma chì thu todhar
Gach taobh air an téid thu,
Mionaichean éisg is innear is smùr;
Ma chì lòn
An deireadh na bàthchadh,
Ás am fàileadh leagadh an cù
— Sin an t-earrach.

Ma chì thu an topag
Ag éirigh 's ag éirigh,
Seinn air an sgéith le caithream sna neòil,
Ma chì thu 'n t-uan òg
A' riagail mu 'mhàthair,
'Deoghal gun tàmh no deocadh an fheòir
— Sin an t-earrach.

Ma chì thu a'ghrian
'S a'chlach-mheallain 'tighinn còmhladh,
Fuachd agus faoilleach 's ciùineachd 's blàths;
Ma chì an geamhradh
'S an samhradh a' còmhstri
Mus cuir sinn cùlaibh ri dùbhlachd na Màirt
— Sin an t-earrach.

If you see cattle
As witnessed by Pharaoh,
Crouched down by a dyke and chewing at shoes
— That's the spring.

If you see a laddie
With lightness of step,
Penning the sheep that have lambs at their feet;
If you see a lassie
With headscarf and coat,
Cleaning her boots for crossing the Minch with
— That's the spring.

If you see a party
With spade and a peatknife,
Digging away in the midst of the bog;
If you see top-peat
And out-peat and dry-peat,
Spread on the field at the end of the day
— That's the spring.

If manure's what you see
Wherever you go,
Intestines of fish and dung and ashes;
If a pool's what you see
In the end of the byre
With a smell that would knock down a dog
— That's the spring.

If the lark's what you see
Rising and rising,
Singing in flight with joy in the clouds,
If the lamb's what you see
New-born and frisking around the ewe,
Tirelessly suckling or sucking the grass
— That's the spring.

If you see sunshine
And hailstones together,
Cold and wolftime and calmness and warmth;
If you see winter
And summer in combat
Before we get rid of the doldrums of March
— That's the spring.

Ma chì thu goirt
Agus ganntrachd is gàgan,
Cruachannan àrd agus niosgaidean leòint';
Ma chì thu gach duine
'S a shùil ris an t-samhradh,
Cromadh gu fann air brochan gun fheòil
— Sin an t-earrach.

Dòmhnall Ailean MacDhòmhnaill (1906–92)

94 *Ceud Fàilt' air Gach Gleann*

Ceud fàilt' air gach gleann
'S air na beanntannan mòr':
Siad a chuimhnich dhomh 'n t-àm
Ghabh mi sannt air bhith beò —
Nuair a bha mi ri fonn
Còmh' ri cloinn, 's sinn ri spòrs
Mu bhruaichean nan allt
'S iad 'nan deann bho gach lòn.

Nuair a dh'éireadh a' ghrian
Bha i riaghladh gach stòr,
A' toirt fàs air an t-sìol,
'S dh'fhàg siud fiachan aic' òirnn
Is gach creutair bhiodh fann
Feadh nam beann air son lòin,
Anns an òg-mhadainn shamhraidh
'S an driùchd feadh an fheòir.

B'e mo mhiann a bhith 'n uair sin
A' fuadach na spréidh
Gu na lèantraichean luachrach
Air son buannachd dhaibh fhéin,
Mi ri biathadh an àil
Nach robh 'n làrach an treud
Leis an fhìor bhainne bhlàth
Gus am fàsadh iad treun.

S iomadh creag agus càrn,
S iomadh gàrradh is bruaich
Aig an do shìn mi ri'n sgàth
A h-uile là bhithinn fuar,

If you see hunger
And shortage and hacks there,
High stacks of peat and ulcerous boils;
If you see everyone
Wishing for summer,
Feebly crouched over gruel without meat
— That's the spring.

Donald Allan MacDonald (Daliburgh, S. Uist)

A Hundred Greetings to Each Glen

A hundred greetings to each glen
And to the high mountains:
They've brought me back to the time
That I got the will to live —
When I was playing
With children, having fun
About the banks of the streams
As they gushed from each pool.

When the sun would arise
She would rule all resources,
Giving growth to the seed,
Leaving us in her debt
And each famished creature
Wandering hills for its food
In the young summer's morning
With dew covering the grass.

What I loved to do then
Was to drive off the cattle
To the rush-covered pastures
For benefit to themselves
As I hand-fed the young
That were apart from the herd
With the finest new milk
Until they grew stronger.

There are many rocks and cairns,
Many dykes and banks
In whose shelter I lay
Every day it was cold,

'S ged bu lìonmhor mo chàirdean,
  Bha pàirt dhiubh gun truas,
'S an té shaothraich ri m' thàladh
  A' cnàmh anns an uaigh.

B' òg chreach am bàs mi,
  Aig aois a dhà no trì,
Cha b' urrainn dhomh bhith dàna
  'N lùib mo chàirdean air son sìth;
Nuair thugadh bhuam mo mhàthair,
  An uair sin dh'fhàgadh mì
Mar neach air thuar a bhith bàite
  Nach b' urrainn snàmh gu tìr.

Nuair a bhuannaich mi aois
  Bha mi saor bho gach bròn:
Na companaich a thaobhainn,
  Gach aon bhiodh le sgòd;
B'e an dùil bhith na b' fheàrr
  Nuair a dh'fhàsadh iad mòr —
Cha bu léir dhuinn an tàire
  Bha aig càch gar toirt beò.

Ghabh mi comhairle gach aon
  'S dh'fhàg siud faoin mi 'nam dhòigh,
Bha mi a' gluasad mar dh'fhaodainn
  Feadh saoghal nam beò;
Chuir mi ùidh anns gach sìon
  A bhiodh a' riarachadh m' fheòil
'S cha robh càs a bh' ann riamh
  Nach robh an triall air mo thòir.

'S cluinnidh mise daonnan
  Aig daoine nach eil òg
Gur léir dhaibh mar tha 'n saoghal
  A' caochladh cho mòr,
'S gur e fìor dhuine dall
  Bhiodh a' samhlachadh stòir
Ri beatha chlann nan daoine
  Nach fhaod fuireach beò.

Ach seo cuimhneachan do m' chàirdean
  An là bheir mi suas,
'S don mhuinntir nì mi fhàgail
  Anns an fhàsaich air chuairt:

And though many were my kin
   Some of them lacked pity
When she who crooned me to sleep
   Lay rotting in the grave.[5]

I was young when death robbed me,
   Just two or three years old,
I couldn't importunately
   Seek solace from my kin;
When my mother was taken from me
   That's when I was left
Like one nearly drowned
   Who couldn't swim to land.

When I grew older
   I got free of all mourning,
The friends that I'd choose
   Were all full of mischief;
They expected to be better
   When they grew to be adults —
We couldn't see the trouble
   Others had to bring us up.

I took everyone's advice
   Which left me foolish in my ways,
I got around as I could
   In the land of the living;
I took a notion for everything
   That satisfied my flesh
And there was never a disaster
   But that I was suspected.

And I always seem to hear
   Among folk who aren't young
That they've noticed how the world
   Is changing so much,
And that it's a man truly blind
   Who'd prefer his possessions
To the life of human beings
   Who've not enough to live on.[6]

Here's a souvenir for my friends
   On the day I expire
And for the people whom I'll leave
   On their journey through the wilds:

Bidh bàrdachd chlann Dòmhnaill
'Na cheòl aig an t-sluagh
Là nach cluinn sibh mo chòmhradh
'S mo chòmhnaidh san uaigh.

Aonghas Caimbeul, 'Am Bocsair' (1908–49)

95   *Caithris nam Bodach*

An Taigh-Tearmainn Hawkhead, 1937

Thug sinn 'n oidhche raoir fo uabhas
An taigh-caoich nan daoine buaireant';
Thug mi 'n oidhche raoir fo uabhas,
    Cha bhi mise buan mar thà mi.

Seall air Eóghain dubh na sròine
'S i cho fada ri sgian ròstaidh —
Thug e grad-leum air mo sgòrnan
    'S mi ri feòrach, "Ciamar thà thu?"

Chì mi thall Iain bochd 'na shuidhe,
Spìonadh fhuilt, a' gul, 's a' mionnan,
'G aslachadh air Rìgh an Dubh-Shluic
    'N ceann a sgiodadh dheth le làmhadh.

Cluinn Seòras Claon is srann aig',
Bhial cho farsaing, caise 's greann air;
'S Alastair ri thaobh sa champa
    Tachais na cois-chaim le steamhaig.

Bheir mi sùil a-null gu Iain
'S e cho reamhar ri muic-bhiadhta,
Mac a' Phearsain an taobh shìos dheth
    Salach, riasach, fionnach, grànda.

'N cluinn thu Iain Dubh is Raibeart —
Nach ann orra fhéin tha sogan!
Sròn a' bhuairidh air Dick odhar,
    Sùil an Deamhain aig' air Pàdraig.

Donald's children's verse[7]
   Will be sung by the people
When you can't hear my chatter
   As I'm living in the grave.

Angus Campbell (Swainbost, Ness, Lewis)

The Old Men's Night-Watch

In Hawkhead Asylum, 1937

We spent last night in horror
In a madhouse of provocateurs;
I spent last night in horror,
   I won't survive too long like this.

Look at black Ewen whose nose
Is as long as a carving knife —
He suddenly leapt at my throat
   When all I asked was, "How are you?"

Over there I see poor John sitting,
Pulling his hair out, weeping, swearing,
Entreating the King of the Black Pit
   To chop his head off with an axe.

Hear Squinting George with all his snoring,
His mouth so wide, short-tempered, surly,
And Alec in the camp beside him
   Scratching his bent leg with a stick.

I take a look across to John
Who's as fat as a pig for slaughter,
While MacPherson down below him
   Is dirty, tousled, hairy, ugly.

Do you hear Black John and Robert —
They're in good form altogether!
Sallow Dick has a nose for trouble
   And has fixed the Demon's eye on Peter.

Pàdraig bochd, cho caol ri lannsa,
'S e cho fuar ri madainn geamhraidh,
Sgeun 'na shùilean 's iad ri dannsa
    Coimhead shamhlaichean is dhràgain.

Seumas crotach air a chliathaich,
Cheart cho greannach ri cat fiadhaich;
Mata gealshuileach 'n taobh shìos dheth —
    Sann air fhéin tha fiamh gun àilgheas.

Seall air Uilleam — thug e leum ás
Chun an ùrlair ás a léine;
S tric mo chridhe 'n drip roimhn bhéist ud
    Ged a dh'éighinn ris, "Bi sàmhach!"

Faic thu O Rourke dubh á Éirinn,
'N geall air sgrios nuair nì e éirigh?
Fuil a' mhortair goil 'na chuislean,
    'S nach ann air tha bus an Nàmhaid.

Seòras Dall, cha sguir e mhionnan
Ged a chnàmhainn ris mo theanga,
'S Iain lapach, mabach, luideach,
    Cheart cho miosa ris an cànan.

'N cluinn thu Dempster fada 'g ùrnaigh —
Sann air fhéin tha brod nan glùinean —
Cumail conas ri Reuben
    'S priobadh na sùl' chlaoin rium Màrtainn?

Mìcheal Mac a' Phearsain (1910–84)

96   *Cumha Mhaighstir Nèill*

Fhuair sinn naidheachd far a' chuain
    Rinn mo ghluasad gu dàn —
Gun do bhàsaich Maighstir Niall,
    'S fois na sìorrachd ann dhà.

Tha sinn 'n-diugh ga chur san ùir
    Far an do lùig e bhith tàmh —
An Cnoc Hàllainn taobh a' chuain
    Far 'n iom' uair thug e sràid.

Poor Peter, as thin as a lance
And as cold as a winter's morning,
Has a startled look in his dancing eyes
    As he sees ghosts and dragons.

Hunchbacked James upon his elbow
Is as surly as a wildcat;
Bright-eyed Matthew down below him
    Suffers fear and knows not pleasure.

Look at William — he has jumped
Onto the floor without his shirt;
That monster often makes my heart stop
    Though I shout at him, "Be quiet!"

D'you see yon black O'Rourke from Ireland
Intent on chaos when he gets up?
A murderer's blood boils in his veins
    And he grimaces like the Devil.

Blind George just won't stop swearing
Even if I wear out my tongue on him,
Pathetic John, confused, dishevelled,
    Is just as foul as him in language.

D'you hear Dempster long at prayer —
He must have terrific knees —
Disputing fiercely with Reuben
    While Martin's squint eye looks at me?

Michael MacPherson (Taobh a' Chaolais, S. Uist)

The Lament for Father Neil

We've heard news across the sea
    That has moved me to compose —
That Father Neil has died,
    May eternal peace be his.

We are burying him today
    Where he wished to lie at rest —
In Hallin Hill beside the sea
    Where so many times he walked.

'S gu bheil sagairt an-seo linn
  A bha dìleas ann dhà,
'S gum bi esan ann 'nan cuimhn'
  A h-uil' oidhch' agus là.

Théid sinn uile nist air glùin
  'S nì sinn ùrnaigh ann dhà
Ris an Òigh as àille snuadh
  'S am Mac a ghuil i le spàirn.

'S bhon tha 'uaigh-san a-nist dùint'
  Chan eil dùil leam gu bràth
Gum faic mi tuilleadh ann a ghnùis
  Ann an dùthaich a ghràidh.

'S gur duilich tha seo linn,
  S truagh an nì mar a thà —
Gu bheil sagart ann gar dìth
  Dhèanadh dìcheall 's gach càs.

Molaidh mi e mar as còir
  Bhon a b' eòlach dhomh à:
Cha do thachair mi ris riamh
  Nach biodh fiamh air le gàir.

'S bha e math dhuinn 's gach nì
  Eadar ìobairt 's gach càs;
S iomadh teagasg thug e dhuinn
  Nam biodh suim againn dhà.

'S fhuair e sgoil dhuinn ann as ùr
  A dh'ainneoin diombaidhean chàich,
'S chaidh an t-ospadal ann suas —
  S esan fhuair e dhan àit'.

Cuideachd Eaglais na Du' Bròin,
  Si Moir' Òigh, tha mi 'g ràdh —
'S bha i riaslach dha bhon stéidh
  Gus 'n do dh'éirich i 'n àird.

Chan e sin obraichean gu léir
  Rinn e fhéin anns an àit' —
Eadar cùirtean 's gach nì,
  Cha ghabh e innse 'nam dhàn.

We have priests with us here now
 Who obeyed him in all things,
In their memory he'll remain
 Every night and every day.

Let us go upon our knees now
 And say for him a prayer
To the Virgin immaculate
 And the Son she mourned so much.

As his grave is now filled in
 I may no more expect
To see his face again
 In the land he loved so much.

This leaves us troubled,
 It's sad the way it is —
That we're missing a priest
 Who did his best in each case.

I will praise him as is right
 Since I knew him so well:
Never did I meet him
 Without a smiling face.

He was good to us in all things
 Both secular and sacred;
Much instruction did he give us
 If we'd only paid attention.

And a new school he got for us
 Despite outside objections,
And the hospital was built there —
 It's he who got it for the place.

And the Church of the Sorrows,
 The Virgin Mary's I mean —
It tried him from foundation
 Till it rose up there on high.

That's not all the achievements
 That were his around here —
What with courts and much else,
 There's not room in my poem.

Ach tha e nochd sa chladh ud shìos
  'S a cholainn dhiadhaidh a' cnàmh,
Ach tha 'anam ann aig sìth
  Far am bì e gu bràth.

Ach cha chan mise nist an còrr
  Mun t-sagart chòir sin an-dràst
Ris an cainte Maighstir Niall
  A rinn deagh ghnìomhanan san àit'.

Somhairle MacGill-Eain (1911–96)

97   *Dàin do Eimhir II: A Chiall 's a Ghràidh*

Ma thubhairt ar cainnt gum bheil a' chiall
co-ionann ris a' ghaol,
chan fhìor dhi.

Nuair dhearc mo shùil air t' aodann
cha do nochd e ciall a' ghràidh,
cha do dh'fheòraich mi mun trian ud.

Nuair chuala mi do ghuth cha d'rinn
e 'n roinneadh seo 'nam chré;
cha d'rinn a' chiad uair.

Ach dhiùchd siud dhomh gun aithne dhomh
is reub e friamh mo chré,
gam sguabadh leis 'na shiaban.

Leis na bha dhomh de bhreannachadh
gun d'rinn mi faileas strì;
gun d'rinneadh gleac le m' chéill.

Bho dhoimhne an t-seann ghliocais seo
sann labhair mi ri m' ghaol:
"Cha diù leam thu, cha diù bhuam."

    Air an taobh a-staigh mo ghaol,
    mo thuigse air an taobh ghrinn,
    is bhristeadh a' chòmhla bhaoth.

Tonight down in yon graveyard
His pious body's wasting,
But his soul is at rest
Where he'll be for ever.

I'll say no more myself
Of that kindly priest just now
That they called Father Neil
Who did good deeds hereabouts.

Sorley MacLean (Oscaig, Raasay)

Poems to Eimhir II: Reason and Love

If our language has said that reason
is identical with love,
it is not speaking the truth.

When my eye lighted on your face
it did not show the reason in love,
I did not ask about that third part.

When I heard your voice it did not make
this division in my flesh;
it did not the first time.

But that came to me without my knowing
and it tore the root of my being,
sweeping me with it in its drift.

With all I had of apprehension
I put up a shadow of fight;
my reason struggled.

From the depths of this old wisdom
I spoke to my love:
"You are not worthy of me, nor from me."

On the inside my love,
my intellect on the elegant side,
and the foolish door was broken.

Is thubhairt mo thuigse ri mo ghaol:
"Cha dhuinn an dùbailteachd;
tha 'n coimeasgadh sa ghaol."

98   Dàin do Eimhir IV: Gaoir na h-Eòrpa

A nighean a' chùil bhuidhe, throm-bhuidh, òrbhuidh,
Fonn do bheòil-sa 's gaoir na h-Eòrpa,
A nighean gheal chasurlach aighearach bhòidheach,
Cha bhiodh masladh ar latha-ne searbh 'nad phòig-sa.

An tugadh t' fhonn no t' àilleachd ghlòrmhor
Bhuamsa gràinealachd mharbh nan dòigh seo,
A' bhrùid 's am meàirleach air ceann na h-Eòrpa
'S do bhial-sa uaill-dhearg san t-seann òran?

An tugadh corp geal is clàr gréine
Bhuamsa cealgaireachd dhubh na bréine,
Nimh bhùirdeasach is puinnsean créide
Is dìblidheachd ar n-Albann éitigh?

An cuireadh bòidhchead is ceòl suaimhneach
Bhuamsa breòiteachd an adhbhair bhuain seo,
Am mèinnear Spàinnteach a' leum ri cruadal
Is 'anam mórail dol sìos gun bhruaillean?

Dé bhiodh pòg do bheòil uaibhrich
Mar ris gach braon den fhuil luachmhoir
A thuit air raointean reòta fuara
Nam beann Spàinnteach bho fhòirne cruadhach?

Dé gach cuach de d' chual òrbhuidh
Ris gach bochdainn, àmhghar 's dórainn
A thig 's a thàinig air sluagh na h-Eòrpa
Bho Long nan Daoine gu daors' a' mhórshluaigh?

99   Dàin do Eimhir X: Theagamh nach eil i 'nam chàs

Theagamh nach eil i 'nam chàs,
Ealain iomaluath an dàin:
   Labhar mar ghleadhraich nan dos,
   Teud-moghanach, no caoin le fois —

And my intellect said to my love:
"Duality is not for us;
we mingle in love."

Poems to Eimhir IV: The Cry of Europe

Girl of the yellow, heavy-yellow, gold-yellow hair,
The song of your mouth and Europe's cry of agony,
Fair, heavy-haired, spirited, lovely girl,
The disgrace of our day would not embitter your kiss.

Would your song and splendid beauty take away
From me the dead loathsomeness of these ways,
The brute and the brigand at the head of Europe
And your proud, red mouth with the old song?

Would white body and radiant forehead
Take away the black, foul chicanery,
Bourgeois venom and poison creed
And the feebleness of our churlish Scotland?

Would loveliness and triumphant music
Put away from me the frailty of this lasting cause,
The Spanish miner leaping in the face of horror
And his great spirit going down untroubled?

What would the kiss of your superb mouth be
Compared with each drop of the precious blood
That fell on the cold uplands
Of Spain's mountains from a column of steel?

What every lock of your gold-yellow head
Against all the poverty, anguish and grief
That will come and have come on Europe's people
From the Slave Ship to the slavery of the masses?

Poems to Eimhir X: Perhaps it's not part of my destiny

Perhaps it's not part of my destiny,
The quicksilver art of poetry:
Loud like the clamour of drones,
Sweet-stringed, or gentle with ease —

Ged a thàrr dhomh uiread gràidh,
Uibhir smuaintean gun tàmh,
Uiread iomagain, uiread cràidh
'S a dh'fhóghnadh do chòmhlan bhàrd,
    'S a dh'fhóghnadh don chòmhlan gun tost
    Gun fhurtachd gun fhoidhidinn gun fhois
    D'am bheil an t-àite seo a-bhos
    Cuide ri Yeats is Uilleam Ros.

100   *Dàin do Eimhir XIII: A' Bhuaile Ghréine*

Do m' shùilean-sa bu tu Déirdre
'S i bòidheach sa bhuaile ghréine;
    Bu tu bean MhicGhilleBhrìghde
    An an àilleachd a lithe.
Bu tu nighean bhuidhe Chòrnaig
'S Mairearad an Amadain Bhòidhich,
    An Ùna aig Tòmas Làidir,
    Eimhir Chù Chulainn, agus Gràinne.
Bu tu té nam mìle long,
Ùidh nam bàrd is bàs nan sonn,
    'S bu tu an té a thug an fhois
    'S an t-sìth bho chridhe Uilleim Rois,
An Audiart a bhuair De Born,
Agus Maebhe nan còrn.

Agus mas eadh as fìor gun d'ràinig
Aon té dhiubhsan t' àilleachd,
Tha fhios gum b'ann le spiorad gràsmhor
Air a dhealbh an aghaidh àlainn.
    Agus uime sin bu chòir dhomh
    'N Dàn Dìreach a chur air dòigh dhut
    A ghlacadh gach uile bhòidhchead
    A las macmeanmna na h-Eòrpa.
Bu chòir nochdadh 'na iomchar
Dìonas na Spàinne gu h-iomlan,
    Geur aigne na Frainge 's na Gréige,
    Ceòl na h-Albann 's na h-Éireann.

Bha còir agam gach uile éifeachd
A thug Lochlann is Éire

Though I've experienced as much love,
As many restless thoughts,
As much worry, as much anguish
As would suffice a band of poets,
  As would suffice the band without rest
  Or relief or patience or peace
  Whose place on this side over here
  Is together with Yeats and William Ross.

Poems to Eimhir XIII: The Sunny Fold

To my eyes you were Deirdre
Beautiful in the sunny cattle-fold;
  You were MacBride's wife
  In her shining beauty.
You were the yellow-haired girl of Cornaig
And the Handsome Fool's Margaret,
  Strong Thomas's Una,
  Cuchulainn's Eimhir, and Grainne.
You were the one of the thousand ships,
Desire of poets and death of heroes,
  You were she who took the rest
  And the peace from the heart of William Ross,
The Audiart who plagued De Born,
And Maeve of the drinking horns.

And if it is true that any one
Of them reached your beauty,
It must have been with a gracious spirit
Shaped in a beautiful face.
  And therefore I ought
  To fashion for you the Dàn Dìreach
  That would catch every beauty
  That has kindled the imagination of Europe.
There ought to appear in its course
The vehemence of Spain complete,
  The acuteness of France and Greece,
  The music of Scotland and of Ireland.

I ought to put every effect
That Norway and Ireland

Is Alba àrsaidh do mo dhaoine
A chur cuideachd an caoine
Agus an ìobairt don iongnadh
Tha geal dealbhte an clàr t' aodainn.

Agus a chionn nach mise aon diubh —
MacGhilleBhrìghde no Naoise,
    Tómas Ua Custuil no MacDhòmhnaill,
    Bertrans no 'n t-Amadan Bòidheach,
Cù Chulainn no Fionn mór no Diarmad —
Se mo chàs-sa an iargain
A ghabhas spiorad nam bàrd cianail
A ghlacadh anns na ranna pianta,
    A thogail 's a chumail mar a b' àill leam,
    Dìreach cuimir anns an dàn dhut,
    Sean agus ùr is lànmhor,
    Cumadh is meanmna gach àilleachd:
Còmhla an ìomhaigh an éibhneis,
Luathghaireach, domhain, leugach,
Geur-aigne na Frainge 's na Gréige,
Ceòl na h-Albann is na h-Éireann.

101 *Dàin do Eimhir XIV: Reic Anama*

Bàrd a' strì ri càs an t-saoghail,
Siùrsachd bhuadhan is an daorsa
Leis na mhealladh mór-roinn dhaoine,
Cha mhise fear a chanadh, shaoil leam,
Gun tugadh reic an anama faochadh.

Ach thubhairt mi rium fhìn, 's cha b' aon-uair,
Gun reicinn m' anam air do ghaol-sa
Nam biodh feum air bréig is aomadh.
Thubhairt mi an diofar sin gun smaointinn
Gum b'e an toibheum dubh 's an claonadh.

Do mhaitheanas dhomh air son na smuaine
Gum b' thusa té a ghabhadh truaghan
De spiorad beag lag suarach
A ghabhadh reic, eadhon air buadhan
T' aodainn àlainn 's do spioraid uallaich.

And old Scotland gave to my people
Together in mellowness
And to offer them to the wonder
That is fair and shapely in your face.

And since I am not one of them —
MacBride or Naoise,
    Thomas Costello or MacDonald,
    Bertrans or the Handsome Fool,
Cuchulainn or great Fionn or Diarmad —
It is my dilemma to seize
In tormented verses the longing
That takes the spirit of sad poets,
    To raise and keep as I would like,
    Direct and well-formed in the poem for you,
    Old and new and full,
    The form and spirit of every beauty:
Together in the image of joy,
Paean-like, deep, jewel-like,
The acuteness of France and Greece,
The music of Ireland and of Scotland.

Poems to Eimhir XIV: The Selling of a Soul

A poet struggling with the world's condition,
Prostitution of talents and the bondage
With which the bulk of men have been deceived,
I am not, I think, one who would say
That the selling of the soul would give respite.

But I did say to myself, and not once,
That I would sell my soul for your love
If lie and surrender were needed.
I spoke this in haste without thinking
That it was black blasphemy and perversion.

Your forgiveness to me for the thought
That you were one who would take a poor creature
Of a little weak base spirit
Who could be sold, even for the graces
Of your beautiful face and proud spirit.

Uime sin, their mi rithist an-dràsta,
Gun reicinn m' anam air do sgàth-sa
Dà uair, aon uair air son t' àilleachd
Agus uair eile air son a' ghràis ud
Nach gabhadh tu spiorad reicte tràilleil.

102   *Dàin do Eimhir XXV: B' fheàrr leam na goid an teine*

B' fheàrr leam na goid an teine
    Á nèamh air sgàth an t-sluaigh,
A' ghad nach d'rinn am milleadh
    Aig sireadh na fhuair —
Gad meallaidh bho do shùilean,
    Beòthachadh ùr an duain.

103   *Dàin do Eimhir XXIX: Coin is Madaidhean-Allaidh*

Thar na sìorraidheachd, thar a sneachda,
Chì mi mo dhàin neo-dheachdte,
Chì mi lorgan an spòg a' breacadh
Gile shuaimhneach an t-sneachda:
Calg air bhoile, teanga fala,
Gadhair chaola 's madaidhean-allaidh
    A' leum thar mullaichean nan gàradh,
    A' ruith fo sgàil nan craobhan fàsail,
Ag gabhail cumhang nan caol-ghleann,
A' sireadh caisead nan gaoth-bheann,
    An langan gallanach a' sianail
    Thar loman cruaidhe nan àm cianail,
An comhartaich bhiothbhuan 'na mo chluasan,
An deann-ruith ag gabhail mo bhuadhan:
    Réis nam madadh 's nan con iargalt
    Luath air tòrachd an fhiadhaich
    Troimh na coilltean gun fhiaradh,
    Thar mullaichean nam beann gun shiaradh:
Coin chiùine cuthaich mo bhàrdachd,
Madaidhean air tòir na h-àilleachd,
    Àilleachd an anama 's an aodainn,
    Fiadh geal thar bheann is raointean,
    Fiadh do bhòidhchid chiùin ghaolaich,
    Fiadhach gun sgur, gun fhaochadh.

Therefore, I will say again now,
That I would sell my soul for your sake
Twice, once for your beauty
And again for that grace
That you would not take a sold and slavish spirit.

Poems to Eimhir XXV: I'd prefer to the stealing of fire

I'd prefer to the stealing of fire
  From heaven for the people's sake,
The theft that caused no damage
  When seeking what was found —
The theft of your eyes' allurement,
  The kindling of poetry anew.

Poems to Eimhir XXIX: Dogs and Wolves

Across eternity, across its snow,
I see my unwritten poems,
I see the spoor of their paws dappling
The august whiteness of the snow:
Bristles raging, bloody-tongued,
Lean greyhounds and wolves
  Leaping over the dykes,
  Running under the shade of the trees of the wilderness,
Taking the narrow defile of glens,
Making for the steepness of windy mountains,
  Their baying yell shrieking
  Across the hard barenesses of the terrible times,
Their everlasting barking in my ears,
Their hot onrush seizing my mind:
  Career of wolves and eerie dogs
  Swift in pursuit of the quarry
  Through the forests without veering,
  Over the mountaintops without sheering:
The mild mad dogs of my poetry,
Wolves in chase of loveliness,
  Loveliness of soul and face,
  A white deer over hills and plains,
  The deer of your gentle beloved beauty,
  A hunt without halt, without respite.

104   *Dàin do Eimhir XXXVIII: Labhair mi*

Labhair mi mu reic anama
     Air do sgàth, a ghaoil:
Toibheum, toibheum, toibheum grànda,
     Toibheum ràbhain bhaoith:
An t-anam a reicteadh air do sgàth-sa,
     Chan e a dh'fhàsadh saor —
An t-anam a reicteadh air do sgàth-sa,
     Sann dh'fhàsadh e daor.

105   *Dàin do Eimhir XLIV: Ged chuirinn dhiom éideadh*

Ged chuirinn dhiom éideadh
     Faireachaidh na cluaineis
'S nam falbhainn lom gleusta
     'Nam chaoir céille buadhmhoir,
Ruiginn an-sin cré-ghaol
     Mo chéille luaidhe
'S liùbhrainn do t' éibhneas
     Caoir na céille buadhmhoir.

106   *Dàin do Eimhir XLIX: Fo Sheòl*

Bha 'm bàt' agam fo sheòl, 's a' Chlàrach
     Ag gàireachdaich fo sròin,
Mo làmh cheàrr air falmadair
     'S an t'éile 'n suaineadh sgòid.

Air dara tobhta 'n fhuaraidh
     Shuidh thu, luaidh, 'nam chòir,
Agus do ròp laist' cuailein
     Mu m' chrìdh 'na shuaineadh òir.

A Dhia, nan robh 'n cùrs' ud
     Gu mo cheann-uidhe deòin,
Cha bhiodh am Buta Leódhasach
     Air fóghnadh do mo sheòl.

Poems to Eimhir XXXVIII: I spoke

I spoke about the selling of a soul
    For your sake, my love:
Blasphemy, blasphemy, ugly blasphemy,
    The blasphemy of a vapid harangue:
The soul sold for your sake
    Would not grow free —
The soul sold for your sake
    Would be enslaved.

Poems to Eimhir XLIV: Should I even strip off

Should I even strip off
    My deceit-proof clothing
And go naked and eager
    As a blaze of supreme reason,
I'd then reach the core-love
    Of my reason for living
And I'd add to your pleasure
    The blaze of supreme reason.

Poems to Eimhir XLIX: Under Sail

My boat was under sail, and the Clarach
    Laughing against its prow,
My left hand on the tiller
    And the other in the sheet's winding.

On the second thwart to windward
    You sat by me, darling,
And your lighted rope of hair
    About my heart, a winding of gold.

God, had that course been
    To my desire's destination,
The Butt of Lewis had not sufficed
    For my boat under sail.

107   Dàin do Eimhir LIII: Gur suarach leam

Gur suarach leam an t-ar-a-mach mór
A dh'fhóghnas do chor nan daoine
On chunnaic mi ìomhaigh na tha còir
'S i dealbhte 'm bòidhchid aodainn.

108   Dàin do Eimhir LIV: Camhanaich

Bu tu camhanaich air a' Chuilithionn
'S latha suilbhir air a' Chlàraich,
Grian air a h-uilinn anns an òr-shruth
Agus ròs geal bristeadh fàire.

Lainnir sheòl air linne ghrianaich,
   Gorm a' chuain is iarmailt àrbhuidh,
An òg-mhadainn 'na do chuailean
'S 'na do ghruaidhean soilleir àlainn.

Mo leug camhanaich is oidhche
   T' aodann 's do choibhneas gràdhach,
Ged tha bior glas an dòlais
   Troimh chliabh m' òg-mhaidne sàthte.

109   Dàin do Eimhir LVIII: A nighean 's tu beairteachadh

A nighean 's tu beairteachadh
   Tacan tha tréigsinn,
Ciamar a bhacar leinn
   Cas-ruith a cheum-shruth?
Ciamar a ghlacar leinn
   Fras-bhlàth a' chéitein?
Ciamar a thasgar leinn
   'M basgaidean leug e?

O nighean 's do mhala gheal
   Laiste le bòidhchid
Mar ris a' chamhanaich
   Laiste le h-òige,
S tu chuireas brasadh air
   M' aignidhean còmhla
'S a ghriosas gu cabhagach
   Marc-shluagh a' cheòlraidh.

Poems to Eimhir LIII: Insignificant to me

Insignificant to me is the great revolution
    Which will grapple with mankind's plight
Since I saw the image of all that is good
    Portrayed in the beauty of a face.

Poems to Eimhir LIV: Dawn

You were dawn on the Cuillin
    And benign day on the Clarach,
The sun on his elbow in the golden stream
    And the white rose that breaks the horizon.

Glitter of sails on a sunlit firth,
    Blue of the ocean and aureate sky,
The young morning in your head of hair
    And in your clear lovely cheeks.

My jewel of dawn and night
    Your face and beloved kindness,
Though with the grey shaft of grief
    My young morning is transfixed.

Poems to Eimhir LVIII: O girl who enriches

O girl who enriches
    The moment that's passing,
How can we stifle
    The swift flow of its current?
How can we capture
    The blossom of maytime?
How can we store it
    In baskets of jewels?

O girl whose bright forehead
    Is lit up with beauty
Along with the dawn
    Lit up with youthfulness,
You cause to quicken
    All my mind's faculties
And bring to a gallop
    My muses' cavalry.

O sheallaidh chiùin fhosgailte,
    Mosgladh na còireid,
Ciamar a chosgar leam
    Dos-bhlàth do ròsan
Agus tu nochdadh dhomh
    Bochdainn mo sheòltachd
'S mi fiachainn ri deocadh ás
    Socrachd a bhòidhchid?

O aodainn shàr-shnaidhte
    Fo t' aighear geal éibhneach,
Ciamar a ghlacar leinn
    Fasan a sheuntachd,
Ciamar a thasgar leinn
    Frasan a leugachd
Mum bi e falaichte
    Thairis an céin-thir?

O aodainn ghlain, aodainn,
    Nach saoirteadh do bhòidhchead
Bho chumhachd gach baothalachd,
    Aomadh is dò-bheairt!
Nach cuimteadh mar fhaodail e
    Caoin air a stòradh,
Am fasgadh gach caomhalachd
    Saoir th' aig a' cheòlraidh!

110   *Dàin do Eimhir LIX: MhicGilleMhìcheil . . .*

MhicGilleMhìcheil, s tric mi smaointinn
    Air gach faodail a fhuair thu,
Agus do shaoibhreas gach aon latha
    Gun charachd gheur gun bhruaillean:
Gun d'fhuair thu àgh is sonas ceòlraidh
    Gun ghleac ri ònrachd 's fuathas,
'S nach ann mar sin a bhitheas dhuinne
    Ri sgal guineach an fhuaraidh.

Ach Alastair MhicGilleMhìcheil,
    Thàinig gun strì dhomh luathghair
Ann an geal mhaise aodann nìghne
    A dh'ainneoin brìgh a bhuairidh;

O calm open vision,
    Awakening of kindness,
How can I use up
    The clustered bloom of your roses
As you reveal to me
    How poor is my skill
In trying to suck out
    Its beauty's tranquillity?

O face perfectly sculpted
    In bright happy cheerfulness,
How can we capture
    The way of its charm,
How can we store
    The showers of its sparkle
Before it is hidden
    In a faraway land?

O face, o pure face,
    Could your beauty but be freed
From the power of all vanity,
    Aberration and vice!
Could it but be kept
    As a gently stored treasure,
Sheltered by each freely-given
    Kindness of the muse!

Poems to Eimhir LIX: Carmichael . . .

Carmichael, I often think
    Of every treasure you chanced on,
And of your wealth every day
    Without bitter wrestling and delirium:
That you got the grace and happiness of the muse
    Without struggle against loneliness and terror,
And that it will be very different for us
    Against the venomous blast to windward.

But Alastair Carmichael,
    There came to me without striving
A paean in the fair beauty of a girl's face
    In spite of its troubling;

Agus air latha thàrladh dhòmhsa
Ealaidheachd òir gun luasgan —
'S i coimhlionta, mar thàinig ortsa,
Gun mheang, an Ortha Bhuadhach.

111   *Dàin do Eimhir LX: Nuair chunna mi*

Nuair chunna mi 'n cùl ruadh a-raoir
    'S a' bhathais aoibhinn bhòidheach,

Sann fo chòta truagh an rìgh
    A leum an cridhe gòrach.

Air na bh' ann a chòmhlan sluaigh
    Cha robh, a luaidh, do sheòrs' ann:

Air na bh' ann a dh'aigne gheur
    B'e thus' thu fhéin mo chòmhlan:

Air na bh' ann a dh'inntinn mhóir
    S tu fhéin a dh'fhóghnadh dhòmhsa:

Air na bh' ann a dhùrachd mhóir
    Cha b'i siud dórainn m' fheòla:

Chunna mi 'n cùl ruadh a-raoir
    'S a' bhathais shaoibhir bhòidheach.

Chunna mi 'n cùl ruadh is dhùisg
    Seann roinneadh ùr 'nam fheòil-sa.

112   *Dàin do Eimhir: Dimitto*

Thalla, a leabhair bhig neo-euchdaich:
Amhairc a-steach 'na sùilean leugach:
Ge bacach thu, chan eil thu breugach:
'N àm sgaoileadh sgiath bidh tu thar shléibhtean.

And one day there came to me
A peaceful golden lyric —
Complete, as came to you,
    Flawless, the Hymn of the Graces.

Poems to Eimhir LX: When I saw

When I saw the red hair last night
    And the joyous lovely countenance,

It's under the king's wretched coat
    That the foolish heart was leaping.

For all the gathering of people there
    Your kind, my love, was not among them:

For all the sharpness of their intellect
    You were my gathering yourself:

For all the great minds that were there
    You alone would be enough for me:

For all the passion that was there
    It brought my flesh no anguish.

I saw the red hair last night
    And the rich lovely countenance.

I saw the red hair and once more
    An old split awoke within my flesh.

Poems to Eimhir: Dimitto

Go, my little unheroic book:
Look into her jewel-like eyes:
You may be lame, but you tell no lies:
When it's time to fly you'll be over mountains.

113   *Dàin Eile I: Ban-Ghaidheal*

Am faca Tu i, Iùdhaich mhóir
    Ri'n abrar Aon Mhac Dhé?
Am fac' Thu a coltas air do thriall
    Ri strì an fhìon-lios chéin,

An cuallach mheasan air a druim,
    Fallas searbh air mala 's gruaidh,
'S a' mhìos chrèadha trom air cùl
    A cinn chrùibte, bhochd, thruaigh?

Chan fhaca Tu i, mhic an t-saoir
    Ri'n abrar Rìgh na Glòir,
Am measg nan cladach carrach siar
    Fo fhallas cliabh a lòin.

An t-earrach seo agus seo chaidh
    'S gach fichead earrach bhon an tùs
Tharraing ise 'n fheamainn fhuar
    Chum biadh a cloinn is duais an tùir.

Is gach fichead foghar tha air triall
    Chaill i samhradh buidh' nam blàth,
'S threabh an dubhchosnadh an clais
    Tarsainn mìnead ghil a clàir.

Agus labhair t' eaglais chaomh
    Mu staid chaillte a h-anama thruaigh,
Agus leag an cosnadh dian
    A corp gu sàmhchair dhuibh an uaigh.

Is thriall a tìm mar shnighe dubh
    A' drùdhadh tughaidh fàrdaich bochd;
Mheal ise an dubhchosnadh cruaidh —
    Is glas a cadal suain a-nochd.

Other Poems I: A Highland Woman

Hast Thou seen her, great Jew
 Who art called the One Son of God?
Hast Thou seen on Thy way the like of her
 Labouring in the distant vineyard,

The load of fruits on her back,
 A bitter sweat on brow and cheek,
And the clay basin heavy on the back
 Of her bent, poor, wretched head?

Thou hast not seen her, son of the carpenter
 Who art called the King of Glory,
Among the rugged western shores
 In the sweat of her food's creel.

This spring and last
 And every twenty springs from the beginning
She has carried the cold seaweed
 For her children's food and the castle's reward.

And every twenty autumns that have gone
 She has lost the golden summer of her bloom,
And the black-labour has ploughed the furrow
 Across the white smoothness of her forehead.

And Thy gentle church has spoken
 Of the lost state of her miserable soul,
And the unremitting toil has lowered
 Her body to a black peace in a grave.

And her time has gone like a black slush
 Seeping through the thatch of a poor dwelling;
The hard black-labour was her inheritance —
 Grey is her sleep tonight.

308   SOMHAIRLE MACGILL-EAIN   AN TUIL

114   *Dàin Eile XVI: Trì Slighean*

Do Ùisdean MacDhiarmaid

Cha b' urrainn dòmhsa cumail fàire
Air slighe chumhang nan àrdbheann
A nochdadh thar cridhe do bhàrdachd:
    Agus, uime sin, MhicDhiarmaid,
    Soraidh leat: ach nam bu mhiann leam
    B' urrainn domh an t-slighe chrìon ud,
    Thioram, ìseal, leantainn tìorail
Th' aig Eliot, Pound agus Auden,
MacNeice, is Herbert Read 's an còmhlan:
    B' urrainn, mur b'e am fiaradh
    A chuireadh 'nam aigne dà bhliadhna
Le m' dhùthaich fhìn is càs na Spàinnte,
Cridhe feargach is nighinn àlainn.

115   *Dàin Eile XVII: 'N e d' mhiann*

'N e d' mhiann bhith eadar sléistean nìghne
'S do bheul air blàth a cìochan
'S an t-Arm Dearg an éiginn àraich
Air a shàrachadh 's a riasladh?

116   **Dàin Eile XVIII: An Dùn Éideann 1939**

A dh'ainneoin ùpraid marbhaidh
    Anns a' Ghearmailt no san Fhraing,
Bidh mo chuimhn' air bòrd san taigh seo
    Dà oidhche 's mi ann.

Am-bliadhna roghainn na h-Albann,
    An nighean ruadh, clàr na gréine;
'S a' bhònuiridh an nighean bhàn,
    Roghainn àlainn na h-Éireann.

Other Poems XVI: Three Paths

For Hugh MacDiarmid

I couldn't keep in sight on the horizon
The narrow mountain path
That appeared over your poetry's heart:
    And so, MacDiarmid,
    Farewell: but if I wished
    I could comfortably follow
    That small, dry, low path
Of Eliot, Pound and Auden,
MacNeice, and Herbert Read and the rest:
    I could, were it not for the bias
    Put for two years in my intellect
By my own land and the plight of Spain,
An angry heart and a lovely girl.

Other Poems XVII: Is it your wish

Is it your wish to be between a girl's thighs
    With your mouth on the blossom of her breasts
While the Red Army's in the heat of battle
    Being pushed back and slaughtered?

Other Poems XVIII: In Edinburgh 1939

In spite of the turmoil of killing
    In Germany or in France,
I'll remember a table in this house
    Two nights that I was there.

This year the choicest of Scotland,
    The redhead, the face of the sun;
The year before last the fair-haired,
    The beautiful choice of all Ireland.

117   Dàin Eile XIX: Gabh a-mach ás mo bhàrdachd

Gabh a-mach ás mo bhàrdachd,
S tu mo chuthach, aodainn àlainn,
　　Trìd nach tug mi 'n t-suim bu chòir dhomh
　　Do churachd is do fhàs nan dòchas
　　No do ghnìomhadh nan rann seòlta.

Cha d'rinn mi leat mar bu chaomh leam
An tuigsinn no atharrachadh an t-saoghail;
　　Cha d'lean mi aon riamh gu crìch leat:
　　Dh'fhàgadh staoin is cam gach strì leat,
　　Agus mi fhìn le rann neo-bhrìoghmhor.

Gabh a-mach ás mo chuimhne,
S tu mo chuthach is mo chuingeadh,
　　Agus mi nis, aig ceann aon tòrachd,
　　Nas failmhe, fainne 's eughmhais dòchais
　　Na na bha mi nuair a thòisich.

Gabh a-mach ás mo bhàrdachd —
S tu mo bhreisleach, aodainn àlainn!

118   Dàin Eile XXI: An Seann Òran

Tha mo chom a' seinn ri d' bhòidhche
　　'S mo chuislean 'g éigheach luathghair:
Tha m' fhuil uile mar fhìon cròiceach
　　A' cur thairis cuaiche.
Fa do chomhair, a thé bhòidheach,
'Na mo cheann dà mhìle smeòrach
　　　Ann an coille òig ri ceileir:
　　　'Na mo chluais deich mìle seillean.

Tha mo chom ri mire-chatha,
　　Armailt fo bhrat buadhach,
Goll is Fionn ag cur an latha,
　　Caoilte 'n tréine 'luathais.
Bhon as tu mo chéille còmhraig
Buaileam le deich mìle pòg thu;
　　　Bhon as tu mo chònspann àraich
　　　Se strìochd do bhuaidh, a thé àlainn.

Other Poems XIX: Get out of my poetry

Get out of my poetry,
You are my madness, lovely face,
   Through which I didn't heed as I ought
   The sowing and the growth of hopes
   Or the construction of skilled verses.

I didn't do with you as I wanted
In intellect or in changing the world;
   I brought none to conclusion with you:
   You left all striving shallow, crooked,
   And myself with insubstantial verse.

Get out of my memory,
You're my madness and my slavery,
   And I, at the end now of one pursuit,
   Emptier, weaker and more void of hope
   Than I was when I began.

Get out of my poetry —
You're my delirium, lovely face!

Other Poems XXI: The Old Song

My breast sings at your beauty
   And my veins cry out for joy:
All my blood's like bubbling wine
   Overflowing a cup.
In your presence, lovely one,
In my head two thousand thrushes
   In verdant forest chorusing:
   In my ear ten thousand bees.

My breast is in a battle-rage,
   Army under victory banner,
Goll and Fionn going into action,
   Caoilte in his speed of valour.
Since you are my battle-spouse,
I'll strike you with ten thousand kisses;
   Since you're the champion of my field
   Yielding's your triumph, lovely one.

Tha m' eich chrodhant air a' mhachair
  Dian an toiseach ruaige:
Ghabh mi 'na shuaicheantas an lasadh
  Tha 'nad rudhadh gruaidhe.
Ge b'e chòmhraigeas am blàr thu,
S tus' as fheàrr na Conall Ceàrnach,
    Na Diarmad, Osgar, no Cù Chulainn —
    Mo bhuaidh-sa tuiteam fo d' bhuillean.

Se am bristeadh a' bhuaidh-làraich
  Ann am blàr an aoibhneis:
Air na thachras sann bhios mànran
  'S òl an talla Maebhe.
O thé bhuidhe, O thé bhòidheach,
Si do ghruag a' bhratach shròiltean,
    Se do chliabh geal am magh éibhneach,
    Buaidh is caithream air a réidhlean.

Tha mo chom a' seinn le sòlas
  Ann am mullach saoibhreis:
Tha cuirm is caithream do bhòidhche
  A' lasadh mìle coinnleir.
Se t' aodann lurach, a ghaoil nìghne,
A' Ghearmailte an ceòl na fidhle,
    Se a' chaoine is an drithleann
    Bh' aig Alba ann an ceòl MhicCruimein.

Tha mo chom a' seinn le faoilte
  'S e air àird a' mhonaidh,
Ag amharc a' cheò ghil a' taomadh
  'Na ghlumagan solais.
O thé bhuidhe, O thé éibhneach,
Annas t' aodainn mo bheinn gréine,
    Agus se do ghiùlan lurach
    M' fhiùran dìreach, mo ghleann giuthais.

Tha mo chom a' seinn le ciùine
  Ann am beul na h-oidhche
Bhon a dh'fhoghlaim e gach iunntas
  Tha san aigne shaoibhir.
O thé bhòidheach, s tu mo shireadh,
Mo sheun, mo ghile na gile,
    Mo shàr cheòl thar séistean àlainn,
    Mo rann faodail thar gach bàrdachd.

My brave horses on the plain
   Are vehement in van of rout:
As a badge I took the flush
   That's in your reddening of cheek.
Whoever opposes you in battle,
You are better than Conall Cearnach,
     Than Diarmad, Oscar, or Cu Chulainn —
     My triumph is falling to your blows.

Defeat is victory out and out
   In the field of pleasure:
Whatever happens there'll be feast
   And drinking in Maeve's hall.
O golden one, O lovely one,
Your hair's the silken banner,
     Your fair breast is the plain of joy,
     Shout of triumph on its surface.

My breast sings with happiness
   In the height of riches:
Your beauty's victory feast and cry
   Lights up a thousand candles.
Your lovely face, O darling girl,
Is a Germany of symphonies,
     It's the polished sparkling music
     That MacCrimmon gave to Scotland.

My breast sings with welcome
   On the summit of the hill,
Watching the white mist cascade
   Into deep pools of light.
O golden one, O joyful one,
My sunny hill is your face's wonder,
     And your lovely bearing
     Is my straight sapling, my pinewood glen.

My breast sings with calmness
   In the mouth of the evening
Since it learned of all the riches
   In the cultivated mind.
O lovely one, you are my holy grail,
My charm, my brightness of brightness,
     My great music over lovely tunes,
     My choice lyric over every poem.

Tha mo chom a' seinn le caoine
  Ann am meadhon oidhche
Bhon a dh'fhoghlaim e gach iongnadh
  As caoimhe coibhneas.
O nighean, s tusa Sgrìob Chloinn Uisnigh
Le bann de rionnagan dùmhail,
    S tu Arcturus agus Bhénus,
    Crios is truaill an t-Sealgair reultaich.

119   *Dàin Eile XXIII: Thug Yeats dà fhichead bliadhna*

Thug Yeats dà fhichead bliadhna
Gu tric 's cruaidh a' fiachainn
  Ri annas aon aodainn
Chur an caoine bhriathran.

Thug mise còrr 's dà bhliadhna
Am faoine a' cheart fhiachainn,
  Agus thàrrla dhòmhsa
Searbhachd, bròn is iargain.

120   *Dàin Eile XXIV: An uair a thig an teannachadh*

An uair a thig an teannachadh
  Air dòchas agus spéis
Agus a dhùineas arraban
  Air farsaingeachd nan speur,
An uair a thig an crioslachadh
  De chreagan dubh' air réis,
Cà bheil an dia bheir faothachadh
  Do aognaidheachd na cré?

A chumas feòil bho chnàmhadh air
  A' bhroilleach mhàbte lom
'S a ghreasas an fhuil shiùbhlach
  Air a cùrsa troimh a' chom:
Cà bheil an dia chur bacadh air
  An t-sacadh a thig trom
No a liùbhras saorsachadh
  Do shaothrachadh nam bonn?

My breast sings with gentleness
In the middle of the night
Since it learned of every marvel
Of most tender kindness.
O girl, you are the Milky Way
With its band of close-packed stars,
You are Venus and Arcturus,
The belt and scabbard of Orion.

Other Poems XXIII: Yeats spent two score of years

Yeats spent two score of years
Trying often and hard
To express in perfection of words
The marvel of one face.

I've spent two years and more
Vainly attempting the same,
And what I've experienced
Is bitterness, sadness and yearning.

Other Poems XXIV: When the tightness comes

When the tightness comes
On hope and on esteem
And anguish encloses
The breadth of the skies,
When the circling comes
Of black rocks on a race,
Where is the god who'll give relief
To the frightfulness of clay?

Who'll keep flesh from corruption
On the tortured naked breast
And who'll urge the speeding blood
On its course through the body:
Where is the god who'll nullify
The loading that weighs heavily
Or who'll deliver freedom
To the toiling of the soles?

121   *Dàin Eile XXVI: An-seo an gaol*

An-seo an gaol
  'na laighe marbh:
  thugaibh air falbh
    a' cholann chré:
càirichibh gu caomhail i,
    a' sgaoileadh gheug
    is talamh dubh
    is fàilean glas;
na fàgaibh dad
    ach feur:
is dèanaibh uaill
gun d'rinn sibh uaigh
    bhios uaibhreach ris an speur.

Fàgaibh an uaigh
  is aig a ceann
  an sadadh gann
    de dh'uabhar geur.
Dìrichibh m'a taobhan i
    le faoine réidh,
  cur samhladh grinn
de chrèadhaich fhann:
na fàgaibh gann
  a sgèimh.
Sin agaibh uaigh
a mhaireas buan
    is suaimhneach ris a' ghréin.

122   *Éisgeachd I: An Dùn 'na Theine*

Ged theab gun do loisgeadh Dùn Bheagain
  Cha robh "theab" an losgadh nan taighean
A loisg MacLeòid a chum Dùn Bheagain
  A chumail uasal air a chreagan.

123   *Éisgeachd II: Air an Adhbhar Cheudna*

Cà bheil Leòdaich gu cur ás
  Smùidreach gharbh na h-aitribh seo?
Chuir an cuan Barrach iadsan ás
  Air cùlaibh Caolas Bhatarsaigh.

Other Poems XXVI: Here is love

Here is love
　lying dead:
　take away
　　the corpse of clay:
place it kindly,
　　clearing branches
　　and black earth
　and green sod of turf;
don't leave anything
　　but grass:
and be proud
that you've made a grave
　　that's splendid to the sky.

Leave the grave
　and at its head
　　the sparing cast
　　of bitter pride.
Straighten it around its sides
　　with smooth vanity,
　　placing a neat symbol
of weak clay:
stint not
　　on its beauty.
There you've a grave
to last forever
　　tranquil to the sun.

Satire I: The Castle on Fire

Although Dunvegan nearly burned down
　There was no "nearly" in the burning of the houses
That MacLeod burned to keep Dunvegan
　In grandeur on its rocks.

Satire II: On the Same Topic

Where are there MacLeods to put out
　The thick smoke of this building?
The sea of Barra put *them* out
　Behind the Kyle of Vatersay.

124 Éisgeachd IV: Do Mgr Niall Mac an t-Seumarlain

Leanaidh t' aodann-sa na h-àlan,
Brath nan Teacach 's nan Spàinnteach
Air a dhealbh 'nad smuiseal grànda.

125 Éisgeachd VI: Don Bhreitheamh a thubhairt ri Iain MacGhill-Eathain gum b'e Gealtair a bh' ann

Chuala mi gàireachdaich nan reultan,
Lasganaich gealaich agus gréine,
　　Mothar a' chruinne-cé 's e 'g iathadh
　　Luime 's farsaingeachd na bliadhna.
Gàireachdaich, lasganaich is éisgeachd
Bho mullaichean gorma anns na speuran,
Mothal gàire aig na béistean
A' magadh ortsa, mo cho-chreutair.

126 Éisgeachd VII: Road to the Isles

Théid mi thun nan Eileanan
is ataidh mi le m' bhaothalachd
mu bhruthan sìth an Canaigh 's Eige,
mu ghusgal ròn an Éirisgeigh,
mu chlàrsaichean 's mu Eilean Bharraigh,
mu Fhir Ghorma 's mu Chaitligich,
mu thaighean dubha 's tràighean geala,
mu Thìr nan Òg 's mun Iùbhraich Bhallaich:
　　cuiridh mi iad ann mo phòcaid
　　air son snaoisean mo shròine,
air son boillsgeadh mo shùilean,
air son gealaich mo rùintean,
　　air son braisealachd goil coire,
　　a thaobh bréige is goileim.
Gabhar dhiom am fìor Ghàidheal
a réir meud mo mhór phàighidh
　　leis na tàlantan diadhaidh
　　a thruis 's a sholair mi 'na chrìochaibh:
gabhar sràid leam an Dùn Éideann
an crios 's am breacan an fhéilidh;
boillsgear follais aig gach céilidh,
càrnar leam tùis, mar dh'fheumar,
air altairean Khennedy-Fraser,
seinnear duanagan . . . . . .

Satire IV: To Mr Neville Chamberlain

Your face will haunt generations,
The betrayal of the Czech and Spanish peoples
Displayed in your ugly muzzle.

Satire VI: To the Judge who told John Maclean
that he was a Coward

I heard the giggling of the stars,
The laughter of the moon and sun,
    The universe's belly-laugh while circling
    The bareness and breadth of the year.
Giggling, laughter and scorn
From blue peaks in the skies,
The belly-laughter of the beasts
Mocking you, my fellow creature.

Satire VII: Road to the Isles

I will go to the Isles
and inflate with my vapidity
about fairy mounds in Canna and Eigg,
about the wailing of seals in Eriskay,
about 'clarsachs' and the Isle of Barra,
about Blue Men and Catholics,
about 'black' houses and white strands,
about Tìr nan Òg and the Speckled Barge:
    I will put them in my pocket
      as snuff for my nose,
as a light to my eyes,
a moon to my desires,
    to make my kettle boil the quicker,
    for lies and chatter.
I will be called the 'true' Gael
according to the extent of my large endowment
    with the holy talents
    I collected and procured in his country:
I will promenade in Edinburgh
in the belted, kilted plaid;
I will shine at every 'ceilidh',
heap incense, as is fitting,
on the altars of Kennedy-Fraser,
I'll sing ditties . . . . . .

127 *Glac a' Bhàis*

Thubhairt Nàsach air choreigin gun tug am Furair air ais do fhir na Gearmailte "a' chòir agus an sonas bàs fhaotainn anns an àraich".

'Na shuidhe marbh an "Glac a' Bhàis"
    Fo Dhruim Ruidhìseit,
Gill' òg 's a logan sìos m'a ghruaidh
    'S a thuar grìsfhionn.

Smaoinich mi air a' chòir 's an àgh
    A fhuair e bho Fhurair
Bhith tuiteam ann an raon an àir
    Gun éirigh tuilleadh;

Air a' ghreadhnachas 's air a' chliù
    Nach d'fhuair e 'na aonar,
Ged b' esan bu bhrònaiche snuadh
    Ann an glaic air laomadh

Le cuileagan mu chlosaich ghlas'
    Air gainmhich lachdainn,
'S i salach-bhuidhe 's làn de raip
    'S de sprùidhlich catha.

An robh an gille air an dream
    A mhàb na h-Iùdhaich
'S na Comannaich, no air an dream
    Bu mhotha, dhiùbhsan

A threòraicheadh bho thoiseach àl
    Gun deòin gu buaireadh
Agus bruaillean cuthaich gach blàir
    Air sgàth uachdaran?

Ge b'e a dheòin-san no a chàs,
    A neoichiontas no mhìorun,
Cha do nochd e toileachadh 'na bhàs
    Fo Dhruim Ruidhìseit.

Death Valley

Some Nazi or other has said that the Fuehrer had restored to German manhood the "right and joy of dying in battle".

Sitting dead in "Death Valley"
    Below the Ruweisat Ridge,
A boy with his forelock down about his cheek
    And his face slate-grey.

I thought of the right and the joy
    That he got from his Fuehrer
Of falling in the field of slaughter
    To rise no more;

Of the pomp and the fame
    That he had, not alone,
Though he was the most piteous to see
    In a valley gone to seed

With flies about grey corpses
    On a dun sand,
Dirty yellow and full of the rubbish
    And fragments of battle.

Was the boy of the band
    Who abused the Jews
And Communists, or of the greater
    Band of those

Led from the beginnings of generations
    Unwittingly to the trial
And mad delirium of every war
    For the sake of rulers?

Whatever his desire or mishap,
    His innocence or malignity,
He showed no pleasure in his death
    Below the Ruweisat Ridge.

128   bho *An Cuilithionn*

S mise Chlio mhór Sgitheanach,
Tha mi ainmeil thar chiadan:
    Tha mi fiosrach feadh an t-saoghail,
    Is eòl dhomh dàn is dàl nan daoine.
Bha mi latha an Srath Shuardail
Agus thànaig gaoir gu m' chluasan:
Chuala mi corranach nan truaghan
A bha am Morair a' ruagadh
Á Boraraig is Suidhisnis uaine
Gu taobh eile nan cuantan.
      Thug mi sùil air Dùis MhicLeòid
      'S cha do mheall a' bhriag mo bhròn.

S mise Clio mhór Leódhais,
Choisich mi cho fad 's a dh'fhóghnadh
Air an t-slighe eathlamh dheònach ud
Á Beàrnaraigh gu Steòrnabhagh.
    S mise Chlio gun chion àrdain
      Oir chunnaic mi Faghaid na Pàirce;
S mise Chlio gheur-chùiseach:
Tha fhios agam co ás gach Dùsgadh.

S mise Clio bhrònach Mhuile:
Chunnaic mi fraineach 'na tuiltean.

S mise Clio na Hearadh:
Phioc mi anns na creagan sear ud.

S mise Clio Innse Gall:
Chunnaic mi allaban is call,
    Chuala mi pìob mhór MhicCruimein
    Agus a' chaora mhaol a' criomadh.

S mise Clio Inbhir Nis:
Sheas mi leam fhìn anns an sgrios
    A bh' air Druim Athasaidh shuas ud
    Nuair a nochd feasgar an uabhais:
Chunnaic mi Teàrlach Ruadh a' teicheadh
Agus Alastair Ruadh 'na chlosaich.

Chualas an corranach 's an caoineadh
Ann am mèilich nan caorach.

from *The Cuillin*

I am the great Clio of Skye,
I am known above hundreds:
    I am well-informed throughout the world,
    I know the fate and dispensation of mankind.
I was one day in Strath Swordale
And a sore cry came to my ears:
I heard the coronach of the poor ones
Whom the Baron was driving
From Borreraig and green Suisnish
To the other side of the oceans.
    I looked at the hand of MacLeod
    And the lie did not deceive my grief.

I am the great Clio of Lewis,
I walked as far as was required
On that keen and ready way
From Berneray to Stornoway.
    I am the Clio that does not lack pride
    For I have seen the Hunt of Park;
I am the shrewd Clio:
I know whence every Revival.

I am the sorrowful Clio of Mull:
I have seen bracken in floods.

I am the Clio of Harris:
I worked the pickaxe among those eastern rocks.

I am the Clio of Innse Gall:
I have seen suffering and loss,
    I heard the great pipe of MacCrimmon
    And the hornless sheep cropping.

I am the Clio of Inverness:
I stood alone in the great destruction
    That was on Drummossie up yonder
    When the evening of horror came in sight:
I saw Charles Roy fleeing
And Alastair Roy a carcase.

I heard the coronach and the weeping
In the bleating of the sheep.

S mise Clio na Galldachd:
S aithne dhomh breòiteachd is dallabhrat,
Chunnaic mi am mèinnear 'na thràill daorsa
Ach chunnaic mi ròs dearg Chluaidh a' sgaoileadh
'Na bhrat cumhachdach mór feirge
'S MacGill-Eain a' togail meirghe.

S mise Clio na h-Éireann:
A Dhia, fhuair mise mo léireadh
Le gort Bliadhna Bhuntàta,
Le fòirneart, bochdainn is ànradh;
Ach a dh'ainneoin na truaighe
S mise Chlio mhór uallach,
Oir chunnaic mi Ó Conghaile 's am Pearsach,
Wolfe Tone, MacGearailt agus Emmet.

S mise Clio mhór Shasainn,
Cha b'e mo chuibhreann-sa a b' fhasa:
Chunnaic mi Tyler is John Ball,
Kett is Dudley olc is More,
Lilburne, 's air Drochaid Àth Bhuirg
MacThómais le daga 's gach dòrn;
Blake is Shelley le'n cràdhlot,
Ioma Pàirc is Dachaigh Stàiteil.

S mise Clio na Spàinne,
Sann agamsa tha fhios air àmhghar:
Bha mi 'm Madrid is Barsalòna,
Chunnaic mi gaisge agus fòirneart,
Gach fulangas agus gach truaighe,
A dh'ainneoin spàirn cridhe 'n uabhair.

S mise Clio na Frainge:
Chunnaic mi 'n t-Ar-a-Mach caillte
'S chunnaic mi La Commune le bròn,
Le h-àmhghar, le gaisge 's le glòir.

S mise Clio na h-Eadailte:
Chunnaic mise sealladh eagalach
Nuair bha 'm Via Appia fo chroisean-ceusta
Spartacus 's nan Tràillean euchdach;
Chunnaic mi de bhòidhche na dh'fhóghnadh,
Agus cuideachd bàs Mhatteoti.

I am the Clio of the Lowlands:
I know sick frailty and blinding illusion,
    I saw the miner a bonded slave
    But I saw the red rose of Clyde spreading
To a great mighty mantle of anger
When Maclean raised a banner.

I am the Clio of Ireland:
O God, I was greatly tortured
    With the famine of Potato Year,
    With tyranny, poverty and anguish;
But in spite of the misery
I am the Clio of great spirit,
    For I have seen Connolly and Pearse,
    Wolfe Tone, Fitzgerald and Emmet.

I am the great Clio of England,
My lot has not been the easier one:
    I saw Tyler and John Ball,
    Kett and evil Dudley and More,
    Lilburne, and on Burnford Bridge
    Thompson with a pistol in each fist;
Blake and Shelley with their anguish,
Many a Park and Stately Home.

I am the Clio of Spain,
It is I who know anguish:
    I was in Madrid and in Barcelona,
    I saw heroism and tyranny,
Every suffering and misery,
In spite of the struggle of the proud heart.

I am the Clio of France:
I saw the Revolution lost
    And I saw the Commune with its grief,
    Its suffering, heroism and glory.

I am the Clio of Italy:
I saw a terrible sight
    When the Via Appia was under the crosses
    Of Spartacus and the militant slaves;
I saw all the beauty that sufficed,
And also the death of Matteoti.

S mise Clio na Gréige,
Chunnaic mi daorsa le creuchdan,
Agus Metaxas na bréige
A dh'ainneoin gliocais is éigse.

S mise Clio nan Innsean:
Chunnaic mi a' ghort nach innsear,
 Chunnaic mi spùilleadh is breugan,
 Nehru is Gandhi 'nan éiginn;
Chunnaic mi bochdainn thar smaointean,
Ceann-crìche a' chinne-daonna.

S mise Clio na Gearmailte:
A Dhia, s mise chunnaic alla-cheò
 Air cor is cridhe nan daoine,
 Liebknecht, Thaelmann is daorsa.

S mise Clio na Sìona:
Fhuair mise mo chuid fhìn dheth;
 Ach ghlac mi slabhraidhean Tatu Hó
 'S chaidh an truaighe 'na glòir.

S mise Clio an t-saoghail:
Shiubhail mi beanntan, glinn is raointean,
Bailtean agus monaidhean faoine,
Ach chan fhacas móran faochaidh.
 Leugh mi Plato is Rousseau,
 Voltaire, Condorcet agus Cobbett,
Kant, Schopenhauer, Hume, Fichte,
Marx, Lenin, Blok, Nietzsche.

S mise Clio an t-saoghail:
Dh'obraich mi m' aiseag air Saothach nan Daoine,
 Bha mi aig Batal a' Chumhaing
 Agus an Leningrad san iomairt
Mun Phàileis nuair thànaig sruth
Dhe na Boilseabhaich 'nan ruith.

Smeòrach mis' air ùrlar Phabail
Ach cha d'fhuair mi móran cadail.

 Seall a-mach, an e 'n là e,
 'S mi ri feitheamh na fàire
  'S mi ri coimhead a' Chuilithinn
 Gus an tulgadh bhith sàsaicht';

I am the Clio of Greece,
I saw slavery and its wound,
And false Metaxas
In spite of wisdom and philosophy.

I am the Clio of India:
I saw famine that cannot be told,
    I saw exploitation and lies,
      Nehru and Gandhi in extremity;
I saw poverty beyond thought,
The ultimate of humanity.

I am the Clio of Germany:
O God, it is I who saw a blinding mist
    On the condition and heart of mankind,
    Liebknecht, Thaelmann and slavery.

I am the Clio of China:
I had my own share of it;
    But I grasped the chains of Tatu Ho
    And the misery changed to glory.

I am the Clio of the world:
I traversed mountains, glens and plains,
Towns and empty moorlands,
But I did not see much respite.
    I read Plato and Rousseau,
    Voltaire, Condorcet and Cobbett,
Kant, Schopenhauer, Hume, Fichte,
Marx, Lenin, Blok, Nietzsche.

I am the Clio of the world:
I worked my passage on the Ship of the People,
    I was at the Battle of Braes
    And in Leningrad in the stir
About the Palace when a stream
Of the Bolsheviks came running.

I am a mavis on the floor of Paible
But I did not get much sleep.

    Look out, is it day,
    As I wait for the horizon
      And I gaze at the Cuillin
    Till the rocking has ceased;

Seall a-mach, an e mhadainn
    A tha balladh nan speuran,
Agus faic an e 'n ròs dearg
    A tha 'g òradh nan sléibhtean?

S mise Clio an t-saoghail:
Tha mo shiubhal sìorraidh, aognaidh.
    Ach gu tric sann dh'éireas an lasair
    A dh'fhàdas eanchainn, cridhe 's anam.
Bha mi 'n Leipzig le ùidh
Nuair sheas Dimitrov air bialaibh cùirt,
    'S chuala mi uiread 's a chuala
    Mi riamh roimhe 'n uair ud.
Chunnaic mi 'na chaoir bheò uile
Spiorad beadarrach an duine,
Anam aigeannach a' churaidh,
Eanchainn eagarra nam mullach,
    Aigne sìor-bhuadhach gun chlaoidh,
    Cridhe geal-ghathach an t-saoi;
Cuibhle na h-Eachdraidh a' dol mun cuairt.
Oirre cha toir an domhan buaidh.

    Théid a' chuibhle mun cuairt
Is tionndaidhidh gu buaidh an càs.
    Nàile, chì mise bhuam
Onfhadh a' chuain gun tràigh;
    Chì mi bàrcadh nan stuadh
Agus bàirlinn le gruaim mhóir àird:
    Bidh an latha sin buan
'S bidh na beanntan fo nuallan àigh.

129   *An t-Àilleagan*

Thàinig thusa, a nì bhuadhmhoir,
Leis an trioblaid tha san t-suaimhneas,
    Agus on a tha thu ciùin is àlainn,
    Còir fosgailte mar òra ghràsmhor
A thasgadh le Alastair uasal
Bho gach càs is ionnsaigh thruaillidh,
    Is o nach urrainn dhomh do shloinneadh
    Air beinn, air cladach no an coille
Mar a b' àbhaist do mo chuideachd
San Eilean Sgitheanach no am Muile

Look out, is it morning
    That dapples the skies,
And see if it is the red rose
    That is gilding the mountains?

I am the Clio of the world:
My wandering is eternal, and chill with death.
    But often there rises the flame
    That kindles brain, heart and soul.
I was in Leipzig, with eager hope,
When Dimitrov stood before the court,
    And I heard as much then
    As I ever heard before.
I saw in one living flame
The surging spirit of man,
The spirited hero soul,
The exact brain of the summits,
    The ever-triumphant irrepressible spirit,
    The white-darting philosophic heart;
The wheel of History going round.
Over it the universe will not prevail.

    The wheel will go round
And the distress will turn to victory.
    Look, I see afar
The surging of the ebbless sea;
    I see the rise of the waves
And a swell with a great high gloom:
    That day will be lasting
And the mountains will shout for joy.

The Little Jewel

You have come, all-conquering one,
With the torment that's in restfulness,
    And because you're calm and lovely,
    Kind and open like some charm of graces
Preserved by noble Alastair
From all misfortune and corrupt attack,
    And since I cannot trace your kin
    On hill, on shore or in a forest
As my people always did
In the Isle of Skye or Mull

No an Ratharsair nan Leòdach
No an Canada air fògradh,
Bheir thu bhuam fhìn mo smuaintean
A chionn nach fhaic mi ort an truaighe
    Chosamhlach a th' air gach aogas
    Eile chunnaic mi an taobh seo.
Tha thu mar nach do mhaoidh ort
Tìm no atharrachadh claoidhte,
    Mar gun seachnadh tu 'mhuir-bhàithte
    Bheir an cuan seo air gach àilleachd.

130   *A' Bheinn*

Dhìrich mi beinn an uabhais
    Nuair a shaoil mi gum b'e t' fheum,
'S cha robh oidhche no latha
    Nach do shracadh mi le d' bheud.

Ged reubadh an-siud m' amhach
    Le cion analach 's le fuachd,
Chum mi orm anns an dìcheall
    Gu fras-mhullach nan cruach.

Bha am biod trom air a' chridhe,
    A' meilleachadh feòla gu goirt,
An aingealach 'nam eanchainn,
    Gun aon dòchas air a thoirt.

Ach cha bu shuarach a' chreachainn
    Ged a bha i mar am bàs:
B' uasal a' chreag am mullach
    Ge b'e an-iochd a càrn.

Siud a' chreag a b' àirde
    A ràinig mo chas-sa riamh,
Ach aig gach òirleach d'a h-àirde
    Tha mo thàmailt mìle shìos.

Or in Raasay of the Clan MacLeod
Or in Canada in exile,
You will take away my thoughts
As I don't see on you the same
    Affliction that's on every other
    Face that I've seen over here.
You are as if never threatened
By time or all-oppressive change,
    As if you might avoid the breakers
    With which this ocean overwhelms all beauty.

The Hill

I climbed the hill of horror
    When I thought it was your need,
And I was neither night nor day
    Untortured by your plight.

Though my throat was torn there
    By breathlessness and cold,
I pressed on with diligence
    To the mountains' highest summit.

The peak was heavy on the heart,
    Destroying flesh with bitter cold,
With numbness in my brain
    No sort of hope was offered.

But the hill-top wasn't mean
    For all that it resembled death:
The summit was a noble rock
    Though merciless its peak.

That was the highest rock
    Ever reached by my foot,
But for every inch of its height
    My shame's a mile below.

131   *Mhag mo reusan*

Mhag mo reusan air mo chridhe
  Air grodadh do mo reul:
Chuir thusa, ghloic, ri àilleachd
  Neo-r-thaing do thuigse fhéin,
Ach chan e an claoidheadh
  A bha 'nad dhùil de bheud.
Bha eagal ort roimh mhaoim-shruth
  An anacothroim ghéir,
Ach cha robh roimh mhaoim-shruth
  An t-suarachais 's nam breug.

132   *Feasgar Samhraidh: Linne Ratharsair*

An ròs eadar Beinn Dianabhaig
Agus Cruachan Suidh Fhinn,
  Currac aotrom air Glàmaig,
  Ainmeachas curraice air Blàthbheinn,
  Sruth an lìonaidh an Caol na h-Àirde,
  Luasgan 's lainnir air a' Chlàraich.

133 bho *Uamha 'n Òir*

Dithis ann an Uamha 'n Òir
a' dol an coinneamh a' bhàis:
fear nach cuala mun chù,
a neart aineolas nan òg;
an dàrna fear le barrachd lùiths
agus an laige thar gach laige
's fhios aige gun robh an cù
de choin uamhalta bhàis
's gun robh a fiaclan cheart cho fada.

Mo dhìth, mo dhìth
le ceithir làmhan,
dà làimh sa phìob
is té san sgiath
is té sa chlaidheamh.

My reason mocked

My reason mocked my heart
  When my star had rotted:
You fool, you added to its beauty
  Despite your own intellect,
But their oppression's not
  The plight you expected.
You feared the terror-burst
  Of bitter adversity,
But not the terror-burst
  Of worthlessness and lies.

A Summer's Evening: The Sound of Raasay

The rose between Beinn Dianabhaig
And Cruachan Suidh Fhinn,
  A light cap on Glamaig,
  Just a hint of a cap on Blaven,
  The filling tide in Caol na h-Airde,
  A sparkling surge upon the Clarach.

from *The Cave of Gold*

Two men in the Cave of Gold
  going to meet death;
  one who had not heard of the dog,
  his strength the ignorance of the young;
  the second with greater strength
  and with the weakness above all weakness,
  knowing that the dog was
  of the eerie dogs of death
  and that her fangs were quite as long.

My lack, my lack
  with four hands,
  two hands to the pipe
  and one to the shield
  and one to the sword.

Mo dhìth, mo dhìth
le ceann is cridhe,
sùil chiar sa cheann
's gun sùil sa chridhe.

Dòmhnall MacDhòmhnaill (1912–89)

134　Òran na Politician

O togaidh mise fonn air an fhonn seo an-dràst'
Air long nan crann caol th' anns a' chaolas a' tàmh —
　　'S on thàinig i on chuan le rud luachmhor air bòrd
　　Tha 'n t-Eilean ann an tuaineal, 's an sluagh air an dòigh.

Air madainn gheamhraidh ghaothar is smùid oirr' on chuan,
Sann thàinig i an taobh seo, long aobhach nam buadh,
　　'S gun cualas an glaodh feadh nan daoine dol suas,
　　"Tha 'n iùbhrach 'na slaod, 's i gun saod aic' air gluas'd!"

Sin nuair thòisich cailleachan ri seanchas 's ri ràdh,
"Nach ann a thug an sealbh fiach an airgid don bhàgh —
　　Tha barrachd innte, a ghalghad, de dh'ìm is de chàis'
　　Na dh'ith iad anns a' Ghearmailt on thòisich am blàr."

Fhuair na bodaich còmhla, 's chaidh òrdain mun cuairt
Sgiobaidhean car dòigheil bhith còmhla 'n ceann uair
　　Air son an t-eathar mòr ud a bhòrdadh gu luath
　　Gun fhios nach fhaighte stòras 's rud còir a thoirt bhuaip'.

Sin far an robh 'n starraban 's an seanchas mun tràigh,
Bodaich agus cailleachan ri searmoin 's ri dàin,
　　Cha chualas uimhir sglàmhachd is rànaich san àit'
　　On thàinig Prionnsa Teàrlach le chabhlach don bhàgh.

'S thog gach eathar cùrsa air long nan crann beur
'S i 'na culaidh smaointinn a' dùnadh nan speur,
　　'S bha sgioladh air na dùirn aig na lùth-ghaisgich threun
　　Is fairge ga spùtadh 'na smùid as an déidh.

'S dh'éigheadh bodach gaoisneach 's e slaodadh air ràmh,
"Tha muillean tunna, Nìll, innt' cho cinnteach 's tha dhà,
　　'S ged a tha sinn cinnteach á prìosain is càin,
　　Nach suarach a' phrìs seach a' phìob a bhith làn!"

My lack, my lack
with head and heart,
dim eye in the head
and no eye in the heart.

Donald MacDonald (Eriskay)

The Song of the Politician

Oh I will raise a tune upon this tune for just a while
To the slender-masted ship that rests there in the kyle —
   Since she came from the ocean with a priceless thing on board
   The Island's in a lather, and delighted are her folk.

On a windy winter's morning with the sea whipped into spray,
The happy ship that brought us luck, that's when she came our way,
   And the cry was heard going up from all the Island's people,
   "The vessel's gone aground, and she's stuck fast on the bottom!"

That's when old wives began to gossip and to say,
"Providence has surely brought good value to the bay —
   There's more, my dear, on board of her of butter and of cheese
   Than they've eaten in all Germany since war was declared."

The old men got together, and the order went around
That crews of fair ability should muster in an hour
   To board that mighty vessel as quickly as they could
   In case there was a cargo of things they could remove.

That led to commotion and excitement by the shore,
With old men and women spouting sermons and poems,
   This much shouting and wrangling was unheard of in the place
   Since Prince Charlie had sailed with his fleet into the bay.

Each boat now set her course for the tall-masted vessel
Which was a thought-provoking sight as she blocked out the heavens,
   And the brave, agile heroes lost the skin from off their palms
   As the sea spouted up in spray and spindrift at their stern.

And some greybeard cried out as he gave his oar a tug,
"There's a million tons in her, Neil, as sure as there are two,
   And although we can be sure of getting prison and a fine,
   It's a small price to pay for the filling of our pipe!"

Bha sealladh ac' air bòrd bheireadh sòlas don t-sùil,
Deiseachan is brògan, pulòbhars is gùin;
   Sgeinean agus spàinean 'nan càrnan 's gach rùm
   'S chaidh na bodaich gòrach a' pòcadh 's gach cùil.

Bha tombaca ruadh ann, fear dualach 's fear bàn,
Fear cho dubh ri ròcais, fear stròicte 's fear slàn;
   Canastairean guamach aig Ruairidh 'na chràig —
   Cha d'chaidil e on uair sin ach air cluasagan siàg.

Thàinig rudan innleachdach prìseil am bàrr,
Eadar cìrean mìne, San Izal, is teàrr,
   Sentaichean, is Lysol, is Glyco, is Sloan's,
   'S gun robh na bodaich bàthte ann an eau de Cologne.

Sin nuair nochd an sìoda 'na phoidhlichean àigh,
Stocainnean rìomhach, bha mìn agus blàth —
   'S thuirt cailleach rium fhìn, 's gun mi 'g innse rud ceàrr,
   "Fhuair mi rudan sìod' bhios car ìosal gan cnàmh."

Bha poplin dubh is ruadh ann is duailean de shnàth,
Calico 'na stiallan 's 'na shìomain 's gach àit';
   Gun robh a h-uile leud an rud fiachmhor an àigh
   Na dhèanadh leddies bhrèagha de cheud cailleach ghrànd'.

Ach am measg an rùidhlich 's na h-ùpraid 's na fuaim
Gun cualas an glaodh feadh na h-iùbhraich dol suas
   Gun d'fhuaras an aon rud san t-saoghal bha bhuap':
   Togsaidean leann, inneal-ciùil — is stuth cruaidh.

Chaidh na bodaich faoin 's iad a' slaodadh am bàrr
Fodha chun nan sùilean, a' grùdach san teàrr,
   'S cha b' fhiach is cha b' fhiù leotha aon fhear no dhà —
   Ach na chumadh smùidean ri'n daoine gu bràth.

'S nuair a fhuair na seòid luchd gach geòl' agus bàt',
Thogadh suas gach seòl, 's bha gach seòlaid dhiubh làn;
   'S chuir gach fear ri rùchan fear slaodanach slàn,
   'S ghabh na gillean smùid mun do shaor iad na ràimh.

Dh'éigheadh bodach ròmach, air tòcadh le òl,
'S e slaodadh pìob òmair le leòm ás a phòc',
   "'Illean, togaibh suas i 's le uaill nì sinn òl
   Deoch-slàint' an duin' uasail chuir am fuadach fo sròin."

Joyous was the sight that met their eyes on board,
Pullovers and gowns, and shoes and suits of clothes;
   In every cabin they could find there were piles of knives and spoons
   And the old men went crazy poking into every nook.

There was red tobacco there, and twisted stuff and white,
There was stuff as black as rooks, and flaky stuff and plug;
   Roddy found enormous tins that looked tiny in his hand —
   He's never slept from that time on but on pillows made of shag.

Expensive manufactured products came to the fore,
Such as fine combs, Sanitary Izal, and tar,
   Perfumes, and Lysol, and Glyco, and Sloan's,
   Till the old men were all drowned in eau de Cologne.

That's when the silk appeared, piled high in all its glory,
Stockings that were fine and warm, and a beauty to behold —
   One old woman said to me, without a lie being told,
   "I've found things made of silk here that are cut pretty low."

There was black and russet poplin there and also twists of thread,
You saw calico in stripes and cords each way you turned your head;
   With sufficient priceless cloth cut in every size and shape
   To make a hundred ugly crones into sophisticated dames.

But amongst all the bustle and uproar and sound
Going up throughout the ship there was heard the mighty shout,
   That the one thing they wanted in all the world was in it:
   Barrels of beer, musical instruments — and spirits.

The old men went mad dragging up from afar,
Immersed to the eyeballs, raking through the tar,
   Of no value or interest to them was just a few —
   For they wanted what would knock them out and their descendants too.

And when the heroes had a cargo on every boat and skiff,
Every sail was hoisted, and soon each harbour was filled;
   A great health-giving gulp rattled down each man's dry throat,
   And the lads had all got tipsy before they'd shipped their oars.

Some hairy fellow roared, all swelled up from the bottle,
As he pulled an amber pipe with pride from out of his pocket,
   "Lads, raise your drams for a toast and with dignity we'll drink
   To the health of the gentleman who caused her bow to sink."

Bha bodaich 's iad le cléibh tarraing sago is jam,
Fir eile dannsa eightsome 's ag éigheach gu trang,
　Cuid eile dhiubh a' beucail, 's a' leum feadh nan stang
　'S a' dèanamh 'Palais Glide' ann an ceann Port an Fhaing.

Dh'éigheadh cailleach chrùbach 's i slaodadh nan cléibh,
"Dùin do bheul, a Dhùghaill, 's tu 'n còmhnaidh mun Haig —
　Sann annad tha 'n t-ùmpaidh, tha 'n caothach ort, a bhéist!"
　Ach mun deach an stuth fon ùir sann bha smùid oirre fhéin.

Calum Iain MacLeòid (1913–77)

135　*An Giùlan*

Bha mi ri muir nuair a dh'fhalbh Seònaid,
　Fada muigh ri tuinn aig cùl Hàisgeir,
Marcan-sìne gu frasach mìngheal
　A' slapadaich ri bial-mór a' bhàta.

Bha e anmoch nuair a lorg mi caladh,
　Bha iargain a' chuain ag ràdh rium,
"Tha eireachdas na ciste 'na sìneadh-breislich,
　Tha a' ghaoth a' gluasad a h-eislinn-càraidh."

Shuidh mi tacan ri taobh mo chaithris,
　Mo bhòtainn-iasgaich fliuch le sàile;
Cha shileadh na deòir ged bha còir ac' —
　B'e cagarsaich an taibh mo mhànran.

Lean mi ceum air cheum an giùlan,
　Cudthrom a duslaich seal 'nam ghàirdean,
Sgalghaoir pìob' a' caoidh mo dhìobhail,
　Sloistreadh nuatharra air mol na h-Àirde.

Ged tha mi 'n-diugh an coilltean céine
　Fada bho nuallan Cladh na Tràghad,
S tric bhios t' ìomhaigh tighinn 'nam fhianais
　'S réilig Bhòsta air chùl nan gàirthonn.

Some of them with creels were fetching sago and jam,
While others did an eightsome reel and cried out as they danced,
    Another group went roaring, leaping through the pools of water
    And doing the Palais Glide at the end of Sheepfank Harbour.

Some lame old wife would shout as she dragged the creels away,
"Shut your mouth, Dugald, you're forever at the Haig —
    You're nothing but a drunken fool, you've gone crazy, you pest!"
    But before the stuff went underground she was sozzled like the rest.

Calum I N MacLeod (Dornie, Kintail)

The Funeral Procession

I was at sea when Janet went,
    Far out facing waves behind Hàisgeir,
A squall showery, smooth and white
    Battering the gunwale of the boat.

It was late when I reached harbour,
    The stress of the sea was saying to me,
"The coffin's elegance is trauma extended,
    The wind is moving its resting-plank."

I sat for a while beside my wake,
    My seaboots wet with brine;
Tears would not flow as they should have done —
    The ocean's whisper was my tune.

Step by step I followed the procession,
    The weight of her dust for a while in my arms,
The cry of a pipe lamenting my loss,
    The Aird shingle gloomily crashing.

Though I'm today in distant forests
    Far from the roar of Cladh na Tràghad,
Often does a vision of you enter my mind
    With the Bosta graveyard behind the breakers.

Carstìona Anna Stiùbhart (1914–83)

136 *Taigh Dubh mo Sheanar*

Bidh taigh dubh mo sheanar an gnàth 'na mo chuimhne
Le teine meadhon-an-làir a bhiodh blàth agus aoigheil,
   Ged bhithinn glé chrosta chan fhaca mi fearg ann,
   Toirt dhomh mo thoil fhìn 's a' toirt brìgh ás mo sheanchas.

Bhiodh Anna san t-sabhal aig a peileir a' suathadh
Is calgan an eòrna dol 'nan ceò mu taobh fuaraidh,
   Mis' anns an doras ag amharc le uabhas
   Gu dé stuth bha 'na casan — 'n e leathar, no luaidhe?

Mo sheanair le sùist aig a dhùbhlan a' bualadh,
Buille bho bhuille ri frasadh nan sguaban,
   Cabar cur charan mu chlaigeann 's mu ghuaillean
   Mar dhrumair Fort Deòrs' leis a' cheòl a' toirt buaidh air.

Latha glanaidh an taighe dheadh teannadh gu ùpraid,
Sguabadh 's a' sgaladh 's a' glanadh nan cùiltean,
   Nigheadh soithichean an dreasair 's am balla ga aoladh
   'S fuaim rothan na muilne air na beingean gan sgùradh.

Se a bhiodh spaideil gus an tigeadh am bùrn air,
Boinneag bho bhoinneag toirt slac air an ùrlar,
   Sruthan an t-silidh air a' bhalla mar sgrìobhadh
   No mar dhealbh air a tharraing ann an cruth Mona Lìsa.

Sann an-siud bha 'n alarm aig àm a bhith dùsgadh,
Cha robh an coileach a' cadal, cha deadh laic air an t-sùil aig',
   Comanndair na spiris ri fair' orra daonnan,
   Cur eòin ann an crannaibh le Guiglidh Gùg Ò!

Catrìona cho brosnaicht' 's i cur a-mach fon an aodach —
Ma théid mis' air mo chasan thàinig deireadh do shaoghail,
   Théid car math 'nad amhaich, 's bidh prais ann le ùilleag
   'S bidh coileach a' Chaimhmein nas traing' na bha dùil aig'.

Ás na thig is na thàinig se latha leagail an t-sùithe,
Bhiodh na h-acair gan sadadh 's na cabair gan rùsgadh —
   Theichinn le cabhaig agus leanadh an cù mi,
   An cat bochd air an starsaich 's a' chasdaich ga mhùchadh.

Christina Stewart (Bayble, Point, Lewis)

My Grandfather's Black House

My grandfather's black house will stay in my memory
With its fire in the middle that was warm and embracing,
  Even were I naughty I never saw anger there,
  I could do what I wanted and got a fair hearing.

Ann in the barn would be foot-threshing furiously
With the beards of the barley in a mist to her windward,
  I'd stand in the doorway watching and wondering
  What she had in her feet — was it leather, or lead?

Grandad with a flail and all his might threshing,
Stroke upon stroke sending sheaves into showers,
  The shaft twisting and turning round his skull and his shoulders
  Like the drummer at Fort George keeping time with the music.

On house-cleaning day things would go into uproar,
With sweeping and scalding and cleansing the corners,
  Washing plates from the dresser and liming the walls
  With noise fit for mill-wheels as benches were scoured.

Wouldn't it look fine till the water was put on it,
Drop after drop splashing down on the floor,
  Streams decorating the wall like inscriptions
  Or a picture drawn like the Mona Lisa.

What an alarm there was when it was time to wake up,
The cock didn't sleep, his eye never slackened,
  The chief of the roost watching over them always,
  Sending birds to the branches with Googly Goog Oh!

Our Katie's so startled she's wetting the bedclothes —
When I get to my feet you've reached the end of your life,
  Your neck will be wrung, there'll be bree in the pan
  And the Cayman cock will be busier than expected.

The day of all days was when the soot was brought down,
The anchors cast off and the rafters revealed —
  I'd run away in a panic with the dog tearing after me,
  While the poor cat on the threshold choked on its coughing.

Air taobh shuas an tallain sreath leapannan dùinte,
Iad sgeadaicht' cho snasail le slatan de chùirtein,
   'S iad bha ion-mhiannaicht' laighe sìos annta cùbhraidh —
   Ged bhiodh oidhch' nan seachd sian ann bhiodh fèath annta 'n còmhnaidh.

Cha robh nì orr' gan còmhdach ach obair na làimhe,
Litear de dh'fhodar, cha robh snàithle de naidhlon;
   Fallas a' mhalaidh air gach plaid' agus cuibhrig,
   Gan càrdadh 's gan toinneamh 's gan snìomh air a' chuibhle.

B'e siud taigh mo sheanar mar b' fheàrr b' aithne dhòmhs' e,
S iomadh oidhch' agus latha chuir mi seachad ann dòigheil —
   Dh'ainneoin innleachd is annas tha againn fo'r spògan
   Sinn ri strì air son tuilleadh *To Keep Up With The Joneses.*

An t-Urr. Coinneach Ros (1914–90)

137   *Fògradh Cogaidh sna h-Innsean*

Cha do sheac a' ghrian ud
no iorghaill nam mìltean beul
fad réis bhliadhnachan
m' aisling òrdha.

Chuir duathar nam beann sgleò
air iomdhath nan làithean
's allt a' Ghlinne ri crònan
an grunnd mo shaoghail.

'Torwood' a' seinn tro chilltean Bhenàres
's manadh Healabhail air Nanga Pàrbat.

138   *O a Ghaidhealtachd Till*

Am bi daoine a-chaoidh 'na do ghlinn,
An gàire luath fo do speur,
   Blàr-mònadh ait air an t-sliabh,
   Cur agus buain agus snìomh?

O a Ghaidhealtachd till
   Air imrich bhuan gu do ghlinn,
Dèan turas á Tìr nan Òg
   Le do shaibhreas làn a-rìst!

Box beds in a row above the partition,
Decorated so nicely with rods for the curtains,
   So enticing were they to lie down in their fragrance —
   However dreadful the night they were like an oasis.

No covers they had that were not made by hand,
With litter of straw and not one thread of nylon;
   The sweat of the brow on each blanket and coverlet,
   They being carded and wound and then spun on the wheel.

That was grandfather's house as I knew it so well,
Many nights and days I spent there in contentment —
   Despite all the appliances we have at our fingertips
   We're still always trying to keep up with the Joneses.

Rev. Kenneth Ross (Glendale, Skye)

Wartime Exile in India

Neither that sun
nor the cacophony of thousands of mouths
throughout a span of years
withered my golden dream.

The mountains' shade obscured
the kaleidoscope of the days
while the burn of the Glen chattered
in the riverbed of my world.

'Torwood' sounding through the temples of Benares
and the spectre of Healaval on Nanga Parbat.

O my Gaeldom Return

Will there ever be folk in your glens,
Their laughter quick under your sky,
   Happy lifting of peats on the moor,
   Sowing and reaping and spinning?

O my Gaeldom return
   To live for good in your glens,
Come back from the Land of the Young
   With your treasure-chest full once again!

Gabh oighreachd air monadh is cuan,
  Na tobhtaichean fuar dèan slàn,
Seinn òrain mhilis nan dual
  Mun cuairt air cagailte gràidh.

Dèan leabhar is dealbh is dàn,
  Biodh do theachdaireachd àrd agus réidh,
Do theanga gleus ri saogh'l ùr,
  Eòlas an smùirnein 's nan reul.

139   *Farmad*

O sguiribh an t-òran
's an ceòl a tha binn,
a chlann-nighean nan làmh-gheal
sa ghàrradh a' seinn,
ur n-anailean maotha
mar ìobairtean cùbhraidh
a' cuibhleadh san àileadh;
cuiribh clos air ur beòil
mus bi farmad sna h-Àirdibh
's na h-ainglean a' còmhstri —
uist-uistibh d'ur ceòlraidh
a ghòragan grinn.

Deòrsa mac Iain Deòrsa (1915–84)

140   *Siubhal a'* Choire

Thog sinn a-mach air a' mhachair uaine,
Chuir sinn a' Gharbhaird ghailbheach, ghruamach,
Leum on iardheas sìontan cruadh oirnn.
  Thog i a ceann ri ceann nam fuarthonn,
  An té dhubh chaol 'nì gaoir 'na gluasad,
  Thog i a seinn is rinn i ruathar.

Shìn i a sgòd le cruas na cruadhach,
Shìn i a taobh ri taobh nan stuadhan,
Shìn i a ceum a cheumadh chuantan.
  Bhuail i beum le 'beul 's i 'tuairgneadh,
  Thug i sad le sgar a guailne,
  Gheàrr i leòn le 'sròin 's i 'luasgan.

Claim inheritance of hill and sea,
   The cold ruins bring back to life,
Sing the sweet traditional songs
   Around a love-giving hearth.

Make book and picture and poem,
   Let your message be loud but calm,
Tune your tongue to a world that's new,
   The knowledge of atom and stars.

Envy

O desist from the song
and the music that's sweet,
my white-handed girls
who sing in the garden,
your delicate breaths
like offerings fragrant
curl through the air;
silence your mouths
for fear of envy on high
with the angels competing —
shush-shush with your muses,
my flittery belles.

George Campbell Hay (Tarbert, Kintyre)

The Voyaging of the Corrie

We lifted out on to the green plain,
We weathered Garvel the tempestuous and scowling,
Hard rain-squalls leaped upon us out of the south-west.
   She raised her head against the heads of the cold waves,
   The black narrow one who makes a clamour as she goes,
   She raised her singing and made an onrush.

She stretched her sheet as hard as steel,
She stretched her side to the sides of the waves,
She stretched her stride to pace the oceans.
   She struck a blow with her gunnel as she buffeted,
   She struck a dunt with the seam of her shoulder,
   She clove a wound with her beak as she lurched.

Eilean Aoidh — bu aoibh a nuallan;
Àird MhicLadhmainn — a gaoir gum b' uaibhreach;
Os cionn na h-Innse sheinn i duanag.
    Cha robh 'nar sùilean ach smùid a stràcan,
    Cathadh is sìoban o chìr nam bàirlinn,
    Cha robh 'nar cluais ach fuaim a stàirneil.

141   *Òran don Oighre*

S ioma gleann a tha fo d' làimh-sa,
    Beanntan 's àilein réidh 'nam bonn,
'S ioma calamh seasgar sìtheil
    'S acarsaid gu dìdean long;
Srathan ìosal, sléibhtean 's coilltean,
    'S coireachan an fhéidh san àird —
Le cinnt 's le ceartas fhuair thu t' fhearann
    O d' shinnsir fhéin, 's gum meal thu à.

Gum meal thu fhéin t' oighreachd fharsaing
    Far nach fhaic thu fear a' tàmh,
Gach tobhta falamh 's fàrdach fhuaraidh
    Is goirtean luachrach gun fhàs;
Seall a-mach, a thriath, á d' uinneig
    Air na bailtean cruinn sa ghleann
Far nach cluinnear guth no gàire —
    Na làraichean gun mhuinntear annt'.

Gum meal thu fhéin do chàs 's do chor-sa,
    Fearann falamh, sporan gann,
Mheud a chosgas tu ga chumail
    'S gun tuath chumas nì riut ann;
Peacadh 'n athar air a chlann-sa —
    Is teann an lagh, 's cha bhacar à,
Is àrsaidh t' oighreachd sin, 's cha ghann i,
    Is ioma gleann a tha fo d' làimh.

142   *An t-Sàbaid*

"Mur cum thu Sàbaid Dhé, a mhic,
    Chan éirich leat gu bràth."
Mo thruaighe, bhris Clann Dòmhnaill i
    Aig Inbhir Lòchaidh là.

Eilean Aoidh — joyous was her roaring;
Ardlamont — haughty was her shouting;
Up off Inchmarnock she sang a ditty.
    In our eyes there was nothing but the smoke of her strokes,
    Spindrift and driven spray from the crests of the billows,
    In our ears there was nothing but the sound of her snorting.

A Song to the Heir

Many a glen is under your hand,
    Mountains with level plains below,
Many a sheltered and peaceful harbour
    And anchorage for ships' protection;
Low-lying straths, and hills and woods,
    And the deer corries far up on high —
With sureness and rightness you got your estate
    From your own predecessors, and may you enjoy it.

May you enjoy your enormous inheritance
    Where never a man alive will you see,
Each empty ruin and deserted dwelling-house
    And little enclosure where nothing but rushes grow;
Take a look, laird, out of your window
    At the townships huddled in the glen
Where no voice or laughter is ever heard —
    Ruined remains with no inhabitants.

May you enjoy your plight and predicament,
    Deserted land and an empty purse,
For despite whatever you spend to maintain it
    There are no tenants to supply you with anything;
The sin of the father upon his children —
    Harsh is the law, and it can't be resisted,
For old is that estate of yours, and vast,
    And many a glen is under your hand.

The Sabbath

Unless you keep God's Sabbath,
    Son, you'll never prosper."
Alas, Clan Donald shattered it
    One day at Inverlochy.

143   *Ceithir Gaothan na h-Albann*

M' oiteag cheòlmhor chaoin 'teachd deiseil 'nam bheitheach samhraidh i,
Mo stoirm chuain, le dìle 'cur still 's gach alldan domh,
A' ghaoth tuath le cathadh sneachda 'nì dreachmhor beanntan domh,
A' ghaoth 'tha 'g iomain m' fhaloisg earraich ri leathad ghleanntaichean.

Duilleach an t-samhraidh, tuil an dàmhair, na cuithean 's an àrdghaoth earraich i,
Dùrd na coille, bùirich eas, ùire 'n t-sneachda 's an fhaloisg i,
Tlàths is binneas, àrdan, misneach, fàs, is sileadh nam frasan i,
Anail mo chuirp, àrach mo thuigse, mo làmhan, m' uilt is m' anam i;
Fad na bliadhna, ré gach ràidhe, gach là 's gach ciaradh feasgair dhomh,
Is i Alba nan Gall 's nan Gàidheal as gàire 's blàths is beatha dhomh.

144   bho *Mochtàr is Dùghall*

Chreic e a chaoraich air na féilltean
Is chuir e a bhathar ri chéile —
Pasgain shìoda fo obair ghréise,
Cotan, bratan-ùrlair, léintean,
Soithichean umha, copain, seunan,
Sgeanan nan cas snaidhte leugach;
Burnuisean Shùsa, 's iad cho eutrom
Ri lìon an damhain-allaidh ghleusta;
Fàinneachan aobrainn 'nan ceudan
'S am pailteas de gach cungaidh-sgèimhe —
An heana, an còhl, luibhean is freumhan;
Coifidh is mìlseanan gun euradh;
Innealan-ciùil is cìrean-feusaig,
Agus Coràin an dathaibh éibhinn,
Le caignidhean is cuairteagan réidhe
A chuireadh le tlachd air mhisg an léirsinn.

Le a shreath chàmhal fon luchd ud
Thog e 'n àird air mochthrath fionnar
Mun do nochd a' ghrian cùl nan tulach
A gharadh nam pàilliuna dubha.
Thuirt e, "An ainm a' Chruithir!"
Is rinn e an cùrsa a chumail
Air Bioscra, 's e air mhearan subhach,
A' tilgeadh os a chionn a mhusgaid
'S ga cheapadh . . .

The Four Winds of Scotland

My melodious gentle breeze blowing from southward in my summer birchwood is she,
My ocean storm, with downpour sending in headlong spate each burn for me,
The north wind with driving snow that makes beautiful the hills for me,
The wind that drives my springtime muirburn up the slopes of glens is she.

Leaves of summer, spate of autumn, snowdrifts and high spring wind is she,
Sough of woodland, roaring of waterfalls, freshness of snow and heather ablaze is she,
Mild pleasantness and melody, angry pride and courage, growth and pouring of showers is she,
Breath of my body, nurture of my understanding, my hands, my joints and my soul is she;
All year long, each season through, each day and each fall of dusk for me,
It is Alba, Highland and Lowland, that is laughter and warmth and life for me.

from *Mokhtâr and Dougall*

He sold his sheep at the markets
And put his wares together —
Rolls of silk worked with embroidery,
Cotton, rugs, shirts,
Vessels of brass, cups, amulets,
Knives with carved jewel-set hilts;
Burnouses from Souse, as light
As the webs of the cunning spider;
Ankle-rings in their hundreds
And an abundance of every beautifying preparation —
Henna, kohl, herbs and roots;
Coffee and sweetmeats without stint;
Instruments of music and combs for the beard,
And Korans in joyous colours,
With interlocking letters and smooth whorls
Which would inebriate the sight with pleasure.

With his string of camels under that burden
He took the road on a cool early morning
Before the sun showed from behind the knowes
To warm the black tents.
He said, "In the name of the Creator!"
And held his course
On Biskra, and he in a delirium of pleasure,
Throwing his musket into the air
And catching it . . .[8]

Oidhche bhiothbhuan san rath-dhorcha,
Bu dùinte dall a mall-uairean gorma.
Bu bhagairt leinn gach cagar 's monmhar
A bh' aig an osaig feadh nan tolman;
Bu ghuth nàmhaid gach gluasad soirbheis,
'S gach ospag ionnsaigh mhèirleach borba.

Is beag a b' fheàirrde sinn ar n-éisteachd
Is cur ar cluasan gus an deuchainn.
Nuair a b' airgead òr nan reultan
'S a ghlas an là am bun nan speuran,
'Na sholas tiamhaidh, fann, air éiginn
A' taisbeanadh dlùth theachd na gréine,
Thug sinn sùil mun cuairt le chéile —
Siud againn sealladh truagh ar léiridh!
Air gach làimh dhinn, 'nan luchd-séistidh,
Feuch na Tuargaich mar fhad éigh dhuinn,
Mar armachd thaibhse no aisling éitigh,
A' gabhail beachd oirnn 's iad 'nan ceudan.

Gu h-obann, a Dhia, le tuiltean òmair
Thar an fhàsaich ghlais gan dòrtadh,
Leum a' ghrian san speur is dreòs dith;
Gach preas is tolman ri h-ògleus
A' seasamh a-mach air a leth-òradh
Air ghrunnd a sgàile gu riochdail beòdha.
Sheall i dhuinn fìor chruth nam bòcan,
Gach aon le 'aodann air a chòmhdach,
Bréid uaine gu bàrr a shròine
Cleas ar maighdeann 's ar ban pòsta.

Bu chosmhail iad 'nan uidheam còmhraig
Ri feachdan àrsaidh Shidi Ocba
Nuair mharcaich e 's an Creideamh còmhla,
Iuchair gach daingnich 'na thruaill òrdha,
Fear-iùil gach bealaich a lann shròiceach
O Chairuàn gu ruig am mòrchuan.
Bha sleaghan aca bu tana corrdhias,
Sgiathan cruinne, claidhnean mòra,
Is bogha aig gach fear den chòmhlan
Air fiaradh cùl slinnein, mar ri dòrlach.
Chan fhaca sinn aon mhusg 'nan dòidibh,
'S bha gunnachan is luaidh gun sòradh

An eternal night in the moon's last quarter,
Shut in and blind were its dragging blue hours.
A threat we thought every whisper and murmur
That the breeze made through the dunes;
The voice of an enemy was each stirring of the wind,
And every gust an onset of wild robbers.

We were little the better of our listening
And the putting of our eyes to the test.
When the gold of the stars was silver
And the day showed pale at the foot of the sky,
A melancholy, feeble light, scarce revealing
The close approach of the sun,
We all threw a glance around together —
And yonder was the wretched sight of our misfortune!
On every side of us, as besiegers,
Behold the Touaregs within shouting distance of us,
Like an army of spectres or a ghastly vision,
Watching us in their hundreds.[9]

Suddenly, oh God, with floods of amber
Pouring over the grey wilderness,
The sun leaped into the sky shedding forth a blaze;
Every fold and dune stood out in its young light
Half gilded, defined and vivid
On the background of its own shadow.
It revealed to us the real appearance of those terrors,
Each one with his face covered over,
A green veil to the top of his nose[10]
In the manner of our maidens and married women.

They were similar in their war-gear
To the antique hosts of Sidi Oqba[11]
When he and the Faith rode together,
The key of every stronghold in his gilded sheath,
His rending sword the guide of every pass
From Kairouan to the great ocean.
They had spears with fine tapering points,
Round shields and great swords,
And each man of the company had a bow
Aslant behind his shoulder, along with a quiver.
We did not see one musket in their hands,
And we ourselves had guns and lead

Againn fhéin; ach thug mi òrdugh
Gun teannadh ri làmhach no ri trògbhail.
Bha am fàsach farsaing mun cuairt òirnne,
Sinn air ar n-aineol, iad air an eòlas.

Treis duinn ann gun ghuth gun ghluasad,
Crùibte, làn iomagain is uathbhais,
Mar chrodh casgraidh ann am buaile,
Is iadsan 'nan grunnaibh fuaimneach
A' marcachd thall 's a-bhos gu luaineach
A' cur an comhairle ri'n uaislean.

An-sin, a chlisgeadh, sguir a' bhruidhinn,
Stad an gluasad, is sheas iad uile
Mar a bh' aca. Sheall mi 's chunnaic
Dithist a' teachd á broilleach grunnain,
Laoch leathann àrd mar ri duinein,
A' dèanamh oirnn gu stàtail ruighinn.
Stad iad suas is iad air ruigsinn
Mar dheich troigh dhuinn. Thog an curaidh
A làmh dheas mar chomharra furain,
Is bheannaich mi fhéin don deamhan fhuilteach.
Shìn e an-sin ri cainnt is glugail
Nach dèanadh Creidmheach beò a tuigsinn,
'S bu rogha dibhearsain e ri 'chluinntinn
Mur b'e am Bàs a bhith ri'r n-uilinn
A' feitheamh ri brosnachadh on bhus ud.
Lean e a' cluich a làimhe 's uchd air
'S a' phlabartaich 'na sruth 's 'na sriut ás;
Bu mhanntach, briste, tùchte, tiugh i
Mar chàrsan duine 's a chìoch-shlugain
Air at 's ga thachdadh. Dh'éist mi gu h-umhail,
'S cha b' fhada gàire 's cha b' fhada gul uam.
Fad an t-siubhail bha mi guidhe:
"A Chruthadair a rinn a chumadh
'S a chuir na th' aige 'chainnt 'na shlugan,
Deònaich dhuinne meadhan tuigsinn,
Air neo cha slàn a bhios mo mhuineal!"

An-sin mhothaich mi don duinein,
'S bha fiamh a' ghàire air an trustar.

Is roghnaiche beul sìoda na tachdadh,
Is cumaidh teanga mheala 's masgall

Without stint; but I gave the order
Not to take to firing or fighting.
The wide desert was around us,
We in a region we did not know, they in a place where they were well acquainted.

A while we passed there without speech or movement,
Crouching, full of apprehension and terror,
Like cattle for the slaughter in a fold,
While they rode to and fro in noisy groups
And strayed hither and thither
Taking counsel with their nobles.

Then, in a clap, their talking ceased,
The movement stopped, and they all stood
Fixed where they were. I looked and saw
Two men coming from the breast of a group,
A tall broad warrior and a wee mannie,
Making towards us at a stately unhurried pace.
They stopped short when they had reached
Ten paces from us. The warrior
Raised his right hand as a sign of greeting,
And I myself greeted the bloody devil.
Then he set to in a gurgling speech
That no Believer living could understand,
And it would have been a choice diversion to listen to it
Had not Death been at our elbow
Waiting to be urged on by that maw of his.
He went on gesturing with his hand and swelling out his chest
While his blabbering streamed and poured from him;
It was stammering, broken, stifled and thick
Like the hoarseness of a man whose uvula
Is swollen and is choking him. I listened humbly,
And neither laughter nor weeping was very far away from me.
All the time I was praying:
"O Creator who fashioned him
And who put such speech as he has in his gullet,
Grant to us means of understanding,
Or else my throat will not be whole and sound!"

Then I noticed the wee mannie,
And there was a smile on the scoundrel's face.

It is better to have a mouth of silk than to be strangled,
And a tongue of honey and flattery will keep

An sgian as géire o na h-aisnibh.
Fhreagair mi ma-tà ceann a' phaca
Le modh 's le cuir bhinn, shlìogach, shnasmhor,
Gun fhios am b' fhiach an cur 'nan altaibh.
Chuir mi mìlsead is deagh bhlas orr'
Le dòchas gun tuigeadh am madadh
A' chiall, gun tuigsinn nam facal.

"Fhir uasail a thàinig o chéin oirnn,
Is binne do chòmhradh na 'n liùt theudach,
Mìneachadh mùinte ollamh na h-Éipheit
Is duain Andalùis le chéile.
Chan fhios domh, air mo cheann 's air m' fheusaig,
An samhlaich mi do chruth 's do bheusan,
Do ghliocas dìomhar domhainn is t' euchdan,
Ri Sultan Stambùil nan steud-each
No ri Rìgh Ghranàda réimeil
Air an innsear a liuthad sgeulachd.
Thug do thadhal beannachd Dhé oirnn
'S — cha cheil mi — an déidh t' fhaicinn 's t' éisteachd
A-chaoidh chan iarr mi feadh nam féilltean
Ach sgeul do bheatha bhith fada éibhinn.
Bu bheairteas leam a bhith 'nam dhéircein
Gad amharc am-feast, a ghnùis na gréine.
Ach seall le truas air t' òglach feumach
Is innis a-nis do thoil mhaith fhéin da."

Chuir an sgiùrsair braoisg is dréin air,
An duinein 's e fhéin a' gnùst ri chéile.

Thionndaidh an duineachan a ghnùis oirnn,
Ghreas e a chàmhal na bu dlùithe,
Bhean e do 'bhathais, rinn e ùmhlachd
Is thòisich e — O anabarr iongnaidh —
An Àrabais cho taghte cùirteil
'S a chluinnear am Bàrdo rìoghail Thùnais.
"Cha ruig thu leas a bhith cùinneadh
Nam briathar òir mar ghibht don bhrùid seo.
Cha dèan cainnt a chraos a dhùnadh,
Ach a lìonadh leis na spùinn e,
'S gur mèirleach air rathaidean na dùthch' e
A nì an deòraidh fhéin a rùsgadh.
Air sgàth aghaidh Allah, na dùisg e.

The sharpest knife away from the ribs.
I answered then the leader of the pack
With courtesy and musical, sleekit, well-turned phrases,
Not knowing whether it was worth my while to joint them together.
I put sweetness and a savoury taste on them
Hoping that the hound would understand
The sense, without understanding the words.

"O noble man that has come from afar to us,
Your converse is more melodious than the stringed lute,
The learned expositions of the sages of Egypt
And the songs of Andalusia all together.
By my head and by my beard, I do not know
If I am to liken your form and your virtues,
Your deep secret wisdom and your prowess,
To the Sultan of Stamboul of the steeds
Or to the King of Granada who reigned so wide
And of whom are told so many tales.
Your visit has brought the blessing of God upon us
And — I will not conceal it — after seeing you and listening to you
Never more will I seek aught throughout the markets
But news that your life is long and joyous.
And it would be riches to me to be a beggar
And gaze upon you forever, O countenance of the sun.
But look with pity upon your needy servant
And tell him now your own good will."

The gallows' bird put a twisted grimace on him
While he and the mannie grunted to one another.

The mannikin turned his face to us,
Nudged his camel closer,
Touched his forehead, made obeisance
And began — oh wonder of wonders —
In Arabic as choice and courtly
As is to be heard in the royal Bardo of Tunis.[12]
"It does not profit you to coin
Words of gold as a gift for this brute.
Speech will not close his maw,
But only its fill of what he has plundered,
For he is a robber of the highways of this region
Who will strip even the pilgrim bare.
For the sake of Allah's countenance, do not rouse him.

Bi iriseal 's na tairg dha dùbhshlan,
Is gheibh sibh bhur beatha leis on ùruisg
Ged sgobadh e uaibh cosnadh bhur cunnraidh.

"Fichead bliadhn' air ais, mo shùilean,
Rinn e mo charabhan a spùinneadh,
Is leis gun robh mi dreachmhor lùthmhor
Rinn e ciomach is tràill gun diù dhiom.
Cnàmhan mo chompanach, a thùirse —
Thog gaoth nan dìthreabh 's ì sìor smùidrich
Gainmhe mìne tòrr is dùn orr'.
Leugh mi mo ghliocas, theann mi 's dh'ionnsaich
An donnalaich cainnt a th' aig na brùidean,
Is tha mi 'n-diugh mar chomhairleach cùirte
'S mar chompanach creiche aig a' chù sin.
Their e rium, 'Is tu a thùras
Gach car glioc 's gach annas ùr dhuinn.
Is tu mo chasan leis an siùbhlainn,
Is tu mo làmhan 's mo sgiathan cliùiteach
Gam thoirt air ite ás mo chrùban.'

"Fhuair mi le sin droch-inbh' a' chùirteir,
'S bu phrìosanaich riamh anns gach cùirt iad.
An e dol ás gun chead bu rùn domh?
Chan fhad' a shìninn riamh an cùrs' ud,
Oir bhiodh am fàsach marbh ga stiùradh,
A' brath mo shlighe 's ga thoirt gam ionnsaigh.
Ghoireadh a' ghaoth ris: 'Tionndaidh! Tionndaidh!
Ghabh e mar sin!' 'S gach bruan ùrach
'S gach clach a dh'fhairicheadh trom mo chùrsain:
'Tha e 'n-seo, an-seo, a dhiùlnaich!'

"*Ya Rabbi, Rabbi!* Féilltean Tùnais,
An caladh, na sràidean sgàile, an lùchairt,
'S an t-iomlan fionnar, sneachdgheal, ùrgheal —
Gu bràth chan fhosgail mo dhà shùil air.
Ach seall a-nis. Tha ceathach mùgach
A' ciaradh aogas grànd' an ùmaidh.
Is leòr dhuinn na thubhairt mi, a rùnaich;
Ach fhuair mi 'n t-òrdan, mar ri bùitich,
Innse dhuit gu bheil an cù sin
Air mhiann ruamhair is rùdhraich
Am measg do bhathair. Sìon as fiù leis
Bidh aige, mar chomharra do dheagh dhùrachd."

Be humble and offer him no defiance,
And you will escape with your life from the monster
Although he will snatch from you the winnings of your trading.

"Twenty years ago, my eyes,
He plundered my caravan,
And as I was handsome and strong
He made me a captive and a slave of no account.
My companions' bones, oh grief —
The wind of the wastes endlessly smoking with fine sand
Has raised a heap and a mound upon them.
I studied my wisest course, set to and learned
The yowling speech of the brutes,
And this day I am a court counsellor
And reiving companion of that dog.
He says to me, 'It is you that devise
Each wise plan and fresh novelty for us.
You are my feet for me to travel,
You are my hands and my famed wings
Bearing me up in flight out of my crouching.'

"And so I have the wretched rank of a courtier,
And they have ever been prisoners in every court.
And should my intent be to escape without his leave?
I would never stretch that course very far,
For the inanimate desert would be guiding him,
Betraying my path and bringing him towards me.
The wind would cry to him: 'Turn! Turn!
He went yon way!' And each particle of earth
And every stone that felt the weight of my charger
Would shout: 'He is here, here, warrior!'

"*Ya Rabbi, Rabbi!*[13] The markets of Tunis,
The harbour, the shadowy streets, the palace,
And all of it cool, snow-white, fresh-white —
Never will my two eyes open on it again.
But see now. A surly mist
Is darkening the ugly face of the boor.
What I have said suffices us, dear man;
But I have had the command, along with threats,
To tell you that the dog
Desires to delve and rummage
Amongst your wares. Everything he thinks of worth
Will be his, as a sign of your good will."

Ged bha an cridh' annam is smùid ás,
Thuirt mi — 's mi dèanamh mìn mo ghnùise —
"Air mo cheann is air mo shùilean."
Thill an duinein le coltas sunndach
A ràdh gum b' onair leam mo spùinneadh.
Thionndaidh mac Iblis a chùl ruinn,
Thog e 'làmh dheas — 's a Dhia, an ùpraid!

Ri bhith bruidhinn an-diugh fhéin air
Thig brat fala air mo léirsinn.
Gum buidhich Allah gnùis an treubh ud!
Cha robh faolchu tana feumach
Do'm bu ghreim 's bu deoch an eucoir
Nach robh 'na fhicheadan 's 'na cheudan
An sàs 'nar seilbh, is iad a' speuradh,
A' tarraing, ag utadh 's a' malairt spéicean.
Gach pasgan againne chaidh 'fheuchainn,
'S a shracadh sìos ás a-chéile.
Rinn iad na tràillean fhéin a dheuchainn,
Gam brodadh 's gan stobadh le'n dubhmheuraibh.
Fad an latha lean na béistean,
Is mi gan amharc á geimhlibh m' éiginn,
Fiamh a' ghàire air mo dheudach.

A mholadh sin do Thriath nan Saoghal,
An Tròcaireach, Truacantach, an t-Aon Dia,
Maighstir na Camhanaich, a shaor sinn
Is a chuir 'nam cheann an smaoin ud.

Anns gach conaltradh mun ghealbhan
Fhuair na Tuargaich an t-ainm sin
Bhith beò gun sògh, air nòs nan ainmhidh,
Beatha chaol air fodar garbh ac',
Air meas buidhe nan craobh-pailme
'S air bainne an gobhar anfhann
A dh'ionailtreadh measg chlach is gainmhe.
Dheasaich mi, ma-tà, is thairg mi
Tì meannta milis don mhèirleach gharg ud,
Dh'fheuch an tigeadh e o 'aintheas
Le tlachd, 's an callaicheadh a bhalg e.
Bhlais e air, a Chruithir m' anma,
Sgob e ás e an aon bhalgam,
Is shìn e air a ghlugail bhalbhain.

Although the heart within me was smoking,
I said — making my countenance smooth —
"On my head and on my eyes."
The mannie returned cheerfully
To say that I held it an honour to be plundered.
The son of Iblis[14] turned his back on us,
And raised his right hand — O God, the uproar!

When I speak of it this very day
A mantle of blood comes over my sight.
May God turn yellow the faces of that tribe!
There was not a thin needy wolf
To whom wrongdoing was food and drink
That was not in his scores and hundreds
Among our possessions, blaspheming,
Tugging, jostling and exchanging blows.
Every bundle we had was tried,
Rent and torn asunder.
Even the slaves themselves were tested,
And they prodded them and jabbed them with their black fingers.
All day long the monsters continued,
And I watched them out of the fetters of my necessity,
Baring my teeth in a smile.

Praise be for it to the Lord of all the Worlds,
The Merciful, the Compassionate, the One God,
The Master of the Dawn, who saved us
And who put in my head the thought.

In every conversation around the fire
The Touaregs had got the name
Of living without any luxury, after the manner of animals,
Having a lean life on rough fodder,
On the yellow fruit of the palm-trees
And the milk of their weakly goats
That browsed through stones and sand.
I made ready, therefore, and offered
Sweet mint tea to the wild robber,
To see if pleasure would give him up
His fury, and if his belly would tame him.[15]
He tasted it, O Creator of my soul,
And drained it in one mouthful,
Then started his dumbie's mouthings.

"Thuirt e," ors an duinein sgeigeil,
"'Is maith a' ghobhar a shil a leithid,
Ge b'e càite no co leis i.'
'S da-rìribh sin na tha e creidsinn."

"A ghrian an fhàsaich," rinn mi freagairt,
"Cha ghobhar dhubh no bhàn ga leigeil
A rinn an deoch, ach luibhean seacte
An ceann uisge, is fodha teine.
Mas toil le d' chridhe leòmhainn, bheir mi
Am pailteas duit den luibh, is fleasgach
A thàirneas gu mion-eòlach ceart i,
Air mhodh gum bi i daonnan deas duit
Nuair as trom an là 's a theas ort."

An déidh ròlais nach do thuig sinn:
"Their grian an fhàsaich," ors an duinein,
"Gur fiach le 'chridhe àrd na chuir thu
'Na thairgse a ghabhail; is, tuilleadh,
An éirig do dhùrachd is an urraim,
An còrr de d' ghibhtean théid a liubhairt
Dhuit mar thà e, is t' òr-sa cuideachd.
(Dh'fhàilnicheadh ar beathaichean fo 'chudthrom.)
An fheadh 's a tha e a' casg a chuideachd
'S gan toirt gu 'shàil, gun amharc umad
Bi falbh gu d' bhathar is cuir cruinn e,
Beannaich Dia is lean air t' uidhe.
Ma chìthear an-seo a-rìst do bhuidheann
Gheibh i an aon rùsgadh dunach.
Soraidh leat, sann duit as buidhe,
Thusa tha falbh nuair tha mi fuireach."

Rug mi fhéin air làimh an duinein,
Sheachain mi 'shùilean, 's iad a' sruthadh.
Thionndaidh e is lean e 'n curaidh,
A bha saodach pac a chuilean
Le crann a shleagha 's rinn a ghutha.

Dh'ullaicheadh an-sin ar triall leinn,
Chuir sinn cruinn na bh' ann de dh'iarmad,
Tràillean is bathar. Dh'fhan mun trian deth.

Làn éibhneis — ar ceann a' snàmh leis
'S ar cridhe a' falbh air sgiathan àrda —

"He said," said the mocking mannie,
"'Good is the goat that gave such milk,
Wherever it might be and whoever might own it.'
And in truth that is what he believes."

"Sun of the desert," I answered,
"It was no goat, black or white, that made the drink
On being milked, but dried herbs
In water, with a fire underneath.
If it pleases your lion heart, I will give you
Abundance of the herb, and a youth
Who will mask it cunningly and rightly,
So that it will always be ready for you
When the day and its heat are heavy upon you."

After some vapouring we did not understand:
"The sun of the desert says," said the mannie,
"That his lofty heart deigns to accept
What you have offered; and, furthermore,
To recompense your good will and the honour,
What remains of your gifts will be restored
To you as it stands, and your gold also.
(Our beasts would fail under its weight.)
While he is restraining his company
And bringing them to heel, without looking about you
Go to your wares and gather them together,
Bless God and continue your journey.
If your company is seen here again
It will get the same disastrous stripping.
Farewell, fortunate that you are,
You who are going while I am biding."

I took the mannie by the hand,
But avoided his eyes, for they were wet with tears.
He turned away and followed the warrior,
Who was herding his pack of whelps
With the shaft of his spear and the edge of his voice.

Then we prepared our departure,
And gathered what remnants were left
Of slaves and goods. About a third remained.

Full of joy — our heads swimming with it
And our hearts away on lofty wings —

Thug sinn ar cùl ris a' ghràisg ud.
Bu teàrnadh gach dìreadh leinn gam fàgail . . .

Bu toil le Òmar spòrs is aighear,
Is toirm nan ceàrrach anns a' chaifidh
'Nan suidh' air bratan-ùrlair alfa
A' cluich air dìsnean 's air na cairtean;
A' giorrachadh nan oidhche fada
Is eallach teth nan latha lasrach
Le tòimhseachain is sgeulachd Antair.
Bhiodh an tambùr 's a' ghàita aca,
Cofaidh na h-Iemen, seinn is aiteas.

Sin far an robh an dòmhlan aobhach
Nach leigeadh durc 'nan còir no daormann —
Clàr-feòirne, còmhradh, feadain chaola,
Uain air biorain is feòil gu saor ann,
An deòiridh 's an déircein a' glaodhach:
"Rudeigin air ghaol Dé, a dhaoine!"
'S an sgeulaiche a b' fheàrr 's a b' aosta
'Na thost nuair thogadh Òmar gaolach
A ghuth an tiugh a' chòmhlain aotruim.
Ach bhiodh a mhac ri làithean maotha
'Òige fhéin a' tighinn daonnan
Air fàidhean is air nithean naomha,
A' dèanamh tarcais air an t-saoghal,
Air foill na beatha is a faoineas . . .

Ciod e a th' annainn, a chlann mo dhùthcha?
Ciod e a th' annainn is a bha 'n Dùghall?
Ciod e tha an dualchas is an dùthchas?
Cainnt is eachdraidh, snàth nan glùinean,
Na ginealaich druim air dhruim a' cùrsachd,
A' cas-ruith a-chéile cleas nan sùghan.
Breith is bàs mar fhàs na h-ùrach,
Àrach, is àbhaistean nach do mhùthadh
Le'r sluagh on rinn e Alb' air thùs deth.
Am b' oighre air guth 's air cumadh gnùis' e
Air faireachdainnean, inntinn, sealladh sùla
Aig daoine a dh'fhàiltich sìos gan ionnsaigh
Luchd am faraire is an giùlain,
Riamh mun d'iarr iad a' bhean-ghlùin da?
Bu Ghàidheal e, 's bu bhlàth a dhùrachd

We turned our back on yon rabble.
Every ascent was a descent to us as we left them . . .[16]

Omar enjoyed recreation and mirth,
The rattle of gamblers in the café
Sitting on carpets of esparto
Playing at dice and playing at cards;
Shortening the long, long nights
And the hot burden of the flaming days
With riddles and a tale of Antar.[17]
They'd have the tambour and gaïta,[18]
Yemen coffee, song and pleasure.

That's where the happy crowd collected
Who'd admit no dagger or curmudgeon —
Chess, conversation, slender flutes,
Lambs on skewers and meat aplenty,
The pilgrim and the beggar crying:
"Something for the love of God, my friends!"
And the best and oldest storyteller
Fell silent when beloved Omar
Raised his voice amidst the genial crowd.
But his son throughout the tender days
Of his own youth invariably spoke
Of prophets and of sacred things,
Disdaining matters of the world,
Life's deceptions and its vanity . . .[19]

Who are we, my country's children?
Who are we and who was Dougall?
What are patrimony and tradition?
Language, history, generations' thread,
With generations coursing wave on wave,
Pursuing each other like the billows.
Birth and death like growth of soil,
Rearing, and customs never changed
By our race since it first created Scotland.
Was he heir to voice and countenance,
To feelings, mind and cast of eye
Of folk who welcomed down towards them
Those who waked them, bore their coffin,
Long before they called his midwife?
A Gael was he, and warm was his regard

Don chànain àrsaidh a rinn a dhùsgadh
O 'chadal creathlach; san d'rinn e sùgradh
Ri leannan anns a' choille chùbhraidh.
B' Albannach e, a fhuair mar dhùthaich
An tìr bheag ghailbheach, ghrianach, chliùiteach
Nach dèan saltairt 's nach gabh lùbadh.
B'ann de Chloinn Àdhaimh rinn Dia dùileach
Fodha Fhéin 's os cionn nam brùid e . . .

Saoghal fa leth mac an duine,
Domhan beò leis fhéin gach urra;
Grian is dorchadas na cruinne,
Siùil mhara 's grianstad san fhuil ann.
Cia mheud glùn a th' ann ar cumadh?
Chan innis sgeul, cha lorg cuimhn' iad,
'S ath-bheirear iad uile cuideachd
San naoidhean, is a shinnsre cruinn ann.
Théid e leò gu ceann a thurais,
'S bidh pàirt dheth beò an déidh a shiubhail.
Chìthear a ghnùis 's e fhéin 'na uirigh;
Faodar gur e a ghuth a chluinnear
Is ogh' an ogha nach fhac' e 'bruidhinn.
Cùis-bhùirt sinn! Ged a thà na h-uile
'Nan taighean-stòir làn fòtais, usgar,
Dhìleab àrsaidh, shubhailc, dhubhailc,
Dh'fhan Clann Àdhaimh fòs 'na struidhear,
Ga sgapadh fhéin gu dall, faoin, fuilteach.

Peacach a thruailleas ùir is adhar,
Duin' òg an salachar a' chatha
Dol ás ri reothairt bhrais a latha.

Brisear an teud, stadar an ceilear,
Nuair bu bhinne, àirde sheinn iad;
Sguirear 's gun am port ach leitheach.

Mìghnìomh a dhallas grian is reultan,
A' chuid as bòidhche dhinn 's as tréine
Ga h-eadarmhort gun iochd, ga ceusadh.
Na h-òganaich gan cur gu deuchainn —
Am feòladair maraon 's an treud iad.
Slòigh an domhain ri oidhche éitigh
A' spealgadh lòchrain càch-a-chéile.

For the old language that awoke him
From his cradle sleep; in which he courted
His sweetheart in the fragrant wood.
A Scot was he, who had for homeland
The little, stormy, sunny, famous land
That tramples not and can't be bent.
It's of Adam's Clan that God of elements
Made him below Himself and above the brutes . . .[20]

A world apart is each son of man,
A living world in himself is every person;
An earth's sunshine and darkness,
Tides and solstices in his blood.
How many generations go to shape us?
No story can tell, and no memory trace them,
Yet they are all reborn together
In the little child, and his ancestry is united within him.
Along with it he goes to the end of his journey,
And a part of him will be alive after he is gone.
His face will be seen when he himself is in his grave;
And it may be that it is his voice that will be heard
When the grandson of the grandson whom he never saw
Is speaking. We are a fit subject for derision!
Though all men are storehouses full of refuse, gems,
Ancient heirlooms, virtues and vices,
Adam's Clan still remains a wastrel,
Squandering itself blindly, foolishly, bloodily.

It is a crime that corrupts earth and air,
A young man amid the filth of battle
Perishing in the headlong springtide of his days.

The string is snapped, the singing stopped,
When their music sounded its sweetest;
They cease with the melody but half played.

It is a misdeed that blinds sun and stars,
The bonniest and the strongest of us
At mutual massacre, slaying and crucifying themselves.
Youth — butcher and flock in one —
Being put to the test.
The nations of the world on a foul night
Shattering one another's bright lanterns.[21]

Chunnaic an dithist seo cur a' chatha;
'S nar leigeadh Dia a leithid fhaicinn
Do ghaolach dhòmhsa, seadh, car aitil,
Ged a b'ann am bruadar cadail.[22]

Ghluais Mochtàr a làmh sa bhruthainn
A shuathadh fallais, a ruagadh cuileig.
Chlisg an Gefreiter, sgaoil e 'bhuille.

Bhàsaich àrdan Ahmaid mhòrail,
Ciùineas Obàïd 's beòchridh' Òmair,
Tró eile le Mochtàr fon mhòrtair.

Bhàsaich am fear a bha ri 'uilinn,
Dhubhadh ás a shinnsreachd uile;
Mhortadh a chlann nach do rugadh.

Chaidh an domhan beag a bhruanadh
A dh'fhàs ann fhéin 'na earrach uaine,
A ghin, gun fhios, na bha mun cuairt dha,
'S a rinn e 'chumadh le a smuaintean
Air na chunnaic e 's na chual' e,
Nuair leig an tuigse air a ghuaillean
A h-eallach duineil, deacair, uasal.
Dà dhomhan iolchruthach luachmhor
A dhubhadh ás gu bràth mun d'fhuair iad
Teachd gu ìre làin, 's a sguabadh
Ás an speur le buille thuairmse.

Mort nam marbh is mort nan naoidhean
Nach do ghineadh — crìoch dhà shaoghal.

145 *Atman*

Rinn thu goid 'nad éiginn,
    Dh'fheuch thu breug gu faotainn ás;
Dhìt iad, chàin is chuip iad thu,
    Is chuir iad thu fo ghlais.

Bha 'm beul onarach a dhìt thu
    Pladach bìdeach sa ghnùis ghlais;
Bha Ceartas sreamshùileach o sgrùdadh
    A leabhar cunntais, 's iad sìor phailt.

These two saw the fighting of battle;
May God never let anyone who is close to me
See such a thing, aye, even a moment's glimpse of it,
Even though it should be in sleep and in a dream.

In the sweltering heat Mokhtâr moved his hand
To wipe away the sweat, to chase away a fly.
The Gefreiter[23] started, and let loose the shot.

There died the angry pride of regal Ahmed,
The gentle meekness of Obayd and Omar's living heart —
They died a second time along with Mokhtâr by the mortar.

There died the man who lay at his elbow,
All his ancestry was blotted out;
His children were murdered unborn.

There was reduced to dust the little world
That grew within him in his green springtime,
Which was created, unknown to him, by everything around him,
Which he formed by his thoughts
On all that he saw and heard,
After understanding had laid
Its manly, difficult, noble burden on his shoulders.
Two complex priceless worlds
Were blotted out for ever before they had attained
The fullness of their being, and were swept
From the sky by a chance blow.

Murder of the dead, murder of children
Never begotten — the end of two worlds.[24]

Atman

You thieved in your need,
    And you tried a lie to get off;
They condemned you, reviled you and whipped you,
    And they put you under lock and key.

The honourable mouth that condemned you
    Was blubberish and tiny in the grey face;
And Justice was blear-eyed from scrutinising
    Its account-books, and they ever showing abundance.

Ach am beul a dhearbhadh breugach,
  Bha e modhail, éibhinn, binn;
Fhuair mi eirmseachd is sgeòil uaith
  'S gun e ro eòlach air tràth bìdh.

Thogte do shùil on obair
  Á cruth an t-saoghail a dheoghal tlachd;
Mhol thu Debel Iussuf dhomh,
  A cumadh is a dath.

Is aithne dhomh thu, Atmain,
  Bean do thaighe 's do chóignear òg,
Do bhaidnein ghobhar is t' asail,
  Do ghoirtein seagail is do bhó.

Is aithne dhomh thu, Atmain:
  Is fear thu, 's tha thu beò,
Dà nì nach eil am breitheamh,
  'S a chaill e 'chothrom gu bhith fòs.

Chan ainmig t' fhallas 'na do shùilean,
  S eòl duit sùgradh agus fearg;
Bhlais is bhlais thu 'n diofar
  Eadar milis agus searbh.

Dh'fheuch thu gràin is bròn is gàire,
  Dh'fheuch thu ànradh agus grian;
Dh'fhairich thu a' bheatha
  'S cha do mheath thu roimpe riamh.

Nan robh thu beairteach, is do chaolan
  Garbh le caoile t' airein sgìth,
Cha bhiodh tu 'chuideachd air na mìolan
  An dubh phrìosan Mhondovì.

Nuair gheibh breitheamh còir na cùirte
  Làn a shùla de mo dhruim,
Thig mi a thaobh gu d' fhàilteachadh
  Trast an t-sràid ma chì mi thù.

Sidna Aissa, chaidh a cheusadh
  Mar ri mèirlich air bàrr sléibh,
'S b'e 'n toibheum, Atmain, àicheadh
  Gur bràthair dhomh thu fhéin.

But the mouth which was found lying
    Was mannerly, cheerful and melodious;
I got sharp repartee and tales from it
    Though it was not too well acquainted with a meal.

Your eye would be raised from your work
    To draw pleasure from the shape of the world;
You praised Jebel Yussuf to me,
    Its form and its colour.

I know you, Atman,
    The woman of your house and your five young things,
Your little clump of goats and your ass,
    Your plot of rye and your cow.

I know you, Atman:
    You are a man, and you are alive,
Two things the judge is not,
    And that he has lost his chance of being ever.

Your sweat is not seldom in your eyes,
    You know what sporting and anger are;
You have tasted and tasted the difference
    Between sweet and bitter.

You have tried hatred and grief and laughter,
    You have tried tempest and sun;
You have felt life
    And never shrunk before it.

Had you been wealthy, and your gut
    Thick with the leanness of your tired ploughmen,
You would not be keeping company with the lice
    In the black prison of Mondovi.

When the decent judge of the court
    Gets the fill of his eye of my back,
I will come aside to welcome you
    Across the street if I see you.

Our Lord Jesus was crucified
    Along with thieves on the top of a hill,
And it would be blasphemy, Atman, to deny
    That you are a brother of mine.

146   *Còmhradh an Alldain*

Na h-aibhnichean móra,
     Ge mórail, mall, leathann iad,
Tàimis is Tìobar
     'S an Nìl, ge aost' a seanchas,
Na chunnaic mi 'nam thuras
     De shruthan mòra 's meadhanach,
Hamìz agus Harrais
     Is Safsaf Sgiogda eatarra,
Seabùs is Buidìma
     Is Picentìno eabarach,
Meidearda Chruimìri,
     Forni, Irno 's Sele leo,
Remel fo Chonstantìna
     Is Lìri a dhearg ar fleasgaichean —
Mas briagh iad, is fheudar dhaibh
     Géilleadh don Alld Bheithe sin.
Ge cian iad no ainmeil
     Is balbhain gun cheileir iad.

Guthan is cluig
     Aig mo shruthan mu na clachan domh,
Cruitean is fuinn,
     Luinneagan labhar ann;
Tiompain is clàrsaichean,
     Gàireachdaich is cagarsaich,
Sùgradh is deasbad,
     Feadain gu faramach.
Crònan sgeap mar dhuis
     Is ceòl brugha troimhn rainich uaith,
Cuairteagan is dannsadh,
     Canntaireachd is caithreaman.
Fàilte leis a' bhruthach
     Is Cumha 'm beul a' chladaich ann:
Glaine, gile, binneas,
     Sruth glinne is ghlacagan.

An linntean a shàmhchair
     Is sgàthan don chraobh bheithe e,
An t-àilleagan achrannach
     Slatagach meanganach.
Bidh a sgàile thar a bhile,
     'S am bricein ga fhalach ann;

The Wee Burn's Talk

The great rivers,
    Though they are majestic, broad and slow,
Thames and Tiber
    And the Nile, though aged be its history,
And all that I saw on my journey
    Of great and middling streams,
Hamîz and Harrash
    And the Safsaf of Skikda among them,
Seybouse and Budjîma
    And the muddy Picentino,
The Medjerda of Kroumiria,
    The Forni, Irno and Sele along with them,
The Rhummel under Constantine
    And the Liri that our youths reddened —
Though they be fine, they must
    Yield to yon Alld Beithe.
Though they be far-off or namely
    They are dumb creatures without melody.

Voices and bells
    Does my wee burn make round the stones for me,
Small harps and tunes,
    And loud ditties in it;
Tympans and great harps,
    Laughing and whispering,
Sweethearting and disputing,
    Chanters sounding out.
A beehive humming like the drones of pipes
    And fairy-knowe music it sends out through the bracken,
Eddying and dancing,
    Canntaireachd and bold war-note sounding.
It sounds a Welcome down the brae
    And a Lament at the lip of the shore:
Pureness, whiteness and melody,
    Stream of the glen and the little hollows.

In the pools of its tranquillity
    It is a mirror for the birch-tree,
The lovely darling of the intricate
    Twigs and branches.
Her shadow lies across its brink,
    And the little trout hides himself in it;

Bidh a faileas air 'uachdar
   'Na lìon duathair is ghathannan,
'S is comhcheòl a cheòlain
   Còmhradh na h-ainnire.

Chan eil guth aig daoine
   O chaoineadh gu cainnt fhanaideach,
Eadar ciùine 's mearan,
   Beannachadh is mallachadh,
Comhairle no searmoin,
   Eirmseachd is sgaiteachas,
Nach cluinnear leis na tuilm
   Feadh nam bulbhag 's nan caiseal uaith.

Cluinnear iongnadh 's mìothlachd,
   Miodal mìn is masgall ann,
'N àm tachairt ris na creagan
   Bidh gearanaich is talach ann;
Brosnachadh is cronachadh,
   Moladh is achmhasan —
Mo shruthan briathrach, bruidhneach,
   Tha guidhe is atach ann.
Tha dàin is duain is ùrnaighean,
   Sgeòil-rùin agus naidheachdan,
Tha salmaireachd is adhradh,
   Tha aoirean is magail ann,
'S an ceòl a chuala mac Laérteis
   Là Céitein ga ghabhail ann.
Mu Shamhain uair bidh donnalaich,
   Ochanaich is casaid ann,
Ceumadh is tailmrich
   Cleas armailt a' faicheachd ann;
Là Lùnaist bidh snàth fuaim aige
   Cleas duanaig aig balachan.

Chan eil eun sléibh no coille
   Nach tug a ghoir 'na leasain uaith,
'S e tiamhaidh, luaineach, ioraltach —
   Tric mar ghairm fheadagan.
Sann aige air tùs
   A dh'ionnsaich iad an gearan ac',
A dh'ùraich ceòl nan Cruimeineach
   Le cuir agus breabadaich,

Her reflection is on its surface
　A net of shade and sunbeams,
And the speech of the maiden
　Sounds in harmony with its music.

There is no tone of voice among men
　From lamentation to derision,
Between placidity and frenzy,
　Blessing and cursing,
Counselling or preaching,
　Or cutting repartee,
That the knowes do not hear from it
　Among its boulders and lynns.

Wonder and displeasure,
　Smooth fawning and flattery are heard in it,
And when it comes against the rocks
　It has girning and complaining in it;
Encouraging and blaming,
　Praising and reproving —
My wordy, talkative wee burn,
　It has supplication and beseeching in it.
There are songs and lays and prayers,
　Secret tales and newsbearing,
There are psalmody and worshipping,
　Satires and mockery in it,
And the music that Laertes' son heard
　Is sung in it on May days.
About Hallowe'en there will be howling,
　And lamentation and accusing in it,
Pacing and clanging
　Like an army marching in it;
And on Lugh's day it will have a thread of sound
　Like a boy singing a little song.

There is no bird of the wood or hill
　That did not learn its cry in lessons from it,
So melancholy, wandering and cunning it is —
　Often like the call of plovers.
It was from it in the beginning
　That they learned their complaining,
Which the music of the MacCrimmons renewed
　With cadences and prancing,

Taorludh agus siubhal
　　A' sruthadh á tuill leadarra.
Cantail is cruitearachd,
　　Ruitheannan ceilearachd,
Fuinn stàtail mar cheud manach
　　An Laideann 'seinn an Fheasgarain.
Saltairt is sitrich
　　'N àm lighe cleas eachraidh ann;
Rothan troma 's drumaichean
　　'S na tuiltean a' greasad air;
Canain air cabhsairean
　　An steallraich gach eas' aige.

Cha teirig cainnt no duain dha
　　'S a' ghrian 's an cuan a' solar dha,
Le'n àlach neòil a' cumail fileantachd
　　Am filidheachd a choilleagan —
Na neòil bheaga 's na baidealan
　　Le frasan a' cur dheoch thuige;
Neòil shneachda àrda thuraideach,
　　Neòil dhubha oillteil thorannach,
Neòil earraich luath an iar-thuath,
　　Neòil chiara dhùmhail fogharaidh,
Neòil an latha 's neòil na h-oidhche
　　A' roinn gun ghainne choireal air.
Tha ceathach, ceò is ceòban
　　A' cumail òran 's oilein ris,
Gach caochan falaich uisge
　　(Mionchuisleannan a' mhonaidh iad),
Gach feadan is gach clais
　　A' cur fala agus sogain ann.
Am fraoch a' crathadh driùchda
　　Nuair dhùisgeas a' ghaoth mhochthrathach,
An raineach is an luachair
　　A' luasgan ris na h-osagan,
'S tha luisreadh ùr na mòintich
　　Ag òstaireachd mhionchopan da.

Òran buan a' teàrnadh
　　Gach ràidh ás na coireachan,
Uair le dùrdan dùsail,
　　Uair le bùirich dhoineannaich;
Ag éigheach 's a' ceasnachadh
　　'S ga fhreagairt fhéin 'na chonaltradh,

Taorludh and siubhal
   Streaming from clangorous chanter holes.
Canticles and crowdering,
   Rippling runs of melody,
Stately tunes like a hundred monks
   In Latin chanting Vespers.
Trampling and neighing
   In time of flood like cavalry;
Heavy wheels and drums
   When the spates hurry it on;
Cannons on causeys
   In the spouting of its every waterfall.

Speech and songs will never fail it
   While the sun and the ocean provide for it,
With their brood of clouds keeping fluency
   In the poesy of its lays —
The little clouds and the stormy battlement clouds
   Sending drinks to it with showers;
The high turreted snow clouds,
   The black awful thunder clouds,
The swift spring clouds from the north-west,
   The dark heavy clouds of autumn,
The clouds of day-time and of night-time
   Giving without stinting tunefulness to it.
The smirr, the mist and the soft rain
   Ply it with instruction and songs unceasingly,
Every hidden runnel of water
   (The tiny veins of the moorland are they),
Every rill and channel
   Send blood and cheer to it.
The heather shaking down the dew
   When the early morning wind awakens,
The bracken and the rushes
   Rocking in the breeze,
And the fresh plants of the boglands
   Play the landlord with tiny cups for it.

An eternal song descending
   Every season from the corries,
At times with a drowsy droning,
   At times with a tempestuous roaring;
Crying out and questioning
   And answering itself in its conversing,

A' brìodal chum na tràghad,
    A' tàladh 's a' coiteachadh,
A' tilleadh don mhuir chéir
    O a chéilidh aig na monaidhean,
Am beòshruth beag as fheàrr
    Na gach sàr abhainn thostach leam.

147 *Bisearta*

Chì mi ré geàrd na h-oidhche
Dreòs air chrith 'na fhroidhneas thall air fàire,
    A' clapail le a sgiathaibh,
A' sgapadh 's a' ciaradh rionnagan na h-àird' ud.

Shaoileadh tu gun cluinnte,
Ge cian, o 'bhuillsgein ochanaich no caoineadh,
    Ràn corraich no gàir fuatha,
Comhart chon cuthaich uaith no ulfhairt fhaolchon,
    Gun ruigeadh drannd an fhòirneirt
On fhùirneis òmair iomall fhéin an t-saoghail;
    Ach siud a' dol an leud e
Ri oir an speur an tostachd olc is aognaidh.

    C'ainm a-nochd a th' orra,
Na sràidean bochda anns an sgeith gach uinneag
    A lasraichean 's a deatach,
A sradagan is sgreadail a luchd thuinidh,
    Is taigh air thaigh ga reubadh
Am broinn a-chéile am brùchdadh toit a' tuiteam?
    Is có a-nochd tha 'g atach
Am bàs a theachd gu grad 'nan cainntibh uile,
    No a' spàirn measg chlach is shailthean,
Air bhàinidh a' gairm air cobhair, is nach cluinnear?
    Có a-nochd a phàigheas
Seann chìs àbhaisteach na fala cumant?

    Uair dearg mar lod na h-àraich,
Uair bàn mar ghile thràighte an eagail éitigh,
    A' dìreadh 's uair a' teàrnadh,
A' sìneadh le sitheadh àrd 's a' call a mheudachd,
    A' fannachadh car aitil
'S ag at mar anail dhiabhail air dhéinead,

Crooning down to the shore,
Coaxing and enticing,
Returning to the dark sea
From its ceilidh with the moorlands,
The little living stream that I love better
Than all the grand silent rivers.

Bizerta

I see during the night guard
A blaze flickering, fringing the skyline over yonder,
Beating with its wings,
And scattering and dimming the stars of that airt.

You would think that there would be heard
From its midst, though far away, wailing and lamentation,
The roar of rage and the yell of hate,
The barking of the dogs from it or the howling of wolves,
That the snarl of violence would reach
From yon amber furnace the very edge of the world;
But yonder it spreads
Along the rim of the sky in evil ghastly silence.

What is their name tonight,
The poor streets where every window spews
Its flame and smoke,
Its sparks and the screaming of its inmates,
While house upon house is rent
And collapses in a gust of smoke?
And who tonight are beseeching
Death to come quickly in all their tongues,
Or are struggling among stones and beams,
Crying in frenzy for help, and are not heard?
Who tonight is paying
The old accustomed tax of common blood?

Now red like a battlefield puddle,
Now pale like the drained whiteness of foul fear,
Climbing and sinking,
Reaching and darting up and shrinking in size,
Growing faint for a moment
And swelling like the breath of a devil in intensity,

An t-Olc 'na chridhe 's 'na chuisle
Chì mi 'na bhuillean a' sìoladh 's a' leum e.
Tha 'n dreòs, 'na oillt air fàire,
'Na fhàinne ròis is òir am bun nan speuran,
A' breugnachadh 's ag àicheadh
Le shoillse sèimhe àrsaidh àrd nan reultan.

148 *An t-Òigear a' Bruidhinn on Ùir*

Seall, a chinne-dhaonna, dlùth air,
   'S gun toir an t-sùil don chuimhne rabhadh.

Seall am fonn a dh'òl ar lotan
   Air a threabhadh leis a' chanan.

Seall na h-achaidhean a shluig sinn
   A' sgeith an duslaich anns an adhar,

Ruidhle aig na cuilbh dhubh' orr'
   Ri drumaireachd nan gunn' a' tabhann.

Air an uisgeachadh le feòlachd,
   Le fuil òigear oidhche 's latha.

Air an ruamhar, air an riastradh,
   Air an cliathadh leis a' chasgairt.

Seall na bothain is na bailtean,
   'Nan cruachan clachaireachd gun fhasgadh.

Seall smùr nam baile pronn san Eadailt
   'S nan clachan leagte thall san Aifric,

Duslach mìn nan taighean marbha,
   Stùr armailt air uaigh nan dachaigh.

Bu chòir gun cruinnicheadh gaoth mhòr e
   Air feadh na h-Eòrpa fada 's farsaing,

Ás an Eòrpa is á Breatainn,
   Ga sguabadh leatha 'na neul gathach,

I see Evil as a pulse
And a heart declining and leaping in throbs.
    The blaze, a horror on the skyline,
A ring of rose and gold at the foot of the sky,
    Belies and denies
With its light the ancient high tranquillity of the stars.

The Young Man Speaking from the Grave

Look closely on it, mankind,
    And let the eye bid the memory take heed.

See the land that has drunk our wounds
    Ploughed by the cannon.

See the fields that swallowed us
    Spewing their dust in the air,

As the black pillars dance a reel on them
    To the drumming of the barking guns.

Watered they are with butchery,
    With the blood of young men night and day.

They have been dug, they have been torn,
    They have been harrowed by the slaughter.

See the cottages and towns,
    Heaps of masonry that give no shelter.

See the dust of the crushed towns in Italy
    And of the villages overthrown in Africa,

The fine dust of the dead houses,
    The stour of armies on the graves of homes.

A great wind should gather it
    Through Europe far and wide,

From Europe and from Britain,
    Sweeping it along in a stabbing cloud,

'S gun séideadh i sna sùilean cruaidhe
Leis nach truagh ar lotan sracte,

Leis nach truagh ar buain earraich,
'S ar n-uaighean feachda air ar n-aineol,

Gan lìonadh le sleaghan duslaich,
Gan cur a shruthadh is gan dalladh,

Ceart mar a thachd an duslach ciar sinn
'S a mhùch e grian òg ar latha.

149   *Meftah Bâbkum es-Sabar?*

Meftah Bâbkum es-Sabar *"Iuchair bhur dorais an fhoidhidinn"* — *sreath á dàn
Àrabach.*

Is cuimhne leam an sùg el-Cheamais,
Sa chaifidh dhorcha is sinn a' deasbad,
Guth cianail, mar ghuth chlag fo fheasgar,
A mhol domh strìochdadh don Fhreastal.
"Mo chridhe fhéin, is faoin bhur gleac Ris,
'S gu bheil gach toiseach agus deireadh
Air an sgrìobhadh Aige cheana."

Sgrùd e bas a làimhe 's lean e:

"Do roinn, do mhanadh, is do sgàile —
Théid iad cuide riut 's gach àite.

"An rud a tha san dàn 's an sgrìobhadh
Is gainntir sin a ghlais an Rìgh oirnn.
Si 'n fhoidhidinn le sealladh ìosal
Iuchair doras ar dubh phrìosain."

Ghin aintighearnas na gréine lasraich
Is ainneart speuran teth na h-Aifric
Gliocas brùite sgìth nam facal.

A ghliocais mar chluig mhall' an fheasgair,
Chan ann duinne do leithid!
Oir sgrìobhadh roghainn fa leth dhuinn:
An t-sìth 's am bàs, no gleac 's a' bheatha.

To blow in the hard eyes
　　That do not grieve for our torn wounds,

That do not grieve for us, mown in the springtime,
　　Or for our campaign graves in a strange land,

To fill them with spears of dust,
　　To set them streaming and to blind them,

Even as the dark dust cloud choked us
　　And quenched the young sun of our day.

Meftah Bâbkum es-Sabar?

Meftah Bâbkum es-Sabar *"Patience the key to your door"* — *a line from an Arabic poem.*

I remember at sûq el-Khemis,
While we argued in the dark café,
A voice, melancholy as the voice of bells when evening falls,
That counselled me to be submissive to Providence.
"My own heart, your struggle against It is in vain,
For every beginning and ending
Has been written by It already."

He gazed at the palm of his hand and went on:

"Your portion, your predestined fate, and your shadow —
These accompany you in every place.

"What is fated and has been written
Is as a dungeon that the Divine King has locked upon us.
Patience with a downcast look
Is the key to the door of our wretched prison."

The tyranny of the flaming sun
And the violence of the hot skies of Africa
Had begotten the bruised, tired wisdom of these words.

Wisdom like the slow bells of evening,
Not for us is your like!
For a choice apart has been written for us:
Peace and death, or struggling and life.

Dh'fhalbh na diasan, dh'fhan an asbhuain?
Thuit na bailtean, chinn an raineach?
A bheil tom luachrach air gach stairsnich?
A shaoghail, tha sinn ann ga ainneoin;
Tha a' ghrìosach theth fon luaithre fhathast.

Na iarraibh oirnn, ma-tà, cur sìos duibh
Draoidheachd cheòlmhor fhacal lìomhta,
Nithean clòimhteach, sgeòil an t-sìthein,
Ceò no òrain air son nìonag,
Òran tàlaidh caillich sìtheil
A' tulgadh a h-ogha 's ga bhrìodal —
Na iarraibh, ach sgal na pìoba.
Beachdan gnàthach, laghach, cinnteach,
Òraid dhàicheil á ceann slìogte,
Nòsan àbhaisteach no mìnead,
Suaimhneas turban geal na h-Ìoslaim,
Foidhidinn Àrabaich ga shìneadh
Fa chomhair Allah fon bhruthainn shìorraidh,
Na iarraibh — tha sinn beò da-rìribh
Agus "Is fuar a' ghaoth thar Ìle
Gheibhear aca an Cinntìre."
Iarraibh gàire, gean is mìghean,
Càirdeas, nàimhdeas, tlachd is mìothlachd.
Iarraibh faileas fìor ar n-inntinn.

Siribh an annas ar làimhe
A' bheatha ghoirt, gharbh, luathghàireach,
Oir thairg am Freastal ré ar làithean
Roghainn na beatha no a' bhàis duinn.

Blàr-cath' ar toile, leac ar teine,
An raon a dhùisgeas ar seisreach,
Stéidh togail ar làmhan 's ar dealais;
An talla a fhuair sinn gun cheilear,
Is far an cluinnear, moch is feasgar,
Ceòl ar sinnsre 's gàir ar seinne;
An leabhar far an sgrìobhar leinne
Bàrdachd ùr fon rann mu dheireadh
A chuireadh leis na bàird o shean ann —
B'e sin ar tìr. No, mura gleacar,
Rud suarach ann an cùil ga cheiltinn
A thraogh 's a dhìochuimhnich sluagh eile.

Are the full ears gone, and only the stubble remaining?
Fallen are the townships, and up has sprung the bracken?
Is there a clump of rushes on every threshold?
O world, we are here and live on in spite of it;
The hot ember is under the ashes yet.

Do not ask us, then, to set down for you
Some musical wizardry of polished words,
Soft downy things, or tales of the fairy knowe,
Mist or songs for young girls,
The lullaby of some peaceful old woman
As she rocks her oe and gives it fondling talk —
Do not ask that, but the scream of the pipes.
Nice, conventional, certain opinions,
A plausible oration from a well-sleeked head,
Customary ways or smoothness,
The tranquillity of the white turbans of Islam,
The patience of an Arab prostrating
Himself before Allah in the eternal sultriness,
Do not ask for them — we are alive in earnest
And "Cold is the wind over Islay
That blows on them in Kintyre."
Ask for laughter, and cheerful and angry moods,
Friendship, enmity, pleasure and displeasure.
Ask for the true reflection of our mind.

Seek in each new work of our hand
Life, sore, rough and triumphant,
For Providence has offered us during our days
The choice between life and death.

The battlefield of our will, the hearthstone we kindle our fire upon,
The field our ploughteam will awaken,
The foundation for the building of our hands and our zeal;
The hall we found without melody,
And where will be heard, early and evening,
The music of our forebears and the clamour of our singing;
The book where we will write
New poetry below the last verse
Put in it by the poets of old —
Such will be our land. Or, if there be no struggle,
A mean thing of no account hidden away in a corner
Which another people drained dry and forgot.

150   bho *Tilleadh Uilìseis*

A' cagnadh 'fheirge, an riochd an déircich
'Na dhùn féin, bu ghailbheach
A shùil-fhiar fo 'mhailghean air cuirm nan tòiseach.

'Na dhéidh bu labhar sreang a bhogha
Is b' fhionnar oiteag a shaighdean
Feadh an talla air gruaidhean na dòmhlachd.

Is iomadh misgear uaibhreach a tholladh
'S a leig 'fhochaid dheth 's a ghàire
'S a shleuchd 'na fhuil 's a làmhan dearg mu 'sgòrnan,

Is suirgheach maoth a fhuair a leagadh
Beul fodha, 's e 'sgeith lod fala
Measg fìon, feòl', arain, chuachan is fhear-feòirne.

151   *Achmhasain*

(Trì Rainn agus Amhran)

Na beanntan àrda, saora
    Dh'fhuilingeas gaoth is grian,
Gar faicinn mar a tha sinn —
    Is achmhasan dhuinn iad.

Glinn nan làrach uaigneach
    Far na bhuadhaich am fiadh,
Na h-achaidhean fo rainich —
    Is achmhasan dhuinn iad.

Ar tìr bha uair 'na leòghann,
    Bha mòr ri trod 's ri sìth,
'Na measan aig sàil Shasainn —
    Is achmhasan dhuinn ì.

Ceangal

Euchdan ar cinnidh dhuinn s achmhasan fìor,
A cheòl 's a bhàrdachd, a chànain 's ar n-òigridh ga dìth;
    Na h-uillt bhrasa 's a' ghaoth thig saor á marannan cian,
    Samhail misneach ar n-athraichean — achmhasain, achmhasain iad.

from *The Return of Ulysses*

Chewing his anger, in the guise of a beggar
In his own *dùn*, stormy was his sidelong glance
Under his brows at the banquet of the chiefs.

And afterwards loud was the string of his bow
And cool was the waft of his arrows
Throughout the hall on the cheeks of the throng.

Many an arrogant drunkard was pierced
And gave over his jibing and laughter
As he bowed down in his blood with his hands red about his throat,

And many a delicate suitor was cast down
Prone on his face, spewing a puddle of blood
Amongst wine and flesh and bread, amongst goblets and chessmen.

Rebukes

(Three Verses and an Envoi)

The high, free mountains
    That endure wind and sun,
That they should see us as we are —
    They are a rebuke to us.

The glens with their lonely ruined village sites
    Where the deer has conquered,
The fields under bracken —
    They are a rebuke to us.

Our land which was once a lion,
    Which was great in war and peace,
A messan at England's heel —
    It is a rebuke to us.

Envoi

The heroic feats of our nation truly are a rebuke to us,
Its music and its poetry, its language which our youth goes lacking;
    The headlong burns and the wind which comes free from far-off seas,
    The image of our fathers' spirit — rebukes, rebukes are they.

152   *Ors a' Bhéist Mhór ris a' Bhéist Bhig*

On s mith thu, ithidh mi thu;
On s mion thu, ithidh mi thu;
Ged s clis thu, ithidh mi thu;
Nuair nach fhios duit, ithidh mi thu;
O nach mis' thu, ithidh mi thu;
Gheibh mi ris thu, 's ithidh mi thu;
Chì mi leis thu, 's ithidh mi thu;
On s treis duit, ithidh mi thu;
On s driop e, ithidh mi thu;
O nach tric seo, ithidh mi thu;
On s a-nis duinn, ithidh mi thu,
Agus, a-rithist, ithidh mi thu.
Se mo ghliocas — ithidh mi thu.

153   *An Ciùran Ceòban Ceò*

Dol sìos an cladach madainn dhomh, 's an t-adhar ann gun deò,
Bha sìth feadh fuinn is mara ann, is taise bho na neòil;
Cha chluinnte feadh a' chiùinis ach fann chiùcharan aig eòin,
Bha gach nichein tostach driùchdach anns a' chiùran cheòban cheò.

Cha robh àird no iùl ann a stiùireadh neach 'na ròd,
Cha robh àit no ùin' ann, ach aon chiùineas domhainn mòr;
Bha 'n saoghal làn den mhaoithe, fo dhraoidheachd is fo chleòc,
Is bann-sìthe air mo shùilean anns a' chiùran cheòban cheò.

Chan fhaicte fonn no fàire, bha sàmhchar air gach nì,
Bha beithich agus dùslaingean 'nan smùid gun dath gun lìth;
Bha cnuic is glacan paisgte ann, is chailleadh muir is tìr,
Bha fois is clos is dùsal anns a' chiùran cheòbain mhìn.

Chaidh sliosan agus leathadan á sealladh anns na neòil,
Cha robh dath no fuaim ann, no uair, no solas lò;
Bha 'n sileadh mall réidh socrach air cnoc, air glaic, air lòn,
'S bha 'm Paiste Beag fo dheataich anns a' cheathach cheòban cheò.

Bha na ciothan ceathaich chiùranaich 's iad dùmhail dlùth, gun ghlòir,
Gu cagarsach, gu cùbhraidh, tais, ùr, gun ghuth gun cheòl,
A' snàmh mu mhill is stùcan, 's a' dùnadh mu gach còs,
Bha tlàths is tlachd a' tùirling anns a' chiùran cheòban cheò.

Said the Big Beast to the Little Beast

Since you're vulgar, I'll eat you;
Since you're small, I'll eat you;
Though you're nimble, I'll eat you;
When you don't know, I'll eat you;
As you're not me, I'll eat you;
I'll catch you at it, and I'll eat you;
I'll see you with it, and I'll eat you;
Since you've had a while, I'll eat you;
As it keeps me busy, I'll eat you;
As this doesn't happen often, I'll eat you;
As it's now for us, I'll eat you,
And, again, I'll eat you.
My wisdom is — I'll eat you.

The Smirry Drizzle of Mist

Going down the shore on a morning, when the air was without a breath of wind,
There was peace throughout land and sea, and a softness from the clouds;
Nothing was to be heard through the stillness but a faint chirping of birds,
Everything was silent and dewy in the smirry drizzle of mist.

There was no airt or direction to guide one on one's way,
There was no place or time there, but one great deep stillness;
The world was full of tenderness, under druidry and under a cloak,
And there was a fairy blindfolding on my eyes in the smirry drizzle of mist.

Land or horizon could not be seen, quietness was over everything,
A smoke was rising from colourless hueless birch groves and thickets;
Hills and hollows were enfolded in it, and land and sea were lost,
There was peace and rest and slumber in the fine drizzle of mist.

Hillsides and slopes were lost to sight in the clouds,
There was no colour or sound there, or hour, or light of day;
The slow caressing rain was on hill, and hollow, and meadow,
And the Wee Patch was in a smoke in the foggy drizzle of mist.

The showers of drizzly mist came closely down, all voiceless,
Whispering and fragrant, soft and fresh, without voice or melody,
They floated about hilltops and cliffs, and closed in about every hollow,
Gentleness and pleasure were drifting down in the smirry drizzle of mist.

154 Uladh

O Shiorramachd Àir gu Ard Macha ghluais sinn fhéin,
Siar 'nar tàintean bochd cràite gun tug sinn ceum;
Is dian a tha làmhach is ràn nam boma 'nar déidh —
A Dhia nan gràs, "is láidir an snaoisín é"!

155 Suas gun Sìos

Suas gun sìos, buaidh gun bhualadh,
   Buannachd gun chall gun dìth;
Nì ùr a th' ann san t-seann shaoghal,
   Buidhinn saorsa le sìth.

156 Ionndrainn na Sìne

Cian am-bliadhna is cian an-uiridh.
Seo an t-àit a bh' ann an-uiridh,
Is bliadhna 's bliadhna 's bliadhna buileach.

A Dhia, am faic mi siud tuille,
Eagan nan sliabh fon drumach?
An t-uisge fiar 's an drumach,
An t-uisge ciar 's an drumach,
An t-uisge liath 's an drumach,
An t-uisge tiamhaidh 's an drumach,
An t-uisge cianail 's an drumach,
'S e 'na fhrasan dian dubha,
'Oir ga riasladh air a thuras,
A' ghaoth a' sianail 's a' tuireadh.
Cha b' ionnan sin riamh is turadh;
Cha b' ionnan 's latha briagh buidhe;
Cha b' ionnan 's grian is bruthainn
An sileadh neolochdach fionnar.
An t-uisge riabhach 'na thuiltean,
Uisge àird an iar 'na dhruma,
Uisge nan sliabh 's an drumach,
Eagan nan sliabh fon drumach.

A Dhia, am faic mi siud tuille?

Ulster

From the Shire of Ayr to Armagh we went,
Westward in poor worn droves we took our step;
Vehement is the firing and the roar of bombs after us —
O God of grace, "it is powerful snuff"!

Up with no Down

Up with no down, victory with no blows struck,
   Gaining with no loss or deprivation;
It is a new thing in the old world,
   Winning freedom by peace.

Longing for the Tempest

Far off this year and far off last year.
This is the place that was there last year,
And year and year and year entirely.

God, will I ever see that again,
The notches of the hills under the downpour?
The slanting rain and the downpour,
The dark rain and the downpour,
The grey rain and the downpour,
The melancholy rain and the downpour,
The lamenting rain and the downpour
And it in vehement black showers,
With its edge tattered on its journey,
The wind screaming and wailing.
Never the same that as dry warm weather;
Not the same as a fine yellow day;
Not the same as sun and sultry heat
The innocent cool fall of rain.
The brindled rain in its torrents,
The rain of the western airt like a drum,
The rain of the hills and the downpour,
The notches of the hills under the downpour.

God, will I ever see that again?

157   *Guidhe an Iasgair*

Fèath is fàbhar agus fortan,
    Pailteas coltais anns gach bàgh,
Reòtach air clàr 's air cliathaich
    'S margadh fial air teachd an là.

158   *Bloigh Lebensraum*

Na muilleanan tha 'n Sasainn fheuraich,
    Is mór á meud iad, uain;
Tha 'd ag iarraidh, mas fìor am beul seo,
    Bloigh Lebensraum mu thuath.

159   *Na Ràtaichean 's a' Bhàrdachd*

"Cìsean is ràtaichean àrda," ors esan rium.
"Ìocaibh 's pàighibh," ors à, "air an teas 's na shluig.
Dìobair a' bhàrdachd o t' fhàrdaich, no creanaidh thu."
Is sìorraidh na dàin, ged bhiodh ràtaichean 'teachd gun sgur.

"Prìsean gan àrdachadh àrd, agus faradh nam bus
A' dìreadh gach ràidh, gun sa bhanca ach tastan tur;
An TV, is na pàistean a' fàs, is an caban 'nan sluic.
V.A.T.," ors à. Dhùisg a' bhàrdachd is chaidil a ghuth.

"Bheil e Crìostail 's mo spàirn gach là ri pathadh 'na mhuir,
Ri ìota nach tràigh, nach sàsaichear aiteal leam,
'S na prìsean 's na pàistean, 's gach ràta ag at 's gam ruith?
Ma bhitheas tu ri bàrdachd gun stàth, gun can mi *Fuich!*

"Deich p air son copan cofaidh is barrachd, fuich!
Trì p air son bogsa mosach lethfhalamh spung.
Dol sìos air an nota, na rocaidean, aillse, an Ruis;
Droch thìde, cion oibre, na robairean, stailcean 's muirt.

"A' phrìs chuirear ort air son bothain mar fhail nam muc;
B.P. a tha coma, air a shocair 's nach abair dìog;
E.E.C. 's an liotar 's an kilo, 's na Pakidhean tiugh;
Cìopras is Doire, an dolar 's an t-Amin ud.

The Fisherman's Prayer

Calm weather and favour and fortune,
    Plenty of traces in every bay,
Frost of fishscales on deck and on hull
    And generous market at break of day.

A Spot of Lebensraum

The millions that are in grassy England,
    They are proud of size, lamb;
They are seeking, if this mouth speak true,
    A spot of Lebensraum up north.

The Rates and Poetry

"Taxes and high rates," said he to me.
"Fork out and pay for heating and the food you have swallowed.
Banish poetry from your dwelling, or else you will pay dearly for it."
Poems are eternal, though rates should come without cease.

"Prices being raised to dizzy heights, and the bus fares
Going up every quarter, with nothing in the bank but a meagre shilling;
The TV, and the children growing, with their gabs a bottomless pit.
V.A.T.," said he. My poetry wakened and his voice fell asleep.

"Is it Christian for me to have to struggle every day with a thirst which is a sea,
With a drouth which will never ebb, and which won't be satisfied by me for an instant,
And the prices and the children, and all the rates swelling up and pursuing me?
If you are engaged on useless poetry, I will say *Fie!*

"Ten p and more for a cup of coffee, fie!
Three p for a miserable half-empty box of matches.
The pound losing value, the rockets, cancer, Russia;
Bad weather, no jobs, the robbers, strikes and murders.

"The price they demand for a hovel no more than a pigsty;
The M.P. doesn't care, takes it easy and won't say a thing;
The E.E.C. and the litre and kilo and Pakis all over the place;
Cyprus and Derry, the dollar and yon Idi Amin.

"Brezhnev is Trotski is Mosco 's mo chasan fliuch;
Na Sìnich is pop is porno is m' ad á cruth;
Gach nìonag cho moiteil 's nach mothaich i aiteal dhuit;
Gun dìth air ball-coise, 's na coin is na capaill a' ruith.

"Tha a' phinnt 'dol an àird aon là, ged a tha i cus.
An ceann mìosa no dhà, 'dol an àird, 's i 'na h-annas dhuinn."
Chrìochnaich e, 's dh'fhàg e am bàr fo phathadh 's fo chruit.
Rinn mi dìochuimhn' air làn a thàsain 's na rainn seo dhuibh.

160   *Dùrachdan Nollaige*

Nuair a thig oirbh an Nollaig
Guma sona a bhitheas sibh,
Agus ré na Bliadhn' Ùire
Móran sunnd is toil-inntinn.

161   *Dùrd a' Ghlinne*

Fonn ciùil bu bhinne dùrd a' ghlinne
'S e dùint' an grinneas chraobh;
Duilleach 's feur is guth nan eun
Là buidhe gréine caomh.

Iain Peatarson (1916–90)

162   *Turas an Ànraidh*

Dh'ainneoin anastachd is riaslaidh
Tillidh Eileanaich gach bliadhna
Dha na ceàrnan creagach riabhach
Far an iarradh iad bhith còmhnaidh.

Is minig chuala mi 'nam phàiste
Mu thursan garbh' a rinn am bàta —
Gun do theab iad a bhith bàthte
'S mar a thàrr iad ás air éiginn.

Ach bidh cuimhn' agam gu bràth air
Nuair dh'fhalbh mi fhéin is Dòmhnall Màrtainn
'S clann nighean 'n Tuairneir á Beàrn'raigh
Liuthad àmhghair bh' againn còmhladh.

"Brezhnev and Trotsky and Moscow and my feet are wet;
The Chinese and pop and porn and my hat's out of shape;
All the lassies so stuck up they don't even notice you;
Still, there's plenty of football, and dogs and the horseracing too.

"A pint is going up one day, although it is too dear.
After a month or two, going up, novel luxury though it is to us."
He finished, and left the bar thirsty and bent.
I forgot the whole of his querulous whining and made these verses for you.

Christmas Greetings

When Christmas comes upon you
   May happiness be yours,
And in the New Year
   Much good cheer and peace of mind.

The Hum of the Glen

The sweetest music is the hum of the glen
   Enclosed in the elegance of trees;
Foliage and grass and the voice of the birds
   On a lovely golden sunny day.

Ian Paterson (Berneray, Harris)

Stormy Voyage

Despite storms and tribulation
Islanders go home each year
To the brindled rocky districts
   Where they'd love to be living.

I often heard as a child
Of heroic journeys made by boat —
Of coming close to being drowned
   And escaping with their lives.

But I'll always remember
When I set off with Donald Martin[25]
And the Turner girls from Berneray[26]
   How much we suffered together.

An Di-Haoine bha mi falbh ás
Bha madainn rosgalach gharbh ann,
A'ghaoth a'séideadh on eardheas
    Mar chuir an seanchas air dòigh dhomh.

Seanchas nan daoine beachdaidh
Bhios ga breithneachadh mar chleachdadh
'Bidh Di-Haoine 'n aghaidh na seachdain' —
    'S cha robh mearachd 'nan cuid eòlais.

Nuair a thàinig fios o Dhòmhnall
Gun robh e fhéin a' falbh còmh' rium
Rinn mi gàirdeachas ri chòmhdhail
    'S e math air òrain, on as bàrd e.

Air dha tighinn a-nuas á Brùsda
Bha mo pheathraichean 'nan ùpraid,
'Dinneadh cheasaichean 's gan dùnadh,
    'S mise rùileach air son bhrògan.

Nuair a fhuair a' chailleach almsadh
Rinn i tàmadh air an fhalachan
'S thug i drama dha na balachain
    Mum biodh iad anfhann le cion spreòchainn.

Dh'fhàg mi beannachd le na càirdean,
Le mo pheathraichean 's le mo mhàthair,
'S on bha 'n aimsir cho ràsach
    Cha d'fhuair mi àmas gu bhith brònach.

Sìos an cladach dol dhan gheòlaidh
Sann a dh'fheumadh tu bhith teòma
No shleamhnaicheadh a' bhòtann
    'S air do thòin thu 'm measg nam bàirneach.

Seonaidh 's Aonghas bha ga h-iomradh,
Dh'anacail iad i sa phlumanaich,
'Cumail sùl' a-mach gu furachail
    Air son nach cuireadh i striodag òirnne.

Nuair a ràinig sinn an t-eathar
Ris a' bhalbhadh b' fheudar feitheamh,
Thàinig uisge lom fo dheireadh
    'S cha robh air ach leum air bòrd innt'.

On the Friday I was leaving there
Rough and blustery was the morning,
The wind blowing from the south-east
    Just as tradition had prepared me for.

The tradition of observant men
Whose custom is assessing it
Is 'Friday goes against the week' —
    And not mistaken was their knowledge.

When word came down from Donald
That he was travelling with me
I was glad to have his company
    He being good at songs, as he's a poet.[27]

When he came down from Brusda
My sisters were going crazy
Packing cases and closing them
    While I scrabbled for shoes.

When my mother got a chance
She made a lunge for something hidden
And gave the lads a dram
    For fear they'd fail from lack of strength.

I bade farewell to my kinsfolk,
To my sisters and my mother,
But the weather being so rough
    I had no chance to be mournful.

Going down to the rowing-boat
You had to cross the shore with care
Or your boot would miss its foothold
    And down you'd sit amongst the limpets.

It's Johnny and Angus were rowing her,[28]
Manoeuvring her in the rising sea,
And maintaining a good lookout
    To ensure no spray would wet us.

When we'd reached the larger boat
We had to wait for a calm spell,
But slack water came at last
    And we simply jumped aboard her.

Cha do dhiùlt an t-inneal-sparraidh,
Thug e leum ás a' chiad tarraing,
'S ri mo bhràthair chòrd am faram
   'S dh'fhuasgladh caran far a mònaids.

Cha robh ann ach leth na h-uarach
Gus do chuir iad air tìr an Uibhist a-Tuath sinn,
'S ás an eathar bha sinn uasal
   Chionns nach d'fhuair sinn steallan sàile.

Fhuair sinn bho na siantan fasgadh
Anns a' bhàthaich aig MacAsgaill,
'S chaidh na h-iollaichean a phasgadh
   'S a chur air ais le fear a' bhàta.

An Loch nam Madadh san taigh òsta
Ghabh sinn làin a shùgh an eòrna,
'S o nach d'chleachd mi bhith 'nam phòiteir
   Cha do dh'òl mi ach a dhà dhiubh.

Nach mairg am fear a dhèanadh dìmeas
'S, nas miosa na sin, a dhèanadh mì-fheum
Dhen an deoch ud tha cho brìoghmhor
   'S a nì gach nì dhut cho òirdhearc.

Thàinig i 'n-iar, a sheachd mhiosad,
Le uisge siar a bha sgriosail;
Cha leigmid a leas grisead —
   Cha robh fhios air cuin a sheòlaist'.

Bha e suas ri deich uairean
Mun deachaidh na ròpan aic' fhuasgladh,
Ach bha Uibhist air a fuaradh
   'S cha do ghluais i far a sàile.

Sean nuair thòisich òrain Ghàidhlig,
Òrain Eachainn is Iain Èirdsidh
'S feadhainn le Calum mac Iain 'ic Phàdraig,
   'S Rodaidh Bàn gan seinn cho ceòlmhor.

Thuirt fear Uibhisteach, "A ghràidhein,
Nach ann tha na h-òrain aig a' Bheàrndrach!"
'S bha mi moiteil dha bhith càirdeach
   'S fhuair e làn a Mhac an Tòisich.

The engine gave no trouble,
But jumped to life with one pulling,
The sound seemed fine to my brother
    So turns were loosened off her moorings.

Only half an hour it took them
To land us in North Uist,
With the boat we were delighted
    Because the brine hadn't wetted us.

We got shelter from the weather
In the byre MacAskill had,[29]
Our rough clothes were parcelled up
    And sent back with the boatman.

In Lochmaddy in the changehouse
We had some drams of barley bree,
But being no great imbiber
    All I drank of them was two.

Woe betide the man who'd scorn
And, worse than that, abuse
That drink which is so potent
    It makes everything seem wonderful.

Westerly it backed, seven times as bad,
With rain across the land that was fearsome;
There wasn't any point in our hurrying at all —
    There was no knowing when she'd be sailing.

It was close to ten o'clock
Before her ropes were untied,
But she kept Uist to windward
    And clung fast to her waters.

That's when Gaelic songs began,
Songs by Hector and Iain Archie[30]
And some by Calum 'Ain Phàdraig,[31]
    With Roddy Bàn singing them masterfully.[32]

A man from Uist said, "My friend,
What songs the fellow from Berneray has!"
And I was proud to be his kinsman
    And he got his fill of whisky.

An Loch Baghasdail bha i rapach,
'S cha deadh a-mach ach sgiobadh tapaidh;
Ach bha earbs' ac' ás a h-acainn —
   'S ged gheibheadh i clatradh, cha bhiodh beud dhi.

Cha robh soitheach 's cha robh coire,
Bòrd no bearraid nach do sgoradh —
Chan ann a chionns gun robh i corrach
   Ach cho molach 's a bha 'n fhairge.

Null gu Canaigh rinn i garraichdeadh
'S na bu doimhne an cladhach fairge,
'S a dh'innse dhut gun robh i garbh ann —
   Cha tigeadh sgarbh ás ach air éiginn.

An domhain dorcha 's i gun mheachainn
Le muir is gaoith ri dibhearsain
Nach robh ac' ach slige-chreachainn
   Dh'fhaodte creachadh nuair a b' àill leo.

Bha an dorchadas gach taobh dhinn
Mar gum biodh i ruinne glaodhaich
Gum bu neoni an cinne-daonna
   Is iad air faondradh gun dòchas.

Anns an dorchadas 'nar n-aonar
Thòisich m' aigne-sa ri saoilsinn
Gun do sgaradh sinn on t-saoghal
   'S gum b'e faoineis bha 'nar seòladh.

Bha sinn gu dearbh air ar tulgadh,
'S leis mar a bha iad air an tunacail
Bha 'chlann-nighean a' cur muinghinn
   Ás na fuirbhirnich threuna.

Nuair a dh'éireadh muir fo 'sliasaid
Bheireadh i ruinnseadh air a cliathaich,
Bhiodh i creanachadh air fad-fiaraidh —
   'S "Och a chiall!" aig luchd a' ghòmaidh.

Nach ann ann a bha 'n t-onfhadh —
Chaith i Dòmhnall far an t-sorchain,
Nuair a thug i aiste 'n gorrochdadh
   Dh'fhàg poit-ghorm air mac-mo-laghachain.

In Lochboisdale it was rough,
It took a skilful crew to go out;
But they could trust her equipment —
    She'd be buffeted hard, but unharmed.

There was neither dish nor kettle,
Tool nor table unsecured —
Not because she was unstable
    But for the roughness of the sea.

Crossing to Canna came a burst of bad weather
And each sea-trench delved ever deeper,
And to demonstrate the extent of its roughness —
    A cormorant could scarcely survive it.

The deep was dark and merciless
With sea and wind amused
To have a little scallop-shell
    For plundering at their whim.

The darkness on each side
Seemed to cry out upon us
That man was a nothingness
    Wandering hopelessly.

In the dark by ourselves
My mind started to imagine
That we'd parted from the world
    And that our voyage was folly.

We were well and truly tossed,
And seeing themselves being jolted
The girls put all their confidence
    In the lads and their courage.

When a sea heaved up her stern
She'd keel over to one side,
Her whole hull would be quivering —
    And "Good grief!" the vomiters cried.

What a hurricane there was —
It threw Donald off his stool[33]
When she made such a lurch
    That my buddy got a shiner.

Chuir nighean òg a ceann troimh uinneig
'S am fear bha còmh' rithe sruth dhen fhuil ás,
Sann a bha an t-iongnadh buileach
    Nach robh tuilleadh air an leònadh.

Ach mun d'ràinig sinne Malaig
Bha iomadh fear a' gearan a stamaig,
'S an-diugh mo dhùrachd dhaibh bhith fallain
    Gun aon smalan mar bu chòir dhaibh.

Ach gabhaibh leth-sgeul mo bhàrdachd —
Chan eil ann ach gearan àilgheis,
Cha b' ionnan 's na lathaichean ànrach
    Nuair nach robh ach ràmh is seòl ann.

Sibhse théid air chuairt dhan àite
Bhios a' tolach air an tàire,
Cuimhnichibh na seana Ghàidhil
    A bha àbhachdach sa chruadal.

163   *Uisge Phìob*

Sann tha 'n othail air na cruinneagan
Tha fuireach anns an eilean seo
Fàgail soraidh aig na cuinneagan
    Bha gan cumail-san cho trang.

Uisge phìob nach teirig ac'
'S chan fhaic na tobair tuilleadh iad
A' taomadh is ag eaghonadh
    Le sgeileidean 'nan làimh.

164   *Bogsa Diùc*

Chuala mi luach tastain de cheòl
    Ann an taigh òil a' chofaidh
Gliongadaich gun dòigh
    'Cur chasan òg' 'nan torainn,
Bras-bhualadh iomadh teud
    Còmh' ri séist neo-chothrom,
Glaodhaich gun bhrìgh gun chéill
    Mar aig na féidh sa mhonadh.

A girl's head went through a window
And the man with her was bleeding,
It was really quite remarkable
    That others weren't injured.

But before we got to Mallaig
Many passengers had bad stomachs
And I wish them now good health
    Without blemish as is proper.

But please forgive my verses —
They're just a fussy complaint,
Quite unlike the days of storm
    When they'd only oar and sail.

You who journey to the place
Murmuring condescendingly,
Don't forget the Gael of old
    Who were cheerful in adversity.

Piped Water

How excited are the lasses
Who're living in this island
Taking leave of the buckets
    That were keeping them so busy.

They've piped water unlimited
And no well again will see them
Emptying and filling
    With skillets in their hands.

Juke Box

I heard a shilling's worth of music
    In the house of drinking coffee
Jangling in a frenzy
    Sending young feet a-tapping,
With many strings twanging
    To a chorus out of key,
Pointless idiotic bawling
    Like the deer do on the moor.

165 Bó Dhearg

Bó dhearg 's i 'na seasamh
Cnàmh a cìre mu thràth eadraidh,
Cnàmhach, cnàmhach, cnàmhach,
    Stad is slugadh.

Bòrlam eile suas o 'goile,
Fiar is connlach air am meileadh,
Cnàmhach, cnàmhach, cnàmhach,
    Stad is slugadh.

Suapadh iorbaill air a caoldruim
Cuileagan caobaidh mach 'nan sgaothan,
Cnàmhach, cnàmhach, cnàmhach,
    Stad is slugadh.

Crathadh cluaise, diosg-leum aithghearr
Chuileagan bun na h-adhairc tha tathaich,
Cnàmhach, cnàmhach, cnàmhach,
    Stad is slugadh.

Priobadh ruisg is iad ga ciùrradh,
O chlach sùla clisgidh tiùrra,
Cnàmhach, cnàmhach, cnàmhach,
    Stad is slugadh.

Breabadh coise suas mu h-ùtha,
Gaoir nan sgiath comh-fhreagairt gnùsaid,
Cnàmhach, cnàmhach, cnàmhach,
    Stad is slugadh.

Crith air feòil chuireas eagal orra,
A-mach air iteig cliath mhollaicht',
Cnàmhach, cnàmhach, cnàmhach,
    Stad is slugadh.

166 Cearcall Hùla

Cearcall hùla, cearcall hùla,
Siud agaibh iorram clann-nighean na dùthcha,
  Cearcall 'na dheannaibh aig gach cruinneig sa bhaile
'S i ga chumail on talamh le meadhanan lùthmhor,

Red Cow

Red cow who's standing there
Ruminates at milking time,
As she chews, chews, chews,
    Stopping to swallow.

Another batch up from her stomach,
Masticating hay and straw,
As she chews, chews, chews,
    Stopping to swallow.

Sweep of tail about her back
And biting flies rise in swarms,
As she chews, chews, chews,
    Stopping to swallow.

Twitch of ear, sudden leap
Of flies that flock where the horn grows,
As she chews, chews, chews,
    Stopping to swallow.

Blink of eyelid as they nip her,
From the eyeball jumps the jetsam,
As she chews, chews, chews,
    Stopping to swallow.

Kicking leg up by her udder,
Buzz of wings to match her grunting,
As she chews, chews, chews,
    Stopping to swallow.

Shaking flesh makes them frightened,
And off they fly, the cursed phalanx,
As she chews, chews, chews,
    Stopping to swallow.

Hula Hoop

Hula hoop, hula hoop,
There goes the chant of the girls of the land,
A hoop kept going round by each lass in the township
Held off the ground by their sinuous midriffs,

Siud agaibhs' an iomairt a thàinig dhan dùthaich
Chumas nigheanan cho tana 's nach aithnicht' o'n cùl iad,
 Sgeadaichte 'n earradh cho cuimir 's cho goirid
'S an cearcall ga thoinneamh le eacarsaich shunndaich
 Timcheall, timcheall, timcheall an caoldruim,
Nas luaithe, nas luaithe fhads a nì 'n lùths e,
 S beag an t-iongnadh no 'n t-annas gun sibh a bhith reamhar,
Gun stad 'na bhur n-anail ach aighearach mùirneach,
 Tha gach maighdeann is caileag cho caol agus tana
'S gun cuir gillean a' bhaile am barrachd a dh'ùidh annt',
 Clann-nighean a' bhaile cumail cearcaill 'na dheannaibh,
Cha robh dùileam ri m' mhaireann gum faicinn an taobh-s' e,
 Cearcall hùla, cearcall hùla,
Siud agaibh iorram clann-nighean na dùthcha.

An t-Urr. Cailein T MacCoinnich (1917–94)

167   *An Seanchaidh*

Tha fear-òraid sa bhaile seo shuas againn
'S chan eil seanchaidh san dùthaich a shuathas ris —
 Bha mi raoir aig' air chéilidh
 'S chuir e 'n tàthadh a-chéile
Na thug barradh gu léir air na chuala mi.

Bha 'bhreithneachadh domhainn gu rannsachadh
Gach gnè chàis mu'm bi daoine ri connsachadh —
 An robh gaiseadh 'thaobh nàdair
 Sa chrodh chaol chunnaic Phàroh,
'S dé tha bacadh muir làin aig na conntraighean?

Fhuair mi eòlas air nithean bha 'n duathar orm —
Mar a chailleadh Clach Sgàin 's mar a fhuaras i,
 Cuin a thogadh Tùr Bhàbail,
 Cia lìon troigh a bha dh'àird air,
'S gun robh cungaidh chum slàinte sa bhuaghallan.

Thug e tarraing air sgeul Mhic an t-Srònaich dhomh,
Mar a bhiodh e am falach 's an tòir ac' air;
 Mar chaidh Eilidh a léireadh
 Le droch chuilbheartain Bhénuis
'S mar thug gaisgich na Gréige á Tròas i.

That is the craze that has come to the country,
Keeping lassies so slim they're not known from behind,
    Dressed in a garment so neat and so skimpy
While the hoop is kept spinning by cheerful exertion
    Around and around and around all their middles,
Quicker and quicker as long as they're strong enough,
    It's not surprising or strange that you aren't fat
As you never draw breath but stay cheerful and merry,
    All the lasses and girls are so slim and so slender
That the lads of the township fancy them better,
    The girls of the township keeping hoops in a spin,
I little thought that I'd see it here in my time,
    Hula hoop, hula hoop,
There goes the chant of the girls of the land.

Rev. Colin N Mackenzie (Taransay, Harris)

The Shennachie

There's an orator in our township up here
That no shennachie in the country can equal —
    I visited him last night
    And what he placed side by side
Quite excelled all I'd ever heard previously.

His mind was profound for dissecting
Each question that folk like to speak about —
    Did the lean cows that Pharaoh saw
    Have some natural failing,
And what holds back the ocean at neaptides?

I found out about things that were unclear to me —
How the Stone of Scone was lost then retrieved again,
    When the Tower of Babel was erected,
    How many feet high it measured,
And how the ragweed was a curative treatment.

He mentioned the story of Stronach to me,
How he hid when pursuers were following him;
    How Helen was tormented
    By Venus' evil intentions
And was brought out from Troy by Greek warriors.

Chuala mi sgeul ás an Ròimh aige
Mun a' Phàp Alexander, 's bu neònach i —
    Gum bu duine mì-bheusach
    A bha riamh anns a' bhéist ud,
'S gur i nighean leis fhéin a bha pòst' aige.

Cia lìon ainmhidh rinn Nòah a shàbhaladh
'S ciamar chùm e rian anns an Àirc orra,
    Mar a thàinig Sliochd Mhìlidh
    Ás an Spàinn roimh an dìle,
'S gun robh coilich gun chìrein am Beàrnraigh ac'.

Nach eil biadh air an t-saoghal as càilmhoire
Na gug' air a ròsladh 's buntàta leis,
    'S gur e adhbhar na Siaraich
    Bhith cho ruiteach san ìomhaigh
Gun robh grùthan na sìolaig 'nam pàistean ac'.

Mar bha treubhantas Shamsoin 'na chiabhagan
'S nach robh 'n Alasdair Ailpein ach spìocaire —
    Nach robh lideadh den fhìrinn
    Anns an leabhar a sgrìobh e,
'S mu Iain Buinean bhith 'm prìosan thaobh fhiach a bh' air.

Rinn e aithris mar sgrìobhadh na h-Àithnteanan
'S mar a fhuair Coinneach Odhar a thàlantan,
    Mar theich Naois agus Déirdre
    Nall o chladaichean Éireann,
'S dé dh'fhàg bodaich á Bréinis cho cànranach.

Cia mar bhiodh Cù Chulainn a' gnàthachadh
San uisg' an gath-bolg a thug Sgàthach dha,
    Co ás bhiodh am maorach
    Air Tràigh Thunga a' taomadh,
'S an robh linntean an t-saoghail do-àireamh dhuinn.

Thug e iomradh air Mort Ghleanna Còmhainn dhomh
'S dé bu chiall don Làimh Dheirg aig na Dòmhnallaich,
    Mar a thachair sa Ghàrradh
    'S gur e taghadh na Gàidhlig
A bh' aig Eubha 's aig Àdhamh a' còmhradh ann.

Gun robh daoin' ann o shean bha 'nam fuamhairean,
'S mar bha rothan an tàthadh an uaireadair;

I heard a story he had from Rome
About Alexander, one of the Popes —
    Such a brute of a man,
    His morals were so bad
That he married a daughter of his own.

He knew how many animals Noah had rescued
And how he had the Ark organised below decks,
    How the Milesians came
    From antediluvian Spain
And that they had cocks without combs in Berneray.

That there's no finer food in creation
Than roast guga along with potatoes,
    And that folk from the west side
    Get their rosy complexions
From being fed sand-eels' livers as babies.

How Samson's valour was in ringlets
And Alasdair Alpin was a skinflint —
    That there was no truth at all
    In the book that he wrote,
And how for debts owed John Bunyan was imprisoned.

He told how the Commandments were written
And how the Brahan Seer got his gifts,
    How Naois and Deirdre eloped
    Here from Ireland's shores,
And why the Breanish men spend their time girning.

How Cù Chulainn would handle
In the ford Sgàthach's 'bag-spear',
    And how all the shellfish
    On Tong Beach used to get there,
And if the ages of the world were incalculable.

He described the Massacre of Glencoe then
And what the Red Hand of the MacDonalds meant,
    And what happened in the Garden
    And the excellence of the Gaelic
Used by Adam and Eve there in converse.

That there were people of old who were giants,
And the interaction of cogs in a timepiece;

Mun a' mhollachd bha tàmhachd
Ann an uaigh Thut-an-Kàmain,
'S mar bha Rasputin 'n sàs aig a' Bhuaireadair.

Thaobh na béist air Loch Nis, gur e ròn a th' ann,
'S gum facas each-uisge an Cròlasta;
　　Mar chaidh Òigh Bhaile Raghnaill
　　Thoirt a-mach le làimh làidir
Air an uinneig a b' àird' an Taigh Ròghadail.

Rinn e iomadh nì soilleir le bhriathran dhomh
A bha folaicht' o dhaoine an dìomhaireachd —
　　Mun iasg mhór a shluig Iònas,
　　Có rinn Càin a phòsadh,
'S cà robh Màiri NicLeòid air a tiodhlacadh.

Nuair a shaoil leam bha chuimhn' air a sàrachadh
Sann a theann e ri innse mu Mhànas dhomh,
　　'S mu na bandiathan bréige
　　Aphrodìte 's Artémas,
'S gun robh Hitler an greim aig an Àbharsair.

Sann a dh'fhaighnich e sin dhomh an cuala mi
Mun Bhàillidh 's mun bhearradh rinn Ruairidh air —
　　Leis mar chaidh e 'na ùpraid
　　'S an taigh òst' air thuar dùnadh,
Dh'fhàg e beum agus sùlag sa chluais aige.

Ciod a dh'éirich don sgioba threun chruadalach
Bh' air a' *Mhàiri Celeste* 's nach d'fhuaradh iad;
　　Mar a sgriosadh gun tròcair
　　Bailtean aingidh a' chòmhnaird
'S mar chuir foghlam Dhuns Scòtuis 'na thuaineal e.

Cia mar chaill sinn an Cath aig Mons Graupius,
'S cho fìor olc 's a bha teaghlach nam Bòrgias,
　　Mar bha ionmhas gun chunntas
　　'N talla mhór Mhontezùma,
'S gun robh dà sheòrsa chrùbag gun spògan ann.

Se mo bharail ged dh'fhanainn gu sìorraidh ann
Nach biodh traoghadh air còmhradh a' chrìostaidh ud,
　　'S gum bi farsaingeachd 'eòlais
　　'Na chùis iongnaidh ri m' bheò leam —
Ged a-nis tha 'chuid mhór dheth air dhìochuimhn' orm!

Of the doom overhanging
　　The tomb of Tutankhamen,
And how Rasputin was the Devil's disciple.

Of Loch Ness, that it's a seal and no monster,
While a water-horse has been seen in Crowlista;
　　How the daughter of Balranald
　　Was forcibly abducted
Through the highest window in Rodel.

With his words he made many things clear to me
That were hidden from people in secrecy —
　　About the fish that swallowed Jonah
　　And just who took Cain as husband,
And where Mary MacLeod's place of burial can be.

When I thought his memory was exhausted
He started to go on about Magnus,
　　And about the false goddesses
　　Aphrodite and Artemis,
And that the Devil had Hitler in thrall.

Then he asked if I'd heard
Of the clip Roddy gave the Factor —
　　How he made such a fuss
　　When Closing Time came up
That he thumped him and gave him an earmark.

What befell those brave hardy crewmen
Who left the *Marie Celeste* in mid-ocean,
　　How the wicked towns of the plain
　　Were so mercilessly razed
And how Duns Scotus' learning confused him.

How we lost the Battle of Mons Graupius,
How corrupt were the tribe of the Borgias,
　　How there was wealth beyond count
　　In Montezuma's great house
And how two sorts of crabs had no claws on them.

I do believe if I'd stayed till eternity
That good man's talk would still not have ebbed on him,
　　And I'll marvel for always
　　At the breadth of his knowledge —
Though I forget quite a lot of it already!

An t-Urr. Iain MacLeòid (1918–95)

168 *Bantrach Cogaidh*

Sgaoil i 'aodach air gàrradh:
briogais bhàn is léine gheal,
crios gorm leathann,
còrd geal caol.
Bha mi air clach ri taobh,
bonaid cruinn air mo cheann:
bonaid m' athar.
Deise ghorm 'na stiallan
mar reub iad bho chorp i
nuair fhuair iad e
fuar bàthte air an tràigh,
air a pasgadh le làmhan gràidh
is cridhe brist':
mar deise rìgh dol gu banais.

Car son tha thu dol uair sa mhìos
don phost-oifis 'nad aodach dubh,
le cridhe trom,
's a' tilleadh feasgar
le leabhar a' pheinsean 'nad làimh?
Car son a thog thu mi 'nad uchd
's do cheann crom,
is fhliuch thu m' aodann le do dheòir
nuair thuirt mi,
"Mhàthair, cà'il m' athair?"

Aon là san sgoil
sheas sinn sàmhach dà mhionaid
a' cuimhneachadh
air laoich a' Chogaidh Mhóir,
is ruith mi dhachaigh 'na mo dheann
a dh'innse dhi,
"Cha bhi cogadh tuilleadh ann."

Oidhche gheamhraidh bha i snìomh;
shuidh mi ri taobh.
Bha ceann dol liath 's i fhathast òg.
An lùib an t-snàth chaidh fuiltean mìn
mar shìoda measg an duibh.

Rev. John MacLeod (Arnol, Lewis)

War Widow

She spread his clothes on a dyke:
light-coloured trousers and white shirt,
a broad blue belt,
a thin white cord.
I was on a stone by her side,
a round bonnet on my head:
my father's bonnet.
Blue uniform in tatters
as they tore it from his body
when they found him
cold drowned on the beach,
folded with loving hands
and broken heart:
like the clothes of a king going to a wedding.

Why do you go once a month
to the post-office in your black clothes,
with heavy heart,
and come back in the evening
with pension book in your hand?
Why did you bury me in your bosom
with your head bent
and wet my face with your tears
when I said,
"Mother, where's my father?"

One day in school
we stood quietly for two minutes
remembering
the heroes of the Great War,
and I ran home pell-mell
to tell her,
"There will be war no more."

One winter's night she was spinning;
I sat down by her side.
Her hair was going grey when she was still young.
Amidst the thread went one fine hair
like silk among the black.

Thuirt i, "Gléidh cuimhn' orms'
nuair chì thu m' fhalt an lùib an t-snàth
's nach bi mi ann."
'S mar thubhairt bhà.

Rinn iad d' uaigh ri taobh nan tonn.
Cha chlisg thu chaoidh aig gaoith no stoirm.
Sibh sin cho réidh, thu fhéin 's an cuan —
cha toir e tuilleadh uat do ghràdh.

Nach math gun tug am bàs thu tràth,
's nach fhac' thu cogadh ùr 'nad là
's nach fhac' thu mise falbh don bhlàr
le deise ghorm is bonaid cruinn
mar bh' air m' athair
nuair fhuair iad marbh e
aig a' Bhràigh.

169   Bàs Baile

Chaidh am fuadach gu cùl a' chladaich
is shlaod iad bith-beò á talamh creagach.
Ged bha muir fiadhaich, bha tràigh fialaidh
is dh'fhàs na balaich mór.

An-dràst' 's a-rithist
thigeadh cairteal tombac'
is leth-bhotal uisge bheath'
agus gu'm màthair bocsa
le aodach aost' mì-fhreagarrach
bho Chomann còir nam Ban Uasal.

Sgrìobh i litir,
toirt taing am Beurla bhriste
gu mnathan a' bhaile mhóir.
Aig céilidh an Dùn Éideann
chaidh a leughadh 's rinn iad fanoid.
'S thuirt mnathan uaisle le gàire,
Cuiridh sinn thuic' bocsa
seann aodaich eile
agus gheibh sinn litir éibhinn
le tuilleadh dibhearsain.

She said, "Remember me
when you see my hair amidst the thread
and I'm not there."
And what she said came true.

They made your grave beside the waves.
You'll never flinch at wind or storm.
You've made your peace there, you and the sea —
no more will it take from you your love.

It's good that death took you quite soon,
that you saw no new war in your day
and did not see me leave for battle
with round hat and blue uniform
like my father was wearing
when they found him dead
at the Brae.

The Death of a Township

They were cleared to the back of the shore
to eke a living out of rocky land.
Though sea was savage, ebb was generous
and the boys grew big.

Now and again
a quarter of tobacco would come
and a half-bottle of whisky
and to their mother a box
of old unsuitable clothes
from the dear Ladies' Association.

She wrote a letter,
sending thanks in broken English
to the ladies of the city.
At a ceilidh in Edinburgh
it was read and they mocked.
And ladies said laughing,
We'll send her another
box of old clothes
and get a comical letter
with more entertainment.

Is ràinig am bocsa sàbhailt'
baile cùl-a'-chladaich:
gùn is seacaid saighdeir,
briogais is còta ministeir,
b'e rud e air son cur bhuntàt'!
Dh'fhalbh litir am Beurla bhriste
is rinn uaislean a' bhaile mhóir gàir'.

Thàinig bìoball teaghlaich Gàidhlig
is searmoinean Spurgeon le litir dhiadhaidh
ag iarraidh orr' bhith riaraicht'
leis na nithean bha làthair.

Mo ghràdh-sa òigridh ar là
'nam fiasaig dhùint' bho chluais gu cluais.
Mun d'ràinig na balaich againn aois fiasaig
no aois smaoineachaidh
dh'éigh iad Cogadh
is chaidh am marbhadh anns an Fhraing.
Bha 'm murt ud laghail.

A' chuid dhiubh a thàrr ás,
fhuair an fhairge iad a' tilleadh dhachaigh
agus dh'fhàg i na cuirp air an tràigh
's b'e marbh-phaisg fhuar an fheamainn.

A' chuid a thill leòinte 's beò,
cha robh gam feitheamh ach geallaidhean briste —
bàtaichean is lìn a' breothadh,
iasg gu leòr sa chuan gun comas thoirt ás.
Bhuain iad mòine, chuir iad buntàta
is chaidh le crodh gu àirigh
is dh'fhàs cnàmhan briste làidir.

Cur seachad oidhche gheamhraidh
chaidh na balaich chun an taigh-sgoile
a dh'fhaicinn dealbhan mu Chanada
le 'magic lantern'. Dé 'n cron a bh' ann?
Is chunnaic iad crodh am feur gu'n cluasan,
caileag bhòidheach 's a h-uchd air geat
le fiamh a' ghàir' is sràbh 'na bial,
is chaidh iad dhachaigh 'g ràdh, Tha sinne falbh.
Thuirt a' chlann-nighean, Thà is sinne.

And the box reached in safety
the back-of-the-shore township:
a gown and a soldier's tunic,
a minister's trousers and jacket,
just the thing for planting potatoes!
Off went a letter in broken English
and the city gentry laughed.

There came a Gaelic family bible
and Spurgeon's sermons with a pious letter
asking them to be content
with what they had.

How I love the modern youngsters
enclosed in beards from ear to ear.
Before our lads reached beard-growing age
or were old enough to think
War was declared
and they were killed in France.
That murder was lawful.

Those of them who survived,
the sea got them on their way home
and left the bodies on the beach
and the seaweed was a cold shroud.

Those who returned wounded and alive,
nothing awaited them but broken promises —
boats and nets rotting,
fish aplenty in the sea without the means to take it out.
They cut peats, planted potatoes
and went with cattle to shieling
and broken bones grew strong.

By way of passing a winter's night
the lads went to the schoolhouse
to see pictures about Canada
with a 'magic lantern'. What was the harm?
And they saw cows up to their ears in grass,
a lovely girl leaning on a gate
smiling with a straw in her mouth,
and they went home saying, We're off.
The girls said, So are we.

Lìon gach màthair ciste le aodach blàth
air son talamh fuar, is bìoball anns gach seotal.
An oidhch' a dh'fhalbh iad
dhìrich sinn an cnoc a b' àirde
is shuidh sinn gun fhocal, sàmhach,
gus an deach ás ar sealladh
solas crann-àrd a' *Mhàrloch*.
Sin thòisich glaodh taigh-fhaireadh
aig tiodhlacadh daoine beò.
An oidhch' ud bhàsaich am bail' againn.

170 *Aideachadh*

Ar cainnt a' call a lùths
is sinne fàs am mórchuis
os cionn chomhairle, bruadarach,
is fuaranan na Gàidhlig
a' dòirteadh uisge ùr.

Riaraichte le bùrn na claise
gun ceum ga thoirt nas fhaisge
air fuaran fìorghlan blasta
is mar an-uiridh Mòd am-bliadhna
le òrain cianalais is molaidh.

Moladh làithean a dh'fhalbh;
ag éigheach fad seachdain,
"Suas leis a' Ghàidhlig."
Cur tàir air comhairle,
a' diùltadh slàinte
's ar feum cho follaiseach.

Sgeadaichte an aodach tartain
cur shìthean ar litearachais
aig bonn clach cuimhn' ar cànain.
Eas-creideamh a' cur na ceiste,
"Am faigh a' Ghàidhlig bàs?"

Eagal aghaidh chur air saoghal
ás aonais taic bhog deoch làidir,
mar dhaoine aig adhlacadh
a' diùltadh creids' san Aiseirigh.

Each mother filled a kist with warm clothes
for a cold land, with a bible in each shottle.
The night they left
we climbed the highest hill
and sat wordless, silent,
till the *Marloch*'s mainmast light
disappeared from our sight.
Then the wake-house cry arose
for the burial of the living.
That night our township died.

Confession

Our speech losing its strength
while we grow in vanity
beyond counsel, dreaming,
while the springs of Gaelic
spout a new water.

Satisfied with ditchwater
without a step to bring it closer
to a fresh sweet-tasting spring
and this year's Mod like last year's
with songs of longing and of praise.

The praise of bygone days;
declaring all week long,
"Up with Gaelic."
Scorning all advice,
rejecting health
when our need's so evident.

Attired in tartan clothes
putting the flowers of our literature
at the foot of our language's memorial.
Agnosticism asking,
"Will Gaelic die?"

Afraid to face life
without soft help from strong drink,
like folk at a funeral
denying belief in the Resurrection.

Dòmhnall Iain MacDhòmhnaill (1919–86)

171   *Òran an Fheamnaidh*

Ochòin, a chiallain, gur mì tha cianail
   'S mi 'n-seo gam riasladh am bial na Cròice:
An todhar fiadhaich 's e doirbh a lìonadh,
   'S chan eil sa chrìostachd na spìonadh ròin' ás.

Nuair nì mi 'n gràpa chur sìos le m' shàil ann,
   Bidh snìomh air cnàmhan mun teàrn e òirleach,
'S nuair gheibh mi 'm bàrr e, 's chan ann gun spàirn dhomh,
   An truaighe snàithl' bhios an sàs 'na mheòirean.

Mum faigh mi dìol dheth 's a'chairt a lìonadh,
   Mo mheòirean piante gun sian ach tòcadh:
Thig stamh na liathaig am bàrr le m' spìonadh
   'S gur ann mu m' bhial a bhios crìoch a bhòidse.

Se mhadainn choirb-fhuair le gaoith 's le stoirm
   A bhith triall a dh'fheamnadh thug searbh-bhlas dhòmhs' air;
'S gum b' fheàrr dhomh falbh ás 's mi phòsadh banacheaird,
   'S bhiodh saoghal soirbh agam 's airgead pòca.

Nach cruaidh an càs dhomh 's do shluagh an àite
   Bhith fuar is pàiteach an sàs am beòshlaint',
'S na nì mi dh'àiteach gus 'n cinn am bàrr ann,
   Cha phàigh e 'm màl dhomh ged s ànrach dhòmhs' e.

Gur bochd ri chunntais g'eil luchd mo dhùthcha
   Fo mhurt 's fo mhùiseig aig dùirn nan rògair,
Is Alba chliùiteach a dhearbh a biùthas
   Fo chealg nan iùdhach 's a stiùir 'nan crògan.

Ged mhaoladh m' fhiaclan ás aonais dìot ann
   Chan fhaod mi lìon chur air iasg Loch Ròdhag
'S gach maor is iarla tha 'n gaoth na crìostachd
   Gum faod iad iasgach gu'm miann fo m' shròin ann.

A Bhrusaich stàtail, nam biodh tu 'n-dràsta
   Ri faicinn càradh nan Gaidheal còire,
Fo bhinn nan tràillean a mhill ar nàisean:
   Tha tìr nan àrdbheann aig pràig fo'm brògan.

Donald John MacDonald (Peninerine, S. Uist)

The Song of the Seaweed-Cutting

Pity me, friend, I'm sad and in misery
  Struggling here at the mouth of the Cròic:
The manure of the wild's so hard to collect,
  No-one in christendom could pluck a hair of it.

When I put the graip down into it with my heel,
  There'll be bones dislocated before it goes in an inch,
And when I get it aloft, by no means without effort,
  The devil a strand is stuck in its prongs.

Before I've enough of it to fill the cart,
  My fingers are tortured with nothing but swelling:
The stem of the tangles comes up with my straining
  Till the end of its voyage is round about my mouth.

It's the cursed cold morning with wind and with storm
  That's made going to get seaweed taste so bitter to me;
I'd be better to leave and marry a tinkeress,
  I'd have an easy life and money in my pocket.

It's the wretched fate of myself and my neighbours
  To be cold and thirsty while making a living,
When all the tilling I do to make the crop grow there
  Will not pay my rent despite all my distress.

It's sad to reflect that the people of my country
  Are mocked and abused by the threats of scoundrels,
While glorious Scotland that's proved her renown
  Is duped by capitalists with her helm in their fists.

Though my teeth are blunted for lack of nourishment
  Not a net may I set for the fish of Loch Roag
While each bailiff and earl ever heard of in christendom
  May fish all they like there right under my nose.

O stately Bruce, could you only see now
  The present plight of the gracious Gael,
Condemned by the trash who've destroyed our nation:
  The land of the mountains trampled by vermin.

Nam biodh ri fhaotainn an déidh mo shaothrach
  Na phàigheadh m' aodach, air ghaol mo chòmhdach,
Cha bhiodh mo shaorsa cho cruaidh 's cho daor dhomh,
  'S cha bhiodh mo shaoghal cho lughdaicht' òg dhomh.

172 *An Guth á Broinn na Màthar*

Teannaibh dlùth is thoiribh cluas dhomh,
  Sibhs' a shluagh a tha 'nur slàint',
Éistibh rium is gabhaibh truas rium
  'S mi air thuar mo chur gu bàs leibh;
Tha mi 'n-seo, 'nam leanabh saidhbhir
  Paisgte cruinn am broinn mo mhàthar,
'S am murtair 'na sheasamh dlùth dhomh
  'S aont' a' Chrùin aige mo smàladh.

Cha téid croich no càin no prìosan,
  Cha téid binn a thoirt le cùirt air,
Ged a mharbhadh e na mìltean
  Tha e caoiteas lagh na dùthchadh;
Nì e mis' a mhurt a-màireach,
  Dh'iarr mo mhàthair air co-dhiù e —
Saoil nach murtair is' i fhéin
  Don aon dìol-déirc a th' air a giùlan?

Cha do rinn mi cron air creutair
  Tha fon ghréin air feadh an t-saoghail,
B'e mo mhiann tighinn còmh' ruib' fhéin ann
  'S a bhith 'g éirigh suas gu aois ann;
Nuair a ghineadh mi le m' mhàthair
  Bha mi 'g ràdha, "Bheir i gaol dhomh."
Ach se sòlas thoirt dh'a feòil
  A bha i 'n tòir air, 's cha b'e maoth-phàist'.

Chan fhaic mise latha samhraidh,
  Laoigh is gamhna ruith sna pàircean,
Chan fhaic mi sòbhrach nan alltan,
  Flùraichean an gleann no 'n gàrradh;
Cha chluinn mi air madainn Chéitein
  Còisir theudach nan craobh àrda,
Cha ruith mi, cha leum le aoibhneas
  Còmh' ri cloinn mar a rinn àsan.

If even I got after all my labour
    The cost of my clothes, just enough to cover me,
My freedom would not be so harsh and restricted,
    My life would not be so lessened when young.

The Voice from the Mother's Womb

Come close and give an ear to me,
    All of you who have your health,
Listen to me and take pity on me
    For you're about to have me killed;
Here I am, a developed child
    Wrapped around in my mother's womb,
And the murderer standing close to me
    With the Crown's consent to snuff me out.

He'll get no gallows, fine or prison
    And no court will sentence him,
Even if he murdered thousands
    He is quit of the country's law;
He will slaughter me tomorrow,
    Anyway my mother has asked him to —
Isn't she herself the murderer
    Of the very waif that's in her womb?

I have never harmed a creature
    Under the sun throughout the world,
All I wanted was to join you there
    And grow up and come of age there;
When my mother had conceived me
    I was saying, "She will love me."
But giving pleasure to her flesh
    Was what she wanted, not a baby.

I'll never see a summer's day,
    Fields alive with calves and stirks,
Nor the primrose of the streamlets,
    Or flowers that grow in glen or garden;
I'll not hear in Maytime morning
    The sweetstringed choir high in the trees,
I won't run, or jump for joy
    With other children as they did themselves.

Chaidh mo chuid-sa chur don t-saoghal
    Nuair a ghineadh maoth gun chlì mi,
'S nam biodh daoine ceart dha chéile
    Cha bhiodh beul fon ghréin is dìth air;
Ach tha cus a' càrnadh stòrais,
    Ag ithe, 's ag òl, 's a' dìobhairt,
'S am bràithrean gun fiù an greim
    A theireadh sgoinn dhaibh tighinn gu ìre.

Chruthaich Dia mi mar a b' àbhaist —
    Se gum fàsainn bha 'na dhòchas,
Cha b'e bha 'na inntinn idir
    Gun robh mise gu bhith chòrr ann;
Chruthaich e m' anam neo-bhàsmhor
    Ged bha peacadh Àdhaimh beò air,
Ach bha Sàcramaid a' Bhaistidh
    Dol a thaisbeanadh na glòir dhomh.

Och mo thruaighe, fàth mo dhòlais,
    Chaidh mo chòir rithe dhòmhs' a dhiùltadh:
Chan eil Baisteadh ann dhomh 'n dòchas
    Mar a dh'òrdaich Rìgh nan Dùl dhomh,
Ach tha fios gun nochd E bàidh rium —
    Neochiontach de phàiste diùmbaidh
Nach fhaigh cead tighinn chun an t-saoghail
    'S cothrom tighinn gu aois ri ùin' ann.

O nach gabh thu truas, a mhàthair,
    Riums', am pàist' a th' air do ghiùlan,
Éist rium agus cluinn mo ràn
    Is gaol na màthar dhomh ga dhiùltadh;
Bhon a ghin thu mi le d' shaor-thoil,
    Thoir don t-saoghal mi le d' dhùrachd,
'S cha bhi m' theang' ag eubhach pian dhut
    Nuair thig Dia thoirt breith na cùirt' ort.

'S thus' tha feitheamh leis an iarann
    Gus mo chrìochnachadh 'nam phàiste,
Cuimhnich, ged nach fhaic mi t' ìomhaigh,
    S mi nach dìochuimhnich gu bràch thu —
Nuair bhios t' anam ort ga iarraidh
    'S tu 'g eubhach, "A Dhia dian bàidh rium,"
Bidh mise agus crùn mu m' cheann
    Ag eubhach, "Sìos don toll an t-Àbharsair!"

All my share came into being
   When, weak and tender, I was conceived,
And if people did right by each other
   No mouth on earth would suffer want;
But too many are amassing wealth,
   Eating, drinking, vomiting,
While their brothers lack even the mouthful
   To give them strength to reach maturity.

God made me in the usual way —
   It was His hope that I would grow,
It wasn't in His mind at all
   That I should be superfluous;
He created my eternal soul
   Though stained by Adam's living sin,
But the Sacrament of Baptism
   Was still going to show me glory.

But alas, my cause of sadness,
   My right to it has been denied:
I've now no hope of the Baptism
   Ordered for me by the King of the Elements,
But of course He will show me love —
   An innocent loveless child
Denied all admittance to the world
   And any chance to mature there in time.

Oh won't you take pity, mother,
   On me, the child that's in your womb,
Listen to me and hear me cry out
   As a mother's love is denied me;
Since you so willingly conceived me,
   Bring me to the world and bless me,
And my tongue won't seek your torment
   When God comes in court to judge you.

And you who're waiting with the knife
   To finish off my childhood,
Mind, though I cannot see your face,
   I won't forget you, never —
When your soul's being sought from you
   And you crying, "God have mercy,"
With a crown about my head
   I'll shout, "Send him down to Hell, the fiend!"

Thuirt an Tighearna, "Na dian marbhadh,"
  Nuair a dhealbhaich E na fàithntean;
Thuirt E, "Their thu gaol gu léir dhomh
  Agus mar dhut fhéin, dha d' bhràthair."
'S sibhse rinn an t-Achd a sgrìobhadh
  A tha murt nam mìltean pàiste,
Mas e 'n ceartas a their buaidh
  Och och mo thruaighe là ur bàis sibh.

173   *Taigh a' Bhàird*

Chunnaic mis' thu Di-Dòmhnaich,
  A thaigh nan òran 's nan rann —
Bha thu fuar dhomh, gun chòmhradh,
  Mar do sheòrsa gach àm,
Ach ruith mo smaointean air sgiathan
  Gu iomadh bliadhn' eil' a bh' ann
Nuair a chruinnicheadh gu d' sheòmair
  Gach aon bha còmhnaidh sa ghleann.

Thug thu fasgadh is coibhneas
  Do Sheonaidh Caimbeul am bàrd,
Bu tu dachaigh an aoibhneis
  Dha fhéin 's do mhaighdeann a ghràidh:
Saoil nach tusa bha 'g ionndrainn,
  Nuair dhùin a shùilean sa bhàs,
An gaol a dh'fhiosraich sibh còmhla
  'S tu fhéin ga theòthadh le d' bhlàths.

Nach iomadh seanchas is òran
  A dh'éist an òige bhon aois
Taobh a' ghealbhain dhe d' chòmhlaidh
  'S an teine mònadh 'na chraos;
Gillean gasta 'nad chéilidh
  A thataidh léirsinn do ghaoil,
'S b'e lasair theine ceann fhòidean
  Bu tric a threòraich na laoich.

Gun robh snigh' air mo ghruaidhean
  Nuair sheall mi suas ort an-dé,
Balla balbh 's e cho fuar dhomh,
  Bha 'n t-anam sguabt' às a chéis:

"Thou shalt not kill" is what the Lord said,
    When He created the commandments;
"You'll give," He said, "all love to me
    And as to me, so to your brother."
And you who put the Act together
    That murders children by the thousand,
If justice triumphs in the end
    I pity you the day you die.

The Poet's House

I saw you on Sunday,
    House of song and of rhymes —
You were cold to me, speechless,
    Like your kind at all times,
But my thoughts flew away
    To many other years then
When there came to your chamber
    All who lived in the glen.

You gave shelter and kindness
    To Johnny Campbell the bard,
You were the home of delight
    To him and his darling:
I have no doubt you missed,
    When his eyes closed in death,
Your love for each other
    As you wrapped him in warmth.

So many stories and songs
    Did youth listen to from age
On the hearth-side of your door
    With the peat-fire ablaze;
Fine lads at your ceilidh
    Whom your love's sight caressed,
It was mostly peat fire flame
    That brought them home to rest.

There were tears on my cheeks
    As I looked up at you yesterday,
A dumb wall so cold to me,
    The soul driven from its body:

Fear an taigh' ann an Tàllann
    'S tus' air t' fhàgail gun fheum —
Saoil an cuala mi ràn bhuat
    A' caoidh a' bhàird agad fhéin?

An tuirt thu rium, "Bhon as bàrd thu,
    Cuir an àirde mo chliù,
Chan eil onair aig càch dhomh,
    Rinn iad m' fhàgail gun diù;
'S bhon tha eadarainn an càirdeas
    Le bann na bàrdachd, co-dhiù,
Inn's do dh'aitreabhan leòmach
    Gun robh mo ghlòir-s' os an cionn!"

Bidh do ghlòir-s' os an cionn-san,
    A sheann taigh chliùitich a' bhàird,
Fhads bhios freumhag an dùthchais
    A' tarraing sùgh air son fàs;
Tog do cheann thar do ghuaillean,
    'S cuimhnich t' uaisle thar chàich
Mar thug thu dachaigh is còmhnaidh
    Do Sheonaidh Dhòmh'll 'ic Iain Bhàin.

174 *Do Mhaighstir Niall*

Dh'éirich suas a' ghrian thar àirde,
Staoileabhal nan stùcan beàrnach;
    Beath' an eilein rinn ath-dhùsgadh —
    De cha d'fhosgail thus' do shùilean.

Dhùisg á suain a' chuach le fàilte,
Fhliuch i teang' am bùrn Loch Hàllainn,
    Dhòirt i glòir a pongan ciùil oirnn —
    De cha d'fhosgail thus' do shùilean.

Shéid an osag iarach bhàidheil
Steach bho Orasaigh na tràghad,
    Dhùisg i bàrr nan raointean flùrach —
    De cha d'fhosgail thus' do shùilean.

Cha bu chòir dhomh cumha chianail
A sgrìobhadh, a Mhaighstir Niall, dhut,
    'S thus' a' mealtainn fiach do shaoithreach —
    Duais an òrdain "Biadh mo chaoirich".

The householder in Hallin,
    And you left unrequired —
Did I hear a cry from you
    Lamenting your own poet?

Did you say, "Since you're a poet,
    Sing my praises on high,
No-one else has respect for me,
    They've abandoned me to die;
And as we two are related
    Through poetry's bond, at least,
Tell sophisticated mansions
    I surpassed them in prestige!"

Your prestige will surpass them,
    Famed old house of the poet,
As long as tradition's root
    Taps sustenance for growth;
Raise your head above your shoulders,
    Assert the honour you command
For providing home and succour
    To Seonaidh Dhòmh'll 'ic Iain Bhàin.

To Father Neil

Up rose the sun upon a height,
Stulaval of the gapped pinnacles;
    The island's life awoke anew —
    But you opened not your eyes.

The cuckoo woke from sleep with welcome,
Wet her tongue in Hallin's water,
    Poured out her glorious notes of music —
    But you opened not your eyes.

The westerly breeze blew its caresses
In from Orosay of the strand,
    Aroused the tips of the flowered fields —
    But you opened not your eyes.

It's no forlorn lament I ought
To be composing, Father Neil, for you,
    As you enjoy your labour's prize —
    The reward of the order to "Feed my flock".

Lorgan buan buil-bhuaidh do dhìchill
Gràbhalaicht' air iomadh inntinn,
    Làthaireachd do phears' a' lìonadh
    Na ceàrn sa 's thu fhéin san t-sìorrachd.

Falbhaidh madainn, feasgar, oidhche,
Ach ri'r beò chan fhalbh á cuimhne
    Cuimhneachain chùbhraidh neo-bhàsmhor,
    Cuimhneachain do-roinnt' am bàs bhuat.

Buaidh do spioraid feadh do chàirdean
Neart do-fhaicsinneach ach làidir —
    Do bhratach thar Uibhist sgaoilte,
    Do ghuth an osag a gaothan.

Dhìrich mi suas leathad Hàllainn,
Bruthach-tasgaidh nan iom'thàlann;
    Shaoil mi meudachadh an glòir ann
    Nuair dh'aonaich thu ris a' chòmhlan.

175   *Geata Tìr nan Òg*

Chì mi bhuam an gàrradh-crìche
    'S geata Tìr nan Òg!
Ceum air cheum a' triall ga ionnsaigh,
Ruith an-dé 's an-diugh don chunntais —
Gann a chì mi air mo chùlaibh
    Iomadh lùb san ròd.

Chì mi bhuam an garradh-crìche
    'S geata Tìr nan Òg!
Air a chùl tha cuan a' tràghadh,
San t-sruth-lìonaidh thig am bàta —
Ma bhios m' ainm-sa sgrìobht' air clàr innt'
    Nithear àit' air bòrd.

Chì mi bhuam an garradh-crìche
    'S geata Tìr nan Òg!
Mach á ceò nan timean àrsaidh
Mhìnich innsearachd an fhàidh dhuinn
Gun robh 'n t-aiseag seo air fàire
    Eadar bàs is beò.

Your labours' lasting effective marks
Are clearly engraved on many minds,
　　Your personality's strength is filling
　　This district though you're in eternity.

Morning, evening, night will pass,
But never in our lifetime will be lost
　　Those immortal fragrant memories
　　Which death can't separate from you.

Your spirit's strength in all your friends
Is a power invisible but strong —
　　Your banner over Uist flying,
　　Your voice whispering in her winds.

I climbed up Hallin's gentle slope,
The storage-bank of many talents;
　　I sensed an increase in their glory
　　When you went to join the gathering.

The Gate of the Land of the Young

I can see the distant march-dyke
　　　　And the gate of the Land of the Young!
Step by step as I go towards it,
Present and past come fast to account —
Scarce do I see when I turn around
　　　　The many bends in the road.

I can see the distant march-dyke
　　　　And the gate of the Land of the Young!
At its back the ocean's ebbing,
As the tide fills the boat will come —
If my name's inscribed in her
　　　　They'll make room on board.

I can see the distant march-dyke
　　　　And the gate of the Land of the Young!
Out of the mist of times gone by
The seer was able to prophesy
That this ferry was on the horizon
　　　　Between death and life.

Chì mi bhuam an garradh-crìche
'S geata Tìr nan Òg!
Madainn ùr bhon ear a' liathadh
Suas á duibhr' na h-oidhche chiar ud —
Mhair a mùgan iomadh bliadhna,
Tric a' biathadh deòir.

Chì mi bhuam an garradh-crìche
'S geata Tìr nan Òg!
Tha mi sgìth san t-slighe bhuain seo
Gun mo chlì mar bha i uairean —
Gun mo cheum cho ealamh uallach
No mo shnuadh cho beò.

Chì mi bhuam an garradh-crìche
'S geata Tìr nan Òg!
Tùs an turais bha 'nam fhàbhar,
Soirbheas-cùil an siùil mo bhàta —
Fearainn ùra 's ubhal a' ghàrraidh
Sàsachadh mo dheòin.

Chì mi bhuam an garradh-crìche
'S geata Tìr nan Òg!
Tha mi feitheamh sruth an lìonaidh
'S am bàt'-aisig tighinn am fianais —
O gum boillsgeadh soillse shìorraidh
Dhuinn thar crìoch nam beò.

Dòmhnall R MacGilleMhoire (1919—)

176   bho *Fàilte don Phrionnsa Teàrlach 's a' Bhana-Phrionnsa
Diàna a dh'Eilean Sgalpaigh na Hearadh, 2.7.85*

Gun seall sinn gach bad dhuibh
Dhan eilean bheag ghlas seo
'S gun lùig sinn sibh a dh'fhantainn a' tàmh ann.

Urras nan rìghrean
Am Breatainn 's 'na Ìmpir'
A' ruith troimh gach sgìr agus cànain.

I can see the distant march-dyke
　　　And the gate of the Land of the Young!
A new morning dawns from the east
Up from the gloom of yon dusky night —
Many a year its dreichness lasted
　　　And many a tear it fed.

I can see the distant march-dyke
　　　And the gate of the Land of the Young!
I'm tired of this perpetual path
Without the strength I sometimes had —
My step not being as light or hardy
　　　Or my colour so alive.

I can see the distant march-dyke
　　　And the gate of the Land of the Young!
The start of the journey was in my favour,
A wind from astern in the sails of my boat —
Pastures new and the apple of the garden
　　　Fulfilling my desire.

I can see the distant march-dyke
　　　And the gate of the Land of the Young!
As I wait for the flowtide rising
The ferryboat's on the horizon —
Oh that a lasting light may guide us
　　　Past the edge of the living world.

Donald R Morrison (Scalpay, Harris)

from *Prince Charles' and Princess Diana's Welcome to the Isle of Scalpay, Harris, 2.7.85*

We will show you each part
Of this little grey island
And we wish you would come and stay here.

The guarantee of kings
In Britain and its Empire
Runs through each district and language.

Bha am freumhan a' dìreadh
O eachdraidh a' Bhìobaill,
O leabhraichean sgrìobhaidh nam fàidhean.

Ach a-nis seo ar miann-ne
Do na buill seo dhen iarmad
Tha 'n-diugh air an triall sa 'nar fàbhar:

Sonas gu sìorraidh
Dhuibh anns a' Chrìostachd
Is seòladh is dìon on Àrd Rìgh.

Fàilte do Theàrlach
Is fàilt' do Dhiàna,
Fàilt' orr' dhan bhaile 's dhan àite.

Fàilte do Theàrlach
Is fàilt' do Dhiàna,
'S guma slàn 's guma fallain a' chàraid.

An t-Urr. Ruairidh MacDhòmhnaill (1920–98)

177   bho *Turas don Ghealaich*

Thog cumhachd do-thomhas nan ceithir dùilibh
    Air bhog a' charbad bhon ùrlar àrd
Le fuaim an tàirneanaich is boillsg an dealanaich.
    Ghabh an luchd-siubhail gu snàmh;
As an déidh bha gaoir a' chrith-thalmhainn,
    Anns an long-iarmailt gach nì bha sàmh.

Ann an reul-chuairt fharsaing nan nèamhan
    Shocraich triùir dhaoine gu triall
Fad sheachd làithean eadar grian is talamh;
    Chaidil is ghabh iad am biadh
Eutrom, os cionn tarraing na talmhainn
    Ann am falamhachd iomlan gun chrìoch.

"Càit a bheil an triùir dhaoin' a' dol?"
    "Chun na gealaich," arsa mo mhàthair chaomh.
"Dé as ciall di an-diugh?" arsa mise,
    "Se 'Theirig a Hiort' as àbhaist dhi ràdh rium —

Their roots have climbed
From the history of the Bible,
From the written books of the prophets.

But now here's our wish
For these scions of the dynasty
Who are today on this visit to grace us:

Eternal happiness
Be yours in Christianity
With the High King as guide and protector.

Welcome to Charles
And welcome to Diana,
They're welcome to the village and the place.

Welcome to Charles
And welcome to Diana,
And may the couple be safe and well.

Rev. Roderick Macdonald (Locheport, N. Uist)

from *Journey to the Moon*

The immeasurable strength of the four elements
    Launched the vehicle from the platform
With the noise of thunder and the glow of lightning.
    The travellers took to swimming;
After them was the earthquake's cry,
    In the spacecraft all was quiet.

In the broad orbit of the heavens
    Three men settled down to travel
For seven days between sun and earth;
    They slept and took their food
In lightness, above the earth's pull
    In total emptiness without end.

"Where are the three men going?"
    "To the moon," said my dear mother.
"What does she mean today?" said I,
    "It's 'Go to St Kilda' she usually says to me —

Bha i a' leughadh an telebhisean,
  Tha sin air a cur bun-os-cionn."

Cha chluinn thu 'Theirig a Hiort' gu bràth tuilleadh —
  Chan eil Hiort ach spitheag air falbh;
Bha dùil aig do sheanair gur e iomall na talmhainn,
  'S nan robh e beò an-diugh bhiodh e balbh.
Ann am maodal neo-chrìochnach a' chruinne
  Triùir dhaoine — an ainm an t-sealbh.

Air feasgar Sàbaid brèagha samhraidh
  Àm reothairt air teachd gu muir-làn,
Seall a' ghealach a' snàmh san iarmailt;
  An creid thu mo sgeul cho dàn' —
Gu bheil triùir de'r fìor cho-chreutairean
  A-nochd air a' ghealaich a' tàmh?

178   *Taibhs*

Chrois e e fhéin
's e a-nis a' dol seachad air a' chladh.
Siud am preas far am faca Bean Mhurchaidh
am boireannach geal
le a ceann fo a h-achlais.
Nach i a ghabh an t-uabhas
is cha robh e mar iongnadh
gun robh i air leabaidh
fad cholaideug
's an uair a dh'fheuch an Dotair Mór
ri chur sìos air pàipeir dé bha ceàrr oirre
sgrìob e a cheann is rinn e osna:
"Chunnaic i taibhs."
Smaoinich e an uair sin
nach leigeadh eòl is ealain leis
sin a sgrìobhadh
's dh'atharraich e e:
"Shaoil leatha gu fac i taibhs."
Seadh, agus a-réist, s cinnteach,
shaoil leatha gun robh i tinn
is shaoil leis an lighiche
gun robh i ann am fiabhras.
Ach cha robh saoilsinn idir

She was reading the television,
    That's what has put her upside-down."

You'll hear 'Go to St Kilda' nevermore —
    St Kilda's just a stone's throw away;
Your grandfather saw it as the edge of the world,
    And were he alive today he'd be dumb.
In the endless paunch of the universe
    Three men — for goodness' sake.

On a fine Sabbath evening in summer
    With the springtide at the full,
See the moon swimming in the sky;
    Do you believe my tale so bold —
That three of our own fellow creatures
    Are living tonight on the moon?

Ghost

He crossed himself
as he was now passing the graveyard.
There's the bush where Murdo's Wife
saw the white lady
with her head in her oxter.
What a fright she got
and it was no surprise
that she took to her bed
for a fortnight
and when the Big Doctor tried
to put down on paper what was wrong with her
he scratched his head and sighed:
"Saw a ghost."
Then it occurred to him
that knowledge and science did not allow him
to write that
and he changed it:
"Thought she saw a ghost."
Yes, and there again, certainly,
she thought she was ill
and the doctor thought
she was in a fever.
And there was no thought at all

aig an stob glainne a chuir e fo a teanga
a nochd an teas a bha 'na com.

A Dhia, dé am fuaim a bha siud
thall aig preas Bean Mhurchaidh?
S fheàrr dhomh mi fhìn a chroiseadh a-rithist
seachd uairean gu bhith tèaraint.
Nach bochd nach tug mi leam mo phaidirean
's gun gabhainn an Ùrnaigh.
Ach an dèanadh sin eadar-dhealachadh?
Thuirt an Dotair Mór ri Bean Mhurchaidh
nach robh ann ach obair a mac-meanmainn,
thug an sagart an aon nì a chreidsinn oirre
agus dh'aontaich am ministeir.
Chan eil ach aon choire agam fhìn
ri chur ás leth an triùir urramach —
chan fhaca duine aca riamh taibhs.

179   *Meirg*

Tha an trompaid air meirgeadh;
chan eil feum oirre tuilleadh.
Theich a' chinnteachd
leis an do chuir i an céill
fìrinnean
anns nach b' urrainn daoine
teagamh a chur,
is 'nan àite thàinig Reusan:
deasbad is ceistean is teagamh
— inntinn fhosgailte, their cuid.
Tha an trompaid air meirgeadh;
cha bhi daoine air am bòdhradh tuilleadh
le fìrinnean nach do thuig iad.

Ach se nàdar na meirge
a bhith a' sgaoileadh,
mar a nì a' chaitheamh.
An dùil càit an tog i ceann
a-màireach.

about the stub of glass that he put under her tongue
which showed the heat that was in her body.

O God, what was that noise
over there at Murdo's Wife's bush?
I'd better cross myself again
seven times to be safe.
Too bad I didn't bring my beads
so that I could say the Rosary.
But would that make any difference?
The Big Doctor said to Murdo's Wife
that it was only the product of her imagination,
the priest convinced her of the same
and the minister agreed.
Personally I have only one criticism
to make of the three gentlemen —
none of them has ever seen a ghost.

Rust

The trumpet has rusted;
it is needed no more.
The certainty has fled
with which it declared
truths
which people could not
doubt,
and in their place came Reason:
debate and questions and doubt
— an open mind, some say.
The trumpet has rusted;
folk will no longer be deafened
by truths which they did not comprehend.

But it's in the nature of rust
to spread,
like consumption.
I wonder where it will appear
tomorrow.

180   *Seotal*

Ann an seotal na ciste
chunnaic mi na criomagan thar luach
a thug m' athair dhachaigh far a' chuain
an uair a sguir e a sheòladh
's a thionndaidh e 'na threabhaiche.

Ann an seotal na ciste
bha dealbhannan nan àiteachan coimheach
's nam bana-choigreach laghach
a thug aoigheachd dha ann am puirt fad ás
mus tug mo mhàthair gu cléir e.

Ann an seotal na ciste
bha cairt Co-Bhann nan Seòladairean
a bhuinig dhaibh luach an saothrachaidh
's an-uiridh a ghairm stailc
a thug air m' athair grìosad.

Ann an seotal na ciste
bha àileadh a bha tur eadar-dhealaichte
bho gach àileadh air an talamh sa,
àileadh a' mholltair phrìomh-amaich
atharail on d'fhuair mi gintinn.

Anns a' chistidh ghualainneach fhada
a dh'fhosglar fa m' chomhair san fheasgar,
a dhùinear a beul 's i am' easbhaidh,
's mo shùilean dùinte gun fhosgladh,
am bi seotal idir sa chistidh?

Màiri M NicGhillEathain (1921—)

181   *Do Bheinn Eubhal*

A spioraid bhuadhmhor na bàrdachd,
Nach tig thu nuas leam an-dràsta,
'S leig leam duanag a thàthadh gu deònach,
'S nì mi luaidh air an àrdbheinn
A rinn mo bhuaireadh 'nam phàiste
Le h-aghaidh chruachanach chàireanach cheòthar,

Shottle

In the shottle of the kist
I saw the precious items
Father brought home from sea
when he stopped sailing
and became a ploughman.

In the shottle of the kist
were photos of the strange places
and of the foreign ladies
who gave him hospitality in far ports
before Mother took him to the altar.

In the shottle of the kist
was the card of the Seamen's Union
which had gained them a decent wage
and which last year called a strike
which made Father swear.

In the shottle of the kist
was a unique smell
different from all other smells on earth,
the smell of the primeval substance
of which I was begotten.

In the long, shouldered kist
which will open before me in the evening,
whose mouth will be closed in my absence,
with my eyes shut forever,
will there be a shottle in that kist?

Mary M Maclean (Grimsay, N. Uist)

To Ben Eaval

All-enabling spirit of poetry,
Please come down now to join me,
Let me build the poem of my dreams,
And I'll praise the high mountain
That entranced me in childhood
With her conical cloud-capped face and her gums,

Le h-aghaidh chiar-chorrach ùdlaidh
Mu'm bi na siantan a' bùirich
Nuair thig i fiadhaich sna dùdlachdan reòdhte;
'S a dh'ainneoin riasladh gach drùdhadh
A chuir gach bliadhna bho thùs ort
Tha thu stéidhichte, dlùth air a' chòrsa.

Gur corrach cas-leacach àrd thu,
Le d' shruthan bras-shligheach gàir-uisgeach
'S iad air taisteal o d' bhàrr chun a' chòmhnaird —
Air am maistreadh troimh bheàrnan
'S iad le tais-ghuth, a' teàrnadh
Gu'n tig iad faisg air an tràigh a tha fòdhpa:
Gur leathann tàbhachdach dùr thu,
'Nad shuidhe sàmhach air ùrlar
An eilein àlainn a dhùisgeas gu ceòl mi,
'S nuair thilleas Màigh-mhìos an driùchda
'S a bheir i fàs air gach flùran,
Gun dèan i fàbhar 's gun crùn i le ceò thu.

'N e bheithir lasrachail liath-gheal
A rinn le fras tigh'nn on iarmailt
'S a rinn do chas-chreagan riabhach a sgròbadh
'S a rinn do bhreacadh 's do stialladh
'S a chuir an sracadh 'nad chliathaich
A bhios ri fhaicinn gu sìorraidh mar leòn ort?
'N e buillean goirte na h-aoise
A thug na rochdaidhean braoisgeach
A tha cho nochdte 'nad aodann tron cheò ort
'S a rinn do lotadh 's do mhaoladh
'S a chuir a' chroit air do chaoldruim
'S a rinn do bhoghtaichean fraochail a shròiceadh?

Ach on thùsaich an saoghal
Ged shiubhail ùin' agus daoine,
Cha tàinig mùthadh no caochladh 'nad chòir-sa,
'S a dh'ainneoin bùirein nan gaothan
Cha dèan thu crùbadh no caoineadh
'S cha chuir am faoileach no 'n dùdlachd gu bròn thu:
Tha thus', Eubhal, an-dràsta
Sa chruinne-ché seo san làraich
San deach do stéidheachadh tràth ann ad' òige,
'S gu'n tig a' chrìoch ás na h-àrdaibh
'S an téid a' ghrian-gheal a smàladh,
Bidh thu 'm fianais, san àite 'sam b' eòl thu.

With her dark-pitted sinister face
Round which elements roar
When the frozen doldrums turn wild;
For all the force of erosion
Each year from the start on you
You remain there, close by the coast.

Pitted, steep-sloped and high are you,
With your swift-flowing, loud-watered streams
That have come from your peak to the plain —
They've been churned through crevasses
And chatter quietly, descending
Till they approach the strand that's below them:
Broad, solid, stubborn are you,
Sitting quietly on the floor
Of the fair island that stirs me to music,
And when May returns with its dew
Bringing growth to each floweret,
It makes a favour and crowns you with mist.

Did some flaming silver-bright firebolt
Come with rain from the sky
To scaur your steep brindled crags
And leave you pockmarked and scratched
With a tear in your side
That will forever be seen as your wound?
Did painful strokes of old age
Make those big leering wrinkles
Seen so clearly through mist on your face
And leave you injured and hairless
With that hump on your shoulders
And rip up your heathery clothes?

But since the creation
Though time and people have passed,
No difference or change has approached you,
Despite the roaring of winds
You don't cringe or complain,
Neither wolftime nor doldrums upsets you:
You, Eaval, are now
In the spot in this universe
Where you were fixed early on in your youth,
And till the end comes from high
And the bright sun's extinguished,
There you'll be, in your accustomed place.

182   *Glòir no Dórainn?*

Ged as greadhnach an saoghal
'S ged as dripeil clann-daoine
'Sireadh mire is maoin agus eòlas,
    Is faoin-bhreaghas gun fheum iad,
    Siùbhlaidh seachad gu léir iad —
Seadh, cha mhair an cruinn-cé, ged as mòr e,
    Oir nuair lìbhrigear 'n àithne
    Théid gach bìdeag dheth smàladh,
Ged bu diongmhalta tàitht' e, gach òirleach;
    Bidh gach nì dol ás àite
    'S bidh na mìltean fo sgànradh
Ri aghaidh rìoghalachd gàirdein Iehòbha.

Bidh na reubalaich bhrùideil
A mheudaich euceart an t-saoghail
Leis gach eucoir bha ùdlaidh is deòmhnaidh
    Air an àithneadh don chùirt ud:
    Siud a' bhàirlinn nach diùlt iad —
Siud an t-àit' 'n téid an rùsgadh gun tròcair;
    Bidh na gadaichean cùilteach
    Bha tric a' seachnadh na sùla
Agus misgeirean mùigeach an òst-thaigh
    'S luchd mionnain, bhreug agus cùl-chain
    Le'm briathran neo-chùbhraidh
Uil' am fianais fo sgrùdadh na Mòrachd.

Ach se cheist dh'fheumar fhuasgladh
Mus tig breisleach na h-uair seo:
Bheil ar teisteanas shuas ann an òrdugh?
    'S nuair bhios am feasgar a' ciaradh
    'S a théid gach freastal ás fianais
Cà' 'm bi seasmhachd na sìorraidheachd mhòir dhuinn?
    'N ann a' seinn le Fear Saoraidh
    Ann an aoibhneas a lùchairt
Gu saoghal nan saoghal ri sòlas?
    No a' plosgail san truaighe
    Bhios a' losgadh 's nach fuaraich
'S fadadh-spuinge an uabhais ga theòdhadh?

Glory or Agony?

Though the world is exuberant
And humankind intent
On seeking pleasure and riches and knowledge,
    They're of no consequence or use,
    They all disappear —
Indeed, the universe won't last, for all its size,
    For when commandment is given
    Every scrap will be destroyed of it,
Though firmly cemented, each inch of it;
    All the bits will be exploding
    And thousands will be terrified
Facing the regal arms of Jehovah.

    All the barbarous rebels
    Who've stoked social injustice
With each crime that's been sinister and evil
    Will be summoned to that court:
    It's the writ they can't refuse —
That's the place where they'll be flayed without mercy;
    The surreptitious thieves
    Who'd not look you in the eye
And all the snarling drunkards of the bar-room
    And blasphemers, liars and defamers
    With all their foul-smelling words
Will all assemble for inspection by the Lord.

    But here's the question to be answered
    Before the trauma of this time:
Is our testament on high all in order?
    And when the night is approaching
    And all help is disappearing
Where will we stand in all eternity?
    Joining in song with the Redeemer
    In the pleasures of His palace
To world without end in contentment?
    Or palpitating in the ghastliness
    Which burns and never cools
With the tinder of horror inflaming it?

Ann an eachdraidh na Fìrinn,
Air an deachdadh gu cinnteach,
Se seo faclan an dìtidh gu sònraicht':
"Cha b' aithne dhomh riamh sibh —
Dèanaibh imeachd ás m' fhianais
Do bhras-theine sìorraidh na dòrainn."
Bidh an sloc tha gun ìochdar
An-sin a' fosgladh le mianan
Chum an glacadh le giallaibh gun tròcair;
Pronnasg lasrach ga bhiathadh,
Cha tig laigs' air a chìocras
Ach ataidh le dian-theas an còmhnaidh.

A' chuid tha 'n taice ri Crìosta,
Ged as lapach gu fìor iad,
Cha bhris nàmhaid no diabhal na còrdan
A tha gu sàbhailt' gan aonadh
Ris an t-Slànaighear chaomh ud
Le a bhàs a dh'ionnlaid an dò-bheart;
Tha iad sàraichte sgìtheil,
Tha peacadh-nàdair a' strì riu,
Tha trioblaidean millteach san fheòil ac',
Ach tha 'n gealladh gràsmhor ag inns' dhaibh
Á lànachd na Fìrinn
Gur h-oighreachan cinnteach air Glòir iad.

Siud an dachaigh bhios éibhneach,
Cha bhi gearain no éigheach,
Caismeachd-bàis cha séidear gu brònach,
Cha bhi cridhe fo phéin ann,
Cha bhi snighe air léirsinn,
Bidh na rìghrean gu léir toirt an glòir ann;
Geatan fosgailt' gun seul orr',
Cha bhi oidhch' ann no reultan,
Solas-coinnle chan fheumar sna seòmair,
'S gathan aoibhneach na gréine —
Cha bhi boillsgeadh dhiubh fhéin ann,
Oir bidh soillse Uan Dhé ann mar lòchran.

In the text of the Scriptures,
   Truthfully written,
Are the following words of damnation:
   "I've never known you at all —
   Go now from my presence
To the swift lasting flames of perdition."
   The bottomless pit
   Will then open with a yawn
To seize them with merciless jaws;
   With burning brimstone to feed it,
   Its hunger won't slacken
But will keep swelling with ferocious heat.

   Those who depend upon Christ,
   Even if utterly weak,
No enemy or devil can break
   The cords that safely unite them
   To that compassionate Saviour
Through his death which cleansed their iniquities;
   They're tormented and wearied,
   With original sin tempting them
And troubles belabouring their flesh,
   But the gracious promise is telling them
   From the fullness of Scripture
That they are definite heirs of Glory.

   That's the home that is blissful,
   Without cry or complaint,
No death-march is mournfully blown,
   No heart will be anguished,
   No eye will shed tears there,
All the kings will invest it with glory;
   Open gates without seal on them,
   Neither night there nor stars,
No candlelight's needed in its rooms,
   And joyful beams of the sun —
   Even *they* will not gleam there,
For the Lamb of God will shine forth as its lantern.

An t-Oll. Ruaraidh MacThòmais (1921—)

183 *Teallaichean*

Ann am meadhon an teallaich òig aoibhnich
chì mi 'nan seasamh taibhsean èibhleag
a ghlèidh an cruth 's an cumadh dom lèirsinn
ged tha 'n taobh a-staigh dhiubh mìn-gheal breòite
a' crìonadh gu luath na meadhon-oidhche
air cagailt sgaoilte brist mo sheòmair.

'S am meadhon an teallaich òig eile
chì sùilean m' eagail tannasgan aoibhneis
nach dùraig mo smuain sàthadh boillsgeach
a dhèanamh annta, air eagal ceòl-gàire
a sgathadh gu lom o cholainn deireil
's a leagail 'na luath air cagailt àmhghair.

184 *Sgòthan*

Brat ciartha air mo shùil
  Air chor 's nach fhaic mi bhuam
Do chaochladh, eilein chiar,
  Is m' iargain ort cho buan.

Ged dh'fhalbh mi uat gun smuain
  Le braise 's gàir na h-òig,
Mo shùil air fàire chian
  'S mo cheuman dian 'na tòir,

Cha robh 'n fhàir' ach 'na bun-sgòth,
  Sgòth air sgòth a' mùchadh lì
Na grèin air muir mo mhiann,
  'S a' chaile-bianain 'na mo chrìdh.

Sgòth air sgòth ga càrnadh suas,
  Toirt a' char asam gach là,
Beanntan Bharbhais air mo bhialaibh,
  'S Mèalaiseal fo ghorm bhlàth.

Mùirneag bheag taobh thall an loch
  Mar gun ruiginn oirr' le ràmh,
Sìthean an Airgid gu deas —
  Cha leig mi leas a bhith fo phràmh.

Prof. Derick Thomson (Bayble, Point, Lewis)

Hearths

In the midst of the fresh joyous hearth
I see set ghosts of embers
that have kept shape and outline as I look at them
though inside they are powder-white and fragile
withering to midnight ash
on the splayed broken hearth of my room.

And in the midst of the other young hearth
my fear's eyes see ghosts of joy,
and my thought does not dare to make
a shining thrust into them, lest laughter
be cut bare from a listless body
and fall as ash on a hearth of pain.

Clouds

Waxed bandage on my eye
So that I do not see
How you have changed, dark island,
Long missed.

Though I left light-heartedly
In youth's brashness and gaiety,
My eye on a distant horizon,
My steps hurrying towards it,

The horizon was only the cloud-base;
Cloud after cloud quenched the sparkle
Of the sun on the sea I wanted,
Of the phosphorescent gleam in my heart.

Cloud piling on cloud,
Tricking me daily,
Barvas Hills before me,
Mèalaiseal in a blue bloom.

Little Mùirneag across the loch
As though I could touch it with an oar,
The Silver Mount to the south —
I need not feel depressed.

Beinn Phabail an-seo ri m' thaobh
Is Hòl 'na chrùban gu tuath —
Ach chaidh mise bhuap air taod
Cho fada 's a thèid gaol bho fhuath.

185   bho *Mu Chrìochan Hòil*

'S air feasgar foghair bhiodh an speal gun sgìths
a' tional bàrr na bliadhna air a bil;
na balaich, a' cur sùil am fearachas,
gu dian a' ceangal sguab, 's an asbhuain ùr
ga saltairt fo am bròig, 's le dìcheall bhuan
a' dèanamh adagan nach maireadh oidhch;
neo a' falach-fead am measg nan cruachan coirc
le cridhe mear an anmoich, 's gaoth on chuan
slìobadh an sliasaid is an druim le gaoir;
mar dhath an lìonaidh tighinn air a' chuan
bha dath a' chrìonaidh tighinn air an fhraoch,
fàsach an abachaidh a' tional neart
a chuireadh e ri freumhan geala 'n fhàis;
socair na h-asaid air gach fonn is sliabh,
is gàir na mnatha-glùine air gach cnoc.
Eathar 'na siubhal air muir dorcha, trom,
muir m' eilein, muir mo bhaile, raon an èisg
'g iarraidh a thadhal is a threabhadh fòs;
fir-chlis na mara, 'n caile-bianan grad,
lasadh mar mhire ann an sùilean òigh'.

Air oidhche gheamhraidh leigt' an ceòl ma sgaoil:
bhiodh faram air an drochaid, danns gu dian
ri ceòl melodeon, eubh is gàir mu seach
is sgiamhail nìonag; bainnsean 's ruith-na-h-oidhch.
Tha leus na gealaich fhathast 'na mo shùil,
is fead na gaoithe daonnan ri mo chluais,
is ionndrainn ga mo bhuaireadh air gach sràid
air geamhradh 's caplaid bheò a' chinne-daonn.
Ri àm an reothaidh cha robh fois no sgìths
air lorg na deighe, 's nuair a thigeadh sneachd
bha 'n saoghal ùr, is dh'fheumaist dhol air fheadh.
Bu mhath an lamp' bhith laist sa mhadainn mhoich,
'nar suidhe aig tràth-bracaist, is bu mhath
solais a' bhaile deàrrsadh air a' chnoc,

Bayble Hill beside me here
   And Hòl crouching to the north —
But I went away from them on a tether
   As far as love goes from hate.

from *In the Vicinity of Hòl*

In the autumn evening the tireless scythe
gathered the year's produce on its blade;
boys, eager to show their manliness,
busily tying sheaves, the fresh stubble
being trampled underfoot, earnestly
making stooks that would not last a night;
or playing hide-and-seek among the stacks
with hearts gay in the twilight, wind from the sea
stroking their thighs and backs, raising gooseflesh;
like colour of filling tide upon the sea
the colour of withering spread on the heather,
wilderness of ripening gathering strength
to put to the white roots of growth;
relief of childbirth in each field and slope,
cry of the midwife on every hill.
A boat coursing on dark heavy seas,
my island's, my village's, the fish field
that needs to be visited and ploughed;
the sea's northern lights, sudden phosphor gleam,
glowing like merriment in a maiden's eyes.

On winter nights music would be unleashed:
a hubbub on the bridge, eager dancing
to melodeon music, call and laugh in turn
and girls squealing; weddings and night-courtship.
The moon's light stays in my eye still,
the wind's whistle always at my ear,
and on each street I miss humanity's
winter and living bustle.
In freezing weather one never tired
seeking out ice, and when the snow came
the world was new and must be visited.
A lamp lit in early morning was good,
as we sat at breakfast, it was fine
to see the village lights shining on the hill,

is lanntairean gan lasadh air an oidhch
aig àm na bleoghainn. Is bu mhath an t-àm
san tigeadh sìneadh air an fheasgar fhann,
's ar sùil ri tuilleadh cleasachd air a' bhlàr.
Bha 'm fonn 'na laighe rùisgte fo ar sùil,
gach lagan 's leathad coisrigte don àm
a dh'fhalbh 's don àm a thigeadh,
lom, mar chaidh a chruthachadh air tùs,
is lom, mar chìteadh e air là na h-as-eirigh,
gun chòmhdach ach a' chuimhne, caoin le caoin
an eòlais ged bha choslas aognaidh fuar.
Nuair thigeadh srannraich gaoithe thar a' chnuic
dh'fhàsadh an talamh cruaidh 's an cridhe mear,
's rachadh an t-anmoch mar am peilear teann
san fheòil a dh'altraim fàs is searg nan ràith.

186 *Na Cailleachan*

Crùbte an-seo fon an t-sian,
's air chùl nam balla tha cumail na gaoithe air ais,
òirlich de thìm bho na sparran,
tha iad 'nan suidhe, ri còmhradh
air crodh 's air daoine,
's ri cur fàd air an teine,
's an sileadh 'na ghlaodh dubh a' dlùthadh.

Se foghar fiadhaich a rinn i
's tha 'n coirc 'na laighe;
cha dàinig iasg an-diugh, nì ach an sgadan,
sgadan saillte 's buntàt', buntàt' is sgadan;
chan eil nì ri dhèanamh ach fàd a chur mun an teine
is bruidhinn air crodh 's air daoine.

'S tha 'n sileadh 'na ghlaodh dubh a' dlùthadh
a-nuas bho na sparran,
a-nuas bhon an tughadh,
is feumar as t-earrach an tughadh a sgaoileadh 'na thodhar
air an talamh-buntàta,
's cha dàinig iasg an-diugh, nì ach buntàt' is sgadan.

Dad ach a' bruidhinn air crodh 's air daoine
's a' cur fàd mun an teine —
O shaoghail, is goirid do chuairt, 's is lom an cridhe,
is tana an sgàile, is dlùth oirnn nimh an fhuaraidh.

and lanterns lit in the evening
at milking time. And we enjoyed
when the wan evening began to grow lighter,
expectant of longer play out in the open.
The land lay bared under our eyes,
each brae and hollow consecrated
both to past and future,
bare as it had been first of all created,
and bare as it would be at the resurrection,
clothed only in the memory, ripe
with knowing's ripeness though it looked cold and forbidding.
When a noisy gust of wind came over the hill
the ground grew hard and the heart merry,
and dusk went like a forceful bullet
into the flesh the seasons' growth and decay had nourished.

The Old Women

Hunched here under the storm,
behind the walls that keep back the wind,
inches of time from the rafters,
they sit, talking
about cows and people,
and putting a peat on the fire,
while the molten soot's black gum comes closer.

It's been a wild autumn
and the corn is lying;
no white-fish came today, nothing but herring,
salt herring and potatoes, potatoes and herring;
there is nothing to do but put a peat on the fire
and talk about cows and people.

And the molten soot's black gum comes closer,
down from the rafter,
down from the thatch,
and in spring the thatch must be spread as manure
on the potato patch,
and no white-fish came today, only potatoes and herring.

Nothing but talking of cows and people,
and putting a peat on the fire —
O life, short is your course, bare is the heart,
frail is the shelter, close to us is the venom of the cold wind.

187   Clann-Nighean an Sgadain

An gàire mar chraiteachan salainn
ga fhroiseadh bho'm beul,
an sàl 's am picil air an teanga,
's na miaran cruinne, goirid a dhèanadh giullachd,
no a thogadh leanabh gu socair, cuimir,
seasgair, fallain,
gun mhearachd,
's na sùilean cho domhainn ri fèath.

B'e bun-os-cionn na h-eachdraidh a dh'fhàg iad
'nan tràillean aig ciùrairean cutach,
thall 's a-bhos air Galldachd 's an Sasainn.
Bu shaillte an duais a thàrr iad
ás na mìltean bharaillean ud,
gaoth na mara geur air an craiceann,
is eallach a' bhochdainn 'nan ciste,
is mura b'e an gàire
shaoileadh tu gun robh an teud briste.

Ach bha craiteachan uaille air an cridhe,
ga chumail fallain,
is bheireadh cutag an teanga
slisinn á fanaid nan Gall —
agus bha obair romhpa fhathast
nuair gheibheadh iad dhachaigh,
ged nach biodh maoin ac':
air oidhche robach gheamhraidh,
ma bha siud an dàn dhaibh,
dhèanadh iad daoine.

188   Srath Nabhair

Anns an adhar dhubh-ghorm ud,
àirde na sìorraidheachd os ar cionn,
bha rionnag a' priobadh ruinn
's i freagairt mireadh an teine
ann an cabair taigh m' athar
a' bhliadhna thugh sinn an taigh le bleideagan sneachda.

The Herring Girls

Their laughter like a sprinkling of salt
showered from their lips,
brine and pickle on their tongues,
and the stubby short fingers that could handle fish,
or lift a child gently, neatly,
safely, wholesomely,
unerringly,
and the eyes that were as deep as a calm.

The topsy-turvy of history had made them
slaves to short-arsed curers,
here and there in the Lowlands, in England.
Salt the reward they won
from those thousands of barrels,
the sea-wind sharp on their skins,
and the burden of poverty in their kists,
and were it not for their laughter
you might think the harp-string was broken.

But there was a sprinkling of pride on their hearts,
keeping them sound,
and their tongues' gutting-knife
would tear a strip from the Lowlanders' mockery —
and there was work awaiting them
when they got home,
though they had no wealth:
on a wild winter's night,
if that were their lot,
they would make men.

Strathnaver

In that blue-black sky,
as high above us as eternity,
a star was winking at us,
answering the leaping flames of fire
in the rafters of my father's house,
that year we thatched the house with snowflakes.

Agus siud a' bhliadhna cuideachd
a shlaod iad a' chailleach don t-sitig
a shealltainn cho eòlach 's a bha iad air an Fhìrinn,
oir bha nid aig eunlaith an adhair
(agus cròthan aig na caoraich)
ged nach robh àit aicese anns an cuireadh i a ceann fòidhpe.

A Shrath Nabhair 's a Shrath Chill Donnain,
is beag an t-iongnadh ged a chinneadh am fraoch àlainn oirbh,
a' falach nan lotan a dh'fhàg Pàdraig Sellar 's a sheòrsa,
mar a chunnaic mi uair is uair boireannach cràbhaidh
a dh'fhiosraich dòrainn an t-saoghail sa
is sìth Dhè 'na sùilean.

189   *Bùrn is Mòine 's Coirc*

"Bùrn is mòine 's coirc" —
facal am beul strainnseir
ann an dùmhlachd a' bhaile,
ann am baile nan strainnsear.
Boile! An cridhe gòrach
a' falpanaich mu na seann stallachan ud
mar nach robh slighe-cuain ann
ach ì.
An cridhe ri bacan, car mu char aig an fheist
's i fàs goirid
's an inntinn saor.
Is daor a cheannaich mi a saorsa.

190   *Am Bodach-Ròcais*

An oidhch' ud
thàinig am bodach-ròcais dhan taigh-chèilidh:
fear caol àrd dubh
is aodach dubh air.
Shuidh e air an t-sèis
is thuit na cairtean ás ar làmhan.
Bha fear an-siud
ag innse sgeulachd air Conall Gulban
is reodh na faclan air a bhilean.
Bha boireannach 'na suidh' air stòl
ag òran, 's thug e 'n toradh ás a' cheòl.

And that too was the year
they hauled the old woman out on to the dung-heap
to demonstrate how knowledgeable they were in Scripture,
for the birds of the air had nests
(and the sheep had folds)
though she had no place in which to lay down her head.

O Strathnaver and Strath of Kildonan,
it is little wonder that the heather should bloom on your slopes,
hiding the wounds that Patrick Sellar, and such as he, made,
just as time and time again I have seen a pious woman
who has suffered the sorrow of this world
with the peace of God shining from her eyes.

Water and Peats and Oats

"Water and peats and oats" —
a word in a stranger's mouth
in the throng of the town,
in the town of the strangers.
Madness. The foolish heart
lapping along these ancient rocks
as though there were no sea-journey in the world
but that one.
The heart tied to a tethering-post, round upon round of the rope
till it grows short
and the mind free.
I bought its freedom dearly.

Scarecrow

That night
the scarecrow came into the ceilidh-house:
a tall thin black-haired man
wearing black clothes.
He sat on the bench
and the cards fell from our hands.
One man
was telling a folktale about Conall Gulban
and the words froze on his lips.
A woman was sitting on a stool,
singing songs, and he took the goodness out of the music.

Ach cha do dh'fhàg e falamh sinn:
thug e òran nuadh dhuinn
is sgeulachdan na h-Àird an-Ear
is sprùilleach de dh'fheallsanachd Geneva,
is sguab e 'n teine á meadhon an làir
's chuir e 'n tùrlach loisgeach 'nar broillichean.

191 Murdag Mhòr ("Mucka")

A' gluasad air rathad corrach
le ceuman troma,
cnap beag dubh,
sùil air bhiod am bodhaig sgìth,
a' tighinn dhachaigh bhon a' chutadh,
's a' bhò ri bleoghan,
buntàta ri phriogadh,
norradh cadail 's a' bhò ri bleoghan,
is rathad Steòrnabhaigh a-rithist.

Bha thu fad air falbh
bho mo thuigse,
eadhon anns an là sin;
tha thu 'n-diugh
mar dhuine bha beò ri linn Chrìosda,
a' feitheamh ri làmhan an lighiche,
ris an ol'-ungaidh,
a' coiseachd troimh do Ghilead,
troimhn a' chàthair rèisgte.

'Na mo thùr aolaichte
bidh uinneag troimh 'm faic mi an sealladh sin:
na biodh mo làmh ro chrìon fhad 's tha ol'-ungaidh agam.

192 Làmhan

Làmhan tha tigh'nn gu mo chuimhne a-nis:
tana, tioram, is cailc orr',
pliutan plaomach le fallas,
meuran odhar le niocotain,
ìnean sgàrlaid air ìghneagan.
Iad sin air iomall na cuimhne;

But he did not leave us empty-handed:
he gave us a new song
and tales from the Middle East
and fragments of the philosophy of Geneva,
and he swept the fire from the centre of the floor
and set a searing bonfire in our breasts.

Murdag Mhór ("Mucka")

Trudging along a rough road
with heavy steps,
dark, small and stocky,
darting eye in tired body,
coming home from the gutting,
the cow to be milked,
the potato patch to be weeded,
a wink of sleep and the cow to be milked,
and the road to Stornoway again.

You were far removed
from my understanding,
even then;
now
you are like someone who lived in the time of Christ,
awaiting the hand of the physician,
the anointing oil,
walking through your Gilead,
through the black skinned peat-land.

In my lime-washed tower
there will be a window from which I can see that sight:
let my hand not be niggardly while I have oil to give.

Hands

Hands are what I remember now:
thin, dry, with chalk on them,
flabby sweaty fins,
fingers yellow with nicotine,
girls with scarlet nails.
These are at the edges of my memory;

'na teis-meadhon
làmhan air amhaich coin,
air ceann balaich,
am muing eich,
air cliathaich bà;
làmhan am picil an sgadain,
an taois nan isean,
air sine, air ràmh,
air gruaidh naoidhein ris a' chìch.

Tha feur a' fàs troimh na làmhan sin,
sàl gan suathadh,
ach fhad 's a mhaireas mise
bidh cuimhne gan slìobadh.

193 *Earrach '74*

Tha crathadh de dh'aol anns an earrach seo
air an talamh dhonn,
com na dùthcha sgìth
le mùchadh sneachda,
"caistealan liath' air an stormadh le iarann",
ach crathadh aoil a-nis.
Ged tha toinneamh anns an fheur,
marbh-bhrat na bliadhna 'n-uiridh,
tha 'm beò anns an ùir,
beò-aol bheir fhathast crathadh oirnn.

194 *Ceud Bliadhna san Sgoil*

Ceud bliadhna san sgoil
is sinn 'nar Gaidheil fhathast!
Cò shaoileadh gum biodh an fhreumh cho righinn?
Dhòirt iad eallach leabhraichean oirnn,
is cànanan, eachdraidh choimheach,
is saidheans, is chuir iad maidse riutha.
O abair lasair
de mhinistearan 's de mhaighstirean-sgoile,
de dhoctairean 's de dh'einnsinidhears,

right in the middle
hands on a dog's neck,
on a boy's head,
in a horse's mane,
on a cow's side;
hands in herring pickle,
in the chickens' mash,
on a cow's teat, on an oar,
on the face of a child at the breast.

Grass grows through these hands,
salt water rubs them,
but as long as I last
memory will stroke them.

Spring '74

The year of the General Election . . . with hindsight, two General Elections

There's a sprinkling of lime this spring
on the brown earth,
the land's breast weary
with suffocating snow,
"grey castles reinforced with iron bars",
but a sprinkling of lime now.
Though the grass is matted,
last year's dead mantle,
there is life in the soil,
quicklime that will shake us yet.

A Hundred Years in School

A hundred years in school
and we're Gaels still!
Who would have thought the root was so tough?
They poured a load of books on us,
languages, foreign history,
science, and put a match to them.
O what a blaze
of ministers and dominies,
doctors and engineers,

profeasairean is luchd-reic-chàraichean,
ach aig ceann nan ceud bliadhna,
an dèidh gach greadain 's gach dadhaidh,
nuair a sguab iad an luath air falbh,
bha a fhreumh ann a-sin fhathast,
fann-bhuidhe an toiseach.
Is minig a chunna sinn craobh a chaidh a losgadh —
A! sann le fun tha mi,
na biodh eagal oirbh, a luchd-stiùiridh an fhoghlaim,
a chomhairlichean na siorrachd, 's a' Bheurla cho math agaibh —
a' fàs —
siud sibh, sguabaibh a' chlann a Steòrnabhagh —
nas braise.

195   *An Crann*

1   Crann ann an ùir mo dhùthcha
cruaidh anns an asbhuain
soc anns a' ghlasach
gorm-thonn a' dol 'na chop dubh
air a' chladach ùr seo,
crann ùr.

Feumaidh e a dhol domhainn,
fon a' chopaig,
troimhn an luachair,
an gorm 's an geal 's an dubh
air am filleadh 's air an toinneamh
anns an tochailt,
anns a' bhogha,
anns an sgrìob dhearg.

Feumaidh na gàirdeanan bhith righinn.

2   Tha fonn aig a' chrann,
iomadh fonn aig crann mo dhùthcha,
fonn iomadh-fhillte air a clàr
mus deach a creachadh.
Feumaidh na meuran a bhith làidir
is gràdhach,
tha sgreab dhubh air clàr mo dhùthcha.

professors and car-salesmen,
but after a hundred years,
after each scorching and singeing,
when they brushed away the ash
the root was there still,
pale-yellow at first.
We have often seen a bush that was burnt —
I'm just joking,
have no fear, directors of education,
county councillors, with your fluent English —
growing —
that's right, centralise education in Stornoway —
faster.

The Plough (or Cross/Mast/Lot/Harp-Key/Saltire etc.)

1   A plough in my country's soil
steel in the stubble
sock in the meadow
green wave turning to black foam
on this new shore,
a new share.

It must go deep,
under the docken,
through the rushes,
green and white and black
entwined and interlaced
in the delving,
in the bow,
in the red furrow.

The arms must be tough.

2   The plough has land / The harp-key has a tune,
my country's harp has many tunes,
it had a many-layered tune
before it was smashed.
The fingers must be strong
and loving,
there's a black scab on my country's skin.

Tha at fo thuinn air mo dhùthaich;
cha dèan sgiùrsadh,
cha dèan plàsd,
cha dèan an lannsa m' annsachd slàn
gu'm bi an leabaidh-shiùbhla làn.

3   Fo na bunan seacte
fon a' bhalla loit'
fon an taigh air grodadh
fo na fhreumhan toinnte
fon an inntinn fhiar
fon a' chridhe ragte
stob a-steach an crann.

4   Sgrìob troimh fhraoch 's troimh luachair,
sgrìob air gualainn donn na beinne,
tha iomadh lot air slios mo dhùthaich
nach fhalaich a-chaoidh an crann-giuthais,
's cha dèan fiaradh feachda fidhchill
falach-fead nuair thig a' mhadainn.

Tha sgreaban dubh' air clàr nam bailtean
nach dèan tarbh-chrann stùrach rèidh,
lot nach leighis craiceann tearra;
gun an fhuil bhith air a glanadh
thig an niosgaid leatha fhèin.

Gheibh sinn pronnastan an earraich
's nì sinn faloisgear dhuinn fhìn
air na cnuic is air na sràidean,
ann an Glaschu 's ann an Eige,
's thig am feur an àird a-rìs.

5   An dèidh a' chruinn an cliathadh,
an dèidh a' chliathaidh a' bheatha ùr,
an ùir bhrisg a' leaghadh
's a' dol 'na cnap nuadh
fon a' ghrèin,
a' tòcadh,
ag at fo shruth cuisle.

There's a swelling under my country's skin;
scourging cannot,
plaster may not,
the lance won't make my darling well
till the bed of birth is full.

3   Under the withered stubble
     under the rotted wall
     under the house in decay
     under the knotted roots
     under the twisted mind
     under the stubborn heart
     thrust the plough in.

4   A furrow through heather and rushes,
     furrow on the brown shoulder of the hill,
     my country's side has many wounds
     that pine trees will never hide,
     the chess army with tortuous moves
     will not play hide-and-seek in the morning.

     There are black scabs on the towns' surface
     that dusty bulldozers cannot smooth,
     wounds that a skin of tar can't heal;
     unless the blood itself has been cleaned
     the boil will keep coming again.

     We'll get sulphur in the spring
     and make a bonfire for ourselves
     on the hills and in the streets,
     in Glasgow and in Eigg also,
     and the grass will show through again.

5   After the plough the harrow,
     after the harrow the new life,
     the friable soil melting,
     forming a new lump
     under the sun's rays,
     rising,
     swelling with a rush from the veins.

Tha cuimhn' agam ort,
ròp mu do ghuaillean a' cliathadh,
's na h-eich gann
is daor.
Bu mhath an là a bheireadh e fhèin ás.

'S bu sheachd mhath a' bhliadhna bheireadh i fhèin ás
bho shìol gu adag,
ach an-diugh
an dèidh aisling Rìgh na h-Èipheit
feumaidh ar sùil bhith air a' choirc ag òradh
fada bhuainn,
is spealan eile ga bhuain.

6   "Se farmad a nì treabhadh" —
feumaidh gun do dh'fhalbh e
ás an sgìre againn,
tha h-uile lota bàn am-bliadhna.

7   Cha dèan farmad,
cha dèan eud,
cha dèan càineadh an talamh rèidh.
Cha dèan "mi fhìn",
cha dèan "mo threubh",
cha dèan "mo chlas" ach plàst is cèir.
Cha chan sagart,
cha chan clèir,
cha chan eaglais dhuinn a' chreud.
Cha chuir eathair,
cha chuir beairt,
cha chuir ola 'n dùthaich ceart
gus an tig fear-saoraidh ùr —
Sir Crannchur MacGilleMhùin?

8   Nuair a thèid an Crann an àird
bidh Seoc an Aonaidh air a mhàs,
nuair a bheir tuath-ghaoth dha crathadh
bidh Seoc bochd ás aonais plathaidh,
bidh rudhadh ann an gruaidhean Seoc
nuair mhaoidheas an Crann air a shoc,
nuair chì sinn a' chrois air a' chrann
nì sinn ri ar dùthaich bann.

I remember you,
rope on shoulder pulling a harrow,
since horses were scarce
and dear.
Taking each day as it came.

Especially glad to see a whole year through
from seed to stack,
but now
after the King of Egypt's dream
we must set our sights on the corn ripening
a long time ahead,
and other scythes reaping it.

6   "Envy makes good ploughing" —
     it must have abandoned
     our parish,
     none of the crofts are worked this year.

7   Envy will not,
     grudging won't,
     slanging can't prepare the ground.
     "I myself",
     "my own clan",
     "my class" are bandages, I've found.
     Neither priest
     nor presbyter
     nor church can say for us the creed.
     New boats will not,
     nor will looms,
     oil won't give us what we need
     till a new redeemer comes —
     Sir Harpsichord MacGillybums?

8   When we run the Saltire up
     the Union Jack will get a bump,
     when the north wind makes it flutter
     Jack's old flaps will sound like butter,
     and Jack's cheeks will blush right red
     when the Saltire's brandished at his head,
     when we see the cross on the flag-tree
     we shall make a band with our land to be free.

9   Ar crann fhìn air ar slinnean,
       taic an fhiodha ri ar druim,
       chan eil dà dhòigh ann
       ma tha dòigh idir ann.
       Chan eil air ach an cnoc a dhìreadh
       a dh'ionnsaigh na sìthe,
       chan eil air ach am fìon
       geur 's ga bheil e
       òl,
       cha dèan Peadar
       cha dèan Pòl
       sinne a dhìon
       no ar beatha a chur ann an suim
       mura bi ar druim
       's ar slinnean ris a' chrann.

196   *Earail air Luchd-Adhraidh a' Bheòil-Aithris*

Air Oidhche Shamhna
iarraidh mi ort do cheann a chur ann am baraille
's leig leamsa m' ubhal ith.

Air Oidhche Shamhna
feuch an tèid thu mhullach an taigh'
's tuit troimhn fhàrlas dhan a' phoit bhrochain.

Air Oidhche Shamhna
bi cinnteach gun cagainn thu do chnothan
gun fhios nach toir thu piseach air neach.

Air Oidhche Shamhna
nuair a chuireas tu ar samhradh dhan an uaigh
na can earrach ri ar geamhradh.

197   *Alba v. Argentina, 2/6/79*

mìos as dèidh Taghadh na Pàrlamaid, 3/5/79

       Glaschu a' cur thairis
       le gràdh dùthcha,
       leòmhainn bheucach
       air Sràid an Dòchais,

9   Our own cross on our shoulderblades,
the support of the wood at our back,
there are no two ways about it
if there's any way out of our loss.
Nothing for it but climb the hill
towards peace still,
nothing for it but drink the wine
even though it is all
vinegar,
Peter cannot
nor can Paul
protect us
or give to our life what it lacks
unless our backs
and shoulderblades are carrying the cross.

A Warning for Folklore Worshippers

On Hallowe'en
I'll ask you to put your head in a barrel
and leave me to eat my apple.

On Hallowe'en
be sure you climb on to the roof
and fall through the smoke-hole into the porridge-pot.

On Hallowe'en
make sure you chew your nuts,
better that than propagate.

On Hallowe'en
when you consign our summer to the grave
do not call our winter spring.

Scotland v. Argentina, 2/6/79

a month after the General Election, 3/5/79

Glasgow erupting
with patriotism,
growling lions
on Hope Street,

an Central
mùchte le breacan,
cop air Tartan bho mhoch gu dubh,
is mùn nam fineachan air a' bhlàr;
iolach-catha a' bàthadh bùrail nam busaichean —
Sco-o-t-land, Sco-o-t-land —
Alba chadalach,
mìos ro fhadalach.

198   bho *Àirc a' Choimhcheangail*

6   *A' Bheatha Mhaireannach*

Bha a' bheatha sin
gu bhith maireannach;
cha tigeadh galar nan còig oidhch' oirr',
no foill caithimh;
cha chuireadh suaile gu grunnd i,
no maor chun na sitig;
bha i tèaraint' bho shàthadh beugaileid,
cha toireadh fiabhras gu ceann i.
Bhiodh i milis
le ìm is iasg,
is carthannachd,
laoidhean is sailm,
coibhneas fo phlaide
is lit sa mhadainn.

7   *Iasgairean*

Iasgairean a bh' annta fhèin
cuideachd.
Bha am muir na b' fhiadhaiche,
bha na creagan aosta greannach
ged a bhiodh grian orr',
ach bha 'n aon mhiann
's an aon acras air an siubhal,
's bha na daoine dha'n innseadh iad an sgeul
a-cheart cho faisg air an talamh
is eòlach air na clachan,
co-dhiù air son ballaist,
is thuigeadh iad buaidh
an Fhir a thionndaidheadh iad gu aran
no a ghluaiseadh tè mhòr dhiubh bho bheul 'uaigh.

the Central
choked with Tartan,
foaming from dawn to dusk,
and clansmen's piss on the battlefield;
the battle-cry drowning the buses' drone —
Sco-o-t-land, Sco-o-t-land —
sleepy Scotland,
a month late.

from *The Ark of the Covenant*

6   *Everlasting Life*

That life
was to be everlasting;
no fifth-night fever would overtake it,
nor wily tuberculosis;
a sea-swell would not put it to the bottom,
nor a ground-officer turn it out of doors;
it was safe from bayonet thrust,
fever would not bring it to a close.
It would be sweet
with butter and fish,
and good company,
hymns and psalms,
favours under the blanket
and porridge in the morning.

7   *They themselves were fishermen*

They themselves were fishermen
too.
The sea was wilder,
the ancient rocks more surly
though the sun shone on them,
but they lived with the same desire
and the same hunger,
and the people to whom they told their story
were just as close to the ground
and familiar with stones,
especially for ballast;
they could understand the power
of One who could turn stones to bread
or move a huge one from the mouth of His grave.

8   *Adhradh mara*

A' dol a-null air an eathar dhan an eaglais,
deise dhorch is lèine gheal is aodann ruiteach,
crògan mòra 's ràimh umhail,
tùis an t-siabain 's tùis na h-ùrnaigh
a' dol 'nan aon,
adhradh bho àite-seòlaidh gu cala.

9   *A' gabhail an Leabhair*

Air ar glùinean,
uilnean air a' bheing,
sìorraidheachd bheag na maidne,
's an cù saor
a' dabhdail air an rathad.
O, nan tigeadh cairt!
An gleoc a' bualadh deich
's mo sheanair a' stobadh fhacal
dhan ghleadhraich;
uiseag
a' bruidhinn ris a' Chruthaidhear;
ràmh ga thoirt air bòrd;
dìosgail bhac sa bhàgh.
"Cluinnidh Tu a h-uile facal a their sinn riut
anns an t-sàmhchair seo,
air do mhadainn naoimh."
Fuaim eagallach aig na h-uighean a' plubraich sa phana.

10   *Bòidhchead air a crosadh*

Bu duilich gun robh bòidhchead air a crosadh:
bha na ballachan dìreach, lom,
bha na h-uinneagan ceithir-cheàrnach,
cha tàinig blàth air an diosteampair,
bha e 'na pheacadh a dhol air do ghlùinean
anns an eaglais,
stòladh ás aonais stùil,
bha na solais geal, is fuar,
ach bha aon chrois ann,
air pìos sìoda air a' chùbainn;
cha robh a' chrois air a crosadh buileach.

8   *Going over to church by boat*

Going over to church by boat,
dark suits, white shirts and ruddy faces,
large fists, obedient oars,
incense of spindrift and incense of prayer
coalescing,
worship from sailing-point to harbour.

9   *Taking the books*

On our knees,
elbows on the bench,
the morning's little eternity,
the dog free
to stroll along the road.
O for a cart!
The clock strikes ten
and my grandfather jabs words
into the racket;
a lark
talking to the Creator;
an oar being shipped;
creaking of rowlocks in the bay.
"You can hear every word we speak to You
in this peace,
in Your sacred morning."
The eggs make a fearful din jumping in the pan.

10   *Beauty forbidden*

It was sad that beauty was forbidden:
the walls were straight and bare,
the windows square,
the distemper had not mellowed,
it was a sin to kneel
in the church,
schooling without stools,
the lights were white and cold,
but there was one cross,
on a piece of silk on the pulpit;
the cross was not entirely forbidden.

Bòidhchead air a smàladh,
falt air theannachadh fon a' phrìne,
ruaig air ghrìogagan,
gach nì ag iarraidh gu dubh
's gu dubhachas,
ach dh'èireadh fiamh a' ghàire,
cho fann ri diosteampair,
aig ceann an t-suidheachain
an àm sgaoilidh,
fàsgadh làmh anns a' phoirdse,
is corra ghàire air a' bhlàr-a-muigh.
Anns a' chàr
dh'fhaodadh tu lachan a dhèanamh,
air do shocair.

Ach air a shon sin
bha an eaglais mar iodhal
ged nach robh sùilean fiar innt',
righte, fuar,
gun charachadh,
duilich suathadh innt',
gun sgàile tionndaidh,
sùil fhuar 'na bathais
air an druim a' dol a-mach á fianais,
màrmor fo phòig,
cridhe cloich innte.

Bha corra dhuine ann
a thug am bòidhchead innte 's aiste
's cha deach i 'na smàl.

11 *Iomradh air an fheadhainn a chaidh dhachaigh*
    (a' chiad Shàbaid de January, 1979)

Iain Chaluim Eòghainn, ás na Fleisirean,
air a leithid seo a latha:
    e fhèin 's a bhean glè ghaolach air a-chèile,
    teaghlach mòr aca, is oghaichean,
    taigh làn 's a' cur thairis,
    fialaidh 'nan gnè,
    pailteas a' sruthadh thuca,
    na Leabhraichean aca moch is anmoch:
    àite falamh anns an dachaigh a-nochd.

Beauty damped down,
hair tightened with pins,
beads banished,
everything tending to black
and melancholy,
but a faint smile would appear,
thin like distemper,
at the pew end
as we dispersed,
a gripping of hands in the porch,
an occasional laugh outside.
In the car
you could laugh outright,
but quietly.

But for all that
the church was like an idol
though it did not have squinting eyes,
stiff, cold,
unmoving,
difficult to touch,
with no shadow of turning,
a cold eye in its temple
on the back going out of sight,
kissed marble,
a heart of stone in it.

There were occasional people
who took their beauty in and out of it
without its going up in flames.

11   *An intimation of those who have gone home / died*
      (*First Sabbath of January, 1979*)

Iain son of Calum son of Ewen, from Flesherin,
on such-and-such a day:
    he and his wife were very loving,
    had a large family, grandchildren,
    a house full and overflowing,
    generous by nature,
    rich in the world's goods,
    they took the Books morning and evening:
    an empty place in the home tonight.

Calum Mhurchaidh Fhionnlaigh, á Pabail,
air an là seo eile:
 duine bha dona gu deoch 'na òige,
 's gu boireannaich,
 mus tàinig caitheamh ann;
 tha mhàthair 's a phiuthar beò fhathast,
 tha iad ag ràdh
 gur iadsan thug a-steach e
 aig na h-òrduighean mu dheireadh,
 cha robh e fada staigh.

Niall Alasdair Thormoid, á Garrabost,
air Là na Bliadhn' Ùire:
 ceannaiche,
 ghlèidh e mhin anns a' Chiad Chogadh
 gus an deach a' phrìs an àird —
 cha robh i buileach air grodadh —
 bha 'n tombac' aige daor
 's bha e trom air;
 càmhail aige gam faicinn anns an trom-laighe,
 fàsach gun bhrat-ùrlair am fianais.

Màiri Eachainn Mhòir, ás a' Chnoc,
a sheachdain gus a-nochd:
 chailleadh an gille bha dol ga pòsadh
 anns an Fhraing,
 deireadh December
 1917 . . .

15 *Air a' Cheist*

Nuair a dh'èireadh tu air a' cheist
bha na suidheachanan fada a' dol á fianais,
sgleò a' tighinn air na deiseachan gorma,
cha robh guth air ad no currac,
a' chùbainn a' dol ás an t-sealladh
's am Bìoball fhèin air a chur an dara taobh,
is bha thu anns a' bhàr sin a-rithist
aig iasgach Shasainn
far an tàine tu aghaidh ri aghaidh
ris a' Chruthaidhear.
Cò chailleadh cuimhn' air a leithid?

Calum son of Murdo son of Finlay, from Bayble,
on another day:
    a man who was heavy on drink in his youth,
    and fond of women,
    until he contracted TB;
    his mother and sister survive him,
    it is said
    it was they who brought him in
    at the last Communions,
    he wasn't a member for long.

Neil son of Alexander son of Norman, from Garrabost,
on New Year's Day:
    a merchant,
    he hoarded meal during the First War
    until the price went up —
    it had not quite gone bad —
    his tobacco was dear
    and he smoked heavily;
    he was seeing camels in his nightmares,
    a desert with no carpet to be seen.

Mary daughter of Big Hector, from Knock,
a week ago tonight:
    the boy who was to marry her was lost
    in France,
    at the end of December
    1917 . . .

15   *When you rose on Question-Day*

When you rose on the question
the long pews disappeared from view,
the serge suits became shadowy,
there was no perception of hats or mutches,
the pulpit slipped out of sight,
and the Bible itself was laid aside,
and you were in that bar again
at the English fishing,
where you came face to face
with the Creator.
Who would forget the like of that?

16   *Se Glaschu an Èipheit a bh' agaibh*

Se Glaschu an Èipheit a bh' agaibh
's chaidh cuid agaibh ann 'nur n-òige
nuair a thàinig a' chaoile air an tìr:
chaidh sibh sìos am measg nan diathan coimheach,
ann an coileid nan sràid
dh'èist sibh ri cainnt nan cinneach
is dh'fhàs sibh suas rith',
bhruidhinn sibh ri siùrsaich an teampaill
air Sràid an Dòchais,
's chuir sibh aodach na tìr ìseil oirbh
feasgar Di-Sathairn,
's thug sibh tarraing air an fhìon aca,
is dh'fhàs am biadh blasta dhuibh.
Ach ghairm ur n-athair air ais gu ur tìr fhèin sibh
ach am biodh a shliochd lìonmhor ann an tìr a' gheallaidh.

17   *Ùrnaigh*

M' ùrnaigh
nach lorgar mi
là-eigin ann am' èiginn
air mo ghlùinean
ag ùrnaigh.

199 bho *Air Sràidean Ghlaschu*

Nuair a chluinneas mi
ban-fhrithealaich á Glaschu
a' dèanamh mion-chòmhradh
mu Pherry Como
no Starsky is Hutch,
no a' gabhail fear de na h-òrain
aig Iain Lennon,
cuimhnichidh mi
gu bheil Ualas
air cùl na còmhla,
is Alastair mac Colla
aig muileann Ghocam-Gò
's an dùthaich agam, le dìth tuigse,
air a dhol a thaigh na bidse.

16   *Glasgow was your Egypt*

Glasgow was your Egypt
and some of you migrated there in your youth
when the lean years came on your land:
you went down among the foreign gods,
in the thronging streets
you listened to strange tongues
and got to know them,
you talked to the temple harlots
on Hope Street,
and dressed in the Lowland fashion
on Saturday afternoons,
tried the taste of their wine
and grew accustomed to their food's flavour.
But your Father called you back to your own land
that His progeny might multiply in the Land of Promise.

17   *Prayer*

My prayer
that I be not found,
one day, in extremity,
on my knees,
praying.

from *On Glasgow Streets*

When I hear
Glasgow waitresses
talking earnestly
about Perry Como
or Starsky and Hutch,
or singing a song
by John Lennon,
I remember
that Wallace
is out the window,
and Alastair mac Colla
at the mill of Gocam-Gò
and my country, for lack of will,
has gone to hell.

Smuaintean ann an cafe an Glaschu

Á iomallan Burma a bha iad,
òg, brèagh, is gàir' air am bilean dealbhach,
pògan tais na grèin' orra fhathast
an dèidh buige a' mhonsoon,
ceòl mìn nach togadh mo chluasan ceart,
's bha beagan aoibhneis 'na mo chridhe riutha —
thuig mi cho duilich 's a tha e dhan SED
iarrtasan nan Gaidheal a thuigsinn.

200 *Madainn Diar-Daoin, ann an Oifis Puist an Glaschu*

Bho shràidean
agus bho chaol-shràidean a' bhaile
chruinnich iad
gu Oifis a' Phuist,
na bacaich agus na ciorramaich:
fear a' slaodadh nan casan càm aige,
duin' òg le sgreaban dubh' air aodann,
fear eile le na sùilean ag at 'na cheann,
boireannach letheach-òg
creachte leis an òl,
seann bhodach 'na shliopairean,
bun-feusaig is falt fada,
is briogais thana,
gach duine 's a shùil air toiseach a' chiudha
's a bhileag 'na làimh,
a' dol gu fuaran an fhàsaich
far an robh a' chuirm,
dall is mar a bhà iad
a' leantainn an t-solais,
bodhar is cluais ri ceòl.
Sheall mi gun fhios nach robh Crìosta
air cùl a' chunntair,
ach bha na bacaich ann a-sin cuideachd.
Mise 'nam sheasamh anns a' chiudha
a' smaoineachadh gun robh mi slàn.

Thoughts in a Glasgow cafe

From distant Burma they were,
young, lovely, with laughter on their shapely lips,
the sun's soft kisses on them still
after the moistness left by the monsoon,
a delicate music my ears could not properly hear,
and I felt some kindness towards them in my heart —
I understood how difficult it is for the SED
to understand the Gaels' wishes.

Thursday Morning, in a Glasgow Post Office

From the streets
and from the back-streets of the city
they converged
on the Post Office,
the lame and the halt:
a man dragging his crooked legs along,
a young man with black scars on his face,
another whose eyes bulged from his head,
a youngish woman
haggard with drink,
an old man in his slippers,
stubbly beard and long hair,
wearing thin trousers,
each one looking to the head of the queue,
holding his slip of paper,
going to the spring in the desert
where the feast was,
blind as they were
and following the light,
deaf and eager for music.
I looked to see if Christ
was behind the counter,
but the halt were there too.
And I standing in the queue there
thinking I was whole.

201   Na h-Iongnan

Nollaig?
Pàpanach?
Se th' againne ar creideamh fhìn,
am Bìoball naomh —
na pìosan a tha sinn a' tuigse,
ag iarraidh a thuigse.
Na cuir dheth an TV:
chan fhaca mi 'm pìos sin de *Dallas*
an turas mu dheireadh.
Tha iad ag ràdh gun lean na h-iongnan a' fàs
greiseag an dèidh bàis.

202   A' Ghaidhealtachd

A' cuimhneachadh Pàirce nam Beathaichean Fiadhaich ann am Bàideanach

Biast-dhubh ann an garadh
sgèan 'na smàl-shùil
a' coimhead troimhn uinneig ghloinne.

Làn-damh a' leigeil air
nach eil e gad fhaicinn
a' togail dhealbh.

Iolaire a' tilgeil nan itean.

Bradan ann an cèids
a' fàs reamhar
air biadh coimheach.

Cat-fiadhaich
a' losgadh mar thìm-bhom
ann an oisean dhe 'chrìon rìoghachd.

The Nails

Christmas?
Papish?
We have our own faith,
the holy Bible —
the parts of it we understand,
that we want to understand.
Don't switch off the TV:
I missed that bit of *Dallas*
the last time it was on.
They say that fingernails go on growing
for some time after death.

The Highlands

Remembering the Wild-Life Park in Badenoch

Otter in a den
alarm in its smouldering eye
as it looks through the glass window.

An antlered stag
pretending it doesn't notice
you taking photos.

An eagle moulting.

Salmon in a cage
growing fat
on alien food.

Wild-cat
burning like a time-bomb
in a corner of its shrunken kingdom.

203 Pioghaid

Tha pioghaid ann
a bhios a' tighinn a ghabhail cuairt,
'na deise Sàbaid, 'na mo leas,
is bidh i cur iongnadh orm
leis cho speiseanta 's a tha i,
an t-aodach dubh gleansach air a bhruisigeadh,
's na bannan geala cho grinn,
ceum Sàbaid aice cuideachd
mar gum biodh i faireachdainn
sùil a' mhinisteir oirre.
Bidh mi feitheamh ach am faic mi
a bheil tastan aice ga chur san truinnsear,
is tha mi cinnteach
gu bheil Bìoball beag eireachdail
aice fo a sgiathan.
Ach feasgar a-raoir
bha gàgail an donais aice fhèin 's aig a h-àl
gu h-àrd anns a' chraoibh sin.
Gabh do roghainn.

204 Deireadh an t-Saoghail

Chan ionnan
deireadh an t-saoghail
ann an Glaschu 's an Ceann Loch Raithneach:
tuitidh an t-adhar 'na chnap
air Sràid Earra-Ghaidheal,
a' cur Boots is Lewis's 'nam màl,
le ìsbeanan is clòimh-cotain
an amhaichean a-chèile,
is peant dearg air an talc,
's bidh na diathan-brèige 'bromadaich
anns a' BhBC 's aig STV,
's gun facal a' tighinn ás am beul.

Ach ann an Raithneach
bidh iad a' togail bàta ùr air an Loch
's a' dol dha na saunas,
's a' dèanamh bùth mhòr den an eaglais
's ag adhradh an Naoimh Terry Wogan.

Magpie

There's a magpie
who comes for a stroll,
in her Sunday best, in my garden,
and it amazes me
how trig she is,
her black shining dress well brushed,
with such elegant white stripes,
walking with a Sunday pace too
as though she felt
that her minister was watching her.
I wait to see
if she has a shilling to put in the plate,
and I'm quite sure
she has a handsome little Bible
tucked under her wings.
But last night
there was a devilish cackling from her and from her brood
up in that tree.
Take your pick.

The End of the World

The end of the world
will come in different ways
in Glasgow and in Kinlochrannoch:
the sky will fall suddenly
on Argyle Street
throwing Boots and Lewis's into confusion,
with sausages getting all mixed up
with cotton-wool,
red paint spilt on the talcum,
and the false gods farting
in the BBC and at STV,
speechless.

But in Rannoch
they will be building a new ship on the Loch
and going to the saunas,
turning the church into a department-store
and worshipping St Terry Wogan.

205 *Teagamh*

Dùil 'am gun robh mi saor ach cha robh:
an geata gu bhith dùint' air fàire,
an leathad na bu chaise na bha dùil,
's nuair a dh'fheuch mi na sìnteagan
thuig mi gun robh 'n spearrach sìoda an-sin fhathast,
agus is dòcha feist mu m' amhaich,
a' phrosbaig cho doilleir ri mo shùil
nuair a ràinig mi 'n rubha;
ach dè 'm feum a th' ann am prosbaig?
fear-saoraidh, ge-tà, dhèanadh esan feum,
is cinnteach,
nam b'e 's gu bheil saorsa ann ach chan eil.

206 bho *Gormshuil*

Sgal aig a' ghaoith ris an uinneig,
na làmhan a' slìobadh an aodaich,
's am muir a' tighinn gu tràigh.

An leabaidh a' fàs cumhang
le bruthadh na h-ùrach,
slacadaich morghain air a' chlàr.

Am feur a' fàs
dùmhail air an talamh,
a' glasadh ann an glasadh an là.

Saoghal air seacadh gu aon seòmar,
gu meud leaptha, gu anail
a' plathcadaich fo na plaideachan.

Ballachan na feòla a' sìor iadhadh
mun a' ghrìosaich,
an èibhleag a' fàs beag,
a' crìonadh gu deirge,
gu lasair sùla,
gu boinne,
gu boinneag
an àite buinne,
dìth cheap air an doras-iadht',
dìth grèine air sruth na fala.

Doubt

Thinking I was free but I wasn't:
the gate on the horizon almost closed,
the hill steeper than expected,
and when I tried to stride it out
the silken shackles were there still,
and perhaps a halter round my neck,
while the telescope was so dull
when I reached the headland;
but what's the good of a telescope?
a redeemer, though, he would work,
surely,
if indeed there is freedom but there isn't.

from *Gormshuil/Blue-Eye*

A blast of wind against the window,
hands stroking the cloth,
the sea coming in to the shore.

The bed grown narrow
with the pressing-in of earth,
clatter of gravel on the board.

The grass growing
dense on the ground,
turning grey with the greying of the day.

A world shrunk to a single room,
to the extent of a bed, to breath
coming in gusts under the blankets.

The walls of flesh constantly closing in
round the hearth,
the ember growing small,
withering to redness,
to a flame in the eye,
to a drop,
to a droplet
instead of a flood,
shortage of turfs for the closing-door,
lack of sun in the blood-stream.

An làmh
sgìth air a' bhòrd,
seacte le socair,
bàn le fois
nam bliadhnachan,
an craiceann an crochadh ris a' bhois,
na h-iongnan grinn.

A' ducail,
a'stobadh meur ann an imleag tìm',
eadar fuireach 's falbh,
glaist' ann am prìosan feòla.

A' dol an coinneamh a' bhàis
gun dòchas, gun eagal,
mar gun tilgeadh tu fàd
air na h-èibhleagan beò,
a' feitheamh gus an tèid e 'na luaithre.

Le làmhan paisgte
a' tighinn bhon a' chomanachadh:
pasgadh na h-àbhaist,
is àbhaist na Càisge,
's an comann, an co-chomann,
an dlùthadh, an sgaradh,
a' chuimhne, an dìochuimhn',
an deuchainn, an t-socair,
an locair, a' chnuimh,
a' chuing, an laoidh,
an Gàrradh, an salm,
an t-òran, an iodhlainn,
an iollach, an t-slabhraidh,
an teine, an gràdh,
an gràs, an teine-dè,
an t-ubhal, Àdhamh,
an leabaidh-phòsta,
an eileatrom.

207 bho *Meall Garbh*

Nam bu dia mi,
a' dèanamh nan riaghailtean cloiche
air an t-sliabh seo,

The hand
tired on the table,
wrinkled with inactivity,
white with the rest
of the years,
the skin suspended from the palm,
the nails neat.

Tapping,
jabbing a finger in time's navel,
halfway between going and coming,
locked in a prison of flesh.

Going to meet death
without hope, without fear,
as though you were to throw a peat
on the living embers,
waiting till it turns to ash.

Hands clasped
coming from communion:
customary clasping,
custom of Easter,
and the company, the companionship,
the nearing, the parting,
memory, forgetfulness,
hardship, ease,
the plane, the maggot,
the yoke, the hymn,
the Garden, the psalm,
the song, the cornyard,
the cry, the chain,
the fire, love,
grace, St Anthony's fire,
the apple, Adam,
the bridal bed,
the bier.

from *Meall Garbh*

Were I a god,
making laws in stone
on this upland,

chuirinn na coigrich dhan an fhàsach —
gu Glaschu 's Dùn Dèagh is Bradford,
Bognor Regis is Hull is Southport,
Comar nan Allt is Milton Keynes is Surbiton —
is chuirinn na Gaidheil 'nan àite,
is compiutair na dhà ac'
a dh'innseadh dhaibh anns a' mhionaid
na chaidh a ghoid orra de bhradain,
de chearcan-fraoich 's de ruadh-bhuic,
agus àireamh nam pacaidean fuadain —
cornflakes is pizza is truileis
de gach seòrs' sa chruinne
a thàinig tuath air na Crìochan
bho chaidh a' Phàrlamaid againn a Lunnainn . . .

Lòchaidh is Dochairt gu'n iar
a' treòrachadh chun na cille finne
air bòrd an locha,
seann àiteachas Chlann an Aba
is dìdean an Deòir;
sinn 'nar deòraidhean 'nar dùthaich fhìn,
riaraichte le dèirce,
deònach an sprùilleach as lugha
a ghabhail bho làmhan coimheach,
toilichte le tarcais,
leagte ri leisgeulan,
leaghte le plìon luchd-poilitics,
adhlaicte ann an dìochuimhn' eachdraidh
's a' ghrian a' dol an-iar oirnn.

208   Seanairean

Seanair a' cuimhneachadh a sheanar:
is dòcha gun canadh cuid
nach eil ann ach rumastaireachd na h-aoise,
ruaimlich smuain ann an reumhaireachd dìochuimhn',
ruagaireachd an t-saoghail a bh' ann,
agus s fheudar aideachadh gu bheil sin ann,
ach tha tuilleadh ann —
boillsgeadh dhen tuil tha gar toirt leatha
thar slèibhtean is còmhnardan eachdraidh,
a' taomadh 's a' tòiceadh 's a' turracail,
's a' sìothladh socair gu sèimhe sanais,
sainnseireachd seanar.

I would send the strangers to the wilderness —
to Glasgow and Dundee and Bradford,
Bognor Regis and Hull and Southport,
Cumbernauld and Milton Keynes and Surbiton —
and I would put Gaels in their place,
with a couple of computers
that would tell them in a minute
the number of salmon that had been stolen from them,
the numbers of grouse and roe-deer,
and the number of foreign packets —
cornflakes and pizzas and rubbish
of every kind in the world
that came north of the Border
since our Parliament went to London . . .

Lochay and Dochart to the west
leading to the white church
on the edge of the loch,
old residence of the MacNabs
and refuge of the Dewar;
we are beggars in our own land,
satisfied with alms,
ready to take the tiniest crumbs
from foreign hands,
satisfied with insult,
ready to accept excuses,
melted by the empty smiles of politicians,
buried in history's forgetfulness
while the sun travels to the west.

Grandparents

A grandfather remembering his grandfather:
perhaps some would call that
merely the rambling of old age,
rumbling of thought in the rovings of forgetfulness,
roaming in search of a lost world,
and admittedly that's part of it,
but not the whole story —
there are glimpses of the flood that carries us
over the mountains and plains of history,
spilling, swelling, swinging,
settling silently to the stillness of a whisper,
a grandfather's gabbling.

209   bho *An t-Anam-Fàis*

Tràigh Ghruineard is tràigh Dhunkerque
a' sùghadh fuil nam marbh
anns an eachdraidh bhrùideil
a tha 'nar dualchas,
as bith cò bu choireach,
Caimbeulach no Leathanach,
Hitler no Churchill,
's a leisgeul aig gach fear dhiubh,
na siantan garbh
a' dùnadh bearradh nam biodag,
is seirm nan rann
a' mùchadh le'n coireal
gleadhraich nan lann
is fead nam peilear.

210   *Ròidean Rwanda*

Ròidean fada Rwanda
a' dol 'nan smùid
fo chasan an eagail 's an dòchais
is priobadh an TV
againn an àite aislingean:
nach ann oirnn a thàinig an dà là.

Ach tha mac an duine,
's an nighean aige cuideachd,
iol-chruthachail;
chan fhada
gus am bi na sùilean dubha sin
a' leum a-rithist
le dòchas
no suainte ann an gràdh
no biorach le gion is gamhlas
's na gàirdeanan lapach
a' snaidhmeadh a' ghaoil,
's gam pasgadh an ùrnaigh,
's a' togail nan gunna,
's am Fear tha gu h-àrd
ag ràdh Ris fhèin,
"Carson nach do dh'ionnsaich mi mun DNA

from *The Vegetative Soul*

Gruineard Beach and the shore at Dunkirk
sucking in the blood of the dead
in the brutal history
we inherit,
whoever was to blame,
Campbells or Macleans,
Hitler or Churchill,
and each one has his excuse,
the rough weather
closing the rents made by daggers,
and the music of verse
drowning with its skirling
the clamour of blades
and the whistling of bullets.

The Rwanda Roads

The long roads of Rwanda
turning to dust
under the feet of fear and hope
while we have glimpses of TV pictures
instead of dreams:
times have changed.

But the son of man,
and his daughter too,
are endlessly resurgent;
soon
these dark eyes
will leap again
with hope
or glaze with love
or sharpen with greed and hate
while the listless arms
encircle love,
are clasped in prayer,
and hold the guns,
while the One on High
says to Himself,
"Why didn't I learn about DNA

agus na modhan-cruthachaidh ùr
gus daoine a dhèanamh
a leanadh mo riaghailt
an àite an rathaid lùbaich
shìorraidh
air a bheil mo shluagh a' gluasad
ás an fhairge
's troimh na craobhan
gu saoghal
nach robh mi ag iarraidh?''

Uilleam Nèill (1922—)

211 bho *Sealg Ulaidh*

Ann an seòmar caol an Dùn Éideann
measg leabhar tiorma dustach
chuala mi duine geur tuigseach
fìor-shìol Ghilleòin na h-Àirde
a' dealbhadh faram nan ràmh
no bualadh-chlaidheamh is guth sgaiteach
air bràigh caisteal Inbhir Lòchaidh.

Is tha mo chridhe a' seinn
a dh'ainneoin balbhachd mo dhùthcha
o nach eil mi gu léir ciontach
dhen bhrathadh dheireannach.

212 *Plus ça change*

Duilich a bhith làn dòchais
   Sna làithean bochd a th' againn,
Gach yuppie le òr 'na phòca
   A' tighinn 'na thighearna tharainn.

Dubhchosnadh shìos an Lunnainn
   Fo sgàil chompiutairean mòra,
Bratach ri chur air dùnan
   Eadar Dùn Phris is Bròra.

and the new forms of procreation
that would produce people
who would obey my laws
instead of following this everlasting
winding road
on which my people move
from the sea
through the trees
to a world
I didn't want?"

William Neill (Ayrshire)

from *Treasure Hunt*

In a narrow room in Edinburgh
amongst dry dusty books
I heard a sharp intelligent man
of the true seed of Gilleoin of the Aird
portraying the sound of the oars
or the clash of swords and a scathing voice
on the castle brae of Inverlochy.

And my heart sings
despite the dumbness of my country
because I am not completely guilty
of the final betrayal.

Plus ça change

Hard to be hopeful
   In these wretched times,
Each yuppie with gold in his pocket
   Coming to laird it over us.

Hard labour down in London
   In the shade of great computers,
Flag to be planted on dunghill
   Between Dumfries and Brora.

Le prìs taigh-beag an Docland
  Gach fear a' ceannach chaisteal
Far an òl iad cocktails
  Le caviar nam praisean.

Nigel is Lucinda
  Ag amharc thar an talamh.
Iad fhéin 's na caoraich
  'S na gleanntan fada falamh.

213 Aghaidh ri Aghaidh

Mar bhalach a-rithist air bruach na h-aibhne
lùb mi ghlùn a dh'fhaicinn a-nuas san doimhneachd.
Cha robh breac, no geadas, no doirbeag tighinn 'nam léirsinn
ach a-mhàin sgàthan dubh doilleir fèathach
is bodach liath teagmhach
a' sealltainn orm gu crosta.
Bha mi gun fhoidhidinn gun do chuir e bacadh
air aodann na b' òige choimhead suas orm
los gun innseadh e ciamar a bha
leithid de dh'aighear annam 's mi òg
is iasg leisg fodham air là brèagha samhraidh.

214 Sealltainn thar Chluaidh

Cuimhne leam oidhche dhorcha ghailleannach
deireadh na Samhna, stoirm a' togail sglèat,
gaoth mhòr bheucach bhagrach
'na deann-ruith seachad air Arainn is cathair Shuibhne
's mi air tràigh eadar m' athair 's mo sheanair
is greim teann aca air gach làmh dhiom.
Ged nach b' urrainn dhaibh m' aodann a dhìon
bho sgiùrsair guineach nam frasan,
le acair daingeann gach taobh dhiom
cha b' urrainn na dùilean mo bhriseadh.

Sin thàinig onfhaidhean eil' orm
bho aigeann dorcha gun ghrunnd
's mi gu léir gun acair,
le làmh neo-chinnteach air an stiùir.

With the price of a loo in Dockland
    Each man buying castles
Where they'll drink cocktails
    With caviare by the potload.

Nigel and Lucinda
    Looking over the land.
They and the sheep
    And the long empty glens.

Face to Face

Like a boy again on the bank of the river
I knelt to see down into the depths.
Neither trout, nor pike, nor minnow came into my sight
but only a mirror, black, obscure and calm,
and a grizzled and doubting old man
looking at me peevishly.
I was annoyed that it prevented
a younger face looking up at me
and telling how I knew
such rapture when young
with a lazy fish under me on a lovely summer's day.

Looking over Clyde

I remember a dark night of gales
at the end of November, a storm lifting the slates,
a great roaring threatening wind
in its mad dash past Arran and Suibhne's chair (Ailsa Craig)
when I was on the shore between my father and grandfather
who had a tight grip on both my hands.
Although they could not keep the stinging whip of the showers
from my face,
with a strong anchor on each side of me
the elements could not break me.

Then other tempests came upon me
from a dark bottomless abyss
and I was completely without an anchor,
an uncertain hand on the tiller.

Ach fhuair mi aig a' cheann thall
sàbhailte gu cala, agus tha fèath ann.

Linne Chluaidh mar sgàthan, ciùin fo m' shùil.

215 *Cumha Bhaltair Cinneide 1450–1508*

Chunnaic mi Bhaltair Cinneide
a' coiseachd troimh chlach mo shùla
fo sgàil a' Chaisteil Dhuibh
aig àm laighe na gréine
is grinneal fo chois
air tràigh liath Dhùn Iubhair.

Ach cha robh e an léirsinn
duine air bith eile:
cha chual' iad a cheum
's cha b' urrainn dhaibh idir
a leabhar a leughadh
ged a shìn e dhaibh e;
chan fhac' a' ghràisg ud
an làrach Ghille Bhrìghde
ach ballachan falamh
air am bu toil leo
graffiti ùr a sgròbail
ann an cànain eile.

216 *Stuth Toirmisgte*

Ma théid mi 'nam sheasamh
an-seo air oirthir Ghallabha
chì mi Eilean Mhanainn
gorm glan air fàire ás an dànaig
an stuth toirmisgte mar bhranndaidh,
shìoda, chlàireat, shaorsa, Ghàidhlig.

But in the end I arrived
safely to harbour, and there is calm.

Firth of Clyde like a mirror, gentle under my eyes.

In Memory of Walter Kennedy 1450-1508

I saw Walter Kennedy
walking through the apple of my eye
under the shadow of the Black Vault
at the time of sunset
and gravel under his feet
on the grey beach of Dunure.

But he was not apparent
to any other person:
they did not hear his step
and they could not
read his book
though he offered it to them;
that gang could see nothing
in Gilbert's ruin
but empty walls
where they were pleased
to scratch new graffiti
in another language.

Contraband

If I stand here
on the coast of Galloway
I can see the Isle of Man
clear blue on the horizon from whence came
contraband such as brandy,
silk, claret, freedom, Gaelic.

Calum Dòmhnallach (1922—)

217   *Gu Dé Thachair dha m' Thìr?*

Na feannagan snasail bha aca sna Bàigh
Bha brìoghmhor is torrach air son coirce 's buntàt',
Gun d'leig iad siud seachad, tha 'n talamh 's e bàn,
'S chan fhaicear air uachdar ach luachair a' fàs.

Chan eil treabhadh neo taomadh air na raointean an-iar,
Chan eil todhar ga sgaoileadh, chan eil an t-saothair 'na fhiach —
Gur beag a bha dùil a'm mun tionndaidhinn-sa liath
Gum faicinn mar bhà e, mar fhàsach nam fiadh.

Tha cuimhn' a'm an còmhnaidh bhiodh mòine ga buain,
An connadh bha blàth nuair a dh'fhàsadh i fuar,
Ach far an deach m' àrach tha àireamh dhan t-sluagh
Nach loisg an-diugh fàd dhith — se as fheàrr leotha 'n gual.

Chan eil cùisean an-dràst' mar a bha e 'nam òig':
Chan eil glag aig an spàl a' cur pàtran air clò,
Chan eil lìon dol a shàl, 's chan eil tàbh neo lìn mhór,
Chan eil cearcan air spàrr 's chan eil bàthach le bó.

An cànan a chleachd mi 's a bha tlachdmhor 'nam chluais
'S a thogadh mo chridhe nuair thillinn air chuairt,
'S a dh'ainneoin gach seann rud chaidh a chall son rud nuadh —
Se Ghàidhlig dol bàs tha gam fhàgail fo ghruaim.

Ach s maite ma-thà gur e siud as fheàrr na bhith strì
Ri talamh 's ri àiteach gu'm fàsar dheth sgìth;
Ach cha leig sinn a leas dhol air ais ann an tìm —
Cha bhi e gu bràth mar a bha e ri m' linn.

Torcuil MacRath (1923—)

218   *Cead Deireannach Àirnis*

1   *Roimhn an Dùnadh*

Sann aig Cailean MacÌomhair tha 'n t-ainm bhith ga riaghladh,
   Ach se 'n Duidseach am balach, 's tha gach duine fo spòig;
Smèididh Brownell, 's nì Cailean air Sasainn —
   Tha 'dhunaidh a' maoidh' air 's tha cheann air a' bhòrd.

Malcolm MacDonald (Manish, Harris)

What's Happened to my Land?

The neat lazybeds which they had in the Bays
That were fertile and fruitful for oats and potatoes,
They've let them go fallow, the land's gone to waste,
And nothing's seen growing on its surface but rushes.

There's no ploughing or tillage on fields to the west,
No fertiliser's spread, it's not worth the trouble —
Little did I think before I'd turn grey
That I'd see how it was, like the wilds of the deer.

I remember how peat always used to be reaped,
The fuel that was warm when the weather grew cold,
But where I was raised there's a number of folk
Who won't burn a lump of it — they'd rather have coal.

Things aren't now how it was in my youth:
There's no clack of the shuttle patterning tweed,
No net goes in brine, there's no hand-net or line
No hens upon roost and no byre with a cow.

The language I used which was sweet to my ears
And lifted my heart when I came back to visit,
And in spite of each old thing displaced by a new one —
It's the dying of Gaelic that leaves me depressed.

But then maybe it's better than constantly struggling
With land and with tillage till it leaves you exhausted;
But there's no point in trying to go backwards in time —
It can't be again how it was in my day.

Torcuil MacRath (Grimshader, Lochs, Lewis)

Last Farewell to Arnish

1   *Before the Closure*

Colin Maciver is supposed to be running it,
   But the Dutchman's the lad, we're all subject to him;
When Brownell beckons, Colin heads for England —
   Disaster awaits him and his head's on the block.

Ach sann air madainn Di-Luain a bha mise sa bhruaillean,
    Sann air madainn Di-Luain a bha 'n t-àite fo sgleò —
Cha robh Iain is Ailig a' bruidhinn ri chéile,
    'S bha mise 'nam éiginn, a' falbh ann an ceò.

Se Ailig an t-àrd-fhear os cionn an luchd-tàthaidh
    'S bidh Iain, mar as àbhaist, a' cur an luchd-plàtaidh fo sprochd:
An e innleachdan Phiollaidh dh'fhàg am paidhir ud an Glumaig
    A' cumail sùil air na gillean tha sgiobalta còir?

Mo bheannachd aig na gillean bha cho sgoinneil ag obair,
    Luchd-tàthaidh is eile a chum an t-àite fo sheòl,
A' slaodadh gach 'seacaid' sìos chun na mara —
    Ma leanas iad orra, bidh Brownell air a dhòigh,

Cha téid Cailean a Shasainn 's chan fhaigh Cailean a dhunaidh,
    Cha bhi guth air an Nazi 's air là mór na Roinn Eòrp';
Á tobar na dòrainn gheibh sinn ar beòshlaint —
    Bidh 'n Duidseach 'na phròbhost 's fear Leódhais 'na thràill.

'S nam faighinn-sa caraid a chuireadh fonn air an luinneig,
    Caraid le guth gus am fuaim chur air dòigh,
Chuirinn-s' an tuilleadh 's an tuilleadh ris an luinneig
    Is seinnidh mo charaid i fhathast aig Mòd.

2   *As déidh an Dùnaidh*

Sann dhòmhsa tha e duilich an còrr dheth aithris,
    Sann dhòmhsa tha e duilich an sgeulachd seo ìnns' —
Thàinig an Duidseach á Sasainn, le sannta 'na anam,
    'S chaidh na balaich a sgapadh thar muir agus tìr.

Chaidh na teintean a mhùchadh 's tha na geataichean dùinte
    'S chuir na balaich gu tùrsach an cùl ris an tìr,
Ach thuirt 'Churchill', le gàire, "Tha beath' as déidh Àirnis,
    Tha obair 's ar sàth dhith an coise sàl a' chuain mhóir."

Shìos ann an Glumaig ma nì thu ann tadhal
    Chì thu aitreabh tha snasail air taobh do làimh chlì,
Ach cha thachair ort ann an duine chuireas fàilt' ort no furan
    Mura bi Cailean anns an uinneig 's e 'na shuidhe leis fhéin.

But on Monday morning I was in a dilemma,
   On Monday morning things were under a cloud —
Iain and Alec weren't speaking to each other,
   Leaving me desperate, not knowing what to do.

Alec's the man that's in charge of the welders
   With Iain, as usual, on the nerves of the platers:
Is it the wiles of the Devil that left that pair in Glumag
   Overseeing the lads who are decent and skilled?

A health to the lads who rose to the challenge,
   Welders and others who kept the place on the move,
Dragging each 'jacket' down to the ocean —
   If they go on like this, Brownell will be pleased,

Colin *won't* go to England and *won't* get the chop,
   We'll hear no more of the Nazi and Europe's big day;
From this well of tears we'll all earn our living
   With the Dutchman as provost and the Lewisman his slave.

If I could find a friend to put a tune to the lyrics,
   Some friend with a voice that could make it sound grand,
I'd continue adding extra words to the poem
   And my friend will perform it some day at a Mod.

2   *After the Closure*

The rest of it's sad for me to relate,
   This story's difficult for me to tell —
The Dutchman came from England, greed in his soul,
   And the lads were scattered over ocean and land.

The fires have been doused and the gates have been closed
   And the lads have sadly turned their backs on the land,
But 'Churchill' said, smiling, "There's life after Arnish,
   There's work and no lack of it upon the ocean wave."

Down there in Glumag if you go for a visit
   You'll see a neat building if you look to your left,
But no-one will meet you to welcome or greet you
   Unless Colin's in the window sitting by himself.

219 *Cor na Tìr*

A-raoir dh'éist mi ri luchd-malairt
   'S ri luchd-pàrlamaid le briathran mìn,
'S ged a chualas mòran fhacal
   Cha d'fhuaireas freagairt air cor na tìr.

Bhruidhinn an luchd-malairt air misneachd,
   Bha 'n Tòraidh 's an Làbarach ri chéil' a' strì,
Iad uile sàsaichte le fìon is annlan
   Ged a tha bochdainn anns an tìr.

Ri taobh na sràide chunnacas truaghan
   Ann am bucas cardbord sìnt',
Ach cha do dh'fhaighnich iad dhan truaghan
   Gu dé a bheachd air cor na tìr.

Saoil am faca mi droch aisling,
   Seann eachdraidh a' tighinn beò as ùr?
Nuair bha mis' 'nam bhalachan casruisgt'
   Sann gann bha cosnadh anns an tìr.

Gnìomhachais a' searg 's a' crìonadh,
   A' fàgail nam mìltean ann an dìth,
Is gus an tàinig cogadh oillteil
   Suarach an cosnadh a bh' anns an tìr.

Niall B MacFhionghuin (1925—)

220 *A' Chlach Ionmhainn*

A chlach ionmhainn,
Lia Fàil neo Clach Sgàin, fàilte!
Chuala mi an naidheachd éibhinn
gum bi thu saor bho ghlas na cathrach,
's gun till thu ruinn a-rithist gun dàil.

A chlach ionmhainn, is ionmhainn leinn thu;
mallachd air an rìgh a ghoid thu.
Se Òrd nan Albannach a bh' aca airsan,
an rìgh a rinn cron oirnn 's a thug sgrios;
fada an leigheas, tha fhios againn.

The Country's State

Last night I listened to tycoons
  And politicians with smooth tongues,
And though I heard a lot of words
  The country's state went unresolved.

The tycoons spoke of confidence,
  The Tory and the Labour man debated,
All full of wine and nourishment
  Though there's poverty in the land.

On the street they showed a homeless man
  In a cardboard box stretched out,
But they didn't ask the homeless man
  What he thought of the country's state.

Could it all have been a nightmare,
  Old history coming back to life?
When I ran barefoot as a boy
  Employment was scarce in the land.

Businesses withering and failing,
  Leaving thousands in want,
And till a dreadful war came along
  There was little work in the land.

Neil B MacKinnon (Mull and Aberdeen)

The Dear Stone

Dear stone,
Lia Fàil or Stone of Scone, welcome!
The joyous news I've heard
that from the coronation chair you'll be set free,
that you'll return to us without delay.

Dear stone, we love you dearly;
cursed be the king who stole you.
The Hammer of the Scots they called him,
who brought harm upon us, wrought destruction;
long the healing, as we know.

Lia Fàil neo Clach Sgàin, fàilte!
Gun till thu dhachaigh a-nis sàbhailte
gum faod féin-riaghladh a bhith againn,
a-chum 's gum bi ar tìr neo-eisimeil;
gun till thu ruinn is sinn a' feitheamh
ceud mìle fàilte a chur ort!
Se mo dhùrachd nach till thu a-chaoidh
gu Lunnainn, a chlach ionmhainn.

Catrìona NicDhòmhnaill (1925—)

221 *Cum Sinn Dlùth*

A Rìgh nan Dùl da'n léir gach neach air thalamh,
    Bi-sa dlùth nuair dh'iadhas duibhre dhorch' —
Tha stoirmean garbh' na beatha cruaidh ri'n giùlan
    'S tha solas geal an dòchais doirbh ri lorg:
Cum sinn dlùth, cum sinn dlùth,
Cum sinn dlùth fo dhìon 's fo sgiath do thròcair chaoimh.

Tha sinn cho fosgailt' do gach seòrsa cunnairt,
    'S có tha foghainteach fa chomhair deuchainn cràidh?
Ach bi-sa dhuinn 'nad sgiath 's cuir sinn 'nad fhasgadh
    'S gun gabh ar cridhe fois, 's ar n-earbs' 'nad ghràdh:
Cum sinn dlùth, cum sinn dlùth,
Cum sinn dlùth fo dhìon 's fo sgiath do thròcair chaoimh.

Nuair dhùmhlaicheas an dorchadas mun cuairt dhinn
    'S nach léir dhuinn 'n ceum a tha fo'r bonn,
Thoir òirnn bhith suidhe sìos gu socair stòlda,
    Ciùinich Fhéin am bruaillean tha 'nar com:
Cum sinn dlùth, cum sinn dlùth,
Cum sinn dlùth fo dhìon 's fo sgiath do thròcair chaoimh.

Tog ar sùilean trom' a-rithist suas gu d' ionnsaigh,
    Sgap na sgòthan chum 's gum faic sinn solas iùil,
Nochd thu fhéin tron chléith o chùl a' bhalla
    'S cluinneamaid do ghuth ag ràdh, "Thig leam."
Cum sinn dlùth, cum sinn dlùth,
Cum sinn dlùth fo dhìon 's fo sgiath do thròcair chaoimh.

Lia Fàil or Stone of Scone, welcome!
Now may you return home safely
that we may govern ourselves once more,
that our land be independent;
return to us for we are waiting
to welcome you a hundred thousand times!
That you may never return to London
is my earnest wish, dear stone.

Catherine Macdonald (Staffin, Skye)

Hold Us Close

O King of the Elements who sees every person on earth,
   Be Thou close when impenetrable darkness surrounds us —
The wild tempests of life are difficult to bear
   And the bright light of hope is hard to detect:
Hold us close, hold us close,
Hold us close protected by Thy gentle mercy's wing.

We are so open to each kind of danger,
   And who is strong enough to face the test of pain?
But be to us a shield and give us Thy protection
   To let our heart find rest, trusting in Thy love:
Hold us close, hold us close,
Hold us close protected by Thy gentle mercy's wing.

When the darkness intensifies around us
   And we cannot see the path that's underneath our sole,
Make us sit down with stoic ease,
   Calm Thou the panic in our breast:
Hold us close, hold us close,
Hold us close protected by Thy gentle mercy's wing.

Raise our drooping eyelids up again to Thee,
   Disperse the clouds to let us see a guiding light,
Show Thyself through the wattle from behind the wall
   And let us hear Thy voice saying, "Come with me."
Hold us close, hold us close,
Hold us close protected by Thy gentle mercy's wing.

Is théid sinn leat, a dh'ainneoin dragh is àmhghair,
　　Ged bhiodh an t-slighe dorcha mar tro cheò —
S Tu an caraid s dlùithe leanas ruinn na bràthair,
　　Truasail, dìleas thar gach duine beò:
Cum sinn dlùth, cum sinn dlùth,
Cum sinn dlùth fo dhìon 's fo sgiath Do thròcair chaoimh.

'S nuair thig an t-àm san ruig sinn ceann na slighe
　　'S a chì sinn sealladh soilleir air gach nì a bhà,
Tuigidh sinn an-sin do Làmh a smachdaich;
　　Ach gus a-sin, ar n-ùrnaigh théid an àird':
Cum sinn dlùth, cum sinn dlùth,
Cum sinn dlùth fo dhìon 's fo sgiath do thròcair chaoimh.

222　*An t-Aoibhneas a tha staigh sa Chridhe*

An t-aoibhneas seo tha staigh 'nam chrìdh
　　Cha dealaich nì air talamh rium,
Se th' ann ach tiodhlac dhomh o Dhia
　　'S air uairean lìonar m' anam leis.

A dh'ainneoin trioblaid agus teinn
　　Bhios tadhal orm sa bheatha seo,
Bidh 'n t-aoibhneas seo gam thogail suas
　　'S gam chur os cionn nan nithean seo.

Chan iarrainn dealach' ris a-chaoidh —
　　Bidh nèamh cho dlùth 's cho aithnicht' dhomh,
Is labhraidh mi ri Fear mo Ghràidh
　　Is innsidh mi gur toil leam E.

Tha Fear mo Ghràidh-sa geal is dearg,
　　Toil-inntinn bhith 'na chuideachd-san,
Is fhuair mi uaithe trusgan ùr
　　Rinn tàillear grinn nam Flaitheanas.

Bidh 'n t-aoibhneas seo gam chur gu ceòl
　　'S b'e sin an ceòl tha barraichte,
Is bristidh e a-mach mar thuil
　　Is togaidh e bhon talamh mi.

And with Thee we will go, despite trouble and anguish,
    Though the way may be dark as if through a mist —
Thou art the friend that stays closer to us than a brother,
    Compassionate, loyal beyond any person alive:
Hold us close, hold us close,
Hold us close protected by Thy gentle mercy's wing.

And when the moment comes for us to reach our journey's end
    And when we clearly get a sight of everything that's been,
Then we'll understand Thy Hand that chastised;
    But till then, it's our prayer that will arise:
Hold us close, hold us close,
Hold us close protected by Thy gentle mercy's wing.

The Joy that is inside the Heart

This joy that lies inside my heart
    Nothing on earth will part from me,
For it's a gift to me from God
    And there are times it fills my soul.

For all the trouble and distress
    That prey upon me in this life,
This joy can lift me up on high
    And set me over things like that.

I'd never want to part from it —
    Heaven's close and known to me,
And I speak to Him I Love
    And tell Him I adore Him.

The One I Love is red and white,
    It's a pleasure to be with Him,
And He gave me a new garment
    Made by Heaven's skilful tailor.

This joy sets me music-making
    And marvellous music it is too,
For it bursts out like a flood
    And lifts me up above the ground.

Ged gheibhte mi 'm measg mhóran sluaigh
    'S nach aithnichinn aon anam dhiubh,
Lasaidh 'n t-aoibhneas seo 'nam chrìdh
    'S e air gach aon dhiubh falaichte.

Air leabaidh trioblaid agus teinn
    Is pian gam fhàgail anshocrach,
Nì 'n t-aoibhneas seo mo chrìdh cho blàth
    'S mo chluasag nì e cofhartail.

Am meadhan ùpraid an t-saoghail
    'S gach nì a bhios cur cabhaig orm,
Nì 'n t-aoibhneas seo mo chur gu sunnd
    'S bidh m' obair aotrom aigeannach.

O ùghdair bheannaichte mo chiùil,
    Uat Fhéin a thàinig m' òran-sa,
'S is e mo thlachd 's mo mhiann gach là
    Do làthaireachd bhith còmhla rium.

Tha sùil agam nuair gheibh mi suas
    Bhith seinn sa chòisir shònraicht' dhut;
An t-àit' as ìsle gheibh mi 'n-siud,
    Se urram mór bhios dhòmhsa ann.

Dòmhnall Aonghais Bhàin (1926—)

223 *Am Faoilteach* (bho *Mìosan na Bliadhna*)

Stoirm is gailleann 's deilge shìontan,
Frasan sneachda 's càblaid fhiadhaich,
Reodh-ghaoth snaidheadh feadh nan crìochan,
                    Aimsir ùdlaidh;
Aingealtachd air fiamh nan speuran,
Splèachdach neòil air aodann gréine,
Connspaid iargailleach ag éirigh
                    Air na dùilean;
Mìos an Fhaoiltich rinn a dhranndail,
Toirt gu chrìch an ràidhe geamhraidh,
Géilleachdainn do thìm 'na deann-ruith
                    Triall a chùrsa.

If I find myself in a crowd of folk
   Without a soul of them known to me,
This joy just lights up in my heart
   Hidden to every one of them.

On bed of trouble and distress
   Where pain leaves me afflicted,
This joy makes my heart so warm
   And brings comfort to my pillow.

Amidst the bustle of the world
   And all that makes me hurry,
This joy serves to bear me up
   And my work is light and cheery.

O blessed subject of my song,
   From Thee has come my music,
My pleasure and desire each day
   Is to have Thy presence near me.

When I go up I hope to sing
   In the special choir for Thee;
The lowest place that I get there
   A great honour will it be to me.

Donald MacDonald (S. Lochboisdale, S. Uist)

January (from The Months of the Year)

Storm and tempest and skewer of hurricanes,
Showers of snow and angry confusion,
Icy wind carving its way through the land,
          Surly weather;
Wickedness in the skies' expression,
Squinting are clouds on the face of the sun,
Warlike dispute comes up to the surface
          Of the elements;
The month of the Wolftime has given its snarl,
Bringing an end to the winter quarter,
Ceding to time in her frantic onrush
          Its momentum.

224   *Moladh Mnathan-Eiridinn Ospadal an Rathaig Mhóir, Inbhir Nis*

Bhon fhuair mi léirsinn is fradharc ùr
Mo pheann gun gleus mi le séist is sunnd,
    'S gun inn's mi càirdeas nam mnathan gràdhach
Chuir geamhradh gràineil 'na ghàrradh fhlùr.

Tha Annag chiatach mar ghrian an àigh,
Is Sìneag rianail nam basan bàn —
    Clann-nighean cliutha á tìr mo dhùthchais
Chuir long deagh-dhùrachd fo shiùil gu sàl.

Tha Maureen rìomhach nam mìltean beus
A thogadh òg am Bail' Ùr an t-Sléibh,
    Tha gaol ri àiteas 'na h-aodann bàidheil
Mar òr a' deàrrsadh am measg nan seud.

Am measg a' chòmhlain tha òrdail grinn
Tha rìbhinn bhòidheach á Rubh' na h-Aoidh,
    Á Eilean Leòdhais an fhraoich 's na mònadh
Far 'n tric bhios òrain le ceòl gan seinn.

Tha té á Sgalpaigh, Raonaid 'IcSuain,
A dh'fhàs mar neòinean feadh chòs nan cluan —
    Mar ghrian san fhaoilteach tha h-ìomhaigh aoigheil
'S a deud mar fhaoileag air bhàrr nan stuadh.

Tha té á Éirinn a-nall thar chuan,
Tìr nan raointean tha daonnan uain',
    'S tha té bheag bhàn ann cho loinneil càirdeil
Ri reul na h-àilleachd san àird a-tuath.

Mo bheannachd bhuan a bhith ac' gu léir,
Gach àit' an gluais iad 's an dèan iad ceum —
    Bidh gaol is càirdeas far 'm bi an tàmhachd
Mar bhoillsgeadh gràsmhor gu bràch nach tréig.

In Praise of the Nurses of Raigmore Hospital, Inverness

Since I got vision and sight anew
My pen I'll wield with music and cheer,
     To speak of the care of those loving girls
Who made of harsh winter a garden of flowers.

Lovely Annie like glorious sunshine,
Unruffled Jeannie of fair white palms —
     Girls of repute from the land of my forebears
Who've put this ship of good wishes to sea.

Beautiful Maureen of thousands of virtues,
In Newtonmore village she was brought up when young,
     Tenderness dwells in her kindly face
Like gold that shines in the midst of jewels.

Among the group that's calm and pretty
Is a beautiful girl from Point of the Eye,
     From the Isle of Lewis of heather and peat
Where so often songs are performed to music.

There's a girl from Scalpay, Rachel MacSween,
Who grew like a daisy in the nooks of the fields —
     Like the sun in the wolftime is her welcoming face
With her teeth like a gull on the tips of the waves.

There's one from Ireland across the sea,
The land of the fields forever green,
     There's a blonde little girl as lovely and kind
As the beautiful star of the northern skies.

May my blessing forever go out to them all,
Wherever they go, every step that they take —
     There'll be kindness and love wherever they stay
Like a graceful gleam that will never fade.

225   A' Mhaighdeann Chriadhadh

Sann madainn Di-Dòmhnaich a chunnaic mi 'n ògbhean
A lìon mi le sòlas 's a chuir dòchas 'nam phàirt:
Bha i cho ùrar ri gàrradh nan ùbhlan
Air an còmhdach le driùchd tigh'nn cho cùbhraidh bhon àird.

Ged shéideadh an tuath-ghaoth le gailleann an uabhais,
Tha còta mu h-uachdar nach lig fuachd 'na a pàirt;
Ged dheàrrsadh a' ghrian oirr' á speuran na h-iarmailt',
Cha loisg i gu sìorraidh rìbhinn chiat' a' chùil bhàin.

Thug mi beannachd na sìth' dhi, le cleamhnas is dìlseachd,
'S ged nach d'fhreagair i mì, cha robh nì mach á àit' —
Si chriadh th' annam fhìn, chan eil teagamh nach fìrinn,
Nuair théid mo shìneadh gu h-ìosal sna clàran.

Tormod Calum Dòmhnallach (1927—)

226   Eathar Angaidh

Cha robh sàs ach an t-sàil aic'
Tigh'nn timcheall Rubha Bhataisgeir,
    Na balaich le greim oirr' gu cruaidh,
Angaidh aig a' chuibhle
Ga stiùireadh tro ghuailnean
    Nan suailean bha bualadh le fuaim.

Am bus aic' ag éirigh
Suas do na speuran,
    Poggy le shròin don ghaoith,
Sky 's e 'na lùban
Ri cunntadh nan crùbag —
    Chan aithne dhomh 'n còrr a dheadh innt'.

Rug iad air poidsear
Muigh air Tràigh Tholastaidh,
    Thug iad gu cùirt e gun dàil,
Ach dé thubhairt an Siorram,
Thubhairt e, "Not proven."
    Tha nise na balaich gun chàil.

The Doll

On Sunday morning I saw a young lady
  Who filled me with joy and gave me some hope:
She was as fresh as a garden of apples
  All covered in dew coming sweet from above.

Should the northerly wind blow a terrible storm,
  She's wrapped in a coat that will keep out the cold;
Should the sun shine upon her from the skies of the firmament,
  Never will it burn that beautiful blonde.

I greeted her warmly, with fellow-feeling and loyalty,
  And though she didn't respond, it was all as it ought to be —
I'll be clay too, there's no doubting the truth of it,
  When I'm laid out below in the boards of my coffin.

Norman Malcolm Macdonald (Tong, Lewis)

Angie's Boat

Erect on her keel
Rounding Vatisker Point,
  The lads held on to her tight,
Angie stood at the wheel
Steering over the mountains
  Of billows pounding with noise.

Her prow going up,
Up to the heavens,
  Poggy's nose to the wind,
Sky bending double
Counting the crabs —
  I know nobody else who'd fit in.

They caught a poacher
On the ebb out at Tolsta,
  And straightaway brought him to court,
But what did the Sheriff say,
"Not proven," he declared.
  Now the lads have no means of support.

Chan eil lìon beag san àite
Air a bhiadhadh cho càilear
 Ri na sreangan aig balaich Àird Thung,
Ach is beag feum nì seo dhaibh
Is bàtan móra làidir
 Ri sgrìobadh a-staigh air a' ghrunnd.

Cha robh sàs ach an t-sàil aic'
Tigh'nn timcheall Rubha Bhataisgeir,
 Na balaich le greim oirr' gu cruaidh,
Angaidh aig a' chuibhle
Ga stiùireadh tro ghuailnean
 Nan suailean bha bualadh le fuaim.

Iain Mac a' Ghobhainn (1928–98)

227 *Tha thu air aigeann m' inntinn*

Gun fhios dhomh tha thu air aigeann m' inntinn
mar fhear-tadhail grunnd na mara
le chlogaid 's a dhà shùil mhóir,
's chan aithne dhomh ceart t' fhiamh no do dhòigh
an déidh cóig bliadhna shiantan
time dòrtadh eadar mise 's tù:

beanntan bùirn gun ainm a' dòrtadh
eadar mise gad shlaodadh air bòrd
's t' fhiamh 's do dhòighean 'nam làmhan fann.
Chaidh thu air chall
am measg lusan dìomhair a' ghrunna
anns an leth-sholas uaine gun ghràdh,

's chan éirich thu chaoidh air bhàrr cuain
a-chaoidh 's mo làmhan a' slaodadh gun sgur,
's chan aithne dhomh do shlighe idir,
thus' ann an leth-sholas do shuain
a' tathaich aigeann na mara gun tàmh
's mise slaodadh 's a' slaodadh air uachdar cuain.

No small-line in the place
Is as temptingly baited
    As the strings of the men from Aird Tong,
But they see little point in it
When boats big and strong
    Are coming in to trawl the sea-bottom.

Erect on her keel
Rounding Vatisker Point,
    The lads held on to her tight,
Angie stood at the wheel
Steering over the mountains
    Of billows pounding with noise.

Iain Crichton Smith (Bayble, Point, Lewis)

You are at the bottom of my mind

Without my knowing it you are at the bottom of my mind
like a visitor to the bottom of the sea
with his helmet and his two large eyes,
and I do not rightly know your appearance or your manner
after five years of showers
of time pouring between me and you:

nameless mountains of water pouring
between me hauling you on board
and your appearance and manner in my weak hands.
You went astray
among the mysterious plants of the sea-bed
in the green half-light without love,

and you will never rise to the surface
though my hands are hauling ceaselessly,
and I do not know your way at all,
you in the half-light of your sleep
haunting the bed of the sea without ceasing
and I hauling and hauling on the surface.

228   Aig a' Chladh

Chunna mi aig a' chladh an-dé iad,
    Le adan dubh orr', 's grian ag éirigh,
Deàrrsadh dhìtheanan mu'n casan
    Is fear a' caitheamh searbh-léine.

Lasair an adhair, cuan a' seinn,
    Dòrtadh fheur, is seasmhachd bheann,
Còmhradh bàsmhor adan dorcha,
    Bàrdachd samhraidh bun-os-cionn.

Latha farsaing fad' air fàire,
    Bìoball a' losgadh ann an làmhan
Gaoithe 's gréine, 's cuan a' tuiteam
    Mar dheise fhalamh air an tràigh ud.

'S tha esan a-nise far a bheil e,
    Mo nàbaidh 'na laighe fon t-seillean
A' crònan am measg dhìthean milis.
    B'e 'm bàs a thug bàs dha 's cha b'e 'm peileir.

Is grian a' dòrtadh, cuan a' dòrtadh,
    Adan dubh' gu dorch a' seòladh
Air cuan ròsan mar a dh'fhalbhas
    Facail bhochd air làn na ceòlraidh.

229   An Litir Àraid

Chuir mi litir gu mo ghaol,
    Pàirt dhith am Beurla 's pàirt an Gàidhlig:
"I love you" air an dara taobh,
    'S air an taobh eile: "Tha mo ghràdh ort."

Ach fhreagair i anns na facail sa:
    "Se a dh'iarrainn na laigheas fon dà chànan,
Bruadairean nan daoine marbh,
    Lainnir a' chuain mhóir 's a ghàire."

At the Cemetery

I saw them yesterday at the cemetery
   Wearing black hats, while a sun was rising,
A glowing of flowers about their feet
   And one wearing a salt shirt.

Glitter of the sky, sea singing,
   Pouring of grass, steadiness of mountains,
Mortal conversation of black hats,
   Poetry of summer topsy-turvy.

A long wide day on the horizon,
   A Bible burning in the hands
Of wind and sun, and a sea falling
   Like an empty dress on that shore.

But he is now where he is,
   My neighbour lying under the bee
That is humming among sweet flowers.
   It was death that killed him and not the bullet.

Sun pouring, sea pouring,
   Black hats darkly sailing
On a sea of roses as there sail
   Poor words on a full tide of music.

The Strange Letter

I sent a letter to my love,
   Part of it in English and part in Gaelic:
"I love you" on the one side,
   And on the other: "Tha mo ghràdh ort."

But she answered in these words:
   "What I would want is what lies under the two languages,
The dreams of the dead,
   The gleam of the great ocean and its cry."

230 *An t-Òban*

1   Tha an t-uisg a' drùdhadh air an Òban,
      's an sarcas air falbh dhachaigh.
      Na leómhannan 's na cait-fhiadhaich
      's na beathaichean eile (chan eil Gàidhlig againn
      air an son-san), dh'fhalbh iad dhachaigh
      troimh na pàipearan, sanasan-reice.
      Tha na seataichean a' fàs falamh
      aig beul na tràghad, beul nan taighean,
      beul an taigh-òsta — uisg a' tuiteam
      troimh mheadhon sàl trom na mara.

2   An tog mi baile de phàipear?
      Le leómhannan dathte air a' bhalla?
      Le tìgearan móra borba,
      's cuibhl' a' chiùil a' cur char dhith?

      An tog mi adhar de phàipear?
      Sgòthan pàipeir, solais gheala?
      An tog mi mi fhìn de phàipear,
      's air pàipear na rainn gan gearradh?

3   Tha am muir a-nochd mar shanas-reice,
      leabhar an déidh leabhair a' deàlradh.
      Tha m' fhaileas a' ruith sìos don chuan.
      Tha mo chraiceann dearg is uaine.

      Có sgrìobh mi? Có tha dèanamh bàrdachd
      shanas-reice de mo chnàmhan?
      Togaidh mi mo dhòrn gorm riutha:
      "Gaidheal calma le a chànan."

4   Dh'fhalbh an sarcas dhachaigh.
      Sguab iad a' mhin-shàibh air falbh.
      Dh'fhalbh dealbhan nam biastan.
      Tha 'n t-uisg a' tuiteam air a' bhàgh.

      Dh'fhalbh a' chuibhle leatha fhéin.
      Tha an seuson a-nis seachad.
      Tha an leómhann a' ruith troimhn ghréin.
      Dh'fhàg e an t-uisg air cùl a chasan.

Oban

1   The rain is penetrating Oban,
and the circus has gone home.
The lions and wildcats
and the other beasts (we have no Gaelic
for them) have gone home
through the papers and advertisements.
The seats are emptying
at the mouth of the shore, in front of the houses,
in front of the pub — rain falling
through the midst of the heavy salt of the sea.

2   Shall I raise a town of paper?
With coloured lions on the wall?
With great fierce tigers,
and the wheel of music spinning?

Shall I raise a sky of paper?
Clouds of paper, white lights?
Shall I make myself into paper,
with my verses being cut on paper?

3   Tonight the sea is like an advertisement,
book after book shining.
My shadow is running down to the sea.
My skin is red and green.

Who wrote me? Who is making a poetry
of advertisements from my bones?
I will raise my blue fist to them:
"A stout Highlander with his language."

4   The circus has gone home.
They have swept the sawdust away.
The pictures of beasts have gone.
The rain is falling on the bay.

The wheel has gone off by itself.
The season is now over.
The lion is running through sunlight.
He has left the rain behind his feet.

5   Thòisich an clag mór a' bualadh.
     Tha an eaglais air a fosgladh.
     Shuidh mi sìos innte 'nam inntinn
     's chunna mi air an uinneig,
     an àite Nàzareth 's an Crìostaidh,
     talamh caithte is min-shàibh,
     leómhann a' falbh air buaile
     spreadhte Phalestine gun tàmh.

231   Na Seanfhacail

Sheòl na seanfhacail
gu cala sàmhach
far an robh na bàtaichean
eile. Far an robh iad uile,
baile de shiùil dhonna
a' tiormachadh anns a' ghréin.

232   Coinnichidh sinn

"Coinnichidh sinn uaireigin,"
ars esan,
"ann an àite gun iomagain,
ann am baile neochiontach
far am bi sìth gun deireadh."

Cha dubhairt i smid.
Dh'fhairich i an reothadh
ás a' bhaile neochiontach sin
's na rionnagan spioradail
a' dèanamh a broilleach fuar.

233   Mas e Ghàidhlig an cànan

1   Mas e Ghàidhlig an cànan
     a bh' ac' ann an Eden,
     an e sin fhéin as coireach
     gu bheil an cionta gar lìonadh
     's gu bheil sinn cho mollaicht'
     's nach fhaic sinn le fìrinn
     air Leódhas beag corrach
     ròsan no frìthean?

5   The big bell began to peal.
The church has been opened.
I sat down inside it in my mind
and saw on the window,
instead of Nazareth and Christ,
worn earth and sawdust,
a lion moving in the explosive
circle of Palestine without cease.

The Proverbs

The proverbs sailed
to a quiet harbour
where the other boats
were. Where they all were,
a city of brown sails
drying in the sun.

We will meet

"We will meet some time,"
said he,
"in a place without anxiety,
in a township of innocence
where there's peace without end."

She said not a word.
She sensed the frost
from that innocent township
with the spiritual stars
making her breast cold.

If Gaelic is the language

1   If Gaelic is the language
that they spoke in Eden,
is that itself the reason
that we're full of guilt
and that we're so accursed
that we can't see with truth
on little rugged Lewis
roses or deer-forests?

2   Mas e Ghàidhlig an cànan
     a bh' ac' ann an Eden
     dé thubhairt Àdhamh ri Eubha
     nuair a chaill e chuid fearainn,
     gach croit agus abhainn,
     an ubhal bu mhath leis,
     có bhiodh 'na h-àite
     is ise gun fhàinne
     is esan an sàs innt'?
     Oir dh'fheumadh e nise
     bhith togail bhuntàta.
     Tha mi cinnteach nach cluinnte
     eadhon an Gàidhlig
     am facal a thubhairt e
     's an dithis a' siubhal bho
     bhòidhchead a' ghàrraidh.
     Ach co-dhiù chuir e 'n cliabh oirr'
     an déidh Pàrrais fhàgail
     's bha i iomadach bliadhna
     a' cliathadh bhuntàta.

3   Mas e Ghàidhlig an cànan
     a bh' ac' ann an Eden
     car son a bha Eubha
     'na suidhe gun aodach
     's a cìochan neo-dhiadhaidh
     cho saor ris na gaoithtean?
     Bha fear dubh ri a cliathaich
     le feusaig 's le Bìoball
     's e uabhasach fiadhaich
     le pathadh gun fhaochadh.

4   Mas e Ghàidhlig an cànan
     a bh' ac' ann an Eden
     dé na facail thubhairt Dia riu
     nuair a chuir e fo sgaoil iad?
     "Bha mi toilicht a-riamh
     a bhith 'g éisteachd ri music
     ach se Mozart as àill leam
     na bhur rannan beag aotrom."

2   If Gaelic is the language
that they spoke in Eden
what did Adam say to Eve
when he lost his land,
every croft and river,
the apple he loved,
who'd have her place
and she with no ring
and he telling her off?
For now he would have to
be lifting potatoes.
Never heard I am sure
even in Gaelic
is the word he said
when the pair were departing
the beauty of the garden.
But anyway he put the creel on her
when Paradise was behind them
and she was many a year
planting potatoes.

3   If Gaelic is the language
that they spoke in Eden
why did Eve
sit without clothes
and her godless breasts
as free as the winds?
A dark man was beside her
with beard and with Bible
looking terribly fierce
from unrelieved thirst.

4   If Gaelic is the language
that they spoke in Eden
what words did God say to them
when He sent them away?
"I was always content
to be listening to *music*
but I'd rather have Mozart
than your light little rhymes."

5   Ars Eubha ri Àdhamh,
"An cluinn thu MacDhòmhnaill?
Tha e 'g ràdh ri càch
gur e Ghàidhlig bu chaomh leinn:
ach tha mi duilich a ràdh
gu bheil mo naidhlons cho surely
ri clòimh a' dol bàs
's nach eil seans' ann air bùithtean."

6   Nuair a ràinig i bùth
sann a fhuair i mascàra
's a-rithist blouse ùr
agus rouge agus clàran
's bha i cho toilicht ri diùc
air Sràid Sauchiehall
a bha uair am measg fhlùr-
annan gucagach Phàrrais.

234 *Innsidh mi dhut mar a thachair*

Innsidh mi dhut mar a thachair.
Bha mi air cabhsair an Glaschu
nuair a chunnaic mi
a' deàlradh air balla
"Gealach abachaidh an eòrna —
bheir i sinne Leódhas dhachaigh."

Bha seo àraidh, nach robh,
aig àm na Nollaig —
cha robh Gaidheal ri fhaicinn,
cha robh càil ann ach craiceann
de gheal 's de dh'uaine 's de dhearg
's mu chuairt orm an t-sràid fhalamh.
Co-dhiù thug e gu m' chuimhne
cruachan-mònach, muir is teine,
etcetera.

'S aon oidhche cuideachd
's mi 'nam laighe 'nam leabaidh
chunna mi an *Caióra* a' seòladh
mar gum b'ann air madainn
samhraidh tarsainn air an dreasair —

5   Eve said to Adam,
"Do you hear MacDonald?
He's saying to the others
that we preferred Gaelic:
but I'm sorry to say
that my nylons are dying
as *surely* as wool
and there's no chance of shops."

6   When she got to a shop
what she bought was mascara
and a new blouse as well
and rouge and some records
and happy as a lord was she
on Sauchiehall Street
who was once among the bud-
ding blooms of Paradise.

I'll tell you how it happened

I'll tell you how it happened.
I was on a pavement in Glasgow
when I saw
shining on a wall
"The moon that ripens the barley —
she will take us home to Lewis."

This was odd, wasn't it,
at Christmastime —
not a Highlander in sight,
there was nothing but skin
that was white and green and red
and round about me the empty street.
Anyway it brought to my memory
peat-stacks, sea and fire,
etcetera.

And one night too
as I lay in my bed
I saw the *Kai-Ora* sailing
as if on a summer's
morning across the dresser —

's an rùm cho geal ri gruth no bainne —
tha sibh a' tuigsinn — leis a' ghealaich.

Ach se bu mhìorbhail i buileach
(tha mi 'g obair ann an oifis)
an àite nam pàipearan
ris am bi mi déiligeadh
chunna mi air madainn Samhain
"An Eala Bhàn" 's e sgrìobhte
air mo dhasc gu fìor dhaingeann.

Uill, tha mi ciallach gu leòr,
se sin co-dhiù mo bharail.
Ach tha e àraidh
a bhith fuireach ann am baile
's a' coiseachd troimh shràidean
cho buidhe 's cho falamh
's a' coimhead òrain dhathte
ach, uill, feumaidh mi innse dhuibh,
chunna mi an-dé fhéin
sgrìobhte gu soilleir air balla
BUY BRITISH BUY HAIG
's os a chionn
     AM BATA DARACH.

235   A' Ghaoth

Tha a' ghaoth a' séideadh anns an t-simileir.
Có air a tha i gearain fad na h-oidhch'?
Gu bheil i gun ainm? Nach eil duine bruidhinn oirre
nuair a tha i sàmhach anns a' choill?
A bheil i air son gun toir sinn an aire dhi?
An e sin as coireach gum bris i ar bàtaichean,
gun cuir i ás do ar taighean màrbhail,
gum bàth i ar seòladairean anns a' chuan?
'S nuair a chì i ùmhlachd 'nar n-aodannan
am fàs i sàmhach a-rithist, an téid i chadal,
le a broinn làn, le a ceann aotrom is ciùin?

and the room as white as crowdie or milk —
you understand — with the moon.

But what was more miraculous still
(I work in an office)
instead of the papers
that I deal with
I saw one November morning
"The White Swan" written
on my desk in all firmness.

Well, I'm sane enough,
that's what I think at least.
But it's odd
to be living in a city
and walking through streets
so yellow and so empty
and seeing coloured songs
but, well, I must tell you,
I saw only yesterday
written clearly on a wall
BUY BRITISH BUY HAIG
and above it
    THE OAKEN STICK.

The Wind

The wind is blowing in the chimney.
What's it complaining about all night?
That it has no name? That no-one talks about it
when it is silent in the wood?
Is it trying to attract our attention?
Is that why it breaks our boats,
destroys our marble houses,
drowns our sailors in the sea?
And when it sees humility in our faces
does it grow quiet again, go to sleep,
with its belly full, its head light and calm?

236   *Aig an Doras*

Ai ai
obh obh
tha na Jehovah's Witnesses aig an doras.
Tha iad a' sgrùdadh mo bheatha
air an latha stoirmeil seo
leis a' Bhìoball aca fhéin.

Tha duslach air an uinneig a th' air an staidhre
(chì mi air an cùlaibh i)
tha a solas doilleir tréigt!

237   *An TV*

Tha a' ghrian ag éirigh gach latha
á faileasan falbhach —
air an TV.

Cha do chreid sinn gun robh Éirinn ann
gus am faca sinn i iomadh oidhche —
air an TV.

Tha e nas fhaisge air Humphrey Bogart
na tha e air Tormod Mór —
on fhuair e an TV.

Arsa Plato —
"Tha sinn ceangailte ann an uaimh" —
se sin an TV.

Thàinig nighean a-steach do rùm
gun bholtrach gun fhiamh —
ás an TV.

Mu dheireadh chaill e an saoghal
mar a thubhairt Berkeley —
cha robh ann ach an TV.

Cheannaich e *War and Peace*,
Tolstoy, tha mi ciallachadh,
an déidh fhaicinn air an TV.

At the Door

Aye aye
oh dear
the Jehovah's Witnesses are at the door.
They examine my life
on this stormy day
with their own Bible.

There's dust on the stair window
(I can see it behind them)
its light is dim, forlorn!

The TV

The sun rises every day
out of fleeting shadows —
on the TV.

We didn't believe Ireland was happening
till we saw it night after night —
on the TV.

He's closer to Humphrey Bogart
than he is to Tormod Mór —
since he got the TV.

Said Plato —
"We are tied up in a cave" —
that's the TV.

A girl came into a room
without scent or colour —
out of the TV.

In the end he lost the world
as Berkeley said —
there was only the TV.

He bought *War and Peace*,
Tolstoy, I mean,
after seeing it on the TV.

Nuair a chuir e ás an TV
chaidh an saoghal ás —
chaidh e fhéin ás.

Cha dàinig a làmhan air ais thuige
no a shùilean
gus an do chuir e air an TV.

Ròs ann am bóla air an TV,
na nithean a th' anns an t-saoghal,
's na nithean nach eil.

Fhuair e e fhéin ann an sgialachd
's chan fhaigheadh e aiste
air an TV.

Bha e anns an sgialachd:
bha e anns an rùm.
Cha robh fhios càit an robh e.

S tù a ghràidh as fheàrr leam
na *Softly Softly*
no *Sportsnight with Coleman.*

An seòmraichean glaiste le geatachan iarainn
ach a ghràidh
a bheil TV annta?

238   *Na h-Eilthirich*

A liuthad soitheach a dh'fhàg ar dùthaich
le sgiathan geala a' toirt Chanada orra.
Tha iad mar neapaigearan 'nar cuimhne
's an sàl mar dheòirean
's anns na croinn aca seòladairean a' seinn
mar eòin air gheugan.

Muir a' Mhàigh ud, gu gorm a' ruith,
gealach air an oidhch', grian air an latha,
ach a' ghealach mar mheas buidhe,
mar thruinnsear air balla,
ris an tog iad an làmhan,

When he put off the TV
the world went off —
he went off himself.

He had not got his hands back
or his eyes
till he put on the TV.

A rose in a bowl on the TV,
the things that are in the world,
and the things that aren't.

He found himself in a story
and couldn't escape from it
on the TV.

He was in the story:
he was in the room.
There was no knowing where he was.

I'd rather have you my love
than *Softly Softly*
or *Sportsnight with Coleman.*

In locked rooms with iron gates
but my love
is there TV in them?

The Emigrants

The many ships that left our country
with white wings for Canada.
They are like handkerchiefs in our memories
and the brine like tears
and in their masts sailors singing
like birds on branches.

That sea of May, running in such blue,
a moon at night, a sun at daytime,
and the moon like a yellow fruit,
like a plate on a wall,
to which they raise their hands,

no mar mhagnet airgeadach
le gathan goirte
a' sruthadh don chridhe.

239   *Dealachadh*

Nuair a dh'fhàg am bàt' an cidhe
thill thu dhachaigh,
do bhonaid air cùl do chinn.

Thog mi mo làmh riut
mar dhuilleag foghair
coltach ris a' bhànrigh
á carbad gorm.

Chaidh thu tarsainn air a' bhruthach.
Dh'éirich am bàta air an tonn.
Bha na féithean uaine
a' tilleadh dhachaigh.

Màiri NicDhòmhnaill

240   *Ghrad-leum cù-geàrd a h-inntinn*

Ghrad-leum cù-geàrd a h-inntinn
is choisich air spògan sàmhach dhan h-uile cùil.
Cha b' urrainn i 'ghreimeachadh na b' fhaide.
Theannaich am bann is rinn e spàirn.
Mach! Mach!
An aghaidh spùilleadair an doirch.
Shuath e
luchd-faire eile na h-oidhch.
A' chomhachag ghlas
a' taibhsearachd a danns.
Sionnach
a' dubhar chraobh.
Conaltradh socair
is thill e dhachaigh,
am bann a-nis sgaoilte,
làmhan tàlaidh
ga cur 'na suain.

like a silver magnet
with piercing rays
streaming into the heart.

Parting

When the boat left the pier
you came home,
your bonnet on the back of your head.

I raised my hand to you
like an autumn leaf
like the queen
from a dark-blue limousine.

You went across the brae.
The boat rose upon the wave.
The green sinews
were coming home.

Màiri Macdonald (Grimsay, N. Uist)

The watchdog of her mind

The watchdog of her mind whiplashed into wakefulness,
began his nightly prowl of soft-padded feet.
The confines of her body could no longer hold him.
Against his tautening leash he strained.
Out! Out!
Out to the dark beyond
to brush against those
other sentinels of the night.
The tawny owl
ghosting its eerie dance.
The vixen
shadowing the larches.
He softly spoke
and turned for home,
the leash now slack
in gentling hands
as she fell asleep.

Cairstìona Anna NicAoidh (1928—)

241   *An t-Earrach*

Oiteag fhionnar trom le nuadhachd beatha,
s cungaidh-leighis i do gach euslaint,
cùbhraidh le blas geur nam meas liomain,
a' sainnsearachd chagairean blàth-chridheach
mu eunlaith is toraidhean fearainn,
a' cur spionnadh a dh'uilnean na fuar-thalmhainn
gu bruthadh gu h-uachdar
lusan is bileagan bha 'm bruaillean cadail
fo gheasaibh aig Rìgh na Reòtachd.

Garbhan MacAoidh (1929—)

242   *Bealltainn ann am Fàcland*

Variazioni sul tema 'Ailein Duinn, Shiùbhlainn Leat'

Gura mise th' air mo sgaradh!
Chan e sùgradh 'nochd th' air m' aire,
Chan e sùgradh 'nochd th' air m' aire
Ach stoirm nan sianta 's meud na gaillinn.

Fuil air feamainn, fuil air fearann,
Air an tràigh is air an tarmac,
Brag nam bom is cnag nan canan —
Bealltainn ann am Fàcland.

Nuair a thill sinn o Phort Stanlaidh,
Eadar Darwin is an drochaid,
Chunnaic sinn na gillean gasta
Marbh air a' mhòintich.

Thàinig cuirp gu tìr am Pebble:
Cha b'e siud ar rogha cladha
Ach Esquel am Patagonia
No Bun Easain ann am Muile.

Christina A MacKay (Achmore, Lochs, Lewis)

Spring

A cool breeze heavy with newness of life,
it is a balm for every sickness,
fragrant with the sharp taste of lemons,
whispering warm-hearted messages
about birds and the fruits of land,
strengthening the elbows of the cold ground
to press to its surface
herbs and shoots that were in a delirium of sleep
enchanted by the King of Frost.

Girvan McKay (Glasgow)

Maytime in the Falklands

Variazioni sul tema 'Ailein Duinn, Shiùbhlainn Leat'

I'm distraught, I'm torn apart!
Mirth's not on my mind tonight,
Mirth's not on my mind tonight
But rainstorm, snow and speed of wind.

Blood on seawrack, blood on land,
On the beach and on the tarmac,
Thud of bombs and crack of fieldguns —
Maytime in the Falklands.

On the way back from Port Stanley,
Between Darwin and the bridge,
We stumbled on the handsome lads
Lying dead upon the moor.

Corpses came ashore at Pebble:
Not the graveyard we'd have chosen
But Esquel in Patagonia
Or Bunessan in the Isle of Mull.

Dh'òlainn deoch ge b' oil le m' chàirdibh,
Cha b'ann a dh'fhìon dearg na Spàinne,
Cha b'ann a dh'fhìon na h-Argentìna
Ach de dheòir na cloinn' 's nam bantrach.

Anthony Dilworth (1929—)

243   bho *Successa Petronia*

Tha iomadach annas ann an Sasainn —
leithid Drochaid Chlifton thar sruth na h-Abhann
ann am Bristol
's fón nan Samaritanach
aig gach ceann dith
ag iarraidh air luchd féin-mharbhaidh
fónadh an toiseach
air son comhairle
an àit' an tilgeil fhéin
na ceudan de throighean a-bhàn
air an dìon-mhullach
a chaidh a thogail os cionn an rathaid mhòir
gus am bacadh bho spreadhadh 's spadadh sgriosail
a sgaoileadh eanchainn, 's gaorr, 's mionach
am measg làraidhean 's chàraichean, 's dhràibhearan,
's iad làn uabhais 's oillt
aig an t-sealladh.

Agus na seann amaran-failcidh Ròmanach
ann am Bath
far eil na mìltean de ghalain de dh'uisge teth
a' ruith gach latha
's iad air a bhith dòrtadh gun sgur
bho chionn bhliadhnachan ciana sìorraidh
fada mus tàinig Cèasar.

Tha Cathair-Eaglais Wells ann,
cho eireachdail 's cho sòlaimte,
làn pròis 's àrdain 's diadhalachd,
agus tì 's cofaidh gan reic
sna clostairean
gus an luchd-turais claoidhte
a chumail a' dol.

I'd drink, whatever my kinsfolk say,
Not of the red wine of Spain,
Nor of wine from Argentina
But of the widows' and the children's tears.

Anthony Dilworth (Edinburgh)

from *Successa Petronia*

There's many a wonder in England —
such as the Clifton Bridge over the river Avon
in Bristol
with the Samaritans' telephone
at each end of it
requesting suicides
to call first
for advice
instead of throwing themselves
down hundreds of feet
onto the canopy
which has been built over the highway
to deter them from destructive bursting and slaughter
which would scatter brains, and gore, and guts
amongst lorries and cars, and drivers,
and they filled with horror and disgust
at the sight.

And the old Roman baths
in Bath
where thousands of gallons of hot water
run every day
which have been pouring without cease
for distant eternal years
long before Caesar came.

There is Wells Cathedral,
so magnificent and solemn,
full of pride and grandeur and godliness,
with tea and coffee being sold
in the cloisters
to keep the exhausted tourists
going.

... Ach b'e do bhàs-sa, Shuccessa Phetronia,
aig aois faisg ceithir bliadhna
bu mhotha dhrùidh orm,
's an carragh beag cuimhne cloiche
a thog do phàrantan muladach dhut
leis gach bliadhna 's gach mìos 's gach latha
de d' bheatha ghoirid
air an cunntadh gu pongail
ann an Laidinn.
Agus dh'fhàg iad a' chlach seo
aig Aquae Sulis
's iad an dùil gum biodh tu gu bràth
fo chùram na Ban-Dé.

An ann Breatannach no Ròmanach
a bha do mhuinntir?
Dé 'chànain a chleachd iad
gus gaol a shealladh dhut
's iad ga do thàladh gu cadal?
Am bu tusa aona shòlas grianach
am beatha,
no an robh clann eil' aca?
Agus bheil caileag òg eil' an-diugh ri mireadh 's ri soideis
's a' goid do leannanachd ort,
's i spaidsearachd 'nad àite
air àrd-shràidean mòralach Bath
le gill' òg nach do dh'fhiosraich thu riamh,
's gun fhios gun fhorfhais aic'
gu bheil i, ma dh'fhaoidte,
càirdeach dhut?

Victor Price (1930—)

244 *An déidh aimhreit*

An déidh aimhreit a chuireadh nàire
air duine fichead bliadhna na b' òige
tha mi faighneachd dhiom fhéin:
— Càit a bheil an gliocas
bu chòir 'thighinn leis an aois?

... But it was your death, Successa Petronia,
at the age of nearly four
that affected me the most,
and the little stone monument
that your grieving parents erected for you
with every year and month and day
of your short life
calculated carefully
in Latin.
And they left this stone
at Aquae Sulis
expecting you to be forever
in the care of the Goddess.

Were your people
Britons or Romans?
What language did they use
to show you their love
as they lullabied you to sleep?
Were you the one bright sunshine
of their life,
or did they have other children?
And is another young girl today flirting and cuddling
and stealing your adolescence
as she parades in your place
on the splendid avenues of Bath
with a young boy that you never met,
neither knowing nor caring
that she is, perhaps,
related to you?

Victor Price (Newcastle, Co. Down, N. Ireland)

After a struggle

After a struggle that would put to shame
a man twenty years younger
I put the question to myself:
— Where is the wisdom
that is supposed to come with age?

'S tha mi smaoineachadh an uair sin:
— Agus nan robh e agad
cha bhitheadh feum ann,
oir tha a' bheatha 'dol air adhart
ach tha sùilean a' ghliocais
air cùlaibh a chinn.

An t-Oll. Dòmhnall MacAmhlaigh (1930—)

245   *Rabhd Eudochais*

Dé nì ceòl no cainnt sgeilmear
no craobh a' fàs craobhach dealbhach
no blàth caomh a' chinnidh daonna
no beul gràidh le còmhradh beatha
no gilead na gréine no leugan na mara
no caoineadh
no sgarrghail rabhaidh
fiosrachadh foghair no samhraidh no earraich
no geamhraidh
dhan an fheadhainn a roghnaich
boidhr' agus doille —
's a tha 'n aghaidh ris a' bhailbhe?

246   *A' Cheiste*

"Carson," their iad,
"a chaitheas tu d' àm a' dèanamh dhàn?
B' fheàrr dhuit, air a' cheann thall,
a bhith ri ceàird eile."

An ceann thall
dhomhsa
a rèir a slat-thomhais-san.

Ghineadh dhomh faillean,
á spàrn dhiamhair;
dh'fhàs e tromham craobhach;
chuir mi romham gum fàsadh e dìreach

gus buil thoirt air slatan fiara.

And I think after that:
— And if you had it
it would be no use,
for life goes forward
but wisdom's eyes
are at the back of its head.

Prof. Donald MacAulay (Bernera, Lewis)

Cry of Despair

What's the use of music or polished diction
or tree that grows branching and shapely
or the gentle blossom of humanity
or loving mouth with talk of life
or the sun's brightness or the sea's jewels
or keening
or warning cry
knowledge of autumn or summer or spring
or winter
to those who have chosen
deafness and blindness —
and are facing dumbness?

Question

"Why," they say,
do you spend your time making poems?
It would benefit you more, in the end,
to practise another trade."

The end
for me
measured by their yardsticks.

A tree was for me engendered
by some mysterious striving;
its branches spread through me;
I decided it should grow undeformed

to overcome deviant yardsticks.

247   Do Fhear-Sgrìobhaidh Ainmeil

Bha na leacan dubha sleamhain;
có a ghléidheadh a chasan
ach fear eòlach air leantainn
sùghadh na tìde-mhara?
— is bha e gun teagamh ealant
air lorg meidh a bhonnan
air binnean gach carragh:

chleachd e a dhol sìos gach àm reothairt
a rùileach am measg nan stabhan
a ghlacadh nan clàimheagan-caoich
's a tharraing ás na crùbagan odhar;

ach fhuair maorach
biathaidh faochadh
bho a dhubhan 's bho 'fhiacaill:
bha e riaraichte
le driamanan crutha a dhanns
air an t-sleamhnachd.

248   Féin-Fhìreantachd

Chan iarr iad orm ach
gal aithreachais peacaidh
nach buin dhomh
's gum faigh mi saorsa
fhuadan nach tuig mi:

ludaradh ann an uisge
an déidh uisge tana, guinteach
am feallsanachd —

agus gun amharas chrochadh iad
an nigheadaireachd anns na nèamhan.

To a Famous Writer

The black slabs were slippery;
who could keep his feet
save a man used to following
the suction of the tide?
— and he was doubtless skilful
at finding the balance of his soles
on the summit of each rock:

he used to go down at each spring tide
to rummage amongst the tangles
and catch the shrimps
and pull out the dun crabs;

but shellfish for bait
received relief
from his hook and from his tooth:
he was satisfied
with the contortions of his dance
on the slipperiness.

Selfrighteousness

They ask of me only
to weep repentance for a sin
that does not concern me
and I shall get in return an alien
freedom I don't understand:

to be drubbed in one thin,
wounding water after another
of their philosophy —

and confidently they would hang
their washing in the heavens.

249 A' Ghiblinn troimh thrì Sùilean

Fo chuibhrig geal an t-sneachd
saoilidh mi gu bheil an talamh
adhbhar-rìgh seo
a' togail a shlat-neirt —
mar gum biodh buig' agus grodadh
teadhradh dheich ginealaichean
sguaibte glan ás
fon an rèidh uailleil —
fo fhar-bhrat.

Tha an solas a' dìsneadh
an làir eadar an dubh-dhuilleach
a' breacadh a' bhaile
bhàin — aisling uaille air a h-inns air;
's a' breacadh m' aigne gu sradadh
ri fùdar ròs-dhearg mo chomhfhaireachdainn
— cha mhór nach dugainn buidheachas
air son crodh ballach.

An-diugh: an latha eadar
earrach is geamhradh
's nach geamhradh 's nach earrach
tha an roth a' cladhach
na h-aon shreath
sìos nìos doimhne:
gun charachadh a' caradh;
ag ithe connadh
feòla is loinne
is gilead rèidh an t-sneachd
is bòidhchead nam breac —
a' caitheamh biadh na clainne:
Cha doir a' Ghiblinn sa
blàth á marbh-thalamh.

250 Soisgeul 1955

Bha mi a-raoir anns a' choinneamh;
bha an taigh làn chun an dorais,
cha robh àite suidhe ann
ach geimhil chumhang air an staidhre.

April through three Eyes

Under the white mantle of the snow
I think the earth
this king-to-be
is raising up his rod of strength —
as if the damp and rot
of ten tethered generations
were being swept clean out
under the vain smoothness —
under extra cover.

The light is dicing
the ground through the dark foliage
dappling the town's
whiteness — its dream of vanity exposed;
and sparking my mind to fire
the rose-red powder of my compassion
— I'd almost give thanks
for dappled cows.

Today: the day between
spring and winter
that's not winter and that's not spring
the wheel is digging
the same furrow
down deeper:
turning without moving;
eating fuel
of flesh and splendour
and the smooth whiteness of the snow
and the beauty of the dapplings —
consuming the children's food:
This April will bring
no blossom from dead ground.

Gospel 1955

I was at the meeting last night;
the house was full, packed to the door,
there was no place for me to sit
but a cramped nook on the stairs.

Dh'éist mi ris an t-sailm: am fonn
a' falbh leinn air seòl mara
cho dìomhair ri Maol Dùn;
dh'éist mi ris an ùrnaigh
seirm shaoirsinneil, shruthach —
iuchair-dàin mo dhaoine.

An uair sin thàinig an searmon
— teintean ifrinn a th' anns an fhasan —
bagairt neimheil, fhuadan
a lìon an taigh le uabhann is coimeasg.

Is thàinig an cadal-deilgeanach 'na mo chasan . . .

Donnchadh MacLeòid (1934—)

251　*Samhla*

Chuala mi searmonaich'
a' lìrigeadh samhla
air Gràs
's Eadar-Mheadhan.

Ars esan,
"Feuch
loch-uisge òil
no researvoir
's ro bheag a threòir
bho ruith an leothaid,

sìor lìonadh tanc
air cnoc,
aig àird
gu ruith 'na mhàl
thoirt dhuibh ur sàs."

S math dhan àl
nach eil an Gràs
cho loma-làn
de riasg
ri bùrn
Loch Mòr a Stàrr.

I listened to the psalm: the tune
transporting us on a tide
as mysterious as Maol Duin's;
I listened to the prayer
a liberating, cascading melody —
my people's access to poetry.

Then we got the sermon
— the fires of hell are in fashion —
vicious, alien threats
that filled the house with confusion and terror.

And I got pins-and-needles in my feet . . .

Duncan MacLeod (Ranish, Lochs, Lewis)

Illustration

I heard a preacher
give an illustration
of Grace
and of Intercession.

Said he,
"Behold
a fresh-water loch
or reservoir
with insufficient pressure
from the angle of the gradient,

steadily filling a tank
on a hill
at a height
to run at speed
and satisfy your need."

It's as well for the brood
that Grace is not
so glutted
with peat
as the water
of Loch Mòr a Stàrr.

Iain Moireach (1938—)

252　*Ar n-Airgead 's ar n-Òr*

Ars fear ceann a' bhùird
is e sgrìobadh a ghlùin
Tha sinn deiseil, tha mi 'n dùil?

Tha.
Tha.
Tha.

Nis, an-uiridh, thurchair
mar tha fhios agaibh uile
gun dh'fheuch fear urchair
air ar dualchas, 's mar chuala sibh
air ar fonn.

— An cù!
— Am madadh!
— An coigreach!

Thubhairt e 's e ri fanaid
gun robh esan air a mhealladh
gun robh sinne — sinne! — a' sgaradh
dàin a thàinig o bheul-aithris
's a' toirt air luchd-seinn
ceòl binn a mhùchadh
's 'na àite bhith brùchdadh
ceòl siùcarach
Sasannach.

— Nach e tha faoin!
— Nach e tha maol!
— Nach e bh' air fuireach aig an taigh.

O, bha 'n duine glic gu leòr
profeasar, neo rudeigin d'a sheòrs'
ann am "Music"
is thàinig e 'n tù sa
chun a' Mhòd.

— A' Mhòd . . .
— A, a' Mhòd . . .
— Ar Mòd . . .

John Murray (Lower Barvas, Lewis)

Our Silver and our Gold

Said the man at the head of the table
as he scratched his knee
We're ready, I think?

Yes.
Yes.
Yes.

Now, last year, it so happened
as you all know
that a man had a go
at our culture, and as you've heard
at our land.

— The dog!
— The hound!
— The alien!

He said in mockery
that he was disappointed
that we — yes we! — were murdering
poems that came from oral tradition
and forcing singers
to smother sweet music
and instead to be belching
music that's clammy
and kitschy.

— Isn't he foolish!
— Isn't he cheeky!
— If only he'd stayed at home.

Oh, the fellow was sensible enough
a professor, or something of the sort
in "Music"
and he came our way
to the Mod.

— The Mod . . .
— Ah, the Mod . . .
— Our Mod . . .

Thàinig e null o thìrean céin
gus am faiceadh e dha fhéin
cruinneachadh binn nan tréibh
nuair chuireadh iad an céill am fonn.
'S cha do chòrd e ris.

— Car son?
— A-réist . . .
— A thàinig e?

Nach e sin, a chàirdean ciatach.
Cha dubhairt e nach robh sinn fialaidh
cha dubhairt e nach robh sinn lìonmhor
gun robh sinn trom air fìon, neo
gun robh ar glùinean bàn.
Ach nach do chòrd ar seinn ris.

— An trosg!
— An damh!
— Am fògarrach, mac an donais —

Ach seasaidh sinne buan ge b' oil leis.
S iomadh cruadal agus onfhadh
a dh'fhuiling sinne le onair.
Tha buinn òir agus airgid a' seinn ar cliù
's ar nàimhdean cealgach anns an ùir
's cha mhór an call dhuinn
esan, cho Gallda,
gun Ghàidhlig aige nas mù.
Bheil sinne dol a dh'éisteachd
ri fear ann am féileadh
a thàinig air chéilidh
's gun Ghàidhlig aige?

— Sinne?
— Mo nàire!
— Dé 'n uair a tha e?

Fhiribh
a-nise:
dé mu dheidhinn britheamh
fear glic a chumas air dòigh sinn?
Chunnaic mi a-bhòindé
duine anabarrach ceòlmhor

He came over from foreign lands
to see for himself
the melodious meeting of the tribes
when they'd strike up their tune.
And he didn't like it.

— Why?
— Then . . .
— Did he come?

Quite so, dear friends.
He didn't say that we weren't hospitable
he didn't say that we weren't numerous
that we were heavy on the bevvy, or
that our knees were white.
But that he didn't like our singing.

— The cod!
— The bullock!
— The beggar, son of the devil —

But we'll stand firm in spite of him.
It's many a hardship and storm
that we've withstood with honour.
Gold and silver medals sing of our fame
while our deceitful foes lie in the soil
and no great problem to us
is he, so Lowland,
nor does he even have Gaelic.
Are we going to listen
to a man in a kilt
who came to call
without any Gaelic?

— Us?
— For shame!
— What time is it?

Men
now:
what about a judge
a wise man to keep us right?
The day before yesterday I saw
an extremely musical fellow

's tha mise làn dòchas
gum bi sibh deònach
e bhith againn air a' Mhòd —
Beethoven?

— Tha.
— Tha.
— Tha.

Uail, siud siud a chàirdean.
S mithich dealachadh an-dràsta.
Suas leis a' Ghàidhlig!

Tha —
ha —
ha.

('Ic 'Ic 'Ic 'Ic Iain, 27/11/65. Abair strutan, ars e fhéin nuair a leugh e an sataidhir geurbhideach uile-a-combaisteachadh a tha seo. Agus shéid e aon choinnlean am measg taip an seòrsasgrìobhadair.)

253 *An t-Acras*

Dà dhealbh, coimhearsnaich
Dà dhuine, coimh-thìrich
Dà thìr
na dithis ag ith
fear ga choimhead fhéin
fichead uair air a cheann dìreach
'aodann draghte, caol, fada
an gloineachan ceòlmhorfalamh
spàinean airgid
a shùilean geur san fheòil
gàire bhean àilleagach 'na chluais
bristeal.

Fear eile a' coimhead 'na chuimhne
fichead caraid air an ceann dìreach
'aodann cruaidh caol fada
trì oidhcheannan gun sòlas cadail,
cupan salach, gunna
a shùilean geur leòinte
casdaich nam peileir 'na chluais
bristeal.

and I'm extremely hopeful
that you'll be willing
for us to have him to the Mod —
Beethoven?

— Yes.
— Yes.
— Yes.

Well, that's that comrades.
It's time to be going now.
Up with Gaelic!

Hear —
He —
haw.

(Of the Son of the Son of the Son of the Son of John, 27/11/65. What a doddle, said
he when he read this sharpstinging all-in-compassing satire. And he blew one
nostril amongst the typewriter keys.)

Hunger

Two images, neighbours
Two men, compatriots
In two countries
both eating
one seeing his self
twenty times tumbled headlong
face dragged long, thin
in tinkling empty glasses
in silver spoons
his eyes smart in his flesh
a bejewelled woman's laugh in his ear
crystal-brittle.

The other's memory reflects
twenty buddies tumbled headlong
his face hard, long and thin
three nights without pleasure of sleep
a dirty cup, a gun
his watchful eyes galled
the bullets' cough in his ear
brittle-crystal.

Tormod MacGill-Eain (1938—)

254   *Maol Donn*

An t-Ùrlar

Bu tu a' chraobh leatha fhéin an lios nan sùl
    'S tu 'gleusadh dhos na pìob' le meòirean grinn;
Bha 'n còmhlan balbh gun deò an talla dhlùth
    Nuair chuir thu bàt' do chiùil le uaill bho thìr.

Shùigh do làmhan pongan dìreach geur
    On Spàinnteach chruaidh a cheannsaich thu le bàidh,
'S mar dh'fhalbhas ceò air beinn roimh theas na gréin'
    Theich draghannan an t-saoghail o m' inntinn chràidht'.

Dhearc sùil mo chuimhn' air làithean geala cian,
    Mo shaoghal socair 's rathad nan dùl mo dhàn —
Co-ionnan leam an t-ùrlar dìreach dian
    Ri tùs mo chuairt neo-chaochlaidich don bhàs.

Gu cinnteach dàna lùb thu 'm port gu d' dheòin
    Is dh'fhuadaich thu 'n teagamh grod o d' chrìdh,
Mar sin air slighe réidh roi-òrdaicht' m' òig'
    Ghluais mi troimhn latha 's shluig mo chiall am brìgh.

An Srathan liath nam fang air Bràigh Loch Iall
    Bha 'r dachaigh seasgair blàth, fo chuip na gaoith',
Gun sgìths 's le furtachd leugh mi leabhar na bliadhn'
    Is fhuair mi fìrinn lom nach dìobradh 'chaoidh.

Cha robh ar teachd-an-tìr san àm ach truagh —
    B'e beachd nan uasal Galld' gur mór ar feum —
Ach fhuair sinn lòn, is dh'fhuadaich sinn am fuachd
    Mun chagailt chòir le gnìomhan ghaisgeach treun'.

Chan fhaicinn iarmailt dhearg aig ceann an là
    'S cha chluinninn sgriach na comhachaig anns a' choill
Gun smaoineachadh air fuil chaidh dhòrtadh tràth
    'S air blàraibh aost' 's cinn-chinnidh meallt' le foill.

Sa gheamhradh dhìleach, talamh is speur 'na cheò,
    B'e m' annsachd riamh mun tein' a' Ghàidhlig chaomh;
Bhiodh 'Fear na h-Eabaid' 's òrain nuadh 'tighinn beò,
    'S an cill mo chuimhn' bha 'n-diugh 's an-dé mar aon.

Norman Maclean (Glasgow)

MacCrimmon's Sweetheart

The Ùrlar (Ground Movement)

You were the only tree in the garden of eyes
    As your nimble fingers tuned the drones of the pipe;
The hall was packed and the silent crowd held their breath
    When you pushed the boat of your music from land with pride.

Your hands extracted notes that were straight and sharp
    From your Spanish hardwood so affectionately tamed,
And as mountain mist dissolves in the heat of the sun
    The cares of the world departed from my anguished mind.

My memory's eye beheld bright far-off days,
    My tranquil world and the hopeful road my theme —
Synonymous to me the straight and vehement ground
    With the start of my unaltering race to death.

With bold assurance you bent the tune to your will
    And gnawing doubt you banished from your heart,
And so on the smooth predestined path of my youth
    I moved through each day and my sense imbibed their sap.

In grey old Strathan of fanks in the Braes of Lochiel
    Was our warm sequestered home, lashed by the gale,
With ease unexhausted I read the book of the year
    And learned the starkness of truth that would never fail.

Our livelihood was wretched for the time —
    Lowland officials felt that great were our needs —
But we found nourishment, and ways to beat the cold
    Around the kindly hearth with brave heroes' deeds.

I couldn't see red sky at the end of the day
    And couldn't hear the screech of the owl in the wood
Without thinking of blood spilt early in life
    And of ancient battles and chiefs treacherously betrayed.

In the rainy winter, with earth and sky a mist,
    What I always loved around the fire was mellifluous Gaelic;
'The Man of the Habit' and new songs would come alive,
    And in the cell of my memory today and yesterday were one.

Uair eile dh'aithnich m' aigne cumhachd Dhé,
    Bha 'n fheadag 'tuiteam sìos on iarmailt fhann;
Bha sàmhchair 'snàmh gu ciùin air loch 's air sléibh
Is ìochdar-druim mo chrìdh aig fois sa ghleann.

Le cùram dh'fhàg do mheur an grunnd 'na dhéidh
    Is leig thu t' eich gu aonach saor gun srian —
B' ionnan leam an taorludh gàireach treun
    Ri làithean m' shaors' san d'fhuair mi fios air pian.

An Taorludh

Bu phròiseil do shiunnsair nuair ghreasaich thu 'n crònan,
Bras-mheòirean ceòl-sturtail glòir-ghleust' ga phògadh —
Taorludh air taorludh gu caithreamach ceòlmhor,
    Thilg thu 'chuing 's leig thu t' sheòltachd fa sgaoil.

Mar dhìreas am fireun gu h-aotrom thar mhòintich
Dh'éirich do spiorad air buillean geur sròiceach,
Bha t' inntinn 'na lasair is t' earbsa 'nad ròidean,
    Dhearc do shùil sgaoilte air deireadh 's air tùs.

Dé 'n smuain bha 'nad inntinn air 'n turas ro-shiùbhlach
Do làmhan glan innleachdach carach ga giùlan?
Dé 'n dealbh o chian chuir do chuimhne roimh t' shùilean
    Nuair ghluais thu le misneachd an taorludh gu crìch?

Rugadh mo nàire ann an lùthchleas is àrd-agal,
Gleadhraich is ùpraid a' bhaile gam thàladh —
Bu ghionach an t-acras is miann rinn mo chràdhlot,
    Dh'òl mi mo shàth de dh'fhìon taitneach an t-saoghail.

Le iuchair ùr-dhèanta ar leam mar an ceudna
Gum feuchainn ri fuasgladh gach ceist rinn mo léireadh,
Bu ghnìomhach mac-meanmain 's mo smuaintean air spéiceadh
    An athbhliadhn 's an-uiridh mo stéidh, seach am-bliadhn'.

Mar dhamh ann an ceò ghluais m' aigne san fhàsach,
Le bhith sireadh na fìrinn' bha mo chré air sàrach';
Ged a theann mi air bàrdachd cha robh càirdeas mar b' àbhaist
    Eadar mise 's na sràidean am baile na strì.

At another time my spirit recognised the power of God,
   With the plover falling down from the languid sky;
Silence floating gently on loch and on hill
   While the very bottom of my heart was at rest in the glen.

With care your finger left the ground behind it
   And you let your horses free to go unbridled to the heights —
Identical to me the brave rumbustious taorludh
   And my days of freedom when I came to experience pain.

The Taorludh (Free Movement)

Proud was your chanter when you quickened the melody,
Swift music-smart glory-trimmed fingers were kissing it —
Taorludh on taorludh triumphantly musical,
      You threw off the yoke and unleashed your skilfulness.

As the eagle soars over moorland so lightly
Your spirit rose upon sharp cutting strokes,
Your mind was aflame and you trusted your paths,
      Your eye looked divided at end and beginning.

What thought were you pondering on the speediest of journeys,
Borne along by your fresh clever dexterous hands?
What film from afar did your memory show you
      As your taorludh was confidently drawn to a close?

My shame was born in agility and eloquence,
For the city's uproar and bustle attracted me —
Intense were the hunger and ambition that drove me,
      And I drank my fill of the world's pleasant wine.

With a modern key I thought in addition
That I'd try to unlock every question that vexed me,
Imagination was active but my thoughts were confined —
      My basis the future and past, not the present.

Like a stag in the mist moved my mind in the wilderness,
Through searching for truth my body was tired;
Though I turned to verse the old friendship was gone
      Between me and the streets and the city of strife.

Bu tric air an oidhche bhiodh m' inntinn am bruaillean,
Ann an dorchadas uaigneach bhiodh an t-eagal gam bhuaireadh,
Mo chorp air a leònadh le faobhar nan cruaidh-lann,
    Glaiste 'na phrìosan bha mo chridhe fo bhròin.

Cha robh tlachd ann an leabhar 's an ceòl-pìob' cha robh tàmhachd,
Ghabhainn ùidh ann an uiread, ach b'e 'n ùine mo nàmhaid;
Ged bhiodh smuaintean a' sruthadh, chan fhaighinn an sàs annt',
    Bu ghuirme leamsa na beanntan fad ás.

Nuair theann thu air 'chrùnludh bha 'm bonn òir 'na do léirsinn,
Le meòirean troma bhuail thu 'm feadan gu gleusta;
Bha thu 'g àinich gu luath mar each sàraicht' cur réise
    Nuair thog thu an crùn air ceann-deiridh do phuirt.

An Crùnludh

    Nuair thug thu ionnsaigh dhéineasach
    Bha airtneal agus éislean ort;
    Ach dh'ainneoin sgìths gun d'éirich thu
        'S thàinig lùths gu d' mheòirean.

    Bu bhinn do phìob mhór acainneach
    'S tu 'n lùib a' chrùnluidh thartaraich,
    Do mheòir mar eich dian astarach
        A' gearradh leum le sòlas.

    Bha dranndan aig duis lìonmharra
    'S bha ribheid gheur gam miadachadh —
    Si phìob nach leig air dìochuimhn thu
        Ged s urramach do sheòltachd.

    O s tù an laoch a chliùthaichinn
    'Nam dhàn le inntinn dhùrachdaich —
    Mar chluich thu 'm port gu fiughantach
        'S mar bhuail thu balbh an còmhlan.

    B' ionnan do cheòl faramach
    'S mo bheatha luaineach caithriseach,
    Nuair bha gach crìoch sìor tharraing uam
        'S an nàmhaid air mo thòrach.

Often at night with my mind in a torment,
In lonely darkness fear would embrace me,
My body was torn by the edge of the swordblades,
    Locked in its prison was my sorrowing heart.

With no pleasure in book nor repose in pipe music,
In so much I'd be interested, but my enemy was time;
Though thoughts would rush by, I couldn't get hold of them,
    The hills farther off were to me always greener.

When you turned to the crùnludh the gold medal seemed close,
As your powerful fingers struck the chanter with skill;
Breathing fast like a hard-pressed horse in a race
    You picked up the crown at the end of your tune.

The Crùnludh (Crown Movement)

When you made a brave effort
You were faint with exhaustion;
Despite tiredness you rose
    And strength came to your fingers.

Sweet was your great accoutred pipe
As you rattled out the crùnludh,
Your fingers like horses strong and swift
    Leaping high with pleasure.

Copious drones humming
With crisp reed augmenting them —
It's the pipe unforgettable
    Though noble's your skill.

You're the warrior I'd celebrate
In my song with earnest mind —
How you played the tune heroically
    And struck the audience dumb.

Synonymous your echoing music
With my restless sleepless life,
Each aim forever eluding me
    And the devil in pursuit.

B'i 'chrìoch bha riamh air m' aire-sa
'S bha mo cheum ro chabhagach,
'S mo léirsinn air a dalladh orm
     Chan fhaicinn feum san lò seo.

Ach theirig smuaintean siùbhlacha
Fo bhuaidh nam ponga lùthmhora
Nuair shìn thu ris an ùrlar dhuinn
     'S tu crìochnachadh gu dòigheil.

An t-Ùrlar

Bu tu a' chraobh leatha fhéin an lios nan sùl,
     Bha 'ghlòir dhuit dlùth 's bha 'phròis ag at do chléibh,
'S nochd thu tiamhaidheachd 'nad anam rùisgt'
     Nuair sheòl thu bàt' do chiùil gu cala réidh.

'M measg sloisreadh chòmhradh 's molaidh 's beucaich àird
     Is sàiltean air an làr a' bualadh cruaidh,
Thug sìol do theisteis rabhadh dhomh air fàs
     Is thuig mi, sann san là seo fhéin tha 'n duais.

Ma mhealas sinn an là seo mar as còir
     'S ma chuireas sinn ar beòil air blàth a' chiùil
Bidh 'n-dé 's an-uiridh dhuinn mar bhruadar glòir
     'S bidh h-uile màireach sìnte ri ar dùil.

Aonghas MacNeacail (1942—)

255   bho *sireadh bradain sicir*

bha mi 'nam dhuin' air
talamh cruaidh
a' dùbhlan fàsaich
a' sireadh bradain
(tromh thobar tiompain)

nuair a bha mi
san t-saoghal eile
bhuail do bhodhran
orm ruithim shìnteach

The end was always in my thoughts
And my step was too hasty,
And since my eyes had been blinded
    I'd see no point in today.

But fleeting thoughts were driven off
By the power of the music
When you brought us back to the ground
    To finish as is proper.

The Ground

You were the only tree in the garden of eyes,
    Glory was close and pride puffed out your chest,
And you revealed the gloom in your naked soul
    As you sailed the boat of your music safe into port.

Midst rumbling conversations, clapping, shouting loud
    And heels being beaten hard upon the ground,
Your testimony's seed brought me a warning about growth
    And I realised how each day brings its own reward.

If we enjoy the present as we should
    And place our mouths upon the music's bloom
Each yesterday will be our dream of glory
    And each tomorrow will be as we hope.

Aonghas MacNeacail (Uig, Skye)

from *seeking wise salmon*

i was a man
upon the land
defying wilderness
in search of salmon
(through a drumming well)

when i was
in the other world
your bodhran beat
on me a striding rhythm

bha mi 'nam shealgair
air thòir a' bhradain
luath-leum sicir
aig meadhoin oidhche
fo shoillse réil

bha mi 'nam iasgair
bha mi 'nam shealgair
a' leantainn ceum
tromh thobar tiompain
gu nèamh nam meang

gun dh'ith mi buidheachas
dhen bhiolair ghorm ann

cha d'fhuair mi cnò
sa chòsan chraobhach

ach thusa dannsa
tromhn àile linneach
d' fheadan seunach
a' braonadh rann
a dhealbh do chreach

bha thu 'nad iasgair
air thòir a' bhradain

256 bho *an cathadh mór*

fann-mhèileadh chaorach 's gul theud-thelefon
leaghadh tromh chéile
geum féidh fo sgàile
            sgiamhail na gaoithe
dùdach luingeis do-fhaicsinn air linne
            brùchdadh mar osann leòinte
tromh chaoineadh sgalach
sgeirean gach taobh fo chobhar fo chathadh
h-uile siùbhlaiche deònachadh dachaigh
(siosarnach shocair aig lòineag air bradhadair)

bhith cruinn mun cuairt cagailt!

a chruinne   chuir thu ort gu bhith lom

i was a hunter
pursuing salmon
swift leap of wisdom
at stroke of midnight
under light of stars

i was a fisher
i was a hunter
followed a path
through the drumming well
to a branched and sacred grove

i ate sufficiency
of green cress there

i found no nut
in that wooded cave

but you dancing
through the channelled air
your flute of spells
distilling phrases
to depict your prey

you were a fisher
in pursuit of salmon

from *the great snowbattle*

feeble bleat of sheep and keening telephone
dissolve into each other
stag's bellow veiled
                    by screaming wind
hoot of hidden shipping on the kyle
                    pours wounded moan
through squalling lamentation
reef on each side under spindrift snowdrift
every wanderer wishing home-shelter
(somewhere sibilant crystals turn steam on the fireglow)

o to be in the circle round a hearth!

earth   you dressed yourself to be bare

gilead mala air bheanntan
gilead cìch air an t-sìthean
gilead brù air a' mhòintich
gilead sléiste san achadh

gruag neòil air do sgorran
agus sgàile air d' aodann

mìorbhail an t-sneachda
gach criostal àraid
gach criostal gun chàraid
meanbh-chlachaireachd
gach lòineag a' tàthadh
saoghal fo chidhis . . .

chan fhaic an t-iasgair ach cobhar
sgorran is sgeirean fo chobhar
sgaothan a' gluasad
    thar na cala
    thar an raoin
    thar an t-sléibh
cha dhearc a shùil air cuan air cala
chan fhaic e ach cobhar nan sgaoth
a' traoghadh air raointean

    an eathar 'na taibhse air teadhair
    a lìn 'nan greasain gheal bhreòiteach
    oillsginn gun anam a' crochadh is
    bòtainnean laighe mar chuirp

sluaighean a' chuain do-ruigsinn . . .

    fuil smeòraich
    ite 'na h-aonar

    làrach spòg cait

whiteness of brow on the mountains
whiteness of breast on the foothills
whiteness of belly on the moorland
whiteness of thigh in the meadow

coif of cloud on your peaks
and a veil on your face

marvel of snow
every crystal unique
every crystal without peer
micro-masonry
every flake cementing
a world beneath its mask . . .

the fisher sees nothing but foam
summits and skerries are under the spray
shoals are moving
     over harbour
     over fields
     across the moors
his eye can not see ocean, anchorage
he sees only foaming shoals
subsiding on meadows

     the boat is a tethered ghost
     his nets white friable webs
     his oilskins hang soulless while
     boots are outstretched corpses

ocean's multitudes are out of reach . . .

     blood of a mavis
     a feather alone

     cat's foot print

257 *teist*

1   anns an dùthaich seo, tha sinn
       cofhartail. chan iarr sinn
       bho'r bàird ach mìlseachd
                    fileantas.

       ach ann an dùthaich eile, dùthaich m' anam-sa
       chan e fileantas tha dh'easbhaidh
             ach fìrinn,
                    dearg rùisgte

2   dh'àraicheadh mis' ann an creideamh dòigheil gun cheist
       an-sin bhà mi glaist'
       gus an tàinig darwin is frazer le iuchraichean móra
       (cha d'fhosgail freud càil nach robh 'nam leasraidh) . . .

       sheinn sinn òran dhut, a luaidh
       chan ann air an aon nì bh' air m' inntinn
       ach air do chùlan bachlach òir
             do ghruaidhean bàn
             do shùilean fìorghorm (sann glas a tha iad)

258 *acras*

       dh'éirich a' mhuir shiabach, le grian mhaidne
       dearg-bhileach, a' tairgsinn dhomh biadh,
       ach shìn i air ais.

       dh'éirich a' mhuir chraobhach aig meadhan-latha,
       bàn-ghruagach, ag ìobairt dhomh gaol,
       ach shìn i air ais.

       dh'éirich a' mhuir sgianach aig àm duibhre
       dubh-shùileach, is sguab i mi, sguab
       i, is chaith i air ais.

testimony

1   in this land we are
comfortable. we seek nothing
from our bards but sweetness
              eloquence.

but in another country, in my soul
it's not eloquence that's lacking
      but truth,
              stark naked

2   i was reared in an orderly unquestioning faith
and there i was locked
till darwin and frazer came with great keys
(freud unlocked nothing that was not in my loins) . . .

we sang songs for you, my love
not on the one thing that was on my mind
but of your golden ringletted hair
        your fair cheeks
        your pure blue eyes (it's grey they are)

hunger

the lathered sea rose, with morning sun
red-lipped, offered me food,
but then she drew back.

the branching sea rose at noon
flaxen-haired, offered me love,
but she drew back.

the bladed sea rose at dusk
dark-eyed, she swept me up, swept
me, and then tossed me back.

259   *an eilid bhàn*

mi gabhail rathad na beinne   àrd
am measg nan tulach liathruadh   toirt
fa-near na h-éilde
            "ag iarraidh a h-annsachd"
tha grian gun chùram
san iarmailt cheana agus spealtag
na seann ghealaich
            dol 'na sìneadh air chùl
an dà sgùrr san fhireach thall a tha
smèideadh ri chéile mar a bha iad riamh

se dh'iarrainn an àite bhith siubhal
bhith dlùthchòmhla riutsa
            m' eilid bhàn
's mi gun dùsgadh fhathast

chan eil sin ri bhith san tràth seo
agus reul dheireannach na h-oidhche dol bàs
tha thu fada bhuam a-nise 's mi siubhal rathad na beinne
gun chinnt a bheil thu 'nad dhùisg
no a bheil àit' agam 'nad bhruadar

"b' eòlach do sheanair," ars na feallsamhna
mar gun cuireadh am briathran stad air an t-sealgair
's mi falbh a shuidh' air chùl deasc
far an tig thu eadar mo pheann 's am pàipear
falach-fead am measg cholbhan craobhach mo leabhair-cunntais
cuiridh do mheall-thighinn buaireachail maill' air a' ghleoc agus
mo mheasrachadh buileach air seachran
bidh mo dhiathad gun tuar no seagh
agus nuair a tha mi ag òl tha fios a'm
nach fhaic mi an cupa
bidh thu 'nad reul air chùl m' aigne
cho deàrrsach 's gun cuir thu a' ghrian air ais

ach sann air an t-sealg eile bhios m' inntinn
far am bi na buill-airm choma gan giùlain
air guailnean luchd-faghaid a tha
gun aithne air d' àilleachd
chan e do chniadachd a tha dhìth orra
ach an t-sealg

the white hind

i take the mountain road   high
amid the grey-red knolls
observing the hind
          "seeking her love"
the carefree sun
is in the sky already and the sliver
of the old moon
          goes to rest behind
the two peaks in the ridge which
beckon to each other as they always have

i'd wish, rather than travel,
to be close to you
          my white hind
and not wakened yet

that's not to be this time
as the last star of night goes out
you are far from me now as i travel the mountain road
uncertain whether you are awake
or whether i have a place in your dreams

"tell us something new," say the philosophers
as if their words could stop the hunter
as i go to sit behind a desk
where you will come between my pen and paper
hide-and-seek among the branched columns of my ledger
your distracting illusory visit will slow the clock and
completely unbalance my judgement
my food will be without appearance or essence
and when i'm drinking i know
i'll not see the cup
you'll be a star at the back of my mind
so bright you'll extinguish the sun

but my thought will be on the other hunt
where the indifferent weapons are carried
on the shoulders of stalkers who
don't know your beauty
not your caresses they want
but the hunt

an t-sealg is
a' bhuille sgoilteach

> o m' eilid bhàn
> o m' eilid bhàn

260 *dàn bealltainn*

1   san àm mus deach tìm
a ghlacadh sa ghainntir
bha 'n aigne 'na craobh
a' sìneadh a geugan
        a-mach
tro bhealach bó féinne
air slighe chlann uisnich

  là buidhe   là guidhe
là buidhe bealltainn

  là guidhe   là buidhe
là guidhe gealltainn

  là laoidheadh na gréine
sgealb-lasrach á darach nan speur
tein'-éiginn nan gruaidh 's nan achadh

  là briseadh nam bonnach
bha drùidht an taois-uighe

  là còmhdach an t-sìl
ann am foirbhreith is feitheamh

  là séideadh a' mhaghair
am beulaibh nan iasg

  là togail tein' air
bharraibh chnoc
aig camhanaich

  là basadh nan gnùis
ann an drùchd

  là dùbhlan donais
an dannsa cruinn
mu chrannaibh bealltainn

the hunt and
the gutting blow

       my white hind
       o my white hind

beltane poem

1   in the time before time
was locked in a dungeon
the mind was a tree
that stretched its branches
           out
through the pass of finn's cattle
on the journey of uisneach's sons

yellow day   praying day
yellow day of beltane

praying day   yellow day
day of prayer for promises

day of hymning the sun
flame-splinter of the oak of space
need-fire of brow and meadow

day to break bannocks
drenched in batter

day to clothe seed
in conjecture and waiting

day to blow bait
into mouths of fish

day to raise fires on
hilltops
at dawn

day to dip faces
in cupped hands of dew

day to challenge demons
in dance around
the beltane tree

2   treas latha bealltainn
là an t-seachnaidh

do nàimhdean
       mar shionnach mar
       iolair mar
       ghailleann

mar shionnach ag èaladh
tro dhoirean do mheamhair
a' cnàmh nam facal
dubh-ollamh nam breug
an cumadh sionnaich
    an t-ollamh breactheangach
    a' callachadh d' anail
    a' bàthadh do ghuth
cur goileam
       an àite do chànain

mar iolaire sgiathadh
thar rìoghachd a sheilbhe
gad sheunadh le
spuirean nan dlighe
       a dheilbh e
air fearann, air cuinn do shaothair
    iolaire chrùin
    iolaire chròich
    iolaire mas fhìor

tha gailleann tha gailleann
an uchd an dadam
an dadam
a' giùlain 'na dhòrn
an gailleann a cheannsaich an duine
an gailleann
'na tharbh a' cadal
an creitheall innleig
's an teadhair a' caitheamh

3   beannachadh bealltainn air
trì creachan uasal nan gàidheal

2   third day of beltane
day of avoiding

your enemies
    like fox
    like eagle
    like storm

like a fox creeping
through the copse of your imagination
consuming the words
black tutor of lies
in the form of a fox
    the chequer-tongued tutor
    taming your breath
    drowning your voice
setting prattle
      in place of your language

like an eagle winging
above his kingdom
bewitching you with
the taloned rights
      he claims
on the soil and coin of your labour
    eagle crowned
    eagle in saffron
    counterfeit eagle

there's storm, storm
in atom's embrace
the atom
bears in its fist
the storm quelled by man
the storm
a sleeping bull
in doll's cradle
as tether wears thin

3   beltane blessings on
the three lawful crimes of the gael

fo sgàthan dubh na h-oidhche
ballan-beothachaidh nan sruth
a' grùdadh fìon a bhith
'na struidh-leum shaor
thar taomadh eas
an t-airgead seangmhear sùghar
a' gabhail a' mhaghair

air brat-raon an rainich
mar fhaileas ruadh fillt'
eadar faileas a phròis
agus peilear a ghuinidh
    dòrn adhairceach fosgailte
    snaimt' ann an àile
    's a' tuiteam
feòil chabrach nam beann

an iolbheusachd slait tha
bàta snaidhte
    nì anam is ainmhidh ghiùlain
    gu leitirean dìon
bothan locairt
    a dhiùltas furan
    do gach fuaradh
bogha lùbte
    sàthadh shaighead
    anns gach sgrìob
    gu'n éirich crann

261 *samhla*

sàth le d' léirsinn an sgàile, tha mise (sùil d' fhaileis) an-seo
an clachan, an coire, an cochall do chridhe
mar phasgadh de shoillse reòit ann an linne céir

tha mi 'nam chidhis de dhathan, ach ged a bhiodh
eallaichean sùghar nan coille 'g abachadh 'nam ghruaidhe
am faic thu 'm madadh liath mireadh gu socair eadar na meuran

am faic thu portan is rodan a' dannsa gu tiamhaidh fon chliabh
is nathair air spiris an ugainn, a' deothal do bhriathran gu'm fiaradh
agus siud, far nach robh dùil, air chùl claiginn, iolaire briathradh

under the black mirror of night
reviving balm in the streams
matures the wine of its being
in free prodigal leaps
over teeming cataracts
succulent wanton silver
taking the bait

on the moor's banner of bracken
a red-brown shadow is folded in
between the shadow of its pride
and the wounding pellet
   an open fist of horn
     tangled in air
     and falling
antlered flesh of the bens

in the unstinting wood
boat finely carved
   will ferry soul or beast to
   sheltering slopes
bothy planed smooth
   never to welcome
   gust or gale
bow bent
   and plunging arrows
   in each furrow
   to grow as trees

appearance

pierce the veil with your vision, i (your shadow's eye) am present
in kirkton, in corrie, in the husk of your heart
like a folding of light in a pool of wax

i am a mask of colours, but even if
the succulent freight of the forest were ripening in my cheek
do you see the grey wolf quietly sporting between the fingers

do you see crab and rat dance solemnly under the rib-cage
the snake that roosts on the collar-bone, sucking your words to skew them
while there, unexpectedly, behind the skull, an eagle swears

gum bi an teist mar a bha, cho cruaidh, cuairteach ri slige cnò
ach, ged nach brist mi tro bhàrr mo ghréidhidh le sùrd
an tàmh tha mi luaineach, an tost tha mi fuaimneach

262   marilyn monroe

òr 'na do ghruaig
òr ann an ìnean do chas
òr ann an ruisg chadalach do shùilean beò
òr 'na do ghruaidhean, 'nam fathann athaidh
òr ruadh do bhilean
òr sa ghualainn mhìn àrd a' fasgadh do smig
òr anns a' bhroilleach ghealltanach
paisgte 'na bhad
òr 'na do chneas seang, air miadan do chruachan
ann an lùb nan sliasaid is
air glùin nan dìomhaireachd
rinn d' adhbrainn òrach
dannsa caol
do gach sùil a shealladh
airgead-beò 'na do chuislean
airgead-beò 'na do chridhe
airgead-beò gu na h-iomaill
dhe d' anam
agus d' osnadh, do ghàire
do ghuth-seinn, do ghuth-labhairt
mar bhraoin de dh'òr

agus do gach fear a chùm
air lios leaghteach nan dealbh thu
òr, o
bhàrr calgach do chlaiginn gu
buinn rùisgte do chas
òr, òr, òr,
beò no marbh

their cuid nach robh thu cho cùbhraidh
's iad a' deothal an t-sùigh
á sporan suilt òrach do bhèin
òr, òr, òr

that the proof will be, as always, hard, enclosing, shell of a nut
but, though i may not burst through the film that embalms me
in stillness i move, my silence gives voice

marilyn monroe

gold in your hair
gold in the nails on your feet
gold in the sleepy lids of your living eyes
gold in your cheeks, in their rumour of a blush
red gold of your lips
gold in the raised shoulder that shelters your chin
gold in your breasts, their promise
enfolded in wisps
gold in your slender waist, on the meadows of your hip
in the curve of thigh and
on your knee of mysteries
your golden ankle gave
slim dances
that any eye could see
quicksilver in your veins
quicksilver in your heart
quicksilver to every corner
of your soul
and your sighs, your laugh
your singing, your speech
like a mist of gold

and to every man who kept you
on the screen's dissolving field
gold, from
the maned top of your skull
to the bare soles of your feet
gold, gold, gold,
alive or dead

some say you weren't so fragrant
as they suck the substance
from the fertile purse of your skin
gold, gold, gold

263 *fòrladh dhachaigh*

bha uair a bha cianalas gam bhàthadh
nuair dh'inntriginn buailtean m' eòlais
's gum faicinn preas eile dhìth
sa mheasghart cheòlar

a-nise tha fearg a' snaidheadh mo bhriathran
gach rann 'na fhaillean san talamh chrìon

biodh e seang
biodh e anfhann
biodh e crom
biodh e pàiteach
se m' fhearg
           tha biathadh a dhuillich
           tha sìneadh a ghasan

264 bho *Sgàthach*

Don àrmann a thug coibhneas do charaid is do choigreach
léine-chròich, bràist' òir, agus làn chòir an caitheamh.

Don àrmann a sheas daingeann an aghaidh sitheadh nàmhaid
sgiath umha, sìol daraich, is comh-lìonadh beatha.

Don àrmann a dh'fhan dìleas nuair bu shùgach cuireadh géillidh
lios bàn, crò làn, agus gealltanas torachd.

Don àrmann nach do thréig ann an gailleann borb na còmhraig
claidheamh iarainn, faobhar mionnan draoidh ann.

Agus dhutsa, Chù Chulainn, ged bu diachainn chruaidh mo ghnè-sa thu,
an duais as àraid òrdha tha 'n còir mo thabhairt,
an duais nach làimhsich ach gaisgeach àraid,
gun coisinn thu mus fàg thu mi.

An Gath Beilge 'na lasair, chuireadh farmad air na diathan:
caithte leis an aon chois, fàgail aon leòn anns a' chliathaich,
trichead riofag sgaoileadh mach tromh chuislean dol an dìobhail —
an gaisgeach a gheibh sealbh air tha bhuaidh 'na dhàn anns an iargall.

home vacation

there was a time nostalgia drowned me
when i entered familiar pastures
when i saw another bush missing
from the orchard of sweet sounds

now rage carves my words
each verse a sapling in the barren earth

though it be slender
though it be weak
though it bend
though it need water
my anger
           will nourish its leaves
           will stretch its branches

from Sgàthach

To the warrior who gave kindness to both friend and to stranger
a saffron shirt, a badge of gold, and full right to wear them.

To the warrior who stood rocklike in the face of sudden onslaught
bronze shield, an acorn, and a life of fulfilment.

To the warrior who stayed faithful when surrender seemed sweet beacon
a clear field, stocked fold, and the promise of plenty.

To the warrior who never yielded in the fiercest storm of battle
sword of iron, sharp as druid's censure.

And to you, Cù Chulainn, sorest test of my good nature,
this rare most precious prize that I can give you,
which the greatest son of war alone can handle,
you will have earned before you leave.

The Fiery Dart is flaming, arousing envy among the great gods:
thrown by the one foot, makes only one wound in the body,
through which thirty barbs spread to ensure the strike is fatal —
the hero who possesses it is destined for great triumphs.

265 bho *An Turas Sìos gu Tìr nam Marbh*

Diarmad: O b' fheàrr leam fhìn bhith mach á seo
          'S air ais an gleanntan m' eòlais —
          Air thòir nam fiadh air raointean glan',
            'S chan ann air sràid an òtraich;
          Cha d'fhuair mi fois no cadal sèimh,
            Ach anshocair is dòlas
          On thug do mhealladh mi bho m' dheòin,
            A' traoghadh brìgh mo dhòchais.

          O b' fheàrr leam fhìn bhith mach á seo
            'S air ais an gleanntan m' eòlais,
          Air thòir nam fiadh air raointean glan',
            'S chan ann air sràid an òtraich;
          Tha beuc nan uidheam cràidhteach dhomh,
            Tha ghleadhraich dhomh 'na dòrainn —
          Is geur beatha staingte theann
            Le té nach eil leam pòsta.

          O b' fheàrr leam fhìn bhith mach á seo
            'S air ais an gleanntan m' eòlais —
          Air thòir nam fiadh air raointean glan',
            'S chan ann air sràid an òtraich.

Gràinne: Nach seall thu dannsa beò an t-sluaigh
           Thar lìomhachd gheal nan cabhsair,
          Is uinneagan nam bùithnean laist'
           Mar dheàlradh ghàrradh samhraidh.

Diarmad: Car son tha mis' an-seo 'nad chois,
           Mar chù a chaill a mhaighstir?
          'S mo sporan nise gu bhith bàn
           On dh'fhàg sinn an taigh òst' ud.

Gràinne: Nan toireadh thusa dhomh do bhlàths
           Cha bhitheadh tu cho diùmbach;
          Dé s ciall dha d' fhàgail aran slàn
           Mar ìobairt eadar-chùba?

Diarmad: Tha 'n t-aran sin 'na theisteanas
           Nach tàinig sinn gu siùrsachd —
          Gach latha chì mi 'na mo cheum
           Am pòsadh a rinn Fionn leat.

from *The Journey Down to the Land of the Dead*

Diarmad: I wish that I were out of here
    And back where I'm at ease with —
Pursuit of deer on cropped green sward,
    Not here on streets like dunghills;
I've had no rest nor slept at ease,
    Just discomfort and sorrow
Since your beguiling led me here,
    Where I am lost and hopeless.

I wish that I were out of here
    And back where I'm at ease with,
Pursuit of deer on cropped green sward,
    Not here on streets like dunghills;
The noise of traffic pains my ears,
    The uproar feeds my anguish —
O sour life in this ditch with you
    To whom I am not married.

I wish that I were out of here
    And back where I'm at ease with —
Pursuit of deer on cropped green sward,
    Not here on streets like dunghills.

Gràinne: But see the living dance of crowds
    Across white shining pavements,
And see the great store windows
    Lit like radiant summer gardens.

Diarmad: What am I doing here with you,
    A dog that's lost his master?
And now I've only pence to rub
    Since leaving that last guesthouse.

Gràinne: If you could give your warmth to me
    You wouldn't be so mournful;
Why do you leave that bread untouched
    Like a bedside sacrifice?

Diarmad: That bread stands as evidence
    We haven't turned to whoring —
Each step I take I see the day
    That you and Finn were married.

Gràinne: A Dhiarmaid MhicilleDhuinn,
sàth mi le d' phòig —
chan iarrainn ach thusa ri m' thaobh
tromh dhubhar na h-oidhche 's geal là;
on dhùisg thu mo ghràdh is mo dheòin
chan aithne dhomh sìochaint no tàmh,
's cha chaidil gu'n laigh ort mo shùil.
Na bi cho tìom:
na fàg mi 'n-seo fuaghal mo bhròin.

Diarmad: O thuirt mi riut is abraidh mi
     Cho fads tha deò 'nam chuimhne:
Nach dubh mi ás gu Latha Luain
     Am pòsadh a rinn Fionn leat.

An Torc: Có ach sinne? Có ach sinne?
Có ach sinne? Sinn na Tuirc!

Diarmad: Cha toil leam seo, bi faiceallach,
tha cron 'na rùn dhan treubh seo.

An Torc: Có ach sinne? Sinn na Tuirc!
     Ithidh sinne pitean 's buid!
Bheir tairbh is reithichean is buic
     Ùmhlachd dhìblidh dha na Tuirc!

Sdt Keith: B'e siud Mala Liath
's a sgioba de mheàirlich —
mura b'e a cuid mì-mhodh
bhiodh na sràidean seo sàbhailt';
bhiodh an saoghal fo'n ceannsachd
nan leigte ma sgaoil iad.

Gràinne: O, bu bheag orm an coltas,
gu h-àraid am bànrainn.

Sdt Keith: Chan eil glaistig cho cruaidh rith'
ri fhaotainn san dùthaich,
ach mo chùram-sa dìon thoirt
do dh'aoighean dhe'r seòrsa —
fiùs le faileas de bhuaireadh,
cuiribh teachdrachd dham iarraidh.

Diarmad: Mach leinne á seo,
gus am faigh sinn còs tèaraint'.

Gràinne: O Diarmad MacilleDhuinn,
pierce me with kisses —
I'd wish only you by my side
through the darkness of night and bright day;
since you woke my love and desire
I know neither peace nor rest,
nor will sleep till my eye lies on you.
Don't be so timid:
don't leave me here weaving my grief.

Diarmad: What I've told you I'll say again
    As long's my memory's breathing:
I can't burn out till great Doomsday
    That you and Finn are married.

The Torc: We're the only! We're the only!
We're the only! Fighting Torc!

Diarmad: I don't like this, be careful now,
this gang are out for trouble.

The Torc: Wha's like us? We're the Torc!
    We eat fannies, we eat cocks!
Every bull and ram and buck
    Cringes when he sees the Torc!

Sgt Keith: You've met Mala Liath
and her squadron of hoodlums —
were it not for their mischief
we'd have peace on our highways;
they'd take on the whole world
if we didn't control them.

Gràinne: God, I hated their manner,
especially their leader.

Sgt Keith: She's the hardest she-devil
in the whole of the country,
but it's my solemn duty
to protect guests such as you are —
just a whisper of trouble,
get a message out to me.

Diarmad: Let's clear off out of here,
better find us safe shelter.

Calum Greum (1942—)

266   *Daoine bha an Leódhas uaireigin*

Bu mhìorbhaileach na daoin' iad,
oighrichean acrach nan cruadalan.

Air an gineadh am bolg saillt na fairge,
bu neo-thruacanta chaidh an snaidheadh
á creagan greannach an coimhearsnachd.

Air an altram an uchd farsainn a' chruthachaidh,
bu luath a dh'fhoghlaim iad a dòighean
an oilthigh a cunnartan:
bu chabhagach am fàs gu fearalas.

Bu tapaidh treun-fèithichte na gàirdeanan
a chreach liosan uisgeach a' ghrunna.

Bu theann an greim-tachdaidh a rinn iad
air sgòrnan neo-ghealltanach an cuibhrinn,
a' fàsgadh ás dòchas is aran
(troimh stoirmean fallasach am beatha
bu tric bha gach cuid dhiubh a dhìth orr').

B' fheàirrd oighrichean sochaireach am buaidh
peann cruaidh an duinealas smiorail
a sgrìobh an cliù cinnteach le onair
air cladaichean fiadhaich Leódhais.

Tormod Caimbeul (1942—)

267   *Mi Fhìn agus a' Revolution agus mo Bhata-Darach*

"Thòisich i ri 'g éigheachd mo chrùisgean 's mo bhata-darach."

1   Bha mi 'n-diugh air Sràid a' Phrionns'
ann an cuan dhathan.
(Hi-ri-o-ri! Thàna mi!
Thàinig fuil is feòil MhicDhuibhne!
Borb is colganta MacDhuibhne!
Garg is borganta MacDhuibhne!

Calum Graham (Garrabost, Point, Lewis)

Lewis Heroes

They were wonderful, those men,
hungry heirs to adversity.

Conceived in the salty womb of the sea,
they were pitilessly hewn
from the harsh rock of their environment.

Nursed in creation's wide lap,
they were quick to learn her ways
in her university of dangers:
abrupt was their passage to manhood.

Powerful, strongly sinewed were the arms
that plundered the watery gardens of the deep.

Tight was the stranglehold they took
of their unpromising portion,
wringing from it both hope and bread
(through their storm-torn, toiling lives
they were often without either).

The privileged heritors of their victory
could do with the hard pen of that spirited manliness
which wrote their certain fame with honour
on the wild shores of Lewis.

Norman Campbell (S. Dell, Ness, Lewis)

Me and the Revolution and my Oaken Stick

"She started shouting my cruisie and my oaken stick."

1   I was today on Princes Street
in an ocean of colours.
(Hi-ri-o-ri! I've come!
Campbell's blood and flesh have come!
Fierce and bristling is Campbell!
Frightening and ferocious is Campbell!

Colganta is borbalta
Gargalta is borganta
MacDhuibhne, mo ghaisgeach!)
Ach bha mi gun sunnd,
gun faram, gun fonn;
cha robh sgeul air na suinn
a chuir smùid ri na Gaill
cho chionn fhada.
Fuich, fuich na Dùbhghallaibh
Fuich is fuich na fuididh.

Bha mi 'n-diugh fo sgàil a' chaisteil
's chuimhnich mi air na gaisgich:
fleasgaich threun nam féileadh
gillean calm' nan geur-lann —
cunbhalach is cinnteach —
cha tric a-nis an cuimhn' 'ad.

Ach a-màireach
A chàirdean
A-màireach a' revolution.

2   Agus bidh a' revolution seo
     fo stiùireadh ar deagh charaid,
     ar tighearna, ar prìomhaire,
     ar gealach, ar grian,
     ar clachan-meallain;
     lìonmhor do chrodh air àirigh, a mhic Mhaol-Onfhaidh!
     lìonmhor an t-aran-eòrna air do bhòrd!
     tlachdmhor do chlàrsach, do chlàrsair 's a cheòl!
     tlachdmhor do bhata-darach, d' òrdag 's do ghunna-fada!
     treunmhor do chlann a-màireach, a mhic Mhaol-Onfhaidh!
     Do mhoraileachd! Do mhoraileachd!
     A' revolution seo . . .
     A mhic Mhaol-Onfhaidh, do mhoraileachd!
     Seo mi 'n caolan mór Dhùn Éideann
     a' séideadh teine
     ag éigheachd, teine agus sgrios agus Dante agus brochan-corc.

     Nach cluinn sibh fuaim nam fear
     fuaim nam fear stuama
     gu h-àrd thar mhonadh

Bristling and fearsome
Frightful and ferocious
Is Campbell, my hero!)
But I was cheerless,
noiseless, tuneless;
gone were the heroes
who knocked spots off the Lowlanders
so long ago.
Yuch to the black Lowlanders
Yuch, yuch, what cowards.

I was today in the castle's shade
and I remembered the champions:
the brave kilted warriors
the bold lads of the sharp blades —
steady and sure —
seldom now are they remembered.

But tomorrow
My friends
Tomorrow's the revolution.

2   And this revolution
will be led by our good friend,
our lord, our leader,
our moon, our sun,
our hailstones;
many are the cattle upon thy shieling, O son of Maol-Onfhaidh!
many are the barley cakes upon thy table!
pleasant are thy harp, thy harper and his music!
pleasant are thy oaken stick, thy thumb and thy forefinger!
valorous are thy children tomorrow, O son of Maol-Onfhaidh!
Thy nobility! Thy nobility!
This revolution . . .
O son of Maol-Onfhaidh, thy nobility!
Here I am in Edinburgh's great intestine
blowing fire
shouting, fire and destruction and Dante and oatmeal porridge.

Don't you hear the noise of the men
of the valiant men
high across moorland

gu h-àrd thar chuantan
gu h-àrd
na fir uasal
('S tha fir nam feusagan gu h-ìosal
's thig sinn o gach taobh orr'
na prabairean, na fuididh)
Ach éist anam,
dùin-do-chab-dà-mhionaid . . .

3   Tha 'n t-uaireadair a' bualadh uair
    Tha ghaoth bho tuath a' tionndadh fuar
    Tha Suaithneas Bàn air cnàmh san uaigh
    ach geallaidh mi gun toir e buaidh
    a dh'aithghearr
    oir tha mac Mhaol-Onfhaidh gu cinnteach gu h-àrd
    's tha trèana mhór Mhalaig an àiteigin,
    's tha mis' an-seo air Sràid a' Phrionns'
    cho dòigheil ri botal Parozone.

4   Cho dòigheil a' danns' mi,
    danns', danns',
    danns' le mo bhata-darach;
    's an uair a thog mi mo cheann
    bha duine cam a' coimhead rium
    (duine mór molach
    le pluicean;
    duine dorch dosrach
    le crògan;
    duine mar dà uircean geamhraidh
    a' gabhail cuairt)
    le gàirdeachas, O àrdachas,
    chuir mi fàilte
    àrd mo chinn air:
    "Hi-ri-o-ri!
    Nach tusa MacCrioman?
    Cà bheil do phìob?
    An-diugh a' revolution!"

    'S thug e dhomh dòrn
    a chuir flat fuar mi
    air son uair a thìde.

high across oceans
high
the noble men
(And the bearded men are down there
and we'll come on them from all sides
the rabble, the cowards)
But listen my friend,
shut-your-trap-for-two-minutes . . .

3   The clock strikes one
The north wind is turning cold
The White Cockade has rotted in the grave
but I promise he will be victorious
soon
for the son of Maol-Onfhaidh is certainly up there
and the great Mallaig train is somewhere,
and I'm here on Princes Street
as happy as a bottle of Parozone.

4   So happily I danced,
danced, danced,
danced with my oaken stick;
and when I raised my head
a man with a squint was looking at me
(a big hairy man
with puffy cheeks;
a dark stubbly man
with great big paws;
a man like two winter's sucking-pigs
going for a walk)
with rejoicing, O highness,
I saluted him
at the top of my voice:
"Hi-ri-o-ri!
Are you not MacCrimmon?
Where is thy pipe?
Today is the revolution!"

And he gave me a thump
that laid me out cold
for a whole hour.

5   Thàna' mi timcheall le brùc
       aig bùth mhór Binn;
       glan-gorm an t-adhar os mo chionn
       le faoileag aonar a' triall tarsainn —
       thusa, thusa, fhaoileig bhòidhich,
       innis dhaibh gu bheil mi seòladh
       am measg bhrògan de gach seòrsa:
       brògan biorach
       brògan breòidhte
       brògan air nach toirinn gròta
       brògan a rinn clabhadh
       air òrdagan bha fàs gu fallain.

       Fallain fàs d' òrdagan, a mhic Mhaol-Onfhaidh!
       Geal-snasail iad air machair air mòinteach air ùrlar do dhachaigh!

       A' revolution seo . . .
       faoileag le sgiathan . . .
       mo bhata-darach . . .

       Nach dèan mi òran còmhnard
       Air Leódhas fuar nan cruachan-mònach
       Leódhas beag maiseach
       Far an d'fhuair mi — O, na can e!
         (Leig d' anail
         séid do shròin
         sgròb do chiabhag . . .
         O, plosgairtich mo chuirp
         aig bùth mhór Binn.)

6   Bu mhiann leam bhith triall leat air sgiathan na h-oidhch'
       Gu Leódhas beag riabhach bha riamh dhomh cho binn;
       Eilean snasail nan àirigh, nan càrn, 's nan crodh-laoigh
       Far am faigh thu deagh chàirdeas bho gach mac agus mnaoi
       Bho gach athair is màthair
       'S gu dearbha gu h-àraidh
       bho Murchadh mór nam mionach
       tha fuireachd anns na glinn.

       Bu mhiann leam, a luaidh, bhith air chuairt leat an-dràst'
       Aig tràighean a-siar eilean ciatach mo ghràidh
       Ann an sàmhchair an t-samhraidh chan eil ann àit' as fheàrr

5   I came round with a belch
      at Binns' department store;
      clear blue was the sky above me
      with a lone seagull flying across —
      thou, thou, lovely seagull,
      tell them I'm sailing
      amidst shoes of all kinds:
      pointy shoes
      rotten shoes
      shoes I wouldn't pay fourpence for
      shoes that crushed toes
      that were growing healthily.

      Healthy is the growth of thy toes, O son of Maol-Onfhaidh!
      How neat and white they are on the machair the moor the floor of thy home!

      This revolution . . .
      a seagull with its wings . . .
      my oaken stick . . .

      Won't I make a steady song
      About cold Lewis of the peat-stacks
      Little lovely Lewis
      Where I got — O, don't say it!
          (Take a breather
          blow your nose
          scratch your head . . .
          O, the panting of my body
          at Binns' department store.)

6   How I'd love to be flying with you on the wings of the night
      To little brindled Lewis which was ever so sweet-voiced to me;
      Charming isle of the shielings, the cairns and the milch cows
      Where you get such warm friendship from each man and each maid
      From each father and mother
      And indeed especially
      from big Murdo of the guts
      who lives in the glens.

      How I'd love, my darling, to walk with you just now
      At the western ebb shores of the fair isle of my love
      In the silence of the summer there's no better place

Chan eil àit' ann cho bòidheach, cho ceòlmhor, 's cho làn
de chrùbagan
de chrùbagan
de chrùbagan.

Ach nì mi co-dhùnadh 's mo shùil air an t-sliabh,
Air na raointean 's na caolais as àillidh fon ghrian;
Se mo mhiann is mo dhùrachd nuair thig mi gu crìoch
Bhith càir'te le m' chàirdean sa mhachair ud shìos —
mi fhìn agus mo bhata-darach
's mo sgealban
mo sgealban
's gun cumadh Dia mac Peodaran
fad' air falbh, fad' air falbh
ceud mìl' air falbh bhuam.

> (Ach bhàsaich esan le brag
> Aig doras-cùil taigh-òsta
> Latha mór nam pinntean)

Anna!
Las do chrùisgean!
Lorgamaid
　　　sgot
　　　　　céill.

Bu chaomh leam facal taing a thoirt dhan duine a sgrìobh 'Am Bruadar a chunnaic Anna' — amhran dealanaich agus amhran tàirneanaich.

Dòmhnall Iain MacÌomhair (1942—)

268　*Mathanas*

Thoir dhomh mathanas 'nad neochiontas
ma chuir mi m' fhuil 'nad chuislean
is m' fheòil air do chnàmhan
is mo pheacadh 'nad anam;
chan eil thu airidh
air truaillidheachd an trusgain sin.
An toir thu dhomh mathanas
nach do dh'ullaich mi an saoghal romhad
's tu togail ort aig tùs do shlighe,

There's no place as lovely, as musical, as full
of crabs
of crabs
of crabs.

But I'll draw to a close with my eye on the hill,
On the loveliest fields and kyles in the world;
My wish and desire when I come to the end
Is to be placed with my kin in yon machair below —
me and my oaken stick
and my limpet hammer
my limpet hammer
and God keep the son of Peodaran
far away, far away
a hundred miles away from me.

> (But he died with a bang
> At the back door of a pub
> On the great day of the pints)

Anna!
Light your cruisie!
Let's find
      a bit
         of sense.

I would like to say a word of thanks to the man that wrote 'The Dream that Anna saw' — a song of lightning and a song of thunder.

Donald John Maciver (Loch Croistean, Uig, Lewis)

Forgiveness

Forgive me in your innocence
if I've put my blood in your veins
and my flesh in your bones
and my sin in your soul;
you don't deserve
the corruption of that mantle.
Will you forgive me
for not preparing the world for you
as you set off to begin your journey,

nach do sguab mi fuath ás na seòmraichean
's nach do las mi teine ùr sa chagailt?
An toir thu dhomh mathanas
air son nan ùbhlan nach do thog mi ás an rathad
air na chaill mi fhìn cho tric mo chasan?
An toir thu dhomh mathanas
air son nan dìleab a fhuair mi fhìn
's mo shìnnsirean
aig tùs ar tòiseachaidh?
An toir thu dhomh mathanas
air son sireadh mathanais,
eadhon air son mathanas
mathanais?

269   *Indira*

Na ràinig do spiorad na diathan
tro cheò do lasraichean,
no 'n robh 'n aiseirigh dèante
nuair thréig an anail na h-asnaichean,
's uaignidheachd do chairbh-theine
a' losgadh mo cheistean
mus d'fhuair mi freagairt dhaibh,
ach dé thuirt na fàidhean
anns an fheallsanachd
a chàraich air an tiùrr thu
's a bha 'na sgàthan air do chreideamh caillte?
Chunnaic mi saoghal maille riut
air àrd-ùrlar do mhòr-lasaidh,
saoghal, dòigh-beatha is cànan
air an sgeadachadh leis a' chamfor,
leis a' chùbhraidheachd mheallta,
a' toirt a chreidsinn
nach robh fàileadh damaite —
samh a' bhàis —
a' ruighinn sròn nan diathan
a bha a' diathalachd os do chionn
mus deach an teine ás,
's an-sin an luath —
cha robh na lasraichean 'nan tàmh,
cha do dh'ith iad aran an dìomhanais,
cha robh iadsan ri fealla-dhà,

for not sweeping hatred from the rooms
and lighting a new fire in the hearth?
Will you forgive me
for the apples that I didn't pick off the road
on which so often I stumbled myself?
Will you forgive me
for the legacies got by myself
and my ancestors
at the start of our beginning?
Will you forgive me
for seeking forgiveness,
even for forgiving
forgiveness?

Indira

Has your spirit reached the gods
through the smoke of your flames,
or was resurrection accomplished
when the breath left the ribcage,
with the privacy of your pyre
burning my questions
before I could get answers to them,
but what did the prophets say
in the philosophy
that placed you on the bier
and mirrored your lost religion?
I saw a world with you
on the platform of your pyre,
a world, way of life and language
decorated with camphor,
with deceptive fragrance,
persuading people
that an accursed odour —
the stench of death —
couldn't reach the nose of the gods
who were shimmering above you
before the fire went out,
and then the ashes —
the flames were not at rest,
they did not eat the bread of vanity,
they were not joking,

's aig crìoch an Armageddoin sin
thog iad thu bho do chagailt,
's chì mi fhathast
saoghal is cànan is dòigh-beatha
a' sìor ghluasad ann am broinn do theine,
agus reòite, air sneachd an-iochdmhor
beanntan Himalaya.

270   *Cladh*

A' coiseachd tron chladh anns a' ghaoith fhuair
smaoinich mi air Gray 's air an 'Elegy',
agus smaointich mi cuideachd
nach b'e cuirp a-mhàin a bh' anns na h-uaighean
ach gun robh taisgt' an-sin cuideachd
iomadh sgeulachd is iomadh cràdh,
iomadh dòrainn is iomadh cliù,
nach fhaca, 's nach fhaic, solas latha gu bràth;

a bheil an cridhe a' bàsachadh cuideachd?
a bheil faireachdainn a' fuireach beò?
dé tha 'g éirigh do na h-aislingean
nuair chàirear an corp fon fhòd?

tha fhios gu bheil a' bheatha cruaidh
don neach tha daonnan dìreadh bheann,
am mullach daonnan fada shuas
's an dìreadh daonnan sgìth is mall;

a' coiseachd tron chladh anns a' ghaoith fhuair
smaoinich mi air beatha 's cha b'ann air bàs,
air na h-ìomhaighean 's air na h-aislingean —
s cinnteach nach e seo crìoch nam blàr,
nam blàr fuilteach 's nam blàr cruaidhe
taisgt' an cistean caol' sna h-uaighean;

chan e, chan e, cha shearg an ìomhaigh,
s buan a mhaireas i gu sìorraidh,
's nuair bhios clach sa chladh le m' ainm oirr'
s cinnteach gur e 'n corp a sheargas;

a' coiseachd tron chladh anns a' ghaoith fhuair
smaoinich mi air a' phian 's air a' chràdh,

and at the end of that Armageddon
they raised you from your hearth,
and I still see
a world and language and way of life
ever-moving in the belly of your fire,
and frozen, on the merciless snow
of the Himalaya.

Graveyard

Walking through the graveyard in the cold wind
I thought of Gray and of the 'Elegy',
and I thought too
that the graves contained not merely corpses
but that also stored away there
were many tales and agonies,
many griefs and reputations,
that never saw, nor ever will, the light of day;

does the heart die too?
does feeling stay alive?
what happens to dreams
when the body's buried?

of course this life is very hard
for one who's always climbing hills,
the summit always further up
while slow and tiring is the climb;

walking through the graveyard in the cold wind
I thought of life and did not think of death,
I thought of images and dreams —
it's certain this is not the end of strife,
of bloody strife and violent strife
stored in narrow coffins in the graves;

no, no, the image will not waste,
for ever and ever will it last,
and when a stone in the graveyard bears my name
it's certainly the corpse that wastes;

walking through the graveyard in the cold wind
I thought of the pain and of the agony,

air an eachdraidh a tha làn de sgeulachdan,
's air mac-talla nach robh freagairt mo dhàin;
gu h-àrd anns an adhar bha còisir a' seinn
's cha chualas air thalamh leam briathran cho binn —

O mairidh, O mairidh na h-aislingean beò,
's cha bhàsaich an cridhe gu sìorraidh,
cha mhùchar an cridhe le teine no ceò
's cha sgriosar gu bràth an ìomhaigh.

271　*Dàin*

Có a leughas na dàin nach do sgrìobh mi?
Nuair bhàsaicheas mi
spìon mo chridhe ás mo chorp,
's le cutaig mhìn
dèan bearradh beag,
is chì thu leabhar
sa bheil sgrìobhte na dàin nach do sgrìobh mi;
fuasgail e gu cùramach
le sùilean caomha, blàth',
tog ás na briathran
aon mu seach
is gheibh thu dealbh
air Eden mar a bha e
mus do nochd an nathair ann.

Maoilios M Caimbeul (1944—)

272　*Dòchas*

Dòchas —
rionnag anns na speuran.

Dùil —
rocaid agus rionnag anns na speuran.

Creideamh —
adhar làn rionnagan.

Cinnt —
grian a' deàrrsadh.

of the history that's full of tales,
and of an echo that didn't match my drift;
up high in the sky a choir was singing
and nowhere have I heard any words so sweet —

O dreams will last, will last alive,
and the heart will never ever die,
the heart won't be quenched by fire or smoke
and the image will never be smashed.

Poems

Who will read the poems that I have not written?
When I die
pluck my heart out of my body,
and with a delicate gutting-knife
make a little incision,
and you will see a book
in which are written the poems which I did not write;
free it carefully
with gentle, warm eyes,
lift out the words
one at a time
and you'll have a picture
of Eden as it was
before the serpent appeared in it.

Myles M Campbell (Staffin, Skye)

Hope

Hope —
star in the skies.

Expectation —
rocket and star in the skies.

Faith —
sky full of stars.

Certainty —
sun shining.

273   *Do Chròcus air a Shlighe a Nèamh*

Srianagan flannach
ann am meadhon a' ghuirm
mar rocaid bhithean iongantach
ann an tìr os cionn ar céill,
a' socrachadh air planaid mo thuigse.
No saoil a bheil thu coltach ruinne,
a' ruighinn 's gun a bhith ruighinn,
gun thu ruighinn ach leth thugainn,
air chall ann an astar do bhith,
sinn le chéile a' siubhal
troimh eadar-fhalamhachd nan reul
a' feitheamh ri slànaighear dhìthean.

Saoghail suaint' ann an saoghail,
d' fhear-sa cùbhraidheachd is dath
mar gum biodh annad strì siubhail
gu inbhe nach eil thu tuigsinn.
No ann an gintinneachd na cruinne
an tàinig an camadh ceàrr ort
's gu bheil thu nise glaist' 'nad thiotan
's 'nad cheann-uidhe, lì is tùis?

— agus ann an aon nì eile,
d' àilleachd.
Air sgàth an àilleachd sin
a th' eadar thusa agus mise,
a' còmhnaidh annadsa no annamsa,
a' sileadh troimh chaol-lìn ar nàdair,
nì mi dhut mar as miann leat,
spìonaidh mi thu á do fhreumhan
agus bheir mi dhachaigh a nèamh thu
am measg nan dia. Bidh tu an-sin
ann a bhàs air mullach a' bhùird
a' moladh agus air do mholadh.

S dòcha nach ruig mise air nèamh
ach ruigidh tusa.
Tha do shìorraidheachd air teachd,
a chompanich-tìm, mo bhràthair.

To a Crocus on its Way to Heaven

Purple streaks
in the middle of the green
like a rocket belonging to strange beings
in a land beyond our sense,
settling on the planet of my understanding.
Or I wonder if you are like us,
arriving and not arriving,
reaching only half to us,
lost in the depth of your being,
together travelling
through the space between the stars
waiting for the saviour of flowers.

Worlds coiled within worlds,
yours one of fragrance and colour
as if there was a striving in you to travel
to a level you do not understand.   .
Or in the generation of the world
did you take the wrong turning
that you are now locked in your moment
and in your destination, hue and incense?

— and in one more thing,
your beauty.
For the sake of that beauty
that is between you and me,
dwelling in you or in me,
pouring through the fine mesh of our nature,
I will do as you desire,
I will tear you from your roots
and take you home to heaven
among the gods. You will be there
in a vase on the table
praising and being praised.

Perhaps I'll not reach heaven
but you will.
Your eternity has arrived,
time companion, brother.

274   *An Referendum air son Pàrlamaid ann an Alba 1/3/79*

Air latha an Referendum

Tha sneachda ga do chòmhdach
mar òigh a' dol gu a banais,
's ged a dhiùltas do ghilead na tràillean
bidh tu ann an ceangal a' phòsaidh
mus bi an oidhche seachad,
Alba bhòidheach dha'n tug mi gràdh.
Tha thu air tighinn gu inbhe,
fàgaidh tu taigh t' athar
agus seasaidh tu ann an comann saor
ris a' chòrr den t-saoghal.
Bidh tu fhéin agus saorsa
'nan càraid a' fàs gu suairce
agus air an latha seo éiridh tu suas
agus canaidh tu, cha dhealaich sinn gu bràth.
Agus cuimhnichidh tu air do latha bòidheach,
air an latha a sheas thu 'nad chulaidh ghil,
agus bidh tu moiteil agus glan agus saor.

ach air an latha an déidh an Referendum

A thruaghain!
'S tu 'nad òigh fhathast
gun saorsa, gun solas, gun ola.
Nach bochd nach tàirngeadh cuideigin thu!
Ach tha eagal orm gum fàs thu
'nad sheann mhaighdeann, gearanach, crosta,
ag éisteachd ris a' ghaoith anns an t-simileir
agus anns na craobhan fàsail,
a' feitheamh ris a' phosta a' tighinn,
a' faicinn do thiormachd anns an sgàthan,
a' tarraing do shàilean an taigh t' athar —
thu 'na thaice gu h-iomlan —
a' smaoineachadh air na seòid
nach tig gu bràth gad iarraidh.
Theich do bhòidhchead.
Cha bhi eòlas agad air gràdh.
Agus càite bheil na mnathan a nì gaoir
no a bhuaileas basan aig do thuireadh?

The Referendum for a Scottish Assembly 1/3/79

On the day of the Referendum

Snow covers you
like a virgin going to her wedding,
and though your whiteness repels slaves
you'll be in the bonds of marriage
before the night is out,
beautiful Scotland whom I have loved.
You have come of age,
you will leave your father's house
and stand in free communion
with the rest of the world.
You and freedom
will be a couple growing civilly
and on this day you will rise up
and you will say, we will never part.
And you will remember your beautiful day,
the day that you stood in your white dress,
and you will be proud and pure and free.

but on the day after the Referendum

You wretch!
A virgin yet
without freedom, or happiness, or oil.
How sad that no-one could nail you!
But I'm afraid you will grow
to be an old maid, complaining, bad-tempered,
listening to the wind in the chimney
and in the desolate trees,
waiting for the postman to come,
seeing your barrenness in the mirror,
dragging your heels in your father's house —
completely dependent on him for support —
thinking of the suitors
who will never come to seek you.
Your beauty has fled.
You'll have no knowledge of love.
And where are the women who will keen
or strike palms at your funeral?

275   *An t-Aran*

An uair a chuireas mi an t-aran
am measg an trealaich,
an uair a shadas mi an leanabh dubh
a-mach gu fir a' ghlanaidh,
smaoinichidh mi air an sanas
a chunnaic mi ann am pàipear-
naidheachd na Sàbaid —
leanabh Innseanach bochd
a' chléibh fhalaimh
agus nam ball dubh-losgadh . . .
Sinne a' coimhlionadh ar crìch àraidh,
a' toirt breith le dìol an arain.

Agus canaidh mi
dé tha thusa dèanamh
a tha 'na do Chrìostaidh?
no mise air a bheil eagal
a bhith 'na mo Chrìostaidh?
air a bheil eagal
a bhith 'na mo pheacach . . .
ann an tìr làn de neoni . . .

na solais dheth
agus Crìost 'na fhaileas lasrach
do-chaigneach air a' bhalla.

276   *Na Liopan*

An uair seo se na liopan a bh' ann
anns a' bhùth-aodaich i 'na seasamh
fa mo chomhair 's mi 'g iarraidh briogais
caileag bhòidheach a' bhodhaig chuimir
na cam-lùban bàn a' tuiteam mu gualainn
's i reic aodach fir.

Bha iad pinc agus cruinn agus deiseil
gu bruidhinn iad cho làn is i
cho diùid cho ciùin cho còir
's mise cho lom a' faireachdainn
fa comhair am measg an aodaich

Bread

When I put the bread
amongst the rubbish,
when I throw the black child
out to the bin-men,
I think of the advert
I saw in the Sun-
day paper —
the poor Indian child
with the empty rib-cage
and the black burning limbs . . .
Here we fulfil our chief end,
judging with the retribution of bread.

And I say
what are you doing
who are a Christian?
or I who am afraid
to be a Christian?
who am afraid
to be a sinner . . .
in a land full of nothing . . .

the lights off
and Christ a flickering fleeting
shadow on the wall.

The Lips

This time it was the lips
as she stood before me in the clothes shop
and I wanting trousers
the pretty trim-bodied girl
fair curls falling on her shoulders
selling men's clothes.

They were pink and round and ready
to speak they so full she
so shy so calm so kind
and I so bare feeling
before her among the clothes

a' ceannach briogais. Seann dheise orm
caran robach 's m' iongnan gun ghearradh
a' faireachdainn salach sean ise
òg cho glan air a h-éideadh
's mise ag iarraidh 'na làthair
còmhdach fa comhair mi lom
ise gun aodach an t-aingeal
le briogais.

277   An t-Eilean 'na Bhaile

Ann an dòigh se baile a th' ann am Muile,
ann am baile tha na treubhan measgte.
Se baile th' ann le sluagh sgapte
mar a tha an saoghal a' fàs gu bhith 'na bhaile,
na seann luachan, treubh is cinneadh,
a' seargadh ann an saoghal gnìomhachais, teicnigeach.

Chunnaic mi dà chloich 'nan seasamh 'nan aonar —
chaidh lianag fhàgail dhaibh anns a' choille ghiuthais,
clachan s dòcha a thogadh nuair a bha a' ghealach naomh,
iad 'nan seasamh mar dhà phrionnsa, no prionnsa 's a ghràdh,
'nan clachan-cuimhne do shìol rìoghail.
Treubh a chaidh á bith.

Chunnaic mi clach eile — Dòmhnall Moireasdan, Àrd Tuna,
ceithir fichead 's a cóig deug, is 'inntinn geur mar sgithinn,
làn de sheanchas is bàrdachd a threubha,
colbh sgairteil de Chlann na h-Oidhche,
agus timcheall air am baile a' fàs —
baile nach tuig e — luachan do-ruigsinn dha chéile.

Tha am prionnsa 'na chloich anns a' choille,
agus treubh ùr air a thighinn.
Chan eil rìgh 'nam measg a dhearbhas
a threòir.
Is tuath iad le cridheachan pàipeir;
pàtaranan faoine a' losgadh.

Cha dèan na mnathan gaoir tuilleadh, is an t-eilean 'na bhaile.

buying trousers. With an old suit
somewhat ragged and my nails uncut
feeling dirty old she
young so cleanly clothed
I wanting in her presence
a covering before her bare
she without clothes the angel
with trousers.

The Island a Town

In a sense Mull is a town,
in a town the tribes are mingled.
It is a town of dispersed people
as the world grows to be a town,
the old values, tribe and kin,
withering in an industrial, technological world.

I saw two stones standing alone —
a lawn was left for them in the pine wood,
stones perhaps raised when the moon was holy,
standing like two princes, or a prince and his love,
memorial stones to a seed royal.
An extinct tribe.

I saw another stone — Donald Morrison, Ardtun,
ninety-five years of age, mind sharp as a knife,
full of the history and poetry of his tribe,
stalwart column of the Children of the Night,
and round him the town growing —
a town that does not understand him — values that cannot be bridged.

The prince is a stone in the wood,
and a new tribe has arrived.
There isn't a king among them to prove
his valour.
They are a peasantry of paper hearts;
empty patterns burning.

The women will lament no more. The island is a town.

278 *An Clamhan*

Muile nam monaidhean farsaing
  Agus nam bailtean gun daoine;
An clamhan air chaithris 'na rìoghachd
  Ag éisteachd ri beul-aithris na gaoithe.

279 *Am Fear-Turais*

Fear-turais á Sasainn —
thàinig e staigh dhan bhàr
aon oidhche ann am meadhan an t-samhraidh,
e bruidhinn mu eòin a chunnaic e
air eilean Threisnis — nach robh e mìorbhaileach!
ceithir seòrsa thar fhichead —
ach aon nas lugha na 'n-uiridh.

'S ann an Sasainn
bhiodh e a' faicinn eòin cuideachd
nuair a gheibheadh e saor
o chosnadh bùirdeasach.
'S thuig mi 'n uair sin
gum bu duine e ás an fhicheadamh linn —
beagan ceart, beagan ceàrr,
beagan bog, beagan air chall,
gun e tuigsinn na bha tachairt,
's ged a thuigeadh, gun e 'na chomas
na h-eòin a bheannachadh ceart.

280 *Glaschu*

An uair a bha mi 'nam leanabh
cha chreidinn gun caochaileadh
mo mhàthair aon latha.
Bha mi dìreach ga àicheadh
gu tur.
Uaireannan dheigheadh i a Ghlaschu —
airs bith cà' robh Glaschu —
agus thilleadh i.
Sin e, nuair a chaochaileadh i
bhitheadh i ann an Glaschu.

The Buzzard

Mull of the spacious moors
   And the deserted townships;
The buzzard wakeful in his kingdom
   Listening to the oral tradition of the wind.

The Tourist

An English tourist —
he came into the bar
one night in midsummer,
talking of birds he had seen
on the Treshnish islands — wasn't it marvellous!
twenty-four varieties —
but one less than last year.

And in England
he would see birds also
when he was free from
his middle-class occupation.
And I understood him then
as someone from the twentieth century —
somewhat right, somewhat wrong,
somewhat soft, somewhat lost,
not understanding what was happening,
and, even if he did, not able
to bless the birds aright.

Glasgow

When I was a child
I couldn't believe
my mother would die one day.
I just wouldn't
believe it.
Sometimes she would go to Glasgow —
wherever Glasgow was —
and return.
That's it, when she died
she would be in Glasgow.

Cha robh mi air tiodhlacadh fhaicinn.
'S ged a tha a-nis,
tha Glaschu fhathast
air oir mo smuain.

Tha e doirbh fàs mór.

281   *Borgh Leódhais*

Eaglais le uinneagan dathte
ri taobh an taigh againn. Eaglaisean
an àiteachan eile, òrdaighean
anns na h-eaglaisean. Ministearan
ann an aodaichean dubha,
busaichean a' tighinn o na h-òrdaighean,
agus sinn a' seinn shalm. Eildearan
ag ùrnaigh 's a' gàireachdainn . . .
agus 'cailleachan' ann am beannagan
aig bòrd a' chomanachaidh.
Taighean geala agus taighean dubha,
tidsearan le strapaichean,
uèirichean an telefon,
agus Di-Sathairne á Steòrnabhagh
drungairean air busaichean,
agus aon rud nach dìochuimhnichinn —
briosgaidean Ròigean, tioram, neo-mhilis,
cho cruaidh ris na crùbagan.

Tha a' mhuir a' seinn an àiteigin,
tha mi a' cluinntinn a monmhair;
fada shìos air cùl nan gàrraidhean,
cho sòlaimte ri òrgan,
a' còmhradh, a' gàirich.

282   *Gealach na Sultain*

Dealbh le Kiyonaga (1752–1815)

Saoil an tig thu a-nochd, a ghràidh,
air feasgar foghair
dhan t-saoghal air bhog seo.
Na dèan maille, Ukiyo,

I hadn't seen a funeral then,
and although I have now,
Glasgow is still
at the back of my mind.

It's hard to grow up.

Borve, Lewis

A church with stained glass
beside our house, churches
in other places, communion services
in the churches. Ministers
in black clothes,
buses coming from the communions,
and we singing psalms. Elders
praying and laughing . . .
and 'cailleachs' in kerchiefs
at the communion table.
White houses and black,
teachers with belts,
telephone wires,
and on Saturday from Stornoway
drunkards on buses,
and one thing I couldn't forget —
Roigean's biscuits, dry and unsweet,
crab-hard.

The sea sings somewhere,
I hear its murmur;
far away behind the walls,
solemn as an organ,
conversing, roaring.

September Moon

A painting by Kiyonaga (1752–1815)

I wonder if you will come tonight, darling,
this autumn evening
to this floating world.
Do not linger, Ukiyo,

agus a' ghealach am bàgh Edo —
fann, cho fann, a fiamh tro sgòth —
agus na bàtaichean-iasgaich,
sradagan anns an dorch.
Na bi fada, Ukiyo.
Fàg do bhean agus thig gu Yoshiwara,
a-staigh air an aon gheata
gu saoghal an t-seilich.
Tha a' ghealach agus mise a' feitheamh.
Feuch gun tig thu
agus mo ghruag fhathast an òrdugh.
Dèan cabhag, a ghaoil,
mus tig Sakata gam shireadh.

283 bho *Haiku*

Tha mo chù
'na bhàrd cho math riums'.
Bidh e a' comhartaich
ri nàimhdean.

284 *A' Càradh an Rathaid*

Oilisgin buidh' orm
's mi càradh an rathaid,
a' lìonadh nan toll
le teàrr agus morghan.
Tha cuimhn' a'm mar a bha an teàrr
a' bristeadh 'na bhuilgein
ann an teas na h-òige.
Sinn a-nise
a' càradh an rathaid
nach eil a' dol a dh'àite.

Thàinig fear a thuirt:
Cuir an-siud i, a charaid —
tha an rathad a' bristeadh fo'r casan.
Teàrr a' chridhe fàs cruaidh,
gun ghrian ann ga thòcadh,
e dìreadh, e teàrnadh,
's gun teàrnadh ann —
an t-aon a dhèanadh feum.

the moon is in Edo bay —
faint, so faint, its gleam through cloud —
and the fishing boats,
sparks in the dark.
Don't be long, Ukiyo.
Leave your wife and come to Yoshiwara,
in by the one gate
to the world of the willow.
The moon and I are waiting.
See and come
while my hair is still in order.
Hurry, love,
before Sakata comes looking for me.

from *Haiku*

My dog
is a poet as well as me.
He barks
at enemies.

Mending the Road

With a yellow oilskin on
I mend the road,
filling the holes
with tar and aggregate.
I remember how the tar
used to break in bubbles
in the sultriness of youth.
Now
we mend the road
that is going nowhere.

One came who said:
Put it there, my friend —
the road is breaking under our feet.
The heart's tar hardens,
no sun to swell it,
climbing, descending,
there is no ascent —
the only one to remedy.

Eun air a' ghéig
's e seinn leis fhéin:
    Ille bhig, ille bhig,
    na biodh dragh ort,
    na biodh dragh ort,
    chan eil rathad anns an adhar,
    car son a tha thu a' càradh
    an rathaid nach eil a' dol a dh'àite?

Tha an rathad cho cùilteach,
gluasadach, lùbach,
fo fhàire fradhairc,
'na lìon-chuislean gun chrìch
ann am bodhaig na cruinne,
aon mhionaid cho slàn,
's an uair sin ga phronnadh.

    Na creid, na creid
    nach eil e dol a dh'àite
    (arsa bodach an rathaid);
    abaichidh gach nì
    's bidh an cridhe sàsaicht'
    le samhla,
    le fuil bhlàth nan cuislean
    's thig gach nì gu àite
    mar anns an toiseach.

An-dràsta lìon na tuill
's bi dol air d' aghaidh:
feumaidh gach duine bhith siubhal —
's a' càradh.

285 *Ceartas Coma a' Bhàis*

Molaidh mi thu, a bhàis,
air son seo,
agus air son seo a-mhàin:
do cheartas coma
a leagas an t-aintighearna gu làr
's nach leig leothasan
mar Sellar is Ceauşescu
a bhith beò gu bràth.

A bird on the twig
singing by itself:
>Little boy, little boy,
>do not worry,
>do not worry,
>there is no road in the sky,
>why do you mend the road
>that is going nowhere?

The road is so creviced,
mobile, tortuous,
below vision's horizon,
the never-ending vein-webs
in the body of creation,
one moment whole,
the next crushed.

>Don't believe, don't believe
>that it goes nowhere
>(said the old man of the road);
>each thing will ripen
>and the heart will be sated
>with a symbol,
>with the veins' warm blood
>and everything will arrive at its place
>as in the beginning.

For the moment fill the holes
and go on your way:
everyone must travel on —
and be mending.

The Indifference of Death

>I will praise you, death,
>for this,
>and for this alone:
>your indifferent justice
>which lays the tyrant low
>and does not allow people
>like Sellar and Ceauşescu
>to live forever.

286   *An Éibhleag*

Sonas a' deàrrsadh
mar an éibhleig bheò.
A-màireach bidh thu dubh —
ach las is loisg is leum a-nochd.

287   bho *Agus mar sin car a' Mhuiltein*

agus dhùisg mi aon uair eile / an turas seo ann am bàta / agus an duine beag 'na
shuidhe anns an deireadh / agus thuirt e / 'Cha bhi thu an-seo a-màireach' / 'O
mo ghràdh ort' / arsa mise / mar gun robh fhios agam cà' robh mi / no cà' 'm
bithinn an ath thiotan / agus rinn mi gàire / ach thuirt e / 'Tha do bhliadhna gu
bhith suas / a-màireach bidh thu air ais ann an Ostabhaig' / 's ged a bha mi
faireachadh màbte / choimhead mi mun cuairt orm / 's bha mi air loch ciùin / cho
ciùin ri Pàrras / 's bha bogha-frois air fàire / os cionn nan craobhan / 's bha eas a'
tuiteam o chreagan àrda / gu mall / gun chùram / mar gum biodh gu sìorraidh /
's bha mi dol a bhruidhinn / a' dol a bhruidhinn ris an duine bheag uaine / ach cha
robh e ann / 'na àite bha an nighean àlainn / sèimh agus ciùin bha a gàire / agus
bha i mar gum biodh 'na pàirt dhen uisge / agus dh'fhairich mise cuideachd ciùin
/ mar phàirt de nàdar / nàdarrach mar a bha nàdar / mar a bha an t-uisge / anns
an eas / gu bràth a' tuiteam / anns an aon àite / agus thuirt an nighean a bha seo /
an nighean leis a' ghràdh 'na sùilean / 'Gabhaidh tu ris' / 's thuirt mise /
'Gabhaidh mi ri dé?' / agus thuirt i a-rithist anns an aon ghuth chiùin / 'Gabhaidh
tu ris / ris an tuil / ris a' chiùine / ris na sìthichean / 's ri daoine' / 's bha a falt bàn
thar a gualainn a' deàrrsadh / 's chaidh mi air son bontainn rithe / air son mo làmh
a chur 'na làimh / ach chaidh i á sealladh / agus mar sin car a' mhuiltein . . .

Iain MacDhòmhnaill (1946—)

288   *Hearach*

Do ghnùis
rocach air a sgoradh
le grian is gaoth is uisge
mar bheanntan d' eilein.

Do chrògan
a dh'fhairich fuachd, teas,
cuideam, reubadh, blàths,

The Ember

Happiness gleaming
like the living ember.
Tomorrow you'll be black —
but light and flame and flare tonight.

from *And so Somersault*

and I woke up once again / this time in a boat / with the little man sitting in the stern / and he said / 'You will not be here tomorrow' / 'O bless you' / I said / as if I knew where I was / or where I would be the next moment / and I laughed / but he said / 'Your year is to be up / tomorrow you will be back in Ostabhaig / and though I felt harassed / I looked around me / and I was on a peaceful loch / as peaceful as Paradise / and there was a rainbow on the horizon / above the trees / and there was a waterfall tumbling down from high rocks / slowly / negligently / as if it were for ever / and I was going to speak / going to speak to the little green man / but he wasn't there / in his place was the beautiful girl / gentle and calm was her smile / and she seemed as if she were a part of the water / and I felt calm too / as if I were a part of nature / natural as was nature / as was the water / in the waterfall / forever falling / in the same place / and this girl said / the girl with love in her eyes / 'You will accept it' / and I said / 'I will accept what?' / and she said again in the same calm voice / 'You will accept it / accept the flood / accept the calmness / accept the otherworld people / and accept human beings' / and her blonde hair over her shoulder was gleaming / and I made a motion to touch her / made a motion to put my hand in hers / but she disappeared / and so somersault . . .

Ian MacDonald (Grimsay, N. Uist)

Harrisman

Your face
lined and scored
by sun and wind and rain
like the mountains of your island.

Your hands
that have felt cold, heat,
weight, tearing, warmth,

gearraidhean is slànachadh,
paisgte air do bheulaibh
mar fhreumhan craoibhe.
Chum iad beò thu.
Tha choltas orra.

Do ghuth
sìtheil cho domhainn
ri locha dorcha, ciùin
am mòintich d' eilein.

289   *Turas*

Thill sinn feasgar
far an robh sinn a' gearradh.
Ràinig sinn am bàgh leis a' gheòla.

An làn a' tighinn
's an fheamainn a' dol air bhog.
Thòisich sinne ga cruinneachadh.

Bha 'n sàl flodach.
Shlaod sinn am ball ri chèile.
Theannaich sinn an ròp aig an oir.

Cha robh e ro mhòr
ach bha e tiugh, dùmhail.
Dhèanadh e buntàta gu leòr dhuinne.

Dh'fhalbh sinn leis
's e ceangailte ri tobhta.
Sheas am badadh 's cha do thruis e.

Bha i air fàs fuar
mun d'ruig sinn, 's lot dearg
a' dol am feabhas san àird an-iar.

Gealach fhann
ag èirigh, còta bàn
sgòthan mu casan, 's muir-làn ciùin.

Oidhch' eile bha siud, bliadhn' eile.

cuts and healing,
folded in front of you
like the roots of a tree.
They kept you alive.
They look it.

Your voice
peaceful and as deep
as a dark, calm loch
in the moors of your island.

Once

We went back in the evening
to where we had been cutting.
We reached the bay in the boat.

The tide having turned
and the seaweed beginning to float.
We began to gather it together.

The salt water was lukewarm.
We pulled the raft of seaweed together.
We pulled the rope tight at the edge.

The raft was not too big
but it was thick, well-packed.
It would grow enough potatoes for us.

We set off with it,
tied to a thwart.
The binding held, didn't run along the rope.

It had grown cold
before we arrived, with a red wound
healing in the west.

A pale moon
rising, a petticoat
of clouds round its feet, and a calm high tide.

That was another night, another year.

290 *An t-Uisge*

Tha 'n t-uisge sileadh
air mo chlaigeann lom
is air mo chnàmhan geal rùisgte,
is mi 'nam shìneadh gu balbh
eadar Uibhist is Ifrinn.

Is a' drùdhadh air cliathaich Eubhal,
air an smùr dhubh mhìn
a tha fuar leis an ùine
o chaidh an fhalaisg às.

Is air grunnan thaighean
shìos ris a' chladach —
clachan is muran is luachair —
is na bheil annta,
muinntir nach toir buaidh,
mar nach tug sinne.

291 *Ainmeannan*

Aonranach ainmeannan àiteachan
aig an stad sinn an-dràsta 's a-rithist,
air an astar fhada eadar dà fhàrdaich
no eadar dà shaoghal:
iadsan gun chaochladh
ge b'e cò 'n taobh a thèid sinne —
suas no sìos, samhradh no sian,
falbh no tighinn.

Aonranach ainmeannan àiteachan —
aognaidh tron ghlainne
'nan litrichean grinne,
'nan solas gun bhlàths,
'nan ciùineachd dealain,
'nan comharran slighe.

The Rain

The rain is falling
on my bare skull
and on my naked white bones,
as I lie dumbly
between Uist and Hell.

And soaking through the side of Eaval,
through the fine black dust
which is cold because the heather fire
went out so long ago.

And through a group of houses
down by the shore —
stones and bent grass and rushes —
and those in them,
people who will not win,
as we did not.

Names

Lonely the names of places
at which we stop now and then,
on the long trail between two dwellings
or between two worlds:
they unchanging
whichever way we go —
up or down, summer or storm,
coming or going.

Lonely the names of places —
bleak through the glass
in their neat letters,
in their light without warmth,
in their electric calm,
signs of the way.

Catrìona NicGumaraid (1947—)

292   *Gealladh Gaoil*

Bha gealladh gaoil anns na duilleagan
  dha'n tug thu breab air an t-slighe
nuair a thill sinn ri chéile
  — 's bha do shùilean cho milis.

Ach nuair a bheir mi sùil thar mo ghualainn
  gu geur tron an t-suirghe,
saoil an e rabhadh tiamhaidh
  bha sa bhreab ud do m' chridhe?

293   *Sireadh*

Choisich mi mach
    air cladaichean ciar mo bheatha
's dh'amhairc mi air creagan mo shòlais . . .

Is an uair sin,
    dìreach mar sin,
        chunnaic mi puill mo dhórainn
— tuinn mo nàdair, sìos is suas,
    gu na rionnagan no gu na h-uaigh,

a' plapail dìreach tiotan bhuam
no sgrìobadh fad air falbh mu Eilean Theàrlais,
    null, thall bhuam, aig Eilean Theàrlais.

Is an uair sin, gille-brìghde
    a' coiseachd gu speirgeach air an tràigh
    gun suim aig'
        —— ochan, ochan,
        brìgh mo bhàrdachd,
        brìgh mo bhròin, m' uallach 's m' ochan.

Ruigeadh m' anam mach gu Eilean Chanaigh
    thar nan ulbhagan gun smaointinn,
    a' flotadh suas mun an Taigh-Sholais,
    sìos seachad Meall a' Ghrìobaidh,
    null an uair sin chun an Stob Iullan,

Catriona Montgomery (Roag, Dunvegan, Skye)

The Promise of Love

There was a promise of love
    in the leaves you kicked in your path
when we returned together and
    your conversation was seductive.

But when I look over my shoulder
    cynically through the courtship,
was there a plaintive warning
    in that kick to my heart?

Seeking

I walked out
    on the dusky shores of my life
and I viewed the rocks of my joy . . .

And then,
    just like that,
        I noticed the pools of my anguish
— the fluctuating waves of my character, rising and falling,
    to the stars or to the grave,

palpitating a little distance from me
or stretching far away by Harlosh Island,
    far, far away, by Harlosh Island.

And then, an oyster-catcher
    arrogantly patrolling the beach
    without concern
      —— my God,
        for the essence of my poetry,
        my anguish, and my sighing.

My soul would wander to the Isle of Canna
    over the waves without concern,
    floating up by the Lighthouse,
    down past Meall a' Ghrìobaidh,
    over then to the Stob Iullan,

a' lorg m' anam is mi a' sireadh,
mi fhéin air chall le tacadh amhaich
    — deòir neònach 'na mo bhroilleach
    nach tuit gu bràth
    gu Lath' na Cruinne,

strì, 's a' strì ri siubhal an Duine,
mi fhìn, mi fhìn 's mi dol á follais
    sìos, sìos chun a' ghrunna,
's a' togail ceann an-dràst 's a-rithist . . .

    O Thì — mise! mise!
    Sgìth! sgìth! mise! mise!

    Dé 'n t-ioghn',
      dé 'n t-ioghn',
        ars an t-isean.

294   An Ceusadh

Air dealbh fhaicinn de 'An Ceusadh' le Mìcheal Angelo: do mo mhàthair fhèin

Thusa 'n-sin a' deuradh na fala,
mis' an-seo a' sileadh nan deur . . .
a' mhàthair a' caoidh a cuid cloinne
a tha fhathast 'na cuideachd 's a dh'fhalbh.

Fearghas MacFhionnlaigh (1948—)

295   An Geiréiniam

tha peatalan a' gheiréiniam
a' deàrrsadh neon-dhearg
's a' crithinn gu h-aotrom
le cniadachadh ciùin an deòthain

agus tha gaganan de ghucagan òga
le amhaichean caola eala-lùbt'
a' crochadh mar chnòthan mun cuairt
a' ghallain mhàthaireil mhòrail

searching for the soul, and seeking
the self who is lost with a choked heart
    — strange tears
    which will never be shed
    till the Day of Judgement,

striving, and striving to follow the Self,
myself, myself as I disappear
    down, down to the dark depths,
my head bobbing up now and then . . .

    My God, my God, I am exhausted,
    I am exhausted.

No wonder,
   no wonder,
      sang the bird.

The Crucifixion

On seeing 'The Crucifixion' by Michelangelo: for my own mother

You there dripping the blood,
I here pouring tears . . .
the mother lamenting her children
who are both in her company and gone.

Fearghas MacFhionnlaigh (Vale of Leven)

The Geranium

the petals of the geranium
shine neon-red
and shake lightly
with the gentle caress of the breeze

and clusters of young buds
with slender swan-curved necks
hang like nuts around
the magnificent motherly sapling

agus a' bogadan
              beagan
a-nis 's a-rithist

feuch se fìor-dhearg a th' ann
gun phriobadh neo dol ás
oir chan eil inntinn
aig an dìthean
a dh'fhulaing amharas

296　*Medusa, an Cuclopach, 's an* Daily Record

air an treas duilleag

cìochan, gam tharraing
mar dhà phól mhaighneid
— déimhneach 's diùltach

sinean, a' cur dealain tromham
mar dhà eleactród
— anód is catód

a chaileag, se craobh-phàrrais a th' annad
is dà mheas Eubha 'nad bhroilleach
— a' buileach eòlais maithe 's eòlais uilc

agus cà bheil a' chraobh-phàrrais
gun nathair 'na duilleach
a' cagarsach peacaidh?

ar leam gur léir dhomh tòrr nathraichean
ri séis mun cuairt do chinn
is cruas mì-chneasta deàrrsadh ás do shùilean

ach ged a chluicheas tu Medusa
a' cur ás dhan fhear a sheallas ort
tha sinn mar-thà air cur ás dhuits (a ghràidh)

le sùil chuclopaich a' chamara

and bob

                            a little

now and again

look it's pure red
without blinking or going out
for the flower
has no mind
to have suffered doubt

Medusa, the Cyclops, and the Daily Record

on the third page

breasts, drawing me
like two magnetic poles
— positive and negative

nipples, electrifying me
like two electrodes
— anode and cathode

O girl, you are a tree of paradise
with Eve's two fruits in your bosom
— bestowing the knowledge of good and evil

and where is the tree of paradise
without a serpent in its foliage
whispering sin?

I think I see a lot of serpents
hissing around your head
with cruel hardship shining from your eyes

but even if you play Medusa
destroying the man who looks upon you
we have already destroyed you (my dear)

with the cyclopean eye of the camera

297 *An Tuagh*

thàinig e oirbh mar shrònadharcach 'na dheann
is sibh a' feitheamh
mar shulu le sleagh

thàinig e oirbh mar tharbh
is sibh a' feitheamh
mar mhatador le claidheamh

thàinig e oirbh mar thanca
is sibh a' feitheamh
mar shaidhdear le greinèid

thàinig e oirbh mar dhragon
is sibh a' feitheamh (gu h-ìoranta tha fhios)
mar an Naomh Seòras

thàinig e oirbh le ulfhartaich chon is Talai-hò
ach bu sionnach sibh
nach teicheadh

thàinig e oirbh mar dhìneosor
ach b' ainmhidh ùr sibh
le Einstein 'nur ceann

thàinig e oirbh mar locomòtaibh fo smùid
is sibh mar dhrochaid
an impis éirigh

thàinig e oirbh
le àrdan Napoleon
le gaoirchatha Genghis Khan
le tàirchainnt Hiotlair fhéin
le ain-iochd Stailinn
le ìmpiricheas Shasainn
le bodhaig de Bohuin

thàinig e oirbh
is sibh 'nur dìollaid
mar iolair air creig
mar leòmhainn air crùban

The Axe

he came at you like a rhinoceros at speed
as you waited
like a zulu with a spear

he came at you like a bull
as you waited
like a matador with a sword

he came at you like a tank
as you waited
like a soldier with a grenade

he came at you like a dragon
as you waited (ironically of course)
like St George

he came at you with the howling of dogs and a Tally-Ho
but you were a fox
that would not flee

he came at you like a dinosaur
but you were a new animal
with Einstein in your head

he came at you like a locomotive under steam
and you were like a bridge
about to rise

he came at you
with the pride of Napoleon
with the battlecry of Genghis Khan
with the invective of Hitler himself
with the cruelty of Stalin
with the imperialism of England
with the body of de Bohun

he came at you
and you in your saddle
like an eagle on a rock
like a crouching lion

thàinig e oirbh
le lanns is sgiath is clogaid is dos
is each is armachd is tàirneanach is fallas
is sitheadh is duslach is ràiteachas is bàs

thàinig e oirbh

ach a chlisge
le gluasad luath
le gradghluasad cruinn
le deasghluasad pongail
le snasghluasad brìoghmhor
san robh an sàs ar n-eachdraidh gu léir

bhoillsg druilinn
ur tuagh sa ghréin
is thuit briosgbhuille a' sgoltadh
clogaid is claiginn

a' leagadh Goliat ùr
'na chairbhinn chun an làir

ach bhriseadh ur tuagh, a Rìgh
is tha t'éile fhathast a dhìth oirnn

298   *Flùrannan*

❀ sìol-mhéinnichean, a' mallspreadhadh
❀ dath-bhomaichean seirceil
❀ lì-fhuarain reòidhte, a' leaghadh gach madainn
❀ muileannan-gaoithe deàrrsach a' sìor shùghadh neachtair
❀ òr-chuachan driogach a' sìor shnigheadh meala
❀ coinfiti air ginideachadh 's air tighinn fo bhlàth
❀ gùc-ghàireachdainn na talmhainn ri fealla-dhà
❀ sròl-bhrataichean nan Nàisean Aonaichte air crainn uaine
❀ heliphuirt nam meanbh-fhrìde le ràdar ultra-bhiolait
❀ factaraidhean foto-cho-chur a' beò-ghlacadh na gréine
❀ ciùineachagan radharcach
❀ solasan trafaig na h-aigne
❀ obairlainn cùbhraidheachd

he came at you
with lance and shield and helmet and plume
and horse and armour and thunder and sweat
and thrusting and dust and boasting and death

he came at you

but suddenly
with a swift movement
with a round quick-movement
with a careful ready-movement
with a substantial neat-movement
upon which our entire history hinged

there flashed out of nowhere
your axe in the sun
and a smart-stroke fell splitting
helmet and skull

knocking the new Goliath
as a carcase to the ground

but your axe was broken, O King
and we still lack another

Flowers

❀ landmines, slowly-exploding
❀ affectionate colour-bombs
❀ frozen colour-wells, melting every morning
❀ shining windmills steadily sucking nectar
❀ gold-goblets of distillation slowly exuding honey
❀ confetti propagated and come into bloom
❀ the bud-laughing of the earth convulsed in mirth
❀ the silk-banners of the United Nations on green flagpoles
❀ insect heliports with ultra-violet radar
❀ photosynthesis factories seizing the sun alive
❀ visible tranquillisers
❀ traffic lights of the psyche
❀ fragrance workshops

❀ crainn-sgaoilidh dhath-theilifis

❀ sbruileach air tuiteam o bheul a' bhogha-froise

❀ coinnlean is tùisearan is uinneagan de ghloine dhathte

❀ cleasan-teine fàs-bheairteach

❀ port-á-beul bith-cheimigeach

❀ bilean boireannta a' sèimhphògadh ar sùilean

299   bho *A' Mheanbhchuileag*

Bha mi 'nam shuidhe uair a' leughadh aig bòrd
nuair a mhothaich mi lìon damhain-allaidh
air taobh a-muigh na h-uinneige
agus meanbhchuileag ri strì innte.
Choimhead mi fhads a nochd an damhan-allaidh.
Chaidh mi air ais gu m' leabhar.
Nach b'e dòigh nàdair sin?
Meanbhchuileag agus damhan-allaidh air lìn.
So-leòntachd agus cumhachd snìomhte le chéile.
Ach chuir e dragh orm.

Tha e a' cur dragh orm
gu bheil a' mhòrchuid den t-saoghal fo shàl,
is leth an latha fo dhorchadas,
is luisreadh an dà Mhul fo dheigh,
is Machu Picchu 'na thobhta,
is an dodo air dol á bith,
is grabhataidh a' cur spàirn ruinn,
is an treas cuid de ar beatha air caitheamh ann an suain,
is dà thrian de ar n-eanchainnean á feum,
is cidhis na cruinne-cé air sleamhnachadh
a-chum nach eil co-chothram ann eadar bòidhchead is fìrinn,
is breugan a' cnàmhadh ar planaid
mar ghithean an corp cait,
's gu bheil a leithid de rud ann idir ris an abrar bàs,
a-chum gur buaine cnàmhan na eanchainn
is plastaig na gaol.

Innsidh mi seo dhuit —
chan e Atlas a th' annam;
chan urrainn dhomh an saoghal a ghiùlain.
Chan eil annam ach atam air druim an domhain,
ri strì eadar fisean is fiùisean.

❀ colour-television transmitting-masts
❀ crumbs fallen from the rainbow's mouth
❀ candles and censers and stained-glass windows
❀ organic fireworks
❀ biochemical mouth-music
❀ female lips gently kissing our eyes

from *The Midge*

I was sitting once reading at a table
when I noticed a spider's web
outside the window
and a midge struggling in it.
I watched as the spider appeared.
I went back to my book.
Was that not the way of nature?
A midge and a spider on a web.
Vulnerability and power woven together.
But it troubled me.

It troubles me
that most of the world is under sea,
and half the day under darkness,
and the foliage of the two Poles under ice,
and Machu Picchu a ruin,
and the dodo extinct,
and gravity fighting against us,
and a third of our lives spent in sleep,
and two thirds of our brain out of use,
and the mask of the universe having slipped
so there is no correlation between beauty and truth,
and lies riddling our planet
like maggots in a cat's corpse,
and there is such a thing as that which is called death,
so that bones are more durable than brain
and plastic than love.

I'll tell you this —
I'm not Atlas;
I cannot bear the world.
I am only an atom on the surface of the globe,
struggling between fission and fusion.

Tha e a' cur dragh orm
a' faicinn dùthaich a' dol fodha
mar chaisteal-gainimh fon làn,
is cànain air tilgeil uainn
mar bhratach phàipeir ghlas,
's weltanschauung air dearmad
mar aisling-latha fhaoin,
is eachdraidh air dol á fianais
mar lorg-coise cloinne air an tràigh.

Innsidh mi seo dhuit —
chan e Fionn a th' annam;
chan urrainn dhomh mo dhùthaich a ghiùlain.
Chan eil annam ach cealla am bodhaig Albainn,
ri strì a bhith 'nam chealla-eanchainn.

Tha mi beag 's tha eagal orm roimh rudan beaga:
a' chealla aillseach a sgriosas bodhaig,
am facal òinseach a sgriosas gaol,
am bonn-airgid a reiceas rìoghachd,
an t-atam sgoilt a sgriosas Hiroisimea,
a' vìoras nimheil, am peilear nàimhdeil,
mearachd ann an inntinn feallsanaich.

Dh'ionnsaich mi rud —
tha mi bàsmhor;
s dòcha gun tig a-màireach ás m' aonais.

Bu toil leam a bhith mar Mhaois,
a' sgrìobhadh bhriathran Dhé;
ach bhriseadh clàr-cloiche am peann plastaig agam.
Agus a bharrachd air sin
chan eil preas loisgeach agamsa
mar choinneil.

Bu toil leam a bhith mar Argas,
a' coimhead air an domhan le ceud sùil;
ach tha an iunaibhears ro àibheiseach dhomh.
Gidheadh mur faic mi a h-uile nì
cionnas a bhios cinnt agam air nì sam bith?
Nach fheum eanchainn an cruinne shlugadh
mus bi i fallain?

It troubles me too
to see a country sink
like a sand-castle beneath the tide,
and a language thrown from us
like a faded paper flag,
and a weltanschauung forgotten
like an empty daydream,
and history disappear without a trace
like a child's footprint on the beach.

I'll tell you this —
I'm not Fionn;
I cannot bear my country.
I am only a cell in Scotland's body,
struggling to be a brain-cell.

I am small and fear small things:
the cancer cell that destroys a body,
the stupid word that destroys love,
the coin that sells a kingdom,
the split atom that destroys Hiroshima,
the poisonous virus, the enemy bullet,
a mistake in the mind of a philosopher.

I learned something —
I am mortal;
maybe tomorrow will come without me.

I would like to be like Moses,
inscribing the words of God;
but a stone tablet would break my plastic pen.
And besides
I have no burning bush
for a candle.

I would like to be like Argus,
gazing on the world with a hundred eyes;
but the universe is too vast for me.
Though if I don't see everything
how will I be certain of anything?
Doesn't a brain have to swallow the universe
before it can be sane?

Uaireannan
chì mi nithean a' tighinn beò
's a' dol 'nan ceò;
a' binndeachadh
's a' leaghadh.

Éist ri srann nan ataman!

A bheil iad ann far an robh iad?
Am mair iad far a bheil iad?
Eil fhios có bhios annad sa mhadainn?

Dé cho daingeann 's a tha iarann?
Dé cho buan 's a tha inntinn?

An dèan thu faileas anns a' ghréin?

Innsidh mi seo dhuit —
chan fhaighear cinnt ach ann am preas loisgeach.

Am bi mi beò a-màireach?
An robh mi beò riamh?
Tha mi taingeil
gun do shlìob mi cat.

Thuirt Giacometti uair
nan robh teine ann an ealainlann
gun teasraigeadh esan cat roimh Rembrandt.
Duine glic.
Cha sgriach peantadh sna lasraichean.

Bha cat againn fhèin a fhuair bàs.

Tha fhios nach eil e iomchaidh
a bhith a' caoidh cait
nuair a bhios
crith-thalmhainn an Sìona,
is tuiltean sa Bhangla Dais,
is goirt feadh leth an t-saoghail.

Ach bha cat againn a fhuair bàs;
agus bha gràdh againn air . . .

Sometimes
objects appear
to disappear;
rematerialise
dematerialise.

Listen to the atoms buzz!

Are they there where they were?
Will they remain where they are?
Are you sure who you'll be in the morning?

How solid is iron?
How stable is mind?

Do you cast a shadow in the sun?

I'll tell you this —
the only certainty is in a burning bush.

Will I be alive tomorrow?
Was I ever alive?
I am thankful
to have caressed a cat.

Giacometti said once
that if there were a fire in an art gallery
he would rescue a cat before a Rembrandt.
A wise man.
A painting will not scream in the flames.

We ourselves had a cat which died.

Of course it isn't proper
to lament a cat
when there are
earthquakes in China,
and floods in Bangla Desh,
and famine throughout half the world.

But we had a cat which died;
and we loved him . . .

Tha mi beag, agus is toil leam na rudan beaga:
an sìol adhlaict' a sgoltas an cabhsair;
an t-sileag uisg' a chaitheas a' chlach;
a' ghainmhein mhìn a thiodhlaiceas am biorramaid;
a' chiad eun a chuireas fàilt' air a' ghréin;
an dùthaich bheag, an cànan beag;
facal na fìrinn as truime na 'n Domhan.

Gu h-obann dh'éirich mi
agus chaidh mi don chidsin,
a' tilleadh le sgian gheur.
Dh'fhosgail mi an uinneag
agus gheàrr mi gu faicilleach
tron lìon mu thimcheall na meanbhchuileig
gus an robh i fuasgailte.
Dh'fhalbh i air iteig,
agus chaidh an damhan-allaidh air ais 'na tholl dorch.

So-leòntachd agus cumhachd;
dòigh na cruinne-cé.

So-leòntachd agus cumhachd;
agus tròcair.

300   bho *Iolair, Brù-Dhearg, Giuthas*

O chionn ochd ceud bliadhna pheant am fear-ealain Sìonach
Ma Yüan dealbh air an tug e an t-ainm
"Bàrd a' dearcadh air a' Ghealaich"

(Agus dé as ciall dhan Ghealaich?
An i sgàthan na Gréine no sgàthan na h-Inntinne?
Càite bheil Cearcall an t-Solais a' tòiseachadh?

Mon Dieu, tu es la lumière de ma vie.
Tu éclaires la nuit
où je suis.)

Os cionn a' Bhàird a tha 'na shuidhe tha Giuthas aost' a' fàs.
Bhàrr géige chithear badan de thrì cuilg
a' tuiteam san t-sàmhchair gun fhiosda sìos.

I am small, and I like the small things:
the buried seed that splits the sidewalk;
the water-drop that devours the stone;
the grain of sand that inters the pyramid;
the first bird that welcomes the sun;
the little country, the little language;
the word of truth that is heavier than the World.

Suddenly I rose
and went to the kitchen,
returning with a sharp knife.
I opened the window
and cut carefully
through the web around the midge
till she was free.
She flew off,
and the spider went back to its dark hole.

Vulnerability and power;
the way of the universe.

Vulnerability and power;
and mercy.

from **Eagle, Robin, Pine**

Eight hundred years ago the Chinese artist Ma Yüan
painted a picture which he called
"A Poet looks at the Moon"

(And what is the meaning of the Moon?
Is it the mirror of the Sun or the mirror of the Mind?
Where does the Circle of Light begin?

Mon Dieu, tu es la lumière de ma vie.
Tu éclaires la nuit
où je suis.)

Above the sitting Poet grows an ancient Pine.
Off a branch a cluster of three needles is seen
falling in silence unknowingly down.

Dé as ciall do thrì cuilg-giuthais a' tuiteam còmhla
san t-sàmhchair fo sholas na Gealaich? — Mas ciall neo-chrìochnach e
dé chanas sinn a-réiste mun Chraoibh-Ghiuthais shlàin?

Agus dé mun Bhàrd a tha 'na shuidhe?
Agus dé mu Ma Yüan a pheant an dà chuid bàrd 's Giuthas?
Agus dé umainn fhèin a chì a déidh ochd linntean a' chùis-chléith?

"Tha fuilteinean bhur cinn uile air an àireamh," thuirt am Mesiah.
" — Chan eil aon ghealbhonn air dhearmad am fianais Dhé."
An giùlain sinn na tha sin de chuideam brìghe?

Gu'm bi mac-talla sìorraidh aig gach facal dìomhain?
— Trì cuilg-giuthais a' tuiteam fo sholas na Gealaich.
Tha mi gan cluinntinn.

Tha mi gan cluinntinn a-nis.
Tha guthan aca.
Tha iad a' seinn.

Gliocas a lorg — chan e sin an duilgheadas. Sann ann an gliocas
a tha sinn beò 's a' gluasad 's a tha ar bith againn.
Se tha duilich ùmhlachd a thoirt dhan Ghliocas a tha sinn air lorg.

Tha aon duilleag mòr gu leòr
gu bhith 'na ràth-teasairginn dhan inntinn.
Éiridh craobh 'na bàta fa ar comhair.

Nì brù-dhearg a' chùis
mar leus-mara dhan aigne.
Fóghnaidh iolair gus neo-chrìochnachd a dhearbhadh.

301 bho *Bogha-Frois san Oidhche*

Tre chreideamh dh'ìobair Abrahàm,
air dha a bhith air a dhearbhadh,
a mhac Isaac . . .

A' meas gum bu chomasach Dia
air a thogail eadhon o na mairbh;
on d'fhuair e e eadhon ann an samhladh.

EABHRAIDHICH 11:17–19

What is the meaning of three pine-needles falling together
in silence under the light of the Moon? — If it's an infinite meaning
what do we say then about the whole Pine-Tree?

And what about the sitting Poet?
And what about Ma Yüan who painted both a poet and a Pine?
And what about ourselves who see after eight centuries the correspondence?

"The hairs of your head are all numbered," said the Messiah.
" — Not one sparrow is forgotten before God."
Do we bear that much importance?

So that every idle word has an eternal echo?
— Three pine-needles falling under the light of the Moon.
I hear them.

I hear them now.
They have voices.
They are singing.

Finding wisdom — that's not the problem. It's in wisdom
that we live and move and exist.
The problem is submitting to the wisdom we have found.

One leaf is big enough
to be a life-raft for the mind.
A tree rises like a boat before us.

A robin will do
as a beacon for the intellect.
An eagle will suffice as proof of infinity.

from *Rainbow in the Night*

By faith Abraham,
when he was tested,
offered up his son Isaac . . .

Considering that God was able
to raise him even from the dead;
from whence, figuratively speaking, he did in fact receive him.

HEBREWS 11:17–19

Getsemane: "Amar-bruthaidh ola"

Ola fhìor-ghlan a' chroinn-ola,
brùite air son an t-solais.

ECSODUS 27:20

Ach b'i toil an Tighearna a bhruthadh;
chuir e fo àmhghar e.

ISAIAH 53:10

Dh'ung thu le ola mo cheann.

SALM 23:5

'Nad thròcair, a Thighearna, ung
ceann brùite ar Duine Staoin-ne
le ola.

OLA

Ola.
Sgaoilte air an rathad fhliuch.
Dathan a' bhogha-frois
taoisgte
air an tarmac
dhubh.

Aig meadhan-là shuidh iad ri taobh an rathaid, an taic uillt bhig, agus dh'fhosgail
Diorbhail a basgaid agus thug i a-mach beagan arain. Thairg i pìos dhan Bhodach-
Ròcais, ach dhiùlt e. "Cha bhi an t-acras orm idir," thubhairt e; "agus tha e
fortanach nach bi. Oir chan eil mo bheul ach air a dhèanamh le peant, agus nan
gearrainn toll ann ach an ithinn, thigeadh a' chonnlach leis a bheil mi air mo lìonadh
a-mach, agus mhilleadh sin cumadh mo chinn." Chunnaic Diorbhail sa bhad gun robh
seo fìor, uime sin cha d'rinn i ach a ceann a ghnogadh agus chum i oirre ag ithe a h-
arain.

L FRANK BAUM, *BUIDSEACH OZ*

Gethsemane: "Oil-press"

Pure oil of the oil-tree,
bruised for the light.

EXODUS 27:20 THE GAELIC BIBLE

But it was the will of the Lord to bruise him;
he has made him sick.

ISAIAH 53:10 RSV FOOTNOTE

Thou anointest my head with oil.

PSALM 23:5

In Your mercy, Lord, anoint
the bruised head of our Tin Man
with oil.

OIL

Oil.
Spilt on the wet road.
Colours of the rainbow
flooding
the black
tarmac.

At noon they sat down by the roadside, near a little brook, and Dorothy opened her basket and got out some bread. She offered a piece to the Scarecrow, but he refused. "I am never hungry," he said; "and it is a lucky thing I am not. For my mouth is only painted, and if I should cut a hole in it so I could eat, the straw I am stuffed with would come out, and that would spoil the shape of my head." Dorothy saw at once that this was true, so she only nodded and went on eating her bread.

L FRANK BAUM, THE WIZARD OF OZ

Iogart Beò

Mean air mhean thill comas-slugaidh Chiarain.
Ged nach b' urrainn dha fhiaclan a dhùnadh buileach glan,
bha comas-cagnaidh aige a-nis chun na h-ìre 's gun gabhadh
biadhan sìmplidh — leithid loiliopop reòthte no iogart — a thoirt dha.
Chan itheadh e gu leòr mar seo, gun teagamh,
agus chaidh a bheathachadh dha-rìribh fhathast
tron tiùb shròn-ghastrach aige.

Co-dhiù, bhon a bha e air a bhith cho tric fo bhuaidh antibiòtaigean,
bha na bactèria ghasta ud a nì feum dhuinn 'nar rianan-cnàmhaidh
air dol á bith san stamaig aigesan.

Bha Dr Lin dhen bheachd gun robh iogart "beò"
math ann an cùisean mar seo
gus "ath-thuineachadh" a dhèanamh air a' mhionach.

A-mach gun do ghabh mi am beul na h-oidhch' an tòir air a' iogart bheò.
Cha robh a leithid a rud ri fhaighinn am feasgar sin.
Mu dheireadh thall dh'fheuch mi an delicatessen a bha seo.
Nuair a chaidh mi a-steach, bha am fear air cùl a' chunntair
a' cabadaich ri cuideigin.
Thug mi sùil tro uinneig a' frids air crogan a dh'iogart Greugach.
Saoil an dèanadh sin an gnothach?
Ri ùine fhuair mi cothrom bruidhinn ri fear na bùtha.

"Do you have any live yoghurt?"

"Hold on while I go out and catch some!" fhreagair e.

Cha d'rinn mi fiamh-ghàire. "Well," lean e air, "it all depends on what you mean
by *live* — all yoghurts are alive to some extent!"

"*Forget it!*" thuirt mi gu guineach, a' tionndadh a dh'ionnsaigh an dorais.

"There's no need to be like *that!*" ars esan.

LIVE YOGHURT

Very gradually Ciaran's ability to swallow returned.
Though he could not yet close his teeth,
he had enough of a chew to deal with simple foods
— for instance an ice-lolly or yoghurt.
Of course, this wasn't enough to keep him going,
so his real nutrition still came
via his nasal-gastric feeding-tube.

Also, since so many powerful antibiotics had been used on him,
even those necessary and useful bacteria of the digestive tract
had been wiped out.

Dr Lin said he was a believer in live yoghurt
as a means of "recolonising" the gut
in cases like these.

So off I went that evening in search of some live yoghurt.
Could I find a shop which had any?
Eventually I tried a particular delicatessen.
When I went in, the fellow behind the counter
was blethering to someone.
I peered through the fridge window at a carton of Greek yoghurt,
wondering whether that might do.
After a while I managed to speak to the shopkeeper.

"Do you have any live yoghurt?"

"Hold on while I go out and catch some!" he replied.

I did not smile. "Well," he continued, "it all depends on what you mean by *live* —
  all yoghurts are alive to some extent!"

"*Forget it!*" I rasped, turning towards the door.

"There's no need to be like *that!*" he said.

AN SEÒMAR-BÌDH

Bha prìomh thrannsa-cheangail an ospadail air leth mì-chàilear.
Seòrsa de chaolan ìochdarach a bh' ann.
Donn. Dorch. Teth. Teann. Claon.
Cha robh làr no mullach no balla réidh.
An-siud 's an-seo stobadh pìob a-mach gus bagairt
a dhèanamh air do cheann.

Bheireadh lioft (nan nochdadh e), no staidhre, suas thu
chun an t-seòmair-bhìdh. (Bhon innidh chun na stamaig?)
A réir coltais cha tàinig e a-steach air cuid dhen
fhoireann-bìdh cho cianail truagh
's a bha feadhainn dhe na pàrantan.
Daoine s dòcha nach robh air greim ithe fad làithean,
a bha air a bhith 'nan suidhe ri taobh leabaidh leanaibh
a bha a' bàsachadh. A shlaod iad fhèin air falbh, s dòcha
gus blasad bìdh a ghabhail. A' fàgail
na codach bu mhò dheth air an truinnsear.

Cha robh clann ceadaichte san t-seòmar-bìdh.
Bha an staidhre, ge-tà, sgeadaichte le dealbhan a rinn clann.
Duilleagan an fhoghair fhathast air cuid dhiubh, tha cuimhn' agam.
Cha mhòr gun tug mi sùil orra.
Ge b'e càit an coimheadainn a là no a dh'oidhche,
bha mo fhradharc lìonte le balach rag air leabaidh.

Là a bha seo dhìrich mi an staidhre seo le Màiri.
Chaidh sinn a-steach dhan rùm-ithe.
Macaroni cheese no *stovies*.
Bha an làr air chrith le inneal-cidsin air choreigin.
Thàinig an tuainealaich orm.
Cur na mara.
Sheas mi air ais 's mo dhruim an taic a' bhalla.
Dhùin mi mo shùilean.

Sann ann an saoghal eadar aisling
agus trom-laighe a bha sinn beò.

The Canteen

The main connecting corridor of the hospital was particularly off-putting.
It was a sort of lower gut.
Brown. Dark. Hot. Constricting. Twisting.
Not a floor nor a ceiling nor a wall was regular.
Here and there a pipe would jut out
and threaten your head.

A lift (if it appeared) or a stairway would take you up
to the canteen. (From bowel to stomach?)
And some of the dining-staff didn't seem to realise
just how distraught
many people were.
Parents who perhaps had not eaten for days.
Who had been sitting at the bedside
of their dying child. Eventually
they'd come to eat something. Only
to leave most of it on the plate.

Children were not allowed in the canteen.
The stairway, though, was decorated with paintings by children.
I remember some collages with autumn leaves.
I really wasn't capable of taking them in.
Wherever I looked, day or night, I saw before my eyes
a paralysed boy on a bed.

One day I climbed these stairs with Mary.
We entered the dining-room.
Macaroni cheese or *stovies*.
The floor reverberated to some kitchen appliance or other.
I felt dizzy.
Sea-sick.
I stepped back and let the wall hold me up.
I closed my eyes.

We lived in a world somewhere
between dream and nightmare.

Dòmhnall Greumach (1949—)

302 *Superloo Steòrnabhaigh*

A-nis, a bhalaich Leódhais, mas e 's gun tig an t-àm
'S gun tadhail sibh air Steòrnabhagh air son bhur pinnt is dram,
Théid a-steach dhan taigh-aolaich anns a' phub fhads bhios sibh ann
Neo bidh sibh coiseachd dhachaigh le bhur casan gu math cam.

Tha dà thaigh bheag sa bhaile sin de sheòrs' nach fhacas riamh
A thàinig 'n àit nan socharan a bh' againne bho chian;
Cha chluinn thu òran Gàidhlig, 's chan fhaigh thu balgam fìon —
Nach truagh a-nis tha cùisean anns na h-Eileanan an-Iar.

Se tha gu bhith duilich anns a' gheamhradh, 's e cho fuar
'Nar seasamh anns a' chiudh tha siud le sneachd is gaoth bho thuath,
A h-uile fear le làmh mu cheann a' cumail air a ghruaig
'S na caileagan a' feitheamh air son sùil thoirt air an gruaidh.

Deich sgillinn tha a dhìth ort mus fhaigh thu steach don àit,
Ach nuair a thig do thùrna sann ort a bhios a' ghàir:
Cha chluinn thu fuaim na mara, neo 'ghuidheachdainn aig càch —
Tha thu nis cho tèarainte 's a bhiodh tu anns an Àirc.

Ach ùine nis chan fhaigh thu ann, 's chan fhad' gu'm feum thu 'thréigs':
Deich mionaidean a th' agad dheth gu'n seachain thu an seuthar
D' aghaidh chur air na siantan agus rithist a-mach dhan ghèil' —
Ach tha thu nise dòigheil, agus frogail thu de cheum.

Chan fhada nis gu'm faic thu iad stéidhte air gach taobh,
Cofhartail sa mhòine an àit nan geugan fraoich,
Fear eile dha na cearcan 's gum faigh sinn uighean maoth —
Is iomadh feum gu'n cuir sinn iad, có thuirt gun robh sinn faoin?

Gheibh luchd-turais faochadh air an t-Sàbaid mar as còir
An àite dhol dhan Ghearraidh Chruaidh 's iad fosgailt' ri na neòil;
Chan fheum iad tuilleadh gearain gu na pàipearan nas motha
Oir tha Leódhas nis cho spaideil ri Eilean uain' a' Cheò.

Donald Graham (North Tolsta, Lewis)

The Stornoway Superloo

Now, O lads of Lewis, if occasion should arise
That you visit Stornoway to have your dram and your pint,
Go to the toilet in the pub while you still have the chance
Or else you will be walking home with your legs at a slant.

There's two toilets in that town of a kind not seen before
That replace the conveniences we've had since long ago;
You'll hear no Gaelic songs, nor get a drop of wine —
That's how everything's gone downhill here in the Western Isles.

What's going to be tough, though, the winter being so cold,
Is standing in yon queue in the north wind and the snow,
Every man reaching round his head to hold on to his hair
While the lassies are all waiting to do a makeup repair.

Ten pence is what you need to get admittance to the place,
But when it comes to your turn you'll have a smile on your face:
You'll hear no people swearing, nor the sound of the sea —
It's like being in Noah's Ark, that's how safe you will be.

But time now you'll not have there, for soon you've got to leave:
It's ten minutes you're allowed till you vacate the seat
To go and brave the elements and out to face the storm —
But lively goes your step now, you're back in your best form.

Soon now you'll see superloos all going up together,
Comfortable at the peats instead of tufts of heather,
With another for the hens to lay us eggs that are smoother —
We'll have lots of uses for them, who said that we were stupid?

Tourists will relieve themselves on Sundays with decorum
And need no longer use the Castle grounds where they're out in the open;
From complaining to the papers they might as well desist
Because Lewis is just as posh now as the green Isle of Mist.

Mòrag NicGumaraid (1950—)

303   *Uaireannan tha eagal orm*

Uaireannan tha eagal orm
nach tuig thu mi,
eadhon thusa a thuig
mo chuid bàrdachd o thùs.
Seadh, tha eagal orm
nach do thuig thu mo chuid bàrdachd o thùs.

304   *Geamhradh*

Ribeagan gaoiseideach
ro lag air son am
boinne driùchd a ghiùlan.
Biastagan liatha
's iad lag, reòidhte.
Cluaran is clachan.
Bogalach is fraoch.
Bileagan a bhàsaich
mus d'fhuair iad aois.

305   *Coilleag ghlan gheal chadalach*

Coilleag ghlan gheal chadalach,
priobadh beag sùil,
's gu mall fosglaidh e,
     gu mall,
cho mall nach mothaich thu dha (cho mall)
gu'm faic thu dà shlige far an robh a h-aon.

306   *Dùisgidh mi aon mhadainn*

Dùisgidh mi aon mhadainn
     is seallaidh mi air a' ghaoith
     is chì mi òran is ceòl.
Ged nach fhairich mi càil
's nach cluinn mi fonn
coimheadaidh mi air mo chùlaibh
     's chì mi bàrdachd.

Morag Montgomery (Roag, Dunvegan, Skye)

Sometimes I'm afraid

Sometimes I'm afraid
you won't understand me,
even you who understood
my poetry from the start.
In fact, I'm afraid
you didn't understand my poetry from the start.

Winter

Hairy strands
too weak to bear the
dewdrop.
Grey insects
that are weak, frozen.
Thistle and stones.
Bog and heather.
Shoots that died
before reaching maturity.

Pure white sleepy cockle

Pure white sleepy cockle,
little blink of an eye,
and slowly it opens,
        slowly,
so slowly you don't notice it (so slowly)
till you see two shells where there were one.

I'll wake up one morning

I'll wake up one morning
        and I'll look at the wind
        and I'll see a song and music.
Though I'll feel nothing
and hear no tune
I'll look behind me
        and see poetry.

Cha bhi feum agam ortsa an uair sin.
Cha bhi mo smuaintean ort
   ged as tu mo cheòl
    's mo bhàrdachd a-nochd.

307   *An t-Amadan*

Thachair mi ri duine
còir
thuirt e le
bròn
"An Salachar!"
thuirt e.
'S a spòg 'na
shròin
's an t'éile 'na
mhiotag
(far am bu chòir dhi).
'S thachair mi ri duine
còir
thuirt e le
spòrs
"Cuiridh mi mo dhòrn 'na do
bhus"
(rud a choisinn thu)
is thuirt an duine eile
còir
"An Salachar!"
thuirt e, a-rithis
's a spòg 'na
shròn
's an t'éile 'na
mhiotag
(mar bu chòir do spòg duine còir).

Is thachair mi ri duine còir
's e ga dhalladh (mar bu nòs)
gun e dèanamh dragh
no fosgladh beòil.
"An t-Amadan" thuirt iad.
Thuirt iad.

I'll have no need of you then.
I'll not think about you
    though you are my music
    and my poetry tonight.

The Fool

I met a gentle
man
he said with
sadness
"Dirt!"
he said.
With his paw in his
nose
and the other one in his
glove
(where it should be).
And I met a gentle
man
he said in
fun
"I'll put my fist in your
face"
(which you deserved)
and the other gentle
man said
"Dirt!"
he said, again
with his paw in his
nose
and the other one in his
glove
(as a gentle man's paw ought to be).

And I met a gentle man
who was drunk (as usual)
and not causing trouble
or opening his mouth.
"The Fool" they said.
They said.

308　*Muilemhàgag*

Tha muilemhàgag 'na cadal air an t-séise
is srann mór aice.
Muilemhàgag 's a craiceann a'
sgagadh le teas na mòine.
Craiceann crocodile.
Buidhe-liath.

I 'na cadal
agus buille a cridhe a' plapadh
mionaid air mhionaid.
S iongantach gu bheil a sùilean fosgailte.
Leth fhosgailt'.
Té dhiubh uaine 's an t'éile cho soilleir
ri éibhleag dhearg.
Cho dearg nach aithnichear
dé tha 'na fhaileas — an éibhleag no 'n t-sùil
a' leigeil a spioraid.

Thàinig fàd mór boireannaich 's shuidh i air
's cha chualar ach dùd mall ciùin
's chan aithnichear dé rinn am fuaim
— a' chailleach, no a' mhuilemhàgag
a' leigeil a spioraid.

Donnchadh MacLabhrainn (1950—)

309　*Clydebank*

Àm na Nollaig is solasan buidhe
'nan sreath thar nan sràidean
mòra, sgapte, an-siud 's an-seo,
sop solais air bhog san duibhre
mar chuimhneachan air an tìd'.

Ann an ceàrn, faisg air Woolies,
creathall bheag, bhìodach, bhochd.
1690 air a sgròbadh thar aodann Muire,
gàir' air a gnùis is smugaid shearbh
'na snigheadh on t-sùil.

Toad

A toad is sleeping on the bench
snoring loudly.
A toad whose skin is
cracking in the heat of the peatfire.
Crocodile skin.
Yellow-grey.

It's asleep
with its heart beating
minute by minute.
Its eyes don't seem to be open.
Half open.
One of them green and the other as bright
as a red ember.
So red you can't tell
which is illusion — the ember or the eye
releasing its spirit.

A great lump of a woman comes and sits on it
and nothing is heard but a slow gentle fart
and there's no way of knowing which made the noise
— the woman, or the toad
releasing its spirit.

Duncan MacLaren (Clydebank)

Clydebank

Christmastime and yellow lights
strung across the main
streets, scattered, here and there,
wisp of light afloat in gloom
as a seasonal memento.

In a corner, close to Woolies,
a little, tiny, modest crib,
1690 scratched on Mary's face,
smile on her countenance and bitter spit
dripping from the eye.

Julian Ronay (1951—)

310 *Bi air t' Fhaiceall*

Tha sinn ro mhodhail.
Ach anns a' chrìch marbhaidh ar modhalachd sinn.
Feumaidh sinn bhith borb 's àrdanach —
le ciùineas, bàsaichidh ar cànain
agus nuair a tha a' Ghàidhlig san uaigh,
fuar, fon fhòd,
bidh a' chànain Chuimreach air a bruidhinn fhathast.
Sin agad an diofar eadar Alba 's a' Chuimrigh.

Tha na nàimhdean 'nar n-inntinnean;
ma tha sinn a' laighe air an làr,
saltairidh gnàthan eile sinn.
Feumaidh sinn bhith gu fasanta, cathach
'nar dòighean:
dìonaidh sin a' Ghàidhlig.

Cuir ar cànain ann an saoghal eile —
na sgrìobh an còmhnaidh,
na bi a' bruidhinn an còmhnaidh,
mu dheidhinn faingean, caoraich 's crodh 's
Maighstir MacDhòmhnaill 's a' cuimhneachadh
air an eilean bhòidheach far an d'fhuair
sinn ar n-àrach òg.
Marbhaidh rudan sgìreachdail an t-àm
ri teachd 's ar spionnadh.

Seall air Cymdeithas yr Iaith Gymraeg:
tha na balaich sin a' cathachadh
    agus sinn a' suidhe.
Eu-comasach a bhith measarra 's reusanta,
no bidh sinn aig ar leabaidh-bhàis.

311 bho *A' Dràibheadh ann an Ameireaga*

Tha gràdh agam air Los Angeles.
Dèanamaid adhradh do L.A., a h-uile là ann an càraichean, le ceòl
binn a' tighinn bhon rédio.
Chan eil sinn a' creidsinn ann an riaghailtean is òrdugh.
Feuchaidh sinne nì sam bith,
chan eil ùghdarras aig pàrantan is tidsearan.

Julian Ronay (Edinburgh)

Be Careful

We are too polite.
But in the end our politeness will kill us.
We must be passionate and proud —
with quietness, our language will die
and when Gaelic is in the grave,
cold, under the sod,
the Welsh language will still be spoken.
That is the difference between Scotland and Wales.

The enemies are in our minds;
if we are lying on the floor,
other practices will trample us.
We must be modern, aggressive
in our ways:
that will protect Gaelic.

Put our language in another world —
do not always write,
do not always be speaking,
about fanks, sheep and cattle and
Mister MacDonald and remembering
the lovely island where we
were reared when young.
Parochial things will kill
the future and our strength.

Look at Cymdeithas yr Iaith Gymraeg:
those boys are battling
    while we sit.
Impossible to be moderate and reasonable,
or we will be at our death-bed.

from *Driving in America*

I love Los Angeles.
Let us worship L.A., every day in cars, with sweet
music coming from the radio.
We don't believe in rules and order.
We will give anything a try,
parents and teachers have no authority.

Tha mi déidheil air bùithean, càraichean is pàrtaidhean.
Gun 'stuthan' is 'corparrachd' bhiomaid falamh,
aonarach le smuaintean, marbhanta is neo-thruaillichte.
Thoir dhomh fuil, bram, is feòil.
Gabhaidh mi dolairean, céiseagan, càraichean ùra 's gàireachdainn.
Chan eil meomhairean agam agus chan eil mi gan iarraidh.

312   *Féin-Mhort, Lunnainn a-Deas*

Anns a' chrìch
cha tàinig duin' a chéilidh ort.
Cha robh ann
ach solas is dorchadas
latha 's oidhche
agus an saoghal taobh a-muigh
a' leaghadh air falbh.

Chaill thu dòchas
a' fuireach leat fhéin
ann an leabaidh-suidhe Lunnainneach,
a' tuiteam a' tuiteam
ás do chiall le aonranachd
ann an ifrinn phrìobhaideach.

An-sin thionndaidh thu air falbh
a' fàgail an t-saoghail
a' dol gu àite
far nach fhaicear thu
àite cho fad air falbh
's nach urrainn do dhuine sam bith
beantainn riut.

Crìsdean Whyte (1952—)

313   *Ro-dh'aithnich mi*

Ro-dh'aithnich mi am bruadar
latha mo bhreitheimh dheireannaich.

Cha robh teine no tròmbaid ann,
no diabhlan le griomairean,

I am nuts about shops, cars and parties.
Without 'products' and 'materialism' we'd be empty,
lonely with thoughts, dull and uncorrupted.
Give me blood, fart, and flesh.
I'll take dollars, cassettes, new cars and laughter.
I have no memories and I don't want them.

Suicide, South London

In the end
no-one came to visit you.
There was only
light and darkness
day and night
with the world outside
melting away.

You lost hope
living by yourself
in a London bedsit,
falling falling
mad with loneliness
in a private hell.

Then you turned away
leaving the world
going to a place
where you'll not be seen
a place so far away
that no-one can
touch you.

Christopher Whyte (Glasgow)

I foresaw

I foresaw my last
judgement in a dream.

There was no fire, no trumpets,
no devils with forks,

cha chuala mi laoidhean mòr'
na cuid a chaidh a shàbhaladh,

cha chuala mi sgairteachadh
nan daoine rachadh am pianadh

a chaoidh. Thachair orm buidheann
fhlathail, shìothchail, fhurachail,

is dh'fheòraich mi (mar gum biodh fios agam
a chean' air brìgh na coinneimh sin):

"Dè an rud a dh'iarradh orm?"
Dh'amhairc iad gu socrach ciùin

air mo luaineachd is m' imcheist
is fhreagair iad: "Chaidh iarraidh ort

clò farsaing, ealant', ioma-dhatht'
fhighe de dh'fhaclan seunta,

sam biodh snàthainn dubh an eu-dòchais
a' coinneachadh ri snàthainn òir

an àigh, is uainead a' ghaoil
ga cur tro ghuirmead na gràin',

coimeasgadh air dearg misneachail
is odhar tràight' na cladhaireachd,

is an clò gu lèir a' co-chòrdadh
a-rèir an tàlainn thugadh dhut . . ."

Dhùisg mi, air iomagain mo bheòil
na briathran: "Bithibh foighidneach.

Fhuair mo theanga fuasgladh
gu h-anmoch, lag, neo-sheasmhach —

chan eil mi ach a' tòiseachadh,
's mo bhilean cearbach teabadach . . ."

I heard no ponderous hymns
from the ranks of the saved,

no screams from those who were
to be tortured to infinity.

I came upon a group of people
who were noble, calm, attentive

and I asked (as if I had already
guessed the meaning of our meeting):

"What was I supposed to do?"
They gazed kindly and steadily

on my fickleness, my lack of faith
and answered: "You were asked to weave

a broad, skilful, many-coloured
cloth of magic words

where the black thread of despondency
would meet the golden thread of joy,

the green of love inter-
twine with the blue of disgust,

courageous red shade into
the drained sallow of cowardice

and the whole possess a harmony
consonant with your talent . . ."

I woke, with on my restless mouth
the words "Be patient. My tongue

was only untied recently,
feebly and uncertainly,

I'm only beginning, my lips
are clumsy and stammering . . ."

314 *Thug thu cead dhomh*

Thug thu cead dhomh,
os cionn gach bacaidh
a fhuair mi bhom theaghlach,
mo sgoilearachd 's mo Dhia

(an Dia sin a sheargaich
rè feasgairean san do thrèigeadh e
am faileasan a rìoghachd dhuibh
mar mheas nach tèid a thrusadh,
a' dol gu mall 'na luaithre
air glaisneulachd nan altairean —
is beag nach do ghabh mi truas ris);

os cionn gach cràidh, gach cruaidh-chàs
a thug na linntean air ar cinnidh,
am foill, am fiamh, an cealgaireachd,
an t-iasad rinn an sàbhaladh,
's iad spaideil ann am breug-riochd;

os cionn mo sgàtha, mo chladhaireachd,
a' ghràidh 's na h-earbs' a bha dh'easbhaidh orm,
gam dhalladh ri mo dhleasdanas,
mo chomas is mo fhreagarrachd.

Ach dè as fàth dhomh bhith ri gearan?
Chaidh m' fhuasgladh is mo chur gu sùnnd,
gu dìcheall is gu dèanadas
's mo chochall air a bhloighdeachadh
aig luathghàir do bhòidhichid.

315 *Fontana Maggiore*

An dèidh dha obair a chrìochnachadh, tha Giovanni Pisano, a dhealbh am fuaran agus a shnaidh na clàir, a' cur a sgeilb a thaobh, agus ag ràdh:

Tha mi air na h-uisgeachan
a chuibhreachadh an cearcall coilionta
de mhàrmor, air dath an t-sneachda is nan ròs,
gu bhith 'na gheata-latha a chuireas srian
is riaghladh air na steallaidhean bhon doimhne,
air sìor-leum ceannairceach nan tobar dorch.

You gave me permission

You gave me permission
beyond the forbidding
I got from my family,
my schooling and my God

(that God who withered
through long, forsaken afternoons
in the shadows of his black kingdom,
like an unpicked fruit,
slowly turning to ashes
above the pallid altars —
I came close to pitying him);

beyond the suffering, the trials
our people suffered through the ages,
their treachery, hypocrisy,
surviving at second hand,
parading themselves in borrowed clothes;

beyond my fear, my cowardice,
my lack of love and confidence,
blinding me to all that I
could and had to do.

But what point is there in complaining?
I've been set free, put to work
diligently, zealously,
now that my husk has been shattered
by your beauty's joyous shout.

Fontana Maggiore

His work finished, Giovanni Pisano, who designed the fountain and carved the panels, puts his chisel down, and says:

I have bound the waters
in a perfect circle of marble,
the colour of snow and roses,
a day gate to bridle and control
the upsurge from the deep,
the eternal, anarchic leaping of dark wells.

Chaidh an t-uisge stiùireadh gus a seo
bho tholmanan tonn-luasganach na dùthcha,
a' plubraich tro ioma-shlighe fheadanan
na dian-ruith dealasaich, neo-fhoighidnich,
gus am brùchd e a-mach 'na mhìorbhail
glain' is fionnarachd am meadhan a' bhaile.

Tuitidh e an toiseach sna soithichean
a ghiùlaineas triùir rìbhinn air an cinn,
a ghlac mi gu sìorraidh ann an dannsa bacta,
an umha a' breugnachadh an sùbailteachd,
deisealachd làmh is sileadh earraidh aotruim.

Is luath ioma-roinnte binn an teàrnadh
a th' aig na h-uisgeachan bho mhèis gu mias,
gach aon nas meudaichte, nas furanaich,
a' gabhail soillse na grèine ann a h-uchd,
ga phronnadh air a h-uachdar is ga stiùireadh
suas a dheàlrachadh air ìomhaighean
is clàir na mèis os a cionn.

            Chuir mi a dh'fhoghlam
's a dh'fheallsanachd an sgeadachadh nan clàr
na dh'fhòghnadh do neach sam bith airson a sheòladh
is àiteachadh gu buan san t-saoghal seo bhos.
Chì e na naoimh 's na h-easbaigean deagh-bheusach,
riochdan nan stàit mun cuairt agus nan caraid,
an droch chlèireach a rinn feall air a' bhaile,
rìghrean an t-Seann Tiomnaidh 's Eaglais na Ròimhe.

Dhealbh mi nan dèidh, air a' mhèis as ìsle,
fògradh ar ciad phàrantan bhon ghàrradh,
stèidheadairean a' bhaile 's a shamhlaidhean,
an iolair, an grìofain is an leòmhann fhèin,
na h-ealainean saora, an reul-eòlas
agus an fheallsanachd, 'na bànrigh air chàch.

Mu dheireadh leughaidh neach, airson a thaitneadh,
saothraichean treabhaidh agus tuathanachais,
air an roinn am measg amannan na bliadhna
fo chomharraidhean nan reul a fhreagras riutha,
air dòigh 's gun aithnich esan àite fhèin
is fheumalachd an co-fhreagairt gach buill.

They led the water here
from the restless hills nearby,
gurgling through a maze of pipes,
rushing, headlong and impatient
to burst forth from this masterwork,
chill and pure in the centre of the city.

First it pours into a dish
three girls carry on their heads
whom I trapped in an eternally frozen dance,
their suppleness a paradox in bronze
of ready hands and light, flowing robes.

Then it falls from basin to basin,
quick, melodious, constantly divided,
each one wider and more welcoming,
gathering the sunlight into itself,
shattering and reflecting it
to gleam on the panels of the basin above.

The learning and philosophy I used
to decorate the panels will suffice
as a guide for any man, to show him
his place for ever in this world below.
He will see saints and virtuous clergymen,
the emblems of our neighbouring states and allies,
the wicked priest who betrayed our city,
the Old Testament kings, and the Church of Rome.

After these, on the lowest basin,
he sees our first parents banished from the garden,
the city's founders and its heraldry,
the eagle, the griffin and the lion,
the liberal arts, astrology
and philosophy, the queen of them all.

Next he can read, just for pleasure,
the labours of tillage and of husbandry
according to the seasons of the year,
with the corresponding constellations,
so that he can recognise his place
and usefulness where all things work together.

Math dh'fhaodte gur fàillinneach na rinneadh leam,
ach is obair e co-dhiùbh as fhiach luaidh.
Bhiodh mòran gam dhì-moladh, ach dh'fhuiling mi
an càineadh le neo-shuim eanchainn is crìdh'.
Agus, a chionn 's nach tèid an cuimhneachan
a chiùrradh aig an nàimhdeas, is gum bi
m' àmhghar air lùghdachadh, 's mo chliù a' dol
nas fharsainge, dearbhadh na nì mo chàineadh
gu suarach, gun toill iad fhèin an crùn.

Bhithinn a' snaidheadh an fhiodha is an òir,
na h-ìobhraidh is an airgid, is cha bhiodh e
'nam chomas rud suarach a choilionadh nam b'e
mo rùn-sa fhèin a dhèanamh. Is uasal
na riochdan a sgeilb mi, is eugsamhail
na cruthan a bhiodh a' freagradh ri mo mhiann.
Aithnicheadh na bhitheas gam beachdachadh
am fiùghantas, is moladh iadsan m' obair.
Gur tròcaireach a sheallas an Slànaighear
air duin' a fhuair a leithid a thàlantan.

316   *An Daolag Shìonach*

Ann an ceàrn àraidh de Shìona,
san iar-dheas, chan fhada bho bheanntan Iunnàn,
tha seòrsa ùbhlan rim faighinn
's iad cho anabarrach taitneach
's gum biodh na h-ìompairean o shean a' cosg
an òir rin ceannach, is gan tairgse
aig fèisdean 's cuirmeannan san àros mhòr.
Ach cha robh dìreach blas nan ubhal aca.
Leugh mi gu robh daolag coireach ri sin,
nach fhaighear ach air craobhan na ceàirn ud,
's a dh'fhàgas uighean airson tràth a' chinntinn
an cridhe nan ubhal. Chan fhan iad ann
gu fad', ach thèid cùbhraidheachd iongantach
a sgaoileadh feadh gach meas. An dèidh don chnuimh
a sgiathan a shìneadh a-mach is teicheadh,
chan fhàgar lorg de fantainn ann ach sgleò
òmarach an lì an ubhail, 's boladh
mìorbhaileach a dh'fhairtlich e
air sgoilearan is gàirnealairean
na cùirt gu lèir a mhìneachadh.

'S e sin a nì mi leis a' chànain seo.

There may be defects in what I have done,
but nevertheless this work merits praise.
Many have slandered me, but I suffered
their mocking with indifferent mind and heart.
And to prevent their hostility
from damaging this memorial, and so
that my pain may be lessened, and my fame
more widespread, let those who criticise
the execution show they could do better.

I have carved both gold and wood,
ivory and silver; if I tried,
I couldn't bring forth something second-rate.
The images I sculpted are majestic,
multiple forms answered my inspiration.
Let anyone who looks at them admit
their worth, and praise my handiwork.
And may Our Saviour look with mercy
on one who was given talents of this kind.

The Chinese Beetle

In a particular part of China,
in the south-west, not far from the mountains of Yunnan,
a species of apple can be found
which is so extraordinarily delightful
that the emperors of old used to spend
their gold to buy them, and offer them
at feasts and banquets in the palace.
But they did not really have the taste of apples.
I have read that a beetle was responsible for that,
which is found only on the trees of that district,
and which leaves eggs for incubation
in the heart of the apple. They do not remain there
long, but a remarkable fragrance
is spread throughout every fruit. When the worm
has stretched its wings and fled,
no trace is left there of its sojourn but an amber
sheen in the apple's hue, and a marvellous
scent that defeated the attempts
of the scholars and gardeners
of the entire court to explain it.

That's what I do with this language.

317 Dà earrainn de *Bho Leabhar-Latha Maria Malibran*

Thachair mi ri Maighstir Rossini 'n-diugh.
Bha mi tighinn a-mach bho bhùth nan ad,
searbhanta 'nam dhèidh, a gàirdeanan
làn de bhogsaichean 's de phacaidean.
Bha fonn math orm, an carbad a' feitheamh
aig oir na sràid, is dìreach air an stairsneach
thachair mi ri gnùis a dh'aithnich mi
gu furasda bho làithean m' òige anns
an Ròimh 's sa' Chathair Nuadh. Bha boireannach
ri thaobh, 's i beagan glas-neulach, is seang.

Thuig mi air ball gur e Olympe a bh' ann,
Olympe Pellissier, nach urrainn dhà
a phòsadh fhad 's a bhios an Colbran beò,
a bhean-chèile chaidh fhàgail anns an Eadailt.
Tha iad a' gobaireachd mun dithis aca
's gach taigh san dèanar cèilidh ann am Paris
is chuala mi nach tèid a fàilteachadh
le boireannaich a tha gam faicinn fhèin
gu moralta 's gun smal. Cha robh mi dìreach
cinnteach am bruidhninn rithe no nach bruidhneadh
's mi cuimhneachadh an fhir-chèil' agam fhìn,
Maighstir Malibran tha beò sna Stàitean
Aonaichte, 's an ceangal cràidhteach ud
gun fhuasgladh leis a' Phàpa gus an là
an-diugh, a dh'aindeoin na thug mi de dh'òr
don chlèir 's do dh'fhir an lagh' airson mo shaoradh.

Chuimhnich mi na bhitheas Charles ag ràdh
mum shuidheachadh neo-thèarainte, na sùilean
gam shìor-leantainn anns gach àit' don tèid mi,
na teangannan cho trang mum dheidhinn-sa,
fhios aig càch nach fhaod mi dol gam fhaoisid
's a liuthad duine ag iarraidh mo sgrios.
Chòrd rudeigin an gnùis Olympe rium,
shìn mi mo làmh a-mach, is thàinig snodha-
gàir' air aodann an fhir-sgrìobhaidh ciùil
as ainmeile tha beò rir làithean-ne . . .

Dè 'm fàth dhomh bhith 'nam bhreugaire? Carson
nach aidichinn e? A luchd-leughaidh chaoimh,
chan iad sin na cuspairean as fheàrr leibh.

Two sections of *From the Diary of Maria Malibran*

I met Maestro Rossini today.
I was coming out of the hat shop,
a maidservant behind me, her arms
full of boxes and packages.
I was in a good mood, the carriage waiting
by the kerbside, and right at the entrance
I met a face I recognised
easily from my girlhood days in
Rome and Naples. There was a woman
at his side, who looked rather pale and slender.

I realised at once it was Olympe,
Olympe Pellissier, whom he cannot marry
during the lifetime of the Colbran,
the wife he left behind in Italy.
Gossip's rife about the two of them
in every Paris salon, and I've heard
that she doesn't receive acknowledgement
from any lady who regards herself
as morally unstained. I was not quite
sure if I should speak to her or not
as my own spouse came into my mind,
Mr Malibran who lives in the United
States, that painful marriage tie of mine
unloosened by the Pope until this very
day, in spite of all the gold I've given
to clergy and to men of law for my release.

I recalled the thing that Charles is fond of saying
about my unprotected state, the eyes
forever following me no matter where I go,
clacking tongues discussing my affairs,
everybody knowing I can't confess myself
and countless people willing my destruction.
Something in Olympe's face appealed to me,
I stretched my hand out, and a smile appeared
upon the face of the most celebrated
composer living in the world today . . .

What use is it for me to be a liar? Why
should I not admit it? My dear readers,
these are not the subjects you prefer.

Nam b' e bhith còrdadh ribh a bha 'nam rùn,
bu chòir dhomh sgrìobhadh air cùis eadar-dhealaicht'.

'S dòch' air an acfhainn a chaidh fhàgail anns
an t-sabhal lem sheanair caoin, tha marbh a-nis,
gach ainm a bh' oirr', 's an dòigh cheart air an robh
gach ball ga chleachdadh, 's mis' a' caoidh na meirg'
a lobhas iad, 's an traidisean air chall.

No mar a tha mi muladach san àm
a bheir an t-aiseag mi air falbh bho thìr
m' eòlais chun a' bhaile mhòir, 's a' chroit
san d' fhuair mi m' àrach òg a' dol 'na smàl
a-mhàin air iomall lèirsinn, gus nach fhaic

mi iadhaire an telebhisein air
mullach an taigh. B' fheàrr leibh a bhith leughadh,
math dh'fhaodt', mun chianalas 's mun chiont a bhios
mi faireachdainn aig deasg na h-oifis àird,
faram na trafaige san t-sràid gam bhòdhradh,

'nam shùil na taighean beaga, is 'nam chluais
faclan na cànain brìoghmhoir' ud a bh' againn
a dhiùltamaid a bruidhinn ris a' chloinn,
's a mholas mi cho fad' 's nach iarr sibh orm
a cleachdadh no bhith sgrìobhadh ach sa' Bheurla.

An àite sin, sgrìobh mi mu bhoireannach
nach robh facal Gàidhlig aice, nach robh
fhios aice, 's dòcha, gu robh cànan ann
den t-seòrsa. Mura bheil mi comasach
air dàintean fìor-Ghàidhealach a sgrìobhadh,

tha sin a chionns nach eil mi 'nam fhìor-Ghàidheal,
a-rèir coltais. Ach, a luchd-leughaidh chaoimh,
tilgidh mi na faclan seo air talamh
nàimhdeil, seasg, neo-mhothachail, is faodaidh
sibh a bhith gam chreidsinn, ged nach e

deudan a th' annta, air neo dèideagan,
aig a' cheann thall tòisichidh iad a' fàs,
cnàmhan is crè is craiceann aig gach fear dhiubh
's an leabhar ùr fa chomhair nan sùl ùr ac',
a sgrìobh mi mu Maria Malibran.

If to be pleasing you were my desire,
I should have written on another topic.

Perhaps about the tools abandoned in
the barn by my dear grandfather, now dead,
each name they had, and of course the proper way
to use each part, while I bemoan the rust
that rots them, and the lost tradition.

Or how I'm melancholy at the time
the ferry brings me over from the land
I know towards the city, with the croft
where I was reared when young becoming just
a blur on the horizon, till I cannot see

the television aerial up there
upon the roof. You'd much prefer to read,
perhaps, about the longing and the guilt
I feel when sitting at the lofty office desk,
deafened by the noise of traffic in the street,

in my eye the little houses, in my ear
the words of yon rich flowing tongue of ours
which we'd refuse to pass on to the kids,
and which I'll praise as long as you don't ask
me to be using it, or writing other than in English.

Instead of that, I wrote about a woman
who'd not a word of Gaelic, and didn't even
know, perhaps, that any tongue existed
of that kind. If I am unable
to write truly Gaelic poems,

that is because I am not a true Gael,
it would seem. But, gentle readers,
I'll cast these words on hostile, barren,
unsympathetic ground, and you can
just believe me, even though they're not

dragons' teeth, nor are they pebbles,
in the long run they will start to grow,
each one of them with bones and flesh and skin
while facing their new eyes is the new
book that I wrote about Maria Malibran.

Aonghas Pàdraig Caimbeul (1954—)

318   *Ràdar Beinn Sheaval*

Air a mullach chì thu daonnan
Sealladh biothbhuan air gach taobh dhith,
Sìos gu deas gu Taobh a' Chaolais,
Mach an-iar gu oir an t-saoghail,
Suas gu tuath gu Beinne Bhadhla,
Null an-ear gu Alba ùdlaidh;
Sìos gu deas chì mi mo dhaoine —
Barraich, Éirisgich, is aon dhiubh,
Uibhisteach ris am b' aithne saoirsneachd,
Iasgach, tàillearachd is crùidheachd,
A bhàsaich bochd, gun duais de shaothair
Ach ràdar dol mu chuairt gun fhaochadh;

Mach an-iar chan eil càil air fàire
Bho mhachair ìosal do-shàsaicht' Hàllainn
Gu cladh Àird Mhìcheil 's gob Rubh' Àisirnis
Ach tobhtaichean is cruitean fàsach
Is bratan dearg an Airm san àile
Fo ghàire ràdar dol mu chuairt gun nàire;

Shuas mu thuath tha 'n t-adhar dorcha
Le gaoth an iarthuath ag iadhadh òirnne
Tarsainn Hiort 's na h-eilein Mhònach
A' sgaoileadh neulan onfhadhach borba
A bhuaileas Beinne Bhadhl' 'nan stoirmean
A dh'ainneoin eararadh ràdar foirfe;

Null an-ear thar a' Chuilthinn chùiltich
Tha beathachan eile a' blasadh na h-ùbhla:
Eadar Beinn Sheaval is mullach na Urals
Tha mìltean de ràdars a' feitheamh ri sprùilleadh
Air cliathaichean mòintich ar leisg 's ar ciùineis —
Air sléibhtean ar coingeis tha freumhan a phuinnsein.

Angus Peter Campbell (S. Boisdale, S. Uist)

The Radar of Beinn Sheaval

On her summit you see always
A view eternal on each side of her,
Down south to Taobh a' Chaolais,
Out west to the world's edge,
Up north to Benbecula,
Over east to gloomy Scotland;
Down to the south I see my people —
Eriskay and Barra folk, and one of them,
A Uistman who practised carpentry,
Fishing, tailoring and shoeing horses,
Who died poor, with no prize for his toil
But radar revolving ceaselessly;

Out west there's nothing to be seen
From the low insatiable plain of Hallin
To Ardmichael's graveyard and Rubh' Ashernish's point
But roofless walls and empty crofts
And the red banner of the Army flying,
Smiled upon by radar shamelessly revolving;

Up to the north the sky is dark
With the north-west wind enfolding us
Crossing St Kilda and the Monach Isles
Scattering wild aggressive clouds
That will strike Benbecula as storms
Despite infallible radar's probing;

Over east by the crannied Cuillins
Other creatures are tasting the apple:
Between Beinn Sheaval and the tops of the Urals
Are thousands of radars waiting for crumbs
On the mountainsides of our sloth and docility —
On the hills of our apathy are the roots of its poison.

319   *Gearraidh na Mònadh á Smeircleit*

Taigh Fhionnlaigh,
taigh a' Bhadhlaich,
taigh Aonghais a' Cheanadaich,
taigh Aonghais 'ac Dhòmhnaill,
taigh Alastair Ruaidh,
taigh Dhomhachainn,
taigh an Ruaidh,
taigh Dhòmhnaill Eachainn,
taigh Sheumais Shlàdair,
taigh Sheòrais,
taigh a' Chlachair,
taigh Sheonaidh Mhóir,
taigh Alastair Dhuibh,
taigh Phàdraig Eoghainn,
taigh Sheonaidh Ailein,
taigh Dhòmhnaill Penny,
taigh Iagain Dhòmhnaill.

Mar a bhà,
's mar a thà,
's mar a bhitheas.

Fad saoghal nan saoghal.

Amen.

320   *Oidhche Chullaig*

A-nochd chuimhnich mi air Oidhche Chullaig:
an t-àgh, an toileachas, an deasalachadh.

Tha mise nochd a' tighinn gur n-ionnsaigh
   A dh'ùrachadh dhuibh na Cullaig;
Cha ruig mi leas a bhith ga innse,
   Bha i ann ri linn mo sheanar.

'S a' chais ga cur mun cuairt,
's na faclan a' bruthadh a-mach:
silidh, ìm, càise ("Mac Eòghainn Mhóir"!), briosgaidean, is "stork" le gàire,

Garrynamonie from Smerclate

> Finlay's house,
> the Benbecula man's house,
> Angus son of the Kennedy's house,
> Angus MacDonald's house,
> Red Alastair's house,
> Domhachann's house,
> A Ruaidh's house,
> Donald Hector's house,
> Seumas Shlàdair's house,
> George's house,
> the Stonemason's house,
> Big Johnny's house,
> Black Alastair's house,
> Patrick Ewen's house,
> Seonaidh Allan's house,
> Donald son of Penny's house,
> Iagan Dhòmhnaill's house.
>
> As it was,
> is,
> and will be.
>
> World without end.
>
> Amen.

Hogmanay Night

Tonight I remembered Hogmanay Night:
the anticipation, the joy, the preparation.

I am coming tonight to you
    To renew for you Hogmanay;
I have no need to tell you of it,
    It existed in the time of my grandfather.

And the skin-strip put round,
and the words pouring forth:
jam, butter, cheese ("Big Ewen's son"!), biscuits, and "stork" with a snigger,

's suas, suas-suas gu Taigh Nìll 'Illeasbaig
's na balaich aig taigh le òran is botal mór,
fear le tastan, fear le leth-chrùn, fear leis a' "Chaiòra".

Mo chaisean Cullaig ann am' phòcaid,
  S math an ceò thig ás an fhear ud:
Théid e deiseil air na pàistean,
  Gu h-àraid air bean an taighe.

'S sìos, sìos seachad air an dìg,
's sìos, sìos seachad air an dìg
(far am b' fheudar dhomh mùn),

mo chaisean Cullaig ann am' phòcaid,
s math an ceò thig ás an fhear ud.

'S cho doirbh 's a bha na faclan deireannach
's tu cho beag (có aig' a Dhia bha fios orra?).

Chì thu nis iad ann an leabhar brèagha
(The Folksongs and Folklore of South Uist),
's mise cho diùid le na briathran móra:

Bean an taighe si as fhiach e,
  Làmh a riarachadh na Cullaig;
Rud beag de shochair an t-samhraidh
  A' cumail geall air aig an aran.

Fosgail an doras is leig a-staigh mi!

Fosgail an doras is leig a-staigh mi!

Fosgail an doras is leig a-staigh mi!

321   *Farpais Réidio nan Gaidheal*

An-diugh
se Taobh a-Deas Loch Baghasdail a tha an aghaidh Sgalpaigh

airson eàrlas clàr cóig nota deug.

and up, up to Neil MacPhee's house
and the boys ashore with a song and a big bottle,
one with a shilling, one with a half-crown, one singing the "Caiòra".

My Hogmanay skin-strip in my pocket,
    And good is the smoke that comes from it:
It will go sunwise round the children,
    And especially round the housewife.

And down, down past the ditch,
and down, down past the ditch
(where I had to have a pee),

my Hogmanay skin-strip in my pocket,
and good is the smoke that comes from it.

And how difficult the last lines were to remember
and you so wee (did anyone know them, O God?).

You can now see them in the beautiful book
(The Folksongs and Folklore of South Uist),
and I so shy with the big words:

'Tis the housewife who deserves it,
    Here is the hand for the 'Hogmanay';
A small thing of the good things of summer
    To keep a promise got with the bread.

Open the door and let me in!

Open the door and let me in!

Open the door and let me in!

The Gaelic Radio Quiz

Today
it's South Lochboisdale versus Scalpay

for a fifteen pound record token.

Màiri NicGumaraid (1955—)

322 *Sgillinn leis nach Ceannaichear Càil*

Nach tog sibh a' Ghàidhlig
      Tha tòrr ga h-ionnsachadh
steach leibh dhan an linn sa
      ach chan eil feum oirr' an-diugh
is gabhaibh i le atharrachadh
      chan fhad a bhios i aig duine
mas e gu feum
      tha i air cus bhuillean a ghabhail
chan eil innt' ach cànan
      an déidh sin, si bh' againn a-riamh
ach se ar cànan a th' innt'
      cha chan sinn nach fheuch
's cha thog duin' eil' i ás a' bhoglach
      nuair a bhios tìd' againn.

323 **Do Dhol-a-Mach**

Chaidh thu dh'Israel
còmh' ri caraid do charaid dhut
a lorg dòigh-beatha
dh'ath-nuadhaicheadh do spiorad.

Chaidh thu gu kibbutz.

Thug thu cruadal ort fhéin
air sgàth adhbhar an t-sluaigh
is talamh nan Iùdhach
a leasachadh.

Rinn thu oidhirp Eabhra ionnsachadh.

Thòisich thu faicinn cho slàn 's a tha teaghlach
a chumas cuimhn' air a-chéile.
Chunna tu Diadhachd a dh'obraicheadh,
shaoil leat gum fac' thu Dia a's an rabaï.

Agus thug thu 'n aire do na laghan.

Mary Montgomery (Arivruaich, Lochs, Lewis)

A Penny that Buys Nothing

Why not take up Gaelic
        Lots of folk are learning it
in with you to this century
        but it's no use today
and use it differently
        it won't be spoken for long
if needs be
        it's had too many setbacks
it's only a language
        on the other hand, we've always spoken it
but it's our language
        we won't say we won't try
and no-one else will lift it out of the bog
        when we have time.

Your Carry-On

You went to Israel
with a friend of a friend
in search of a lifestyle
offering spiritual renewal.

You went to a kibbutz.

You submitted to hardship
for the people's cause
and also to develop
the land of the Jews.

You made an effort to learn Hebrew.

You started to see how sound are a family
that remember each other.
You saw a Theology that worked,
you thought you saw God in the rabbi.

And you observed the laws.

Thuit fallas is deòir bhuat
do dh'ùir an Talaimh Naoimh,
talamh a chaill a dhaoine —
chitheadh tu làraich seann dòigh-beatha.

'S do theachd-a-steach —
Bog thu fhéin gu math,
crath smùir bho do chasan
mun till thu dhachaigh.

Tog d' oighreachd fhéin, 'Ghaidhil,
's till dhachaigh.

324   *Soraidh Leibh*

Soraidh leibh
nuair a thig oirbh
a dhol a Cheann Trá a sheasamh
ris an tAmhrán Náisiúnta
's a dh'aideachadh
gun do dh'fhàg sibh a' Bhànrigh aig an taigh

A bheil amhran agaibhs'
dh'fhaighnich fear an taighe
Tha
Chan eil
Tha
Dé fear?
'Flower of Scotland'
O chan e
Nach e?
Dé eile?
'Soraidh Leibh
is Oidhche Mhath Leibh'
is mise còmh' ribh
le beag nàire
'na mo laige leis a' ghàire

Cha b'e sin a bha iad ag iarraidh
an Ceann Trá an Contae Chiarraí
ach se fhuair iad
's sheas iad ris

You shed sweat and tears
into the Holy Land's soil,
a land that lost its people —
you'd see the ruins of an old way of life.

And your carry-in —
Immerse yourself well,
shake dust from your feet
before you come home.

Take up your own inheritance, Gael,
and come back home.

Farewell

Farewell
when your day comes
to go to Ventry and stand
for the National Anthem
and admit
you've left the Queen at home

Do you have an anthem
asked the master of ceremonies
Yes
No
Yes
Which one?
'Flower of Scotland'
Oh no
No use?
What else?
'Soraidh Leibh
is Oidhche Mhath Leibh'
and me along with you
embarrassed
and quaking with laughter

That wasn't what they wanted
in Ventry in County Kerry
but it's what they got
and they stood for it

cho modhail balbh
's rinn sinne falbh
mar fhògarraich

Is iadsan 'Laochra Fáil
Atá faoi gheall ag Éirinn'
Is sinne sluagh na dàil
A tha ro mhall ag éirigh

ach thog sinn 'Flùr na h-Alba' an Tamhlacht
agus leag sinn an taigh

Meg Bateman (1959—)

325   *Dealbh mo Mhàthar*

Bha mo mhàthair ag innse dhomh
gun tig eilid gach feasgar
a-mach ás a' choille dhan achadh fheòir —
an aon té, s dòcha,
a dh'àraich iad an-uiridh,
's i a' tilleadh a-nist le a h-àl.

Chan e gràs an fhéidh fhìnealta
a' gluasad thar na leargainn
a leanas ri m' inntinn, no fòs
a dà mheann, crùbte còmhla,
ach aodann mo mhàthar 's i 'bruidhinn,
's a guth, cho toilicht', cho blàth.

326   *Do Sgoilear Àraidh*

Mar chat
a' cluich le luch
gun ghlacadh oirre

mar ghreann na gaoithe air an loch
a' sìneadh gu grad
's cho luath a' tarraing air ais

tha an sgoilear a' teagasg
a' gluasad air leth-chunntas.

so quiet and polite
and off we went
like refugees

They're 'The mighty warriors of Fate
Who're under oath to Ireland'
While *we're* the people who procrastinate
And are too slow in rising

but we sang 'Flùr na h-Alba' in Tallaght
and brought the house down

Meg Bateman (Edinburgh)

Picture of my Mother

My mother was telling me
that a hind comes every evening
out of the wood into the hay-field —
the same one, probably,
they fed last year,
returning now with her young.

It isn't the grace of the doe
moving across the slope
that lingers in my mind, nor yet
the two fawns huddled together,
but my mother's face as she spoke,
and her voice, so excited, so warm.

To a Certain Academic

Like a cat
playing with a mouse
without catching it

like the ripple of the wind upon the loch
suddenly extending
and as quickly drawing back

the academic teaches
progressing through understatement.

327 *Ceist*

Bheirinn a' ghrian dhut 's a' ghealach
  's na rionnagan gu tur —
Ciamar mar sin as leòr dhomh
  mi fhìn a thoirt dhut?

328 *Cìocharan*

An glasadh an latha
tha thu ag òl gu dian,
do shùilean ag amharc bhuat,
gun bhrìgh 'nan duinne dhomh;
tha ùghdarras sa ghreim
a tha aig do dhà làimh air a' chìch,
is d' òrdagan a' pronnadh mo bhlian
ri caismeachd dhìomhair.

Feasgar nì thu brìodal:
nì thu dinneadh air an t-sine
's nì thu gàire 's i ag éirigh,
nì thu caogadh ri Dad mun cuairt oirre
is briosgaid 'na do dhòrn.

Ach a dh'oidhche
cha chuilean meata thu —
cha tàlaidh pòg air do bhilean thu
no duanag ga cagairt 'na do chluais —
spìonaidh do chorragan mo ghùn
agus, le raoic asad dhan dorchadas,
agraidh tu do chòir mar bu dual.

329 *Ath-Chruthachadh*

(dha m' leanabh)

Bha mi air m' aineoil sa bhaile ghlas seo
mus tàinig thusa;
bu bheag a tharraing mo shùil ann,
ach bithidh tusa a' cur seachad
ùine mhór aig an uinneig, 's tu coimhead
nam fork-lifts 's nan làraidhean fodhad.

Question

I'd give the moon and the sun to you
    and all the stars —
How then is it enough for me
    to give you myself?

Breastling

In the grey of the dawn
you drink intently,
your eyes gaze ahead,
their brownness tells me nothing;
there is authority in the hold
of your two hands on the breast,
your toes knead my belly
to a rhythm of their own.

In the evenings you grow fond:
you press in the nipple
and laugh as it rises,
peeping round it at Dad
with a biscuit in your fist.

But at night
no tamed pup you —
no kiss on the lips can soothe you
or ditty whispered in your ear —
your fingers tear at my gown
as, roaring at the darkness,
you claim your hereditary right.

Transformation

(to my child)

I was strange in this grey town
till you came;
little drew my eye,
but you stand at the window
for ages, watching
the fork-lifts and lorries below.

A-raoir choimhead sinn a' ghealach
'na lainnir air na sglèatan,
is sa mhadainn dhùisg mi ri
"Solas! Solas!"
an t-àite ath-chruthaichte
le grian dhearg a' gheamhraidh.

Ach is buaine òradh
do chuid sonais air an àite —
air gach lòn sa chabhsair sgàinte,
air a' chladh 's an scrapyard
a chì mi bhuam tron uinneig
a bhris thu 'nam sheasgachd.

330   *Cuireadh dhan Bheatha*

Cha chuireadh dhan bheatha e seo —
bhith glacte eadar diomb
agus an t-uisge glas a-muigh.
Lìonaidh iargall an telebhisein
an neonitheachd a-staigh.
Chan eil càil coisrigte san taigh seo —
thruaill an fhearg gach rud.
Seachnaidh sinn a-chéile san leabaidh —
tòn fhuar no glùn gheur —
's an leanabh stobte eadarainn,
a throighean 'nan cadal 'nam làmhan.

Cha robh mi an dùil ri seo do dhuine againn
's is goirt nach eil nas fheàrr agam
dhan leanabh aig a bheil a ghàire
'na cuireadh gu beatha dhomh gach ùine.

331   bho *Do Fhear-Pòsta*

Fad a' gheamhraidh chùm thu ceileireadh ris na h-eòin,
ach a-nist, 's mi dràibheadh tron fhline ris a' chosta,
aithnichidh mi nach eil ann ach an luimead seo.
Chan fhaigh mi lorg air ais dhan choille
far an dèanainn mo shìneadh sa chùbhraidheachd.

Last night we watched the moon
skinkling on the slates,
and this morning I woke to
"Light! Light!"
the place transformed
by the red winter sun.

But more lasting your delight's
gilding of the place —
of every puddle in the cracked pavement,
of the cemetery and scrapyard
that I see through the window
you breached in my barrenness.

Invitation to Life

This is no invitation to life —
to be trapped between resentment
and the grey rain outside.
The tumult of the telly
fills the silence in the flat.
Nothing is sacred here —
anger has defiled all.
In bed we avoid each other —
cold bum and sharp knee —
with the baby a barricade between us,
his feet sleeping in my hands.

I never wanted this for any of us
and it hurts I have nothing better
for the child whose smile
is my constant invitation to live.

from To a Married Man

All winter you kept the birds singing,
but now, as I drive through the sleet by the coast,
I realise there is only this bleakness.
I can find no way back to the woods
where I'd stretch out in fragrance.

Eadarainn tha na monaidhean is an cur is an cathadh
's ged nach àichinn fasgadh an taoibh thall dhut,
's ged nach àichinn càil a bharrachd dhut,
cha robh mi 'n dùil ri tost an earraich sa
no ri nimh na h-aonaranachd a tha gam tholladh.

Rody Gorman (1960—)

332 *Air Bàs Charles Bukowski*

Chuala mi
gun do chaochail Charles Bukowski

nuair a bhruidhinn mi ris a' phost
air a chuairt

a' lìbhrigeadh nan litrichean
's nam pàipearan an-diugh sa mhadainn

's bhuail e orm an uair sin
gun robh Bukowski fhéin 'na phost ri 'linn

's gur h-e e fhéin a bha freagarrach
seach am post air a bheil mi eòlach

a bhith romham an-diugh sa mhadainn
a' lìbhrigeadh nan litrichean

's e a' cantail: Madainn mhath — s mise am post ùr
's chaochail mi an-dé

ach mairidh mo chliù 'na mhìr
-naidheachd mun a' chruinne-ché.

333 *Ìomhaighean*

Se an obair a chuir mi romham an-dràsta
ìomhaighean a thoirt còmhla

de shaoghal an là an-diugh
's den àm a dh'fhalbh

Between us are the hills with their snow and drift
and though I would not deny you their shelter,
though I would not deny you a thing,
I was not prepared for the silence of this spring
or the bitter loneliness blowing through me.

Rody Gorman (Dublin, Ireland)

On the Death of Charles Bukowski

I heard
that Charles Bukowski had died

when I was speaking to the postie
on his round

delivering the letters
and newspapers this morning

and it occurred to me then
that Bukowski himself used to be a postman in his day

and that it would have been more appropriate
rather than the postie I know

for *him* to be standing there before me this morning
delivering the letters

saying: Good morning — I'm the new postman
and I died yesterday

but my fame shall last
like a story throughout the universe.

Images

The task I have set myself just now
is to bring images together

of the world today
and of yesterday

mar ìomhaigh
de Kim Basinger

's i 'na Sìle nan Cìoch
am meadhan *Mayfair.*

334 *Ubhal*

Aon dhe na làithean
agus caraid agam bhon sgoil
air chuairt againn gu biadh
's beul gu math àilgheasach air,
dh'innis a mhàthair dha mo mhàthair
dé chòrdadh 's nach còrdadh ris,
's cha ghabhadh esan a h-uile càil
a ghabhadh sinn fhìn gun taghadh
's fhuair esan ubhal 's cha d'fhuair sinne ann.

'S as déidh an rud
sann a ghabh sinn farmad
's tha mi fhìn
air a bhith lorg a' bhlais
a bh' air an ubhal ud riamh on uair sin.

335 *Deich Bliadhna*

Tha mi fhìn 's mo bhean
a' comharrachadh
deich bliadhna de phòsadh

's tha a' chlann
san lobhta-làir fodhainn 'nan laighe
's gun de dh'fhuaim air feadh an taighe
ach an dithis againn a' gabhail ar biadh.

— Tha seo math fhéin —
arsa mise — Se goulash a th' ann, nach e?

like one
of Kim Basinger

as a Sheila-na-Gig
in the centre pages of *Mayfair*.

An Apple

Once upon a time
when a pal of mine from school
was at our house for his tea
who had a very fussy appetite,
his mother told my mother
what he liked and didn't like,
and he wouldn't take everything
that we were obliged to take
and he got an apple and we didn't.

And after that
we were full of envy
and personally
I've been looking for the taste
of that apple ever since.

Ten Years

Myself and the wife
are celebrating
our tenth wedding anniversary

and the kids
are all asleep on the ground floor below us
and there isn't a noise about the house
but the two of us eating.

— This is really good —
I said — It's goulash, isn't it?

336 *Leumadair Bungee*

Thug mi leum asam far bile na creige
gus am faighinn ma sgaoil bhuat fhéin
's gun d'rachadh mo chall

ach ciamar a bhiodh comas agam
air a' chùis is gun agam de dh'uidheam
ach uidheam leumadair-bungee
's, ge b' oil le m' amhaich,
nach d'rachadh agam ach air tighinn
air ais dha d' ionnsaigh
'nam chnap air a' cheann thall?

337 *Rodeo*

Seo mi fhìn a-rithist,
beul ri dhol suas air do mhuin
'nam mharcach-rodeo;

shaoileadh tu, as déidh
na dh'fhiosraich mi san t-suidheachadh ud,
gun robh mi air faighinn
an uachdar air a' ghnothach

ach, fhathast,
nuair a dh'éireas mi dhan diallaid,
tha fhios agam glan gur h-e tha romham
o ba ba bó ró hùrdaibh hó ró
tuiteam.

338 *Gnìomhair is Cuspair*

"Nothing may separate the verb and its subject." R D Clement, 'Gaelic', ann an
Trudgill, Peter, ed., 1977, *Language in the British Isles*, Cambridge etc.

Bha mi 'nam ghnìomhair aice uair
's i fhéin agam 'na cuspair
's, a dh'ainneoin 's gu bheil riaghailt
is rian 'san cumar a-mach
nach gabh na dhà dhiubh a sgaradh,

Bungee Jumper

I jumped off the edge of the cliff
so as to be free of you
and get lost

but how could I manage it
when all the equipment I had
was bungee jumper's equipment
so that, with the best will in the world,
all I could manage was to come
back to where you were
in a lump at the end?

Rodeo

Here I am again,
about to mount you
like a rodeo rider;

you would think, after
all my experience in that position,
that I would have got
on top of the situation

but, still,
when I get up into the saddle,
I know fine that what I'm going to do
o ba ba bó ró hùrdaibh hó ró
is fall.

Verb and Subject

"Nothing may separate the verb and its subject." R D Clement, 'Gaelic', in Trudgill, Peter, ed., 1977, *Language in the British Isles*, Cambridge etc.

She had me as a verb once
while she was my subject
and, for all that there's a rule
and a system that maintain
that these two can't be separated,

sann a sgar sinn, le cinnt;
seadh, cha tuig mi ciamar,
ach sgaradh, se sin a thachair.

339 *An Oidhch' Ud*

Rinn mi meòrachadh iomadach sin turas
air an oidhch' ud a thug thu ás

nuair a dh'éirich gaoth cho àrd mun dùthaich
's gun do sheas na craobhan fhéin gun charachadh.

Peadar Morgan (1960—)

340 *Dùn Dà Làmh*

Dùn Dà Làmh
a' gramachadh cuimhne
air sluagh am falach 'nar fuil
a' togail meirghe
nach eil air mheomhair.

Dùn dà bhàrr
a' sealltainn thairis
air a rìoghachd am measg nam beann
a' caitheamh crùn
nach leaghar le tìm.

Dùn dà shrath
a' bristeadh gu h-ìseal
air sròn na daingnich mar thuinn
a' srùbadh eachdraidh
sìos chun na mara.

Dùn dà chreideamh
fos cionn Bhràigh Spé
Craichidh gun chroitear an-diugh
gun Phròstanach
gun Chaitligeach
gun Chrìostalachd a-rithist.

we separated, sure enough;
yes, I don't understand how,
but separation, that's what happened.

That Night

I have thought so many times
about that night you left

when a wind got up so strong round the country
that the very trees stood motionless.

Peadar Morgan (Dundee)

Dùn Dà Làmh

Fort of Two Hands
grasping memory of a people
hidden in our blood
raising a standard
that is forgotten.

Fort of two peaks
looking over its kingdom
amongst the hills
wearing a crown
that time won't melt.

Fort of two straths
breaking below on the point
of the fortress like waves
sucking history
east to the sea.

Fort of two beliefs
above the Spey's upper reaches
Crathie crofterless today
without Protestant
without Catholic
without Christianity again.

Dùn dà latha
os cionn Srath Mhathaisidh
dachaigh a' bhàird fo sgàil,
an dàn seo
air a' mhullach
anns a' ghréin.

341   *Coinneal*

Tha aislingean
a' lasadh
siobhag mo dhòchais

agus a' caitheamh
coinneal mo bheatha.

342   *Trafaig Oidhche*

Faoileag an solas na sràide
sguabadh na soillse roimhpe
carbad adhair a' saor-ghluasad
le bruthach ciùin na gaoithe
sgoth na h-oidhche seòladh
air stuadh an t-saoghail
chun an dorchadais.

Dòmhnall Rothach (1962—)

343   *Madainn Sneachda*

Thàinig an sneachd gu sàmhach,
gile gu sàmhach air gile,
air a' choille, air an fheurach, air a' mhuir,
gu coma.

Bha reodhadh na linne do-mhothaichte,
doilleireachadh sùla
's an corp a' ragadh.
Chòmhdaich an sneachd i
gu coma, mar bhrat.

Fort of two fates
above Strathmashie casting shade
on the home of the bard,
this poem
on the summit
in the sun.

Candle

Visions
are burning
the wick of my hope

and consuming
the candle of my life.

Night Traffic

Gull in the streetlight
sweeping the glow before it
an aerial vehicle ever moving
down the calm slope of wind
the night-time skiff sailing
on the billow of the world
into the darkness.

Donald Munro (Glasgow)

Snowy Morning

The snow came in silence,
whiteness silent on whiteness,
on the forest, on the meadow, on the sea,
indifferently.

The pool's freezing was imperceptible,
the dulling of an eye
and the body stiffening.
The snow covered it
indifferently, like a blanket.

Tha darach air tuiteam
air an leathad gheal,
ceud samhradh a' crìonadh
san t-solas fhann,
a' feitheamh ri sàbh
ann an làmhan meilichte.

A' srannail mar dhràgonan aig a' gheata,
na bà air am buaireadh leis an fhuachd,
mì-fhoidhidinn 's an t-acras gan iomain:
an àiteigin bidh na laoigh air chrith,
neo-challaichte is aineolach,
fon raineach.

Tha na caoraich neo-ghluasadach,
a' coimhead gun chaogadh on bhruthach,
a' leigeil deatach lag anns an àile reòta:
fo thughadh sneachda,
cnàmh-losgadh na beatha
'na sàmhchair so-leònte.

Cailein MacFhionghain (1963—)

344 *Cothrom Peanais*

Mar Chuimhneachan air Jock Stein

An oidhch' ud
an déidh naidheachd do bhàis
sann shil deòir a' bhròin 'nan sruth
troimh làrach deòir an aoibhneis
air aodainn do luchd-leanmhainn
gun smaointinn no gun suathadh.

Ach bidh cuimhn' ort gu bràth, Jock,
oir thug thu misneachd do na mìltean
agus na seòid anns na cearclan uaine,
's chan fhacas an leithid bhon uair sin.

Bu tu 'n gaisgeach, Jock, a thairg gu h-iomlan
do chorp fhéin is d' inntinn
gus an dùthaich umhail seo a chur an àird;

An oak has fallen
on the white slope,
a hundred summers wasting
in the wan light,
waiting for a saw
in chilled hands.

Snorting like dragons at the gate,
the cows distracted by the cold,
impatience and hunger driving them:
somewhere the calves will be shivering,
untamed and unknowing,
under the bracken.

The sheep are motionless,
looking unblinking from the slope,
releasing weak breath in the frozen air:
under a thatch of snow,
making life decompose
into vulnerable silence.

Colin MacKinnon (S. Uist)

Penalty

In Memory of Jock Stein

That night
after the news of your death
the tears of grief poured in streams
through the traces of the tears of joy
on the faces of your followers
unfeigned and unwiped.

But you will always be remembered, Jock,
for you inspired thousands
and the warriors in the green hoops,
and their like has not been seen since then.

You were the hero, Jock, who devoted completely
your own body and your mind
to lifting up this humble land;

's gu dearbh cha robh sinn airidh ort
a dh'eug gu glòrmhor, grad,
an déidh faochadh fadalach
an oidhch' ud.

Alasdair Barden (1963–98)

345   *An Teaghlach Sìonach*

Teaghlach Sìonach, a' bruidhinn Cantonìos,
Ag ith' an taigh-bìdh Sìonach, a h-uile h-aon aig sìth;
    Bha iad cho riaraicht' am measg an daoine fhéin
    'S an gille-frithealaidh a' déiligeadh ri'n uile feum:

Esan cuideachd a' bruidhinn Cantonìos,
Ach bruidhinn anns a' Bheurla rium ag iarraidh orm prìs
    A' bhiadh a bha mi feitheamh air, 's mi 'n dòch's gum biodh e fad'
    A' tighinn gus an éistinn riu 's an cànan ciùin a bh' ac'.

Bha trì ginealaich dhan teaghlach ann a-shin —
Bho sheanair sìos gu oghaichean bha ceithir fichead bliadhn';
    Ach nan éisteadh tu nas fhaisge riutha, chluinneadh tu le pian
    Nach ann an Cantonìos a bha na h-oghaichean a' bruidhinn.

Bu truagh leam nach b' urrainn dhaibh tuigsinn Cantonìos,
'S am measg an cuideachd fhéin thuirt iad, "I'll have some chow mein please."
    Bha mi duilich air an son a th' ann an dùthaich chéin —
    Ach smaoinich mise air na Gaidhil. Tha sinn 'nar dùthaich fhéin.

Dòmhnall Uilleam Stiùbhart (1967—)

346   *Bu tu mo mhuir gun stiùireadh*

Bu tu mo mhuir gun stiùireadh
Bu tu mo thalamh bàn gun treabhadh
Bu tu rathad nan lùb cumhang
Bu tu mo chagailt' fhuaraidh
Bu tu mo chlàrsach chreachte
Bu tu mo bheithe chrìon, 's a dosrach

Nach géilleadh do m' bhàrc.
Mì-thorrach, breun, gun bhàrr.
Do bhaile dùinte fàs.
'S a gealbhan air cnàmh.
'S na teudan rùisgt', gun ghàir.
Leagailte mu làr.

and indeed we didn't deserve you
who died gloriously, suddenly,
after belated relief
that night.

Alasdair Barden (Haddington)

The Chinese Family

A Chinese family, speaking Cantonese,
Eating in a Chinese restaurant, everyone at peace;
   They were so contented among their own people
   With the waiter attending to their every need:

Cantonese was what he was speaking as well,
But he spoke English to me in totting up the bill
   For the food I had ordered, and I hoped it wouldn't come
   For a while so I could listen to their quietly spoken tongue.

There were three generations of the family gathered there —
From grandad down to grandchildren was all of eighty years;
   But if you listened closer you could hear, and it was shocking,
   That it wasn't Cantonese that the grandchildren were talking.

I was sorry that they couldn't understand Cantonese,
And among their own people they said, "I'll have some chow mein please."
   I felt sorry for them being in foreign parts —
   But I thought of the Gael. It's in our own land we are.

Dòmhnall Uilleam Stiùbhart (Col, Lewis)

You my unsteerable sea

You my unsteerable sea	Unweathered by my barque.
You my unploughed wasteland	Barren, bare, unsown.
You the narrow track twisting	To a closed deserted village.
You my chilly hearth	Its embers quenched.
You my plundered harp	Shorn of strings, without laughter.
You my withered birch, its leafage	Felled upon the ground.

Ach b' fheàrr leam thu ri m' ghualainn
'Nam bhall-teanga measg nan cailleach
Seach bhith sgrìobhadh nan rannghal
Aig na gallbhodaich chrìona

'S mi 'm làn-bheòil a' bhaile,
Gach seann sgròig san eilean,
'S gun annt' ach cnàimh-chagnaidh
Bhios ri rùrach san oilthigh.

347   *Latha Eadar-Dhà-Shian*

Trì latha, 's cha chualas ach sgread is geumnaich
    An ànraidh, 's e uile-chruinnicht' oirnn an Leòdhas —
Bòrd-luadhaidh lom a' bhannail chruaidh-ghreimich —
    Mar ghràisg ri ràiteachas 's ri earra-ghlòir.

Uspartaich an t-sàil mu bhonn nan creagan,
    Ri cruinnleum, ri car-a-mhuiltein feadh na tràghad;
Smùid na mara ga fhroiseadh 's ga leagail
    'Na fhir-chlis ghrian-last', lasanta, gun smal.

Ach thog a' ghaoth. Is thàinig an latha a-mach ciùin,
    An latha eadar-dhà-shian. Agus bha a' chruitheachd fo thàmh,
Mar altachadh ga ghabhail san aibheis shuas,
    No 'n t-sàmhchair bu dual do bheannachadh bàird.

Nis molam an dealan-dé fo làn aodach,
    'S e taobhadh na machrach, a' beatadh ris a' bhruthaich.
Molam an seillean, trom-luchdaicht' le 'chuid faodail,
    Ri crònan 'iorraim chréicealaich troimhn driùchd.

Fead fann, 's an gnog fad ás sa mhadainn chulmaich,
    Canntaireachd thopag, luathghaireach san speur:
Molam iad. Gu bheil poc' nan uspag dùinte;
    Gu bheil sinn tèarainte — dreiseag fhathast — bhon t-sreup.

Anna Frater (1967—)

348   *Aon Phòg*

Dé feum a bh' ann an aon phòg
aig àm dealachaidh
ach breisleach a dhùsgadh
agus aithreachas
nach do rinn thu sin a' chiad latha
nuair a ràinig mi thu?

But rather you by my shoulder
A byword amongst old women
Than be knocking out rat-rhymes
To the withered old codgers

And me the talk of the township,
Every crone in the island,
And them only of interest
Rummaging around the university.

A Day Between Two Storms

Three days, with nothing heard but the shriek and bellow
    Of the tempest, gathered upon us in Lewis —
The bare board of the brawny waulking band —
    Like a ranting, hollering rabble.

The brine panted about the base of the cliffs,
    Galloped and somersaulted about the beach;
Sea spray was threshed and flung down
    Into a sunlit aurora, ablaze, faultless.

But the wind lifted. And the day came out calm,
    The day between two storms. And the creation was at rest,
As if a grace were said in the abyss above,
    Or the silence accorded a poet's blessing.

Now let me praise the butterfly under full sail,
    Coasting the machair, beating up the brae.
Let me praise the bee, heavy-laden with its trove,
    Grumbling a rowing song through the dew.

A faint whistle, and the distant knock in the morning haze,
    Larks' canntaireachd, joyful in the sky:
Let me praise them. The bag of squalls is closed;
    And we're safe — a while yet — from the strife.

Anne Frater (Bayble, Point, Lewis)

One Kiss

What use was one kiss
at the time of parting
except to wake confusion
and regret
that you didn't do that on the first day
when I reached you?

349 *Clann a-Màireach*

"*A mhàthair, co ás a thàinig mi?*"

Dé chanas tu ris?
An innis thu an fhìrinn, gun do thagh thu air pàipear
na buadhan a b' fheàrr leat
air son do phàist',
's gun do lorg thu 'athair
ann an catalog
gun fiù 's làmh a chur ri 'aodann
no bruidhinn ris
no 'phògadh?
An innis thu mar a thug thu dhachaigh
am botal glainne
a dhèanadh trom thu,
's gun do chuir thu do leanabh
mar a chuireadh tu snèap,
a' leantainn comhairle
nan dotairean-tuathanach?
Dh'fhuirich thu le foighidinn
gu'n tigeadh am foghar
's gum faiceadh tu an lus.

Bha thu ag iarraidh leanabh
mar a dh'iarras leanabh dola,
agus cheannaich thu e
mar phacaid sìol
gun guth air gaol no pòsadh.
Mo thruas air do mheas
mura h-eil e co-ionnan
ris an dealbh air a' phacaid.

350 *Bill*

Crith 'na do ghuth 's tu a' bruidhinn
air an dachaigh anns nach robh thu riamh
ach 'nad shrainnsear;
bruidhinn air an eilean le gaol
a tha lìonadh do chridhe 's do shùilean:
an gaol a dh'ionnsaich thu aig glùin d' athar
anns a' chànan chùbhraidh
a bha 'na mhìlseachd air do theanga
mus deach am blas a chall

Tomorrow's Children

"Mother, where did I come from?"

What will you tell him?
Will you tell the truth, that you chose on paper
the qualities you wanted
in your child,
and that you found his father
in a catalogue
without so much as touching his face
or talking to him
or kissing him?
Will you tell how you took home
the glass bottle
which would make you pregnant,
and that you planted your child
like you would plant a turnip,
following the instructions
of the farmer-doctors?
You waited patiently
for autumn
so that you could see the harvest.

You wanted a child
as a child wants a doll,
and you bought him
like a packet of seeds
without word of love or marriage.
Pity on the fruit
that does not match
the picture on the packet.

Bill

Your voice trembles as you talk
of the home where you were always
but a stranger;
speaking of the island with a love
that fills your heart and your eyes:
the love that you learned at your father's knee
in the fragrant language
that was a sweetness on your tongue
before the taste was lost

le sgoilearachd is aois;
an gaol a thug thu seachad
ann am bliadhnachan a' chogaidh,
agus a chùm thu blàth 'nad chridhe —
a' buaireadh do shìth.

B'i Leòdhas a' bhean a fhuair thu
air an taobh sa den Chuan Siar,
agus cha do thréig thu leannan d' òige
ged nach do thill i leat.
'S ged a phòs thu t'éile
tha 'n t-eilean beag donn
fhathast 'na chuan
fo fhraoch do shùilean,
fo na speuclairean dorcha,
fon bhonaid *baseball*,
a' cumail a' ghrian bho d' shùilean:
grian a tha 'deàlradh
air bodach àrd tapaidh
ann an léine le gàirdeanan goirid
agus dealbh éibhinn air a mhionach,
briogais ghoirid
agus brògan canabhais,
's blàth a' ghàire a' fosgladh
ann am blàths a ghnùis.

Grian a tha 'falachd air an fhìrinn
gum feumadh an tilleadh
pòsadh eaglais
agus aodach dubh
agus aodann dorch,
's gum bàsaicheadh an gaol.

351 *Ceist*

Am feum mi bhith a' sgrìobhadh
mus leugh thu mi?
A bheil do cheann cho làn
de dh'fhacail Ghallda
's de litreachas
nan cànanan caillte
nach urrainn dhut
teachdaireachd mo shùilean
a thuigsinn?

with age and education;
the love that you gave
during the war years,
and which you kept warm in your heart —
troubling your peace.

Lewis was the wife that you found
on this side of the Atlantic,
and you did not abandon the sweetheart of your youth
although she did not return with you.
And though you wed another
the little brown island
is still a sea
under the heather of your eyes,
behind the sunglasses,
under the baseball cap,
keeping the sun from your eyes:
a sun that shines
on a tall sturdy man
wearing a T-shirt
with a cartoon on the stomach,
shorts
and canvas shoes,
and laughter's blossom opening
in the warmth of his face.

A sun that conceals from him the truth
that the return would need
wedding the church
and black clothes
and a gloomy face,
and that the love would die.

Question

Do I have to write
before you can read me?
Is your head so full
of foreign words
and of the literature
of lost languages
that you're unable
to understand
the message of my eyes?

Notes to Poems

1 (p. 212) Alternatively *Ag éisdeachd* 'Listening to' (*Ugam agus Bhuam*) [*UB*] or *A' faighinn* 'Obtaining' (Lachlan Morrison).

2 (p. 214) *UB* has *Tha ar dòchas 's e daingheann mu laithean na Calluig / Gu ruig sinn Iostambuil ged is fhad' tha e thall* ('Our hope is firm around the days of New Year / That we'll reach Istanbul though it's far over there').

3 (p. 214) Instead of *le òran nach gann* the *UB* version has *'s iad victorious ann* ('and they victorious there')!

4 (p. 214) This seems hypermetric, and in fact *UB* and Lachlan Morrison have *an òigh a tha grinn* 'the girl that's pretty', rhyming with *'toirt sòlas gu cuimhn'* 'bringing joy to mind' in the last line.

5 (p. 281) The poet's mother, Mary Ann MacLeod, *nighean Aonghais Choinnich* (1879–1910). When the poet was barely three years old she died at Daliburgh on 25 Jan. 1910, aged 31, within hours of giving birth to her fourth daughter, Mary Ann. The poet's father was left with five children, and on 22 Sept. 1911, at Howmore, he married Joan Laing, who is said to have told her mother-in-law that the young Dòmhnall Ailean 'did not accept her and was unkind to her'; after bearing him three more children (Donald John, Mary Kate , Samuel), she died in 1920. The poet's father himself died in 1932. (Macdonald, thesis, 307.)

6 (p. 281) Fr Macdonald's translation 'only the blindest of men would put wealth before the life of the children of men who are not permitted to stay alive' (thesis 128, book 111) suggests an anti-abortion message. I find this a little anachronistic for 1928. I see it as referring principally to the decline in communal charity which was one result of the shift from joint tenancies to crofting — 'every man for himself, and let the Devil take the hindmost'.

7 (p. 283) Or 'the poetry of Clan Donald', as Fr Macdonald points out (thesis 130, book 113). But the poet is referring here mainly to himself and his sisters, and their father was indeed called Donald.

8 (p. 349) Author's trl., but I have set out his English prose to correspond with the lines of the original. *Mochtàr is Dùghall* 13, 50; Byrne's thesis 410–11.

9 (p. 351) Here Hay's translation (*Mochtàr is Dùghall* 53) adds: "Neither hand nor mouth was stirred by them." I suppose in the original this would have been *Cha do ghluaiseadh làmh no beul leo.*

10 (p. 351) The *tagelmoust* veil, worn by male Touaregs, and removed only for sleeping (Byrne's thesis 178).

11 (p. 351) Islamic general who took part in the conquest of North Africa and attempted to quash Berber resistance; killed in battle at Sidi 'Okba, near Biskra, AD 683 (Byrne's thesis 178).

12 (p. 355) The winter residence of the Beys of Tunisia.

13 (p. 357) "O My Lord, My Lord!" (Byrne's thesis 178).

14 (p. 359) Satan.

15 (p. 359) Byrne (thesis 179) remarks that Hay may perhaps have had access to Henri Lhôte's *Les Touaregs du Hoggar* (Paris 1944), which states (p. 237) that 'for drink they take only water . . . and milk; in the last fifty years they have grown accustomed to drinking green tea in the Arab manner, flavouring it with mint or certain aromatic plants of the Hoggar'.

16 (p. 363) Author's prose trl. *Mochtàr is Dùghall* 19–26, 52–6; Byrne's thesis 417–26.

17 (p. 363) Stories about Antar, an Arab hero, poet and lover, have been circulating since the 6th century AD and were ultimately set down by a courtier of Haroun al Rashid, filling 32 volumes. The stories speak of the desert and its people, and their message is that strength and courage are only of real value when allied to generosity and respect. See Diana Richmond (ed.), *Antar and Abla: A Bedouin Romance* (London 1978).

18 (p. 363) Gaïta: the bagpipe of the Maghreb.

19 (p. 363) Editor's trl. *Mochtàr is Dùghall* 31–2; Byrne's thesis 432.

20 (p. 365) Editor's trl. *Mochtàr is Dùghall* 40; Byrne's thesis 441.

21 (p. 365) Author's prose trl. Hay, 'An Duine agus an Cogadh', *Gairm* 76 (Am Foghar 1971) 330 (Gaelic); *Mochtàr is Dùghall* 60 (English); Byrne's thesis 447–8 (Gaelic and English).

22 (p. 366) Dr Byrne has asked me to point out that he reconstructed the original Gaelic of this quatrain from a stray pencilled note beginning *Chunnaic thu bhith cur a' chatha* ('You saw the fighting of battle').

23 (p. 367) German infantryman of rank equivalent to lance-corporal.

24 (p. 367) Author's prose trl. *Mochtàr is Dùghall* 60, 44–5, 59 (ten lines of original missing from *Chunnaic an dithist seo* to *fon mhòrtair*); Byrne's thesis 448–9. The missing ten lines, beginning *Chunnaic Mochtàr cur a' chatha*, were taken by Byrne from a manuscript source.

25 (p. 393) A seaman in the merchant navy. Excessively fond of a dram, he died young.

26 (p. 393) The Turner sisters are now Mrs Cathy Murray, Edinburgh, and Mrs Jean Rodger, Lochmaben.

27 (p. 395) Donald MacKillop, composer of the song 'Coille an Fhàsaich'.

28 (p. 395) The poet's brother John (d. 1968) and perhaps Angus MacKillop, *Aonghas Dhòmhnaill Anna*.

29 (p. 397) Angus MacAskill, a crofter at Newton Ferry, N. Uist.

30 (p. 397) The Berneray poets Hector MacKinnon and Iain Archie MacAskill, q.vv.

31 (p. 397) Malcolm MacAskill (1825–1903), MacKinnon's predecessor as Berneray's pre-eminent poet. For a full edition of his work see Alick Morrison (ed.), *Òrain Chaluim* (Glasgow [1965]).

32 (p. 397) Roderick MacKillop, who still lives in Berneray.

33 (p. 399) Mr Donald MacKillop (*Dòmhnall Bàn*), a seaman. Still living in Berneray.

CÙL-CINN / BACKGROUND
including acknowledgements

Catherine Macfadyen (Catrìona NicPhàidein) 1819–1913

Catherine Macfadyen was born 4 April 1819 in Tiree, a daughter of Neil Macfadyen, tailor, and his wife Euphemia (Oighrig, Effie) Maclean. In 1841 she married Archibald MacDonald, crofter-fisherman, Milton, Caolas, Tiree. Among their children were two poets, Euphemia (*Oighrig nì 'Illeasabaig*, born 1842) and Donald (born 11 January 1858). She died at Caolas aged 94 on 25 May 1913, 'a very fine old lady, respected and revered by all who knew her' (Cameron, *Bàird Thirisdeach* 288).

Cregeen and MacKenzie say (*Tiree Bards and their Bardachd* (Isle of Coll 1978) 12): "A family called MacDonald at Caolas, who were crofters, was wholly characteristic in producing three successive generations of practising poets, including Mrs Archibald MacDonald, her son Donald, her daughter Euphemia, and two grandchildren, Alasdair MacDonald and Joseph Hardy." For the biography and poetry of all five individuals see *Bàird Thirisdeach* 288–306. Donald Meek, a native of Caolas who is Professor of Celtic in the University of Aberdeen, points out to me that Oighrig nì 'Illeasabaig made an elegy to John Macdonald, his great-grandfather's youngest son, when he was killed in France in 1917; it appears at *Bàird Thirisdeach* 304–5.

1 *Am Peinsean* ('The Pension'). Editor's trl. *Bàird Thirisdeach* 288. Cameron singles out this song in his introduction, p. xxii: "I would especially commend for neatness of expression and style, as well as true poetic feeling, the verses composed by that charming old lady, the late Mrs MacDonald, Milton, on her receiving the Old Age Pension." Cregeen and MacKenzie call the poem 'a short lyric, deceptive in its simplicity' and a 'telling, epigrammatic song' (*Tiree Bards* 22). Old Age Pensions were introduced in 1908 at a rate of 5s a week, see also poem 9. Lloyd George's great Budget of 1909–10, which paid for the measure, is praised by the Lewis poet Murdo Macleod in 'Òran a' Bhudget', see Angus Duncan and Jane Mary Duncan (eds), *Bàrdachd Mhurchaidh a' Cheisdeir* (Edinburgh 1962) 39.

Alexander Carmichael (Alastair MacGilleMhìcheil) 1832–1912

Alexander Carmichael was born 1 December 1832 in Taylochan, Lismore, ninth and youngest child of Hugh Carmichael, farmer, from Lismore (*Eoghann Greusaiche, Eoghann Ghilleasbaig*, 1783–1862), and his wife Elizabeth (Betty) MacColl, from Balliveolan, Lismore (1791–1863), the others being Cathrine, Archibald, Donald, Mary, Alexander, Dugald, Bell and Cathrine (again). *Greusaiche* ('Shoemaker') appears to have been Hugh Carmichael's nickname and not his trade: he farmed first in Balegrundail, where the family lived until about 1823, subsequently at Cruit an Lochain, and finally at Killandrist. He appears to have kept a public house or dram shop, of which the Rev. Ian Carmichael pointed out (*Lismore in Alba* (Perth 1947) 164) that the island had 'a more than sufficient supply', adding: "When one remembers how busy the industry of illicit distilling was at one time, the need for so many retail shops will be readily appreciated." It may have been knowledge thus gained that led Alexander (*Sandaidh Eoghainn Greusaiche*) to his subsequent profession, although he himself preferred to point out that his family had once held the title of Baran Taigh an Sgurrain.

Alexander was educated at Lismore parish school, and had the advantage of living next door to the schoolmaster, Samuel MacColl, an Appin man, whose name is still well remembered in the island. It has been said that he continued his education in Greenock and Edinburgh, but no evidence has been furnished for this to date, other than that his sister Mary and her husband (her cousin Duncan Carmichael) lived in Greenock 1846–52, and that Alexander may have attended schools in both places as part of Civil Service training. The Census of 30 March 1851 finds him, at age 18, living as a ploughman with his elderly parents at Killandrist, the rest of the family absent, although Mary and her husband were to return in due course to farm at Killandrist. Alexander had hoped to join the army, but was accepted instead by the Civil Service and became an exciseman, serving in Greenock, Dublin, Islay, Cornwall, Skye, Uist, Oban, Uist again, and finally Edinburgh.

It was when stationed in Islay in 1860 and at Carbost in Skye in 1861 that his career as a folklore collector began, as can be seen from his correspondence of that period with John Francis Campbell of Islay, editor of the monumental *Popular Tales of the West Highlands* (1st edn 1860–2, 2nd edn repr. Hounslow 1984). Two stories that he heard in Islay are in vol. 3, pp. 119–26, while his report on the Ossianic question is in vol. 4, pp. 209–27. Telling Campbell that he had travelled his home districts of Kingairloch, Appin, Benderloch and part of Lorne without hearing a single old tale, he placed the blame for it upon the shoulders of alien landlords, farmers, factors and some of the clergy, especially of the Free Church.

In 1868, when stationed at Lochmaddy, Alexander Carmichael married Mary Frances Urquhart Macbean (1841–1928), a civil engineer's daughter from the Black Isle. They had met on a visit to the lighthouse at Barra Head. Their marriage took place in Edinburgh, and their first home was Trumisgarry Manse, the minister (Neil Macquarrie, who died in November that year) being a bachelor. In 1871 they moved to Creagorry in Benbecula. Following unsuccessful attempts to lease a farm in North Uist, they went to live in Scolpaig House in that island in 1879 or 1880, finally leaving for Edinburgh in 1882. During these fourteen years in the Isles their four children were born — Alexander and Elizabeth (Ella) at Killandrist, Eoghan at Iochdar in South Uist, Iain at Scolpaig. All of them, like their father but not their mother, grew up as Gaelic speakers. Ella (1871–1928) married William J Watson, Donald Mackinnon's successor in the University of Edinburgh's Chair of Celtic, and the Chair was filled in turn by their son James Carmichael Watson, who lived from 1910 to 1942.

For the last thirty years of his life Carmichael was the doyen of Edinburgh's Gaelic intellectual community. He published the first two volumes of *Carmina Gadelica [CG]* in 1900, and received the honorary degree of LLD from the University of Edinburgh in 1909. He died in Edinburgh on 6 June 1912, and was buried in St Moluag's churchyard in Lismore.

It was in Uist, as Professor Mackinnon put it, that Carmichael 'reached his full development and got to know, as few have ever known it, the inner life of the people' (*CG* 4: xxii). This was of course in spite of his profession; indeed a couple of stories are still to be had in Uist of smugglers getting the better of him (Dòmhnall Eàirdsidh Dòmhnallach, 'Alasdair Mac Gille Mhìcheil (1832–1912)', in Ruaraidh MacThòmais (ed.), *Ainmeil an Eachdraidh* (Glasgow 1997) 51–64: 60). But he was loved for his kindness and generosity — the day he left Uist, he is said to have paid bills of nearly £100 for food and clothes that he had given to the poor — and he was able to collect not only a vast store of words, songs, stories and traditions, but also the hymns, prayers, charms, incantations and cures which constituted the most intimate part of the people's inheritance.

This stands in apparent contrast to the reluctance of the Lismore people to speak of him. Michael Carmichael and James Carmichael Watson once spent several days in the 1930s walking through the island, and found no-one who could — or would — tell them about their grandfather, yet the light of many of his time who had done rather less to bring credit to Lismore shines bright there to this day. This reticence is recalled by the present generation in the island but no longer fully understood. The conundrum is resolved if we view Carmichael as what used to be called a "ladies' man": one who got into a scrape in his youth, perhaps, and fell foul of church and community. He was by all accounts a man of great charm, physically strong, attractive and courageous. Unusually for a folklorist, he liked to cross the gender boundary. Campbell's informants for *Popular Tales of the West Highlands*, whose field-workers were all men, were preponderantly male — 102 males, 21 females. When one then turns to the table in *CG* 2: 374–81 showing informants consulted in person by Carmichael, it is startling to find that the number of males is almost identical at 103, but that the number of females has shot up to 112.

Even after going to live in Edinburgh, Carmichael was constantly walking the highways and bridle-paths of the Highlands and Islands, and his exploits as a traveller were legendary. Kenneth Macleod (q.v.) wrote: "What he failed to get in Uist he searched for in Glen Garry; what he lost in Kintyre he tracked in Sutherland. He might fail in the morning to get what he wanted, but there was still the evening to come, and another day, and another week, and another year; and sooner or later, he found, sure enough, the word or the line or the rite he sought" (*CG* 4: xxxiii).

Carmichael's contribution to Gaelic antiquarian studies may be found in the *Transactions of the Society of Antiquaries of Scotland*, J F Campbell's *Leabhar na Féinne* (1872), Alexander Nicolson's *Gaelic Proverbs* (1881), the *Transactions of the Gaelic Society of Inverness*, W F Skene's *Celtic Scotland*, the *Report* of the Napier Commission, and *The Celtic Review* (of which his daughter Ella and Professor Mackinnon were co-editors). His greatest monument is however *CG*. The first two volumes, edited by himself with Ella's help, made an immediate impact. Into their pages, wrote Macleod (*CG* 4: xxvii), 'the author breathed much of his own remarkable personality', while Tessa Ransford has described the work as 'the Parnassian Spring of poetry in Scotland' (*The Scotsman*, 5 December 1992). These volumes were re-edited and reissued by Ella in 1928. Volumes 3 and 4, edited by her son James, appeared in 1940 and 1941, while volumes 5 and 6, edited by Angus Matheson and his brother William, appeared in 1954 and 1971. Still more material remains in the Carmichael-Watson Collection in Edinburgh University Library; a small sample of it was published, with an analysis of the editorial process which it appeared to have undergone, by the present editor in *The West Highland Free Press*, 24 June 1994.

Between 1976 and 1992, in fact, the authenticity of *CG* provided Scottish Gaelic studies with its liveliest debate of the century, a debate akin in some ways to the Ossianic controversy 200 years before. Carmichael was accused by Mr Hamish Robertson in *Scottish Gaelic Studies* of being a fabricator. This elicited the classic rejoinder from the late Dr J L Campbell that *Carmina* was conceived as 'a literary and not as a literal presentation of Gaelic folklore'. Further damaging evidence of editorial interference was provided by the late Dr Alan Bruford. The debate is set to continue if or when Mr Robertson presents his full analysis; in the meantime, a single-volume condensed edition of vols 1–5, published by Floris Books of Edinburgh in 1992, includes an essay by Dr John MacInnes which sets out the debate in a lucid and balanced manner. My own published view is there clearly stated (p. 18): "Ronald Black . . . is well aware that Alexander Carmichael's writings can lead astray the unwary. Even so, he declares that '*Carmina Gadelica* is by any standards a treasure house . . .'"

It is thus as an unrepentant admirer of Alexander Carmichael's achievement as an ethnologist that I am also willing to acknowledge here, just once, his achievement — and his influence — as a creative artist. In his *Scotsman* obituary Kenneth Macleod said that Carmichael 'was more of the bard and of the seer than of the scientist', but he is not generally thought of as a poet, and I know of no poems of which he claimed authorship. I choose 'Ora nam Buadh' because it is, as Dr MacInnes says, 'probably the single most famous charm in the whole of *Carmina Gadelica*', and because, to quote him again, 'perhaps few texts in *Carmina* are totally free of some editorial repair-work and some, including the "Invocation of the Graces", may have it to a very high degree' (Floris edn pp. 15–17).

I am grateful to Michael Carmichael BSc MRCVS, Fort William (1914–98), son of Alexander's son Eoghan, for much information, kindness and friendship over many years, and for unhesitatingly permitting me to reprint 'Ora nam Buadh' in such an ambiguous context.

2   ***Ora nam Buadh*** **('The Invocation of the Graces').** Carmichael's trl. *CG* 1 (2nd edn 1928) 6–11; Floris Books edn (1992) 36–8, 575–6. In his introduction to the poem (*CG* 1: 6–7, cf. 2: 374) Carmichael refers to it as being got from Duncan Maclellan, crofter, Carnan, S. Uist, who heard it from Catherine Macaulay in the early years of the nineteenth century; he also refers to a fragment sent to him in 1888 by John Gregorson Campbell, taken down from Margaret Macdonald, Tiree. "The poem must therefore have been widely known. In Tiree the poem was addressed to boys and girls, in Uist to young men and maidens. Probably it was composed to a maiden on her marriage." Kenneth Macleod wrote of it (*CG* 4: xxxiv–xxxv): "One of Dr Carmichael's fording adventures deserves special mention. He was crossing, after nightfall, from South Uist to his home in Benbecula, by what is called the South Ford. The night was one of black mistiness, the ford what is known in Uist as 'the ford of the coming storm', and as Mr Carmichael, as he then was, waded nearly breast-high through one salt stream after another, all he was conscious of was the roll and the singing of waters, and the rhythm of a poem he had taken down a few hours before.

Is sùilean thu dh'an dall,	Eyes art thou to the blind,
Is crann dh'an deòraidh thruagh.	A staff to the pilgrim lone.

This poem, rescued on shore and nearly lost at sea in one and the same evening, was none other than *Ora nam Buadh*, 'The Invocation of the Graces', a composition said to be unique in the literature of Europe."

I print Carmichael's text and translation without alteration of any kind. See poems 110, 129.

Katherine Whyte (Catrìona NicGhille-Bhàin) 1845–1928

Katherine Whyte was born 11 April 1845 as Catherine Whyte in Oban, fifth of twelve children of Henry Whyte, from Bonawe (1807–75), and his wife Mary MacIsaac, from Oban (b. 1817?), the others being William, three boys who died in infancy, Christina, Charles, Dugald Malcolm, Mary Henrietta, Henry Robert, Marion Jane and Duncan MacGregor. Since 1843 Henry Whyte had been a schoolteacher and Congregational lay missionary in Appin, and in 1855 he succeeded his younger brother Charles (1817–99) as minister to the Congregational church of Appin and Lismore. Strangely, perhaps, given that Henry and Charles were Gaelic speakers, Henry's children were not brought up with the language. This appears to be at variance with the philosophy of the Highland Congregational missionaries, who were highly supportive of education in the native tongue, as was shown by Donald Meek in 'Evangelical Missionaries in the Early Nineteenth-Century Highlands', in *Scottish Studies* 28 (1987) 1–34. Neither of Katherine's brothers William (1838–66, missionary in Madras) nor Charles (1851–1939, minister at Nairn and in Australia) is given in William D McNaughton's *The Scottish Congregational Ministry 1794–1993* (Glasgow 1993) as a Gaelic speaker.

Between 1848 and 1851 the family appear to have moved to Granite Lodge in Appin, where on 11 September 1863 Katherine married William Grant (1836–66, son of James Grant, tanner, and his wife Mary Gordon) from Huntly in Aberdeenshire. Grant was then working as a journeyman tailor from Argyle Square, Oban. The ceremony was conducted by Katherine's uncle Charles, now Congregational minister in Oban. The marriage was short and tragic. Their only child, Mary, was born 19 July 1865 at their home, Craigmore Place in Oban. William Grant contracted TB and, no doubt to avoid passing it on to the child, went home to Huntly where he died on 17 November 1866. Katherine returned to Granite Lodge where three months later, on 17 February 1867, little Mary died of hydrocephalus.

Thus widowed and childless at the age of 21, Katherine Whyte may, like many another Victorian lady in her position, have begun a career as a governess, though this point remains to be investigated. What is certain is that like her first cousins John Whyte ('MacMharcuis', 'IBO' [Iain Bàn Òg?], 1842–1913) and Henry Whyte ('Fionn', 1852–1913), and the latter's daughter Annetta Campbell Whyte (1889–1950), she eventually became a prolific writer and editor of what may be called 'Gaelic ephemera' — articles, essays, songs, stories, short plays and translations in both English and Gaelic. A list of her writings from 1886 to 1913 is given in Lachlan Macbean's *The Celtic Who's Who* (Kirkcaldy 1921) 52–3. She wrote much for children, her kinderspiel 'Dùsgadh na Féinne' being described as ground-breaking (*An Deo-Gréine* 9 (1913–14) 168). Her paper 'Peasant Life in Argyllshire in the End of the Eighteenth Century', in *Scottish Historical Review* 16 (1919) 144–52, offers a fascinating account of traditional life as related to her many years before by her maternal grandmother, who was born a MacCallum in Barichreil, Nether Lorn, in 1774; the account bears some resemblance to 'Duilleag á Linn mo Sheanamhar' in *Aig Tigh na Beinne* 150–69.

Katherine Whyte appears to have travelled extensively, and, as is the way of these things, the experience deepened her thoughts about her people and their language. In an introductory note to her Gaelic version of Schiller's 'Wilhelm Tell', which she translated direct from German and published in *Transactions of the Gaelic Society of Inverness* 17 (1890–1) 302–51 (it had previously appeared in *The Northern Chronicle*), she tells us that part of her purpose was 'to learn to think in Gaelic, and thus be able to speak Gaelic fluently'. She became an enthusiastic supporter of An Comunn Gaidhealach, and her work features prominently in its journal *An Deo-Gréine* from its inception in 1905. Her book *Aig Tigh na Beinne*, by 'K. W. G.' (Oban and Glasgow 1911), is a substantial collection of her stories, essays, translations and poems. She was awarded a Civil List Pension in 1914 'in recognition of the merits of her writings in the Gaelic tongue' (*An Deo-Gréine* 9 (1913–14) 168). She died in Oban on 18 August 1928.

I am grateful to Professor Donald Meek for information.

3   From *Cèilidh Dhùn-Ì* ('The Ceilidh of Dùn-Ì'). Editor's trl. *Aig Tigh na Beinne* 199–201.
        Contains 147 lines, of which lines 41–75 are printed here. Coibhi the Druid, Oisean the poet and
        Calum Cille (St Columba) meet on top of Dùn-Ì, the highest hill in Iona, to discuss progress in
        the world since they departed it.

4   *Iomram Bean na Bainnse* ('The Bride's Oar-Song'). Editor's trl. *Aig Tigh na Beinne* 222–3.

5   *Briseadh na Fàire* ('The Breaking of the Dawn'). Editor's trl. *Aig Tigh na Beinne* 227–9. The
        new century dawned disastrously for Britain, the seemingly unstoppable Boers threatening the
        Cape. In January 1900 Field-Marshal Lord Roberts of Kandahar (1832–1914) went to South
        Africa to take personal charge of the campaign against them. An overrated but competent
        general, he relieved the besieged towns of Kimberley, Ladysmith and Mafeking, captured
        Cronjé and his army, marched through the enemy's countries, seized their capitals, scattered
        their forces, and drove their leaders and officials into exile or out to the veld. "He was in firm
        control of all the means of communication and supply and, agriculture excepted, of all the
        wealth-producing resources of the former republics. And he had done all this in less than a year"
        (Byron Farwell, *The Great Boer War* (London 1977) 317). In December he set off for home,
        returning to Cape Town by way of Durban in order to visit the grave of his son, a casualty of the
        campaign. Imagining the war to be over when in fact it had merely entered its guerrilla phase,
        the British public was delighted with its elderly hero. The poem was printed with the following
        introduction (here translated): "On his way home from Africa, Earl Roberts sent word that he
        would land at Port Elizabeth at six o'clock in the morning, and that he would have to return to
        the vessel at nine. The town and the fleet in Algoa Bay put themselves in festival array to do
        honour to the Victor, and to the Commander-in-Chief of the British Army. Blacks, Indians and
        Malays joined the white people as one in their carnival costumes waiting to greet him; but the
        great sight of the day was the children of the town, on a broad field on the summit of the slope
        upon which the town is built. Here the young people of the Sunday School, each group of
        children under the care of their teacher, had gathered in their hundreds. They were put into a
        single big circle, with a high dais in the middle for the conductor. Earl Roberts entered the circle
        in his carriage, and went around it, speaking words of wisdom and love to the infants and the
        young people. They sang in unison: 'God save the Queen,' etc. And when the carriage turned to
        go, the children gathered around it like bees to shake his hand and get his autograph."
            It is clear, then, that the poem was written for performance in a children's play or tableau. It
        is sub-headed 7 December 1900. The poet may have been an eye-witness to the scene: in *An Deo-
        Grèine* 3 (1907–8) 94–5 is a list of technical terms associated with women's work with which she
        won a prize at the 1900 Mod, 'sent, if we remember well, all the way from the Antipodes'.
        Perhaps she was visiting her brother Charles, who had been in Newcastle, N.S.W., since 1885.
        For metre see notes on poem 64.

Alexander Cameron (Alasdair Camshron) 1848–1933

Alexander Cameron, 'Bàrd Thùrnaig', was born 12 April 1848 at Inverasdale, Gairloch, sixth
and last child of Roderick Cameron, agricultural labourer and (after 1849) crofter, from Contin
(*Ruairidh mac Ruairidh*, 1804x5–81), and his wife Mary Maclennan, from Kernsary
(*c.*1811–*post*1891), the others being Roderick, Murdo, Janet, Mary and Catherine. The family
appears to have moved a short distance to Midtown when the poet was about one year old, and
he was reared there till the age of eight. One of his earliest memories was of how, as a child being
brought to the peatcutting in a creel, he was praised and touched by a woman, Barabal, who was
reputed to have the evil eye. As soon as he climbed out he fainted and began to vomit, no doubt
thanks to the jolting motion of the creel on the way uphill. His mother promptly brought him
home on the breast. She was advised by a neighbour that the only cure for his condition was *an
t-uisge-airgid*, water into which a piece of silver had been dipped. The water was to be drawn in
the name of the Glorious Trinity, each Person of the Three separately named. He was given the
water to drink. His hands and forehead were bathed in it, and he fell asleep.

When he awoke he was as right as rain, but there came a pillar of the Church. "Is this the child
that I heard was sick?"

"Yes," said his mother.

"He got better quickly. Do you know what was wrong with him?"

"I believe it was a *cronachadh.*"

"What is that, woman?"

"It is a *beum-sùla*, a stroke of the evil eye, because under the Almighty's hand it is *uisge-airgid* that has helped him."

"Oh woman, woman, what did He have to do with it?"

"The silver did the trick."

"Oh how I despair of ever making you wise."

The poet lived all his life on the shores of Loch Ewe, whether at Inverasdale, Naast, Poolewe or Tournaig. His first school was a Gaelic-medium one of the type ultimately swept away by the Education Act of 1872 (see poem 194), with the result that by the age of five he could read the Gaelic New Testament fairly well. The Gaelic school was replaced about 1854 by a theoretically English-medium Free Church one in which, despite being in a class of 85, the poet was enabled to make good progress by a 'pupil teacher', whose help he repaid by posting his love letters for him four miles away at Poolewe. About 1867 he went to live and work as a shepherd at Tournaig on the Inverewe estate, which belonged to Osgood Mackenzie (1842–1922), celebrated creator of the Inverewe Garden and author of *A Hundred Years in the Highlands* (1st edn 1921). Mackenzie it was who really taught him English, giving him the run of his library and encouraging him to memorise and recite long pieces from the poets of the past, a task in which he delighted. After ten years' service he became Mackenzie's sheep manager, and he also speaks in one of his letters (*Am Bàrd* 189) of journeys made to Skye, Mull, Uist, Harris and Inverness to build up the estate's herd of Highland cattle.

In 1880 he married Jessie Macpherson (1851–*pre*1934). A daughter of the Tournaig blacksmith Alexander Macpherson and his wife May Fraser, she was a maid to Osgood's mother (the Dowager Lady Mackenzie) at Inverewe. Osgood acted as witness. The couple had five children: Elizabeth (Lizzie), Mary Ann, Roderick, Alexander and Murdo.

A lifelong champion of the Gaelic language, Alexander Cameron was a member of An Comunn Gaidhealach from its foundation in 1891 until his death, and his poems and other writings appeared in various journals. Papers consisting of his songs, the first read by him in person in 1906, were published in *Transactions of the Gaelic Society of Inverness* 26 (1904–7) 351–68 and 432–48. He carefully avoided satire, unlike his neighbour Duncan Mackenzie (*Bàrd Cheann Loch Iù*, 1831–1907), who was a master of the art. (See J H Dixon, *Gairloch* (Edinburgh 1886, repr. Gairloch 1974) 192–4; Coinneach Dòmhnallach, 'Bàrd Cheannlochiù', *Gairm* 72 (Am Foghar 1970) 347–60.)

Osgood Mackenzie refers to our poet in *A Hundred Years in the Highlands* as 'my old sheep manager, Alexander Cameron, better known to his many friends as the Tournaig Bard on account of his being such a good Gaelic poet and improvisatore'. Late in life he became the friend, tutor and correspondent of an enthusiastic Gaelic learner, Captain Ian A Moffatt-Pender — 'Iain an Fhéilidh', 'Iain Mór nan Creag', for whom see *Gairm* 18 (An Geamhradh 1956) 134–5, and p. 822 below. In 1926, under Moffatt-Pender's editorship, his collected works appeared under the title *Am Bàrd: Òrain, Sgrìobhaidhean agus Litrichean Bàrd Thùrnaig (Alasdair Camshron)*, published by W M Urquhart of Edinburgh, and consisting of five essays (one of which is 'Eòlas-Aimsir nan Gaidheal', see below), 25 poems and songs, and a series of 28 letters, full of old-fashioned dignity, written to 'Iain Mór nan Creag' between 1919 and 1925. He died at Achadhmor, Londubh, Poolewe, on 5 December 1933, and at Moffatt-Pender's instigation a cairn was erected in his memory at Inverewe in 1952, for which see 'Tuireadh Bàrd Thùrnaig', *Gairm* 31 (An t-Earrach 1960) 208–9.

I am grateful to Roy Wentworth, Erradale, Gairloch, for information, and to Mrs Annie MacKintosh, Conon Bridge (the poet's eldest surviving grandchild), for information and permission to reprint:

6   *An Sgàileagan* (**'The Umbrella').** Editor's trl. *Am Bàrd* 154–5, there entitled 'Rathad Mor gu Ceann Loch Iubh'. Set to the tune 'Gabhaidh sinn an Rathad Mór'. Composed on receipt of an umbrella from the management of *The People's Journal* in Dundee. The poet's series of five articles in Gaelic on the theme of weather lore, 'Eòlas-Aimsir nan Gaidheal' (later reproduced more or less complete in *Am Bàrd* 45–60), appeared in the Inverness and North Counties edition of *The People's Journal* between 19 August and 16 September 1916, and it may be assumed that an umbrella was considered the appropriate reward. It was Cameron's habit to thank the paper in Gaelic verse for such gifts. His thanks for a cruet set had appeared on 17 June that year, and for a copy of *The Celtic Annual* on 24 June.

The penultimate stanza refers to the celebrated poem 'An Dubh-Ghleannach' by Alexander MacKinnon (1770–1814), for which see John Mackenzie (ed.), *Sàr-Obair nam Bàrd Gaelach* (4th edn Edinburgh 1877) 341, 346–7. The *Dubh-Ghleannach* ('Dark Lady of the Glen') was a pleasure-boat belonging to Alexander Macdonald of Glenaladale, who erected the monument to Prince Charles at Glenfinnan.

Mhionnaich Neiptiun agus Aeòlus	Neptune and Æolus swore
Bhon chaidh gaoth is cuan fo'n òrdugh	As they'd control of wind and wave
Nach do mhaslaicheadh cho mòr iad	That they'd never been so scorned
Bho linn na h-Àirce bha aig Nòah	Since the time of Noah's Ark
Gun robh an Rìgh as àirde còmhnadh	As by the King of highest succour
A' dion 's a' sàbhaladh Chloinn Dòmhnaill.	Protecting, saving the Clan Donald.

See also poem 56.

Archibald Macintyre (Gilleasbaig Mac an t-Saoir) 1854–1922

Archibald Macintyre was born in 1854, second(?) child of Alexander Macintyre, shepherd (d. 1860), and his wife Mary Fletcher (?1827–1874), who were married on 22 January 1852. He had an elder sister Catherine, born 1853. He spent his life as a shepherd in the upper Loch Fyne area of Argyll. On 19 June 1879, at the Free Church in Glencroe, he married Barbara Sinclair, from Lochgoilhead (1848x9–1929), daughter of Archibald Sinclair, another shepherd. They settled at Dunderave, where they raised four sons: Alexander ('Sandy', 1881–1972), Archibald (1883–1963), Donald (188?–1945) and Peter (1887–1963).

Little else is known of 'Old Archie' save what is contained in 'Òran Ghlinne Chrò'. He died 24 February 1922 at Stank by Loch Lubnaig, Callander; his Sunday plaid of shepherd's tartan, still in immaculate condition, remains in the care of his granddaughter, Mrs L Galbraith, 6 Auchagoil, Minard, and was exhibited at the Dalmally Show in 1996.

For the full poem and further information see Iain Rothach, 'Cuimhneachain Bràigh Cnuic', *Gairm* 88 (Am Foghar 1974) 338–43. I am grateful to Mrs Rae MacGregor, Inveraray, and Mr Angus Dickson, Bridge of Allan, for information, and to the poet's grandson Calum Macintyre, Brig o' Turk, for information and permission to reprint:

7   **From *Òran Ghlinne Chrò* ('The Song of Glen Croe').** Editor's trl. *Gairm* 88 (Am Foghar 1974) 342–3. Preserved in a commonplace-book kept by Sandy, now in the possession of Sandy's eldest son Calum, who lives at Benmore, Brig o' Turk. The occasion of the poem was the removal in 1913–14 of the sheep from Sir Andrew Noble's farm at Clachan, Loch Fyne — of which Old Archie, then living at Cuil, was shepherd — to make room for deer. The first eleven stanzas (not printed here) describe the final drove to Macdonald Fraser's mart at Stirling; how the sheep went under the hammer of Paton the auctioneer; how Old Archie bought the mart assistants a drink; and how, good shepherd that he was, he wept for the lambs he would never see. The song was composed in Glen Croe on his solitary (and jobless) way home, 10 March 1914.

The Glen contains little today but a trunk road and forestry, and it is chilling to note that within two years of the composition of the song, on 21 January 1916, three of Old Archie's grandsons (Sandy's sons Alexander, Archie and Calum) were respectively killed, maimed and injured there by a car from Inveraray, when Sandy and his family were living in the shepherd's cottage at the foot of the 'Rest and be Thankful'. The following report of the accident appeared in *The Oban Times*, 29 January 1916:

MOTOR CAR FATALITY. — On Friday evening, as an Inveraray motor car was proceeding through Glen Croe on the way to the town, and when passing the house in the glen of Mr Alex. Macintyre, shepherd, a distressing accident occurred. Mr Macintyre's children were near the roadway, and two of them suddenly darted in front of the car. One of them, Alexander, aged two years, was run over and killed; another, Malcolm, five years of age, was knocked down and seriously injured about the head. The occupants of the car did all they could to render assistance, and then drove off to Inveraray and reported the matter to Sergeant Mackinnon, County Constabulary. Dr Stewart was called, and he proceeded to Glen Croe, and attended to the injured boy. Much sympathy is felt all over the district for Mr Alex. Macintyre and his wife in their great sorrow.

Donald Maciver (Dòmhnall MacÌomhair) 1857–1935

Donald Maciver (*Dòmhnall Iain Ruaidh, Am Ma' Sgoile Ruadh*) was born 4 August 1857 in Crowlista, Uig, Lewis, third child of John Maciver from Carnish (*Iain mac Aonghais*, 1815–1904) and his wife Christina Macaulay, a crofter's daughter from Crowlista (*Carstiona nighean Dhòmhnaill Thormoid*, 1823–1902), the others being Angus, Margaret, John and Alexander. By the time Alexander was born in 1863 the family was living in Valtos. The poet's father Iain mac Aonghais, a tenant farmer, was the son of an army pensioner whose croft had been in Carnish, which was cleared in 1852–3; Iain mac Aonghais had received a good formal education, and was appointed in 1869 as Gaelic schoolmaster to the parish of Uig, his school probably being the one at Islivig. At some point he was appointed to the school at Sgigersta in Ness, and that is where he is found with his family by the Census of 1881.

The poet's sister Margaret married Kenneth Macmillan, Lemreway, Lochs, and he himself married Margaret Macaulay from Islivig (*Mairead nighean Thormoid 'ic Dhòmhnaill*, 1856–1924); they had ten children, Christina Anne, Mary Anne, Angus, Murdina, Norman, Annie, Johanna (Joan), Donald, Margaret (Madge) and Henrietta (Etta). The poet took up his father's profession, his first school being at Lemreway, where he lived with his married sister; their father came to join them and is said to be buried at Gravir.

The poet returned to Uig in 1883 to teach at Breasclete, moving finally in 1896 to become headmaster of Bayble School in Point, which he forged into one of the most successful schools in the Western Isles. A Fellow of the Educational Institute of Scotland, he was a tireless proponent of bilingualism in education, and in 1900 published a *Bilingual Text Book*, the stated aim of which was 'to facilitate the teaching of English in the Upper Division of his own school'. He retired in 1922 to live at Glennan, Garrabost, and was succeeded by James Thomson, q.v. He won many Mod prizes for his poetry, and six of his songs appear in Iain N MacLeòid (ed.), *Bàrdachd Leódhais* (Glasgow 1916, repr. Stornoway 1998). His own work *Place-Names of Lewis and Harris* was published in Stornoway in 1934.

Donald Maciver died at Garrabost on 28 September 1935. Most of his papers were regrettably destroyed when Glennan was dismantled. His remaining manuscripts, all in Gaelic, are in the possession of Norman MacSween, Head of Jeddore, Nova Scotia, a son of his daughter Johanna.

I am grateful for information to Mrs Effie Macdonald, Registrar, Stornoway; Mrs Catherine Stewart, Vatisker, Back, a great-granddaughter of the poet's sister Margaret; Norman MacSween; Annie MacSween, North Dell; Donald MacIver, Crowlista, a great-grandson of the poet's mother's sister Rachael Macaulay; Bill Lawson, Northton, Harris; and, last but not least, Mrs Lorna Steven (*née* MacGillivray), Kirklands Farm, Haddington, E. Lothian, daughter of the poet's eldest daughter Christina Anne. I am grateful to Mrs Steven for her kindness and for permission to reprint:

8   *An Ataireachd Àrd* **('The Sea's Lofty Roar').** Editor's trl. *An Deo-Gréine* 1 (1905–6) 60; *Bàrdachd Leódhais* 171–3. The tune may be found in, among other places, James Thomson and Duncan MacDonald (eds), *Eilean Fraoich: Lewis Gaelic Songs and Melodies* (2nd edn, ed. by Duncan M Morison *et al.*, Stornoway 1982) 17, and Alexina Ghreumach and Alma NicShimidh (eds), *Sùil ri Cladach* (Stornoway 1992) 26. The genesis of the song is as follows. The poet had an uncle, his father's brother Donald Maciver (1817–95), called Dòmhnall Bàn Crost due to his mischievous temperament. When a boy he lived at Carnish. One day when walking the shoreline at Crowlista he came upon Donald Macaulay, *Dòmhnall Aonghais Buachaille*, who was famed for his feats of strength (see Murchadh MacLeòid, 'Dòmhnall Aonghuis Buachaille', *Gairm* 17 (Am Foghar 1956) 51–4). Dòmhnall Aonghais Buachaille was standing rock-fishing, not being able to sit due to a large festering boil on his buttock. Knowing this, Dòmhnall Bàn Crost came up stealthily behind him, kicked him in the boil and ran away. He was eventually caught and soundly beaten, and said afterwards that he learned a few lessons that day. He married Mary Buchanan from Carnish, and they emigrated to the Eastern Townships of Quebec with their family in 1852 when Carnish was cleared. He returned for a visit about 1888 when the poet was at Breasclete; the two men, uncle and nephew, went to Carnish, and when standing on the ridge high above Tràigh Leire watching the Atlantic breakers rolling in through Camas Ùig to the Tràigh Mhór, Dòmhnall Bàn said, *Chan eil nì an-seo mar a bhà, ach ataireachd na mara air an tràigh.* 'Nothing here is as it was except the surge of the sea on the strand.'

The story, or at least that part of it leading to the punch line, was told by the poet himself in his introduction to the poem as published in *An Deo-Gréine*. Inspired by his uncle's words lingering in his mind, Maciver composed 'An Ataireachd Àrd' as an entry for the poetry competition in the 1905 National Mod, which it won. It was subsequently set to music by John Macdonald, a native of one of the inner isles who had attended the first Mod in Oban in 1892, and who went on to compose many songs such as 'Athchuinge' and 'Bean a' Chotain Ruaidh' in the 1920s, and to conduct the Oban Gaelic Choir until 1946 (Frank Thompson, *The National Mod* (Stornoway 1979) 50). The combined effect of Maciver's words and Macdonald's melody is breathtaking.

John Campbell (Seonaidh Caimbeul) 1859–1947

Seonaidh Caimbeul was born 13 June 1859 in S. Lochboisdale, S. Uist, fourth child of Donald Campbell, cottar and stonemason, who was from Boisdale although born in Eriskay (*Dòmhnall mac Iain Bhàin*, 1821–94), and his wife Mary Gillies, from S. Lochboisdale (*Màiri nighean Iain Fhionnlaigh*, 1831–66), the others being John A, Catherine (died in infancy), Mary (died in infancy), Alexander (died in infancy), Catherine, and Flora (died in infancy). They were of the Campbells known in S. Uist as *Caimbeulaich an Urrais*. Donald Campbell's work as a stonemason has stood the test of time — Capt. Angus Edward MacInnes, who was born in one of the houses he built, wrote in 1997, "It is now well over one hundred years old and is still standing and habitable" (*Eriskay Where I Was Born* (Edinburgh 1997) 101).

Seonaidh grew up as a herdboy, and started attending school at age nine or ten, but did not learn to read either Gaelic or English at that time. Poetry ran in his family. His elder brother, also John (known as Iain, 1855–1934), was a particularly good poet as well as an accomplished stonemason who built hotels in Oban and the Catholic church in Castlebay; most of Iain's songs are now lost, having died with his son, the late James Campbell from S. Lochboisdale, *Seumas Iain 'ic Dhòmhnaill 'ic Iain Bhàin*, in 1979. However, three more of Iain's five sons, Roderick, Aonghas Iain and Iain (who died in New Zealand), were talented songmakers, Roderick in particular. Known locally as *Ròidseag* and further afield as *An Case* (because where others bought a bottle of beer on leaving a bar he bought a whole case), Roderick composed songs such as 'A Pheigi a Ghràidh' (for which see *Gairm* 6 (An Geamhradh 1953) 109) and 'Òran na h-Airship'. Thanks to his boisterous life on the high seas, these were learnt by his sailing companions and are now known and sung throughout the Western Isles. See Margaret Fay Shaw, *Folksongs and Folklore of South Uist* (2nd edn Oxford 1977) 269; Rev. Fr John A Macdonald, 'The Songs of Donald Allan MacDonald' (M.Litt. thesis, Aberdeen 1983) 11–15 = Rev. Fr John A Macdonald, *Òrain Dhòmhnaill Ailein* (Benbecula 1999) 40–3; MacInnes, *Eriskay Where I Was Born* 101; notes on poem 134.

Seonaidh spent his life as a fisherman, learning the trade from a Golspie skipper to whose Gaelic he gradually became accustomed, and eventually acquiring his own boat. In winter, although he spoke little English (J L Campbell described him in 1939 as a monoglot Gaelic speaker), he would go to Glasgow to work in the shipyards or gasworks. When fishing for lobsters at Canna he learned to read from the schoolteacher there. In 1892 he married Margaret MacFarlane (*Peigi Aonghais 'ic Phàrlain*, 1864–1947), who was born at Auratote but whose forebears had come from Skye in the 1820s to work as shepherds — first at Balranald, then to Vallay in the 1830s, Askernish about 1839, and Uisgebhagh about 1850. By 1892, the MacFarlane home was at Caolas Stadhlaigh on the lonely east coast of S. Uist, a place much frequented by fishermen, and the poet got to know her through her father's hospitality.

Seonaidh and Peigi had no children. Their home on *Am Meall* in S. Lochboisdale (5 N. Glendale, a croft created in 1919) became a popular *taigh-céilidh*; indeed 'Òran Sheonaidh', the first song ever composed by Donald Allan MacDonald (q.v.), was made there in Seonaidh's absence in 1922 (Macdonald, thesis, pp. 99–100, 238, 265, 292–4, and *Òrain Dhòmhnaill Ailein* 80–1, 205, 230). It is celebrated in Donald John MacDonald's 'Taigh a' Bhàird', poem 173. "Seonaidh was the nicest man I ever met," recalls Dòmhnall Aonghais Bhàin, q.v. (personal communication, 14 August 1998). "Even in old age he was so nice and kind, no matter how difficult things would be, Seonaidh would crack one of his jokes."

During 1930–5 Seonaidh was one of those who provided Margaret Fay Shaw with the material which ultimately appeared in *Folksongs and Folklore of South Uist*, see especially pp. 10–17, 26–8 and 269 and plates 5b and 15 of that book. On 28 November 1933 he gave her 'Duan na Càisg', which she quickly published in *Scottish Gaelic Studies* 4 (1935) 150–2, stating that Seonaidh was a native of Loch Carnan, where he had learnt it as a child. This statement, which appears to be at variance with John MacInnes's information (confirmed by his birth certificate, GRO 1859/118/3/31) that Seonaidh was born in S. Lochboisdale, was then repeated in *Folksongs and Folklore of South Uist*.

Seven or eight of Seonaidh's songs had been written down by Fr Allan McDonald (1859–1905) and his friend Dr George Henderson (1866–1912) before Fr Allan's translation in 1894 from Daliburgh to Eriskay. A manuscript of the songs exists among Henderson's papers in Glasgow University Library. Before 1914 Malcolm MacPhee, schoolmaster in Garrynamonie, had begun to write down the songs before he left for Benbecula and then the War. The late John MacInnes, Daliburgh (*Iain Pheadair Iain 'ic Sheumais*, referred to above), recommended the task in 1934, but his own work as a fisherman often interrupted it, and it was not until Dr John Lorne Campbell (1906–96) became involved that 48 out of almost 100 of Seonaidh's songs (amounting to about 4,500 lines) taken down by MacInnes were finally published, with an account of the poet's life, as *Òrain Ghàidhlig le Seonaidh Caimbeul* (1936). Two songs had already appeared in *Scottish Standard*, August 1935. The book was reviewed in, among other places, *An Gaidheal* 32 (1936–7) 109. In October 1935 Campbell and MacInnes brought Seonaidh to Glasgow, where his speech was recorded by the BBC for a record of Scottish dialects. Raconteur as well as poet, some of his traditional stories were published in the journal *Outlook* and in J L Campbell's *Sia Sgialachdan* of 1939.

Seonaidh died at Locheynort (where he had two nephews) on 8 February 1947, and is buried in Cnoc Hàllainn. I am grateful for information to Dòmhnall Aonghais Bhàin (q.v.) and to Bill Lawson, whose *Croft History: Isle of South Uist, Volume 3* (Northton, Harris 1997) provides much valuable information, see especially pp. 130 and 160.

9   **Òran a' Pheinsean ('The Song of the Pension').** Editor's trl. *Òrain Ghàidhlig le Seonaidh Caimbeul* 75–9. Old Age Pensions were introduced by Lloyd George, then Chancellor of the Exchequer, in 1908 (see poem 1), but this song presumably dates from 1929, the year of the Wall Street Crash, when the poet reached the qualifying age of 70. It includes a nod in the direction of Ronald Laing's splendid 'Òran na Féille' (*c*.1890), in which the poet sets off with a *damh* ('bullock') and is confronted one at a time at the fair by his creditors, including — in the fullest surviving version — factor, creelmaker, mason, shoemaker, tailor, Lowland traveller and smith, in that order. See *Folksongs and Folklore of South Uist* 124–7 and *Tocher* 40 (1986) 242–6.

       Ruairidh in the first stanza is Roderick Macmillan, S. Uist District Clerk. There are references in the last stanza to the dole, which was then being paid at a rate of 15 weeks' benefit for 12 weeks' National Insurance contributions, and to 'transitional' unemployment benefit, which was paid after insurance payments were exhausted, and was subject to a means test. The poet's final comment refers to the principle, then rapidly gaining ground, that benefits should be paid irrespective of means or of contributions.

Angus Morrison (Aonghas Moireasdan) 1865–1942

Angus Morrison was born 15 November 1865 in Ullapool, Ross-shire, son of Roderick Morrison, shoemaker, and his wife Mary Mackenzie, whose marriage had taken place on 10 February 1843. The 1871 Census shows the family living at Shore Street and comprising parents Roderick (56) and Mary (48), daughters Mary (15) and Donaldina (12), and sons Simon (10) and Angus (5). No doubt there were also sons and daughters born between 1843 and 1855. Angus was a first cousin of the poet John MacLennan, see Hugh Barron, 'Notes on Bards', in *Transactions of the Gaelic Society of Inverness* 50 (1976–8) 201–36: 217.

The poet became a tea and coffee merchant. By 1900 he was living at Union Street, Inverness, and he served as Secretary and Treasurer of the Gaelic Society of Inverness from *c*.1904 to 1907. After that he appears to have moved south, but he may have travelled a great deal — presumably by train, boat, and hired pony and trap — in the course of business; indeed his poems are set in many different parts of the Highlands. As well as an assiduous maker of rhymes he was a collector and publisher of songs and pipe tunes. His *Òrain nam Beann* (for which see p. liii above) first appeared in Glasgow in 1913, and *Dàin agus Òrain Ghàidhlig* [*DOG*], a very substantial collection of his own poems, was published in Edinburgh in 1929.

In his later years the poet began compiling a book of Gaelic placenames, and contributed occasionally to *An Gaidheal*. At the time of his death he was a vice-president of the Highland Pipers' Society and a member of Comunn Tìr nam Beann. True to his trade, his playlet 'Dà Unnsa Tea' (1941) rises to a climax with such verses as

Air tuiteam oidhche 's an lainntir soillseach   By the light of the lamp at the fall of night
Mo ghean is m' aoibhneas 'phoit tea bhith còmh' rium   My wish and delight's the teapot beside me

(*An Gaidheal* 36 (1940–41) 130). He died, unmarried, aged 77 on 10 December 1942 in his house at 13 Brandon Terrace, Edinburgh, and his obituary in *The Ross-shire Journal* of 18 December that year states that he was to be interred in Clachan Burying Ground in Ullapool.

I am grateful to Hugh Barron for information.

10   From *Alba Saor* ('Scotland Free'). Editor's trl. *DOG* 171–4. The poem consists of nine stanzas, of which 1–7 are printed here. Stanza 6 refers to the Scottish National Party, founded in 1928.

11   *Nam biodh agam moisein bodaich* ('If I had an old meanie of a mannie'). Editor's trl. *DOG* 358. Sounds like a variation on the *port á beul* (mouth tune) 'Nam biodh trì sgillinn agam', see James Thomson and Duncan MacDonald (eds), *Eilean Fraoich: Lewis Gaelic Songs and Melodies* (2nd edn, ed. by Duncan M Morison *et al.*, Stornoway 1982) 114, or on the lines *Nam biodh agam bodach prabach . . .*, by Donald Morrison ('Geinidh'), see Tormod MacLeòid (ed.), *Bàrdachd á Leódhas* (Glasgow 1969) 58.

12   From *Smuaintean air Mórachd Ìmpireachd Bhreatainn* ('Thoughts on the Greatness of the British Empire'). Editor's trl., with assistance from Kenneth MacDonald. *DOG* 378–9. The poem consists of 194 lines of iambic pentameters; the first 34, printed here, are pretty representative of the whole.

13   *Madainn na Sàbaid* ('The Sabbath Morning'). Editor's trl. *DOG* 392–4. Changing attitudes to the Sabbath epitomise the social history of the Highlands and Islands, and throughout the twentieth century respect for the Sabbath, rather than for the language, remained the principal marker of Gaelic identity, but the battlegrounds of 'Fortress Sabbath' gradually moved further north and west (see poems 78, 198). Morrison was old enough to remember how ten local men were arrested on Sunday 3 June 1883 for preventing the movement of goods on the Sabbath by occupying the pier at Strome Ferry, then the western terminus of the Dingwall–Skye railway; they were sentenced to four months in Calton Jail, Edinburgh. See David McConnell, *The Strome Ferry Railway Riot of 1883* (Dornoch 1993).

The condition of the Sabbath between the Wars was summed up thus in *The Monthly Record of the Free Church of Scotland* 26 (1926) 114: "There is every year some new encroachment on the sanctity of the Lord's Day. With the bait of reduced fares, railway and steamboat facilities for pleasure travelling on the Lord's Day to country districts and coast towns have multiplied during the year, and the scenes witnessed at some railway stations and summer resorts, as a result of the running of trains and the sailing of steamers, have been most disgraceful. In some country parishes the people on their way to church, and at their homes, are greatly disturbed by gangs of noisy trippers who arrive in char-a-bancs, and by other pleasure seekers in the form of motorists of all types, and these strangers are quite regardless of the rights of the many who highly value the quiet that is traditionally associated with the Sabbath in Scotland. Wise efforts were made to induce the parties running the motor-bus service from Inverness to Dingwall to desist from the practice of maintaining that service on the Lord's Day, but without avail. There are many people in the cities and country towns who seek to make the Sabbath a day of additional profits, by opening shops and places of amusements, and this particular form of Sabbath desecration is yearly on the increase . . . The sale of newspapers on the Lord's Day grows apace, to the great annoyance of many of the community, and this is one of the many evil consequences of the Great War."

Amongst Sabbatarian *causes célèbres* in the 1920s were the dismissal in 1927 of the assistant keeper of Toward Lighthouse on the Clyde for refusing to take part in the testing of a radio link on the Sabbath, and the popular success of the Skye Sabbath Defence League, which was launched in 1929 by Kenneth MacRae, FC minister of Kilmuir, in an attempt to persuade the London Midland and Scottish Railway Co. to abandon a plan to run Sunday excursions from

Inverness to Kyle so that day-trippers could then cross on hired boats to Skye. (The line had been extended from Strome Ferry to Kyle in 1897.) The whole issue of public transport was a vexed one: in a special poll in 1926, for example, the ratepayers of Rothesay voted by a large majority in favour of the running of tramcars on the Sabbath. The poet also draws attention to the Socialist and Communist Sunday Schools which were a cause of much political soul-searching in Britain throughout the 1920s. He would no doubt have agreed with the Chairman of the Education Committee of London County Council who, when asked in 1928 about his party's opposition to the use of LCC property for Socialist Sunday Schools, replied that the policy 'was not dictated by any fear of a rising of the juvenile proletariat, but by consideration of the harm which would be done to the juvenile proletariat by the pernicious institutions to which the question related' (*The Times*, 1 February 1928).

Angus Mackechnie (Aonghas MacEacharna) 1870–1944

Angus Mackechnie was born 8 January 1870 at Cuilbhuirg, Iona (his mother's family home), eldest son of Donald Mackechnie from Kenovay, Tiree, carpenter and poet (*Dòmhnall Bàn mac Iain 'ic Eoghain*, 1846–1923, for whom see Cameron's *Bàird Thirisdeach* 209–16), and his wife Catherine Macphail from Iona (*Catrìona nighean Aonghais 'ic Dhonnchaidh 'ic Aonghais*, 1848–1919). At that time the poet's father was working as a carpenter in Glasgow, but when the poet was ten years old the family returned to Tiree and settled in Hynish, his father becoming postman for the south end of the island.

Angus excelled at school in Tiree to the extent of learning Greek. He became a pupil teacher, but relinquished this for the post of telegraph clerk and assistant postmaster in Tiree. Then he went to sea. He rose to the position of master, and commanded a number of vessels for various companies, including latterly the Clyde steamers operated by the LMS Railway.

In 1892 he had married Janet Maccorkindale (*Seònaid nighean Donnchaidh 'ic Dhòmhnaill 'ic Àdhaimh*, 1865–1958), who was of a Gaelic-speaking Kintyre family that had come to Coll to run the post office there in the 1870s; the story of their early courtship is told by their granddaughter, Mrs Jo Currie, formerly of Edinburgh University Library, in 'Mull People', *The Scottish Genealogist* 44 (March 1997) 15–24: 16–17. They had seven children: Donald, Catherine, Duncan, Angus, Elizabeth, Iain and Janetta. They lived for a time at Campbeltown, and when the poet retired from the sea they took over the Post Office at Bunessan in Mull. 'Dùthaich nan Gaisgeach', also known as 'Tìr Mhaiseach nan Cruach', won the poet the Bardic Crown at the National Mod in Fort William in 1927 (see p. 821), and seventeen of his songs and poems are in *Na Bàird Thirisdeach*. He died in Bunessan on 10 December 1944.

I am grateful to Mrs Currie for information and permission to reprint:

14   *Iorram nan Ìtheach* (**'The Iona Boatsong'**). Editor's trl. Cameron (ed.), *Bàird Thirisdeach* 382–3. Gribun is a high part of the Mull coast to the north-east. Kentra, the shore of the Ross opposite the north end of Iona, breaks the force of a nor'-easterly bearing down on the Sound. The Reilig (*Réilig Òdhrain*, dedicated to St Oran) is the Iona burial-ground. 'George' is Captain George Ritchie, and 'MacPhail' is Angus MacPhail, Postmaster at Iona, d. 1932.

Rev. Kenneth Macleod (An t-Urr. Coinneach MacLeòid) 1871–1955

Kenneth Macleod (*Coinneach a' Mhaighistir*, 'the Schoolmaster's Kenneth') was born 2 February 1871 in the schoolhouse, Sanna Bheag, Isle of Eigg, sixth child of Donald Macleod (*Dòmhnall mac Coinnich*, 1831x2–93) and his wife Janet (Jessie) Humphrey (1837–77), the others being Marion, Christina, Williamina, Felina, David, Euphemia and Ishobel. Their father, a native of Uig in Skye, was parish schoolmaster of the Small Isles, having previously served at Drumbeg in Assynt and Tongue in Sutherland, while their mother was a daughter of David Humphrey, farmer and local factor at Cul-Cinn in Assynt. The Humphreys were a local family in Assynt who believed themselves descended from an English soldier stationed in Inverness in Cromwell's time. The MacLeods to whom the poet belonged were known in Skye as *Clann a' Chomhairlich*, 'the Counsellor's Family'; a branch of the MacLeods of Fasach in Glendale, they had been celebrated as tradition-bearers.

Kenneth's mother died of TB in 1877, when he was six, and his father's sister, Janet Macleod, came to Eigg to keep house and help rear the family. Janet possessed a great wealth of inherited knowledge which she delighted in passing on to her fosterchildren; we meet her at the schoolhouse in Eigg in vol. 5 of *Carmina Gadelica* (pp. 60–5), being questioned about the great waulking-song 'Seathan Mac Rìgh Éireann' by Kenneth Macleod and Alexander Carmichael (q.v.) in January 1905. In addition, the collective oral memory of the 300-strong Eigg community was constantly in action at ceilidhs, waulkings and weddings. "The writer was fortunate enough to spend his boyhood in Eigg just before the old order of things had quite passed away. Several of the folk could boast that their parents had been taught a little reading and writing, and a great deal of poetry, by *Raoghall Dubh*, son of the famous bard, *Alastair Mac Mhaighstir Alastair*" (*The Road to the Isles* 75). Between the ages of 6 and 16, therefore, Kenneth imbibed the traditions of the Skye MacLeods from his family and of the Clanranald MacDonalds from his friends and neighbours.

Thanks to a bursary, Kenneth went in 1885 to Raining's School, Inverness. Shortly after this, his father retired to live in Oban and then in Taynuilt; he died in Oban in 1893. In 1887 Alexander Macbain, the philologist headmaster of Raining's, encouraged Kenneth to tour Skye and Uist in search of folklore, and the results were published in the school magazine and in Macbain's *Celtic Magazine*. In 1888, recommending Kenneth for a university bursary, Macbain wrote: "He speaks and writes the best Gaelic I know of; he is full of Gaelic lore and folk-literature — especially folk tales" (*SCML* x).

Kenneth attended the University of Glasgow, but ill health prevented him taking his degree, and in 1893 he became a lay missionary of the Church of Scotland, serving successively in S. Uist, Stornoway, N. Uist, Morvern, Campbeltown, Lochboisdale, Kilberry, Kyleakin, Lochboisdale (again), Mallaig, Glenquoich, Morvern (again), Straloch, Crianlarich, Straloch (again), Ardchattan, and Boat of Garten. As a lay missionary he performed all the duties of a parish minister except administering the sacraments and officiating at marriages. Licensed to preach in 1917 by special permission of the General Assembly, he served as minister of Colonsay 1917–23 and of Gigha and Cara until his retirement in 1947. He was a gentle, unworldly man, diffident but a good preacher. He never married.

Between assignments Macleod spent much time in Edinburgh, where he attended University classes in Celtic and became the youngest member of the Gaelic intellectual community presided over by Carmichael. Thanks to the authority this gave him, for most of the first half of the century, following Carmichael's death in 1912, he was the icon of the Gaelic literary world (in a very similar way to Sorley MacLean in the second half). He was thus, for example, able to block the publication of George Campbell Hay's poems in 1939 (Michel Byrne, 'Bàrdachd Mhic Iain Dheòrsa', Edinburgh PhD 1992, 45–9).

Between 1908 and 1929, in collaboration with Marjory Kennedy-Fraser, Macleod published the four-volume *Songs of the Hebrides*, in which Gaelic music was rendered fit for the concert platform according to the fashion of the day. It was an enterprise that matched his talents. As T M Murchison wrote (*SCML* xxxiv), "From his own store of folksong he supplied much of the material, both words and music. He composed new Gaelic verses and also made new English versions and verse-translations of the old songs." Having struck a popular seam, consisting of traditional material mixed freely with his own imagination and expressed through English prose and verse, Macleod continued to mine it in *The Road to the Isles* (1927) and *The Road to Iona* (1933). It is difficult to believe that he was the same Kenneth Macleod who declared at the 1912 Mod, *Tha An Comunn an dèidh bliadhna air fhichead de cheòl a thoirt duinn — nach toir e dhuinn a-nis bliadhna air fhichead de Ghàidhlig?* "An Comunn has given us 21 years of music — will it please now give us 21 years of Gaelic?" (*SCML* 55; Frank Thompson, *History of An Comunn Gaidhealach: The First Hundred (1891–1991)* (Inverness 1992) 36). This disjunction between heart and head earned him the lash of Sorley MacLean's satire (poem 126).

Macleod wrote a good deal of Gaelic prose in a style steeped in idiomatic rhythms of speech, and a collection of his essays and stories, edited by T M Murchison, was published by the Scottish Gaelic Texts Society as *Sgrìobhaidhean Choinnich MhicLeòid [SCML]* in 1988. He is best remembered in English for his song 'The Road to the Isles', written, as he said himself, 'for the lads in France during the Great War'; his Gaelic poetry is less well known, and it is probably true to say that, as well as working to a stereotype, he deliberately cultivated an elusive quality in his work. He wrote of himself: "From the cradle you were unconsciously drinking in a life and thoughts that had all but died out elsewhere. The result would be, that if you began to write a book, say twenty or thirty or forty years after, you could not always be certain whether this thought or that verse was really your own, or something out of the past. Not that it greatly matters . . ." (*The Road to the Isles* 8).

He received the degree of DD from the University of St Andrews in 1932. He died in Edinburgh on 9 July 1955, and was buried in his father's grave in the parish churchyard of Muckairn at Taynuilt. He was summed up by Dr John Lorne Campbell (personal communication, ?7 December 1970) as 'a delightful man, but his feet weren't really on the ground'. For more detailed biographies in Gaelic and English see Niall MacGille Sheathanaich, 'Coinneach MacLeòid', *Gairm* 13 (Am Foghar 1955) 81–3; Aonghas MacDhonnchaidh (Angus Robertson, q.v.), 'B' Aithne Dhomh Coinneach MacLeòid', *Gairm* 19 (An t-Earrach 1957) 257–61 and *Gairm* 20 (An Samhradh 1957) 325–7; and *SCML* i–xlii. See also *Gairm* 34 (An Geamhradh 1960) 143–5.

15   *An Fhuar-Bheinn* (**'The Cold Hill'**). Editor's trl. Thomson (ed.), *An Dìleab* 3; Mackinnon (ed.), *Cascheum nam Bàrd* 73.

Rev. Neil Ross (An t-Urr. Niall Ros) 1871–1943

Neil Macleod Ross was born 24 September 1871 at Fasach, Glendale, Skye, first child of Kenneth Ross, from Glendale (*Coinneach mac Nèill*, 1842–1908), and his wife Margaret Macleod, who was originally from Forse by Loch Varkasaig (*Mairead nighean Thormoid*, 1846–1923), the others being Alexander, Norman (father of Rev. Kenneth Ross, q.v.), Calum, Kate and Christina. Neil Ross was a cousin of the poet Neil Macleod (1843–1913), author of *Clàrsach an Doire* (1883). His father was a well-known builder, with sixty bridges and many houses in the west of Skye to his credit.

The poet was educated at Glendale School, in Aberdeen, at the High School of Glasgow and at Edinburgh University (MA, BD). A lifelong enthusiast for all things Gaelic (including, for example, pipe music and the wearing of Highland dress), he was a competitor — and prizewinner — at the very first Mod, held in Oban in 1892. Things went very badly at first that day, and the organisers feared disaster. One of them, Sheriff John MacMaster Campbell, recalled: "It was not till, in the tartan of his clan, Neil Ross stepped upon the platform, that our courage began to grow; and when, by-and-bye, the audience rose like one man to his bold declamation of 'Cha'n fhaigh an Ghàidhlig bàs' ['Gaelic shall not die'], we felt that our first Mòd was saved" (*An Deo-Gréine* 7 (1911–12) 183).

Ross served as minister of St James's, Kirkcaldy (1907–11), Rosemount, Aberdeen (1911–13), Buccleuch, Edinburgh (1913–23), and Laggan, Badenoch (1923–43). In 1907 he married Helen Annand Smith (1885–1959), a native of Alyth, and they had five children: Janet Morag, Kenneth David (who died in infancy), Neil, Norman Macleod and Roderick Sutherland. He was President of An Comunn Gaidhealach for four years and edited its journal *An Gaidheal* from 1923 to 1936. He also served for many years as Inverness-shire county councillor and member of the Education Committee.

Ross's academic labours were indefatigable. In 1914, on the death of Professor Donald Mackinnon, he had been a candidate for the Chair of Celtic in Edinburgh University, a post which eventually went to William J Watson, son-in-law of Alexander Carmichael, q.v. His Edinburgh University DLitt thesis 'Material for Drama in Gaelic Literature' was rejected. His next submission, on 'Heroic Poetry from the Book of the Dean of Lismore', succeeded, however, and was published under the same title by the Scottish Gaelic Texts Society in 1939. His son Roderick writes (personal communication, 2 September 1998): "Every year my father would go to Skye for a month; and my mother saved up and made sure he went, for Glendale gave him spiritual refreshment — especially when he visited Waterstein and Neist, where his psychic certainty indicated to him that bardic oratory and heroic poetry were taught there, possibly in 6th–9th centuries."

Neil Ross was made a Companion of the British Empire in 1933 and received the honorary degree of Doctor of Divinity from the University of Glasgow in 1934. He died in Edinburgh on

17 December 1943, and was buried at Laggan. *Armageddon: A Fragment* was published by his
widow in 1950.

I am grateful to the poet's sons Mr Neil Ross and Dr Roderick S Ross (both of Edinburgh) for
information and for permission to reprint:

16   Dunkirk (from *Armageddon*). Author's trl. *Armageddon* 104–11. Determined to produce a
Gaelic epic on a huge scale, the poet eagerly followed the events of 1939–40 from his study in the
Manse of Laggan and rendered them into heroic verse. As the work progressed he read it to his
family. His sons (who still possess the original manuscript) vividly recall the effect on them of
the long unbroken Homeric lines and the added emphasis with which their father declaimed the
fourth line of each stanza. His intention was to describe the entire course of the War, but due to
his last illness and death the work breaks off at the end of the Battle of Britain (July–Oct. 1940).
The poem as it stands thus consists of 288 stanzas (1,152 lines) describing the British Empire
and its Nazi foe, the Battle of the River Plate, the Norway Campaign, the Fall of France and the
Battle of Britain. The stanzas printed here are nos. 203–16.

The Dunkirk evacuation took place between 26 May and 4 June 1940. Cut off from the rest of
the Allied armies by the rapid advance of Hitler's forces, 300,000 soldiers of the British
Expeditionary Force and the French 1st Army were plucked to safety by a flotilla of small craft
from the port of Dunkirk. Churchill called the evacuation 'a miracle of deliverance'. See poem 209.

Angus Robertson (Aonghas MacDhonnchaidh) 1871–1948

Angus Robertson was born 6 October 1871 in Breakish, Skye, third child of Donald Robertson,
fisherman (*Dòmhnall Sheumais*, 1835–84?), and his wife Ann, also a Robertson (*Anna Aonghais*,
1838–??), the others being James, Ann, Mary and Neil. He left home early to make his way in
Glasgow, but realised that he had given up his education too soon, and returned to school in
Breakish for a couple of years before joining a Glasgow publishing firm about 1890. He threw
himself into the Highland and Gaelic life of the city. Poet, songmaker and publicist, by 1907 he
had founded the weekly illustrated paper *St Mungo*. Probably at Ruaraidh Erskine of Mar's
suggestion, he adapted his story 'Black Alpin' which had appeared in *St Mungo*, and thus three
instalments of his historical novel *An t-Ogha Mór* appeared in the periodical *An Sgeulaiche*
(1909–10). The complete 226-page novel was published in Glasgow in 1913, an English
translation, *The Ogha Mor*, following in 1924. It is a lexical tour-de-force, 'valuable,' as a *Herald*
obituarist put it, 'if only for the mine of ready phrase and words that were on the eve of passing
out of ken which it contains and preserves'.

During the First World War Robertson was Controller of Publicity in the Ministry of
Information. As President of An Comunn Gaidhealach (1922–7) he established the Bardic
Crown (see pp. 821–2) and went to America to promote the idea of a Gaelic university in Iona. In
1898 he married Rachel Cormack Donaldson (1873–1956). They had two sons (Donald and
Weston) and five daughters (Donalda, Rachel, Roberta and two who died in infancy). Weston
joined the RAF, was shot down over France, and died as a result of his injuries; his father's lament
for him, 'An Sgaradh', appeared in *An Gaidheal* and was also issued as a bilingual edition (*An
Gaidheal* 37 (1941–2) 99, 116; 40 (1944–5) 27).

Robertson spent the years 1927–45 in business in London. In 1933 he published a collection
of essays, *Children of the Fore-World*, described by one reviewer as 'a teeming book' in which he
'buttonholes his reader and pours forth a wealth of curious information'. He followed it in 1938
with *Òrain na Céilidh*, containing nine songs, of which a writer in *An Gaidheal* 34 (1938–9) 36
remarked, *Bha fhios aig cuid againn o chionn fada gu robh fiacail aig ar caraid Aonghas
MacDhonnchaidh nuair a rugadh e. Cha bhi mar sin ionghnadh sam bith air muinntir a' Chomuinn
Ghaidhealaich gun chuir Aonghas a mach leabhar òran.* "Some of us have long known that our
friend Angus Robertson was born with teeth. Members of An Comunn Gaidhealach will thus not
be the least bit surprised that Angus has produced a book of songs." It is reviewed in, among
other places, *An Gaidheal* 34 (1938–9) 46–7. Finally, Robertson's *Cnoc an Fhradhairc* (Glasgow
1940) consists of the 47-page title-poem ('an attempt at an eclogue in Gailig') along with 28 much
lighter poems and songs, some pieces in English, and an introduction in which Robertson
characteristically sums up the work as 'an unconscious effort of mine during the present ungodly

atmosphere of ethnological distortion, to escape from the sibilant belching of the Blatant Beast and his consort, the Red Laugh of death'. It was reviewed in, among other places, *An Gaidheal* 36 (1940–1) 53–4. A generous giver to Gaelic causes and to the Iona Community, Robertson died in Bearsden on 21 October 1948.

Angus Robertson had a lifelong love of books, of reading and of writing. His granddaughter, Mrs Mairi Renwick, Invergowrie, remembers him returning in triumph from the Glasgow 'barras' with his bargains. His home was always full of stimulating conversation, everything from discussion to argument, and his obituary in the *Glasgow Evening News* declared: "He had a fitting and precise sense of words, and as a keen conversationalist himself was inclined to bemoan the decline of the art among the younger generation. In any company, wherever Angus was, that was the head of the table! He had the dignity of a Highland chieftain, the courtesy also, but was quick to resent mere facetiousness, and liked on all occasions to preserve a certain formality."

I am grateful to Mrs Renwick for information and permission to reprint the following. At her request, spelling and punctuation have been left exactly as published in 1940.

17   *An Dà Latha* ('The Two Days'). Editor's trl. *Cnoc an Fhradhairc* 70–1.
18   *Maorach is Feamannadh* ('Shell-Fishing, Seaweed-Cutting'). Editor's trl. *Cnoc an Fhradhairc* 72–3. For the use of seaweed as fertiliser etc. see also poems 113, 171, 289.

Roderick Mackay (Ruairidh MacAoidh) 1872–1949

Roderick Mackay was born 16 November 1872 in Geàrraidh Chnoc an Torran, Paible, N. Uist, eldest child of Alexander Mackay, *an Saighdear Ruadh*, from Knockline (*Alastair mac Ruairidh mhic Eachainn*, 1846–1926), and his wife Ann Macaulay, from Knockintorran (*Anna nic Iain mhic Nèill*, 1845–1919), the others being Mary, John, Alexander (Alick), Neil, and Mary Flora. The *Saighdear Ruadh* is described by the Census as a 'staff sergeant of Militia' and was presumably, like the grandfather of Donald Maciver (q.v.), an army pensioner; his father, Ruairidh mac Eachainn, had been a grasskeeper or boundary shepherd, and he himself was variously employed as cattle herd, labourer, fisherman and *maor* (ground officer). The family had no croft, but lived at the east end of the township, between the glebe and the present main road. They subsequently moved to Ceann Àrd, in 1898 to Eilean Vorogay, and in 1904 the short distance to Aird Illeray, all within the district of Claddach Illeray.

The poet's father and brother Alick also composed verse, but nothing is known to survive of their work. He himself first started making songs when he was 13. He joined the Cameron Highlanders during the First World War but was discharged due to an asthmatic condition. At one point he served on the crew of Andrew Carnegie's yacht (see p. xxvii). For some years he was clerk to the factor of the North Uist estate; this involved collecting the crofters' rents. He went round the island on a regular basis, often staying overnight with relatives and friends. He never married. His collected songs and poems, 63 in number, were edited by Hector MacDougall and published in Glasgow in 1938 under the title *Oiteagan á Tìr nan Òg* for the Uist and Barra Association (see p. xxii). The book was reviewed in, among other places, *An Gaidheal* 34 (1938–9) 124–5. He was living in Aird Illeray by 1939, and died there on 9 February 1949.

Roderick Mackay was both a bearer of tradition and the model of a traditional poet. George Mackenzie's introduction to *Oiteagan á Tìr nan Òg* draws attention, first, to the importance of his work as a storehouse of vocabulary seldom heard by then even in Uist, and second, to the qualities of his verse: intellect, emotion, humour expressed in smoothly-flowing stanzas, the poet seamlessly piecing together in words the picture that is in his mind, be it in elegy, eulogy, love-song, comic song or satire.

I am grateful to Norman Johnson (Lochmaddy), Donald MacDonald (Aird Illeray) and William MacDonald (Sgoil Lionacleit) for help and information, and to the poet's nieces Mrs Ann Morrison (Gerinish, S. Uist) and Mrs Morag Anderson (Livingston, W. Lothian) for information and permission to reprint:

19   *Òran aig Toiseach Cogadh Mór na h-Eòrpa* ('Song at the Start of the Great European War'). Editor's trl. *Oiteagan á Tìr nan Òg* 42–4. 'Crucifier' is the literal meaning of *Ceusfhear*, a Gaelic spelling of *Kaiser*.

20   **Òran na Caillich Bhuana ('The Song of the Cailleach of Harvest').** Editor's trl. *Oiteagan á*
Tìr nan Òg 49–51. No poem demonstrates better than this one the changed atmosphere at the
threshold of the twentieth century. The *cailleach* or 'wife' was traditionally a sheaf clothed like a
woman, embellished with dockens, ragweed stocks and threads of various colours, and perhaps
given a *bréid* or married woman's headdress and a pair of slippers to wear. Representing her
maker's own harvested corn, she was deposited in someone else's uncut fields as a sinister
warning of famine, and could only be passed on to a neighbour whose reaping was still further
behind. This was of course both feared and resented, and could lead to violence if the bringer of
the cailleach were caught — instances are on record from Uist and Eigg of cailleach-bearers
being variously pursued, killed, shot at, shaved and stripped naked, and the hill in South Uist
called *Cnoc na Cailliche* got its name from a battle fought over the dropping of a cailleach.

During the nineteenth century, with the change from communal to individual tenancies, the
custom softened, but the cailleach was still being put in lazy crofters' corn in North Uist in 1896,
and in South Uist she might still go from person to person till she rested with the last man to
finish reaping, but it was treated as a bit of fun, the man shown to be behind was helped by his
neighbours, and the only lasting result would be a few vituperative verses addressing the
cailleach as an ugly old woman.

Our poem is a little stronger than that. The people of Carnach in the Aird, on the shore
opposite Samhla in the tidal island of Baleshare, seem genuinely upset about the cailleach as well
as being unsure about where she has came from. Allan likens her to a streetwise herring-girl on
the way north to Lochmaddy with a sickle on her hip for self-defence, and indeed this latter-day
cailleach-bhuana seems to have had at least as much metal in her as straw. The main objection to
her seems to be that people now have plenty of food, including meat, and are willing to share it
with their neighbours. Morag's crop may be behind, but that is because, in the new way of
things, she has received a food-parcel from relatives in Glasgow as well as salting away a sheep
for the winter, while Angus, her son, has slaughtered a cow that he bought in Locheport and has
given Morag the innards to make puddings with. In short, this crofting community is no longer
dependent upon its corn-harvest, but is still insecure enough, as the new century dawns, to
worry about an ancient symbol of starvation.

Charles MacNiven (Tearlach MacNimhein) 1874–1944

Charles MacNiven was born 15 January 1874 in the schoolhouse at Carnach, Scoraig, in the
parish of Lochbroom, Ross-shire, one of fifteen children of Archibald MacNiven, schoolmaster
and poet (1826–98), a native of the parish of Kilchoman in Islay. Archibald's father, also
Archibald, was married to Flora Brown and was tenant farmer at Craigens and tacksman at
Corsapol in Kilchoman. The younger Archibald and his four brothers are all believed to have
attended Edinburgh University. Two of them are understood to have become schoolmaster-
missionaries, one dying in Jamaica and one in the Gold Coast, both young and both from fever.
Another, Malcolm, became schoolmaster at Ardlussa in Jura.

In February 1853, in Ullapool, Archibald the poet married Elizabeth (Betsy) Macdonald,
daughter of Angus Macdonald (a turner in the village) and his wife Ann (a native of Assynt in
Sutherland). At that time he was living at Achendrain in Strathmore at the head of Lochbroom.
The couple then moved to Arnisdale in Glenelg, where he had been appointed master of the
Gaelic School (see p. xxii). In addition to acting as sewing-mistress, Betsy there gave birth to at
least four children: Alexander or Angus, Flora Ann, Catherine (Katie) and Archibald (who died
of TB when a student in 1883).

About 1863 the family moved again to the school at Scoraig in Lochbroom, where Betsy gave
birth to at least nine more children: Hughina, Hugh (who became schoolmaster in Jura and died
young, see *Bàird Chill-Chomain* 7, 158–9), Henrietta, Malcolm, Duncan (who died of bronchitis
in 1879), Mary, Charles (the poet), John, and another Duncan (the poet, q.v.). There were also
apparently two daughters whose place of birth is unknown, Jessie and Belle.

Archibald's splendid elegy 'Och is mis' tha cianail fàilinneach', on his brother Alexander who
died in Demerara, was published in Glasgow in 1879 in Archibald Sinclair's anthology *An
t-Òranaiche* (pp. 520–2). The 1891 Census finds him as a 'retired schoolmaster' visiting his
brother Malcolm in Jura, and family tradition has it that he suffered serious injury when knocked
down by a horse and carriage in Glasgow. He died in Inverness District Asylum on 12 July 1898,

his residence being given in the death certificate as Scoraig Public School, his occupation simply as schoolteacher.

Charles was 24 when, following his father's sad death, his mother came to Islay; he may well have preceded her. He never married, and little is known of his life save that he worked as a cattleman and competed at Islay mods. Eighteen of his poems were published in Glasgow in 1936, along with 82 of his brother Duncan's, in a volume entitled *Bàird Chill-Chomain: Òrain agus Dàin le Donnchadh agus Teàrlach Mac Nimhein, Ìle [BCC]*. The book was edited by Hector MacDougall with a foreword in Gaelic by Neil Shaw, who points to the personal encouragement given to the brothers by the Skye poet Neil Macleod (1843–1913), and to the influence of their father, and, more especially, their mother: "These brothers heard croons and lullabies on their mother's knee which still ring in their ears today. Like music from the otherworld (*mar cheòl á sìth-bhrugh*) these tunes surface every so often . . . and bring beauty and form to the poets' words." The book was reviewed in, among other places, *An Gaidheal* 32 (1936–7) 46.

Charles's verse has a keener satirical edge than Duncan's. Latterly, at least, he lived with certain of his unmarried brothers and sisters in Lochbroom Cottage, Rockside, near Bruichladdich. He died at Kilchoman on 10 May 1944. At Easter 1989 a cairn was erected by the road at Rockside with the inscription: "Erected by many friends to the memory of Duncan and Charles MacNiven, the Kilchoman Bards."

I am grateful to Mrs Jean Hunter (Port Charlotte), Mrs Margaret MacDougall (Assistant Registrar, Lochgilphead) and Linda Carmichael (Assistant Registrar, Bowmore) for information, and to Mrs Etta Shaw (Furnace), a granddaughter of the poets' elder sister Henrietta, for information and permission to reprint:

21   *Òran Bainnse* ('Wedding Song'). Editor's trl. *BCC* 146–7. Macarthur (3rd-last stanza) was
      the innkeeper at Bridgend, *Beul an Àth*.
22   From *Seinnidh mis' an duanag* ('I'll sing the lovesong'). Editor's trl. *BCC* 150. This is the last
      of four 16-line stanzas.
23   *Banais Chòrsabuil* ('The Wedding at Corsapol'). Editor's trl. *BCC* 156.

Duncan Livingstone (Donnchadh MacDhunléibhe) 1877–1964

Duncan Livingstone was born 30 March 1877 in his grandfather's house at Reudle (*Raodal, Rogh'dal*), Torloisk, Mull, third of seven children of Donald Livingstone, journeyman joiner and mason (*Dòmhnall mac Alastair 'ic Iain 'ic Dhòmhnaill 'ic Dhonnchaidh*, 1843–1924), and his wife Jane Macintyre (*Sine nighean Donnchaidh mhic Iain*, 1845–1938), the others being Elizabeth (Lizzie, b. 1872), John (b. 1874), Alexander (Alex, b. 1879), Mary (b. 1881), Neil (b. 1885) and Donald (b. 25 August 1887). The outlines of the house in which the poet was born can still be seen today.

The poet's great-great-great-grandfather and namesake, Duncan Livingstone, was at Culloden (1746) with his father (who was killed there), brothers and brother-in-law. It is believed that this Duncan eloped with (?)Ann MacLean, that they were granted the mill at Ensay, Treshnish, by MacLean of Torloisk, and that the traditional song 'Mo Rùn Geal Dìleas' was composed for her, presumably therefore by Duncan. Ann's father Hector was the disinherited eldest son of Donald, 10th chief of the MacLeans of Coll, and Isobel, only daughter of Ruairi Mear (1635–64), 17th chief of the MacLeods of Dunvegan. Hector was widely regarded in Coll and Mull, especially by the Livingstones, as the rightful MacLean of Coll. Our poet was particularly proud of this part of his pedigree. In addition, his grandfather Alexander Livingstone (himself a farmer) was understood to have been an uncle of the explorer Dr David Livingstone (1813–73), a descendant of one of the brothers who fought at Culloden, while his mother Jane Macintyre, a native of Ballachulish, was thought to have been a great-niece or great-grand-niece of Donnchadh Bàn Macintyre (1724–1812), one of the greatest of all makers of Gaelic songs; her father Duncan, a Macintyre of Glen Noe (from whom our poet appears to have been named), was born at Fearnach, Taynuilt, and became a journeyman mason and farm manager.

The poet's parents were married in 1872 in Glasgow, where his mother had been a domestic servant. His father had had several spells in Canada working on the construction of timber houses. When Duncan was about 18 months old the family moved to Tobermory, and that is where he was educated. "The scholars of my day," he wrote in a letter published in *An Gaidheal* 37 (1941–2) 83, "were thrashed if they spoke Gaelic in the school or its environs." When he was 16 they went to live at 126 Talisman Road in Glasgow. He became a clerk, then a mason's apprentice, using every opportunity to study in the evenings at the Technical College. Moving on to London, when the Boer War broke out and he heard that the Laird of Torloisk was raising a cavalry regiment he enlisted; an undated cutting in his niece's possession describes his departure.

> Lord Alwyne Compton's troops of Imperial Yeomanry left Colchester this morning for the Royal Albert Docks to embark for South Africa. The men wore khaki, and looked very smart. They took their horses with them, and were enthusiastically cheered by a large concourse of people as the special trains left the station.

Duncan took a bullet in the ankle and returned, lamed, to Glasgow to resume his trade. It was at this time that he carved the lintel of the main door of St Columba's Church of Scotland, St Vincent Street, Glasgow, with its black-letter inscription *Tigh Mo Chridhe, Tigh Mo Ghràidh* ('The House Of My Heart, The House Of My Love'), shown in Derick Thomson's *Companion to Gaelic Scotland*, p. 164.

Deciding to return to South Africa, the poet sailed from Southampton on the SS *Staffordshire* on 3 March 1903. He never returned, and indeed his brothers John (a master joiner like their father) and Alex (a mason like Duncan) came out too. There was a great need for housing on the Reef, and together the three brothers built a series of houses in Denver, Johannesburg, Heidelberg and elsewhere. Following differences in policy, however, they disbanded their company in 1910 and joined the Public Works Department.

As a Clerk of Works to the government, during 1910–13 Duncan had overall charge of the masonry in the construction of the Union Buildings in Pretoria, seat of government of the new Union of South Africa. It was a task in which he took enormous pride (poem 30). Many of the stonemasons were from Scotland, Alex among them. John, who had enjoyed an apprenticeship amongst the woods of Loch Etiveside, was responsible for much of the outstanding timberwork. Among the many items he turned out in his little workshop in the basement were presentation caskets for foreign dignitaries. (John went on to prosper from gold-mining, while Alex became a sugar-farmer in Zululand.) It was in this period that Catriona (Katie) MacKenzie MacDonald, daughter of William MacDonald of Torrans Farm and Kinloch Hotel near Pennyghael in Mull, came out to be Duncan's wife. They were married in 1911, but had no family.

After living in central Johannesburg for a while Duncan and Katie returned to Pretoria, where he built a home called Aros at 789 Schoeman (Park) Street, Arcadia. Completing his Public Works career as Master of Works at Bloemfontein, he retired in 1937, and joined the Transvaal Provincial Administration in 1938. Katie died in September 1951; Duncan, who was devoted to her, never recovered from the blow. Ultimately he went to live in a hotel. He retired again in 1958, but agreed to supervise the construction of the Pretoria Technical College at Arcadia, which was completed on his 83rd birthday in 1960. He spent his retirement writing and playing bowls, and died on 25 May 1964 in Pretoria, where he is buried in Rosetta Street Cemetery.

As is pointed out in his biography in *Gairm* 10 (An Geamhradh 1954) 123, there was a lively Highland community in Pretoria when the poet first settled there. He, his wife and his two brothers were active and hospitable in Scottish and Gaelic circles. Duncan and Alex edited a Gaelic page in the Caledonian Society's journal, *The Caledonian*. Duncan founded the Celtic Society of Pretoria, a literary association boasting 40 members of Scottish, Irish and Welsh origins, and he and his friend Seán Breanach established a Celtic section in the State Library, Pretoria, which consisted by 1954 of about a thousand books.

Livingstone's Gaelic writing was doubtless stimulated by the Gaelic broadcasts from South Africa which he began making for the BBC in the 1930s. Among his earliest poems to be published were 'A' fàgail Aifric' in *Crois Tàra* 12 (June 1939), three in *An Gaidheal* (1940–3) on the topic of the War, and a lament (in imitation of Sìleas na Ceapaich's 'Alastair á Gleanna Garadh') for his nephew, Pilot Officer Alasdair Fergusson Bruce (a son of his sister Elizabeth), who was killed over Germany in 1941, in *The Caledonian* (August 1942) 20. The bulk of his

Gaelic poetry and essays appeared still later in his life, between 1953 and 1964, mostly in *Gairm*, but also in the Canadian journals *Teangadóir* and *Irisleabhar Ceilteach*. There are poems on African political themes and also a fine lament, 'Cràdh', for Katie in *Gairm* 25 (Am Foghar 1958) 71.

Livingstone left his books and papers to the State Library, Pretoria, while his unpublished work survives as MSB 579 in the South African Library, Cape Town. This manuscript contains nearly 140 poems, mainly in Gaelic but including a few in Scots and English, dating from 1931–50, a time of personal contentment for the poet which was shattered by Katie's death in 1951. It is, in the main, community poetry, a kindly commentary on births and marriages, deaths and retirements, visits and accidents amongst the Gaelic- and Scots-speaking people of the Rand. There is also private verse expressing the poet's profound love for his wife, while the events of the Second World War figure strongly in the third quarter of the manuscript. Of the other peoples of South Africa there is but little sign: a clerkess with a very English name is thanked in English for her Gaelic typing, a district engineer with an Afrikaner one is congratulated in English on his retirement, Katie's black maid Dolly is praised in Gaelic upon her death. The impression one gets is that Katie's death snapped the poet's last link with a lost world. After 1951 his horizons expanded as Africa changed: his verse is suddenly full of politics and social concern, and is sent abroad for immediate publication rather than being kept nostalgically in a commonplace-book.

For assessments of Livingstone's work by Derick Thomson (q.v.) see his *An Introduction to Gaelic Poetry* (London 1974) 255–7 and 'Donnachadh Macdhunlèibhe', *Gairm* 119 (An Samhradh 1982) 257–68. I am grateful to Mrs Sheila Rowan (Assistant Registrar, Lochgilphead), Ms Joan Stent (State Library, Pretoria), Mr Karel Schoeman (Head of Special Collections, South African Library, Cape Town), Mr Attie Mackechnie of Fionnphort in Mull, Mr Ronald MacLean of Edinburgh (great-grandson of Charles MacLean and his wife Mary Livingstone, b. 1801, sister of the poet's grandfather Alexander Livingstone, b. 1802), Prof. Donald Livingstone of Stockport in Cheshire (son of the poet's brother Alex), Prof. Ian Livingstone of Norwich (son of the poet's youngest brother Donald), Mrs Kay Fuller of Morningside in Kwa-Zulu-Natal (Catriona MacKenzie Livingstone, Alex's daughter), Mrs Edith Hodgen of New Zealand (Alex's granddaughter), and Mr Alasdair Silver of Dysart in Fife (grandson of the poet's sister Lizzie) for information, and to Mrs Helen Reynolds of Thornhill in Dumfriesshire (*née* Bruce, Lizzie's daughter) for information and permission to print:

24   From *Cogadh agus Sìth* ('War and Peace'). Editor's trl. MSB 579 pp. 123–6. No doubt written *c*.1940, this operetta (which takes up pp. 119–28 of the manuscript) is dedicated *Do an chaileag a dh'fhàg mise a dhol gu cogadh*, 'To the girl I left to go to war' — presumably the poet's wife Katie.

25   *Rannan Callainne* ('Festive Verses'). Editor's trl. MSB 579 p. 137. *Callainn*, literally 'kalends', is a term for the New Year, cf. poem 320. The great shinty matches of the past were played on winter holidays, see for example Hugh Dan MacLennan, *Not an Orchid* (N. Kessock 1995).

26   *Cath Fairge Monte Video* ('The Battle of the River Plate'). Editor's trl. MSB 579 p. 138. On 13 December 1939 the British cruisers *Achilles*, *Ajax* and *Exeter* engaged the German battleship *Admiral Graf Spee* in the Plate estuary between Uruguay and Argentina. The action ended on 17 December when the *Graf Spee* was scuttled off Montevideo by her captain.

27   *Am Bullaphant* ('The Bullaphant'). Editor's trl. MSB 579 p. [151]. Another wartime poem. The *Oxford English Dictionary* gives *bullimong* 'a mixture of various kinds of grain sown together (as oats, pease, and vetches) for feeding cattle', but the poem describes a cake. Exhaustive enquiries in Britain and South Africa have failed to reveal the solution — or the recipe. There are tantalising echoes of John Buchan (1874–1940), another Boer War veteran, who gave two characters — father and son — in his Richard Hannay novels the name Bullivant. Livingstone would have read and re-read these. It is a mystery worthy of *The Thirty-Nine Steps*.

28   *Feasgar an Duine Ghil* ('The Evening of the White Man'). Editor's trl. *Gairm* 33 (Am Foghar 1960) 69–70. Ghana was the first British colony in Africa to gain independence (1957). Egypt and Syria forged a short-lived 'United Arab Republic' 1958–61, but the dream of Arab unity has remained just that.

29   *Bean Dubh a' Caoidh a Fir a Chaidh a Mharbhadh leis a' Phoileas* ('A Black Woman Mourns her Husband Killed by the Police'). Editor's trl. *Gairm* 34 (An Geamhradh 1960) 141–2. On the Sharpeville Massacre, 21 March 1960. *Baba Inkòsi Sikelele* 'God Save Us'. The poet's nephew Prof. Ian Livingstone writes (personal communication, 16 Feb. 1999): "I visited Duncan (from Uganda) at his hotel (Union Hotel, Pretoria) in 1959. He was resident there.

Later, when I was back in Uganda, he sent me a very long poem, in English (10 pages?) on Sharpeville, where some 77 Africans had been shot dead by police (mostly in the back). This had obviously affected him greatly. Unfortunately, I don't have the copy any more." See p. xxxvi.

30   *Togalach an Aonaich* ('The Union Buildings'). Editor's trl. *Gairm* 51 (An Samhradh 1965) 280–2. The poem is dated 12 June 1962. Sending it to *Gairm* shortly after the poet's death, Seán Breanach remarked: *Is le linn na tógála a tháinig a bhean Caitríona chuige ó Albain, "An Òighe Mhuileach" mar deir sé sa dán, agus tá a aigne ag rith siar don am a dtugaidís araon cuairt ar an bhFoirgneamh agus ar na gáirdíní áilne atá in a thímpal.* "It was while construction was under way that his wife Katie came to him from Scotland, 'the girl from Mull' as he says in the poem, and his mind goes back to the time they walked together around the Buildings and the surrounding gardens."

Angus Y MacLellan (Aonghas MacGill-Fhaolain) 1879–1962

Angus Y MacLellan was born 31 January 1879 in S. W. Margaree (*Bràigh na h-Aibhne*), Cape Breton, N.S., Canada, the seventh of twelve children (eight sons, four daughters) of John MacLellan (*Iain mac Iain 'ic Caluim*) and his wife Mary Gillis, who were married at Broad Cove (*An Caolas Leathann*) on 14 February 1871. The 'Y' in his name was a product of his own imagination. His grandfather John MacLellan had emigrated from Morar, settled in S. W. Margaree, and married Mary MacFarlane.

Angus Y was educated to the fifth grade at the local school in S. W. Margaree, serving as altar boy in St Joseph's R.C. Church, and initially worked on the land. In August 1904 he married Margaret MacDougall (1879–1975), who was born in Broad Cove Marsh, and whose forebears came from Lorne. (Her grandfather, Ronald MacDougall, had emigrated from Lorne and settled at Broad Cove; he married Florence MacNeil, and their son Sandy married Mary MacEachern, who bore him a large family, including Margaret.) They had six sons (Alex Dan, John James, Murdock Alexander, Duncan Hugh, John Thompson and Hugh Lawrence, of whom the last-named died in infancy) and two daughters (Mary Margaret and Lauranna).

In 1912 Angus Y became keeper of the lighthouse on Margaree Island, where he remained for 34 years. It is an almost treeless rock, about a mile long by half a mile wide, three miles off the west coast of Cape Breton between Margaree Harbour and Inverness. The lighthouse was erected in 1854. The family's link to the mainland was an open 24-foot motor boat. They were cut off from January to May by drift ice, which occasionally formed a walkable (but dangerous) 'bridge'; while idyllic in summer, in winter the sense of isolation could be overwhelming. The first child to sight a bird in spring would tear off to the house with the news: *Chunnaic mi eun an-diugh!* "I saw a bird today!" *O, dé seòrs' a bh' ann?* "Oh, what kind was it?" It meant that summer had come; another week and the island would be full of birds, while in two weeks a score or so of fishermen would be building their shanties on the shore.

Angus Y's visits to his mainland friends, especially Donald D MacFarlane, stimulated his compositions; indeed it was to indulge his love of reading, writing and making songs that he had taken the job on the island in the first place. He had taught himself to read and write Gaelic, and in addition to short stories he wrote letters in Gaelic and English to many people throughout the world. The family raised sheep, spun wool, kept a vegetable garden and made their own cheese and soap. When the children reached school age they left the island, boarding at Dunvegan or Broad Cove. During 1931–6 they left the island for the winter, leaving Angus Y and Alex Dan to tend the light. In 1936 a resident tutor was hired.

Angus Y retired in 1946 when the twelve kerosene lamps were replaced by an automatic system, and the family moved to Inverness; he died there on 27 December 1962 and is buried at Broad Cove. He was a gifted poet, musician and raconteur whose published stories may be said to mark the stirrings — regrettably still-born — of a modern Gaelic literature in Cape Breton. An informant said of him in 1989 to John Shaw, *Dheanadh e ceathramh 's e 'na sheasamh a' bruidhinn riut.* "He'd compose a verse while standing talking to you." Five songs by him, and one about him, appeared in Eachann MacDhùghaill (ed.), *Smeòrach nan Cnoc 's nan Gleann* (Glasgow 1939); they include his popular song in praise of Margaree Island, 'An Innis Àigh'.

I am grateful to Mrs Karen E McKay, Halifax, and Dr John Shaw, Edinburgh, for information; and to the poet's son Duncan (born January 1917 at Broad Cove and now living in Halifax, a fluent speaker, reader and writer of Gaelic) for texts, information, and permission to print:

31 *An Sgiobair Ùr* ('The New Skipper'). Editor's trl. Helen Creighton and Calum MacLeod (eds), *Gaelic Songs in Nova Scotia* (Ottawa 1964) 209–11. Composed in honour of Angus L MacDonald (1890–1954), a native of Inverness County, C.B., when elected Premier of Nova Scotia in 1933 at the age of 43.

32 *Fàilte na h-Aimsir do D.D.* ('Season's Greetings to D.D.') Editor's trl. *Smeòrach nan Cnoc 's nan Gleann* 141. 'D.D.' is the poet's friend, the schoolmaster (and poet) Donald D MacFarlane.

33 *Am Bùth aig Maitiu* ('Matthew's Shop'). Editor's trl. Text kindly supplied by the poet's son, Duncan MacLellan.

James MacLeod (Seumas MacLeòid) 1880–1947

James MacLeod was born 2 January 1880 in Scalpay, Harris, eighth and last child of William Macleod, crofter-fisherman, from Scalpay (*Uilleam mac 'An 'ic Nèill 'ic Uilleim*, 1833–82), and his wife Effie Martin, from Scalpay (*Oighrig Ruairidh Thormoid Dhuinn*, 1843–82), who were married in 1864. His sister Joan married Robert McCaig, and their son Norman (1910–96) went on to become Scotland's leading poet in the English language.

On leaving Scalpay Primary School, James went to work as a herdboy in the island of Taransay, off the west coast of Harris. He then got employment in a shop in Glasgow, eventually acquiring a shop of his own. He built Torman House ('An Torman') in Scalpay in 1912–13, setting up in business there as a clothier and woollen manufacturer. He was in the Army in the First World War. In Edinburgh in 1930 he married Jane Iona Campbell (1903–44), daughter of Dr Kenneth Campbell, a medical practitioner in Oban, and they had one son, James Ivor. Iona (as she was known) died of cancer in the Lewis Hospital, Stornoway, in June 1944; James Ivor was brought up largely in Oban.

James MacLeod is of much greater importance as a novelist than as a poet. He wrote his novels in Scalpay in the 1920s. *Cailin Sgiathanach* (in Gaelic) appeared in 1923, and *Highland Waif* (in English) in 1928; there was also an unpublished work, 'Torman'. He died in the Lewis Hospital, Stornoway, on 12 February 1947.

Donald R Morrison (q.v.) quotes the words of James's niece on visiting Torman House shortly after his death: *Bha 'n-sin de sgrìobhaidhean, duilleag air muin duilleig, cruach dhiubh, agus botal mór inc agus peann ri'n taobh. Feumaidh gum b'e leabhar eile a bha e sgrìobhadh.* "There were so many writings there, page upon page like a stack of peats, with a bottle of ink and a pen beside them. It must have been another book he was writing" (Dòmhnall R Moireasdan, 'Seumas MacLeòid', *Gairm* 108 (Am Foghar 1979) 353–4). This picture was confirmed to me by the late Norman MacCaig, who vividly recalled paper flying in all directions as his uncle worked, and indeed set the memory in verse:

> Mad on his small island
> he scribbled by lamplight, fluttering down
> great snowflakes of paper
> on to the drift at his feet.
>
> Fishermen dug his potato patch,
> fetched stores from the pier, hung
> on his door handle
> small bombs of fish.
>
> Behind barricades and shutters
> he listened to them, his eyes
> sore with terror. They prowled
> in the darkness of his mind.
>
> When men came and took him away,
> mad king of his small island,
> he left behind him his people
> buried, dead, in the paperdrifts.

('Uncle Seumas', Norman MacCaig, *Collected Poems* (new edn, London 1990) 190; cf. Marjory McNeill, *Norman MacCaig* (Edinburgh 1996) 4.) I am grateful to Donald R Morrison, Miss Morag MacLeod and Bill Lawson for information, and to Mr Ewen McCaig for permission to reprint the above and the following:

34   *A' Cheist* ('The Question'). Editor's trl. Thomson (ed.), *An Dìleab* 25–6. In the last stanza I have made two emendations from the *An Dìleab* text: *àilb* (meaningless) to *àill* ('spirit') and *'comhcheangal* ('its covenant') to *'r comhcheangal* ('our covenant'). The poem confirms the recollections of the Scalpay people that the poet's wife Iona left him and went home to Oban. This must have happened at an early stage, given that the marriage took place on 31 January 1930 and the poem was published in 1932. Iona was 24 years younger than her husband. It should be noted however that she died in the Lewis Hospital, 'his' territory, not 'hers'.

Duncan MacNiven (Donnchadh MacNimhein) 1880–1955

Duncan MacNiven, a younger brother of Charles (q.v.), was born 23 January 1880 in the schoolhouse at Scoraig, in the parish of Lochbroom, Ross-shire. Brought up in Scoraig, he would have been 18 when his mother moved to Islay after his father's death, and it may perhaps be assumed that he moved to Islay at that point and not before. Lachlan Macbean's *Celtic Who's Who* of 1921, which calls him *am Bard Ileach*, gives his address as Rockside, Bruichladdich, Islay, and his date of birth as 23 January 1883, which is clearly contradicted by his birth and death certificates.

Duncan MacNiven worked as a general labourer, and won many Mod prizes. *Bàird Chill-Chomain* [BCC], published in Glasgow in 1936, includes 82 of his poems. His name is given in the form 'Donnchadh Mac Ghille-Naoimh' in *An Gaidheal* 35 (1939–40) 14. He was a prolific versifier, latterly in English as well as in Gaelic. About 1947 he contracted gangrene and lost a leg. He was measured — and re-measured — for an artificial one which, however, never fitted properly, and the result is this priceless glimpse of the earliest days of our National Health Service:

> If there's a place on earth I hate
> That place's in Sauchiehall Street,
> I visited that place of late —
> The gates of Hell I call it;
> A well-known name above the door,
> "The Ministry of Pensions",
> While every rogue within its walls
> Should all be in detentions.
>
> I went a poor and limbless man
> To have a leg adjusted,
> They kept me waiting for a year
> And now the leg is rusted;
> In there they seemed like fiends from Hell,
> Their faces even twisted:
> They call them servants of the Crown —
> Such men should ne'er be trusted.

He continued however to walk miles every day around Lochgorm on his crutches, chatting to anyone he met, and in 1953 he had a part in Ealing Studios' film *The Maggie*. He died in Bowmore on 12 March 1955.

I am grateful to Mrs Etta Shaw for information, copies of some of the later poems, and permission to reprint the above and also:

35   *Cadal* ('Sleep'). Editor's trl. *BCC* 100–1.
36   *Far 'n do chaith mi 'n oidhch'* ('Where I spent last night'). Editor's trl. *BCC* 134–5.

Christina Macleod (Ciorstai NicLeòid) 1880–1954

Kirsty Macleod was born 30 July 1880 at 40 Upper Bayble, Point, Lewis, youngest of nine children of Hector Macleod, crofter-fisherman, from Lower Bayble (*Eachann Bàn Iain Phàraig*, 1838–1913), and his wife Catherine Macdonald, from 30 Upper Bayble (*Catriona Chaluim Pìobair* or *nighean Chaluim Thormoid*, 1838–1913), the others being Matilda, Annie, Henrietta, Donald, Effie, Margaret (Peigi), Kate and Mary. Eachann Bàn had been allocated five acres of virgin land at 40 Upper Bayble, in an area known as Geilir, and it is said that he used to fish from Port Lidhir during the day and break in his land for cultivation by moonlight. In 'Seanachas', *Gairm* 7 (An t-Earrach 1954) 264–5, the poet recalls memories of the family shieling at Cnoc a' Choilich.

Kirsty was the only one of the nine children who obtained a secondary education. She achieved this at Bayble School by becoming a 'monitor' at age 13, with pay of £5 p.a., and a 'pupil teacher' at age 14, her pay rising to £15 by age 18. She went on to serve as an 'uncertificated teacher' at Airidhantuim on the west side, then as a 'certified teacher' at Melvich in Sutherland and at Fishcross School in Alloa.

In 1907 she married Kenneth Macleod from Tolsta Chaolais (*Coinneach a' Bhocs*, 1884–1971), then Classics Master at Lasswade Academy. She settled smoothly into the role of schoolmaster's wife, and they had six children, Mairi, Catherine Louise, Kenneth Iain (Eachann), Alan, Tormod and Christina Margaret (Hazel). Following headmasterships at Portnahaven in Islay and at Ullapool, in 1913 her husband was appointed Rector of Fortrose Academy in the Black Isle. During the First World War he served with the 4th Seaforth Highlanders in France and Mesopotamia, and was demobilised with the rank of Captain in 1919.

In her 36 years in Fortrose the poet's enthusiasm and forthright personality earned her great respect. Her door was always open, and generations of pupils warmed to her kindness. An enthusiast for all things Gaelic, she formed a choir and taught the language in the school. She was a self-taught piano player, and staged fundraising ceilidhs, concerts and children's plays, taking a particular delight in waulking songs and in 'action songs' for children, which she liked to compose herself. Her children's play 'Na Ràithean' was published in 1926, while three of her action songs appeared in *An Gaidheal* between 1934 and 1937.

In 1943 she published *Ceòlradh Cridhe* (original melodies with Gaelic and English words, some with accompaniment by her son Kenneth). This was followed in 1952 by her collected poems, *An Sireadh*. Her spirited independence of mind shines through these 43 poems; some of the later ones, especially, display her very twentieth-century determination not to believe something which she could not understand. This questioning of the nature of God sets her apart from the many Lewiswomen of her generation who passively accepted the doctrines of the Free Church. Also of great importance is the fact that as wife, mother and teacher she had known ten years of World War — her verse is representative of all those who knew only worrying and waiting. One further poem appeared in *Gairm* 6 (An Geamhradh 1953) 180; others remain unpublished.

On Kenneth Macleod's retirement in 1949 he and his wife travelled to Australia, where three of her sisters lived, and to South Africa to see their son Tormod, taking in Ceylon and Rhodesia on the way. They then settled in Inverness, where the poet died on 19 July 1954. A month before her death she wrote: "I lived really two lives, an everyday life which was seen and a spiritual life which is more real to me than the outward life which could be observed. I grew up in that life too and I still live in it."

In 1971–2 the poet's great-niece Catherine M Macdonald (later Mrs C M Dunn), who was born and brought up on the same croft in Bayble as herself, wrote a dissertation on her poetry (MA, Celtic, Aberdeen). An abridged version of this was published as 'The Poems of Christina MacLeod', *Transactions of the Gaelic Society of Inverness* 49 (1974–6) 97–134. It offers a detailed thematic study of Christina Macleod's work, pointing out, for example, that the poet's 'typical reaction to war was made up of feelings of fear, anxiety, hope, grief, and pride'.

Kenneth I E Macleod included a number of his mother's poems, set to music, in his *Music from the Heart* (Leeds 1972); the poet's American great-grandchildren hope to reprint *Ceòlradh Cridhe*. *Music from the Heart* was reviewed in *The Stornoway Gazette*, 28 April 1973, and can still (1999) be obtained from Gairm Publications. Many of the songs in both books are still performed by two of the poet's grandchildren, Dr Deirdre Jean (Macleod) Loughlin, of Worcester, Mass., and Frances (Wilson) Milne of Nairn, and by one of her great-grandchildren, Siobhan Margaret-Jean (Loughlin) Petrella of Worcester, Mass.

For the poet's family history see Bill Lawson, *Croft History: Isle of Lewis, Volume 2* (Northton, Harris 1992) 72. I am grateful to Mrs Dunn for information, and to Kenneth I E Macleod (who died in 1998) and his daughter Dr Loughlin for information and permission to reprint:

37   *Cuimhneachan 1914–1918* ('In Memory of 1914–1918'). Editor's trl. *An Sireadh* 18–19.
38   *An Dubhsgaile* ('The Blackout'). Editor's trl. *An Sireadh* 45–7.

Murdo Macleod (Murchadh MacLeòid) 1881–1907

Murdo Macleod was born 28 March 1881 in Scalpay, Harris, son of Malcolm Macleod, fisherman (*Calum Dhòmhnaill Thormoid Pìobaire*, 1851–1912), and his wife Christy Martin (*Carstìona nighean Mhurchaidh Ruairidh Thormoid Dhuinn*, b. 1857), a first cousin of James MacLeod, q.v. Their other children were Donald, Kenneth, Christina, Rachel, Rachel Ann and Euphemia.

Murdo attended the island's school from the age of six. At the age of 17 he left home to become a merchant seaman, spending four years on Clyde steamers sailing out of Glasgow, and two years on ocean-going vessels between London and such distant destinations as Australia and New Zealand. Although mindful at first of his responsibilities to his family, he latterly fell into bad habits, particularly with regard to drink.

His last, fatal voyage to New Zealand was a particularly stormy one, and he received an injury from which he never recovered. He was brought to a hospital in a foreign port and left there without a penny. He somehow made his way back to Scalpay, and was welcomed home by his father as a prodigal son to be nursed by his mother for the last four years of his life. For the first two of these years he believed that he would recover, but experienced spiritual agony followed by conversion, which came to him in the form of the words, *Is leòr mo ghràs-sa air do shon.* "My grace is enough for you."

The last two years, in this state of grace, he spent in prayer and in the composition of a remarkable series of hymns and religious poems. Following sixteen days on his deathbed he died of tuberculosis aged 26 on 13 November 1907. In accordance with his wishes, his hymns were published in 1908 (as *Laoidhean agus Dàin Spioradail*). The volume's editor, the Rev. Malcolm MacLennan, points out that Macleod's verses afford glimpses of a soul refined by suffering and transfigured by grace. "As poetry," he adds, "they deserve honourable mention in Gaelic literature."

In addition to his hymns the poet composed at least one secular piece, 'Air fa la la lo', a love song to a girl called Mairead Fhionnlaigh Ailein. I am grateful to Miss Morag MacLeod for information.

39   *Gràdh m' Fhear-Saoraidh* ('The Love of my Redeemer'). Editor's trl. *Laoidhean agus Dàin Spioradail* (Edinburgh 1908, repr. 1966) 5–8.

Duncan Johnston (Donnchadh MacIain) 1881–1947

Duncan Johnston was born 20 August 1881 at Lagavulin, Islay, fourth child of John Johnston, farm servant (*Iain Muileach*, 1843x4–1904), and his wife Isabella Gillespie, domestic servant, from Gruinart (*Iseabail nighean Dòmhnaill*, 1844x5–1902), the others being John, Alexander, Donald and Isabella. His paternal grandparents were natives of Sgurr in the Ross of Mull, and two of his forebears on his father's side, Donald and Dugald Johnston, were builders and owners of Laphroaig Distillery; he spoke of Donald as *bràthair mo shinseanar*, 'my great-grandfather's brother'. His mother's people were noted musicians, she herself (a farmer's daughter) being a gifted storyteller who passed on to him a great deal of traditional knowledge.

After leaving Ardbeg School in 1895 Duncan spent fourteen years working with his father as a roadman, but his passions were Gaelic language and tradition and the need for their preservation. He was a founder member of the Kildalton and Oa branch of An Comunn Gaidhealach. From age 18 he was holding Gaelic classes in Port Ellen, making verses for Christmas and New Year cards (some of which survive), composing serious poetry such as 'Marbhrann do Niall MacLeòid', and writing short humorous plays which were acted by a drama club. Lachlan Macbean's *Celtic Who's Who* of 1921 lists six such publications by him during 1909–14, such as 'Fàilte an Eilthirich' which appeared in *The Oban Times* in 1910; his dialogue 'Ceist nan Ceist' appeared in *Guth na Bliadhna* in spring 1914 and was reprinted in An Comunn Gaidhealach's *Ceithir Còmhraidhean* of 1931.

Johnston served as a volunteer in the 3rd Highland and Mountain Artillery Brigade 1900–7 and in the Territorial Force (8th Argyll and Sutherland Highlanders) 1910–16. Before departure on active service in 1914 he married Mary Bell (*Màiri NicilleMhaoil*, daughter of Angus and Flora Bell, Glenegedale); they had five children, Flora, Isabella, Iain, Duncan and Alistair. Rising to the rank of sergeant, in 1916 he was invalided home as a severe asthmatic after being gassed at the Front (cf. poems 49, 50). In 1918 he left Islay again with his wife and family to take up a position as attendant at the Department of Natural Philosophy in Glasgow University.

For the rest of his life Johnston, in his modest, unassuming way, took an active part in the Gaelic cultural life of Glasgow. As well as poet and musician he was recognised as historian, genealogist and tradition-bearer, and he served as librarian of the Glasgow Islay Association. 'Don Ghealaich' won him the Bardic Crown at the National Mod in Perth in 1929 (see p. 821). His collection *Crònan nan Tonn* (Glasgow 1938) contains 28 poems, 21 of them with music; it was reviewed in, among other places, *An Gaidheal* 34 (1938–9) 78. Having retired in 1945, he died in Glasgow on 20 July 1947, and is buried in Kilnaughton Cemetery, Islay.

Johnston's obituarist, Duncan MacDougall, remarked that 'Don Ghealaich' was not his best piece, and that the longer 'An Guth' (*Crònan nan Tonn* 1st edn 61–3, 2nd edn 65–7) was 'in the opinion of many, the best Gaelic poem written in the last half-century' (*An Gaidheal* 42 (1946–7) 149). It is an interesting judgement but not one that has stood the test of time. 'Don Ghealaich' has, at least, the virtue of being free of pious sentimentality. Johnston is in fact best remembered as the composer of great songs like 'Sìne Bhàn', 'Birlinn Ghoiridh Chròbhain' and 'Birlinn Cholla Chiotaich', many of which are sung at gatherings in Islay to this day. To celebrate the 50th anniversary of his death a plaque was unveiled on 19 July 1997 at Lagavulin Distillery, a concert was held the same evening at Port Ellen, and *Crònan nan Tonn* was reprinted with four extra poems; it is available from the publishers, Dun Eisdein, 198 Culduthel Road, Inverness IV1 2AE.

I am grateful to the poet's daughter-in-law, Mrs Catherine Johnston, Bruichladdich, for information and permission to reprint:

40   **Càrn air a' Mhonadh ('A Cairn on the Moor').** Editor's trl. *Crònan nan Tonn* 38–40 (1st edn), 42–4 (2nd edn). Johnston's note: "Tradition has it that towards the end of the 16th century Angus of Arran, with a company of his men, came to Isla to assist his kinsmen, the MacDonalds of Isla, in their struggle with the MacLeans of Mull. Angus was mortally wounded in battle, but ere he died he commanded his clansmen to lift his body and carry him back home, and not to let the bier touch the earth until his beloved Arran was in sight. His faithful men obeyed the wish of their Chief to the letter. They carried him for nearly 20 miles, until, when coming over the top of Ben Bhàn, the hills of Arran could be seen, far away in the distance, towering over the peninsula of Cantyre. Having fulfilled this much of their dead Chief's wish they let the bier down, and rested and refreshed themselves. But ere they moved away again they built a huge cairn to mark the spot on which the bier had rested. This cairn can be seen to the present day, and is known as *Càrn Aonghais Arannaich* — Angus of Arran's Cairn. We composed this little song in order to preserve such an interesting tradition."

Rev. Angus MacKinnon (An t-Urr. Aonghas MacFhionghain) 1885–1957

Angus MacKinnon was born 22 February 1885 in Galtrigil, Borreraig, in the parish of Duirinish in Skye, eighth and youngest child of John MacKinnon, crofter-fisherman, from Galtrigil (*Iain Beag mac Dhòmhnaill*, 1833–1911), and his wife Rachel MacPherson, from Holmisdal, Glendale (*Raghnaid Phàdraig*, 1843–1923), the others being Annie, Katie, Maggie, John, Peter, Ewen and Donald. During the 1880s John MacKinnon was a foreman on the building of the Glasgow–Mallaig railway, whose conditions of employment — typically for that era — prevented him returning home more than three times in nine years, given the length of time it took to get from Glasgow to Glendale; his wife, the poet's mother, had to go to visit him instead. The gift of poetry clearly came through her, as she was related to four of the most prominent poets of the day, Mary Macpherson (*Màiri Mhór nan Òran*, 1821–98), Donald Macleod (*Dòmhnall nan Òran*, 1787–1873), and his sons Neil (1843–1913) and John (for whom see Neat's *Voice of the Bard* 296–301, 344–5). In keeping with traditions about great Gaelic poets of the past, Angus is said to have composed impromptu verses when still a small boy, such as this confession after stealing some peats:

Sùil gu deas agus sùil gu tuath,	Glance to the south and glance to the north,
Làmh a' bùrach anns a' chruaich —	A hand delves in the peatstack —
S math tha fios aig an Tì tha shuas	The Lord above knows perfectly well
Gu bheil i 'n cruach mo nàbaidh!	It's in the stack of my neighbour!

Angus was short but very strong. As a lad he learned to swim and dive like a fish, indeed in one extraordinary incident he gripped a six-foot skate which pulled him up from the bottom and along the surface of the sea. After leaving school in Glendale he crewed on herring boats for several seasons, and it was on a particularly long and stormy voyage that he began to feel close to his Maker. Emigrating to Canada in 1908, he had spells of employment as a labourer in Montreal docks, fishing on schooners on the Grand Banks and in Hudson Bay, laying tracks for the Canadian Pacific Railway, and in the warehouses and lumber yards of Vancouver. It was in Vancouver that he experienced the dynamic change within himself that led to his vocation.

About 1912 Angus received an injury from a falling log which seriously affected his eyesight for the rest of his life. Returning to Skye, he took to shopkeeping and became a lay preacher, and when he joined the army in 1914 he was made a postal courier. Curiously, his war service was most remarkable for a life-altering experience of which he was entirely unaware even though he was its cause. The following is related by a Baptist minister:

> I was in a company of soldiers in training on an army base in the south of England. We were led into a barrack room, about thirty of us in all in the long hut. It was the time for retiring, and the room was full of young soldiers, each in various stages of getting ready for bed. There was continual banter and a great deal of profanity. I had come from a devout evangelical Christian home. But here I was in another world as it were, the real world. And I thought to myself that I would just have to leave my religion back home and be part of this. There was this constant noise, as I said, swearing and cursing all part of it as if this was the way of it.
>
> Suddenly a silence spread right through the hut. I looked up to the further end. There at his bunk, a soldier was kneeling. His head was bowed forward, his hands clasped in prayer. All eyes were turned towards the praying soldier on his knees. I remember how the profane language of young men close to me faded away, so that you could feel the hush over the whole company. Faces, each a mirror of their thoughts, signalled the profound effect this soldier had made on the company. Yet he had not spoken a word. (*Highland Minister* 104–5)

After the war our 'praying soldier' got himself a higher education at Edinburgh University and the Free Church College. In 1924 he became FC minister of the large parish of Aultbea and Poolewe in Wester Ross, and two years later he married Catherine Matheson, from Stoer in Sutherland (*Catrìona nighean Aonghais*, 1900–82). They had nine children, Rachel Mary, Ian Angus, Katie, Catherine, Angus Matheson, Ina, Joan, Donalda Munro (Alda) and Helen (who died in infancy).

Angus MacKinnon's ministry was of the heroic Highland type of the past, modified only a little by the use of a motor-car to get around his huge parish — rooted deep in a Sabbath that demanded as many as four services in two languages, supported by patriarchal elders who were prodigious in their memory of scripture and tradition, punctuated by huge seasonal communions, and driven throughout by the intense freedom and joy of evangelical love. In addition to Aultbea he frequently had the care of neighbouring Gairloch; for twenty years he served as a county councillor, and during the Second World War he was presbyterian chaplain to a huge naval base on his doorstep at Loch Ewe. He retired in 1955, died after a long illness at Kildary on 22 December 1957, and lies buried in the cemetery at Mellon Charles in Aultbea.

The poet was himself blessed with that remarkable memory that was so characteristic of generations of Highland people reared on food for the ear in church and ceilidh-house. Once when a favourite minister had been preaching and a member of the family had been too sick to attend, he said: "Would you like to hear his sermon?"

"Did you write it down?" was the surprised response. Writing on Sunday was considered sinful.

"No, but I can remember it." And he proceeded to repeat the entire sermon, word for word.

Poetry was in MacKinnon's soul, as his soul was in his poetry. Regrettably, one Saturday night at Aultbea when the womenfolk were safely out in the byre milking the cows, he took his substantial collection of secular verse — 'all those daft poems I made,' as he put it — and consigned it to the flames of the big kitchen range. His preaching clearly possessed some of the qualities referred to by Sorley MacLean (*Ris a' Bhruthaich* 108–9) in his description of the 'great prose' that Gaelic once had — a prose now lost because divinely inspired and not written. His religious poems first appeared in the *Free Church Monthly Record* during the First World War. Many of them are in *Highland Minister: The Life and Poems of Rev. Angus MacKinnon, Aultbea*, an intimate biography by his son Angus Matheson MacKinnon, published by the Catalone Press (Sydney, N.S.) in 1997.

I am grateful to the Rev. Angus M MacKinnon, Louisburg, C.B., for permission to quote from *Highland Minister*; to Mrs Mary Mackenzie, Galtrigil (daughter of the poet's brother Donald), for information; and to Mrs Rachel Gollan, Lochcarron (the poet's eldest daughter), for information and permission to reprint:

41   ***Deireadh Òrdugh Ghleann Dail*** ('The End of the Glendale Communion'). Editor's trl. *Highland Minister* 115–16. A loving description of one of the great outdoor communions before the First World War. The communion 'season' lasts from Thursday to Monday. The *teampall* or man-made church to which the poet returns is bare of all symbolism — God has been encountered in His own church, the open air. The *pàilliun* or 'tent' at this period would have been a small wooden shelter which protected the preachers and the Bible from the elements (an example may be seen in the Museum of Scotland, Edinburgh); in earlier times it might have been no more than a sail stretched over some oars. *Fear na cuirm*, 'the controller of the feast', is the parish minister, while Moses, Elias, Mephibosheth, Paul and Timothy appear to be the five colleagues whom he has invited, in the traditional manner, to assist him. 'Paul' and 'Timothy' dispense the Sacrament on the Sabbath, Timothy deferring to Paul as the senior minister present; in the final stanza, Paul is described giving the 'action' sermon.

42   ***Am Mac Stròdhail*** ('The Prodigal Son'). Editor's trl. *Highland Minister* 83–5. According to the Rev. Angus M MacKinnon, this is the 'signature poem' which describes the poet's conversion in Vancouver.

Donald Sinclair (Dòmhnall Mac na Ceàrdaich) 1885–1932

Donald Sinclair was born 5 December 1885 in Ledaig, Castlebay, Barra, fifth child of Donald Sinclair, fisherman, from Ledaig (*Dòmhnall Dhonnchaidh Cìobair*, 1838–1910), and his wife Catherine MacKinnon from Kentangaval (*nighean Chaluim Mhurchaidh Fhionnlaigh*, 1848–1926), the others being Duncan, Màiri, Murdo, Neil, Mary and Annie. The poet's grandfather, Donnchadh Cìobair (1805–74), had come from Argyll to work for the Barra Estate as a shepherd in Vatersay and Berneray; through his father, Donald Sinclair from Appin, or his mother, Ann MacLachlan from Lismore, Donnchadh Cìobair is said to have been a near relation of Alexander Carmichael, q.v. Young Donald's grandfather on his mother's side, Malcolm MacKinnon, was a poet, but his songs appear to have passed from memory.

Donald attended school in Castlebay, becoming a pupil teacher; he was already making humorous and satirical rhymes and songs which were popular in Barra by the time he left. After fishing with his father for a few seasons he was sent to Edinburgh at age 18 to become an apprentice electrical draughtsman in the firm of Bruce Peebles.

Donald became caught up in the city's Gaelic movement, and was strongly influenced by its patriarchs Alexander Carmichael and Neil Macleod (1843–1913). He enjoyed mixing with the Edinburgh literati, and became a personal friend of the Scots poet Christopher Grieve ('Hugh MacDiarmid', 1892–1978), who wrote:

"What Gaelic needs," says Donald Sinclair, "is a tremendous recovery of idiom. A great deal of the language has gone dead through disuse. It must be revived." . . . He visited Barra once a year, and his holiday there always gave him a fresh harvest of quaint sayings and pithy idioms from the lips of the older people, which he afterwards drew upon with fine effect in his compositions. These owe many of the archaic and dialect words with which they abound to that source . . . His longest poem, 'Latha nam Seochd Sian' [sic], is a very powerful descriptive poem in seven parts, dealing with the conflict of the elements. He was also a delightful essayist on Nature themes and subjects of Gaelic traditions, and short-story writer, while he was a keen advocate of Scottish Nationalism on aspects of which he wrote several trenchant papers from a definitely Sinn Fein angle . . . Apart from the 'settled order in his mind' and the consequent classicality of his work, he was tirelessly alert to the problems of the present and the future of Gaelic literature, and I had conversations of absorbing interest with him on Scottish and Irish politics, on the disintegration of the Gaelic into dialects and on the problems of synthesis that exist also in regard to the Scots vernacular, and the necessity in both of a resurrection of great amounts of 'dead vocabulary', and the like. I have known almost all the Scottish writers who have been alive within the past quarter of a century or are still alive, and I found him perhaps the most charming and interesting of them all. (Hugh MacDiarmid, *At the Sign of the Thistle* (London [1934]) 25, 84, 87)

'Là nan Seachd Sìon' ('The Day of the Seven Elements') was published in parts in *Guth na Bliadhna* in 1915–16, and clearly influenced the work of Donald Macintyre, see poems 56 and 64 below. A prose translation of 'Slighe nan Seann Seun' is the sole representative of twentieth-century Gaelic verse in MacDiarmid's *Golden Treasury of Scottish Poetry* [*GTSP*], first published in 1946. Sinclair produced altogether twenty or thirty songs and poems, scattered about such publications as *The Celtic Review, Guth na Bliadhna, An Ròsarnach* and *The Pictish Review*; his work is touched on by Derick Thomson, *An Introduction to Gaelic Poetry* (London 1974) 254, but remains to be fully assessed. In so doing, he should not be confused with his namesake and contemporary, Donald Sinclair of Barrapol in Tiree, nineteen of whose hymns appear in John Campbell's *Laoidhean Soisgeulach* (Glasgow 1922).

The principal achievement of our Donald Sinclair appears in fact to have been as a dramatist — he wrote six plays, two of them for children, and five of which were performed at various locations in the islands and in the Gaelic communities in Canada. One of his earliest plays, 'Domhnull nan Trioblaid', was performed in his old Castlebay schoolroom under his own direction in 1912, when he was 26. See Edward MacCurdy, 'The Plays of Donald Sinclair', in *Transactions of the Gaelic Society of Inverness* 41 (1951–2) 68–92.

Also in 1912, Sinclair went to Manchester to become an engineer's draughtsman at Metropolitan Vickers. He had a calm approach to his duties, says MacDiarmid, 'and changed back in his leisure hours as calmly to the work of a Gaelic bard, in much the fashion that, in Corkery's *Hidden Island* [sic], field-workers all day regained the scholarship and subtle interests of the Bardic Colleges in their nightly gatherings' (*At the Sign of the Thistle* 85).

In 1918, in Castlebay, the poet married Margaret Campbell from Kentangaval (*Maighread nighean Ruairidh Chaluim Dhòmhnaill*, 1890–1937), whose parents were originally from Mingulay. She came to live with him at Wembley in Middlesex (where his work as an electrical engineer had brought him during the War) and subsequently in Manchester. They had seven children, Mary, Elizabeth, Morag, Eithne, Donald, Catriona and Gormshuil. He died in Manchester on 5 May 1932, and is buried in St Brendan's, Barra. I am grateful to Mrs Màiri Sinclair, Ledaig, widow of his only son Donald, for information and permission to reprint:

43   ***Slighe nan Seann Seun* ('The Way of the Old Spells').** Editor's trl. *An Ròsarnach* 4 (Glasgow 1930) 29–30; *Gairm* 7 (An t-Earrach 1954) 224–5. I made my translation before seeing MacDiarmid's, and have left it unchanged. MacDiarmid's ('The Path of the Old Spells') was first published in *Voice of Scotland*, see *GTSP* xl, 18–19. For my 'Rich is the stomach of the stacks' he had 'Rich the body of the hills', *cruach* being both a stack of corn, hay or peats and a square, stack-shaped hill. In the first line of the 5th stanza *Gairm* has *ùir* for *àis*. This would allow an alternative translation 'O days that took away a whole new generation of my people', referring to the First World War. MacDiarmid has 'O days that departed with the time-store of the wisdom of my people'. For a definitive interpretation of the poem we must await a full study of Sinclair's work. Says MacDiarmid, *GTSP* 373–4: "Much of Sinclair's poetry is difficult owing to his use of much obsolete or obsolescent Gaelic, and many localisms of the island of Barra." Amen to that.

Hector MacKinnon (Eachann MacFhionghain) 1886–1954

Hector MacKinnon was born 26 December 1886 in Berneray, Harris, eldest child of Finlay MacKinnon, from Dervaig in Mull (*Fionnlagh Bàn*, 1855–1937), and his wife Mary MacLeod, from Berneray (*Màiri Bhàn Alastair Ruaidh*, 1857–1952), the others being Alexander, John, Duncan, Lachlan and Neil (twins), Grace, and Roderick. Finlay MacKinnon, a stonemason, had met his wife when he came to work on the same farm in the Isle of Bute where she was employed. After marriage she brought him to Berneray, where he got the job of farm manager at Borve — until 1900 the people all lived at Ruisgarry in the other end of the island. He built the family home in the new township at Borve and also built houses there in due course for his sons Hector, Lachlan and Roderick.

Hector, Duncan and Neil were all in the Navy in the First World War, and Roderick saw action in the Royal Engineers in the Second. Duncan and Neil were lost. Duncan's body came ashore at Ramsgate and was buried there. Hector experienced religious conversion when his ship, the *Ermine*, was sunk by enemy action in the Dardanelles.

O liuthad gill' uasal suairc is ceanalt'	O so many fine lads that were decent and kind
Le snuadh bu mhaiseach air sràid	And good-looking to see in the street
Tha 'na shìneadh sa chuan, 's gur fuar a leabaidh	Are lying in the ocean, and cold is their bed
Fo stuaghannan caithriseach àrd'. (*NL* 84)	Under the high restless waves.

He spent the rest of his life at home in Berneray, becoming the island's postman, a position which he filled until 1951. In 1921 he married Catherine MacLeod (*Ceit Ruairidh Chùbair*, 1897–1964), and they had four children, Nellie, Roderick, Mary (Mrs Mary Macleod) and Duncan; Mrs Macleod's son Sgt Hector MacKinnon MacLeod, an RAF air electronics operator who took part in the Gulf War of 1991, is named after him.

Hector MacKinnon was related on his father's side to the Tiree poet John MacLean (*Bàrd Thighearna Chola*, 1787–1848), and may have been related on his mother's side to the even more celebrated Mary MacLeod (*Màiri nighean Alastair Ruaidh*, c.1615–c.1707), who made many songs in praise of Sir Norman MacLeod of Berneray. A Church of Scotland elder and lay preacher, he is the sole representative in this anthology of the type once known as *na Daoine*, 'the Men', commonly defined as lay guardians of the faith, powerful in prayer, venerated for their piety and often possessed of the gift of prophecy, whose practice was to wander the country speaking to the question at fellowship meetings, supporting godly ministers and opposing laxity in all its forms.

Before his experience of conversion he had composed a number of secular songs, many of which survive, but afterwards he restricted his talents solely to spiritual verse, always set to well-known Gaelic tunes. He certainly possessed the gift of prophecy: as Angus Macfarlane points out (*NL* ix; I translate), "He was a person who was very spiritual in his mind, and who was often found in the Lord's company both in private and in public. As a result of that the Lord revealed to him beforehand things that were to take place."

The poet died in Berneray on 22 December 1954, and, as his daughter Mary has pointed out to me (personal communication, 20 October 1998), one of his prophecies concerned his burial. "My father always said he would never be buried in the local cemetery. It was an old place closed now, and we didn't know what he meant. They were making a new cemetery in Shiabaidh, but [it] was not finished or opened when he died, so the local minister, a Rev. William MacLennan, phoned Inverness for permission to get him buried in the new place, and he did so. My father was the first person there. I don't know why this happened, as there was a place in the old cemetery beside his parents and brother Neil.

"So there must have been some connection, as there was no word of this new burial place when he said he would never be buried in the old one."

Despite a deep personal humility, Hector MacKinnon was an irrepressible evangelist for the word of God in all its orthodox purity, as his poems show. "He was effective and persuasive in his prayers and his preaching," says Macfarlane (*NL* x, translated), "both in church and in worshipping along with the prisoners of hope, and even out in the hills." This last point is corroborated by Murdo MacSween in his elegy to the poet (*NL* 238):

Bu tric a rinn e àros Dhé	He often made God's dwelling
De dh'òb ri taobh na tràigh	Of a creek beside the strand
No de dh'aonaranachd an t-sléibhe,	Or of the moorland solitude,
'S làth'reachd Dhé dha anns gach àit'.	Knowing God's presence everywhere.

MacKinnon is referred to and quoted in Alick Morrison (ed.), *An Ribheid Chiùil* (Glasgow 1961) 19–23. His collected verse was published in 1990 by the Stornoway Religious Bookshop under the title of his best-known hymn, *An Neamhnaid Luachmhor* ('The Pearl without Price') [*NL*]. There is a biographical foreword by the Rev. Angus Macfarlane. The sheer size of the collection, 98 poems by MacKinnon himself plus five elegies addressed to him (of which MacSween's is one, pp. 236–9), testifies to his stature as poet and saint. Many of his hymns are, as the Rev. Roderick MacLeod points out, 'virtually sermons in verse on biblical themes or inspired by scenes from the world of nature' (Nigel Cameron (ed.), *Dictionary of Scottish Church History and Theology* (Edinburgh 1993) 524). There are also 21 elegies, five addresses to living individuals, several hymns in celebration of particular meetings and communions, and, more exceptionally, one hymn each on the First World War (quoted above) and on Hitler (1940), in the latter of which he returns via startling imagery to his all-motivating image of drowning sailors (*NL* 195).

Mar fhalaisg sa Mhàrt chuir thu 'n t-àit ri teine	Like the heather in March you set fire to the land
'S cha bhàth thu lasair dhe d' dheòin,	And you can't drown its flame should you want to,
Le d' adhaircean àrd' gan sàthadh annainn	With your towering horns being thrust into our flesh
'S gun bhàidh ri anam tha beò,	Without love for a living soul,
Cur bhàtaichean ùr' le do *U* dhan ghrinneal	Sending new-launched boats by your *U* to the bottom
Le criuth' 's le acfhainn air bòrd,	With crew and equipment on board,
Le d' innleachdan bàis tha gràineil salach,	With your weapons of death so repugnant and filthy
Tha nàr ri'n aithris an clò.	That it's shameful to list them in print.

I am grateful to Mrs Mary Macleod, Borve, Berneray, for information, and to herself and her brothers for permission to reprint the above and:

44   *Fuath an t-Saoghail* ('The World's Hatred'). Editor's trl. *NL* 183–5. See Luke 21: 17, "And ye shall be hated of all men for my name's sake." Composed 1937. The words of Sorley MacLean (q.v.) on the Elect are worth quoting here. "There's been an awful lot of exaggeration of a kind of self-righteousness, because those people were not self-righteous. I mean, in all fairness, there might have been some cases of hypocrites and all that, but there would be in anything. So you see . . . especially in the Thirties when a lot of people were talking and finding all the faults of Scotland in Calvinism, I was saying, 'What the devil do all these people, writers and all those, know about Calvinism?' . . . One has to be fair. Among those people, there are so many I know who were saintly, just saintly men . . . I didn't find those people hypocrites, because the whole business of this sinfulness, the desperate wickedness of the human heart, precluded self-righteousness." (From interview with Donald Archie MacDonald, in *Sorley MacLean: Critical Essays*, ed. Raymond J Ross and Joy Hendry (Edinburgh 1986) 217–18.)

45   *Lìon an Damhain-Allaidh* ('The Spider's Web'). Editor's trl. *NL* 185. Composed 1937.

Donald Macdonald (Dòmhnall Ruadh Chorùna) 1887–1967

Dòmhnall Ruadh was born 9 July 1887 in the township of Corùna on Claddach Baleshare, North Uist, son of Flora Macdonald, a domestic servant (*Flòraidh Fhionnghala Dhòmhnaill 'ic Mhurchaidh 'ic Iain 'ic Mhurchaidh*, 1858–1923), and of Donald Macdonald, a seaman. There were three others in the family, two boys and a girl.

Flòraidh Fhionnghala's father, also Donald Macdonald (*Dòmhnall mac Ailein 'ic Chaluim*, 1829–62), is also known to have been a merchant seaman. He was likewise the grandfather of Donald Allan MacDonald (q.v.), and Flòraidh Fhionnghala was thus a half-sister of the latter's father, Dòmhnall na Bainfhighich. Poetry was in Dòmhnall Ruadh's blood — Dòmhnall mac Ailein 'ic Chaluim is said to have been a songmaker, as was his sister Maighread, composer of "Ille dhuinn, is toil leam thu'. Dòmhnall mac Ailein died aged 33 as a result of injuries suffered while performing a heroic feat of seamanship. In 1861 he was aboard the Admiralty survey ship HMS *Porcupine* off St Kilda when there arose a gale of such ferocity that the captain, Henry C

Otter, asked for a volunteer to be tied to the wheel. Dòmhnall mac Ailein was lashed to the wheel for twelve hours, and saved the ship. When he was finally released only two spokes remained unbroken, and by the time he got home he was coughing blood. He never worked again. The story is believed to have been told by Captain Otter in a book or article called 'The Hero of the Isles', but this has not been traced.

Dòmhnall Ruadh's maternal great-grandfather, Donald Fergusson (*Dòmhnall mac Mhurchaidh 'ic Iain 'ic Mhurchaidh*, 1780–1845), fought at Corunna in 1809, and his great-grandmother, a Skyewoman called Marion Campbell (1791–1866), was also present at the battle — her husband, a Skye MacLeod, was killed, so Dòmhnall mac Mhurchaidh brought her home to Uist, married her, and named their home for the battle. As Fred Macaulay points out, the poet's background thus contained a certain glorification of war which was to expire forever in the mud of France (*DRC2* xxv, xxxiv).

Dòmhnall Ruadh attended school in Carinish, but never learned to write Gaelic. His first verses were composed at the age of 13. Realising his talent, his mother made him promise never to make satires or scurrilous songs. It was a promise he kept, and this lack of a satirical tendency, along with the introspection induced by his experience of war, seems to have set him a little apart from his own community as well as distinguishing him from such contemporaries as the other Dòmhnall Ruadh (Donald Macintyre, q.v.). See p. xxv.

Like so many others of his time, Dòmhnall Ruadh Chorùna enlisted in the Militia at the age of 17. He joined the Camerons on the outbreak of war in 1914, and was badly wounded on the Somme in 1916. Though restored to reasonable health, he was no longer fit for front-line duty, and spent the rest of the War with the West Riding Field Regiment.

The years following the War were filled with emptiness, economically as well as personally. There was little living to be had in Uist other than from the poacher's gun. In 1922, however, he married Annie Macdonald (*Anna Ruairidh 'ic Nèill*, 1890–1971), and they had two children, Mary and Malcolm, both of whom died in 1965. Dòmhnall Ruadh had become a stonemason, and went on to build more than thirty houses in different parts of Uist. Experiencing a degree of prosperity for the first time in his life in the years after the Second World War, the Voice of the Trenches, as we may call him (see p. xxiv), became a prolific poet once more, but subsequently suffered a great deal from illness. He died in Lochmaddy on 13 August 1967.

Fortunately, at the instigation of Fred Macaulay of the BBC, most of Dòmhnall Ruadh's poems and songs had been written down from his dictation shortly before his death by John Alick Macpherson (see p. 822), who was at that time a teacher at Paible. They were first published by Gairm Publications in 1969 in an all-Gaelic edition prepared by Macpherson, *Dòmhnall Ruadh Chorùna* [*DRC1*]. This edition contains 12 poems and songs from 1914–20, 17 from 1920–45, and 28 from 1945–66: 57 items in all, though it should be noted that the later poems are, on average, much shorter than the earlier ones. It was followed in 1995 by an illustrated bilingual edition [*DRC2*], again entitled *Dòmhnall Ruadh Chorùna*, this time edited by Macaulay himself and published by Comann Eachdraidh Uibhist a-Tuath. Thanks to the excellent memory of the poet's cousin Maggie Boyd (Mrs John MacQuarrie, who died in 1994), to whom Dòmhnall Ruadh liked to sing each new composition as soon as it was made, the new edition contains 61 items along with extra fragments.

For further assessment of the poet's work see reviews in *Gairm* 68 (1969) 284–6 and *Scottish Book Collector* 4, no. 11 (1995) 28, along with Derick Thomson's very surprising comments in *An Introduction to Gaelic Poetry* (London 1974) 259, and the verse tribute to him by Donald John MacDonald (q.v.) now published in *Chì Mi* 262–5.

Mhol thu 'n eala bhàn gu ciatach	You praised the white swan with elegance
Ann am briathran brèagha bàidheil,	In splendid loving words,
Dh'inn's thu dhuinn mu 'liuthad deuchainn	You told us of how many trials
Tron deach thu ri beulaibh nàmhaid;	You survived in going against the foe;
Mhol thu 'n tìr a dh'àraich òg thu,	You praised the land that reared you young,
Uibhist bhòidheach bheag a' chrà-gheoidh . . .	Lovely little sheldraked Uist . . .

I have to thank Mr Macaulay for his generous assistance and for his comments on my translations, which were made before the publication of his own in *DRC2*. I have now (I hope) adjusted my translations wherever his work showed them to be inaccurate. Any remaining errors are mine. I am also grateful to Mrs Maggie Morrison, Sollas, Mr Lachlan MacLeod, Lochmaddy, and Mr William MacDonald, Sgoil Lìonacleit, for further information; and to Miss Mary M Campbell, Mr Neil Campbell and Mrs Fay Buesnel, all of Jersey in the Channel Islands (the poet's next-of-kin, being the children of his wife's niece Mrs Maggie Campbell), for permission to reprint:

46   *Òran Arras* **('The Song of Arras').** Editor's trl. *DRC*1 22; *DRC*2 28–9; Trevor Royle (ed.), *In Flanders Fields: Scottish Poetry and Prose of the First World War* (Edinburgh 1990) 68–9. *Tìr nan geug*, literally 'the land of the branches' (stanza 5), evokes the age-old 'vegetal' image of the warrior as part of a tree, cf. *fearann nan geug* (same meaning) in poem 50.

47   *Air an Somme* **('On the Somme').** Editor's trl. *DRC*1 23; *DRC*2 30–1; *In Flanders Fields* 70–1.

48   *Dh'fhalbh na gillean grinn* **('Off went the handsome lads').** Editor's trl. *DRC*1 24–5; *DRC*2 36–9.

49   *Òran a' Phuinnsein* **('The Song of the Poison').** Editor's trl. *DRC*1 26; *DRC*2 40–1. Poison gas was first used on 22 April 1915. The *New York Tribune* of 27 April 1915 reported: "The gaseous vapour which the Germans used against the French divisions near Ypres last Thursday, contrary to the rules of The Hague Convention, introduces a new element into warfare. The attack of last Thursday evening was preceded by the rising of a cloud of vapour, greenish grey and iridescent. That vapour settled to the ground like a swamp mist and drifted toward the French trenches on a brisk wind. Its effect on the French was a violent nausea and faintness, followed by an utter collapse . . . The work of sending out the vapour was done from the advanced German trenches. Men garbed in a dress resembling the harness of a diver and armed with retorts or generators about three feet high and connected with ordinary hose pipe turned the vapour loose towards the French lines." See also notes to poem 58.

50   *Nam bithinn mar eun* **('Were I like a bird').** Editor's trl. *DRC*1 30–1; *DRC*2 50–3. Fred Macaulay points out to me that *céinnt* in the first stanza appears to be a variant of *cian, céin*, 'distance': *an sliabh le céinnt*, 'foreign hills', 'the alien heath'. The second stanza lists N. Uist's highest hills, which stretch in a line down the east side of the island: N. Lee, S. Lee, Eaval (for which see poems 181, 290) and the mountainous island of Ronay.

51   *Tha mi duilich, cianail, duilich* **('I am sorry, anguished, sorry').** Editor's trl. *DRC*1 20–1; *DRC*2 24–7.

52   *Cha b'e gunna mo nàmhaid* **('It was not my enemy's gun').** Editor's trl. *DRC*1 17–19; *DRC*2 12–17. As shown at the beginning, each couplet is sung twice. *Beinn na Coille* ('the Hill of the Wood') is a mile east of Corùna. The image of the poet's gun as his sweetheart is traditional: to take just one example, Donnchadh Bàn Macintyre (1724–1812) named his gun *NicCòiseim* after the man in Glen Lochay from whom he purchased it, *MacCòiseim* ('Son of Constantine'). But Dòmhnall Ruadh develops the image skilfully.

53   *Òran an H-Bomb* **('The Song of the H-Bomb').** Editor's trl. *DRC*1 82; *DRC*2 154–5. The first hydrogen bomb was exploded by the USA in November 1952. Dòmhnall Ruadh's detailed account of how he was seriously wounded on the Somme at the end of autumn 1916 (see stanza 2) appears in *DRC*2 32–5.

54   *Motor-Boat Heillsgeir* **('The Heisgeir Motor-Boat').** Editor's trl. *DRC*1 54; *DRC*2 94–5. Describes a five-mile voyage from Port Roy in Heisgeir to Maskeir on the shore at Paible, the nearest part of the N. Uist mainland. For Heisgeir see also pp. 747–8.

James Thomson (Seumas MacThòmais) 1888–1971

James Thomson was born 27 July 1888 in Aird Tong, Lewis, son of Donald Thomson, fisherman (*Dòmhnall mac Alastair 'ic Sheumais*, 1841–1904), and Mary Campbell (known as *Màiri nighean Chaluim* or *Màiri Chiorstaidh Mhurchaidh*, 1853–1926, her father having died in 1859). The Thomsons had come to Lewis from Speyside in the eighteenth century.

    The poet was educated at Tong School, the Nicolson Institute (Stornoway) and Aberdeen University; he taught at Whithorn and in the Nicolson Institute, and served in the army in France in the First World War. On the retirement in 1922 of Donald Maciver (q.v.) he became headmaster of Bayble School, Point, Lewis. Remaining in that post until his retirement 31 years later, he became one of the island's most prominent figures. Crowned Bard in 1923 at the National Mod (see p. 821), he prepared the 1932 anthology *An Dìleab* (see p. xxxix) and helped collect and publish the melodies in *Eilean Fraoich* (first edn 1939). His own collected poems were published as *Fasgnadh* (Stirling 1953), and, having retired in 1953 to live in Edinburgh, he edited *An Gaidheal* 1958–62. He also translated plays, contributed to periodicals, and broadcasted. His recollections of Lewis life, serialised as 'Uisge an Fhuarain' in *Gairm* 178–85 (1997–8), form a valuable contribution to Gaelic ethnography, see appreciation in *Gairm* 187 (An Samhradh 1999) 281. A trailblazer in cultural and economic matters in Lewis, his obituary in *The Stornoway Gazette* describes him as 'dapper in his person, precise in his movements as in thought'.

In 1916 he married Christina Smith, from Keose in Lochs, Lewis (*Tìneag Aonghais Alastair Bhig*, 1887–1968). A schoolteacher like himself, she was of a family richly endowed with traditional knowledge and songs. They had two sons: James (who taught in Plockton, Golspie and Grantown on Spey, where he now lives) and Derick, q.v.

The poet died in Glasgow on 18 September 1971. The principal assessments of his verse are by John A ('Jake') MacDonald in *Gairm* 6 (An Geamhradh 1953) 183–5, by Sorley MacLean (q.v.) in *Lines Review* 5 (1954) 30–1, and by his son Derick in *An Introduction to Gaelic Poetry* (London 1974) 254–5.

I am grateful to Professor Derick Thomson for information and permission to reprint:

55   *A' Ghaoth* ('The Wind'). Editor's trl. with Derick Thomson's help. *Fasgnadh* 63.

Donald Macintyre (Dòmhnall Mac an t-Saoir) 1889–1964

Dòmhnall Ruadh was born 1 October 1889 at Snishival, South Uist, the seventh of eight surviving children of Angus Macintyre, crofter, Snishival (*Aonghas Ruadh mac Nill 'ic Dhòmhnaill 'ic Dhòmhnaill 'ic Iain*, 1853–1929), and his wife Catherine (Kate) Maclean (*Ceit Ruadh nighean a' Phìobaire Bhàin*, 1855–1940), the others being Flora (mother-in-law of Donald Allan MacDonald, q.v.), Kate, Una, Margaret (mother of Donald John MacDonald, q.v.), Neil, Angus and Catherine. The poet's father was a quiet, scholarly man who could read English; the poet's mother, a stronger influence, passed on to him a rich linguistic, literary and musical legacy, including in particular prayers, proverbs and the singing of pipe tunes. Dòmhnall Ruadh believed that he was descended from Macintyres who had come from Skye as bowmen to Clanranald, the most notable being a certain Gille Pàdraig Dubh who was said, in the spirit of William Tell, to have been made by his chief to shoot at an egg on his own son's head.

Dòmhnall Ruadh attended school until he was 14, but his real education came from his mother and from Finlay MacCormick, from whom he learned waulking songs and much else of value; this in turn he passed on, while herding cattle, to the receptive ear of another celebrated native of Snishival, *Màiri nighean Alastair 'ic Dhòmhnaill 'ic Dhòmhnaill 'ic Iain* (Mearag or Màireag), 24 years his senior, from whom K C Craig recorded the waulking songs published as *Òrain Luaidh Màiri Nighean Alasdair* in 1949. Much later in life Dòmhnall Ruadh placed his knowledge — and collections — of waulking songs, charms and so on at the disposal of scholars such as Calum Maclean and Dr John L Campbell, see for example the Floris Books edition of Carmichael's *Carmina Gadelica* (1992) 16 and J L Campbell (ed.), *Hebridean Folksongs* 1 (Oxford 1969) xi.

Dòmhnall Ruadh is thought to have received some training as a stonemason and to have practised that trade in Harris, but his first love was lobster-fishing. When not long out of his teens he was elected to represent the Snishival crofters in a celebrated case, tried at the courthouse in Lochmaddy, which resulted from an attempt made by the proprietrix of Benbecula, South Uist and Barra (Lady Gordon Cathcart) to prevent her tenants keeping dogs without a licence. Not only did the crofters win their case, but Donald made his name as a promising young poet out of his two songs on the affair, 'Òran nan Con' and 'Triall gu Cùirt nan Con'.

Dòmhnall Ruadh did not have a good singing voice, but was an excellent debater and a prizewinning piper and dancer. He served for some years as a militiaman in the Cameron Highlanders, becoming Lochiel's piper, and rejoined the regiment as piper on the outbreak of war in 1914. He took part in the Battle of Loos.

After the War Dòmhnall Ruadh returned to crofting at Kildonan, to where his father had moved as part of the repopulation of the middle district of S. Uist. But like many others he had to spend the period between the Wars taking work wherever he could get it. In his case this meant working successively in Lord Leverhulme's drifter fleet, as a telephone linesman in Lochaber, and on building sites in Perthshire. At Callander he learned bricklaying, a trade which served him well when he moved on to Greenock, Glasgow, and finally Paisley, where he made his home. In 1930 he married Mary, daughter of Gilbert Maclellan from S. Uist (*Gille Brìghde mac Dhòmhnaill Mhóir 'ic Ghille Bhrìghde*), and they had four children, Morag, Angus, Catherine and Anne.

Dòmhnall Ruadh was a prolific poet, dedicated to his craft. He won the Bardic Crown at the National Mod in Glasgow in 1938 with 'Aeòlus agus am Balg', one of the judges hailing it as 'the Gaelic poem of the century'. Some of his verse was published during his lifetime in *An Gaidheal* and in *Gairm*, a journal to which he gave an enthusiastic welcome in 1952, but various proposals to publish his work during his lifetime came to nothing; during his last illness, concluding that the world had no real interest in his songs, he got ready to consign his work to the flames, but was fortunately prevented from doing so by his daughter Morag. Soon after this he fell and fractured his skull. He died a week later on 7 January 1964, and was buried in Hawkhead Cemetery, Paisley.

Four years later his poems, edited by the Rev. Somerled MacMillan, were published by the Scottish Gaelic Texts Society as *Sporan Dhòmhnaill* [*SD*], this being the title of one of his best-known songs. The corpus amounts to 84 items (of which 'Còmhradh eadar an t-Seann Té 's an Té Ùr', 'Tómas Seanntair', 'An Dà Chù' and 'Loch nan Geàrr' are translations, mainly from Burns), a total of 9,862 lines. It was reviewed in, among other places, *Scottish Gaelic Studies* 11 (1966) 265–6 and *Gairm* 65 (An Geamhradh 1968) 89–93, and briefly discussed by Derick Thomson in *An Introduction to Gaelic Poetry* (London 1974) 257. Dòmhnall Ruadh is the subject of a fine elegy by his nephew Donald John MacDonald (*Chì Mi* 218–23), e.g.:

Dh'fhàg thu dìleab tha luachmhor	You left a legacy that's priceless
Mar bheath' a dh'inntinn an t-sluaigh tha dhe d' nàisean —	To feed the minds of your compatriots —
Beairteas litreachais phrìseil	A wealth of valuable literature
'S e gu gibhteil leat sgrìobht' ann am bàrdachd;	Which you wrote giftedly in verse;
Chuir do sheirbheis 's gach cuspair dhith	Your work in each of its subjects
Fuil bu deirg' ann an cuislean na Gàidhlig,	Put reddest blood in the veins of Gaelic,
'S bidh air mhaireann do bhriathran	And your words will remain
Ged bhios do cholainn a' crìonadh am Pàislig.	Though your body decays in Paisley.

A cairn in memory of both poets was unveiled at Snishival on 10 October 1996, see *Chì Mi* pp. [ii], xii and [xxxiv]. I am grateful to Bill Innes for his help with translations, and to Mrs Morag Cumming for information and permission to reprint:

56   **From Aeòlus agus am Balg ('Æolus and the Bellows').** Editor's trl. *SD* 71–2. The poem was clearly inspired by Donald Sinclair's 'Là nan Seachd Sìon' (see p. 737) and by Alexander Mackinnon's 'An Dubh-Ghleannach' (for which see notes to poem 6), particularly the lines

Bha Neiptiun agus Aeòlus eudmhor —	Neptune and Æolus were jealous —
D'iarr iad builg nan stoirm a shéideadh,	They ordered the storm-bellows blown,
Dh'òrdaich iad gach bòrd dhith reubadh	Commanded each plank of her torn
'S na siùil a shracadh 'nam bréidean	And the sails to be ripped into shreds
Le borb-sgread is fead na reub-ghaoith	By the wild howl and whistle of the tearing wind
'Cur siaban thonn 'na steoll sna speuran.	Sending spindrift of waves in a spout to the skies.

Our poem has 712 lines, in nine sections: Æolus orders the bellows; Æolus boasts; Neptune arises; Neptune boasts; Neptune to Æolus; Æolus to Neptune; the storm in Uist; a Norwegian ship; the following morning. Given the timescale of the poem's composition (1920–38) it is difficult not to see in it a prophetic allegory on the rise and ultimate defeat of Mussolini and Hitler. In the final section the ship is saved by prayer to God, to whose will Æolus and Neptune must yield.

The lines reprinted here are 301–52. They are from the central 'storm' section, which is headed *Mocheirigh Phàdraig Mhóir sa mhadainn air an t-siathamh latha deug dhen Mhàirt sa bhliadhna naoi ceud deug agus am fichead* ('The early rising — or 'brutal awakening'? — of Pàdraig Mór on the morning of 16 March 1920'). March 1920 was unprecedentedly wet and stormy in the islands, and during St Patrick's week there were heavy gales from the west and north-west. Ships were stormbound, and there were reports of starvation in Skye. Uist was also hard hit, but the following report from there reached the *Oban Times* of 27 March 1920: "BENBECULA. — During the past week landholders were busy collecting sea-weed. As a result of the persistent gales several dwellings and outhouses have very materially suffered in this district. Early on the morning of the 17th ult. part of the dry stone wall of the dwelling-house occupied by Mr Roderick McLellan, Cean-loch, Moor of Aird, fell to the ground, causing a considerable portion of the roof to fall in. Mr McLellan and his wife, who had been dubious as to their safety, were sitting at the fire at the time of the occurrence. Fortunately they were able to crawl from underneath the debris to the front door, and made their way in the darkness to a neighbour's house about a mile away. Mr MacLellan is not in robust health, and he will find it a difficult task to rebuild his dwelling-house without financial help. Anyone desirous of helping may do so by corresponding with Mr MacLellan direct."

57   **Thug mi 'n oidhche raoir glé shàmhach ('I spent last night very quiet').** Editor's trl. *SD* 129–31. For a general introduction to this poem see my article '"I spent last night very quiet"', *West Highland Free Press*, 13 January 1989: "Macintyre . . . is believed to have composed it after visiting *Taigh Aonghais Mhóir*, Angus Macintosh's house at Loch Eynort, and it seems to me he is basically complaining that he found all the *content* of a ceilidh but none of the *form*." For notes on people and places cited see *SD* 356–8. With reference to stanza 7 I would add that the ride of Michael Scot was through the sky to Rome in the tale 'Mar a fhuair Micheal Scot fios na h-Inid ás an Ròimh' ('How Michael Scot brought the knowledge of Shrovetide from Rome'), for which see for example John MacInnes, 'Sgeulachd Mhìcheil Scot / The Tale of Michael Scot', in *Scottish Studies* 7 (1963) 106–14; and that, according to John Gregorson Campbell, "*Nial Scrob* (Neil the Scrub), a native of Uist, was on certain days lifted by the Fairies and taken to Tiree, and other islands of the Hebrides, at least so he said himself" (*Superstitions of the Highlands and Islands of Scotland* (Glasgow 1900) 69). He was, in other words, some inveterate wanderer who gained credit by attributing his journeys to supernatural intervention. For the 'Crest from Hell' (stanza 9) see my article 'The biggest animal in the world?', *West Highland Free Press*, 12 March 1999, and the references provided in Donald Meek (ed.), *The Campbell Collection of Gaelic Proverbs and Proverbial Sayings* (Inverness 1978) 149. Cf. poem 167 and p. lii above.

58   **Aoir Mhusolinidh ('In Dispraise of Mussolini').** Editor's trl. *SD* 262–5. In *SD*, which no doubt reflects the poet's manuscript, the pairs of short lines are laid out as single long ones and the poem is not broken into sections. With Mrs Cumming's permission, I have reorganised that self-effacing layout in order to lend more visibility to the astonishing rip of the poem's rhyme and rhythm. It is satire of a very high order and must be allowed room to breathe.

     The fascist dictator Benito Mussolini, 'il Duce' (1883–1945), became leader of Italy in 1922. His invasion of Abyssinia (Ethiopia) in 1935 was carried out with ruthless disregard for world opinion and included the use of poison gas, cf. poems 49, 63. A journalist by training, he relied on bluff and bluster to achieve his political aims, and failed to build his army into an effective military machine. He foolishly declared war on France on 10 June 1940 when that country was about to surrender to Germany, thus abandoning the neutrality which was the best safeguard of his regime. His attack on Greece was beaten back in 1941, and Italy was invaded by the Allies in 1943. His end came on 28 April 1945 when, trying to take refuge in Switzerland after being released from prison with his mistress Clara Petacci, he was caught and lynched by Communist partisans at Giulino di Mezzegra near Lake Como. The description of his demise in poem 80 appears to have been prophetic.

59   **Òran na Cloiche ('The Song of the Stone').** Editor's trl. *SD* 147–52. The Stone of Destiny or *Lia Fàil* (also called *Clach Sgàin*, the Stone of Scone), the symbol of Scottish nationhood, was taken from Scotland by Edward I in 1296 and placed under the Coronation Chair in Westminster Abbey, from which it was daringly removed early in the morning of Christmas Day 1950 by three Glasgow University students (Ian Hamilton, Gavin Vernon and Alan Stuart) and a young Gaelic-speaking teacher from Inverasdale in Gairloch (Kay Matheson). For other Gaelic verse on the Stone see poems 60 and 220, and the chapter 'Litreachas' in Dòmhnall Iain MacÌomhair (q.v.), *A' Chlach* (Glasgow 1993) 62–83. The poet traces the legendary history of the stone: its origin (st. 5) as Jacob's pillow (Gen. 28: 12), how it was brought via Spain (st. 9) to Ireland (st. 18), where it was possessed by various heroes (st. 6), and thence to Scotland in the time of the Picts (st. 3). The reference in st. 17 to the *Fir Bholga* (?'Bag-Men', from whom presumably are Caesar's *Belgae* and today's Belgians) is a little obscure, but the poet probably knows his *De Bello Gallico* and is thinking of them as repositories of divine inspiration — druids. See Pat Gerber, *The Search for the Stone of Destiny* (Edinburgh 1992).

60   **Nuair chaidh a' Chlach a Thilleadh ('When the Stone was Returned').** Editor's trl. *SD* 153–5. Ian Hamilton has written: "So far as I am aware, the Government resolutely refused to negotiate, while at the same time dropping hints that if it were returned openly, sympathetic consideration would be given to the Stone's retention in Scotland" (*The Taking of the Stone of Destiny*, 1992 edn, London, p. 196). The decision to release the Stone was made by John

MacCormick (1907–61), the Mull man who was chairman of the Scottish Convention and the leading Nationalist of his day. It was passed into the care of the General Assembly of the Church of Scotland by being deposited at the site of the high altar of Arbroath Abbey on 11 April 1951. It was immediately secured by the police and returned to Westminster Abbey. Says Hamilton (199–200): "They swooped on the Stone in a panic. They locked it over-night in a police cell as though it had been common loot, and they sneaked it back over the Border at dead of night while a great roar of protest went up in Scotland . . . Of course we were bitterly criticised by many people for returning it. For years I had to endure the taunts of people that I had traded it for my freedom." See poems 59, 220.

61   **Bùth Dhòmhnaill 'IcLeòid ('Donald MacLeod's Pub').** Editor's trl. *SD* 160–3. The establishment in question was near Paisley Road Toll in Glasgow. Bill Innes points out to me that a 'Happy Day' (stanza 8) was a drink — apparently a mixture of ales. The reading *camhach* 'talkative' in the same line was given to him by Morag Cumming; *SD* has *reamhar* 'fat'.

62   **From Fàilte an Diabhail don Droch Dhuine ('The Devil's Welcome to the Bad Man').** Editor's trl. *SD* 193–4. The poem consists entirely of a monologue by the Devil. It has 18 stanzas, of which the first seven are printed here, chosen for their sea imagery. 'From the Leac Bhàn to Sìg nan Cuaran' delineates South Uist and Eriskay, I think, as Sìg nan Cuaran is in Iochdar and the Leac Bhàn may be a reference to Leac na Banaraich, the 'Dairymaid's Slab' at the south end of Eriskay. The Devil goes on to discuss his, and the Bad Man's, relationship to God, and through extended use of tree imagery breaks to the Bad Man more and more bad news about the nature of Hell, finishing (*SD* 197):

Se do choire fhéin da-riribh	It's your own sin altogether
Rinn do libhrigeadh 'nam làmhan	That's delivered you into my hands
Gus bhith ròstadh air mo bhranndair,	For roasting on my gridiron
Teadhraichte le slabhraidh phràisich.	Tethered with a chain of brass.

63   **From Aoir an Luchd-Riaghlaidh ('The Satire of the Ruling Class').** Editor's trl. *SD* 271–6. The poem has 45 stanzas, of which nos. 23–43 are printed here. The first half consists mainly of a series of tabloid-style comparisons between those who have wealth or influence (including academics, publicans and film stars as well as financiers and politicians) and those who do not. In the second half the poet settles down to food and politics in particular, reserving his bitterest satire for Neville Chamberlain, cf. poem 124; Mussolini's attack on Abyssinia is also mentioned, cf. poem 58. 'Norman' (*MacThormaid*) is Montagu Colet Norman, Governor of the Bank of England 1920–44.

64   **Nuair a thàinig am Buroo do Dhùthaich nam Beann ('When the Buroo came to the Land of the Mountains').** Editor's trl. *Gairm* 39 (An t-Earrach 1962) 211–14; *SD* 211–15. The poet reminds the Uist people of the grinding poverty which they suffered down to the start of the twentieth century. Far from their using wheeled vehicles, even the *càrn* ('slipe' or horse-drawn sled) was rare, he says, while the greatest feast of the year was the *srùthan*, a Michaelmas cake made of egg, butter, cream, berries and all the grains of the harvest. He refers in particular to 'the Year the Potatoes Rotted', 1846. The Hann is a bay on the north side of Loch Eynort in S. Uist. The shellfish imagery derives from Sinclair, see p. 737. The 'buroo' of the title (also 'broo', 'brew') is the 'unemployment bureau' (subsequently euphemised as 'labour exchange', then 'job centre'), thus also the unemployment benefit or dole itself. To be 'on the brew' in Scotland is to be unemployed. The usage dates from the 1930s; poem 9, being earlier than that, has *dòl* ('dole').

The metre is an old one which has variously been called 'strophic', 'bairdne' — and even 'bàrdachd', given its centrality to poetry's basic function of praising the warrior. Eighteenth- and nineteenth-century anthologists always printed it in separate triplets, and this tradition was continued in the twentieth century by Prof. Watson and all other academic editors. In poem 5 Katherine Whyte grouped the triplets attractively in pairs. By contrast, later twentieth-century poets such as Macintyre usually grouped the triplets into 12-line stanzas without indents, thus (in my opinion) detracting from the dignity of the metre and losing its resonances. However, it is clear that the 12-line units represent the poet's semantic building-blocks, the 'chapters' of the poem, and after much thought I have decided to retain them, while employing indents in the style of Katherine Whyte to display the metre. As with poem 58 — which employs an interesting variant of the same metre — this gives the verse a little more room to breathe.

65   **O, faighibh suas an Cogadh ('O, get ye up the War').** Editor's trl. *SD* 291–2. Evokes, with superbly controlled irony, a period in 1950–1 when General Douglas MacArthur (1880–1964), as Supreme Commander of UN forces in Korea, pursued an aggressive military strategy aimed at total victory over North Korean and Chinese forces and the reunification of the country. As a

socialist, the poet is sceptical of the demonisation of the Russian, Chinese and Korean communists, and of the hero-worship of MacArthur by the American public. For *rùisg* 'strip' in the sense 'rape' see e.g. John Mackenzie (ed.), *Sàr-Obair nam Bard Gaelach* (4th edn Edinburgh 1877) 373. MacArthur was dismissed by President Truman in April 1951 for publicly criticising his policy of restoring the division of Korea at the 38th parallel. Korea remains divided today.

Hugh Laing (Ùisdean Laing) 1889–1974

Born 11 October 1889 in Stoneybridge, S. Uist, of Protestant stock, Hugh Boyd Laing was fourth child of Donald John Laing, crofter (*Dòmhnall-Iain Anndra 'ic Dhòmhnaill 'ic Anndra*, 1857–1906), and his wife Ann Boyd, from Liniclett, Benbecula (*Anna nighean Dhòmhnaill Alastair*, 1854x5–94). The other surviving children were Rachel, Donald Archie, Andrew, John and Flora. Both the Laings (*Clann Anndra*) and the Boyds were of N. Uist origin, see Rev. William Matheson, 'Notes on North Uist Families', in *Transactions of the Gaelic Society of Inverness* 52 (1980–2) 318–72: 333–5, 347–8. Matheson says that the poet's grandfather, Andrew, was the first Laing to settle in South Uist, but the poet's great-grandfather, Donald, appears in Howmore in the Census of 1841.

When Hugh was four his mother died nine days after giving birth to twins, Ronald Norman and Norman, who died aged 18 days and 16 days respectively. His father died when he was 14. Hugh was educated in North Uist, at Kingussie High School and at Glasgow University. In 1910 he taught at Skerry's College, Edinburgh, and during 1912–13 he studied Semitic languages at Glasgow University with a view to training for the ministry. Feeling however that he was not cut out to be a clergyman, he emigrated to Western Australia, arriving there on the *Orontes* on 9 December 1913. He entered the teaching profession, starting at Scotch College before joining the State Education Department in 1915. He taught at Goldfields High School in Kalgoorlie until 1918, being rejected four times for active service because of a minor physical disability. He then taught for seven years at Perth Modern School before moving to Bunbury High School in 1925.

In April 1927 he was involved in a curious incident. Three coloured seamen from South Africa had jumped ship at Bunbury from the SS *Erica*. The Immigration Act then in force prescribed a dictation test for undesirable aliens, and Laing was asked to administer the test in Gaelic. One of the men, Gabriel Clarivette, was spirited enough to declare 'that he could write in any ordinary language, bar the one they gave him', and Laing was highly impressed by the phonetic correctness of his transcription. Nevertheless all three were deemed to be prohibited immigrants and deported, and Laing came to regret the part he had played. (See R MacilleDhuibh, 'The Bunbury Incident', *West Highland Free Press*, 23 May 1997.)

In 1929 he moved to Albany High School as First Assistant and head of English, and in the same year married Marion Stibbs, daughter of Arthur John and Christina Stibbs of Collie, W. Australia. They had four children, Marjorie Jean, Ragnhild Christine (Rae), Lesley Marion and Ian Arthur Finegal. He served as Headmaster at Albany 1942–3, at Northam High School 1944–9, and at Albany again until his retirement in 1954. During 1954 he was Acting Superintendent of English in Secondary Schools, and for a further ten years served on the examining panel for Leaving Certificate English. He was an outstanding teacher whose craggy appearance, quizzical sense of humour and unusual accent made him the butt of jokes, which he took in good part: his nickname, from *Ùisdean*, was Whizz-Bang or Whizzy.

Laing had a wide knowledge of European languages, ancient and modern. His translations, poems, short stories and historical writings in English and Gaelic appeared in Scotland in *Gairm*, *An Gaidheal*, *Guth na Bliadhna*, *An Ròsarnach*, *Life and Work*, *Glasgow University Magazine*, *The Glasgow Herald*, *The Stornoway Gazette*, *The Oban Times*, etc., in Australia in *The Sydney Bulletin*, *Westerly*, *The West Australian*, etc., in Canada in *The Toronto Globe and Mail*, and in Ireland in *Timire an Chroí Naofa*; he also wrote a regular column in *The West Australian Teachers' Journal* from 1961 to 1971.

After retirement Laing returned to Uist as often as he could. A selection of his work (free translations from and into Gaelic verse, original verse in English and Gaelic, and Gaelic stories, including a full account of the *Erica* incident) was published in 1965 by the Stornoway Gazette Ltd as *Gu Tìr mo Luaidh: Dàin Eilthireach, Sgeulachdan agus Eachdraidh*, and in the same year he was crowned Bard at the National Mod in Largs (see p. 822). In 1974 a further collection, *An*

Sealgair Naomh agus Dàin Eile (consisting of translations into Gaelic verse and six original Gaelic poems), was published in Berneray, Harris. He died in Perth on 22 September 1974 and is buried there in Karrakatta Cemetery — as is Iain Archie MacAskill, q.v.

I am grateful to Margaret Medcalf and the Australian National University, Canberra, for permission to draw upon Miss Medcalf's draft entry on Laing for the forthcoming *Australian Dictionary of Biography*, vol. 15; to Mrs Rachel Wilson, Aberdeen (a granddaughter of the poet's sister Rachel), for information; and to Miss Jean Laing, Shenton Park, W. Australia (the poet's daughter), for information and permission to reprint:

66   **Seann Éipheiteach ann an Tìr Airsnealach ('An Ancient Egyptian in a Weary Land').** Editor's trl. *Gairm* 50 (An t-Earrach 1965) 104; *Gu Tìr mo Luaidh* 26. The *Gairm* version is used here. The *Gu Tìr mo Luaidh* version differs from it as follows: title merely *Ann an Tìr Airtnealach* 'In a Weary Land'; line 4 *gheal* 'white' omitted; stanzas 3 and 4 transposed; stanza 5 *Tha mi mar shealgair dian nam fiadh / A stadas grad a' faicinn bian / Is cròic air sliabh a' cnàmh* 'I'm like the bold hunter of the deer / Who stops short on seeing hide / And antlers on hillside rotting'. Jean Laing writes (personal communication, 26 February 1997): "I hunted through my father's 1925 edition of *Anthology of Ancient Egyptian Poems* compiled by C Elissa Sharpley. The book is one of the Wisdom of the East series edited by L Cranmer-Byng and Dr S A Kapadia. The closest I could find was a fine poem believed to have been written about 2000 BC entitled, 'Song of a Man Who was Weary of Life'. If this is the original, my father's translation is certainly 'free'! To quote the compiler in her introduction, 'Although the outlook of this weary man was sorrowful exceedingly, he sorrowed not as those who have no hope.' My father's weary man I feel was a good deal more pessimistic."

Peter Morrison (Pàdraig Moireasdan) 1889–1978

Peter Morrison was born 17 October 1889 in Yellow Point (*An Rubha Buidhe*), Grimsay, N. Uist, the first child of Archibald Morrison, tailor and crofter-fisherman, from Eilean Steaphain (*Gilleasbaig mac Phàdraig 'ic Iain*, 1853–1931), by his wife Mary Campbell from the Rubhaichean (*Màiri Dhòmhnaill Òig*, 1853–1940), the others being Neil, Mary (mother of the poet Màiri Macdonald, q.v.) and Mary Flora. The oldest of the siblings was however their half-brother Donald John Campbell, a maker of humorous songs, none of which survive. Màiri Dhòmhnaill Òig herself composed songs and hymns, of which one survives — 'Òran mu Chogadh Aifriga' (*UB* 113).

Typically for his time, Peter grew up imbibing the singing of his mother and the learning of the ceilidh house, especially *taigh Clann Chaluim Big 'ic Mhathain* in the Rubhaichean, thus described by Donald Archie MacDonald (*UB* x, translated):

It was one of the old thatched longhouses with the fire in the middle of the floor. There were two brothers and two sisters living there and they had all reached a good age by this time. A quern was still being used in that house — as indeed was the case in many other houses at the time — and Peter saw the old oil lamp, the *crùisgein* or cruisie, burning there too. Night after night the house would be full of *céilichean*, some of them making their way home on a dark winter's night by the light of a peat — a living ember showering sparks, which the old men watched warily for fear the thatch or the hay be set ablaze. Peter told me a great deal about the ceilidhing of those houses that neither time nor space will allow me to set down here.

For English learning there was the school, which Peter attended until he was 14, and ultimately he became a fluent reader and writer of both Gaelic and English.

Again like many of his time, Peter's first experience of a world outside the islands was provided by the summer camps of the Territorial Army, in his case the 3rd Cameron Highlanders at Inverness. During 1908–10 he worked on the railways in Gourock, and he followed this with four years at sea. When war was declared in 1914 he joined the Lovat Scouts, and served with them in Gallipoli, Egypt, Salonika and France, reaching the rank of corporal. In later life he liked to tell how he fed large numbers of starving troops at Salonika by setting up a quern (*UB* 85–90; Donald Archie MacDonald, 'Bleith Sailoiniga (The Salonika Milling)', *Scottish Studies* 32 (1998) 38–49).

Returning to Grimsay to work as a crofter-fisherman, in 1922 he married Flora

Maccorquodale from Kallin, Grimsay (*Flòraidh Lachlainn 'ic Iain*, 1895–1972). They had four children, Lachlan, Mary Flora, Annie and Archie. During most of the years to 1930 the family lived in the Lowlands, where Peter took whatever factory or shipyard work he could get. He spent 1932–9 at home, and 1939–45 on the move between construction jobs in Glasgow and spring and autumn work on the croft. After the War the family spent four years farming Heisgeir, a fertile island off the west coast of North Uist (see poem 54): happy years of hunting and fishing for Peter, but he failed to persuade any other families to join them, and eventually they returned to Sandbank in Grimsay, the house he had acquired in the 1930s. He died in Kallin on 7 July 1978.

Peter was a remarkably active and versatile man, equally at home on land and on sea, in prose and in verse; he was full of traditional tales and songs, and was interested in everything. His work was published in *The People's Journal*, *An Gaidheal* and *Gairm*. Donald Archie MacDonald made many recordings of him (some of which were broadcast), and published some transcripts and translations in *Tocher* 16 (1974) 303–22 and 20 (1975) 156–7. *Ugam agus Bhuam* [*UB*] appeared in 1977, containing 25 of Peter's stories and 13 of his songs. An album of some of the stories was issued in 1978 by Tangent Records, and re-issued as a cassette in 1995 by Greentrax Recordings of Cockenzie, with accompanying booklet.

I am grateful to the poet's niece, Màiri Macdonald (q.v.), for information, and to his son Lachlan Morrison, Sandbank, for information and permission to reprint:

67   *Òran don Chogadh* ('A Song to the War'). Editor's trl. Composed at Suvla Bay, Gallipoli, 1915. There are two published versions. One (chorus and five stanzas) appeared in *The People's Journal*, Inverness and North Counties Edition, 2 September 1916, p. 12. The other (chorus and seven stanzas) was recorded from the poet by Donald Archie MacDonald in 1973 and is now SA 1973/172/A1 in the Sound Archive of the School of Scottish Studies; it was published by MacDonald, first in *Tocher* 16 (1974) 305–7, then in *UB* 92–3. There are many minor differences between the versions. With the exception of the sixth stanza, I have basically used the *People's Journal* version, adding to it the two stanzas which appear only in the *UB* version, i.e. those beginning *Nuair thòisicheas buaireas* and *Bidh peileirean*. The song remains popular in Grimsay, and I am very grateful to Lachlan Morrison and Ian MacDonald (q.v.) for their comments. I have used Lachlan's version of the sixth stanza, in which the *People's Journal* has:

> Chan ionann 's nuair b' òg mi bhith seòladh na geòla
> 'S na companaich còir le'm bu deòin a bhith leam,
> Le m' ghunna glan bòidheach 's mo chù air an t-sàile —
> Nuair dhèanainn-sa làmhach bhiodh Dòmhnall 'na dheann.

("Not at all like my youth when out sailing my boat / With agreeable companions who desired to be with me, / Or my lovely smart gun and my dog at my heel — / When I fired a shot it's Donald would run.") There need be little doubt but that Lachlan's is the correct version. His father would go out by boat with his next-door neighbour, his second cousin Donald Campbell (who was killed in the War), to hunt cormorants. "They would go ashore on a *rubha* (headland) and shoot them on the wing," Lachlan told me. The *UB* version agrees with Lachlan's save that it has *geal* 'white' for *glan* 'smart' — it is sometimes sung like this, confirms Lachlan, in reference to his father's white-barrelled gun.

John Munro (Iain Rothach) 1889–1918

John Munro was born 10 December 1889 in Swordale, Point, Lewis, son of John Munro, fisherman, and his wife Margaret Macleod. He grew up in Aignish. He was educated at Knock School (where he spent some years as a pupil-teacher) and at the Nicolson Institute, where he was a friend and contemporary of Murdo Murray, q.v. Gifted with enormous enthusiasm for every task he undertook, he read deeply in English literature, and became dux of the school. After graduating MA from the University of Aberdeen in 1914 he decided to train for the ministry, but his studies were interrupted by the outbreak of war.

He went to France with the 4th Seaforth Highlanders in October 1914 and served with them in the trenches throughout the War. He was commissioned as a 2nd Lieutenant in June 1916. At Wytschaete on 13 April 1918, during the German spring offensive, his platoon was almost surrounded, but fought its way out of the trap. He was awarded the Military Cross for the skill and heroism with which he held back the enemy while the rest of the battalion regrouped to mount a successful counter-attack. Three days later, on 16 April, he was killed in action. He is commemorated in Panel 9 of the Ploegsteert Memorial in Berks Cemetery Extension, 12.5 kilometres south of Ieper (Ypres) town centre on the N365 leading to Ploegsteert and Armentières.

The three poems here printed appear to be all that survive of Munro's output. Murdo Murray believed that they represent only a small part of his work, of which one portion was lost in France, and another placed in the hands of an unknown individual (LS 84). According to Murray, 'Ar Tìr' and 'Ar Gaisgich a Thuit sna Blàir' formed a single composition. This conflated version was printed in Trevor Royle's *In Flanders Fields: Scottish Poetry and Prose of the First World War* (Edinburgh 1990) 89–93, along with a translation by Derick Thomson (q.v.) which had originally appeared (with very favourable comment) in *An Introduction to Gaelic Poetry* 252–4. Murray appears to have had the poet's own manuscript before him when he reproduced the poems in *Luach na Saorsa* [*LS*], but as *An Dìleab* appears nevertheless to have many of the fuller and more reliable readings, I have preferred it.

I am grateful to the Scottish National War Memorial and the Commonwealth War Graves Commission for information. See also pp. xxiv and xxxix above.

68   *Ar Tìr* (**'Our Land'**). Editor's trl. Thomson (ed.), *An Dìleab* (1932) 12; cf. *LS* 85. According to Murray, Munro wrote 'Ar Tìr' on the train to Kyle of Lochalsh when going home on leave after more than a year in the trenches.

69   *Ar Gaisgich a Thuit sna Blàir* (**'Our Heroes who Fell in Battle'**). Editor's trl. *An Dìleab* 35–6. The principal differences in the version in *LS* 85–7 are: *deas-làmhach* 'dexterous' added at end of line 1; last seven lines of poem placed after *fairich, cluinn* ('feel, hear', 19 lines from end).

70   *Air sgàth nan sonn* (**'For the sake of the warriors'**). Editor's trl. *An Dìleab* 43. In the version in *LS* 87–8 the lines *air adhart, air adhart; / seo an rathad, / cuir a' Bhratach an sàs / daingeann àrd / air Sliabh Glòrmhor Deagh-Sìth!* (poem 69) appear at the end of this poem also, while our lines 22–5 (*air an sgàth-s'* to *an àir —*) are missing.

Murdo Murray (Murchadh Moireach) 1890–1964

Murdo Murray was born 2 March 1890 at 18 Back, Lewis, fourth surviving child of Roderick Murray, master shoemaker, from Back (*Ruairidh Dhòmhnaill Nèill Iain Dròbhair*, 1858–1930), and his wife Mary Maciver, from Coll (*Màiri Mhurchaidh Chaluim Aonghais*, 1862–98), the others being Calum, Iain, Ceit, Marion (Mòr) and two who died in infancy. He left school at age 14, then re-entered education a year later and became dux of the Nicolson Institute in 1909. He graduated MA from the University of Aberdeen in 1913, and taught successively in Tolsta and Bayble (Lewis), in Uist, and in Lairg (Sutherland).

On the outbreak of the First World War he joined the 4th Seaforth Highlanders. He crossed to France with his battalion in February 1915 and first saw action at Neuve Chapelle, where the Seaforths fought alongside units of the Indian Expeditionary Force. During these two days his battalion suffered 150 casualties. He recorded life in the trenches in a diary written in Gaelic and English, for which portions relating to 1915 and 1917 survived, including notably the battle of Ypres, 16 June 1915. He was commissioned Lieutenant in December that year. Shortly before the end of the war he received a serious arm wound from which, fortunately, he recovered. Resuming his teaching career, he was at Foyers to 1925 and at Beauly to 1928, in which year he was appointed an Inspector of Schools for Ross and Cromarty.

In 1921 he married Jean Macinnes, a schoolteacher from Sleat in Skye, and they settled at Viewfield, Strathpeffer. They had no family. He died at home in Strathpeffer on 30 May 1964. His war diary, along with a few poems, geographical essays and literary criticism, including an essay on John Munro (q.v.), were published in Alasdair I MacAsgaill (ed.), *Luach na Saorsa* (Glasgow 1970). It was reviewed in, among other places, *Scottish Gaelic Studies* 12 (1971) 127–30, and the verse received some comment in Derick Thomson's *An Introduction to Gaelic Poetry* (London 1974) 252. Two of the poems were reprinted, with translations, in Trevor Royle (ed.), *In Flanders Fields: Scottish Poetry and Prose of the First World War* (Edinburgh 1990) 109–13.

I am grateful to Mrs Mary MacIver, Back (daughter of the poet's brother Iain), for information and permission to reprint:

71   *Luach na Saorsa* **('The Value of Freedom').** Editor's trl. Thomson (ed.), *An Dìleab* (1932) 20; *Luach na Saorsa* 73–4. First published in *An Deo-Gréine* 10 (1914–15) 126 with author's note: "15th Platoon, 4th Gordon Highlanders, / British Expeditionary Force, / 17th April, 1915 / . . . Dear Sirs, / Below are a few Gaelic verses which I wrote the other day in the trench . . . / Murdo Murray (1376, L.-Corpl.)."

Duncan Finlayson (Donnchadh Fionnlasan) 1897–1966

Duncan Finlayson was born 7 February 1897 at Aird Bernisdale, South Snizort, Skye, son of John Finlayson, crofter and merchant seaman, from Aird Bernisdale (*Iain Dhonnchaidh 'c Iain Gobha*, b. 1851), and his wife Catherine Shaw, also from Aird Bernisdale (*Ceit nighean Iain 'ic Theàrlaich 'ic Caluim*, b. 1862), who were married in 1892. His father, a grandson of the blacksmith at Sconser, was once shipwrecked on Anticosti Island in the Gulf of St Lawrence. Duncan himself saw action in the First World War as a deck-hand in the Royal Naval Reserve, mainly in the Mediterranean, and subsequently worked as a fisherman. For a very short period he served like his father in the merchant navy. He also spent some time in the Territorial Army (the Cameron Highlanders). Most of his life however was spent quietly working his croft: he lived with his sister Mary, did not drink, and never married.

During the years following the Clydebank blitz Duncan and Mary shared their home with three young relatives, Morag, Chrissie and Kenneth Campbell. According to Morag's son, Richard Campbell, Bishopbriggs (personal communication, 13 March 1997), "They remember Duncan as being a great storyteller with many of the old tales — alas all lost now."

With the outstanding exception of 'Òran Hitler', most of Duncan's songs were local in nature. Although he had not been taught how to write Gaelic, he attempted to transfer them to paper as best he could, either phonetically or with the aid of a dictionary. He sang them to melodies of his own composition, but these were never written down. Some of the songs were transcribed over a number of years by Flora MacDonald, Skinidin, Glendale, who had come to teach the school at Bernisdale in 1947. In 1956 she returned to Bernisdale with her husband Hugh Mackenzie, the headmaster, and he resumed the work.

Duncan died in Aird Bernisdale on 31 October 1966. In 1988 Mary Finlayson passed the Mackenzies' versions of nine songs, along with two transcribed anonymously and eight in Duncan's own hand, to Richard Campbell. Following further editing by Dr Alasdair Maclean, Aird Bernisdale (a brother of Sorley MacLean, q.v.), three of the 19 poems appeared in *Gairm* from 1987 to 1992. These were 'Mórag', 'Òran Hitler' and 'Òran a' Chamain', of which the last-named appeared twice under different titles in nos. 145 and 158.

Duncan's best-known songs are probably 'Breacan Màiri Ùistein' and 'Na Brògan Ùra'. Kenneth Campbell recalled that someone from Harris claimed 'Breacan Màiri Ùistein' as his own, that Duncan was extremely angry, and that letters appeared in the press about it. According to Richard Campbell the same fate befell 'Na Brògan Ùra', with various persons claiming ownership at different times.

I am grateful to Mr Campbell for information and permission to reprint:

72   *Òran Hitler* **('The Song of Hitler').** Editor's trl. *Gairm* 143 (An Samhradh 1988) 221–3.

Rev. Angus Finlayson (An t-Urr. Aonghas Fionnlasan) 1897–1973

Angus Finlayson was born 24 October 1897 in Marvig, Lochs, Lewis, second child of John Finlayson, mason and fisherman, from Marvig (*Seonaidh Ruairidh*, 1861–1951), and his wife Catherine MacFarlane, also from Marvig (*Ceit Alastair Thormoid*, 1862x3–19??), the others being Peter, Margaret, Alan, Roddy, Murdy, Betty, Jean and John. His parents had married in Peterhead in August 1888 when his father, himself a boatbuilder's son, was working as a fisherman and his mother as a domestic servant. His poetic gift appears to have come from his father. A keen piper, the poet enlisted in the Army at the outbreak of the First World War, and soon became a member of the regimental pipe band. During 1914–16 he served in France and during 1916–18 in India, where he took great pleasure in the beauty of the Himalayan foothills and won several awards for solo piping. He remained in the Army until 1927.

Angus was of a Free Church family of the scrupulous kind, his father having declined to approach the table on sacramental occasions until quite advanced in years, and while a soldier he seems to have been, in the words of the Rev. Prof. Donald MacLeod, 'no stranger to the more sombre aspects of religious experience' (NMS 7). This grew more marked as the years passed, and in 1924 he became a communicant member of Duke Street Free Church in Glasgow. He was admitted as a candidate for the ministry in 1927 and, following his studies at Skerry's College, Glasgow University and the Free Church College in Edinburgh, received licence to preach in 1935. He laboured as parish minister of Struan (Skye) 1936–8, Scalpay (Harris) 1938–48, and North Tolsta (Lewis) 1948–72.

North Tolsta had been disjoined from Back as recently as 1945, and his first duty and lasting memorial there was the erection of a permanent church building, which was finally achieved in 1957. Also in 1957 he married Isabella Morrison from Cross in Ness (1912—). They had no family. Amongst his travels in the service of the Church was a journey to British Columbia in 1962. His career was crowned in 1964 by his appointment for that year as Moderator of the FC General Assembly.

The poet retired in October 1972, but continued to preach every Sabbath. He died suddenly and unexpectedly in Stornoway on 30 March 1973; in his widow's words, however (NMS 5), "In the last week of his life there was a peculiar urgency about all that he did and about his message in particular, which his hearers did not fail to notice. The glory of God and the felicity of the after-life of all Christ's redeemed were his constant theme and joy." It may be that he had been granted some of that foreknowledge which is a special gift of those devoted both to prayer and to poetry. At least two Gaelic elegies to him were published: A NicLeòid, 'Marbhrann don Urramach A Fionnlasdan', The Stornoway Gazette, 18 August 1973, and 'Marbhrann don Urr. Aonghas Fionnlasdan', in Iain MacRath, Tuireadh agus Dìoghlum (Habost, Lochs, Lewis 1982) 15–16.

Just as he had carried the pipes as a soldier, Angus Finlayson bore all the dignity of the Church in his intellect and demeanour. In his early years his preaching was full of drama, to the extent that furnishings such as pulpit-lamps might be sent crashing by the sweep of his hand. In his maturity his delivery became cool and calm while no less robust in content. He placed due emphasis on the Law and its sanctions, the glory of the person of Christ with the mysteries of priesthood and atonement, and the nature of everyday spiritual experience. His secular heroes appear to have been Lord Macaulay and Sir Winston Churchill. As an individual he was warm and genial, while his lifelong devotion to music and poetry are evidence of a character belying the modern stereotype of the FC minister; in Prof. MacLeod's words (personal communication, 13 November 1998), "Angus Finlayson was a fascinating man, not least because of the contrast between his dour exterior and his warm, affectionate and playful spirit."

His poetic output was considerable, and not all of it was religious. An anonymous tribute to him (by the Rev. James Morrison, who was 40 years FC minister of North Uist) in The Stornoway Gazette, 28 April 1973, lays stress on his preoccupation with the temptations of the believer:

> In no area was his analytical skill as a steward of the ministries of God more pronounced than when dealing with the entrance of the law in conversion, at the beginning of the Christian life, and again when dealing with the same ministry in all the manifold afflictions and trials of the saints of God throughout their wilderness journey. One could always sense the throb of his comprehensive and heartfelt knowledge of these temptations of God's choice people in such areas of their experience. And how deftly he could weave the end-product of all such fiery trials, the sentence of death in mind and heart, into the pattern of one whole trust in God who raiseth the dead! Indeed his expertness in this was at times awe-inspiring, for he could at every turn distinguish grace from nature with singular precision; and with similar accuracy of judgement he recognised what was of God 'under every garb and every weakness' . . . But he was ever anxious to be of help to all mourners in Sion, and whenever he was assured of his administering comfort to the 'broken in heart' and the 'crushed in spirit', it was a real joy to his generous heart. Even his frequent recourse to poetical composition had invariably the believer's afflictions and joys in the way, as his theme of song.

In 1975 his widow privately published No More Sea: Sermons and Addresses of the Rev. Angus

Finlayson [*NMS*] (the reference is to Rev. 21: 1), including a biographical introduction by Prof. MacLeod, then minister of Partick Highland Free Church. The book's only Gaelic content is our poem. I am grateful to Prof. MacLeod, the Rev. Angus M MacKinnon (Louisburg, C.B.), and the Rev. Donald Nicolson (Stornoway) for information, and to Mrs Finlayson, her sister Mrs Agnes MacLeod, and the poet's niece Mrs Katie Belle MacLeod for information and permission to reprint:

73   ***Dùrachd Teachdaire Chrìost*** **('The Wish of a Messenger of Christ').** Editor's trl. *NMS* 69–71. In 1964, the poet's moderatorial year, the Rev. Angus Matheson MacKinnon, then FC minister of Strathpeffer and Garve, had asked him to send copies of as much as possible of the work of his own late father the Rev. Angus MacKinnon (q.v.), who, as we have seen (p. 736), had burnt his verse. The present poem was included in the packet, and was duly published in 1997 in Angus M MacKinnon's book *Highland Minister*, pp. 458–61, on the understanding that it was his father's work. It is remarkable for its eloquent admission of doubt, a virtue lacking in the verse of many evangelical laymen like Hector MacKinnon, q.v. It thus reflects Finlayson's experimental preaching: as MacLeod points out (*NMS* 9), Finlayson undoubtedly preached from his own experience, recognising that the Lord's people had experiences, and that the pulpit must take cognisance of them, and that this was especially true in the problem of assurance — 'or the lack of it'. Angus M MacKinnon's comment on the poem (*Highland Minister* 458) may now fairly be applied to Finlayson: "Though a minister, he knew the reproach of Christ his master, in the assaults of the prince of darkness, his own vulnerability to doubt, and the normal negative experiences shared by all in a life lived by faith."

Iain Archie MacAskill (Iain Èirdsidh MacAsgaill) 1898–1933

Iain Archie MacAskill was born 19 February 1898 in Berneray, Harris, second child of Donald MacAskill (*Dòmhnall Tharmaid Shaighdeir*, 1873–1955), and his wife Anne Morrison (*Anna Chaluim Dhòmhnaill, Anna Chaluim Moireasdan*). Their other children were Norman, Alexander, Effy, Malcolm, Morag, John, Mary and Kate.

Iain Archie was brought up at No. 3 Borve by his mother's parents. He left school in 1912 to become the township herd, and in 1914 enlisted as a piper in the Cameron Highlanders. At the age of 17 he took part in the battles of Festubert and Givenchy, and was one of the pipers who led the 5th Camerons into action at Loos in September 1915; of these pipers, three were killed and eighteen wounded, but though the ribbons were torn off his pipes, Iain Archie emerged unscathed. From 1919 to 1923 he was a constable in the City of Glasgow Police (and a prize-winning piper), after which he returned to Berneray to work his father's croft. It was at this point that his career as a poet began.

In the winter of 1924 Iain Archie made up his mind to take advantage of a Government scheme to settle 75,000 emigrants in five years in Western Australia. It was a decision he was to regret. He received a 1,500-acre wheat farm (which he named Borvedale) at Lake Varley, a hundred miles east of Fremantle; he 'had a house, a lorry, a horse called "Prince Charlie", and a native servant who appeared to be in league with some wandering tribes of Aborigines' (*RC* 52).

His brother Malcolm joined him in 1928. From that year on, however, the Depression made wheat production in Western Australia uneconomic; as is shown by his songs, most of which were composed in this period, he became profoundly disillusioned, and wished only to return to the happy life he had known in Berneray and Glasgow. He had always been fond of a dram, but this did not help him now. In June 1933, at the age of 35, he died of pneumonia at Perth. He is buried in Grave No. 377 in Karrakatta Cemetery — also the last resting place of Hugh Laing, q.v.

Alick Morrison's biography of the poet in *An Ribheid Chiùil, being the Poems of Iain Archie MacAskill* (Glasgow 1961) [*RC*] 7–34 and 51–6 provides a detailed and important picture of an island upbringing at the turn of the twentieth century. The contrast between the school (pp. 13–14) and the ceilidh-house (p. 17) is crucial. "Gaelic culture reigned supreme all over the island except at one spot; it stopped dead at the threshold of Berneray Public School." The book was reviewed in, among other places, *Lines Review* 17 (1961) 62–4, *Gairm* 36 (An Samhradh 1961) 373–5, and *An Gaidheal* 56 (1961) 81.

I am grateful to Mr Alick Morrison for information, and to Mr John MacAskill, Cnoc na Gréine, Berneray (the poet's brother) and his son Norman for information and permission to reprint:

74   *Mì-Chliù nan Daoine Dubha, 1930* ('The Ill-Fame of the Black Men, 1930'). Editor's trl.,
       with help from the late Rev. Roderick Macdonald, q.v. *RC* 86–8. The Tailor of stanza 12
       (Archibald MacLeod, *Gilleasbaig Tàillear*, 1844–1931) is amply and lovingly described by
       Morrison in *RC* 111. In a traditional Highland community such as Berneray, tailoring was one
       of the few crafts practised on a full-time basis, and tailors (being peripatetic) were often at the
       heart of tradition and tradition-bearing. Gilleasbaig was frequently the butt of his customers'
       practical jokes, but responded in kind. When he had finished an article for one of his tormentors
       he would say, *A Dhia, seo dhuit i a-nis! Tha i cho math 's ged a thigeadh i á bùtha á Glascho!*
       "Well, here it is now! It's as good as if it had come from a shop in Glasgow!" And it would be
       short in the arm or wide in the leg. *Pàdraig* of the last stanza is Peter Munro, *Pàdraig mac
       Chaluim mhic Ghilleasbaig* (1866–1950), an outstanding character who was Berneray's 'prince of
       mirth'; old Archibald the tailor was his perfect foil (fully described in *RC* 13, 27–9).

Joan MacKenzie (Seonag NicCoinnich) 1900–72

Joan MacKenzie was born 27 April 1900 in Scarista, Harris, youngest of eight children of John
MacKenzie, farm servant (*Iain Fhionnlaigh Aonghais 'ic Fhionnlaigh*, 1846–1933), and his wife
Mary Paterson, a dairymaid from Berneray, Harris (*Màiri Thormoid Òig Alastair 'ic Thormoid*,
1855–1929), the others being John, Chirsty, Kate, Norman (died in infancy), Norman (again),
Donald (killed in action), and Finlay. Joan was a great-niece of the celebrated religious poet John
Morrison (*Gobha na Hearadh, c.*1796–1852). In 1925 she married Donald Alexander MacSween
from Meavaig, Harris (*Dòmhnall Alastair mac Dhòmhnaill MhicSuain*, 1889–1969), who came to
live in Scarista, and they had eight children, Donald, Mary (died in infancy), Catherine, Mary
Kate, Johan, Norman, Donald John and John. She died on 30 October 1972.
    I am grateful to Donald John MacSween for information and permission to reprint:

75   *Òran Clach Stèineagaidh* ('The Song of Steinigie Stone'). Editor's trl. [Bill Lawson (ed.),]
       Chì Mi 'n Tìr (Northton, Harris 1996) 27–8. Steinigie Stone is at Scarista in Harris. The fourth
       verse reflects the Highland tradition that Fionn mac Cumhaill still sleeps under places like this,
       waiting for the call to arms that will bring him out with his warband to save the Gael in one last
       battle. It is a tradition commonly associated with Tomnahurich at Inverness and Craigiehowe in
       the Black Isle. In the Lowlands the figure in question is usually Thomas the Rhymer, while in
       England and Wales it is King Arthur.

Murdo MacFarlane (Murchadh MacPhàrlain) 1901–82

Murdo MacFarlane was born 15 February 1901 in Melbost in the district of Eye, Lewis, fifth
child of Malcolm Macfarlane, fisherman, from Melbost (*Calum Dhòmhnaill Chaluim
Dhòmhnaill*, 1862–1955), and his wife Johanna (Hannah), also a MacFarlane from Melbost
(*Hannah Mhurchaidh Dhòmhnaill*, 1863–1952), the others being Jessie, Mary, Annie, Donald and
Christina. According to the poet, the MacFarlanes had come north from the parish of Lochs
when Park was cleared, but Hannah's aunt Catherine was baptised in Melbost in 1811, and that
is a very early date for a clearance in Park.
    Murdo was educated in Knock School, where he was taught English, Latin and a little French
but not Gaelic; in later life he taught himself to read and write Gaelic up to a point. His earliest
employment was on the ambitious schemes of Lord Leverhulme, who owned Lewis in the 1920s.
When these collapsed, Murdo was one of the many young people who left the island for Canada
on three ships belonging to the Canadian Pacific Railway (see notes on poem 169). He returned,
disillusioned, from the prairies of Manitoba in 1932, and this experience led to his most popular
song, 'Fali, Fali, Fali Oro'.
    He spent the rest of his life as a crofter, save for army service 1942–5, and never married.
Murdo became nationally known in the 1960s as a composer of popular songs, one of which
achieved first prize in the Pan-Celtic Festival in Killarney. As pointed out by Fr John A
Macdonald ('The Songs of Donald Allan MacDonald' (MLitt thesis, Aberdeen 1983) 29 = *Òrain
Dhòmhnaill Ailein* (Benbecula 1999) 54), Murdo was the outstanding example of a traditional
poet who adapted his art by composing songs specifically for the new Gaelic folk movement. The
groups Na h-Òganaich and Na Siaraich owed their initial success to songs composed by him for

them to sing at Mod competitions, and Na h-Òganaich went on to achieve commercial success with several of his compositions. His thoughts on the long-standing custom of composing Gaelic verse to existing tunes are on record in *Tocher* 38 (1983) 74–5:

> To compose poetry to an old tune is all right, but it takes a first-rate poet to eradicate the old song, the words of the old song to the same tune — his composition has to be exceptional before he can put the old one out of circulation. And besides, I don't think it's right to try and destroy an old thing. Now, I make the effort nowadays, I try with the things I compose, the little that I compose, to be able to say, "Well, this is new, not only words but music."

Murdo died at Tong on 7 November 1982. His collection *An Toinneamh Dìomhair* was published in Stornoway in 1973, and *Dàin Mhurchaidh* (this time with tunes for the songs, and a cassette) in 1986. Among reviews of his work are those in *The Stornoway Gazette*, 14 April 1973, *Sruth* (published in *The Stornoway Gazette*), 28 April 1973, and *Gairm* 84 (Am Foghar 1973) 377–8. His elegy by Donald John MacDonald (q.v.) in *Chì Mi* 322–5 draws attention to

Toinneamh dìomhair na h-inntinn —	The subtle skein of the mind —
Seadh, inntinn bha sònraicht',	Yes, a mind extraordinary,
Inntinn Ghaidhealach bhàrdail,	A Gaelic poetic mind,
Inntinn bhàidheil ri deòraidh.	One that cherished the underdog.

I am grateful to Bill Lawson for information, and to the poet's cousin Mrs M F Campbell, Tong, for information and permission to reprint:

76　　*Naoi Ceud Deug 's a Ceithir Deug* ('Nineteen Fourteen'). Editor's trl. *An Toinneamh Dìomhair* 62–4. The First World War began for Britain on 4 August 1914. *A' Bhruach*, the Bruach, is the east-coast port of Fraserburgh.

Malcolm Nicolson (Calum MacNeacail) 1902–78

Calum Ruadh was born 19 March 1902 in Gedintailor, Braes, Portree, Skye, one of ten children of John Nicolson, crofter-fisherman, from Gedintailor (*Iain mac Uilleim*, 1856–1945), and his wife Annie Macleod, from Balmeanach (*Anna Dhòmhnaill Ruaidh*, 1861–1942), whom he married in 1883. One of Calum's brothers, Donald, who survived him, was also a poet. They inherited their talent from both sides of the family, their mother in particular being famous in her day for her songs (see *Gairm* 18 (An Geamhradh 1956) 143).

Calum took up crofting and salmon-fishing at Camustianavaig. In 1934 he married Margaret Mary (Peggy), daughter of Alexander MacCallum, a boat hirer at Camustianavaig, and during the Second World War he served in the RAF. In the 1960s he was extensively recorded by the Danish musicologist Thorkild Knudsen in an attempt to answer the questions, "Who is the bard, why does he compose and sing, and how?" The material was presented in a seminar in the School of Scottish Studies on 13 June 1968, and published in 1978 as a record and booklet under the title *Calum Ruadh: Bard of Skye* (Scottish Tradition 7).

Calum held strong views about many things, including the rightful importance and dignity of the poet in Gaelic society, but Knudsen was particularly interested in his unusual musical technique. In much the same way as the traditional Gaelic poet deploys a semi-finite range of verbal motifs, so apparently did Calum deploy a semi-finite stock of musical motifs. Instead of picking an existing melody (or devising a new one) and fitting words to it, as most poets would have done, he seemed to reach out and select different snatches of melody that might be circling around in his unconscious memory at the same time in order to use them as the most effective vehicle for his words. "I never composed any song on anyone else's tune, perfect," he told Knudsen. "I take bits of it. I've got to sing songs in my own fashion, in my own way, in my own manner, and I'm damned if I'm going to do any other thing."

Calum published his songs in *An Gaidheal* and *Gairm*. His collected poems, 41 in number, were published in Glasgow as *Bàrdachd Chaluim Ruaidh* in 1975, and reviewed in *Gairm* 93 (An Geamhradh 1975–6) 93–6. He died in Broadford on 25 February 1978 while production of the album of his work was in its final stages. It was reissued on cassette by Greentrax Recordings of Cockenzie in 1994. For an illustrated account of his life, along with three of his songs, see Neat's *Voice of the Bard* 217–29, and for a definitive discussion of his musical technique see Dr John MacInnes's essay 'The Bard through History' at pp. 321–52 (esp. 347–8) of the same work. "In reality," says MacInnes, "Calum Ruadh used three or four melodies, drawn from older songs, and moved more or less at will among them."

I am grateful to the poet's widow and his nephew Mr Donald Michie, Camustianavaig, for information and permission to reprint:

77   *Cùmhnantan Sìthe Pharis* **('The Paris Peace Treaties').** Editor's trl. *Bàrdachd Chaluim Ruaidh* 24–5. The victorious Allies met at the Paris Peace Conference from 29 July to 15 October 1946 to hammer out treaties with Italy and other defeated nations. The fate of Germany was not under discussion, as the country was already divided and agreement between the USA and USSR (Russia) was impossible. The Russian delegation was led by the veteran Foreign Minister, Vyacheslav Molotov (1890–1986), while the initial British one was led by the Prime Minister, Clement Attlee, and (in the absence through illness of the Foreign Secretary, Ernest Bevin) Hector McNeil (1907–55), who was of Barra extraction: then Under-Secretary of State for Foreign Affairs, he later became Secretary of State for Scotland. Thanks to the doctrine of International Revolutionary Communism, Molotov had given his name to the 'molotov cocktail', cf. notes to poem 13.

78   *Blàr Chaol Àcainn* **('The Battle of Kyleakin').** Editor's trl. *Bàrdachd Chaluim Ruaidh* 44–5. The battle in question was the result of an attempt by about 50 demonstrators (led by the Rev. Angus Smith, then Free Church minister of Snizort) to frustrate the operation of the first Sunday ferry from Kyle of Lochalsh to Kyleakin in Skye, 6 June 1965. The event generated strong feelings on both sides and attracted a great deal of media interest. It was a defining moment in the history of the Sabbath, the keeping of which was (and is) considered by many to be the principal marker of Gaelic identity, cf. poem 13. The demonstrators were forcibly moved by over 30 police led by Andrew McClure, chief constable of Inverness-shire. In a symbolic gesture characteristic of the period, Smith sat down in front of the cars coming off the ferry. He had to be carried away bodily. He and 13 others were charged with breach of the peace and detained for half an hour before being released; he was driven home to Snizort in a police car. On 22 June the procurator fiscal at Portree decided that no proceedings should be taken against the 'Kyleakin Fourteen', and freed them of all charges.

The views expressed by Calum Ruadh are characteristically trenchant, and reflect a traditional poetic function of exposing hypocrisy. "That was a lot of damn nonsense, that Kyleakin incident," he told Knudsen. "I disapproved of that, terrible." His mention of rusty swords is interesting, but was certainly not borne out by the events on the day; his accusations of drunkenness may be slightly nearer the mark. It is true, as he implies, that many Free and Free Presbyterian congregations were encouraged to defend the Sabbath by shunning tourists on that day. It is also true that 'such people are thin on the ground here', most of the demonstrators having been from north Skye. The reference in the same stanza to 'people far better than themselves' is Calum Ruadh's way of pointing to the irony that those who believed themselves to be of the Elect were nevertheless willing to regard their Gaelic language and crofting lifestyle as inferior to the language and lifestyle of their visitors. His views were informed by his own position as a FC adherent who persisted in composing secular songs, thereby cutting himself off from the Means of Grace. When asked by an elder to stop making songs, he refused. "I don't see any sin in them provided you don't put lies in them. I believe that the gift is from God."

Donald Grant (Dòmhnall Grannd) 1903–70

Donald Grant was born 25 January 1903 in Camuscross, Sleat, Skye, the youngest of three children of Donald Grant, seaman, Camuscross (*Dòmhnall 'c Dhòmhnaill 'ic Iain 'ic Dhòmhnaill*, 1860–1906) and his wife Christina Macpherson, Camuscross (*Cairistìona Ghilleasbaig [Ruaidh] Sheumais Chaluim*, 1867–1919), the other children being Catherine and Angus. The poet's father died in Rouen in France after taking ill at sea, possibly with appendicitis, but this did not have as great an effect on him as the subsequent death of his mother when he was 16.

He was educated at Duisdale School, Portree High School, Glasgow University (MA, EdB), Jordanhill College of Education, and (later) London University (BA). He won a Blue for shinty at Glasgow University and later captained the Glasgow Skye team. Entering the teaching profession in 1926, he taught first at Lochgilphead High School, then in Glasgow primaries, becoming headmaster successively at Washington Street, Eastbank and Broomhill. In 1935 'An Uilebheist is na Foghlamaich' won him the Bardic Crown at the National Mod in Edinburgh (see p. 821 below). In 1936 he married Margaret MacInnes, Cardross, whose parents belonged to Camuscross and Knoydart. They had two children, Innes and Kirsteen.

In 1951 he won first prize in the Gaelic poetry competition of the Arts Council of Great Britain (see p. 783 below). During 1951–4 he was seconded, part-time, as lecturer in Gaelic at Jordanhill. He became active in Gaelic drama (winning one Best Actor award and two first prizes for a new play) and in conducting choirs such as the Knightswood Gaelic Choir. Among his many official positions were Secretary and President of the Glasgow Skye Association, President of the Highlanders' Institute 1958–60, President of An Comunn Gaidhealach 1965–8, and Secretary and President of the Celtic Congress. During the 1960s he was a frequent broadcaster and newsreader on Gaelic radio. He edited school-books for An Comunn Gaidhealach and also their journal *An Gaidheal* 1962–4, and contributed to *Sruth* and *Gairm*. He retired in 1968 and returned to Skye, but died on holiday in Ibiza on 1 February 1970. A selection of his work, including short stories, plays and poetry, was published in Glasgow as *Tìr an Àigh* in 1971. His widow now lives in Helensburgh after 22 years in their retirement home at Camuscross; their daughter Kirsteen is well known as a Gaelic singer.

I am grateful to Kirsteen Grant and her mother for information and permission to reprint:

79   From *An Uilebheist is na Foghlamaich* ('The Monster and the Experts'). Editor's trl. *Tìr an Àigh* 229–32. The poem contains 37 stanzas, of which nos. 3–14 are printed here; the final 23 describe how the 'experts' try to hunt and kill the beast, and how she gets the better of them. The 'monster fever' of 1933–9 provided a welcome distraction from political and social misery. It was launched by a report in the *Inverness Courier* of 2 May 1933 from Alex Campbell — a man steeped in Gaelic tradition who happened to be the Loch Ness water-bailiff and the paper's Fort Augustus correspondent — that a creature which he variously described as a 'water kelpie' and 'a fearsome-looking monster' had been seen in the loch, thus provoking dozens of 'sightings' in that period alone. In terms of folklore the Monster appears to be an amalgamation of three strands of belief — the *each uisge* or water-horse, the *Cìrean Cròin* or sea-serpent (for which see poem 57), and the spirit of the loch, in this case *an Niseag*, see my article 'Nessie: water-horse, *Cìrean Cròin* and loch spirit', *West Highland Free Press*, 26 March 1999. As the folklorist Calum Maclean, brother of Sorley MacLean (q.v.), pointed out in his book *The Highlands* (Inverness 1959) 108, "Local opinion supports the belief that the monster is really there and that it has been there for a very long time."

Roderick MacLeod (Ruairidh MacLeòid) 1903–65

Roderick MacLeod was born 15 March 1903 in Kyles Stockinish, Harris, second child of Alexander Macleod, fisherman, from Kyles Stockinish (*Alastair Ruairidh Iain Mhóir a' Chaolais*, 1865–1942), and his wife Catherine (Kate), also a Macleod, from Leacklee (*Ceiteag Thormoid Bhig Iain 'ic Thormoid Òig*, 1867–1948), the others being Alexander and Norman. After leaving Stockinish school he worked for a short time as a labourer on Lord Leverhulme's construction schemes in the island. He then spent the rest of his life in the merchant navy. He made many songs, most of them witty and some known only to his Gaelic-speaking shipmates, although he was a good scholar who left a great deal of his work in manuscript; his 'Oran a' Chòta' appears in *Chì Mi 'n Tìr: Òrain ás na Hearadh* (Bill Lawson Publications, Harris 1996) 42–3. He was widely known as 'Harris', and also (thanks to the family nickname *Cunnartach*, in their case denoting cleverness) as 'Ruairidh Cunnartach'. He died tragically in 1965 when working for the City Line, as a result of falling into the hold of his ship off the Canaries. He is buried at Las Palmas.

I am grateful to Bill Lawson for information, and to the poet's nephew, Finlay MacLeod, Stockinish, for information and permission to reprint:

80   *An Cùlaibh Éirinn* ('At the Back of Ireland'). Editor's trl. Alexina Ghreumach and Alma NicShimidh (eds), *Sùil ri Cladach: Cruinneachadh de dh'Òrain Mhara* (Stornoway 1992) 34–5 (with music). The poet brings to the depiction of modern warfare a fundamental technique of traditional verse: the story is not systematically told but hinted at through glimpses of heightened reality.

Angus Campbell (Aonghas Caimbeul, 'Am Puilean') 1903–82

Angus Campbell, 'Am Puilean', was born 9 October 1903 in Swainbost, Ness, Lewis, third child of Alexander Campbell from Habost (*Alastair Mhurchaidh Òig*, 1865–1948) and his wife Christina (Chirsty) Maclean (*Cairistìona Aonghais MhicillEathain, Cairistìona Reubain*, 1868–1930), the others being Mary, Murdo, Norman, Angus ('Am Bocsair', q.v.) and Margaret (Peggy). Alastair Mhurchaidh Òig was related to the poet Murdo Morrison (*Murchadh a' Bhocs*, 1884–1965, Shader and Niagara Falls), author of a collection *Fear Siubhal nan Gleann* (Glasgow 1923). Swainbost was a new settlement, consisting of crofters evicted in 1842 from Uig; expected to emigrate, they were reluctantly given land in Ness to avert a threat of violence.

On the origin of the Puilean's nickname his son Donald John comments, "Many Ness nicknames have no meaning, as appears to be the case here" (personal communication, 24 April 1997). He attended the 300-pupil Cross School from 1909 to 1918, and this (translated) is his view of the education he received (*SIR* 22): "A Lowlander, who had not a word of Gaelic, was the schoolmaster. I never had a Gaelic lesson in school, and the impression you got was that your language, people and tradition had come from unruly, wild and ignorant tribes and that if you wanted to make your way in the world you would be best to forget them completely. Short of the stories of the German Baron Münchhausen, I have never come across anything as dishonest, untruthful and inaccurate as the history of Scotland as taught in those days."

His father having obtained the post of missionary in the Free Church, in 1918 the family moved to Berneray, Harris. The journey took them through Stornoway; at the age of 14, it was the poet's first ever visit to that town. His first job in Berneray was as a cowherd, and he spent some time as a handyman and boatman in the islands of the Sound of Harris in the service of the Stewarts of Ensay. In 1924 he left to crew on luxury yachts, visiting such places as the French Riviera: an experience which fuelled his radical social views.

He then enlisted in the Seaforth Highlanders for seven years, most of which were spent in India. His first poetry was composed on the voyage out. He saw action on the North-West Frontier — noting the common experience of Pathan and Gael — but also enjoyed the life of relative luxury afforded to British troops. He heard Mahatma Gandhi speak, and saw the aviator Amy Johnson. In 1932 he returned to Swainbost to invest his earnings in a shop. In 1933 he married Mary Mackay from Eoropie (*Màiri na Pòlaig*, 1909–83), and they had seven children: Donald John, Christine, Alasdair, Angus, Marion, Murdina and Norman. It was during these years that the 'bothans' of Ness first grew up in response to the social needs of the younger men, the Puilean being one of the moving spirits behind the first of them. Times were hard, however, and he got work for a while in Fairfield's shipyard in Glasgow.

As a member of the Territorial Army, the Puilean rejoined his old regiment on the outbreak of war in 1939. His experience was very like that of Donald John MacDonald (q.v.): he saw action in France, was captured at St Valéry in 1940, and spent the rest of the war in prison camps in Poland, frequently doing agricultural labour. His description in *SIR* of a three-month forced march from Stalag Thorn to Magdeburg before the advancing Russians, January–April 1945, is particularly graphic. He was liberated on 11 April 1945, and returned to shopkeeping in Swainbost. He retired during the 1960s, and his collected verse, *Moll is Cruithneachd* [*MC*], was published in Glasgow in 1972. The book was reviewed by, among others, Donald John MacDonald, in *Gairm* 80 (Am Foghar 1972) 374–7; for further assessment see Derick Thomson, *An Introduction to Gaelic Poetry* (London 1974) 260–2, and Roy Wentworth, 'Ath-Sgrùdadh (12): Bàrdachd Aonghais Chaimbeil (Am Puilean)', *Gairm* 138 (An t-Earrach 1987) 118–28. The poem 'Smuaintean am Braighdeanas am Pòland, 1944' ('Thoughts on Bondage in Poland, 1944') is published with English translation in Michael Davitt and Iain MacDhòmhnaill (eds), *Sruth na Maoile* (Edinburgh and Dublin 1993) 14–17.

In 1969 the Gaelic Books Council announced a prize of £200 for a biography or autobiography; the Puilean won it with *Suathadh ri Iomadh Rubha* [*SIR*], published in Glasgow in 1973. It is a remarkable achievement, consisting as it does of the memoirs of an exciting life, woven together with a forthright personal philosophy and much detailed ethnological commentary on tradition and change in island communities during the twentieth century, all steeped in a solution of anecdote, sometimes brilliantly funny. It is the twentieth century's leading work of Gaelic non-fictional prose.

The Puilean died in Stornoway on 28 January 1982. I am grateful to his son Donald John for information and permission to reprint:

81   **Deargadan Phóland ('The Fleas of Poland').** Editor's trl. with Donald John Campbell's assistance. *MC* 47–9. Composed 1944, according to *MC*, but the poem's origins seem to date from 1941, when the poet was one of 28 PoWs outhoused from 'Fort 17' in Nazi-occupied Poland as agricultural labourers. Sleeping as they did with hay and pigeons above them, and stock of all kinds on either side, they were tormented by fleas. "We called them the *Freiceadan Dubh* ('Black Watch'), and any man they didn't reduce to cursing and swearing deserved a place in the courts of the saints. I made a satirical poem on them at the time, but that didn't take the strength out of their frames or the sharpness out of their sting" (*SIR* 295–6, translated).
      Buanna ('layabout') in the 5th-last stanza is in origin a mercenary or billeted soldier, a word with resonances of the Norse occupation of Lewis, see my articles 'The daddy of all couch potatoes' and '"Butcher-meat — or else"', *West Highland Free Press*, 15 and 29 January 1999.

82   **Ciod E? ('What is He?').** Editor's trl. *MC* 95–6. Composed 1970. The title may equally mean 'What is It?' — the poem is a plea for freedom of conscience.

John Nicolson (Iain MacNeacail) 1903–99

John Nicolson was born 30 October 1903 in Sheader, Uig, Skye, sixth of eight children of William Nicolson, from Sheader (*Uilleam Alastair Chaluim*, 1853x4–1931), and his wife Marion Campbell, also from Sheadar (1865x6–1953), the others being Christina Ann, Christina (Kirsty), Isabella, Donald, Alexander, Malcolm and Mary. William Nicolson was a crofter who worked part-time as coachman on the Uig estates (then owned by John Urquhart), and his wife was an outstanding singer and storyteller. At the age of six the poet started attending Uig school, where he appears to have got his lifelong nickname, 'Skipper', from wearing a sailor's cap or the like. He was not taught Gaelic at school, but neither was he punished for speaking it. In due course he taught himself to read and write the language.

In 1910 the Uig estates were bought by the Congested Districts Board. Glenconon was divided into crofts, one of which was obtained by William Nicolson, and the family moved across the river. They were now able to enjoy the luxury of housing their cows in a separate byre instead of keeping them, as was traditional, under the same roof as themselves. While still at school the poet got work at Earlish helping on a croft — herding, fetching water and cleaning the byre. He left school in 1918 at the age of 14, and it was around this time that he made his first song, 'Òran an Tombaca', which he was to sing again from memory for Thomas McKean after a gap of almost 70 years. He worked for some time at Linicro as an assistant in the blacksmith's forge, then spent the period from about 1924 to 1936 running a croft for Alexander Matheson in Glen Hinnisdale and crewing occasionally on a herring boat. Like Donald Allan MacDonald (q.v.), he had placed his poetic gift at the service of his community through the making of songs of entertainment, of commentary and of praise; since Glenconon and Glen Hinnisdale were full of crofting families at that time and ceilidhing was commonplace, this was his most productive period.

From 1936 on there was no work left at home, however. The poet was forced to tread the well-worn trail in search of employment on the mainland, and spent nearly three years planting trees on Sir John Stirling Maxwell's Corrour estate in Rannoch Moor. The outbreak of war in 1939 found him working on roads and dams in the Dalwhinnie area for Balfour Beatty. He was called up, and joined the Royal Scots Fusiliers — an unfortunate choice, as it was a regiment with few Gaelic-speakers and therefore very little that could make life bearable through the stimulation of his talents. He saw active service in Italy, France, Belgium, Holland and Germany.

In 1945 the poet returned to Glenconon to help his brother with the family croft, and in 1947 he married Mary Munro from Glen Hinnisdale (*Màiri Dhonnchaidh Ruaidh*, 1920—), granddaughter of his father's old employer John Urquhart. The couple went to live at Cuidrach to act as caretakers of Cuidrach House and to manage the stock there. They made their home in the converted stables nearby, gradually built up their own stock, and raised a family of eight — Duncan, Morag, Willie, John Angus, Jessie, Jenny Mabel, Stanley and Isobel.

In 1980 Nicolson and his fellow Uig poet Angus Fletcher (1896–1982) were recorded in Dundee by Catriona Montgomery (q.v.) for a cassette and booklet issued in that year as *Òrain Aonghais agus an Sgiobair*. Fletcher, a maker of humorous songs, provided the froth to Nicolson's more full-bodied malt; both were capable of keen satire, but our poet preferred to keep his most vituperative work, such as 'An cuala sibh mun ghàrlach ud?', well under wraps (see p. xxv above).

In 1988 he was visited for the first time by a young American PhD student from Edinburgh University, Thomas McKean. They were introduced by Dr Margaret Bennett, a native of the district who was at that time a lecturer in the School of Scottish Studies. As one of the last of the old-style township poets, Nicolson was the perfect focus for a first-hand study of the context of a corpus of traditional verse. Over several years McKean made extensive recordings, resulting in a thesis, 'The Life and Songs of Iain "an Sgiobair" MacNeacail and the Function of Song in a Hebridean Community' (1993), and a book, *Hebridean Song-Maker: Iain MacNeacail of the Isle of Skye* (Edinburgh 1997, with CD) [*HSM*]. The latter was reviewed in *Scottish Book Collector* 5, no. 11 (1998) 36 and *Cothrom* 15 (1998) 48–52, among other places.

Nicolson was able to recall some 30 of the 100 or so songs that he had made, and McKean embeds them for us in the poet's recollections of the events and environment that produced them. The act of composition was involuntary, for example, but was aided by some form of regular motion such as cycling or walking along the road (see p. xlv above). Being cast straight into the oral environment without the intervention of writing, the survival of songs depended on their reception. "They were for the time being, just." If popular, they were remembered by others, even decades later, and the poet's own recollection of them was shored up by frequent performance; if not, they might perish forever. The song's social context was thus all-important, and songs of the type made by Nicolson were still part of the social currency of the generation that grew up between the Wars. *Rinn e òran dhan a chuile nighean òg mun àm sin a bha san àite*, said Mrs Isabel Ross. "He made a song to every young girl in the area at that time." And his son Stanley reported occasional knowing looks being exchanged at ceilidhs when a song called 'A Mhàiri, a Mhàiri' was sung (*HSM* 97, 116, 199).

John Nicolson died on 17 May 1999, and tributes to him by Tom McKean and Aonghas MacNeacail (q.v.) appeared in *The West Highland Free Press*, 28 May 1999. MacNeacail remarked significantly that he 'may have been the last of his kind, whose poetry was made to be heard across a room'. The poet did not live to see the illustrated account of his life, along with two of his songs, published on 18 August 1999 in Neat's *Voice of the Bard* 229–35, 347–8.

I am grateful to Dr Thomas McKean for permission to quote from *HSM*, and to the poet and his wife Mary for information and permission to reprint:

83   ***An t-Each Iarainn* ('The Iron Horse').** Editor's trl. *HSM* 36–7. With regard to ghosts (stanza 3), it was widely believed that horses had the second sight and were much troubled by spirits and apparitions. See for example John MacInnes, 'The Seer in Gaelic Tradition', in Hilda Ellis Davidson (ed.), *The Seer* (Edinburgh 1989) 10–24: 14.

84   ***Nochd gur luaineach mo chadal* ('Fitful's my sleep tonight').** Editor's trl. *HSM* 61–2. In the 5th stanza the horrible reality of war is strikingly dovetailed with some of the traditional imagery which glorifies it. The shorthand *fuil chraobhach* 'tree-blood' calls up a set of concepts which are both ancient and complex. The tree is the genealogical one of nobility and breeding; the blood rises red in white cheeks like sap, but may also spread in branch-like streams on the ground. The last stanza reinforces the traditional assumption that a song will be passed home from the battlefield by word of mouth, the numbers of those who have it multiplying each time it is sung along the way. One of the many advantages of conveying a message in this way is that verses could be sung selectively as appropriate to the audience. A poet may hope for example to alert the menfolk at home to the brutality of a war without giving undue anxiety to his mother.

85   ***Òran do Teonaidh Hellinga* ('Song to Johnnie Hellinga').** Author's trl. *HSM* 85–7. Early in 1978 Donald MacDonald of Waternish, who was by then resident in Budhmor Home for the Elderly in Portree, put the Waternish Estate on the market. In March that year it was bought by Johannes Hellinga, an extrovert Dutch cattle dealer with a shady reputation. Hellinga launched his extraordinary reign on 31 May by throwing a party for his crofting tenants in the Dunvegan Hotel, announcing from the stage that he had sold the township of Lochbay to its tenants for £200. For ten more years his unorthodox business methods and rowdy lifestyle were much to the fore in the national press, and he was ultimately confirmed as just another of the irresponsible landowners who blotted the history of the Highlands in the twentieth century — he was simply a speculator who had no use for crofting land. The poet was impressed by him, however, as he was meant to be. "I've seen him here, he bought my lambs, and he sold them in Portree for so much and he lost £200 on them. 'Oh,' I says, 'Hellinga, . . . I'll need to make some of that up to you.'... 'Away, be quiet,' he says, 'I make ... that in a quarter of an hour!'" (*HSM* 86). Hellinga had telephoned the poet once, seemingly in connection with the party in the Dunvegan Hotel. The poet did not go, but composed this song for him anyway, along with an English version in case he came to call (*HSM* 132). The full English version has nine verses, in a slightly different order from the surviving Gaelic one, which has only six; I have rearranged the sequence of the English verses (and dropped three) in order to provide a facing translation. The difficult issue of land reform fell to the new Scottish Parliament in 1999.

Norman MacLeod (Tormod MacLeòid) 1904–68

Norman MacLeod, also known as 'Contair', 'Tommy' or 'Tommy Contair', was born 15 June 1904 in Portvoller, Point, Lewis, second child of Murdo Macleod from Bayble (*Murchadh 'An Chòcair*, 1882?–1942) and his wife Johanna Mackenzie (*nighean Thormoid Choinnich*, 1874–1957), the others being Margaret, Christina, Murdo, Iain, Margaret (Mairead Bheag), Seonag, Uilleam, Iain (Seonaidh), Eiric and Dollag (who died in infancy). His mother was a seventh daughter of a seventh daughter and therefore had the cure of the King's Sickness, *Tinneas an Rìgh*. Educated at Aird Primary School, the Nicolson Institute, Glasgow University and Jordanhill College of Education, he taught in a succession of Lewis schools: Gravir (Lochs) 1930–31, Fidigarry (Lochs) 1931–5, Loch Croistean (Uig) 1935–43, Knock (Point) 1943–52 and Lionel Junior Secondary (Ness) 1952–68. In 1932 he married Marion Macleod from Ranish (*Mòr Iain Mhurchaidh Chaluim*, 1908–82), and they had four children, Dolina, Murdo John, Norman and George. During the Second World War he served in the Home Guard.

At Lionel the poet was head of the Gaelic Department and Deputy Headmaster. A much-loved dominie known fondly to his pupils as the Bodach, he could teach almost any subject on the curriculum, communicating it with warmth and humour, but his particular interest was in the language, literature, folklore and music of the Gael. He was behind the School's lively magazine *Tàintean* with its strong Gaelic content. Convivial but a rebel by nature, he was a life-long socialist and member of the Labour Party, as well as an indefatigable collector and preserver of words, traditions, songs and poetry. His daughter says (personal communication, 17 March 1997): *Saoilidh mi gu bheil mi fhathast a' cluinntinn brag, agus abair brag, na h-aon chorraig air an typewriter sgriosail ud, a bha dol a latha agus a dh'oidhche, agus a theab na bha staigh a chur às an ciall. Bu shuarach aige.* "I feel I can still hear the rattle, and what a rattle, of the one finger on that accursed typewriter, which would be going day and night, and nearly driving everyone at home out of their minds. He didn't care."

He died in Lionel after a long illness on 14 November 1968, the year before he was due to retire, and is buried in the Eye cemetery on the Bràighe in Point. An enthusiastic contributor to *Gairm* under the characteristically self-mocking byline 'Am Bàrd Bochd', part of his collection of Lewis verse was published by Gairm Publications in 1969 as *Bàrdachd á Leódhas*. A substantial collection of his own work remains in typescript but deserves to be published; it ranges widely in nature from delicate short lyrics to satire of startling ferocity. His work is briefly assessed in Derick Thomson, *An Introduction to Gaelic Poetry* (London 1974) 262–4.

I am grateful to the poet's daughter, Mrs Dolina Gunn, Stornoway, for information, a copy of his typescript 'Rabhdan a' Bhàird Bhochd' [RBB], and permission to print:

86   **Raoir chunna mi ('Last night I saw').** Editor's trl. with assistance from Mrs Gunn. RBB 18.

87   **An 'Sus' a Shàraich Mi ('The "Sus" that Vexed Me').** Editor's trl. *Gairm* 38 (An Geamhradh 1961) 180–1; RBB 27–8.

88   **Bàgh Leumrabhaigh ('Lemreway Bay').** Editor's trl. RBB 44.

89   **Faoin Achain ('An Idle Wish').** Editor's trl. RBB 36. Mention of Nikita Khrushchev, Dwight D Eisenhower ('Ike') and Harold Macmillan suggests a date for the poem of 1960.

90   **Dubh is Geal ('Black and White').** Editor's trl. RBB 66. *Loch Bhat an Dìb* is Loch Vatandip, three miles west of Stornoway where the B8010 to Breasclete parts company from the A858 to Garynahine and Uig.

91   **An t-Àite bho Dheireadh ('The Last Place').** Editor's trl. RBB 81. There are countless euphemisms in Gaelic for God, the Devil, Heaven and Hell. Further examples may be found in poems 74 (*am fear sgiathach*, 'the winged one'), 95, 167, 172, 218 and 252. Swearing in the language is based almost entirely on religion, and to name the Devil or Hell directly is to use very strong language indeed. See Aonghas Caimbeul, *Suathadh ri Iomadh Rubha* (Glasgow 1973) 36.

92   *Thuit mo leannan* ('My love's fallen'). Editor's trl. RBB 96.

George Morrison (Seòras Moireasdan) 1906–88

George Morrison was born 6 October 1906 in North Tolsta, Lewis, first surviving child of John Morrison, crofter/fisherman, from Tolsta (*Iain Sheòrais, Iag*, 1877–1945), and his wife Catherine Macdonald, also from Tolsta (*Catrìona Mhurchaidh Bhuidhe*, 1885–1961), the others being Murdo, Donald, John, Angus, Ishbel, Mary-Anne, Etta and Kate-Anne. He was educated at Tolsta Public School, the Nicolson Institute and Glasgow University, graduating with Honours in Classics. He spent most of his life teaching Latin and Greek in Glasgow. In 1936 he married Jane Macintosh Wood (1906–71), a primary school teacher from Stevenston in Ayrshire (they had probably met as teacher and pupil at Gaelic evening classes), and they had three children, Ian, Anne and Kenneth.

In 1941 or so Morrison joined the Royal Naval Volunteer Reserve. Serving in the Atlantic and Indian Oceans, he was commissioned and reached the rank of Lieutenant. "He impressed the naval commission board with Tolsta Public School, the connotation of Public being different in England," says his son Ian (personal communication, 10 March 1997). "A fellow Lewis matelot used to laugh at the Gazette Brevities without knowing that the author was swinging in the hammock beside him."

George Morrison was indeed an extremely funny man as well as an erudite one, and was best known to a generation of Lewis people as 'The Breve', writer of the 'Brevities' column, which ran in *The Stornoway Gazette* from the mid-1930s, with occasional intermissions, for nearly 40 years. His achievement is well summed up by the editor of his poems, Mrs Catherine Grant, wife of *Gazette* editor James Shaw Grant (*ÒB* [vi], translated): "It may not be going too far to say that it was easier for the people of the Island to accept the changes on all sides of them because they were reading George's writings every week — a mixture of loyalty to the past, hatred of fanaticism and intolerance, support for social improvement, contempt for snobbery, and distaste for vanity and showing off — all wrapped up in a humour which is incisive and at times scathing." He was a great friend of that other comic poet, Norman MacLeod, q.v., whose third son is George Morrison MacLeod.

George Morrison retired as headmaster of Whitehill Senior Secondary School in 1967, but continued to live in Glasgow. Selections from his 'Brevities' were published in 1978 as *One Man's Lewis*, and 26 of his poems in 1985 as *Òrain a' Bhritheimh* [*ÒB*]. It was reviewed in, among other places, *Gairm* 137 (An Geamhradh 1986–7) 91–4. He died in Glasgow on 17 September 1988, and is buried in North Tolsta.

I am grateful to the late James Shaw Grant, Inverness, for information, and to the poet's son, Mr Ian Morrison, New Tolsta, for information and permission to reprint:

93   *An t-Earrach* ('The Spring'). Editor's trl. *ÒB* 12–13. Says Ian Morrison (pers. comm., 10 March 1997): "My father told me, possibly more than once, that autumn was his favourite season, which seemed strange till the explanation that that was the time of plenty food, compared with the poverty of spring. No Safeway in Stornoway then, with everything from *Glasag de Sturgeon* to luxury toilet tissue."

Donald Allan MacDonald (Dòmhnall Ailean MacDhòmhnaill) 1906–92

Donald Allan MacDonald was born 19 December 1906 in Daliburgh, S. Uist, fourth child of Donald MacDonald (*Dòmhnall na Bainfhighich* or *Bainich*, 1862–1932) and his wife Mary Ann MacLeod (1879–1910), the others being Ann, Mary, Jessie and Mary Ann. The family was of protestant North Uist stock, the poet being first cousin to Dòmhnall Ruadh Chorùna, q.v. Dòmhnall na Bainfhighich had been brought up in the house of his maternal grandmother Ann Stewart, *née* Laing (1811–89), who was a *bainfhigheach* or weaveress; he became a carpenter, and lived with his family till 1910 in Glebe Cottage, Daliburgh, the property of the Church of Scotland.

The bereavements described in note 5 at p. 708 above gave the poet a strong sense of the transience of life and of its fundamental values. He enjoyed poaching, and worked in the summer as a herdboy. He attended school at Daliburgh from age 6 to 14, but never learned to write Gaelic. He worked for six months in 1923 as a farm-servant at Barnabuck in Kerrera before returning home to be apprenticed to his father.

For the next twenty years he had to take employment where he could get it. He thus worked as carpenter, builder's labourer and even barman at a variety of locations including Harris, Barra, Kinlochleven and Glasgow. Following service in England as a gunner in the Royal Artillery during 1943–5, and further spells of seasonal employment, he worked for 12–15 years for South Uist Estates as joiner, handyman, water-bailiff and gamekeeper, acquiring a croft at Kildonan.

In 1932 he had married Catherine (Kate) Macintyre, who was a niece of Donald Macintyre (q.v.) and a cousin of Donald John MacDonald (q.v.); her mother was Flora, Macintyre's eldest sister, mentioned in his 'Òran nan Easgannan' (*Sporan Dhòmhnaill* 235). They had eight children, Donald, Angus, Catriona, John, Flora, Mary Ann, Catriona and Neil. In 1959 he won the Bardic Crown at the National Mod in Dundee with 'Aiseirigh a' Bheachain' (see p. 822 below). On retirement in 1971 he and Kate moved to Inverness to be closer to many of their family. He died there on 23 February 1992, and is buried at Cnoc Hàllainn.

Donald Allan's poetry is almost entirely local in nature, his best-known work being the love-song 'Gruagach Òg an Fhuilt Bhàin', composed *c.*1928. He was not blessed with a particularly good memory, and relied on appreciative ceilidh-house audiences for the preservation of his work. When such audiences ceased to exist after the Second World War, he largely lost interest in poetry, and there are many gaps in the corpus of 35 songs laboriously assembled during 1976–80 by Fr John Angus Macdonald. *Tha iad aig muinntir Uibhist*, he would say (thesis 35, book 67), "The Uist people know them", but by then this was not altogether the case. He may well have been the last Scottish Gaelic poet who composed within the oral tradition and remained aloof from any adaptations of that tradition. See Rev. Fr John A Macdonald, 'The Songs of Donald Allan MacDonald' (MLitt thesis, University of Aberdeen, 1983), 'The Poetry of Donald Allan MacDonald', *Transactions of the Gaelic Society of Inverness* 58 (1992–4) 32–50, and, last but not least, *Òrain Dhòmhnaill Ailein Dhòmhnaill na Bainich: The Songs of Donald Allan MacDonald 1906–92* (Benbecula 1999, the 'book of the thesis'). Around 150 people squeezed into the former school at Kildonan in South Uist, now a museum, on 2 August 1999 to launch the book with songs and speeches, and plans are being made for a memorial to the poet at the Daliburgh cross-roads.

I am grateful to the poet's eldest son, Donald MacDonald, Heatherlea, Lochboisdale, for information and permission to reprint:

94   **Ceud Fàilt' air Gach Gleann ('A Hundred Greetings to Each Glen').** Editor's trl. John A Macdonald, thesis 125–9 (text), 278–9 (notes), 368–9 (melody), book 108–113 (text), 210 (notes), 235 (melody). The song was made in 1928 for a mod in Daliburgh. The poet recalled that he was fishing at a loch in the hills a couple of days before the event was to take place when he was approached by Alexander Fraser, the Daliburgh schoolmaster. *Tha fhios gu bheil thu a' dol a chur rudeigin chun a' Mhòid.* "I assume you're going to enter something for the mod." The poet, who was 22 at the time, had given the mod not the slightest thought, and replied, *Chan eil sion agams' as fhiach a chur ann co-dhiù.* "But I've nothing to enter." *Ach,* replied Fraser, *cuir ann rud air choreigin, tha iad ag iarraidh òrain nach deach a sgrìobhadh riamh.* "Put in something or other, they want songs that have never been written down." The makings of our song had been in his head for some time. He completed it, had it written down and submitted it. According to his own account, it won first prize for poetry, and when he sang it he won first prize for singing (thesis 278–9, book 210). All his life he took delight in the fact that he beat John Campbell (q.v.) into second place in three sections of the competition (thesis 58, book 6).

Angus Campbell (Aonghas Caimbeul, 'Am Bocsair') 1908–49

Angus Campbell, 'Am Bocsair', was born 3 September 1908 in Swainbost, Ness, Lewis, a younger brother of Angus Campbell, 'Am Puilean', q.v. It was relatively common for brothers to receive the same name in this way, nicknames solving most difficulties except the receipt of mail. It was the consequence of genealogical custom, the elder Angus in this case being named for his mother's father, *Aonghas Reuban*, the younger for his mother's brother.

The Bocsair first attended Cross School, where he received his nickname from his ability with his fists. The family moved to Berneray, Harris, in 1918, and then to Bernera, Lewis, in 1926; by the time he had left school in Berneray the Bocsair had begun making a name for himself with his songs and rhymes, and he became a very good singer whose talents were much in demand at weddings and ceilidhs. He spent the years of the Depression back and forth between shopkeeping in Ness and whatever work could be had in Glasgow, but finally qualified in 1934 as a nurse in Hawkhead Mental Asylum, now known as Leverndale Hospital (he gained exceptional marks in the examination, being the first at Hawkhead to obtain a Pass with Distinction). Like the police and the prison service for men, and general nursing and domestic service for women, it was an occupation taken up by many Gaelic speakers from the islands around this time.

In 1937 the Bocsair married Mary Murray from South Dell (1909–95), whose mother was a sister of the poet Donald Macdonald, *Dòmhnall Chràisgein* (1861–1916), author of the collection *Bàrd Bharabhais* (Glasgow 1920), for whom see pp. xxiv and lxix (n. 74) above. They had four children, Donald, Alasdair (the playwright), Norman (q.v.) and Christina.

It was in Glasgow that the poet first contracted the tubercular condition which ultimately killed him. In 1940 he brought his family to live at South Dell, where he built a house and resumed the trade of shopkeeper. He also served as an effective District Councillor for a number of years. Eighteen of his poems were published as *Òrain Ghàidhlig* in 1943. About 1946 he had an experience of conversion, and he died in South Dell after a two-year sickness on 15 December 1949.

The Puilean's moving tribute to him will be found on pp. 346–8 of *Suathadh ri Iomadh Rubha*. A fresh edition of his poems, brought together by Norman MacLeod (q.v.) and introduced by the Puilean, was finally published in Loanhead as *Bàrdachd a' Bhocsair* in 1978; it contains 66 items ranging from philosophical themes through verses on love and nature to comic songs. It was reviewed in, among other places, *Gairm* 106 (An t-Earrach 1979) 171–4 and *Lines Review* 68 (1979) 37–9.

I am grateful to the poet's son Norman for information and permission to reprint:

95 *Caithris nam Bodach* (**'The Old Men's Night-Watch'**). Editor's trl. *Bàrdachd a' Bhocsair* 89–90. Humour does not come blacker than this. The air is that of Kenneth Macleod's very popular 'Maighdeannan na h-Àirigh':

Thug mi 'n oidhche raoir 's mi bruadar	I spent last night in my dreams
Mar ri nighneagan na buaile —	With the young girls of the cowfold —
B' fhìnealt' uasal mìn na gruagaich	Maidens fine, noble and gentle
'Seinn nan duanag anns an àirigh.	Singing lovesongs in the shieling.

Symptomatically, there is a remarkable crop of by-names for the Devil in this poem: *Rìgh an Dubh-Shluic* ('the King of the Black Pit'), *an Deamhan* ('the Demon'), *an Nàmhaid* ('the Enemy'), cf. poem 91.

Michael MacPherson (Micheal Mac a' Phearsain) 1910–84

Michael John MacPherson (*Micheal Ruadh, Micheal Alastair Bhig*) was born at Taobh a' Chaolais, East Kilbride, in the south end of South Uist, 26 April 1910, eldest son of Alexander Macpherson, crofter, from Borve, Barra (*Alastair Beag Mhicheil Alastair*, 1873–1954), and his wife Peggy MacInnes, from Eriskay (*Peigi Iain 'ic Alastair*, 1879–1952), the others being Donald John, Morag, Mary Ann, Theresa and Ealasaid. Most Uist and Barra Macphersons appear to be descendants of the MacMhuirichs who had served the Kings of the Isles and the MacDonalds of Clanranald as poets for five hundred years, ultimately anglicising their name as Macpherson for no better reason than that the mainland *Clann Mhuirich* — an unrelated but much larger kindred — had done so before them, see for example John MacPherson, *Tales of Barra told by the Coddy* (ed. J L Campbell, Canna 1960) 14–15. A more recent book, Capt. Angus Edward MacInnes's *Eriskay Where I Was Born* (Edinburgh 1997), has much to say (pp. 94–5) about the poet's more immediate family, and especially his father Alastair Beag.

The MacPhersons in East Kilbride could compose songs. Iagan Bachd, so called because he belonged to that part of the west side of Barra, and his brother, Alasdair Bheag [*sic*], were orphans brought over from Barra by their auntie Eal[a]said, who married an Eriskay man at the Balla. Alasdair Bheag married an auntie of mine. Iagan never married.

They moved over to East Kilbride when it was crofted. If you were in their house and asked how their song-making was going, auntie Peggy would say, "Oh, they are waiting for someone to die."

Iagan composed a nice song once about how he would be out fishing with a small boat and he used to get a tow from the bigger boats to Castlebay. Between Iagan Bachd and Michael Ruadh, his nephew, they must have composed a thousand songs.

MacInnes goes on to explain that Alastair Beag was no poet but a clever man to have in a boat in a crisis. He had an old fishing-boat, the *St Theresa*, which sprang a leak.

I heard Alasdair Bheag talking about it years later, telling how he had a knife in the leak to keep the water pressure out. I was only young at the time this happened, but I was once in the Marine School in South Shields, when one day a designer was brought in to give the boys a lecture on what to do if wooden lifeboats were damaged in any way or were leaking badly. He was lecturing on with half the class dozing off when he came to talk of the knife and the pressure of water. I looked at him right away, saying to myself, that fellow must have been to East Kilbride on holiday and got some tutoring from Alasdair Bheag.

After leaving Garrynamonie School, Mìcheal Alastair Bhig became a fisherman himself, and subsequently a merchant seaman. In 1935 he married Mary Ann MacLean from South Boisdale (*Màiri Anna Sheonaidh Aonghais*, 1915—) and they had a family of three: Iain Alasdair (deceased), John (who is married in Canada), and Margaret Ann, who married Cathelus Campbell and now lives in the paternal home. Mrs Campbell recalls her father telling bed-time stories of how his boat just missed being torpedoed during the Second World War, while Capt. MacInnes speaks of meeting him in Bayonne, New Jersey, in 1943.

The R.F.A. (Royal Fleet Auxiliary) tanker, *Blue Ranger*, with half her deck crew belonging to my part of the world, came alongside. It was great to hear Gaelic being spoken again . . . My first cousin, Michael Ruadh MacPherson, was one of her crew, and I was to hear the first song he composed. He must have composed hundreds afterwards, but this one was his first after being in a Russian convoy. (*Eriskay Where I Was Born* 175–6)

Returning to Uist after the War, Mìcheal Ruadh settled down to life as a crofter-fisherman, and when I made his acquaintance in 1970 he was working on the new road into Glendale behind his native township. In his daughter's words, his main hobby was composing songs, and he particularly enjoyed house ceilidhs. Being unable to write Gaelic, he took to using a cassette tape-recorder in composition to ensure that his work would not be lost, genially commandeering the services of those blessed with a Gaelic education, such as myself, to write down the words for him, with the result that several of his compositions appeared in *Gairm* between 1970 and 1983.

Mìcheal Ruadh died in Glasgow on 23 December 1984, and is buried at Cnoc Hàllainn. I am grateful to Mrs Campbell for information and permission to reprint:

96   *Cumha Mhaighstir Nèill* ('The Lament for Father Neil'). Editor's trl. *Gairm* 123 (An Samhradh 1983) 229–31. Monsignor Neil Mackellaig died in 1982 after 48 years in the priesthood, most of them in Bornish and Daliburgh, S. Uist. See poem 174. The futuristic Church of Our Lady of the Sorrows at Garrynamonie was completed in 1964.

Sorley MacLean (Somhairle MacGill-Eain) 1911–96

Sorley (Samuel) MacLean was born 26 October 1911 at Oscaig, Raasay, second of seven children of Malcolm Maclean, tailor, from Raasay (*Calum mac Chaluim 'ic Iain 'ic Tharmaid Mhóir 'ic Iain 'ic Tharmaid*, 1880–1951), and his wife Christina Nicolson, also from Raasay (*Ciorstaidh Shomhairle Mhóir Iain 'ic Shomhairle Phìobaire 'ic Iain 'ic Eóghain*, 1886–1974), the others being John, Calum, Alasdair, Norman, Ishbel and Mary. Both his Maclean and his Nicolson forebears included tradition-bearers on all sides. He was thus exposed to the riches of Gaelic cultural experience in both song and story, and although his gifts did not include a singing voice they did include a superb memory: "I made up for my lack of pitch in music by having an inability to forget the words of any Gaelic song I liked, even if I heard it only once" (from interview with Donald Archie MacDonald, 'Some Aspects of Family and Local Background', in *Critical Essays*, 211–12: 217–18). Two further elements made up the mix — the radicalism of a people battered by clearance and emigration but enthused by the relative success of the struggle for land that began with the Battle of the Braes in 1882 and ended with the Crofters' Act of 1886, and the evangelical fervour of Free Presbyterianism in the very island in which it had been born in 1893.

MacLean attended Raasay Primary School from 1918 to 1924, and Portree Secondary School (now Portree High School) from 1924 to 1929. He graduated from Edinburgh University with first class honours in English in 1933, following this up with a year at Moray House Teachers' Training College. He taught English at Portree High School (1934–7), Tobermory Secondary School (1938) and Boroughmuir Secondary School, Edinburgh (1939–40); while awaiting conscription he taught evacuees for a few months in Hawick. As shown at pp. xxix–xxxiv above, the intellectual and emotional turbulence of MacLean's life throughout the 1930s gave rise to the single greatest outpouring of Gaelic verse that the twentieth century experienced. The end of this period was marked by the publication in January 1940 of the first issue of *17 Poems for 6d*, jointly written with Robert Garioch.

MacLean joined the Signals Corps in September 1940. From December 1941 he was on active service in Libya and Egypt. Seriously wounded at the battle of El Alamein on 2 November 1942, he was restored to health in hospitals at Burg el Arab, Cantara, Suez, Baragwanath, Netley and Raigmore (Inverness), from where he was discharged in August 1943. It was the same hospital in which he died 53 years later. Once again a sea-change in his life was marked by the publication of his work: *Dàin do Eimhir agus Dàin Eile* appeared in November 1943.

At the end of that year MacLean returned to his old job at Boroughmuir, becoming principal teacher of English in 1947. He met Renee Cameron in 1944, and they were married on 24 July 1946; they raised a family of three daughters, Ishbel, Mary and Catriona (who predeceased him). He and Renee, with her kindly and devoted tolerance, were the perfect match, the most back-handed compliment he ever received being from a writer who declared that the most striking thing about him was the beauty of his wife's pale blue eyes.

In 1956 the poet left the congenially literary atmosphere of Edinburgh behind him to begin a new life with his family as headmaster of Plockton Secondary School in Ross-shire. Things were difficult at first.

> MacLean himself taught most of the English and history classes, teaching for thirty-three periods out of forty, while also having to perform his administrative role as headmaster. For his first three and a half years, he was also without secretarial assistance. (Aonghas MacNeacail, 'Questions of Prestige', in *Critical Essays*, 201–10: 205)

It was a far from unfulfilling period, however, as can be recognised in the brilliant papers on Gaelic literature which he continued to present to the Gaelic Society of Inverness. He took a leading role in the successful campaign for a Higher Leaving Certificate in Gaelic for Learners, a crucial step in the development of Gaelic education from which much of benefit to the language has subsequently flowed. He delighted in his pupils, loved Plockton and its people (many of them distant relatives of his own), found time to walk the Kintail hills, and, last but not least, indulged his lifelong passion for shinty — he reintroduced it to his school, and is a figure of note in the annals of the game.

Many of his pupils at Plockton in the 1960s did not realise that their headmaster was a poet, however, and in a sense he was not. The bibliography of critical work (below) falls revealingly silent between 1960 and 1971. In his Boroughmuir period he had sent new poems to *An Gaidheal* and then to *Gairm* nos. 1, 7 and 8, culminating in summer 1954 with 'Hallaig', which is regarded by many as his greatest poem and was certainly stimulated by the new all-Gaelic magazine and its editors' untiring requests for 'more, more'. But after describing a working trip to Bavaria in March 1955 in *Gairm* 12, he fell silent. A flurry of creativity began in 1960–2 after the reappearance of four of his poems in Norman MacCaig's *Honour'd Shade* (Edinburgh 1959), leading to some new poems and prose in *Gairm* 31, 35 and 40, along with part of 'An Cuilithionn'. The death of his folklorist brother Calum at the age of 44 in 1960 was marked by 'Cumha

Chaluim Iain MhicGill-Eain'; completed in 1968, it is, again, widely regarded as one of his greatest achievements.

It is a source of some perplexity to me that these movingly elegiac works of MacLean's maturity should be regarded as in some way superior to the poems of the 1930s, which seem so totally engaged with the present moment that they make the blood run faster, and form such a natural extension of the tradition of spiritual verse represented by Angus Finlayson, q.v. MacLean certainly speaks in both for the whole of humanity, but while in the late poems he speaks for the Gael and the dead, in the early ones he speaks for the young and the living. I myself was greatly helped by these poems as a young man, and it came as no surprise to me at all when in January 1998 I was asked for a translation of MacLean's early poem 'Reothairt' by Edinburgh CID, who had found a scribbled copy of it at a crime scene.

In 1972 MacLean retired to live at Peinchorrain in the Braes of Portree in Skye, looking across the Clàrach to his native Raasay. It was a good time for him to retire, as his work had just been discovered by the non-Gaelic-speaking world. The process of discovery was greatly aided by the growth of a national and international circuit of poetry readings (see pp. xlii–xliii above). Thanks to the astonishing cadences of his voice and his droll mastery of the stage, MacLean swept all before him. He became a poet again. He began to receive honours, all accepted with his unique blend of modesty and flair. In 1968 Iain Crichton Smith had started the process of publishing translations from *Dàin do Eimhir* which culminated in his *Poems to Eimhir* (Newcastle 1971, repr. with originals as *Eimhir*, Stornoway 1999). *Lines Review* devoted an issue to his work in 1970, through which he released three 'Dàin do Eimhir' poems hitherto held back. He was Creative Writer in Residence in Edinburgh's Department of English Literature (1973–5) and *Filidh* (Poet in Residence) at Sabhal Mór Ostaig in Skye (1975–6). In addition to a remarkable clutch of prizes, fellowships, chiefships and freedoms, he received honorary degrees from Dundee University (1972), the National University of Ireland (1979), the universities of Edinburgh (1980) and Grenoble (1989), the Open University (1989), Anglia Polytechnic University (1994), and Glasgow (1996). In 1981 his life was commemorated in a major exhibition in the National Library of Scotland (see catalogue *Somhairle MacGill-Eain: Sorley MacLean*, ed. by Ann Matheson), and in the same year he was featured in words and drawings in *Seven Poets*, published by Glasgow's Third Eye Centre. His life and work inspired two films, Douglas Eadie's 'Sorley Maclean's Island' (1974) and Tim Neat's 'Hallaig' (1984); among other films in which he appeared is David Halliday's 'Uamh an Òir / Songs of the Land' (1994).

His collected criticism and prose writings, edited by Professor William Gillies, were published in 1985 by Acair of Stornoway as *Ris a' Bhruthaich*. His 75th birthday in 1986 was marked by the publication of Ross and Hendry's *Sorley MacLean: Critical Essays*, which includes a substantial biography by Hendry and important contributions by 16 other writers including Smith and MacNeacail. In 1990 he was Edinburgh University's Alumnus of the Year, and was awarded the McVitie's Prize as Scottish Writer of the Year and the Queen's Gold Medal for Poetry, while in 1991 he received the Saltire Literary Award for Scottish Book of the Year. His 80th birthday in 1991 was marked by a book with a modern Highland perspective, *Somhairle: Dàin is Deilbh*, edited by Angus Peter Campbell (q.v.) and including verse by eight of the poets represented in *An Tuil* — William Neill, Norman Malcolm Macdonald, Smith, John Murray, MacNeacail, Myles Campbell, Angus Peter Campbell himself and Mary Montgomery — as well as a new poem, 'A' Ghort Mhór' ('The Great Famine'), by MacLean himself.

On top of all this, and in addition to his huge influence on younger Gaelic poets, MacLean had become virtually a 'cult' figure in Ireland, a cult marked by the Claddagh Records LP 'Barran agus Asbhuain' (1973), an interview in the poetry magazine *Innti* 10 (1986), and Máire Ní Annracháin's full-length critical exploration *Aisling agus Tóir: An Slánú i bhFilíocht Shomhairle MhicGill-Eain* (An Sagart, Maynooth 1992). In other words, he was being recognised not only as one of the greatest Scottish Gaelic poets who had ever lived, but as the greatest Gaelic poet of his day in either Scotland or Ireland.

Shortly before his 85th birthday, in an interview with Angus Peter Campbell (*The Scotsman*, 24 October 1996), MacLean summarised the century for us. "For ill, but perhaps not absolutely for ill, the Great War. For bad, the Great Depression. For sheer amount of misery, the Second World War. For good, the government of Attlee, which was continued to a certain extent by Macmillan and people like that, which did an awful lot for the good of the country, and which was undone by the government of Thatcher." He died in Raigmore Hospital after a short illness on 24 November 1996, thus missing by less than a year two events of 1997 which would have cheered him greatly, the return of a Labour government and the referendum which has brought Home Rule to Scotland. An unedited film of his last stage appearance, in the 1996 Edinburgh Festival, is in the possession of the Scottish Film Archive, provisionally titled 'An Turas Seo'. Among his latest works are the poems 'An t-Ascalon' ('Escallonia') and 'Festubert' (on the First World War), first published in 1992 in Wales and Skye respectively but brought together with earlier material in *Pervigilium Scotiae* (Etruscan Books, Buckfastleigh 1997), and a Gaelic foreword to R Black, W Gillies and R Ó Maolalaigh (eds), *Celtic Connections: Proceedings of the 10th International Congress of Celtic Studies* (E. Linton 1999), which we understand was the last thing he wrote.

In addition to *17 Poems for 6d* and *Dàin do Eimhir* [*DE*], substantial selections of MacLean's poems appeared as: Tom Scott (ed.), *Four Points of a Saltire* [*FPS*], with George Campbell Hay (q.v.), William Neill (q.v.) and Stuart MacGregor (Edinburgh 1970); Donald MacAulay (ed.), *Nua-Bhàrdachd Ghàidhlig* [*NBG*], with George Campbell Hay, Iain Crichton Smith, Derick Thomson and Donald MacAulay (Edinburgh 1976), including discussion of the poets' work; *Reothairt is Contraigh, Spring Tide and Neap Tide: Selected Poems 1932–72* [*RC*] (Edinburgh 1977); the English-only *Poems 1932–82* (Philadelphia 1987); and finally *O Choille gu Bearradh: From Wood to Ridge* [*CB*] (Manchester 1989, new edn Manchester and Edinburgh 1999). In 1977, between *NBG* and *RC*, the poet changed the spelling of his English surname from Maclean to MacLean.

Other poems survive in manuscript. A complete scholarly edition of all the poet's work is greatly to be desired, and in this connection (as in others) the untimely death on 22 July 1999 of Donald Archie MacDonald, who became his near neighbour and literary executor after his retiral from the School of Scottish Studies in 1994, is a very great loss.

Entries on Sorley MacLean will be found in histories of (and companions to) Scottish and Gaelic literature, for which see p. 820 below. The principal work of assessment is Raymond J Ross and Joy Hendry, *Sorley MacLean: Critical Essays* (Edinburgh 1986). It contains footnote references but no bibliography. For further assessment see: Iain Crichton Smith, 'The Poetry of Sorley Maclean', *An Gaidheal* 53 (1958) 99–100, 109–10; Iain Crichton Smith, 'Homage to Sorley Maclean', *Saltire Review* 5, no. 15 (1958) 37–40; Gordan MacGill-Fhinnein, 'Somhairle MacGill-Eathain: File Mór na Nua-Ghàidhlig', *Comhar* vol. 19 nos. 9 and 11, and vol. 20 nos. 1 and 3 (1960); Iain Crichton Smith, 'A Note on Sorley Maclean's *Dàin do Eimhir*', *Stand* 12, no. 2 (1971) 8; John MacInnes, *The Listener*, 2 September 1971; Iain Crichton Smith, 'The Poetry of Sorley Maclean', *The Glasgow Review* 4, no. 3 (1973) 38–41; Breandán Ó Doibhlin, 'Mórfhile Ghael Albain', in his *Aistí Critice agus Cultúir* (Dublin 1975); John MacInnes, 'Sorley Maclean's "Hallaig": A Note', *Calgacus* 1, no. 2 (1975) 29–32; John Herdman, 'The Poetry of Sorley Maclean: A Non-Gael's View', *Lines Review* 61 (1977) 25–36; Brendan Devlin, 'On Sorley Maclean', *Lines Review* 61 (1977) 5–19; John MacInnes, 'A Radically Traditional Voice: Sorley MacLean and the Evangelical Background', *Cencrastus* winter 1980; Raymond J Ross, 'Sorley MacLean: A Bard to All People', *The Scotsman*, 24 October 1981; John Montague, 'A Northern Vision', in Seán Mac Réamoinn (ed.), *The Pleasures of Gaelic Poetry* (London 1982) 161–74; John Herdman, 'Sorley MacLean's "Calbharaigh"', *Akros* 17, no. 51 (1983) 26–8; Ray Burnett, 'Sorley MacLean's *Hallaig*', *Lines Review* 92 (1985) 13–22; Iain Crichton Smith, 'Gaelic Master: Sorley MacLean', in his *Towards the Human* (Loanhead 1986) 123–131; James B Caird, 'Sorley MacLean', *Edinburgh Review* 74 (1986) 57–62; Colin Nicholson, 'To Sing a People's Fate . . .', *The Scotsman*, 25 October 1986; Robert Crawford, 'Recent Scottish Poetry and the Scottish Tradition', *Verse* 4, no. 2 (1987) 36–46; Terence McCaughey, 'Somhairle MacGill-eain', in Cairns Craig (ed.), *The History of Scottish Literature, Vol. 4, Twentieth Century* (Aberdeen 1987) 147–63; Christopher Whyte, 'The Cohesion of *Dàin do Eimhir*', *Scottish Literary Journal* 17, no. 1 (1990) 46–70; J Derrick McClure, 'Douglas Young and Sorley MacLean', in Derick Thomson (ed.), *Gaelic and Scots in Harmony* (Glasgow 1990) 136–48; Pádraig Ó Fuaráin, 'Somhairle Mac Gill-Eain agus Seán Ó Riordáin: Friotal, Creideamh, Moráltacht' (MA dissertation, Maynooth 1994); Piotr Stalmaszczyk, 'Alba's Major Voice: Somhairle MacGill-Eain', *Celtic Pen* 10 (1996) 8–10; Christopher Whyte, 'A Note on *Dàin do Eimhir* XIII', *Scottish Gaelic Studies* 17 (1996) 383–92; Alasdair MacRae, 'Sorley MacLean in a Context beyond Gaeldom', *Études Écossaises* 4

(1997) 19–30; Máire Ní Annracháin, 'Vision and Quest in Somhairle MacGill-Eain's "An Cuilithionn"', *Lines Review* 141 (1997) 5–11; and Henri Gibault, 'Sorley MacLean (1911–1996)', *Études Écossaises* 4 (1997) 11–17.

Book reviews of particular interest will be found in, among other places, *Poetry Scotland* 2 (1945), *Gairm* 76 (Am Foghar 1971) 379–84, *The Scotsman* 15 February 1975, *The Glasgow Herald* 21 April 1977, *The Scotsman* 23 April 1977, *The Times Literary Supplement* 9 September 1977, *Gairm* 101 (An Geamhradh 1977–8) 94–6, *The Scotsman* 23 December 1989, *Gairm* 150 (An t-Earrach 1990) 186–8, and *Lines Review* 112 (1990) 40–5.

I am grateful to the late Donald Archie MacDonald for much good advice and help with translations, to Mrs Renee Maclean and the Scottish Film and Television Archive for information, and to Mrs Maclean and (where relevant) Carcanet Press Ltd for permission to reprint the following. Other than in minor matters of orthography and punctuation, I have preferred earlier versions of both text and translations, setting out English prose to correspond with the lines of the original. The density of reference in poems 100, 118 and 128 is such that I have decided it is best not to try to provide detailed annotation for them here.

97   *Dàin do Eimhir II: A Chiall 's a Ghràidh* ('Reason and Love'). Author's trl. *DE* 11; *RC* 6–7; *CB* 4–7. Composed May 1932.

98   *Dàin do Eimhir IV: Gaoir na h-Eòrpa* ('The Cry of Europe'). Author's trl. *DE* 12, 97; *NBG* 74–7; *RC* 12–13; *CB* 8–9. *Long nan Daoine*, 'the Slave Ship' (also *Saothach nan Daoine* as in poem 128), refers to an attempt made in 1739 to kidnap people from MacLeod estates in Skye and Harris and sell them into slavery in America. Sir Alexander MacDonald of Sleat and Norman MacLeod of Dunvegan appear to have colluded in the affair. See Norrie MacLennan, 'Highland slavers escaped justice' and 'How the Soitheach nan Daoine affair sent ripples through high society', *West Highland Free Press*, 12 and 19 May 1989.

99   *Dàin do Eimhir X: Theagamh nach eil i 'nam chàs* ('Perhaps it's not part of my destiny'). Editor's trl. *DE* 13.

100   *Dàin do Eimhir XIII: A' Bhuaile Ghréine* ('The Sunny Fold'). Author's trl. *DE* 14–15; *RC* 14–17; *CB* 12–15.

101   *Dàin do Eimhir XIV: Reic Anama* ('The Selling of a Soul'). Author's trl. *DE* 16; *RC* 16–19; *CB* 14–15.

102   *Dàin do Eimhir XXV: B' fheàrr leam na goid an teine* ('I'd prefer to the stealing of fire'). Editor's trl. *DE* 26.

103   *Dàin do Eimhir XXIX: Coin is Madaidhean-Allaidh* ('Dogs and Wolves'). Author's trl. *DE* 30, 98; *NBG* 78–81; *RC* 36–7; *CB* 134–5.

104   *Dàin do Eimhir XXXVIII: Labhair mi* ('I spoke'). Editor's trl. *DE* 34.

105   *Dàin do Eimhir XLIV: Ged chuirinn dhiom éideadh* ('Should I even strip off'). Editor's trl. *DE* 37. Here more than elsewhere, my translation represents the beginning of informed discussion, not its end. The phrases *éideadh faireachaidh na cluaineis*, *mo chéille luaidhe* and *liùbhrainn do t' éibhneas* are particularly rich in ambivalence. 'Of my reason for living' is a catch-all interpretation: *mo chéille luaidhe* may represent 'of my beloved darling', 'of my darling intellect', or even, as Donald Archie MacDonald pointed out, 'of my leaden intellect'. The poem is a jewel that must be held up to the light, a perfect example of MacLean's mischievous, probing subtlety.

106   *Dàin do Eimhir XLIX: Fo Sheòl* ('Under Sail'). Author's trl. *DE* 39, 100; *RC* 52–3; *CB* 150–1. The Clarach is the southern part of the Sound of Raasay. See p. xxxiv above.

107   *Dàin do Eimhir LIII: Gur suarach leam* ('Insignificant to me'). Editor's trl. *DE* 43.

108   *Dàin do Eimhir LIV: Camhanaich* ('Dawn'). Author's trl. *DE* 43, 100; *NBG* 72–3; *RC* 54–7; *CB* 156–7.

109   *Dàin do Eimhir LVIII: A nighean 's tu beairteachadh* ('O girl who enriches'). Editor's trl. *DE* 48–9.

110   *Dàin do Eimhir LIX: MhicGilleMhìcheil . . .* ('Carmichael . . .'). Author's trl. *DE* 49; *CB* 164–7. 'The Hymn of the Graces' is poem 2.

111   *Dàin do Eimhir LX: Nuair chunna mi* ('When I saw'). Editor's trl. *DE* 50.

112   *Dàin do Eimhir: Dimitto.* Editor's trl. *DE* 50.

113   *Dàin Eile I: Ban-Ghaidheal* ('A Highland Woman'). Author's trl. *DE* 53, 101; *NBG* 104–7; *RC* 76–9; *CB* 26–9. For the use of seaweed as fertiliser etc. see also poems 18, 171, 289.

114   *Dàin Eile XVI: Trì Slighean* ('Three Paths'). Editor's trl. *DE* 82.

115   *Dàin Eile XVII: 'N e d' mhiann* ('Is it your wish'). Editor's trl. *DE* 82. "Munich in

September 1938 and the Nazi occupation of Czechoslovakia and Franco's victory in Spain in early 1939 convinced me that the only hope of Europe was the Red Army of Russia, and I believed that all the anti-Soviet propaganda, or most of it, came from Fascist or pro-Fascist sources" (*CB* 63). See pp. xxxi–xxxii above.

116   *Dàin Eile XVIII: An Dùn Éideann 1939* ('In Edinburgh 1939'). Editor's trl. *DE* 83.

117   *Dàin Eile XIX: Gabh a-mach ás mo bhàrdachd* ('Get out of my poetry'). Editor's trl. *DE* 83.

118   *Dàin Eile XXI: An Seann Òran* ('The Old Song'). Editor's trl. *DE* 86–7.

119   *Dàin Eile XXIII: Thug Yeats dà fhichead bliadhna* ('Yeats spent two score of years'). Editor's trl. *DE* 90.

120   *Dàin Eile XXIV: An uair a thig an teannachadh* ('When the tightness comes'). Editor's trl. *DE* 90.

121   *Dàin Eile XXVI: An-seo an gaol* ('Here is love'). Editor's trl. *DE* 91.

122   *Éisgeachd I: An Dùn 'na Theine* ('The Castle on Fire'). Editor's trl. *DE* 94. The fire which gutted one wing of Dunvegan Castle took place in November 1938. "From far and near the neighbours gathered to help to fight the fire and to save the contents of the castle, much of which they carried away for safe keeping and as carefully returned. It was a tribute to the love and esteem with which the MacLeods of MacLeod were regarded" (I F Grant, *The MacLeods: The History of a Clan* (1981 edn, Edinburgh) 588).

123   *Éisgeachd II: Air an Adhbhar Cheudna* ('On the same topic'). Editor's trl. *DE* 94. The *Annie Jane*, carrying emigrants from Skye, went down in the Kyle of Vatersay, see *Ris a' Bhruthaich* 20.

124   *Éisgeachd IV: Do Mgr Niall Mac an t-Seumarlain* ('To Mr Neville Chamberlain'). Editor's trl. *DE* 94. Chamberlain (1869–1940) was UK Prime Minister 1937–40. The poem refers to his failure to support the Spanish Republic when it was attacked by Franco's fascists in the Civil War of 1936–9, and to his signing of the Munich Pact of September 1938, which ceded the Sudetenland (part of Czechoslovakia) to Hitler's Germany. Chamberlain also appears, with his much-derided umbrella, in poem 63.

125   *Éisgeachd VI: Don Bhreitheamh a thubhairt ri Iain MacGhill-Eathain gum b'e Gealtair a bh' ann* ('To the Judge who told John Maclean that he was a Coward'). Editor's trl. *DE* 94. The poet writes (*CB* 315): "John Maclean (1879–1923) was a schoolteacher and member of the Social Democratic Federation, who believed passionately in workers' education (his teaching of 'Marxian economics' attracted classes of over one thousand at times). He was anti-militarist, and was imprisoned four times between 1916 and 1921. His position as a socialist and a nationalist is unequalled in Scottish political history." He is also referred to in poem 128.

126   *Éisgeachd VII: Road to the Isles*. Author's trl. *DE* 95, 103. Refers principally (but not exclusively) to the Rev. Kenneth Macleod, q.v., whose *The Road to the Isles* appeared in 1927. The inverted commas in MacLean's translation suggest that he regarded 'clarsach', 'black house' and 'ceilidh' as upstarts in the English language, and patronising ones at that. The islands mentioned are Catholic ones. For the *Fir Ghorma* — 'Blue Men' or fairies of the sea — see J G Campbell, *Superstitions of the Highlands and Islands of Scotland* (Glasgow 1900) 199. The *Iùbhrach Bhallach* or 'Speckled Barge' (the topic of a Kennedy-Fraser song) features in the tale 'Gaisgeach na Sgéithe Deirge', a favourite of Macleod's, see J F Campbell (ed.), *Popular Tales of the West Highlands* 2 (2nd edn, Paisley 1890, repr. Hounslow 1983) 454, and T M Murchison (ed.), *Sgrìobhaidhean Choinnich MhicLeòid* (Edinburgh 1988) 64, 153. Cf. p. lvii and poem 196.

127   *Glac a' Bhàis* ('Death Valley'). Author's trl. *FPS* 140–1; *NBG* 106–9; *RC* 120–3; *CB* 210–13.

128   From *An Cuilithionn* ('The Cuillin'). Author's trl. *CB* 110–117. Written 1939, see *CB* 63. The poem as published in *CB* has a short introduction and seven sections, totalling 1,220 lines. Each section presents a variation on the same theme, i.e. the narrator looks out from the Cuillin over the past and present condition of Skye, the West Highlands, Europe, and the world. Reprinted here are lines 854–993, from the middle of the longest section, no. 6. It is the poem's political climax, following the great lyrical climax (*Eich mhóir a' chuain / Mo ghaol do ghruaim* . . . 'Great horse of the sea, / My love your gloom . . .') in section 5. A tight unity is imparted to our extract by the poet's device of having Clio (one of the nine muses, the inventor of historical and heroic poetry) speak for each place in the first person. The line *Smeòrach mis' air ùrlar Phabail* is taken from 'Smeòrach Chlann Dòmhnaill' by the N. Uist poet John MacCodrum (1693–1779), see W Matheson (ed.), *The Songs of John MacCodrum* (Edinburgh 1938) 44–5:

> Smeòrach mis' air ùrlar Phaibil,   A mavis I on Paible's flat,
> Crùbadh ann an dùsal cadail . . .   Huddled in a drowse of sleep . . .

The following couplet, *Seall a-mach, an e 'n là e, / 'S mi ri feitheamh na fàire*, is the beginning of a song on the drowning of Iain Garbh MacLeod of Raasay, see MacLean, *Ris a' Bhruthaich* 304, and Alexander MacDonald, *Story and Song from Loch Ness-Side* (Inverness 1914, 1982) 289. The last eight lines of the extract are an evocation of the so-called 'Òran Mór Mhic Leòid' by Roderick Morison (*c.*1656–*c.*1714), see W Matheson (ed.), *The Blind Harper: An Clàrsair Dall* (Edinburgh 1970) 58: *Chaidh a' chuibhle mun cuairt / Ghrad thionndaidh gu fuachd am blàths . . .* ("The wheel has gone round, / The warmth has suddenly turned cold . . ."). So the narrator's voice returns, and Clio's is heard again only momentarily in section 7.

129 **An t-Àilleagan ('The Little Jewel').** Editor's trl. *An Gaidheal* 41 (1945–6) 24.

130 **A' Bheinn ('The Hill').** Editor's trl. *An Gaidheal* 41 (1945–6) 35.

131 **Mhag mo reusan ('My reason mocked').** Editor's trl. *An Gaidheal* 41 (1945–6) 74. In assisting me with the translation, Donald Archie MacDonald pointed out that this poem is a reflection on 'Dàin do Eimhir LI: Crìonnachd' (*DE* 41, 100; *RC* 54–5; *CB* 152–5). The term 'terror-burst' is the poet's own. In his 'prose' translation of 'Crìonnachd' in *DE* 100 he rendered the line *le maoim-shruth nan speur* as 'with the terror-burst of the skies'. For line-by-line versions he altered this to 'when the skies burst and stream with terror'.

132 **Feasgar Samhraidh: Linne Ratharsair ('A Summer's Evening: The Sound of Raasay').** Editor's trl. *Poetry Scotland* no. 4 (1949) 29.

133 **From Uamha 'n Òir ('The Cave of Gold').** Author's trl. *CB* 298–301. This underrated poem is, I believe, as good as anything composed by the poet after 1950. It has 302 lines, of which I reprint the last 18, which form a helpful summary. The poem is highly symbolistic and appears to be autobiographical. It is in three sections: the entry of the first piper (young man); the entry of the second piper (older man); reflections. The story of a piper entering a cave to meet the Devil is widespread, and has been localised in many different places, see Daniel F Melia, 'The Lughnasa Musician in Ireland and Scotland', *Journal of American Folklore* 80 (1967) 365–73, David Buchan, 'The Legend of the Lughnasa Musician in Lowland Britain', *Scottish Studies* 23 (1979) 15–37, esp. 36, Alan Bruford, 'Legends Long Since Localised or Tales Still Travelling?', *Scottish Studies* 24 (1980) 43–62, esp. 44–5, and 'Three Fairy Songs', *Tocher* 47 (1993–4) 279–89 — to which I may add that the legend was the subject of protracted correspondence in the *Oban Times* in 1915.

Donald MacDonald (Dòmhnall MacDhòmhnaill) 1912–89

Donald MacDonald was born in Eriskay on 8 May 1912, eldest of fourteen children of Hector Macdonald, fisherman, from Eriskay (*Eachann mac Dhòmhnaill 'ic Aonghais 'ic Eoghainn 'ic Eachainn 'ic Dhòmhnaill Chruinn*, 1880–1960), and of his wife Kate MacKenzie from Uist (*Ceit Maiseig*, 1890–1982). He was educated at Eriskay Primary School, Daliburgh Junior Secondary School, Lochaber High School (Fort William) and Glasgow University (MA in Latin and Gaelic 1935), followed by a year's teacher training at Jordanhill College. In *Eriskay Where I was Born* (Edinburgh 1997) 33, Capt. Angus Edward MacInnes offers this racy vignette of the poet's youth:

> I think being brought up in an atmosphere of hearing old timers spouting and arguing about seamanship, and what great guys they were when they could show anyone anything from a needle to an anchor, killed off any ambition young ones had other than being good seamen. You might get one in a thousand like our next-door neighbour, Donald MacDonald, who went through University and gained his M.A. degree with Honours. It is a mystery to me how that man managed to study with all the buzz going on around him, as there must have been about thirty school children in and out of the house shouting, screaming and carrying on between their own crowd and those of their neighbours. The grown-ups, too, could shout and argue, especially the MacMillans next door, Ian, Fairy and Peggy, who were past masters at arguing, and there would be Donald in the middle of the melee with his nose in a book. How he managed to concentrate is beyond me.
> With the limited amount of money which was available through bursaries, schoolmasters were rated as high as anyone in our islands could reach. Having one in the family would be someone for relations to boast about as everything connected with a schoolmaster was held sacred.

In summer 1933 the poet had collected traditional stories in Eriskay for Trinity College, Dublin. He carried out similar work in Uist the following summer for An Comunn Gaidhealach, some of the results being published from 1940 in their journal *An Gaidheal*. Between 1934 and 1951 An Comunn also published his Gaelic translations of several one-act plays, including 'Clann Rìgh

Lochlainn'. He taught in Barra for eleven years, initially at Eoligarry (1936–7) and then for ten years at Castlebay, and in 1947 he returned to Eriskay as headmaster.

In 1949 he married Kate MacKinnon from Barra (*Ceit Nill 'Illeasbaig Nill Eòin*, 1922—). They had four children, Catriona, Neil, Allan and Margaret. 'An Ròn' won him the Bardic Crown at the National Mod in Inverness in 1949 (see p. 822). He retired in 1977 and was awarded the Silver Jubilee Medal by the Queen. His collected verse was published as *Rannan á Eilean na h-Òige* in 1981, consisting of 13 poems, 10 children's songs and translations of 6 hymns. Among his books for children published by Acair are *Banrigh na Mara*, *Reubadair a Staca* and *An Gille Gallda*. Some of his work in prose — his 1933 collection of stories, and at least one children's book — remains unpublished. He died on 23 May 1989, and is buried in Eriskay.

I am grateful to the poet's widow Kate and his son Allan for information and permission to reprint:

134   *Òran na* **Politician** ('The Song of the **Politician**'). Editor's trl. *Rannan á Eilean na h-Òige* 28–31. For the tune see Alexina Ghreumach and Alma NicShimidh (eds), *Sùil ri Cladach* (Stornoway 1992) 44. On the morning of 5 February 1941 an 8,000-ton cargo vessel, the SS *Politician*, bound from Liverpool for Jamaica and New Orleans, ran aground in the Sound of Eriskay. Among her cargo were a quarter of a million bottles of whisky. What happened next became the subject of a song 'Òran na *Politician*' by Roderick Campbell (nephew of John Campbell, q.v.), published in Margaret Fay Shaw, *Folksongs and Folklore of South Uist* (2nd edn, Oxford 1977) 88–90; of Compton Mackenzie's best-selling *Whisky Galore* (1947); of the Ealing Studios film of the same name, shown in America as *Tight Little Island* (1949); of Roger Hutchinson's book *Polly: The True Story behind 'Whisky Galore'* (Edinburgh 1990), in which Campbell's song is reprinted at pp. 122–5; and of our poem. One of the first people on the scene was Dòmhnall Aonghais Bhàin (q.v.), see Timothy Neat, *The Voice of the Bard* (Edinburgh 1999) 30–2. Hutchinson points out (*Polly* 33) that the vessel's holds were filled with 'the usual hastily assembled miscellany of goods which might realise hard cash in the United States, and with essential items for the West Indian colonies': cotton, machetes, flycatchers, confectionery, motor-cycle hubs, enamelware, oil-burning stoves, cutlery, exercise books, plumbing equipment, cigarettes, tobacco, soap, medicines, carpets, baths, mirrors, pineapple cubes, biscuits. The whisky, by contrast, was destined for the Texas 'millionaire market', and the islanders found it to be wonderfully non-toxic: "You could drink it all day and all night and you would never have a headache after it." That is because, as Hutchinson remarks, 'its brand names were beyond parody' — The Antiquary, Haig's Pinch, VVO Gold Bar, Ballantine's Amber Concave, White Horse, King's Ransom, Victoria Vat, Johnnie Walker Red and Black Label, Mountain Dew, King William IV, McCallum's Perfection, King George IV, PD Special, Old Curio, Spey Royal. The ship was formally salvaged between 15 February and 12 March, and Hutchinson says that everything possible was removed at that point except alcoholic liquids, presumably on the basis that 'undutied, damaged cases of spirits, which were now floating in an unpleasant compound of oil and water' were worthless. But the people of the islands moved in gratefully from all directions, and the evidence of Hutchinson's own account and of our poem is that not only the whisky remained but much else besides.

Calum I N MacLeod (Calum Iain MacLeòid) 1913–77

Calum Iain Nicholson MacLeod was born 12 March 1913 in the Schoolhouse, Dornie, Kintail, only child of John Nicholson Macleod, a farmer's son from Kilmuir in Skye (1880–1954), and his wife Annie (*Anna nighean Chaluim*, 1885–19??), a daughter of Malcolm Macleod, missionary, Breaclete, Bernera, Lewis. The poet's father, a schoolmaster, had taught for three years in Bernera before moving successively to Larkhall, Gladsmuir, Dornie, Errogie (Stratherrick) and Knockbain, finally retiring to Beauly; an enthusiastic participant in the affairs of An Comunn Gaidhealach, he contributed to Gaelic periodicals, wrote plays, and edited the important anthology *Bàrdachd Leódhais* (1916), but is perhaps best remembered for his column 'Litir á Beàrnaraigh', which ran in *The Stornoway Gazette* from 1917 to 1954 under the pseudonym 'Alasdair Mór' and resulted in the collection *Litrichean Alasdair Mhóir* (1932). "The letters," remarked a *Gazette* obituarist, "were not only a contribution to modern Gaelic literature, they were a faithful mirror of the thoughts, habits and outlook of the people of the Western Isles in the first half of the twentieth century." See also T M MacCalmain, 'Iain N. MacLeòid ("Alasdair

Mór"), Sàr-Sgrìobhadair Gàidhlig', *Gairm* 11 (An t-Earrach 1955) 243–50.

Calum Iain was educated at Stratherrick, Knockbain and Inverness Royal Academy, then studied Gaelic at Glasgow University under the Rev. Dr George Calder before matriculating at Edinburgh University, where he studied Celtic under Professor W J Watson, graduating MA in Celtic in 1939. In 1937 'An Cuan Siar' won him the Bardic Crown at the National Mod in Dundee (see p. 821 below). He served in the Intelligence Corps of the British Army from 1940 to 1946, rising to the rank of major, and in 1942 married Iona MacDonald, 'Ardalanish', Inverness, daughter of Donald Macdonald from Ardalanish in Mull, himself a prominent member of An Comunn Gaidhealach. (The wedding was celebrated in Gaelic verse in *An Gaidheal* 38 (1942–3) 59–60 by Iain MacLennan, Brisbane, Australia.)

In 1949 Calum Iain MacLeod settled in Cape Breton Island as Gaelic Adviser for the Province of Nova Scotia, moving in 1958 to Antigonish to establish the Celtic Studies Department at St Francis Xavier University. He was highly regarded in Canada as a scholar, and widely respected as a promoter of Scottish culture and as teacher and judge of piping at various Highland games. His widow points out that 'on campus he was known to always wear his kilt to class even throughout the cold Antigonish winter'. He published *Simplified Gaelic Lessons for Beginners* (Glace Bay, N.S., 1950), and he and his wife also produced a long-playing record *Scottish Gaelic for Beginners*, issued jointly in Canada and Scotland about 1955. In the form of *Gaelic Songs in Nova Scotia* (with Helen Creighton, 1964), *Sgeulachdan á Albainn Nuaidh* (1969), and *Bàrdachd á Albainn Nuaidh* (1970), he was responsible for gathering together a great deal of the Gaelic literature of Nova Scotia. His own collected poems were published at Glace Bay in 1952 as *An t-Eilthireach: Original Gaelic Poems and Melodies*, reviewed in *Gairm* 2 (An Geamhradh 1952) 89; his collected prose, mostly written in Kirkhill, appeared in 1977 as *Sgial is Eachdraidh*.

Major Calum Iain MacLeod died on 16 June 1977 and lies in Glenbard Cemetery, close to the first and most celebrated of Cape Breton's Gaelic poets, John Maclean (1787–1848). I am grateful to his widow, Mrs Iona MacLeod, Antigonish, for information and permission to reprint:

135   *An Giùlan* (**'The Funeral Procession'**). Editor's trl. *Gairm* 17 (Am Foghar 1956) 78. The poem appears to describe the vision of a coffin seen at sea off Bernera, its *eislinn-càraidh* — the part on which the body is laid — ruffled by the wind. It turns out not to be a portent of the poet's own death, or of his wake, but an intimation that a woman called Janet has died. For such experiences see e.g. J L Campbell and Trevor Hall, *Strange Things* (London 1968), esp. pp. 249–329. By Hàisgeir I take it that the poet means Harsgeir (*hardhsker*, 'hard skerry'), the most westerly of the Bernera islands. The names in the last two stanzas are of places in Bernera itself: *Cladh na Tràghad*, the 'Beach Graveyard', is at Bosta on the north shore.

Christina Stewart (Carstìona Anna Stiùbhart) 1914–83

Chrissie Anne Stewart was born 19 September 1914 in Upper Bayble, Point, Lewis, eldest of seven children of Malcolm Stewart, fisherman (*Calum Uilleim Iain 'An Sheòrais*, 1890–1973), and his wife Margaret Nicolson (*Maighread Mhurchaidh Fhionnlaigh*, 1892–1970), the others being Colina, William John, Murdina, Margaret, Henrietta and Dolina. She attended Bayble School 1920–31 under the headmasterships of Donald Maciver (q.v.) and James Thomson (q.v.), receiving a bursary in 1928 and the MacAulay Cup for Gaelic in 1929, the first year in which it was awarded.

James Thomson obtained work for her in Stornoway Post Office, but the cost of lodgings there would have run away with most of her salary. She spent some time as a herring girl (cf. poem 187), then obtained employment in a Glasgow hotel. During the Second World War she worked as a clerkess in a Dumfries munitions factory. On 21 January 1947, at 20 Upper Bayble, she married Murdo Macleod, also from Upper Bayble (*Murchadh Iain Mhurchaidh Chaluim*, 1911–81), and they had a son, John (1947–86), and a daughter, Barbara Margaret (Mrs Barbara Hamilton, Montrose, 1951—). She died in Bangour Hospital, West Lothian, on 13 September 1983.

The life of Chrissie Anne Stewart serves to remind us what the word 'community' means. Her father was from 28 Upper Bayble. Her mother was from 20 Upper Bayble, although the family lived as cottars on 20a. She herself married a man from 43 Upper Bayble, and they raised a family at 1a Upper Bayble, a split croft inherited and passed on to them by her only brother-in-law.

She did not begin composing until late in life when her children had left home. To the best of her daughter's knowledge there were no other songmakers in the family, but then she had the advantage of belonging to what must surely be regarded as the poetry capital of the world (see p. lxx, n. 101). Three of her songs appear in *Gairm* 102 (An t-Earrach 1978) 173–9 under the title 'Bardachd á Pabail le Carstìona Anna NicLeòid'. Her song 'Am Mac Stròdhail', addressed to her son John, who was killed in an accident in Edinburgh in 1986, remains popular in Lewis. Another, 'Call an *Ivy Rose*', is dedicated to her brother-in-law, Donald John Macleod, who was lost at sea.

For the poet's family history see Bill Lawson, *Croft History: Isle of Lewis, Volume 2* (Northton, Harris 1992) 25, 50, 76. I am grateful to her sister, Mrs Dolina Graham, Knock, for information, and to her daughter Mrs Hamilton for information and permission to reprint:

136   *Taigh Dubh mo Sheanar* ('My Grandfather's Black House'). Editor's trl. *Gairm* 102 (An t-Earrach 1978) 176–7. For the annual spreading of soot-impregnated thatch on the fields see poem 186. The thatch was secured on the roof by means of heather-rope weighted with stones (*acair*, 'anchors').

Rev. Kenneth Ross (An t-Urr. Coinneach Ros) 1914–90

Kenneth Ross was born 3 December 1914 at Fasach, Glendale, Skye, eldest of eleven children of Norman Ross, crofter, from Glendale (*Tormod Choinnich Thormoid 'ic Thormoid 'ic Mhurchaidh*, 1871–1959), and his wife Marion Macneill, from Borreraig (*Mòr nighean Aonghais 'ic Sheumais*, 1891–1955). Norman Ross was a brother of the Rev. Neil Ross, q.v. Amongst Kenneth's siblings were Margaret (better known as the actress Mairead Ros) and the late James Ross of the School of Scottish Studies.

Kenneth Ross attended school at Borrodale in Glendale from 1919 to 1929. After service as a Warrant Officer with the RAF in India, Burma and elsewhere (1935–45) he continued his education at Edinburgh University, Moray House, and Trinity College, Glasgow. He became minister of Gigha and Cara in 1957, ten years after the retiral from the same parish of Kenneth Macleod (q.v.), and subsequently served at Lochgelly Churchmount (1960–1), Lismore (1961–6), Gigha and Cara again (1966–9), Kirkmichael and Tomintoul (1969–77), and Northmavine in Shetland (1978–80).

In 1962 he married the artist Mary (Mamie) Parker, a native of Northumberland; following his retirement in 1980 they went to live in that county, where he died suddenly at home in Haltwhistle on 29 December 1990. He is buried in St Peter's churchyard, Newbrough, Northumberland. He contributed essays and poetry in Gaelic to *Gairm* and to the Gaelic Supplement of *Life and Work*, and in English to *Life and Work* and the *Hexham Courant*. A volume of his essays was published in 1972 as *Aitealan Dlù is Cian*. His translation of Pär Lagerqvist's novel *Barabbas* (Stockholm 1950, English translation 1951) survives in manuscript.

I am grateful to the poet's brother Alasdair Ross, Drumnadrochit, for information, and to his widow for information and permission to reprint:

137   *Fògradh Cogaidh sna h-Innsean* ('Wartime Exile in India'). Editor's trl. *Gairm* 56 (Am Foghar 1966) 314; *Aitealan Dlù is Cian* 11. 'Torwood' is one of the tunes to which Gaelic psalms are sung; Healaval Beg and Healaval More, 'MacLeod's Tables', are the mountains behind Glendale.

138   *O a Ghaidhealtachd Till* ('O my Gaeldom Return'). Editor's trl. *Gairm* 51 (An Samhradh 1965) 268.

139   *Farmad* ('Envy'). Editor's trl. *Gairm* 56 (Am Foghar 1966) 314.

George Campbell Hay (Deòrsa mac Iain Deòrsa) 1915–84

George Campbell Hay was born 8 December 1915 in Elderslie, Renfrewshire, second child of John MacDougall Hay (1881–1919), minister of Elderslie 1909–19, and his wife Catherine Campbell, from Cowal (1883–1975). The poet's elder sister Sheena lived from 1911 to 1989. Their father — a native of Tarbert (Loch Fyne), a fishing merchant's son, and a former headmaster of Lionel School, Ness, Lewis — was author of the novel *Gillespie* (1914), which paints an extraordinarily powerful picture of life and society in his native village. Their mother, a Free Church minister's daughter and a semi-fluent Gaelic speaker, had connections with Islay, Knapdale and Tarbert itself.

Following his father's death from tuberculosis when he was four, George was raised in Tarbert before being sent to school in Edinburgh in 1925 at the age of ten. The older generation in the village still spoke Gaelic amongst themselves, and he began to acquire the language from his mother, from his aunts, from the men congregated in Dougie Leitch's boatshed, and, later on, during his holidays from Fettes, as a crewman on Calum Johnson's fishing-boat. Having received a scholarship as the son of a deceased minister, he was at John Watson's until 1929, when he went on to Fettes, then in 1934 to Corpus Christi College, Oxford. Throughout this time he continued acquiring languages, for which he had a phenomenal gift. In 1940 he wrote (Byrne, thesis 23): "I can speak Gaelic, Danish and English, and read also Swedish, Icelandic, Irish, Modern Greek, Greek, Latin, French, and with a lot of dictionary thumbing Welsh and Spanish."

From fishing in Loch Fyne Hay moved on to yachting trips in Clyde and Hebridean waters, hillwalking and poaching, and a voyage to Scandinavia on a coal-boat. On graduation from Oxford in 1938 he threw himself into Nationalist politics. When war broke out in 1939 he saw it from a purely Scottish viewpoint: "It has to be admitted," he wrote (in Gaelic) to Robert Rankin in August 1940 (Byrne, thesis 22), "that the English are getting the worst of it, and it's right that they should. They took for themselves all the resources, wealth, fame and honour that belonged to the three kingdoms, and now let them have all the bombs, bullets and shells. To tell the truth, I'm not sorry for them. They've never been anything but mean, and their leaders are incompetent old men who should be in the grave. Many's the brave young Scot who met a sudden death on account of those old dodderers, and it's my hope and desire that they won't have died in vain."

Willing to defend Scotland but not England, Hay spent the period from October 1940 to May 1941 on the run in the hills of Argyll. He was caught at Arrochar, imprisoned for a few days in Saughton Jail, and finally agreed to his call-up for the sake of his mother, who was being hounded by the CID. He spent the War, from June 1942, as a clerk in the Royal Army Ordnance Corps — first at Catterick, then, from November that year, in Algeria and Tunisia. A rather unusual private, he enjoyed a fairly leisurely time, reading, writing, thinking and worrying about Scotland, talking to Italian PoWs, Arab civilians and anyone else who came his way, and imbibing their languages and modes of thought. In June 1944 his unit moved to Italy, where he worked mainly as an instructor and interpreter. Ideas which had germinated in Algeria now came to fruition, and over the next 18 months Hay produced some of his finest work.

He was coming to terms with his situation. Promotion to corporal, then sergeant, in spring 1945 was followed by a period of leave in Scotland in the autumn, then a transfer to the Army Education Corps. In January 1946 he was posted from Italy to Kavalla in northern Greece, where once again there was little to do. The result, unfortunately, was a violent incident which led, directly or indirectly, to the mental illness which blighted the rest of his life. This is how he described it in 1980 to Angus Martin (Byrne, thesis 32–3): "I was an education sergeant and I was sent to Macedonia. And there had been the civil war in Greece, and the right-wing were on top. I was left-wing in my sentiments. In Macedonia I used to hob-nob with working-class people (I spoke Greek) and the right-wing people noticed this, and I was in a place called Kavalla, and they got a notion I was a communist, and that was death in Greece at that time — I mean, the right wing were on top. There was a terrific to-do, knives and carabines and all the rest — and that's the origin of my getting my pension . . . I wasn't shot. I missed it narrowly."

Hay was invalided out of the Army with 'nervous trouble'. It was in fact a chronic schizophrenic condition which prevented him ever taking up full-time employment again. Most of the rest of his life was spent in and out of the Royal Edinburgh Hospital, where his elder sister Sheena had been a patient since 1938 (she died at St Margaret's Nursing Home in Edinburgh on 2 December 1989). Hay was never forgotten by his friends, however, and indeed his poetry — in Gaelic, Scots and English — made him hard to forget. *Fuaran Sléibh* [FS] appeared in 1947, *Wind on Loch Fyne* in 1948, and *O na Ceithir Àirdean* [OCÀ] in 1952. The 1950s were a particularly dark time, but thereafter he wrote a great deal when he was well enough. He contributed to numerous periodicals, and the anthologies *Four Points of a Saltire* of 1970 and *Nua-Bhàrdachd Ghàidhlig* [NBG] of 1976, which includes discussion of his work, brought him firmly back to public notice. The astonishing *Mochtàr is Dùghall* appeared in 1982, then, after a brief return to Tarbert, he died in Edinburgh on 25 March 1984.

Entries on George Campbell Hay will be found in histories of (and companions to) Scottish and Gaelic literature, for which see p. 820 below. For further assessment see: William Neill, 'The Poetry of George Campbell Hay', *Scotia Review* 8 (1974) 50–6; Angus Martin, 'George Campbell Hay: Bard of Kintyre', in his *Kintyre: The Hidden Past* (Edinburgh 1984) 48–71; Derick Thomson, 'George Campbell Hay: A Tribute', *Scottish Review* 35 (1984) 42–4; Donald E Meek, 'Land and Loyalty: The Gaelic Verse of George Campbell Hay', *Chapman* 39 (1984) 2–8; John Burns, 'Generous Spirited Heart: The Poetry of George Campbell Hay', *Cencrastus* 18 (1984) 28–30; John Burns, 'George Campbell Hay', *Radical Scotland* 9 (1984) 25; Robert A Rankin, 'George Campbell Hay as I Knew Him', *Chapman* 40 (1985) 1–12; Uilleam MacGillÌosa, 'Ath-Sgrùdadh (11): Deòrsa Caimbeul Hay', *Gairm* 135 (An Samhradh 1986) 262–9 and *Gairm* 136 (Am Foghar 1986) 331–9; Iain Crichton Smith, 'George Campbell Hay: Language at Large', in his *Towards the Human* (Loanhead 1986) 108–15; Derick Thomson, 'The Passion and Involvement of George Campbell Hay', *Radical Scotland* 21 (1986) 38; and Christopher Whyte, 'George Campbell Hay: Nationalism with a Difference', in Derick Thomson (ed.), *Gaelic and Scots in Harmony* (Glasgow 1990) 116–35. *Seeker Reaper*, an illustrated edition of Hay's Scots poem of that name, was published by the Saltire Society, Edinburgh, in 1988. See also pp. xxxvi–xxxix above.

The poet's surviving papers were purchased by the National Library of Scotland. The rights to his verse were acquired by Robin Lorimer (the original publisher of *Nua-Bhàrdachd Ghàidhlig*) in 1985, and now belong to the W L Lorimer Memorial Trust, to whom I am grateful for permission to reprint the following poems. Michel Byrne's Edinburgh University PhD thesis 'Bàrdachd Mhic Iain Dheòrsa: The Original Poems of George Campbell Hay', which includes a substantial biography, was completed in 1992, and I am deeply grateful to Dr Byrne for permission to draw upon it here in advance of publication in 2000 of his two-volume edition of Hay's poems by Edinburgh University Press for the Lorimer Trust, which is eagerly awaited. I am also grateful to Dr Byrne for reading and commenting on this section of the anthology. My readings (both text and translation) are based on Byrne's thesis and on some of the earlier published editions.

140   *Siubhal a' Choire* **('The Voyaging of the *Corrie*').** Author's trl. Byrne's thesis 141 (notes), 303 (text); his sources: *FS* 12, *NBG* 118–19, manuscripts (1936–83). Composed 1936. The locations are in the Firth of Clyde.

141   *Òran don Oighre* **('A Song to the Heir').** Editor's trl. Byrne's thesis 142 (notes), 305 (text); his source: *The Voice of Scotland* I/4 (March–May 1939) 14. Composed 1936.

142   *An t-Sàbaid* **('The Sabbath').** Editor's trl. Byrne's thesis 143 (notes), 307 (text); his sources: *An Gaidheal* 43 (1947–8) 7, *OCÀ* 65. Composed Tarbert 1936? Montrose and the MacDonalds famously defeated the Campbells at Inverlochy on a Sunday, 2 February 1645.

143   *Ceithir Gaothan na h-Albann* **('The Four Winds of Scotland').** Author's trl. Byrne's thesis 159 (notes), 359 (text); his sources: *FS* 33, *NBG* 120–121, manuscript (1974). Composed *c.* 1940.

144   From *Mochtàr is Dùghall* **('Mokhtâr and Dougall').** Author's and editor's trl., see p. 708 notes 8, 16, 19, 20, 21, 24. Byrne's thesis 174–80 (notes), 400–49 (text); his sources: *The Voice of Scotland* IV/2 (Dec. 1947) 26–9, *Edinburgh Evening Dispatch* 6 December 1947, *OCÀ* 44, *Gairm* 10 (An Geamhradh 1954) 155, *Gairm* 76 (Am Foghar 1971) 330, *Mochtàr is Dùghall*, manuscripts (1944–83). The poem was composed 1944–7, in Italy, at Kavalla (Greece), and in Tarbert, but its locus is eastern Algeria, e.g. Biskra, and northern Tunisia, e.g. Kairouan (Qairwan), Souse (Susa). See p. xxxviii above.

145   *Atman.* Author's trl. Byrne's thesis 181 (notes), 450–1 (text); his sources: *Comhar* (Eanáir 1946) 3, *OCÀ* 11–13, *Four Points of a Saltire* 102–3, *NBG* 128–31, manuscripts (1945–74). Dated Nocera, Italy, 11 August 1944. Jebel Yussuf, 'Joseph's Mountain', is in Algeria, and Mondovi is a small Algerian market town; to the Moslems *Sidna Aissa*, Our Lord Jesus, was one of the prophets.

146   *Comhradh an Alldain* **('The Wee Burn's Talk').** Author's trl. Byrne's thesis 181–2 (notes), 454–7 (text); his sources: *Alba* (1948) 27–9, *OCÀ* 4–9, manuscripts (1944–83). Composed Villa Morese, Italy, 31 October 1944. The Hamîz, Harrash, Safsaf, Seybouse, Budjîma, Medjerda and Rhummel are rivers in Algeria and Tunisia; Skikda (Philippeville) and Constantine are towns in

Algeria; the Picentino, Forni, Irno and Sele are rivers south of Salerno in Italy; the Liri is a river below Cassino, between Naples and Rome; and the Alld Beithe ('Birch Burn') is south of Tarbert, Loch Fyne. "Laertes' son" is Ulysses, cf. poem 150, and "Lugh's day" is Lammas, 1 August.

147   *Bisearta* **('Bizerta').** Author's trl. Byrne's thesis 183 (notes), 463–4 (text); his sources: *Modern Scottish Poetry* (1946) 78–9, *OCÀ* 39–41, *NBG* 122–5, manuscripts (1945–83). Composed Bône (Algeria) and Italy, 1943–5. The metre is taken from a medieval Italian religious poem by Fra Girolamo Savonarola, see his *Poesi*, ed. Piccoli, 5 (Turin 1927) 53. Byrne points out (thesis 183) that Tunisia was trapped in Allied–German crossfire in the last months of the North African campaign, from November 1942 to May 1943, the last of the German resistance being based around Bizerta and Tunis. He quotes Peter Calvocoressi, *Total War* (2nd edn, London 1989) 394: "Tunisian towns and villages were bombed in a war which Tunisians could not by any stretch of the imagination regard as their own."

148   *An t-Òigear a' Bruidhinn on Ùir* **('The Young Man Speaking from the Grave').** Author's trl. Byrne's thesis 186 (notes), 475–6 (text); his sources: *An Gaidheal* 40 (1944–5) 87, *FS* 40–1, *NBG* 126–9, manuscripts (1945–74). Dated 30 March 1945.

149   *Meftah Bâbkum es-Sabar?* Author's trl. Byrne's thesis 186–7 (notes), 477–9 (text); his sources: *Scots Independent* 257 (Jan. 1948) 2, *OCÀ* 22–5, *NBG* 132–7, manuscripts (1945–83). Dated May 1945, Salerno, Italy. In the third-last section, the 'oe' in Hay's translation is Gaelic *ogha* 'grandchild', while the saying *Is fuar a' ghaoth thar Ìle / Gheibhear aca an Cinntire*, 'Cold is the wind over Islay / That blows on them in Kintyre', appears to reflect a couplet in the Annals of Tigernach, *Is uar in gáeth dar Ile / dofuil oca i Cínd tire . . .* Whitley Stokes translated it as 'Cold is the wind over Islay; / there are warriors [óca] in Kintyre . . .' ('The Annals of Tigernach: Third Fragment', *Revue Celtique* 17 (1896) 119–263); A O Anderson agreed with him (*Early Sources of Scottish History* 1 (Edinburgh 1922) 148), but Hay, it seems, did not. See Byrne's thesis 186–7.

150   *From Tilleadh Uilìseis* **('The Return of Ulysses').** Author's trl. Byrne's thesis 187 (notes), 481–2 (text); his sources: *FS* 45, manuscripts (1945–74). Dated Salerno, Italy, 23 May 1945. On Ulysses' slaughter of the suitors who have been pestering his wife Penelope during his absence upon the Odyssey. The poem is in three parts, of which the last only is printed here.

151   *Achmhasain* **('Rebukes').** Author's trl. Byrne's thesis 190 (notes), 492 (text); his sources: *Scots Independent* 236 (April 1946) 5, *Catalyst* 2/2 (Spring 1969), manuscripts (1946–74). Dated Kavalla, Greece, 3 February 1946. 'Messan' (*measan*) in st. 3 is a lapdog.

152   *Ors a' Bhéist Mhór ris a' Bhéist Bhig* **('Said the Big Beast to the Little Beast').** Editor's trl. Byrne's thesis 210 (notes), 550 (text); his source: *Scots Independent* 355, 31 December 1960. A note published with the poem, probably written by Hay himself, states that the big beast is England, and the little one Scotland.

153   *An Ciùran Ceòban Ceò* **('The Smirry Drizzle of Mist').** Author's trl. Byrne's thesis 217 (notes), 574–5 (text); his sources: *Gairm* 67 (An Samhradh 1969) 227–8, *NBG* 138–9, manuscripts (1969–75). Dated 25 February 1969. Version in Scots published as 'The Smoky Smirr o Rain' in Tom Scott (ed.), *Four Points of a Saltire* (Edinburgh 1970) 77. Seems to have emerged from the line *Tha ceathach, ceò is ceòban* ('The smirr, the mist and the soft rain') in poem 146. *Am Paiste Beag*, the Wee Patch (st. 4), is a field on the long-deserted farm of Lagan Ròaig, which lies on the shore halfway between Tarbert and Skipness (Byrne's thesis 217). It is not given, however, in a list of fishermen's place-names on that stretch of coast in Angus Martin, *The Ring-Net Fishermen* (Edinburgh 1981) 244–7. See p. xxxvi above.

154   *Uladh* **('Ulster').** Author's trl. Byrne's thesis 230 (notes), 618 (text); his sources: *Scots Independent* 68 (Nov. 1976) 8, manuscript. The quote is in Irish, see T O'Rahilly, *Búrdúin Bheaga* (Dublin 1925) 24.

155   *Suas gun Sìos* **('Up with no Down').** Author's trl. Byrne's thesis 229 (notes), 619 (text); his sources: *Scots Independent* 68 (Nov. 1976) 8 (headed 'The Ballot not the Bullet — A Victory with no Defeated'), manuscript.

156   *Ionndrainn na Sìne* **('Longing for the Tempest').** Author's trl. Byrne's thesis 230 (notes), 620 (text); his sources: *Scotia Review* 17 (Summer 1977) 51–2, manuscripts (1976–7). Composed 1976.

157   *Guidhe an Iasgair* **('The Fisherman's Prayer').** Editor's trl. Byrne's thesis 231 (notes), 622 (text); his sources: *Gairm* 101 (An Geamhradh 1977–8) 29, manuscripts (1976–7). Composed 1976.

158   *Bloigh Lebensraum* **('A Spot of Lebensraum').** Author's trl. Byrne's thesis 232 (notes), 624 (text); his source: manuscript (1977). *Lebensraum* was the principle of 'living space' used by Hitler to justify German expansionism.

159   *Na Ràtaichean 's a' Bhàrdachd* **('The Rates and Poetry').** Author's trl. (stanzas 1–4, 7); editor's trl. (stanzas 5–6). Byrne's thesis 232–3 (notes), 627–8 (text); his sources: *Gairm* 105 (An

Geamhradh 1978–9) 31–2, manuscripts (1978). We may picture the poet here in his 'local', Bennett's Bar opposite his flat at 6 Maxwell St., Morningside, Edinburgh. 'Rates' was the popular term for the tax levied by local government. Mrs Thatcher replaced it in 1989 with a still less popular Poll Tax or 'Community Charge' which led to civil unrest. This gave way in due course to 'Council Tax'. 'V.A.T.' is Value Added Tax, levied throughout the 'E.E.C.' — the European Economic Community, now the European Union. Among other topical causes of complaint are the replacement of pints and gallons with litres and of miles with kilometres; the prevalence of Pakistani shopkeepers; and the Ugandan dictator Idi Amin. While Leonid Brezhnev (1906–82) certainly remained Soviet leader in 1978, the grouse about the Bolshevik revolutionary Leon Trotsky (1879–1940) is a little out of date. But then, that is the nature of the poem's humour.

160   *Dùrachdan Nollaige* ('Christmas Greetings'). Editor's trl. Byrne's thesis 250 (notes), 690 (text). From a Christmas card, ?1982.

161   *Dùrd a' Ghlinne* ('The Hum of the Glen'). Editor's trl. Byrne's thesis 250 (notes), 690 (text); his sources: *Gairm* 126 (An t-Earrach 1984) 166, manuscript (1983).

Ian Paterson (Iain Peatarson) 1916–90

Ian Paterson was born at Ruisgarry, Berneray, Harris, 16 January 1916, son of Finlay Paterson, shopkeeper and ferryman, from Berneray (*Fionnlagh Aonghais 'ic Iain 'ic Shomhairle*, 1876–1953), and his wife Christina MacCuish, also from Berneray (*Cairstìona Iain 'ic Fhionnlaigh*, 1884–1968). There were six in the family: Christina, John Angus, Bessie, Ian, Catriona and Ruairidh. The first Paterson is believed to have come to Berneray as a butler or tutor in the retinue of the celebrated Sir Norman MacLeod, who died in 1705.

Ian was educated at Berneray Primary School, Inverness Royal Academy, Glasgow University and Jordanhill College. He served in the Royal Navy from 1940 to 1946. He took part in Atlantic convoys and the landings at Salerno and Anzio, but his closest brush with death came on 10 December 1941, three days after Pearl Harbor, when his ship, the *Prince of Wales*, was attacked off Malaya by Japanese aircraft. When the battleship went down Ian spent some time in the water but was rescued by an escort vessel; he was thus luckier than those of his comrades who drowned or were picked up by the Japanese, but it was an experience of which he seldom spoke.

From 1947 to 1966 he taught in Fife, eventually becoming head-teacher of Coaltown of Balgonie Primary School. Being very likeable but shy in nature, it was with some relief that in 1966 he accepted a post as transcriber of Gaelic tapes for the Sound Archive of Edinburgh University's School of Scottish Studies. He retired as a Lecturer in 1983 and died, unmarried, on 29 January 1990. He is buried in Berneray Old Cemetery. He was not a singer, and his poems, though strongly rooted in the community life of Berneray, were a private hobby of his own, shared only with the readers of *Gairm*, in which they appeared regularly from 1953 to 1961.

I am grateful to the poet's sister Miss Christina Paterson, Edinburgh, for information, the loan of the poet's manuscript book of poems 'Leabhar nam Prannag' [LP], help with translations, and permission to print:

162   *Turas an Ànraidh* ('Stormy Voyage'). Editor's trl. *Gairm* 30 (An Geamhradh 1959) 137–40; LP 28–32. The journey took place in August 1957. Nowadays the first leg is done by car, a causeway from Berneray to North Uist having been completed in spring 1999.

163   *Uisge Phìob* ('Piped Water'). Editor's trl. LP 55, dated August 1961.

164   *Bogsa Diùc* ('Juke Box'). Editor's trl. LP 55, dated '1957 or 1958'.

165   *Bó Dhearg* ('Red Cow'). Editor's trl. LP 56, dated '1956(?)'.

166   *Cearcall Hùla* ('Hula Hoop'). Editor's trl. LP 73, dated '1955(?)'. The hula-hoop craze pre-dated mini-skirts by ten years. The skimpy dresses referred to are the knee-length fashions of the post-war era, as compared for example to the traditional drugget skirts of the island women, which reached to the ground, or at least to their boots.

Rev. Colin N Mackenzie (An t-Urr. Cailein T MacCoinnich) 1917–94

Colin Norman Mackenzie was born 27 August 1917 in Glasgow to Colin John Mackenzie and Rachel Brindle. He had one brother, Angus. He was brought up in his mother's home in the island of Taransay, Harris, attending school in the island from 1922 to 1931. His mother's people were steeped in Gaelic tradition — songs, stories, creative talent — and much of this was true of the island community as a whole. "Poetry, sung or recited," he recalled (in notes headed 'The Writer's Art', for a copy of which I am grateful to his widow), "was popular, revered in the community." So he began writing poetry at age 12–14: it was in his blood — a fact of which, he says, he was constantly reminded.

He completed his formal education at Kingussie Secondary School (1934–8) and the University of St Andrews (Arts and Divinity, 1938–44) and went on to do supply work in the islands until 1947 — 'informative years', as he called them — but his literary awakening came in 1947 when he succeeded another poet, Malcolm Laing from N. Uist, as minister of Howmore in S. Uist. He suddenly found himself at the interface between individuals in his parish who possessed a rich store of tradition, vocabulary and idiom: men and women like Duncan Macdonald and his son Donald John (q.v.), Donald Macintyre (q.v.), Angus MacMillan (*Aonghas Barrach*), for whom see Calum I MacGillEathain, 'Aonghus agus Donnchadh', *Gairm* 10 (An Geamhradh 1954) 170–4, and Màireag, for whom see Kirkland C Craig's *Òrain Luaidh Màiri Nighean Alasdair* (1949) — and those who were now coming in search of these 'treasures of our race', as he called them, such as the Rev. William Matheson, Calum Maclean, K C Craig, the Rev. Donald MacKenzie, and his old fellow-student Dr Alex MacLean.

In 1952 he won the Bardic Crown at the National Mod in Rothesay (see p. 822 below), and in the same year he married Christina (Chrissie) Monk from Benbecula. Their family consisted of five children, Catherine, Nan, Alexander Angus, Colin Iain and Lilian. He subsequently served as minister of Kilwinning Erskine (latterly linked with Fergushill) 1955–75, Kirkhill 1975–82, and Carinish, N. Uist, 1982–5, followed by six years of locum work before he finally retired.

In 1956 he won a prize of ten guineas offered by *Gairm* for a short story, and prose became his favourite medium. He is best known for highly atmospheric mystery stories employing strong shafts of humour and a prose rich in traditional vocabulary and idiom; similar qualities are to be found in his verse. The prose appeared in *Oirthir Tìm* 1969, *Mar Sgeul a dh'innseas Neach* 1970, *An Leth Eile* (a novel underrated by critics) 1971, and *Nach Neònach Sin* 1973; the verse remains in *Gairm*. He was constantly writing, and produced several books in the years after 1973, some of which received Gaelic Books Council awards, but none of which were published. They include a novel 'An t-Olc Eòlach', a biography 'Tasdan an Rìgh', a children's adventure story 'Uamh an Òir', and 'Nì E Chùis', described in his notes as 'a survey of complacency in the Hebrides'. For a critical assessment of his work see Dòmhnall E Meek, 'Ath-Sgrùdadh (5): Cailein T. MacCoinnich', *Gairm* 123 (An Samhradh 1983) 237–47.

The poet died in Daliburgh, S. Uist, on 30 January 1994. I am grateful to his widow for information and permission to reprint:

167 *An Seanchaidh* ('The Shennachie'). Editor's trl. *Gairm* 52 (Am Foghar 1965) 309–11. On the Stone of Scone (st. 3) see poems 59, 60, 220. On the outlaw *Mac an t-Srònaich* or Stronach (st. 4), a native of Garve in Ross-shire who was a fugitive in Lewis 1831–8, see Alex. Urquhart, 'Mac an t-Srònaich', *Transactions of the Gaelic Society of Inverness* [*TGSI*] 38 (1937–41) 46–62, and Donald Macdonald, *Lewis: A History of the Island* (Edinburgh 1978) 136. The Milesians of Spain (st. 6) were the legendary ancestors of the Gael, cf. notes to poem 59. 'Guga' in st. 7 is the young of the solan goose, see John Beatty, *Sula: The Seabird-Hunters of Lewis* (London 1992). The book referred to in st. 8 is Alasdair Alpin MacGregor, *The Western Isles* (London 1949), in which the people of the Western Isles were slandered; a vigorous defence was mounted in the newspapers by Dr J L Campbell of Canna and others, and Donald Macintyre (q.v.) joined in with a magnificent satire, 'Òran do dh'Alasdair Suarach' (*Sporan Dhòmhnaill* 175–84). For Cù Chulainn and Sgàthach (st. 10) cf. poem 264.

On the abduction of Balranald's daughter (st. 13) see Donald Archie MacDonald, 'The Balranald Elopement in Fact and Fiction', *TGSI* 56 (1988–90) 52–112, and 'Songs of the Balranald Elopement', *TGSI* 57 (1990–2) 1–57. Mary MacLeod in st. 14 is the poet Màiri nighean Alastair Ruaidh (*c*.1615–*c*.1707); she is said to be buried in the south transept of St Clement's church, Rodel, see J C Watson (ed.), *Gaelic Songs of Mary MacLeod* (Edinburgh 1934, repr. 1965) xix. The Magnus of st. 15 is the hero of an Ossianic lay and prose tale, see for example J F Campbell (ed.), *Popular Tales of the West Highlands* 3 (2nd edn Paisley 1892, repr. Hounslow 1984) 363–95. In st. 17 what the poet probably has in mind is how the arguments of the Scottish theologian Duns Scotus (1265?–1308?) were of such excessive subtlety that his name, in the form 'dunce', came to mean a blockhead.

The place-names in the poem are mainly in Lewis (Breanish, Tong, Crowlista) and Harris (Berneray, Rodel). Among bynames cited for the Devil are *am Buaireadair* 'the Tempter' and *an t-Àbharsair* 'the Adversary', cf. poems 91, 95.

I discussed this poem in 'The Eclectic Tradition-Bearer', *West Highland Free Press*, 31 May 1996. Perhaps my conclusion bears repeating: "The poem is a satire and a brilliant bit of fun, and no doubt some of this shennachie's *seanchas* came out of schoolbooks in the first place, but I believe it is one of many building-blocks that can help us build up a full picture of the traditional ceilidh-house. Dòmhnall Ruadh's poem [57] is another, and Carmichael's introduction to *Carmina Gadelica* is another. The point is that here was a general education. Among the subjects our poem mentions, we have already met biblical studies, tides, Scottish history, medicine, Lewis history, classical mythology, Celtic mythology and poultry. It also ranges through the history of the Papacy, gastronomy, contemporary issues, nonconformism, natural history, horology, Egyptology, 20th-century Europe and the supernatural. And we encounter the *Marie Celeste*, Duns Scotus and Montezuma."

Rev. John MacLeod (An t-Urr. Iain MacLeòid) 1918–95

John MacLeod was born 14 January 1918 in Arnol, Lewis, second son of Norman Macleod (*Tormod Choinnich*, 1883–1919) and his wife Christina, also a Macleod (*Carstiona a' Cheannaiche*, 1884–1933). His elder brother, Norman, was born 14 January 1915. Their father was one of the returning servicemen who died in the *Iolaire* tragedy, see p. xxii and poem 168. Their mother died in Arnol aged 49 in 1933, and an aunt, Mrs Hull, returned from Canada to Arnol to take care of the boys for a year.

Norman emigrated to Canada and spent his life there, while John remained in Lewis to complete his secondary education in the Nicolson Institute. He matriculated at Glasgow University in 1937, spent the years 1940–3 as a Navy telegraphist on HMS *Ganges* and HMS *Eglinton*, and graduated MA in 1943, subsequently serving for two years as assistant minister of St Columba's, Copland Road, Glasgow, before being licensed to preach by the Presbytery of Glasgow in 1945. He was ordained as a chaplain in the Royal Navy in May of the same year, and served the Presbyterian Church of Canada in Ontario and Alberta from 1947 to 1960 while obtaining the additional degrees of BD (Montreal) and BEd (Calgary).

In 1948, in Canada, he married Dolena MacKenzie from Stornoway (*Doileag Dhòmhnaill Ùistein*, 1918—). They had two daughters, Christeen (1949–65) and Kathreen (1956—). They returned to Scotland in 1960, the poet being inducted to St Paul's, Newington, Edinburgh, in 1961, and subsequently to Kilmore and Kilbride Oban Old Church in 1967, from which he retired in 1983, although he continued to conduct the monthly Gaelic service.

His poems and articles appeared regularly in *Gairm*, in the Gaelic Supplement of *Life and Work*, and in the *Eilean an Fhraoich* annual, and for many years he was Gaelic columnist of *The Oban Times*. He was a writer and translator of Gaelic hymns, a number of which were published in *Seinnibh dhan Tighearna* (1986). He died in Oban on 7 December 1995, and is survived by his widow and his daughter Kathreen, who now lives in Campbeltown.

I am grateful to Mrs Dolena MacLeod, Oban, for information and permission to reprint:

168　*Bantrach Cogaidh* ('War Widow'). Editor's trl. Tormod Calum Dòmhnallach, *Call na h-Iolaire* (Stornoway 1978) 70–1. HMY *Iolaire* sank at the entrance to Stornoway harbour on New Year's morning 1919; 205 lives were lost, 79 were saved. (My thanks to Mrs Dolena MacLeod and Mr Dan Morrison for these figures.)

169　*Bàs Baile* ('The Death of a Township'). Editor's trl. *Gairm* 91 (An Samhradh 1975) 276–8. In the 1920s Lewis was suffering mass unemployment. In April 1923 the *Metagama* sailed to Canada with 300 emigrants. In April 1924 the *Marloch* took 290, and a few weeks later the *Canada* took 270. Most of these were young people who had never been out of the island before. See Jim Wilkie, *Metagama: A Journey from Lewis to the New World* (Edinburgh 1987).

170　*Aideachadh* ('Confession'). Editor's trl. *Gairm* 97 (An Geamhradh 1976–7) 81.

Donald John MacDonald (Dòmhnall Iain MacDhòmhnaill) 1919–86

Donald John MacDonald was born 7 February 1919 in Peninerine, S. Uist, third child of Duncan Macdonald, crofter and stonemason, from Snishival (*Donnchadh mac Dhòmhnaill 'ic*

Dhonnchaidh, 1882–1954), and his wife Margaret Macintyre, also from Snishival (*Mairead nighean Aonghais Ruaidh 'ic Nill 'ic Dhòmhnaill 'ic Dhòmhnaill 'ic Iain*, 1880–1952). His parents' marriage had taken place in 1913; their other children were Dòmhnall Eòin, Catherine (Ceit) and Ann (Anna).

The poet's cultural background and pedigree were second to none. His father was possibly the outstanding storyteller of his generation in Western Europe — William Matheson (for whom see poem 211) said of him (*SE* xii), *Cha do thachair duine eile rium-sa a riamh a bha cho fiosrach ris anns gach nì a bhuineas do dhualchas nan Gàidheal, agus sin uile o bheul-aithris.* "I have never met anyone else who knew as much as he did about everything to do with Gaelic tradition, and all of it from oral sources." He was of MacDonalds who appear to have been in fact MacRyries, a family which had served the MacDonalds of Sleat as hereditary poets and historians (*SE* ix–x, 148–9). The poet's uncle Neil, a shy man who lived with them and worked at home as a joiner, was an even greater influence, and, as pointed out by Bill Innes in *Chì Mi* viii, his knowledge of Gaelic tradition may have been even richer than his brother's. Duncan's (and Neil's) aunt Mearag or Màireag (Mary MacCuish, *Màiri nighean Alastair 'ic Dhòmhnaill 'ic Dhòmhnaill 'ic Iain*) had a rich store of waulking-songs, some of which were published by K C Craig as *Òrain Luaidh Màiri Nighean Alasdair* in 1949. The poet's mother came of a family notable for historical tales, songs and music, and was an elder sister of Donald Macintyre, q.v. It is no surprise, therefore, that Donald John was making rhymes and songs from an early age.

When he left school at age 14 he started work with his father on their croft at Peninerine. In 1937 he joined the Territorial Army (4th Battalion Cameron Highlanders), and his first ever trip to the mainland was to their camp at Nairn in the summer of that year. The summers of 1938 and 1939 were spent at their camp at Barry in Angus. As a Territorial, Donald John was called up immediately upon the outbreak of war in 1939, and after training at Inverness and Aldershot was sent to France in January 1940. He tells this part of the story in 'A' Srùdhan', *Gairm* 128 (Am Foghar 1984) 301–4. He was taken prisoner on the surrender of the 51st (Highland) Division at St Valéry, 12 June 1940, and brought to Germany. He spent four-and-a-half-years doing forced labour in various prison camps, working mostly in quarries and salt-mines; he recalls these experiences in harrowing detail in *Fo Sgàil a' Swastika* (Inverness 1974), of which a new bilingual edition by Bill Innes is to be published shortly by Acair of Stornoway.

Demobbed in 1946, he returned to work four crofts in Peninerine and Snishival, a total of 80 acres. He later gave away the most inaccessible one to a Stoneybridge man who could reach it more easily. In 1948 he won the Bardic Crown at the National Mod in Glasgow with 'Moladh Uibhist', one of a number of poems and songs which he had composed in Germany (see pp. 821–2 below). His courtship of Mary M Maclean (q.v.) began around this time; they were engaged in 1949. At this time he also became an active folklore collector, and the eminent folklorist Calum Maclean (a brother of Sorley, q.v.) wrote of him in 1954, *Gun aon teagamh, 's e Dòmhnall Iain . . . am fear is fheàrr air cruinneachadh beul-aithris a thàinig 'nar measg an Albainn san linn so.* "Without any doubt, Donald John . . . is the best folklore collector that has come amongst us in Scotland in this century." Calum had advised him to tape and transcribe everything his father had — a tall order — and the result was that in the last short year of his father's life he managed to transcribe over 1,500 pages of his stories (Calum I MacGillEathain, 'Aonghus agus Donnchadh', *Gairm* 10 (An Geamhradh 1954) 170–4).

Mary Maclean having broken off their engagement, in 1954 Donald John married his neighbour Neilina MacNeil. Neilina's father, *Ruairidh Flòraidh*, was from Earsary in Barra, but she was known locally as *Nellie Alastair Thàilleir*, having been brought up by her grandparents in Stoneybridge after her mother died in childbirth. Their only child, Margaret, was born in 1955. Forty-six of his poems were published as *Sguaban Eòrna* [SE] in 1973, and his brief account of the history and folklore of his native island appeared under the title *Uibhist a Deas* in 1981. Latterly his health was poor, broken by a life of physical toil both at home and as a PoW. He died in Glasgow on 2 October 1986.

A full edition of Donald John MacDonald's verse, with parallel English translation, was published by Birlinn of Edinburgh in 1998 as *Chì Mi / I See: Bàrdachd Dhòmhnaill Iain Dhonnchaidh / The Poetry of Donald John MacDonald*, edited by Bill Innes. It contains 108 poems, including 14 hymns and a Gaelic translation of Gray's 'Elegy' — a task also attempted by Duncan Livingstone, q.v.

The work of Donald John MacDonald represents a powerful combination of deep traditional knowledge and modern Gaelic literacy. A cairn in his memory and that of his uncle Donald Macintyre was erected at Snishival in 1996, see *Chì Mi* [ii], xii and [xxxiv]. I am grateful to Capt. Bill Innes for information and help with translations (which were prepared before *Chì Mi* appeared), to Mrs Margaret Campbell, Peninerine, for information, and to Mrs Nellie MacDonald, Peninerine, for permission to reprint:

171 *Òran an Fheamnaidh* ('The Song of the Seaweed-Cutting'). Editor's trl. *SE* 105–6, *Chì Mi* 82–5. Sung to the tune 'O nach àghmhor a-nis bhith fàgail'. The *Cròic* is the bay next to Peninerine, a favourite place for collecting seaweed. *Cròic* is itself a word denoting seaweed-covered rocks and anything of comparable shape, e.g. a deer's antlers. The phrase *Fo chealg nan iùdhach* in the 6th stanza means literally 'Under the deceit of the jews'; the lower-case *i* is the poet's own. Innes translates the line as 'Defrauded by the misers who grasp her helm'. For *Bhrusaich* in the 8th stanza the poet's manuscript reads *Bhrusail*, perhaps in error. For the use of seaweed as fertiliser (and to supply the alginates industry) see also poems 18, 113, 289.

172 *An Guth á Broinn na Màthar* ('The Voice from the Mother's Womb'). Editor's trl. Cf. *Stornoway Gazette*, 29 December 1973, and *Chì Mi* 224–7, 367–8. My thanks to Ferdia McDermott for passing on to me this copy of the song, obtained in South Uist, where it was circulating in manuscript. It corresponds quite closely to the *Gazette* version except for some re-ordering of stanzas. It differs in certain respects from the version printed by Innes from the poet's final draft: in particular, the poet omitted stanzas 6 and 7, which in my opinion are integral to the poem and fully worthy of it. The last stanza refers to the Abortion Act of 1967, which resulted from a Private Member's Bill introduced by David Steel MP, who in 1999 became the first Presiding Officer of the new Scottish Parliament.

173 *Taigh a' Bhàird* ('The Poet's House'). Editor's trl. *Crann* 3 (Comunn Ceilteach Oil Thigh Obair Dheadhain, 1977) 9–10; Fr John Angus Macdonald, 'The Songs of Donald Allan MacDonald' (MLitt thesis, Aberdeen 1983) 542–3; *Chì Mi* 260–3. The house is that of John Campbell, q.v. The 3rd stanza refers to the practice of taking a peat from the fire to light one's way home at night.

174 *Do Mhaighstir Niall* ('To Father Neil'). Editor's trl. *Gairm* 127 (An Samhradh 1984) 265, *Chì Mi* 314–15. Elegy on Monsignor Neil Mackellaig, who died in 1982 after 48 years in the priesthood, most of them in Bornish and Daliburgh, S. Uist. See poem 96.

175 *Geata Tir nan Òg* ('The Gate of the Land of the Young'). Editor's trl. *Gairm* 137 (An Geamhradh 1986–7) 45–6; *Chì Mi* 330–3. See p. lvii above.

Donald R Morrison (Dòmhnall R MacGilleMhoire) 1919—

Donald R Morrison was born 5 November 1919 in Scalpay, Harris, son of Donald Morrison, shopkeeper, from the Rubha Glas in Scalpay (*Dòmhnall mac Ruairidh Iain 'ic Alastair*, 1894–1952), and his wife Kirsty, also a Morrison from Scalpay (*Ciorstaidh nighean Fhionnlaigh Ailein*, 1882–1972). He went to England to join the Navy but was rejected on grounds of poor eyesight, and was in the RAF during the end of the Second World War. He spent some time herring-fishing in his father's boat. He became assistant to his father in the general store in Scalpay and continued running the shop after his father's death. He never married.

Songs started coming to Donald Morrison when in school, but he did not start writing them down until afterwards. He decided to start sending them away on the grounds that if he kept them all at home they might be put in the fire, and his poems have therefore appeared in a great variety of anthologies, newspapers and magazines such as *An t-Eilean a Tuath* (ed. Dòmhnall Iain MacLeòid), *The Stornoway Gazette*, *Sruth*, *Crann*, *Gairm*, *Dé Tha Dol?*, *An Gaidheal*, the *Monthly Record* of the Free Church, and *The West Highland Free Press*, in addition to being deposited in the archives of the National Library of Scotland, the Mitchell Library, Stornoway Town Library, An Comunn Gaidhealach (Inverness), the Lewis and Harris Association, and the BBC in Glasgow. His poem about a fishing-boat called the *Màiri Òg* won him the Bardic Crown at the Inverness Mod in 1957 (see p. 822 below).

For many years the poet has been a prolific contributor to *Gairm* of anecdotes and photographs, and an overall assessment of his work is long overdue. I am grateful to him for information and permission to reprint:

176 From *Fàilte don Phrionnsa Teàrlach 's a' Bhana-Phrionnsa Diàna a dh'Eilean Sgalpaigh na Hearadh, 2.7.85* ('Prince Charles' and Princess Diana's Welcome to the Isle of Scalpay, Harris, 2.7.85'). Editor's trl. *Gairm* 132 (Am Foghar 1985) 360. Prince Charles, the heir to the throne, married Diana Spencer (b. 1 July 1961) on 29 July 1981. They were divorced in August 1996. Diana was killed in a car crash in Paris with her friend 'Dodi' al-Fayed on 31 August 1997, and her death caused an extraordinary outburst of public grief. The poem consists of 22 three-line stanzas, each with end-rhyme on *à*, originally arranged in pairs in the manner of poem 5 (for metre see poem 64). Only the last 7 stanzas are reprinted here, as they sum up the poem well.

Rev. Roderick Macdonald (An t-Urr. Ruairidh MacDhòmhnaill) 1920–98

Roderick Macdonald was born 14 June 1920 in Locheport, N. Uist, eldest child of Donald John Macdonald (*Dòmhnall Iain Aonghais 'ic Ruairidh, 1890–1979*) from Berneray, Harris, and his wife Mary, also a Macdonald (*Màiri nighean Eachainn 'ic Ruairidh, 1884–1977*) from Locheport, their other children being Hector (1922–94) and Angus (1925—). As the poet's father (formerly a merchant seaman, see poem 180) had become a Church of Scotland missionary, subject to quinquennial transfers, the family attended various primary schools in N. Uist (Loch Portain, Locheport and Grimsay).

The poet got his secondary schooling at Bayhead (Paible) and the Nicolson Institute, Stornoway. He graduated MA at Glasgow University in 1941, staying on to gain a Diploma with Distinction in the Faculty of Divinity in 1944. After being licensed to preach in Glasgow Cathedral, he served with Church of Scotland Canteens in the 15th (Scottish) Division in France and Germany. In 1945 he was locum in Dunvegan for four months, then from 1946 to 1967 he was minister of St Columba's, Stornoway. For these twenty years he preached weekly in Gaelic and English in Stornoway and throughout the Western Isles; he also served as Clerk to the Presbytery, as a JP, as chairman of Lewis District Education Committee, and as Territorial Army chaplain, gaining TD and bar. In 1954 he spent a sabbatical year as chaplain at St Andrew's, Karachi, Pakistan.

In 1946 the poet married Margaret Whyte Currie from Glasgow, and they had four children, Iain, Deirdre, Lewis and Lindsay. From 1967 to 1983 he was minister of Insch in Aberdeenshire, and he continued to serve as clerk to the presbyteries of Garioch and Gordon for a few years after his retirement. He died at Insch on 10 June 1998. Less than a year later his son Lewis was elected Labour member for Aberdeen Central in the Scottish Parliament.

Throughout his life from 1946 Roderick Macdonald wrote, published and translated in Gaelic. In 1978, in addition to taking part in a tour of Ireland by Scottish poets and musicians (for which see p. xliii above), he became the last of the crowned bards of An Comunn Gaidhealach at the National Mod in Golspie (p. 822 below). From 1983 to 1996, as 'Ruairidh Eile', he wrote the lively and popular 'Litir Ruairidh' which appeared weekly in *The Stornoway Gazette*, a worthy successor to Tom Murchison's 'Còmhradh Cagailte' of 1955–83. His publications include *Leth-Cheud Bliadhna* (1978), *Laoidhean Molaidh* (1983), *Ceud Òran le Raibeart Burns* (1990), *Seinn an Duan Seo* (1990), *Traoghadh is Lìonadh* (1991), *Bàrdachd Raibeirt Burns* (1992) and *Trilingual Poetry* (1995). His work also appeared in numerous journals, and he lectured widely on Gaelic poetry, particularly on 'Burns and Gaelic'. In 1992 he established the Burns-Gaelic Trust, the aim of which is to foster closer links between the Gaelic and Scots cultures. Not only did he translate the whole of Robert Burns's poetry into Gaelic, he turned it into fluent Gaelic verse that retained the rhythms of the original — a remarkable achievement. Among reviews of his work are those in *Gairm* 106 (An t-Earrach 1979) 177–9 and *Gairm* 161 (An Geamhradh 1992–3) 92–3.

I am grateful to the poet and his widow for information and permission to reprint:

177 From *Turas don Ghealaich* ('Journey to the Moon'). Editor's trl. *Gairm* 76 (Am Foghar 1971) 320; *Leth-Cheud Bliadhna* 11–15. These are the first five of 20 stanzas, the others consisting mainly of reflections on the question, *Càit eil Dia?* "Where is God?"

The moon landing took place on 20 July 1969. The poem puts what is known in journalism as a 'Gaelic spin' on the event, and would be memorable even if only for its illustrations of how people grope for idioms adequate to express technological change — *leughadh an telebhisean*, for example, 'reading the television'. To frighten a child that was misbehaving people used to say things like: *Cuiridh mi Hirt air muin mairt thu!* "I'll send you to St Kilda on a cow's back!" See W J Watson, *History of the Celtic Place-Names of Scotland* (Edinburgh 1926) 99.

178   *Taibhs* ('Ghost'). Editor's trl. *Gairm* 116 (Am Foghar 1981) 321; *Traoghadh is Lionadh* 49. An *Dotair Mór*, 'the Big Doctor', was the nickname of Dr Alexander John MacLeod, who served as GP in N. Uist from 1932 to 1974.

179   *Meirg* ('Rust'). Editor's trl. *Gairm* 158 (An t-Earrach 1992) 124; *Trilingual Poetry* 18–19.

180   *Seotal* ('Shottle'). Author's trl. *Leth-Cheud Bliadhna* 10; *Trilingual Poetry* 16–17.

Mary M Maclean (Màiri M NicGhillEathain) 1921—

Mary Margaret Maclean was born 3 June 1921 at Knockqueen, N. Uist, daughter of Catherine Cameron, Knockqueen, and William Maclean, grocer, Carinish. The family moved to Grimsay in July 1935. She attended Glaic Primary School, Claddach Carinish, then undertook further education by various correspondence courses, including one with the Writing School, Clun, Shropshire.

On the outbreak of War in 1939 she joined the Auxiliary Territorial Service. She trained in Edinburgh and served in a clerical capacity in Thurso, Wick, Orkney and Inverness. After the War she was employed as a secretary in Oban, first with Cefoil (a seaweed processing company), then with the Admiralty Repair Base. In 1950 she came home to Grimsay to care for her elderly grandmother; she stayed with her until her death in 1963, and continues to live in Grimsay.

In 1947 she published *Sunbeams and Starlight*, a booklet of poems in English and Gaelic. She went on to win the Bardic Crown at the National Mod in Edinburgh in 1951 with 'Do Bheinn Eubhal' (see p. 822 below). It was the first time an attractive young woman had won the prize, and she found herself 'the darling of an excited Press' (Frank Thompson, *The National Mod* (Stornoway 1979) 20). In the same year the then Scottish Committee of the Arts Council of Great Britain had offered a number of prizes for Gaelic poetry in connection with the Festival of Britain. "Many of the Crowned Bards were invited to contribute an entry," she recalls (personal communication, August 1997). 'Am Fear-Ciùil' won her the then very substantial sum of £15 for second place equal in the competition for a poem in the *òran mór* tradition, the first prize of £30 being won by Donald Grant, q.v. At the end of that triumphant year she was appointed Bard to the Clan MacLean Association, while on occasional trips to Glasgow she made recordings for the BBC programme 'Sgeul na h-Aon Oidhche'.

During this time she was courted by Donald John MacDonald (q.v.) from Peninerine in South Uist, who made many arduous journeys across the sea-ford that still separated Benbecula from North Uist to visit her. They were engaged in 1949 (*VB* 54). In July 1951 when she brought her grandmother to Glasgow for a stay of five or six weeks in hospital, he wrote to her twice a week. According to Bill Innes (*Chì Mi* x–xi) they became engaged *after* she won the Bardic Crown, but she broke off the engagement 'after five years' and never married. MacDonald married in 1954. Three fine songs full of traditional imagery and one intensely personal poem which he made to her have now been published: 'An Rìbhinn Uasal', 'Do Mhàiri NicIllEathain', 'Mo Chridhe fo Leòn', and 'Thusa' (*Chì Mi* 108–17, 122–5).

Mar chaineal ùr no cìr-mheala fhlùran	Like fresh cinnamon or honeycomb of flowers
Tha t' anail chùbhraidh, a rùin nam mnà.	Is your fragrant breath, O darling of women.

Mary Maclean's collection of short stories *Lus-Chrùn á Griomsaidh* appeared in 1970 and her novel *Gainmheach an Fhàsaich* in 1971. Her poems, short stories and articles have appeared in *An Gaidheal, The Clarion of Skye, Gairm, The Stornoway Gazette, The Scotsman, The Free Church Monthly Record* and *Am Pàipear* (Uist). For an illustrated account of her life, along with versions of three of her poems, see Timothy Neat's *Voice of the Bard* [*VB*] 34–63. I am grateful to her for information and permission to reprint:

181   *Do Bheinn Eubhal* ('To Ben Eaval'). Editor's trl. *Am Pàipear*, September 1998. For metre see poem 64. This is a shorter and substantially different version of the poem of the same name which won the Bardic Crown in 1951 and was published in Mackinnon's *Bàird a' Chomuinn* 1–4

and (in part) in *VB* 56–9. Eaval (347 m.) is the highest hill in N. Uist, cf. poems 50, 290. "It's a mountain whose presence is always with me," says the poet (*VB* 55), after telling a story of how as a little girl she once sheltered behind a rock there in a storm. With its anthropomorphic touches like the adjective *càireanach* ('displaying toothless gums', line 6), the poem captures to an extraordinary degree the flavour of a little girl's view of an old man such as her grandfather. The tendency to personify a beloved mountain is a longstanding one in Gaelic verse and may represent something very ancient. The *fàbhar* of st. 8 is a favour in the sense of a knot of ribbons or flowers worn in the hair, often given by a sweetheart in token of love, cf. the traditional couplet

Is math thig boineid le fàbhar   Well does bonnet with favour
Air fear àrd a' chùil chlannaich.   Suit the tall man with wavy hair.

182   *Glòir no Dòrainn?* **('Glory or Agony?').** Editor's trl. *The Stornoway Gazette*, 8 March 1969. For metre see poem 64. A vision of the Day of Judgement. A shorter English version of this poem appears in *VB* 47–8, along with the poet's explanation that it attempts to express the emotions she felt in 1954 when she broke off her engagement to Donald John MacDonald and entered the Free Church.

Prof. Derick Thomson (Ruaraidh MacThòmais) 1921—

Derick Smith Thomson was born 5 August 1921 in Stornoway, a son of the poet James Thomson, q.v. Educated in Bayble, Stornoway, Aberdeen, Cambridge and Bangor (N. Wales), he served with the RAF 1942–5 before resuming his studies. He went on to become Assistant Lecturer in Celtic (Edinburgh 1948–9), Lecturer in Welsh (Glasgow 1949–56), Reader in Celtic (Aberdeen 1956–63), and Professor of Celtic (Glasgow 1963–91), presiding with great authority over two successive university departments during a remarkable 35-year period of development and change.

As poet, academic and father of modern Gaelic publishing, it was widely recognised during the 1960s and 1970s that Derick Thomson had (in George Campbell Hay's words) 'done more for Scottish Gaelic than any other man living' (Daiches, *Companion to Scottish Culture* 376). He co-founded the quarterly *Gairm* in 1952 and has been sole editor of it (and head of Gairm Publications) since 1964. Imprints for which he has been responsible — Gairm Publications, the Celtic Departments of Aberdeen and Glasgow, and, from 1979, his own Clò Chailleann — have published about 150 titles. He inaugurated the Historical Dictionary of Scottish Gaelic in 1966 and founded the Gaelic Books Council in 1968. He edited *Scottish Gaelic Studies* from 1962 to 1976, and was for many years president of the Scottish Gaelic Texts Society. His long list of academic and educational writings begins with the definitive *Gaelic Sources of Macpherson's Ossian* (1952) and bristles with seminal works such as articles on MacMhuirichs (1963) and learned orders generally (1968), *An Introduction to Gaelic Poetry* (1974), the translation of a biology textbook (1976), the most usable English–Gaelic dictionary (1981), and the indispensable *Companion to Gaelic Scotland* (1983, 1994). The last decade of the century saw *Bàrdachd na Roinn Eòrpa an Gàidhlig* (1990), *The MacDiarmid MS Anthology* (1991), and *Mac Mhaighstir Alasdair, Selected Verse* (1996).

Thomson's own verse has been published in seven collections: *An Dealbh Briste* [*DB*] ('The Broken Picture', 1951); *Eadar Samhradh is Foghar* [*ESF*] ('Between Summer and Autumn', 1967); *An Rathad Cian* [*RC*] ('The Far Road', 1970); *Saorsa agus an Iolaire* [*SI*] ('Freedom and the Eagle', 1977); *Creachadh na Clàrsaich* [*CC*] ('Plundering the Harp', 1982), which also includes the first four collections; *Smeur an Dòchais* [*SD*] ('Bramble of Hope', 1991); and *Meall Garbh* [*MG*] ('The Rugged Mountain', 1995). The poet's English translation of *An Rathad Cian* was published under the title *The Far Road* in New York in 1972, while a selection of his poems (and discussion of his work) appeared in Donald MacAulay's anthology *Nua-Bhàrdachd Ghàidhlig* [*NBG*] (Edinburgh 1976).

In 1952, the year in which *Gairm* was founded, Derick Thomson married the Mod Gold Medallist Carol Galbraith from Campbeltown, and they have six children (Dòmhnall Ruaraidh, Daniel, Cairistìona, Ranald, Roderick and Calum). They have continued to live in Glasgow following his retirement from the Chair of Celtic in 1991.

The poet was the first recipient of the Ossian Prize (Hamburg, 1974). He was elected a Fellow of the Royal Society of Edinburgh in 1977 and of the British Academy in 1992, and received honorary degrees from the universities of Wales (1987) and Aberdeen (1994). Vol. 17 of *Scottish Gaelic Studies* (1996), a collection of studies by 38 scholars edited by Donald MacAulay, James Gleasure and Colm Ó Baoill for presentation to him, includes a fuller biography and complete list of his publications to 1992. See also pp. xl–xliv above.

Entries on Derick Thomson will be found in histories of (and companions to) Scottish and Gaelic literature, for which see p. 820 below. For further assessment see: Iain Crichton Smith, 'Two Poems by Derick Thomson', *An Gaidheal* 61 (1965) 52–3; Donald MacAulay, introduction to 'The Far Road', *Lines Review* 39 (1971) 3–12; Iain MacDhùghaill, 'An Dealbh Briste: Ath-Sgrùdadh', *Gairm* 97 (An Geamhradh 1976–7) 55–61; Iain Crichton Smith, 'Derick Thomson's "Clann Nighean an Sgadain"', *Akros* 17, no. 51 (1983) 42–4; Christopher Whyte, 'Derick Thomson: Reluctant Symbolist', *Chapman* 38 (1984) 1–6; Fearghas MacFhionnlaigh, 'Borbhan Comair: Ath-Sgrùdadh air Bàrdachd Ruaraidh MhicThòmais', *Gairm* 131 (An Samhradh 1985) 259–71; Iain Crichton Smith, 'The Poetry of Derick Thomson', in his *Towards the Human* (Loanhead 1986) 136–43; Iain Crichton Smith, 'Derick Thomson: Concern with Gaelic Culture', *Radical Scotland* 23 (1986) 38; Iain Crichton Smith, 'A Sensuous Perception: One Aspect of Derick Thomson's Poetry', *Scottish Gaelic Studies* 17 (1996) 356–61. Substantial reviews of his work include those in *Ossian* (1968) 47–51 (by Calum Graham, q.v.), *Scottish Gaelic Studies* 12 (1971) 135–6, *Gairm* 74 (An t-Earrach 1971) 179–84, *Gairm* 82 (An t-Earrach 1973) 188–92, *Lines Review* 65 (1978) 27–30, *Gairm* 105 (An Geamhradh 1978–9) 89–92, *Scottish Review* 29 (1983) 41–3, *Gairm* 122 (An t-Earrach 1983) 183–6, *Lines Review* 85 (1983) 11–20, *Scottish Gaelic Studies* 14 (1983) 136–8, *Lines Review* 112 (1990) 5–11, *Gairm* 159 (An Samhradh 1992) 278–81, *Lines Review* 127 (1993) 48–51, and *Gairm* 173 (An Geamhradh 1995–6) 87–9.

I am grateful to the poet for information and permission to reprint:

183   *Teallaichean* ('Hearths'). Author's trl. *DB* 53; *CC* 60–1.

184   *Sgòthan* ('Clouds'). Author's trl. *ESF* 11; *NBG* 156–9; *CC* 66–7. The hills mentioned are in Lewis.

185   From *Mu Chrìochan Hòil* ('In the Vicinity of Hòl'). Author's trl. *ESF* 15–17; *CC* 72–5. The poem has 124 lines, consisting of introduction, four seasons and conclusion; nos. 57–105 (autumn and winter) are reprinted here. Hòl is a small hill behind the schoolhouse at Bayble.

186   *Na Cailleachan* ('The Old Women'). Author's trl. *Gairm* 1 (Am Foghar 1952) 75; *ESF* 24, 74–5; *CC* 84–7. For the spreading of thatch as manure, see poem 136 and my article 'Spreading Thatch as Manure', *West Highland Free Press*, 14 June 1991.

187   *Clann-Nighean an Sgadain* ('The Herring Girls'). Author's trl. *ESF* 26, 76–7; *NBG* 150–3; *CC* 88–9. From *c.*1851 to 1939 girls from the Western Isles would travel in large numbers to fishing ports as far away as Yarmouth and Lowestoft to work as herring-gutters, see e.g. Tormod Calum Dòmhnallach (q.v.) and Leslie Davenport, *Clann-Nighean an Sgadain* (Stornoway 1987).

188   *Srath Nabhair* ('Strathnaver'). Author's trl. *ESF* 36, 79–80; *NBG* 152–3; *CC* 94–7. Kildonan and Strathnaver in Sutherland were ruthlessly cleared of people between 1813 and 1819 by Patrick Sellar (1780–1881), cf. poem 285.

189   *Bùrn is Mòine 's Coirc* ('Water and Peats and Oats'). Author's trl. *RC* 6; *NBG* 162–3; *CC* 130–1.

190   *Am Bodach-Ròcais* ('Scarecrow'). Author's trl. *RC* 18; *NBG* 164–5; *CC* 140–1.

191   *Murdag Mhòr* ("Mucka"). Author's trl. *RC* 41; *CC* 162–3.

192   *Làmhan* ('Hands'). Author's trl. *RC* 44; *CC* 164–7.

193   *Earrach '74* ('Spring '74'). Author's trl. *SI* 8, 50; *CC* 198–9.

194   *Ceud Bliadhna san Sgoil* ('A Hundred Years in School'). Author's trl. *SI* 9; *CC* 198–9. On the Education Act (Scotland) of 1872, which established universal primary education through the medium of English; also on a more recent phenomenon, the closure of rural schools and secondary units (Scottish schools are run by local Education Authorities). Cf. p. 714 above.

195   *An Crann* ('The Plough (or Cross/Mast/Lot/Harp-Key/Saltire etc.)'). Author's trl. *SI* 15–18, 54–8; *CC* 208–15. A multi-storeyed poem. *Crann* is basically anything pole-shaped, including even an oil-rig. The poem was composed in the era of the SNP's "It's Scotland's oil!" campaign of the mid-1970s, when oil wealth and political independence appeared to be synonymous concepts. There are puns on many other words than *crann*, e.g. *cliathadh* in section 5 is the copulation of chickens as well as harrowing. The reference to *Sir Crannchur*

MacGilleMhùin is sarcastic. An alternative translation might be 'Sir Lottery MacGillyPiss'. The name evokes that of the late Sir Andrew Gilchrist (*Sir Anndra MacGilleChrìost*), chairman of the Highlands and Islands Development Board 1970–6. As his *Gairm* editorials show, Thomson was bitterly disappointed that non-Gaels with little understanding of the needs of Highland communities — men such as Gilchrist — were routinely appointed to the most senior positions in the HIDB.

196   **Earail air Luchd-Adhraidh a' Bheòil-Aithris ('A Warning for Folklore Worshippers').** Author's trl. *CC* 260–1. See p. lvii and poem 126. The 'smoke-hole' reference evokes countless stories of practical jokes on Hallowe'en, such as in Neil Gunn's novel *The Serpent* (1969 edn, Inverness) 48: "Down through the hole came the goat and landed four-footed in the fire. Its hair went up in a singeing lowe and with a leap the demented brute was among the women."

197   **Alba v. Argentina, 2/6/79 ('Scotland v. Argentina, 2/6/79').** Author's trl. *CC* 264–5. In the General Election of 1979, Mrs Thatcher came to power, SNP representation in the House of Commons was reduced from eleven to two, and all hopes that the Scotland Act might still become law (see poem 274) were finally dashed. A month later, amidst patriotic fervour whipped up by 'Ally's Tartan Army', the Scottish football team faced Argentina (and lost).

198   **From Àirc a' Choimhcheangail ('The Ark of the Covenant').** Author's trl. *CC* 272–9. See pp. xliii–xliv above. In Highland presbyterian churches, 'adherents' may outnumber communicant members by as many as ten to one. This results partly from the ascetic lifestyle expected of those who have experienced God's saving grace. Communion takes place only once or twice a year, but the 'communion season' lasts from Thursday to Monday. Friday of the communion season is Question Day; the principal service on that day is an opportunity for communicants to answer, from their own knowledge and experience, some such question as: "How does one distinguish between the hope of the hypocrite and the hope of the child of God?" The poem has 17 sections; of those not reprinted here, 1–5 acknowledge respectively the power of certainty, strength, tradition, intimacy and familiarity that underlie Highland religion, while 12–14 offer two more cameos, preceded by an extraordinary prayer of the type that might well be heard on Question Day, ending:

Sinne th' air moglachadh 'na do lìon,   We who are entangled in Your net,
na caomhn do sgian oirnn.   do not spare the knife on us.

199   **From Air Sràidean Ghlaschu ('On Glasgow Streets').** Author's trl. *SD* 14–15. The poem is in 18 parts, each a closely-observed cameo depicting some part of the rainbow of humanity to be found in my native city. Parts 6 and 7, reprinted here, have been chosen for their cultural commentary, and are not particularly typical. Perry Como (1912—) was a well-known American crooner, *Starsky and Hutch* a popular American police series that ran on TV from 1975 to 1979; John Lennon (1940–80) was a member of the influential English rock group called The Beatles. It was prophesied of the MacDonald hero Alasdair mac Colla (*c.*1610–47) that when he found himself at the mill of Gocam-Gò his time would be up, see Angus Matheson, 'Traditions of Alasdair Mac Colla', *Transactions of the Gaelic Society of Glasgow* 5 (1958) 9–93: 66–9. The 'SED' is the Scottish Education Department. Cf. poem 207.

200   **Madainn Diar-Daoin, ann an Oifis Puist an Glaschu ('Thursday Morning, in a Glasgow Post Office').** Author's trl. *SD* 26–7.

201   **Na h-Iongnan ('The Nails').** Author's trl. *SD* 32–3. *Dallas* was a hugely popular American TV series that ran from 1978 to 1991.

202   **A' Ghaidhealtachd ('The Highlands').** Author's trl. *SD* 58–9.

203   **Pioghaid ('Magpie').** Author's trl. *SD* 80–1.

204   **Deireadh an t-Saoghail ('The End of the World').** Author's trl. *SD* 82–3. Boots and Lewis's are department stores. Rannoch is a beautiful part of the central Highlands with a more than usually high proportion of timeshare and holiday-home owners; Terry Wogan (1939—) is an ageing but engaging TV and radio personality — very popular among middle-class viewers — who owns land in the Highlands himself. It is hard to know whether the ship reference is intended to be sinister, but there is a sinister precedent for it, see W J Watson (ed.), *Scottish Verse from the Book of the Dean of Lismore* (Edinburgh 1937) 224–33, and W Gillies, 'Courtly and Satiric Poems in the Book of the Dean of Lismore', *Scottish Studies* 21 (1977) 35–53: 46–7.

205   **Teagamh ('Doubt').** Author's trl. *SD* 100–1.

206   **From Gormshuil ('Gormshuil/Blue-Eye').** Author's trl. *SD* 130–3. The poem is in 14 parts, of which nos. 4–8 (the central part of this central-sounding allegory) are reprinted here.

207   **From Meall Garbh.** Author's trl. *MG* 62–5, 66–7. Written early in 1988, the poem is in 18

parts, and consists of the poet's reflections on the unpeopled — or rather de-peopled — landscape that confronts him when climbing this Perthshire mountain. It is clearly intended as a counterpoise to poem 199. Reprinted here are the second half of part 11 and the second half of part 14.

208   *Seanairean* ('Grandparents'). Author's trl. *MG* 104–5.
209   From *An t-Anam-Fàis* ('The Vegetative Soul'). Author's trl. *MG* 108–11. The poem is in 8 parts and consists of reflections on the nature of memory and the passage of time; part 5 is reprinted here.
210   *Ròidean Rwanda* ('The Rwanda Roads'). Author's trl. *MG* 114–15. In 1994 a wave of ethnic violence swept Rwanda in central Africa. Between 200,000 and 500,000 people were slaughtered. In one 48-hour period in July more than a million Rwandans crossed into neighbouring Zaïre — the greatest mass flight of refugees in modern times.

William Neill (Uilleam Nèill) 1922—

William Neill was born 22 February 1922 in Prestwick, Ayrshire, son of Thomas Neill from Ballantrae and his wife Mary Carswell Auld from Kilmarnock, who died during his infancy. His father later spent some years in Canada, and as a boy William spent much time with relations in the strongly Scots-speaking rural community that lies in the triangle between Auchinleck, Mauchline and Ochiltree. He was educated at Ayr Academy, suffering the then familiar Scottish experience of being thrashed for speaking his native language — in his case, Scots.

He served in the RAF from 1938 to 1966, graduated MA in Celtic and English at Edinburgh University in 1970, and gained his teacher's certificate at Jordanhill College in 1971 after studying under the late John A ('Jake') MacDonald. His spoken Gaelic was learned mostly from urban Gaels in Edinburgh and Glasgow, and he won the Bardic Crown at the National Mod in Aviemore in 1969 (see p. 822 below). He taught English at Castle Douglas High School till his retirement in 1981, and now lives in the village of Crossmichael in Galloway with his second wife Doris. He has two daughters by his first marriage, Alisoun and Deborah.

Neill is a prolific poet and translator in Gaelic, Scots and English. His work has appeared in *Scotland's Castle* (1969), *Poems* and *Four Points of a Saltire* (1970), *Despatches Home* (1972), *Buile Shuibhne* (1974), *Galloway Landscape* (1981), *Cnù à Mogaill* (1983), *Poems in Three Leids* and *Wild Places* (1985), *Blossom, Berry, Fall* (1986), *Making Tracks* (1988), *Straight Lines* (1991), *Tales frae the Odyssey* (1992), *A Caledonian Canto* (1993), and *Selected Poems 1969–1992* [SP] (1994), as well as in the journals *Gairm, Chapman, Lines Review, Spectrum, The Dark Horse, Northwords, Poetry Wales*, and *Poetry Ireland Review*. Awards for his poetry have included The Grierson Verse Prize and Sloan Prize (1970) and a Scottish Arts Council Book Award (1985), and his work in Scots and English has been the subject of a thesis — Emanuela Zocca, 'Seguendo le Tracce: Incontro con la Poesia di William Neill', Bologna 1997. Reviews of his Gaelic work include those in *Gairm* 128 (Am Foghar 1984) 378–9, *Gairm* 144 (Am Foghar 1988) 377–80, and *Lines Review* 133 (1995) 56–8. Much of his poetry is directed against the cultural anglicisation of Scotland. His abiding interest in our complex linguistic identity is also revealed in frequent letters to leading Scottish newspapers, and his Gaelic essays have appeared in *The Scotsman*.

I am grateful to the poet for information and permission to reprint:

211   From *Sealg Ulaidh* ('Treasure Hunt'). Editor's trl. *Cnù à Mogaill* (Glasgow 1983) 46. The poem is in three parts, of which the third is reprinted here. The first two deal with the loss of the poet's Gaelic legacy and his search for it in Ireland. *Seòmar caol an Dùn Éideann* is presumably the Rev. William Matheson's room on the 13th floor of the David Hume Tower in Edinburgh University. Matheson (1910–95) taught in the University's Department of Celtic from 1952 to 1980. He was descended, as the poet says, from an 11th-century figure called Gilleòin na h-Àirde, see Donald Archie MacDonald, 'William Matheson', *Tocher* 35 (1981) 283–347: 283. Matheson played an important part in preparing the third edition (1959) of W J Watson's *Bàrdachd Ghàidhlig*, and the texts which the poet recalls run consecutively at pp. 213–19 of that book: Iain Lom's 'Latha Inbhir Lòchaidh' (cf. note 87 on p. lxix and poem 142) and Murchadh Mór's 'An Làir Dhonn' (cf. p. xxxiv above), with its words

Chluinnte faram nan ràmh	The sound of the oars would be heard
On charraig a' snàmh . . .	Echoing from the rock . . .

212   *Plus ça change.* Editor's trl. *Gairm* 151 (An Samhradh 1990) 217. The Thatcherite 1980s —
epitomised by a new financial district created in London's Dockland — were boom years for
south-east England, distorting UK property values and giving rise to a new breed of young
upwardly-mobile professionals, 'yuppies'.

213   **Aghaidh ri Aghaidh ('Face to Face').** Editor's trl. *Gairm* 139 (An Samhradh 1987) 209–10; *SP*
142–3.

214   **Sealltainn thar Chluaidh ('Looking over Clyde').** Author's trl. *Chapman* 47/48 (1987) 121;
SP 122–3.

215   **Cumha Bhaltair Cinneide 1450–1508 ('In Memory of Walter Kennedy 1450–1508').**
Author's trl. *Gairm* 159 (An Samhradh 1992) 216; *SP* 80–1. Kennedy, who inspired William
Dunbar's 'Flyting of Dunbar and Kennedie', represents the lost Gaelic civilisation of the district
of Carrick in Neill's native Ayrshire. Gaelic ceased to be a living language there in the
seventeenth century.

216   **Stuth Toirmisgte ('Contraband').** Author's trl. Previously unpublished.

Malcolm MacDonald (Calum Dòmhnallach) 1922—

Malcolm MacDonald (*Calum Sham*) was born 24 July 1922 in Manish in the Bays, Harris, eldest
of three children of Samuel MacDonald, then a cottar, from Manish (*Somhairle mac Ruairidh 'ic
Dhòmhnaill 'ic Eoghainn 'ic Dhòmhnaill*, 1891–1976), and his wife Mary MacLeod, also from
Manish (*nighean Dhòmhnaill 'ic Aonghais 'ic Ruairidh Bhàin Dròbhair*, 1892–1974), the others
being Sarah and Donald John. When the poet was 14 the family moved to a croft at Horgabost
over in the machair of the west side, land having been purchased there for crofting by the
Department of Agriculture.

     In 1939 the poet was called up. He joined the 4th (which subsequently became the 2nd)
Camerons at Fort George. Following training in Shetland and elsewhere he was graded 'A1 Plus'
(super fit). He served in Egypt and Italy, and at Monte Cassino on 18 March 1944 he was very
seriously wounded by an exploding shell, losing several ribs. He spent a month in a field
ambulance, followed by long periods in hospital in Naples and Worcester. When the War ended
in 1945 he was in Buckinghamshire training to be a prisoner-of-war guard. Remaining in
England, he worked first in iron foundries, then became a guard on British Railways. He settled
in Manchester (where he still lives), and shortly afterwards married Mary (Molly) Moxon, from
Manchester; they have two children, Mary and Roderick. Now long retired, he is an enthusiastic
gardener and reads a great deal of history.

     Calum Sham is an outstanding example of a traditional poet whose creativity was not stifled
but stimulated by exile and social change. Prior to the War his output consisted of occasional
humorous verses in the oral tradition about events in the township. He made no war poems at all,
preferring to avoid the reliving of traumatic events. Afterwards, however, he composed as many
as 50 songs. He worked mainly on trains running the length of England, and the songs would
come to him in the guard's van while the green of the landscape or the black of the night rolled by.
These were, however, inspired not by life in England but by holidays in Harris.

     As an annual visitor to the island the poet was struck by the pace of change. He was particularly
disturbed by the coming of television. He and his brother Donald (*Dòmhnall Sham*), who has
raised a family in the island and is well known as a singer and songmaker, have remained faithful
to traditional values, and their songs are still frequently sung in island homes, so the victory of
television over the ceilidh cannot be said to be complete.

     Although very few of the brothers' songs have been published, many have now been written
down and brought together, thanks to the enthusiasm and hard work of Donald's daughter Joina,
who has a degree in Celtic from Glasgow University. I am grateful to her for information, and to
the poet for permission to reprint:

217   **Gu Dé Thachair dha m' Thìr? ('What's Happened to my Land?').** Editor's trl. [Bill Lawson
(ed.),] *Chì Mi 'n Tìr* (Northton, Harris 1996) 32. *Todhar* in the sense of manure consisting of
dung, straw and seaweed gave way to *todhar Gallda*, artificial ('Lowland') fertiliser, but even
this, the poet appears to say, is no longer applied.

Torcuil MacRath 1923—

Torcuil MacRath was born 25 November 1923 in Grimshader, Lochs, Lewis, third child of Kenneth Macrae, crofter-fisherman, from Grimshader (*Coinneach [Beag] Choinnich [Mhóir] 'c Iain 'c Ìomhair*, 1882–1946), and his wife Wilina Macleod, also from Grimshader (*Wilina nighean Alastair 'ic Iain 'ic Mhurchaidh 'ic Choinnich 'ic Dhonnchaidh*, 1885–1975), the others being Kenina and Joan. His father's great-grandfather Evander (*Ìomhar*) had come out from Kintail. At Grimshader School he was subjected to a form of education which he has described with justifiable bitterness in his essay 'Hidden Memories'.

He served in the Navy during the Second World War, following which he spent thirty years working for the Post Office at Grimshader, but left in the 1970s when cuts began to bite; he also ran cattle and sheep, since, as he says (personal communication, 28 March 1997), *Cha robh BSE ann: se sannt bu choireach gun tàinig an galar sin.* "There was no BSE: it's greed that brought that disease." He spent some time working in Lewis and elsewhere as a bricklayer before taking up work as a labourer at the oil platform construction yard at Arnish near Stornoway.

Torcuil continued until recently to work his croft at Grimshader, and remains very active. He is a frequent contributor in Gaelic to *Gairm* and in Gaelic and English to *The Stornoway Gazette*. In 1995 he published his first collection of essays in the two languages, *A' Bhuaile Fhalaich*. He has been working on a second book, as he says, *a' sabaist ri typewriter agus tha e gus a' chùis a dhèanamh ormsa* — 'struggling with a typewriter and it's nearly beating me' (pers. comm., 24 March 1997). It will be published by Acair as *An Cearcall*. One aspect of his education is very typical among his generation of Gaelic speakers:

> We were never told that there was such a thing as Gaelic grammar. Certainly, the language was not banned, but you received the impression that it was of little or no value. The old folk, however, spoke the language fluently and correctly. Some of it must have rubbed off on us. Later, when I made an effort to write in Gaelic, I was surprised how easy it was; words I had heard long ago would come flooding back. There is, I think, a memory bank somewhere, though access to it is not always easy. (*A' Bhuaile Fhalaich* 29–30)

I am grateful to the poet for information and permission to reprint:

218   *Cead Deireannach Àirnis* (**'Last Farewell to Arnish'**). Editor's trl. Part 1 appeared in *Gairm* 137 (An Geamhradh 1986–7) 42–4 under the title 'Luinneag'. The whole poem, minus the stanza beginning *Cha téid Cailean*, appeared in *The Stornoway Gazette*, 2 September 1989, under the title 'Cead Deireannach Arnish'.

The Lewis Offshore yard at Glumaig, Arnish, south of Stornoway, was established in 1974 by Heerema UK Ltd. Following a string of industrial disputes it was closed down in 1988 with the loss of 450 jobs. In the issue of *The Stornoway Gazette* in which the poem appeared, Calum Macdonald MP was reported as accusing Heerema of asset-stripping; he listed the equipment removed and described the company's activities as 'vandalism'. The yard reopened following a management buy-out in 1990 and provided as many as 500 jobs for part of the 1990s.

The poet's introduction to 'Luinneag' is as follows (translated): "Monday morning was never pleasant, but that one was terrible. In the oil construction yard at Arnish things were not going well. Trouble was afoot. The man in charge of the welders and the man in charge of the platers — both Lowlanders — had fallen out with each other. To cut a long story short, I was between a rock and a hard place. I didn't know whether I was coming or going. On the way home that evening, while driving over the moor road, one or two verses came to me like a stone from the sky. I made a little ditty about Arnish — here it is! More about Arnish can perhaps be seen in it than in the *Gazette* or the *Free Press*."

In st. 1, Colin Maciver is the manager (and a future member of the management buy-out team), 'the Dutchman' is Heerema chairman Pieter Heerema, and Norman Brownell is managing director of Heerema UK. *Piollaidh* in st. 3 is one of the Devil's bynames, see poem 91. Heerema were said to have worked for the Nazis during the War constructing submarine shelters (that, at any rate, was what the poet was told by a young Dutch employee), hence the 'Nazi' reference in st. 5.

219   *Cor na Tìr* (**'The Country's State'**). *A' Bhuaile Fhalaich* 42–3.

Neil B MacKinnon (Niall B MacFhionghuin) 1925—

Neil Bruce MacKinnon was born 12 January 1925 in Aberdeen, eldest child of Neil MacKinnon, from Quinish, Mull (*Niall mac Nèill 'ic Nèill*, 1891–1936), and his wife Andrewina Macintosh MacKenzie, who had Skye and Inverness-shire connections (1897–1976); the other children were Ronald Lee and Norma Gillies (Mrs John Watson). Their father, an oil company superintendent, won the Gold Medal for singing at the National Mod in Perth in 1924, and their grandfather was farm manager at Quinish, being awarded the long service medal of the Royal Highland and Agricultural Society of Scotland in 1918 for 45 years' service to the estate.

The poet was educated at Aberdeen Grammar School, and served in the Navy during the Second World War. He subsequently worked for the United Africa Company in Nigeria and in educational publishing in Canada. In 1955 he married Louise Reid from Aberdeen, and they have two sons, Alasdair and Robert. After graduating with Honours in Celtic Studies from Aberdeen University in 1966 he became a teacher, and now works as an independent researcher and translator (mainly from German). He began writing Gaelic poetry in 1966, most of his work (including translations of German verse) having been published in *Gairm*. I am grateful to him for information and permission to reprint:

220 *A' Chlach Ionmhainn* ('The Dear Stone'). Author's trl. *The Scotsman*, 26 July 1996. A version of the poem, entitled 'Clach Sgàin', appeared in *The Scots Independent*, August 1996. The Stone of Destiny (for which see poems 59, 60) was ceremonially returned to Scotland on St Andrew's Day 1996 (700 years after its capture by Edward I) by Michael Forsyth, last Conservative Secretary of State for Scotland, in a vain attempt to stave off demands for Home Rule. The event was celebrated with delightful sarcasm in 'lia fàil' by Aonghas MacNeacail (q.v.), see *Chapman* 85 (1996) 3–5, which includes a translation into Scots by William Neill, q.v.

Catherine Macdonald (Catrìona NicDhòmhnaill) 1925—

Mrs Catherine Macdonald was born Catherine MacLeod on 3 December 1925 in Digg, Staffin, Skye, eldest child of Murdo MacLeod, from Digg (*Murchadh Theàrlaich*, 1886–1945), and his wife Marion MacKinnon, also from Digg (*Mòrag Dhòmhnaill Iain Theàrlaich*, 1900–82), the others being Donald, Charles John, Murchadh (who died in infancy) and Annie. Before his marriage Murdo MacLeod was a railway worker, latterly he was employed in the aluminium factory in Fort William.

The poet was brought up in Digg. She left school at 14 and subsequently entered domestic service, looking after an elderly lady in nearby Kingsburgh. She then moved first to Inverness, where she worked at the Mayfield Home of Rest, then to Arran, where she worked in the post office at Lochranza, then to Glasgow, where she worked as a nurse at Stobhill Hospital. It was there, in 1948, that she married Donald Macdonald, from Glasphein, Staffin (*Dòmhnall nan Crannag*, 1920–92). His father Donald (1890–1934) having died when he was 14, he had left school to work the family croft and help his mother, and by 1948 he was working on the pleasure boats at Craigendoran. They moved back to Staffin, where they raised a family of four at Glasphein: Chris Ann, Morag, Donald and Murdella.

Mrs Macdonald is a member of the Church of Scotland congregation in Staffin. She began composing hymns in 1972, around the time when her children were leaving home. She makes verse in both Gaelic and English, and has composed a number of tunes, some of which, such as 'Abba' and 'Harmony', are used in the churches today. With the encouragement of Allan MacDonald — himself a maker of humorous songs, at that time headmaster of Staffin school and a FC lay preacher — her first collection, *Sgeul na Réite* ('The Story of the Atonement'), was published by the Stornoway Religious Bookshop in 1981. It contains 32 hymns, beautifully crafted. A second and still stronger collection containing exactly the same number of hymns, *Na Bannan Gràidh* ('The Bonds of Love'), was issued by the same publisher in 1987.

Mrs Macdonald, who still lives in Glasphein, now has five grandchildren, Catherine, Margaret, Dòmhnall Alasdair, Bruce and Dòmhnall Seosamh, and two great-grandchildren, Alisdair and Eilidh.

I am grateful to the poet and her son Donald for information and permission to reprint:

221   **Cum Sinn Dlùth ('Hold Us Close').** Editor's trl. *Na Bannan Gràidh* 24–5. This beautiful hymn
       reminds us that in the first half of the century people still confronted physical darkness much
       more than now. It also evokes the often flimsy wattled partitions within the traditional island
       home.

222   **An t-Aoibhneas a tha staigh sa Chridhe ('The Joy that is inside the Heart').** Editor's trl. *Na
       Bannan Gràidh* 35–6. The alleged dourness of Highland presbyterianism is a matter of exterior
       perception. It is a religion that brings ineffable pleasure to the believer. The 4th stanza reflects
       Song of Solomon 5: 10, *Tha fear mo ghràidh-sa geal agus dearg, sònruichte am measg dheich mìle*,
       a favourite theme of Gaelic hymn-makers — it runs like brightly-coloured threads through
       almost every line of an entire hymn of 16 stanzas by UFC catechist John Smith, from Bernera,
       Lewis (*Iain Chaluim Ruaidh*, 1857–1924), ending:

> Tha Crìosta geal-dearg 's e neo-sheargta gu bràth,
> Bidh geal-dearg aige 'n còmhnaidh anns a' ghlòir a tha àrd,
> Bidh geal-dearg ann ri deàrrsadh do gach pàirtidh 'na ghràdh,
> Bidh geal-dearg ann gu sìorraidh, 's duine 's Dia ann ri tàmh.

("Christ is white-red and unwithering for ever, / He'll always have white-red in glory on high,
/ White-red shines in Him for all who partake in His love, / White-red's in Him forever, being
both man and God.") See Iain Chaluim Ruaidh, *A' Chulaidh as Fheàrr* (Stornoway 1983) 27.

Donald MacDonald (Dòmhnall Aonghais Bhàin) 1926—

Dòmhnall Aonghais Bhàin was born 12 December 1926 in S. Lochboisdale, S. Uist, fourth child
of Angus Macdonald, crofter-fisherman, from S. Lochboisdale (*Aonghas Bàn mac Iain 'ic
Aonghais Mhóir*, 1874–1927), and his wife Catherine (Kate) Mackellaig from Kilpheder (*Ceit
Dhòmhnaill 'IcEilleig*, 1891–1966), the others being Ewen, Donald John and Christina. He
attended S. Lochboisdale Primary School, known locally as *Sgoil Ghlaic Ruairidh*, leaving in 1940
at the age of 14. He says (personal communication, 10 March 1997):

> Before my mother married she used to be at the herring gutting and she had all the songs which were
> so common in those days, and although we were brought up very poor we had a happy home, but not
> much luxury. The ceilidh house was going strong in my young days and many's a song and story I
> heard. There was quite a few bards in the glen at that time. It's difficult for my age group to get used
> to the new style of living. I would never like to see the hard times which I experienced myself, but I
> still miss some of the old way of life.

Even for the minority of individuals who inherit one, a croft is seldom capable of providing
more than half an income, and Dòmhnall Aonghais Bhàin's biography is representative of the
West Highland experience in the twentieth century. After leaving school he took odd jobs cutting
peat and working for the other crofters. Then he had a spell at the fishing and doing odd jobs in
between. There followed a succession of jobs mostly away from home: at a tweed mill in Oban,
on a building site in Easdale, on a hydro-electric scheme near Inveraray, with the Forestry
Commission at Barcaldine, on a water scheme in Uist, on a hydro scheme in Ross-shire, and
finally with contractors at Lochboisdale and Benbecula, including work on the controversial
Rocket Range. He then spent five years looking after his invalid mother and nine years at the
alginates factory; when it closed down he spent a year on a job-creation scheme, but never worked
again. Suffering ill health of various kinds, he has endured countless stays in six different
hospitals. "It's difficult to explain the kindness I got in all these places," he says (pers. comm.,
August 1997). "I did my best to pay back the nurses with poems and songs. I had five operations
in that time, but other people got it much worse."

Chief among the poets and storytellers of his youth were *clann Dhòmhnaill 'ic Iain Bhàin*, of
whom John Campbell (q.v.) was one, but Dòmhnall Aonghais Bhàin was also greatly influenced
by his schoolteacher, Annie Macphee, who loved poetry of a different kind and introduced him
to Byron, Shelley and Keats. The result is that he has never been a public poet of the type so well
represented by Donald Allan MacDonald, q.v. His first songs and poems were composed in
secret and, if written down, subsequently burnt. For many years he has used a cassette tape-

recorder both as an aid to composition and also to record what he has composed. As Fr John Angus Macdonald has said of him,

> The structures within which his verse, and indeed the compositions of all local bards in Uist, would be orally transmitted have all but disappeared within the community. And so, Donald MacDonald seeks and finds an audience for his verse amongst the readers of *Am Pàipear* and the *Stornoway Gazette* to which he submits regular contributions of transcriptions of recordings of his own poetry. ('The Songs of Donald Allan MacDonald' (MLitt thesis, Aberdeen 1983) 17, cf. Fr Macdonald's *Òrain Dhòmhnaill Ailein* (Benbecula 1999) 44)

Since the 1960s Dòmhnall Aonghais Bhàin has poured out an astonishing stream of closely-focused verse celebrating the beauty of womanhood and of the natural environment of South Uist. This has appeared mainly in *The Stornoway Gazette*, *Am Pàipear* (the Uist community newspaper), *Gairm*, and *The Scotsman*. A long-promised collected edition has yet to appear, and is much to be desired. For an illustrated account of the poet's life, along with six of the poems (including one, 'An Rocaid', in free verse, and another, 'Camilla's Picture', written in English only), see Neat's *Voice of the Bard* 3–33; for his family history see Bill Lawson, *Croft History: Isle of South Uist, Volume 3* (Northton, Harris 1997) 142–3.

I am grateful to the poet for information and permission to reprint:

223   *Am Faoilteach* ('January') from *Mìosan na Bliadhna* ('The Months of the Year'). Editor's trl. *The Stornoway Gazette*, 17 February 1990. I distinguish *Faoil(t)each* in its modern sense of the calendar month of January from *faoil(t)each* in its traditional sense of what I call 'wolftime', the cold stormy period of two weeks on either side of *Latha Fhéill Brìghde*, 1 February. In line 9 the two senses seem to combine; see also st. 5 of poem 224.

224   *Moladh Mnathan-Eiridinn Ospadal an Rathaig Mhóir, Inbhir Nis* ('In Praise of the Nurses of Raigmore Hospital, Inverness'). Editor's trl. *Gairm* 171 (An Samhradh 1995) 208. The poet comments (pers. comm., 11 November 1998): "I had a big operation in the Royal Infirmary for an ulcer which was giving me trouble for a long number of years, till at last it burst and I was lucky to be alive. It was other people's blood that saved me and among them was a woman. So I should write nice things about women."

225   *A' Mhaighdeann Chriadhadh* ('The Doll'). Editor's trl. *Am Pàipear*, November 1998. Literally translated, the poem's title means 'The Maiden of Clay'. The poet writes (pers. comm., 11 November 1998): "The Doll was the toy of a young girl that was sitting beside me in church when the holiday people were at home. The girl's mother gave me a strange look when she saw me giving the Doll the hand-shake of peace during Mass."

Norman Malcolm Macdonald (Tormod Calum Dòmhnallach) 1927—

Norman Malcolm Macdonald was born 24 July 1927 in Thunder Bay, on the shores of Lake Superior, Canada, eldest child of Finlay Macdonald, civil servant, from Aignish (*Fionnlagh Chaluim Mhurchaidh Phortair*, 1897–1959), and his wife Mary Ann MacLeod, from Tong (*Màiri Anna Thormoid Chaluim Dhòmhnaill Ghlais*, 1900–94), the others being George, Iain, Donald, Maretta and Finlay. His parents had emigrated in 1920 and 1923 and married in 1925, but the Great Depression obliged them to return to Lewis when he was three years old. He was thus brought up on his grandfather's croft in Tong (where he still lives) and attended Tong School and the Nicolson Institute.

Norman Macdonald spent some time in New Zealand and worked variously as labourer, clerk and journalist. Following a spell in 1972–3 as a mature student at Newbattle Abbey College, he became administrator and writer for the touring Gaelic theatre company Fir Chlis. For four years from 1982, following Sorley MacLean (q.v.), he was *Sgrìobhadair* (Writer in Residence) at Sabhal Mór Ostaig in Skye, and he subsequently became Dramatist in Residence with the National Gaelic Arts Project and An Comunn Gaidhealach. In 1983 he married Màiri Macdonald, q.v.

The poet began writing in his thirties and has been a full-time playwright, screenwriter and novelist since 1984. Through fairly equal doses of fact and fiction, and of English and Gaelic, he has succeeded uniquely in documenting the Lewis experience throughout the twentieth century. His work includes the novels *Calum Tod* (1976) and *An Sgàineadh* (1993), the 26 poems in *Fàd*

(1978), and three illustrated non-fictional accounts: *Creach Mhór nam Fiadh* (1973), on the Park Deer Raid of 1887; *Call na h-Iolaire* (1978), on the loss of the *Iolaire* in 1919 (see poem 168); and *Clann-Nighean an Sgadain* (with Leslie Davenport, 1987), on the herring-girls, for whom see poem 187. *Fàd* was reviewed in, among other places, *Gairm* 107 (An Samhradh 1979) 281–3.

The poet has also written many plays in both languages, including 'Slàinte' (Fir Chlis, 1978), 'The Brahan Seer' (Eden Court Theatre, Inverness, 1986), 'The Shutter Falls' (TV, 1986), 'Anna Campbell' (Traverse Theatre, Edinburgh, 1987), 'The Teuchter's Tale' (Mull Theatre, 1993) and 'Portrona' (community play, Stornoway, 1996). His 'Beul nam Breug' ('Mouth of Lies'), suggested by the life and work of the seventeenth-century poet Màiri nighean Alastair Ruaidh and of the piper Pàdraig MacCruimein, was toured in Britain by Tosg in 1998. I am grateful to him for information and permission to reprint:

226   ***Eathar Angaidh* ('Angie's Boat').** Editor's trl. *Fàd* 24–5. Angie's is the last of the village boats which had fished in Broad Bay for 200 years until it was denuded of its rich haddock and plaice fisheries by illegal trawling. The poem was written to commemorate this lost aspect of Lewis community life, and the scores of local fishermen drowned in the Bay. Angie is still (1999) working as a fisherman there after fifty years or more.

Iain Crichton Smith (Iain Mac a' Ghobhainn) 1928–98

Iain Crichton Smith was born 1 January 1928 in Glasgow, second of three children of John Smith, merchant seaman, from 52 Upper Bayble, Point, Lewis (*Iain Iain Iain Dhòmhnaill* or *mac Iain Sheoc*, 1871–1931), by his second wife Christina Campbell, who was from the neighbouring township of Garrabost (*Carstìona nighean Iain Chaluim Ruaidh*, 1889–1969), the others being Alex John and Kenneth William Crichton. No. 52 was a croft created in 1875 and obtained in that year by the poet's great-grandfather, 65-year-old John Smith (*Seoc Dhòmhnaill*, 1810–94); it was promptly subdivided to help provide a living for both of Seoc Dhòmhnaill's sons and their families.

The poet's father had previously been married to Effie MacMillan from 49 Upper Bayble (*nighean Mhurchaidh Choinnich*, 1878–1913), and they had a daughter Chrissie (Mrs Arnott, Glasgow). He died when Iain was three years old, and the family returned to Lewis, where Iain attended Bayble School and the Nicolson Institute. Being dependent on a Widow's Pension, the family was in very poor circumstances, and the poet's mother, a deeply religious woman who had been a herring-girl (cf. poem 187), struggled against heavy odds to raise the four children.

The first train that the poet could recall seeing was the one that brought him to Aberdeen University in 1945. He graduated with Honours in English in 1949 and, following teacher training at Jordanhill College, Glasgow, did his National Service as a sergeant in the Education Corps. He taught English from 1952 to 1955 in Clydebank High School, and from 1955 to 1977 in Oban High School, living in a flat in Combie Street which he had bought for himself and his mother. Her death in 1969 came as a devastating blow, as she had been what he called an 'overwhelming presence' in his life, although he could not believe in her unforgiving God. In his *Herald* obituary of the poet, Lorn Macintyre calls her 'a figure of constancy as she sat by the fire, waiting in her ear muffs to go to the Free Church while her son tapped out yet another poem on his typewriter'.

In 1977, the same year in which he left teaching to become a full-time writer, he married Donalda Logan, *née* Gillies, a nurse from Arisaig, who brought him a ready-made family in the form of her sons Alisdair and Peter. They settled in Taynuilt, near Oban. By then he was a leading Scottish novelist and poet in two languages, writing novels in Gaelic and English, short stories in Gaelic and English, poems and plays in Gaelic and English, and criticism, mainly in English. He became renowned for the quantity as well as the quality of his output: Grant F Wilson's *A Bibliography of Iain Crichton Smith* (1988) runs to 228 pages, and reveals that even then he had already written over 900 poems. In English he produced ten novels, six collections of short stories and thirteen volumes of verse, including his posthumously-published poem to his wife, *The Leaf and the Marble* (1998). His novel *In the Middle of the Wood* (1987) received particular praise for the honesty with which it portrays the poet's spell of mental illness. He was, certainly, a man who lived on the edge of madness: but it could be a joyous madness, as witness his love of oxymoron, his infectious laughter, the delight with which he pricked pomposity, and the hilarious existentialism of his character Murdo (who began life as Murchadh in the pages of *Gairm* 106–9 in 1979).

It is undoubtedly fair to say that Smith the storyteller has had a greater impact on Gaelic literature than Smith the poet. His Gaelic verse collections are *Bùrn is Aran*, 1960 [*BA*], *Biobuill is Sanasan-Reice*, 1965 [*BSR*], *Rabhdan is Rudan*, 1973, *Eadar Fealla-Dhà is Glaschu*, 1974 [*EFDG*], *Na h-Ainmhidhean*, 1979, *Na h-Eilthirich*, 1983 [*NE*], and *An t-Eilean agus An Cànan*, 1987. He was one of the five poets whose work appeared, with critical assessment, in Donald MacAulay's 1976 anthology *Nua-Bhàrdachd Ghàidhlig: Modern Scottish Gaelic Poems* [*NBG*]. An Irish translation of 'An Cànan' by Paddy Bushe appeared as *Teanga* in 1990 (Coiscéim, Dublin). His Gaelic prose may be found in *Bùrn is Aran*, 1960, *An Dubh is an Gorm*, 1963, *Maighstirean is Ministeirean*, 1970, *An t-Adhar Ameireaganach*, 1973, and *Na Guthan*, 1991 (short stories); *Tormod 's na Dolaichean agus Màiri 's an t-Each Fiodh*, 1976, and *Little Red Riding Hood agus An Dorus Iaruinn*, 1977 (children's stories); and *Iain am measg nan Reultan*, 1970, *An t-Aonaran*, 1976, *Am Bruadaraiche*, 1980, *Na Speuclairean Dubha*, 1989, *Turas tro Shaoghal Falamh*, 1991, *An Dannsa mu Dheireadh*, 1992, *An Rathad gu Somalia*, 1994, and *A Pheigi a Ghràidh*, 1994 (short novels for children, teenagers or adults). He was also a prolific reviewer, and a collection of his critical work, including essays on Sorley MacLean (q.v.), George Campbell Hay (q.v.), Derick Thomson (q.v.) and Donald MacAulay (q.v.), may be found in his *Towards the Human* (Edinburgh 1986).

Among the poet's honours were: OBE; FRLS; honorary doctorates from the Universities of Aberdeen, Dundee and Glasgow; ten Scottish Arts Council awards; award for Gaelic television play; PEN Silver Pen Award 1970; Poetry Book Society recommendations 1972, 1975, 1989, 1994; *The Scotsman* Short Story Award 1983; Poetry Book Society Choice 1984; prizes for Gaelic plays 1984, 1986; Commonwealth Poetry Prize 1986; Saltire Award 1992; Forward Award 1994; and Cholmondeley Award 1996.

The poet died at home in Taynuilt, after a battle with throat cancer, on 15 October 1998, and was cremated at Helensburgh. Both of his brothers had predeceased him: Alex John had spent a good part of his life in charge of the education of blacks and whites in Zimbabwe, and died in Canada, while Kenneth had died in Australia. In the BBC 'EX-S' film *The Journey* (1997) Smith spoke of how he scattered Kenneth's ashes in the sea at Bayble, and declared:

> *Life sparkles and passes.* It comes from a poem that I wrote for children many many years ago in which I was comparing life to the spinning of a bicycle wheel sparkling in the sunshine . . . Life does pass. In my judgement there is no punishment and there is no reward, and it's simply a series of moments passing. One tries to hold on to these moments by writing about them.

Entries on Iain Crichton Smith will be found in histories of (and companions to) Scottish and Gaelic literature, for which see p. 820 below. For further assessment see: Frederic Lindsay, 'Disputed Angels: The Poetry of Iain Crichton Smith', *Akros* 12, no. 36 (1977) 15–26; Alan Titley, 'Iain Mac a' Ghobhainn, Scríbhneoir', *Comhar* 47, no. 4 (1988) 15–25; Douglas Gifford, 'Deer on the High Hills: The Elusiveness of Language in the Poetry of Iain Crichton Smith', in Derick Thomson (ed.), *Gaelic and Scots in Harmony* (Glasgow 1990) 149–62; Carol Gow, *Mirror and Marble: The Poetry of Iain Crichton Smith* (Edinburgh 1992); and, above all, Colin Nicholson (ed.), *Iain Crichton Smith: Critical Essays* (Edinburgh 1992), which includes Derick Thomson, 'The Gaelic Poetry', pp. 1–10. See also pp. liv–lv above.

For the poet's family history see Bill Lawson, *Croft History: Isle of Lewis, Volume 2* (Northton, Harris 1992) 82–3. I am grateful to the poet and his widow for information and permission to reprint:

227   **Tha thu air aigeann m' inntinn ('You are at the bottom of my mind').** Author's trl. *Gairm* 2 (An Geamhradh 1952) 87; *BA* 59; *BSR* 13, 57; *NBG* 168–71.
228   **Aig a' Chladh ('At the Cemetery').** Author's trl. *BA* 65; *BSR* 16, 60; *NBG* 170–3.
229   **An Litir Àraid ('The Strange Letter').** Editor's trl. *BA* 69.
230   **An t-Òban ('Oban').** Author's trl. *BSR* 23–4, 64; *NBG* 176–9.
231   **Na Seanfhacail ('The Proverbs').** Editor's trl. *EFDG* 8.

232   **Coinnichidh sinn ('We will meet').** Editor's trl. *EFDG* 9.
233   **Mas e Ghàidhlig an cànan ('If Gaelic is the language').** Editor's trl. *EFDG* 11–13.
      'MacDonald' is perhaps Alastair mac Mhaighstir Alastair (*c*.1698–*c*.1770), who composed
      'Moladh an Ùghdair don t-Seann Chànain Ghàidhlig' ('The Author's Praise for the Old Gaelic
      Tongue'), see Derick Thomson (ed.), *Alasdair Mac Mhaighstir Alasdair: Selected Poems*
      (Edinburgh 1996) 75–82. Sauchiehall Street is in Glasgow.
234   **Innsidh mi dhut mar a thachair ('I'll tell you how it happened').** Editor's trl. *EFDG* 20–1.
      'An Eala Bhàn' is by Dòmhnall Ruadh Chorùna, q.v., and the *Kai-Ora* is celebrated in a song of
      that name, see notes on poem 320.
235   **A' Ghaoth ('The Wind').** Editor's trl. *EFDG* 37.
236   **Aig an Doras ('At the Door').** Editor's trl. *EFDG* 41.
237   **An TV ('The TV').** Editor's trl. *EFDG* 43–4. The English philosopher Bishop George Berkeley
      (1685–1753) maintained that the objects we perceive are only ideas in our minds, and that the
      whole of reality consists of ideas in the mind of God. Humphrey Bogart (1899–1957) was an
      American film star. *Softly Softly* (a police series) and *Sportsnight with Coleman* were two of the
      most popular shows on BBC TV in the early 1970s.
238   **Na h-Eilthirich ('The Emigrants').** Author's trl. *NBG* 186–7; *NE* 5; Ian Stephen (ed.), *Siud
      an t-Eilean: There goes the Island* (Stornoway 1993) 42–3.
239   **Dealachadh ('Parting').** Editor's trl. *NE* 27.

Màiri Macdonald (Màiri NicDhòmhnaill)

Màiri Macdonald was born in Grimsay, North Uist, second child of Roderick William
Macdonald, crofter (*Ruairidh Uilleam Ghilleasbaig Ruairidh mhic Èirdsidh*, 1894–1953), and his
wife Mary Morrison (*Màiri Ghilleasbaig Phàdraig 'ic Iain*, 1895–1982), the others being Lachlan
and Maggie (Mairead). The poet's great-great-great-grandfather Archibald Macdonald was
cleared from Sollas to Locheport, and her great-grandfather, Gilleasbaig Ruairidh mhic
Èirdsidh, moved to Grimsay. Her father's maternal grandfather, John Maclean, came from Mull
to Uist as a teacher for the Society in Scotland for the Propagation of Christian Knowledge, and
married and settled there. Her mother was a sister of Peter Morrison, q.v.

Màiri was educated at Grimsay School, Paible Junior Secondary and Portree High School.
Following a period of office work in Glasgow she trained as a primary teacher at Jordanhill
College, 1965–8, being greatly influenced by John A ('Jake') MacDonald, who inspired in her a
great love of Gaelic poetry. She taught at Riddrie (Glasgow) 1968–9, as sole teacher in Grimsay
1969–72, and at Woodcroft Special School (Glasgow) 1972–3. Her first poem (unpublished) was
written in 1972 following the break-up of her marriage and subsequent divorce. It was in English,
but there is now a Gaelic version too.

From 1973 Màiri taught at Kilmuir in Skye (a two-teacher school), moving on in 1975 (as sole
teacher) to Glen Etive, where she lived alone and wrote a great deal, surrounded by the
mountains where the poet Duncan Bàn Macintyre (1724–1812) once hunted: probably her
happiest period. During 1981–2 she cared for her invalid mother in Grimsay. In 1982 she became
head teacher at Kensaleyre in Skye, and in 1983 met and married Norman Malcolm Macdonald
(q.v.), then *Sgrìobhadair* at Sabhal Mór Ostaig. In 1986–8 she worked as a Gaelic teacher at the
College before returning to live in Lewis with her husband.

Màiri Macdonald is not a prolific poet. She has to be emotionally moved: by *cianalas*, by death,
by separation. Her collected poems, illustrated by herself, were published as *Mo Lorgan Fhìn* in
1985, and reviewed in (among other places) *Books in Scotland* 18 (1985) 37–8, *Chapman* 43–4
(1986) 177–8, and *Gairm* 136 (Am Foghar 1986) 377–9. More of her verse has appeared in
Chapman, in *An Anthology of Scottish Women Poets* (1991), in *Siud an t-Eilean* (1993), and in
school anthologies. A collection of her Gaelic short stories was published by Acair as *Grima* in
1990; she has also written stories for radio. She received a Scottish Arts Council bursary in 1992.
I am grateful to her for information and permission to reprint:

240   **Ghrad-leum cù-geàrd a h-inntinn ('The watchdog of her mind').** *Mo Lorgan Fhìn* 18–19.
      Author's English version, with line-breaks changed to make it correspond a little more closely to
      her Gaelic poem. Composed in Glen Etive.

Christina A MacKay (Cairstìona Anna NicAoidh) 1928—

Christina MacKay was born 23 December 1928 in Achmore, Lochs, Lewis, youngest of five children of John R MacKay from Achmore (*Seonaidh Nèill Iain*) and his wife Marion, also a MacKay from Achmore (*Mòr Nèill Aonghais Chaluim*). She was educated at the school in Achmore and in the Nicolson Institute, Stornoway, where her love of Gaelic poetry was engendered through study of John Mackenzie's classic anthology *Sàr-Obair nam Bard Gaelach*, systematically taught by the late Alex Urquhart, who was for many years head of the Gaelic Department.

After completing a three-year course at Aberdeen Teachers' Training Centre in 1951, she taught in various schools throughout Lewis, including Lionel, Lemreway, Breasclete, and Stornoway Primary. In 1961 she married John MacIver (Croix de Guerre 1945) from Callanish (*Iain Aonghais Ruairidh Aonghais Òig*). She was widowed in 1981 and has a son, Iain A R, and a daughter, Marion Kay. She retired from teaching in 1991.

During her teaching career she composed numerous children's poems, still unpublished. Some of her occasional adult poems have appeared in *Gairm* over the years under the name Cairstìona Anna NicIomhair. In 1995 she won First Prize in the William Ross Award for Gaelic writing with 'Do mo Chéile Nach Maireann'. I am grateful to her for information and permission to reprint:

241   *An t-Earrach* ('Spring'). Editor's trl. *Gairm* 144 (Am Foghar 1988) 307.

Girvan McKay (Garbhan MacAoidh) 1929—

Girvan Christie McKay was born 14 August 1929 in Todos Santos del Chaparé, Bolivia, son of William Fulton McKay (who was then working as a missionary) and his wife Janet Girvan Fisher; he has one sister, Margarita. He is of Sutherlandshire ancestry, but his father's family had settled in Glasgow. The family moved on to Spain and then (following the outbreak of the Civil War) Portugal. He was educated in Oporto 1937–9 and at Hillhead High School, Glasgow, 1940–6. After the War the family returned to Portugal where Girvan earned a living variously as graphic artist, office clerk and roving buyer of gramophone records; he also wrote a great deal of poetry, still unpublished.

Given this background, it was natural that Girvan should possess linguistic gifts, and on leaving Portugal in 1954 it was these that he fell back upon. He worked as English teacher, translator and broadcaster in Germany, then as manager of a language school in Manchester. It was there that he first attended Gaelic classes, and in so doing met Máire Coxon, whom he married in 1959; they have three sons, Ruairidh Lachlan, Conall Ailpein and Somhairle Eoghan. They spent some time in the joint post of missionary-teacher in Fair Isle, between Orkney and Shetland, after which Girvan studied for the Church of Scotland ministry in Aberdeen 1965–9. From 1969 until 1974 he served as a minister at Buenos Aires, indulging his passion for travel by visiting Patagonia and other far-flung parts of Argentina. He was minister of Strath, Skye, 1974–7, since when he has served various congregations in the Irish Republic. He now lives in Tullamore, Co. Offaly.

His articles, stories and poems have appeared regularly in *Gairm* since 1960, and he has contributed to other Gaelic publications. He also writes in Esperanto and is correspondent in Ireland for the Esperanto-language news magazine *Monato*, which is printed in Antwerp. Most of his writing activity has consisted of translations from various languages. He is the author of the English–Gaelic Key to Dwelly's Dictionary (1975). His Gaelic translations of poetry have been included in the anthology *Bàrdachd na Roinn Eòrpa* (Glasgow 1990) and in *Zapovyit* ('Testament'), a commemorative volume honouring the Ukrainian national poet Shevchenko (Kiev 1989). His autobiography, 'Guirme Chnoc Ciana', appeared in *Gairm* 124–31 (1983–5). At the end of it he wrote: "If I have found out one truth throughout my life, it is not in religion or in philosophy that I found it but in music and in poetry. *B' fheàrr leam bhith 'nam bhàrd na 'na mo dhiadhair.* I would rather be a poet than a theologian."

I am grateful to the poet for information and permission to reprint:

242   **Bealltainn ann am Fàcland ('Maytime in the Falklands').** Editor's trl. *Gairm* 120 (Am Foghar
       1982) 312. 'Ailein Duinn' is said to have been composed by Annie Campbell, Scalpay, Harris,
       for her drowned sweetheart in 1786, see e.g. J L Campbell (ed.), *Hebridean Folksongs* 1 (Oxford
       1969) 44–9, 161–2. The Falkland Islands, Las Malvinas, were seized by Argentina on 3 April
       1982 and retaken by British troops on 14 June. Port Stanley, Darwin and Pebble Island are all in
       the Falklands.

Anthony Dilworth, 1929—

Tony Dilworth was born 3 October 1929 in Bolton, Lancashire, fourth child of Henry Dilworth,
grocer and hotelier, and his wife Rose O'Connor (the others being Joan, Mark and Basil). He was
brought up in Edinburgh, the family having moved there when he was one month old.

Independently of each other, Mark and Tony both took up Gaelic during the Second World
War when they were pupils at the Abbey School in Fort Augustus (where Mark eventually
became Abbot). Gaelic was not taught in the school at that time — Fr Cyril Dieckhoff, author of
A Pronouncing Dictionary of Scottish Gaelic (1932), was retired, and there were no Gaelic-
speaking monks in the community until Fr Ninian MacDonald (from Fort Augustus) returned
from the United States in 1945, followed by Fr Andrew MacDonnell (from Glen Garry) who
returned from Canada in 1953. So Tony began by using MacLaren's *Gaelic Self Taught* and
conversing with Neil MacEachen (a classmate from Arisaig) and two men who worked around
the Abbey, Peter MacLaren from Whitebridge in Stratherrick and John Urquhart from the Black
Isle.

The end of the War saw a number of Gaelic speakers returning to the village, one in particular
with whom the poet got conversation practice being Big Allachan, a MacLean who had been a
policeman at the gates of the House of Commons; such men could be heard speaking Gaelic on
the Canal Bridge, but when he returned in 1954 for the Gaelic Section of the Linguistic Survey of
Scotland, they had stopped.

After National Service with the Parachute Regiment in Germany, the poet graduated with
Honours in Celtic at Edinburgh University in 1954. In that year, too, he married Miriam Sherry
from Fort Augustus. They have three children, Mark, Paul and Catriona. During 1954–7 he
carried out fieldwork for the Survey in Perthshire, N. Argyll, mainland Inverness-shire, the
Small Isles and Wester Ross, travelling large distances by bicycle. He encountered ambivalent
attitudes to Gaelic, unstinted hospitality, and a rich variety of usage, which he summarised in his
Mainland Dialects of Scottish Gaelic (Abbey Press, Fort Augustus 1958).

Following teacher training in Aberdeen, Tony Dilworth taught in Edinburgh primary and
secondary schools. He broke off in 1964–6 to teach English in Tanzania, an experience which
greatly informed his teaching of Gaelic. In 1975 he was appointed head of St Francis' RC Primary
School, and in his letters to *The Scotsman* around this time he became a scourge of the educational
establishment. Now retired, he helps in the production of *Tocher* as a voluntary worker in the
School of Scottish Studies, and has long been active in Gaelic adult education in Edinburgh. He
is currently chair of the board of Comann an Luchd Ionnsachaidh (CLI) and secretary of the
Edinburgh branch of the Saltire Society. He is co-author (with Morag MacLeod) of *A Structural
Approach to Learning Scottish Gaelic* (Abbey Press, 1980), and author of numerous articles in *The
Scotsman, Gairm, Cothrom* and *Scottish Language*, and of a Gaelic distance-learning course for
Edinburgh's Telford College. His poems have appeared in *Gairm* (1952–8, 1993—), *Crann* and
Cothrom. I am grateful to the poet for information and permission to reprint:

243   **From Successa Petronia.** Editor's trl. with author's assistance. *Gairm* 170 (An t-Earrach 1995)
       158, 160. The poem has 111 lines. In the central section, omitted here, the poet recalls some of
       the wonders of London, Devon, Sandhurst, etc., but thoughts of Successa Petronia draw him
       back to Bath.

Victor Price, 1930—

Victor Price was born 10 April 1930 in Newcastle, Co. Down, N. Ireland, and educated at
Methodist College and Queen's University, Belfast. A linguist by inclination and training, he

took his degree (1951) in French and German, but added other languages later. After a short spell of teaching in Ireland and Germany he joined BBC Northern Ireland in 1956 and, following three years in Hong Kong (where he started writing novels), spent the rest of his working life in the World Service in London, retiring as head of its German Service in 1990. He has two sons from his first marriage, and now lives with his second wife in Belfast.

His publications in English include: the novels *The Death of Achilles* (about the Cyprus emergency), *The Other Kingdom* (about a middle-distance runner) and *Caliban's Wooing* (about schoolmasters); the poetry collections *Overkill*, 1980 (an Ulsterman Publications pamphlet) and *Two Parts Water*, also 1980 (several items in which first appeared in *Lines Review*); and the translated *Plays of Georg Büchner* (with introduction). He has also written novels as yet unpublished: *Chinese Opera*, set in Hong Kong in the early 1960s, and *The Ninety-Eight*, about the rebellion of 1798, set in Co. Down and culminating in the battle of Ballynahinch. For a period in the 1990s he was London theatre critic for *The Scotsman*, and his play 'An Artist in the Family' was read at the Traverse Theatre, Edinburgh, in October 1996.

Victor Price learned Scottish Gaelic in the 1970s from Anna Morrison (Ness and Bearsden). He first started writing poetry in 1974, and a number of his Gaelic poems were published in *Gairm* from then until 1979. He chose Scottish Gaelic in preference to Irish because, he says, for an Ulster Protestant, learning Irish is making a political statement, which he had no intention of doing, and because (despite his Welsh surname) he is at least ninety per cent Scots-Irish in any case: "My mother was a Purdy, hers a McDowell and hers a Spence. There are also McKibbins and Gordons galore among my relatives. My father's mother was Reid . . ."

I am grateful to the poet for information and permission to reprint:

244　　*An déidh aimhreit* ('After a struggle'). Editor's trl. *Gairm* 97 (An Geamhradh 1976–7) 79.

Prof. Donald MacAulay (An t-Oll. Dòmhnall MacAmhlaigh) 1930—

Donald MacAulay was born 21 May 1930 in Bernera, off Lewis. He was educated at Bernera School, the Nicolson Institute (Stornoway), Aberdeen University (Celtic and English, 1953) and Emmanuel College, Cambridge (Section B of the Archaeology and Anthropology Tripos, i.e. Celtic and Teutonic — Old English and Old Norse — Languages, literatures and histories, 1955). He did his National Service in the Royal Navy's Russian Language section, 1955–7. In 1957 he married Ella Murray Sangster, from Cairnie, Aberdeenshire, and they have two children, Cathlin (b. 1958) and Iain (b. 1962).

Professor MacAulay's university posts were in English Language and General Linguistics, Edinburgh, 1958–60; Irish, Trinity College Dublin, 1960–3; Applied Linguistics, Edinburgh, 1963–7; Celtic, Aberdeen, 1967–91 (as Senior Lecturer, Reader and Head of Department); and finally Celtic, Glasgow, 1991–6 (as Professor and Head of Department). He has been chairman of the Gaelic Panel of the Scottish Examination Board, of the Gaelic Committee of the Consultative Committee on the Curriculum for the Scottish Education Department, of the Governors of Catherine MacCaig's Trust, and of the Gaelic Books Council. His poetry appeared as *Seòbhrach as a' Chlaich* (Glasgow 1967) [*SC*]. He has been the editor of *Nua-Bhàrdachd Ghàidhlig: Modern Scottish Gaelic Poems* (Edinburgh 1976) [*NBG*], in which he was one of the five poets featured, along with critical assessment (in his case, self-assessment); of *Oighreachd agus Gabhaltas* (Aberdeen 1980), an important collection of essays on the land troubles of the late nineteenth century; of the periodical *Scottish Gaelic Studies*; and, finally, of *The Celtic Languages* (Cambridge 1992).

There has been no definitive collection of MacAulay's work since 1967; it has appeared in *Gairm* and in anthologies such as *Sruth na Maoile* of 1993. His verse is characterised by a highly polished and yet fractured style that draws deep upon the vagaries of the mind and on the rich vocabulary and idiom of Bernera Gaelic. It is, on the whole, a bare, cerebral verse that avoids excesses of symbolism and prefers to present the bigger picture through painstaking contemplation of the smaller one. Ambiguities and uncertainties lurk everywhere. One is tempted for example to suggest that of all the Gaelic poets of the century, MacAulay is the one whose work is tied most strongly to the printed page, least strongly to performance. Yet when one thinks of his habit of leaving lines blank to show a pause, one begins to realise that his verse may be defined as the mode of expression that occupies the territory between normal thought and normal speech. It is thus as much a performance art as a Shakespearian soliloquy, and requires the possibility of speech to realise its potential. All in all then, many aspects of his verse can be shown to be very traditional in nature even though uncompromisingly modern in form. His work is still much read and a collected edition is very much to be desired, though the presence of translations would be a mixed blessing; notes and a glossary might be a better idea. The very fact that the majority of his work is still untranslated has become part of his poetic identity: in an era of credit cards, instant access, 'user-friendliness' and glib interpretations, the most difficult of our major poets must be accessed by his audience on his own terms and through his own language.

Entries on Donald MacAulay will be found in histories of (and companions to) Scottish and Gaelic literature, for which see p. 820 below. Among more substantial reviews of his work are those in *Gairm* 63 (An Samhradh 1968) 277–81, *Scottish International* 3 (1968) 59–60, and *Lines Review* 26 (1968) 37–8. For further assessment see Iain Crichton Smith, 'A Poem by Donald MacAulay', *An Gaidheal* 60 (1965) 128–9, and Iain Mac a' Ghobhainn, 'Ath-Sgrùdadh — An Dotair Leòinte: Bàrdachd Dhòmhnaill MhicAmhlaigh', *Gairm* 125 (An Geamhradh 1983–4) 68–73, or its translated version, 'The Modest Doctor: The Poetry of Donald MacAulay', in Smith's *Towards the Human* (Loanhead 1986) 116–22.

I am grateful to the poet for information and permission to reprint:

245   *Rabhd Eudochais* ('Cry of Despair'). Editor's trl. *SC* 11.
246   *A' Cheiste* ('Question'). Author's trl. *SC* 11, 86.
247   *Do Fhear-Sgrìobhaidh Ainmeil* ('To a Famous Writer'). Editor's trl. *SC* 15; Derick Thomson, *An Introduction to Gaelic Poetry* (London 1974) 280–1.
248   *Féin-Fhìreantachd* ('Selfrighteousness'). Author's trl. *SC* 21; *NBG* 194–5.
249   *A' Ghiblinn troimh thrì Sùilean* ('April through three Eyes'). Editor's trl. with much help from author. *SC* 25.
250   *Soisgeul 1955* ('Gospel 1955'). Author's trl. *NBG* 192–5. Maol Dùin was a miraculous navigator in early Gaelic literature.

Duncan MacLeod (Donnchadh MacLeòid) 1934–

Duncan MacLeod was born 17 June 1934 in Ranish, Lochs, Lewis, third son of Murdo MacLeod (*Murchadh Mhurchaidh Aonghais Dhòmhnaill*, 1897–1956) and his wife Catherine, also a MacLeod (*Catrìona Dhonnchaidh 'ic Mhurchaidh 'ic Thormoid 'ic Mhurchaidh Thuilm*, 1897–1936), both from Ranish. The other surviving brother is the Rev. Alex M MacLeod, Kinloch, Lewis. Orphaned as a child by the death of his mother, the poet's continuing sense of loss and disruption is reflected in poems such as 'Ionndrainn' and 'Dh'fhàg thu mi'.

After secondary education in the Nicolson Institute and two years in the Army, he worked in the Civil Service and the United Kingdom Atomic Energy Authority; then, following a spell with An Comunn Gaidhealach in the late 1960s, he spent a few years in industry before going into banking and insurance. He retired following a heart attack at the age of 47, but returned to work as director of the Celtic Film and Television Association until a recurrence of the early ailment forced retirement again in 1993. An occasional Gaelic broadcaster over many years, he was closely associated with developments in that field, especially during his time with the CFTA. As founding Chairman of *Féisean nan Gaidheal* he guided the formulation of policy and a strategy for the establishment of that group.

In 1962 he married Catherine Morrison MacDonald, daughter of Marion MacRae (*Mór Alastair Sheòrais*) from Ranish and of Norman MacDonald (*Tormod Darky*) from Habost, Ness, a cousin of Murdo Morrison (*Murchadh Alastair Eachainn*), composer of 'An Caióra', for which see notes on poem 320. Their first home was in Thurso, and they have lived in Inverness since 1966, bringing up a family of four (Murdoch, Norman, Alex and Sharon). While *Gairm* has been the main outlet for his work, some has appeared in *Sruth na Maoile* and elsewhere. His collection *Casan Rùisgte* appeared in 1985, and was reviewed by Iain Crichton Smith (q.v.) in *Gairm* 132 (Am Foghar 1985) 383. I am grateful to the poet for information and permission to reprint:

251   *Samhla* ('Illustration'). Editor's trl. with author's assistance. *Casan Rùisgte* 21–2.

John Murray (Iain Moireach) 1938—

John Murray was born 27 March 1938 in Lower Barvas, Lewis, the third child of Finlay Murray, crofter and joiner, from Barvas (*Fionnlagh mac Iain 'ic Uilleim 'ic Iain 'ic Thormoid Gobha*, 1890–1970), and his wife Jessie Ann MacLeod, schoolteacher, from Duart Drumbeg, Assynt (1907–92), the others being Neil John, Alexander MacLeod, and Mairi. He was educated at Barvas School, the Nicolson Institute, Edinburgh University and Moray House College.

In 1961 he married Nora MacIver from Borve, Lewis (*Nora Chaluim a' Phuins, Nora Chaluim 'ic Tharmoid 'ic Caluim 'ic Caluim 'ic Caluim Phàdraig*); they have no children. From 1961 to 1969 he taught English in Musselburgh Grammar School. In 1969 he became the first Editorial Officer of the Gaelic Books Council in Glasgow, being succeeded in that post in 1976 by Ian MacDonald (q.v.), the writer Ian MacLeod having worked part-time for the Council during 1975–6. Returning to live in Barvas, he was successively Director of the Bilingual Education Project for Primary Schools (1975–8), Assistant Director of Education, Comhairle nan Eilean (1978–84), producer, BBC Gaelic Radio (1984–7), and Editor of BBC Radio nan Gaidheal (1987–93). In 1993 he left full-time employment to pursue his personal interests in writing, community development, broadcasting, etc., but is currently acting as Gaelic Development Adviser to Lews Castle College. He has served on numerous boards and committees since 1976 in the general area of Gaelic cultural and community development.

A highly versatile writer, John has published many plays, short stories and children's books as well as poetry, and has written a great deal for both radio and television. His outstanding achievement is probably the short stories collected as *An Aghaidh Choimheach* (1973); with its publication, in the same year as *Suathadh ri Iomadh Rubha* by Angus Campbell ('Am Puilean', q.v.), it became possible for a while to say that prose had overtaken poetry as the leading medium of literary expression in Gaelic. His career epitomises the Gaelic cultural dilemma, however: serious literary activity for adults comes a poor second when the most able hands are required to man the pumps of education, administration and the media. The alternative is that, albeit with flags flying, the ship will sink under the waves.

John Murray's poetry has been published in *Gairm*, *Kunapipi* and other periodicals and in the anthologies *Somhairle, Dàin is Deilbh* (1991), *Siud an t-Eilean* (1993) and *Sruth na Maoile* (1993); his 'Turas an Asainde' (1994), composed following the death of his mother, was exhibited in Inverness as a poster poem with accompanying glasswork by Stephanie Bouvier, thus exemplifying his cross-media instincts. When not engaged in this dazzling variety of activities, *Bidh mi ag obair sa ghàradh agus a' ruith as déidh rabaidean*, he says — *feadhainn dha-rìribh agus feadhainn shamhlachail.* "I work in the garden and run after rabbits — real ones and metaphorical ones" (personal communication, 12 March 1997). I am grateful to him for information and permission to reprint:

252 **Ar n-Airgead 's ar n-Òr ('Our Silver and our Gold').** Editor's trl. with author's advice. *Gairm* 54 (An t-Earrach 1966) 182–4.
253 **An t-Acras ('Hunger').** Author's trl. *Gairm* 55 (An Samhradh 1966) 268–9.

Norman Maclean (Tormod MacGill-Eain) 1938—

Born 26 December 1938 in Ibrox, Glasgow, Tormod is a son of Neil Maclean (*Niall Mòr mac Iain Eoghain Ruaidh*, 1901–51) from Tiree and his wife Peggy Mackinnon (*Peigi Bheag nighean Thormoid 'ic Ailein*, 1907—) from Claddach Baleshare, N. Uist. During the Second World War he was evacuated first to Srathan, Loch Arkaig, Lochaber, home of his maternal grand-uncle James Macdonald (*Seumas Mòr mac Aonghais 'ic Iain Mhòir*, of whom he speaks eloquently in *VB* 285–7), then to Benbecula where he attended Torlum School.

On returning to Glasgow he completed his education at Bellahouston Academy and Glasgow University, becoming a teacher of English and mathematics. In 1967 he won both the bardic crown and the gold medal for singing at the National Mod in Glasgow (see p. 822). He has composed tunes for the bagpipe and songs and poems in both Gaelic and English. Three of his songs are in *Sruth na Maoile* (1993). From 1976 to 1991 he was a popular stand-up comedian and all-round entertainer at home and abroad — in theatres, on television (ratings for his light entertainment series *Tormod Air Teilidh*, 1978, were especially high) and in cabaret. He has contributed, on both sides of the camera, to Gaelic language programmes for Grampian Television, Scottish Television and the BBC.

In recent years the multi-talented Tormod has taken to writing ground-breaking Gaelic novels. His first, *Cùmhnantan* (1996), is (in his own words) a snigger at the greed and opportunism of the Gaelic TV community; he tells us in *VB* with characteristic modesty that sales of it 'have surpassed those of any Gaelic book in the last fifty years except the Bible'. Insofar as it is autobiographical it depicts the freewheeling Tormod of the 1990s. His second, *Keino* (1998), is stronger and darker, and contains extended descriptions of both sex and violence. It is set largely in the derelict schoolhouse at Srathan, and in the last chapters the narrator, 'Eachann MacPhàil', recalls anguished childhood memories of his father, 'Niall Mòr', who was accidentally drowned in Glasgow's King George V Dock (the poet's father actually died of a heart-attack on a Govan pavement). *Keino* has been made into a short film.

Tormod is married to, though separated from, Peggy Martin from Back, Lewis (*Peigi Dhòmhnaill 'Dhouble'*). He is at present based in the Bellahouston district of Glasgow. For a vintage selection of his colourfully-expressed thoughts and memories see Timothy Neat (ed.), *The Voice of the Bard* (Edinburgh 1999) [*VB*] 268–91.

I am grateful to the poet for information and permission to reprint:

254 Maol Donn ('MacCrimmon's Sweetheart'). Editor's trl. *Sruth*, 5 October 1967. The translation of portions of 'Maol Donn' published in *VB* 279–81 was prepared by the present editor in September 1996 for *An Tuil*. 'Maol Donn' is a pipe tune known in English as 'MacCrimmon's Sweetheart'. The sweetheart in question is thought to have been MacCrimmon's favourite cow — Maol Donn, 'Brown Hornless', being a common name for a cow — and the MacCrimmon in question is stated in one source, Glen's Collection, to have been Dòmhnall Ruadh. 'Fear na h-Eabaid' (st. 8) is a traditional tale.

Aonghas MacNeacail, 1942—

Aonghas MacNeacail, widely known as *Aonghas Dubh*, was born 7 June 1942 in Uig, Skye, son of Alexander Nicolson, merchant seaman, from Idrigil, Uig (*Alasdair Aonghais Shomhairle*, 1907–51), and his wife Catherine Stewart (*Catrìona Chaluim Stiùbhairt*, 1906–90). He has a younger sister, Margaret. He grew up in Idrigil, said to have been the birthplace of *Màiri Mhór nan Òran* ('Great Mary of the Songs', 1821–98). Iain MacNeacail, 'The Skipper' (q.v.), was a distant relative, as is Alasdair Nicolson, composer, for whom Aonghas wrote 'Sgàthach'. His father's cousin, *Dòmhnall Iain Shomhairle*, is said to be the composer of 'Òran a' Ghramaphon', still occasionally heard on Gaelic radio. Aonghas himself has a growing reputation as a maker of songs, but is no singer; he is, however, first cousin, on his mother's side, to Calum Ross, a Mod Gold Medallist and fine ceilidh singer.

The poet's upbringing was not untypical of his community and times: a father, of economic necessity absent for most of the time (even after he left the sea to spend more time with his family), who died before his son's ninth birthday, and a widowed mother who combined small-scale crofting with diligent adherence to the doctrines of the Free Church, and cushioned her children from hardships as far as humanly possible. Primary school in Uig (1947–54) introduced him to the world of English, which became thereafter the language of all authority; at secondary level, in Portree High School (1954–8), his native language was taught to native speakers, by a native speaker, through the medium of English. He can only recall two text-books, *Bàrdachd Ghàidhlig*, an anthology of Gaelic poetry carrying little work more recent than the early nineteenth century, and none at all more recent than the early twentieth; and *Rosg Gàidhlig* ('Gaelic Prose', of which, he says, there seemed to be no great variety to choose from beyond the religious and the homiletic). After school the sea beckoned; but he was distracted by other things, and his first job, from 1959, was in a British Rail office, during which period he began to write poetry — in English.

In 1968 Aonghas matriculated as a mature student at Glasgow University, where he became a member of Philip Hobsbaum's seminal Writer's Group, alongside such figures as Tom Leonard, James Kelman, Alasdair Gray and Liz Lochhead. After four years in a central London housing office he returned to Skye in 1977 as *Sgrìobhadair* at Sabhal Mór Ostaig, the Gaelic College, and he has lived by his writing ever since. In that same year he was advised by the Post Office that his name in the telephone directory must be in the English form which appeared on his birth certificate, but that the Gaelic version could be included (on payment of a supplementary charge) as an 'additional entry'; he resolved their difficulties by reclaiming his Gaelic name as the only one by which he should be known.

Having written predominantly in English, he wrote poetry only in Gaelic for the next fifteen years. His Gaelic verse has been widely published in Europe, America and Australia, and has taken him on recital tours of North America, various European countries, Israel and Japan. He has writtten scripts for radio, television and film as well as stage, and has collaborated with various visual artists and musicians. His first English collection, *Rock and Water*, was mostly written in the early 1970s but not published till 1990, while his long poems *Sireadh Bradain Sicir: Seeking Wise Salmon* (1983) and *An Cathadh Mór: The Great Snowbattle* [CM] (1984) were both illustrated by Simon Fraser and published by Balnain Books of Nairn. His first full collection, *An Seachnadh agus dàin eile: The Avoiding and other poems* [AS], appeared in 1986, and another, *Oideachadh Ceart agus dàin eile: A Proper Schooling and other poems* [OC], in 1996. For *OC* he won the Stakis Scottish Writer of the Year award for 1997 and was shortlisted for the Paul Hamlyn Poets Award of the same year. The operas 'An Turas' and 'Sgàthach', for which he wrote the librettos, were performed in 1997–8 to considerable critical acclaim. Among more substantial assessments of his work are reviews in *Gairm* 126 (An t-Earrach 1984) 191, *Gairm* 138 (An t-Earrach 1987) 188–90, *Lines Review* 101 (1987) 41–5, *Lines Review* 141 (1997) 43–9, and comments by Iain Crichton Smith (q.v.) in 'Recent Gaelic Poetry', *Scottish Language* 8 (1989) 21–33. The poet has held Writer's Fellowships with An Comunn Gaidhealach in Oban (1979–81), with Ross and Cromarty District Council (1988–90), and in a joint Fellowship at Glasgow and Strathclyde Universities (1993–5), and he was again *Sgrìobhadair* at the Gaelic College 1995–8. His use of lower-case letters in his poetry derives, he says, from the recognition that capital letters are *pronounced* no differently from the others.

> Poetry being, first and foremost, an aural art, the absence of capitals asks the reader (*and* the writer) to listen to the sense of what is heard, and written. I like to think that poetry is alphabetically democratic, in its search for sense, harmony, or whatever other objective it pursues. (Personal communication, 31 July 1997)

In 1980 Aonghas MacNeacail married the actress Gerda Stevenson. Their son, Somhairle Rob, was born in 1988 and their daughter Galina Edith in 1998. They live at Carlops in the Scottish Borders. I am grateful to the poet for information and permission to reprint:

255   from **sireadh bradain sicir** ('seeking wise salmon'). Author's trl. *Sireadh Bradain Sicir* 15–19. The poem has 230 lines, of which nos. 82–111 are reprinted here. It has strongly mythic qualities, with elements of love as well as of nature. In search of 'wise salmon' the narrator variously takes the form of hunter and fisher, of dancer and seal, and much of this appears to be synthesised in the chosen extract.

256   from **an cathadh mór** ('the great snowbattle'). Author's trl. *CM* 14–18, 29, 48. The poem has 286 lines, of which nos. 21–44, 124–37 and 260–2 are reprinted here. "The blizzard becomes personified as a kind of monstrous power, or being, against which all nature fights. From out of the swirling whiteness memories rise and visions, premonitions, hopes. We are in a world of conflicting dualities, where white spreads its own darkness, where innocence wounds, where the 'real' strives to dominate the imagined . . ." (*CM* 7)

257   **teist** ('testimony'). Author's trl. *AS* 26–7.

258   **acras** ('hunger'). Author's trl. *AS* 38–9.

259   **an eilid bhàn** ('the white hind'). Author's trl. *AS* 90–3.

260   **dàn bealltainn** ('beltane poem'). Author's trl. *OC* 24–31. Beltane, 1 May (the summer quarterday), was often called *Latha Buidhe Bealltainn*, 'Yellow (Lucky) Beltane Day', probably to distinguish it from 3 May. The poem looks as if it was inspired by Thomas Pennant, *A Tour in Scotland in 1769* (3rd edn, Warrington 1774, repr. Perth 1979) 97–8:

> A *Highlander* never begins any thing of consequence on the day of the week on which the 3d of *May* falls, which he styles *La Sheachanna na bleanagh*, or the dismal day. On the 1st of

May, the herdsmen of every village hold their Bel-tein, a rural sacrifice. They cut a square trench on the ground, leaving the turf in the middle; on that they make a fire of wood, on which they dress a large caudle of eggs, butter, oatmeal and milk; and bring, besides the ingredients of the caudle, plenty of beer and whisky; for each of the company must contribute something. The rites begin with spilling some of the caudle on the ground, by way of libation: on that, every one takes a cake of oatmeal, upon which are raised nine square knobs, each dedicated to some particular being, the supposed preserver of their flocks and herds, or to some particular animal, the real destroyer of them: each person then turns his face to the fire, breaks off a knob, and flinging it over his shoulders, says, *This I give to thee, preserve thou my horses; this to thee, preserve thou my sheep*; and so on. After that, they use the same ceremony to the noxious animals: *This I give to thee, O Fox! spare thou my lambs; this to thee, O hooded Crow! this to thee, O Eagle!*

The poet refers in addition to *Slighe Chlann Uisnich* ('the Path of the Children of Uisneach') and what was I think traditionally called *Bealach Bó Finne* ('the Pass of the White Cow'), two names for the Milky Way, see my article 'From the Harvest Moon to the Milky Way', *West Highland Free Press*, 27 September 1996; and to the 'three lawful crimes of the Gael': *breac á linne, slat á coille, 's fiadh á fireach*, 'a trout from a pool, a stick from a wood, and a deer from a hill', see Alexander Nicolson, *Gaelic Proverbs* (Edinburgh 1882) xxi, 70. The *tein' éiginn* or 'need-fire' was kindled afresh, without the use of iron, to ward off disease, and Beltane fires were kindled in the same way.

261   *samhla* ('appearance'). Author's trl. *OC* 36–7.
262   *marilyn monroe*. Author's trl. *OC* 54–5. The film actress Marilyn Monroe lived from 1926 to 1962.
263   *fòrladh dhachaigh* ('home vacation'). Author's trl. *OC* 62–3.
264   from *Sgàthach*. Author's trl. Unpublished libretto, 1998, pp. 35–6. The opera is mythological in character and is in 22 scenes; the extract is from scene 15. The female warrior Sgàthach is said to have taught Cù Chulainn the martial arts at Dùn Sgàthaich in Sleat, Skye. Her greatest gift was a mysterious weapon usually called the *gath bolga* (literally 'bag spear'?), for which see also poem 167.
265   from *An Turas Sìos gu Tìr nam Marbh* ('The Journey Down to the Land of the Dead'). Author's trl. Paragon Ensemble, programme notes (1998) 30–2. This three-act opera is a fascinating mixture of mythological and modern elements. Gràinne, Finn's wife, seduces Diarmad, his best friend, and they flee to the city, with its bright lights and seedy hotels, its gangs and corrupt policemen. Diarmad places unbroken bread in the bed between them as a symbol of chastity. In the end Gràinne succumbs to drugs. The first two acts are set in the country, the third in the city; our extract is from the beginning of Act 3.

Calum Graham (Calum Greum) 1942—

Calum Roderick Graham was born 29 August 1942 in Garrabost, Point, Lewis, son of Donald Graham, 'Stately', from Garrabost (*mac Ruairidh Chaluim 'ic Chaluim*) and his wife Mary Bell Smith from Aird, Point (*Màiri Bell Dhòmhnaill Ruaidh Chaluim Ghobha*); he has one brother, Murdo. He was educated at Bayble School, the Nicolson Institute and Glasgow University. In 1992 he married Catherine MacKinnon (*nighean Dhonnchaidh Sheumais Alasdair*) from Swordale, Skye. They live in London, where he works as a pensions trustee and consultant and is active in several Gaelic-related organisations. He has one son, Donald, by a previous marriage. His occasional poetry has appeared in *Gairm*, and he is the co-author (with Duncan Gillies) of *Thall 's a-Bhos* (1991), a collection of classic short stories translated into Gaelic.

I am grateful to the poet for information and permission to reprint:

266   *Daoine bha an Leódhas uaireigin* ('Lewis Heroes'). Author's trl. *Gairm* 57 (An Geamhradh 1966) 15; *Edinburgh Review* (1991) 144–5; Ian Stephen (ed.), *Siud an t-Eilean: There goes the Island* (Stornoway 1993) 90–1.

Norman Campbell (Tormod Caimbeul) 1942—

Norman Campbell was born 7 October 1942 in South Dell, Ness, Lewis, third child of the poet Angus Campbell, 'Am Bocsair', q.v. He attended Cross School and the Nicolson Institute. He worked in factories in Glasgow and spent two years with British Railways in Edinburgh before going on to Edinburgh University and Jordanhill College of Education. He describes this part of his career thus (personal communication, 18 March 1997):

> Oilthigh, no mar a thuirt fear a bha còmh' ri Alasdair mo bhràthair ann an Obar Dheathain, òlthaigh! (Sandy Bells, Charles Tavern, Hole in the Wa', Greyfriars Bobby's, Hall Bar etc.) Glaschu (a-rithist!) — Cnoc Iòrdain agus an tuilleadh slòpraich air Byres Road.

He survived, however, to teach Gaelic and English in Glasgow, South Uist and Lionel School in Ness, and has also spent a total of four years as *Sgrìobhadair* (Writer in Residence), two with Comhairle nan Eilean in the Western Isles and two at Sabhal Mór Ostaig in Skye. His highly poetic *Deireadh an Fhoghair* (1979), which views an island community through the eyes and minds of its last surviving inhabitants, is certainly the most stylish piece of sustained prose ever written in Gaelic; uncompromisingly modern in form yet traditional in sympathy, it can still probably be reckoned the best novel ever written in the language. Of his other work, *Dòmhnall MacDhòmhnaill MacDhòmhnaill* (1980) is a lively children's novel, while *An Naidheachd bhon Taigh* (1994) is a substantial collection of poems and stories; between these he produced *Uilleam agus an Iolair, Aisling Chatrìona, Cathal Garg agus a' Hearach, Doileag Anna Mhìcheil* and *Hostail*, all save the last for children.

I am grateful to June Ellner for information and to the poet for information and permission to reprint:

267 **Mi Fhìn agus a' Revolution agus mo Bhata-Darach ('Me and the Revolution and my Oaken Stick').** Editor's trl. with author's advice. *Gairm* 60 (Am Foghar 1967) 312–16. *Clann MhicMhaol-Onfhaidh* were the Camerons. In part 5, Binns is now Fraser's, at the west end of Princes St., and there is an echo of 'An *Caióra*', for which see notes on poem 320.

O se thusa, fhaoileag bhòidheach   O it's you, lovely seagull
Tha ri seòladh os mo chionn . . .   That is flying overhead . . .

Donald John Maciver (Dòmhnall Iain MacÌomhair) 1942—

Donald John Maciver was born 12 November 1942 in Laxdale near Stornoway, Lewis, son of Norman Maciver, schoolmaster, from Lochganvich (*Tormod Thormoid an Tàilleir*), and his wife Annie Morrison from Kirkibost in Bernera (*Anna Dhànaidh*). He has one sister, Norma. He grew up at Loch Croistean, Uig, and (from age 11) at Airidhantuim on the west side. He was educated at The Nicolson Institute and Aberdeen University (Honours in Celtic Studies). In 1969 he married Alice MacLeod, and they have one son, Morris Rae.

He taught Gaelic for 21 years at The Nicolson Institute (16 years as Principal Teacher), and is now Languages Adviser in the Education Department of Comhairle nan Eilean Siar. He is a member of the Executive Committee of An Comunn Gaidhealach, and was President of An Comunn Gaidhealach from 1985 to 1990. He has also been an editor of *Sruth*, a director of Acair Ltd, and a member of the Gaelic Books Council and of the National Gaelic Arts Project.

He has originated and compiled many school texts in Gaelic — Jacobite songs, crossword puzzles, humorous stories/anecdotes/jokes, and other texts based directly on the Gaelic curriculum for learners and fluent speakers. His main publications are *Camhanaich*, 1982, and *Grian is Uisge*, 1991 (collections of original short stories), *Eadar Peann is Pàipear*, 1985 (an anthology of short stories with a comprehensive introduction), *Coinneach Odhar*, 1990 (prophecies of the Brahan Seer), *Cò Rinn E?* of 1992 (a whodunit), and *A' Chlach*, 1993 (an account of the Stone of Destiny). His poems, and many stories, have appeared in *Gairm*, with poems also in *Northwords*. He has been a winner of poetry, short story, article, and new drama competitions at National Mods, and many of his stories have been broadcast on BBC Radio. Since 1997 he has been writing articles, stories and reviews in a regular Gaelic column for the *Stornoway Gazette* (in succession to the Rev. Roderick Macdonald, q.v.); he is Gaelic consultant to *An Gàidheal Ùr*, to which he also contributes material. A collection of his verse is much to be desired.

I am grateful to the poet for information and permission to reprint:

268   *Mathanas* (**'Forgiveness'**). Editor's trl. *Gairm* 128 (Am Foghar 1984) 324.

269   *Indira*. Editor's trl. *Gairm* 131 (An Samhradh 1985) 249. Mrs Indira Gandhi was prime minister of India 1966–77 and 1980–4. She was assassinated by a Sikh extremist in 1984.

270   *Cladh* (**'Graveyard'**). Editor's trl. *Gairm* 146 (An t-Earrach 1989) 115–16. 'Elegy in a Country Churchyard' by the English poet Thomas Gray (1716–71) was a staple of Scottish education for over a hundred years. Describing his schooldays in Colonsay *c.* 1850, Prof. Donald Mackinnon (1839–1914) wrote:

> The pupil's equipment was not hard to carry. A grey slate with some attempted calculations on it, writing-paper as cheap as the egg-wife could get in Greenock, ink from the sap of the oak-tree, a pen from the feather of the solan goose, Gray, the Shorter Catechism, a Gaelic Bible covered with sheepskin, and a good shinty-stick. (Lachlan Mackinnon (ed.), *The Prose Writings of Donald Mackinnon* (Edinburgh 1956) 267, translated)

271   *Dàin* (**'Poems'**). Editor's trl. *Gairm* 146 (An t-Earrach 1989) 116.

Myles M Campbell (Maoilios M Caimbeul) 1944—

Myles MacInnes Campbell was born 23 March 1944 in Staffin, Skye, fourth and youngest child of Donald Campbell, from Lionel, Ness, Lewis (*Dòmhnall Choinnich Thormoid*, 1899–1991), and his wife Effie MacInnes from Flodigarry, Skye (*Oighrig Mhaoilis*, 1904—), the others being Peter, Mary Ann and Kenann. As their father was a Free Church missionary, the family moved from parish to parish, and the poet's formative years were spent in Staffin, Uig (Skye), Borve (Lewis), Waternish (Skye), Portree High School (Skye), Glenelg (Inverness-shire) and Achmore (Lewis). He attended various schools, the last being Lewis Castle College, where he studied Navigation.

     The poet joined the merchant navy at 16. His first boat was the MV *Lairdsloch*, plying between Glasgow's Broomielaw docks and Derry, and he spent altogether three-and-a-half years on tankers and cargo boats, visiting such countries as Japan and Australia. Leaving the sea in 1964, he became successively wages clerk and prison officer in Inverness and wages clerk in Edinburgh before gaining Highers in night school (it was at this stage that he learned to write Gaelic) and going to Edinburgh University, where he graduated BA (Celtic, History, English) in 1976. After Jordanhill College he became Gaelic teacher in Tobermory High School in Mull.

     In 1971 he married Margaret Forrest Hutchison from Edinburgh and they had one son, Alasdair. They were divorced in 1992. During 1984–7 he was a Gaelic Development Officer with the Highlands and Islands Development Board in Inverness. In 1992 he moved to Skye, and now teaches Gaelic in Gairloch High School, commuting home to Flodigarry at weekends. He points out that a permanent thread runs through this constant change of scene — his determination to write and to view himself as a writer first and foremost. Writing, particularly the poetry, is for him an expression of inner exploration and development.

     His verse has appeared in journals such as *Gairm, Lines Review, Poetry Ireland Review, Comhar, Orbis* and *Gairfish*; in anthologies such as *Twenty of the Best* (1990), *An Aghaidh na Sìorraidheachd* (1991), *Siud an t-Eilean* (1993) and *Scotland o Gael and Lawlander* (1996). His poetry collections are *Eileanan* (Glasgow 1980), *Bailtean* (Glasgow 1987), *A' Càradh an Rathaid* [*CR*] (Dublin 1988) and *A' Gabhail Ris* [*GR*] (Glasgow 1994). He has also written novels for children and teenagers: *Clann a' Phroifeasair* (1988), *Talfasg* (1990), *Mèirlich nam Bradan* (1991), *Á Ulbha gu Geelong* (1992), *Murt ann an Diùranais* (1993), and *Iain agus na Drogaichean* (1993). His poetry has twice won Gaelic Books Council awards. He was scriptwriter for the team which produced the support materials (books and audio tapes) for series 2, 3 and 4 of the Gaelic learners' television series *Speaking Our Language*. Among more substantial assessments of his work are reviews in *Gairm* 115 (An Samhradh 1981) 279–83, *Gairm* 140 (1987) 381–4, *Lines Review* 137 (1996) 55–8, and comments by Iain Crichton Smith (q.v.) in 'Recent Gaelic Poetry', *Scottish Language* 8 (1989) 21–33. An edition of his collected work is much to be desired.

     I am grateful to the poet for information and permission to reprint:

272   Dòchas ('Hope'). Editor's trl. Eileanan 31–2.
273   Do Chròcus air a Shlighe a Nèamh ('To a Crocus on its Way to Heaven'). Author's trl.
        Gairm 100 (Am Foghar 1977) 373–4; Meic Stephens, Derick Thomson and Seán Ó Tuama (eds),
        International Poetry Review, Celtic Issue (Greensboro N.C. 1979); Eileanan 29–30.
274   An Referendum air son Pàrlamaid ann an Alba 1/3/79 ('The Referendum for a Scottish
        Assembly 1/3/79'). Editor's trl. with author's assistance. Eileanan 14–15. Devolution was
        debated with much more passion in the 1970s than in the 1990s, and this is a much more
        passionate poem than, say, Derick Thomson's 'Pàrlamaid an Dùn Èideann' (Gairm 188 (Am
        Foghar 1999) 305):

            Pàrlamaid an Dùn Èideann?   A parliament in Edinburgh?
            Ruigidh each mall muileann   A slow horse reaches a mill
            is tòisichidh am bleith.   and the grinding starts.

Although the Labour government's Scotland Act of 1978 provided a much weaker measure of
devolution than did that of 1998, Labour MP George Cunningham successfully moved in the
House of Commons that an assembly could only be created if 40% of the electorate voted 'yes' in
the Referendum. Given the excitement of the times and the likelihood of a high turnout,
nationally-minded people did not seriously doubt but that this would be achieved, and the
powdering of snow which covered Scotland on the morning of 1 March 1979 is ingrained in our
memories in the same way that we remember where we were when we heard the news of John F
Kennedy's assassination or of the Dunblane Massacre. In the event, 51.6% voted 'yes' and 48.4%
voted 'no', but the proportion of the electorate that had voted 'yes' was only 32.9%, so despite
Scotland voting in favour of it, devolution was lost.
        Votes were counted regionally, and the pattern that emerged is of cultural interest. The six
regions that voted 'yes' were those most strongly left-wing, urban, or Celtic: Western Isles,
Highland, Strathclyde, Central, Fife and Lothian. The six that voted 'no' were those with larger
rural or non-Celtic populations: Shetland, Orkney, Grampian, Tayside, Dumfries & Galloway,
and the Borders.
        There was some hope that devolution could still be saved, but amidst considerable bitterness,
the SNP withdrew their support for the Government, and Margaret Thatcher's Conservatives
swept into power in the ensuing election (see poem 197). On 11 September 1997 the next Labour
government held another referendum on devolution; this time every region voted 'yes', and the
40% hurdle was passed even though none had been imposed. But for many, the bitter taste of
disenfranchisement had lasted nearly twenty years, and is impossible to forget. This poem
reflects that feeling.
275   An t-Aran ('Bread'). Editor's trl. with author's assistance. Eileanan 32–3.
276   Na Liopan ('The Lips'). Author's trl. Gairm 114 (An t-Earrach 1981) 127; Bailtean 14–17.
277   An t-Eilean 'na Bhaile ('The Island a Town'). Author's trl. Bailtean 20–3. For Donald
        Morrison, Ardtun, see Eric Cregeen and Donald W MacKenzie, 'Donald Morrison', Tocher 24
        (1976–7) 289–319. Clann na h-Oidhche 'the Children of the Night' — from the fifteenth-century
        forename Mac na h-Oidhche — was the byname of those Morrisons descended from Ó
        Muirgheasáin poets, see Derick Thomson (ed.), Companion to Gaelic Scotland 219.
278   An Clamhan ('The Buzzard'). Author's trl. Bailtean 24–5.
279   Am Fear-Turais ('The Tourist'). Author's trl. Bailtean 30–1.
280   Glaschu ('Glasgow'). Author's trl. Bailtean 34–7.
281   Borgh Leódhais ('Borve, Lewis'). Author's trl. Bailtean 40–1. Borve is on the west side. For
        'black' houses (i.e. built of undressed stone, originally thatched, chimneyless, and with the fire
        originally in the middle of the floor) see note on poem 126. Strapaichean, 'belts', were leather
        straps or tawses for corporal punishment, normal in Scottish schools until the 1970s.
282   Gealach na Sultain ('September Moon'). Author's trl. CR 32–3.
283   From Haiku. Editor's trl. CR 48–9. Just one of twenty 3- or 4-line haikus in which Mull, the
        Far East and humanity speak to each other. Here's another: Thàinig na Mongolaich / oirnne
        cuideachd / ach càit an taiphun? "The Mongols came /upon us too / but where's the typhoon?"
284   A' Càradh an Rathaid ('Mending the Road'). Author's trl. CR 94–7.
285   Ceartas Coma a' Bhàis ('The Indifference of Death'). Editor's trl. with author's assistance.
        GR 22. The Stalinist dictator of Romania, Nicolae Ceauşescu (1918–89), who had impoverished
        and enslaved his people, was violently deposed by popular revolution and executed on
        Christmas Day 1989; for Patrick Sellar see poem 188.
286   An Éibhleag ('The Ember'). Editor's trl. with author's assistance. GR 28.
287   From Agus mar sin car a' Mhuiltein ('And so Somersault'). Editor's trl. with author's

assistance. *GR* 45–6. This prose-poem is a dream sequence in ten parts, each ending in some form of collapse with the words *agus mar sin car a' mhuiltein* . . .: (1) returning from Ronald's wedding in Ostavaig the narrator comes across Peggy Anna's horse, mounts it, goes off at a gallop and is thrown; (2) he climbs a stair into the night sky where he is surrounded by every full stop he has ever seen in books; falling, he is surrounded by sheep, who give him a dram; (3) he is brought by little green otherworld people into their *sìthean*; (4) a beautiful woman makes love to him; he faints again, and when he wakes up she has turned into a crab with its claws in his flesh; (5) in another room, amidst drinking and dancing, he meets the otherworld queen, who promises that after a year and a day he will return to Ostavaig; he tries to escape; (6) everything seems to have turned to stone, he lies as if in the grave and lines of verse come to him such as *far am biodh còmhradh, is tea, is blàths* ('where there would be talk, and tea, and warmth') from Derick Thomson's 'Cisteachan-Laighe' ('Coffins'); (7) he is attacked and torn apart by witches in Hell; (8) he wakes up sober at a temple door and is tended by men in black cloaks who bring him to *seòmar na tobrach*, the well-room; (9) the passage printed; (10) he wakes up in Ostavaig where he fell off the horse; it is the start of another day, and the sheep must be fed.

Ian MacDonald (Iain MacDhòmhnaill) 1946—

Ian MacDonald was born 25 June 1946 in Scalpay, Harris, his mother's island, and did not see his 'native' place of Grimsay, North Uist, for some days. He is the eldest child of Alick MacDonald, crofter-fisherman-carpenter, from Kallin in Grimsay (*Ailig Iain*, 1907—), and his wife Bella Morrison, from Scalpay (*Beileag Iain Thormoid*, 1911–96), the others being Mary and Effie Anne. He attended primary school in Kallin, Grimsay, and secondary school in Bayhead (N. Uist) and Inverness. He took an MA at Glasgow University during 1964–8 — a period of considerable misery, he says — and at Jordanhill College during the following year gained a certificate to teach Gaelic and English. He intended to teach eventually, but during 1969–73 took a variety of labouring jobs in Birmingham, Essex and Glasgow, usually working in Grimsay during the summer. He joined the Civil Service in London in January 1974, but became Editorial Officer of the Gaelic Books Council, Glasgow, in succession to John Murray (q.v.) in October 1976, and is there still, although his title is now Director.

Most of Ian MacDonald's writing was done in the 1960s, in Gaelic and English. The English largely remained unpublished, but Gaelic poems and stories have appeared in *Gairm* (mostly in the 1970s) and in a few other publications, such as the anthology of contemporary Gaelic verse in *Akros* vol. 11, no. 31 (August 1976). With Michael Davitt, he compiled the Scottish–Irish poetry anthology *Sruth na Maoile* (Canongate Press and Coiscéim, 1993), and he has silently edited many other books. He has translated several children's books, including *Am Mabinogi* (Club Leabhar, 1984), a Gaelic version of a modern re-telling of the medieval Welsh tales.

I am grateful to the poet for information and permission to reprint:

288 *Hearach* (**'Harrisman'**). Author's trl. *Open Space* 8 (Winter 1977) 5–6; *Gairm* 68 (Am Foghar 1969) 343.
289 *Turas* (**'Once'**). Author's trl. *Gairm* 68 (Am Foghar 1969) 343–4. For the use of seaweed as fertiliser (or to supply the alginates industry) see also poems 18, 113, 171.
290 *An t-Uisge* (**'The Rain'**). Author's trl. *Gairm* 92 (Am Foghar 1975) 364. For Eaval see poems 50, 181.
291 *Ainmeannan* (**'Names'**). Author's trl. *Gairm* 111/112 (Samhradh/Foghar 1980) 252.

Catriona Montgomery (Catrìona NicGumaraid) 1947—

Catriona Montgomery was born 22 March 1947 in Roag, Dunvegan, Skye, fifth of seven children of Murdo Montgomery (1901–73) and his wife Mary Beaton (1909—), the others being Alasdair (who died in childhood), Murdo, Donald, Thomas (who died in infancy), Flora, and the poet Morag, q.v. Her mother, along with others in the township, had many old songs, and she started composing Gaelic songs herself when in her teens. She was educated in Vatten Primary School, Portree High School, Glasgow University (where she graduated in Celtic and Scottish History), and Jordanhill College of Education.

At university she was deeply influenced (like many other young people of her era) by the poetry of Sorley MacLean, q.v.; it is an influence which is much to the fore in her early work — love poetry of which she says (*AAS* 140), *Chan e rud a bu toigh leam a dhèanamh, ach a dh'fheumainn a dhèanamh, a bh' innte.* "It was not something I enjoyed doing, but something I had to do." After two years teaching Gaelic and Modern Studies in a Glasgow school, she went to Sabhal Mór Ostaig, the Gaelic college in Skye, as its first *Filidh* or Writer in Residence. In 1975 she married Thomas McLaughlin and has lived since then in Dundee (where she taught for two years in an Assessment Centre) and now in Glasgow, where she works as an actress and writes scripts for radio and television. She has two children, Eilidh and Rob.

Her verse has appeared in the periodicals *Gairm* (1970–8), *Cencrastus* and *Lines Review*, in the joint collection *A' Choille Chiar* (with her sister Morag, 1974), in the anthologies *An Aghaidh na Sìorraidheachd* [*AAS*] (1991), *An Anthology of Scottish Women Poets* (1991) and *Sruth na Maoile* (1993), and in her own collection *Rè na h-Oidhche* [*RO*] (1994). Among the more substantial reviews of her work are those in *Gairm* 92 (Am Foghar 1975) 380–3, *Chapman* 78–9 (1994) 191–3, *Scottish Book Collector* 4, no. 5 (1994) 31, and *Lines Review* 137 (1996) 55–8; for a broader assessment see Meg Bateman, 'Women's Writing in Scottish Gaelic since 1750', in Douglas Gifford and Dorothy McMillan (eds), *A History of Scottish Women's Writing* (Edinburgh 1997) 659–76: 668–9. Over the years most of her poetry has become more public and less personal in nature, the exception being her religious verse.

I am grateful to the poet for information and permission to reprint:

292 **Gealladh Gaoil ('The Promise of Love').** Author's trl. *A' Choille Chiar* 14, *AAS* 144–5, *RO* 56–7.
293 **Sireadh ('Seeking').** Author's trl., slightly adapted. *A' Choille Chiar* 24, *RO* 36–9. The poet appears to be looking due south from Roag through Loch Bracadale to Canna and the Hyskeir Lighthouse.
294 **An Ceusadh ('The Crucifixion').** Author's trl. *RO* 66–7.

Fearghas MacFhionnlaigh, 1948—

Fearghas MacFhionnlaigh was born 25 November 1948 in the Vale of Leven, Dunbartonshire, eldest son of Stuart McKinlay and his wife Catherine Nugent. The family emigrated to Ontario in 1950, and two brothers were born in Toronto — Stuart, who is on the editorial staff of *The Herald*, and Neil, who is a Presbyterian minister in Australia. Two sisters, Catriona and Mhairi, were born after the family returned to the 'Vale' in 1958. Their father worked as a plater in shipyards around the Clyde.

Fearghas was educated at the Vale of Leven Academy, at Duncan of Jordanstone College of Art, Dundee, and at Jordanhill College of Education. After qualifying, he worked for three years as a 'Travelling Secretary' with the Inter-College Christian Fellowship. He now lives in Inverness with his wife Mary (Glasgow-born of Lewis parentage) and two children, Ciaran (16) and Cara (15), both Gaelic-speakers. He teaches art at Inverness Royal Academy; for a few years he also taught Gaelic-medium art at Millburn Academy, Inverness.

Fearghas understands that one of his great-grandmothers on his mother's side was a Gaelic speaker from Argyll, but his own parents had no knowledge of the language. His own interest in Gaelic grew in his teens, partly stimulated by the place-names around Loch Lomond, but also in reaction to the English syllabus at school, with its tacit message that Scottish language and literature were (apart from some Burns) irrelevant to education.

Converted to Christ when he was sixteen, Fearghas has been greatly influenced by the cultural and philosophical writings of Dutch Calvinist thinkers like Van Til and Dooyeweerd. Scottish (and particularly Gaelic) Calvinism was, he believes, early infected with Gnostic anti-materialism, and needs to be thoroughly critiqued. In this context he enjoys the story about Salvador Dali who, when asked what the difference was between himself and the other surrealists, answered, "The difference is that I *am* a surrealist!"

It was in his teens also that Fearghas formed his solid conviction that Scotland should be an independent republic. He formally gaelicised his name in 1983 by amending his birth certificate. This was his way of declaring a 'republic of the mind'.

Poetic influences on Fearghas include T S Eliot's *Wasteland*, Hugh MacDiarmid's *A Drunk*

Man Looks at the Thistle, Bob Dylan's Highway 61 Revisited, and early Gaelic nature poetry. His work has appeared in various Scottish and Irish magazines, pre-eminently Gairm — the early and ongoing support of Derick Thomson (q.v.) was a crucial encouragement — but also Chapman, Inniu, Comhar, Puente, Poetry Ireland Review and International Poetry Review. He has work in the anthologies An Aghaidh na Sìorraidheachd (1991) and Sruth na Maoile (1993), and has translated the Spanish of Pablo Neruda in Bàrdachd na Roinn Eòrpa (1990). His main works are an early children's novel Có Ghoid am Bogha-Froise? (1978) and three poem sequences: A' Mheanbhchuileag (Glasgow 1981), of which his own English translation appeared as 'The Midge' in Cencrastus 10 (Autumn 1982); Iolair, Brù-Dhearg, Giuthas (Glasgow 1991), in memory of his mother; and Bogha-Frois san Oidhche (Carberry 1997), a 'journal' of three harrowing months with his son in Edinburgh's Royal Hospital for Sick Children in 1990. He has twice participated in the annual Gaelic poets' tour of Ireland. Assessments of his work include reviews in Gairm 115 (An Samhradh 1981) 279–83, Lines Review 121 (1992) 45–7, Cencrastus 60 (1998) 26, and comments by Iain Crichton Smith (q.v.) in 'Recent Gaelic Poetry', Scottish Language 8 (1989) 21–33.

I am grateful to the poet for information and permission to reprint:

295   An Geiréiniam ('The Geranium'). Editor's trl. Gairm 97 (An Geamhradh 1976–7) 34.

296   Medusa, an Cuclopach, 's an Daily Record ('Medusa, the Cyclops, and the Daily Record'). Editor's trl. Gairm 100 (Am Foghar 1977) 333. Medusa was a beautiful girl who violated the temple of Athene, for which Athene turned her hair into serpents and made her face so ugly that all who looked on it were turned to stone. A Cyclops ('circular-eye') was a one-eyed giant whose work was to forge iron for Vulcan. Following the example of Rupert Murdoch's The Sun, every day from the early 1970s to the early 1990s Scotland's best-selling newspaper, The Daily Record, printed a photograph of a semi-naked girl on page 3.

297   An Tuagh ('The Axe'). Editor's trl. Gairm 106 (An t-Earrach 1979) 167–8. The first incident of Bannockburn, 23 June 1314. "To vanquish the king of Scots himself in single combat: such a feat of chivalry did not often come the way of an ambitious knight. Henry de Bohun rode at Bruce, lance at rest. Bruce pulled himself out of the path of the oncoming lance, so that, in Barbour's memorable line, 'Schir Henry myssit the nobill kyng'. As he drew level, Bruce raised himself up in his stirrups and with a mighty effort swung his axe downward so fiercely that the blade pierced Bohun's helmet and split his head in two. Bohun's body fell to the earth beside him, and Bruce was left holding the stump of his axe-shaft, shattered by the tremendous impact . . . The incident ought never to have occurred; yet its effect on the highlanders, islesmen and others in the king's brigade can be imagined and the story, as it spread back through the rest of the army, would lose nothing in the telling" (Geoffrey Barrow, Robert Bruce (2nd edn, Edinburgh 1976) 312).

298   Flùrannan ('Flowers'). Editor's trl. Gairm 106 (An t-Earrach 1979) 168–9.

299   From A' Mheanbhchuileag ('The Midge'). Author's trl. A' Mheanbhchuileag 5–8, 32; Cencrastus 10 (Autumn 1982) 28, 33. I reprint the beginning and end. Machu Picchu, high in the Peruvian Andes, is a fortress city of the Incas; probably their last stronghold following the Spanish Conquest, it was rediscovered virtually intact in 1911. The Japanese city of Hiroshima was destroyed by an atomic bomb on 6 August 1945. Argus in Greek mythology was a many-eyed monster who guarded Io, princess of Argos, when Zeus had turned her into a heifer. Alberto Giacometti (1901–66) was a Swiss sculptor, painter and poet. See p. lix above.

300   From Iolair, Brù-Dhearg, Giuthas ('Eagle, Robin, Pine'). Editor's trl. Iolair, Brù-Dhearg, Giuthas 13–15. Reflections on the death of the poet's mother, who died of cancer in November 1989, aged 59. The poem has 448 lines, of which nos. 214–49 are reprinted here. It is referred to in Bogha-Frois san Oidhche 158–9 at a point where Ciaran is recovering rapidly:

> Cha dèan mi a' chùis idir an oidhch' ud air dàn mo mhàthar.
> Mearachdan gun stad leis a' chlò-sgrìobhadair.
> A' tòiseachadh a-rithist 's a-rithist . . .

('I don't make any headway in the evening with my mother's poem. / Endless typing errors. / Restarting again and again.') See p. lix above.

301   From Bogha-Frois san Oidhche ('Rainbow in the Night'). Author's trl. Bogha-Frois san Oidhche 146–53. In January 1990 the poet's son Ciaran, then aged 7, was struck down by a brain virus which paralysed him for three months and threatened him with severe mental and physical

handicap. The poet struggles to find words with which to come to terms with the event. The poem has c.1,885 lines, not counting additional matter such as frequent quotations from scripture and *The Wizard of Oz*. It is in four sections, 'Preface', 'Dusk', 'Night' and 'Dawn'. I reprint the beginning of 'Dawn'; the scene is the Sick Children's Hospital in Edinburgh. See p. lix above.

Donald Graham (Dòmhnall Greumach) 1949—

Born 4 November 1949 in Stornoway, Donald Graham ('Jumbo') is a nephew of the poet Duncan Graham ('Dod'); his maternal grandfather (Murdo Murray) and aunts also wrote songs. He attended the Nicolson Institute 1961–7, and subsequently worked as bricklayer, then bonus clerk, with MacLeod of Skye. He married in 1976 and has two sons, Murray Angus and David. He attended Sabhal Mór Ostaig, the Gaelic-medium Business Studies college in Skye, then worked in Inverness for Highland Region translating books for schools. He returned to North Tolsta in 1990 to become a self-employed bricklayer, and is now also a part-time Gaelic teacher, writer and song collector. He has produced countless songs both comic and serious, and points out that although his chosen medium is often referred to as *bàrdachd baile* ('village poetry') as opposed to *bàrdachd cheart* ('real poetry'), it is far from clear whether such terms have any meaning. His 'Bodaich Ghorm' a' Chuain Sgì' is available commercially on tape, sung by D A Matheson; however, few of his 'songs' are actually set to music. Several of his short stories have been published in *Gairm*. He compiled *Rola Urram Tholastadh*, and his *Fealla-Dhà no Trì* (a joke book) and *Cleasan agus Ceistean* (a puzzle book) were published by Leabhraichean Beaga in 1993 and 1997 respectively.

I am grateful to the poet for information and permission to reprint:

302   *Superloo Steòrnabhaigh* (**'The Stornoway Superloo'**). Editor's trl. with author's advice. Published in *The Stornoway Gazette*, 12 May 1990, under the title 'Furtachd' ('Relief').

Morag Montgomery (Mòrag NicGumaraid) 1950—

Morag Montgomery was born 18 January 1950 in Roag, Dunvegan, Skye, sister of the poet Catriona Montgomery, q.v. She was educated in Vatten Bridge School and Portree High School, and spent a year at Glasgow School of Art before returning home to run the croft, with fifteen head of cattle, during her father's terminal illness. She was married in 1972 and went to live in Glendale where she had two sons, Murchadh (b. 1973) and Roy (b. 1979). Her eldest brother Murdo had suffered brain damage as a result of a motor accident in 1962 and was nursed at home by her mother; as the latter's health declined, the responsibility of caring for both her mother and brother fell on Morag's shoulders until they both went into a nursing home in 1989. The following year her son Russell was born and she and her sons moved to Sleat, Skye, where she attended a course at Sabhal Mór Ostaig. They then spent five months in Galway where she trained as a TV puppeteer and consequently wrote scripts and performed the character of Ceiti for the TV series *Mire Mara*.

Morag has read her poetry all over Scotland and Ireland and has been three times on the Scottish–Irish arts tour (see p. xliii). Her life and poetry were featured in a docudrama series in Germany directed by Hardy Kruger and filmed in 1990. Her poetry has appeared in *Gairm* (1970–5), in the joint collection *A' Choille Chiar* (with her sister Catriona, 1974), and in the anthology *Sruth na Maoile* (1993). She continues to live in Sleat with her sons, and has been writing and illustrating a children's novel. Tragically, in 1998 her son Roy was killed in a road accident.

I am grateful to the poet for information and permission to reprint:

303   *Uaireannan tha eagal orm* (**'Sometimes I'm afraid'**). Editor's trl. *Gairm* 82 (An t-Earrach 1973) 158.
304   *Geamhradh* (**'Winter'**). Editor's trl. *Gairm* 85 (An Geamhradh 1973) 48.
305   *Coilleag ghlan gheal chadalach* (**'Pure white sleepy cockle'**). Editor's trl. *A' Choille Chiar* 47.
306   *Dùisgidh mi aon mhadainn* (**'I'll wake up one morning'**). Editor's trl. *A' Choille Chiar* 48.
307   *An t-Amadan* (**'The Fool'**). Editor's trl. *Gairm* 89 (An Geamhradh 1974–5) 26–7.

308   *Muilemhàgag* ('Toad'). Editor's trl. *Gairm* 89 (An Geamhradh 1974–5) 27–8.

Duncan MacLaren (Donnchadh MacLabhrainn) 1950—

Duncan MacLaren was born 22 March 1950 in Dumbarton, and brought up in Clydebank. He is of Gaelic-speaking Perthshire stock, but the language had petered out in the family two generations before, so he had to reacquire it. He studied Celtic and German at Glasgow University and, much later, graduated MTh in theology and development studies from New College, Edinburgh University. He has variously been a researcher for the Historical Dictionary of Scottish Gaelic; a researcher in the House of Commons for SNP MPs; national press officer for the SNP; and the first director of Scotland's only aid and development agency, the Scottish Catholic International Aid Fund. He now works in Rome as Head of International Relations for Caritas Internationalis, the largest network of relief, development and social service agencies in the world.

Duncan's Gaelic poetry, short stories and articles have been published in many journals, but his more recent writing has mostly been on political, development, and theological topics, in English. He appears in *Sruth na Maoile* (1993) and *The Radical Tradition: Saints in the Struggle for Justice and Peace* (DLT 1992), recently translated into Hungarian. He is a founder member of the Glasgow Lay Dominicans, attached to the Roman Catholic Order of Preachers.

I am grateful to the poet for information and permission to reprint:

309   **Clydebank.** Editor's trl. with author's advice. *Gairm* 115 (An Samhradh 1981) 227; *Sruth na Maoile* 146–7. 'Woolies' is a Woolworth's store, and 1690, the date of the Boyne, is a sectarian war-cry in the urban west of Scotland. This poem is one of a pair; in the other, Clydebank is imagined as a Gaelic-speaking place and, concludes the poet, *thigeadh lughdachadh air / do bhochdainn chràidh*: 'your grinding poverty / would be diminished'.

Julian Ronay, 1951—

Born 16 December 1951 in Musselburgh, Julian is the son of Julian Ronay, naval officer, of Herne Hill, London, and his wife Marjory Doyle. His maternal grandmother, Jessie Miller, of Ulbster, Caithness, was a full cousin of the novelist Neil M Gunn. Educated at Edinburgh Academy, he has lived in London, Brighton and Paris, and has had various jobs, mainly working in bookshops and doing unskilled gardening work. Self-taught in Gaelic and (in his own words) 'still very much a learner', his Gaelic poems have been appearing consistently in *Gairm* since 1974, while his poems in English have been published in *Understanding, Breakthrough, Melting Pot, Beyond Diagnosis, Inspirations from Scotland*, etc. His main love and interest, he says, is Gaelic poetry.

I am grateful to the poet for information and permission to reprint:

310   **Bi air t' Fhaiceall ('Be Careful').** Editor's trl. *Gairm* 89 (1974–5) 25. Cymdeithas yr Iaith Gymraeg ('the Welsh Language Society') was formed in response to the poet Saunders Lewis's impassioned appeal of 1962 to 'go to it in earnest and without wavering to make it impossible to conduct local authority or central government business without the Welsh language'. Its activities provide a model for minority-language activists. See Robert Owen Jones, 'The Welsh Language', in R Black, W Gillies and R Ó Maolalaigh (eds), *Celtic Connections* (Edinburgh 1999) 425–56: 433.

311   **From A' Dràibheadh ann an Ameireaga ('Driving in America').** Editor's trl. *Gairm* 144 (Am Foghar 1988) 308. The poem has 67 lines, of which nos. 16–27 are reprinted. It goes on to offer an equally gentle critique of the triumph of style over substance.

312   **Féin-Mhort, Lunnainn a-Deas ('Suicide, South London').** Editor's trl. *Gairm* 170 (An t-Earrach 1995) 162.

Christopher Whyte (Crìsdean Whyte) 1952—

Christopher Whyte was born 29 October 1952 in the West End of Glasgow. Of his grandparents, three had emigrated from Ulster: a MacAloon from Glenties in County Donegal, a Fergusson from Newry in County Down and a MacCrossan from Killiclogher in County Tyrone. In medieval Ireland *crosánaigh* were satirical rhymers who performed scurrilous verses at funerals. Perhaps some of that spirit survives in their distant offspring. His father's father was of Scottish Protestant stock and may well have been a Highlander.

After studying at St Aloysius' College, Glasgow (an institution which bears a suspicious resemblance to St Ignatius' Academy in his first novel, *Euphemia MacFarrigle and the Laughing Virgin*, 1995), he took an English degree at Pembroke College, Cambridge, in 1973, and left for Italy, where he spent most of the period until 1985. He was a language teacher and a university lector in both Rome and Bari, and it was in Rome that he began the serious study of Gaelic, helped by a summer spent washing dishes at Ord House Hotel in Sleat, Skye. An important part of his apprenticeship involved translating the larger part of the poetry of Sorley MacLean (q.v.) into Italian, mainly for private satisfaction (though a part has been published).

Translations into Gaelic of the work of Cavafis and Ritsos (one of which has since been attributed to Iain Crichton Smith, q.v.) appeared in *Gairm* in 1982, but it was not until 1987 that Whyte attempted original composition in the language. Professor Derick Thomson (q.v.) provided constant support and encouragement during these years, as well as supervising the PhD on the poetry and prose of Uilleam MacDhunléibhe (1808–70) which Whyte submitted to Glasgow University in 1991. By that time he was lecturing in the Department of Scottish Literature at Glasgow, having taught between 1986 and 1989 in the Department of English Literature in Edinburgh.

His first collection *Uirsgeul / Myth* (1991) was joint winner of a Saltire Award in 1992, and since then his work has appeared regularly in Scottish magazines, as well as being translated into Croatian, Albanian and Italian. An extended cycle 'An Tràth Duilich', composed in winter 1989–90, has been published only in part (*Chapman* 74–5, 1993), while a third long sequence, 'Bho Leabhar-Latha Maria Malibran', appeared in two successive issues of *Gairm* in 1996. Another, 'Fontana Maggiore', is still incomplete. Among reviews of his verse are those in *Lines Review* 121 (1992) 45–7 and *Gairm* 158 (An t-Earrach 1992) 181–3.

In 1991 the poet edited the anthology *An Aghaidh na Sìorraidheachd: Ochdnar Bhàrd Gàidhlig / In the Face of Eternity: Eight Gaelic Poets*. He benefited from the advice of Ian MacDonald (q.v.) of the Gaelic Books Council in preparing the text for publication, and since then MacDonald has often been the first person to read, and comment upon, his original verse in Gaelic. In 1995 he embarked upon a successful career as a fiction writer in English; his second novel, *The Warlock of Strathearn* (1997) won a Scottish Arts Council Award, while his third, *The Gay Decameron*, appeared in paperback in 1999.

I am grateful to the poet for information and permission to reprint:

313   *Ro-dh'aithnich mi* ('I foresaw'). Author's trl. *Uirsgeul* 10–13.
314   *Thug thu cead dhomh* ('You gave me permission'). Author's trl. *Uirsgeul* 30–3.
315   *Fontana Maggiore*. Author's trl. *Uirsgeul* 78–83. This sequence takes as its starting point the fountain in the main square of Perugia, Italy, built by Nicola and Giovanni Pisano in 1272–3. The final paragraphs of the opening section incorporate inscriptions from a range of the monuments left by Giovanni.
316   *An Daolag Shìonach* ('The Chinese Beetle'). Editor's trl. with author's assistance. *Gairm* 172 (Am Foghar 1995) 326.
317   Two sections of *Bho Leabhar-Latha Maria Malibran* ('From the Diary of Maria Malibran'). Editor's trl. with author's assistance. *Gairm* 175 (An Samhradh 1996) 272–3; *Gairm* 176 (Am Foghar 1996) 371–2. Malibran (1808–36), an opera singer, was a close friend of both Rossini and Bellini. Flaubert and Turgenev were assiduous members of the salon which her sister Pauline Viardot subsequently held in Paris. The poem is part fact, part fiction. As published in *Gairm* it has 744 lines, of which nos. 63–98 and 705–44 are reprinted here. The first extract conveys something of the flavour of the 'diary', which combines gossip and memories, lyric force and dramatic tension; the second is the poem's conclusion, the italics being the poet's own.

Angus Peter Campbell (Aonghas Pàdraig Caimbeul) 1954—

Angus Peter Campbell was born 29 April 1954 in South Boisdale, South Uist, son of Ewan Campbell from Ludag (*Eòghainn Mòr Aonghais Nìll Aonghais Iain Mhòir*) and his wife Christina MacDonald from Garrynamonie (*Ciorstaidh Eòghainn Mhòir 'ic Dhòmhnaill 'ic Aonghais 'ic*

Alastair). His name often appears in the form *Aonghas-Phàdraig*, as used in the district. His uncle was Neil Campbell (*Niall Mòr*), well known as the long-serving ferryman between Ludag, Eriskay and Barra. On his mother's side he is a second cousin to the famous piping brothers from Glenuig, Angus, Allan and Iain MacDonald.

Angus Peter was brought up in Garrynamonie. After leaving primary school there he went at age 12 to Oban High School, where his English teacher was Iain Crichton Smith, q.v. He is grateful to Smith for exposing him to international literature when such exposure was not fashionable in Scottish schools. Hamlet one day, Donnchadh Bàn the next, then Lowell the day after was, he says, the fine seed that Smith sowed. At Edinburgh University he obtained an Honours degree in Politics and History while doing a 'secret' degree in literature, being particularly interested in the modern American poetry of Roethke, Stevens, Hugo and the Latin-American work of such as Marquez. He was also greatly influenced by a visiting tutor from UCLA, Richard Ashcroft, a declared Marxist, and by Sorley MacLean (q.v.), who was the University's Writer in Residence at that time.

On leaving university Angus Peter joined the *West Highland Free Press* as its first-ever Gaelic-speaking journalist, then moved on to BBC Radio and Grampian Television, again as that station's first-ever Gaelic-speaking reporter. In the late 1980s he became a well-known Christian activist, turning his back on the media world to live and work in the housing estates of Muirhouse and Pilton in Edinburgh. He returned to the Gaidhealtachd in 1990 as *Sgrìobhaiche* at Sabhal Mór Ostaig, where he now lectures on Gaelic culture and media. He is married to Lyndsay Howieson, a sculptor, and has four daughters, Shona, Màiri, Steaphanaidh and Brìghde.

Through the 1980s Angus Peter's poetry appeared periodically in *Gairm*. His first published collection, *The Greatest Gift* (1992), was in English, and was well received, being described by Sorley MacLean as 'a masterpiece'. *Cairteal gu Meadhan-Latha*, a novel for teenagers, appeared in the same year, and another collection, *One Road*, including several Gaelic poems, in 1994. His outstandingly honest and ground-breaking novel for teenagers, *Gealach an Abachaidh*, was produced by Acair in 1999 for use in schools by Comhairle nan Eilean Siar. It is to be followed by one for younger children, *Am Motorbaidhseagal agus Sgàthan*.

The poet is also working on an epic Gaelic novel for adults which concerns itself with the abuse of power across the twentieth century. He points out that his verse primarily concerns itself with disintegration, the disintegration of Gaelic language and tradition serving as parables for the wider human disintegration that is evident wherever one turns, be it Vietnam or Croatia; and that his poetry, while consciously rooted in the local, has universal resonances, and vice versa. He discusses his background and questions of identity in 'Cò Mi agus Co As? / Who am I and From Whence?', *Cothrom* 19 (Earrach 1999) 10–12. Reviews of *One Road* appeared in, among other places, *Edinburgh Review* 93 (1995) 226–9; *Lines Review* 132 (1995) 55–7; and (by Iain Crichton Smith) *Cencrastus* 51 (1995) 33.

I am grateful to the poet for information and permission to reprint:

318   *Ràdar Beinn Sheaval* ('The Radar of Beinn Sheaval'). Editor's trl. *Gairm* 121 (An Geamhradh 1982–3) 58–9. From 1956 to 1999 Benbecula and S. Uist were home to a rocket range and a number of tracking stations. The presence of the Army in the Western Isles was bitterly controversial at first, and led to the film *Rockets Galore*, but as long as the 'Cold War' lasted it brought the islands a measure of prosperity in the form of jobs and facilities.

319   *Gearraidh na Mònadh á Smeircleit* ('Garrynamonie from Smerclate'). Author's trl. *One Road* 34–5.

320   *Oidhche Chullaig* ('Hogmanay Night'). Author's trl. *One Road* 98–101. *Cullaig* is the S. Uist variant of *Callainn* ('New Year'), for which see poem 25. The principal elements in the traditional celebration of New Year's Eve in Gaelic Scotland are: (1) the scapegoat — a band of young men parades round the houses, one dressed in an animal's skin and being beaten with sticks; (2) a specific rhyme is recited at the door of each house, followed by such words as: *Fosgail an doras is leig a-staigh mi!*; (3) the singed dewlap (*caisean uchd*, here reduced to *cais*) of a sheep is passed around and sniffed for good luck by each person present; (4) small gifts are given. All of these elements are present to some extent in the poet's recollections except the first. The three quatrains in the poem are traditional and are taken from Margaret Fay Shaw (ed.), *Folksongs and Folklore of South Uist* (2nd edn, Oxford 1977) 24. For the Lewis song 'An Caióra' by Murdo Morrison (d. 1932) see James Thomson and Duncan MacDonald (eds), *Eilean Fraoich: Lewis*

Gaelic Songs and Melodies (2nd edn, ed. by Duncan M Morison *et al.*, Stornoway 1982) 185–6; see also poem 267.

321 **Farpais Réidio nan Gaidheal ('The Gaelic Radio Quiz').** Author's trl. *One Road* 120–1.

Mary Montgomery (Màiri NicGumaraid) 1955—

Mary Montgomery was born 23 March 1955 in Arivruaich, Lochs, Lewis, youngest of three children of the late Iain Montgomery, who was born in Canada (*Iain Dhòmhnaill 'An Tàilleir*, 1917–79), and his wife Jessina Martin, from Melbost, Point (*Jessina Sheonaidh Eòghainn*, 1924—), the others being Jessie Anne and Donald. Jessie Anne died tragically as the result of a road accident in Croy, outside Inverness, in 1986, leaving four children. She was 40. Donald, a year younger, is a director at Johnston's mill in Elgin and a frequent traveller abroad. He is married with three of a family.

Mary's grandfather, Donald Montgomery, had emigrated to Canada from Balallan at the beginning of the twentieth century and worked as a sheep farm manager outside Calgary, Alberta, later returning with his three surviving children to Lewis where he established himself as a grocer, tweed merchant and fish salesman. Following his death the business passed to his son Iain, who retained Canadian citizenship throughout his life. Altogether six out of seven members of Donald's family emigrated to the New World, leaving Mary's paternal relatives thoroughly dispersed and global.

By contrast, although some of her Martin relatives are featured in *Pioneers of the West* (Edmonton, Alberta 1995?), the core and extended links of her mother's family remain firmly embedded in south Lewis and Harris, where thanks to sheer numbers (and her mother's strong interest in genealogy) Mary's awareness of having an identity within a close but evolving community was fostered from a very early age. She enjoyed a materially secure upbringing against the backdrop of a rural community which offered much in the way of artistic and spiritual experience. She points out that writing became part of the traditional process of learning, providing expression as well as experimentation of ideas, and the exploring of ideas remains at the heart of her reasons for writing poetry.

Her work has appeared in two collections, *Eadar Mi 's a' Bhreug* (1988) and *Ruithmean 's Neo-Rannan* (1997), both published by Coiscéim of Dublin and including translations into Irish, and in anthologies and periodicals such as *An Aghaidh na Sìorraidheachd*, *Sruth na Maoile*, *Gairm* and *Chapman*. Her *Clann Iseabail* (Stornoway 1993) has been described as the best Gaelic novel since Norman Campbell's *Deireadh an Fhoghair* of 1979. Among the more substantial reviews of her verse are those in *Chapman* 54 (1988) 88–90 and *Gairm* 145 (An Geamhradh 1988–9) 90–2; for broader assessments see Fearghas MacFhionnlaigh, '"Leth-Shealladh den Leth-Sgeul" — Màiri NicGumaraid', in *Gairm* 160 (Am Foghar 1992) 363–7, and Meg Bateman, 'Women's Writing in Scottish Gaelic since 1750', in Douglas Gifford and Dorothy McMillan (eds), *A History of Scottish Women's Writing* (Edinburgh 1997) 659–76: 669–70. Since leaving Aberdeen University in 1976 she has worked mainly in Gaelic development and broadcasting. Her most recent position has been that of lecturer in Lews Castle College's Communications Section.

Mary has remained unmarried since her divorce from John Cameron of Stornoway in the mid-1980s, but has two children (twins) from her relationship with Iain MacLeod of Habost, Lochs: Donald Montgomery MacLeod and John Martin MacLeod, born 1996. At present, caring for Donald and John is her main preoccupation.

I am grateful to the poet for information and permission to reprint:

322 **Sgillinn leis nach Ceannaichear Càil ('A Penny that Buys Nothing').** Editor's trl. *Gairm* 100 (Am Foghar 1977) 363–4.

323 **Do Dhol-a-Mach ('Your Carry-On').** Editor's trl. *Gairm* 104 (Am Foghar 1978) 340–1.

324 **Soraidh Leibh ('Farewell').** Editor's trl. *Ruithmean 's Neo-Rannan* 34–7. Reflects events on a Gaelic poets' tour of Ireland in 1990 (see p. xliii), and compares Scottish confusion with Irish confidence in matters of linguistic identity. The Irish national anthem 'Amhrán na bhFiann', quoted in Irish in the penultimate section, is never sung other than in Irish. There is no Scottish Gaelic national anthem as there is not considered to be a Scottish Gaelic nation. Formal gatherings at the start of the century might have concluded with 'God Save the King' sung in English or Gaelic; by the middle of the century, following An Comunn Gaidhealach's non-

political ethos, John MacFadyen's 'Soraidh Leibh is Oidhche Mhath Leibh' ('Farewell and Goodnight be with you') was more likely, though it is a poor song compared even to 'Auld Lang Syne'. It was composed in 1907, see *Gairm* 11 (An t-Earrach 1955) 244. In recent years 'Flower of Scotland' has become very popular throughout Scotland, sung in the language in which it was composed, English. Various Gaelic versions of it have been published, but there is no standard, universally recognised Gaelic version.

Meg Bateman, 1959—

Vivienne Margaret Bateman was born in Edinburgh on 13 April 1959 of two English geneticists. Though her parentage was scientific, her grandfather, John Bateman, had published a collection of poems, *The Passing of Youth*, in 1921. Meg's upbringing in the New Town with three other children (now a hospital manager, a shepherd and an architect), by a mother who was open to all sorts of suggestions and a father who possessed enormous *joie de vivre*, was largely blissful. Her only misgivings took the form of a yearning for a community that was not class-based, for a way of life that was less technological, and for a mode of expression that came more easily than piano-playing.

The imperative to express the discrepancy between what is felt and what can be spoken she felt from an early age, but poetry did not become its outlet until her mid-twenties. When the question of university arose, she sought to realise the first two of these ideals and went to study Gaelic at Aberdeen University. She spent a year in West Kilbride in South Uist with Mary Kate and Peter Morrison (*Pàdraig Aonghais Dhùghaill Bhàin*), to whom she is indebted for much more than the language. She graduated in Gaelic Studies and went on to do a PhD in Classical Gaelic Religious Poetry. It was during this period of unfocused research that Meg started writing in Gaelic, for it was Gaelic poetry that had shaped her literary sensibilities during university. While finding the process of writing fascinating, and the result something of a life-line, she stopped writing for five years with doubts about her exhibitionism and self-obsession. The birth of her son, Colm, gave her a new zest for life, and the release from an unhappy relationship with his father returned her energies to her. She taught at Aberdeen University from 1991 to 1998, and now lectures at Sabhal Mór Ostaig in Skye.

Meg's poetry has been published in the collections *Òrain Ghaoil* (Dublin 1990) and *Aotromachd agus Dàin Eile* (Edinburgh 1997), in the anthologies *Fresh Oceans* (1988), *Other Tongues* (1989), *Twenty of the Best* (1990), *An Anthology of Scottish Women Poets* (1990), *An Aghaidh na Sìorraidheachd* (1991), *Internal Landscapes* (1991), *Dreamstate* (1993), *Sruth na Maoile* (1993), and in the magazines *Gairm*, *Chapman*, *Lines Review*, *Verse* etc. *Aotromachd*, her second collection, was short-listed for the Stakis Prize in 1997 and won a Scottish Arts Council book award. Among the most substantial reviews of her work to date are those by Derick Thomson in *Gairm* 155 (An Samhradh 1991) 285–6 and *Gairm* 179 (An Samhradh 1997) 283–4, and by Christopher Whyte in *Lines Review* 141 (1997) 43–9.

I am grateful to the poet for information and permission to reprint:

325   **Dealbh mo Mhàthar ('Picture of my Mother').** Author's trl. *Òrain Ghaoil* 76–7; *Other Tongues* 60–1; *An Aghaidh na Sìorraidheachd* 16–17.

326   **Do Sgoilear Àraidh ('To a Certain Academic').** Editor's trl. *Gairm* 141 (An Geamhradh 1987–8) 42–3.

327   **Ceist ('Question').** Editor's trl. *Gairm* 141 (An Geamhradh 1987–8) 43; cf. *Òrain Ghaoil* 86–7.

328   **Cìocharan ('Breastling').** Author's trl. *Aotromachd* 78–9.

329   **Ath-Chruthachadh ('Transformation').** Author's trl. *Aotromachd* 82–3.

330   **Cuireadh dhan Bheatha ('Invitation to Life').** Author's trl. *Aotromachd* 84–5.

331   From **Do Fhear-Pòsta ('To a Married Man').** Author's trl. *Aotromachd* 94–5. The poem has seven parts; this is part 3.

Rody Gorman, 1960—

Born 1 January 1960 in Dublin, Rody Gorman has been in Scotland since 1987 when he came to Sabhal Mór Ostaig. During 1989–92 he was Assistant Director, and during 1992–5 Director, of its Gaelic Terminology Database Unit, overseeing the publication of its first volume (*An Stòr-*

Dàta Briathrachais Gàidhlig, Leabhar I) in 1993. In 1998 he graduated MA in Gaelic Studies from the University of Aberdeen, and was appointed Writer-in-Residence at Sabhal Mór Ostaig.

He began writing Scottish Gaelic poetry in 1994, and his collection *Fax and Other Poems* was published by Polygon in 1996, the same year in which he took part in a tour of Ireland by Scottish poets and musicians (see p. xliii). Another collection, *Cùis-Ghaoil*, was published by Diehard of Edinburgh in 1999. Some of his verse in Irish has been published in the anthology *An Chéad Chló* (Cló Iar-Chonnachta 1997), and a collection *Bealach Garbh* is to be published by Coiscéim of Dublin. His poetry has featured in *Scratch, Seam, The Rialto, Cencrastus, Verse, Chapman, Lines Review, New Writing Scotland, Gairm, Poetry Ireland Review, Innti, The Honest Ulsterman, Cyphers* and other periodicals and anthologies, and has been translated by William Neill (q.v.) and others. Since 1997 he has been Gaelic editor of *New Writing Scotland*, and since 1998 of *Poetry Scotland*. He has won various literary prizes. Among more substantial reviews of his work are those in *Cencrastus* 58 (1997) 29–30 and *Lines Review* 141 (1997) 43–9.

I am grateful to the poet for information, for sending a pre-publication draft of *Cùis-Ghaoil*, and for permission to print:

332 **Air Bàs Charles Bukowski ('On the Death of Charles Bukowski').** Author's trl. *Fax* 24–5. The American poet Charles Bukowski (1920–94) worked variously as dishwasher, truck driver and postman while learning his craft. A cult success as an underground writer, he evoked a world of low-lifers through his pared-down style and sardonic sense of humour.

333 **Ìomhaighean ('Images').** Author's trl. *Fax* 32–3. Kim Basinger (1953—) is a Hollywood actress. Sheila-na-gigs are nude female figures with genitals prominently exposed. They are to be found carved in stone in medieval buildings (especially churches) throughout western Europe, but especially in Ireland, see James O'Connor, *Sheela na Gig* (Fethard Historical Society, Co. Tipperary 1991). Gorman's *Síle nan Cìoch*, Irish *Síle na gCíoch* ('Sheila of the Breasts'), comes with the authority of the *Oxford English Dictionary*, but more recent research suggests that the term is correctly *Síle na Díg* or *Gíg* 'Sheila of the Vulva' and that the figures, far from being obscene, represent the act of childbirth. I am grateful to Dr Barbara Freitag, Dublin, for pointing this out.

334 **Ubhal ('An Apple').** Editor's trl. *Fax* 36.

335 **Deich Bliadhna ('Ten Years').** Author's trl. *Fax* 48–9.

336 **Leumadair Bungee ('Bungee Jumper').** Editor's trl. with author's assistance. *Cùis-Ghaoil* 15. The expression *ge b' oil le m' amhaich* means literally 'though my neck didn't like it'.

337 **Rodeo.** Editor's trl. From draft of *Cùis-Ghaoil*, omitted in published book.

338 **Gnìomhair is Cuspair ('Verb and Subject').** Editor's trl. *Cùis-Ghaoil* 48. A more literal translation for *gnìomhair* 'verb' might be 'doing word'. *Cuspair* 'subject' also means 'target'; in the sense of the object of the poet's affections it is a common term in love songs.

339 **An Oidhch' Ud ('That Night').** Editor's trl. *Cùis-Ghaoil* 58.

Peadar Morgan, 1960—

Peadar Morgan was born 13 February 1960 as Alexander Peter Morgan to a local family in Broughty Ferry, Dundee. Four years later the family moved to North London, and as holidays were always spent with his mother's family in Kingussie, it is with Badenoch that he identifies most and there that he first came into contact with Gaelic. He returned to Scotland to attend Aberdeen University, after which interest became passion and he learnt the language. He later attended Sabhal Mór Ostaig as a student. He has worked collecting oral history in Badenoch and as a journalist on the local paper, as Assistant Director of the Gaelic Terminology Database Unit, and as Learners' Development Officer with Comunn na Gàidhlig. He is now Director of Comann an Luchd Ionnsachaidh (CLI). He married another learner, Dawn Adamson, in 1996.

He started composing Gaelic verse while still learning the language, and his poems have been published in *Gairm*, in *Northwords* and in *Verse*. He claims that 'the muse got fed up waiting for more and left'. He is the author of various Gaelic articles and published translations, among the latter being *Asterix the Gaul*. He is editor of CLI's highly successful bilingual quarterly *Cothrom*.

I am grateful to the poet for information and permission to reprint:

340 **Dùn Dà Làmh.** Author's trl. *Gairm* 152 (Am Foghar 1990) 317–18. Dùn da Làmh [*sic*] is a

vitrified fort in Badenoch. At the time of the poem it was not known whether 'Two-Handed Fort' referred to the hill's two peaks or to the two straths below it. In any case Peadar Morgan now prefers 'Fort of Hands', following the interpretation of the name as older *Dùn inda Làmh* by Roibeard Ó Maolalaigh, 'Place-Names as a Resource for the Historical Linguist', in Simon Taylor (ed.), *The Uses of Place-Names* (Edinburgh 1998) 12–53: 20. Crathie was a crofting township where the two types of Christianity met. It was deserted by the last person in 1952. Lachlan MacPherson, tacksman of Strathmashie (*c.*1723–*c.*1767), was a renowned Gaelic poet.

341   **Coinneal ('Candle').** Author's trl. *Gairm* 154 (An t-Earrach 1991) 154.

342   *Trafaig Oidhche* **('Night Traffic').** Author's trl. *Gairm* 156 (Am Foghar 1991) 326.

Donald Munro (Dòmhnall Rothach) 1962—

Born 4 May 1962 into a family of 'Glasgow Highlanders', Donald Munro was raised in Kirkintilloch and Balerno. As in many such families, Gaelic was spoken in the home and the house was filled with Gaelic music, but the language was not passed on to the children; nevertheless, as he points out in the words of the saying, "You couldn't buy or sell him in it." He studied at Glasgow University. He has worked as a historian with the Scottish Urban Archaeological Trust and has taught Creative Writing for Glasgow University as a part-time lecturer. He currently lives in Knapdale, working as a software engineer. Again, like many of his background, the effort of working in Gaelic often seemed disproportionate, but he felt a compelling need to write in that medium. His Gaelic verse has been published in *Gairm, Chapman, Northlight, New Writing Scotland 1993* and in the anthology *Siud an t-Eilean*. His short stories in English have appeared in *Chapman, An Cànan*, and the Scottish Arts Council collection *The Laughing Playmate*. I am grateful to him for information and permission to reprint:

343   *Madainn Sneachda* **('Snowy Morning').** Editor's trl. *Gairm* 155 (An Samhradh 1991) 272–3.

Colin MacKinnon (Cailein MacFhionghain) 1963—

Colin MacKinnon was born 25 July 1963 in Daliburgh, S. Uist. Both his parents are from S. Uist: his father a schoolmaster, his mother a nurse. He has an Honours degree in Celtic from the University of Edinburgh, and is now working as a television reporter with BBC Scotland in Glasgow. He has published only one other piece of poetry ('Peacadh?', *Gairm* 155, An Samhradh 1991), but would like to spend more time writing. I am grateful to him for information and permission to reprint:

344   *Cothrom Peanais* **('Penalty').** Editor's trl. *Gairm* 133 (An Geamhradh 1985–6) 42. Jock Stein, legendary Celtic manager and then manager of Scotland, died of a heart attack at a World Cup qualifying match in Cardiff, 10 September 1985. Scotland were awarded a penalty right at the end of the match while losing 1–0. From the resulting goal — 'late relief' — they secured their place in the World Cup, but at the expense of their manager's life. See Ruaraidh (Òg) MacThòmais, 'Jock Stein (1920–1985)', in Ruaraidh MacThòmais (ed.), *Ainmeil an Eachdraidh* (Glasgow 1997) 65–70.

Alasdair Barden, 1963–98

Alasdair Barden was born 28 December 1963 in Nairobi, Kenya, son of Dr Patrick Barden from Eastbourne in Sussex and his wife Dr Elizabeth Marsh from Bristol. At the age of four and five years, however, he spent some time in Skye. His father was then working in Uig, setting up Skye's Artificial Insemination Service for Cattle, affectionately known as *an Tarbh air Ceithir Cuibhlichean*, 'the Bull on Four Wheels'. Though Gaelic was not spoken at home, Alasdair was taught the language by his father, who was himself learning while in Uig, and by Miss Màiri Robertson, the headmistress at Uig, who was keen that Alasdair should be conversant with the Gaelic reader *Alasdair agus Màiri* before he went to school. Subsequently brought up in Haddington, East Lothian, when his mother worked as a doctor in Edinburgh, Alasdair was educated there at Haddington Primary and Knox Academy (where he was dux); he forgot his Gaelic however and was horrified to discover at the age of 19 or 20, when he found *Alasdair agus Màiri* in a cupboard at home, that he could no longer read a word of the language.

Inspired by the music of Runrig, he studied Gaelic again in his spare time while a medical student at Edinburgh University, reaching fluency by attending conversation classes run by Johanna Campbell, *Seonag Toronto*, from Callanish in Lewis. At her classes she not only taught the pure Callanish Gaelic of the late nineteenth century but also confirmed in Alasdair his desire to live and work in a Gaelic-speaking area. He began at this time to precent the psalms at the Gaelic services in Greyfriars' Kirk. He had taken degrees in science and surgery as well as in medicine, and despite the attractions of hospital work and research, he became a general practitioner in Stornoway. In 1993, in St Kilda, he married Donna Campbell from Mill House, Breasclete (*nighean Dòmhnaill Iain na Muilne, nighean Dòmhnaill Iain Chaluim Bhig*) who worked in Gaelic television. Their wedding made headlines as the first in St Kilda for 67 years; guests were brought to it, rather uncomfortably, in fishing boats. Their sons Dòmhnall Alasdair and Teàrlach were born in 1994 and 1997.

Several of Alasdair Barden's poems and short stories had been published in *Gairm*, mostly under the name Ali-B, his nickname at school. In 1994 he won the Duncan Johnston Trophy for singing *puirt á beul* at the National Mod in Dunoon. He was a member of the Gaelic Broadcasting Committee, an accomplished broadcaster, chairman of the Western Isles SNP constituency association, and BMA representative for the Western Isles. He and Donna were enthusiastic sponsors of the revival of shinty in Lewis, and in 1996 they helped to found *Comann Camanachd Leòdhais*.

In his initial draft for this biography Alasdair Barden wrote: "As well as his interests in Gaelic and medicine Alasdair has built a car and then a gyrocopter in his own garage, attaining his private pilot's licence in 1996 on the aircraft he built." He liked to point out that the drive from his home at Gearraidh Ghuirm to Stornoway Airport was more dangerous than his gyrocopter flights. On 13 June 1998, however, he was tragically killed at Col on just such a flight. The popularity of this friendly young GP in his adopted island was such that his funeral was attended by about 2,000 people, and his coffin was borne in continuous relay by over 800 men from the High Church in Stornoway to the cemetery at Gress.

I am grateful to Dr Patrick Barden (Rumbling Brig, Kinross-shire) for information and to the late Dr Alasdair Barden for information and permission to reprint:

345   **An Teaghlach Sìonach ('The Chinese Family').** Editor's trl. *Gairm* 139 (An Samhradh 1987) 273. Written when the poet was a student in Edinburgh, after witnessing a scene one night in a Chinese restaurant near his lodgings.

Dòmhnall Uilleam Stiùbhart, 1967—

Dòmhnall Uilleam Stiùbhart was born 15 May 1967 in Inverness, eldest child of Dòmhnall Alasdair Stiùbhart (*Dòmhnall Alasdair mac Dhòmhnaill Alasdair Dhòmhnaill Ruaidh*), from Col in Lewis, and his wife Jessie Mowatt, who is from Glasgow of Fraserburgh stock. He is the elder brother of twins Robert and Kate. Brought up in Glasgow, Aberdeen and Gearraidh Ghuirm in Col, he was educated at the Nicolson Institute, then at Magdalen College, Oxford, where he read Greats (Classics, Ancient History and Philosophy). He went on to Edinburgh University, where he graduated PhD in 1997 with his thesis 'An Gàidheal, a' Ghàidhlig agus a' Ghàidhealtachd anns an t-Seachdamh Linn Deug'.

As well as poetry and articles about Highland history, Dòmhnall Uilleam has written and co-written a number of plays. He has made sporadic appearances as an actor both on stage and before the camera, for example in the television soap *Machair* and in the films *Às an Eilean, Roimh Ghaoith a' Gheamhraidh*, and *Am Pòsadh Hiortach*. In 1998 he won the William Ross Award for Gaelic writing. I am grateful to him for information and permission to print:

346   **Bu tu mo mhuir gun stiùireadh ('You my unsteerable sea').** Author's trl. Previously unpublished.

347   *Latha Eadar-Dhà-Shian* (**'A Day Between Two Storms'**). Author's trl. Previously
       unpublished.

Anne Frater (Anna Frater) 1967—

Anne Catherine Frater was born 5 July 1967 in Stornoway, Lewis, second child and only
daughter of Bert Frater (*Mac Uilleag Dòdo*) and his wife Christina Mary MacKenzie (*Ciorstaidh
Mary Ìomhair 'Ain Ìomhair*), her brothers being Ivor, Robert and Craig. The Frater name came
to Lewis with Anne's father, who was born in Melrose in the Borders. (His mother, Willena
MacKenzie (*Uilleag Dòdo*) from Portvoller, Point, Lewis, was a nurse in Dingleton Hospital in
Melrose, where she met and married Robert Frater, the hospital clerk. Widowed when Bert was
very young, she moved back to Lewis with him.)
    Anne was brought up in Upper Bayble, Point, and educated at Bayble School, the Nicolson
Institute and Glasgow University, where she graduated MA in 1990 with first-class Honours in
Celtic and French, and PhD in 1995 with her thesis 'Scottish Gaelic Women's Poetry up to 1750'.
She says she 'first started writing poetry in sixth year in school (unless you count "Bayble means
Beautiful", composed at age 11!)'. Her work has appeared in the journals *Gairm*, *Chapman* and
Verse since 1985; in the anthologies *An Aghaidh na Sìorraidheachd* (1991), *An Anthology of
Scottish Women Poets* (1991), *Siud an t-Eilean* (1993) and *Dream State* (1994); and in her
collection *Fon t-Slige* (1995). *Fon t-Slige* was awarded a prize at the National Mod in Blairgowrie
in 1996 as the best adult Gaelic book published in 1995–6. Among the more substantial reviews
of her work are those in *Gairm* 174 (An t-Earrach 1996) 183–5 and *Lines Review* 137 (1996) 55–8;
for broader assessments see Fearghas MacFhionnlaigh, '"M'Aodann ris an Uinneig": Anne
Frater', *Gairm* 160 (Am Foghar 1992) 367–71, and Meg Bateman, 'Women's Writing in Scottish
Gaelic since 1750', in Douglas Gifford and Dorothy McMillan (eds), *A History of Scottish
Women's Writing* (Edinburgh 1997) 659–76: 670–1. This book also contains (at pp. 1–14) Anne's
own essay 'The Gaelic Tradition up to 1750'.
    Anne now works in the Gaelic television industry under various guises, ranging from
researcher to scriptwriter to subtitler — and maybe more. I am grateful to her for information and
permission to reprint:

348   *Aon Phòg* (**'One Kiss'**). Author's trl. *Gairm* 158 (An t-Earrach 1992) 156; *Fon t-Slige* 38–9.
349   *Clann a-Màireach* (**'Tomorrow's Children'**). Author's trl. *Fon t-Slige* 12–13.
350   *Bill.* Author's trl. *Gairm* 152 (Am Foghar 1990) 354; *Fon t-Slige* 90–1.
351   *Ceist* (**'Question'**). Editor's trl. with author's assistance. *Gairm* 158 (An t-Earrach 1992) 156.

General Bibliography

Baragab: Bàrdachd agus Rosg an Gàidhlig agus Beurla, An Comunn Gaidhealach, Stornoway 1991

Cameron, Rev. Hector, ed., *Na Bàird Thirisdeach: The Tiree Bards*, Glasgow 1932

Campbell, John, ed., *Gaelic Hymn Book: Laoidhean Soisgeulach*, Glasgow 1913, 1922

Carrell, Christopher, ed., *Seven Poets*, Glasgow, Third Eye Centre, 1981

Chì Mi 'n Tìr: Òrain às na Hearadh, Có Leis Thu?, Northton, Harris 1996

Craig, Cairns, ed., *The History of Scottish Literature: Volume 4, Twentieth Century*, Aberdeen 1987

Cregeen, Eric, and MacKenzie, Donald W, *Tiree Bards and their Bàrdachd*, Isle of Coll 1978

Creighton, Helen, and MacLeod, Calum I N, eds, *Gaelic Songs in Nova Scotia*, Ottawa 1964

Crowe, Thomas Rain, ed., *Writing the Wind: A Celtic Resurgence*, Cullowhee N.C., 1997

Daiches, David, ed., *A Companion to Scottish Culture*, London 1981

Davitt, Michael, and MacDhòmhnaill, Iain, eds, *Sruth na Maoile: Modern Gaelic Poetry from Scotland and Ireland*, Edinburgh and Dublin 1993

Ferguson, Mary, and Matheson, Ann, *Scottish Gaelic Union Catalogue: A List of Books Printed in Scottish Gaelic from 1567 to 1973*, Edinburgh 1984

Ghreumach, Alexina, and NicShimidh, Alma, eds, *Sùil ri Cladach: Cruinneachadh de dh'Òrain Mhara*, Stornoway 1992

Gifford, Douglas, and McMillan, Dorothy, eds, *A History of Scottish Women's Writing*, Edinburgh 1997

International Poetry Review, vol. 5, no. 1, Scottish issue, Greensboro N.C., Spring 1979

Ludwig, Hans-Werner, and Fietz, Lothar, eds, *Poetry in the British Isles*, Cardiff 1995

MacAulay, Donald, ed., *Nua-Bhàrdachd Ghàidhlig: Modern Scottish Gaelic Poems*, Edinburgh 1976

— 'On Some Aspects of the Appreciation of Modern Gaelic Poetry', *Scottish Gaelic Studies* 11 (1966) 136–45

MacFhionghuin, Lachlann, ed., *Bàird a' Chomuinn*, Glasgow 1953

MacLeod, Donald John, *Twentieth Century Publications in Scottish Gaelic*, Edinburgh 1980

— 'A Description of Twentieth-Century Gaelic Literature', unpublished PhD thesis, Glasgow 1969

Macleod, Rev. Malcolm, and Macleod, Robert, eds, *An Laoidheadair: The Gaelic Hymnary*, Edinburgh 1934

MacLeòid, Iain N, ed., *Bàrdachd Leódhais*, Glasgow 1916, Stornoway 1999

MacLeòid, Tormod, ed., *Bàrdachd á Leódhas*, Glasgow 1969

MacMhaoilein, Iain, ed., 'Bàrdachd Uibhist-a-Deas', *Gairm* 66–113 (1969–81)

MacNeacail, Aonghas, 'A Long Road to Now: A Snapshot Survey of Gaelic Poetry', *Verse* 11/2 (1994) 29–36

Neat, Timothy, with MacInnes, John, *The Voice of the Bard: Living Poets and Ancient Tradition in the Highlands and Islands of Scotland*, Edinburgh 1999

Orbis 58–9, Scottish issue, Nuneaton, Autumn–Winter 1985

Poetry Australia 63, Gaelic issue, Sydney N.S.W., May 1977

Royle, Trevor, *The Macmillan Companion to Scottish Literature*, Basingstoke 1983, 2nd edn published as *The Mainstream Companion to Scottish Literature*, Edinburgh 1993

Scott, Tom, ed., *Four Points of a Saltire*, Edinburgh 1970

Seinnibh dhan Tighearna: Cruinneachadh Laoidhean, Kevin Mayhew, Bury St Edmunds 1986

Smith, Iain Crichton, 'Modern Scottish Gaelic Poetry', *Scottish Gaelic Studies* 7 (1953) 199–206

— 'The Future of Gaelic Literature', *Transactions of the Gaelic Society of Inverness* 43 (1960–3) 172–80

— *Towards the Human: Selected Essays*, Loanhead 1986

— 'Recent Gaelic Poetry', *Scottish Language* 8 (1989) 21–33

— 'The Internationalism of Twentieth-Century Gaelic Poetry', *Scottish Literary Journal* 18/1 (1991) 82–6

Stephen, Iain, ed., *Siud an t-Eilean: There Goes the Island*, Stornoway 1993

Stoddart, John, ed., *Cerddi Gaeleg Cyfoes*, Cardiff 1986

Thomson, Derick, 'La letteratura Gaelica Scozzese', *Il Bimestre* 22/23 (1972) 31–50

— *An Introduction to Gaelic Poetry*, London 1974, Edinburgh 1990

— *The New Verse in Scottish Gaelic: A Structural Analysis*, Dublin 1974

— ed., 'An Anthology of Recent Gaelic Verse', *Akros* 11, no. 31 (August 1976) 3–45

— 'Gaelic Writers in Lowland Scotland', *Scottish Literary Journal* 4, no. 1 (1977) 36–46

— 'Tradition and Innovation in Gaelic Verse since 1950', *Transactions of the Gaelic Society of Inverness* 52 (1982–4) 91–114

— ed., *The Companion to Gaelic Scotland*, Oxford 1983, Glasgow 1994

Thomson, James, ed., *An Dìleab: Gaelic Verse for Advanced Divisions*, Glasgow [1932]

Watson, Roderick, *The Literature of Scotland* (London 1984) 442–52

— ed., *The Poetry of Scotland, Gaelic, Scots and English, 1380–1980*, Edinburgh 1995

Whyte, Christopher, ed., *An Aghaidh na Sìorraidheachd / In the Face of Eternity: Ochdnar Bhàrd Gàidhlig / Eight Gaelic Poets*, Edinburgh 1991

Williams, J E Caerwen, ed., *Literature in Celtic Countries*, Cardiff 1971

The Bardic Crown

In 1923, following the example of the Welsh Eisteddfod, An Comunn Gaidhealach simplified the structure of its annual poetry competitions into a single contest for a Bardic Crown (*Crùn na Bàrdachd*), the winner to be acknowledged as Bard of An Comunn (*Bàird a' Chomuinn Ghaidhealaich*) for the coming year. The man behind the move, not surprisingly, was Angus Robertson (q.v.), then president of An Comunn. Offering a distinctive middle path between traditional and modern verse, the competition produced much work of note which deserves to be put in perspective. The following list of winning poems and the places where they can be found is therefore offered in the hope that it will stimulate research. (Many subsidiary prizes remained; Sorley MacLean won a junior one in 1928, while in 1946 Derick Thomson won a gold medal as the most distinguished entrant in the literary competitions generally.)

The Bard was crowned each year at the closing concert of the Mod. Astonishingly, unlike in Wales, the winning poem itself formed no part of the proceedings. In Frank Thompson's view the ceremony was 'on many occasions a literal show-stopper and at times caused much embarrassment' (*History of An Comunn Gaidhealach: The First Hundred* (Inverness 1992) 126). This may have been true in the competition's declining years, but winning the Crown gave Mary M Maclean (1951), for example, the best day of her life and brought tears to the eyes of her old teacher, who remembered beating her in school when she caught her writing a poem — "And now she is crowned bard of all Scotland!" (Neat's *Voice of the Bard* 37, 62).

In 1978 no award was made because no entry was of adequate quality. It was the second time in five years that this had happened, and in March 1979 An Comunn announced that the Bardic Crown would no longer be awarded.

AG An Gaidheal; *BC Mackinnon's Bàird a' Chomuinn*; *DG An Deo-Gréine*; *SG Stornoway Gazette*

1923 (Inverness). Seumas MacThómais (James Thomson, Tong, Lewis). *Buaidh an Laoich* ('The Hero's Triumph'). *AG* 19 (1923–4) 62–3; Thomson, *Fasgnadh* (1953) 14; *BC* 88–92.

1924 (Perth). Iain MacPhàidein (John MacFadyen, Mull). *Aitealan on Iar* ('Breezes from the West'). *AG* 20 (1924–5) 7; *BC* 85–7.

1925 (Greenock). Iain MacCormaig (John MacCormick, Fionnphort, Mull). *Blàr Inbhir Chéitein* ('The Battle of Inverkeithing'). *AG* 21 (1925–6) 28–32; *BC* 73–85.

1926 (Oban). Calum MacRath (Malcolm Macrae, Skeabost, Skye). *Cuairt Mhaidne a' Bhuachaille* ('The Herdsman's Morning Round'). *AG* 22 (1926–7) 37; *BC* 71–3.

1927 (Fort William). Aonghas MacEacharna (Angus Mackechnie, Hynish, Tiree). *Tìr Mhaiseach nan Cruach* ('The Lovely Land of the Stacks'). *AG* 23 (1927–8) 43; *BC* 68–71.

1928 (Inverness). Pàdraig Caimbeul (Peter Campbell, Bragar, Lewis). *An Uiseag* ('The Lark'). *AG* 24 (1928–9) 7–8; *BC* 65–8.

1929 (Perth). Donnchadh MacIain (Duncan Johnston, Lagavulin, Islay). *Don Ghealaich* ('To the Moon'). *AG* 25 (1929–30) 39; Johnston, *Crònan nan Tonn* (1938) 58–60; *BC* 62–5; Johnston, *Crònan nan Tonn* (1997) 62–4.

1930 (Dunoon). Ruairidh Caimbeul (Roderick Campbell, Bragar, Lewis). *Cor is Leas na Dùthcha* ('The Condition and Benefit of the Country'). *AG* 26 (1930–1) 26–7; *BC* 59–62.

1931 (Dingwall). Seòras E Marjoribanks (George E Marjoribanks, Sonachan, Argyll). *Sealladh air Cruachan Beann* ('A View of Ben Cruachan'). *AG* 27 (1931–2) 75–6; *BC* 56–9.

1932 (Fort William). Dòmhnall MacillÌosa (Donald Gillies, Snizort, Skye). *Cuireadh do na Gaidhil* ('An Invitation to the Gael'). *AG* 28 (1932–3) 117–8; *BC* 51–6.

1933 (Glasgow). Dòmhnall MacilleMhaoil (Donald MacMillan, Kinlocheil, Lochaber). *Tobar a' Chreachainn* ('The Mountain Well'). *AG* 29 (1933–4) 13–14; *BC* 49–51.

1934 (Oban). Catrìona Fionnghal Urchadan (Mrs Catherine F Urquhart, Leurbost, Lewis). *Soillse agus Sgleò* ('Brightness and Obscurity'). *AG* 30 (1934–5) 19–20; *BC* 45–8.

1935 (Edinburgh). Dòmhnall Grannd (Donald Grant, Camuscross, Skye). *An Uilebheist is na Foghlamaich* ('The Monster and the Experts'). *AG* 32 (1936–7) 68–9, 85, 100; *BC* 36–45; Grant, *Tir an Àigh* (1971) 229–39; poem 79 above.

1936 (Inverness). Eachann MacDhùghaill (Hector MacDougall, Isle of Coll). *An Càrn* ('The Cairn'). *AG* 32 (1936–7) 36–7; *BC* 32–5.

1937 (Dundee). Calum Iain MacLeòid (Calum I N MacLeod, Dornie, Kintail). *An Cuan Siar* ('The Western Ocean'). *AG* 33 (1937–8) 36–7; *BC* 29–31.

1938 (Glasgow). Dòmhnall Mac an t-Saoir (Donald Macintyre, Snishival, S. Uist). *Am Bàrd* (= *Aeòlus agus am Balg*). *AG* 34 (1938–9) 43–4, 107–8; *BC* 23–9; Macintyre, *Sporan Dhòmhnaill* (1968) 61–83; poem 56 above.

1939 (no location — Mod cancelled). Ìomhar MacSporain (Edward Pursell, Campbeltown). *Moladh Màiri* ('In Praise of Mary'). *AG* 35 (1939–40) 27; *BC* 21–3.

1940–5 No Mod, no award.

1946 (Aberdeen). Iain A MacLeòid (John A MacLeod, Shawbost, Lewis). *Radharc Céin* ('Distant View'). *BC* 18–20.

1947 (Perth). Dòmhnall MacGilleathain (Donald Maclean, Braes, Skye). *Don Chuilithionn* ("To the

Cuillins'). *AG* 43 (1947–8) 102; *BC* 16–17.

1948 (Glasgow). Dòmhnall Iain MacDhòmhnaill (Donald John MacDonald, Peninerine, S. Uist). *Moladh Uibhist* ('In Praise of Uist'). *AG* 44 (1949) 116–8; *BC* 10–16; MacDhòmhnuill, *Sguaban Eòrna* (1973) 15–21; MacDonald, *Chì Mi* (1998) 20–31.

1949 (Inverness). Dòmhnall MacDhòmhnaill (Donald MacDonald, Eriskay). *An Ròn* ('The Seal'). *BC* 77–10; MacDhòmhnaill, *Rannan á Eilean na h-Òige* (1981) 28–31.

1950 (Dunoon). Aonghas MacMhathain (Angus Matheson, Staffin, Skye). *Bodach an Stòirr* ('The Old Man of Storr'). *BC* 5–6.

1951 (Edinburgh). Màiri M NicGhillEathain (Mary M Maclean, Grimsay, N. Uist). *Do Bheinn Eubhal* ('To Ben Eaval'). *AG* 46 (1951) 99–100; *BC* 1–4; Neat (ed.), *The Voice of the Bard* (1999) 56–9; cf. poem 181 above.

1952 (Rothesay). An t-Urr. Cailein T MacCoinnich (Rev. Colin N Mackenzie, Taransay, Harris). *An Cliseam* ('The Clisham'). *AG* 47 (1952) 95–6.

1953 (Oban). Iain Camshron (John Cameron, Inverasdale, Gairloch). *An Saighdear* ('The Soldier'). *AG* 48 (1953) 83–5.

1954 (Perth). Raghnall MacLaomainn (Ronald Lamont, Saddell, Kintyre). *Luath air a' Chagailt* ('Ashes on the Hearth'). *AG* 49 (1954) 83–4.

1955 (Aberdeen). Seonaidh Moireasdan (John Morrison, Scalpay, Harris). *An Dealbh* ('The Picture'). *AG* 50 (1955) 101–2; Moireasdan, *Tiugainn do Sgalpaigh* (Northton, Harris 1999) 44–7.

1956 (Largs). Iain M Moffatt-Pender (Iain A Moffatt-Pender, Auchterarder, Perthshire). *Oidhche na Leargaidh* ('The Battle of Largs'). *AG* 51 (1956) 103–6.

1957 (Inverness). Dòmhnall R MacGilleMhoire (Donald R Morrison, Scalpay, Harris). *Màiri Òg*. *AG* 52 (1957) 104–5.

1958 (Glasgow). An t-Oll. Urr. Tómas M MacCalmain (Rev. Dr Thomas M Murchison, Kylerhea, Skye). *Buaidh air na Famhairean* ('Defeating the Giants'). *AG* 53 (1958) 115–6.

1959 (Dundee). Dòmhnall Ailean MacDhòmhnaill (Donald Allan MacDonald, Daliburgh, S. Uist). *Aiseirigh a' Bheachain* ('The Resurrection of the Bee'). *AG* 55 (1960) 4; Rev. Fr John A Macdonald, 'The Songs of Donald Allan MacDonald' (MLitt thesis, Aberdeen 1983) 213–20 etc.; Rev. Fr John A Macdonald, *Òrain Dhòmhnaill Ailein* (1999) 194–201 (text and trl.), 224–5 (notes), 253 (melody).

1960 (Edinburgh). Alastair Iain Mac'IlleMhaoil (Alex John MacMillan, Inverness). *Ar Cainnt mar Chraobh-Dharaich* ('Our Language like an Oak-Tree'). *AG* 56 (1961) 2–3.

1961 (Stirling). Seonaidh Ailig Mac a' Phearsain (John A Macpherson, N. Uist). *An t-Slabhraidh* ('The Chain'). *AG* 56 (1961) 76–7, 88–9.

1962 (Oban). Aonghas MacAonghais (Angus MacInnes, Clarkston). *Crannag a' Mhinisteir*

('The Minister's Pulpit'). *AG* 57 (1962) 134–6.

1963 (Perth). Seumas MacCoinnich (James Mackenzie, Glasgow). *Beachd, Smuain is Teagamh* ('Opinion, Thought and Doubt'). *AG* 58 (1963) 138–9.

1964 (Aberdeen). Dòmhnall Iain MacLeòid (Donald John MacLeod, Ardhasaig, Harris). *Beatha Làn* ('A Full Life'). *AG* 59 (1964) 134.

1965 (Largs). Ùisdean Laing (Hugh Laing, Stoneybridge, S. Uist). *Am Fiabhras nach faigh Bàs* ('The Fever that does not Die'). *AG* 60 (1965) 136–7; Laing, *Gu Tìr mo Luaidh* (1965) 42–3.

1966 (Inverness). No award.

1967 (Glasgow). Tormod MacGill-Eain (Norman Maclean, Glasgow). *Maol Donn* ('MacCrimmon's Sweetheart'). *Sruth*, 5 October 1967; Neat (ed.), *The Voice of the Bard* (Edinburgh 1999) 279–81; poem 254 above.

1968 (Dunoon). Dòmhnall Iain MacDhùghaill (Donald John MacDougall, Barra). *Druim an t-Saoghail* ('The Rim'). *Sruth*, 17 October 1968.

1969 (Aviemore). Uilleam Nèill (William Neill, Ayrshire). *Dòchas air an Tràigh* ('Hope on the Shore'). *Sruth*, 30 October 1969; cf. *Sòlas air an Tràigh*, Nèill, *Cnù à Mogaill* (1983) 29–30.

1970 (Oban). Mòrag Herdman (Mrs Marion Herdman, Blantyre). *Fuaim na Pìoba* ('The Sound of the Pipes'). *Sruth*, 15 October 1970.

1971 (Stirling). Iain Aonghas Macleòid (John Angus MacLeod, Harris). *Fhir na Deifir* ('O Man of Haste'). *Sruth* (in *SG*) 16 October 1971; MacLeòid, *Luinneagan Mhicleòid* (Edinburgh 1973) 5–8.

1972 (Inverness). Alasdair MacAonghais (Alasdair MacInnes, Glencoe). *Dà Shealladh* ('Second Sight'). *Sruth* (in *SG*) 28 October 1972; MacAonghais, *Tron Bhogha-Froise* (Teangue, Skye 1999) 98–9.

1973 (Ayr). Murchadh Moireasdan (Murdo Morrison, Borve, Lewis). *Uilleam Uallas aig Blàr Dhrochaid Shruighlea* ('William Wallace at the Battle of Stirling Bridge'). *Sruth* (in *SG*) 9 March 1974 (24 lines published out of 300).

1974 (Dundee). No award.

1975 (E. Kilbride). Iain MacDhùghaill (Iain Mac-Dougall, Sollas, N. Uist). *Sopan Sìobaidh* ('A Wisp for Wiping'), *Beul nam Bil* ('The Mouth of the Lips'), *Làn Tràigh Bhàlaigh — Reoghart na h-Alba* ('High Tide at Vallay — Scotland's Spring-Tide'). *Gairm* 93 (1975–6) 40–5, 62–5.

1976 (Aberdeen). Sìne Cooper (Miss Jean M Cooper, Aberdeen). *Taigh Falamh* ('Empty House'), *Air Bruach na h-Aibhne* ('On the River Bank'), *Bithidh an Ùine air Ruith* ('The Time will Pass'). All unpublished.

1977 (Golspie). An t-Urr. Ruairidh MacDhòmhnaill (Rev. Roderick Macdonald, Locheport, N. Uist). *Cearcal Cuain* ('Sea Cycle'), *Fios-Freagairt* ('Responses'), *An Aon Dealbh* ('The One Picture'). MacDhòmhnaill, *Leth-Cheud Bliadhna* (1978) 25–6, 33–4, 43–4; cf. *SG*, 15 October 1977, and *Sruth* (in *SG*) 3 December 1977.

1978 (Oban). No award.

Index to Poems

*part poem

A Chiall 's a Ghràidh 288
A nighean 's tu beairteachadh 300
A' Bheinn 330
A' Bhuaile Ghréine 292
A' Càradh an Rathaid 612
A' Cheist 88
A' Cheiste 540
A' Chlach Ionmhainn 502
A' Dràibheadh ann an Ameireaga* 656
A' Ghaidhealtachd 480
A' Ghaoth 148
A' Ghaoth 526
A' Ghiblinn troimh thrì Sùilean 544
A' Mhaighdeann Chriadhadh 512
A' Mheanbhchuileag* 632
Achmhasain 384
acras 566
Aeòlus agus am Balg* 150
Aghaidh ri Aghaidh 494
Agus mar sin car a' Mhuiltein* 616
Aideachadh 416
Aig a' Chladh 516
Aig an Doras 528
Ainmeannan 620
Air an Adhbhar Cheudna 316
Air an Somme 124
Air Bàs Charles Bukowski 688
Air sgàth nan sonn 218
Air Sràidean Ghlaschu* 476
Àirc a' Choimhcheangail* 468
Alba Saor* 28
Alba v. Argentina, 2/6/79 466
Am Bodach-Ròcais 454
Am Bullaphant 70
Am Bùth aig Maitiu 86
Am Faoilteach 508
Am Fear-Turais 608
Am Mac Stròdhail 112
Am Peinsean 2
An Ataireachd Àrd 18
an cathadh mór* 562
An Ceusadh 624
An Ciùran Ceòban Ceò 386
An Clamhan 608
An Crann 460
An Cuilithionn* 322
An Cùlaibh Éirinn 252
An Dà Latha 48
An Daolag Shìonach 666
An déidh aimhreit 538
An Dubhsgaile 100
An Dùn 'na Theine 316
An Dùn Éideann 1939 308
An Éibhleag 616
an eilid bhàn 568
An Fhuar-Bheinn 44

An Geiréiniam 624
An Giùlan 338
An Guth á Broinn na Màthar 420
An Litir Àraid 516
An Oidhch' Ud 694
An Referendum air son Pàrlamaid ann
    an Alba 1/3/79 602
An Seanchaidh 404
An Seann Òran 310
An Sgàileagan 14
An Sgiobair Ùr 82
An 'Sus' a Shàraich mi 268
An t-Acras 552
An t-Àilleagan 328
An t-Àite bho Dheireadh 272
An t-Amadan 652
An t-Anam-Fàis* 490
An t-Aoibhneas a tha staigh sa Chridhe . . . 506
An t-Aran 604
An t-Each Iarainn 260
An t-Earrach 274
An t-Earrach 534
An t-Eilean 'na Bhaile 606
An t-Òban 518
An t-Òigear a' Bruidhinn on Ùir 378
An t-Sàbaid 346
An t-Uisge 620
An Teaghlach Sìonach 700
An Tuagh 628
An Turas Sìos gu Tìr nam Marbh* 580
An TV 528
An uair a thig an teannachadh 314
An Uilebheist is na Foghlamaich* 246
An-seo an gaol 316
Aoir an Luchd-Riaghlaidh* 188
Aoir Mhusolìnidh 156
Aon Phòg 702
Ar Gaisgich a Thuit sna Blàir 214
Ar n-Airgead 's ar n-Òr 548
Ar Tìr 214
Ath-Chruthachadh 684
Atman 366
B' fheàrr leam na goid an teine 296
Bàgh Leumrabhaigh 270
Ban-Ghaidheal 306
Banais Chòrsabuil 62
Bantrach Cogaidh 410
Bàs Baile 412
Bealltainn ann am Fàcland 534
Bean Dubh a' Caoidh a Fir a Chaidh a
    Mharbhadh leis a' Phoileas 74
Bho Leabhar-Latha Maria Malibran* 668
Bi air t' Fhaiceall 656
Bill 704
Bisearta 376
Blàr Chaol Àcainn 244

Bloigh Lebensraum 390
Bó Dhearg 402
Bogha-Frois san Oidhche* 640
Bogsa Diùc. 400
Borgh Leódhais 610
Briseadh na Fàire. 10
Bu tu mo mhuir gun stiùireadh. 700
Bùrn is Mòine 's Coirc. 454
Bùth Dhòmhnaill 'IcLeòid 180
Cadal 90
Caithris nam Bodach. 282
Camhanaich. 300
Càrn air a' Mhonadh. 110
Cath Fairge Monte Video 68
Cead Deireannach Àirnis 498
Cearcall Hùla. 402
Ceartas Coma a' Bhàis 614
Céilidh Dhùn-Ì* 6
Ceist (Meg Bateman) 684
Ceist (Anna Frater) 706
Ceithir Gaothan na h-Albann. 348
Ceud Bliadhna san Sgoil 458
Ceud Fàilt' air Gach Gleann. 278
Cha b'e gunna mo nàmhaid 138
Cìocharan 684
Ciod E? 258
Cladh 596
Clann a-Màireach 704
Clann-Nighean an Sgadain. 452
Clydebank 654
Cogadh agus Sìth*. 64
Coilleag ghlan gheal chadalach 650
Coin is Madaidhean-Allaidh 297
Coinneal. 696
Coinnichidh sinn. 520
Còmhradh an Alldain 370
Cor na Tìr 502
Cothrom Peanais. 698
Cuimhneachan 1914–1918 96
Cuireadh dhan Bheatha. 686
Cum Sinn Dlùth 504
Cumha Bhaltair Cinneide 1450–1508 496
Cumha Mhaighstir Nèill. 284
Cùmhnantan Sìthe Pharis 240
Dàin 598
dàn bealltainn 570
Daoine bha an Leódhas uaireigin 584
Dealachadh 532
Dealbh mo Mhàthar 682
Deargadan Phóland. 254
Deich Bliadhna 690
Deireadh an t-Saoghail 482
Deireadh Òrdugh Ghleann Dail. 110
Dh'fhalbh na gillean grinn 126
Dimitto 304
Do Bheinn Eubhal. 438
Do Chròcus air a Shlighe a Nèamh. 600
Do Dhol-a-Mach. 678
Do Fhear-Pòsta* 686
Do Fhear-Sgrìobhaidh Ainmeil 542
Do Mgr Niall Mac an t-Seumarlain 318
Do Mhaighstir Niall 426
Do Sgoilear Àraidh 682

Dòchas. 598
Don Bhreitheamh a thubhairt ri Iain
   MacGhill-Eathain gum b'e Gealtair
   a bh' ann 318
Dubh is Geal 272
Dùisgidh mi aon mhadainn. 650
Dùn Dà Làmh. 694
Dunkirk 44
Dùrachd Teachdaire Chrìost. 224
Dùrachdan Nollaige 392
Dùrd a' Ghlinne 392
Earail air Luchd-Adhraidh a' Bheòil-
   Aithris 466
Earrach '74. 458
Eathar Angaidh 512
Fàilte an Diabhail don Droch Dhuine* 184
Fàilte don Phrionnsa Teàrlach 's a'
   Bhana-Phrionnsa Diàna a dh'Eilean
   Sgalpaigh na Hearadh, 2.7.85* 430
Fàilte na h-Aimsir do D.D. 84
Faoin Achain 272
Far 'n do chaith mi 'n oidhch' 94
Farmad 344
Farpais Réidio nan Gaidheal. 676
Feasgar an Duine Ghil 72
Feasgar Samhraidh: Linne Ratharsair 332
Féin-Fhìreantachd 542
Féin-Mhort, Lunnainn a-Deas. 658
Flùrannan 630
Fo Sheòl 298
Fògradh Cogaidh sna h-Innsean. 342
Fontana Maggiore 662
fòrladh dhachaigh 578
Fuath an t-Saoghail 116
Gabh a-mach ás mo bhàrdachd 310
Gaoir na h-Eòrpa. 290
Gealach na Sultain. 610
Gealladh Gaoil 622
Geamhradh 650
Gearraidh na Mònadh á Smeircleit. 674
Geata Tìr nan Òg 428
Ged chuirinn dhiom éideadh 298
Ghrad-leum cù-geàrd a h-inntinn 532
Glac a' Bhàis 320
Glaschu 608
Glòir no Dórainn? 442
Gnìomhair is Cuspair 692
Gormshuil* 484
Gràdh m' Fhear-Saoraidh. 102
Gu Dé Thachair dha m' Thìr? 498
Guidhe an Iasgair 390
Gur suarach leam 300
Haiku* 612
Hearach 616
Indira 596
Innsidh mi dhut mar a thachair 524
Iolair, Brù-Dhearg, Giuthas* 638
Ìomhaighean 688
Iomram Bean na Bainnse 8
Ionndrainn na Sìne 388
Iorram nan Ìtheach 42
Labhair mi 298
Làmhan 456

Latha Eadar-Dhà-Shian 702
Leumadair Bungee 692
Lìon an Damhain-Allaidh 120
Luach na Saorsa. 220
Madainn Diar-Daoin, ann an Oifis Puist
    an Glaschu 478
Madainn na Sàbaid 38
Madainn Sneachda 696
Maol Donn 554
Maorach is Feamannadh 50
marilyn monroe 576
Mas e Ghàidhlig an cànan 520
Mathanas 592
Meall Garbh* 488
Medusa, an Cuclopach, 's an *Daily Record*. . 626
Meftah Bâbkum es-Sabar? 380
Meirg 436
Mhag mo reusan 332
MhicGilleMhìcheil 302
Mi Fhìn agus a' Revolution agus mo
    Bhata-Darach 584
Mì-Chliù nan Daoine Dubha, 1930 228
Mochtàr is Dùghall* 348
Moladh Mnathan-Eiridinn Ospadal an
    Rathaig Mhóir, Inbhir Nis 510
Motor-Boat Heillsgeir 146
Mu Chrìochan Hòil* 448
Muilemhàgag 654
Murdag Mhòr 456
'N e d' mhiann 308
Na Cailleachan 450
Na h-Eilthirich 530
Na h-Iongnan 480
Na Liopan 604
Na Ràtaichean 's a' Bhàrdachd 390
Na Seanfhacail 520
Nam biodh agam moisein bodaich 34
Nam bithinn mar eun 132
Naoi Ceud Deug 's a Ceithir Deug 236
Nochd gur luaineach mo chadal 262
Nuair a thàinig am Buroo do Dhùthaich
    nam Beann 196
Nuair chaidh a' Chlach a Thilleadh 176
Nuair chunna mi 304
O a Ghaidhealtachd Till 342
O, faighibh suas an Cogadh 206
Oidhche Chullaig 674
Ora nam Buadh 2
Òran a' Pheinsean 22
Òran a' Phuinnsein 130
Òran aig Toiseach Cogadh Mór na h-Eòrpa 52
Òran an Fheamnaidh 418
Òran an H-Bomb 144
Òran Arras 122
Òran Bainnse 58
Òran Clach Stèineagaidh 234
Òran do Teonaidh Hellinga 264
Òran don Chogadh 212
Òran don Oighre 346
Òran Ghlinne Chrò* 16
Òran Hitler 220
Òran na Caillich Bhuana 54
Òran na Cloiche 166

Òran na *Politician* 334
Ors a' Bhéist Mhór ris a' Bhéist Bhig 386
Pioghaid 482
Plus ça change 492
Rabhd Eudochais 540
Ràdar Beinn Sheaval 672
Rannan Callainne 68
Raoir chunna mi 266
Reic Anama 294
Ro-dh'aithnich mi 658
Road to the Isles 318
Rodeo 692
Ròidean Rwanda 490
Samhla 546
samhla 574
Sealg Ulaidh* 492
Sealltainn thar Chluaidh 494
Seanairean 488
Seann Éipheiteach ann an Tìr Airsnealach . . 210
Seinnidh mis' an duanag* 62
Seotal 438
Sgàthach* 578
Sgillinn leis nach Ceannaichear Càil 678
Sgòthan 446
Sireadh 622
sireadh bradain sicir* 560
Siubhal a' *Choire* 344
Slighe nan Seann Seun 114
Smuaintean air Mórachd Ìmpireachd
    Bhreatainn* 36
Soisgeul 1955 544
Soraidh Leibh 680
Srath Nabhair 452
Stuth Toirmisgte 496
Suas gun Sìos 388
Successa Petronia* 536
Superloo Steòrnabhaigh 648
Taibhs 434
Taigh a' Bhàird 424
Taigh Dubh mo Sheanar 340
Teagamh 484
Teallaichean 446
teist 566
Tha mi duilich, cianail, duilich 134
Tha thu air aigeann m' inntinn 514
Theagamh nach eil i 'nam chàs 290
Thug mi 'n oidhche raoir glé shàmhach 152
Thug thu cead dhomh 662
Thug Yeats dà fhichead bliadhna 314
Thuit mo leannan 274
Tilleadh Uilìseis* 384
Togalach an Aonaich 78
Trafaig Oidhche 696
Trì Slighean 308
Turas 618
Turas an Ànraidh 392
Turas don Ghealaich* 432
Uaireannan tha eagal orm 650
Uamha 'n Òir* 332
Ubhal 690
Uisge Phìob 400
Uladh 388